Handbook of Research on Contemporary Theoretical Models in Information Systems

Yogesh K. Dwivedi
Swansea University, UK

Banita Lal
Nottingham Trent University, UK

Michael D. Williams
Swansea University, UK

Scott L. Schneberger
Principia College, USA

Michael Wade
York University, Canada

INFORMATION SCIENCE REFERENCE

Hershey • New York

Director of Editorial Content:	Kristin Klinger
Senior Managing Editor:	Jamie Snavely
Managing Editor:	Jeff Ash
Assistant Managing Editor:	Carole Coulson
Typesetter:	Jennifer Johnson, Carole Coulson
Cover Design:	Lisa Tosheff
Printed at:	Yurchak Printing Inc.

Published in the United States of America by
Information Science Reference (an imprint of IGI Global)
701 E. Chocolate Avenue,
Hershey PA 17033
Tel: 717-533-8845
Fax: 717-533-8661
E-mail: cust@igi-global.com
Web site: http://www.igi-global.com/reference

and in the United Kingdom by
Information Science Reference (an imprint of IGI Global)
3 Henrietta Street
Covent Garden
London WC2E 8LU
Tel: 44 20 7240 0856
Fax: 44 20 7379 0609
Web site: http://www.eurospanbookstore.com

Library of Congress Cataloging-in-Publication Data

Handbook of research on contemporary theoretical models in information systems / Yogesh K. Dwivedi ... [et al.], editors.
  p. cm.
 Includes bibliographical references and index.
 Summary: "This book provides a comprehensive understanding and coverage of the various theories, models and related research approaches used within IS research"--Provided by publisher.
  ISBN 978-1-60566-659-4 (hbk.) -- ISBN 978-1-60566-660-0 (ebook) 1. Information technology--Research. I. Dwivedi, Yogesh Kumar.
  T58.5.H353 2009 658.4'038011--dc22
                    2008055725

British Cataloguing in Publication Data
A Cataloguing in Publication record for this book is available from the British Library.

Dedication

To my wife, Anju, who encouraged me in this endeavour, supported me during the long hours, and helped me to achieve this.
Yogesh K. Dwivedi

To my parents: Resham and Santosh Lal Ahir.
Banita Lal

To my parents. Pauline and Alan.
Michael D. Williams

To Prof. Ephraim R. McLean, PhD, mentor extraordinaire.
Scott Schneberger

To Heidi, Christopher, and Benjamin, for your love, patience, and encouragement.
Michael Wade

List of Contributors

Table of Contents

Section I
Theory Development and Extension

Chapter I
Brent Furneaux, York University, Canada
Michael Wade, York University, Canada

Chapter II
Marlei Pozzebon, HEC Montréal, Canada
Eduardo Diniz, Fundaçao Getulio Vargas, Brazil
Martin Jayo, Fundaçao Getulio Vargas, Brazil

Chapter III
Susan Gasson, The iSchool at Drexel, Drexel University, USA

Chapter IV
Sven A. Carlsson, Lund University, Sweden
Chapter V
Nicholas Roberts, Clemson University, USA
Varun Grover, Clemson University, USA

Section IV
Management Theories

Section V
Marketing Theory

Section VI
Sociological and Cultural Theories

Detailed Table of Contents

Section I
Theory Development and Extension

Section I includes six chapters dedicated to understanding new theory development and the extension of existing theory. The first chapter presents a broad perspective on the nature of the constructs and relationships explored in IS research and to develop a nomological network of the most salient relationships. The second chapter proposes a multilevel framework particularly useful for research involving complex and multilevel interactions. Chapter III provides a brief introduction to the grounded theory (GT) approach to research, discussing how it has been used in information systems (IS) research, and how GT studies may be conducted to provide a significant theoretical contribution to the management information systems (MIS) field. Chapter IV puts critical realism forward as an alternative philosophical underpinning for IS research. This chapter also provides examples of how critical realism have been used and can be used in research aiming at generating new IS theory, IS evaluation research, and IS design science research. The fifth chapter focuses on theory development but from quantitative perspectives. This chapter reviews previous applications of structural equation modeling (SEM) in IS research and recommends guidelines to using SEM for theory development. Finally, chapter VI proposes and describes an evidence-based "health information system theory."

Chapter I

Brent Furneaux, York University, Canada
Michael R. Wade, York University, Canada

Constructs and the relationships between them are widely considered to be central to theory development and testing. Over time, information systems (IS) researchers have identified and explored an extensive set of relationships amongst a broad range of constructs. The result of these initiatives is a body of literature that can be considered to represent the cumulative learning of the discipline. Based on the premise that this cumulative learning is capable of providing valuable guidance to future theory development, the authors present a review and analysis of a large sample of empirical research published in two leading IS journals. The objective of this endeavor is to offer a broad perspective on the nature of the constructs and relationships explored in IS research and to develop a nomological network of the most salient relationships that can then serve to guide future research and to lend support new and existing theory.

Chapter II

Marlei Pozzebon, HEC Montréal, Canada
Eduardo Diniz, Fundaçao Getulio Vargas, Brazil
Martin Jayo, Fundaçao Getulio Vargas, Brazil

The multilevel framework proposed in this chapter is particularly useful for research involving complex and multilevel interactions (i.e., interactions involving individuals, groups, organizations and networks at the community, regional or societal levels). The framework is influenced by three theoretical perspectives. The core foundation comes from the structurationist view of technology, a stream of research characterized by the application of structuration theory to information systems (IS) research and notably influenced by researchers like Orlikowski (2000) and Walsham (2002). In order to extend the framework to encompass research at the community/societal levels, concepts from social shaping of technology and from contextualism have been integrated. Beyond sharing a number of ontological and epistemological assumptions, these three streams of thinking have been combined because each of them offers particular concepts that are of great value for the kind of studies the authors wish to put forward: investigating the influence of information and communication technology (ICT) from a structurationist standpoint at levels that go beyond the organizational one.

Chapter III

Susan Gasson, The iSchool at Drexel, Drexel University, USA

This chapter provides a brief introduction to the grounded theory (GT) approach to research, discussing how it has been used in information systems (IS) research, and how GT studies may be conducted to provide a significant theoretical contribution to the management information systems (MIS) field. The subject is of particular interest at a time when GT attracts frequent criticism for a lack of rigor. This chapter deals with what makes for a rigorous contribution to "grounded" theory in MIS. It addresses developments and controversies in the generation of grounded theories, examining the use of GT as a coding method vs. the use of GT as a method for generating theory. The discussion focuses mainly on the constructivist/interpretive perspective adopted in most qualitative data studies, as this is the way in which GT has been used most often in MIS. The chapter concludes with a roadmap for the use of GT in MIS research and a discussion of the contribution made by GT studies in MIS.

Different strands of non-positivistic research approaches and theories, for example, constructivism, grounded theory, and structuration theory, have gained popularity in the information systems (IS) field. Although, they are managing to overcome some problems with positivism and structural theories they are not completely without problems. This chapter puts critical realism forward as an alternative philosophical underpinning for IS research. Critical realism starts from an ontology that identifies structures and mechanisms, through which events and discourses are generated, as being fundamental to the constitution of our natural and social reality. The chapter presents critical realism and how it can be used in IS research. Examples of how critical realism have been used and can be used in research aiming at generating new IS theory, IS evaluation research, and IS design science research are provided.

Structural equation modeling (SEM) techniques have significant potential for assessing and modifying theoretical models. There have been 171 applications of SEM in IS research, published in major journals, most of which have been after 1994. Despite SEM's surging popularity in the IS field, it remains a complex tool that is often mechanically used but difficult to effectively apply. The purpose of this study is to review previous applications of SEM in IS research and to recommend guidelines to enhance the use of SEM to facilitate theory development. The authors review and evaluate SEM applications, both component-based (e.g., PLS) and covariance-based (e.g., LISREL), according to prescribed criteria. Areas of improvement are suggested which can assist application of this powerful technique in IS theory development.

Chapter VI

The aim of this chapter is to bridge the gap between what is known about IS theory and the specific characteristics of health to develop an evidence based health information systems theory. An initial background first sets the significance for the need to have a solid information systems theory in health and then argues that neither the information systems literature nor the health sector have been able to provide any satisfactory pathway to facilitate the adoption of information systems in health settings. The chapter further continues by reviewing the common pathway to develop information systems theory and the knowledge foundations used in the process, and then proceeds to highlight how this theory was developed. Subsequently, the building blocks (constructs, premises, supporting evidence and conclusions) that underpins the constructs and a brief explanation of the relationships between them is included. A discussion and limitation section is then followed by a conclusion.

Section II
Information System Development

Section II includes four chapters dedicated to understanding the process and practice of information systems development. The first chapter (Chapter VII) presents the language-action perspective (LAP) as an alternative foundation for analyzing and designing effective information systems. This is followed by chapter VIII analyzing recent developments linking design science to systems analysis and design research and the growing area of the work system method. The third chapter (Chapter IX) within this section attempts to quantify the value of flexibility in systems analysis and design research. To achieve this goal, the authors proposed a real options-based framework to value IT investments, taking risk into account. Finally, chapter X presents a detailed discussion on the theory of deferred action for explaining the effect of emergence on the rational design of information systems.

The Language-action perspective (LAP) provides an alternative foundation for analyzing and designing effective information systems. The fundamental principle of the LAP approach is people perform actions through communication; therefore, the role of information systems is to support such communications among people to achieve business goals. Basing on linguistic and communicative theories, the LAP approach provides guidance for researchers to gain understanding on how people use communication to coordinate their activities to achieve common goal. Web services, a leading technology to develop information systems, aims to support communication among services to achieve business goals. The close match between fundamental principles of Web services and the LAP approach suggests that researchers can use the LAP approach as a theoretical guidance to analyze and resolve Web service problems. This chapter provides a comprehensive starting point for researchers, practitioners, and students to gain understanding of the LAP approach.

In this chapter the authors analyze recent developments linking design science to systems analysis and design research and the growing area of the work system method. As a result, possible directions in a research agenda related to the incorporation of work system method ideas in systems analysis and design are provided. These follow the conceptual framework for IS research developed by a previous study.

Though IT investments are risky by nature, most of the traditional investment valuation models do not have risk in account, leading to erroneous choices. This chapter bases itself in the dogma that flexibility is the key to handle the uncertainty and risk of the future, and therefore is also a philosophy that must be in the very foundations of IT investments, since IT is the basic foundation of so many businesses. Having the previous dogma as a basis, the authors state that flexibility is a vaccine against risk. As such, this flexibility must have a value. The problem the authors attempt to solve in this chapter is the quantification of such value. To achieve this goal, the authors proposed a real options-based framework to value IT investments, having risk in account.

Chapter X

The problem addressed is how to design rationally information systems for emergent organization. Complexity and emergence are new design problem that constrains rational design. The reconciliation of rationalism and emergence is achieved in the theory of deferred action by synthesizing rationalism and emergence. Theories on designing for normal organisation exist but most of them are borrowed from reference disciplines. The theory of deferred action is based in the information systems discipline and is presented as a theory to inform practice to improve the rational design of information systems for emergent organisation. It has the potential of becoming a reference theory for other disciplines in particular for organisation studies. As emergence is a core feature of complexity, the base theory for the theory of deferred action is complexity theory. The theory of deferred action explains the effect of emergence on the rational design of information systems. As a theory to inform practice it provides guidance in the form of design constructs on how to design rationally information systems for emergent organization

Section III
Innovation, Adoption and Diffusion

This section has five chapters addressing theoretical issues concerning adoption and diffusion of technological innovations. The first chapter (Chapter XI) integrates the two theories diffusion of innovation and capability theory for understanding adoption of new applications such electronic government in the context of developing country. The next chapter (Chapter XII) aims to establish whether evolutionary diffusion theory (EDT) could offer an instrument for determining acceptance levels of innovative technologies. The chapter suggests that EDT offers remarkable explanatory depth, applicable not only to analyzing the uptake of complex, multi-user technologies in organizational settings but to any e-business investigation requiring a system-wide perspective. The next chapter, chapter XIII, analyzes four alternative theories (theory of cognitive dissonance, social judgment theory, theory of passive learning, and self-perception theory) in light of the technology acceptance model (TAM) and suggests that these theories provide a reverse relationship in contrast to the traditional attitude-behavior relationship in TAM. The fourth chapter in this section (Chapter XIV) introduces diffusion of innovations (DOI) as a research problem theory applied to examining a business case involving the replacement of enterprise systems by a large risk-averse public sector university in Australasia. Finally, chapter XV explores the technology acceptance model and other theories of user acceptance.

Mahmud Akhter Shareef, Carleton University, Canada

Vinod Kumar, Carleton University, Canada

Uma Kumar, Carleton University, Canada

Ahsan Akhter Hasin, Bangladesh University of Engineering & Technology, Bangladesh

E-government (EG) enables governments to provide citizens easier and electronic access to information and modernized services through personal computers, kiosks, telephones, and other resources. Information and communication technology (ICT) is the prime driving force of EG. Therefore, before implementing an EG project, it is vital to investigate the capability of developing countries to adopt ICT and research the impact of adopting ICT in that society. The authors argue that the purposes of implementing EG can only be accomplished and the full benefits of EG realized if a majority of the population of developing countries has the ability to adopt ICT, the main driver of EG. Therefore, it is essential for policy makers of developing countries to study the adoption capability of ICT of citizens prior to launching EG. Otherwise, there is the strong possibility that EG projects could not accomplish the purpose of its implementation and could fail to reduce the digital divide, establish equal rights for all citizens, and promote good governance.

Linda Wilkins, RMIT University, Australia

Paula Swatman, University of South Australia, Australia

Duncan Holt, RAYTHEON, Australia

Improved understanding of issues affecting uptake of innovative technology is important for the further development of e-business and its integration into mainstream business activities. An explanatory theory that can provide a more effective instrument for determining acceptance levels should therefore be of interest to IS practitioners and researchers alike. The authors aimed to establish whether evolutionary diffusion theory (EDT) could offer such an instrument, developing a set of axioms derived from the EDT literature and applying these to an in-depth review of two e-business implementations: a G2B document delivery system introduced by the Australian Quarantine Inspection Service (AQIS) across a number of industry sectors; and an enterprise-wide system implementation in a local government instrumentality. The authors found EDT offered remarkable explanatory depth, applicable not only to analysing uptake of complex, multi-user technologies in organisational settings but to any e-business investigation requiring a system-wide perspective.

Ahmed Y. Mahfouz, Prairie View A&M University, USA

Based on the theory of reasoned action, the technology acceptance model (TAM) has been one of the most widely used theories in management information systems research. This chapter proposes several alternative theories from the literature to TAM. Four theories are showcased that actually reveal a reverse relationship in contrast to the traditional attitude-behavior relationship in TAM. These four theories are theory of cognitive dissonance, social judgment theory, theory of passive learning, and self-perception theory. Other alternatives to TAM and other popular theories are flow theory, cognitive load theory, capacity information processing theory, and information processing theory. These theories are applicable in e-commerce, online consumer behavior, online shopping, immersive gaming, virtual social interactions, and cognitive research. Pragmatic examples are shown for the theories.

Chapter XIV

The literature review on case study design does not explain how the complex relationships (the issues) in a case study are identified. A top down approach, borrowing from argumentation theory, is a distinct contribution of this chapter which introduces the diffusion of innovations (DOI) as a research problem theory applied to the examination of a business case involving the replacement of enterprise systems by a large risk-averse public sector university in Australasia. The business case document is intended to diffuse the innovation to upper management for funding. But, there is a lack of diffusion study about the business case stage (the process) and the business case document (the outcome) as the construct that affects the innovation and its diffusion. A crucial component of the said diffusion research is designing the case study and mitigating the risks of theory-practice inconsistencies. Critical to mitigating that threat are the complex relationships (issues) that should be thoroughly identified. The context of the research provides experiential practical knowledge and analytical lenses to understand the essential components of a case study and the controversies affecting the rigour in the research design. This makes the top down approach of identifying the issues a good methodological base of designing a single-case study in a particular context. It can be useful to post-graduate and PhD students.

As global business markets become increasingly competitive, firms look to information technology to manage and improve their performance. Timely and accurate information is a key to gaining performance efficiency. Yet, firms may invest in technology only to find that their users are not willing to accept and use the new technology. This chapter explores the technology acceptance model and other theories of user acceptance.

Section IV
Management Theories

There are five chapters included within this section. The first chapter (Chapter XVI) provides a resource-based perspective on information technology, knowledge management, and firm performance. The second chapter in the section (Chapter XVII) analyses electronic marketplaces by using transaction cost theory. Chapter XVIII presents a conceptual framework in which social networking plays a mediating role in

Chapter XVI

     Clyde W. Holsapple, University of Kentucky, USA
     Jiming Wu, California State University–East Bay, USA

The resource-based view of the firm attributes superior firm performance to organizational resources that are valuable, rare, non-substitutable, and difficult to imitate. Aligned with this view, the authors contend that both information technology (IT) and knowledge management (KM) comprise critical organizational resources that contribute to superior firm performance. The authors also examine the relationship between IT and KM, and develop a new second-order variable – IT-KM competence – with IT capability and KM performance as its formative indicators. Thus, this chapter contributes not only by investigating the determinants of firm performance but also by broadening our understanding of the relationships among IT, KM, and firm performance.

Chapter XVII

     Cecilia Rossignoli, University of Verona, Italy
     Lapo Mola, University of Verona, Italy
     Antonio Cordella, LSE-London School of Economics and Political Science, UK

The aim of this chapter is to analyse electronic marketplaces from an organisational point of view. These marketplaces are considered as a particular form of electronic network and are analysed from the perspective of transaction cost theory. This chapter considers the three classical effects identified by Malone et al. (communication effect, electronic integration effect, electronic mediation effect), and also evaluates a fourth effect on the grounds of empirical evidence; this effect is defined by Wigand as "the strategic electronic network effect." Adopting the case study approach, the chapter describes how ICT affects marketplace organisation, and reshapes relationships among the actors involved in this particular type of electronic network.

Chapter XVIII

     Qun Wu, University of Arkansas-Little Rock, USA
     Jiming Wu, California State University, East Bay, USA
     Juan Ling, Georgia College & State University, USA

While some studies have found a significant link between information technology (IT) and firm performance, others have observed negative or zero returns on IT investments. One explanation for the mixed findings is that the causal link from IT to firm performance may be mediated. However, previous information system (IS) research has paid relatively little attention to such mediators. In this chapter, the authors develop a conceptual framework in which social network plays a mediating role in the relationship between IT usage and firm performance. Specifically, IT usage helps organizations strengthen inter- and intra-organizational networks, which, in turn, enhance firm performance.

Chapter XIX

John McAvoy, University College Cork, Ireland
Tom Butler, University College Cork, Ireland

Information system development, like information systems adoption, can be considered to be a change process; yet problems arise when change is introduced. Resistance to the change can develop and the reasoning behind the resistance needs to be determined in order to address it. Resistance can be straightforward, where the change threatens a person's job or creates stress for individuals, yet resistance can also be hidden and complex. Individuals may describe themselves as supporting a change, yet they work against that change (even if they are unaware that they are doing so). When this is happening, competing commitments can be at play; a competing commitment is where an individual professes a commitment to a course of action yet works against that commitment in different, usual subconscious, ways. The competing commitments process is a means of identifying why resistance is occurring even though individuals profess support.

Chapter XX

Tom Butler, University College Cork, Ireland
Ciaran Murphy, University College Cork, Ireland

Recent studies have highlighted the utility of the resource-based view (RBV) in understanding the development and application of IT capabilities and resources in organisations. Nevertheless, IS research has inadvertently carried over several fundamental problems and weaknesses with the RBV from reference disciplines. This chapter proposes an integrative theory, model and research propositions that draws on dynamic capabilities theory from the resource-based view of the firm in institutional economics, and commitment theory in institutional sociology, to explain and understand the process by which IT capabilities and resources are developed and applied in organizations. In so doing, this study addresses the paucity of theory on the role of IT capabilities in building and leveraging firm-specific IT resources. The chapter also addresses the aforementioned problems and weaknesses to build a logically consistent and falsifiable theory, with relatively superior explanatory power, for application in both variance and process-based research, whether positivist or interpretivist in orientation.

Section V
Marketing Theory

There are two chapters in Section V. The first chapter (Chapter XXI) reviews past research around information systems facilitating customer services and identifies the technical and social attributes of IT-enabled customer service systems, as well as the functionalities of customer service systems enabled by these attributes. Finally, chapter XXII presents expectation-confirmation theory (ECT) suggesting that satisfaction is determined by the interplay of prior expectations and perception of delivery. This chapter provides an overview of ECT applications in IS research and demonstrates how polynomial regression analysis allows for a more robust set of models.

Chapter XXI

Tsz-Wai Lui, Cornell University, USA
Gabriele Piccoli, Universitá di Sassari, Italy

As the use of customer service as a tool to create customer value and differentiation continues to increase, the set of customer services that surround the product rather than the product alone will increasingly become a source of competitive advantage and one of the most critical core business processes. However, there is a lack of a strong conceptual foundation for a service economy and a lack of theoretical guidance for optimal customer service systems design. In this chapter, the authors review past research around information systems facilitating customer services and identify the technical and social attributes of IT-enabled customer service systems, as well as the functionalities of customer service systems enabled by these attributes. Moreover, given the key role of customers as co-producers of the customer service experience, the authors address the role of customers' characteristics in IT-enabled customer service systems. Finally, they identify existing research gaps and call for future research in these areas.

Chapter XXII

James J. Jiang, University of Central Florida, USA & National Taiwan University, ROC
Gary Klein, The University of Colorado at Colorado Springs, USA

Expectation-confirmation theory (ECT) posits that satisfaction is determined by interplay of prior expectations and perception of delivery. As such, there are many applications in research and practice that employ an ECT model. The descriptive power allows independent investigations manipulating either of the components and a format to examine just why clients are satisfied (or not) with a particular product or service. However, the use of ECT can be impeded by a seeming lack of analysis techniques able to handle the difficulties inherent in the model, restricting information system (IS) researchers to limit the model to less descriptive and analytical accuracy. This chapter provides an overview of ECT applications in IS research and demonstrates how polynomial regression analysis (PRA) allows for a more robust set of models.

Section VI
Sociological and Cultural Theories

This section includes five chapters. The first chapter (Chapter XXIII) presents various aspects (including background, premises, key concepts and ideas, and critique) of the prominent sociological theory actor network theory. The next chapter (Chapter XXIV) presents various dimensions of another prominent social theory called social capital theory. Chapter XXV reviews the origins, approaches and roles associated with using cultural historical activity theory in information systems research. The fourth chapter (Chapter

XXVI) performs a citation analysis on Hofstede's Culture's Consequences in IS research to re-examine how IS research has used Hofstede's national culture dimensions. Finally, chapter XXVI introduces and discusses domestication theory and its relevance and importance to information systems research.

Actor network theory is a sociological theory that emerged as a useful vehicle to study technology and information systems. This chapter gives the reader some background about the development and emergence of this sociological theory. It reviews some of the premises of the theory and introduces the reader to key concepts and ideas. It also presents some of the critique of the theory, ANT authors' response, and the implication on IS research. This chapter also gives the reader an overview of the application of ANT in different streams of IS research.

Social capital represents resources or assets rooted in an individual's or in a group's network of social relations. It is a multidimensional and multilevel concept which has been characterized by a diversity of definitions and conceptualizations which focus on the structure and/or on the content of the social relations. A common conceptualization of social capital in information systems research consists of a structural, relational and cognitive dimension. The structural dimension represents the configuration of the social network and the characteristics of its ties. The relational dimension represents assets embedded in the social relations such as trust, obligations, and norms of reciprocity. The cognitive dimension represents a shared context which facilitates interactions and is created by shared codes, language and narratives. For a single or multiple members of a network, social capital can be a source of solidarity, information, cooperation, collaboration and influence. Social capital has been and remains a sound theory to study information systems in research areas affected by social relations and the assets embedded in them.

This chapter reviews the origins, approaches and roles associated with the use of cultural historical activity theory (CHAT) in information systems (IS) research. The literature is reviewed and examples are discussed from IS and related fields of human-computer interaction (HCI), computer supported cooperative work (CSCW) and computer supported collaborative learning (CSCL), to illustrate the power of CHAT in IS research as well as its link to appropriate research methods. After explicating the value of its use, the chapter concludes by discussing theoretical and methodological implications of applications of CHAT in examining real-world problems in IS research.

In this chapter, the authors performed a citation analysis on Hofstede's Culture's Consequences in IS research to re-examine how IS research has used Hofstede's national culture dimensions. The authors give a brief history of Hofstede's research, and review Hofstede's cultural dimensions and the measurement of them. They then present the results from a previous study (Ford, Connelly and Meister 2003) and follow-up citation analysis. The authors examine the extent to which Hofstede's national culture dimensions inform IS research, what areas of IS research have used them, and what changes have occurred since the original citation analysis.

This chapter introduces and discusses domestication theory - essentially about giving technology a place in everyday life - and its relevance and importance to information systems (IS) research. The authors discuss domestication within the context of the social shaping of technology and critique use and adoption theories more widely found in IS studies. The chapter illustrates how domestication theory underpins studies of how Irish households find ways of using computers (or not) in their everyday life and research into the use of ICTs in UK gendered households.

Section VII

Psychological and Behavioral Theories

The final section on psychological and behavioral theories includes four chapters. The first chapter (Chapter XXVIII) outlines personal construct theory as a psychological theory and discusses current applications of methodologies based in the theory. It also explores the positioning of the theory within a broader taxonomy of IS theory. The next chapter (Chapter XXIX) presents coping theory, its underlying assumptions and inherent components, discusses its application, highlights the complementarities with existing models and theories currently used in IS research, and provides several areas for future research. Chapter XXX uses and tests vocational theory and personality traits of information technology professionals. Finally, chapter XXXI describes and illustrates the use of the theory of planned behavior and the theory of reasoned action for predicting technology adoption behavior.

The development of any discipline is related to the strength of its underpinning theoretical base. Well-established disciplines have a diversity of clearly stated and competing theoretical frameworks to describe and explain theoretical constructs. Information systems (IS) is a relatively new discipline; many well-known IS theories (such as the technology acceptance model, theory of reasoned action and theory of planned behaviour) are borrowed from disciplines such as economics and psychology. This chapter outlines personal construct psychology, a psychological theory. Current applications of methodologies based in personal construct theory are discussed, and the positioning of the theory within a broader taxonomy of IS theory is explored.

New information technology implementations, as major modifications to existing ones, bring about changes in the work environment of individuals that trigger an important adaptation process. Extant research on the adaptation process individuals go through when a new IT is implemented in their working environment is rather limited. Furthermore, variance theories and models useful to explain IT adoption and use are not well suited to study the dynamics underlying the adaptation process. Coping theory, because it links antecedents, adaptation behaviors, and outcomes altogether, provides a rich lens through which we can study individuals' IT-related adaptation process. A better understanding of this process will enable researchers and practitioners to understand and predict IT acceptance and related behaviors and thus to better manage them. This chapter presents coping theory, its underlying assumptions and inherent components, discusses its application, highlights the complementarities with existing models and theories currently used in IS research, and provides several areas for future research in this area.

Drawing on Holland's (1985, 1996) vocational theory and based on a sample of 9,011 IT professionals, two research questions were investigated. On what personality traits do IT professionals differ from other occupations and which of these are also related to their career satisfaction? Five traits met both these criteria—emotional resilience, openness, tough-mindedness, and customer service—for which IT professionals had higher scores, and conscientiousness, for which they had lower scores. IT career satisfaction was also positively related to extraversion, agreeableness/teamwork, assertiveness, optimism, tough-mindedness, work drive, and visionary style. Results are discussed in terms of the fit of these traits with IT work and the value of these insights for personnel-management functions like selection, training, professional development, and career planning.

Mahmud Akhter Shareef, Carleton University, Canada
Vinod Kumar, Carleton University, Canada
Uma Kumar, Carleton University, Canada
Ahsan Akhter Hasin, Bangladesh University of Engineering & Technology, Bangladesh

Research related to the impact of individual characteristics in their acceptance of online systems driven by information and communication technology (ICT) observed that dissimilarities among individuals influence their adoption and use of the systems. Thus, research streams investigating this issue generally follow the traditions of the theory of reasoned action (TRA) or the theory of planned behavior (TPB). Research reveals that individual characteristics, mediated by beliefs, affect attitudes, which affect intentions and behaviors. These two major behavioral theories related to technology acceptance and the intention to use technology might provide significant theoretical paradigms in understanding how online system adoption and diffusion, driven by information technology, can vary globally. In this study, the authors' first objective is to understand TRA and TPB as they study ICT-based online adoption and diffusion globally. Then, based on that theoretical framework, their second objective focuses on developing a theory of ICT adoption and diffusion as an online behavior.

Foreword

Theoretical models, and the underlying theories, are important in research because they help us, as researchers, to "organise our thoughts, generate coherent explanations and improve our predictions" (Hambrick, 2007). Indeed, it has been suggested by many (e.g., McKay and Marshall, 2001), that theory is indispensable to research, that research without theory is an oxymoron. In similar vein, Kurt Lewin (1945, p.129), has observed that "there is nothing so practical as a good theory." However, "the obverse is also true: nothing is as dangerous as a bad theory" (Ghoshal, 2005, p.86)! The extent to which a theory is good or bad, practical or impractical, safe or dangerous, is both a matter of degree and a function of a researcher's sensitivity to the application context. Furthermore, theories do not constitute an end in themselves, but are merely means to an end. If they help us to understand and describe a phenomenon more accurately and comprehensively, if we can rely on theories as to predict behaviour more consistently, then their usefulness is demonstrated. If, however, they obfuscate that understanding, then their value would be in jeopardy.

It is widely recognised that the appropriate application of theory is desirable in IS research. However, while a number of theories and the associated theoretical models have attracted strong (even excessive) levels of interest, until recently there has been no single source of information where interested researchers, and in particular research students, could access a range of these theories and models illuminated by empirical data sourced from different contexts and interpreted according to the dictates of different epistemological persuasions. With this handbook, the situation has changed. I fully expect that the handbook will prove to be an invaluable and influential guide to theoretical models in IS research. In reading the various chapters in this edited volume, readers will encounter a range of theories and models illustrated through different contexts. These chapters are persuasive accounts of how theory can be applied and how theoretical models can be drawn up to predict relationships. In this respect, the handbook is most useful.

However, I caution researchers to pay particular care to the process of selecting a theory for a specific context and indeed to evaluate it against competing theories that may be more practical, useful or relevant for their given context. The practicality, usefulness or relevance of a theory is a key point here: theories can (and should) not only be tested and re-validated, but also extended, modified, rescoped or refuted. Researchers have an obligation to apply theories carefully, and to consider the need for a theory to be revised according to their interpretation of its application. As Karl Weick (1989, 1999) has commented, we need theories that are useful, relevant to practice and that help us to understand phenomena more effectively. Such *relevant to practice* theories will ideally help us to take action so as to cause positive consequences.

Dr. Robert M Davison,
City University of Hong Kong, Hong Kong

REFERENCES

Ghoshal, S. (2005). Bad management theories are destroying good management practices. *Academy of Management Learning and Education, 4*(1), 75-91.

Hambrick, D. (2007). The field of management's devotion to theory: Too much of a good thing? *Academy of Management Journal, 50*(6), 1346-1352.

Lewin, K. (1945). The research center for group dynamics at Massachusetts Institute of Technology. *Sociometry, 8*, 126-136.

McKay, J., & Marshall, P. (2001). The dual imperatives of action research. *Information Technology & People, 14*(1), 46-59.

Weick, K.E. (1989). Theory construction as disciplined imagination. *Academy of Management Review, 14*(4), 516-531.

Weick, K.E. (1999). Theory construction as disciplined reflexivity: Tradeoffs in the 90s. *Academy of Management Review, 14*(4), 797-806.

Robert Davison *is an associate professor of information systems at the City University of Hong Kong. His current research focuses on virtual knowledge management and collaboration in the Chinese SME context. He has published over 50 articles in a variety of journals. Davison holds editorial positions for the Electronic Journal of Information Systems in Developing Countries, the Information Systems Journal, Information Technology & People and MIS Quarterly. He has also edited special issues of the IEEE Transactions on Engineering Management (Cultural Issues and IT Management), the Communications of the ACM (Global Application of Collaborative Technologies), Information Technology & People (Virtual Work, Teams and Organisations) and the Information Systems Journal (Information Systems in China). For more details see: http://www.is.cityu. edu.hk/staff/isrobert*

Foreword

The oft-quoted dictum of Kurt Lewin in 1945 that "nothing is so practical as a good theory" remains relevant today. A good theory is practical because it helps us to systemize knowledge in ways that are fruitful for both research and professional practice. In research a good theory assists with the cumulative building of knowledge, as it shows areas in which there is some consensus on what is known or agreed and also points to directions where further work is required. Expressing theory explicitly also provides opportunities for researchers to test the theory and make further advances. Good theory also systemizes knowledge in ways that make it easier to disseminate that knowledge and have it widely understood so that it can be used to inform or be acted upon in practice. Further, a good theory has some credibility: it has stood the test of time to some degree and has been assessed against empirical evidence so that we are willing to trust its applicability.

To illustrate what we can hope for in a good theory in the social sciences we can look at the example of the theory of the *Diffusion of Innovations*, originally developed by Everett Rogers in his book released in 1962. Rogers based his theory on his own work studying the adoption decisions of farmers and also on a review of many other studies of innovations of different types in many different contexts. Thus, the theory drew on a strong empirical base, which added to its credibility. The theory has lessons for practice in that it provides advice that can be acted upon by change agents wishing to introduce innovations. A sign that Rogers' theory has been influential is that his work is one of the most highly cited books in the social sciences.

Despite such good examples there remains some lack of understanding of what is meant by theory and how we should theorize. In management there has been debate for a period of time, with issues in the *Academy of Management Review* (1989, Vol. 14, No. 4) and the *Administrative Science Quarterly* (1995, Vol. 40, No. 3) devoted to problems with theorizing. In the social sciences there is also an acknowledgement that consensus on theoretical positions might be more difficult to obtain than in the natural sciences (see Glick et al., 2007).

The field of information systems has problems of its own in relation to theory. The fields of study relating to information technology are relatively new and there is not a long tradition to draw on to explain what is meant by theory and theorizing. As information systems is also inherently an interdisciplinary field, concerned with both the study of technology and the study of human behavior, there are problems in that there are a number of competing traditions jostling for out attention. In information systems we have scholars with backgrounds in diverse fields, from mathematics to management and the natural sciences, all of whom have grown up with their own particular perspectives on the knowledge creation process and theorizing. In my own work I have endeavored to reconcile some of these different views by pointing out that we can have different types of theory, depending on our goals: whether to analyse, explain, predict or to guide design and action (Gregor, 2006).

Further, possibly because of the newness of the field of information systems, we are still finding our way with the development of strong mature theory that is distinct from other disciplines. Weber (2003) makes a good argument for our "own" theory that will characterize our field. Regrettably, it appears that we are still struggling to identify these strong theories that are unique to information systems.

Given this background the publication of the present volume is more than timely, as it addresses a number of difficult but important issues. Foundational work is included that addresses issues such as the nomological network for information systems theory, the use of structuration theory to cope with different levels of analysis and the grounded theory approach. Other chapters show how theory can be developed for a number of our important problem areas in information systems.

The authors and editors of the book are to be commended in undertaking this initiative and giving greater prominence to the valuable work that is being done to advance the state of information systems theory.

Professor Shirley Gregor
The Australian National University, Australia

REFERENCES

Glick, W.H., Miller, C.C., & Cardinal, L. (2007). Making a life in the field of organization science. *Journal of Organizational Behavior, 28*, 817-835.

Gregor, S. (2006). The nature of theory in information systems. *MIS Quarterly, 30*(3), 611-642.

Lewin, K. (1945). The research centre for group dynamics at Massachusetts Institute of Technology. *Sociometry, 8*, 126-135.

Rogers, E. (1962). *Diffusion of Innovation* (1st Ed.). New York: The Free Press.

Weber, R. (2003). Editor's comments. *MIS Quarterly, 27*(2), iii-xi.

Shirley Gregor *is the ANU Endowed Chair in Information Systems at the Australian National University, Canberra, where she heads the National Centre for Information Systems Research. Professor Gregor's research interests include the adoption and strategic use of information and communications technologies, intelligent systems and the philosophy of technology. Professor Gregor spent a number of years in the computing industry in Australia and the United Kingdom before beginning an academic career. She obtained her PhD in information systems from the University of Queensland. Dr Gregor's publications include publications in journals such as Management Information Systems Quarterly, Journal of the Association of Information Systems, European Journal of Information Systems, Journal of Strategic Information Systems, International Journal of Electronic Commerce and the International Journal of Human Computer Studies.*

Foreword

From its early days in the 1970s to present day, information systems (IS) research has undergone a huge metamorphosis from descriptive explorations to theory building efforts. Along the way, vast improvements have been made in methodological rigor and instrumentation design. Many researchers have contributed to the field by defining and providing guidelines for conducting positivistic and interpretive research, as well as explicating various methodologies in the IS context (e.g., surveys, case studies, experimentation, grounded theory, historical analysis, and design science).

A common denominator in the past thirty five years has been the need to base our research on theoretical foundations and build theory so that it allows cumulative work and has sustainable value. While many strides have been made, we are still in infancy in our understanding of theory and its proper use in IS research. From personal experience, not too long ago, while teaching a doctoral seminar, I was confronted with something as simple explaining the different types of research models to my students. It turned out to be a challenge and we had to develop a taxonomy of research models ourselves (Palvia, et al., 2006). It is therefore heartening to note that the editors of this book have taken a very positive step in providing the IS research community the latest and state-of-the-art knowledge about theoretical foundations in IS research.

I have examined the collection of chapters in this volume. I am impressed both by the breadth and the depth of the material included in the book. The book is comprehensive. The contributions have been made by experts in various domains. In the early chapters, the authors describe the process of theory building and extension. Later, they investigate specific theories and their applicability in the IS context. The IS field is interdisciplinary. In my view, therefore, it must be open and willing to embrace existing knowledge and theories from other disciplines. The editors have carefully included theories from various disciplines, such as management, marketing, sociology, culture, and psychology. They have cast a wide net to the benefit of our readers and the IS research community.

I am sure this book will be an excellent source of knowledge for IS researchers and will have a long shelf life as a useful reference.

Professor Prashant Palvia
The University of North Carolina at Greensboro, USA

REFERENCES

Palvia, P., Midha, V., & Pinjani, P. (2006). Research models in information systems. *Communications of the Association for Information Systems, 17*, 1042-1063.

Prashant Palvia *is Joe Rosenthal Excellence Professor and director of the McDowell Research Center in the Bryan School of Business & Economics at the University of North Carolina at Greensboro (UNCG). Dr. Palvia served as department head from 2000 to 2004 and Information Systems PhD Director from 2003 to 2008. Prior to 25 years in academics, he had 9 years of industry experience. He received his PhD, MBA and MS from the University of Minnesota and BS from the University of Delhi, India. Prof. Palvia received UNCG's senior research excellence award in 2005. He is a leading authority in the field of Global Information Technology Management (GITM) and chairs the annual GITMA world conference, the next one being in Mexico City, Mexico in June 2009. Professor Palvia is the editor-in-chief of the Journal of Global Information Technology Management (JGITM), and is on editorial board of several journals. His research interests include global information technology management, virtual teams, open source software, electronic commerce, media choice theory, and trust in exchange relationships. He has published over eighty journal articles including in MIS Quarterly, Decision Sciences, Communications of the ACM, Communications of the AIS, Information & Management, Decision Support Systems, and ACM Transactions on Database Systems, and over one hundred and fifty conference articles. He has co-edited four books on global information technology management; the last one was published in May 2007.*

Foreword

I've spent 40 years conducting information systems research and publishing in academic journals. During this time, I've seen many changes:

- There are more publication outlets for IS research. In particular, there are a large number of specialty journals, such as *Decision Support Systems*. But while this is the case, research-oriented universities still expect faculty to publish in the top-tier journals. This often translates into publishing in *MISQ*, *ISR*, and *JMIS*.
- The number of IS academics has grown. As a result, more scholars are trying to get their research published in a limited number of top-tier journals.
- Research is more specialized. Most of the articles in the top journals are of interest only to the people doing research in that area. There are fewer articles that appeal to a broad audience.
- Academic journals have higher expectations about the rigor of the research methods and data analysis methods used. Case studies are now rare and research studies with extensive multivariate data analyses are common.
- The "packaging" of research is more structured and important. Journals expect manuscripts to be organized and written in specific ways.
- Reviewers are more demanding. Manuscript reviews may be as long as the manuscript itself. And even after revisions are made, there is no guarantee that the manuscript will be accepted for publication.

Theses changes have consequences. It is more difficult and time consuming to conduct and publish research, especially in the leading journals. Junior faculty find it challenging to publish a sufficient quantity of high-quality research to beat the tenure clock. Some people worry that the value of more rigorous, specialized research comes at the cost of decreased relevance to practitioners.

There is another significant change that has taken place: the emphasis on theory-based research. Doctoral programs now require significantly more theory-oriented coursework. The leading journals expect research to either make a significant contribution to theory building or theory testing. This is a significant departure from the past when the only research requirement was to use the literature to show that the research question was important and that the research study and methods were an appropriate way to study the phenomenon under investigation.

There are many excellent reasons for making IS research theory based:

- The use of theory helps build a cumulative body of knowledge. New theories can be developed. Existing theories can be tested or extended. Without theory, there is greater risk that studies are fragmented and provide inconsistent findings. This was a frequent lament before IS research utilized theory more.

- Theory provides researchers with a better starting point. With theory, there is already a model or framework that identifies relevant constructs, variables, and casual relationships. As one of my colleagues, Dale Goodhue, describes it, "a theory is 'a stool' that you stand on to get a better view."
- Theory building and testing are the "gold standard" for research in the social sciences and other business disciplines. Scholars in other fields view IS research as more credible when it is consistent with the research norms in their disciplines. This is important for IS faculty when promotion and tenure decisions are made.

This book provides an excellent coverage of theory, both for learning about theories and how to apply them and as a reference book for conducting theory-based research. Many of the leading theories used in IS research are discussed and illustrated, and there are many excellent chapters that explore how to conduct theory-based research.

Though theory offers many benefits, it should be recognized that there are potential downsides to its use in IS research. Most specifically, it can negatively affect the relevancy of the research. Let's explore this concern.

Any theory, whether it is transaction cost theory or the resource-based theory of the firm, provides a particular "lens" though which a phenomenon is viewed. The problem occurs when the lens is inappropriate for the interests of practice. How the research question is framed and the questions asked are not aligned with practitioners' interests. It sometimes seems that the use of theory is driving the research questions rather than allowing the researcher to investigate the questions that are really of interest to practitioners.

Appropriate theory may not exist for some new, interesting topics. Several years ago when I was conducting research on executive information systems, I became convinced that the inclusion of "soft" information (e.g., interpretations of data) is positively associated with EIS success. I had even collected and analyzed data that supported the contention. When I presented the research at practitioner conferences, I drew large audiences that reacted well to the findings. But when I tried to publish the research in a leading journal, I encountered problems. There wasn't any theory that provided a satisfactory framework for the research. The research was ultimately published in a lesser journal that was less concerned about the lack of theory.

The requirements for doing high-quality, theory-based research results in long cycle times, which limits the timeliness of the research. It takes time to identify appropriate theory, apply the constructs, refine the items for the constructs, test the instrument(s), collect and analyze the data, and write up the study findings. Add to this long review and revise cycles and it is easy to understand why IS research typically lags the needs of practice. In fact, it isn't usually wise to investigate temporal issues because the research isn't likely to be published before less rigorous, practitioner research becomes the conventional wisdom.

Though there are downsides to the use of theory, I'm not suggesting that theory should not be used. The potential benefits are too great. Rather, I believe that the academy should be more flexible in terms of the kinds of theory that are deemed acceptable. Interesting, important research should not be rejected just because the theory base is not deemed to be strong enough.

I believe that a way to increase the relevancy of IS research is for the academy to be more supportive of "Little t" research. Let me discuss the concept of "Big T" versus "Little t" theory, which Alan Dennis and Joe Valacich first introduced to me.

A Big T is a well-recognized theory, such as the theory of reasoned action. It contributes to our ability to understand and predict a phenomenon and can be applied to multiple settings. It provides a solid foundation for building a research model and other research can build on the theory. It adds to the power of specific research findings when the theory is substantiated.

By way of contrast, a Little t is often a new and less developed theory. Some people may not even view it as a theory. It may be as simple as a list of steps, such as Kotter's organizational transformation model or a 2X2 matrix like the strategic grid. A Little t is the type of theory or model that is often taught in classes. A Little t is often phenomenon specific and may be used to either frame or be the output of research.

If the academy was more accepting of Little t research, it would make IS research more approachable and relevant to the business community. Studies could be framed in ways that are more relevant to practice. The time required to conduct the research would be reduced. The research methodologies and statistical methods used might be less difficult for practitioners to understand.

I'm not arguing against Big T research. We need research that transcends the temporal issues of the day and develops understandings that can be applied to new but related phenomenon. However, what I would like to see is more of a balance. Let's also support research that can be readily used by the business community and taught in our classes.

Whether theories are big T or little t, they guide our thinking as they guide our research. This book is a comprehensive and valuable resource for anyone interested in the theoretical underpinnings of information systems research. It includes papers that explore the formation, development, testing, and extension of theory within the field. The authors come from 49 universities in 13 countries, and thus represent a cross-section of contemporary thinking about theory. I believe that theory should be relevant to all our stakeholders – researchers, students, and practising managers – and this book provides value to each of these groups.

Professor Hugh J. Watson
The University of Georgia, USA

Hugh J. Watson *is a professor of MIS and a holder of a C. Herman and Mary Virginia Terry Chair of Business Administration in the Terry College of Business at the University of Georgia. Watson is a leading scholar and authority on decision support, having authored 22 books and over 100 scholarly journal articles. He is a fellow of The Data Warehousing Institute and the Association for Information Systems and is the senior editor of the Business Intelligence Journal. For the past 20 years, Watson has been the consulting editor for John Wiley & Sons' MIS series.*

Preface

Theory is generally considered to be the bedrock of academic research, the foundation upon which scientific enquiry is organized and built. Yet, for many of us, theory is a 'black box', something that we know must be present in research, but for which very little guidance is provided. Indeed, when research papers are rejected by journals, or challenged at conferences, it is more often than not due to problems with theory (or a lack of theory). We have seen many examples of this in our own careers as journal and conference editors. While there are well established norms and guidelines to remedy problems with statistical methods and research design, issues with theory are much less obvious to diagnose and resolve. Thus, the objective of this Handbook is to address the following question – How can the use of theory be improved in IS research?

To answer such a question, it is important to examine the diversity of the various theories and models used in IS research. In particular, IS research draws heavily upon theories developed in a variety of complementary disciplines, such as Computer Science, Psychology, Sociology, Management, Economics, and Mathematics. IS research has developed or appropriated theories to examine central disciplinary themes such as IS development, adoption, implementation, training, and application, as well as strategic, social and political factors. The ISWorld wiki site[1] 'Theories Used in IS Research' has listed more than fifty such theories and models. While this resource provides a very useful starting point to locate and learn about various theories, it does not provide the kind of depth that many researchers require when deciding whether or not to use a particular theory in their research. Links provided to articles that have used a theory can be helpful, but once again, these papers may not present a full account of the theory, or they may offer a slightly modified and fragmented version.

Indeed, finding information about theory can be difficult and intimidating for new researchers. We have seen multiple instances of submissions either lacking theory or using it inappropriately. Even if a researcher manages to identify an appropriate theory for undertaking research, he or she may struggle to determine an appropriate research design that complements the identified theory. Or worse, a researcher may begin with the research design and then try to retrofit a theory after the fact.

The above discussion suggests that despite its ubiquity throughout IS research, there is much that remains unknown about theory. In our view, many of the theories used in IS research are not particularly well understood by IS researchers. For instance, there are few frameworks that have been developed to organize the various theories employed in IS research, and there has been less than extensive work conducted to date on the categorization of the conceptual variables used in IS research. Furthermore, there is a general paucity of work that establishes theoretical ties between IS research and research in other disciplines. Consequently, the correct identification and application of theory becomes particularly challenging for all researchers, and particularly those who may be at the start of their academic careers. By rigorously studying and documenting the theories that have been developed and used within IS research, we believe that it is possible to advance the discipline.

The need for greater understanding of theory in IS research suggests that a literary and meta-analytic collection of IS-related theories and models not only provides a significant contribution to IS knowledge, but also provides a valuable aid to IS researchers. Therefore, the overall mission of the *Handbook of Research on Contemporary Theoretical Models in Information Systems* is to provide a comprehensive understanding and coverage of the various theories, models and related research approaches used within IS research. Specifically, it aims to focus on the following key objectives:

- To examine in detail a number of key theories and models applicable to studying IS/IT management issues;
- To provide a critical review/meta-analysis of IS/IT management articles that have used a particular theory/model;
- To link theories with appropriate research designs;
- To provide examples of real world applications of theories based on empirical analysis;
- To provide an understanding of traditional and contemporary methods for building and testing theory.

This Handbook contributes to a number of theories, models and research approaches. The theoretical contribution of this book is that it synthesizes the relevant literature in order to enhance knowledge of IS theories and models from various perspectives. Included in the Handbook is an extensive list of theories and models, including detailed descriptions of: actor-network theory, capability theory, commitment theory, coping theory, critical realism, cultural historical activity theory, diffusion of Innovations theory, domestication theory, evolutionary diffusion theory, dynamic capability theory, expectation-confirmation theory, grounded theory, Hofstede's cultural consequences, institutional theory, language action perspective, media richness theory, personal construct theory, the resource-based view of the firm, social network theory, social capital theory, structuration theory, the technology acceptance model (TAM), the theory of deferred action, the theory of competing commitments, the theory of planned behavior (TPB), the theory of reasoned action (TRA), transaction cost theory, the value of flexibility, vocational theory, the work systems life cycle (WSLC) model, as well as structural equation modelling (SEM). These theories and approaches have multi-disciplinary origins, suggesting that this Handbook not only contributes to the body of knowledge within the IS discipline but also to its contributing disciplines.

The Handbook is organized into 31 chapters, co-authored by 63 contributors from 49 different institutions/organizations located in 13 countries (namely, Australia, Bangladesh, Brazil, Canada, Ireland, Italy, New Zealand, Norway, Portugal, South Korea, Sweden, the United Kingdom, and the United States of America). Such geographical and institutional variety indicates that the Handbook has drawn on a collection of wide and diverse perspectives. The 31 chapters have been organized into seven sections, namely: Theory Development and Extension (6 Chapters); Information System Development (4 Chapters); Innovation, Adoption and Diffusion (5 Chapters); Management Theories (5 Chapters); Marketing Theories (2 Chapters); Sociological and Cultural Theories (5 Chapters); and Psychological and Behavioral Theories (4 Chapters).

Considering the richness and depth of the content, we firmly believe that this Handbook will be an excellent resource for readers who wish to learn about the various theories and models applicable to IS research, as well as those interested in finding out when and how to apply these theories and models in order to investigate diverse research issues. The chapters included in the Handbook are also useful for readers who are interested in learning about how various research approaches and methods fit with different theories. The target audience for the Handbook includes researchers and practitioners within the management disciplines in general, and within the IS field in particular.

We sincerely hope that this Handbook will provide a positive contribution to the area of Information Systems. In order to make further research progress and improvement in the understanding of theories and models, we would like to welcome feedback and comments about this handbook from readers. Comments and constructive suggestions can be sent to the Editors care of IGI Global at the address provided at the beginning of the handbook.

Sincerely,

Yogesh K. Dwivedi, Swansea University, UK
Banita Lal, Nottingham Trent University, UK
Michael D. Williams, Swansea University, UK
Scott L. Schneberger, Principia College, USA
Michael Wade, York University, Canada

November 26th, 2008

ENDNOTE

[1]   http://www.fsc.yorku.ca/york/istheory/wiki/index.php/Main_Page

Acknowledgment

A number of people have extended their help in the development of the ideas presented in this handbook. We take this opportunity to convey our regards and thanks to those who have helped and supported us at various stages in completion of this work.

This handbook would not have been possible without the cooperation and assistance of the authors, reviewers, editorial advisory board, our colleagues and the staff at IGI Global publishing. The editors would like to thank the people at IGI Global, namely: Kristin M. Klinger for handling the handbook proposal, Jan Travers for managing the contract, Jessica Thompson and Julia Mosemann for managing this project especially for answering queries and keeping project on schedule. A special word of thanks goes to the members of the Editorial Advisory Board for their continuous guidance and support in the editorial processes. A special word of thanks also goes to reviewers for their useful and constructive comments that have been incorporated in the final versions of the chapters. We are highly grateful to *Dr. Robert M Davison, Professor Shirley Gregor, Professor Prashant Palvia* and *Professor Hugh J. Watson* for providing the foreword.

Last but not least, we bestow our unbounded gratitude and deepest sense of respect to our families whose blessing, concerted efforts, constant encouragement and wholehearted co-operation enabled us to reach this milestone.

Yogesh K. Dwivedi, Swansea University, UK
Banita Lal, Nottingham Trent University, UK
Michael D. Williams, Swansea University, UK
Scott L. Schneberger, Principia College, USA
Michael Wade, York University, Canada

Section I
Theory Development and Extension

Section I includes six chapters dedicated to understanding new theory development and the extension of existing theory. The first chapter presents a broad perspective on the nature of the constructs and relationships explored in IS research and to develop a nomological network of the most salient relationships. The second chapter proposes a multilevel framework particularly useful for research involving complex and multilevel interactions. Chapter III provides a brief introduction to the grounded theory (GT) approach to research, discussing how it has been used in information systems (IS) research, and how GT studies may be conducted to provide a significant theoretical contribution to the management information systems (MIS) field. Chapter IV puts critical realism forward as an alternative philosophical underpinning for IS research. This chapter also provides examples of how critical realism have been used and can be used in research aiming at generating new IS theory, IS evaluation research, and IS design science research. The fifth chapter focuses on theory development but from quantitative perspectives. This chapter reviews previous applications of structural equation modeling (SEM) in IS research and recommends guidelines to using SEM for theory development. Finally, chapter VI proposes and describes an evidence-based "'health information system theory'."

Chapter I
Theoretical Constructs and Relationships in Information Systems Research

Brent Furneaux
York University, Canada

Michael Wade
York University, Canada

ABSTRACT

Constructs and the relationships between them are widely considered to be central to theory development and testing. Over time, information systems (IS) researchers have identified and explored an extensive set of relationships amongst a broad range of constructs. The result of these initiatives is a body of literature that can be considered to represent the cumulative learning of the discipline. Based on the premise that this cumulative learning is capable of providing valuable guidance to future theory development, the authors present a review and analysis of a large sample of empirical research published in two leading IS journals. The objective of this endeavor is to offer a broad perspective on the nature of the constructs and relationships explored in IS research and to develop a nomological network of the most salient relationships that can then serve to guide future research and to lend support to new and existing theory.

INTRODUCTION

The management and information systems (IS) literature provides IS researchers with numerous perspectives on the nature, use, and importance of sound theory to the conduct of rigorous research (e.g. Bacharach, 1989; Gregor, 2006; Sutton & Staw, 1995; Whetten, 1989). The views expressed in this literature have increasingly served to guide research inquiries such that the use of substantive theoretical foundations has become an essential hallmark of work considered suitable for publication in leading journals. Although our understanding of what is meant by good theory is the subject of at least some measure of controversy (Weick, 1995), the importance of constructs and relationships to theory development and testing appears to be widely accepted by both IS researchers and by those working in other disciplines. Some have gone so far as to argue that constructs and their relationships form the very essence of theory (Bacharach, 1989). Although others have argued that good theory must go beyond this to provide sound explanations for the relationships that are posited (Sutton & Staw, 1995; Whetten, 1989), they continue to maintain that constructs and relationships are essential to much of what we call theory.

Inadequate attention to the nature of the constructs and relationships underpinning a theory can have severe negative implications for its application and ultimate success. The importance and relevance of a theory that fails, for example, to adequately identify and define its constructs can be difficult or impossible to ascertain. Similarly, without a clear depiction of the nature of the relationships posited by a theory it can be difficult to elucidate the substantive implications that it may hold for practice or future research. Scientific philosophy argues further that our confidence in the validity of a theory is increased by subjecting its posited relationships to repeated empirical testing (Popper, 1992). Such efforts can be significantly hampered when constructs and relationships remain ambiguous or undefined with the result being needless impediments to subsequent theory development.

The centrality of constructs and relationships to the theory development process is highlighted by research methods that call for a thorough exploration of their essence as the basis for the development of new theory (e.g., Glaser & Strauss, 1967). The objective of these methods is, among other things, to ensure that theory more faithfully reflects actual circumstance rather than being a product of researcher bias. Drawing upon the spirit of such perspectives, we aim in the following discussion to report upon an extensive examina-

tion of the empirical findings in two leading IS journals during the period from the start of 1999 to the end of 2007. Rather than seeking to support or refute a particular theory or collection of theories, this examination seeks to depict what the empirical literature says about the many constructs and relationships that have been explored by IS researchers. Our analysis is based on the premise that over time the results of empirical testing yield a growing body of knowledge that can serve to underscore those theoretical explanations that are proving most robust, to identify empirically supported relationships that are in need of more substantive theoretical explanation, and to draw attention to those areas where both theory and empirical testing are lacking.

In the following discussion the reader is urged to take a step back and reflect on the wider findings of the IS discipline, in particular those findings that extend beyond the constraints of individual theoretical perspectives, in an effort to better understand the broader framework upon which the discipline rests. We commence our discussion with a presentation of the conceptual background for our work. Subsequent to this presentation we describe the methodology that was used to acquire and analyze our data and then report on the key findings that stem from this analysis. Finally, we conclude with a discussion of some of the implications of our analysis, an assessment of key limitations, and some closing remarks.

BACKGROUND

Theoretical Constructs and Relationships

Theoretical considerations guide many facets of the research that is conducted and reported upon in the field of information systems including research conceptualization and choice of methodology. Despite such attention and the frequent calls for more and better theorizing (Weber, 2003), the meaning of the term 'theory' remains the subject of considerable discussion (Gregor, 2006). Numerous conceptualizations of theory have been offered in the literature including perspectives that view it as a guide to future action and those that see it as offering a description of the state of some phenomenon or group of phenomena (Gregor, 2006). Although this diversity of perspectives suggests considerable discord in our understanding of what is meant by the term theory, the five conceptualizations of theory identified by Gregor (2006) suggest that the notion of a construct is fundamental to theory in its many forms. The centrality of constructs to theory highlights the potential opportunity that a thorough examination of the constructs used by IS researchers holds for improving our understanding of the nature and use of theory in the discipline.

Constructs have been defined in many ways though a definition that sees them as "hypothetical concepts that are not directly observable, whose existence remains in the world of conception" (Morgeson & Hofmann, 1999, p. 25) appears to capture the essence of what is meant by the term. Variables, in contrast, are the directly observable phenomena that are frequently used to measure or provide an approximate understanding of constructs (Bacharach, 1989). Thus, although constructs are conceptually distinct from variables, it is important to recognize that the variables used by researchers to measure and understand constructs can significantly impact the practical meaning of these constructs. The importance of recognizing such impacts is heightened by the considerable latitude that exists for ambiguity and error in the conceptualization, definition, and measurement of theoretical constructs. For example, constructs identified using different terms cannot actually be considered conceptually distinct if they are measured using the same set of variables. In addition, an important source of error in the interpretation of research results is the error that arises as a consequence of the imprecise representation of constructs by variables (Bacharach, 1989). These

and other challenges related to the distinction between theoretical constructs and the variables used to measure them serve to underscore the importance of considering both when conducting analysis aimed at better understanding the nature of a set of constructs. In the present context, consideration for the explicit and implicit meanings underlying IS research constructs helps to ensure that our analysis is not needlessly clouded by the presence of seemingly distinct constructs that are, in essence, the same.

In addition to the clear identification of theoretical constructs, a second important element of much theory development work involves the assertion of some form of relationship or association between constructs (Doty & Glick, 1994; Gregor, 2006). Bacharach (1989, p. 498) argues, for instance, that a theory is "a statement of relationships between units observed or approximated in the empirical world." Although a number of authors have argued that theory requires more than variables or constructs connected by relationships (e.g., Markus & Robey, 1988; Sutton & Staw, 1995; Whetten, 1989), there appears to be little question regarding the significance of relationships to both theory and much of the theory development and testing conducted by IS researchers.

Relationships are generally conceived of as describing the nature of the causal linkages among constructs (Markus & Robey, 1988; Whetten, 1989) though the manner in which these linkages are characterized varies considerably depending on the phenomena of interest and the conception of theory that is being invoked. They can, for instance, be described as linear or curvilinear when positivist variance-oriented theory is being presented or they can be linked to a temporal dimension as is typically the case in the context of process-oriented theories (Bacharach, 1989; Markus & Robey, 1988; Mitchell & James, 2001). In less positivist perspectives, relationships are more likely to be characterized in terms of associations or as contributing factors whereby causal antecedents may or may not lead to specified outcomes (Gregor, 2006). Bacharach (1989) further notes that relationships need not be unidirectional with dialectical and reciprocal relationships being among the possible alternative specifications. Despite the potential complexity of relationship structure that is suggested here, the identification of some form of relationship between a pair of constructs or the failure to find any form of relationship can provide important guidance to future inquiry irrespective of research paradigm.

Reflecting on the literature that has emerged from several decades of IS research, one is presented with a substantial body of empirical observations surrounding the relationships among a broad range of theoretical constructs. Since every journal acceptance decision serves, to some extent, to define a discipline (Benbasat & Zmud, 2003; Power, 2003), journal publications come to represent an implicit if not explicit understanding of the constructs, relationships, and theories of importance to that discipline (Kuhn, 1970). This publication record can therefore be drawn upon to develop a broad understanding of the theoretical focus of a discipline and to highlight those aspects of its theoretical foundations that have withstood empirical scrutiny. Thus, building on the richness of the extant IS literature, we undertake to explore the constructs and relationships that have been examined in the empirical work within the field. The objective of this initiative is to provide researchers and theorists with improved understanding of the empirical foundations upon which IS theory rests.

Nomological Networks

Empirical support for a theoretical perspective can be improved by linking it to other theories through what have been referred to as a boundary spanning constructs (Bacharach, 1989). Boundary spanning constructs are constructs that are shared by multiple theories and, as such, they are of considerable importance to the theories which share them. In essence, the theoretical links es-

tablished by boundary spanning constructs foster the creation of a network that brings the weight of the empirical evidence for each theory to all other theories connected to the network (Bacharach, 1989). The power of such networks and the significance of boundary spanning constructs to them suggests the value of exploring IS research constructs to identify those that either serve or could potentially serve as boundary spanners between the theories used by IS researchers.

Closely related to the notion of a boundary spanning construct is that of a nomological network (Cronbach & Meehl, 1955). Nomological networks are constructed by linking theoretical constructs into a network of established relationships. Since the relationships in a nomological network are generally well established, the validity of new constructs is often assessed by evaluating the extent to which they fit within such networks (Mayer, Roberts, & Barsade, 2008). Thus, in an effort to extend the utility of our analysis, we draw upon on our data to develop and present a set of nomological networks for the IS discipline. The objective of this effort is to provide empirically grounded guidance to future research and theory development. Using these networks researchers can, for instance, improve the strength of their theory development and validation efforts by connecting their work to other empirical work within the discipline.

Recent literature attention has been directed specifically toward the network of relationships surrounding what has been referred to as the IT artifact (Benbasat & Zmud, 2003; Orlikowski & Iacono, 2001). Benbasat and Zmud (2003) argue, for instance, that the IT artifact and its immediate nomological network should form the core of the IS discipline. Toward this end they identify the inclusion of constructs only distantly related to the IT artifact and the exclusion of the IT artifact as two key errors that should be avoided by IS researchers. Despite some disagreement surrounding this position (e.g. Alter, 2003), the importance of the IT artifact to the IS discipline appears to have general support. Irrespective of any differences, discrepant positions are often seen as continuing to place significant emphasis on the IT artifact (e.g. Wu & Saunders, 2003). Given such emphasis, we expect that the IT artifact will be a particularly significant construct in the IS literature and will play a central role in the nomological networks that we develop. This expectation is therefore explored in the following analysis with the broad conclusion being that the IT artifact is, as expected, a richly developed construct of central importance in the large sample of research that we examine. We now proceed with a discussion of the methods used to acquire and analyze the data that led to this and other conclusions.

ANALYSIS OF EMPIRICAL INFORMATION SYSTEMS RESEARCH

Method

A dataset of constructs and relationships that have received recent empirical attention from IS researchers was assembled via an archival study of the articles published in *Information Systems Research* and *MIS Quarterly* during the nine year period from the beginning of 1999 to the end of 2007. These two journals have been consistently ranked as the leading journals in the field (Ferratt, Gorman, Kanet, & Salisbury, 2007) and were therefore thought to be appropriate to a study that seeks to develop some understanding of the most significant constructs and relationships in IS research. In order to ensure that our analysis reflects the current state of the discipline, the time period under consideration included the most recent period possible. Similarly, examination of a relatively large time period was intended to ensure that findings could be considered reasonably representative of the discipline rather than being excessively influenced by highly topical research

or by the content of occasional special issues that focus on restricted topic domains.

Data collection commenced with the identification of all articles published in the target journals during the selected time period. The resulting collection of 432 articles was then examined to identify those articles incorporating a substantive empirical investigation of constructs and their relationships. This preliminary screening process sought to eliminate articles such as research commentaries, reviews, opinion pieces, and measurement development work. No attempt was made to exclude articles based on either research paradigm or choice of methodology in order to help ensure that findings would reflect the diversity of the discipline as faithfully as possible (Vessey, Ramesh, & Glass, 2002). The result of this pre-screening process was the identification of a total of 238 relevant articles. The full text of these articles was examined by the authors to identify those constructs and relationships in each article that had been subjected to some form of empirical testing. All direct relationships between constructs were added to a relationship dataset though a certain degree of inference was necessary in the case of those studies that were ambiguous in their reporting of constructs or relationships. In addition to recording constructs and their relationships, the direction of each relationship was recorded where this was appropriate and an indication was made as to whether empirical support was found for the relationship. A subsequent review of a subset of the coded data found that the results of the initial coding effort were largely satisfactory.

Although the terms antecedent and consequent are not entirely suited to all research paradigms, in the interests of improved readability the following discussion will use the term antecedent to refer to any construct that was intended by an article to assume a position of causal or temporal precedence to its related construct. Similarly, the term consequent will be used to refer to those constructs that were conceptualized as being outcomes or temporally subsequent to their related constructs. Hence, in these terms, antecedents and consequents of each relationship in the relationship dataset were assessed by returning to the source articles to review construct definitions and empirical operationalizations. Based on the information obtained from this process it was possible to consolidate some constructs and thereby reduce the number of distinct constructs in the dataset while still remaining true to researcher intentions. For instance, two constructs with distinct names were merged if a review of their variable measures suggested that they were examining essentially the same notion. This process of assessment and consolidation was repeated twice for every antecedent and consequent resulting in a reduction from 1295 distinct constructs in the initial dataset to 690 constructs following the consolidation process.

Subsequent to the process of construct consolidation, all relationships were reviewed to ensure that the process did not introduce errors or inconsistencies. The results of this review indicated that the consolidation effort had yielded a satisfactory, consistent set of constructs. Once this had been established, it became evident that constructs frequently consisted of two components, a core construct that was central to what was being examined and some form of qualifier. For instance, the construct "Decision Quality" can be seen to consist of the core construct "Decision" and a qualifier to identify that it is the "Quality" of the decision that is of interest. This recognition led to a final review of all constructs in the relationship dataset to break them into these two components with the objective being to further facilitate efforts to understand the essence of the constructs and relationships of interest to the IS discipline. Following completion of this review the dataset was analyzed using a variety of standard summary statistical techniques and network diagram tools.

Results

The Use of Constructs in IS Research

A total of 690 distinct constructs were identified among the 1512 relationships included in the final dataset. Table 1 provides a list of the 18 constructs from this dataset that were posited as an antecedent or consequent in at least 20 relationships. Also included in the table are brief descriptions of these constructs and an indication of the number of times that each was included in a relationship. The 18 constructs listed in Table 1 account for less than 3% of all constructs in the dataset though they account for 27% of all relationship antecedents and consequents and can therefore be considered of central importance to the field.

Separating constructs into those posited as antecedents and those posited as consequents yielded a list of 502 distinct antecedents and a list of 339 distinct consequents. It should be noted here that the discrepancy between the total construct count and the sum of the antecedent and consequent counts is indicative of the extent to which consequents are also theorized as antecedents and vice versa. Similar to Table 1, Table 2 and Table 3 enumerate those constructs that were posited as an antecedent or consequent a minimum of 20 times. The constructs in these two tables account, respectively, for 1.4% and 2.7% of the antecedent and consequent constructs while also accounting for 19.3% and 22.8% of relationship antecedents and consequents.

The diversity of research conducted in the field appears evident based on the extent to which research attention is distributed across a wide range of constructs. However, to some degree this characterization reflects an incomplete understanding since it focuses on very specific individual constructs without adequate consideration for their dimensionality. A review of the constructs included in the dataset indicates, as noted previously, that many of these constructs consist of a core notion or concept such as "Tech-

Table 1. Usage frequency and description of most prevalent constructs

Construct	Description	Frequency
Technology Use	The actual use of some form of IT artifact including such things as the use of a web site, a spreadsheet, or a decision support system	124
Technology Usefulness	Measures of the extent to which an IT artifact is considered useful	99
Technology Use Intention	Measures of the extent to which an individual, group, or organization intends to use an IT artifact	87
Technology Ease of Use	Measures of the extent to which an IT artifact is considered easy to use	72
Technology Capability	Functional abilities associated with an IT artifact such as a search functionality or support for e-commerce	66
Individual Trust	Individual willingness to rely on an IT artifact or any other person or thing	49
Technology Use Scope	Evaluations of the extent to which an IT artifact is being used	39
Technology Implementation Success	An evaluation of the extent to which the implementation of an IT artifact is considered a success	34
Information Presentation Format	The format in which information is presented including formats that do not rely on the use of an IT artifact	32
Organizational Performance	Measures of organizational performance including such things as return on investment and profitability	32
Technology Satisfaction	Measures of the level of satisfaction with an IT artifact	30
Social Norms	Assessments of social rules, conventions, or expectations including assessments that are strictly perceptual	28
Task Performance	Evaluations of performance on a task	27
Purchase Intention	Measures of the extent to which an individual, group of individuals, or an organization intends to purchase a product or service	23
Technology Use Attitude	Any assessment of attitudes toward the use of an IT artifact	23
Vendor Trust	Evaluations of the willingness of individuals, groups of individuals, or organizations to rely on the integrity or ability of a vendor or supplier	23
Computer Self-Efficacy	Determinations of the level of confidence held in relation to abilities to effectively use IT artifacts	22
Personalization	The extent to which an IT artifact has been or can be adjusted to reflect the needs, wants, and desires of individual users	20

nology" that has been qualified to refer to various dimensions of this core such as its "Use," "Use Intention," "Ease of Use," and "Usefulness." In an effort to assess the impact of this situation on our understanding of the discipline, each construct in the dataset was separated into these two components resulting in a total of 1322 distinct construct components. The frequencies with which these components appeared in relationship antecedents or consequents are reported in Table 4 for the 20 most common components.

Contrary to the impression given by the sheer range of constructs examined by IS researchers,

Table 4 highlights the apparent importance of a limited set of phenomena to the IS discipline. The four relatively distinct notions of technology, information and knowledge, organizations, and tasks are incorporated into 45% of the antecedents and consequents included in the relationship dataset. In particular, some dimension of technology was incorporated into 28.4% of all antecedents and consequents. Since the technology construct is largely synonymous with the notion of the IT artifact, we conclude that the IT artifact has been reasonably well represented in recent IS research. The apparent salience of the IT artifact

Table 2. Usage frequency of most prevalent antecedents

Antecedent	Frequency
Technology Use	74
Technology Capability	50
Technology Usefulness	46
Technology Ease of Use	43
Information Presentation Format	32
Individual Trust	24
Technology Use Scope	23

Table 3. Usage frequency of most prevalent consequents

Consequent	Frequency
Technology Use Intention	85
Technology Usefulness	53
Technology Use	50
Organizational Performance	32
Technology Ease of Use	29
Task Performance	25
Individual Trust	25
Technology Implementation Success	24
Technology Satisfaction	21

Table 4. Usage frequency of most prevalent construct components

Construct Component	Frequency
Technology	859
Information	189
Intention	147
Use	137
Organization	117
Task	100
Performance	99
Usefulness	99
Knowledge	97
Trust	82
Functional Role	80
Ease of Use	72
Capability	71
Satisfaction	64
Individual	62
Quality	57
Vendor	54
Product	53
Purchase	50
Communication	48

in our dataset when compared to the findings of earlier work seems to suggest that IS researchers have been heeding calls for greater emphasis on the centrality of this artifact to our research and theory (Benbasat & Zmud, 2003). This finding might therefore be considered a relatively positive note on the responsiveness of the IS discipline to calls for change.

Finally, an attempt was made to develop a better understanding of the IT artifact through an examination of the dimensions of the technology construct component. All dimensions of this construct component were therefore extracted from the construct component list and reviewed. The most prominent of the dimensions identified are summarized in Table 5 which also includes the frequency with which each dimension was used in connection with the technology construct component. The dimensions included in this table account for 80.7% of the technology constructs in the dataset and can thus be considered to provide

a reasonably comprehensive depiction of how this construct is dimensionalized in the discipline.

Relationships in IS Research

Prior to commencing with an analysis of the relational structure of the constructs examined in the preceding section, it should be noted that the nature of the relationships to be discussed are not strictly positivist in orientation. For instance, a link between two constructs may indicate that one construct is a necessary and sufficient cause of the other or it may simply indicate that one construct contributes to or is associated with the other. Relatively positivist terminology will, however, be used in the interests of readability and to maintain focus on the essential messages that our set of empirical findings provides about the relational structure of IS constructs. Given that the vast majority of the relationships reported in the literature were positivist in orientation, the

Table 5. Usage frequency of the most prevalent dimensions of technology construct

Dimension	Frequency
Use	124
Usefulness	99
Use Intention	87
Ease of Use	72
Capability	66
Use Scope	39
Implementation Success	34
Satisfaction	30
Use Attitude	23
Integration	19
Investment	17
Compatibility	16
Type	14
Complexity	12
Assimilation	11
Governance Structure	10
Knowledge	10
Outsourcing	10

negative implications of this simplification are thought to be relatively small.

The final dataset included a total of 1512 relationships that were subsequently reviewed to identify 1172 distinct relationships. Of the 1172 distinct relationships, 961 received empirical support while 289 were unsupported by empirical evidence. This imbalance between supported and unsupported relationships almost certainly reflects biases in favor of publishing supported findings (Rosenthal, 1979). The discrepancy between the total number of supported and unsupported relationships and the high quantity of distinct relationships is indicative of a small number of relationships that were both supported and unsupported by empirical findings. The most common empirically supported relationships are presented in Table 6 along with an indication of the frequency with which each was found in the dataset.

As would be anticipated given the prominence of the IT artifact among the constructs of interest to IS researchers, a review of the list of relationships receiving the most empirical support also indicates a central role for technology. This ob-

servation, in conjunction with literature calls to make the IT artifact central to any nomological network of the IS discipline (Benbasat & Zmud, 2003), prompted us to build a series of networks based on the empirically supported relationships included in the dataset. Since only empirically supported relationships were included in these networks, they can be expected to offer a view of the discipline that is built from the ground up, irrespective of theoretical arguments.

In an effort to better understand how the most salient dimensions of the IT artifact are interrelated, a nomological network was constructed that included all of the "technology" constructs listed in Table 1. The result of this process is presented in Figure 1. Relationships were mapped in this figure with antecedents being shown as either "increasing" or "reducing" consequent values where empirical evidence suggested that some indication of relationship direction was warranted. In cases where directional inferences were not possible or seemed inappropriate, relationships were simply designated as "impacts." As with the previous findings on the most prominent constructs in the discipline, Figure 1 serves to highlight the salience

Table 6. Frequency of the most prevalent supported relationships

Antecedent	Consequent	Frequency
Technology Usefulness	Technology Use Intention	17
Technology Ease of Use	Technology Usefulness	12
Technology Ease of Use	Technology Use Intention	9
Normative Pressures	Social Norms	8
Technology Capability	Technology Implementation Success	6
Expertise	Explanation Selection	5
Public Announcements	Stock Market Returns	5
Social Norms	Technology Use Intention	5
Technology Usefulness	Technology Satisfaction	5
Technology Usefulness	Technology Use Attitude	5
Individual Trust	Relationship Effectiveness	4
Individual Trust	Technology Use Intention	4
Technology Capability	Organizational Performance	4
Technology Use Attitude	Technology Use Intention	4

of the Technology Acceptance Model (TAM) and related theoretical frameworks in IS research (Venkatesh, Morris, Davis, & Davis, 2003).

While useful to better understand the dimensions of the IT artifact, an isolated nomological network of these dimensions tends to overlook the presumed objective of information systems. Since this objective is often seen as some form of performance outcome (DeLone & McLean, 1992, 2003), Figure 1 also incorporates the performance oriented constructs identified on Table 1. Only two performance constructs emerged from the data

Figure 1. A Nomological Network of the IT artifact and associated performance outcomes

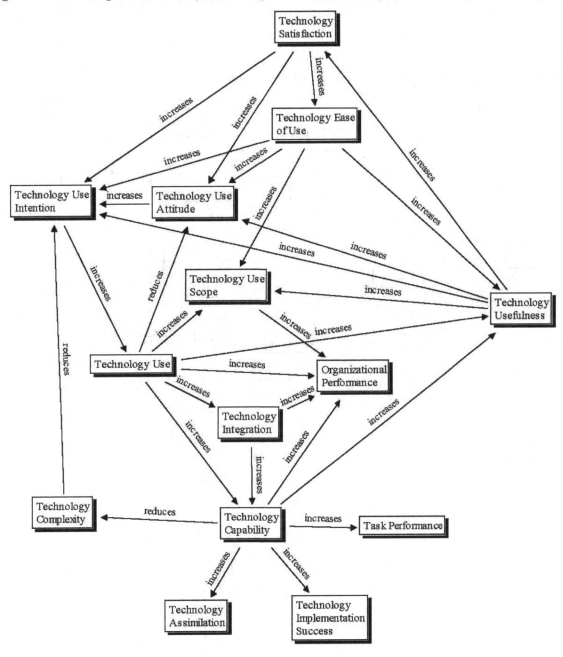

with any degree of prominence: organizational performance and task performance. As Figure 1 shows, organizational performance was found to be related to technology use, use scope, integration, and capability while task performance was only related to technology capability. Subsequent to the development of Figure 1, a nomological network was constructed that included all of the constructs in Table 1 in order to present a network of all of the most salient constructs and relation- ships in IS research as suggested by analysis of our dataset. This network is presented in Figure 2 with relationship labels removed to improve readability. Figure 2 can be contrasted with Fig- ure 1 by recognizing that Figure 1 includes only technology and performance related constructs while Figure 2 includes all constructs that our dataset suggests are prominent in IS research. In the following section we offer a brief discus- sion of some of the implications that the results

Figure 2. A Nomological Network of the IS Discipline

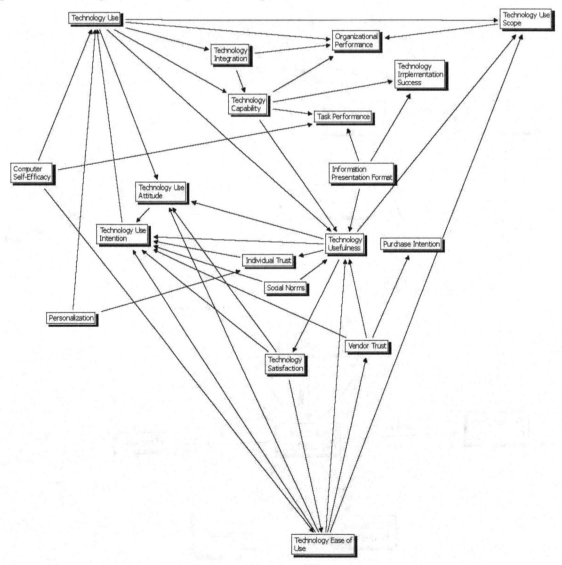

reported here may have for the development and application of theory in the field.

DISCUSSION

An examination of Table 1 highlights the salience of the IT artifact in IS research conducted over the past decade. It is evident that IS researchers are exploring many dimensions of this artifact including its use, usefulness, ease of use, use intention, implementation success, and satisfaction. Perhaps not surprisingly, a significant number of the most common constructs in IS research are closely linked to TAM. The prominence of this stream of research is also evident in the antecedent and consequent lists. Although these lists indicate that constructs such as organizational performance and task performance are posited as consequents with some degree of frequency, the most common consequents relate to technology use intention, usefulness, and use. This finding suggests that IS researchers may be placing greater emphasis on ensuring that the IT artifact is used then they are on ensuring that it drives performance outcomes. Hence, there appears to be some opportunity for theory development and testing in the latter domain.

Two key forms of performance appear to play prominent roles in IS research. The first of these is organizational performance which has been operationalized in many ways. Most of the operationalizations observed in the dataset tended, however, to be financial measures such as profitability and return on assets. In contrast with many of the measures used in the technology adoption stream, organizational performance measures also tended to be objective rather than perceptual. The second form of performance of some salience in our dataset was task performance which was often used in the context of decision support systems research and collaborative systems use. It is interesting to note that the link between task performance and organizational performance appears to have received limited attention. Thus, it would seem that there is a need to more clearly link the task performance gains from IS use to organizational performance gains. There also appears to be a need to more fully explore the task and other performance consequences of IS use in relation to a broader range of systems. Research in this stream would be considered essential by practitioners seeking to justify IS acquisition decisions and such research would benefit greatly from improved theory of general relevance.

One of the challenges faced in our coding and analysis was the extensive use of distinct terms to refer to what appeared to be largely identical constructs and the frequent use of construct names that either inadequately represented the construct or completely misrepresented it. These findings suggest that issues of content validity exist within the field. Problems of this sort impede progress of the discipline on many fronts. For instance, it becomes difficult to link theories into a nomological network when each theory uses a different term to denote a similar concept. Recognizing that this practice is driven, to some extent, by the need to establish unique contribution, we suggest that reviewers give special attention to scrutinizing the research constructs presented in the papers that they review with a view toward ensuring that disciplinary progress is not impeded by needless confusion.

Our analysis further suggests a need for more consistency and clarity in the manner in which research is reported in journal articles. In this chapter we were interested in collecting data on the basic building blocks of empirical research: constructs, relationships, and the empirical support (or lack thereof) that was found for these relationships. Yet, in a substantial proportion of the papers that we reviewed this information was either not easy to identify or was completely absent. We thus believe that the inclusion of two basic elements in all empirical research papers would greatly enhance their usefulness to researcher and practitioner communities. The first of these is a summary table or figure of posited constructs and relationships. The inclusion of this element helps the reader to frame the scope of the study and to assess its relevance to his or her needs. The second element is a summary table of all findings. This element could take the form of a table summarizing hypotheses results or a figure showing the magnitude and significance of posited paths. Surprisingly, at least one of these two elements was missing from a large number of papers thereby making it difficult to establish either which constructs and relationships were being tested or whether tested relationships were empirically supported.

In the interests of improving the clarity of the constructs used in the discipline, we suggest a need for further efforts to establish common terminology and to dimensionalize constructs along the lines of what we present. Considerable opportunity exists for researchers to review the most salient construct dimensions used by IS researchers and to more fully dimensionalize important constructs. Such efforts can be expected to improve our understanding of these constructs and to improve the cohesiveness of research within the discipline. Initiatives of this type would also help to illuminate construct dimensions that have been overlooked or under explored and the incumbent opportunities for new theory development and testing. Based on the results of our study, we would suggest that such efforts commence with the concepts of technology, knowledge and information, organizations, and tasks. Beyond the opportunities that lie in more fully developing the dimensions of these concepts, our empirically grounded results suggest that they may form some sort of core for the discipline and we therefore believe that there may be merit in further exploration of this possibility.

Stepping back from specific findings, we can identify four theory development initiatives that stem from the results and analysis reported here. First, readers may wish to test the veracity of the nomological networks that we present in an effort

to ensure that IS researchers have a sound basis upon which future theory development and testing can be built. Second, efforts to better place future research within the context of the networks that have been presented can serve to increase the rigor of this research and our confidence in it. This work can simultaneously support other theory development work by yielding important extensions to the networks that we offer. Third, researchers who are uncomfortable with the current framing of the discipline may seek to extend the nomological network to place greater emphasis on other constructs or incorporate new constructs. Finally, there is a need in a number of cases to develop and link the theoretical explanations that we use to account for the empirical evidence depicted in these nomological networks (Sutton & Staw, 1995; Whetten, 1989).

Limitations and Future Research

Although we endeavored to conduct a through, rigorous study that would be capable of yielding useful insights on the nature of the information systems discipline, certain limitations presented themselves owing to the nature of the research and the subject matter. Salient among these are the publications selected for inclusion in the study and the time period under consideration. Although the publications used in the study are widely considered the most prominent in the discipline, future research could attempt to incorporate the results of an analysis of additional high quality publications. An extension to the time period under consideration might also yield additional insights though the relatively large time period considered and the inclusion of recent publications would seem to suggest that this limitation may be less significant.

Additional attention to the richness of the relationship structures described in the literature could be expected to yield some interesting perspective. This attention could, for instance, explore the temporal dimension of relationships, their strength, moderating influences, and the role of causal agency. Considerations such as these were not made in the current study in the interests of making the analysis tractable and to avoid obscuring key messages by further complicating the already complex networks that are presented. Nonetheless, a separate study holds the potential to be highly informative. It would, however, almost certainly be complicated by the ambiguity of some research reports as was the case with the current initiative.

As with any subjective undertaking, the construct groupings reflect, at least to some extent, the perspective of the researchers. We have, however, sought to emphasize only the most salient results in order to avoid reporting findings that are more a result of the unique perspective of the researchers than having a substantive basis in the literature. Similarly, although our results indicated the presence of relationships that were unsupported and those that received conflicting support, we opted to emphasize supported relationships. This emphasis was based on our intention to present a network of empirical evidence that can support future theory development and testing.

Since it was not our intention to develop multilevel theory (Klein, Tosi, & Cannella, 1999), we have presented the relationships as reported in the literature without consideration for the numerous challenges associated with levels of analysis. Nonetheless, we feel that this is a rich topic area that is worth further examination and we suggest that the networks presented here may be useful in this regard given their empirical basis. Among the many possibilities, researchers might opt to inquire as to the theoretical nature of an apparent change in level of analysis in one of these networks (Chan, 1998). The development of theory in this vein would certainly be useful to researchers seeking to understand, for instance, how individual outcomes arising from IS use contribute to higher level organizational outcomes.

Finally, it must be remembered that the analysis and networks offered here are intended to facilitate further theory development rather than as a stricture upon the dynamic evolution of the field. In an effort to better elucidate the broad themes of the empirical literature, only the most salient constructs and relationships were included and these networks cannot, therefore, be considered to exhaustively represent all constructs and relationships of interest to the discipline. They do, however, provide some framework for understanding the nature of existing theory within IS research and for recognizing what remains to be done.

CONCLUSION

After several decades of theory development and empirical testing within the field of information systems, we have argued in this chapter that there is considerable merit in pausing to reflect upon the current state of the discipline. Building on the premise that the empirical findings reported in the IS literature provide a valid and useful record of the constructs and relationships of importance to IS researchers, we have presented a review and analysis of these findings over a nine year period. The aim of this review was to develop some understanding of the most significant constructs and relationships in IS research and to provide a broad-based nomological network of the discipline that relies on empirical results rather than any particular theoretical perspective.

As an overview of an extensive body of literature, the findings reported here offer potentially valuable assistance to those seeking to test theory and potentially useful guidance to those readers interested in theory development and refinement. As such, this chapter serves as a useful starting point for subsequent chapters that seek to focus more specifically on individual theoretical perspectives. As has been noted, good theory requires that substantive theoretical explanations be offered for why relationships between constructs exist and under what circumstances they are most and least likely to be found (Sutton

& Staw, 1995; Whetten, 1989). It is this challenge that we present to you the reader. We encourage you to read further in this volume in pursuit of more and better theory.

REFERENCES

Alter, S. (2003). 18 reasons why IT-reliant work systems should replace "the IT artifact" as the core subject matter of the IS field. *Communications of the Association for Information Systems, 12*(23), 366-395.

Bacharach, S. B. (1989). Organizational theories: Some criteria for evaluation. *Academy of Management Review, 14*(4), 496-515.

Benbasat, I., & Zmud, R. W. (2003). The identity crisis within the IS discipline: Defining and communicating the discipline's core properties. *MIS Quarterly, 27*(2), 183-194.

Chan, D. (1998). Functional relations among constructs in the same content domain at different levels of analysis: A typology of composition models. *Journal of Applied Psychology, 83*(2), 234-246.

Cronbach, L. J., & Meehl, P. E. (1955). Construct validity in psychological tests. *Psychological Bulletin, 52*, 281-302.

DeLone, W. H., & McLean, E. R. (1992). Information systems success: The quest for the dependent variable. *Information Systems Research, 3*(1), 60-95.

DeLone, W. H., & McLean, E. R. (2003). The DeLone and McLean model of information systems success: A ten-year update. *Journal of Management Information Systems, 19*(4), 9-30.

Doty, D. H., & Glick, W. H. (1994). Typologies as a unique form of theory building: Toward improved understanding and modeling. *Academy of Management Review, 19*(2), 230-251.

Ferratt, T. W., Gorman, M. F., Kanet, J. J., & Salisbury, W. D. (2007). IS journal quality assessment using the author affiliation index. *Communications of the Association for Information Systems, 17*, 710-724.

Glaser, B. G., & Strauss, A. L. (1967). *The discovery of grounded theory: Strategies for qualitative research*. Chicago: Aldine Publishing.

Gregor, S. (2006). The nature of theory in information systems. *MIS Quarterly, 30*(3), 611-642.

Klein, K. J., Tosi, H., & Cannella, A. A., Jr. (1999). Multilevel theory building: Benefits, barriers, and new developments. *Academy of Management Review, 24*(2), 243-248.

Kuhn, T. S. (1970). *The structure of scientific revolutions*. Chicago: University of Chicago Press.

Markus, M. L., & Robey, D. (1988). Information technology and organizational change: Causal structure in theory and research. *Management Science, 34*(5), 583-598.

Mayer, J. D., Roberts, R. D., & Barsade, S. G. (2008). Human abilities: Emotional intelligence. *Annual Review of Psychology, 59*(1), 507-536.

Mitchell, T. R., & James, L. R. (2001). Building better theory: Time and the specification of when things happen. *Academy of Management Review, 26*(4), 530-547.

Morgeson, F. P., & Hofmann, D. A. (1999). The structure and function of collective constructs: Implications for multilevel research and theory development. *Academy of Management Review, 24*(2), 249-265.

Orlikowski, W. J., & Iacono, C. S. (2001). Research commentary: Desperately seeking "IT" in IT research - a call to theorizing the IT artifact. *Information Systems Research, 12*(2), 121-134.

Popper, K. R. (1992). *The logic of scientific discovery*. New York: Routledge.

Power, D. J. (2003). The maturing IS discipline: Institutionalizing our domain of inquiry. *Communications of AIS, 2003*(12), 539-545.

Rosenthal, R. (1979). The "file drawer problem" and tolerance for null results. *Psychological Bulletin, 86*(3), 638-641.

Sutton, R. I., & Staw, B. M. (1995). What theory is not. *Administrative Science Quarterly, 40*(3), 371-384.

Venkatesh, V., Morris, M. G., Davis, G. B., & Davis, F. D. (2003). User acceptance of information technology: Toward a unified view. *MIS Quarterly, 27*(3), 425-478.

Vessey, I., Ramesh, V., & Glass, R. L. (2002). Research in information systems: An empirical study of diversity in the discipline and its journals. *Journal of Management Information Systems, 19*(2), 129-174.

Weber, R. (2003). Theoretically speaking. *MIS Quarterly, 27*(3), iii-xii.

Weick, K. E. (1995). What theory is not, theorizing is. *Administrative Science Quarterly, 40*(3), 385-390.

Whetten, D. A. (1989). What constitutes a theoretical contribution? *Academy of Management Review, 14*(4), 490-495.

Wu, Y. A., & Saunders, C. (2003). The IS core – VI: Further along the road to the IT artifact. *Communications of the Association for Information Systems, 12*(36), 562-567.

KEY TERMS AND DEFINITIONS

Construct: An abstract concept that describes an idea or phenomenon that is not directly observable.

IT Artifact: A specific bundle of hardware and software that is assembled to fulfill information needs.

Nomological Network: A mapping of the relationships among a set of constructs.

Paradigm: A specific view on the nature of reality and how knowledge is acquired.

Positivism: A view of reality that sees phenomena as being governed by fundamental laws.

Relationship: An association or connection between entities and/or concepts.

Variable: A tangible phenomena that is directly observable and therefore measurable.

Chapter II
Adapting the Structurationist View of Technology for Studies at the Community/Societal Levels

Marlei Pozzebon
HEC Montréal, Canada

Eduardo Diniz
Fundaçao Getulio Vargas, Brazil

Martin Jayo
Fundaçao Getulio Vargas, Brazil

ABSTRACT

The multilevel framework proposed in this chapter is particularly useful for research involving complex and multilevel interactions (i.e., interactions involving individuals, groups, organizations and networks at the community, regional or societal levels). The framework is influenced by three theoretical perspectives. The core foundation comes from the structurationist view of technology, a stream of research characterized by the application of structuration theory to information systems (IS) research and notably influenced by researchers like Orlikowski (2000) and Walsham (2002). In order to extend the framework to encompass research at the community/societal levels, concepts from social shaping of technology and from contextualism have been integrated. Beyond sharing a number of ontological and epistemological assumptions, these three streams of thinking have been combined because each of them offers particular concepts that are of great value for the kind of studies the authors wish to put forward: investigating the influence of information and communication technology (ICT) from a structurationist standpoint at levels that go beyond the organizational one.

INTRODUCTION

Understanding the influence of *information and communication technology (*ICT) in social life is complex, no matter what lens is adopted to study it. In the information systems (IS) field of research, a range of different social theories have been borrowed and adapted in order to gain insight into the interaction of ICT (its design, adoption, implementation and use) and people at different levels (individual, group, organizational and macro). We found institutional theory (Avgerou, 2000), structuration theory (Barley, 1986), critical social theory (Doolin, 1998; Yetin, 2006), actor network theory (Sarker et al, 2006), social construction of technology (Williams, 1997) and symbolic interactionism (Gopal & Prasad, 2000) to be among the most influential social theories applied in IS research.

A number of recent papers have outlined the particular importance of one of these social theories in IS research: structuration theory. Although structuration theory is not specific to IS, but is rather a general social theory, it has been argued it is used in IS research more than in other areas of organizational research (Pozzebon & Pinsonneault, 2005). In a recent and comprehensive review, Jones and Karsten (2008) noted that structuration theory has been cited substantively in more than 330 IS papers to date, including conceptual and empirical studies. What's more, the contribution and potential of structuration theory in general, and more particularly of the structurationist view of technology, for gaining insights on ICT phenomena, is widely accepted.

In this paper, we propose a multilevel framework that extends the structurationist view of technology to investigate the adoption, implementation and use of ICT at the community/societal levels. In line with Burton-Jones and Gallivan (2007), we apply the term multilevel to refer to a type of framework that entails more than one level of conceptualization and analysis. However, where we differ from the latter authors

is regarding the ontological stance. While they place multilevel research within an organization science perspective that adopts a functionalist, positivist and variance-oriented stance (p. 3), we place our multilevel framework within a constructivist tradition that views any social research as processual and *inherently multilevel.*

We also argue that most studies that use the structurationist view depict technology as reinforcing or transforming the institutional properties *of organizations,* i.e., that can be associated with research at the organizational level. Jones and Karsten (2008) highlight such a limitation and identify opportunities for future structurationist IS research to address the relationship between ICT and people in broader contexts than just the specific organizational setting. Greater effort should be made to "broaden the scope of IS research from its traditional focus on phenomena associated with computer-based information systems at the individual, group, and organizational levels, to address the broader institutional and social developments in which IS are increasingly implicated" (Jones & Karsten, 2008, pp. 150).

The organizational level of analysis has hitherto dominated discussion not only in IS but, to a large extent, in management research which arguably correlates with the power held by corporations that occupy a privileged place in the economic world. Nonetheless, t*he importance of studies at the community/societal level is rising, as researchers worldwide become more aware that, as* a society, we will be incapable of dealing with important issues such as social welfare, social equity and sustainability if we continue to focus merely on doing what we are currently doing more efficiently, research included. New forms of social and economic relations as well as new ways of balancing human needs and natural resources are likely to emerge. These needs transcend those organizational problems that IS researchers have traditionally focussed on: productivity, performance, risk, satisfaction and other constructs related to the impact of IT at the organizational or inter-organizational levels. Although these areas remain relevant, their dominance has overshadowed other levels of analysis, and the dynamics of ICT at the community/societal level remains comparatively ill-defined and under-researched. The emergence of theoretical frameworks that address these levels should help to resolve the current imbalance.

In this light, the conceptual framework proposed in this chapter is particularly useful for research involving complex and multilevel interactions between individuals, groups, organizations and networks at the community/societal level. The presence of multiple levels of analysis, from individual to macro, draws attention to the linkage between individual micro-level actions and institutional macro-level contexts. However, the design and application of a multilevel framework cannot preclude serious challenges. How can a structurationist view of technology be applied to more purposively understand the influence of ICT on change or permanence at the community/societal level without drawing attention away from individual practices? What other alternatives could contribute to addressing such a difficult theoretical question?

BACKGROUND

The multilevel framework is influenced by three theoretical perspectives: structurationist view of technology, social shaping of technology and contextualism. In this section, we present and discuss the fundamental premises and concepts of each of these perspectives.

Structuration Theory and Structurationist View of Technology

Structuration is seen as a promising theory for resolving the longstanding debate concerning the relationship between structure and agency, a challenge not confined to ICT or even to organization theory, but having a place among the most ubiq-

uitous and difficult issues in the whole of social theory (Giddens & Pierson, 1998). Rather than opposing objective-subjective or voluntarist-determinist dimensions, Giddens (1984) challenged the premise of mutual exclusivity and assumed the duality of structure and action, proposing the *theory of structuration* and offering a form of social analysis that goes beyond dualistic ways of thinking and helps to bridge micro and macro levels of analysis. Other well known alternatives to historical dualistic views are Bourdieu's (1977) interplay between objectivism and subjectivism, Bernstein's (1983) move beyond objectivism and relativism, Bhaskar's (1989) account of positivism and postmodernism, and Fay's (1996) discussion of science versus hermeneutics. Pozzebon (2004) argues that these accounts are not really competing but alternatives to structuration theory, and that the choice among these alternatives is often a matter of ontological affinity.

Structuration theory has received significant attention, making British sociologist Anthony Giddens one of the world's most-cited sociologists (Jones & Karsten, 2008). It is not our purpose in this chapter to provide a complete overview of Giddens's structuration theory, as a number of comprehensive and authoritative texts on the topic already exist (e.g., Cohen, 1989; Giddens, 1984, 1989, 1990; Giddens & Pierson, 1998; Held & Thompson, 1989). Instead, we have chosen to highlight the stream of IS research applying structuration theory that we term the *structurationist view of technology*, its implications for empirical research and the *main concepts articulated to compose a multilevel framework*.

The *structurationist view of technology represents a chief stream within IS research, and has been analyzed and revised in detail by* Pozzebon and Pinsonneault (2005). It encompasses the work of authors like Barrett and Walsham (1999), Heracleous and Barrett (2001), Montealegre (1997), Ngwenyama (1998), Nicholson and Sahay (2001), Olesen and Myers (1999), Orlikowski (1991, 1992, 1993, 1996, 2000), Orlikowski and Yates (1994),

Sahay (1998), Sahay and Robey (1996), Walsham (2002), Walsham and Han (1993), and Yates and Orlikowski (1992). Although the way structuration theory has been interpreted and applied by these authors varies, they can be distinguished as a group when compared to another influential stream of IS research claiming to espouse structurational concepts, the *adaptive structuration theory* or AST (DeSanctis & Poole, 1994). AST has been widely applied by IS researchers like Chin et al. (1997), Fulk (1993), Majchrzak et al. (2000), Maznevski and Chudoba (2000), and Miranda and Bostrom (1993-1994, 1999). While DeSanctis and Poole's (1994) original elaboration of AST draws on Giddens' main concepts, its subsequent application in empirical studies has departed from the fundamental premises of Giddens' theory. This explains why most studies recognized as AST studies are based on nomothetic assumptions and use survey and experimental methods to test causal models (Pozzebon & Pinsonneault, 2005).

Two authors have been particularly influential in shaping the path of the *structurationist view of technology* stream: Orlikowski and Walsham. The work of Orlikowski is widely recognized as relevant not only in IS but also in organization studies. Two seminal papers published in *Organization Science* in 1992 and 2000 respectively mark two different phases of her influential work.

In the first phase, seeking to extend the understanding of IT from the structuration point of view, Orlikowski (1992) proposed a structurational model of technology. The model posits that IT is simultaneously the product and the medium of human action, and that existing institutional properties (knowledge, resources and norms) influence human actions when interacting with IT. Concurrently, when human actors interact with IT, they act upon institutional structures either to sustain or change them. "Technology embodies and hence is an instantiation of some rules and resources constituting the structure of an organization" (Orlikowski, 1992, pp. 406). Technology is created and changed by human

action at the same time that human action is mediated by existing technologies. Such a recursive notion of technology is what Orlikowski termed the *duality of technology.*

In the second phase, Orlikowski (2000) challenged her own previous work on the structurational model and developed concepts that address the role of emergence and improvisation in technology and *technology-in-use* or *technology-in-practice*. She emphasizes appropriation of the structures inscribed in the technology, and moves towards a more proactive and practical lens that focuses on emergent rather than embodied structures and replaces appropriation with enactment (Orlikowski, 2000). Adopting such an alternative view, Orlikowski points out that there are always boundary conditions on how to use physical properties of artifacts, and that people always can (even if they do not) redefine the meaning, properties and application of a given technology after development or implementation. Her practical lens focuses on human agency and the open-ended set of emergent structures that may be enacted through the recurrent use of a technology.

We selected **technology-in-practice** as a central concept in a multilevel framework aimed at investigating the influence of ICT at a community/societal level. The focus is on the enactment of technology, outlining that there are always boundary conditions on how people redefine the meaning, properties and applications of a given technology during and after implementation, and allowing a better understanding of the emergence or non-emergence of new social structures.

Our view of Walsham's contribution to the structurationist view of technology lies in his emphasis on understanding the influence of ICT in social life, not only as embedded within its organizational context but also within wider social systems, such as those at the nation state level (Walsham, 1993; Walsham & Ham, 1993). In his leading book about interpretivism in IS research, Walsham (1993) combines elements from structuration theory and critical theory, raising concepts such as power and control. More recently, Walsham (2002) put particular emphasis on culture and cross-cultural studies, once again applying structuration theory to macro analyses of social change and encouraging IS researchers to enlarge their scope of analysis, as advocated in this chapter.

In summary, the studies identified here as belonging to the *structurationist view of technology* have offered worthwhile contributions to increasing our understanding of interactions between individuals and groups and ICT within organizations but still fail, except for Walsham's attempts, to purposively address mixed levels of analysis with complicated networks of players. In a collection of constructivist studies on technology, which adopts a purposive political account and integrates macro and historical analyses, we found concepts that help extend the structurationist perspective. They sharpen the focus by incorporating a broader and more heterogeneous set of players.

Constructivist Approaches and Social Shaping of Technology

The second source of theoretical foundation comes from social shaping approaches, which can be divided into two broad categories: socio-economic shaping of technology (e.g., MacKenzie & Wacjman, 1985; Williams 1997) and social construction of technology (SCOT) (e.g., Pinch & Bijker, 1984; Bijker & Law, 1992), the latter category being *strongly influenced by sociology of knowledge (Berger &Luckmann, 1967)*. The special issue of *Technology Analysis & Strategic Management* (volume 12, number 1, 2000) and the book *Innovation, Organizational Change and Technology* (edited by McLoughlin & Harris, 1997) provide a set of papers on technology and political processes within management and organizations that are centered on the social shaping of technology. They adopt a political account and integrate macro and historical analyses.

Like Orlikowski's *technology-in-practice*, social shaping studies outline opportunities in which technology can be interpreted or reinterpreted in different ways. *Aiming at overcoming the rather deterministic conception of technology often found in* mainstream *technology management literature*, which tends to take technology for granted as a well-defined tool (Dawson et al., 2000), social shaping studies *view technology implementation as the outcome of social processes of negotiation between networks of social actors.* Strongly influenced by social constructivist approaches, this *view pays special attention to the diversity of actors' interpretations of the meaning and content of technology (technological frames) and emphasizes the identification of opportunities where decisions and actions regarding technology management and change may be undertaken.* In order to *identify occasions, spaces and mechanisms* that are open for negotiation and change, they incorporate a *broader, complicated and heterogeneous network of diverse players* (Clausen & Koch, 1999; Koch, 2000). *We retain three important concepts from social shaping studies: ICT implementation and use as a negotiation process, relevant social groups and technological frames.*

ICT implementation and use is seen as a **process of negotiation**, where not *only the content of the technology itself, but also the different interests, commitments, perspectives and positions of the network of players interacting with the technology, will influence the process and outcomes of technologies-in-practice and the emergent social structures. The identification of* **occasions, spaces and mechanisms** *open for negotiation and change becomes crucial.*

The implementation of a new ICT in a community or region can be seen as an opportunity to change information flow, resource allocation and responsibility attributions. "IS are drawn on to provide meaning, to exercise power, and to legitimize actions" (Walsham, 2002, p. 362). For this reason, by implementing a new ICT, people can reproduce, transform, adapt and even reinvent their daily practices. In order to take into account a broader, complicated and heterogeneous network of diverse players interacting in a given community or region, we delineate the concept of relevant social groups. The meaning of community merits a separate discussion in itself, and a huge number of different definitions of community can be found in literature and the Internet, e.g., geographic communities, communities of culture, communities of interest, etc. In this chapter, we adopt the concept of community as it has been traditionally defined in sociology: a group of interacting people sharing a common geographical or virtual territory (these people interact in networks and can take part in coalitions, teams, organizations, associations, etc.).

Relevant social groups *refer to a set of people who share a common geographical space or occupy the same functional boundaries. In addition, from a constructivist point of view, relevant social groups also share a set of assumptions about a given subject of interest, for example, the expected benefits of the implementation of a new technology (Sahay and Robey, 1996). Subgroups and alliances between groups form social spaces and play important roles in the choice of management strategy and use of technology.*

The assertion that people within a social group are likely to share a set of assumptions leads to the concept of interpretive frames. People act in the world on the basis of how they interpret and re-interpret it. *Interpretive frames are mental models that shape people's interpretations, influencing their actions and decisions.* The idea of interpretive frames is similar to those of *interpretive schemes* (Giddens, 1984; Bartunek, 1984), *technological frames* (Orlikowski & Gash, 1994; McLoughlin et al., 2000), and *provinces of meaning* (Ranson et al., 1980; Weick, 1993). Table 1 shows previous research on interpretive frames.

Orlikowski and Gash (1994) suggested that technological frames are particularly useful for examining how and why people act around ICT, describing their approach as cognitive and establishing a distinction between cognitive and political perspectives. Accordingly, while the former helps explain contradictory outcomes due to different interpretations of a technology, the latter helps explain particular outcomes due to the loss or gain of power. In this vein, Davidson (2002) also adopted technological frames as a socio-cognitive perspective complementary to analysis of power.

Other authors do not corroborate such a disconnection between cognitive and political dimensions, believing that interpretation and power cannot be separated. Gallivan (1995), Giddens (1984), McLoughlin et al. (2000), and Ranson et al. (1980) are some examples. What Orlikowski and Gash (1994) call "frame incongruence" and "divergent technological frames," McLoughlin et al. call "frame dominance" and "competing ac-

Table 1. Concepts related to interpretive frames

Denomination	Examples of studies
Cognitive maps	Bougnon et al. (1977); Eden (1992)
Interpretive schemes	Bartunek (1984); Giddens (1984)
Interpretive frames	Bartunek and Moch (1987)
Frames	Goffman (1974)
Mental models	Argyris and Schon (1978); Schutz (1970)
Provinces of meaning	Ranson et al. (1980); Weick (1993)
Technological frames	Gallivan (1995); McLoughlin et al. (2000); Orlikowski and Gash (1994); Yoshiota et al. (1994); Davidson (2002)

counts," essentially because interpretive frames represent competing or converging accounts, which can be related to competing or converging interests regarding the outcomes of the implementation of a new technology. *This view of the inseparability of cognitive and political aspects is supported by Giddens: although separated for analytical purposes, meaning and power are intrinsically related - frames of meaning incorporate differentials of power.*

Similarly, *Ranson et al. (1980) propose that people create "provinces of meanings," which represent the basis of their orientation (Ranson et al., 1980).* Although individually held, interpretive frames, *articulated with value preferences and sectional interests,* are shared across groups (Gallivan, 1995). Therefore, different stakeholder groups are likely to have diverse interpretive frames, which not only reveal different perceptions and knowledge, but different expectations and interests as well. *The resolution of competing frames hinges on dependencies of power and domination. In other words, the results of conflict among groups holding conflicting perspectives will depend in part on the comparative power of these groups to make their perspective heard (Ranson et al., 1980).*

Technological frames refer to basic assumptions, beliefs, and expectations that people hold about a specific technological application (Davidson, 2002), including not only the nature and role of the technology itself, but the specific conditions, applications and consequences (intended and unintended) of that technology in particular contexts (Orlikowski & Gash, 1994). Technological frames might be shared within a relevant social group because members are likely to share common perceptions, expectations and interests regarding the implementation and use of a given ICT application. Similarly, technology frames might differ between different relevant social groups.

Although social shaping of technology and the structurationist view of technology share several common premises (both are strongly influenced by constructivism) and have some overlapping areas (for example, the concept of technological frames was borrowed by structurationist studies from social shaping ones), they also have distinctiveness that justify their inclusion in and complementarity with our framework. Among the most important contributions of social shaping studies, when combined with structurationism, is their familiarity with macro level analysis and their capability of broadening the scope of IS research.

Contextualism

The contextualist approach was first introduced by Pettigrew (1985, 1987, 1990) and has gained significant attention among IS researchers (Ngwenyama, 1998; Orlikowski, 1996; Walsham, 1993). Arguing that much research on organizational change is non-processual and non-contextual in character, Pettigrew (1985, 1990) emphasizes three elements: context, process and content. Pettigrew claims that these three elements are equally important and should be considered in concert. He also outlines how different levels of analysis are interconnected and interdependent.

Contextualism is depicted in IS research like a "theory of contextualism" (Karyda et al., 2005), as a methodology (Walsham & Sahay, 1999) and as a type of organizational change framework (Klein & Myers, 1999). Despite these different ways of referring to contextualism, all the IS studies reviewed emphasize similar properties of such a theoretical foundation: it allows the examination in detail of actions and perceptions of human actors without neglecting the historically situated context within which these actions took place and perceptions are formed (Walsham & Sahay, 1999). As Pettigrew (1990, p. 269) explains, when applying a contextualism lens, we look for "continuity and change, patterns and idiosyncrasies, the actions of individuals and groups, the role of contexts and structures, and processes of structuring" over time. Adapting context, process and content to ICT, we consider that:

- Context refers to the social setting where the ICT application is being implemented and used. It helps define the boundaries of the investigation and includes the identification of different relevant social groups interacting in a given social and cultural setting that makes up the research context. It also includes identification of technological frames for each social group, allowing the recognition of shared and conflicting perceptions, expectations and interests that characterize the context.

- Process refers to understanding how the IT application is implemented and with what kinds of consequences (intended and unintended). The analysis of the process focuses on how relevant social groups, and the identified technological frames, influence the negotiation taking place around the implementation and use of ICT. It also includes the identification of occasions, spaces and mechanisms open to negotiation and change.

- Content refers to the socio-technical characteristics of the IT application being implemented, as used by particular actors at a given level of analysis. The technologies-in-practice resulting from the process of negotiation are considered here.

The contextualism approach did not add new concepts to the framework, but it was valuable for proposing a **frame in which** to organize the four selected concepts in terms of three dimensions: **context, process and content.**

MAIN FOCUS OF THE CHAPTER

The *multilevel framework* combines the structurationist view of technology, social shaping of technology and contextualism. It is multilevel because it incorporates inextricably linked levels of analysis: individual, group and local community.

It combines four central concepts: technology-in-practice, negotiation, relevant social groups and technological frames. These concepts are linked according to three interconnected dimensions, as posited by contextualism: content, context and process. This multilevel framework aims at helping to identify occasions, spaces and mechanisms for implementing and using ICT applications at a community/societal level. Each of these concepts, selected to set out the framework, is important for different reasons.

First, because the level of analysis of our framework combines individual (e.g., local people coming from a low income population), organizations (e.g., firms, cooperatives, etc.) and networks of organizations within a region or local community (e.g., associations of cooperatives, arrangements between firms, ICT providers serving a group of firms), we look at ways to take into account actors in a multilevel context. Between individuals and community, there is the group level, which is articulated through the key concept of *relevant social groups*. It is a way to conceptualize and make sense of how people interact within a given community, whether individually or as part of a group, an organization or a network. The notion of relevant social groups allows us to recognize individuals and groups without reducing the complexity of intra- and inter-group relationships.

Second, because of our focus on ICT, the concept of *technological frames* helps us to recognize what kind of interests, assumptions and expectations different social groups attach to the adoption and use of a given technological artifact. Convergence or divergence, dominance or conflict among technological frames reveal important mechanisms in negotiations among relevant social groups.

The identification of relevant social groups within a given community, as well as the individuals that we consider representative of these groups, and the identification of the technological frames attached to these relevant social groups (shared and conflicting perceptions, expectations and interests), define the initial boundaries of the investigation and help establish the *context* in which the implementation and ICT use are being negotiated.

Third, the *negotiation* itself is the next concept that underlies our process-based approach. The negotiation is the *process* (contextualism) that corresponds to the identification of occasions, spaces and mechanisms by which relevant social groups interact over time.

Finally, the concept of *technology-in-practice* can be considered one of Orlikowski's main contributions to the application of structuration theory in the investigation of ICT phenomena. In our framework, we pay particular attention to technology-in-practice as the result of the negotiation process among different social groups, in order to recognize the interests or assumptions

that have prevailed in the implementation and use of ICT, those *characteristics* in terms of use that have prevailed, and the *consequences*, both intended and unintended, for the different social groups involved. Because technology-in-practice represents the ongoing results that grow out of the actual use of an ICT, allowing recognition of socio-technical, political and cultural characteristics of ICT in use, we characterize it as representing the contextualist dimension of *content*.

The result of the combination of the four concepts organized in terms of the three interconnected dimensions of the contextualist frame is presented in Figure 1. The arrows indicate that context influences the process, which influences the content, which influences the context and so on. The framework respects the core characteristics of process theory as earlier defined by Orlikowski and

Figure 1. A structurationist and multilevel framework

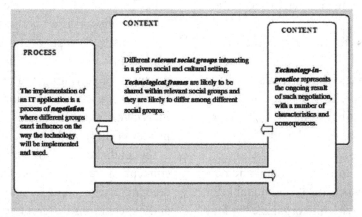

	Context		Process	Content
Individual level	The connection between individuals and the local community goes through the **relevant social groups** interacting in a given social and cultural setting.	People build their **technological frames** over time. This implies the identification of *assumptions, expectations and interests* attached to the implementation and use of a given technology.	The implementation and use of ICT is a **negotiation** where different groups exert influence on how the artifact will be implemented and used. Implies the identification of *occasions, spaces and mechanisms* open for negotiation.	**Technology-in-practice** represents the ongoing results of such negotiation, with a number of *characteristics and consequences (intended and unintended)*.
Group level				
Community level (could be extended to societal level)				

Robey (1991); it accommodates multiple levels of analysis, is contextually and temporally situated, and avoids the blinders of non-historical accounts of social phenomena.

It is multilevel because it incorporates inextricably linked levels of analysis: individual, group and community. The community represents a network of social groups interacting in a given geographical or virtual space and having in common the fact that they are involved in a process of implementation or use of a given technology. The community level could be extended to the societal one if, for instance, the investigation entails implementation and use of ICT at a national level. However, the aim of an investigation applying the multilevel framework is to build a macro account of broader interactions among a network of players without neglecting everyday interactions within relevant social groups. The line that commonly separates macro and micro levels of analysis is removed, rendering it difficult to understand the macro without plunging into the micro level. The actors, individually, through their daily actions, reproduce or reinforce structured rules, norms and meanings (Orlikowski, 1992). By their articulation within subgroups, they constitute social spaces and play important roles in the choice regarding management and use of technology (Clausen & Koch, 1999). In effect, changes in community or societal levels emerge from individual practices and groups or coalitions.

We call this a conceptual framework for "analytical induction" because no hypotheses or propositions are offered but only a framework that will guide the empirical work. Although key concepts are identified (e.g., relevant social groups and technological frames), their relationship and interaction with particular contexts remain to be discovered. Recently, researchers have used analytical induction with important results (Lapointe & Rivard, 2006). The use of this model has the goal of increasing understanding of "how" IT applications are drawn upon to provide meaning

and to legitimize certain outcomes to the detriment of others in different contexts.

Because understanding of the process is seen as fundamental, their relationship and interaction in particular contexts remain to be discovered during data collection and analysis. The goal is to start with a general theoretical model and to distil such a model within an iterative process that does not take the initial model for granted but allows us to recognize new categories and refine existing ones in such a way as to enrich our understanding of the research problem (Patton, 2002).

FUTURE TRENDS

More discussion is needed to refine the proposed multilevel framework as well as to offer alternatives that seek to engage seriously in broader levels of analysis than the organizational one. For instance, as the combination of micro and macro levels of analysis is not an easy task, Pozzebon et al. (2006) have proposed a multilevel frame to identify occasions and opportunities for breaking down ICT rhetorical closure at three levels of analysis: individual, organizational and segment. At the individual level, opportunities were associated to daily users' practices, depending on empowerment and training. At the organizational level, opportunities were related to ongoing organizational decisions and negotiations regarding ICT adoption and implementation. Finally, at the segment level, opportunities were related to forming coalitions, networks and groups of users.

Articulating three levels of analysis, the authors were able to identify occasions and opportunities to help decision-makers preserve their ability to make informed choices at both the micro (e.g., investing in skilled and capable employees) and macro (e.g., networking with other firms) levels. Likewise, Burton-Jones and Gallivan (2007) have proposed a multilevel perspective of system usage. They argue that although the relevance of multilevel issues when studying IT is widely accepted nowadays, the conceptual and methodological tools to conduct multilevel research have only recently matured and so only recently has in-depth multilevel research become feasible. These recent articles suggest that great opportunities exist to extend exploration of multilevel accounts in IS research.

The concepts related to technological frames—cognitive maps, interpretive frames, provinces of meaning—evoke Weick's (1993) paper titled *The Collapse of Sensemaking in Organizations: The Mann Gulch Disaster.* In this seminal paper, Weick analyzes a tragedy that occurred in 1949 in the rugged mountains of Montana, where 13 forest service smokejumpers died trying to battle a violent forest fire that burned fiercely in very difficult terrain. Weick uses this event to examine how the sensemaking processes of highly trained groups break down when the orderliness of the universe is called into question because both understanding and procedures for sensemaking collapse together (Lawrence, 2005). Although this perspective has influenced well-known IS researchers, as was the case with Ciborra (1999), we can argue that the potential of sensemaking theory has not yet been significantly explored in IS research.

Finally, regarding the identification of occasions, spaces and mechanisms open for negotiation, we believe that future research should include a better articulation of emergent action-based lenses in the examination of the negotiation phase. We believe that theoretical approaches like negotiated order (Heracleous & Marshak, 2004), situated-action (Ciborra & Willcocks, 2006) and actor-network (Pentland & Feldman, 2007) could be of great value in providing operationalized concepts that help to recognize, as contextualism wish, the details of actions and perceptions without neglecting the richness of historically situated contexts.

CONCLUSION

It may be argued, i.e., Jones and Kartsten (2008), that IS researchers using structuration theory have done so in a wide variety of ways, and that they should seek to explore the full scope of theories they borrow from other disciplines. We are trying to engage seriously in structuration theory without neglecting the contribution of complementary approaches. As the influence of ICT on social life broadens in scope, heterogeneity in terms of actors involved, diversity of interests and technological views, IS researchers need to rely on conceptual approaches so as to build a multilevel understanding of the technological phenomena. The multilevel approach proposed in this chapter is still under construction, though. Since any conceptual approach is only valid to the extent to which it is adopted by a significant number of researchers and is validated by relevant empirical analysis, the effective contribution of this presented multilevel approach to the IS research field must be proven under use. And as we believe that technology takes shape only after being adopted in practice, we also believe that the evolution of our proposed approach will have a definitive shape only when other researchers have adopted it and contributed to its evolution.

REFERENCES

Argyris, C., & Schon, D. (1978). *Organizational learning.* Englewood Cliffs, NJ: Prentice-Hall.

Avgerou, C. (2000). IT and organizational change: An institutionalist perspective. *Information Technology & People, 13*(4), 234.

Barley, S. R. (1986). Technology as an occasion for structuring: Evidence from observations of CT scanners and the social order of radiology departments. *Administrative Science Quarterly, 31*(1), 78.

Barrett, M., & Walsham, G. (1999). Electronic trading and work transformation in the London insurance market. *Information Systems Research, 10*(1), 1-21.

Bartunek, J. M. (1984). Changing interpretive schemes and organizational structuring: The Example of a religious order. *Administrative Science Quarterly, 29*, 355-372.

Bartunek, J. M., & Moch, M. (1987). First order, second order, and third order change and organization development interventions: A cognitive approach. *Journal of Applied Behavior Science, 23*(4), 483-500.

Berger, P. L., & Luckmann, T. (1967). *The social construction of reality: A treatise on the sociology of knowledge.* Garden City, NY: Anchor.

Bernstein, R. (1983). *Beyond objectivism and relativism: Science, hermeneutics, and Praxis.* Philadelphia: University of Pennsylvania Press.

Bhaskar, R. (1989). *Reclaiming reality: A critical introduction to contemporary philosophy.* London: Verso.

Bijker, W. E., & Law, J. (1992). *Shaping technology/building society: Studies in socio-technical change.* Cambridge, MA: MICT Press.

Bougnon, et al. (1977). Cognition in organizations: An analysis of the Utrecht Jazz Orchestra. *Administrative Science Quarterly, 22*(4), 606-639.

Bourdieu, P. (1977). *Outline of a theory of practice.* Cambridge, MA: Cambridge University Press.

Burton-Jones, A., & Gallivan, M. J. (2007). Toward a deeper understanding of system usage in organizations: A multilevel perspective. *MIS Quarterly, 31*(4), 657-679.

Chin, W. W., Gopal, A., & Salisbury, W. D. (1997). Advancing the theory of adaptive structuration: The development of a scale to measure faithfulness of appropriation. *Information Systems Research, 8*(4), 342-367.

Ciborra, C. (1999). Notes on improvisation and time in organizations. *Accounting, Management & Information Technologies, 9*(2), 77-94.

Ciborra, C., & Willcocks, L. (2006). The mind or the heart? It depends on the (definition of) situation. *Journal of Information Technology, 21*(3), 129-140.

Clausen, C., & Koch, C. (1999). The role of space and occasions in the transformation of information technologies - lessons from the social shaping of ICT systems for manufacturing in a Danish context. *Technology Analysis and Strategic Management, 11*(3), 463-482.

Cohen, I. J. (1989). *Structuration theory: Anthony Giddens and the constitution of social life.* New York: St Martin's Press.

Davidson, E. (2002). Technology frames and framing: A socio-cognitive investigation of requirements determination. *MIS Quarterly, 26*(4), 329-358.

Dawson, P., et al. (2000). Political processes in management, organization and the social shaping of technology. *Technology Analysis and Strategic Management, 12*(1) 5-15.

DeSanctis, G., & Poole, M. S. (1994). Capturing the complexity in advanced technology use: Adaptive structuration theory. *Organization Science, 5*(2), 121-147.

Doolin, B. (1998). Information technology as disciplinary technology: Being critical in interpretive research on information systems. *Journal of Information Technology, 13*(4), 301-311.

Eden, C. (1992). On the nature of cognitive maps. *Journal of Management Studies, 29*(3), 261-265.

Fay, B. (1996). *Contemporary philosophy of social science: A multicultural approach.* Oxford, UK: Blackwell.

Fulk, J. (1993). Social construction of communication technology. *Academy of Management Journal, 36*(5), 921-951.

Gallivan, M. J. (1995). Contradictions among stakeholder assessments of a radical change initiative: A cognitive frames analysis. In W. J. Orlikowski, et al. (Eds.), *Information technology and changes in organizational work*. London: Chapman and Hall.

Giddens, A. (1984). *The constitution of society*. Berkeley, CA: University of California Press.

Giddens, A. (1989). A reply to my critics. In D. Held & J. B. Thompson (Eds.), *Social Theory of Modern Societies: Anthony Giddens and His Critics* (pp. 249-305). Cambridge, MA: Cambridge University Press.

Giddens, A. (1990). *The consequences of modernity*. Stanford, CA: Stanford University Press.

Giddens, A., & Pierson, C. (1998). *Conversations with Anthony Giddens; Making sense of modernity*. Cambridge, MA: Polity Press.

Goffman, I. (1974). *Frame analysis*. New York: Harper and Row.

Gopal, A., & Prasad, P. (2000). Understanding GDSS in symbolic context: Shifting the focus from technology to interaction. *MIS Quarterly, 24*(3), 509-546.

Heracleous, L., & Marshak, R. J. (2004). Conceptualizing organizational discourse as situated symbolic action. *Human Relations, 57*(10), 1285-1312.

Heracleous, L., & Barrett, M. (2001). Organizational change as discourse: Communicative actions and deep structures in the context of information technology implementation. *Academy of Management Journal, 44*(4), 755-778.

Jones, M. R., & Karsten, H. (2008). Giddens's structuration theory and information systems research. *MIS Quarterly, 32*(1), 127-157.

Karyda, M., Kiountouzis, E., & Kokolakis, S. (2005) Information systems security policies: A contextual perspective. *Computers & Security, 24*(3), 246-255.

Klein, H. K., & Myers, M. D. (1999). A set of principles for conducting and evaluating interpretive field studies in information systems. *MIS Quarterly, 23*(1), 67-99.

Koch, C. (2000). Collective influence on information technology in virtual organizations – emancipatory management of technology. *Technology Analysis and Strategic Management, 12*(3), 357-368.

Lapointe, L., & Rivard, S. (2005) A multilevel model of resistance to information technology implementation. *MIS Quarterly, 29*(3), 461-491.

Lawrence, C. (2005). From Milan to Mann Gulch: Reflections on the intellectual contributions of Professor Claudio Ciborra. *European Journal of Information Systems, 14*(5), 484-495.

McLoughlin, I., et al. (2000). Rethinking political process in technological change: Socio-technical configurations and frames. *Technology Analysis and Strategic Management, 12*(1), 17-37.

MacKenzie, D., & Wajckman, J. (1999). *The social shaping of technology* (p. 462). Open University Press.

Majchrzak, A., Rice, R. E., Malhotra, A., King, N., & Sulin, B. (2000). Technology adaptation: The case of a computer-supported interorganizational virtual team. *MIS Quarterly, 24*(4), 569-600.

Maznevski, M. L., & Chudoba, K. M. (2000). Bridging space over time: Global virtual team dynamics and effectiveness. *Organization Science, 11*(5), 473-492.

Miranda, S. M., & Bostrom, R.P. (1993-1994). The impact of group support systems on group conflict and conflict management. *Journal of Management Information Systems, 10*(3), 63-95.

Montealegre, R. (1997). The interplay of information technology and the social milieu. *Information Technology and People, 10*(2), 106-131.

Ngwenyama, O. N. (1998). Groupware, social action and organizational emergence: On the process dynamics of computer mediated distributed work. *Accounting, Management and Information Technology, 8*, 127-146.

Nicholson, B., & Sahay, S. (2001). Some political and cultural issues in the globalization of software development: Case experience from Britain and India. *Information and Organization, 11*, 25-43.

Olesen, K., & Myers, M. D. (1999). Trying to improve communication and collaboration with information technology: An action research project which failed. *Information Technology and People, 12*(4), 317-332.

Orlikowski, W. J. (1991). Integrated information environment or matrix of control? The contradictory implications of information technology. *Accounting, Management and Information Technology, 1*(1), 9-42.

Orlikowski, W. J. (1992). The duality of technology: Rethinking the concept of technology in organizations. *Organization Science, 3*(3), 398-427.

Orlikowski, W. J. (1993). CASE tools as organizational change: Investigating increment. *MIS Quarterly, 17*(3), 309-340.

Orlikowski, W. J. (2000). Using technology and constituting structures: A practice lens for studying technology in organizations. *Organization Science, 11*(4), 404-428.

Orlikowski, W. J. (1996). Improvising organizational transformation over time: A situated change perspective. *Information Systems Research, 7*(1), 63-92.

Orlikowski, W. J. & Gash, D. C. (1994). Technological frames: Making sense of information technology in organizations. *ACM Transactions on Information Systems, 12*(2), 174-207.

Orlikowski, W. J. & Yates, J. (1994). Genre repertoire: The structuring of communicative

practices in organizations. *Administrative Science Quarterly, 39*(4), 541-574.

Patton, M. Q. (2002). *Qualitative evaluation and research methods.* Thousand Oaks, CA: Sage Publications.

Pentland, B. T., & Feldman, M. S. (2007). Narrative networks: Patterns of technology and organization. *Organization Science. 18*(5), 781-797.

Pettigrew, A. M. (1990). Longitudinal field research on change: Theory and practice. *Organization Science, 1*(3), 267-292.

Pettigrew, A. M. (1985). Contextualist research and the study of organizational change processes. In E. Mumford, et al. (Eds.), *Research methods in information systems.* New York: North Holland.

Pettigrew, A. M. (1987). Context and action in the transformation of the firm. *Journal of Management Studies, 24*(6), 649-670.

Pinch, T. F., & Bijker, W. E. (1984). The social construction of facts and artifacts: Or how the sociology of science and the sociology of technology might benefit each other. In W. E. Bijker, et al. (Eds.), *The social construction of technology systems. New directions in the sociology and history of technology.* The MICT Press.

Pozzebon, M. (2004). The influence of a structurationist perspective on strategic management research. *Journal of Management Studies, 41*(2), 247-272.

Pozzebon, M., & Pinsonneault, A. (2005). Challenges in conducting empirical work using structuration theory: Learning from ICT research. *Organization Studies, 26*(9), 1353-1376.

Pozzebon, M., Titah, R., & Pinsonneault, A. (2006). Combining social shaping of technology and communicative action theory for understanding rhetorical closure in IT. *Information Technology & People, 19*(3), 244-271.

Ranson, S., Hinings, B., & Greenwood, R. (1980). The structuring of organizational structures. *Administrative Science Quarterly, 25*, 1-17.

Sahay, S. (1998). Implementation of GIS technology in India: Some issues of time and space. *Accounting, Management and Information Technologies, 8*(2-3), 147-188.

Sahay, S., & Robey, D. (1996). Organizational context, social interpretation, and the implementation and consequences of geographic information systems. *Accounting, Management and Information Technology, 6*(4), 255-282.

Sarker, S., Sarker, S., & Sidorova, A. (2006). Actor-networks and business process change failure: An interpretive case study. *Journal of Management Information Systems, 23*(1), 51-86.

Schutz, A. (1970). *On phenomenology and social relations*. Chicago: University of Chicago Press.

Walsham, G. (1993). *Interpreting information systems in organizations*. Cambridge, MA: John Wiley and Sons.

Walsham, G. (2002). Cross-cultural software production and use: A structurational analysis. *MIS Quarterly, 26*(4), 359-380.

Walsham, G., & Chun, K. H. (1991). Structuration theory and information systems research. *Journal of Applied Systems Analysis, 17*, 77-85.

Walsham, G., & Sahay, S. (1999). GIS for district-level administration in India: Problems and opportunities. *MIS Quarterly, 23*(1), 39-56.

Weick, K. (1993). The collapse of sensemaking in organizations: The Mann Gulch disaster. *Administrative Science Quarterly, 38*(4), 268-282.

Williams, R. (1997). Universal solutions or local contingencies? Tensions and contradictions in the mutual shaping of technology and work organization. In I. McLoughlin & M. Harris (Eds.), *Innovation, organization change and technology* (pp. 170-185). International Thomson Business Press.

Yates, J., & Orlikowski, W.J. (1992). Genres of organizational communication: A structurational approach to studying communication and media. *Academy of Management Review, 17*(2), 299-336.

Yetim, F. (2006). Acting with genres: Discursive-ethical concepts for reflecting on and legitimating genres. *European Journal of Information Systems, 15*(1), 54-69.

Yoshioka, T., Yates, J., & Orlikowski, W.J. (1994). Community-based interpretive schemes: Exploring the use of cyber meetings within a global organization. *AMJ Best Papers*.

KEY TERMS AND DEFINITIONS

Actor Network Theory: Also known as ANT, this is a sociological theory developed by Bruno Latour, Michel Callon and John Law. It is distinguished from other network theories in that an actor-network contains not merely people but objects and organizations. These are collectively referred to as actors, or sometimes as actants.

Adaptive Structuration Theory: DeSanctis and Poole adapted Giddens' theory to study the interaction of groups and organizations with information technology, and called it Adaptive Structuration Theory, also known as AST. This theory is formulated as "the production and reproduction of the social systems through members' use of rules and resources in interaction".

Critical Social Theory: Critical research focuses on the oppositions, conflicts and contradictions in contemporary society, and seeks to be emancipatory, i.e. helping to eliminate the causes of alienation and domination. The main task of critical research is seen as social critique, whereby the restrictive and alienating conditions of the status quo are brought to light.

Institutional Theory: Institutional theory attends considers the processes by which structures, including schemas, rules, norms and routines, become established as authoritative guidelines for social behavior. It examines how these elements are created, diffused, adopted, and adapted over space and time; and how they fall into decline and disuse.

Social Construction of Technology: Also referred to as SCOT, this is a theory advocated by social constructivists that contends that technology does not determine human action, but, rather, that human action shapes technology. It also argues that the ways in which a technology is used cannot be understood without understanding how that technology is embedded in its social context.

Structuration Theory: The theory of structuration was proposed by British sociologist Anthony Giddens in a number of articles in the late 1970s and early 1980s, culminating in the publication of The Constitution of Society in 1984. It is an attempt to reconcile theoretical dichotomies such as agency/structure, subjective/objective, and micro/macro. The approach does not focus on the individual actor or societal totality "but social practices ordered across space and time."

Symbolic Interactionism: Represents a major sociological perspective derived from American pragmatism and particularly from the work of George Mead, who argued that people's selves are social products, but that these selves are also purposive and creative.

Chapter III
Employing a Grounded Theory Approach for MIS Research

Susan Gasson
The iSchool at Drexel, Drexel University, USA

ABSTRACT

This chapter provides a brief introduction to the grounded theory (GT) approach to research, discussing how it has been used in information systems (IS) research, and how GT studies may be conducted to provide a significant theoretical contribution to the management information systems (MIS) field. The subject is of particular interest at a time when GT attracts frequent criticism for a lack of rigor. This chapter deals with what makes for a rigorous contribution to "grounded" theory in MIS. It addresses developments and controversies in the generation of grounded theories, examining the use of GT as a coding method vs. the use of GT as a method for generating theory. The discussion focuses mainly on the constructivist/interpretive perspective adopted in most qualitative data studies, as this is the way in which GT has been used most often in MIS. The chapter concludes with a roadmap for the use of GT in MIS research and a discussion of the contribution made by GT studies in MIS.

INTRODUCTION

The Grounded Theory (GT) research method has grown more popular in recent years. This is partly in response to an increasing awareness of the limitations of applying *a priori*, deductive theo-ries to human transactions embedded in a social context, and partly in response to the immaturity of Management Information Systems (MIS) as a discipline. The GT approach is used to generate a *substantive theory* – a theory that is grounded in specific mechanisms, contexts or environments.

This fits well with the need to produce in-depth empirical studies that develop a dynamic body of theory that evolves with the MIS field itself. The construction of a *grounded theory* relies on a systematic analysis of qualitative data, to theorize about "what is it that is happening here?" The result is a theory that is grounded in empirical evidence, rather than developed from existing conceptual frameworks. The GT approach may be used to analyze qualitative data to produce quantitative data that are analyzed statistically, or it may employ a qualitative, interpretive data analysis throughout. The latter approach is the most frequently encountered in MIS and so this chapter will focus mainly on these studies.

Grounded theories are situated, not only in "the data," but also in the context in which data was collected. They may be considered *idiographic theories,* that are "concerned with the individual [case], pertaining to or descriptive of single or unique facts and processes" (Dey, 1999, pg. 217). Quality criteria for idiographic theories of action emphasize transferability or adaptation to different contexts, rather than the generalizability concerns that are applied to nomothetic or formal theories (S. . Gasson, 2003; Lincoln & Guba, 2000). The GT approach may be used over time to generate formal (nomothetic) theories, that are more generalizable as they are derived from multiple studies and contexts. This requires a substantial amount of time and relies on researchers who are capable of reflexive theoretical abstraction. The majority of GT studies contribute idiographic theories that provide deep insights into the research problem for a limited number of situations or contexts.

The aim of this chapter is to provide an overview of the GT method, to address controversies and issues surrounding its use, and to provide some guidance on how it may be used to contribute meaningfully to MIS research. The chapter is organized as follows. First, some background is provided on the GT approach to research and the GT "method." Secondly, I discuss controversies and developments in both the approach to, and

the methods for Grounded Theory generation. Thirdly, the contribution of the GT approach to MIS is demonstrated by means of illustrative studies. The fourth section presents a roadmap for GT research in MIS, examining the unique challenges that our field presents to GT researchers, discussing the constraints presented by seed categories and *a priori* theoretical models, ethics, boundaries, and scope in MIS research, and issues of generalizability. The chapter concludes with a brief discussion of the contribution of GT to the MIS field.

BACKGROUND

The Grounded Theory Method

The Grounded Theory (GT) research method (Glaser & Strauss, 1967) was devised "to develop and integrate a set of ideas and hypotheses in an integrated theory that accounts for behavior in any substantive area" (Lowe, 1996). GT researchers avoid proposing a theory at the beginning of their study, instead deriving and refining the theory through cycles of data collection, analysis, and synthesis, as shown in Figure 1. This model provides an overview of the structured process underlying the Grounded Theory research method. It is synthesized from multiple texts by the originators of the GT approach (Glaser and Strauss, 1967; Glaser, 1978; Strauss and Corbin, 1990; Glaser, 1992; Strauss and Corbin, 1998). The dotted line box in Figure 1 refers to a stage introduced by Strauss and Corbin (1990), which many researchers find useful, but which was rejected by Glaser (1978, 1992).

At its simplest, the core GT method relies on specific processes that are not found in other approaches to constructing theory (Glaser & Strauss, 1967). Both Bryant (2002) and Urquhart (2002) differentiate between the GT *coding method* and the GT *method of generating theory.* It is the combination of these two elements that makes the GT method unique:

- **The Grounded Theory coding method.**
Data are categorized according to an emergent set of *open codes* (category labels) that the researcher identifies to define key elements of the situation. Through iterative cycles of coding and analysis, data-categories are combined or split to define selective (*theoretical*) *codes*: abstract concepts that describe or explain themes related to the research phenomena of interest. Repeated iterations of coding result in an emerging theory which can be defined in terms of abstract conceptual categories, properties of conceptual categories, and relationships between categories, and/or their properties.

- **The Grounded Theory method of generating theory.** A substantive theory is generated when the researcher can define a core conceptual category in the data, and identify key patterns of relationships between the various theoretical and conceptual categories that apply across data samples. These patterns are made explicit through the generation of *theoretical memos* as the analysis proceeds. Analytical codes, relationships, and attributes are constantly compared across and between further data samples to understand how the emerging theory is reinforced or altered by new evidence. This process of *constant comparison* also guides further data collection, as inductive analysis suggests specific contexts or conditions in which the theory may apply, or reveals discrepancies between data samples that need clarification. Data collection and analysis continue in an iterative fashion until the researcher feels that *theoretical saturation* (the point of diminishing returns from further data analysis) has been reached.

In MIS research, most data collection is guided by the formulation of hypotheses that direct which "variables" in a situation should be measured or

Figure 1. The Grounded Theory Research Method

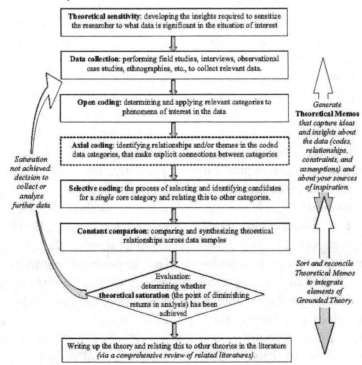

assessed. Even in qualitative, interpretive studies, the research design tends to employ a literature-derived conceptual framework to guide the collection and analysis of data. When employing a GT approach, a literature review is conducted mainly for the purposes of identifying research questions that remain to be answered. The researcher collects any and all empirical data that are relevant to the phenomena or situation of interest (interviews, observations, documents, etc.), then analyzes that data systematically, to derive a conceptual framework or theory by which we may explain, predict, or manage these real-world situations. By evaluating the emerging theory against more and more data, adapting the theory as new insights are realized, and testing these insights against previous data, we can generate theoretical concepts and models that are transferable to similar contexts. The emergent theory is developed by performing a secondary literature review, that searches for theoretical research employing similar concepts to those found in the data. In this way, a GT researcher formulates a *substantive theory* that makes an innovative contribution to knowledge because it is grounded in a specific situation and extended across comparable situations. We terminate the analysis at the point of diminishing returns, when no important insights are provided by analyzing additional data.

The term *grounded theory* has been misused in some studies to denote an absence of method or the generation of a theoretical contribution on the basis of vague inductive reasoning (Babchuk, 1996; A. Bryant, 2002). The following two core elements define the Grounded Theory research method:

- Generation of theoretical concepts and/or models through systematic data analysis, *and*
- Development and evaluation of the emerging theory by means of constant comparison across data samples until theoretical saturation is reached.

DEVELOPMENTS IN THE GROUNDED THEORY METHOD

This section covers the ways in which the Grounded Theory method has developed over time – and also addresses some issues, controversies, and problems encountered along the way. Definitions of the GT "method" have evolved and diverged as authors who espouse diverse research paradigms and philosophies of method experiment with and develop their own approach to generating theory which is grounded in an analysis of the data collected. In response to perceptions that the GT method as described in Glaser and Strauss (1967) was too ill-defined and open-ended to employ practically, both Glaser and Strauss presented developments of the method that they had evolved individually:

- Glaser presented a more systematic process for moving from open coding to selective coding (during which a theory of action is formulated). He suggested eighteen coding paradigms, that could be used to analyze different types of theory, spanning contingency-based theories of action, process theories, causal models, various forms of factor model, structural models, pictorial models, relational theories, and temporal ordering theories. This work described how a process of writing and sorting *theoretical memos*—memos that contain definitions of theoretical relationships between categories of data—are useful to clarify the emerging theory by making explicit the meanings of categories, their properties, and relationships between them. The aim was to both explain the process of GT analysis and to ensure reliability by making the process of theory development auditable (Glaser, 1978).
- Meanwhile, Strauss was working on a social and transactive theory of action, based on symbolic interactionism (Blumer, 1969; Mead, 1934). He argued that social order

can be seen as a trajectory of interactions between actors, or with various situational contingencies (Strauss, 1983). Strauss, in collaboration with Juliet Corbin, produced a detailed exposition of how to use the GT method *systematically* in order to deal with the reliability problems of interpretive, qualitative research. Strauss and Corbin explained how GT analysis can be used to develop theories of social agency by focusing on transaction-based action and interaction strategies, their causal conditions, and their consequences. They introduced an additional stage of analysis—*axial coding*—and suggested the framework shown in Figure 2, around which the search for a core category of human transactional behavior could be structured (Strauss & Corbin, 1990).

The publication of the Strauss and Corbin (1990) book initiated the well-known debate between Glaser and Strauss about what constituted the GT "method." Differences between the two have been analyzed by a number of authors (Annells, 1996; Babchuk, 1996; Dey, 1999; Smit & Bryant, 2000). The key differences between Glaser and Strauss appear to relate to two issues, one ontological (relating to beliefs about how we know reality) and the other methodological (relating to how the GT method should be structured).

The Ontological Issue

The ontological issue is whether the theory that is uncovered by means of a GT approach exists independently of the researcher and the specific context of the research, or whether it is socially-situated and subjective. Annells observes that Glaser (1978, 1992, 2002) appears to adopt a critical realist ontology, where the external world is viewed as existing independently of the researcher and capable of apprehension, albeit imperfectly. Strauss and Corbin, on the other hand, appear to adopt a relativist ontology, where reality is

interpreted by the researcher (Annells, 1996). So we have two distinct worldviews applying in the two texts. Glaser (1978, 1992, 2002) argues that a grounded theory can be "discovered" in "the data," while Strauss and Corbin (1990, 1998) apply their method to the interpretation of a theory that reflects the prevailing consensus on what has occurred. Glaser emphasizes objective abstraction as the means by which we produce a "scientific" theory. He is concerned with data "accuracy," viewing the aim of constant comparison as triangulating data from multiple sources (Glaser, 2002). Strauss and Corbin emphasize the interpretive nature of the data collected and see the aim of constant comparison across data samples as providing a *relative* "verification" of the theoretical model between sources.

The Methodological Issue

The methodological issue was concerned about how the GT method should be structured to provide a systematic method for analysis. Glaser (1978) disagreed with what he saw as an unnecessary over-structuring of the method of generating theory by Strauss and Corbin (1990), who introduced an axial coding stage to integrate the fragmented categories produced by open coding. They suggested that this analysis should employ a conceptual framework based on Strauss' social and transactive view of human agency and interaction (Strauss, 1978, 1983). This is shown in Figure 2.

Glaser (1992) argued that the use of this framework resulted in "forcing" the data into a single paradigm and compared this to the eighteen paradigms that he had suggested (Glaser, 1978). The second edition of the Strauss and Corbin book reduced their axial coding framework to three processual elements: Conditions → Action/ Interaction → Consequences (Strauss & Corbin, 1998). The less structured approach reflected Strauss's search for "fluid organizational elements of negotiations" (Clarke, 2003, p. 556), permit-

Figure 2. Axial Coding Framework, Adapted From Strauss and Corbin (1990)

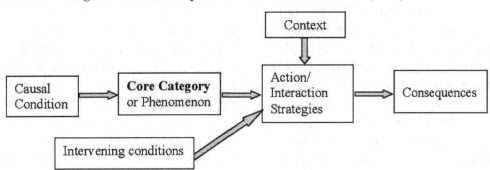

ting a wider set of analytical lenses to be applied to the emerging theory. It is clear that the major difference is that Strauss and Corbin envisaged dynamic theories of human agency and interaction resulting from their method, whereas Glaser's eighteen coding paradigms present a relatively static set of theoretical structures.

Constructivist Grounded Theory

Because of his less structured approach to theoretical coding, Glaser's variant of the GT method has been viewed as more amenable to constructivist theory generation. Glaser himself does not share this view. In a chapter that caused much controversy, Charmaz (2000) argues that the GT method is a particularly good fit with constructivist theory-building. She argues that the GT coding process is capable of reflecting an explicit acknowledgement of multiple actors' perspectives on what is the social reality in a situation. She suggests that a constructivist account of how data were collected, how they were analyzed, and how the resulting theory was derived would avoid the privileging of one subject's account over others (echoing a key concern of Klein & Myers, 1999), and would help identify researcher bias. Charmaz argues that an analysis process that relies on commonalities between accounts for "triangulation" of the data allows the researcher to avoid examining how they arrived at their definition of key categories and to avoid evaluating whether their findings would

be meaningful to their subjects (Charmaz, 2000). Glaser (2002) misinterprets the constructivist position in his response to this view. He argues that the use of constant comparison discovers a "latent pattern" that is common to multiple research subjects or situations and that this, rather than accounting for differences between subject perspectives, resolves the "worrisome accuracy" problem of qualitative data collection. Glaser appears to equate a constructivist approach to imposing researcher subjectivities on the perspectives of research subjects:

So we can see that constructivism—joint build of an interactive, interpreted, produced data – is an epistemological bias to achieve a credible, accurate description of data collection – sometimes. But it depends on the data. If the data is garnered through an interview guide that forces and feeds interviewee responses then it is constructed to a degree by interviewer imposed interactive bias. But, as I said above, with the passive, non structured interviewing or listening of the GT interview-observation method, constructivism is held to a minimum. (Glaser, 2002, para 10).

Multi-Grounded Theory

The positivist/constructivist debate is not the only development that is relevant to the use of a GT approach for MIS research. More recently there have been calls to generate *multi-grounded* theories of action in the MIS field (Lind & Goldkuhl, 2006; Tan & Hall, 2007). These approaches generally combine qualitative data collection with both qualitative and quantitative analysis. They employ a post-positivist approach to data analysis, using objectivist data coding (categorization) techniques to "convert" qualitative data to a form that may be analyzed quantitatively, or supplementing qualitative data with quantitative data (for example, supplementing interview findings with large-scale survey data). Findings from a quantitative data analysis are triangulated against findings from the qualitative data analysis, to provide a pragmatic approach to theory evaluation. This is a useful way of collecting large-scale support for a formal theory in a short period of time. But there are dangers that this approach may lead to reductionist theories of action, where only those elements of a theory that are capable of being assessed quantitatively are included in the theory, so this approach should be considered carefully to understand its contribution.

EXEMPLAR GT STUDIES IN MIS

The Grounded Theory (GT) method would seem to be particularly appropriate to MIS, which is a relatively new discipline and is thus in a position to welcome well-supported theories of action. But the GT approach has so far been used more as a *coding method* in MIS than as a *method of generating theory* through constant comparison across data samples until theoretical saturation has been achieved (Urquhart, 2002). This may well be because of the dominance of objectivist, "scientific method" criteria for evaluating rigor in MIS research studies. These criteria may lead many GT studies to be rejected for publication, or post-rationalized in ways that make them *appear* to be based on extant theory (A. Bryant, 2002). Yet it is clear that the approach generates original theory in MIS research, a critical issue as the field widens to embrace constructivist, situated,

and community-oriented theories of action. As MIS journals become more open to qualitative and interpretivist studies, GT seems increasingly popular as a research approach in MIS. This section presents an overview of exemplar GT studies in MIS, discussing how a variety of studies have employed or developed the GT method. The discussion of these studies reflects applications of the GT approach in MIS over time.

A groundbreaking paper by Orlikowski (1993) raised the profile of the GT method in MIS. This study was awarded the MISQ best paper award for that year, legitimizing the use of the GT method for the field. Orlikowski studied the adoption and use of CASE tools in three organizations, to develop a theory that explains how organizational issues affect technology introduction. She categorized contextual and process elements to understand similarities and differences between CASE adoption and use in two different firms, concluding that differences between their experience of introducing CASE tools could be attributed to variations in the change process, the organizational context, and the intentions and actions of key organizational actors. Different impacts of CASE tool adoption and use were experienced according to whether the change was intended to be incremental or radical, and whether the objective of introducing the CASE tool was to affect the firm's products or processes. These distinctions led to identifiable variations in emphasis and project outcomes (Orlikowski, 1993). This study followed the Glaser & Strauss (1967) method, emphasizing iterative data collection, coding and analysis, and constant comparison of findings across samples and between data sources to triangulate findings (Orlikowski, 1993). An interesting aspects of the study is that the author explains how "the iterative approach of data collection, coding, and analysis was more open-ended and generative" at the first research site than at the second site, as the emerging theoretical constructs guided data collection at the second site. While the process is also related to the open vs. axial coding stages of Strauss &

Corbin (1990), none of the other concepts from this variant of the method make an appearance, leading to the conclusion that the distinction between open and axial coding was made to frame the iterative emergence of conceptual categories. However, the paper provides an excellent discussion of the iterative GT research method and its contribution to a theory that helps us to explain and manage a complex MIS problem.

At about the same time, Pries-Heje (1992) performed an investigation of the use of software tools in IS development projects across 19 firms in Scandinavia. His analysis revealed the existence of three barriers to the continued use of software tools: (i) a developer must have sufficient information to be able to evaluate its potential contribution (and to judge it positively), (ii) they must have a situation for which it will be useful (e.g. a project that requires automation, for a software automation tool), and (iii) the tool must fit with a variety of organizational or project-specific factors, e.g. be compatible with other software tools (Pries-Heje, 1992). This study provides an excellent exemplar of a systematic GT analysis, following the Strauss & Corbin (1990) method. The narrative describes the author's process of analysis in great detail that is really useful for the GT "novice." The author provides multiple examples to explain how he categorized interview data to derive categories, how he grouped and sorted categories to understand key concepts in the use of software tools for IS development, and how he developed a grounded theory through multiple iterations of conceptual analysis.

A paper by Galal and McDonnell (1997) proposed using the GT method as a method for requirements analysis in defining organizational knowledge-based systems (KBS). They argue that statements of both requirements and assessed outcomes from a KBS prototype may be viewed as substantive theories of action. A GT approach can therefore be employed systematically to derive formulations about system requirements and change outcomes. GT core categories could be used to construct "vision scenarios" for the KBS, and system prototypes could be formally evaluated against these scenarios. This is an intriguing idea that builds on the use of ethnographic data (for example in human-computer interface research). As GT can be used to construct theories that explain how knowledge is used in organizations, this approach might have a great deal of potential if used reflectively.

Gasson (1999) explored the reasons for a non-user-centered outcome in a project based upon a user-centered development approach. The analysis compared the intended and the actual processes of development then explored reasons for the differences and an understanding of project constraints in interviews with project participants and managers. Gasson employed a critical incident analysis of the project (Flanagan, 1954), triangulating across informant interviews and supplementing these with an analysis of project documentation to avoid recall bias, then employed the GT method (Glaser & Strauss, 1967) to iteratively analyze interview data and guide identification of critical incidents to be explored in further interviews. The iterative coding, analysis, and constant comparison process identified a set of themes that were based upon the analyst's interpretation of participant perspectives and validated in further interviews with informants. The findings identified two barriers to participation that were experienced by user-representatives and explicitly controlled by technical systems developers. The first barrier was one of system visibility, where technical developers were able to hide the evolving system specification from users because of their control of prototype releases. The second barrier was one of participation legitimacy, where technical developers were able to redefine team participation roles because of interdependencies between user representative tasks and system development tasks (S. Gasson, 1999).

Urquhart (1999, 2001a) analyzed differences in the frames of reference employed by IT system requirements analysts vs. system users.

From this analysis she constructed a theory that demonstrated how various organizational influences (such as management reporting needs), professional relationships (such as age and power differentials), and interactions between these direct the requirements agenda. Urquhart's work is groundbreaking as it takes a constructivist approach to data analysis, following Schwandt (1994) in arguing that "reality" is the product of complex interactions that reflect different individual constructions of meaning. While Urquhart cites both Glaser (1978, 1992) and Strauss & Corbin (1990) as her influences in these articles, in a later discussion of the GT method she describes how she found that Glaser's less structured approach to analysis helped her to evolve an emergent theory. Following Klein and Myers (1999), she asserts that the key task of research is to seek meaning in context. Urquhart suggests that Dey's (1999) explanation of the method as describing, categorizing, and connecting was helpful in achieving this, fuelling the realization that there was a difference between description (identifying elements of the data through assigning descriptive codes) and analysis (the iterative process of identifying relationships between categories of data—which may include families or groups of "open" codes—and developing more complex thematic codes to understand these relationships). This aided her in progressing between the various levels of abstraction required to generate a multi-level conceptual model of situated user-analyst interactions (Urquhart, 2001b, 2002).

A relatively recent study by Hansen and Kautz (2005) on the same topic as the Pries-Heje (1992) paper (the use of IS development tools by practitioners) develops the analytical coding techniques used in GT by using visualization tools to support inductive theory construction. The authors performed twelve semi-structured interviews with systems developers, project managers and staff in three IS development projects in the same organization, to investigate the use of software development tools. The authors followed the Strauss and Corbin (1998) method in using open coding, axial coding, and selective coding to derive categories of interest from a large quantity of qualitative data (interview transcriptions). However, rather than defining a single core category, they used a variety of visualization techniques (arranging categories on posters, color-coded according to the respondent, for various stages of coding) and debate/brainstorming between the two researchers to guide data analysis, constant comparison of data, and to guide further data collection following the analysis of initial interviews. In this, they appear to be following the original Glaser and Strauss (1967) thematic analysis method, supplemented with their own visual analysis techniques. The visualizations allowed them to identify "constellations of results," which sensitized them to relationships between five core categories (universality of the development tool, confidence in project progress, individual's experience of development, co-determination of needs by managers and developers, and method introduction), and 16 sub-categories in their data. The use of visualization techniques permitted the research team to synthesize analytical categories and themes into four "lessons learned," that had more of a process focus. For example, the lesson that the use of software development methods is adjusted in action, so no universal method exists (Kautz, Hansen, & Jacobsen, 2004).

Levina & Vaast (2008) employed a GT method when investigating how differences in country context and organizational context affected collaboration between offshore project team members. Citing Glaser and Strauss (1967), they describe how data collection and analysis were intertwined. Analytical field notes were produced after each interview that focused on what was learned. These notes provided emergent conceptual themes and propositions that were explored by adding new interview questions for subsequent informants who were chosen to confirm or challenge perspectives collected so far, so that they could confirm, explain, or deny emergent propositions. This stage ended when theoretical saturation was reached, in obtaining a set of context-related issue categories. The second stage of analysis complicated the emerging theory by generating and analyzing short descriptions of each project to generate a set of analytical themes. These were used to code the interviews, which generated new themes. The results were shared with key informants and academic colleagues; their feedback led to further data collection and analysis until theoretical saturation was reached. This approach demonstrates the iterative, exploratory nature of GT by using specific process examples and provides a rich description of how theoretical relationships and themes were validated and developed as part of GT data collection and analysis (Levina & Vaast, 2008).

So we see a trajectory of GT studies in MIS, from Orlikowski's (1993) legitimation of the method and Pries-Heje's (1992) discussion of the difficulties in identifying a core category, through Galal and McDonnell's (1997) appropriation of the method as a way to generate situated ontologies for knowledge management systems. This is followed by Gasson's (1999) use of the method to identify critical incidents that guided further data collection, and Urquhart's (1999, 2001a) use of GT to identify processes and issues in understanding between IS analysts and their clients. More recently, we see Hansen and Kautz (2005) supplementing a textual GT analysis with visualization techniques to sensitize them to relationships between categories of data, and to synthesize analytical categories and themes relating to software development processes. Levina and Vaast (2008) employed two cycles of GT analysis, based on different views of their data, to generate and cross-validate themes and relationships between contextual issues and categories of collaboration. This set of studies illustrates the diversity and richness of GT applications in our field and demonstrates how attitudes and understandings of the GT method have developed over time.

THE UNIQUE CHALLENGES OF MIS FOR GT RESEARCHERS

Publishing Conventions and Genres in MIS

As the field of MIS is relatively new, the tensions between MIS as an established "discipline" and MIS as an evolving field of knowledge can make it difficult to publish GT studies. When GT studies are presented as journal papers—the usual MIS genre—they suffer from limitation imposed by the paper length. When a very complex study is described in a single paper, there is often not space for a complete description of how the analysis led to the findings. When a comprehensive description of the analysis is provided, the findings frequently appear superficial, as so much space was devoted to the analysis rather than the complexity and depth of the findings. The MIS field has also evolved a theory-driven approach to formalizing research studies that can make it hard to reconcile the findings of GT studies with the expectations of journal editors and reviewers. This is because GT studies generate substantive theories rather than the formal theories emphasized in the majority of the MIS literature, and because the conventions of structure employed by MIS journals do not permit authors to communicate the emergent nature of GT.

In addition, most MIS journals employ a convention of presenting research as progressing from the conceptual underpinnings arising from a detailed review of literature, through a description of the research method, followed by a presentation of findings, and an interpretation of findings in the light of the original literature. While the majority of journals and conferences in our field are generally accepting of studies based on either deductive (hypothesis-testing, quantitative) or inductive (exploratory, qualitative) data analysis, they are less accepting of studies whose narrative follows a different genre of presentation. As a consequence, most GT studies are presented as conventional qualitative research, where protocols or schema for both data collection and analysis are based on an *a priori* conceptual framework. As discussed above, this conforms with the GT method when that framework is defined at a sufficiently high level that it acts as a data collection guide, rather than a constraining framework for analysis. But this results in the GT process becoming hidden from view and a confusion about what constitutes "grounded theory" in our field. It would be very easy to misunderstand the GT method from published work, as the narrative conventions enforced by editors and reviewers conceal the process by which a new theory was derived.

Descriptions of the search for theoretical relationships and core categories, and the development of an emergent theory through constant comparison between data samples are extremely rare. Even when these are included, they tend to raise objections from reviewers who see this process as "unstructured." This was the case with a paper by De Vreede et al. (1999), that is discussed by Bryant (2002). In a footnote, Bryant tells how the authors communicated to him that they wanted to present their findings as emergent, but were forced to relate their findings to an extant theory of user intentions (the Technology Acceptance Model) by the paper's reviewers (A. Bryant, 2002). The author of this chapter has experienced reviewer objections to even including a reference to Strauss and Corbin (1998), as this "has overtones of the lack of rigor communicated by the use of Grounded Theory." This is a critical issue if we are to develop the potential of our field for innovation and synthesis across disciplines and conventions. A systematic data analysis and synthesis does not rely exclusively on deductive thinking. Instead, it relies on a hermeneutic circle of understanding the whole by decomposing it into individual parts, then understanding those parts and the relationship between them to move to a new understanding of the whole (Gadamer, 1975). The GT method systematizes these cycles of deductive-inductive thinking. While the GT

research method draws on relevant literature, this is generally achieved once an emergent theory has been identified, to relate the findings to theoretical accounts in similar fields or situations. The GT method is most useful for situations where there *is* no extant theory – or in situations where existing theories are perceived as inadequate. Accounts of theory generation in all fields, including the physical sciences most closely associated with deductive methods, abound with references to the theorist's process innovation as a result of their refusal to think within existing paradigms. Perhaps we need more editors and reviewers in MIS who are willing to acknowledge the role of serendipity and induction in generating new theories in our field.

Employing *A Priori* Theoretical Models and Seed Categories

The GT method provides an excellent way of investigating areas of the emerging MIS field that have not yet been explored. This approach to data collection and analysis is not a good fit with theory testing or modification. Yet the conventions of leading MIS journals require that findings are related to existing paradigms and knowledge. This leads to frequent variations of a "grounded" theory method that depends upon seed categories or *a priori* theoretical models.

A GT study on the use of IS development tools and methods was performed by Fitzgerald (1997). This study was unusual in that its author—an experienced software developer—used the concept of "seed categories" to derive an interview protocol, following the Miles and Huberman (1994) approach to qualitative data collection. This study analyzed semi-structured interviews of one IS manager and one IS developer from each of eight organizations, pre-defining the two core categories of interest as *Formalized methodology vs. Methodology in action*, and *Methodology usage*. The use of seed categories to guide data collection was also employed in a study by

Hughes and Wood-Harper (1999). This appears to conflict with Glaser's argument that analytical categories should not be forced (Glaser, 1992). But if one sees these two abstract categories in terms of Glaser and Strauss' (Glaser & Strauss, 1967) *data collection guide* that defines topics of interest for the research study, the seed categories simply focus data collection rather than analysis. (Glaser & Strauss, 1967). Eisenhardt (1989) argues that an *a priori* definition of constructs can shape the initial design of [grounded] theory-building research and can guide data collection. The key issue appears to lie in whether the research method supports processes of research for generating theory, or whether it generates theory by logical deduction from preexisting assumptions

This is not the case when an *a priori* framework is used to direct the *analysis of data*. For example, Bryant criticizes a study by De Vreede et al. (1999), which reported using the GT method to extend a pre-existing theory: the Technology Acceptance Model (TAM). Bryant suggests that this study is flawed because the authors were relating their findings to an existing theory. He argues that this type of reconciliation de-sensitizes the researcher to alternative theories that might be applied to the situation and that use of an *a priori* theoretical framework to determine which data are "significant" or not reflects the positivist, deductive approach of traditional methods, rather than the inductive construction of knowledge claimed for the GT method (A. Bryant, 2002). A similar approach is employed by Maznevski and Chudoba (2000) in their study of the processes and performance of three virtual, global teams over time. After reviewing the literature, they defined "open" codes by means of a coding template that was based on their initial literature review. They performed a second-level, axial coding analysis to "uncover relationships among categories and subcategories," then they performed a third-level analysis that "looked for changes, adaptations, and evolutions, and tried to discern patterns associated with global virtual team effectiveness"

(Maznevski & Chudoba, 2000, pg. 479). The authors argue that the use of an *a priori* conceptual framework permits a comparison across multiple case studies to be conducted more rapidly than is usual with the GT method. This critique is not intended to deride the process reported in this paper, which reflects a deeply insightful and explicit account of their analytical process. But as the resulting theory was grounded in the literature, it is difficult to see this as a "grounded" theory, even if the authors employed the constant comparison method of analysis. While Maznevski and Chudoba employ the construct of theoretical saturation to explain how to determine the point at which to stop adding new cases to the study, this reflects the use of theoretical saturation as the gold standard in evaluating qualitative research reported by (Guest et al. (2006). The paper develops a discussion of how to develop theory across multiple case studies from a straightforward inductive, qualitative analysis, rather than employing the GT mechanisms of category abstraction, theoretical sampling, constant comparison, and core-category identification. In common with Bryant (2002), I am skeptical about the degree to which a research design that is predicated on an *a priori* conceptual framework can be said to generate a grounded theory. On the one hand, the use of an *a priori* framework permits data collection and analysis to be constrained and directed so that it is clear what is being analyzed. But this also closes off the possibility that *unexpected* phenomena, processes, or structures will be identified.

Ethics, Boundaries, and Scope in MIS Research

Bryant (2001) argues that GT in its original form as conceptualized by Glaser and Strauss (1967) tends towards an objectivist ontology that ignores the major subjective concerns of our field. These include the ethical implications of selecting one boundary for analysis over another (which may include or exclude key stakeholders or activities), a failure to address issues of "knowledge-power and social transformation" (Flood, 1999, p. 72), and taking account of social actors, acting in social contexts, as key constituting factors (A. Bryant, 2002). Bryant suggests employing a *systemic* philosophy of inquiry (Checkland & Holwell, 1998; Churchman, 1979), that makes explicit judgments that affect the boundary of analysis and what is – or is not – relevant to a grounded theory. As Charmaz (2000) notes, initial descriptions of the GT method have the implication that there is only *one theory* to be fitted to the "facts" of the situation and that empirical data is somehow collected objectively, with no judgments of relevance, or fit with the emerging theoretical framework of the researcher. While Urquhart (2002) argues that GT can be ontology-neutral, MIS researchers tend to privilege objectivity in documenting and accounting for their data analysis process (a key success factor in publishing MIS research). Bryant's point is a good one: the GT "method" (in its original form) does not include processes that are explicitly designed to engage the researcher in reflection about value-judgments or boundary decisions (Antony Bryant, 2001; 2002).

A systemic philosophy of inquiry often reveals emergent relationships between phenomena that are absent if we see boundaries of action or analysis as predefined. For example, we can view the Sarbanes-Oxley Act of 2002 as a response to a number of recent accounting scandals. But if we take a longer-term, historical view of the legislation as part of a larger pattern of interaction, we see that there were many problems with corporate accountability calls for regulation for many years prior to the scandals and that legislation and regulation tended to favor whichever interest group was dominant at any point in time. The Sarbanes-Oxley Act of 2002 generated a conflict between the interests of financial controllers and directors (whose activities and claims about their companies were subject to greater oversight), independent auditor firms (for whom a broad interpretation of the legislation brought additional

business income), and corporate IS managers (who incurred extra work and costs in developing systems to support broad interpretations of the legislation). From this perspective, the Sarbanes-Oxley legislation is no longer pivotal in restoring consumer confidence, but just one element in a trajectory of interactions between members of various interest groups (Latour, 1987). In this context, the legislation becomes one more "immutable mobile" that is employed and then subverted by corporate directors, accounting professionals, and IS professionals in their attempts to align the need for corporate accountability with their professional interests. This sheds new light on more recent calls by large companies for the SEC to implement the legislation less rigorously – and on the reasons why the Sarbanes-Oxley Act of 2002 failed to rein in the investment misrepresentations that led to the wider economic problems of 2008. The resulting view depends on the boundary of analysis. A *systemic* inquiry, reflecting multiple perspectives of problem-situation boundaries and "ideal world" solutions allows situations to be viewed in a broader context, experimenting with alternative boundaries in order to develop a deeper theory of action than is usual with MIS research (Checkland & Holwell, 1998). This permits explicit recognition of the emancipatory, critical theory research paradigm, identified as noticeably absent from research that employs the Grounded Theory method (Annells, 1996; Charmaz, 2000).

A ROADMAP FOR GT RESEARCH IN MIS

Employing The GT Coding Method vs. The GT Method of Generating Theory

When not discussing specifics of the Glaser or Strauss method in this chapter, I have used the term GT *approach*, rather than GT *method*. This is because the "method" has been the subject of so much debate between its originators -- and because the method itself has developed and evolved with various authors and over time (Dey, 1999). Many studies in MIS claim to employ a grounded theory method without following the systematic abstraction and theory-generation process that is characterized by Glaser and Strauss (1967) as the GT research method. Bryant observes that many recent studies which claim to use a GT method do not follow the later systematic methods of either Glaser (1978, 1992) or Strauss and Corbin (1990, 1998), but employ a process of "loose induction" to derive their findings. He argues that this is an indicator of sloppy research that has no place in MIS, potentially leading to weak theories being derived in these studies (A. Bryant, 2002). Urquhart responds that the GT approach has so far been used more as a *coding* method than as a *research analysis* method, in that researchers infer theoretical relationships between data categories without employing the constant comparison approach to data collection and analysis, or without structuring their theory around a single core category. She observes that this is a valid use that evolves the method: it is still possible to be systematic in one's analysis without employing the GT research method in full (Urquhart, 2002). But it could be argued that without employing the constant comparison method of evaluating and developing emergent theory, the researcher is applying an inductive, qualitative research method for *bricolage* (Denzin & Lincoln, 2005), rather than employing a grounded theory method for systematic analysis. Of course, the GT method has evolved through many different applications in many fields, so that it can no longer be viewed through the epistemological lens of its originators (A. Bryant, 2002). This is demonstrated vividly in the discussion of exemplar studies, above. But the differentiating aspects of the GT *research analysis* method appear to lie in the combination of: (i) the generation of theoretical concepts and/or models through systematic data analysis, and (ii) development

and evaluation of the emerging theory by means of constant comparison across data samples until theoretical saturation is reached.

Many MIS researchers struggle to follow the GT method of generating theory. This may be because researchers who are new to GT tend to read the earlier works by each author, attempting to understand the rather rambling descriptions of Glaser and Strauss (1967), whose book was more a defense of this approach to generating theory than a detailed workbook. Novice GT analysts may attempt to fit their work into one of Glaser's (1978) eighteen coding families without understanding the differences between these, or attempt to conform to Strauss and Corbin's (1990) initial theoretical framework without understanding that this is intended to represent a transactional, dynamic theory of action at a *really* abstract level. Later descriptions of the GT process present the GT method of generating theory in terms of iterative cycles of:

i. **Coding**: Categorizing data to ask "what is going on here?"
ii. **Analyzing**: Moving from open codes to selective codes by combining and relating data-categories to produce useful concepts or models, followed by splitting/redefining conceptual codes where these don't work;
iii. Generating theoretical memos to record the rationale and origin of themes and relationships discerned in the data;
iv. **Evaluating**: Comparing the emerging concepts and models against further data.

These cycles employ constant comparison between data samples and end at the point of theoretical saturation. Dey (1999) provides an excellent overview of how to "do" Grounded Theory analysis and why some things work better than others for specific types of question.

One of the most problematic aspects of the GT method of generating theory lies in identifying a single core category. Pries-Heje describes his experience using the Strauss and Corbin (1990) method of data analysis, during which he constructed and discarded multiple theoretical models. He tells of his many unsuccessful attempts at identifying a single core category, with a great deal of iteration between the three coding stages, before "all the pieces fell into place and I could formulate a consistent theory" (Pries-Heje, 1992, pp. 122-124). While both Glaser and Strauss emphasize the identification of a single core category, recent work in GT questions whether this is really necessary, arguing that complex theories of social action may involve *multiple* core categories, especially when focused at the community level. For example, Dey argues that the identification of a single core category allows the researcher to limit the analysis, but questions whether this resolves the trade-off between complexity and parsimony that is a core aim of GT (Dey, 1999, pp 42-43). My own experience would indicate that this is a matter of abstraction. Defining a single core category is difficult when one is categorizing the data at too detailed a level. If you can conceptualize an overarching theme in the data, defining a core category is much easier. For example, in analyzing IS development processes, you can view these as a set of stages that produce different outputs: a business specification, a functional requirements specification, a logical design, a physical design, a set of software modules, or an integrated information systems. If you think about what all these outputs have in common (for the research objective of understanding IS development as a coherent process), it is possible to define all of these process outputs in terms of partially-realized instantiations of an "IS design structure." So the definition of a core category relies on puzzling over what is the research objective at a high level of abstraction, as well as puzzling over what your multiple "core categories" have in common. But it may be that the subsequent theory becomes too complex to understand, with abstractions that are too abstract to be useful. So there could be a good argument

for retaining multiple core-categories, that reflect instances of a meta core category.

Generalizing From Grounded Theories

Focusing on a substantive theory of action introduces problems in generalizing studies across contexts. It is helpful for GT researchers in MIS to focus on transferability rather than generalizability. The findings of a study performed in one context may be transferred to a different context where key elements of the context are similar (Lincoln & Guba, 2000). As GT studies investigate the same research problem in different contexts, a formal theory may be defined by comparison across contexts and across studies. Generalizability concerns should not deter MIS researchers from employing a GT approach to their study. Rather, they should focus on the relationships between the phenomena, actions, and interactions analyzed in the study, and the properties of the *context* of that study, to develop a framework for the transferability of findings. When studying context, it is helpful to ask the following questions, to determine what data to collect and the extent to which those data are situated within a specific community of practice:

- **Situation:** What is the situation within which the study is located?
- **History:** What is the history of this situation and of the phenomena under study?
- **Language:** How do specific language terms control or define the meaning of phenomena or actions for participants?
- **Membership:** Which community of practice is significant in defining local meanings; who is a member of this group and who is excluded from membership?
- **Culture:** What are the community's conventions, norms, values, genres of communication, and expectations, and how do

these affect members' interpretations of the situation?

- **Boundaries**: What boundaries do participants in the situation see as relevant to their own work and what is included or excluded by applying these boundaries?
- **Practices**: What work-processes are viewed as relevant to the local community of practice and how does the group define that these should be performed?

For example, in arguing that their results were generalizable, Orlikowski and Gash (1994) argued that their data was collected from members of two communities of practice – technologists and technology-users – who otherwise shared a common culture. Members of both groups worked for a high-tech company, performed similarly complex work involving similar customers, and shared common genres of communication, norms of work, and value-systems. Therefore, the only differentiating factor in their attitude to technology was their role in respect of either developing or using technology.

Evaluating Grounded Theory In MIS Studies

The evaluation of theory is especially difficult when applying a GT approach, as there is no design research, in the traditional, top-down sense, so there can be no feel for what are the "expected findings." The original work by Glaser and Strauss (1967) was an attempt to legitimize the generation of theories from qualitative data within the positivist standards of scientific proof that were current at that time. In academia generally, but especially in the MIS field, the acceptance of alternative research ontologies such as interpretivism and critical theory has been accompanied by a recognition of alternative criteria for evaluation (Lincoln & Guba, 2000). The original work on GT argued that validity in its traditional sense was inappropriate as an evaluation criterion for

qualitative findings that were derived inductively (as distinct from the deductive processes of statistical sampling and analysis). Glaser (1992) suggests that an effective GT should satisfy six key criteria that are concerned with the theory generated:

- **Fit**: does the theory fit with the data collected?
- **Work**: does the theory work in explaining behaviors or phenomena in the study?
- **Relevance**: is the theory relevant to the concerns of participants in the situation studied?
- **Modifiability**: Is the theory amenable to modification when new data is compared with prior data – and is it the result of modification through the constant comparison of data?
- **Parsimony**: Does the theory explain the data without unnecessary complications and alternative scenarios?
- **Explanatory scope**: Can the theory be applied to other, similar situations?

Strauss and Corbin, on the other hand, discuss a set of evaluation criteria that support a reflexive research process and theoretical product. They suggest two sets of evaluation criteria:

- *Criteria for the research process* are presented as a set of questions that are concerned with the approach to theory generation. These are concerned with the grounding/rationale, and the development of criteria for theoretical sampling, data analysis, and theory-construction.
- *Criteria for the empirical grounding of the study* guide how the researcher may evaluate the theoretical concepts, their relationships, the conditions under which the theory may vary, processes embedded in the theory, and the significance of the theory. (Strauss & Corbin, 1998, pp. 268-272)

Very few Grounded Theory studies discuss evaluation criteria explicitly. This is probably due to the problems of fitting a GT study within the length constraints of a standard journal article, but may also be a result of the general perception discussed above – that the GT method is weak and so one should not draw attention to its limitations. A notable exception is a fascinating paper by Guest et al. (2006) that discusses how many qualitative interviews are "enough" for theory generation. The authors argue that guidelines for determining non-probabilistic sampling strategies are virtually nonexistent and so they explore the question by analyzing the records from a GT study. The paper is so interesting because its authors observe that the GT concept of *theoretical saturation* has become the "gold standard" in qualitative research, regardless of whether a GT approach is employed. However, the concept of theoretical saturation is frequently not operationalized in ways that can be understood by novice researchers. In a search for evaluation criteria, the two lead researchers documented and analyzed the development of a GT coding scheme after analyzing each of ten rounds of six interviews, split evenly across female subjects of two nationalities (Ghanaian and Nigerian). The interview protocol included six structured questions collecting demographic information, sixteen open-ended main questions, and fourteen open-ended sub-questions, providing a total of 60 interviews A codebook was developed by two data analysts, with the lead analyst creating a content-based coding scheme for each set of six interviews. Intercoder agreement was assessed for every third interview, with coding discrepancies discussed and resolved by the analysis team. Code changes were documented as these occurred.

So how many interviews were enough? The authors discovered that the team had created 92% (100) of the total number of codes developed for the first national group after **twelve** interviews. At this point, they had 88% (114) of the final codes for both national groups, and had identified all of the "most important" codes used in reporting the findings. The second national group (set of 30 interviews) added 5 new codes, bringing the total to 119. But the number of interviews required for theoretical saturation was relatively small because the study focused on a relatively homogeneous population (the two national groups were close in culture) and had a fairly narrow focus which provided a well-structured coding scheme. While their analysis at the end of *six* interviews had identified the four overarching themes that emerged from their findings, the authors comment that the researcher-team were unlikely to be sufficiently sensitized to the importance of these themes to identify them at this point. It was the process of analyzing, comparing, and collaboratively puzzling over sixty interviews that provided the deep insights required to interpret the significance of their themes.

Guest et al. also observe that theoretical saturation may require a great deal more analysis for those researchers who typically develop hundreds of codes from a micro-analysis of the data, then painstakingly analyze patterns and relationships, grouping, discarding, then regrouping categories to derive themes in the data. Theoretical saturation is reached more quickly for analyses that employ a loose inductive process to detect a few broad-brush themes. But the former researchers are more likely to arrive at deep insights and theories that explain the interior workings of a situation than the latter. So while a broad-brush analyst might well have arrived at a working theory after six interviews, this would have been less insightful – and less credible – than the process of iteratively analyzing the whole sample. Unsurprisingly, the authors' answer to "how many interviews is enough for theory construction?" is that it was twelve interviews for them, but that this small number could only be justified for the type of purposive sampling underlying "quick and dirty" research (Guest et al., 2006). The requisite sample size for a GT analysis depends upon what type of theory you want – and also how much effort you are prepared to invest in theory construction.

CONCLUSION: THE CONTRIBUTION OF GT TO MIS RESEARCH

The chapter discussed the Grounded Theory (GT) method and also covered research approaches that are based on the GT method, found in the MIS literature. Differences between the two originators' operationalizations of the method were covered, together with issues and controversies related to the use of the GT method. Key exemplars from the MIS literature were discussed, to give an overview of how its use has been developed an evolved in our field. A discussion of the unique challenges of MIS for GT researchers was followed by a roadmap of how GT may be used to generate rigorous, substantive theories in MIS research.

The adoption of a GT approach is best suited to situations where there is no extant theory, or where existing theory is felt to be insufficient for the contingencies of the situation being studied. As an emergent field of research, MIS has many research problems for which there is no accepted theory. One of the challenges – but also one of the rewards – of working in a field such as MIS is that the absence of a single disciplinary paradigm provides an opportunity to explore alternative theories of action to those suggested by prior research. MIS researchers often tackle research problems that have not previously been explored. The GT approach provides a way for researchers to make truly original contributions to the field. There is a tradition of systematic method in MIS research that is often absent from other fields, where narrative accounts of research are more usual. What distinguishes the GT approach from bricolage is the systematic, painstaking analysis that the GT approach requires.

Given the conventions of our field, it can be difficult to justify the timescales of a qualitative, grounded theory study in MIS. The typical expectation is that most research studies will be performed with much shorter timescales than those required for GT research. While it may take a few weeks to complete a quantitative survey, or an applied study of MIS, it may take several months or years to complete the iterative cycles of data collection, open coding, theoretical coding, and constant comparison that are required for grounded theory generation. This chapter has demonstrated that writing up qualitative GT research presents a fresh set of challenges for MIS researchers. The method is complex and so it can be difficult to fit the required explanations within a standard journal article page-count. This approach to theory generation requires a high degree of commitment to rigor of process and a good understanding of what granularity of analysis is required for the type of contribution envisaged. While quantitative research has its shorthand ways of communicating reliability or validity, citing specific statistical tests in 3-4 words, a GT article can take 1-2 pages to satisfy reviewers and readers that the findings are dependable, confirmable, and were arrived at through a rigorous process of analysis. This requires journals and editors who are tolerant of the longer papers that GT necessitates. The deep understanding of phenomena that accrues from GT research cannot be underestimated. It has been said that qualitative researchers live, breathe, and dream of their data. In addition to all of these, the GT researcher nurtures and raises their findings until they reach the age of independence(!).

As discussed, qualitative GT studies do not follow the narrative conventions of a typical MIS study, meaning that a choice must be made between producing a narrative that reflects the GT process, or employing a normative article structure that falsely implies links between extant theories and the research design. Major decisions about the boundary of analysis and the philosophical stance to be taken to the research must be made and then revisited as new findings emerge. Such reflexive decisions are especially pertinent to our field, where theory increasingly relies upon a systemic approach to situated data analysis and to appreciating the study's wider impact. The future of theory-generation in MIS lies in making unique contributions to knowledge that are not feasible in other academic fields. We are privileged that our field permits the synthesis of ideas, concepts, and theories across the boundaries of disciplines. Grounded Theory has an important role to play in this synthesis, as we struggle to understand the MIS world and the place of human action, interaction, and knowledge within that world.

REFERENCES

Annells, M. (1996). Grounded theory method: Philosophical perspectives, paradigm of inquiry, and postmodernism. *Qualitative Health Research, 6*(3), 379-393.

Babchuk, W. (1996, October 17-19). *Glaser Or Strauss?: Grounded theory and adult education.* Paper presented at the Proceedings of Midwest Research-to-Practice Conference in Adult, Continuing, and Community Education, University of Nebraska-Lincoln.

Blumer, H. (1969). *Symbolic interactionism: Perspective and method.* Englewood Cliffs, NJ: Prentice-Hall.

Bryant, A. (2001). A constructive/ist response to Glaser. *Forum: Qualitative Social Research, 4*(1). Retrieved from http://www.qualitative-research.org/fqs-texte/1-03/1-03bryant-e.pdf

Bryant, A. (2002). Re-grounding grounded theory. *The Journal of Information Technology Theory and Application, 4*(1), 25-42.

Charmaz, K. (2000). Grounded theory: Objectivist and constructivist methods. In N. K. Denzin & Y. S. Lincoln (Eds.), *Handbook of qualitative research* (2nd. ed.) (pp. 509-535). Thousand Oaks, CA: Sage.

Checkland, P., & Holwell, S. (1998). *Information, systems and information systems: Making sense of the field.* Chichester, UK: John Wiley & Sons.

Churchman, C. W. (1979). *The systems approach.* New York: Dell.

Clarke, A. E. (2003). Situational analyses: Grounded theory mapping after the postmodern turn. *Symbolic Interaction, 26*(4), 553-576.

De Vreede, G.-J., Jones, N., & Mgaya, R. J. (1999). Exploring the application and acceptance of group support systems in Africa. *Journal of Management Information Systems, 15*(3), 197-220.

Denzin, N. K., & Lincoln, Y. S. (2005). Introduction: The discipline and practice of qualitative research. In N. K. Denzin & Y. S. Lincoln (Eds.), *The Sage handbook of qualitative research* (3rd ed.) (pp. 1-32). Thousand Oaks, CA: Sage.

Dey, I. (1999). *Grounding grounded theory.* San Diego, CA: Academic Press.

Eisenhardt, K. M. (1989). Building theories from case study research. *Academy of Management Review, 14*(4), 532-550.

Fitzgerald, B. (1997). The use of systems development methodologies in practice: A field study. *Information Systems Journal, 7*(3), 201-212.

Flanagan, J. C. (1954). The critical incident technique. *Psychological Bulletin, 51*(4), 327-358.

Flood, R. L. (1999). *Rethinking the fifth discipline: Learning within the unknowable.* New York: Routledge.

Gadamer, H. (1975). Hermeneutics and social science. *Cultural Hermeneutics, 2*(4).

Galal, G. H., & McDonnell, J. T. (1997). Knowledge-based systems in context: A methodological approach to the qualitative issues. *AI & Society, 11*(1-2), 104-121.

Gasson, S. (1999). The reality of user-centered design. *Journal of End User Computing, 11*(4), 3-13.

Gasson, S. (2003). Rigor in grounded theory research: An interpretive perspective on generating theory from qualitative field studies. In M. Whitman & A. Woszczynski (Eds.), *Handbook for information systems research*. Hershey, PA: Idea Group Publishing.

Glaser, B. G. (1978). *Advances in the methodology of grounded theory: Theoretical sensitivity*. Mill Valley, CA: The Sociology Press.

Glaser, B. G. (1992). *Basics of grounded theory analysis: Emergence vs. forcing*. Mill Valley, CA: The Sociology Press.

Glaser, B. G. (2002). Constructivist grounded theory? *Forum: Qualitative Social Research, 3*(3).

Glaser, B. G., & Strauss, A. L. (1967). *The discovery of grounded theory*. New York: Aldine Publishing Company.

Guest, G., Bunce, A., & Johnson, L. (2006). How many interviews are enough? An experiment with data saturation and variability. *Field Methods, 18*(1), 59-82.

Hansen, B. H., & Kautz, K. (2005). *Grounded theory applied - studying information systems development methodologies in practice*. Paper presented at the 38th Hawaii International Conference on System Sciences (HICSS 2005). Retrieved from http://csdl2.computer.org/comp/proceedings/hicss/2005/2268/08/22680264b.pdf

Hughes, J., & Wood-Harper, A. T. (1999). Systems development as a research act. *Journal of Information Technology, 14*(1), 83-94.

Kautz, K., Hansen, B. H., & Jacobsen, D. (2004). The utilization of information systems development methodologies in practice. *Journal of Information Technology Cases and Applications, 6*(4), 1-20.

Klein, H. K. K., & Myers, M. (1999). A set of principles for conducting and evaluating interpretive field studies in information systems. *MIS Quarterly, 23*(1), 67-94.

Latour, B. (1987). *Science in action*. Cambridge, MA: Harvard University Press.

Levina, N., & Vaast, E. (2008). Innovating or doing as told? Status differences and overlapping boundaries in offshore collaboration. *MIS Quarterly, 32*(2), 307-332.

Lincoln, Y. S., & Guba, E. G. (2000). Paradigmatic controversies contradictions and emerging confluences. In N. K. Denzin & Y. S. Lincoln (Eds.), *The handbook of qualitative research* (pp. 163-188). Beverly Hills, CA: Sage Publications.

Lind, M., & Goldkuhl, G. (2006). How to develop a multi-grounded theory: The evolution of a business process theory. *Australasian Journal of Information Systems, 13*(2), 69-86.

Lowe, A. (1996). *An explanation of grounded theory*. Swedish School of Economics and Business Administration.

Maznevski, M., & Chudoba, K. M. (2000). Bridging space over time: Global virtual team dynamics and effectiveness. *Organization Science, 11*(5), 473-492.

Mead, G. H. (1934). *Mind, self and society*. Chicago: University of Chicago Press.

Miles, M. B., & Huberman, A. M. (1994). *Qualitative data analysis*. Newbury Park, CA: Sage Publications.

Orlikowski, W. J. (1993). CASE tools as organizational change: investigating incremental and radical changes in systems development. *MIS Quarterly, 17*(3), 309-340.

Orlikowski, W. J., & Gash, D. C. (1994). Technological frames: Making sense of information technology in organizations. *ACM Transactions on Information Systems, 12*(2), 174-207.

Pries-Heje, J. (1992). Three barriers for continuing use of computer-based tools in information systems development: A grounded theory approach. *Scandinavian Journal of Information Systems, 4*, 119-136.

Schwandt, T. A. (1994). Constructivist, interpretivist approaches to human inquiry. In N. K. Denzin & Y. S. Lincoln (Eds.), *Handbook of qualitative research* (pp. 118-137). Newbury Park, CA: Sage.

Smit, J., & Bryant, A. (2000). *Grounded theory method in IS research: Glaser vs. Strauss* (Working Paper IMRIP 2000-7). Retrieved from http://www.leedsmet.ac.uk/inn/2000-7.pdf

Strauss, A. L. (1978). A social world perspective. In N. K. Denzin (Ed.), *Studies in symbolic interaction* (Vol. 1, pp. 119-128). Greenwich, CT: Jai Press Inc.

Strauss, A. L. (1983). *Continual permutations of action*. New York: Aldine de Gruyter.

Strauss, A. L., & Corbin, J. (1990). *Basics of qualitative research: Grounded theory procedures and techniques*. Newbury Park, CA: Sage Publications.

Strauss, A. L., & Corbin, J. (1998). *Basics of qualitative research: Techniques and procedures for developing grounded theory* (2nd ed.). Newbury Park, CA: Sage.

Tan, M. T. K., & Hall, W. (2007). Beyond Theoretical and methodological pluralism in interpretive IS research: The example of symbolic interactionist ethnography. *Communications of AIS, 2007*(19), 589-610.

Urquhart, C. (1999). Themes in early requirements gathering: The case of the analyst the client and the student assistance scheme. *Information Technology and People, 12*(1), 44-70.

Urquhart, C. (2001a). Analysts and clients in organisational contexts: A conversational perspective. *The Journal of Strategic Information Systems, 10*(3), 243-262.

Urquhart, C. (2001b). An encounter with grounded theory: Tackling the practical and philosophical issues. In E. Truath (Ed.), *Qualitative research in IS: Issues and trends* (pp. 104-140). Hershey, PA: Idea Group Publishing.

Urquhart, C. (2002). Regrounding grounded theory? - Or reinforcing old prejudices? A brief reply to Bryant. *The Journal of Information Technology Theory and Application, 4*(3), 43-54.

KEY TERMS AND DEFINITIONS

Grounded Theory: A theory that is generated from patterns in, and relationships between, elements of the data collected, rather than based upon extant theories of action. The Grounded Theory *method* is based upon Glaser and Strauss (1967) and requires two key process elements:

1. Data are categorized (or coded) according to an emergent set of categories that define key elements of the situation. These are related together by means of code integration to derive families of codes, or code splitting to derive sub-categories. A substantive theory is generated when the researcher can define core categories in the data and important patterns of relationships between categories, that apply across data samples. These patterns are made explicit through the generation of theoretical memos as the analysis proceeds.

2. A constant comparison method is employed to analyze which elements of the emerging theory apply across multiple data samples, at which point the emerging theory may change. Constant comparison ends when theoretical saturation is reached (see below).

Epistemology: Our beliefs about the nature of knowledge and our relationship to the "real world" (i.e. *how* we know reality). The most common positions are:

- **Interpretivist:** Reported experience, phenomena, and observations are seen as social constructions: filtered through the interpretations that result from the individual's prior experience. This approach attempts to account for interpretations by research subjects and the researcher, in suggesting findings from a research analysis. The resulting theories are seen as contestable and context-specific, providing explanatory power, rich descriptions, and in-depth understanding of how and why to act, rather than providing prescriptive rules for action.
- **Positivist:** Observable, measurable experiences can contribute to knowledge. Theories result from the application of scientific methods of analysis to data, resulting in a research approach that emphasizes quantitative data collection and statistical analysis methods to ensure the validity of findings.
- **Post-Positivist:** Based on the belief that most knowledge is conjectural, this research paradigm emphasizes deductive logic, or warrants, in supporting theory generation. .Post-positivism admits reported experience (for example, surveys), sociological or psychological experiments (where the data must be inferred from other phenomena) and observed human behavior as data. Because of the wider criteria for data acceptability than is the case for positivism, post-positivism is often used to describe an approach to research where large amounts of qualitative data are categorized to produce quantitative data to be analyzed using statistical methods.

Idiographic: An approach to research knowledge that is concerned with the study of individual or specific cases, pertaining to contingent and often subjectively-perceived phenomena that relate to an identifiable context. This may be contrasted with the **nomothetic** approach most usually employed in positivist research studies which are seen as representing a population of individuals and focus on the variables and behaviors that characterize a generalizable set of contexts.

Ontology: Related to how we view the nature of the external world. The two extreme positions are:

- **Realist:** Where the individual views the external world as having an existence independent of their own.
- **Social Constructivist:** Where the individual views the external world as represented by a set of names, concepts, and labels that are used to structure reality. We understand the world by socially-situated processes of framing and filtering that employ consensus concepts, names, and labels. *Very few people ever adopt these extreme positions in totality.* For example, researchers who describe their position as social constructivist would admit to some parts of physical reality as having an existence independent of their own. Similarly, researchers who describe their position as realist (the epistemological term "positivist" is more often employed), admit to some elements of their understanding of the external (to them) world as resulting from subjective perceptions.

Substantive Theory: A theoretical model that provides a "working theory" of action for a specific context. A substantive theory is considered *transferable*, rather than generalizable, in the sense that elements of the context can be transferred to contexts of action with similar characteristics to the context under study (for example, studies of small-group IS design in US management consultancy companies). This contrasts with **Formal Theory**, which is based upon validated, generalizable conclusions across multiple studies that represent the research population as a whole, or upon deductive logic that uses validated empirical theories as its basic axioms.

Systemic Inquiry: This is a philosophy of research and action that relates elements of the situation together, viewing a problem-situation as an interrelated set of cause-effect relationships or phenomena. This philosophy was proposed by Churchman (1979) and operationalized in the Soft Systems approach advocated by Checkland (Checkland and Holwell, 1998).

Theoretical Saturation: The point at which analysis of additional data through constant comparison across data samples, cases, or situations provides no new insights into the substantive theory of action generated from the data.

Chapter IV
Critical Realism

Sven A. Carlsson
Lund University, Sweden

ABSTRACT

Different strands of non-positivistic research approaches and theories, for example, constructivism, grounded theory, and structuration theory, have gained popularity in the information systems (IS) field. Although, they are managing to overcome some problems with positivism and structural theories they are not completely without problems. This chapter puts critical realism forward as an alternative philosophical underpinning for IS research. Critical realism starts from an ontology that identifies structures and mechanisms, through which events and discourses are generated, as being fundamental to the constitution of our natural and social reality. The chapter presents critical realism and how it can be used in IS research. Examples of how critical realism have been used and can be used in research aiming at generating new IS theory, IS evaluation research, and IS design science research are provided.

INTRODUCTION AND BACKGROUND

Positivism seems to be dead in contemporary philosophy of sciences, but it is still very influential in the Information Systems (IS) field. Scholars have investigated the IS field and found that the field is dominated by research approaches and theories based in positivism (Arnott & Pervan, 2005; Chen & Hirschheim, 2004; Schultze & Leidner, 2003). Several IS scholars have pointed out weaknesses in these approaches and theories and in response different strands of post-modern theories and research approaches have gained popularity. The approaches and theories argued for include interpretivism, ethnography, grounded theory, and theories like Giddens' (1984) structuration theory and Latour's (1987) actor-network theory. For simplicity, in this chapter we refer to these different approaches and theories as "post-approaches" and "post-theories" when distinction is not required. Although these approaches and theories overcome some of the problems noted with positivistic approaches and theories, they have some major weaknesses and limitations—these weaknesses and limitations are discussed in the next section. For elaborate critiques of post-approaches and post-theories, see Lòpez and Potter (2001) and Archer, Bhaskar, Collier, Lawson, and Norrie (1998).

An alternative to traditional positivistic models of social science as well as an alternative to post-approaches and post-theories is critical realism (CR). Critical realism argues that social reality is not simply composed of agents' meanings, but that there exist structural factors influencing agents' lived experiences. CR starts from an ontology that identifies structures and mechanisms, through which events and discourses are generated, as being fundamental to the constitution of our natural and social reality.

Critical realism was primarily developed as an answer to the positivist crisis. In 1975 Roy Bhaskar's work "A Realist Theory of Science", with "transcendental realism", was published. In "Possibility of Naturalism" (1979) Bhaskar focused the social sciences and developed his "critical naturalism". These two major works present a thorough philosophy of science project and later "critical realism" and "critical naturalism" were merged to "critical realism". A concept also used by Bhaskar. Through the 80's Bhaskar primarily developed his position through sharpening arguments, etc. The late 70's and early 80's also saw a number of other CR scholars publishing influential works, for example, Margaret Archer's "Social origins of educational systems" (1979) and Andrew Sayer's "Method in social science" (1984). Most of CR's early critique was targeting positivism, but later critique is targeting alterna-

tives to positivism, for example, postmodernism and structuration theory. CR is a consistent and all-embracing alternative to positivism and different postmodernistic strands.

This chapter presents critical realism and shows how it can be used in IS research. We will show how it can be used in behavioral IS research as well as how it can be used in IS design science research.

WHY CRITICAL REALISM?

In response to the cry for the use of post-approaches and post-theories in IS research, researchers have used, for example, research approaches like constructivism, qualitative and intensive approaches, and grounded theory as well as theories like Anthony Giddens' structuration theory—for different IS-examples, see, Lee et al. (1997), Trauth (2001), Whitman and Woszczynski (2004), and Myers (2009).

We will not do an exhaustive review of different post-approaches and post-theories, but will point out limitations and weaknesses in: 1) one approach for generating theories, grounded theory, 2) one "theory" (description) of human action and social organization, structuration theory, and 3) the suggestions to integrate and combine different approaches in IS research, for example combining positivist and interpretive approaches. The choice of the examples is based on that grounded theory is increasingly used by IS-researchers and is a good example of a post-approach. Structuration theory is also gaining increased presence in the IS-literature and is a good example of a post-theory.

Several IS-scholars have suggested the use of grounded theory (Gasson, 2004) and a number of IS studies using grounded theory have been published—for a good example, see Urquhart (2001). Generally, grounded theory (GT) is an approach to the analysis of qualitative data aiming at generating theory out of research data by achieving a close fit between the two (Glaser & Strauss, 1967). Said Strauss and Corbin, "... theory that was derived from data, systematically gathered and analyzed through the research process. In this method, data collection, analysis, and eventual theory stand in close relationship to one another." (Strauss & Corbin, 1998). One of the weaknesses in grounded theory is its concentration on micro phenomena: "The very fixity of this concentration is a factor which prevents grounded theory from attending to historical matters of macro structure as a means of enriching contemporary or, as I [Layder] shall call them, present-centred forms of research on micro phenomena. It should be possible to augment the processual and dynamic analyses of interactional phenomena by a parallel focus on the historically antecedent forms that provide their institutional backdrop." (Layder, 1993). Macro phenomena have no validity to IS-researchers using grounded theory unless these macro phenomena emerge directly from the field data. IS-research suggests that macro phenomena, like national culture, influence IS-designers (Hunter & Beck, 1996) and how IS are used and evaluated (Tan et al., 1995; Leidner et al., 1999; Leidner & Carlsson, 1998). Macro phenomena (structural/systemic factors) can hardly emerge in IS research focusing on agents' perceptions, meanings, and actions. Other problems with GT

pointed out by Layder and other researchers include its flat treatment of power and its rejection of the use of prior theory. Grounded theory focuses situated and interpersonal aspects. This means that a researcher using GT will most likely miss the importance of power "behind the scenes" of situated activities, that is, an IS-researcher using GT will most likely miss the structural (systemic) aspects of power. GT points out that prior theory, in the form of constructs and theoretical frameworks, should play no formal role in empirical studies and analysis. Not using prior theory means overlooking and ignoring constructs and frameworks that have, in the past, proven themselves to be fruitful.

A theory having gained popularity among IS-researchers is Anthony Giddens' (1984) structuration theory—for a good review of the use of structuration theory in IS-studies, see, Jones and Karsten (2008). Most notably is Orlikowski's work on applying structuration theory to the development and use of IS in organizations (Orlikowski, 1992, 2000). Figure 1 depicts Orlikowski's structurational model of technology and shows the relationship between technology, human agents, and institutional properties.

According to Orlikowski (1992), technology is identified as the "product of human action" (arrow a), coming into existence and being sustained

Figure 1. Orlikowski's structurational model of technology

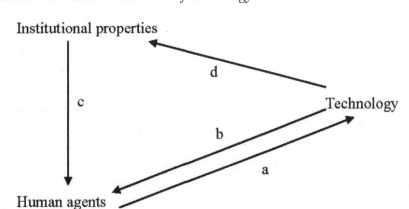

through human action, and being constituted through use. Only through the appropriation of technology by humans does it exert influence. However, technology is also "the medium of human action" (arrow b). Technology constrains and enables social practices. Institutional properties influence human agents (arrow c)—"institutional conditions of interaction with technology." Arrow d reflects the influence of technology in reinforcing or transforming organizations' institutional properties—"institutional consequences of interaction with technology."

Structuration theory overcomes some of the problems associated with structuralism, but Giddens' view on agency and structure is problematic when studying artifacts like ICT-based IS. Giddens' conception of agency and structure means that structure cannot be separated from agency. It is an attempt to treat human action and social structure as a duality rather than a dualism; action and structure are seen as two aspects of the same whole (a duality). According to Reed, it is "a single-level social ontology that conflates 'agency' and 'structure' in such a way that they are analytically rendered down to localized social practices bereft of any institutional underpinnings or contextualization. The ontological status and explanatory power of 'structure'—i.e., as a concept referring to a relatively enduring institutionalised relationships between social positions and practices located at different levels of analysis that constrain actors' capacities to 'make a difference'—is completely lost in a myopic analytical focus on situated social interaction and the local conversational routines through which it is reproduced." (Reed, 1997). Jones after reviewing IS research based on Giddens' structuration theory concludes: "…it is evident that the specific attempts to adapt structuration to incorporate material aspects of IS have encountered a number of serious problems which remain as yet unresolved." (Jones, 1999). And Jones and Karsten add: "A number of aspects of the duality of technology would seem similarly at odds with Giddens's account of structuration.

(Jones & Karsten, 2008). In the section on how to use CR in IS research we will present Volkoff, Strong, and Elmes's (2007) CR-based theory generating study that overcomes the problems noted with structuration theory.

Some IS-scholars advocate that IS-researchers should integrate or combine positivist and interpretive approaches (Lee, 1991; Trauth & Jessup, 2000), integrate case study and survey research methods (Gable, 1994), or combine qualitative and quantitative methods (Kaplan & Duchon, 1988). These suggestions seem to have some similarities with what critical realism writers suggest in terms of using a multi-methodology approach (including the use of multi-methods and multi-techniques), but there is one major difference. Critical realism writers are based in a specific philosophy of social science and in discussing how to use different methods and techniques in research they start from the ontology of critical realism. Generally, IS-writers arguing for integrating and mixing different methodologies, methods, and techniques do this without discussing the underlying ontologies.

Summarizing, from an IS research perspective we can identify at least four major problems with the use of different strands of post-approaches and post-theories as well as the idea to integrate and combine different methodologies and methods. First, the post-approaches and post-theories fascination with the voices of those studied (a focus on agents) has led to an increase in IS research as mere reportages and local narratives. In some cases this has led to what can best be described as an interpretive morass—"any narrative will do." Second, their focus on agency leads to that they ignore the structural (systemic) dimension. Third, their rejection of objectivist elements leads to problem when researching artifacts like ICT-based IS. Fourth, the idea to integrate and combine different methodologies and methods, founded in different and incompatible ontologies, are suggested without an elaborate discussion of how to "handle" the incompatible ontologies. We are not claiming that the criticized post-approaches and post-theories cannot be useful in IS-research, but that they have a number of limitations and that they certainly not are panaceas.

To overcome some of the noted problems some IS scholars have argued that the development of a "position" based on critical realism could be a valuable avenue to explore in IS research. Next section presents critical realism.

CRITICAL REALISM

Different philosophies of science have different ontological views. Idealists have the view that reality is not mind-independent. Idealism comes in different forms reflecting different views on what is man created and how it is created. Realists have the view that reality exists independently of our beliefs, thoughts, perceptions, discourses etc. As for idealism, realism comes in different forms. Today most philosophies of science are based on realism. Bhaskar says that it is not a question of being a realist or not, but what type of realist (Bhaskar, 1991).

Critical realism was developed as an alternative to traditional positivistic models of social science and as an alternative to post-approaches and post-theories, e.g. constructivism and structuration theory. The most influential writer on critical realism is Roy Bhaskar (1978, 1989, 1998). Unfortunately, Bhaskar is an opaque writer, but

good summaries of CR are available in Archer et al. (1998), Sayer (2000), and Dean, Joseph, and Norrie (2005) and key concepts and main developments are presented in Hartwig (2007). In Archer et al. (1998) and Lòpez and Potter (2001) some chapters focus on different aspects of critical realism, ranging from fundamental philosophical discussions to how statistical analysis can be used in critical realism research.

Critical realism can be seen as a specific form of realism: "To be a realist is to assert the existence of some disputed kind of entities such as gravitons, equilibria, utility, class relations and so on. To be a scientific realist is to assert that these entities exist independently of our investigation of them. Such entities, *contra* the post modernism of rhetoricians, are not something generated in the discourse used in their investigation. Neither are such entities, *contra* empiricists, restricted to the realm of the observable. To be a *critical* realist is to extend these views into social science." (Fleetwood, 2002). CR's manifesto is to recognize the reality of the natural order and the events and discourses of the social world. It holds that "we will only be able to understand——and so change—— the social world if we identify the structures at work that generate those events and discourses … These structures are not spontaneously apparent in the observable pattern of events; they can only be identified through the practical and theoretical work of the social sciences." (Bhaskar, 1989). Bhaskar (1978) outlines what he calls three

Table 1. Ontological assumptions of the critical realist view of science (adapted from Bhaskar, 1978). Xs indicate the domain of reality in which mechanisms, events, and experiences, respectively reside, as well as the domains involved for such a residence to be possible.

	Domain of Real	Domain of Actual	Domain of Empirical
Mechanisms	X		
Events	X	X	
Experiences	X	X	X

domains: the *real*, the *actual*, and the *empirical* (Table 1). The *real* domain consists of underlying structures and mechanisms, and relations; events and behavior; and experiences. The generative mechanisms residing in the real domain exist independently of, but capable of producing, patterns of events. Relations generate behaviors in the social world. The domain of the *actual* consists of these events and behaviors. Hence, the actual domain is the domain in which observed events or observed patterns of events occur. The domain of the *empirical* consists of what we experience; hence, it is the domain of experienced events.

Bhaskar argues that "...real structures exist independently of and are often out of phase with the actual patterns of events. Indeed it is only because of the latter we need to perform experiments and only because of the former that we can make sense of our performances of them. Similarly it can be shown to be a condition of the intelligibility of perception that events occur independently of experiences. And experiences are often (epistemically speaking) 'out of phase' with events—e.g. when they are misidentified. It is partly because of this possibility that the scientist needs a scientific education or training. Thus I [Bhaskar] will argue that what I call the domains of the real, the actual and the empirical are distinct." (Bhaskar, 1978). Critical realism also argues that the real world is ontologically stratified and differentiated. The real world consists of a plurality of structures and generative mechanisms that generate the events that occur and do not occur. From an epistemological stance, concerning the nature of knowledge claim, the realist approach is non-positivistic which means that values and facts are intertwined and hard to disentangle.

The literature on the philosophy of science discusses the differences between positivism, constructivism, and critical realism; for example, discussions on their ontological views. Good discussions in terms of doing real world research based on the different philosophies of sciences are

available in Robson (2002) and Bryman (2001). Robson summarizes a critical realism view of science:

1. There is no unquestionable foundation for science, no 'facts' that are beyond dispute. Knowledge is a social and historical product. 'Facts' are theory-laden.
2. The task of science is to invent theories to explain the real world, and to test these theories by rational criteria.
3. Explanation is concerned with how mechanisms produce events. The guiding metaphors are of structures and mechanisms in reality rather than phenomena and events.
4. A law is the characteristic pattern of the activity or tendency of a mechanism. Laws are statements about things that are 'really' happening, the ongoing ways of acting of independently existing things, which may not be expressed on the level of events.
5. The real world is not only very complex but also stratified into different layers. Social reality incorporates individual, group and institutional, and societal levels.
6. The conception of causation is one in which entities act as a function of their basic structure.
7. Explanation is showing how some event has occurred in a particular case. Events are to be explained even when they cannot be predicted."

Critical realism is a well-developed philosophy of science, but on the methodological level, it is less well-developed. The writings of Layder (1993, 1998), Kazi (2003), and Pawson (2006) as well as some of the chapters in Ackroyd and Fleetwood (2000) and Fleetwood and Ackroyd (2004), can serve as guidelines for doing critical realism research. Layder addresses how to do research from a critical realist perspective. Layder writes: "Put very simple, a central feature of realism is its attempt to preserve a 'scientific' attitude towards social analysis at the same time recognizing the importance of actors´ meanings and in some way incorporating them in research. As such, a key aspect of the realist project is a concern with causality and the identification of causal mechanisms in social phenomena in a manner quite unlike the traditional positivist search for causal generalizations"(Layder, 1993). Layder developed his philosophy and framework primarily to be used in theory development and elaboration.

Layder suggests a stratified or layered framework of human action and social organization. The framework includes macro phenomena, e.g. structural and institutional phenomena, as well as micro phenomena, e.g. behavior and interaction. Figure 2 depicts Layder's framework and describes levels (elements/sectors) of the potential areas of interest in research including IS research.

We will briefly present the different elements, starting, for convenience, with the self and working towards the macro elements. The first level is *self*, which refers "... primarily to the individual's relation to her or his social environment and is characterized by the intersection of biographical experience and social involvements." (Layder, 1993). Self focuses on how an individual is affected by and responds to social situations. When encountering social situations, individuals use strategies and tactics, based on their "theories" (mental models), to handle these situations. In general, the self and situated activity have as their main concern "...the way individuals respond to particular features of their social environment and the typical situations associated with this environment." (Layder, 1993).

In a *situated activity*, the focus is on the dynamics of social interaction. The area of self focuses on how individuals are affected by and respond to certain social processes, whereas situated activity focuses on the nature of the social involvement and interactions. This means that interactions and processes have features that are the result of how the participating individuals' behaviors intermesh and coalesce.

Figure 2. Research map (Adapted from Layder, 1993)

Research Element	Research Focus
CONTEXT	*Macro social organization* e.g. gender, national.culture, international and national economic situation, national IT policy
SETTING	*Intermediate social organization* e.g. organization, department, team. Can be an ERP-implementation team.
SITUATED ACTIVITY	*Social activity* Face-to-face activity involving symbolic communication by skilled, intentional participants implicated in the above contexts and settings. Includes also ICT-mediated communication
SELF	*Self-identity and individual's social experience* Can include a person's perception of his/hers ICT skills or a person's perception of an ERP-system

HISTORY

The focus in *setting* is on the intermediate forms of social organization. A setting provides the immediate arena for social activities. A setting can be constituted by things like the culture of the organization, artifacts like ICT-based IS which are used in situated activities, and power and authority structures. It should be stressed that setting is not just a particular pattern of activity. The wider macro social form that provides the more remote environment of social activity is referred to as the *context*. Although there is no clear border between settings and context, with some social forms straddling the two elements, it can be fruitful to distinguish them. In general, context refers to large-scale, society-wide features.

Viewing the design, development, implementation, and use of IS as layers of human activity and social organizations that are interdependent has two major advantages. It enables a researcher to be sensitive to the different elements and their distinctive features. Critical realism and Layder's framework both stress that the layers operate on different "time scales". This means that a researcher has to view the operation of the elements not only vertically, but also horizontally.

Having presented critical realism we will now move to how it can be applied in IS research

USING CRITICAL REALISM IN INFORMATION SYSTEMS RESEARCH

As noted above, CR has primarily been occupied with philosophical issues and fairly abstract discussions. In recent years attention has been paid to how to actually carry out research with CR as a philosophical underpinning. This section presents how CR can be used in IS research. Gregor (2006) argues that five interrelated types of IS theories can be distinguished: (1) theory for analyzing, (2) theory for explaining, (3) theory for predicting, (4) theory for explaining and predicting, and (5) theory for design and action. The five types can

be clustered into two main types: "traditional" natural/social research (first four types) and design science (fifth type). Below we exemplify how CR can be used in both main types of research. We will: (1) present how Layder's adaptive theory can be used in IS research, (2) present a study that, based on CR, generated a new theory of technology-enabled organizational change, (3) present a CR-based IS evaluation approach, and (4) present CR-based design science. Throughout, we will give examples of actual IS-research.

CR-Based Development of IS-Theories

Bhaskar says that explanations (theories) are accomplished by the RRRE model of explanation comprising a four-phase process: "(1) Resolution of a complex event into its components (causal analysis); (2) Redescription of component causes; (3) Retrodiction to possible (antecedent) causes of components via independently validated normic statements; and (4) Elimination of alternative possible causes of components." (Bhaskar, 1998). This is a rather abstract description of explanation (theory) development. Here we will instead use Layder's (1998) less abstract "adaptive theory." It is an approach for generating theory in conjunction with empirical research. It attempts to combine the use of pre-existing theory and theory generated from empirical data. The elements of the research process are: (1) choice of topic/problem, (2) theoretical deliberations, (3) methods and techniques, (4) sampling, coding and memos, and (5) data analysis and theorizing. There is not some necessary or fixed temporal sequence. Layder stresses that theorizing should be a continuous process accompanying the research at all stages. Concerning research methods and research design, CR is supportive of: (1) the use of both quantitative and qualitative methods, (2) the use of extensive and intensive research design, and (3) the use of fixed and flexible research design.

To exemplify how Layder's adaptive theory can be used in IS-research, we will use a project on the use of Executive Information Systems (EIS). The project was done together with Dorothy Leidner.[1] Here a new discussion of the research is carried out.

Layder's adaptive theory approach has eight overall parameters. One parameter says that adaptive theory "uses both inductive and deductive procedures for developing and elaborating theory." (Layder, 1998). The adaptive theory suggests the use of both forms of theory-generation within the same frame of reference and particularly within the same research project. We, based on previous EIS theories and Huber's (1990) propositions on the effects of advanced IT on organizational design, intelligence, and decision making generated a number of hypotheses (a deductive procedure). These were empirically tested. From a CR perspective the purpose of this was to find patterns in the data that would be addressed in the intensive part of the study. (For a discussion of the use of statistics in CR-studies, see, Mingers (2003).) We also used an inductive procedure. Although, previous theories as well as the results from the extensive part of the project were fed into the intensive part we primarily used an inductive approach to from the data generate tentative explanations (theories) of EIS development and use. The central mode of inference (explanation) in CR research is retroduction. It enables a researcher, using induction and deduction, to investigate the potential causal mechanisms and the conditions under which certain outcomes will or will not be realised. The inductive and deductive procedures led us to formulate explanations in terms of what mechanisms and contexts could lead (or not lead) to certain outcomes—outcomes being types of EIS use with their specific effects.

Another parameter says that adaptive theory "embraces both objectivism and subjectivism in terms of its ontological presuppositions"(Layder, 1998). The adaptive theory conceives the social world as including both subjective and objective aspects and mixtures of the two. In our study, one objective aspect was the ICT used in the different EIS and one subjective aspect was perceived effects of EIS use.

Two other parameters say that adaptive theory "assumes that the social world is complex, multi-faceted (layered) and densely compacted" and "focuses on the multifarious interconnections between human agency, social activities and social organization (structures and systems)" (Layder, 1998). In our study we focused the 'interconnections' between agency and structure. We addressed self, e.g., perceptions of EIS, situated activity, e.g., use of EIS in day-to-day work, setting, e.g. organizational structure and culture, and context, e.g., national culture and economic situation. Based on our data we hypothesized that national culture can affect (generate) how EIS are developed and used and how they are perceived. We also hypothesized that organizational 'strategy' and 'structure' as well as 'economic situation' can affect (generate) how EIS are developed and used and how they are perceived.

Our study and the results (theory) were influenced by, e.g. Huber's propositions, the 'theory' saying that EIS are systems for providing top-managers with critical information, and Quinn's competing values approach (Quinn et al., 1996). The latter theory was brought in to theorize around the data from the intensive (inductive) part of the study. Adaptive theorizing was ever present in the research process. In line with CR, we tried to go beneath the empirical to explain why we found what we found through hypothesizing the mechanisms that shape the actual and the events. Our study led to that we argued that it is a misconception to think of EIS as systems that just provide top-managers with information. EIS are systems that support managerial cognition and behavior—providing information is only one of several means—as well as it can be one important means in organizational change. Based on our study, we "hypothesize" that "tentative" mechanisms are, for example, national culture, economic development, and organizational strategy and culture. We also hypothesized how the mechanisms together with different actors' decisions and actions, based on their desires, beliefs, and opportunities, lead to the development and use of different types of EIS. For example: (1) EIS use for personal productivity enhancement respectively EIS use for organizational change, and (2) EIS use for organizational change respectively EIS use for control and stability.

A CR-Based Theory of Technology-Enabled Organizational Change

A classical concern in the IS-field is "explanatory theories for technology-mediated organizational change." Various theories on how technology leads to or enables organizational change have been proposed. The research and the theories can be categorized as having a deterministic view or an emergent view. They can also be classified as having an agency view or a structural view (including a technology view). As discussed above, CR focuses both structure and agency and has an emergent view. It separates structure and agency, whereas other "perspectives" either ignore agency (institutional theory), ignore structure (behavioral approaches), or conflate the two (structuration theory and ANT) (Archer, 1995). (The problems with the other "perspectives" were

presented and discussed in the section "Why critical realism?").

Volkoff, Strong and Elmes (2007) responded to the research question: "how does technology mediate organizational change." They did this by developing a new theory based on the philosophy of CR. The longitudinally studied the implementation and use of an Enterprise Resource Planning (ERP) system. Their specific view on technology-mediated organizational change is based on Archer's (1995) morphogenetic approach which is conceptualized as a cycle consisting of three phases: 1) structural conditioning, 2) social interaction, and 3) structural elaboration. The "concept morphogenesis indicates that society has no preferred form ... but is shaped and re-shaped by the interplay between STRUCTURE and AGENCY." (Archer, 2007, p. 319). The middle phase of social interaction is the one which may appear to be where human agency has its greatest role, but this is not the case, as human agency is implicated in and embedded within all phases of the cycle. The structural conditioning phase incorporates the critical realist assumption that structure pre-dates action(s) which transform it. Structural elaboration post-dates those actions (Figure 3). The structural elaboration phase of the model, which flows out of the social interactions in phase two can have one of two characteristics: structural elaboration/morphogenesis where people and structures are transformed and struc-

Figure 3. Archer's morphogenetic approach

66

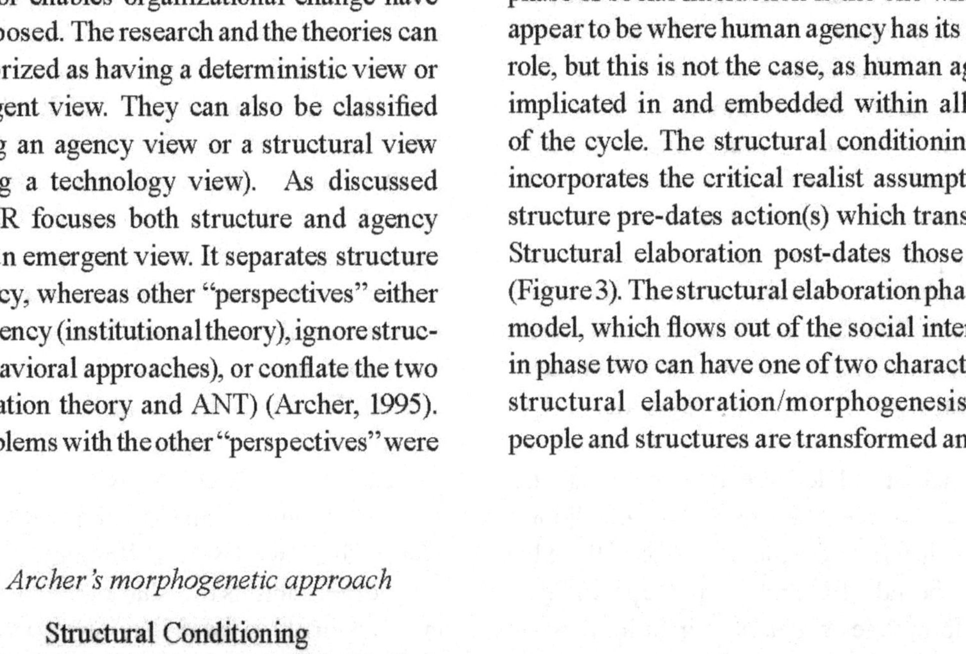

tural reproduction/morphostasis where people and structures are largely reproduced. Said Archer: "Although, all three lines are in fact continuous, the analytical element consists in breaking up the flows into intervals determined by the problem in hand." (Archer, 2007, p. 319).

Volkoff et al. view ERP as "...a source of structural conditioning that is relatively independent and enduring, existing materially in the real domain, rather than primarily as a malleable structure, existing only in the empirical domain at the moment of instantiation. Using a critical realist perspective, we [Volkoff et al.] can discuss the interplay between structures and human agents, and examine the generative mechanisms or mediators through which agents affect structure and, of greater importance for this study, how structures shape agency." (Volkoff et al., 2007, p. 835).

Volkoff et al. based their study on the work of Feldman and Pentland on organizational routines (Feldman & Pentland, 2003; Pentland & Feldman, 2005). They used their distinction between ostensive (structural) aspects of routines and the performative (agentic) aspects of routines. Volkoff et al. found that "in addition to ostensive and performative aspects, routines also have a material aspect that is embedded in the technology." and "material aspect of routines plays a critical and direct role in the change process." Their study resulted in a critical realist theory of technology-mediated organizational change..

CR-Based Information Systems Evaluation Research

The development and expansion of evaluation theory and practice is at the core of several different disciplines. It is important to scrutinize theories, approaches, and models used in evaluation (research) as well as evaluation research approaches' philosophical underpinnings. Stufflebeam (2001) provides a good example. He identified and evaluated twenty-two different generic program evaluation approaches. IS evaluation and IS evaluation

research have been stressed as critical means in advancing the IS-field (Bjørn-Andersen & Davis, 1988). Generally, IS evaluation is concerned with the evaluation of different aspects of real-life interventions in the social life where IS are critical means in achieving the interventions' anticipated goals. IS evaluation research can be considered a special case of evaluation research.

Driving CR-based IS evaluation research, which we call realistic IS evaluation, is the aim to produce ever more detailed answers to the question of why an IS initiative—IS, types of IS, or IS implementation—works for whom and in what circumstances. This means that evaluation researchers attend to how and why an IS initiative has the potential to cause (desired) changes. Realistic IS evaluation research is applied research, but theory is essential in every aspects of IS evaluation research design and analysis. The goal is not to develop theory per se, but to develop theories for practitioners, stakeholders, and participants.

A realistic evaluation researcher works as an experimental scientist, but not according to the logics of the traditional experimental research. Said Bhaskar: "The experimental scientist must perform two essential functions in an experiment. First, he must trigger the mechanism under study to ensure that it is active; and secondly, he must prevent any interference with the operation of the mechanism. These activities could be designated as 'experimental production' and 'experimental control'." (Bhaskar 1998). Figure 4 depicts the realistic experiment adapted to the context of IS initiative/intervention.

Realistic evaluation researchers do not conceive that IS initiatives "work". It is the action of stakeholders that makes them work, and the causal potential of an IS initiative takes the form of providing reasons and resources to enable different stakeholders and participants to "make" changes. This means that a realistic evaluation researchers seek to understand why an IS initiative (IS implementation) works through an

Figure 4. The IS initiative/intervention " experiment"

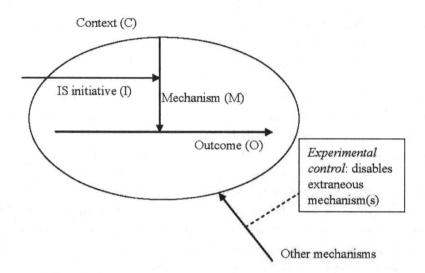

understanding of the action mechanisms. It also means that a realistic evaluation researcher seeks to understand for whom and in what circumstances (contexts) an IS initiative works through the study of contextual conditioning.

Realistic evaluation researchers orient their thinking to context-mechanism-outcome pattern configurations—called CMO configurations. This leads to the development of transferable and cumulative lessons from IS evaluation research. A CMO configuration is a proposition stating what it is about an IS initiative (IS implementation) which works for whom in what circumstances. A refined CMO configuration is the finding of IS evaluation research—the output of a realistic evaluation study.

Realistic evaluation researchers examine outcome patterns in a theory-testing role. This means that a realistic evaluation researcher tries to understand what are the outcomes of an IS initiative (IS implementation) and how are the outcomes produced. Hence, a realistic evaluation researcher is not just inspecting outcomes in order to see if an IS initiative (IS implementation) works, but are analyzing the outcomes to discover if the conjectured mechanism/context theories are confirmed.

In terms of generalization, a realistic evaluation researcher through a process of CMO configuration abstraction creates "middle range" theories. These theories provide analytical frameworks to interpret differences and similarities between types of IS initiatives (IS implementations).

Realistic IS evaluation based on the above may be implemented through a realistic effectiveness cycle. Figure 5 depicts the cycle adapted to IS evaluation. The starting point is theory. Theory includes proposition on how the mechanisms introduced by an IS invention into pre-existing contexts can generate outcomes. This entails theoretical analysis of mechanisms, contexts, and expected outcomes. This can be done using a logic of analogy and metaphor. The second step consists of generating "hypotheses". Typically the following questions would be addressed in the hypotheses: (1) what changes or outcomes will be brought about by an IS intervention, (2) what contexts impinge on this, and (3) what mechanisms (social, cultural and others) would enable these changes, and which one may disable the intervention. The third step is the selection of appropriate data collection methods—as stressed, realists are committed methodological pluralism. In this step

Figure 5. The Information systems evaluation cycle—based on Pawson and Tilley's (1997) and Kazi's (2003) realistic effectiveness cycle

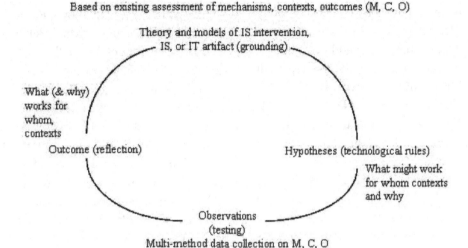

Based on existing assessment of mechanisms, contexts, outcomes (M, C, O)

Theory and models of IS intervention, IS, or IT artifact (grounding)

What (& why) works for whom, contexts

Outcome (reflection)

Hypotheses (technological rules)

What might work for whom contexts and why

Observations (testing)

Multi-method data collection on M, C, O

it might be possible to provide evidence of the IS intervention's ability to change reality. Based on the result from the third step, one may return to the programme (the IS intervention) to make it more specific as an intervention of practice. Next, but not finally, one returns to theory. The theory may be developed, the hypotheses refined, the data collection methods enhanced, etc.

Enterprise Systems Implementation Evaluation

To illustrate realistic IS evaluation research we will use an evaluation study of Enterprise Systems Implementations (Dobson, Myles, & Jackson, 2007)—the article can be considered research in progress. In the study CR was used as the underlying philosophy for the research. The specific type of system addressed is automated performance measurement systems (APMS). APMS are a fairly recent evolution within the context of enterprise information systems. They deliver information to senior managers through automatically collecting operational data from integrated IS to generate values for key performance indicators. APMS are

a consequence of the Sarbanes-Oxley Act (SOX) and similar legislation. The study investigated a number of APMS implemenations with varying degree of success and failure. In reflecting on their research, Dobson et al. say: "In the context of the APMS research, it became evident that contextual issues were paramount in explaining the success and failure of the implementations. … This emphasis on context impacted the underlying research focus. The critical realist focus on retroductive prepositional-type questioning led to a contextual basis for the study seeking to answer 'Under what conditions might APMS implementation prove successful?' rather than 'What are the (predictive) critical success factors for an APMS implementation?' A simplistic critical success factors approach tends to deny the heavy contextuality and complexity of large-scale systems implementation." (Dobson et al., 2007, p. 143)

Dobson et al.'s study has six major phases. The first phase was a literature review including the use of DeLone and McLean's IS success models (DeLone & McLean, 1992, 2003) and Wixon and Watson's data warehousing success model (Wixom & Watson, 2001). The purpose of the review was to develop an APMS success model. The literature review followed Pawson's (2006) suggestions on how to conduct systematic reviews to make sense of a heterogeneous body of literature. The review was driven by a focus on context-mechanism-outcome and how outcome can be "produced". Using Pawson's approach means that it is possible to move away from the many one-off studies and instead learn from fields such as medicine and policy studies on how to develop evidence-based IS design knowledge. In order to guide practitioners, researchers should analyze previous research based on the assumption that one can draw more powerful conclusions from the collective wisdom of previous research.

In the second phase, the developed success model was then used as the basis for generating questions for semi-structured, qualitative interviews. In the third phase, the generated questions were used in a focus group interview. The focus group was composed of IS industry experts, active in the performance measurement system area. The generated data and the first developed model were analyzed and a revised model (Model 1) was developed. In the fourth phase, this model will be tested against a case study with further refinements to the model resulting in Model 2. In the fifth phase, a number of reviews and case interviews will be done. These will lead to the refinements of the model (Model 3 & 4). A final model will be synthesised and will be included in Myles' doctoral thesis.

Dobson et al.'s study illustrates the realistic IS evaluation research well. The study has a focus on unpacking the mechanisms of how complex IS implementations work in particular settings and contexts. The focus is on what is it about this IS implementation that works for whom in what circumstances. With the study's emphasis on deep understanding of contexts, settings and mechanism it shows how realistic IS evaluation research can be a very good alternative to simplistic critical success factors studies.

CR-Based Information Systems Design Science

Above we have presented how CR can be used in IS research being "truth-driven". Below we address Gregor's fifth type of theory: theory for design and action. Research generating this type of theories is solution driven and called IS design science. In order to increase the relevance and bridge the gap between scholarly IS research and IS practice scholars argue for IS design science. Two major IS design science research schools have emerged (O. A. El Sawy, personal communication, August 2006): 1) information systems design theory (cf. Walls et al. 1992, 2004), and 2) design science research (Hevner et al. (2004). The schools share a focus on the IT artifact. Some scholars argue for a third "school". These scholars argue that IS is a socio-technical discipline and that: "design science and the research that builds that body of knowledge must acknowledge that IS is fundamentally about human activity systems which are usually technologically enabled, implying that the context of *design* and *use* is critical, and that research paradigms, practices and activities must embrace such a worldview." (McKay & Marshall, 2005, p. 5).

The primary constituent community for the output of IS design science is the professionals in the IS field. This means primarily professionals who plan, manage and govern, design, build, implement, operate, maintain and evaluate different types of IS initiative and IS.

Using van Aken's (2004) classification we can distinguish three different types of designs an IS professional makes when designing and implementing an IS-initiative: (1) an *object-design*, which is the design of the IS intervention (initiative), (2) a *realization-design*, which is the plan for the implementation of the IS intervention (initiative), and (3) a *process-design*, which is the professional's own plan for the problem solving cycle and includes the methods and techniques to be used to design the solution (the IS intervention) to the problem. IS design science research should produce knowledge that can be used by the professionals in the three types of designs.

We suggest that the outcomes of IS design science can take the form of, for example, algorithmic or heuristic design propositions, design exemplars, or stories and narratives. The outcomes should be useful and applicable to IS practitioners. We have in the last years in a number of projects developed IS design knowledge for what we call "IS use and management" in the form of, for example, design propositions. We have argued for that such research can be developed based on an approach having four major research activities (Figure 6): (1) identify problems and desired outcomes, (2) review (kernel) theories and previous research, (3) propose/refine design theory and (4) test design theory. Carlsson et al. (2008) and Hrastinski et al (2007) present how design knowledge based the approach have been developed for three areas: knowledge management, e-learning, and IS integration.[2]

CONCLUSION

Although, CR has influenced a number of disciplines and fields, it has until recently been almost invisible in the IS-field. CR's potential for IS research has been argued by, for example, Carlsson (2003, 2004), Dobson (2001), Mingers (2003, 2004), Mutch (2002). CR-based empirical research can be found in, for example, Morton (2007), Volkoff et al. (2007) Dobson et al. (2007), and De Vaujany (2008). CR has also critical and emancipatory components (Bhaskar, 2002). Wilson and Greenhill (2004) and Longshore Smith (2005) address how CR in IS research can work critically and emancipatory. CR's potential for IS design science has been argued by Carlsson (2006, 2009) and Lyytinen (2008). CR-based IS design science can be found in Carlsson et al. (2008) and Hrastinski et al. (2007).

It seems that CR-based research overcomes some of the problems with IS research underpinned by positivism or constructivism as well as with research based on theories like structuration theory and ANT.

It should be noted that doing CR-based IS research is not without "problems". For example, due to its open system view and that it recognizes social systems' complexity it will generate theories that are provisional, fallible, incomplete, and extendable. In other words, CR-based IS research will not produce simple theories and "quick fix" results. Based on the few examples of CR-based IS research it seems that doing this type of research is not for the novice.

ACKNOWLEDGMENT

I would like to thank Pertti Järvinen and Erkki Koponen for a number of valuable suggestions and comments.

REFERENCES

Ackroyd, S., & Fleetwood, S. (Eds.). (2000). *Realist perspectives on management and organisations*. London: Routledge.

Figure 6. IS design knowledge development (Hrastinski et al., 2007)

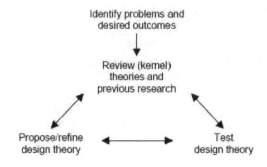

Archer, M. S. (1979). *Social origins of educational systems*. London: Sage.

Archer, M. S. (1995). *Realist social theory: The morpohogenetic approach*. UK: Cambridge University Press.

Archer, M. S. (2007). Morphogenesis/morphostatis. In M. Hartwig (Ed.), *Dictionary of critical realism* (p. 319). London: Routledge.

Archer, M., Bhaskar, R., Collier, A., Lawson, T., & Norrie, A. (Eds.). (1998). *Critical realism: Essential readings*. London: Routledge.

Arnott D., & Pervan, G. (2005). A critical analysis of decision support systems research. *Journal of Information Technology, 20*, 67-87

Bhaskar, R. (1978). *A realist theory of science*. Sussex, UK: Harvester Press.

Bhaskar, R. (1989). *Reclaiming reality*. London: Verso.

Bhaskar, R. (1991). *Philosophy and the idea of freedom*. Oxford, UK: Basil Blackwell.

Bhaskar, R. (1998). *The possibility of naturalism* (3rd ed.). London: Routledge.

Bhaskar, R. (2002). *Reflections on meta-reality: Transcendence, enlightenment and everyday life*. London: Sage.

Bjørn-Andersen, N., & Davis, G. B. (Eds.). (1988). *Information systems assessment: Issues and challenges*. Amsterdam: North-Holland.

Bryman, A. (2001). *Social research methods*. UK: Oxford University Press.

Carlsson, S. A. (2003). Advancing information systems evaluation (research): A critical realist approach. *Electronic Journal of Information Systems Evaluation, 6*(2), 11-20.

Carlsson, S. A. (2004). Using critical realism in IS research. In M. E. Whitman & A. B. Woszczynski (Eds.), *The handbook of information systems research* (pp. 323-338). Hershey, PA:IGI Global Publishing.

Carlsson, S. A. (2006): Towards an information systems design research framework: A critical realist perspective. In *Proceedings of the First International Conference on Design Science in Information Systems and Technology (DESRIST 2006)*, (pp. 192-212).

Carlsson, S. A. (2009). Design science in information systems: A critical realist approach. In A. Hevner & S. Chatterjee (Eds.), *Design science research in information systems*. New York: Springer.

Carlsson S. A., Henningsson, S., Hrastinski, S., & Keller, C. (2008, May 7-9). Towards a design science research approach for IS use and management: Applications from the areas of knowledge management, e-learning and IS integration. In *Proceedings of the Third International Conference on Design Science Research in Information Systems & Technology* (DESRIST 2008), Atlanta, GA.

Carlsson, S. A., Leidner, D. E., & Elam, J. J. (1996). Individual and organizational effectiveness: Perspectives on the impact of ESS in multinational organizations. In P. Humphreys, L. Bannon, A. McCosh, P. Migliarese & J. C. Pomerol (Eds.), *Implementing systems for supporting management decisions: Concepts, methods and experiences* (pp. 91-107). London: Chapman & Hall.

Chen, W., & Hirschheim, R. (2004). A paradigmatic and methodological examination of information systems research. *Information Systems Journal, 14*(3), 197-235.

De Vaujany F.-C. (2008). Capturing reflexivitiy modes in IS: A critical realist approach. *Information and Organization, 18*, 51-71.

Dean, K., Joseph J., & Norrie, A. (2005). Editorial: New essays in critical realism. *New Formations, 56*, 7-26.

DeLone, W. H., & McLean, E. R. (1992). Information systems success: The quest for the dependent variable. *Information Systems Research, 3*(1), 60-95.

DeLone, W. H., & McLean, E. R. (2003). The DeLone and McLean model of information systems success: A ten-year update. *Journal of Management Information Systems, 19*(4), 9-30.

Dobson, P. J. (2001). The philosophy of critical realism—an opportunity for information systems research. *Information Systems Frontier, 3*(2), 199-201.

Dobson, P., Myles, J., & Jackson, P. (2007). Making the case for critical realism: Examining the implementation of automated performance management systems. *Information Resources Management Journal, 20*(2), 138-152.

Feldman, M. S., & Pentland, B. T. (2003). Reconceptualizing organizational routines as a source of flexibility and change. *Administrative Science Quarterly, 48*, 94-118.

Fleetwood, S. (2002). Boylan and O'Gorman's causal holism: A critical realist evaluation. *Cambridge Journal of Economics, 26*, 27-45.

Fleetwood, S., & Ackroyd, S. (Eds.). (2004). *Critical realist applications in organisation and management studies.* London: Routledge.

Gable, G. (1994). Integrating case study and survey research methods: An example in information systems. *European Journal of Information Systems, 3*(2), 112-126.

Gasson, S. (2004). Rigor in grounded theory research: An interpretive perspective on generating theory from qualitative field studies. In M. E. Whitman and A. B. Woszczynski (Eds.), *Handbook for information systems research* (pp. 97-102). Hershey, PA: Idea Group Publishing.

Giddens, A. (1984). *The constitution of society.* Cambridge, UK: Polity Press.

Glaser, B. G., & Strauss, A. L. (1967). *The discovery of grounded theory.* Chicago: Aldine.

Gregor, S. (2006). The nature of theory in information systems. *MIS Quarterly, 30*(3), 611-642.

Groff, R. (2004). *Critical realism, post-positivism and the possibility of knowledge.* London: Routledge.

Hartwig, M. (Ed.). (2007). *Dictionary of critical realism.* London: Routledge.

Hevner, A. R., March, S. T., Park, J., & Ram, S. (2004). Design science in information systems research. *MIS Quarterly, 28*(1), 75-105.

Hrastinski, S., Keller C., & Carlsson, S. A. (2007, May 13-15). Towards a design theory for synchronous computer-mediated communication in e-learning environments. In *Proceedings of the 2nd nternational Conference on Design Science Research in Information Systems & Technology (DESRIST 2007)*, Pasadena.

Huber, G. P. (1990). A theory of the effects of advanced information technologies on organizational design, intelligence, and decision making. *Academy of Management Review, 15*(1), 47-71.

Hunter, M. G., & Beck, J. E. (1996). A cross-cultural comparison of 'excellent' systems analysts'. *Information Systems Journal, 6*(4), 261-281.

Jones, M. (1999). Structuration theory. In W.L. Currie & B. Galliers (Eds.), *Rethinking management information systems* (pp 103-135). UK: Oxford University Press.

Jones, M. R., & Karsten, H. (2008). Giddens's structuration theory and information systems research. *MIS Quarterly, 32*(1), 127-157.

Kaplan, B., & Duchon, D. (1988). Combining qualitative and quantitative methods in information systems research: A case study. *MIS Quarterly, 12*(4), 571-586.

Kazi, M. A. F. (2003). *Realist evaluation in practice*. London: Sage.

Latour, B. (1987). *Science in action*. Milton Keynes, UK: Open University Press.

Layder, D. (1993). *New strategies in social research*. Cambridge, UK: Polity Press.

Layder, D. (1998). *Sociological practice: Linking theory and social research*. London: Sage.

Lee, A. S. (1991). Integrating positivist and interpretative approaches to organizational research. *Organization Science, 2*(4), 342-365.

Lee, A. S., Liebenau, J., & DeGross, J. (Eds.) (1997). *Information systems and qualitative research*. London: Chapman & Hall.

Leidner, D. E., & Carlsson, S. A. (1998). Les bénéfices des systèmes d′information pour dirigeants dans trois pays. *Systèmes d'Information et Management, 3*(3), 5-27.

Leidner, D. E., & Elam, J. J. (1995). The impact of executive information systems on organizational design, intelligence, and decision making. *Organization Science, 6*(6), 645-665.

Leidner, D. E., Carlsson, S. A., Elam, J. J., & Corrales, M. (1999). Mexican and Swedish managers′ perceptions of the impact of EIS on organizational intelligence, decision making, and structure. *Decision Sciences, 30*(3), 633-658.

Longshore Smith, M. (2005). *Overcoming theory-practice inconsistencies: Critical realism and information systems research* (WP134). Department of Information Systems, London School of Economics.

Longshore Smith, M. (2006). Overcoming theory-practice inconsistencies: Critical realism and information systems research. *Information and Organization, 16*(3), 191–211.

Lòpez, J., & Potter, G. (Eds.). (2001). *After postmodernism: An introduction to critical realism*. London: Athlone.

Lyytinen, K. (2008, May 7-9): Design: "shaping in the wild". Keynote speech at the *Third International Conference on Design Science Research in Information Systems & Technology (DESRIST 2008)*, Atlanta, GA.

McKay, J., & Marshall, P. (2005, November 29–December 2) A review of design science in information systems. In *Proceedings of the 16th Australasian Conference on Information Systems*, Sydney.

Mingers, J. (2003). A critique of statistical modelling from a critical realist perspective. In *Proceedings of the 11th European Conference on Information Systems*.

Mingers, J. (2004). Re-establishing the real: Critical realism and information systems. In J. Mingers & L. Willcocks (Eds.), *Social theory and philosophy for information systems* (pp. 372-406). Chichester, UK: Wiley.

Morton P. (2006). Using critical realism to explain strategic information systems planning. *Journal of Information Theory and Application, 8*(1), 1-20.

Mutch, A. (2002). Actors and networks or agents and structures: Towards a realist view of information systems. *Organizations, 9*(3), 477-496.

Myers. M. (2009). *Qualitative research in business & management*. London: Sage.

Orlikowski, W. J. (1992). The duality of technology: Rethinking the concept of technology in organizations. *Organization Science, 3*(3), 398-427.

Orlikowski, W. J. (2000). Using technology and constituting structures: A practice lens for studying technology in organizations. *Organization Science, 11*(4), 404-428.

Pawson, R. (2006). *Evidence-based policy: A realist perspective*. London: Sage.

Pawson, R., & Tilley, N. (1997). *Realistic evaluation*. London: Sage.

Pentland, B. T., & Feldman, M. S. (2005). Organizational routines as a unit of analysis. *Industrial and Corporate Change, 14*, 793-815.

Quinn, R. E., Faerman, S. R., Thompson, M. P., & McGrath, M. R. (1996). *Becoming a master manager* (2nd ed.). New York: John Wiley & Sons.

Reed, M.I. (1997). In praise of duality and dualism: rethinking agency and structure in organizational analysis. *Organization Studies, 18*(1), 21-42.

Robson, C. (2002). *Real world research* (2nd ed.). Oxford, UK: Blackwell.

Sayer, A. (1992). *Method in social science: A realist approach* (2nd ed.). London: Routledge.

Sayer, A. (2000). *Realism and social science.* London: Sage.

Schultze, U., & Leidner, D. E. (2003). Studying knowledge management in information systems research: Discourses and theoretical assumptions. *MIS Quarterly, 26*(3), 213-242.

Strauss, A. L., & Corbin, J. M. (1998). *Basics of qualitative research: Techniques and procedures for developing grounded theory.* Thousand Oaks, CA: Sage.

Stufflebeam, D. L. (2001). Evaluation models. *New Directions for Evaluation, 89*(Spring), 7-98.

Tan, B. C. Y., Watson, R. T., & Wei, K.-K. (1995). National culture and group support systems: Filtering communication to dampen power differentials. *European Journal of Information Systems, 4*, 82–92.

Trauth, E.M., (Ed.). (2001). *Qualitative research in IS: Issues and trends.* Hershey, PA: Idea Group Publishing.

Trauth, E., & Jessup, L. (2000). Understanding computer-mediated discussions: Positivist and interpretive analyses of group support system use. *MIS Quarterly, 24*(1), 43-79.

Urquhart, C. (2001). An encounter with grounded theory: Tackling the practical and philosophical issues. In E. M. Trauth (Ed.), *Qualitative research in IS: Issues and trends.* Hershey, PA: Idea Group Publishing.

Van Aken, J. E. (2004) Management research based on the paradigm of design sciences: The quest for field-tested and grounded technological rules. *Journal of Management Studies, 41*(2), 219-246.

Volkoff, O., Strong, D. M., & Elmes, M. B. (2007). Technological embeddedness and organizational change. *Organization Science, 18*(5), 832-848.

Walls, J. G., Widmeyer, G. R. & El Sawy, O. A. (1992). Building an information systems design theory for vigilant EIS. *Information Systems Research, 3*(1), 36-59.

Walls, J. G., Widemeyer, G. R., & El Sawy, O. A. (2004). Assessing information system design theory in perspective: How useful was our 1992 initial rendition? *Journal of Information Technology Theory and Application, 6*(2), 43-58.

Whitman, M. E., & Woszczynski, A. B. (eds.) (2004). *Handbook for information systems research.* Hershey, PA: Idea Group Publishing.

Wilson, M., & Greenhill, A. (2004): Theory and action for emancipation: Elements of a critical realist approach. In B. Kaplan, D. Truex III, D. Wastell, T. Wood-Harper & J. DeGross (Eds.), *Information systems research: Relevant theory and informed practice* (pp 667-675). Amsterdam: Kluwer.

Wixom, B. H., & Watson, H. J. (2001). An empirical investigation of the factors affecting data warehousing success. *MIS Quarterly, 25*(1), 17-41.

KEY TERMS AND DEFINITIONS

Constructivism (or Social Constructivism): Asserts that (social) actors socially construct reality.

Context-Mechanism-Outcome Pattern: Realist evaluation researchers orient their thinking to context-mechanism-outcome (CMO) pattern configurations. A CMO configuration is a proposition stating what it is about an IS initiative which works for whom in what circumstances. A refined CMO configuration is the finding of IS evaluation research.

Critical Realism: Asserts that the study of the social world should be concerned with the identification of the structures and mechanisms through which events and discourses are generated.

Empiricism: Asserts that only knowledge gained through experience and senses is acceptable in studies of reality.

Positivism: Asserts that reality is the sum of sense impression. In large, equating social sciences with natural sciences. Primarily using deductive logic and quantitative research methods.

Postmodernism: A position critical of realism and rejects the view of social sciences as a search for over-arching explanations of the social world. Has a preference for qualitative methods.

Realism: A position acknowledging a reality independent of actors' (incl. researchers') thoughts and beliefs.

Realist IS Evaluation: Evaluation (research) based on critical realism aiming at producing ever more detailed answers to the question of why an IS initiative works (better) for whom and in what circumstances (contexts).

Retroduction: The central mode of inference (explanation) in critical realism research. Enables a researcher to investigate the potential causal mechanisms and the conditions under which certain outcomes will or will not be realised.

ENDNOTES

[1] See Leidner & Elam (1995), Carlsson, Leidner & Elam (1996), Leidner & Carlsson (1998) and Leidner, Carlsson, Elam & Corrales (1999).

[2] A design proposition can be expressed as: In situation S and context C, to achieve consequence (outcome) O, then do (something like) A (action). Examples: "If you want to enhance "cognitive" participation to provide deep learning, then support asynchronous communication" (e-learning), "If the company frequently engages in M&As and needs to develop a strong IS integration capability, using internal IS professionals and not consultants can enhance that capability" (IS integration) , and "If you want the sharing initiative to have a positive impact on operations, then link knowledge use to operational decision-making and action taking" (KM).

Chapter V
Theory Development in Information Systems Research Using Structural Equation Modeling:
Evaluation and Recommendations

Nicholas Roberts
Clemson University, USA

Varun Grover
Clemson University, USA

ABSTRACT

Structural equation modeling (SEM) techniques have significant potential for assessing and modifying theoretical models. There have been 171 applications of SEM in IS research, published in major journals, most of which have been after 1994. Despite SEM's surging popularity in the IS field, it remains a complex tool that is often mechanically used but difficult to effectively apply. The purpose of this study is to review previous applications of SEM in IS research and to recommend guidelines to enhance the use of SEM to facilitate theory development. The authors review and evaluate SEM applications, both component-based (e.g., PLS) and covariance-based (e.g., LISREL), according to prescribed criteria. Areas of improvement are suggested which can assist application of this powerful technique in IS theory development.

INTRODUCTION

Structural equation modeling (SEM) has become an important and widely diffused research tool for theory development in the social and behavioral sciences. One reason for the substantive use of SEM is that it enables researchers to conduct a single, systematic and comprehensive analysis by modeling relationships among multiple independent and dependent variables simultaneously (Kline, 2005). Additionally, in contrast to exploratory methods, SEM allows for the specification of a precise model that is driven by theoretical considerations (Bollen, 1989). Finally, SEM also permits researchers to model higher-order latent variables (Edwards, 2001). These inherent advantages provided by SEM have caused many researchers in the information systems (IS) field to use it for measuring constructs or developing and testing IS theories.

Despite SEM's numerous advantages, the relative sophistication of SEM also makes it prone to misuse (Anderson & Gerbing, 1988). Moreover, theory development relies upon the effective use of empirical research methods (Van Maanen, Sorensen, & Mitchell, 2007). Invalid theory development could greatly inhibit the building of a cumulative tradition of research. Thus, we believe it is important to take stock of how this powerful technique has been applied in IS research.

To strengthen ties between theory and empirical IS research, this study provides an in-depth review and analysis of a critical mass of SEM applications in three top-tier IS journals. Based on our review, we suggest specific areas for improvement. To the best of our knowledge, no comprehensive survey of contemporary SEM applications in the IS field has been reported in the literature.

OVERVIEW OF STRUCTURAL EQUATION MODELING

To provide a basis for subsequent discussion, we present a brief overview of SEM. SEM is a technique used to specify, estimate, and evaluate models of linear relationships among a set of observed variables in terms of a generally smaller number of unobserved variables. Figure 1 depicts a basic latent variable model. A circle is used to represent each of the four latent variables, and the boxes represent associated manifest or indicator variables. The relationships between the latent variables and their indicators are often referred to as a "measurement" model, in that it represents an assumed process in which an underlying construct determines or causes behavior that is reflected in measured indicator variables.

Within this context, it is important to note that the arrows go from the circles to the boxes, which is consistent with the process noted above. Thus, each factor serves as an independent variable in the measurement model, and the indicator variables serve as the dependent variables. Each indicator is also potentially influenced by a second independent variable in the form of measurement error, and its influence is represented as a cause of the indicator variable through the use of a second arrow leading to each of the indicators. Finally, the model shown in Figure 1 includes correlations (double-headed arrows) among the three exogenous constructs (LV1–LV3) and regression-like structural parameters linking exogenous and endogenous constructs (e.g., LV3, LV4). The model also acknowledges that there is unexplained variance in the endogenous latent variable. The part of the overall model that proposes relationships among the latent variables is often referred to as the structural model.

Often using a maximum likelihood function, covariance-based SEM techniques attempt to minimize the difference between the sample covariances and those predicted by the theoretical model. As a result, the parameters estimated by this procedure attempt to reproduce the covariance matrix of the observed measures. Observed measures are assumed to have random error variance and measure-specific variance components that are not of theoretical interest. Hence, this error variance is modeled separately. Following this, the covariances among the latent variables are adjusted to reflect the attenuation in the observed covariances due to excluded error variance components. Because of this assumption, "the amount of variance explained in the set of observed

Figure 1. Basic Latent Variable Model

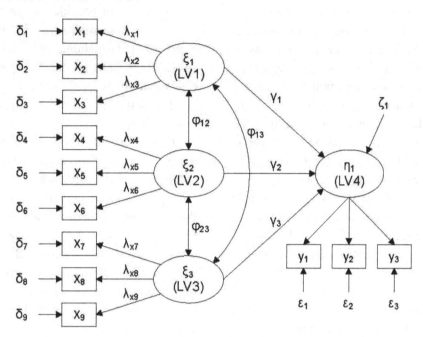

measures is not of primary concern" (Anderson & Gerbing, 1988, p. 412). Thus, covariance-based SEM techniques provide parameter estimates that best explain the observed covariances. Moreover, covariance-based SEM techniques also provide the most efficient parameter estimates (Joreskog & Wold, 1982) and an overall test of model fit.

In contrast to reproducing the covariance matrix of the observed variables, a component-based SEM approach focuses on maximizing the variance explained by the structural model (Chin, 1998). Based on a principal-component model, no random error variance or measure-specific variance is assumed. Parameter estimates are obtained based on the ability to minimize the residual variances of dependent variables (Fornell & Bookstein, 1982). Fit is assessed on the basis of the percentage of variance explained in the regression equations. Component-based SEM techniques also estimate latent variables as linear combinations of their observed measures, thereby providing an exact definition of component scores. This advantage of precise definitions in

conjunction with explaining a large percentage of the variance in observed measures is valuable in accurately predicting individuals' standings on the components (Anderson & Gerbing, 1988).

CONCEPTUALIZING THE ROLE OF SEM IN THEORY DEVELOPMENT

The importance of theory to the advancement of scientific knowledge in the IS field cannot be overstated. Theory allows researchers to understand and predict outcomes of interest, even if only probabilistically (Cook & Campbell, 1979). Theory also allows researchers to describe and explain a process or series of events (Mohr, 1982). As Hall and Lindzey (1957) noted, the function of theory "is that of preventing the observer from being dazzled by the full-blown complexity of natural or concrete events" (p. 9). Thus, the purpose of theory is twofold: to organize (parsimoniously) and to communicate (clearly).

Many scholars define theory in terms of relationships between independent and dependent variables. For instance, Bacharach (1989) defines theory as "a statement of relations among concepts within a set of boundary assumptions and constraints" (p. 496). Theories range from guesses, conjectures, or speculation to more formal propositions, hypotheses, or models, with those that are more formal more likely to appear in print (Weick, 1995). Theory development can be conceptualized as a discourse between generating explanations for phenomena and using appropriate methods to evaluate their validity (Van Maanen et al., 2007). Because the advancement of theory partially rests on methodological tools used to help define ideas and test their conclusions (Blalock, 1969), it is important to match research methods to stages of theory development.

SEM techniques are useful for establishing relationships between constructs (Bollen, 1989). Specifically, SEM techniques leverage knowledge gained from case studies because they allow researchers to examine patterns of relationships across individuals, groups or organizations. For example, partial least squares (PLS) is a component-based SEM technique that centers on establishing that relationships exist and maximizing the variance explained by the structural model (Wold, 1982). PLS's emphasis on relationship building and variance explanation makes it well suited for theory building (Joreskog & Wold, 1982). Covariance-based SEM techniques are also useful in this stage for three reasons: (1) when theory suggests competing models exist, researchers can use SEM techniques to model and test alternative models with the same data set (Anderson & Gerbing, 1988); (2) modification indices can provide insight into plausible alternative explanations for relationships among constructs (MacCallum, 1986); and (3) SEM results are replicable and reusable, thereby providing researchers with opportunities to independently confirm results and evaluate alternative models (Kline, 2005).

Theory building is followed by theory testing, a stage in which rigorous tests are conducted to determine whether hypothesized relationships among constructs actually exist. Appropriate theory testing methods include SEM techniques, regression, and analysis of variance (ANOVA). These methods allows researchers to estimate relationships and make inferences based on statistical analysis. SEM techniques are especially powerful in that they enable researchers to test complete research models (Anderson & Gerbing, 1988). Because covariance-based SEM techniques focus on maximizing the "fit" of the theoretical model to the observed data, they are considered valuable for evaluating nomological nets (Bollen, 1989; Gefen, Straub, & Boudreau, 2000). Table 1 details our discussion of research methods that support various stages of the theory development process.

LITERATURE REVIEW

This study assesses the diffusion and use of SEM techniques in the IS field. We reviewed applications of SEM techniques in three well-established

Table 1. Research methods and stages of theory development

Theory Development Stage	Supporting Research Method	Outcome
Exploratory	In-depth case studies, exploratory interviews	Identification of key concepts and issues, evidence that a phenomenon is important
Theory Building	Multi-site case studies, SEM techniques	Construct definitions, explanations for relationships among constructs, initial tests of relationships, search for alternative models
Theory Testing	SEM techniques, ANOVA, regression	Omnibus tests of theoretical relationships, evaluation of nomological networks

IS journals: *Information Systems Research* (ISR), *Journal of Management Information Systems* (JMIS), and *MIS Quarterly* (MISQ). Consistent with prior research (Gefen et al., 2000), all issues of these journals published over the period 1990-2007 were searched for empirical SEM applications. Theoretical papers addressing issues related to SEM and papers using ANOVA, exploratory factor analysis, path analysis, and regression were excluded from the sample. Table 2 shows the number of articles collected from each journal. Table 3 displays the number of articles using either component-based or covariance-based SEM.

A total of 171 articles satisfied our selection criteria (see Table 2). One apparent trend is that the use of SEM in IS research steadily increased over the period 1998 to 2007. The SEM applications were evenly distributed across the three major IS journals. Another trend is that use of component-based techniques rose substantially starting in 2003 (see Table 3).

METHODOLOGICAL SEM ISSUES

Figure 2 depicts the recommended sequence of activities that need to be performed to conduct effective SEM analysis: (1) model specification, (2) data screening, (3) model estimation and assessment, and (4) model respecification (Kline, 2005; Hair et al. 2006). Each stage consists of a set of salient methodological issues. For instance, researchers need to consider indicator selection, formative/reflective approaches, model identification, and sample size issues in the model specification stage. For each SEM analysis stage

Table 2. Applications of SEM in IS research

	ISR	JMIS	MISQ	Total	(%)
1990	1	0	0	1	0.6
1991	2	1	1	4	2.3
1992	0	1	1	2	1.2
1993	0	1	1	2	1.2
1994	3	1	2	6	3.5
1995	3	2	2	7	4.1
1996	2	2	0	4	2.3
1997	3	0	3	6	3.5
1998	1	0	2	3	1.8
1999	3	5	1	9	5.3
2000	3	2	6	11	6.4
2001	2	4	3	9	5.3
2002	9	5	2	16	9.4
2003	3	6	6	15	8.8
2004	5	7	3	15	8.8
2005	6	6	6	18	10.5
2006	5	6	10	21	12.3
2007	6	10	6	22	12.9
Total	57	59	55	171	
(%)	33.3	34.5	32.2		

Table 3. Applications of SEM in IS research

	Component	Covariance	Total	(%)
1990	0	1	1	0.6
1991	3	1	4	2.3
1992	1	1	2	1.2
1993	0	2	2	1.2
1994	2	4	6	3.5
1995	4	3	7	4.1
1996	3	1	4	2.3
1997	4	2	6	3.5
1998	1	2	3	1.8
1999	4	5	9	5.3
2000	6	5	11	6.4
2001	4	5	9	5.3
2002	4	12	16	9.4
2003	8	7	15	8.8
2004	7	8	15	8.8
2005	13	5	18	10.5
2006	14	7	21	12.3
2007	18	4	22	12.9
Total	96	75	171	
(%)	56.1	43.9		

we describe methodological issues, evaluate the current state of IS research with respect to those issues, and provide recommendations for future research. We also note key differences in these points for component-based and covariance-based SEM approaches.

Model Specification Issues and Recommendations

We cover four issues related to model specification: (1) indicator selection, (2) formative/reflective, (3) model identification, and (4) sample size.

Indicator Selection

A critical decision in survey-based research involves how many indicators can be explicitly related to a latent variable (i.e., construct). Technically, a latent variable may be assessed with only two indicators under certain conditions. However, models with low indicator-to-construct ratios often cause problems with identification and convergence. Hence, scholars recommend that each construct be measured with at least three indicators (Anderson & Gerbing, 1988). In the theory building stage, guidelines suggest that researchers have at least four or five indicators per latent variable, as it is often necessary to drop some indicators in order to achieve construct validity (Churchill, 1979) and arrive at a well-fitting measurement model (Kline, 2005). In either case, it is important that researchers use appropriate indicators to capture the domain space of the construct (Little, Lindenberger, & Nesselroade, 1999).

Figure 2. Methodological issues categorized by stage of SEM analysis

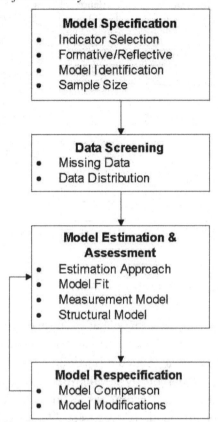

Evaluation and Recommendation: Table 3 provides descriptive statistics regarding the issue of indicator selection. Overall, the median number of indicators across all SEM applications was 26 and the median number of constructs was 6, resulting in a median ratio of indicators to constructs of approximately 4.3. The median ratios of indicators to constructs were 4.3 and 4.8 for component-based SEM and covariance-based SEM, respectively.

A notable proportion of SEM applications in IS research used single indicator constructs when multiple indicators per construct is desirable. The use of single indicator constructs is not recommended because single indicator constructs ignore measurement unreliability, which is one of the problems that SEM was specifically designed to circumvent (Gefen et al., 2000). Researchers must also consider issues regarding indicator selection and model identification. If a standard confirmatory factor analysis (CFA) model with a single factor has at least three indicators, the model is identified. If a standard CFA model with two or more factors has at least two indicators per factor, the model is identified. Bollen (1989) referred to the latter condition as the two-indicator rule. However, models with factors that have only two indicators are more prone to estimation problems, especially when the sample size is small (Kline, 2005). Hence, a minimum of three indicators per factor is recommended.

Formative/Reflective

The distinction between formative and reflective indicators has recently gained attention in the IS field. Constructs are usually viewed as causes of indicators, meaning that variation in a construct leads to variation in its indicators (Bollen, 1989). Such indicators are termed reflective because they represent reflections, or manifestations, of a construct (Fornell & Bookstein, 1982; Gefen et al., 2000). For example, behavioral intention to use a system is often operationalized with three reflective indicators (e.g., Davis, Bagozzi, & Warshaw, 1989; Venkatesh, Morris, Davis, & Davis, 2003). Hence, an individual's change in the latent behavioral intention construct results in corresponding changes in each manifest indicator of intention. Constructs can also be viewed as being formed by their indicators (Blalock, 1971; Bollen & Lennox, 1991). Such constructs are termed formative, meaning the construct is formed or induced by its measures (Fornell & Bookstein, 1982; Gefen et al., 2000). Formative constructs are commonly conceived as composites of specific component variables or dimensions (Edwards & Bagozzi, 2000). For example, if information quality is defined in terms of accuracy, completeness, currency and format, its value may vary with changes in any one of its indicators (Nelson, Todd, & Wixom, 2005).

Table 4. Analysis of model specification issues

	Component (n=96)	Covariance (n=75)	Overall (n=171)
Model Specification			
Number of indicators	29	24	26
	(20, 37)	(17.5, 38)	(19, 37)
Number of constructs	6.5	5	6
	(4, 8)	(3, 7)	(4, 8)
Ratio of indicators to constructs	4.3	4.8	4.3
	(3, 5.7)	(3.4, 9.8)	(3.2, 7.3)
Percentage of models containing at least one single-indicator construct	21	11	16
Percentage of models containing at least one formative construct	46	24	36
Sample size (median)	179	256	212
	(99, 267)	(161, 409)	(128, 355)

Evaluation and Recommendation: While an assessment of the proper use of formative constructs is beyond the scope of our investigation, we did find that 36 percent of all SEM applications had at least one formative construct in the research model. Furthermore, 46 percent of the component-based SEM applications had at least one formative construct, while 24 percent of covariance-based SEM applications had at least one formative construct. While SEM scholars have noted the importance of appropriately conceptualizing and testing constructs as either formative or reflective (Jarvis, Mackenzie, & Podsakoff, 2003; Petter, Straub, & Rai, 2007), we also note that formative representations are fraught with problems like interpretational confounding and external consistency (Howell, Breivik, & Wilcox, 2007). Furthermore, properly specifying the nature of relationships between constructs and their indicators is important because these relationships constitute a secondary theory that bridges the gap between abstract theoretical constructs and measurable empirical phenomena. Without this secondary theory, the mapping of theoretical constructs onto empirical phenomena is ambiguous, and theories cannot be meaningfully tested (Blalock, 1971).

Model Identification

Once a theoretical model has been specified, it is necessary to consider whether or not it is statistically identified. A model is said to be identified when it is theoretically possible to derive a unique estimate of each parameter (Kline, 2005). An underidentified model creates problems because it is possible for two distinct sets of parameter values to yield the same population variance-covariance matrix. In other words, two different solutions for the same structure with widely differing theoretical implications can account for the data equally well. Thus, it is important to address identification issues.

Evaluation and Recommendation: Our review found that very few researchers discuss whether they checked for model identification. This might be due to two reasons. First, journal space is a scarce resource, and second, most SEM computer software packages provide a warning message when a model is underidentified. A simple rule to avoid underidentification is that the number of freely estimated parameters should not exceed the number of distinct elements in the variance-covariance matrix of the observed variables (Sharma, 1996). Formally, the number of free parameters must be less than or equal to the number of observations (i.e., model degrees of freedom ≥ 0). The number of observations equals $v(v+1)/2$, where v is the number of observed variables.

Sample Size

When using covariance-based SEM techniques, small sample sizes can cause nonconvergence and biased parameter estimates (Anderson & Gerbing, 1988; Fornell, 1983), thereby inhibiting theory development. Simulation studies show that small samples are not compatible with maximum likelihood estimation of covariance structure models (Boomsma, 1982). Anderson and Gerbing (1984) suggest that a sample size of 150 or more will typically be needed to obtain parameter estimates that have standard errors small enough to be of practical use. Other scholars recommend a minimum sample size of 200 for SEM analysis (Hair, et al., 2006). Alternately, Bentler and Chou (1987) argue that, under normal distribution theory, the ratio of cases to free parameters should be at least 5:1 to calculate reliable parameter estimates and higher (at least 10:1) to conduct meaningful significance tests.

One advantage of component-based SEM is that it is relatively robust to small sample sizes. Since component-based SEM estimates regression equations sequentially, the sample size needs to meet the demands of the most complex regression equation in the model. The most complex regression will involve either (1) the construct with the greatest number of indicators or (2) the construct with the greatest number of antecedent constructs. Sample size requirements can be calculated by multiplying ten times (1) or (2), whichever is greater (Barclay, Higgins, & Thomson, 1995).

Evaluation and Recommendation: Table 3 shows that the median sample size for all SEM applications is 212. Furthermore, the median sample size for covariance-based SEM applications is 256, which exceeds the conservative minimum sample size of 200 recommended by SEM scholars. The

median sample size for component-based SEM applications is 179, which provides evidence that component-based SEM may be used more often than covariance-based SEM when sample size is smaller. However, researchers should not blindly use component-based SEM in all cases when sample size is small (Marcoulides & Saunders, 2006). IS researchers should take into account a number of factors when determining the appropriate sample size, such as the psychometric properties of the constructs, the strength of the relationships among the constructs, the complexity and size of the model, and the amount of missing data.

Data Screening Issues and Recommendations

The second stage in SEM analysis involves screening the data for missing values, normality, and outliers. We discuss data screening issues in the following sections.

Missing Data

The raw data should be carefully screened before a variance-covariance matrix is computed. It is important to ensure that there are no coding errors and that missing values have been appropriately addressed. Virtually all methods of statistical analysis are plagued by problems with missing data, and SEM is no exception. The use of inappropriate methods for handling missing data can lead to bias in parameter estimates (Jones, 1996), bias in standard errors and test statistics (Glasser, 1964), and inefficient use of the data (Afifi & Elashoff, 1966).

Evaluation and Recommendation: We found that IS researchers do not report missing data issues very often. Only 19 percent of all SEM applications discussed missing data. Again, this may be due to limited journal space. There are a number of ways to handle missing data. Conventional "deletion" methods include listwise deletion and pairwise deletion. Another general approach to missing data is to make some reasonable guesses for the values of the missing data and then proceed to a traditional analysis of the real and imputed data. However, conventional imputation methods that use some form of the mean for data imputation lead to underestimates of standard errors (Little & Rubin, 1987). We recommend that IS researchers consider recent advances in missing data imputation techniques, such as maximum likelihood imputation and multiple imputation. These advanced methods have much better statistical properties than traditional methods (e.g., listwise deletion, pairwise deletion, mean imputation) (Allison, 2003).

Normality

Outlier detection and normality of the data distribution should also be assessed. The most widely used estimation methods in covariance-based SEM applications assume multivariate normality, which means that "(1) all the univariate distributions are normal, (2) the joint distribution of any pair of the variables is bivariate normal, and (3) all bivariate scatterplots are linear and homoscedastic" (Kline, 2005, pp. 48-49). Using data that severely departs from the assumption of normality may lead to one of two problems (Cohen, Cohen, West, & Aiken, 2003). First, parameter estimates may be biased. Specifically, estimates of the path coefficients, R^2, significance tests, and confidence intervals may all be incorrect. Second, the estimate of the standard error of the path coefficients may be biased. In such cases, the estimated value of the path coefficient is correct, yet hypothesis tests may not be correct.

Component-based SEM is robust to non-normal data distribution (Chin, 1998). Similar to the sample size issue, researchers should not consider component-based SEM as a silver bullet for handling non-normal data (Marcoulides & Saunders, 2006). However, we note that EQS 6.1 provides analyses which are robust to non-normal

data distribution (Byrne, 2006). In particular, EQS provides a robust chi square statistic called the Satorra-Bentler scaled statistic (Satorra & Bentler, 1988) and robust standard errors (Bentler & Dijkstra, 1985), both of which have been corrected for non-normality in large samples. These robust estimates have also been applied in IS research (Swanson & Dans, 2000). We may find that future advances in other covariance-based SEM software packages, such as AMOS and LISREL, provide options that allow researchers to conduct reliable covariance-based analyses of non-normal data.

Evaluation and Recommendation: Only 11 percent of all SEM applications tested for multivariate normality. Fifteen percent of covariance-based SEM papers tested for normality, and only 7 percent of component-based SEM papers tested for normality. While minor, this distinction may be due to the fact that component-based SEM is robust to non-normality. We found a number of papers that, after testing for normality and finding a non-normal distribution of their data, decided to conduct a component-based SEM analysis instead of a covariance-based SEM analysis. We recommend that IS researchers report tests for multivariate normality when using SEM applications.

Model Estimation and Assessment Issues and Recommendations

The next stage in SEM analyses involves estimating the model and assessing the results. We discuss four methodological issues: (1) estimation approach, (2) assessment of model fit, (3) assessment of measurement model, and (4) assessment of structural model.

Estimation Approach

SEM techniques allow researchers to simultaneously estimate measurement and structural models (Bollen, 1989). The ability to do this in a one-step analysis approach, however, does not imply that it is the best way to conduct SEM analyses. Scholars recommend that researchers take a two-step estimation approach, where the measurement model is assessed prior to the estimation of the structural model (Anderson & Gerbing, 1988). The measurement model provides an assessment of convergent validity and discriminant validity (Campbell & Fiske, 1959). Once convergent and discriminant validity meet required thresholds, the test of the structural model then constitutes an assessment of nomological validity (Cronbach & Meehl, 1955).

Evaluation and Recommendation: Table 5 provides descriptive statistics on model estimation and assessment. Our review finds that a majority of SEM applications in IS take a two-step approach. However, 35 percent do not take a two-step approach, opting instead to simultaneously estimate measurement and structural models in a one-step approach. There is much to gain in theory development from separate estimation of the measurement and structural models (Anderson & Gerbing, 1988; Gefen et al., 2000). Hence, we recommend that IS researchers use a two-step approach in estimating SEM applications.

Assessment of Model Fit

Fit refers to the ability of a model to reproduce the data, that is, the observed variance-covariance matrix. Model fit indices are either absolute or incremental. Absolute fit indices, such as chi square statistics and root mean square error of approximation, evaluate the degree to which the model reproduces the observed covariance matrix (Kline, 2005). Incremental fit indices, such as comparative fit index and normed fit index, assess the relative improvement in fit when the model is compared with a restricted, nested baseline model (Hu & Bentler, 1998). There is no single "magic index" that provides a gold standard for all models; thus, researchers should report multiple model fit indices in order to adequately assess how well the model fits the observed data.

Evaluation and Recommendation: Table 5 shows that 88 percent of covariance-based SEM applications reported multiple measures of model fit. Thus, a small minority (12 percent) failed to report two or more measures of model fit. Component-based SEM applications do not attempt to reproduce the observed variance-covariance matrix. As a result, component-based SEM does not provide measures of "model fit" similar to its covariance-based SEM counterpart.

The availability of so many different fit indexes presents a number of problems: (1) different fit indexes are reported in different articles; (2) different reviewers of the same manuscript may request indexes that they know about or prefer; (3) a researcher may report only those fit indexes

Table 5. Analysis of model estimation and assessment issues

	Component (n=96)	Covariance (n=75)	Overall (n=171)
Model Estimation & Assessment			
Percentage of two step applications*	68	61	65
Percentage of applications that reported multiple measures of model fit	NA	88	NA
Percentage of models for which construct reliability were reported	94	97	95
Percentage of models for which convergent and discriminant validity were reported	75	85	80
Percentage of models for which structural coefficients were provided	98	85	92
Percentage of models for which R^2 for structural equations were reported	92	52	74
* These statistics include only SEM applications with structural models.			

with favorable values; and (4) a preoccupation with overall model fit may distract researchers from other important information, such as whether or not parameter estimates and variance explained values make sense. SEM scholars recommend a minimal set of fit indexes that should be reported and interpreted when reporting the results of SEM analyses (Boomsma, 2000; Gefen et al., 2000; Kline, 2005; McDonald & Ho, 2002). These statistics include: (1) the model chi-square, (2) the Steiger-Lind root mean square error of approximation (RMSEA, Steiger, 1990) with its 90% confidence interval, (3) the Bentler comparative fit index (CFI, Bentler, 1990), and (4) the standardized root mean square residual (SRMR). Finally, we also recommend IS researchers to be wary of recommended cutoff values for fit indices as universal "golden rules" that must be strictly adhered to (Marsh, Hau, & Wen, 2003).

Assessment of Measurement Model

The measurement model is usually assessed in terms of construct reliability and construct validity (Bagozzi, Yi, & Phillips, 1991). Reliability assesses the internal consistency of construct indicators (Nunnally & Bernstein, 1994). In the IS field, construct reliability is often assessed by computing Cronbach's alpha (Straub, Boudreau, & Gefen, 2004).

Construct validity refers to the extent to which an instrument measures what it is supposed to measure (Cronbach & Meehl, 1955). Construct validity consists of convergent validity and discriminant validity. Convergent validity assesses the extent to which different indicators for the measure refer to the same construct, and discriminant validity assesses the extent to which a measure is adequately distinguishable from related constructs (Campbell & Fiske, 1959). Convergent validity can be assessed with a number of techniques, such as multi-trait multi-method (MTMM), exploratory factor analysis (EFA), and confirmatory factor analysis (CFA) (Straub et al.,

2004). When using CFA, one assesses convergent validity by testing the significance of estimated factor loadings. Discriminant validity is also assessed with MTMM, EFA and CFA techniques. When using CFA, discriminant validity can be obtained through the use of a chi square difference test (Venkatraman, 1989).

Evaluation and Recommendation: As indicated in Table 5, 95 percent of all SEM applications reported assessments of construct reliability. However, 20 percent of all SEM applications did not report evidence of construct validity (i.e., both convergent and discriminant validity). Twenty-five percent of component-based SEM applications did not report evidence of construct validity, while only 15 percent of covariance-based SEM applications failed to report evidence of construct validity. Theory development in IS research rests on the effective conduct of our empirical research. Furthermore, the conceptual domain of a construct must be effectively converted into the operational domain in order to conduct empirical research (Straub et al., 2004). Thus, assessing convergent and discriminant validity is critical to the advancement of our understanding of IS-related phenomena. We encourage IS researchers to effectively and adequately assess construct reliability and validity in their empirical work, especially when using SEM applications.

Assessment of Structural Model

The structural model is assessed by investigating the sign, size and statistical significance of the structural coefficients. It is also important to assess the level of variance explained in the dependent variables (i.e., predictive validity). As noted earlier, the structural model should also be assessed in terms of model fit when using covariance-based SEM techniques.

Evaluation and Recommendation: The vast majority of SEM applications in IS research (92 percent) assess the sign, size and statistical significance of the structural coefficients.

Furthermore, 74 percent of all SEM applications report the variance explained (R^2) by the model. However, one interesting finding is that 52 percent of covariance-based SEM applications reported R^2 values, while 92 percent of component-based SEM applications reported R^2 values. Thus, in addition to reporting model fit and confirmation issues, IS researchers should still report R^2 values regardless of SEM technique used.

Model Respecification Issues and Recommendations

The final stage in SEM analyses involves specifying alternative models. When an initial model of interest does not provide a good approximation of real world phenomena (as evidenced by good model fit), researchers often alter the model to improve its fit to the data. Modification of a hypothesized model to improve its parsimony and/or fit to the data is termed a "specification search" (Long, 1983; MacCallum, 1986). A specification search is designed to identify and eliminate errors from the original specification of the hypothesized model.

Jöreskog and Sörbom (1996) describe three model specification (and evaluation) strategies: (1) strictly confirmatory, where a single a priori model is studied, (2) model generation, where an initial model is fit to the data and then modified (frequently with the use of modification indices) until it achieves adequate fit, and (3) alternative models, where multiple a priori models are studied. The "strictly confirmatory" approach is quite restrictive and does not leave the researcher any leeway if the model does not work. The model generation approach is troublesome because of the potential for abuse, results that lack validity (MacCallum, 1986), and high susceptibility to capitalizing on chance (MacCallum, Roznowski, & Necowitz, 1992). The third approach, specifying alternative models, is useful in theory building because it gives the researcher alternative perspectives concerning the focal phenomena.

Evaluation and Recommendation: In our review, 19 percent of all SEM applications reported making model comparisons. Of the models that were changed post hoc, only 30 percent of these model changes were supported with theoretical arguments. Hence, 70 percent of the model changes were performed based on data-driven reasons (e.g., recommendations based on specification searches). We recommend that IS researchers compare alternate a priori models to discover the model that the observed data support best rather than use specification searches. Moreover, all model changes should be guided by theory since there is always the danger of capitalizing on chance (MacCallum et al., 1992).

RECOMMENDATIONS

The popularity of SEM techniques has rapidly increased in recent years. We take stock of the current state of SEM research in the IS field and suggest ways in which IS researchers can better use these powerful techniques to improve IS theory. Based on our review of SEM applications in three leading IS journals between 1990 and 2007, we provide some general guidelines in which IS researchers can take full advantage of SEM techniques:

Specification: Model specification issues should be considered prior to conducting data collection efforts. Specifically, researchers should consider the number of indicators necessary to ensure construct validity, formative/reflective approaches, model identification, and requisite sample size. We recommend a minimum of three indicators per construct in order to conduct reliable analyses of parameter estimates, standard errors, and model identification. IS researchers should also undertake a careful examination of whether each construct should be modeled as formative or reflective. Since covariance-based SEM techniques require large sample sizes, researchers should consider component-based SEM as an alternative when they are confronted with small sample sizes.

Screening: As in most empirical research, careful screening of raw data is necessary before estimating and testing the hypothesized model. Since missing values, outliers, and non-normal data could cause several problems in estimating structural models (e.g., nonconvergence and biased parameter estimates), data screening should be carefully considered. Since conventional data deletion and mean-based imputation methods often produce unreliable results, IS researchers should consider advanced data imputation techniques (e.g., maximum likelihood imputation, multiple imputation) when faced with missing data problems. We also note that, while component-based SEM is robust to non-normal data, recent advances in covariance-based SEM software packages provide estimates which are robust to non-normal data.

Estimation/Assessment: In order to gain greater confidence in their empirical findings, IS researchers should follow a two-step approach when estimating SEM applications. A two-step approach estimates the measurement model and the structural model separately. We also recommend that IS researchers report multiple measures of model fit. Doing so provides greater insight into how well the model reproduces the observed variance-covariance matrix. Theory development depends upon the valid translation of the conceptual realm to the operational realm. Hence, IS researchers should always assess reliability, convergent validity, and discriminant validity. Finally, we recommend that IS researchers report the sign, size and statistical significance of all structural coefficients, the variance explained in endogenous variables by exogenous variables, and multiple measures of model fit. Our review showed that covariance-based SEM research often concentrates on assessment of model fit, much to the expense of findings related to predictive validity (i.e., variance explained).

Respecification: One advantage of SEM is the ability to compare alternative models, thereby providing multiple views of a phenomena and enhancing theory development. However, post hoc changes to an initial model should be guided by theory rather than data-driven considerations.

We note that while our objective is to provide guidelines to improve the quality of future SEM applications in IS research, we do not recommend blind adherence to the individual guidelines. It is possible that other evidence presented in individual studies (e.g., strong theoretical support) can more than offset any single quality criteria. Furthermore, these criteria could be argued to vary depending on the purpose of the study. Yet consistent violation of multiple criteria will likely result in a poor application of the technique, subsequently hindering theory development in the IS field.

CONCLUSION

It appears as though SEM is here to stay in the IS field, at least for the foreseeable future. SEM's ability to improve measurement reliability in multi-indicator constructs and investigate theoretical frameworks with complex relationships in a single analysis make it a powerful technique. These attributes, along with sophisticated yet relatively easy-to-use software, make it highly probable that the use of SEM will persist. Additionally, SEM is another tool that helps IS researchers strengthen the link between the conceptual realm and the operational (statistical) realm when developing theory. In particular, SEM techniques are useful for (1) establishing relationships exist between constructs, (2) modeling and testing alternative models with the same data set, and (3) confirming and replicating results. By maximizing the fit of the theoretical model to the observed data, covariance-based SEM techniques are especially useful for evaluating comprehensive nomological nets. Thus, SEM is a powerful technique which can be used throughout the theory development process.

However, as our results suggest, astute use of this technique is necessary in order to take full advantage of its ability. In particular, IS researchers should be wary of issues related to model specification, data screening, model estimation and assessment, and model respecification. Based on our review of the IS literature and extant SEM methodological research, we provided guidelines to aid IS scholars in addressing these issues. We hope that our review of prior SEM applications will further enhance the quality of empirical research in the IS field and ultimately contribute to better development of IS theory.

REFERENCES

Afifi, A. A., & Elashoff, R. M. (1966). Missing observations in multivariate statistics: I. Review of the literature. *Journal of the American Statistical Association, 61*(315), 595-604.

Allison, P. D. (2003). Missing data techniques for structural equation modeling. *Journal of Abnormal Psychology, 112*(4), 545-557.

Anderson, J. C., & Gerbing, D. W. (1984). The effect of sampling error on convergence, improper solutions, and goodness-of-fit indices for maximum likelihood confirmatory factor analysis. *Psychometrika, 49*(2), 155-173.

Anderson, J. C., & Gerbing, D. W. (1988). Structural equation modeling in practice: A review and recommended two-step approach. *Psychological Bulletin, 103*(3), 411-423.

Bacharach, S. B. (1989). Organizational theories: Some criteria for evaluation. *Academy of Management Review, 14*(4), 496-515.

Bagozzi, R. P., Yi, Y., & Phillips, L. W. (1991). Assessing construct validity in organizational research. *Administrative Science Quarterly, 36*(3), 421-458.

Barclay, D., Higgins, C., & Thomson, R. (1995). The partial least squares approach (PLS) to causal modeling, personal computer adoption and use as an illustration. *Technology Studies, 2*(2), 285-309.

Bentler, P. M. (1990). Comparative fit indexes in structural models. *Psychological Bulletin, 107*(2), 238-246.

Bentler, P. M., & Chou, C. P. (1987). Practical issues in structural modeling. *Sociological Methods and Research, 16*, 78-117.

Bentler, P. M., & Dijkstra, T. (1985). Efficient estimation via linearization in structural models. In R. Krishnaiah (Ed.), *Multivariate analysis VI* (pp. 9-42). Amsterdam: North Holland.

Blalock, H. M. (1969). *Theory construction: From verbal to mathematical formulations.* Englewood Cliffs, NJ: Prentice-Hall.

Blalock, H. M. (1971). Causal models involving unobserved variables in stimulus-response situations. In H. M. Blalock (Ed.), *Causal models in the social sciences* (pp. 335-347). Chicago: Aldine.

Bollen, K., & Lennox, R. (1991). Conventional wisdom on measurement: A structural equation perspective. *Psychological Bulletin, 110*(2), 305-314.

Bollen, K. L. (1989). *Structural equations with latent variables.* New York: John Wiley.

Boomsma, A. (1982). The robustness of LISREL against small sample sizes in factor analysis models. In K. G. Joreskog & H. Wold (Eds.), *Systems under indirect observation: Causality, structure, prediction* (pp. 149-173). Amsterdam: North Holland.

Boomsma, A. (2000). Reporting analyses of covariance structures. *Structural Equation Modeling, 7*, 461-483.

Byrne, B. M. (2006). *Structural equation modeling with EQS* (2nd ed.). Mahwah, New Jersey: Lawrence Erlbaum Associates.

Campbell, D. T., & Fiske, D. W. (1959). Convergent and discriminant validation by the multi trait multi method matrix. *Psychological Bulletin, 56*(2), 81-105.

Chin, W. W. (1998). The partial least squares approach to structural equation modeling. In G. A. Marcoulides (Ed.), *Modern methods for business research* (pp. 295-336). Mahwah, NJ: Lawrence Erlbaum Associates.

Churchill, G. A. (1979). A paradigm for developing better measures of marketing constructs. *Journal of Marketing Research, 16*(1), 64-73.

Cook, T. D., & Campbell, D. T. (1979). *Quasi-experimentation: Design and analysis issues for field settings*. Boston, MA: Houghton Mifflin Company.

Cronbach, L. J., & Meehl, P. E. (1955). Construct validity in psychology tests. *Psychological Bulletin, 52*(4), 281-302.

Davis, F. D., Bagozzi, R. P., & Warshaw, P. R. (1989). User acceptance of computer technology: A comparison of two theoretical models. *Management Science, 35*(8), 982-1003.

Edwards, J. R. (2001). Multidimensional constructs in organizational behavior research: An integrative analytical framework. *Organizational Research Methods, 4*(2), 144-192.

Edwards, J. R., & Bagozzi, R. P. (2000). On the nature and direction of relationships between constructs and measures. *Psychological Methods, 5*(2), 155-174.

Fornell, C. (1983). Issues in the application of covariance structure analysis. *Journal of Consumer Research, 9*, 443-448.

Fornell, C., & Bookstein, F. L. (1982). Two structural equation models: LISREL and PLS applied to consumer exit-voice theory. *Journal of Marketing Research, 19*(4), 440-452.

Gefen, D., Straub, D. W., & Boudreau, M.-C. (2000). Structural equation modeling and regression: Guidelines for research practice. *Communications of the Association Information Systems, 4*(7), 1-77.

Glasser, M. (1964). Linear regression analysis with missing observations among the independent variables. *Journal of the American Statistical Association, 59*(307), 834-844.

Hair, J. F., Black, W.C., Babin, B., Anderson, R. E., & Tathem, R. L. (2006). *Multivariate data analysis* (6th ed.). Upper Saddle River, NJ: Prentice Hall.

Hall, C. S., & Lindzey, G. (1957). *Theories of personality*. New York: Wiley.

Howell, R. D., Breivik, E., & Wilcox, J. B. (2007). Reconsidering formative measurement. *Psychological Methods, 12*(2), 205-218.

Hu, L., & Bentler, P. M. (1998). Fit indices in covariance structure modeling: Sensitivity to under-parameterized model misspecification. *Psychological Methods, 3*(4), 424-453.

Jarvis, C. B., Mackenzie, S. B., & Podsakoff, P. M. (2003). A critical review of construct indicators and measurement model misspecification in marketing and consumer research. *Journal of Consumer Research, 30*(2), 199-218.

Jones, M. P. (1996). Indicator and stratification methods for missing explanatory variables in multiple linear regression. *Journal of the American Statistical Association, 91*(433), 222-230.

Joreskog, K. G., & Sorbom, D. (1996). *LISREL 8: User's reference guide*. Chicago: Scientific Software International.

Joreskog, K. G., & Wold, H. (1982). The ML and PLS techniques for modeling with latent variables: Historical and comparative aspects. In K. G. Joreskog & H. Wold (Eds.), *Systems under indirect observation: Causality structure and prediction* (Vol. 1, pp. 263-270). Amsterdam: North Holland.

Kline, R. B. (2005). *Principles and practice of structural equation modeling* (2nd ed.). New York: The Guilford Press.

Little, R. J. A., & Rubin, D. A. (1987). *Statistical analysis with missing data*. New York: John Wiley & Sons.

Little, T. D., Lindenberger, U., & Nesselroade, J. R. (1999). On selecting indicators for multivariate measurement and modeling with latent variables: When "good" indicators are bad and "bad" indicators are good. *Psychological Methods, 4*(2), 192-211.

Long, J. S. (1983). *Covariance structure models: An introduction to LISREL*. Beverly Hills, CA: Sage.

MacCallum, R. C. (1986). Specification searches in covariance structure modeling. *Psychological Bulletin, 100*(1), 107-120.

MacCallum, R. C., Roznowski, M., & Necowitz, L. B. (1992). Model modifications in covariance structure analysis: The problem of capitalization on chance. *Psychological Bulletin, 111*(3), 490-504.

Marcoulides, G. A., & Saunders, C. (2006). PLS: A silver bullet? *MIS Quarterly, 30*(2), iii-ix.

Marsh, H. W., Hau, K.-T., & Wen, Z. (2003). In search of golden rules: Comment on hypothesis-testing approaches to setting cutoff values for fit indexes and dangers in overgeneralizing Hu and Bentler's (1999) findings. *Structural Equation Modeling, 11*(3), 320-341.

McDonald, R. P., & Ho, M.-H. R. (2002). Principles and practice in reporting structural equation analyses. *Psychological Methods, 7*, 64-82.

Mohr, L. B. (1982). *Explaining organizational behavior*. San Francisco: Jossey-Bass.

Nelson, R. R., Todd, P. A., & Wixom, B. H. (2005). Antecedents of information and system quality: An empirical examination within the context of data warehousing. *Journal of Management Information Systems, 21*(4), 199-235.

Nunnally, J. C., & Bernstein, I. H. (1994). *Psychometric theory* (3rd ed.). New York: McGraw-Hill, Inc.

Petter, S., Straub, D., & Rai, A. (2007). Specifying formative constructs in information systems research. *MIS Quarterly, 31*(4), 623-656.

Satorra, A. C., & Bentler, P. M. (1988). *Scaling corrections for chi-square statistics in covariance structure analysis*. Paper presented at the Proceedings of the Business and Economics Sections, Alexandria, VA.

Sharma, S. (1996). *Applied multivariate techniques*. New York: John Wiley & Son, Inc.

Steiger, J. H. (1990). Structural model evaluation and modification: An interval estimation approach. *Multivariate Behavioral Research, 25*(2), 173-180.

Straub, D., Boudreau, M.-C., & Gefen, D. (2004). Validation guidelines for IS positivist research. *Communications of the Association for Information Systems, 13*(24), 380-427.

Swanson, E. B., & Dans, E. (2000). System life expectancy and the maintenance effort: Exploring their equilibration. *MIS Quarterly, 24*(2), 277-297.

Van Maanen, J., Sorensen, J. B., & Mitchell, T. R. (2007). The interplay between theory and method. *Academy of Management Review, 32*(4), 1145-1154.

Venkatesh, V., Morris, M. G., Davis, G. B., & Davis, F. D. (2003). User acceptance of information technology: Toward a unified view. *MIS Quarterly, 27*(3), 425-478.

Venkatraman, N. (1989). Strategic orientation of business enterprises: The construct, dimensionality, and measurement. *Management Science, 35*(8), 942-962.

Weick, K. E. (1995). What theory is not, theorizing is. *Administrative Science Quarterly, 40*(3), 385-390.

Wold, H. (1982). Soft modeling: The basic design and some extensions. In K. G. Joreskog & H. Wold (Eds.), *Systems under indirect observation* (pp. 1-47). New York: North Holland.

KEY TERMS AND DEFINITIONS

Construct Validity: The extent to which a given test is an effective measure of a theoretical construct

Factor analysis: A statistical approach that can be used to analyze interrelationships among a large number of variables and to explain these variables in terms of their common underlying dimensions (factor)

Latent Variable: Research construct that is not observable or measured directly, but is measured indirectly through observable variables that reflect or form the construct

Measurement Model: Sub-model in structural equation modeling that specifies the indicators for each construct and assesses the reliability of each construct for estimating the causal relationships

Reliability: Extent to which a variable or set of variables is consistent in what it is intended to measure

Structural Equation Modeling: Multivariate technique combining aspects of multiple regression (examining dependence relationships) and factor analysis (representing unmeasured concepts with multiple variables) to estimate a series of interrelated dependence relationships simultaneously

Structural Model: Linkages between research constructs (or variables) that express the underlying structure of the phenomenon under investigation

Theory: A statement of relations among concepts within a set of boundary assumptions and constraints

Chapter VI
An Evidence–Based Health Information System Theory

Daniel Carbone
University of Melbourne, Australia

ABSTRACT

The aim of this chapter is to bridge the gap between what is known about IS theory and the specifics characteristics of health to develop an evidence based health information systems theory. An initial background first sets the significance for the need to have a solid information systems theory in health and then argues that neither the information systems literature nor the health sector have been able to provide any satisfactory pathway to facilitate the adoption of information systems in health settings. The chapter further continues by reviewing the common pathway to develop information systems theory and the knowledge foundations used in the process, and then proceeds to highlight how this theory was developed. Subsequently, the building blocks (constructs, premises, supporting evidence and conclusions) that underpins the constructs and a brief explanation of the relationships between them is included. A discussion and limitation section is then followed by a conclusion.

BACKGROUND

The importance of having information systems theories that will be conducive to the adoption of new technologies in health settings cannot be underestimated. To place it in context, the health-care sector is not only one of the world's most knowledge-intensive industries but also one of the largest employers; for example the National Health Service (NHS) in the UK is the largest employer of staff in Europe and third largest in the world (Herzlinger & Ricci, 2002; Leitch, 2008).

More important is the worldwide, current and urgent need to improve the uptake of technology in health settings to improve clinical care and associated costs through the use of technology, as clearly defined in the literature (AIHW, 2006; Department of Health and Aged Care, 2003; Grol et al, 1998; Gross et al., 2003; HealthConnectSA, 2007; Nader, 2007; Schuster et al., 2003; WHO, 2008). This is currently occurring despite mounting evidence suggesting positive clinical care improvements due to the introduction health information systems (Celler et al., 2003; WHO, 2008).

This current failure to adopt technology in health settings appears to point to gaps in the understanding of technology implementation and adoption in the health sector.

The current literature on health information systems implementation and adoption suggests that perhaps the health sector suffers from a fixation with 'technology driven implementations' to the detriment of other factors (Aarts et al., 2004; Bates, 2005; Chaudhry et al., 2006; Humber, 2004). That is, the focus of change management strategies to implement these technologies in health settings is seen almost exclusively as a technical (computer/technology system) issue. Moreover, most information technology applications have centered on administrative and financial transactions rather than on the core business of health: the delivery of clinical care (Audet et al., 2004). The concept of clinical care is the central principle associated with the field of health and known these days as Evidence-Based Medicine (EBM). The most important aspect associated with Evidence-Based Medicine is the measure of clinical improvement on patients or a term also known as health outcomes (Heckley, 2004).

In summary, the health sector appears to lack solid theoretical knowledge in organizational change, workflow redesign, human factors, and project management issues involved with realizing benefits from health information technology to tackle the clinical and financial burdens in current health systems (Chaudhry et al., 2006). Moreover, and central to this paper, the health specific literature on information systems implementations appears to fail to acknowledge the role of Evidence-Based Medicine (and health outcomes specifically) in the implementation process.

Perhaps, the solution is to consult the information systems literature in search for theoretical foundations that would support the adoption of technology in health settings.

The Information Systems (IS) literature on the other hand, mainly focused on the business sector and having left much of the 'technology-driven' approaches failures behind, has long benefited from a much more humanistic and contextualized appreciation of non-technological factors (i.e. Human, environmental, Social, etc) to improve adoption; However, in spite of the availability of more than fifty information systems theories and many others form other fields to inform practitioners, implementation failures in health settings still continue unabated to this day (HealthConnectSA, 2007; Schneberger & Wade, 2006). It would appear that even the existing broad knowledge in the IS sector is still not enough to affect effective technological uptake in health settings. What appears to be missing is 'specific' knowledge that would support the adoption of technology in health settings.

As a conclusion, the preceding and very brief literature review suggests that neither the health nor the information systems sectors have succeeded in developing solid theoretical knowledge that would lead to the successful implementation and adoption of information systems in health settings.

This chapter will advance some theoretical constructs regarding observed phenomena that might help bridge the gap between existing knowledge and new knowledge gained in the field and through relevant information systems research in health settings by the author. This examination leads the author to believe that perhaps there is a misalignment in the understanding of current information systems theories and health constructs; more specifically, that existing theories do not specifically focus on the 'core businesses of health' (Evidence-Based Medicine).

It must be also noted that this paper is not meant produce a definitive full-fledged theory, but contribute to the beginning of a theoretical discourse in information systems for health specific settings. Although initially built from an existing theoretical framework; it is intended to go above and beyond the founding theoretical frameworks as suggested recently by the editors of MIS Quarterly (Markus & Saunders, 2007).

THE KNOWLEDGE FOUNDATIONS OF INFORMATION SYSTEMS THEORY

The most common approach to developing or building on theory in the discipline of information systems is to use an established theory (authoritative knowledge) from a reference discipline, develop and adapt it to the information system context by 'trial and error'; this is also known as 'the logic of science' (Popper, 1979). In this approach, an established theory is used to categorize and classify information systems phenomena through a deductive approach (Lind & Goldkuhl, 2006).

Another approach is the inductive analysis of empirical data for the creation of a theory; Grounded theory is perhaps the most widely known methods of inductive theory building (Glaser & Strauss, 1967). This form of theory building was called 'logic of inquiry' by philosopher John Dewey in 1938 (Dewey, 1938), and involves the idea of 'application' grounding, including observational grounding to develop theory (Lind & Goldkuhl, 2006). This method has lead to the creation of concepts and theory useful for practical workplace change and is in line with the notion of a 'practical theory' (Cronen, 2001). However, the lack of relationship to other existing

theories and unclear epistemological basis have been sited as criticism of this approach (Bryant, 2002; Charmaz, 2000).

There is, yet another closely related logic called 'logic of discovery' and it seems to underpin abductive reasoning (Popper, 1979; Wirth, 2008). Wirth (1998) defines abduction as 'the process of adopting an explanatory hypothesis' and covers two operations: the selection and the formation of plausible hypotheses. He goes on further to explain that 'as a process of finding premises, it is the basis of interpretive reconstruction of causes and intentions, as well as of inventive construction of theories' (Wirth, 2008). It is motivated by the observation of a surprising fact or an anomaly that disappoints an expectation; abductive reasoning is a strategy of solving problems and discovering relevant premises. It is "inference to the best explanation". However, from a logical point of view, Pierce (1958) suggested that reasoning backwards is no valid form of inference. It is conjectural, or presumptive thinking, aiming at matching pragmatic standards of plausibility, guided by the reasoner's guessing instinct (Peirce, 1958; Wirth, 1998).

Further epistemological and ontological strengths and weaknesses of every approach can be discerned in a number of other resources (Bryant, 2002; Charmaz, 2000; Urquhart, 2001; Wirth, 2008).

Bob Zmud (1998), ex editor-in-chief of MIS Quarterly, suggested that to truly contribute to theory building, it is necessary to develop and describe a rich conceptual understanding of an information systems phenomena so that it serves to enhance the field's collective understanding of the phenomena and as a basis for future empirical and theoretical work (Zmud, 1998).

More importantly —as the basis for the development of the particular theory to be examined in this chapter stands solely on the author understands of the phenomena, it is imperative that the phenomenon's constructs are augmented compellingly (Zmud, 1998). Arguments, for the purpose of this paper, are defined as set of one or more declarative sentences (or propositions) known as the premises along with another declarative sentence (or proposition) known as the conclusion. Premises are those statements that are taken to provide the support or evidence and the conclusion is that which the premises allegedly support (Fieser & Dowden, 2008). Furthermore, arguments can be deductive and inductive; according to Fieser and Dowden (2008), a deductive argument is an argument in which it is thought that the premises provide a guarantee of the truth of the conclusion. Conversely, an inductive argument is an argument in which it is thought that the premises provide reasons supporting the probable truth of the conclusion. In an inductive argument, the premises are intended only to be so strong that, if they are true, then it is unlikely that the conclusion is false. Moreover, Fieser and Dowden further clarify that even if the author of the argument does not think that the truth of the premises definitely establishes the truth of the conclusion, but nonetheless believes that their truth provides good reason to believe the conclusion true, then the argument is inductive (Fieser & Dowden, 2008).

Zmud (1998) further suggested a four step development pathway to developing sound theory including: (1) the description of the phenomenon, (2) the construct creation, development and explication, (3) the identification of key relationships and (4) the development, justification and articulation of these relationships. (Zmud, 1998). These headings will be used to develop the theoretical discourse.

The Context of the Emerging Phenomena

The first stage in this examination evolved as the observation of emerging facts and anomalies (abductive approach) as a result of the development of the author's PhD information system framework (Carbone, 2008); from where a set of new con-

structs or 'by-products' of the PhD emerged. The PhD study began its own development as a conceptual framework; a product of adapting existing theoretical constructs (authoritative knowledge) and the researcher's own field experience and observations (abductive reasoning). Socio-technical theory provided the theoretical framework to guide the research processes (Clegg, 2000; Land, 2000; Liehr & Smith, 2001; Mumford, 2003, 2006a, 2006b; Williamson, 2002). The testing process itself was inductive in nature (logic of inquiry), aiming at the empirically provable coherence between the premises and experience, in order to derive a probable generalization (Wirth, 2008).

The PhD research focussed specifically on developing an information systems framework to support the prevention and management of chronic conditions (i.e. Asthma and Diabetes) in general practice following a pre-determined deduction/induction pathway. While this was satisfactory for the needs of the PhD study, it left a number of wider emergent constructs outside its limited scope. The limitation included the focus to just chronic conditions and to general practice settings only, even though the emergent premises observed were seen to be applicable to the wide clinical care continuum and other health settings as well.

The following graph in Exhibit 1 represents the knowledge foundations and research pathway just described above down to the emerging premises discovered in the study.

Phenomena Description

Successful implementation and adoption of information systems within the scope of chronic conditions and general practice were formally examined within the PhD study. Similar successful adoptions were observed by the author's own work role as an IS practitioner in a variety of other health settings like Hospitals and Community Health Centres. Furthermore, the practical implementation of information systems outside

Exhibit 1.

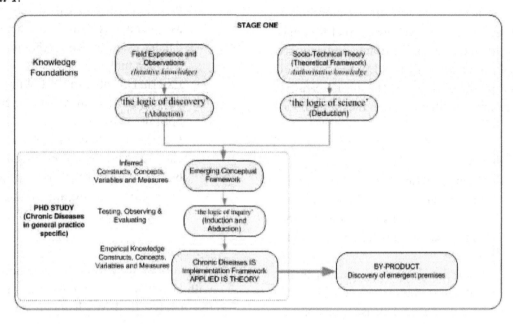

the realm chronic conditions provided additional opportunities to observe the same phenomenon in action.

This 'logic of discovery', based on abductive principals, requires a process of adopting an explanatory hypothesis covering the selection and the formation of plausible hypotheses (Wirth, 2008). To this effect a plausible hypothesis to explain the emerging phenomenon under examination here suggests broadly that:

Health settings will adopt information systems if a clear alignment of its core business with the proposed system outcomes is facilitated through the proper mechanisms.

More specifically, any implementation strategy must take into account the hierarchical socio-technical and clinical values exclusive to every health setting and the system development must be facilitated by catalyst that can clearly understands and align their value structures to the intended information systems.

Construct Creation, Development and Explication

Within this phenomenon, three distinct constructs are identified: The catalyst; the sub-system hierarchy and the evidence-based system. To strengthen the claim for each of these constructs, and avoid being based solely on the author's understanding of the phenomena, inductive arguments will provide reasons (premises) supporting (via varied sources of evidence) the probable truth of the conclusions.

Due to space limitations, and bearing in mind that, as suggested earlier, this examination is not meant to be exhaustive or conclusive (but is meant to begin dialog and further empirical work), premises (or propositions) will be reduced down to short list of declarative sentences and its supporting evidence will also be presented in succinct table format to further reduce the length of the explanations. The conclusions are also provided in short declarative sentences (propositions).

The Catalysts Construct

This construct relates directly to individuals (acting as change/external agents) that find and analyse the evidence and facilitate and support the whole implementation and optimization of subsystems in health settings. The specific catalyst functions are identified through the argumentation that follows:

- *Premises*:
  - o The skills required to find (research), analyse and feed-back empirical evidence to clinicians (decision makers) are not readily available in health settings.
  - o Research and information management skills are needed to produce evidence to drive change and measure outcomes.
  - o Access to health seating electronic health records is necessary for local evidence.
  - o External agents specifically trained have the skills but not the access to clinicians and health setting databases.

  - o Most health settings have 'key' individuals (in health called referred to as 'champions') that have access to databases and the ears of the clinicians/decision makers.
  - o External agents can work with champions produce local evidence and optimise subsystems.
  - o External agents can train champions and other health setting members to become trainers of other members and improve monitoring and maintenance of the sub-systems.

- *Conclusions*:
  An external agent working in conjunction with health setting champions is an effective catalyst to drive change management strategies, development, maintenance and evaluation of health information systems.

The Sub-System Hierarchy Construct

The first phenomenon observed was perhaps not a new theoretical construct per se, but perhaps an extension of existing Socio-technical theory; nev-

Exhibit 2.

The Supporting Evidence			
Premise	Intuitive knowledge (by author – field experience)	Empirical knowledge (Tested over 28 cases in PhD Study)	Authoritative knowledge (Literature Evidence)
1	✓	✓	(Grimshaw et al., 2004; Haigh, 2001)
2	✓	✓	(Grimshaw et al., 2004; Horak, 2001); (Bates, 2000; Bates et al., 1995); (Hummers-Pradiera et al., 2008); (Australian Institute of Health Policies Studies & VicHealth, 2008; Australin Institute of Health Policies Studies & VicHealth, 2008)
3	✓	✓	(Horak, 2001); (Grimshaw et al., 2004); (Richards et al., 1999); (Chaudhry et al., 2006); (Hummers-Pradiera et al., 2008)
4	✓	✓	(HealthConnectSA, 2007); (Hummers-Pradiera et al., 2008)
5	✓	✓	(GPDV & GPT, 2007; HealthConnectSA, 2007)
6	✓	✓	(Horak, 2001); (GPDV & GPT, 2007); (HealthConnectSA, 2007)
7	✓	✓	(Horak, 2001); (GPDV & GPT, 2007); (HealthConnectSA, 2007); (GAO, 2003)

ertheless, the construct is seen as new in the sense that it exclusively applies to health context.

Socio-technical systems theory is theory about the social aspects of people and society and technical aspects of machines and technology. Socio-technical refers to the interrelatedness of social and technical aspects of an organisation. Socio-technical theory therefore is about joint optimization, with a shared emphasis on achievement of both excellence in technical performance and quality in people's work lives (Ropohl, 1999).

The contribution by socio-technical theory should be self-evident albeit with some specific tweaks to reflect the 'fit' to health settings. The recognition of the need to harmonise all existing sub-systems has always been the cornerstone of the socio-technical approach (Schneberger & Wade, 2006). This authoritative knowledge was well supported during the testing phase in twenty eight case studies and well supported by the literature. The following premises were discerned during practice throughout the chronic diseases study further supporting the literature in informing the conclusions and augments in this construct:

- *Premises*:
  - o All health settings are unique (i.e. structural and cultural complexity and variation)
  - o There are many subsystems in health settings.
  - o Sub-systems are interdependent in different measures to their own contexts
  - o All subsystems need attention to maximise optimization.
  - o Not all sub-systems are valued equally by everyone in health settings.
  - o There is a well defined hierarchy apparent in health settings.
  - o Patient Care is the most valued subsystem (a kind of health 'bottom-line').

- *Conclusions:*
  Every health setting possesses a number of interdependent sub-systems that need to be optimised; that are value laden and unique to their context; and the most important is the 'Patient Care' sub-system.

Exhibit 3.

The Supporting Evidence			
Premise	Intuitive knowledge (by author – field experience)	Empirical knowledge (Tested over 28 cases in the Chronic Disease study)	Authoritative knowledge (Literature Evidence)
1	✓	✓	(Dickinson, 2002); (Fithgerald, 2002; HealthConnectSA, 2007); (Davis et al., 2004); (Grol & Wensing, 2004); (Cockburn, 2004)
2	✓	✓	(Hillestad et al., 2005); (Bates, 2005); (Sturnberg et al., 2003); (Sturnberg et al., 2003); (Dickinson, 2002);
3	✓	✓	(Lorenzi, 2003); (HealthConnectSA, 2007)
4	✓	✓	(Cherns, 1976); (Clegg, 2000); (Mumford, 2003, 2006a, 2006b); (Hillestad et al., 2005); (Bates, 2005)
5	✓	✓	(Audet et al., 2004); (Schuster et al., 2003); (Grol & Wensing, 2004); (Grol, 2000 ; Grol & Grimshaw, 2003 ; Grol & Wensing, 2004)
6	✓	✓	(Audet et al., 2004); (Ministry of Health, 2007)
7	✓	✓	(HealthConnectSA, 2007); (Ministry of Health, 2007)

Evidence Based System Construct

The concept of evidence is not new to health settings; however in health the use is normally reserved for medico-clinical endeavours only. The findings from this examination and the relevant authoritative literature suggest evidence to be the key conduit or foundation pathways where information system implementation are quickly accepted and sustainably adopted. The arguments are drawn on the following premises and conclusions:

- *Premises*:
  - o Health settings are owned and/or run by clinicians (decision makers).
  - o Patient care (sub-system) shortcomings are important motivating factors to clinicians.
  - o Other sub-systems (risk management, financial, etc) are also of concern to decision makers.
  - o Clinicians are trained in scientific thought (empirical-rational methods).
  - o Empirical-rational change management strategies exist.
  - o Empirical-rational methods influence clinical practice (behavioural change/ motivational drive).
  - o Evidence of care deficit in clinical practice is found in the local (electronic) health records.
  - o Empirical-rational change management strategies using local data (evidence) affects behavioural change positively.
  - o Sustainability of change and further change depends on the evidence of success.
  - o Local empirical evidence and analyses is needed to measure success (patient health outcomes).

- *Conclusions:*
  Clinicians need empirical evidence that highlights care gaps to affect behavioural change in their clinical practice. Clinicians also need concrete evidence that their efforts are benefiting their patients (health outcomes) and all other subsystems are working efficiently.

Exhibit 4.

The Supporting Evidence			
Premise	Intuitive knowledge (by author – field experience)	Empirical knowledge (Tested over 28 cases in PhD Study)	Authoritative knowledge (Literature Evidence)
1	✓	✓	(Bodenheimer, 1999); (HealthConnectSA, 2007); (AMWAC, 2005)
2	✓	✓	(HealthConnectSA, 2007); (Schuster et al., 2003); (Grol & Wensing, 2004); (Grol, 2000 ; Grol & Grimshaw, 2003 ; Grol & Wensing, 2004)
3	✓	✓	(HealthConnectSA, 2007); (Schuster et al., 2003); (Grol & Wensing, 2004); (Grol, 2000 ; Grol & Grimshaw, 2003 ; Grol & Wensing, 2004)
4	✓	✓	(HealthConnectSA, 2007); (Hendy et al., 2005); (Littlejohns et al., 2003); (Grol & Wensing, 2004 ; Piterman, 2000)
5	✓	✓	(Chin & Benne, 1969); (HealthConnectSA, 2007); (Nickols, 2006)
6	✓	✓	(HealthConnectSA, 2007); (Chaudhry et al., 2006); (Piterman, 2000)
7	✓	✓	(HealthConnectSA, 2007); (Ward, 2003); (HealthConnect, 2005)
8	✓	✓	(HealthConnectSA, 2007); (Haines & Donald, 1998)
9	✓	✓	(Horak, 2001); (Britt, 2007); (Donabedian, 1988)
10	✓	✓	(Davenport & Pursak, 2001); (Ward, 2003); (Ward, 2003): (DoHA, 2008); (Chaudhry et al., 2006)

The Identification of Key Relationships

A sound theory must offer —besides arguments and conclusions for each construct, a compelling discussion on the phenomena resulting from the relationship between these constructs (Zmud, 1998). A complete discussion is in the scope of this paper is clearly limited; however a concise emergent dialog will follow:

The relationships between the three main constructs identified earlier can be readily represented as the analogy of a computer system: two concentric operating and application software systems over a set of interconnected hardware. As per diagram shown in Exhibit 5.

Where the evidence based system construct represents the core business of health (patient care). Identifiable by its twin concerns: input task (drivers) and output task (outcomes). It can be thought of clinical task (business) that needs to be performed or improved (though the adoption of information systems) like the management,

prevention or treatment of clinical problem in any health setting. As such it subsumes all other concerns in this theory. The bottom line, to borrow a business term is: 'the clinical improvement of patient care'.

The catalyst, as with an operating system is the enabler of that overall "clinical ncare" task. However, along the way (from input to output) the catalyst, like an operating system, must make sure that a set of circumstances or optimisation occurs to allow the clinical (input) task —driven by the expectation of improving the health of an individual or population is satisfactorily carried out (output), known in the health field as a clinical outcome. The tasks carried out by the catalyst (operating system) to enable the evidence-based system to succeed are multiple: for example, just to name a few of the potential sub-systems in health settings, it must allow members of the clinical team (Doctors, Nurses, staff, etc) to communicate with each other; it must make sure that risk management systems exist to follow up on patients that might

Exhibit 5.

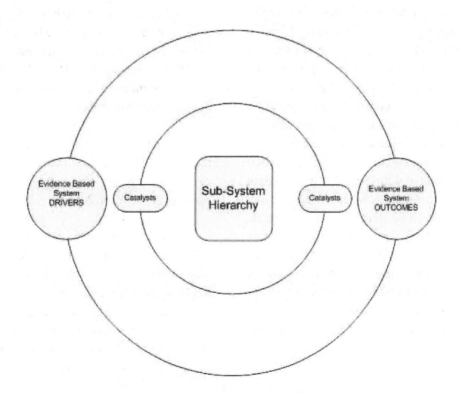

miss out on clinical care; it must ensure that there is a sound financial systems underpinning the work being carried out and it must be capable of providing clinical information required on-time/ every time to assist with clinical tasks. Perhaps the most important task that an operating system engages in a computer system is in "bootstrapping" (booting/starting) the system; this analogy essentially matches the first of the two principal role of the catalyst. The first task of this external (or internal if existing) change agent is to kick start the system by providing the initial "momentum" (data feedback) of what clinical business is at hand (what clinical care needs improving at the health setting by analysing gaps in care within its own patients). The second principal role is to measure the success in achieving that original task (improvement in health outcomes).

The hierarchical set of sub-systems construct represents in this analogy, the existing sub-systems that need to be optimized to allow for the core business (patient care) to be carried out successfully (outcomes). At this point in time, many of this sub-systems exist, however they can be paper-bases (in the case of financial records, recall and reminder letters, appointment books, to name but a few). It is important at this stage to recognize that any system being replaced must be "better", whatever the meaning for users (time efficient, error free, economical, etc) than existing ones. This also will include having the skills and broad knowledge to affect clinical, financial, legal and organisational systems including the provision of education and training. Many important sub-systems, in the author experience, do not exists and need to be developed from scratch. More importantly, every setting is completely unique in almost every aspect (governance, culture, workforce, etc), hence the catalysts must be always willing to adapt and customize solutions that might not optimize a system, but will make individuals feel in control of their setting and their culture.

A key aspect of this theory is the relationship between catalysts and the human/workforce sub-system. This relationship needs to be built around principles of mutual trust and purposeful action between individuals that appear to share a common 'end' goal (health outcomes improvements). This connection between the catalyst and health setting is not always evident as sometimes 'individual's short term goals' might no be the same; for example, the IS practitioner (catalyst) might be more concerned with training and technical processes while the practice champion might be more compelled to be financially and workforce savvy; each sharing their expertise to create a contextually customised and optimized health information system. This explanation is by no means comprehensive, but begins to discuss the basic assumptions behind the constructs' relationship.

Development, Justification and Articulation of these Relationships

Presenting a complete theoretical treatise in the space of single chapter is at best misguided. However an attempt will be made to succinctly summarise the main thrust of this emerging theory.

The simplest approach to do this to follow the suggestion made by one of the greatest mind of our century when he said:

... unless a theory has a simple underlying picture that the layman can understand, the theory is probably worthless...
Einstein (Pescovitz, 2005)

The following graphic in Exhibit 6 represents the main components in this emergent theory, including some of the sub-systems and potential hierarchy. Further explanation follows.

While a picture can paint a thousand words, a misinterpreted picture can lead future researchers down the wrong path. In "reading" this conceptual framework it is important to define the

Exhibit 6.

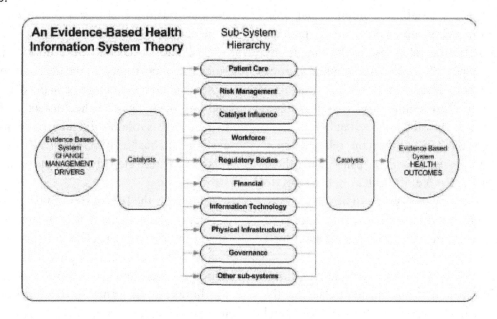

development and articulation of the relationships in this theory as it would apply to a "real world" situation. Let not forget that this theory is based on 'real' observed successful implementation and adoptions.

To start with, the intended implementation and consequent adoption of an information system in a health setting, according to this theoretical model, depends on the potential for that system to improve patient health. However, this position assumes that health settings are aware of their own deficiencies in patient care. In the author's experience, via a purposeful PhD study and everyday observations, there has never been a single case when a clinician has been aware of such deficiencies. In this circumstance, possessing a great solution to a problem that is not perceived to exist is next to useless.

The key to this model then does not start with "the solution", but finding "the problem". That is having access to or securing access to the health setting's medical records. This is in itself is a challenging task, particularly in countries like Australia where patient health data in well

protected by law and clinician's own concerns for its use.

This has implications not just for being able to carryout further validating research in practice, but also for policy at the governmental level; as it suggests that health settings need to be supported by dedicated and well trained health information systems professionals to achieve any degree of success in implementing information systems in health settings. The amount of time resources needed by a well trained catalyst to support the health setting adopt information systems, including education and training and software support are considerable, although easily offset by the gains in health outcomes at the population level.

This is where the catalyst construct comes into its own, particularly as recognised earlier on, that there are no individuals in health settings that possess the multiplicity of skills needed to retrieve, review and analyse their own clinical data. This is further exacerbated when it is considered that there are financial, legal, communication and organisational skills still to be used in the optimization of all remaining sub-systems.

The catalyst would also have to build a high level of trust to be allowed impute (and optimization) in every sub-system; this is perhaps achieved in time as relationships develop. In my own experience it has taken me sometimes three to four years to develop enough rapport in some cases to truly affect the more sensitive sub-systems systems (i.e. financial and governance).

Perhaps the most important relationship a catalyst will make is with a "champion"; these individuals are more often than not the key to fully access every sub-system in health settings. These can be managers, nurses, doctors or staff members; they are the most valuable asset for a catalyst.

When looking at the sub-system hierarchical list on the diagram, it must be made clear that the hierarchy will change form setting to setting and country to country, and is probably time specific as certain development occurs (for example, laws might be passed that incline a health setting to value risk management more than patient care). In Australia for example general practices are private businesses, so there will be a lot more emphasis on financial sub-system outcomes compared to other countries where clinicians are paid a fixed fee.

DISCUSSION AND LIMITATIONS

There is a general awakening in the health sector that sustained behaviour change in clinical practice cannot be brought about solely by traditional dissemination methods (Peer-reviewed journals and re-education). Theoretical approaches to clinical change management require efficient and wide ranging change processes and implementation processes and procedures. These implementations must integrate the individual and existing inter-related human networks. These theoretical approaches must also acknowledge that organisations exist in unique contexts with unique structures and processes all supported by information

systems of one type or another; all underpinning the 'core business' (clinical patient care) through evidence-based medicine.

The author sees in these developments an emergent opportunity for the field of information systems to take a leading role in the development and improvement of the health sector. However, to achieve this role, a solid theory of information systems in health is essential. This emergent theory is a small step towards a more empirically strong theory.

However, the limitations of this examination are many, the content of this chapter was never meant to be comprehensive or conclusive, what it does do however, is to begin a discourse in the hope that others join in its future development. Of the three constructs that were exposed here, only marginal coverage was provided with many premises (if not all) needing further research and critical appraisal; particularly over a broader population than originally studied (general practices). Although there is an emergent authoritative literature supporting some of the premises and conclusions in the constructs; the use of evidence to influence change and validate success and patient outcomes needs further investigation; as does the critical discussion of the extent and role and influence of the catalysts along the artisans-technician and internal-external consultant continuums. Furthermore, the proposition of hierarchical nature of socio-technical sub-systems in health settings needs further verification.

This theory would be better served by further purposeful quantitative and qualitative research that would test every construct down to every single premise. It should focus on a variety of health settings and across a number of countries and across a number of health conditions to better generalise its potential usefulness.

In summary, what was concisely offered here is the beginning of a unique discourse (Hassan, 2006); a theoretical introduction to a multidisciplinary fields not well understood by the information system discipline. In essence an evidence-based health information systems theory holds that: "an information system implementation approach in health setting must be guided, first and foremost by clinical evidence supporting the need for such change in that specific health setting. This evidence is predominantly focused on discovering gaps in local patient care populations to drive change management strategies. Secondly there is a hierarchical necessity to focus on the optimization of all contextual and interdependent subsystem. And thirdly, any measure of success must also be based on the evidence of specific patient health outcome and all other subsystems, keeping in mind their hierarchical importance to the health setting. The facilitation process for all this to happen is through the collaboration of an IS field expert and a site 'champion' that share common goals and objectives".

CONCLUSION

The chapter provided a succinct summary of the context, immediacy and significance for the need to successfully implement information systems in health settings. It briefly discussed the need to consider the core business of health (patient care). The chapter also pointed to the influence that evidence-based medicine (EBM) exerts on health settings and physicians. It suggested mainly a lack of theoretical understanding in the fit between EBM and how it interacts with prospective information systems that are used to research and analyse patient data to improve patient clinical care.

The chapter continued providing the context and foundations for the new constructs discovered in the author's own PhD study to then finally submitting the beginnings of a theoretical foundation to discuss the potentials for the further development of a new evidence-based health information theory. The emerging trends in the health literature suggest many opportunities for the information systems field if solid theories are

developed. Future research needs to strengthen the findings that were outlined as well as the need to further expand on this exploratory chapter. It also suggested that a longer treatise with multiple and international contributors is perhaps a more desired approach for further development.

REFERENCES

Aarts, J., et al. (2004). Understanding implementation: The case of a computerized physician order entry system in a large dutch university medical center. *J Am Med Inform Assoc, 11*(3), 207-216.

AIHW. (2006). *Chronic disease and associated risk factors in Australia, 2006.* Canberra: Australian Government, Department of Health and Ageing.

AMWAC. (2005). *The general practice workforce in Australia: Supply and requirements to 2013.* Australian Medical Workforce Advisory Committee.

Audet, A. M., et al. (2004). Information technologies: When will they make it into physicians' black bags? *MedGenMed, 6*(2).

Australian Institute of Health Policies Studies, & VicHealth. (2008). *A platform for advancing the health of all Australians.* Australian Institute of Health Policies Studies, Melbourne, Australia.

Bates, D. W. (2000). Using information technology to reduce rates of medication errors in hospitals. *British Medical Journal, 320,* 788-791.

Bates, D. W. (2005). Physicians and ambulatory electronic health records. *Health Affairs, 24*(5), 1180-1189.

Bates, D. W., et al. (1995). Incidence of adverse events and potential adverse drug events: Implications for preventions. *JAMA, 274,* 29-34.

Bodenheimer, T. (1999). The American health care system; The movement for improved quality in health care. *N Engl J Med, 340,* 488-492.

Britt, H. (2007). The quality of data on general practice: A discussion of BEACH reliability and validity. *Australian Family Physician, 36*(1/2).

Bryant, A. (2002). Re-grounding grounded theory. *The Journal of Information Technology Theory and Application, 4*(1), 25-42.

Carbone, D. (2008). Information systems in general practice: A framework to implement the management and prevention of chronic diseases. Unpublished doctoral dissertation, Victoria University.

Celler, B. G., et al. (2003). Using information technology to improve the management of chronic disease. *MJA, 179*(5), 242-246.

Charmaz, K. (2000). Grounded theory: Objectivist and constructivist methods. In N. K. Denzin & Y. S. Lincoln (Eds.), *Handbook of qualitative research*. Thousands Oaks, CA: Sage.

Chaudhry, B., et al. (2006). Systematic review: Impact of health information technology on quality, efficiency, and costs of medical care. *Annals of Internal Medicine, 144*(10).

Cherns, A. (1976). The principles of sociotechnical design. *Human Relations, 29*(8), 783-792.

Chin, R., & Benne, K. (1969). The planning of change. In *General strategies for effecting changes in human systems* (2nd ed.) (Vol. 1). New York: Holt, Rinehart & Winston.

Clegg, C. W. (2000). Sociotechnical principles for systems design. *Applied Ergonomics, 31*, 463-477

Cockburn, J. (2004). Adoption of evidence into practice: Can change be sustainable? *MJA, 180*, S66-S67.

Cronen, V. (2001). Practical theory, practical art, and the pragmatic-systemic account of inquiry. *Communication theory, 11*(1).

Davenport, T. H., & Pursak, L. (2001). Information ecology: Mastering the information and knowledge environment. *Business History Review, 3*(75), 15-61.

Davis, D. A., et al. (2004). Solving the information overload problem: A letter from Canada. *MJA, 180*, S68-S71.

Department of Health and Aged Care. (2003). *Practice incentive payments*. Retrieved November, 2003, from http//: www.health.gov.au/pip/index.htn

Dewey, J. (1938). *Logic: The theory of inquiry*. New York: Henry Holt.

Dickinson, J. (2002). General practice. *MJA, 176*(1), 17.

DoHA. (2008). National primary care collaboratives. Retrieved April 28, 2008, from http://www.npcc.com.au/

Donabedian, A. (1988). The quality of care. How can it be assessed? *JAMA, 260*, 1743-1748.

Fieser, J., & Dowden, B. (2008). *Deductive and inductive arguments*. Retrieved from http://www.iep.utm.edu/

Fithgerald, P. (2002). General practice corporatisation: The half-time score. *MJA, 177*(2), 90-92.

GAO. (2003). *Information technology: Benefits realized for the selected health care functions*. Report to the Ranking Minority Member. US Senate.

Glaser, B. G., & Strauss, A. L. (1967). *The discovery of grounded theory: Strategies for qualitative research*. Chicago: Aldine.

GPDV & GPT. (2007). *Outcomes of the CQI in information management workshop*. Melbourne: General Practice Victoria and General Practice Tasmania.

Grimshaw, J., et al. (2004). Effectiveness and efficiency of guideline dissemination and implementation strategies. *Health Technol Assess*.

Grol, R., et al. (1998). Attributes of clinical guidelines that influence use of guidelines in general practice: Observational study. *British Medical Journal, 315*, 418-421.

Grol, R. (2000). Implementation of evidence and guidelines in clinical practice: A new field of research? *International Journal for Quality in Health Care, 12*(6), 455-456.

Grol, R., & Grimshaw, J. (2003). From best evidence to best practice: Effective implementation of change. *Lancet, 362*, 1225-1230.

Grol, R., & Wensing, M. (2004). What drives change? Barriers to and incentives for achieving evidence-based practice. *MJA, 180*, S57-S60.

Gross, P. F., et al. (2003). Australia confronts the challenge of chronic disease. *MJA, 179*(5), 233-234.

Haigh, T. (2001). Inventing information systems: The systems men and the computer, 1950-1968. *Business History Review, 3*(75), 15-61.

Haines, A., & Donald, A. (1998). Getting research findings into practice: Making better use of research findings. *British Journal of General Practice, 317*(7150), 72-75.

Hassan, N. (2006). *Is information systems a discipline? A Foucauldian and Toulminian analysis.* Paper presented at the 27th International Conference on Information Systems, Milwaukee, WI.

HealthConnect. (2005). *About HealthConnect.* Retrieved June 04, 2005, from http://www7.health. gov.au/healthconnect/about/index.htm

HealthConnectSA. (2007). *GP change management strategy: Engagement with general practice.* South Australian Department of Health.

Heckley, P. H. (2004). Evidence-based medicine in 2006: A survey of health plan leaders identifies current and emerging stratgies. *Healtcare Informatics,* (April 2004).

Hendy, J., et al. (2005). Challenges to implementing the national programme for information technology (NPfIT): A qualitative study. *BMJ, 331*, 331-336.

Herzlinger, R. E., & Ricci, R. J. (2002). Dr. know: Can physicans share their experience? *Think Leadership Magazine from IBM.*

Hillestad, R., et al. (2005). Can electronic medical record systems transform health care? Potential health benefits, savings and costs. *Health Affairs, 24*(5), 1103-1117.

Horak, J. B. (2001). Dealing with human factors and managing change in knowledge management: A phased approach. *Topics in Health Information Management, 21*(3), 8-17.

Humber, M. (2004). National programme for information technology. *British Medical Journal, 328*, 1145-1146.

Hummers-Pradiera, E., et al. (2008). Simply no time? Barriers to GPs' participation in primary health care research. *Family Practice,* 1-8.

Ingelse, K. (1997). *Theoretical frameworks.* Retrieved January 6, 2008, from http://jan.ucc.nau. edu/~kmi/nur390/Mod2/theoretical/lesson.html

Lammy, D. (2008). *David Lammy - Leitch and healthcare.* Retrieved April 28, 2008, from http://www.dius.gov.uk/speeches/lammy_ leitch_020408.html

Land, F. (Ed.). (2000). *Evaluation in a socio-technical context.* Boston: Kluwer Academic Publishers.

Liehr, P., & Smith, M. (2001). Frameworks for research. Retrieved January 6, 2008, from http://homepage.psy.utexas.edu/homepage/class/ Psy394V/Pennebaker/Reprints/Liehr%20Class. doc

Lind, M., & Goldkuhl, G. (2006). How to develop a multi-grounded theory: The evolution of a business process theory. *Australasian Journal of Information Systems, 13* (2).

Littlejohns, P., et al. (2003). Evaluating computerised health information systems: Hard lessons still to be learnt. *British Medical Journal, 326,* 860-863.

Lorenzi, N. (2003). *Strategies for creating successful local health information infrastructure initiatives.* Tennessee: Dept of Biomedical Informatics, Vanderbilt University.

Markus, M. L., & Saunders, C. (2007). Looking for a few good concepts…and theories…for the information systems field. *MIS Quarterly, 31*(1), 3-6.

Ministry of Health. (2007). *How to monitor for population health outcomes: Guidelines for developing a monitoring framework.* Wellington, New Zealand: Ministry of Health.

Mumford, E. (2003). *Redesigning human systems.* Hershey, PA: IRM Press.

Mumford, E. (2006a). Researching people problems: Some advice to a student. *Information Systems Journal, 16*(4), 383-389.

Mumford, E. (2006b). The story of socio-technical design: Reflections on its successes, failures and potential. *Information Systems Journal, 16*(4), 317-342.

Nader, C. (2007, November 9). Expert warn of a health 'tsunami'. *The Age.*

Nickols, F. (2006). *Change management 101: A primer.* Retrieved March 29, 2008, from http://home.att.net/~nickols/change.htm

Peirce, C. S. (1958). Collected papers. In C. Hartshorne & P. Weiß (Eds.), (pp. 1931-1935). Cambridge, MA: Harvard University Press.

Pescovitz, D. (2005). HOWTO write a theory of everything. Retrieved April 2, 2005, from http://www.boingboing.net/2005/08/04/howto-write-a-theory.html

Piterman, L. (2000). Methodological/ethical issues and general practice research. *Australian Family Physician, 29*(9), 890-891.

Popper, K. (1979). *Objective knowledge - an evolutionary approach.* Oxford.

Richards, B., et al. (1999). *Information technology in general practice: A monograph commissioned by the general practice branch of the Commonwealth Department of health and Ageing.* Commonwealth Department of Health and Ageing.

Ropohl, G. (1999). Philosophy of socio-technical systems. In *Society for philosophy and technology* (Vol. 4).

Schneberger, S., & Wade, M. (2006). *Theories used in IS research.* Retrieved from http://www.istheory.yorku.ca

Schuster, D. M., et al. (2003). Involving users in the implementation of an imaging order entry system. *American Medical Informatics Association, 10*(4), 315-321.

Sturnberg, J., et al. (2003). Rethinking general practice for the 21st century: The patient counts! *Australian Family Physician, 32*(12), 1028-1031.

Urquhart, C. (2001). An encounter with grounded theory: Tackling the practical and philosophical issues. In E. M. Trauth (Ed.), *Qualitative research in IS: Issues and trends.* Hershey, PA: Idea Group Publishing.

Ward, M. H. (2003). What's happening with IT in general practice? *GPEA,* 6-7.

WHO. (2008). *What works: The evidence for action.* Retrieved January 8, 2008, from http://www.who.int/chp/chronic_disease_report/part3_ch2/en/index13.html

Williamson, H. (2002). *Research methods for students, academics and professionals: Information management and systems* (2nd ed.). Wagga Wagga, Australia: Charles Sturt University.

Wirth, U. (1998). Abductive inference. In P. Bouissac (Ed.), *Encyclopedia of semiotics*. Oxford, UK: Oxford University Press.

Wirth, U. (2008). What is abductive inference? from http://user.uni-frankfurt.de/~wirth/inferenc. htm

Zmud, B. (1998). MISQ: Editor's coments. *MIS Quarterly, 22*(2), 1-3.

KEY TERMS AND DEFINITIONS

Abduction: Is the process of adopting an explanatory hypothesis (CP 5.145) and covers two operations: the selection and the formation of plausible hypotheses. As process of finding premises, it is the basis of interpretive reconstruction of causes and intentions, as well as of inventive construction of theories.

Concepts: A term or label to describe aspects of reality that can be consciously sensed or experienced; the term or description given to events, situations or processes. Evidenced that is sense-based or grouped together through thought connections.

Conceptual Framework: This is a structure of concepts and/or theories which are pulled together as a map for the study as opposed a ready made map (Theoretical Framework).

Constructs: Is a term or label invented by the researcher for a specific purpose to describe a phenomenon or group of phenomena. In other words, it is a summary of thoughts related to a phenomenon.

Deduction: Determines the necessary consequences, relying on logically provable coherence between premises and conclusion. Induction is aiming at empirical provable coherence between the premises and experience, in order to derive a probable generalization.

Empirical-Rational theory of Change Management: People are rational and will follow their self-interest - once it is revealed to them. Successful change is based on the communication of information and the offering of incentives. People can be persuaded AND 'bought' ('carrot' side of carrot-and-stick) (Chin & Benne, 1969).

Induction: Is aiming at empirical provable coherence between the premises and experience, in order to derive a probable generalization. Yet, induction only classifies the data.

Inductive Argument: Asserts that the truth of the conclusion is supported by the premises. (a deductive argument asserts that the truth of the conclusion is a logical consequence of the premises).

Theoretical Framework: This is the structure of concepts which exists in the literature, a ready-made map for the study; it provides the structure for examining a problem; serves as a guide to examine relationships between variables (Liehr & Smith, 2001).

Theory: A theory is an organized and systematic articulation of a set of statements related to questions in a discipline that are communicated in a meaningful whole. Its purpose is to describe (set forth what is -Descriptive), explain (account for how it functions - Explanative), predict (under what conditions it occurs), and prescribe (under what conditions it should occur) (Ingelse, 1997).

Section II
Information System Development

Section II includes four chapters dedicated to understanding the process and practice of information systems development. The first chapter (Chapter VII) presents 'the language-action perspective (LAP)' as an alternative foundation for analyzing and designing effective information systems. This is followed by Chapter VIII analyzing recent developments linking design science to systems analysis and design research and the growing area of the work system method. The third chapter (Chapter IX) within this section attempts to quantify the value of flexibility in systems analysis and design research. To achieve this goal, the authors proposed a real options-based framework to value IT investments, taking risk into account. Finally, Chapter X presents a detailed discussion on the theory of deferred action for explaining the effect of emergence on the rational design of information systems.

Chapter VII
Language–Action Perspective (LAP)

Karthikeyan Umapathy
University of North Florida, USA

ABSTRACT

The Language-action perspective (LAP) provides an alternative foundation for analyzing and designing effective information systems. The fundamental principle of the LAP approach is people perform actions through communication; therefore, the role of information systems is to support such communications among people to achieve business goals. Basing on linguistic and communicative theories, the LAP approach provides guidance for researchers to gain understanding on how people use communication to coordinate their activities to achieve common goal. Web services, a leading technology to develop information systems, aims to support communication among services to achieve business goals. The close match between fundamental principles of Web services and the LAP approach suggests that researchers can use the LAP approach as a theoretical guidance to analyze and resolve Web service problems. This chapter provides a comprehensive starting point for researchers, practitioners, and students to gain understanding of the LAP approach.

INTRODUCTION

Through their article, "Doing and speaking in the office," Flores and Ludlow challenged the conventional notion that communication is merely the transmission of information or symbols and argued that people are linguistic beings who use language to perform actions (Flores & Ludlow, 1980). Through this article, they provided awareness and relevance of communication theories for the information systems field. Goldkuhl and Lyytinen (Goldkuhl & Lyytinen, 1982) coined the term "Language Action View" to describe an approach for designing information systems from the perspective of how people use communication to perform actions. Building on this perspective, Winograd and Flores (Winograd & Flores, 1986) presented a new foundation for designing information systems by conceptualizing actions performed through communications as recurrent communicative patterns. The revolutionary work of Winograd and Flores inspired a wave of diverse Language-action perspective (LAP) based applications in the last two decades (Weigand, 2006). They all have in common the fundamental agreement that language is not only used for exchanging information, as in reports or statements, but also to perform actions such as promises, orders, declarations, etc (Schoop, 2001; Weigand, 2003). LAP emphasizes that such actions should be the foundation for creating effective information systems.

In contrast, traditional approaches consider information systems as repositories for storing representations of facts about the real world (Yetim & Bieber, 2003). According to these approaches, the important goal of information systems is to process stored facts and provide required information for managerial and decision making purposes (Connors, 1992; Davis & Olson, 1984). Therefore, information systems development is considered a process of manipulating information to meet the requirements of a specific business task (De Michelis et al., 1997). Moreover, requirements for developing systems were based on simplified assumptions and heuristics that capture known properties of the real world while ignoring unknown properties (Oreskes, Shrader-Frechette, & Belitz, 1994). Thus, traditional information systems are seen as 'mirrors of reality', where users are provided with abstractions of the reality (Flores, Graves, Hartfield, & Winograd, 1988; Goldkuhl & Lyytinen, 1982). Therefore, each user has a 'local view' of the real world, that is the individual's slice of the reality seen through an information system (Goldkuhl & Lyytinen,

1982). Several researchers within the information systems field have challenged this notion of information systems as an image of reality (Goldkuhl & Ågerfalk, 2000; Hirschheim, Klein, & Lyytinen, 1995; Winograd & Flores, 1986).

On the other hand, the LAP approach presumes that the purpose of an information system is to support communication among people to help them perform actions together (Flores et al., 1988; Goldkuhl & Lyytinen, 1982). LAP considers communication to be a form of action performed by the participants (Winograd, 2006). Therefore, LAP recognizes the importance of communication in an organizational context and focuses on how communicative aspects are used for performing business actions (Mulder & Reijswoud, 2003). Thus, according to the LAP approach, people are part of a community, who interpret the world and coordinate their actions together in that world (Goldkuhl & Lyytinen, 1982). The user is seen as a participant in the community of interpretation and information is contextualized for a community of interpreters (Goldkuhl & Lyytinen, 1982). Thus, appropriate level of analysis for the LAP approach is group and organization.

In spite of significant progress in the past two decades (Weigand, 2006), the LAP approach has not become a significant part of mainstream computing movement to address organizational computing problems (Lyytinen, 2004). Thus, the motivation for this chapter comes from the challenge put forth by Kalle Lyytinen (Lyytinen, 2004) to make LAP part of mainstream of organizational computing.

As organizational computing paradigm shifts away from object-orientation to service-orientation, I argue that the LAP approach provides appropriate theoretical foundations for designing and developing service-oriented Information systems (Umapathy, 2007; Umapathy & Purao, 2007b). The LAP approach would be a good theoretical framework, because it was developed in the context of coordinating communications among organizational entities (which can be considered as services) to achieve organizational goals (Umapathy & Purao, 2007a). Therefore, it is important for IS researchers to have good understanding on diverse theoretical frameworks such as LAP. The objective of this chapter is to provide a comprehensive starting point for information systems researchers, practitioners, and students to gain understanding of the LAP approach.

BACKGROUND

LAP emphasizes how people communicate with others; how language is used to create a common shared reality, and how people use communication to coordinate their activities (Schoop, 2001). Therefore, LAP is grounded in the linguistic and social rules that govern the use of the language. The main theoretical foundation for the LAP approach is the Speech act Theory (Austin, 1962; Searle, 1969). However, the LAP approach is also influenced by the Theory of Communicative Action (Habermas, 1984), Conversation Analysis (Sacks, 1995), and Organizational Semiotics (Stamper, 1996). This section provides overview of the Speech act Theory.

Speech Act Theory

Speech act Theory was first introduced by Austin (Austin, 1962), and further developed and formalized by Searle (Searle, 1969). The underlying theme of the theory is that the use of language is not only to describe a situation or fact, but also to perform certain kinds of actions (Goldkuhl & Ågerfalk, 2000). For instance, the utterance of the statement, "You passed the test," is considered the performance of a declarative action as opposed to making a statement that may be judged true or false. Thus, according to speech act theory, speaking is acting and by speaking, the speaker performs a 'speech act' (Bach & Harnish, 1979).

A speech act is the basic unit of communication that expresses the intention of the speaker, such as

making a promise or asserting a claim (Auramaki, Lehtinen, & Lyytinen, 1988). The meaning of a speech act is understood based on the propositional content and context of its occurrence that includes the speaker, hearer, time, place, and other factors relevant to the performance of communication. The main characteristic of speech act theory is that every speech act consists of four levels of action. Suppose that a speaker succeeds in saying something to a hearer in a given context, then the following acts can be distinguished (Austin, 1962; Moore, 2001):

- **Utterance act** is the act of uttering something. Utterance act refers to the action of the speaker uttering something to the hearer in the given context.
- **Locutionary act** is the act of saying something meaningful. Locutionary act refers to the actual action of the speaker saying something to the hearer in the given context.
- **Illocutionary act** is the act of doing something in saying it. Illocutionary act refers to the action of doing something by the speaker in the given context in virtue of having performed an utterance act.
- **Perlocutionary act** is the act of affecting the hearer by saying it. Perlocutionary act refers to the effect on the hearer's feelings, thoughts, or actions in virtue of the speaker having performed the illocutionary act in the given context.

Of the above four acts, the illocutionary act is critical for the successful performance of the speech act because it expresses the communicative intent of the speaker (Traum, 1999). The illocutionary act can be further decomposed into (i) the illocutionary force, that specifies the type of action and (ii) the propositional content, that specifies the details of action (Austin, 1962). The illocutionary force represents the speaker's intention in producing an illocutionary act. An illocutionary force is the combination of the basic purpose of a speaker in making an utterance, including particular presuppositions, and the attitudes of the speaker (Searle & Vanderveken, 1985). For example, if the speaker says, "You have passed your defense," then the speaker is declaring to the hearer that he or she passed defense. Thus, in this statement the speaker's intention is to make a declaration. However, if the speaker says, "Have you passed your defense," then it can be considered that the speaker is asking a question to the hearer. Therefore, in this statement the speaker's intention is to ask a question. Thus speakers can perform different actions with the same proposition.

Bach and Harnish (Bach & Harnish, 1979) developed six major categories of speech acts based on the correlation between illocutionary acts and illocutionary forces. These categories of speech acts are constatives, directives, commissives, acknowledgments, effectives, and verdictives. Constatives represent the speaker's beliefs, intentions, desires, or experiences. Directives represent the speaker's attempt to get the hearer to perform the action indicated in the propositional content. Commissives represent the speaker's intention to perform the action indicated in the propositional content. Acknowledgements represent the speaker's feelings or psychological attitudes regarding the state of affairs represented by the propositional content. Effectives represent the speaker's effects to change the state of affairs of an institution. Verdictives represent the speaker making an official judgment relevant to the institutional state of affairs that is social binding in the given context. Bach and Harnish have developed about fifty illocutionary forces based on the above speech act classifications.

Speech act frameworks and classifications can be used for decomposing communicative messages into smaller entities (Kimbrough & Moore, 1997). Thus they provide good foundations for interpreting and representing communicative messages (Auramaki et al., 1988). Speech acts can also be used to create larger wholes such as well-formed discourses and conversations (Hirschheim, Iivari, & Klein, 1997). For instance, if the speaker asks a question to the hearer, the hearer may follow up with an answer or a request for clarification, a refusal to answer or a counter-question. Thus set of speech acts can be ordered in a sequence to form a logical whole (Auramaki et al., 1988).

LAP-BASED APPLICATIONS

The LAP approach is not merely a philosophical framework but has stirred the development of a number of methodologies and computer based tools for solving specific organizational problems (Lyytinen, 2004; Weigand, 2006). The LAP approach has been applied in diverse fields such as computer supported co-operative work (CSCW), workflows, business process modeling, business process re-design, e-commerce, electronic negotiations, software agents, and virtual communities (Lyytinen, 2004; Weigand, 2006). This section provides a review of several LAP-based applications.

Coordinator

The Coordinator is one of the earliest applications of the LAP approach (Schoop, 2003). This application was developed based on the observation by Winograd and Flores (Winograd & Flores, 1986) that in the most work environments the coordination of activities are of central importance and these coordinated activities are facilitated by conversations among participants (Beeson & Green, 2003). Winograd and Flores named these conversations as "Conversations for Action" (Winograd & Flores, 1986). Through the coordinator application, they provide a mechanism that utilizes a network of speech acts to model conversations that are directed towards explicit cooperative action (Winograd & Flores,

1986). This mechanism uses circles to represent a possible state in the conversation, heavy circles for termination states, and lines connecting the states to represent speech acts that indicate actions taken, see Figure 1 for an example of a simple conversation for action.

Speech-Act-Based Office Modelling aPprOach (SAMPO)

The Speech-Act-based office Modelling aPprOach (SAMPO) provides a methodology for modeling organizational information systems (Auramaki et al., 1988). The SAMPO approach considers the purpose of information systems development is to support communication among people to perform their activities (Lyytinen, Lehitnen, & Auramäki, 1987). Therefore, the SAMPO approach considers the process of modeling organizational information systems as a process of modeling organizational discourses (Auramaki et al., 1988). A network of speech acts can be arranged in systematic order to model a discourse that establishes, controls, and coordinates organizational activi-

ties (Lyytinen et al., 1987). SAMPO provides a methodology and a graphical tool for modeling complete and coherent organizational discourses by logically structuring the sequence of speech acts (Auramaki et al., 1988).

Dynamic Essential Modelling of Organizations (DEMO)

Dynamic Essential Modelling of Organizations (DEMO) (Dietz, 1994, 2001) is an information systems development methodology that offers concepts and modeling techniques for re-engineering business processes. According to DEMO, an organization has three levels: documental, informational, and essential (Dietz, 1994). At the documental level, actions such as gathering, storing, transmitting, and reproducing information are performed. At the informational level, actions such as deducting or deriving information are performed, preferably using computers. At the essential level, business transactions are executed by human actors. Actions performed at the essential level are considered authentic busi-

Figure 1. Simple conversation for action (Adapted from Winograd & Flores, 1986, pg 65)

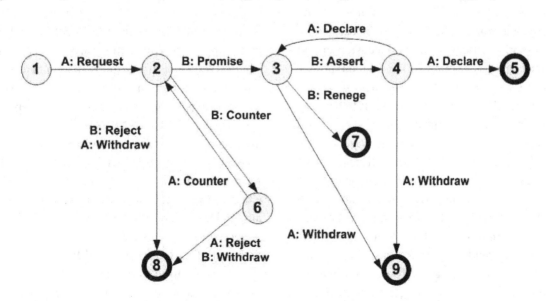

ness actions, while actions performed at the documental and informational levels are categorized as supporting actions (Dietz, 1994). Therefore, business transactions performed at the essential level are the core of the DEMO methodology and are typically performed by two actors: the initiator and the executor (Dietz, Rijst, & Stollman, 1996). Business transactions are divided into three phases under DEMO: the Order (O) phase, the Execution (E) phase, and the Result (R) phase (Dietz, 2001; Dietz et al., 1996). In the O-phase both actors reach an agreement about the execution of some future action. Then, in the E-phase, the executor performs the negotiated future action. During the R-phase, both actors come to agreement on the facts that were accomplished as a result of the execution of the negotiated future action. Albani and Dietz apply DEMO methodology to model enterprise ontology for the strategic supply network development in the strategic purchasing domain (Albani & Dietz, 2006). Through this case example, they illustrate how to use DEMO methodology to identify business components and creating ontological models for developing information systems.

Business Action Theory (BAT)

Business Action Theory (BAT) (Goldkuhl, 1996, 1998) provides a generic framework for describing business interactions between the customer and the performer. The framework is divided into six phases (Goldkuhl, 1998); (1) Business prerequisites phase, (2) Exposure and contact search phase, (3) Contact establishment and proposal phase, (4) Contractual phase, (5) Fulfillment phase, and (6) Completion phase. The BAT-model emphasizes the idea that a business action involves both material and communicative actions; however, it presumes that material actions can be characterized as communication (Goldkuhl, 1996). The framework provides a graphical model to describe the inherent business logic and business processes as communicative exchanges, with exception to

phase 1 (Goldkuhl, 1998). As shown in the Figure 2, phase 2 involves the exchange of interest, phase 3 involves the exchange of proposals, phase 4 involves the exchange of commitments, phase 5 involves the exchange of values, and phase 6 involves the exchange of claims or acceptance (Goldkuhl, 1998).

Layered Pattern Approach

Weigand et al. (Weigand, Heuvel, & Dignum, 1998) argues that in electronic commerce business transactions, participants would interact with each other electronically in multiple forms. However, traditional Electronic Document Interchange (EDI) protocols, that provide implementations for converting paper forms to electronic versions, cannot provide adequate support for e-commerce transactions (Weigand et al., 1998). Weigand and Heuvel, building on the notion of pattern analysis, proposed a layered pattern approach for conducting analysis on e-commerce business transactions (Weigand & Heuvel, 1998). This approach consists of five layers, that are the speech act, the transaction, the workflow loop, the contract, and the scenario (Weigand & Heuvel, 1998). The speech act is used to represent intentional action performed through message exchange in the transaction (Weigand & Heuvel, 1998; Weigand et al., 1998). Thus, speech acts are the basic unit of analysis in this approach. Transactions are considered the smallest sequence of possible actions constituting a business interaction (Weigand et al., 1998). A transaction is formed by compile a set of speech acts (Weigand & Heuvel, 1998). Workflow loops are sets of related transactions aimed towards a goal. Therefore, a set of transactions are grouped to form a workflow loop (Weigand & Heuvel, 1998). Contracts represent obligations and authorizations among business partners (Weigand et al., 1998). A contract is established by interrelating two or more workflow loops (Weigand & Heuvel, 1998). Scenarios are used to describe multiple interactions across contracts that run concurrently among

Figure 2. Business Action Theory Framework (Modified based on Goldkuhl, 1998)

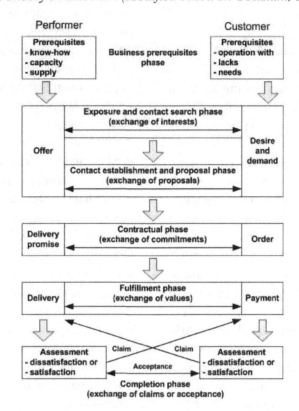

multiple parties (Weigand et al., 1998). A set of related contracts form a scenario (Weigand & Heuvel, 1998).

Generic Layered Pattern Approach

Lind and Goldkuhl (Lind & Goldkuhl, 2001) critically analyzed each layer of the layered pattern approach proposed by Weigand et al. (Weigand & Heuvel, 1998) to show their shortcomings. Lind and Goldkuhl proposed an alternative framework, called the Generic Layered Pattern Approach for any kind of inter-organizational electronic business transaction (Lind & Goldkuhl, 2001), unlike the layered pattern approach that focuses only on e-commerce transactions (Weigand & Heuvel, 1998). The Generic layered pattern approach consists of five layers: the business act, the action pair, the exchange, the business transaction, and

the transaction group (Lind & Goldkuhl, 2001). Except for the business act, each layer is derived based on its preceding layer (Lind & Goldkuhl, 2001). A business act can be a communicative and/ or a material action (Goldkuhl & Lind, 2002). An action pair represents the grouping of business acts as patterns of triggers and responses (Lind & Goldkuhl, 2001). An exchange constitutes one or more action pairs representing the contribution of one actor in return of the other actor's contribution (Goldkuhl & Lind, 2002). A business transaction represents a pattern built from different types of exchanges related to each other (Lind & Goldkuhl, 2001). Business transactions can be thought of as having different phases involving exchanges that lead to states that satisfy the needs of both the customer and the performer (Goldkuhl & Lind, 2002). A transaction group represents recurrent business transactions framed for a long-term agreement aimed at establishing relationships (Lind & Goldkuhl, 2001).

Atoms, Molecules, and Matters

Analogous to the three layers distinguished in Physics, Dietz suggests three conceptual layers to understand business processes (Dietz, 2003). Compared to the layered pattern model (Weigand & Heuvel, 1998) that focuses on electronic commerce, and the generic pattern model (Lind & Goldkuhl, 2001) that focuses on inter-organizational interactions; Dietz's 'atoms, molecules, and fibers' model focuses on both inter and intra-organization interactions (Dietz, 2002, 2003). This model is comprised of three layers: atoms, molecules, and fibers, that capture the business of an organization (Dietz, 2003). Atoms consist of coordination acts and action rules (Dietz, 2003). Coordination acts are facilitated by communicative actions. By performing coordination acts, individuals enter into and comply with commitments directed towards achieving material actions. Constraints on 'Atoms' are provided by action rules, which contain possible acts and how the choice about actions should be made. Molecules consist of transactions and actor roles (Dietz, 2003). Transactions represent finite sequences of coordination acts between two actors directed towards achieving common objectives. Actor roles define the roles played by actors as sets of action rules. Fibers consist of business processes that are considered to be compositions of interconnected transactions (Dietz, 2003).

Agent Communication Languages

A software agent is a computer system that acts autonomously on behalf of a user or a program in a given environment in order to meet its design objectives (Nwana, 1996; Wooldridge, 2002). To be useful, an agent should be able to interact with its environment, user, and/or other agents (Wooldridge, 2002). Agent interactions are very complicated because agents need to maintain and share their knowledge, goals, and commitments (Labrou, Finin, & Peng, 1999). In order to maintain and use knowledge, beliefs, and intentions, agents typically exchange messages through certain agreed knowledge representation languages, collectively referred to as agent communication languages (Labrou et al., 1999). There are two well known and widely used languages, the Knowledge Query and Manipulation Language (KQML) (Finin, Labrou, & Mayfield, 1994) and the Foundation for Intelligent Physical Agents—Agent Communication Language (FIPA-ACL) (FIPA-ACL, 2002). Both languages were developed based on the speech act theory, following the fundamental philosophy of language as action (Labrou et al., 1999). These languages used speech act theory to develop appropriate semantics that allow agents to affect other agents' knowledge, beliefs, and intentions (Pitt, Guerin, & Stergiou, 2000). These languages prescribe speech act based message exchanges to facilitate agents to perform actions upon receiving messages (Colombetti & Verdicchio, 2002).

Formal Language for Business Communication (FLBC)

A main problem in the field of business-to-business electronic commerce is the lack of formal schemes to encode messages for business communication (Weigand & Hasselbring, 2001). Standards, such as EDIFACT, are too costly, do not provide the required expressiveness, and are not flexible enough to cope with the dynamics of the new economy (Weigand et al., 1998). Moore developed the Formal Language for Business Communication (FLBC) based on speech act theory (Moore, 2001). FLBC defines broad range message types that express the speaker's intentions while distinguishing those intentions from type of message content. FLBC utilizes the illocutionary force from speech act theory to provide separation between message types and message contents (Weigand & Hasselbring, 2001). This clear distinction makes it easier for e-commerce applications to interpret and respond to messages (Moore, 2001). FLBC message syntax was developed using XML (XML, 2006), a markup language for self-descriptive data.

Other Notable Applications

Other applications based on the LAP approach that were developed based on inspiration provided by the above applications are mentioned here. eXtensible Language for Business Communication (XLBC), drawing on FLBC (Moore, 2001), semantic network of the multilingual thesaurus and layered pattern approach (Weigand & Heuvel, 1998) provides an extensible communication infrastructure that permits message exchanges to be grouped into different aggregation levels of conversation (Weigand & Hasselbring, 2001). Milano provides a system for supporting multimedia conversations within a work process (De Michelis & Grasso, 1994). Action Technologies extended the Conversation for Action concept (Winograd & Flores, 1986) to develop a business modeling approach known as the Action Workflow Loop, that consists of four basic steps—proposal, agreement, performance, and satisfaction (Medina-Mora, Winograd, Flores, & Flores, 1992). Negoisst is a negotiation support system for conducting complex electronic negotiations over the Internet using both structured message exchanges and cooperative document exchanges (Schoop, Jertila, & List, 2003). Negoisst used the LAP approach to create its architecture and to structure message and document exchanges (Schoop, 2003). Johannesson provides a speech act theory based information systems development framework that reconciles the representation-based and communicative-based approaches to systems development (Johannesson, 1995). This framework shows how to model communications as discourses, and, at same time, view discourses

as sequences of events. Cooperative Information Agents (CIA) is a communication system for the business-to-business application domain that allows software agents to query for required information and also to negotiate based on the information the agent can provide (Verharen, Dignum, & Weigand, 1996). CIA uses speech act theory to model message exchanges among agents.

Regardless of the continued development of diverse LAP-based applications, the LAP computing movement has not penetrated mainstream organizational computing (Lyytinen, 2004). For example, LAP concepts are not taught in most universities or in computing textbooks (Schoop & Kethers, 2000), and there is no example of extensive uptake of LAP-based applications in industry (Dumay, Dietz, & Mulder, 2005). Thus, the LAP movement has been confined to academic scholars, and is not widely known nor practiced outside the narrow borders of the LAP community (Lyytinen, 2004).

CRITICISMS ON LAP APPROACH

While the previous section showcases diverse applications to demonstrate the wide variety of interest in the LAP approach, LAP has also received some criticisms. Most of these criticisms are aimed specifically towards the use of speech act theory, but some focus on the general use of the LAP approach (Schoop, 2001). These criticisms are presented in this section along with solutions intended to counter them.

Bowers (Bowers, 1992) provides a critical attack on the LAP approach, specifically on the Coordinator, that heavily relies on formal speech act based representation for expressing networks of communication structures. He attacks the notion of formal representations, that claims to make a task easier and clearer (Schoop, 2001). He argues that the notion of formalism includes the possibility of forcing people to behave according to representations, thus, leading to situations of centralized power, where certain users can unduly influence others (Bowers, 1992). Therefore, Bowers claims that communication structures developed using the speech act theory oppress users because these structures enforce disciple and control (Schoop, 2001). Typically users are not aware of the vocabulary and intentions behind each speech act, hence, formalisms should be decentralized and kept open to critical assessment (Bowers, 1992). Schoop suggests that one strategy to achieve this goal is to use a participatory design to develop speech act based formalisms (Schoop, 2001).

Building on Bower arguments, Suchman provides the most challenging attack on the LAP approach (Suchman, 1994). She argues that LAP focuses on the speaker's utterance and the hearer's reaction rather than the interaction between the two, where the actual meaning and intentions emerge (Suchman, 1994). She further argues that predefined communication structures act as a plan with a set of actions to be executed, however, these actions are performed depending upon certain contexts and they are loosely connected to the plan (Suchman, 1994). She suggests that systems, instead of forcing predefined plans on to users, should keep track of actions and warn users of potential breakdowns (Suchman, 1994). Similar criticism of the LAP approach, in particular on speech act taxonomies, was provided by Ljungberg and Holm (Ljungberg & Holm, 1997) and suggested alternative criteria for classifying speech acts. Allwood (Allwood, 1977) suggests that the classification of speech acts should be based on communicative functionalities and context (Schoop, 2001).

As a result of these criticisms on the usage and shortcomings of speech act theory, many later applications based on the LAP approach used Habermas' theory of communicative action (Habermas, 1984) in addition to speech act theory (Schoop, 2001). Habermas criticizes the shortcomings of the speech act theory, while agreeing on

its fundamental philosophy that communication is used to perform actions (Yetim & Bieber, 2003). Habermas developed his own version of speech act theory to provide a framework for understanding social interactions as coordination of speech acts (Cecez-Kecmanovic & Webb, 2000). Habermas suggests that social interactions should be viewed from three dimensions (Goldkuhl, 2005; Habermas, 1984; Yetim & Bieber, 2003): (i) an ontology of three worlds (objective, subjective, and social); (ii) the pragmatics of language (representation, expressivity, and appellative); and (iii) the concept of validity claims (truth, normative rightness, sincerity, and comprehensibility). Habermas' theory of communicative action provides a foundation for understanding and analyzing social interactions as the coordination of communicative actions towards achieving mutually agreed upon goals (Klein & Huynh, 2004). This theory also provides a framework for identifying and addressing breakdowns in social interactions (Yetim, 2002). Like any other theory, the use of theory of communicative action in information systems was agreed upon by some researchers (Goldkuhl, 2000; Hirschheim, Klein, & Lyytinen, 1996; Klein & Huynh, 2004; Reijswoud, Mulder, & Dietz, 1999; Yetim, 2002) and criticized by others (Brooke, 2002; Doolin & Lowe, 2002; Introna, 1996; Ljungberg & Holm, 1997).

SERVICE COMPUTING: OPPORTUNITY AND CHALLENGE

Over the past few years, the computing paradigm has been shifting from the current mainstream object-oriented perspective (Booch, 1993) to the service-oriented perspective (Papazoglou & Georgakopoulos, 2003). This type of change occurs when an existing paradigm reaches its limits to deal with increasing levels of software complexity. With the advent of Internet-based technologies, organizations are redesigning their information systems to support their business activities over the Internet (Su, Lam, Lee, Bai, & Shen, 2001; Waldt & Drummond, 2005). Business applications that are implemented over heterogeneous Internet technologies need to be loosely coupled, dynamically bound, and interoperable within and across organizations (Jain & Zhao, 2003). The object-oriented paradigm provides inadequate support for implementing applications over the Internet because object-oriented applications are rigid and hard to evolve (Henders, 1998). The advent of the Service-oriented computing (SOC) paradigm, on the other hand, is intended to facilitate business collaboration and application integration through open Internet standards (Papazoglou & Georgakopoulos, 2003). The SOC paradigm, is therefore considered the appropriate infrastructure for conducting seamless and automated business over Internet (Alonso, Casati, Kuno, & Machiraju, 2004).

Web service is the most promising technology based on the SOC paradigm (Curbera, Nagy, & Weerawarana, 2001; Stal, 2002). A common goal of Web service architecture and its associated standards is to support and coordinate communication among services to achieve particular business goals (Gottschalk, Graham, Kreger, & Snell, 2002; Papazoglou, 2003; Umapathy & Purao, 2007a). However, fundamental shift in the computing paradigm has produced new challenges and problems that must be addressed by Web services to support business activities over the Internet (Khalaf, Mukhi, & Weerawarana, 2003; Tsai, 2005; Umapathy & Purao, 2007b). Some of the central concerns of Web services are precisely those addressed by the LAP approach— segregating of key functionalities, coordinating communication among services to support complex business interactions, and developing communication-oriented design methodologies and principles. The LAP approach, with its essential qualities of communication and coordination, is an appropriate candidate that Web services researchers can use to address its challenges (Umapathy & Purao, 2007a). However, the LAP approach is

founded on human communication theories, on the other hand, Web services primarily support communication among machines. Therefore, Web service researchers must adopt LAP constructs with caution and tailor it towards Web services.

A good starting point to view Web services from the LAP perspective is to compare Web service standards stack against to LAP layered business process models-layered pattern approach (Weigand et al., 1998); generic layered pattern approach (Lind & Goldkuhl, 2001); and atoms, molecules, and matter approach (Dietz, 2003). Umapathy and Purao have mapped the layers of the LAP business process models to the layers of Web service stack (Umapathy & Purao, 2004). Their analysis indicated that none of the LAP business process models alone satisfies needs of Web service stack; however, if models are combined they would cover entire spectrum of the Web service stack. Umapathy and Purao in another study, develop a theoretical reference framework for Web services based on the LAP literatures (Umapathy & Purao, 2007a). The reference framework includes three major layers each containing sub levels within it. Bottom most layer is communication platform which provide preconditions to make message exchanges between services successful. Communication platform includes channel, messaging, and guarantee as its sub levels. Middle layer is communicative act layer which provides conditions for creating commitments between participating services. Communicative act layer includes capability exposure, capability search, proposal and negotiation, and contract establishment as its sub levels. Top most layer is rational discourse which provides conditions for coordinating commitments and interactions among services to achieve business goals. Rational discourse layer includes exchange, transaction, relationship management, and managing multiple contracts as its sub levels. The reference framework is assessed against to stacks for WSDL-based, semantic Web-based, and ebXML Web services to provide recommendations and insights for these three Web service architectures.

CONCLUSION

The Language-action perspective (LAP) approach provides a norm-based and interpretive alternative to analyze and design information systems—using language as it is constituted in social life (Umapathy & Purao, 2007a). The LAP approach has developed into a new foundation for constructing effective information systems with two key principles. First, linguistic communication should be the basis for understanding and designing information systems (Winograd, 2006). Second, people perform actions through communication; therefore, the main role of an information system is to support organizational communications (Schoop, 2001).

The LAP approach was first introduced by Flores and Ludlow (Flores & Ludlow, 1980) who challenged the conventional notion that communication is merely transmission of information or symbols and argued that people are linguistic beings and use language to perform actions (Schoop, 2001). The LAP approach argues that language is not only used for exchanging information, (as in reports or statements etc.) but also to perform actions (as in promises, orders, requests, and declarations etc) (Schoop, 2001; Weigand, 2003). Thus, LAP considers communication to be a form of action performed by the participants (Winograd, 2006).

The LAP approach considers that purpose of an information system is to support communication among people to perform their actions together (Flores et al., 1988; Goldkuhl & Lyytinen, 1982). Therefore, LAP recognizing the importance of communication in an organizational context, focuses on how communicative aspects are used for performing business actions (Mulder & Reijswoud, 2003). The LAP approach, thus, emphasizes how people communicate with others;

how language is used to create a common shared reality and how people use communication to coordinate their activities (Schoop, 2001). Therefore, the LAP approach is grounded in linguistic and social rules that govern the use of the language (Goldkuhl & Lyytinen, 1984).

According to the LAP approach, organizations are social systems with actors that communicates to achieve mutually agreed goals (Dietz, 2003). The aim of Web services is to support communication among services to achieve business goals (Umapathy & Purao, 2007a). Therefore, there is close match between Web services and the LAP approach. This core mapping presents an opportunity for information systems researchers to use the LAP approach as their theoretical guidance to solve Web service problems, thus, help LAP reach mainstream computing paradigm.

REFERENCES

Albani, A., & Dietz, J. L. G. (2006). The benefit of enterprise ontology in identifying business components. In D. Avison, S. Elliot, J. Krogstie, & J. Pries-Heje (Eds.), *The past and future of information systems: 1976–2006 and beyond* (Vol. 214/2006, pp. 243-254). Boston: Springer.

Allwood, J. (1977). A critical look at speech act theory. In Ö. Dahl (Ed.), *Logic, pragmatics and grammar* (pp. 53-99). Lund, Sweden: Studentlitteratur.

Alonso, G., Casati, F., Kuno, H., & Machiraju, V. (2004). *Web services: Concepts, architectures and applications*. Berlin: Springer-Verlag.

Auramaki, E., Lehtinen, E., & Lyytinen, K. (1988). A speech-act-based office modeling approach. *ACM Transactions on Information systems (TOIS)*, 6(2), 126-152.

Austin, J. L. (1962). *How to do things with words*. Cambridge, MA: Harvard University Press.

Bach, K., & Harnish, R. M. (1979). *Linguistic communication and speech acts.* Cambridge, MA: MIT Press.

Beeson, I., & Green, S. (2003, April 9-11). *Using a language action framework to extend organizational process modelling.* Paper presented at the UK Academy for Information systems (UKAIS) Conference, University of Warwick.

Booch, G. (1993). *Object-oriented analysis and design with applications* (2nd ed.). Indianapolis, IN: Addison-Wesley Professional.

Bowers, J. (1992). The politics of formalism. In M. Lea (Ed.), *Contexts of computer-mediated communication* (pp. 232-261). New York: Harvester Wheatsheaf.

Brooke, C. (2002). What does it mean to be 'critical' in IS research? *Journal of Information Technology, 17*(2), 49-57.

Cecez-Kecmanovic, D., & Webb, C. (2000). Towards a communicative model of collaborative Web-mediated learning. *Australian Journal of Educational Technology, 16*(1), 73-85.

Colombetti, M., & Verdicchio, M. (2002). *An analysis of agent speech acts as institutional actions.* Paper presented at the International Conference on Autonomous Agents, Bologna, Italy.

Connors, D. T. (1992). Software development methodologies and traditional and modern information systems. *ACM SIGSOFT Software Engineering Notes, 17*(2), 43-49.

Curbera, F., Nagy, W. A., & Weerawarana, S. (2001). *Web services: Why and how.* Paper presented at the Workshop on Object-Oriented Web services held with the ACM Conference on Object-Oriented Programming, Systems, Language and Applications (OOPSLA), Tampa, Florida, USA.

Davis, G. B., & Olson, M. H. (1984). *Management information systems: Conceptual foundations, structure, and development* (2nd ed.). New York: McGraw-Hill.

De Michelis, G., Dubois, E., Jarke, M., Matthes, F., Mylopoulos, J., Papazoglou, M. P., et al. (1997). Cooperative information systems: A manifesto. In M. P. Papazoglou & G. Schlageter (Eds.), *Cooperative information systems: Trends & directions.* Academic Press.

De Michelis, G., & Grasso, M. A. (1994). *Situating conversations within the language/action perspective: the Milan conversation model.* Paper presented at the ACM conference on Computer supported cooperative work, Chapel Hill, NC, USA.

Dietz, J. L. G. (1994). *Business modeling for business redesign.* Paper presented at the Hawaii International Conference on System Sciences (HICSS), Maui, Hawaii.

Dietz, J. L. G. (2001). Coherent, consistent and comprehensive modeling of communication, information, action and organzation. In M. Rossi & K. Siau (Eds.), *Information modeling in the new milennium* (pp. 9-33). Hershey, PA: IGI Global Publishing.

Dietz, J. L. G. (2002). *The atoms, molecules and matter of organizations.* Paper presented at the International Working Conference on the Language-action perspective on Communication Modelling (LAP).

Dietz, J. L. G. (2003). The atoms, molecules and fibers of organizations. *Data & Knowledge Engineering, 47*(3), 301-325.

Dietz, J. L. G., Rijst, N. B. J. v. d., & Stollman, F. L. H. (1996). *The specification and implementation of a DEMO supporting CASE-Tool.* Paper presented at the International Workshop on Communication Modeling - The Language/Action Perspective (LAP), Tilburg, The Netherlands.

Doolin, B., & Lowe, A. (2002). To reveal is to critique: Actor-network theory and critical information systems research. *Journal of Information Technology, 17*(2), 69-78.

Dumay, M., Dietz, J., & Mulder, H. (2005). *Evaluation of DEMO and the language/action perspective after 10 years of experience.* Paper presented at the International Working Conference on the Language-action perspective on Communication Modelling (LAP), Kiruna, Sweden.

Finin, T., Labrou, Y., & Mayfield, J. (1994). *KQML as an agent communication language.* Paper presented at the International Conference on Information and Knowledge Management (CIKM), Gaithersburg, MD, USA.

FIPA-ACL. (2002, December 06). *FIPA ACL message structure specification.* Retrieved February 2, 2007, from http://www.fipa.org/specs/fipa00061/

Flores, F., Graves, M., Hartfield, B., & Winograd, T. (1988). Computer systems and the design of organizational interaction. *ACM Transactions on Office Information systems (TOIS), 6*(2), 153-172.

Flores, F., & Ludlow, J. (1980). Doing and speaking in the office. In G. Fick & R. H. Sprague (Eds.), *Decision support systems: Issues and challenges* (Vol. 11, pp. 95-118). New York: Pergamon Press.

Goldkuhl, G. (1996). *Generic business frameworks and action modelling.* Paper presented at the International Working Conference on the Language-action perspective on Communication Modelling (LAP).

Goldkuhl, G. (1998). *The six phases of business processes - business communication and the exchange of value.* Paper presented at the International Telecommunications Society (ITS) Conference - Beyond Convergence: Communication into the Next Millennium, Stockholm, Sweden.

Goldkuhl, G. (2000). *The validity of validity claims: An Inquiry into communication rational-

ity.* Paper presented at the International Workshop on the Language-action perspective on Communication Modelling (LAP), Aachen, Germany.

Goldkuhl, G. (2005). *The many facets of communication – a socio-pragmatic conceptualisation for information systems studies.* Paper presented at the International Workshop on Communication and Coordination in Business Processes, Kiruna, Sweden.

Goldkuhl, G., & Ågerfalk, P. J. (2000). *Actability: A way to understand information systems pragmatics.* Paper presented at the International Workshop on Organisational Semiotics, Staffordshire University, Stafford, UK.

Goldkuhl, G., & Lind, M. (2002). *Continuing the dialogue: Generic layer for business interaction.* Paper presented at the International Working Conference on the Language-action perspective on Communication Modelling (LAP).

Goldkuhl, G., & Lyytinen, K. (1982). A language action view of information systems. In *Proceedings of the International Conference on Information Systems.*

Goldkuhl, G., & Lyytinen, K. (1984). Information system specification as rule reconstruction. In T. A. Bemelmans (Ed.), *Beyond productivity - information systems for organizational effectiveness* (pp. 79-95). New York: North-Holland.

Gottschalk, K., Graham, S., Kreger, H., & Snell, J. (2002). Introduction to Web services architecture. *IBM Systems Journal, 41*(2), 170-177.

Habermas, J. (1984). *The theory of communicative action: Reason and the rationalization of society* (T. McCarthy, Trans. Vol. 1). Boston: Beacon Press.

Henders, R. A. (1998). An evolutionary approach to application development with object technology. *IBM Systems Journal, 37*(2).

Hirschheim, R., Iivari, J., & Klein, H. K. (1997). A comparison of five alternative approaches to information systems development. *Australian Journal of Information Systems, 5*(1), 3-29.

Hirschheim, R., Klein, H. K., & Lyytinen, K. (1995). *Information systems development and data modeling: Conceptual and philosophical foundations.* UK: Cambridge University Press.

Hirschheim, R., Klein, H. K., & Lyytinen, K. (1996). Exploring the intellectual structures of information systems development: A social action theoretic analysis. *Accounting, Management and Information Technologies (AMIT), 6*(1/2), 1-64.

Introna, L. D. (1996). Commentary on the intellectual structures of information systems development by Hirschheim, Klein and Lyytinen. *Accounting, Management and Information Technologies (AMIT), 6*(1/2), 87-97.

Jain, H., & Zhao, H. (2003). *A conceptual model for comparative analysis of standardization of vertical industry languages.* Paper presented at the MIS Quartely Special Issue Workshop on: Standard Making - A Critical Research Frontier for Information systems.

Johannesson, P. (1995). Representation and communication - a speech act based approach to information systems design. *Information systems, 20*(4), 291-303.

Khalaf, R., Mukhi, N., & Weerawarana, S. (2003). *Service-oriented composition in BPEL4WS.* Paper presented at the International World Wide Web Conference (WWW), Budapest, Hungary.

Kimbrough, S. O., & Moore, S. A. (1997). On automated message processing in electronic commerce and work support systems: Speech act theory and expressive felicity. *ACM Transactions on Information systems (TOIS), 15*(4), 321-367.

Klein, H. K., & Huynh, M. Q. (2004). The critical social theory of Jürgen Habermas and its implications for IS research. In J. Mingers & L. Willcocks (Eds.), *Social theory and philosophy for*

information systems (pp. 157 - 237). West Sussex, England: John Wiley and Sons Ltd.

Labrou, Y., Finin, T., & Peng, Y. (1999). Agent communication languages: The current landscape. *IEEE Intelligent Systems and Their Applications, 14*(2), 45-52.

Lind, M., & Goldkuhl, G. (2001). Generic layered patterns for business modelling. In *Proceedings of the International Working Conference on the Language-action perspective on Communication Modelling (LAP).*

Ljungberg, J., & Holm, P. (1997). Speech acts on trial. In *Computers and design in context* (pp. 317-347). Cambridge, MA: MIT Press.

Lyytinen, K. (2004). *The struggle with the language in the IT -- why is LAP not in the mainstream?* Paper presented at the International Working Conference on the Language-action perspective on Communication Modelling (LAP), New Brunswick, NJ.

Lyytinen, K., Lehitnen, E., & Auramäki, E. (1987). SAMPO: A speech-act based office modelling approach. *ACM SIGOIS Bulletin, 8*(4), 11-23.

Medina-Mora, R., Winograd, T., Flores, R., & Flores, F. (1992). *The action workflow approach to workflow management technology.* Paper presented at the ACM conference on Computer-supported cooperative work, Toronto, Ontario, Canada.

Moore, S. A. (2001). A foundation for flexible automated electronic communication. *Information systems Research, 12*(1), 34-62.

Mulder, H., & Reijswoud, V. v. (2003). *Three ways of talking business and IT design: Similarities and differences between three approaches.* Paper presented at the The World Multi-Conference on Systemics, Cybernetics and Informatics, Orlando, USA.

Nwana, H. S. (1996). Software agents: An overview. *Knowledge Engineering Review, 11*(2), 205-244.

Oreskes, N., Shrader-Frechette, K., & Belitz, K. (1994). Verification, validation, and confirmation of numerical models in the earth sciences. *Science, 263*(5147), 641-646.

Papazoglou, M. P. (2003). Web services and business transactions. *World Wide Web, 6*(1), 49-91.

Papazoglou, M. P., & Georgakopoulos, D. (2003). Service oriented computing. *Communications of the ACM, 46*(10), 24-28.

Pitt, J., Guerin, F., & Stergiou, C. (2000). *Protocols and intentional specifications of multi-party agent conversions for brokerage and auctions.* Paper presented at the International Conference on Autonomous Agents, Barcelona, Spain.

Reijswoud, V. E. v., Mulder, H. B. F., & Dietz, J. L. G. (1999). Communicative action-based business process and information systems modelling with DEMO. *Information Systems Journal, 9*(2), 117-138.

Sacks, H. (1995). *Lectures on conversation.* Hoboken, NJ: Blackwell.

Schoop, M. (2001). An introduction to the language-action perspective. *ACM SIGGROUP Bulletin, 22*(2), 3-8.

Schoop, M. (2003). A language-action approach to electronic negotiations. In *Proceedings of the International Working Conference on the Language-action perspective on Communication Modelling (LAP).*

Schoop, M., Jertila, A., & List, T. (2003). Negoisst: A negotiation support system for electronic business-to-business negotiations in e-commerce. *Data & Knowledge Engineering, 47*(3), 371-401.

Schoop, M., & Kethers, S. (2000). *Habermas and Searle in University: Teaching the language-action perspective to undergraduates.* Paper presented at the International Workshop on the Language-action perspective on Communication Modelling (LAP).

Searle, J. R. (1969). *Speech acts: An essay in the philosophy of language.* UK: Cambridge University Press.

Searle, J. R., & Vanderveken, D. (1985). *Foundations of illocutionary logic.* UK: Cambridge University Press.

Stal, M. (2002). Web services: Beyond component-based computing. *Communications of the ACM, 45*(10), 71-76.

Stamper, R. (1996). Signs, information, norms and systems. In B. Holmqvist, P. B. Andersen, H. Klein, & R. Posner (Eds.), *Signs of work: Semiotics and information processing in organisations* (pp. 349-397). Berlin: Walter de Gruyter & Co.

Su, S. Y. W., Lam, H., Lee, M., Bai, S., & Shen, Z.-J. M. (2001). *An information infrastructure and e-services for supporting Internet-based scalable e-business enterprises.* Paper presented at the IEEE International Enterprise Distributed Object Computing Conference (EDOC).

Suchman, L. (1994). Do categories have politics? The language/action perspective reconsidered. *Computer Supported Cooperative Work (CSCW), 2*(3), 177-190.

Traum, D. R. (1999). Speech acts for dialogue agents. In M. Wooldridge & A. Rao (Eds.), *Foundations of rational agency* (Vol. 14, pp. 169-202). Kluwer Academic Publishers.

Tsai, W. T. (2005). *Service-oriented system engineering: A new paradigm.* Paper presented at the International Workshop on Service-Oriented System Engineering (SOSE).

Umapathy, K. (2007). *A study of language-action perspective as a theoretical framework for Web services.* Paper presented at the IEEE Congress on Services, Salt Lake City, Utah, USA.

Umapathy, K., & Purao, S. (2004). *Service oriented computing: An opportunity for the language-action perspective?* Paper presented at the International Working Conference on the Language-action perspective on Communication Modelling (LAP).

Umapathy, K., & Purao, S. (2007a). A theoretical investigation of the emerging standards for Web services. *Information Systems Frontiers, 9*(1), 119-134.

Umapathy, K., & Purao, S. (2007b). *Towards a theoretical foundation for Web services - the language-action perspective (LAP) approach.* Paper presented at the IEEE International Conference on Services Computing (SCC), Salt Lake City, Utah, USA.

Verharen, E., Dignum, F., & Weigand, H. (1996). A language/action perspective on cooperative information agents. In *Proceedings of the First International Workhshop on Communication Modeling.*

Waldt, D., & Drummond, R. (2005). *EBXML - the global standard for electronic business.* Retrieved February 19, 2005, from http://www.xml.org/xml/waldt_ebxml_global_standard_ebusiness.pdf

Weigand, H. (2003). The language/action perspective. *Data & Knowledge Engineering, 47*(3), 299-300.

Weigand, H. (2006). Two decades of the language-action perspective: Introduction. *Communications of the ACM, 49*(5), 44-46.

Weigand, H., & Hasselbring, W. (2001). An extensible business communication language. *International Journal of Cooperative Information systems, 10*(4), 423-441.

Weigand, H., & Heuvel, W.-J. v. d. (1998). *Meta-patterns for electronic commerce transactions based on FLBC.* Paper presented at the Hawaii International Conference on System Sciences (HICSS).

Weigand, H., Heuvel, W.-J. v. d., & Dignum, F. (1998). *Modelling electronic commerce transaction - a layered approach.* Paper presented at the International Workshop on the Language Action Perspective on Communication Modelling (LAP), Stockholm.

Winograd, T. (2006). Designing a new foundation for design. *Communications of the ACM, 49*(5), 71-74.

Winograd, T., & Flores, F. (1986). *Understanding computers and cognition: A new foundation for design.* Boston: Addison-Wesley Professional.

Wooldridge, M. (2002). *An introduction to multiagent systems.* Chichester, UK: John Wiley & Sons.

XML. (2006, September 29). *Extensible markup language (XML) 1.0.* Retrieved February 2, 2007, from http://www.w3.org/TR/REC-xml/

Yetim, F. (2002). *Designing communication action patterns for global communication and cooperation: A discourse ethical approach.* Paper presented at the European Conference on Information systems (ECIS), Information systems and the Future of the Digital Economy, Gdansk, Poland.

Yetim, F., & Bieber, M. P. (2003). *Towards a language/action theoretic approach to relationship analysis.* Paper presented at the European Conference on Information systems (ECIS), Naples, Italy.

KEY TERMS AND DEFINITIONS

Communicative Action: Actors engage in discussion to reach understanding and coordinate their activities to achieve their common goal.

Language-Action Perspective (LAP): Linguistic and communicative theories based alternative approach to design and analyze information systems.

LAP Approach: An approach for designing and analyzing information systems with a pre-supposition that role of information systems is to support communication among people to help them perform actions together.

Service Computing: A computing paradigm to develop software applications as "services", which are autonomous, platform-independent computational entities which can be combined in numerous ways to achieve business goals.

Speech Act: A basic unit of communication that expresses intention of the speaker.

Speech Act Pattern: Set of speech acts arranged in sequence to represent a communication or action performed.

Web Services: A software system that provides set of standards to support communication and coordination among services over a network, such as Internet, to achieve their goals.

Chapter VIII
Research Directions on Incorporating Work System Method Ideas in Systems Analysis and Design

Ram B. Misra
Montclair State University, USA

Doncho Petkov
Eastern Connecticut State University, USA

Olga Petkova
Central Connecticut State University, USA

ABSTRACT

In this chapter, the authors analyze recent developments linking design science to systems analysis and design research and the growing area of the work system method proposed by Steven Alter. As a result, possible directions in a research agenda related to the incorporation of work system method ideas in systems analysis and design are provided. These follow the conceptual framework for IS research developed in 2004 by Hevner, March, Park and Ram.

INTRODUCTION

Due to the multi-disciplinary nature of the information systems (IS) field, there has been a long debate (e.g. see Lee, 2000, Orlikowski and Iacono, 2001, Hirschheim and Klein, 2003) about its core knowledge and scope. Hirschheim and Klein (2003) present a multidimensional analysis of the state of the IS discipline. Their chapter points at the richness of information systems development as a field for exploration by IS researchers. Related issues are explored in Iivari, Hirschheim and Klein (2004). Lee (2000) suggested the idea of practicing **design science** as a potential direction for revival of the IS discipline. Hevner et al (2004) presented seminal directions for work in design science in IS research. These lead subsequently to an increased interest in research in **Systems Analysis and Design** (SA&D) (see Bajaj et al., 2005; Iivari et al., 2005; Harris et al., 2006). The importance of Systems Analysis and Design for any program of study in information systems is well summarized by Harris et al. (2006:242). Among the most important aspects of the relevance of SA&D they list the development of analytical and problem solving skills and the development and implementation of information systems (see Harris et al., 2006).

The growing interest in SA&D was evolving in parallel with a renewed interest in the applicability of systems thinking to Information Systems as a discipline (see Alter, 1999, Alter, 2004; Mora et al., 2007, Mora et al., 2008). Throughout these developments the ideas of Steven Alter on the **work system method** played persistently an important role (e.g. see Alter and Browne, 2005, Alter, 2006c). The work system method has emerged over the last decade as a theory for understanding the role of information systems in organizations and is gaining popularity among IS researchers (see Alter, 2006c; Korpela et al., 2004; Siau et al., 2004; Petkov and Petkova, 2008). In spite of that, we feel that there is a need for more work on the diffusion of work system method ideas in Systems Analysis and Design. This is the motivation for the work presented here.

We suggeste here possible research directions for incorporating work system method related ideas in Systems Analysis and Design. These are an extension of the research by Alter and Browne (2005) and Alter (2006c) and they are in line with the recent revival of research in that area as advocated in Bajaj et al (2005). The chapter proceeds with an overview of the work system

method (WSM) and related research, a review of recent work in systems analysis and design as well as design science, which are followed by the proposed directions for future work on applying WSM in SA&D followed by a conclusion.

THE WORK SYSTEM METHOD AND RELATED RESEARCH

The work system method is one of the two existing theoretical frameworks to support teaching of information systems at present. The other approach to introduce the IS field (used predominantly with MBA students) is the IS Interaction Model which focuses on the relationships between IS, their environment and the organization (see Silver et al. (1995). The Work System Method (Alter, 2006c), however, can be used both for IS teaching and research. That distinguishes it from the Interaction Model and makes it suitable for exploring its role in systems analysis. The work system method is an approach for understanding and analyzing systems in organizations including Information Systems (Alter, 2002). Petkov and Petkova (2008) published the results from a controlled experiment showing that it helped students in an introductory IS course to understand better an IS implementation problem.

The Work System Method

The work system method provides a rigorous but non-technical approach to any manager or business professional to visualize and analyze systems related problems and opportunities (Alter, 2006a). A very detailed justification for the work system method and how to apply it to define a work system, analyze it, formulate recommendations for improvement and guide its evolution is presented in Alter (2006c). The work system method (Alter, 2006c) has two major components: the work system framework, representing a static description of the work system and the work system life cycle, focusing on the dynamics of a work system. Detailed definitions of the components of the work system framework are presented in Alter (2002a) and Alter (2006c). The interrelationships between the various elements of a work system are useful for generating an analysis of a specific business problem.

Both the **work system framework** (the static view of a work system) and the **work system life cycle** (the dynamic view how a current or proposed system evolves over time) have a complementary role (see Alter (2002a, 2006c). Table 1 defines several basic terms underlying the work system method, including the notion of work system. The latter does not necessarily include an information system and aims to describe how work is performed. Further elaboration on important definitions of related concepts is presented in Alter (2002a, 2006b).

The **work system framework** consists of 9 elements, 4 internal and 5 external. The four *internal elements*, considered part of the work system, include work items, processes to accomplish those work items, participants (direct and indirect both) to execute processes to perform those work items, technology needed to enable completion of processes and hence work items, and information or knowledge base needed. The five *external elements*, considered not part of

the work system yet are important for its functioning, include strategy (both business and IS/IT), infrastructure needed to support the work system, environmental factors, product/services, and customers (internal, work system users and external, end customers).

The Work System Method and IS Research

Information systems constitute a special case of work systems in which the business processes performed and the products and services produced are devoted to information (Alter, 2002a:95). Information systems exist to support other work systems and there could be some overlap with them. Various possible relationships between an IS and a work system are described in Alter (2002:96). Guidelines for analyzing work systems are presented in Alter (2002, 2006c). Recently Alter extended his approach to the area of service oriented organizations (see Alter, 2007b).

Alter (2006c) stresses that past dominance of single ideas like Total Quality Management and Business Process Reengineering are not sufficient to influence profoundly the IS field. The WSM is more broadly applicable than techniques "designed to specify detailed software requirements and is designed to be more prescriptive and

Table 1. Some basic terms underlying the work system method (Adapted after Alter, 2002 and Petkov and Petkova, 2008)

Basic Term	Definition
Work system	A view of work as occurring through a purposeful system
Work system framework	Model for organizing an initial understanding of how a particular work system operates and what it accomplishes.
Organization	Multiple work systems coordinated to accomplish goals that these work systems cannot accomplish individually
Static view	How a work system operates, based on a particular configuration
Dynamic view	How a work system's configuration evolves over time
Work system life cycle	Process through which a specific work system is created and changes over time through planned and unplanned changes.

more powerful than domain-independent systems analysis methods such as soft system methodology" (Alter, 2002a). We may note that making comparisons between the work system method and soft systems methodology (see Checkland, 1999) requires a broader investigation of their philosophical assumptions and scope which is beyond the scope of this chapter.

The systemic nature of the work system method and its applicability to understanding business and IS problems is its most distinctive and important characteristics (Petkov and Petkova, 2008). Though the work system method has a relatively short history and a small but growing group of followers for now, the multifaceted scale of Alter's work, bringing together systems ideas with methods for deeper understanding of work systems and IS, has strong appeal. Petkov et al. (2008) have concluded that the WSM could be used to *change the attitudes of clients in managerial and operational user roles in combination with* other relevant methods for the purpose of developing better understanding of organizational problems and to improve the communication between clients and software developers.

The practical value of the WSM emerges more strongly through the introduction in its most recent version in Alter (2006c) of three problem solving steps:

- **SP—Identify the system and problems:** Identify the work system that has the problems that launched the analysis. The system's size and scope depend on the purpose of the analysis.
- **AP—Analyze the system and identify possibilities:** Understand current issues and find possibilities for improving the work system.
- **RJ—Recommend and justify changes:** Specify proposed changes and check the recommendation.

Within each step there are three levels of detail in which the issues are explored: at level one takes place a rough definition, at level two are explored a number of specific questions for each step providing additional information and perspectives on the problem situation while at level 3 are employed a number of diverse techniques and any other relevant data that can provide deeper understanding of the problem situation.

Alter's proposal for work systems to replace the IT artifact as the focus of the IS discipline is an interesting innovative idea that has been considered to a degree already by others (see Alter, 2003; Jasperson et al., 2005; and Alter, 2006b). Alter (2002b) considers the four elements of an IT artifact that include information technology, the tasks, task structure, and task context within which it is used and shows "that the term IT artifact seems to encompass almost anything IT touches or affects directly, and is too unclear to serve as a basic concept for defining the IS field. IT artifact verges on being a synonym for the clearer term *IT-reliant work system*" (Alter, 2002b:496). Since the nature of the IT artifact is a central issue in IS research, it indirectly affects possible future work on the WSM and Systems Analysis and Design.

Most of the work related to the work system method has been related to the potential application of its concepts (e.g. see Siau et al., 2004, Casey and Brugha, 2005 and others). There have been very few attempts for a critical analysis of the WSM (see Korpela et al., 2004) or for linking it to other methods like the "work practice approach" (see Petersson, 2005).

The WSM was explored as a teaching tool only by a few authors discussed briefly in Alter (2006c). Ramiller (2005) is one of the few currently published sources on applying WSM ideas. It describes the use of the work system concept for understanding the notion of business processes in an undergraduate IS course. A few cases are discussed in Alter (2006a). An elaborate detailed case study of WSM application can be found in Cox et al. (2002). Alter (2006c) provides evidence that work system ideas provide support for better understanding of business and systems problems when used with masters students who usually have a broader IT background (see Alter, 2006c). A detailed discussion of pitfalls in analyzing systems in organizations based on investigating 200 master's projects is presented in Alter (2006b). Petkov and Petkova (2008) explored the role of the work system framework for improvement of student understanding of an IT related work system problem in an introductory business course on IS. They measured student learning through assessment of a team project and concluded that the Work System Framework has a positive impact on student understanding of business situation involving a complex IS problem. To the best of our knowledge no publication addresses currently all issues related to how the work system method can be applied in the teaching of systems analysis and design and that is an open area for research.

RECENT IDEAS IN DESIGN SCIENCE AND SYSTEMS ANALYSIS AND DESIGN

The renewal of interest in Systems Analysis and Design is related to a considerable degree to the publication of Hevner et al (2004) - a fundamental contribution to IS research that aimed to restore the balance between the two inseparable areas of IS research: behavioral research and design science research. Hevner et al (2004) raised a number of theoretical and practical aspects of stimulating research in design science, one of the two fundamental paradigms in IS research. They provide a conceptual model of IS research that integrates important considerations on relevance and rigor. At the same time they show the complementary role of design science and behavioral science approaches in IS research. They assert the role of design science within the

dual understanding of design as a process and as an artifact. According to Hevner et al. (2004:79) behavioral science deals with the development and justification of theories that explain or predict the phenomena related to the identified business need while design science addresses research through the building and evaluation of artifacts that meet the business need. They define further that the knowledge base in their model provides the raw materials from and through which IS research is accomplished.

The aspects of design science research discussed by Hevner et al (2004) had a direct impact on the growing interest in Systems Analysis and Design teaching and research (see Bajaj et al., 2005 and Iivari et al., 2005). Alter and Browne (2005) were among the first to provide their contribution to the debate on the need for more research in SA&D. They note that existing definitions of SA&D like the one by Iivari et al. (2005) focus on the role of SA&D in the early stages of software development. Alter and Browne (2005) provide a much broader view of Systems Analysis and Design that captures better the diverse extent of the change in work practices by a particular activity requiring SA&D and the range of focus from technical to social aspects of the project. They define as a result six contexts of distinct SA&D situations:

- SA&D for SW/HW maintenance and bug fixes;
- SA&D for SW/HW upgrades involving work practices;
- SA&D for monitoring and patching work practices via process improvement and Six Sigma;
- SA&D for creation or major modification of IT-enabled work systems involving creation of new application software;
- A&D for creation or major modification of IT-enabled work systems involving configuration and installation of commercial application software;

- SA&D for organizational change and reengineering.

Alter and Browne (2005) focus also on two Information Systems development Performance Processes (following Iivari, Hirschheim and Klein, 2004): organizational alignment and requirements construction. Thus they focus on areas that are closely related to the core of Information Systems as a discipline, leaving out aspects of project management and software design as they are perceived to be closer to software engineering. As a result of the interweaving of the work system method with numerous other existing approaches to organizational alignment and requirements construction they provide a broad and systematic range of research issues in SA&D (see Alter and Browne, 2005).

Bajaj et al (2005) outline the characteristics of the gap between teaching and research in systems analysis and design and provide possible factors that contribute to that. Then they proceed to discuss how the conceptual model of IS research proposed by Hevner et al (2004) applies to Systems Analysis and Design. According to them:

SA&D touches on several areas of the IS research framework….. In the knowledge base section, SA&D contributes by providing the models used to represent requirements and systems, and the methodologies used to develop systems drawing from several theories such as cognitive theories, frameworks…and ontologies …. In the IS Research Section, the framework identifies artifacts as a product of IS research, where artifacts can range from initial system requirements, to formal representations of systems, and to actual software. SA&D feeds the knowledge base via the creation of several IS artifacts. SA&D research can employ various research strategies such as laboratory experiments, field study, case study, action research, simulation, and analytical methods. SA&D also touches the Environment section given that SA&D research can be done in an organizational

environment and incorporates the effects of personal or organizational characteristics. (Bajaj et al. (2005:481).

We agree fully with the research directions on using the work System Method provided by Alter and Browne (2005). At the same time we feel that it is possible to formulate further directions for research on the Work System Method and SA&D by using as an organizing framework along the ideas of Hevner et al (2004) and Bajaj et al (2005 as shown in the next section.

POSSIBLE FUTURE RESEARCH DIRECTIONS INCORPORATING WORK SYSTEM THEORY IN SYSTEMS ANALYSIS AND DESIGN

Our suggestions are framed following the conceptual model for IS research and design science research according to Hevner et al (2004) and following some ideas in Bajaj et al. (2005).

On SA&D and the WSM as Part of the Knowledge Base of IS Research

Further work is needed *on identification of the philosophical base* of the Work System Method since currently very little is known about it apart from a certain link between it and pragmatism as suggested by Alter (2007) and Alter (2006c). Another possible direction for investigation is *whether the WSM can embrace more fully systems concepts* (see Bertalanffy, 1962). According to Alter (2007), evaluation of WSM in relation to general systems theory is all the more difficult because WSM was not developed as an application of general systems theory but as a set of ideas and tools that business professionals can use when trying to understand and analyze systems from a business viewpoint. Alter (2007) provides as an answer to this question a challenging reply in the form of "weak maybe". According to us there is a scope for further work on showing how the *systems concepts that currently are incorporated in the WSM provide practical benefits to IS researchers* along some of the directions suggested in Alter (2004) that distinguish the role of the WSM in the knowledge base of Information Systems as a discipline.

Alter (2006c) proposes Sysperanto as an **ontology** in applying the work system method. It is an open issue to *investigate both the theoretical and practical value of Sysperanto compared to other ontologies suggested in the IS research literature* like Wand and Weber (2002) and others.

The work system concept is used also in the socio-technical systems and in other strands of IS research. To the best of our knowledge there is *a need for an analysis of any differences between the way how the notion of "work system" is used by Alter and those researchers working in other areas of IS or between notions like work system and "human activity system" (see Checkland, 1999) or purposeful systems* as used in other systems thinking sources.

Another fundamental issue that deserves a broader discussion is *whether the work system should replace the **IT artifact*** as the focus of IS research as is argued by Alter (2002b) and Alter (2003). The finer details on how that notion is used require further discussion possibly as demonstrated by the debate in Jasperson et al (2005) and Alter (2006a).

A recent direction in IS research is associated with service oriented systems (Alter, 2008) provides an interesting perspective on service system fundamentals and his ideas on how the work system framework, the work system snapshot and the service value chain framework can be applied to service system management can *stimulate comparative analysis with other frameworks explaining service systems and practical implementation case studies on the relevance of the service value chain framework.*

On the Interplay of SA&D and the WSM as Part of IS Research in the Conceptual Model for Design Science Research

The main artifacts that the work system method provides to IS research are the work system framework and the **work system life cycle**. We have mentioned the limited current research on the applicability of work system ideas in Information Systems Research and teaching like the cases described by Ramiller (2005) and Alter (2006b) or the field experiment discussed in Petkov and Petkova (2008). There is a *need to provide evidence from further case studies, laboratory experiments and field experiments on the applicability of the WSM in SA&D*. This requires changes in the way how SA&D is taught at undergraduate level, in postgraduate courses and in professional development courses. There is a need to *investigate how the WSM is taught at universities and to disseminate the experience with it to a wider audience of IS educators through conference and journal papers* along similar concerns about SA&D research in general as found in Bajaj et al. (2005).

The utility of the main artifacts of the WSM, mentioned above, to practicing information systems developers with respect to improving their understanding of the work system and the systems analysis tasks is an open issue. It is interesting to explore their potential in providing a balance between agility and discipline in IS development (see Boehm and Turner, 2004), along the suggested research directions in Bajaj et al. (2005).

On SA&D and the WSM and Their Role for Analyzing the IS Environment

Alter (2003; 2006c) points that the practical reasons for developing the work system ideas were associated with the needs to provide clients with a better way to express their understanding of their work environment and IS requirements. Alter (2006b) has demonstrated the pitfalls associated with poor expression of those issues. Alter and Browne (2005) show how the WSM can be applied for investigating the IS environment which they justify with many published accounts of under-performing information systems. As is indicated in Iivari et al. (2005) and Bajaj et al (2005), the investigation of people, organizations and technologies are central to SA&D. Hence we may conclude that *more analytical and case study work on the integration of the WSM in SA&D for the analysis of the environment of information systems development may contribute to higher rate of IS success.*

CONCLUSION

We set out to identify possible research directions for incorporating work system method (see Alter, 2002a) in systems analysis and design. These research directions are further extensions to what has been previously proposed by Alter and Browne (2005) and Alter (2006c), and are along the lines recommended by Bajaj et al (2005). Our suggestions are framed following the conceptual model for IS research and design science research defined in Hevner et al (2004) and used in Bajaj et al. (2005). We identify the following possible areas of research:

- Identification of the philosophical base of the Work System Method.
- Investigation into whether the WSM can embrace more fully systems concepts.
- Investigate both the theoretical and practical value of Sysperanto compared to other ontologies suggested in the IS research literature.
- Analysis of any differences between the way how "work system" is used by Alter and those researchers working in other areas of IS or between notions like work system and "human activity system".
- Developing a broader discussion on whether the work system should replace the IT artifact as the focus of IS research as argued by Alter (2002b), Alter (2003).
- Investigation into the applicability of WSM for service systems.
- Provide evidence from case studies, laboratory experiments and field experiments on the applicability of the WSM in SA&D.
- Establish the utility of the main artifacts of the WSM mentioned above to practicing information systems developers with respect to improving their understanding of the work system and the systems analysis tasks. Further issues relate to their potential in providing a balance between agility and discipline in IS development, along the suggested SA&D research directions in Bajaj et al. (2005).

We would like to underline that the Work System Method (Alter, 2006c) is an important theoretical development that emerged within the IS discipline. The evidence from the research related to it so far indicates its potential to contribute both to relevance and rigor in IS research. We hope that our suggestions may facilitate further theoretical and practical work on using the Work System Method in Systems Analysis and Design.

REFERENCES

Alter, S. (2002a). The work systems model and its role for understanding information systems and information systems research, *Communications of the Association for Information Systems, 9,* 90-104.

Alter, S. (2002b). Sidestepping the IT artifact, scrapping the IS silo and laying claim to "systems in organizations". *Communications of the Association for Information Systems, 12,* 494-526.

Alter, S. (2003). 18 reasons why IT-reliant work systems should replace 'the IT artifact' as the core subject matter of the IS field, *Communications of the Association for Information Systems, 12*(23), 365-394.

Alter, S. (2004). Desperately seeking systems thinking in the information systems discipline, In *Proceedings of the Twenty Fifth ICIS Conference (pp.* 757-769).

Alter, S., & Browne, G. (2005). A broad view of systems analysis and design: Implications for research. *Communications of the Association for Information Systems, 16*(50), 981-999.

Alter, S. (2006a). Work systems and IT artifacts: Does the definition matter? *Communications of the Association for Information Systems, 17*(14), 299-313.

Alter, S. (2006b). Pitfalls in analyzing systems in organizations. *Journal of Information Systems Education, 17*(3), 295-303

Alter, S. (2006c). *The work system method: Connecting people, processes, and IT for business results.* Larkspur, CA: Work System Press.

Alter, S. (2007). Could the work system method embrace systems concepts more fully? *Information Resource Management Journal, 20*(2), 33-43.

Alter, S. (2008). Service system fundamentals: Work system, value chain, and life cycle. *IBM systems journal, 47*(1).

Bajaj, A., Batra, D., Hevner, A., Parsons, J., & Siau, K. (2005). Systems analysis and design: Should we be researching what we teach? *Communications of the AIS, 15*, 478-493.

Bertalanffy, L. V. (1962). General system theory - a critical review. *General Systems, 7*, 1-20.

Boehm, B., & Turner R. (2004). *Balancing agility and discipline - a guide for the perplexed.* Boston: Addison –Wesley.

Casey, D., & Brugha, C. (2005). From fighting fires to building bridges: The role of metaphor in systems requirements. In *Proceedings of the International Professional Communication Conference, 2005. IPCC 2005.*

Checkland, P. (1999). *Systems thinking, systems practice.* Chichester, UK: Wiley.

Cox, S., Dulfer, R., Han, D., Ruiz ,U., & Alter, S. (2002). TDG engineering: Do we need really another upgrade? *Communications of the Association for Information Systems, 8*, 232-250

Harris A. L, Lang, M., Oates B., & Siau, K. (2006). Systems analysis & design: An essential part of IS education, *Journal of Information Systems Education,17*(3), 241-248.

Hevner, A. R., March, S. T., Park, J., & Ram, S. (2004). Design science in information systems research. *MIS Quarterly, 28*(1), 75-105.

Hirschheim, R. & Klein, H. K. (2003). Crisis in the IS field? A critical reflection on the state of the discipline. *Journal of the Association of Information Systems, 4*(5), 237-293.

Iivari, J., Hirschheim, R. & Klein, H. (2004). Towards a distinctive body of knowledge for information systems experts: Coding ISD process knowledge in two IS journals. *Information Systems Journal, 14*, 313-342.

Iivari, J., Parsons, J., & Hevner, A. R. (2005). Research in information systems analysis and design: introduction to the special theme papers. *Communications of the AIS, 16*, 810-813.

Jasperson, J., Carter, P. E., & Zmud, R. W. (2005). A comprehensive conceptualization of post-adoptive behaviors associated with information technology enabled work systems,*MIS Quarterly, 29*(3), 525-557.

Korpela, M., Mursu, A., Soriyan, A., Eerola, A., Häkkinen, H., & Toivanen, M. (2004). Information systems research and development by activity analysis and development: Dead horse or the next wave? In B. Kaplan, D. P. Truex III, D. Wastell, A. T. Wood-Harper, J. I. DeGross (Eds.), *Information systems research. Relevant theory and informed practice* (pp. 453-471). Boston: Kluwer Academic Publishers.

Lee, A. (2000). Systems thinking, design science, and paradigms: Heeding three lessons from the past to resolve three dilemmas in the present to direct a trajectory for future research in the information systems field. *Keynote Address at the 11th International Conference on Information Management,* Taiwan. Retrieved from, http://www.people.vcu.edu/aslee/ICIM-keynote-2000

Mora, M., Gelman, O., Forgionne, G., Petkov D., & Cano, J. (2007). Integrating the fragmented pieces in IS research paradigms and frameworks – a systems approach. *Information Resource Management Journal, 20*(2), 1-22.

Mora, M., Gelman, O., Frank, M., Paradice, D., Cervantes, F., & Forgionne, G. A. (2008). Towards an interdisciplinary engineering and management of complex IT intensive organizational systems: A systems view. *International Journal on Information Technologies and the Systems Approach, 1*(1), 1-24.

Orlikowski, W. J., & Iacono, C. S. (2001). Research commentary: Desperately seeking the "IT" in IT research - a call to theorizing the IT artifact. *Information Systems Research, 12*(2), 121-134.

Petersson, J (2005). Aren't the fundamental concepts of work systems about actions? In *Proceedings of the Fifth Conference for the Promotion of Research in IT at New Universities and University Colleges in Sweden,* Borlänge.

Petkov, D., Edgar-Nevill, D., Madachy, R., & O'Connor, R. (2008), Information systems, software engineering and systems thinking – challenges and opportunities. *International Journal on Information Technologies and the Systems Approach, 1*(1), 62-78.

Petkov, D., & Petkova, O. (2008). The work system model as a tool for understanding the problem in an introductory IS project. *Information Systems Education Journal, 6*(21).

Ramiller, N. C. (2005). Animating the concept of business process in the core course in information systems. *Journal of Informatics Education Research, 3*(2).

Siau, K., Sheng, H., & Nah, F. (2004). The value of mobile commerce to customers, In *Proceedings of the Pre ICIS SIGCHI Symposium.*

Silver, M., Markus, M. L., & Beath, C. (1995). The information technology interaction model: A foundation for the MBA core course. *MIS Quarterly, 19*(3), 361-390.

Wand, Y., & Weber, R. (2002). Research commentary: Information systems and conceptual modeling – a research agenda. *Information Systems Research, 13*(4), 363-376.

KEY TERMS AND DEFINITIONS

Systems Analysis and Design: The approach to the development of information systems that encompasses the first four phases of the systems development cycle (SDLC): Planning, Analysis, Design and Implementation (Harris et al., 2006)

The Work System Method: Provides a rigorous but non-technical approach to any manager or business professional to visualize and analyze systems related problems and opportunities (Alter, 2006a).

Chapter IX
The Value of Flexibility

Rodrigo Castelo
OutSystems, Portugal

Miguel Mira da Silva
Instituto Superior Técnico, Portugal

ABSTRACT

Though IT investments are risky by nature, most of the traditional investment valuation models do not have risk in account, leading to erroneous choices. This chapter bases itself in the dogma that flexibility is the key to handle the uncertainty and risk of the future, and therefore is also a philosophy that must be in the very foundations of IT investments, since IT is the basic foundation of so many businesses. How do we value a risky IT investment is the underlying subject of this chapter. Having the previous dogma as a basis, the authors state that flexibility is a vaccine against risk. As such, this flexibility must have a value. The problem they attempt to solve in this chapter is the quantification of such value. To achieve this goal, the authors propose a real options-based framework to value IT investments, having risk in account.

INTRODUCTION

The pure Taylorism saw its end on October 24, 1929 – the Black Thursday – when the Wall Street Stock Market crashed yet again, this time with violence (Henin, 1986).

Years later, in the 80's, Michael Porter popularized the ideas of the value chain, focused on maximizing value creation and minimizing costs (Porter, 1985) which, in the end, were exactly the same goals of Taylor.

As an example, the Ford Motor Company applied Taylor's methodology and was able to implement a Just-In-Time production, so called "Dock to Factory Floor" since it demanded an almost inexistent warehouse stock.

Now what is wrong with Taylorism or Porter's value chain? Nothing. The problem is not with the models, but rather on how Ford and others applied them. Among other problems, Ford failed to create a value chain starting at the customer and ending at the suppliers, culminating in a super production crisis.

Japan understood this chain issue back in the 50's, and met an astonishing growth in the 60's, known as the Japanese Miracle.

As an example, by the middle of the past century, the Toyota Motor Company implemented a new methodology for building cars also with smaller economic lot sizes but, more important, targeted for flexible factories capable of shifting production in a matter of days.

More recently, we have other success examples, such as Zara, which was able to create a flexible production, parameterized by its costumers' demand, collected on a daily basis.

As odd it might seem, usually only marketing disciplines have this market or customer-oriented value chain as a basic pillar. Only with this view, a competitive advantage can be sustained.

Even odder, we are constantly assisting a dummy first mover's dictatorship. For instance, take the example of the third generation (3G) mobile communications. As soon as the first communications operator introduced 3G services, all the others followed, investing heavily on the infrastructure. However, there is still no market demand for 3G (Hearts, 2002; 3G.co.uk., 2004).

Bottom line, companies need to be flexible to provide customers with products that meet their ever changing needs. Unfortunately, mankind doesn't deal well with flexibility, or it wouldn't have only started accentuating its evolution 10,000 years ago, when it got sedentary, and thus more stable, in Neolithic.

Context

In the context of the Information Technology (IT) world, we have now been creating applications for over 50 years.

In that time, we have evolved our processes and tools, creating a broad range of methodologies, nevertheless almost all of them seem to have high rates of failure.

In 1995, the Standish Group published a survey, called "The Chaos Report", showing that, on average, only *16%* of the IT projects succeeded, ending on budget, on time, and with all the requirements implemented. If we only account for large companies, this rate dropped to *9%*.

One might think that from 1995 to nowadays some evolution was achieved, and it was. The Standish Group updated this report on 2001, publishing the "Extreme CHAOS Report". This latter report showed that, on average, *28%* of the projects were then succeeding. Therefore, in 6 years, with all the great advances in processes and tools, we were not even able to double the success rate of IT projects.

When compared to other engineering fields, IT won't even qualify as a wannabe. For instance, the first documented civil engineer dates from 2550 BC and contains the schemas for the Imhotep stepped pyramid of King Zoser, located at Saqqarah, which still stands today (Penwell et al., 1995). The Unified Modeling Language (UML) development, if you like, only started in the 90's.

This is why it is so tempting to compare IT with civil engineering and why we hear it so often. Nonetheless, is quite an erroneously comparison. Imagine that when building a bridge, the stakeholders change, on a daily basis, the number of cars the bridge must support, or even the river it must be built on. No bridge will come on budget and on time under such scenario.

However, even if the comparison with civil engineering is wrong, this is no excuse for the ever-repeating failures of IT projects. If it is possible to have flexible automobile or cloths productions, then it must also be possible to have a flexible software production.

When an IT project starts, there is often an unclear vision of the requirements the system must support, an internal resistance to change, or even no top management support. Therefore, it might look that IT projects become mainly sociological projects, and that the barriers to their success tend to be non-technological. This awareness is also stated in the Standish Group reports in which we can see that successful projects have clear statement of requirements, high rates of user involvement, and top management support. In contrast, failing projects don't have this microenvironment. Nevertheless, most important, the reports showed that failed projects had incomplete and constantly changing requirements.

There it is again, the inability to properly handle flexibility. If when building a bridge it would be there for several years without the need for changes, when building Information Systems (IS) this is not true. Companies are facing an ever-increasing strategic change pace. New demands, new competitors, new business models, new rising super powers, new frontiers, new regulations, new problems, new solutions… ISs are the basic tools companies have to handle their businesses, therefore such tools must keep up with the business change pace; they must be flexible both in development and in production time.

Flexibility exists to handle risk. A risky business must be flexible enough for the stakeholders to abandon it or shift in a different direction, otherwise it may become a dead end. When building ISs for companies pressured to change in some way, we must have in account it is not possible to have a clear definition of the requirements upfront. Apart from core systems, the requirements for today will most certainly not be similar in a month, and will for sure be completely different in a year.

This is one of the reasons why IT projects are risky. Technologies that ignore this fact will only be able to survive if they are used for building core systems or pre-doomed projects.

Ultimately, technologies that can handle risk by being flexible enough to deal with constant changes in already incomplete requirements have more value than others, as only this way they can provide any return on the IT investments. However, this will only be a better starting point, since most of the previously cited problems are non-technological.

Problem

As explained, nowadays software projects are high risky investments (Standish Group, 1995; Standish Group, 2001). Therefore, it becomes vital to quantify this risk in order to be able to value the investments. However, this quantification is hard to perform since it enters the futurology realms. As such, how do we handle risk in IT investments?

The answer to this question was already given: we must accept and embrace the uncertainty of the future. Rather than keep thinking in all the possible scenarios and respective needs, which ultimately only leads to an increasing delay in solving the present needs, we should try to be flexible enough to handle the upcoming scenarios while addressing yesterday's needs.

This chapter bases itself in the dogma that flexibility is the key to handle the uncertainty and risk of the future, and therefore is also a philosophy that must be in the very foundations of IT investments, since IT is the basic foundation of so many businesses.

However, most of the traditional investment valuation models do not have risk in account, leading to erroneous choices. Most often, when comparing different technologies to implement a given project, managers have the tendency to choose the ones with smaller upfront costs. Unfortunately, these kick-off costs are just the tip of a huge iceberg. Then how do we value a risky IT investment?

This latter question is the subject of this chapter. Having the previous dogma as a basis, we state that flexibility is a vaccine against risk. Therefore, this flexibility must have a value. The quantification of this value is the problem we will address.

BACKGROUND

Traditional Valuation Models

For several reasons, the measurement of the IT investments value has been increasing dramatically in the past few years. From 2000 to 2001, the importance of this measurement increased for *80%* of the organizations (Hayes, 2001).

Typically, pre implementation measurements are used to compare different alternatives (King et al., 1978) and post implementation measurements are used to cut costs and close projects (Kumar, 1990).

Investment Analysis

Nowadays, the value of IT investments is mainly based on Cost-Benefit Analysis (CBA) (Dupuit, 1844; Marshall, 1920) mingled with the Time Value of Money (TVM) formula (Goetzmann, 2003) with some Weighted Discount Rate (WDR), such as the Interest Rate (IR) or the organization's Weighted Average Cost of Capital (WACC), that feed a Net Present Value (NPV) formula. See Box 1.

However, the value of an investment means nothing by itself, since it must be relativized to the environment where it occurs. As such, companies usually value IT investments by calculating the Return on Investment (ROI), which is the ratio of the gained value compared to a given basis, such as the value of a system before the new IT investment.

$$return\ on\ investment_{arithmetic} = \frac{final\ value - basis\ value}{basis\ value}$$

$$return\ on\ investment_{\log arithmic} = ln\left(\frac{final\ value}{basis\ value}\right)$$

As investing in something includes the cost of not investing on something else, companies may also value the investment by comparing it with the average organization's investment, thus obtaining the Economic Value Added (EVA) (Magretta et al., 2002). See Box 2.

Costs and Benefits

In contrast to the general CBA theory, which is based on strongly accepted principles, the elicitation of the costs and benefits and their valuation is by itself an area of research.

In 1992, DeLone and McLean produced an extensive taxonomy to measure the IT effective-

Box 1.

$$CBA\ value = \sum_i benefit_i - \sum_j cost_j$$

$$future\ value = p\,resent\ value\ (1 + weighted\ discount\ rate)^{years}$$

$$net\ present\ value = \sum_i benefit\ present\ value_i - \sum_j cost\ present\ value_j =$$

$$= \sum_i \frac{benefit\ future\ value_i}{(1 + weighted\ discount\ rate)^{years_i}} - \sum_j \frac{cost\ future\ value_j}{(1 + weighted\ discount\ rate)^{years_j}}$$

Box 2.

$$economic\ value\ added =$$
$$= investment\ profits - (weighted\ discount\ rate\ x\ investment\ \cos ts) =$$
$$= \sum_i benefit_i - weighted\ discount\ rate \sum_j cost_j$$

ness, which can be used as a basis list of costs and benefits, since the effectiveness of a system comes from its benefits. DeLone and McLean's research was later extended by Scott (1995) to even include Structural Equation Models (SEM), such as the Multiple Indicator Multiple Cause (MIMIC) model that can correlate a set of indicators and causes, e.g. costs and benefits, with one given dependent variable, e.g. the IT investment value.

Nowadays, for the purpose of eliciting all the costs and benefits of an IT investment, there are, among others, the Total Costs of Ownership (TCO) and the Total Benefits of Ownership (TBO) approaches. The TCO includes all the system costs and respective values, for instance, its licensing costs and maintenance costs (Ellram, 1993). Conversely, the TBO is a list of all the benefits and respective values of a given IT system, for instance, its adoption rate and usability.

However, the elicitation of the costs and benefits and their valuation is a large area of research, and no simple solution has yet been presented. The time dependency, the need to prove the correlation between the selected costs and benefits and the resulting IT investment value, and finally the valuation of the costs and benefits, all increase the complexity of the models. Furthermore, the gathering of data to predict the costs and benefits values is not only expensive but also time consuming. This is particularly true for the benefits, as the costs already have industry accepted average values.

Traditional Valuation Framework

There is currently a strong use of NPV, ROI and EVA models in the IT industry and, for some

years, stakeholders generally agree on their CBA principles to measure the value of IT investments (Sassone, 1988).

For a limited set of benefits and costs, this framework is more than enough to measure the value of IT investments. However, when dealing with risk and flexibility, we cannot rely on these models to value IT investments, either because they become too hard to use, or because they become invalid.

Risk must be accounted for, when measuring the value of an IT investment, but it is neither a cost nor a benefit. Risk stands outside the CBA and represents a kind of global accuracy of the calculated IT investment value. Being even harder to measure, it should be used to classify the investment. However, these models only account for risk in a very rudimentary fashion, embedded in the WDR, for instance.

Also, it is not realistic nor interesting to assume organizations will hold passively to their IT investments. In most scenarios, an investment creates options and opens new paths over future decisions that managers can take advantage of. These options may add value to investments that cannot be easily calculated by this framework.

For handling these factors, we must use more advanced valuation frameworks.

Options-Based Valuation Models

The value of an IT investment is often used to support the decision of whether or not we should make that investment. However, there may exist other hidden options, as we will see.

Figure 1. A Traditional Framework for Valuing IT Investments

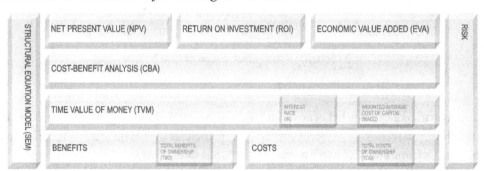

Decision Trees

When you invest, you limit your future options in several ways: you lose the option to invest on something else with the same capital, you win the option of putting the investment on the market, or even to abandon it at a given time, etc.

Hence, when trying to value an investment, we must account for all the decisions we can subsequently make. This is why, when measuring the value of an investment, you must remember this value is the result of the several decisions you make over time, which increase and decrease the value of the investment.

Decision Trees are used to model this type of decisions, not only to help you visualize how the value of your investment will vary with each decision, but also to clarify the set of possible future decisions opened by each one. Many managers use these simpler models to base their decisions, since they can be mingled with dynamically and with low effort, in order to cover a wide range of scenarios (Copeland et al., 2004).

Call and Put Options

There are two types of options. A call option is a contract that gives the holder the right but not the obligation to buy the underlying asset for a certain price at a certain date. A put option is a contract that gives the holder the right but not the

obligation to sell the underlying asset for a certain price at a certain date (Hull, 1992).

The price in the contract is known as exercise price or strike price, and the date is known as expiration date, exercise date or maturity.

Technically, the value of an option is called payoff and does not account for its price, it simply accounts for its exercise price and its underlying market price (Brealey et al., 2003). If we include the initial cost of buying the option, we get its profit. Also, the exercise price and the underlying asset market price are values in the future, therefore to estimate the option future profit you must estimate the future value of the present option profit. See Box 3.

Options Value

At a first glance, it is intuitively understandable that, for a fixed exercise price, the value of a call option increases with the increase of the underlying asset price.

From the option seller perspective, it also comes naturally that the option price should be similar to the underlying asset price less the exercise price. This would give origin to a zero-loss option for the seller and a zero-profit option for the buyer.

However, if the underlying asset price rises much above the exercise price, one can assume

Box 3.

$$call\ option\ future\ profit =$$
$$= underlying\ asset\ market\ price - exercise\ price - call\ option\ future\ price$$
$$put\ option\ future\ profit =$$
$$= exercise\ price - underlying\ asset\ market\ price - put\ option\ future\ price$$

that the call option holders will exercise them. In this scenario, the holder is in fact buying on credit as he will acquire the underlying asset "for sure" but has chosen to finance part of that operation by borrowing. Therefore, for the holder, the delay of the payment to exercise the call may be very valuable if the interest rates or the option exercise date are high. This is so because we can use the amount of money needed to exercise the option to perform other investments and therefore gain more. This is also true for the option seller that can do the same with the collected option price.

Given this, it comes naturally a call option whose underlying asset price has a strong probability of increasing is more valuable than an option whose underlying asset is unlikely to change.

Additionally, if the underlying asset market price is a random walk (Kendall, 1953) then its variance increases linearly with time (Spitzer, 2001).

random walk variance $= \sigma^2 t$

Therefore, the price of the underlying asset varies more with time. Hence, an option value increases both with the variance or volatility of the underlying asset price, and with the exercise date.

Risk

Assuming the price of the underlying asset is a random walk, we were able to associate the value of its call option with the volatility and exercise date, and show that options over riskier assets are more valuable than options over safer ones.

As when you buy a call option, you are actually acquiring the underlying asset without paying for

it immediately, the option is always riskier than the underlying asset. To know how much riskier the option is, we must look at its exercise price and underlying asset price. The more these values are similar, the less risky the option is. The increase of the underlying asset price increases the option value and reduces its risk. Conversely, the decrease of the underlying asset price reduces the option value and increases its risk. As the market price of the underlying asset changes on a daily basis, so does the value and risk of an option to buy that asset.

Bottom line, based on the large numbers probability and statistics theory, the more risky the option is, the more valuable it becomes (Brealey et al., 2003), contrarily to the reasoning we might have when deciding to go ahead with an IT investment over another.

The Five Variables

Table 1 summarizes the five variables that concur to the value and risk of an option, and Table 2 presents a set of rules that relate the value and risk of an option with each one of the five variables, assuming that all the other four variables are fixed.

Replicating Portfolio Technique

As can be noticed, standard discount formulas become very hard to use to value an option, namely because the price of the underlying asset follows a random walk. Fortunately for us, in 1969, Myron Scholes and Fischer Black found the trick to value an option (Black, 1987).

Imagining the price of the underlying asset can go up and down by a known amount, if instead of buying the option you bought an amount of the underlying asset, and borrowed a certain amount of money from the bank, then you could get the exactly same payoffs.

If the payoffs of these investments are equal then both must have the same value. Therefore the value of the call option should be equal to the value of the bought underlying asset, less the repayment of the loan.

This way you have just created a homemade option by buying its underlying asset and borrowing money in such a way that you replicated the payoff of the option. This is called the replicating portfolio technique. The quantity of the underlying asset you must buy to replicate a call option, is called the hedge ratio or option delta. See Box 4.

Binomial Method

Another way to value options is using the binomial method (Cox et al., 1979). The method assumes that, for a given period, only two possible changes can occur in the underlying asset's price of an option. That is, the underlying asset price can go up or down in a given period, with a given probability. In these formulas t is the number of years per period and σ the underlying asset's volatility.

$$P \begin{cases} uP, \text{ with probability } q \\ dP, \text{ with probability } 1\text{-}q \end{cases} \qquad \begin{aligned} u &= e^{\sigma \sqrt{t}} \\ d &= \frac{1}{u} = e^{-\sigma \sqrt{t}} \end{aligned}$$

Table 1. The Five Variables, Value and Risk (Brealey et al., 2003)

#	Variable	Name
1	Underlying Asset Price	P
2	Exercise Price	EX
3	Underlying Asset Volatility	σ
4	Interest Rate	r_f
5	Time to Expiration	t
6	Option Value	V
7	Option Risk	R

Table 2. Options Value and Risk Synthesis (Based on Brealey et al. (2003) reasoning)

#	Rule	Value	Risk
1	The value of an option increases with the increasing of the underlying asset price. The risk of an option increases with the decrease of the underlying asset price.	$P\uparrow \vdash V\uparrow$	$P\downarrow \vdash R\uparrow$
2	The value of an option increases with the decrease of the exercise price. The risk of an option increases with the increase of the exercise price.	$EX\downarrow \vdash V\uparrow$	$EX\uparrow \vdash R\uparrow$
3	The value of an option increases with the increase of underlying asset price volatility. The risk of an option increases with the increase of the underlying asset price volatility.	$\sigma\uparrow \vdash V\uparrow$	$\sigma\uparrow \vdash R\uparrow$
4	The value of an option increases with increase of the interest rate. The risk of an option increases with the decrease of the interest rate.	$r_f\uparrow \vdash V\uparrow$	$r_f\downarrow \vdash R\uparrow$
5	The value of an option increases with increase of the expiration date. The risk of an option increases with the increase of the expiration date.	$t\uparrow \vdash V\uparrow$	$t\uparrow \vdash R\uparrow$

Box 4.

$$option\ delta = \frac{possible\ option\ prices\ spread}{possible\ underlying\ asset\ prices\ spread}$$

$$call\ option\ value = option\ delta \times underlying\ asset\ price - bank\ loan$$

Box 5.

$$call\ option\ value =$$
$$= option\ delta \times underlying\ asset\ price - bank\ loan =$$
$$= N(d_1)P - N(d_2)PV(EX)$$
$$d_1 = \frac{log\left(\frac{P}{PV(EX)}\right)}{\sigma\sqrt{t}} + \frac{\sigma\sqrt{t}}{2}$$

$N(d)$ = Cumulative normal probability density function.

$PV(EX)$ = Option's exercise price discounted at the interest rate r_f.

t = Number of periods to exercise date or years to maturity.

P = Underlying's asset present price.

σ = Standard deviation of continuously compounded rate of return.

However, this model is still not practical for a real scenario, since the underlying asset price should vary several times.

Black-Scholes-Merton Formula

For accurate results, we would have to chop the periods on smaller and smaller slices, making the calculation of the option's value very costly. Fortunately, Robert Merton, Myron Scholes and Fischer Black conceived a formula to solve this problem and calculate the value of any option (Black et al., 1973; Black, 1987). See Box 5.

Real Options

After embracing a given investment, organizations are in most scenarios also acquiring options over future decisions, which can be used to increase the value of the investment or minimize losses. Moreover, these options add more value to risky investments whose outcomes are more uncertain in the present.

The Real Options Theory applies the previously presented financial option models to real assets. It covers the scenarios in which an organization invests money now to create expansion opportunities in the future (Copeland et al., 2004).

After having calculated the value of a real option, that is, the value of the option a particular investment creates, we can then calculate the Adjusted Net Present Value or just Adjusted Present Value (APV) of that investment. The APV, simply extends the basic NPV to account for related investments that have impact on the organization's capital structure. Recently, it was proposed that this value is more accurate than the one given by WACC (Cigola et al., 2005). See Box 6.

The APV, gives us a future vision of the investment value, eventually turning an investment that seems unprofitable at first, actually profitable if we account for the options it creates in the future.

Box 6.

> *adjusted present value =*
> *= base net present value + net present value of related investments*

Figure 2. A real options framework for valuing IT investments

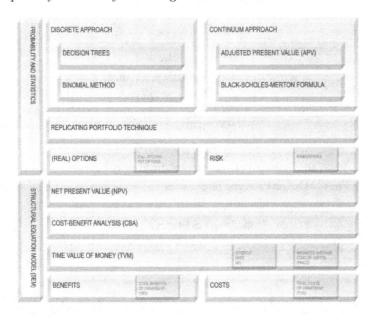

Real Options Valuation Framework

In Figure 2 we extend the traditional investment valuation framework to have risk and future options in account.

This framework includes two advanced modeling approaches that should be used according with the objective of the valuation. The discrete approach uses the Binomial Method and Decision Trees that, although they give approximate results, are a lot more tunable and usable when dealing with compound options, therefore providing more power and understandability to managers (Copeland et al., 2004). The continuum approach uses the Black-Scholes-Merton formula and is more appropriate for single decisions where it's

harder to get accurate estimates, namely for the value of the underlying asset.

This framework includes risk as one of its basic assumptions. Moreover, it assumes that organizations do not hold passively to their investments but, instead, rely heavily, even if not quantitatively supported, on options reasoning, always increasing their investments and aiming for future growth opportunities.

When engaging in a new investment we must account for future related investments. Traditional valuation models are not applicable to these scenarios and eventually cause managers to avoid negative NPV projects, although they could open doors for future investments, which would give a positive APV.

FLEXIBILITY VALUATION

Our goal is to value the flexibility introduced and created by investments on software development. We explained why traditional investment valuation models are insufficient for this purpose, and introduced the advantages of real options models. We are now ready to propose a model to calculate the value of flexibility.

What is Flexibility

The flexibility of software is intuitively expressed as the easiness to adapt it to new requirements. This easiness has multiple metrics, like the time needed to perform changes or the number of changes per unit of time. Usually, the more complex the software is, the less flexible it becomes. Flexibility can then be defined as the changes introduced in a software application over a given time period, as measured by its complexity. Hence, this complexity must be quantified.

As we will see, some of the metrics for software complexity were developed to measure the programmers' productivity, but all of these models can be straightforwardly applied as Software Complexity Metrics (SCM).

In 1974, Wolverton proposed a metric based on the number of code lines. As there were many criticisms to its plainness, other metrics were proposed. For instance, McCabe (1976) argued the complexity of a program could be obtained by the minimum number of paths it defined when seen as a graph.

Other researchers, such as Halstead et al. (1976), proposed easier but still acceptable metrics, such as the number of operators, operands, usage, and similars. As software programs follow the pattern expressed by the Zipf's law (1949) which states that in the natural language a few words occur very often while many others occur rarely, these findings were extended to programming languages and its operators, operands, and to the combinations of them, thus validating Halstead's model (1977).

Only in 1979, Albrecht introduced the now widely used Function Points Analysis (FPA) to measure the size and complexity of IT systems. This analysis is based on Function Points (FP) which are a measure of the size and complexity of computer applications, obtained from a functional perspective by objectively measuring functional requirements. This proposal is therefore independent of the programming language or technology used.

By the late 80's, models to measure the complexity of IT systems using Object-Oriented (OO) languages were also proposed. Some researchers argue that FPA is not applicable to OO languages, and proposed other models to measure the complexity of objects, such as the Object Workload Analysis Gauge (O-WAG) (Rains, 1991), which is somewhat similar to the Halstead's model, since instead of focusing on the object function to measure its complexity, it accounts for its attributes, operations, exceptions, and the like. Nevertheless, there are other models that still use or extend FPA to measure the complexity of OO based IT systems (Antoniol et al, 1999).

Proposed Valuation Model

As we will see, for software applications that have a well defined metric of complexity we can apply the Real Options Theory to value the option of changing or adding one of these Software Complexity Units (SCUs). Hence, we can build a model applicable to any software technology to calculate the value of flexibility, defined as the option to change or add one of its SCU.

The Option to Change

Let us give some examples to explain our approach. On September 2005, Quark unveiled its new corporate identity. The words of Glen Turpin (Quark's director of corporate communications) about this change were (Dalrymple, 2005): "We have changed so much that we felt it was time to send a signal to the world […]. It's not about just changing the look, it's about reflecting externally what has been happening internally and laying the path for everything we are going to do."

Some time ago, Quark created its official Web site on top of some technology. Along with the selection of the technology to use, Quark also implicitly bought the option to change its Web site in September 2005. Assuming the first Quark's Web site was the result of a single project with a given cost, we can say the value of this investment is floored by the cost of the project itself, otherwise the investment would never have been made. Years later, Quark completely changed the face of its original Web site without increasing its software complexity, thus, exercising the option bought before.

Using a SCM for the technology used to build Quark's Web site, we can say that the first Quark's Web site had a given number of SCUs. As there were no changes in complexity, the current Web site also has the same number of SCUs, being therefore the result of changing some of those SCUs.

We have then a first project with a given cost that originated a custom application with some SCUs, and a second project with another cost that changed the SCUs of the first project.

As such, we are in the presence of an option to change Quark's Web site. The exercise price of this option is simply the cost of the project that changed Quark's Web site. The underlying asset in this example is the Web site itself, so its price is at least the cost of the project that originally created it. For simplicity, this assumes, without any value judgment, that Quark's site value equals at least its cost.

From a post implementation perspective, we can calculate the value of the option that Quark received when they first created the initial Web site. As we have seen before, the elicitation of costs and benefits of a given investment is hard to perform and often involves several assumptions and value judgments. However, if we look

at the previous Quark's investments on its Web site from a strictly technological perspective, we can value the option of changing the SCUs of this Web site without any of these problems, relying only in a SCM.

Generalizing this example, we are calculating the option to change a given number of SCUs of a technology. Empirically, we can, for any technology, define a SCM and then gather data from several projects. With that data we can calculate the value of the options at stake in all these projects and correlate their values to obtain the value of the option to change one SCU of that technology, from a strictly technological perspective.

Note this valuation is strictly technological because with this model we can only value the option of changing a SCU of a given technology, and nothing more. We are not arguing that this option adds value to the business. Most important, we are not arguing that technologies with greater values for the option of changing one of its SCUs are better than others, because we made no assumptions on the relation between requirements or benefits and their implementation SCUs, and we established no relation between the SCMs of each technology.

Therefore, we are simply presenting a model that, for a given SCM, can provide managers with a value for the option to change one of its SCUs. The decision on how to interpret this value, e.g. to relate it with the value of other technologies, must be done carefully.

Having said that, this issue could be solved if we used a normalized and inter-technology comparable SCM for all technologies, such as FPs.

The Option to Extend

In most scenarios, applications tend to be extended in functionality, therefore increasing their complexity and their number of SCUs.

As an example, let's look at Amazon. Jeff Bezos started Amazon back in 1995 and, at that time, the site only sold books. Again, along with the selection of the technology, Jeff Bezos also bought the option to change and extend the site. When in 2000 Amazon began selling products from other retailers like eBay, Amazon managers were actually exercising an option Jeff Bezos had bought five years before, back in 1995: the option to extend the site with new services.

In this scenario we have then the initial project with a given cost that originated Amazon's first site, and a second project that extended that site, therefore increasing its number of SCUs. In this case, if we assume the original site functionalities remained unchanged, then so their corresponding SCUs remained unchanged.

The option in this example is similar to the Quark's example, except for the fact that Amazon added new SCUs, while maintaining the existing SCUs intact. The exercise price of this option was once again the cost of the project that implemented the new functionalities and the underlying asset is the application itself, so its price is at least also the cost of the project that originally created it.

Flexibility Valuation Model

Figure 3 generalizes three possible scenarios for a given application regarding its evolution. We have an initial project that costs P and creates an application with N SCUs. Then we have the option to change or extend the initial application, resulting in an application with M SCUs. This option's exercise price is the cost of the project that will perform that change or extension over the initial application. The first alternative is to change the initial application without increasing its SCUs. The second alternative is to extend the initial application with more SCUs, without changing the original ones. Finally, the third and more realistic alternative is to both change and extend the initial application.

With this modulation, we created scenarios to value the several evolution options of an application without the need to make any assumption or value judgment about the benefits of the application. This way, we can apply the model to different

Figure 3. Evolution of software complexity units

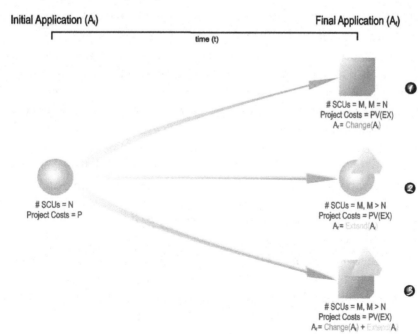

Table 3. Options Theory variable mappings

#	Name	Options Theory Variable	Options Applied to Software Changes		
1	P	Underlying Asset Price	Project Cost of Creating Application with N SCUs		
2	EX	Exercise Price	Project Cost of Changing / Extending Original Application to M SCUs		
3	σ	Underlying Asset Volatility	Needed Changes / Extensions Volatility		
4	r_f	Interest Rate	Risk Free Interest Rate		
5	t	Time to Expiration	Time Between the Two Projects.		
6	V	Option Value	1	Option Value of Changing N SCUs.	
			2	Option Value of Adding M-N SCUs.	
			3	Option Value of Changing N SCUs and Adding M-N SCUs.	

Figure 4. Flexibility Valuation Black-Box Model

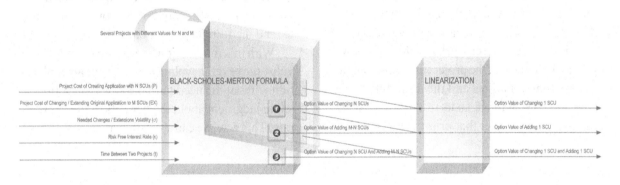

technologies and SCMs to obtain the value of the options to change or add one of its SCUs, from a strictly technological perspective.

Moreover, if we use a normalized and inter-technology comparable SCM, we can provide managers with change and extension option values for different technologies and therefore help on the selection of the technology to choose for implementing a new application.

This model can be applied to any technology as a black-box for each one of the scenarios described in Figure 3. As it will surely happen with most technologies, the option's exercise price will not be linear with the number of SCUs being changed or added. Most probably, when the application starts to grow in complexity, it will become harder to change or extend, and therefore

the value of the option to perform that change or extension will decrease.

In order to obtain the value of the option to change or add a single SCU of an application implemented with a given technology, we will need to linearize those values over the number of SCUs. Also, a valid and applicable linearization model should be chosen for each technology on analysis, since it will depend on how the technology scales with complexity.

Case Study

As a proof of concept, we applied the proposed model to the OutSystems technology in order to calculate the value of the options to change or add one of its SCU.

Each row in Table 4 represents a specific Custom Enterprise Application (CEA) developed for a particular customer. As explained, *P* is the cost of the initial project that originated the first version of the application with a given complexity of *N* SCUs. After *t* months, this application was changed, being its complexity increased to *M* SCUs. The project that introduced those changes represents an investment of *EX*. Note the costs below only account for the required one year term licenses and the services that delivered the project.

In the first scenario, the changes introduced in the applications were merely visual updates or business logic changes that did not cause the resulting application to be more complex since no new functionality was added. Therefore, the resulting *M* SCUs are the same initial *N* SCUs, which in the presented examples were changed in some way.

In the second scenario, only new features were added to the application, while the existing ones remained equal and untouched, causing the application to increase its complexity. Hence, the final application has a complexity of *M* SCUs, higher than the initial *N* SCUs.

With this data we can apply the model with different volatility percentages to obtain the option values of the two scenarios under evaluation, dividing the value of the second project option by the number of changed or added SCUs.

Valuation Model Output

The explained reasoning can be applied to the CEAs listed in Table 4, with different volatilities, as presented in Table 5.

The different volatilities are a measure of the CEA's stability. If you are handling a core application, it is expected it won't change that often, having therefore a low volatility. Conversely, if you are handling a non-core application to support fuzzy business process, ad-hoc activities, and so on, it is expected this application to require a lot more changes as time passes, having therefore a high volatility.

Managers should pick what they feel is an appropriated volatility for a given application, to valuate its flexibility in a particular technology.

From these calculations, we can extract both the value of the option to change one SCU and

Table 4. Projects data

Scenario	CEA	P	EX	t (months)	N	M
1	1.1	$7,400	$3,200	1.23	10,000	
	1.2	$33,500	$9,600	1.68	25,000	
	1.3	$59,400	$25,600	0.91	30,000	
	1.4	$96,700	$44,800	1.59	65,000	
	1.5	$171,200	$38,400	2.91	80,000	
	1.6	$218,400	$134,400	3.18	120,000	
	1.7	$352,800	$134,400	6.18	120,000	
2	2.1	$52,400	$28,800	0.68	20,000	35,000
	2.2	$52,400	$36,100	2.91	20,000	35,000
	2.3	$70,320	$56,320	4.00	20,000	35,000
	2.4	$52,400	$38,400	0.91	20,000	45,000
	2.5	$85,000	$68,700	2.73	30,000	55,000
	2.6	$248,000	$127,500	3.41	80,000	125,000
	2.7	$712,500	$384,000	9.09	195,000	280,000

Table 5. CEAs' Flexibility Option Values for a WDR of 10%

Scenario	CEA	N	M	V, σ = 10%	V, σ = 20%	V, σ = 40%	V, σ = 60%	V, σ = 80%
1	1.1	10,000		$0.4231	$0.4231	$0.4231	$0.4231	$0.4231
	1.2	25,000		$0.9611	$0.9611	$0.9611	$0.9611	$0.9611
	1.3	30,000		$1.1328	$1.1328	$1.1328	$1.1328	$1.1328
	1.4	65,000		$0.8071	$0.8071	$0.8071	$0.8071	$0.8074
	1.5	80,000		$1.6710	$1.6710	$1.6710	$1.6710	$1.6710
	1.6	120,000		$0.7279	$0.7279	$0.7286	$0.7368	$0.7575
	1.7	120,000		$1.8737	$1.8737	$1.8737	$1.8760	$1.8890
2	2.1	20,000	35,000	$1.5837	$1.5837	$1.5837	$1.5837	$1.5838
	2.2	20,000	35,000	$1.1416	$1.1416	$1.1463	$1.1768	$1.2337
	2.3	20,000	35,000	$1.0507	$1.0531	$1.1160	$1.2424	$1.3949
	2.4	20,000	45,000	$0.5711	$0.5711	$0.5712	$0.5741	$0.5841
	2.5	30,000	55,000	$0.7109	$0.7115	$0.7412	$0.8106	$0.8988
	2.6	80,000	125,000	$2.7535	$2.7535	$2.7536	$2.7601	$2.7894
	2.7	195,000	280,000	$4.1794	$4.1794	$4.1976	$4.3109	$4.5163

the value of the option to add one SCU to a CEA built with our selected technology.

Table 6 shows those values for several volatilities. Note that no advanced linearization process was used to reach these results, which are the simple average and deviation.

Seeming there is absolutely no relation with the number of changed or added SCUs and their value, what can we conclude from this gathered data? Simply that the model applies. Why? Well, we hoped that it would be possible to generally obtain the values for the options to change or add one SCU. However, for this to be possible, it would mean that the prices of the underlying asset, in our case the CEAs, wouldn't follow a random walk. Moreover, if this was the case, the Options Theory couldn't be applied. The results show the values of the options vary a lot from project to project. These findings further enforce our initial idea that IT investments are risky and empirically prove the Options Theory can be applied to value IT investments.

As you could have noticed, we were trying to obtain the value of a call option over any stock!

If that was possible, the stock market would collapse. However, there is in fact a relation between risk, flexibility, and complexity, but it varies from IT project to IT project, as the stock options values vary from stock to stock. That relation can be quantified and predicted using the Options Theory.

Also, the gathered data is relative to very different projects, from different industries, and with different purposes. Hence, it was expected the options values to be highly scattered.

Nonetheless, for a particular industry and vertical CEAs we feel the constructed model can be used to calculate the applications' price volatility, the same way financial engineers calculate the volatility of stocks in order to value their options, because in this situation the underlying asset would be the same or similar, although its price could and should vary.

This feeling is supported by the evidence shown in Figure 5, which makes visually clear there is, for each CEA, a strong relation between its initial price, its initial SCUs, the price of the second project which introduces the changes or

Table 6. General Flexibility Option Values for a WDR of 10%

Scenario	Option	$V, \sigma = 10\%$	$V, \sigma = 20\%$	$V, \sigma = 40\%$	$V, \sigma = 60\%$	$V, \sigma = 80\%$
1	Change one SCU	$1.085 +/- 52.1%	$1.085 +/- 52.1%	$1.085 +/- 52.0%	$1.087 +/- 52.0%	$1.092 +/- 52.1%
2	Add one SCU	$1.713 +/- 130.7%	$1.713 +/- 130.7%	$1.730 +/- 130.4%	$1.780 +/- 132.0%	$1.857 +/- 136.4%

Figure 5. CEAs' Variables Correlation for a Volatility of 20% and a WDR of 10%

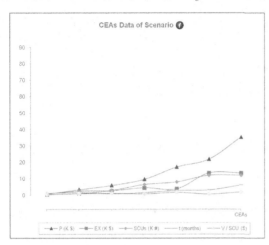
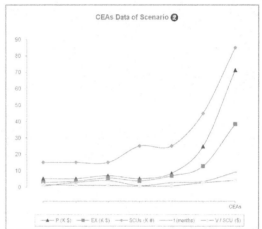

additions, the time between the two projects, and the value of the option to change or add one SCU. In fact, all these variables grow together in both scenarios. Therefore, for a particular type of CEA, in the scope of a given industry and concrete objectives, it should be possible to apply the created model, since these correlations exist, as evidenced.

Given all the above, instead of trying to obtain the value of any stock option, we can instead try to obtain the value of flexibility as a percentage of the initial project, thus relativizing it uniquely to the project and removing the need for external variables.

Output Analysis

Working with the samples of our case study, we can reach some interesting conclusions about the technology being evaluated.

First, we can say the selected technology handles risk quite well, possibly due to its intrinsic capabilities or the methodology it enforces. If we look at Table 5 we can see that for each CEA, the values of the options don't change much across different volatilities. We mapped this volatility with the volatility of the CEA's needed changes and extensions because the underlying price of the CEA varies with these two variables. The more changes and extensions are needed, the more costly the CEA will be, and therefore the volatility of such changes and extensions are a measure of the CEA's price volatility.

In Table 7 we present the averages and deviations of the options values for the several presented volatilities. As you can see, the deviations of the values of the option to change one SCU of a specific CEA are all lower than *1.3%* and the deviations of values of the option to add one SCU to a specific CEA are all lower than *14.7%*.

Table 7. CEAs' Flexibility Option Values Averages and Deviations

Scenario	CEA	N	M	V Average for σ = {10%, 20%, 40%, 60%, 80%}	V Deviation for σ = {10%, 20%, 40%, 60%, 80%}
1	1.1	10,000		$0.4231	0.0%
	1.2	25,000		$0.9611	0.0%
	1.3	30,000		$1.1328	0.0%
	1.4	65,000		$0.8072	0.0%
	1.5	80,000		$1.6710	0.0%
	1.6	120,000		$0.7357	1.3%
	1.7	120,000		$1.8772	0.7%
2	2.1	20,000	35,000	$1.5837	0.0%
	2.2	20,000	35,000	$1.1680	4.0%
	2.3	20,000	35,000	$1.1714	14.7%
	2.4	20,000	45,000	$0.5743	0.6%
	2.5	30,000	55,000	$0.7746	8.0%
	2.6	80,000	125,000	$2.7620	1.6%
	2.7	195,000	280,000	$4.2767	14.5%

This is a highly important remark because it means that for this selected technology, no matter how much volatile the requirements of a project are, or in other words, no matter how much risky the project is, the values of the options to change or add one SCU remain almost the same. This justifies the prior conclusion of this technology handling risk very well.

Albeit the gathered data for this case study is relative to very different projects in their nature, making somehow their comparison non significant, in fact, they all rest within the realms of a specific technology. Therefore, for this technology, and assuming the gathered data is significant for the universe of projects done with it, the mentioned intervals are relevant.

Also worth noticing is the higher *14.7%* deviation, which indicates the scenarios where new functionality is added to the CEA are riskier. This is intuitively expected, since these scenarios increase the complexity of the CEA.

Given the prior conclusion that the selected technology is almost immune to volatility, that is, to risk, the average options values of Table 7 can be used to extrapolate significant intervals for the values of the options to change or add one SCU, that is, the value of flexibility.

Hence, for the selected technology in case study, the value of the option to change one SCU of a specific CEA is within the interval *[$0.4231; $1.8772]* and the value of the option to add one SCU to a specific CEA is within the interval *[$0.5743; $4.2767]*.

With these intervals, we can obtain the value of flexibility as a percentage of the initial project, that is, we can obtain the values of the options to change or add one SCU as a percentage of the price per SCU of a given CEA.

In Table 8 we present the price per SCU of each CEA, by dividing P (the price of the underlying asset) by N (its number of SCUs).

Comparing these prices per SCU with the average option values presented in Table 7, we obtain the value of the options as a percentage of the CEA's initial price per SCU.

Table 8. CEAs' Flexibility Option Values as Percentage of Initial Price per SCU

Scenario	CEA	P	N	Price per SCU	V Average	V / Price per SCU
1	1.1	$7,400	10,000	$0.740	$0.4231	57.2%
	1.2	$33,500	25,000	$1.340	$0.9611	71.7%
	1.3	$59,400	30,000	$1.980	$1.1328	57.2%
	1.4	$96,700	65,000	$1.488	$0.8072	54.3%
	1.5	$171,200	80,000	$2.140	$1.6710	78.1%
	1.6	$218,400	120,000	$1.820	$0.7357	40.4%
	1.7	$352,800	120,000	$2.940	$1.8772	63.9%
2	2.1	$52,400	20,000	$2.620	$1.5837	60.4%
	2.2	$52,400	20,000	$2.620	$1.1680	44.6%
	2.3	$70,320	20,000	$3.516	$1.1714	33.3%
	2.4	$52,400	20,000	$2.620	$0.5743	21.9%
	2.5	$85,000	30,000	$2.833	$0.7746	27.3%
	2.6	$248,000	80,000	$3.100	$2.7620	89.1%
	2.7	$712,500	195,000	$3.654	$4.2767	117.0%

Therefore, we conclude that for this technology, the option to change one SCU of a particular CEA is worth between *40.4%* and *78.1%* the price of that CEA's SCUs and the option to add one SCU to a particular CEA is worth between *21.9%* and *117.0%* the price of that CEA's SCUs.

The interest of this particular conclusion is that we can now estimate intervals for the values of the options to change or extend a given CEA in this technology, knowing only the CEA's initial price and number of SCUs.

Imagine you have an application that cost *$8,500* and has a complexity of *20,000* SCUs. In the worst scenario, the option to change your application is worth *40.4% $8,500 = $3,434*, and in the best scenario *78.1% $8,500 = $6,639*. Hence, the option to change your application is in the interval *[$3,434; $6,639]*. This means that, accounting with the option's value, your application's APV is in the interval *[-$5,066; -$1,861]*, instead of its initial NPV of *-$8,500*.

As for the option to extend your application, in the worst scenario it is worth *21.9% $8,500 = $1,862* and in the best scenario *117.0% $8,500*

= *$9,945*. Therefore, the option to extend your application is in the interval *[$1,862; $9,945]*. This means the APV of your investment is in the interval *[-$6,638; $1,445]*, having some probability to be positive by itself!

FUTURE TRENDS

The main problem with the proposed model is that it requires a lot of input data. Even for vertical solutions it would be needed an effort from vendors to obtain significant statistical data to properly value the flexibility of their technologies.

A bigger obstacle to implement industry wide this or a similar model is related with the market itself. Each technology has its own advantages and disadvantages, and vendors often see no value in being compared numerically, as they would lose the option to exalt their advantages and hinder their disadvantages. As such, the quest for an inter-technology normalized Software Complexity Metric (SCM) is far from being obtained, though academic studies on this area will surely continue. Nevertheless, Function Points (FPs) are quite widely accepted.

The linearization issue of the proposed model should be further investigated, since the value of the options to change or add one Software Complexity Unit (SCU) does not scales equally from technology to technology, nor even inside the same technology with the complexity of the Custom Enterprise Application (CEA).

The third CEA evolution scenario, not addressed in the case study, where the application is both changed and extended is the most real one, but the most difficult to model. With proper data it could be sliced in two compound options of changing one SCU and adding one SCU. However, more advanced models must be built for this research to handle such scenario properly and be useful, since such data is never available.

A topic not addressed in this research but worth mentioning is how metrics related with the changes performed over a CEA can be converted into risk evaluation. To answer this question a taxonomy of changes would have to be created, using, for instance, flexi-points (Rymer et al., 2007). After categorization, such change metrics could be converted into risk evaluation, thus providing a matrix to evaluate the risk of IT investments. However, such taxonomy could also make the proposed model more expensive to apply, since all the foreseen changes would need to be elicited upfront.

Finally, but not less important, a taxonomy to classify CEAs must be built to properly be able to catalog them by similarity and therefore compare what is comparable. When this is done, IT managers will be able to have real numbers to make informed decisions over what technologies to choose for what projects.

CONCLUSION

This chapter intended to value the flexibility in custom software development. The premises to prove were that IT investments are risky, and that flexibility is a tool to handle that risk.

We hope to have proven that IT investments are intrinsically risky and that the Real Options Theory is applicable to value these investments. Also, we expect to have made clear that flexibility is an appropriate way to handle risk in IT.

Several traditional investment valuation models were presented and their inability to handle risk was properly evidenced. We described the Options Theory, particularly, the Real Options Theory, and disserted on how it can be used to value investments having risk in account.

A model was iteratively developed based on the premise there is a strong relation between the costs of a Custom Enterprise Application (CEA) and its complexity. This model outputs the value of the options to change or add one unit of complexity of or to a CEA, and can be used to value the flexibility of any technology.

One of our empirical proofs is that the base premise of the model is correct but that this relation is not linear, as it should depend on several factors particular to the microenvironment were the application exists, namely, the industry, its purpose, the need for specific integrations, and so on. This finding by itself supports the idea that IT investments are risky. Moreover, it empirically proves that the Options Theory can be applied to value these investments, and therefore that the model is valid for an appropriated universe.

The acceptance of risk in IT investments, rather than pretending it doesn't exist, must still be done while the IT industry fails to minimize it. The main tool to handle that recurring risk is flexibility, which therefore has a commensurable value in IT. Using the theory we presented and the model we proposed, managers can quantify and predict risk, and value the flexibility of a given technology before choosing it to implement a CEA.

In the lack of data to feed the model, we expect at least to have contributed to provide IT managers with an options-based reasoning, encouraging them to look further ahead and use flexibility to deal with risk, which is an unavoidable reality of IT investments.

As a proof of concept, we validated the proposed model with real data against the Out-Systems technology. The model allowed us, for this specific technology, to reach four important conclusions.

Firstly, we concluded the selected technology is almost immune to risk. Secondly, that the scenarios where new functionality is added with this technology are riskier than the ones where existing functionality is changed. Thirdly, we concluded the value of the option to change one Software Complexity Unit (SCU) within this technology is in the interval *[$0.4231; $1.8772]*, and the value of the option to add one SCU within the interval *[$0.5743; $4.2767]*. Fourthly, and finally, we were able to obtain intervals for the values of the above options, knowing only the initial status of a CEA. We concluded that the value of the option to change a CEA built with the case study technology is within *[40.4%; 78.1%]* its initial price, and the value of the option to extend a CEA within *[21.9%; 117.0%]*, having a wider range since it is a riskier investment.

For this selected technology, we can now use these findings to adjust the Net Present Value (NPV) of a project, accounting with the value of the options that project creates in the future.

REFERENCES

3G.co.uk. (2004, December 15). *3G adoption a few more years*. Retrieved December 3, 2005, from http://www.3g.co.uk/PR/December2004/8830.htm

Albrecht, A. J. (1979). Measuring applications development productivity. In *Proceedings of the IBM Application Development* (pp. 83-92).

Antoniol, G., Lokan, C., Caldiera, G., & Fiutem, R. (1999, September). A function point-like measure for object-oriented software. *Empirical Software Engineering, 4*(3), 263-287.

Black, F., & Scholes, M. (1973, May-June). The pricing of option and corporate liabilities. *The Journal of Political Economy, 81*(3), 637-654.

Black, F. (1987, August). Goldman Sachs and Company. *Essays of an Information Scientist, 10*(33), 16.

Brealey, R. A., & Myers, S. C. (2003). *Principles of corporate finance* (7th ed.). McGraw Hill.

Cigola, M., & Peccati, L. (2005, March). On the comparison between the APV and the NPV computed via the WACC. *European Journal of Operational Research, 161*(2), 377-385.

Copeland, T., & Tufano, P. (2004, March). A real-world way to manage real options. *Harvard Business Review, 82*(3), 90-99.

Cox, J. C., Ross, S. A., & Rubinstein, M. (1979, September). Options pricing: A simplified approach. *Journal of Financial Economics, 7*(3), 229-264.

Dalrymple, J. (2005, September 9). Quark adopts new corporate identity. *MacWorld*. Retrieved November 20, 2005, from http://www.macworld.com/news/2005/09/09/quarkchange/index.php

DeLone, W. H., & McLean, E. R. (1992, March). Information systems success: The quest for the dependent variable. *Information Systems Research, 3*(1), 60-95.

Dupuit, J. (1844). De la mesure de l'utilité des travaux publics. *Annales de Ponts et Chaussées, 8*(2).

Ellram, L. M. (1993). A framework for total cost of ownership. *The International Journal of Logistics Management, 4*(2), 49-60.

Goetzmann, W. N. (2003, October). *Fibonacci and the financial revolution* (Working Paper N° 03-28). Yale International Center for Finance.

Halstead, M. H., Elshoff, J. L., & Gordon, R. D. (1976). On software physics and GM's PL/I programs. *GM Research Publication GMR-2175, 26.*

Hayes, M. (2001, August). Payback time: Making sure ROI measures up. *InformationWeek.* Retrieved October 1, 2005, from http://www.informationweek.com/showArticle.jhtml;?articleID=6506422

Hearts, J. (2002, November 25). Can 3G adoption gather pace? *IT-Director.* Retrieved December 3, 2005, from http://www.it-director.com/article.php?articleid=3377

Henin, P.-Y. (1986). Desequilibria it the present day. In *macrodynamics: A study of the economy in equilibrium and disequilibrium* (pp. 404). Routledge Kegan Paul.

Hull, J. (1992). *Options, futures and other derivatives* (2nd ed.). Prentice Hall.

Kendall, M. G. (1953). The analysis of economic time series – part I: Prices. *Journal of the Royal Statistical Society, 96,* 11-25.

King, J. L., & Schrems, E. L. (1978, March). Cost-benefits analysis in information systems development and operation. *ACM Computing Surveys, 10*(1), 19-34.

Kumar, K. (1990, February). Post implementation evaluation of computer-based information systems: Current practices. *Communications of the ACM, 33*(2), 203-212.

Laemmel, A., & Shooman, M. (1977). *Statistical (natural) language theory and computer program complexity* (Tech. Rep. POLY/EE/E0-76-020). Brooklyn, New York: Department of Electrical Engineering and Electrophysics, Polytechnic Institute of New York.

Magretta, J., & Stone, N. (2002, April). *What management is: How it works and why it's everyone's business* (1st ed.). Simon & Schuster Adult Publishing Group.

Marshall, A. (1920). *Principles of economics* (8th ed.). Macmillan and Co., Ltd. Retrieved October 1, 2005, from http://www.econlib.org/library/Marshall/marP.html

McCabe, T. J. (1976). A complexity measure. In *Proceedings of the 2nd International Conference on Software Engineering (ICSE '76)* (p. 407).

OutSystems. (n.d.). Retrieved November 20, 2005, from http://www.outsystems.com

Penwell, L. W., & Nicholas, J. M. (1995, September). From the first pyramid to space station - an analysis of big technology and mega-projects. In *Proceedings of the AIAA Space Programs and Technologies Conference.*

Porter, M. E. (1985). The value chain and competitive advantage. In *Competitive advantage: Creating and sustaining superior performance* (pp. 33-61). Free Press.

Rains, E. (1991). Function points in an ADA object-oriented design? *ACM SIGPLAN OOPS Messenger, 2*(4), 23-25.

Rymer, J. R., & Moore, C. (2007, September). *The dynamic business applications imperative.* Forrester Research.

Sassone, P. G. (1988, April). Cost benefit analysis of information systems: A survey of methodologies. In *Proceedings of the Conference Sponsored by ACM SIGOIS and IEEECS TC-OA on Office information systems* (Vol. 9, pp. 126-133).

Scott, J. E. (1995, February). The measurement of information systems effectiveness: evaluating a measuring instrument. *Data Base Advances, 26*(1), 43-61.

Spitzer, F. (2001, January). *Principles of random walk* (2nd ed.). Springer.

The Standish Group International, Inc. (1995). *The CHAOS report.* The Standish Group International, Inc.

The Standish Group International, Inc. (2001). *Extreme CHAOS report*. The Standish Group International, Inc.

Wolverton, R. W. (1974, June). The cost of developing large-scale software. *IEEE Transactions on Computers, 23*(6), 615-636.

Zipf, G. K. (1949). *Human behaviour and the principle of least effort.* Cambridge, MA: Addison-Wesley.

KEY TERMS AND DEFINITIONS

Adjusted Present Value (APV): The APV extends the basic NPV to account for related investments that have impact on the organization's capital structure. Is usually calculated adding the basic NPV of the investment and the related investments NPV.

Custom Software Development: The process by which an information system is developed, not recurring to any pre-existing package or solution sold as a product. Used when the required information system is too specific for any pre-existing product to be applicable, or when the information system needs to be flexible to cope with change or fuzzy requirements.

Flexibility: The ability to adapt to expected and unexpected changes in the environment. In the context of this chapter, flexibility is quantifi-able by the amount of changes introduced in a custom enterprise application over a given time period, as measured by its complexity.

Net Present Value (NPV): Is the present value of an investment in the future, usually calculated by the difference between the present monetary values of the costs and the benefits of the investment.

Option: Is a contract that gives the holder the right but not the obligation to buy or sell the underlying asset for a certain price at a certain date.

Real Option: An opportunity that becomes available after a particular investment is made. The opportunity can be exercised or not, thus leading to impacts on the investment value or not.

Risk: Denotes the potential impact on an attribute of value that a future event may cause. In finances, represents the variability of returns a given investment may have. In the context of this chapter, risk is reflected, among other variables, in the uncertainty of the requirements a custom enterprise application may need to fulfill in the future.

Volatility: A measure of the variation a given asset may have on its price over a given time period. In the context of this chapter, volatility is the percentage of needed changes or extensions a custom enterprise application may need, when compared with its initial state.

Chapter X
The Theory of Deferred Action:
Informing the Design of Information Systems for Complexity

Nandish V. Patel
Brunel University, UK

ABSTRACT

The problem addressed is how to design rationally information systems for emergent organization. Complexity and emergence are new design problem that constrains rational design. The reconciliation of rationalism and emergence is achieved in the theory of deferred action by synthesizing rationalism and emergence. Theories on designing for normal organisation exist but most of them are borrowed from reference disciplines. The theory of deferred action is based in the information systems discipline and is presented as a theory to inform practice to improve the rational design of information systems for emergent organisation. It has the potential of becoming a reference theory for other disciplines in particular for organisation studies. As emergence is a core feature of complexity, the base theory for the theory of deferred action is complexity theory. The theory of deferred action explains the effect of emergence on the rational design of information systems. As a theory to inform practice it provides guidance in the form of design constructs on how to design rationally information systems for emergent organization.

INTRODUCTION

We have been designing, developing, and using information systems in business organizations using computers and lately information tech-nology for nearly sixty years. But what is our understanding of an information system? The practice of information systems has been driven by the invention of digital technology, computers, information technology and lately information and communication technology. Many advances in our knowledge of how to develop information systems have come from practitioners. Practitioners have also built actual information systems that have become the object of study for researchers. These include transaction processing systems, decisions support systems, expert systems, and recently ebusiness systems and enterprise resource planning systems.

Some advances in our understanding have come from researchers. Early understanding of an information system as a technological system improved with knowledge of information systems as socio-technical systems, acknowledging the human social context in which information systems are developed and used. Researchers now define an information system as composing people, organisation and information technology. Some theories on information systems have been proposed (Walls, et al., 1992). Markus, et al., (2002) propose , a design theory for systems that support emergent knowledge processes, (179-21). But we lack good theoretical understanding of information systems.

What is a simple information system and what is a complex information system? When is it simple to design information systems for a business organisation and when is it complex? It is simple when there is no design uncertainty. Possibly when what is wanted is perfectly known, and when complete and predictable information and knowledge is available to organize the available resources to achieve it. Information on available resources should be complete too. This kind of simplicity is not available to designers because there is much design uncertainty in organizations. Designers do not have complete and perfect information and knowledge about the artifact they design because organizational members themselves lack the knowledge. Designers work with incomplete knowledge of want is wanted, imperfect information about how to design and develop, as well as incomplete information on available resources and how to organize them. The

cause of this design uncertainty is complexity.

The predictive capacity of designers is central. Prior to design the purpose of the organisation is knowable to a large extent but it can and does change unpredictably after the organisation has been setup. Commercial companies' purpose of maximizing shareholder value has changed to consider the impact on the natural environment. Consequently, new information on carbon accounting is obtained by adding new information systems or making adjustments to existing ones. An information system is simple when the organisation and the information required to manage it can be predetermined, its design and development is also relatively simple. When design is predictable there is an absence of complexity. Uncertainty about the information required to manage the organisation arises when aspects of the organisation cannot be predetermined. The core of this uncertainty is highly unpredictable situations that arise in the course of organizational life. The absence of the predictive capacity of designers is the essence of design complexity.

Business organisation as a social system is complex. The functions of information systems for a business organisation are far from simple. Functionality is complex not only because of design uncertainty but also because the social system itself is complex (unpredictable). Structure and resources of the organisation are unpredictable (Feldman, 2000; 2004). Patterns of communication between humans within the organization, and between humans and information systems, cannot be completely predetermined for design purposes. As patterns of human communication within the organisation are highly complex it is not simple to determine the necessary information flows. Patterns of information flows between the organisation and its environment are similarly not pre-determinable completely. Also the situations in which information will be used are not pre-determinable exhaustively.

The question of whether the business organisation needs a simple or complex information system is important because most information systems projects are thought to be entirely predictable. Simple information systems are those that can wholly be predicted. Credit control and payroll systems are examples. In actuality many projects, especially organisation-wide information systems like enterprise resource planning systems, are complex in the sense that complete knowledge of required functionality over the life of the system is not possible. Such projects are not only unpredictable during development (the design phase) but later too when the information system is in use. The situational use of the information system reveals purposive and functional shortcomings. A corollary of the question is what level of complexity is needed? These questions and the question of how to design information systems that have no predetermined structure and function but when such structure and function takes form in situ is addressed by the theory of deferred action presented in this chapter.

METHODOLOGICAL APPROACH

We propose complexity theory for developing design science theories capable of informing practice. Design is a scientific field of enquiry particularly important for humans. Design scientists can use complexity as a theory of design to advance and improve design quality. The epistemological methodology of complexity can be used to understand emergence in socio-technical systems like information systems and knowledge management systems, and design processes. And it can be used to propose suitable design constructs and design processes for emergent organisation.

Emergence is a defining characteristic of the ontology of complex adaptive systems. The ontology of such a system cannot be predetermined, predefined because of emergence. A particular event affects other events in non-determinable ways in complex adaptive systems, in a chain of events in which initial causes are untraceable to eventual effects. This epistemology is relevant for understanding and designing systems for emergent organisation. Knowledge systems are such complex adaptive systems. The processes for creating knowledge are intertwined in non-determinable emergent paths.

Emergence is the keystone of complexity theory. Complexity is characterized as constant 'phase change' arising from emergence. Emergence requires social systems to adapt, resulting in complex adaptive systems (McMillan, 2004). Responses to emergence necessitate 'self-organizing systems' that are complex adaptive systems. Complexity in turn requires appropriate concepts and constructs of knowledge. Adaptableness and self-organisation become aspects of organizations that are not generally considered in knowledge and information management theories, strategies and programmes.

SYSTEMS AND COMPLEX ADAPTIVE SYSTEMS

'Systems are objects with varying degrees of complexity, although they are always acknowledged as containing elements that interact with one another.' (Bertuglia and Vaio 2005:3). The staying together of the elements is a defining feature of a system. Social phenomena like the scientific enterprise, economy, population, organisation, and information systems, are such systems. The elements of an information system are people, organisation and information technology. Their coming and staying together composes an information system.

A system that self-organizes in response to its environment is a complex adaptive system. It acquires information on its environment and on its own interaction with that environment. This information is structured into regularities and then condensed into a schema or model for acting in the real world. Adaptation of the system to its environment occurs when it changes itself and its schema when they are inappropriate for being in the real world (Gell-Mann, 2004).

Self-organisation is the response of a system to some random change that causes the system to become unstable. An existing order is disturbed by the change. The stability is then restored by the system self-organizing without some external causative factor. The restored stability is an emergent order. Emergence is intrinsic to self-organizing system. It results in a new structure that is intrinsic to the system and that is not caused by an external factor. A business organisation is self-organizing if no external influences do the self-organizing for it.

Humans are complex adaptive systems that generate other complex adaptive systems. Humans design certain organizations and its information systems as complex adaptive systems. Other examples of complex adaptive systems are cultural evolution, evolution of organizations and societies, evolution of economies and global economies. The global information system, the World Wide Web, is a highly complex adaptive system generated by humans. Strategic information systems and inter-organizational information systems are also generated complex adaptive systems. These are socio-technical systems that tend to be open systems because they are affected by their environment.

If we want to act with some measure of certainty in a complex adaptive system how should we act? Since information is affected by emergence in a complex system it is not possible to act solely by planned action. That is, it is not possible to act according to some completely predetermined design. Designed action in a complex system cannot solely be planned action because human behavior and the functions of information systems need to be modified in response to emergence. So, how can emergence be accounted for in rational design? Complexity theory explains emergent phenomenon, but as design scientists we seek more than an explanation of emergence. We seek to design for emergence.

The structure of the internal elements and their relations distinguish a complex adaptive system from its environment and this structure and internal relations is termed complexity. The complexity of information systems is not investigated or well understood. Complexity, self-organisation, emergence and adaptation are features of certain information systems, for example strategic information systems and the Web. Even less well understood is how to design socio-technical systems rationally to cater for complexity.

An organisation, its management, and information systems are examples of complex adaptive systems that are generated (rationally designed) by humans. What is normally termed 'uncertainty', 'change' and 'changing organisation' or 'creeping requirements' and 'information systems failure' in the literature is better explained in terms of complex adaptive systems. Much instability and uncertainty pervades organizational life, whether it is a charitable, governmental or business organisation. Such uncertainty or indeterminacy is a central feature of complex adaptive systems. It is termed emergence in complex adaptive systems and it is a core feature of complexity.

DESIGN SCIENCE AND COMPLEXITY THEORY

Design is a scientific field of enquiry particularly important for humans. Herbert Simon defined design as: 'Everyone designs who devises courses of action aimed at changing existing situations into preferred ones' (Simon, 1996: 111). The aim of design science is to develop theories of how designers think and work. It also aims to develop methodologies and tools to support designers' work. Some strands of design science, particularly in information systems, aim to develop 'IT artifacts' that are derived from design science investigations (Walls, et. el, 1992). Organisation and its information systems are such 'artificial' or synthetic systems.

Figure 1. Reasoning in the design cycle

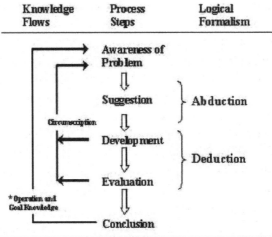

Takeda et al. (1990) have analyzed the reasoning that occurs in the course of a general design cycle, illustrated in Figure 1. Abduction is used for the creative process and deduction is used for the development and evaluation process. This diagram can be interpreted as an elaboration of the *Knowledge Using Process*. It shows the flow of creative effort and the types of new knowledge that arise from design activities.

Consideration of complexity in design has recently been recognized by researchers and research funding bodies (Johnson et al., 2005). The UK's Engineering and Physical Sciences Research Council fund research that seeks to 'embrace' complexity in design.

Design scientists can use complexity theory as a theory of design to advance and improve the quality of design. The epistemological methodology of complexity can be used to understand social systems like organisation, socio-technical systems like information systems, and the design process. Since information systems need to operate in complex social systems, as they are embedded in organisation, complexity can be used to better conceptualize the design ontology of complex information systems.

The description of a complex system can be done of its structure, function or behavior (Zamenopoulos and Alexiou, 2005). Structurally, a complex system is a set of structured elements and the aim is to describe and explain this structure. To describe an emergent property in the structure of the system an exponential function Power Law, $P(s) \propto s^{-\gamma}$, is used. It maps the frequency distribution of some quantity (s). The complexity of the World Wide Web can be described using a Power Law. Functionally, a complex system can be modeled as a function that produces an output with given input. In cybernetics a machine is characterized as 'trivial' or 'non-trivial' depending on the problematic of describing its input-process-output pattern (Von Foerster, 2003). Behaviorally, a complex system can be modeled as a dynamical system.

A complex adaptive system is responsive to its environment. It adapts to sustain itself. When humans design a business organisation and its information systems they are behaving as complex adaptive systems. As complex adaptive systems, humans generate other complex adaptive systems, the organizations and information systems they design and develop. Three out of the five characteristics of complex adaptive systems are to do with information. (Bertuglia and Vaio, 2005: 276-7).

Casti (1986) distinguishes between design complexity and control complexity. Design complexity is concerned with the processes involved in design and how interconnected these processes are. Control complexity is concerned with how control can be maintained in complex designs. Our aim is to include both in developing a theory to support the design of artifacts for emergent organization. To improve control over synthetic complex systems like organisation, its management and information systems. This is possible with deferred action.

Emergence is a central property of complex systems. Emergence is the sudden and unpredictable occurrence of events. As such events cannot be predicted they are said to emerge. Emergent complexity is a characteristic of design too. A particular design is not entirely pre-determinable. Its final form is the result of many iterations until an agreeable from emerges.

The theory of deferred action is a design science theory and draws on complexity as a theory of design. It makes use of the structural, functional and behavioral features of complex systems to understand socio-technical systems like information systems and knowledge management systems. Knowledge management systems particularly have significant emergent properties and they can be better designed if we understand these emergent properties as complex systems. The empirical research leading to the theory of deferred action was from the perspective of information systems development. But because information systems frameworks could not explain the empirical data on emergence in information systems, the deferred systems design and deferred system constructs were proposed. These were further theorized to define the coherence and generality of the theory of deferred action.

OUR DESIGNED ACTIONS AND COMPLEXITY

We rationally determine our designed actions as in the design of purposive organisation. The design and development of information systems is also such designed action. The rational element of designed action is centrally important. Rationality enables us to keep control of our future. Through rationality we can measure our efforts, whether we have achieved our aim, and how well we have performed, as well as other measures.

Aspects of our designed actions can be planned. Such planned action works well in contexts that are stable and predictable. High measure of certainty can be achieved in such contexts. Certain operational information systems can are relatively stable and predictable, for example the central purchasing organisation in a manufacturing business (but over the very long term this can become unstable too). But design by planned action solely is unable to cater for emergence in social systems.

Our designed actions however meticulously planned are not simple to enact. Simple here means an absence of complexity. They are not simple because they are not entirely predictable, and unpredictability (emergence) is a major feature of complex systems. Designed actions are not simple to enact because new organizational situations emerge, requiring new information to act, that could not have been predicted for design purposes. Consequently, the information systems we require to complete our designed actions are not simple too.

Is it possible to design rationally the kind of complex adaptive systems that humans (themselves complex adaptive systems) generate? How can emergence be factored into the rational design of complex adaptive systems like certain information systems? In general, how can emergence be factored in the design of socio-technical systems like information systems and ebusiness systems? The Theory of Deferred Action is proposed to cater for emergence in rationally designed information systems that are characterized as complex adaptive systems.

Complex Organisation

Empirical evidence supports the thesis of emergent organisation. Emergent organizations experience frequent, unpredictable change because of fluctuations in the organisation itself and in the external environment. The change commonly is sudden and unexpected resulting in structures, processes, and resources becoming unstable and difficult to predict. Therefore the efficacy of planning is limited (but it is still necessary). The impact on information systems development projects is therefore logically complex as the challenge of successful definition, adoption, and diffusion is exacerbated. Consequently, emergence clearly has an effect on the generation, distribution and application of information to improve products and services with a direct impact on the efficiency and effectiveness of organizational performance.

Emergent organisation is 'a theory of social organisation that does not assume that stable structures underpin organizations' (Truex et al, 1999: 117; Truex and Klein 1991). Emergence affects structure, processes, and resources. Empirically, organizational structure and processes are emergent. Feldman (2000) studied organizational routines to reveal that even routines are a source of continuous change. Feldman (2004) later revealed that organizational structure is emergent and, importantly, it effects organizational resource allocations. Emergent organisation assumes that organizational structure and processes are fluid (Baskerville et al., 1992). It assumes that 'organizations are always in process; they are never fully formed.' 'Emergent' acknowledges the 'possibility of a current state being a stage to a possible outcome and always arising from a previous history and context.' (Truex et al, 1999; 117) Emergence affects actors' need for information and knowledge

of organisation and organizing (Truex et al., 1999; Markus, 2002; Patel, 2002).

Emergence has implications for information systems where information is characterized as contextually dependent. It becomes problematical to *structure* information in emergent organisation. Truex et al (1999), referring to information systems development, state that there are limited means to address information management in emergent organisation. Similarly, given emergence, our ontological understanding of information and its use to design and support business processes needs revising. As knowledge processes in organisation are effected by emergence (Truex et al. 1999; Patel, 2005), emergence must be considered theoretically as a dimension of information and knowledge. Patel's (2005) study of sales and client relationships in an insurer's company reveals that emergence results in *deferred action* in 'situations that are confusing, unclear, lacking knowledge or unfamiliar' (p.356).

Emergence is intrinsic to social systems (organization). It has non-repeating patterns that arise from interactions and communications between actors, between actors and knowledge management systems *in situ*, and located in various organizational settings over time. Its prime characteristic of unpredictability makes it un-specifiable and therefore problematical to manage. 'Emergence is an unpredictable affect of the interrelatedness of multifarious purposes and the means to achieve them that is characteristic of social action. By implication, emergence is the non-specifiable constraint on rational design because it cannot be determined as design objects, it is off-design' (Patel, 2006:12). An emergent organisation is a complex adaptive system and its enabling and supporting information systems are complex adaptive systems.

For analytical purposes an organisation, processes and information systems, can be divided into two parts. Normal organisation has definable structure, processes and resources, and therefore its data and information can be pre-determined for design purposes. This is termed predictable design in which the artifact to be designed is completely knowable in advance. A manufacturing production process and credit control process are examples. Emergent organisation has indefinable structure, processes and resources, and therefore its data and information cannot be pre-determined for design purposes. This is termed unpredictable design in which the artifact is not completely knowable in advance. Industrial innovation processes and strategy formation are examples. Any organisation is both normal and emergent, and as a whole it is emergent.

Data, Information and Knowledge in the Context of Emergent Organisation

Our understanding of data, information and knowledge is that it has stable properties that are predictable. In applying complexity theory to data, information and knowledge, we ask what is the effect of emergence on data, information and knowledge?

Data are facts about the world and are relatively stable. Data can be identified, structured and processed. The effect of emergence on data is relatively less. Names of customers, their address or the product manufactured do not change often.

The effect of emergence on information is relatively greater. Information is normally defined as processed data (Data + algorithm = information). The meaning that humans attach to data is here interpreted as 'algorithm'. Some kinds of managerial information depends on emergent situations. We re-define information as processed data in the context of emergence. (Data + emergence + [contextual] algorithm = information). New and unpredictable organisational situations arise in the course of organisational life which make information dependent on emergence.

Applying complexity theory to information systems, we learn that information and knowledge

have emergent properties. These emergent properties make information dynamic. Emergence affects the kind information managers need. In emergent contexts information is changeable. Where does the customer live now? Not at the address shown in the company's database but somewhere else. In emergent contexts information has the qualities of uncertainty and unpredictability.

We assume the phenomenon of organisational information has elements that are static and emergent. The static elements are knowable and predictable and therefore they can be specified for design purposed. Transaction processing systems are examples. Information required to manage a motor cycle production process can be predetermined. It can be specified to design and develop the appropriate module for an enterprise resource planning system.

The emergent elements are not knowable, emergent events occur suddenly and unpredictably. Information required to manage sudden announcement of companies merger cannot be predetermined. It cannot be specified in advance. Information systems that are affected by emergence include strategic information system and decision support systems. At the societal level they include the World Wide Web.

The dichotomy of knowledge as explicit knowledge and tacit knowledge is established (Polanyi, 1966). We add as a core third element emergent knowledge. Emergence affects the kind of knowledge managers need in purposive organisation. Knowledge and the processes used to generate knowledge have emergent properties.

INFORMATION SYSTEMS IN EMERGENT ORGANISATION

A source of conceptual models of information system is business and management. Earlier applications of computers in business were in business operations. Routine procedures like inventory control, sales and accounting were automated using computers. Reports produced by these systems were used by management to manage business operations. Additionally, computers were applied to support management decision making resulting in decision support systems. The transaction processing systems and management information systems were designed for normal organisation. Therefore, the concept of information system was that it was predictable.

A strand of information systems research exposed deficiency in the concept of information system as predictable. Researchers applied social science theories such as Actor Network Theory and Structuration Theory to interpret organisational information systems. A prime outcome of this research added the notion of 'meaning' to concept of information system. Humans attach meaning to information in order to make sense of it in particular organisational contexts. What meanings humans will attach to information cannot be predicted.

Other subtle sources contributing to the concept of information systems are science and engineering. A focal conceptual model is inadvertently based on physical 'linear system'. The idea of a linear system is that the phenomenon of interest is represented as a mathematical model to demonstrate casual relationships and therefore to make predictions. Cause and effect and predictability are core features of physical linear systems. Information systems design and development too is broadly conceptualised in terms of cause-effect and predictability. The 'cause' being tools, methods and methodologies for designing and developing information systems and the 'effect' being the information systems product. This is essentially the approach of engineering design.

This evolved concept of information system is suitable for normal organisation. It needs further enhancement to be useful for emergent organisation. Little attention has been given to the effect of emergence on information systems. The 'system' in the term 'information system' is presumed to be a stable and predictable. These are strong features in conceptualisations of information system and in its development process. It is presumed that an information system is a stable and predictable entity (it has known data items and information outputs) and that it operates in a stable environment (the knowable organisation). It is also presumed that the information systems development process is stable and predictable. Predictability in the information systems development process is the expectation that by following some method of development, usually a information system development methodology, the result will be the expected information system product.

Stability, cause-effect and predictability are problematical in the rational design of information systems. Designers and developers encounter problems with stability and predictability in the early stages of information systems development. So-called 'users' are expected to state the functions for a new information system as 'requirements', but often they can only give broad indications, and they tend to change their minds during the development process. Information systems development methods and methodologies become less predictable in the actual context of development. User participatory and prototyping methods have been developed as a response but they too retain the essential core elements of linear systems – stability, cause-effect and predictability.

Being developed for human use and by being placed in human organisation, an information system is a socio-technical system. Stability, cause-effect and predictability are not characteristic of socio-technical systems. A better characterisation of socio-technical systems is complexity. Complex systems are unstable, unpredictable, and adapt to their environment over time. Such systems are termed complex adaptive systems.

Our problem is how to design rationally information systems for emergent context. Emergent contexts include emergent business processes, emergent knowledge processes, emergent organisation structure, and emergent resource needs. We are concerned with the design of information systems with emergent properties. Such complex information systems are embedded in social bodies like organisations and society. Organisation-wide information systems should be designed to have emergent properties (functions). Since aspects of organisation like structure, processes and procedures are emergent, information systems that enable or support them should also be capable of adapting to emergent situations. ERP systems should have emergent properties.

DESIGNING EMERGENT ARTEFACTS RATIONALLY

The problematic of designing information systems rationally by necessity was recognised early (Parnas and Clements 1986). An information system, its development process, and the use of the information system, are all construed to be objects that are created entirely rationally. By rational is meant that designers are expected to be able to explain satisfactorily their design activities. Such rational design assumes explicit purposive action, specifiable business processes, data and information. This is termed information systems specification formalism in the theory of deferred action. The quintessential example of specification formalism is information systems development methodologies.

As noted the meaning that humans attach to information is central to information systems. An information system is much more than rationally specifiable objects. As a socio-technical system, an information system is embedded in a social system (organisation). Since the social system is a complex adaptive system it responds to its environment by changing in an emergent way. Such emergent change is unpredictable. Therefore, information in an emergent organisation cannot be accounted for solely by specification formalism.

Specification formalism fails to recognise emergence and how people, information systems designers and developers and organisational members who make use of the information system

artefact, behave relative to emergence in purposive organisations. Emergence constrains the degree to which an information system can be specified. The scope for designing specification formalism itself is constrained by emergence.

DEVELOPING THE THEORY OF DEFERRED ACTION

Some background leading to the development of the theory of deferred action is discussed in this section. Principles and frameworks for developing information systems conceptualise an information systems as a product and recommend that the product should be developed systematically as phases of an information systems development project. Such phases are well embodied in information systems development methodologies. As no credible alternatives are available, the actual practice of information systems development attempts, rather unsuccessfully, to implement these principles and frameworks. Their success varies greatly but in the main so-called 'users' of information systems are disappointed.

The term 'system' in information systems is not emphasised in the conceptualisation or development frameworks for information systems. Design science research was designed (1) to investigate how an information 'system' is developed and used in organisation and (2) to propose information 'system' design concepts and principles. Four information systems development projects were studied using the case study method in different organisations. When the collected data was analysed it was found that the actual practice of developing information systems differed from the extant principles and frameworks. In some cases and situations the actual use of the information systems by organisational members differed greatly from the intended use. The data could not be interpreted in the available frameworks. The important construct that the data revealed which could not be explained by the frameworks is *emergence*.

To make sense of this emergence data complexity theory was invoked. A core tenant of complexity is emergence. The emergence data was interpreted in terms of complex adaptive systems. The interpretation resulted in conceptualising the information system development process as *deferred systems design* and an information system as a deferred information system (*deferred system*). The design principle of *deferred design decisions* was proposed to implement deferred systems. This principle is designed to raise the level of abstraction of the software artefacts to enable people who use the information system in context to tailor its functions. This reduces the need for an elaborate specification of functionality during design and development. A deferred system is an emergent system. Its systems architecture is designed by reflective designers (professional IT systems developers) but its operational functionality is determined by active designers (people who use the information system) in actual organisational situations.

The deferment construct is a "rich insight" or "second order concept". It is a concept that emerges from the data but through the interpretation of the researcher. It explains how to design information systems rationally for emergent environments like business organisations. The generalisation power of deferment is great. It has been extended to other areas like organisation design (deferred organisation) and to learning in education (deferred learning technology). The generalisability of the deferment construct for designing artefacts that are embedded in social systems was further developed as the Theory of Deferred Action.

THE THEORY OF DEFERRED ACTION

The theory of deferred action (Patel, 2006) is a generic artefact design theory. In Gregor's (2006) terms, it is a theory for action and design. Nomo-

thetically, it explains and suggests effective models of information and knowledge management for emergent organization, by accounting for IT-based information and knowledge systems as embedded in social systems. Its applied aspect helps to explain and improve informational and knowledge artefact design in emergent organization. How can such artefacts cope with organizational change and the uncertainty much characteristic of emergent organization? How can it cope with 'emergent business processes' found in innovation work, jobbing, unit and one-off processes? What kind of taxonomy of knowledge has greater generalisation power and can cope with scaling up? What is an effective model of knowledge capable of accounting for emergent organization? Such questions are addressed by the theory.

The theory assumes business organisations *rationally* seek and pursue some purpose and plan to attain it. A plan is any devise or artefact whose purpose is to construct the future. However, it also assumes *actual* human and organisational behaviour is determined by emergence and sociality in the context of complexity. Therefore, rational behaviour is tempered by emergent behaviour that needs to be catered *actively* in the rational plan. A further assumption is that actuality takes precedence over plans. Actuality is affected by emergence. Therefore, plans need to be evolving to cater for actuality. The main constructs of the theory are: planned action, emergence, and deferred action. A construct in social science refers to an idea that is invented for specific research or theory-building. Constructs are built from other concepts. Normally, constructs are not directly observable but are deduced from relevant empirical observation.

Theorising requires 'creative inspiration' (Rosenthal and Rosnow, 2008). How can the effect of emergence on information and knowledge not only be explained but the theoretical explanation also used to prescribe what action should be taken? This is the design science problem. Given emergent organisation, how can the design of informational and knowledge artefacts be accomplished rationally? The theory of deferred action seeks an answer to this question. It explains emergence in information systems and proposes how to design rationally for emergence. It contributes significant knowledge of how to design socio-technical systems for emergent organisation and improves our understanding of information systems as complex adaptive systems adapting to an emergent environment.

The base theory for the theory of deferred action is complexity theory as expounded previous sections. Emergence is characteristic of complex adaptive systems. The deferment construct explains courses of rationally design human action (organisation to achieve collective purpose and its information systems) suitable for emergent environments. The theory permits analysis of the context of information system to determine the kind of information systems suitable for predictable and unpredictable contexts.

Meta-Design Dimensions

The pre-determined (rational) designability of information systems is affected by emergent organisation. Emergence is a non-specifiable constraint on rational design. It cannot be determined as design objects - it is off-design. When designing and developing information systems, emergence cannot be specified because it is unpredictable. So, what is the rational design of information system for unpredictable environment? Planned action, emergence, and deferred action constructs are meta-design dimensions for designing informational and knowledge artefacts for emergent organisation.

Planned Action

Planned action looks at future states of knowledge. But plans make use of existing available information and knowledge bases. Drawing on established information and knowledge bases is necessary to undertake any planned action aimed at developing future states of knowledge. The innovation of a new electronic product draws on existing electronic information and knowledge bases such as circuit gates, modularisation, and limits to miniaturisation.

Planned action (design) is necessary but not sufficient. Planned action is organisational behaviour devised from some formalism, 'it prescribes actual action as predetermined moves' (Patel, 2006:73) and, therefore, assumes stable organisational structure and processes. Planned action is undertaken centrally. It may be some plan, design, or strategy. Planned action is prescribed action by design and enacted regardless of actuality. For example, a three-year strategic plan or formal systems design for a knowledge management. Planned action characterises human action and organised activity exclusively as rational act and results in specification formalism – formalism used to obtain requirements for and design some IT artefact. Action is rational, purposeful and intentional. It is useful for design problems that can be well-structured based on explicit knowledge and declarative knowledge.

Emergence

Emergence is concerned with the locale - present, contextual, and situational aspects of information. The process of creating future states of knowledge (new knowledge) from information is subject to emergence. While working from an existing electronics information database (planned action), new problems need to be solved that requires new know-how (knowledge). Such information and knowledge has an emergent element. The innovation of a new electronic product draws on the existing knowledge base, but how existing knowledge components are combined while solving new problems is emergent information and knowledge, resulting in some innovative design.

Emergence is 'the occurrence of unplanned and unpredictable human events out of bounds of rational analysis and therefore off-design.' (Patel, 2006: 116) Emergence is the patterns that arise through interactions of actors, and interactions between actors and artefacts, and their environment. Emergence is a becoming aspect of design. It is intrinsic to social organized action. It is an affect of interrelatedness of multifarious purposes and means to achieve them characteristic of social action. In complexity science, emergence is 'the phenomenon of the process of evolving, of adapting and transforming spontaneously and intuitively to changing circumstances and finding new ways of being.' (McMillan, 2004:32). Most examples of emergence are in the natural sciences. There are few concrete business and management examples and no information systems examples. One example relevant to knowledge management is self-organising learning teams. Emergence causes self-organising. Such teams are found in strategic management, where open-ended issues are identified, clarified, and progressed by self-organising networks in an organisation (Stacey, 2003).

In design, planned action prescriptions need to cater for emergence. We postulate that the root of 'wicked problems' (Rittle and Weber, 1984) or wicked information and knowledge problems is emergent organisation. It is necessary to relate by synthesis planned action and emergence to design informational and knowledge artefacts for emergent organisation. Planned action and emergence are related design dimensions when designing for emergent organisation.

Deferred Action

Contextual information happens within a plan (planned information systems) but it cannot be entirely dictated by details of the plan. The electronic product innovation programme (plan) is the goal, but since the actual process of innovation is subject to emergent factors an adequate response to local working situations is necessary – deferred action. Such deferred action is within the programme but enacted in the emergent, rich context of the knowledge generation process, using existing information systems and catering well for creativity. Adaptableness and self-organisation characteristic of complex systems, are aspects of knowledge that are facilitated by deferred action.

Deferred action is the synthetic outcome of relating planned action and emergence. Deferred action results in emergence, space (location), and time being represented in planned action. It enables the enactment of some pre-determined planned action (formal design) by contextualizing it in unpredictable, emergent situations. Deferred action is actual, situational action within some formal design. The formal design is the context in which actual (deferred) action happens. Since emergence is unpredictable actors should be enabled to respond to it in particular organizational situations. Deferred action is the synthesis of planned action and situated action. It enables actors to modify an information system within the context of its use. So an information system is conceptualized as a continuous design and development process, rather than a time-bound product.

Deferred action formally relates emergent actual action with planned action or formal design (Patel, 2006: 96). Deferred action is undertaken locally in the emergent context. It is derived from *natural design* – what humans do naturally to achieve some natural purpose such as sustain and house themselves. Natural design assumes mind and body holistic human action. It is not entirely subject to rationality (planned action or rational design). The three meta-design dimensions and deferred constructs are related and depicted in Figure 2.

The relationships among these constructs, or dimensions of information and knowledge, are stated in Table 1. The dimensions and their interrelationship model *actuality*. Actual situations are never sympathetic to plans or purely rational. They are subject to emergent factors which require an adequate embodied and situational response. In

Figure 2. Deferred action constructs

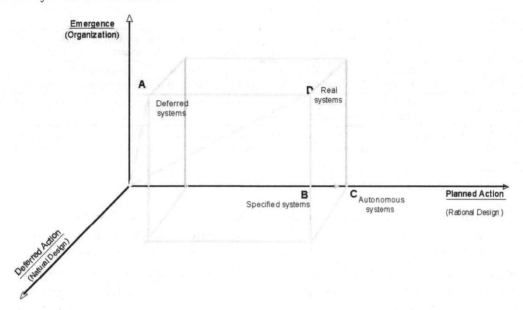

rational design, this response is deferred action. Deferred action differs from *situated action* as propounded by Suchman (1987) because the latter negates plans, while deferred action is the synthesis of planned action and emergent situations. In situated action the situation itself is a given but in deferred action the situation is emergent. Also, situated action lacks enduring structures while planned action builds enduring structures within which deferred action takes place.

Ontology of Information Management

The deferred ontology of data, information and knowledge is determinable, emergent and tailorable. Determinable things are explicitly known to reflective designers, such as stock, costs, and prices. Emergent things are unknown as when competitors bring out new products or when consumers' preferences change. Data, information and knowledge is tailorable in the sense that active designers can tailor operational functionality to suit actual action required in context. They ascribe meaning to it in context. Tailorability

enables operationalisation of tacit knowledge and other deep human traits.

Application of the theory to information management results not only in additional dimensions of information but a new construction of information that contributes to our existing understanding discussed in the introduction. Information can be interpreted in terms of the three constructs and their interrelationships. To illustrate with the example of industrial innovation:

Most usefully, the theory may be used for interventions to inform knowledge-based competition strategy. An example of knowledge-based competition strategy that is well explained by the theory is Google. Knowledge and its creation are important for Google's pre-eminence as a technology leader. Google's mission is to organize the world's information and make it universally accessible and useful. In terms of the theory of deferred action, Google's organisation has the three deferred action dimensions of knowledge. Google has an IT infrastructure (planned action) that is 'built to build', providing the flexibility needed in emergent context. This infrastructure is designed to enable further building by expan-

Table 1. Deferred action dimensions of knowledge

Construct	Description
Planned action	Rational planning is necessary for effective and efficient organisation to build enduring structures and processes that result in some quality product or service for consumption.
Emergence	Emergence creates emergent situations or locale. It makes situations unpredictable. Emergence affects KMS design. Emergence requires KMS design and organisation design to be *continuous*.
Deferred action	Deferred action is the synthesis of planned action and emergence. Deferred action takes place within planned action in emergent locale.
The synthesis of these constructs results in four system types: deferred systems (point A), specified systems (point B), autonomous systems (point C), and real systems (point D) in Figure 1. These types can also be generic design types and organisation types.	

sion and adaptation (emergence) to market needs. Google executives realise that they are not best placed to know the emergence, so they actively enable employees to take action when they consider it appropriate (deferred action). Employees are given 10% of their time for creative work. Thus a Google employee blogger reveals how easy it was for him to write software code and have it implemented in Google's gmail application because he disliked a certain aspect of it. So, Google's organisation is a deferred organisation and its IT systems are deferred systems, as depicted in Figure 2.

The theory contains other theoretical categories summarised in Table 2. These terms arise from application of the theory to the use of IT in business organisations to manage data, information and knowledge. The diffused management category in the table is the logical consequence of emergent organisation. Since emergence is organisation-wide its management in relation to knowledge needs to be diffused in the organisation as in Google's case. The result of the synthesis of the dimensions of knowledge and the categories is the production of informational and knowledge IT artefacts.

GENERIC DEFERRED ACTION DESIGN TYPES

Based on the synthesis of planned action and emergence, organisational action can be mapped

in terms of four generic design types: specified design, real design, deferred design and autonomous design depicted in Figure 3 (also explained in Table 1). Each quadrant names the generic design type, gives example of type of knowledge management best suited for that design type, names the type of organisation and system design, and names the type of work best suited for the design type.

Deferred Design

A deferred system contains design uncertainty and cannot be completely pre-specified because of emergence - the rich human and organizational context in which it functions. Operational needs emerge in this context. Deferred systems contain specifiable and non-specifiable operational design. Systems functionality cannot be completely pre-defined because of emergence. Deferred systems are significant for modern organizations exposed to constant change.

A deferred system is characterised by high emergence, high level of deferred action, and low capacity to plan system functionality and information needs centrally. The operational functionality of a deferred system is a function of its environment. Its form is not predetermined but evolves in response to emergent factors. It exhibits emergent functionality that is not pre-specified (planned) but arises from the intentions of individuals or groups who interact with it in context. Therefore, a deferred system is deferred until the

Table 2. Categories from applying deferred action to IT

Category	Description
Human (behaviour)	Humans use IS and KMS in context. (They are distinguished from professional IS developers but in a sense they design the systems).
Organisation design	Organisation is composed of people, structure, processes, IS and KMS. Organisation is emergent. *Organising* is normal.
IT artefact	IT artefact is any information or knowledge artefact created with the use of information technology. IS and KMS design depends on people, organisation, and emergence. IS and KMS design is affected by emergence. IS and KMS design requires deferred action.
IS and KMS design	IS and KMS design depends on people, organisation, and emergence. IS and KMS design is affected by emergence. IS and KMS design requires deferred action.
Diffused management	Diffused management of local situations is necessary because of emergence. It caters for self-organisation and adaptive behaviour. Centralised management of local situations is ineffective in emergent organisation.

Figure 3. Deferred action taxonomy

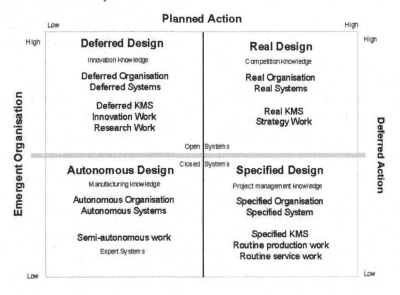

actor decides what the system will become. The actors design decisions are taken through the operational principle of deferred design decisions. An operational principle is 'any technique or frame of reference about a class of artifacts or its characteristics that facilitates creation, manipulation and modification of artifactual forms' (Dasgupta, 1996; Purao, 2002).

The dominant property of deferred system is emergence which requires the use of deferred design decisions principle. A deferred system is

deferred until active designers (actors) decide what it becomes in actuality. *Deferred systems are co-designed by reflective designers (professional designers) and active designers (actors).* Reflective designers make structural time-specific design decisions and active designers make design decisions that are influenced by emergence. They decide the operational functionality as revealed by emergence. Deferred design is not constrained by prior design decisions of reflective designers. Active designers make design decisions in pursuit of objectives and come to <u>own</u> systems. Deferred decisions happen in context in the situation where they are imperative and necessary. Table 3 lists properties of exemplar deferred systems.

Ontologically, data, information and knowledge in deferred systems are tailorable. Data structures and data processing algorithms used to produce information can be tailored to suite particular emergent organisational situations.

Deferred systems are suitable for design domains where specification of operational functionality is ineffective and complete requirements gathering is not possible because of emergence. An example is a knowledge management system to support innovation.

Real Design

Real systems are co-designed in real-time by reflective designers (professional designers) and active designers (actors). Reflective and active designers' design decisions are effective in real-time. Real systems architecture and functionality is not pre-determined design but designed during use in actuality. (This may be required in deferred systems too, but it is not necessary.) Active designers determine design of real-time deferred structure and details of operational functionality. Deferred architectural form and operational functionality is shaped in real-time in context by active designers' deferred design decisions. Such decisions determine much of the operational system architecture.

A real system is enacted in the situation by active developers with the overall objectives set as plans by reflective developers. It acknowledges high emergence, high level of deferred action, and high need to plan. Its overall design is planned to achieve specific objectives but active developers determine the details of these.

Active designers enact a real system. It is not used as a delivered product like other systems types. They come to <u>own</u> the system. Real systems exhibit high emergence, deferred action, and importance of central planning and local action. Therefore they contain much structural and operational design ambiguity. Structure and operational functionality are minimally designed

Table 3. Properties of deferred systems

Deferred System Properties	Spreadsheet	World Wide Web	eXtensible Mark-up Language (XML)
Emergent	√	√	√
Reflective Developer	√	√	√
System-System Environment Interface (S-SEI)	√	√	√
Deferred Design Decisions (DDD)	√	√	√
Action Developer	√	√ Partially, if trained (Extradeferment)	√ (Intradeferment)
Tailoring Tools (Ttools)	√ (micro-Ttools)	√(micro-Ttools & Meso-tailoring)	√ (meso-Ttools)
Non-SDLC Developed	√	√	√

Source: Patel N V (2006) Organisation and Systems Design: The Theory of Deferred Action, Palgrave Macmillan

because they are enacted, rather than placed, in context. Real systems take shape, form and change by deferred action.

Systems architecture is divided into specified structure and deferred structure. Like building construction design process, deferment of structure is possible in real design. The architecture of real systems emerges. Requirements for deferment structure can be determined by specification. Structure too does not have to be specified it can be deferred. Reflective designers design specified structure. Specification design is to achieve specific objectives as planned action. Reflective designers cannot predict all the structural form and no operational form because of emergence. The capability to design for real-time by specification is minimal in emergent organisation.

The dominant property of real system is emergence requiring the principle of real design decisions. Real systems are enactive. Active designers enact real systems during action. Reflective and active designers jointly make structural and functional design decisions. Reflective designers make initial structural design decisions based on requirements specification. When the system is live active designers make structural and operational functionality design decisions by deferment design in real-time.

Real systems data, information and knowledge ontology is similar to deferred systems. It differs because it emerges and it is determined and implemented in real-time. Design issue in real design decision is the same as in deferred design. The difference is that real design decisions need to be implemented in systems in real-time, using technology that delivers real-time data, information and knowledge. The same design principle as for deferred systems applies to reflect deferred action in formal systems design.

Real systems are suitable for design domains where specification of real-time structure and operations is not possible, where they emerge and need to be realised in context in real-time. So they require deferred action. An example is 'comput-

ing on the edge of network' military systems and aspects of learning systems. Real systems are of interest to military organizations, educationalists and companies. Modern theatre of war poses new problems for military strategists to achieve objectives because strategy alone cannot account for the actual field of operation. Central planning becomes redundant in actual contexts because of unknown variables and emergent situations. Understanding interrelations among specification design, emergence, and deferred action and deferred design can provide a framework for designing appropriate action to achieve aims.

Specified Design

A specified system is designed and shaped prior to operation in actuality. It is assigned artificially to design domains by reflective designers. Complete design knowledge is assumed. Specified systems admit no emergence and assume high capability for specification design. So systems architecture and operational functionality is specified with specification formalism. Operational functionality is assumed to be knowable, specifiable by 'users' prior to use and assumption of stable systems 'environment' is made. The dominant property of specified systems is predetermined structure and functions resulting in the dominant design principle of specified design decision.

Specified systems are imposed. Reflective designers are exclusive designers. Design is based on specification of information and knowledge needs 'captured' from potential 'users'. Such design requires complete 'requirements gathering', 'specification' and 'engineering' by reflective designers. Specification formalism is used to develop elaborate systems models to represent design domains. Formal specification details systems architecture and operational functionality. Reflective designers then design systems models and implement them. Such designing is presumed capable using information systems development methodology or other practice conforming to SDLC main phases.

A specified system has predefined functionality designed into it by reflective developers who 'capture' requirements from potential users. Systems strategists and system designers assume that system functionality is knowable and the system environment is stable. Consequently, specified systems admit low emergence and low deferred action, and assume high capacity for system planning. Specified systems are suitable for application domains that are unambiguous and completely specifiable, and do not require deferred action. They assume perfect knowledge, stable system functionality and system environment. Early applications of IT to business were of this type, and most strategic system planning is in this quadrant.

Reflective designers only make specified design decisions. Only they can design systems. Design of large-scale software particularly relies on specified design and is termed 'software engineering'. Reflective designers make all the design decisions in metaphorical 'clean rooms' detached from experiences of 'users' and actual context of use. The design issue is how to determine formal systems specification for reflective designers' use to code systems.

Business workers simply use designed systems. Deferred action necessary for contextual information needs from systems is constrained by prior reflective designers' specified design decisions, which explains research that finds systems are not used or tend to disappoint. Changes required to systems to make them relevant to context are relayed and managed by reflective designers as 'change control'.

Ontologically, data, information and knowledge are objects existing independently. They are knowable, determinable, stable, fixed and independent of 'developers' and 'users'. Specified design decisions are based on ontology of information as mechanical artefact (Shannon, 1948). Specified systems do not admit meaning attribution to information.

Specified systems are suitable for completely specifiable, certain and unequivocal design domains. Emergence is not present. So, they do not require deferred action. Early applications of computers to business were of this type, and most strategic system planning is done as specified design.

Autonomous Design

An autonomous system makes use of intelligent software to predefine system design choices for users. The autonomous agent is the autonomous software. Emergence is not explicitly acknowledged in autonomous systems design. Two types of autonomous systems can be distinguished based on control given to 'users'. Reflective designers predefine systems functionality embedded in intelligent agents enabled to make design decisions autonomously and independently of business workers and reflective designers. Some designs are based on formalism derived from the situated action thesis. Intelligence inside machines is dominant design principle. Presently they admit low emergence, low capacity for specification design and low deferred action. There are no real examples of such systems, but researchers and designers are exploring multi-agent systems for many organizational processes. Autonomous systems have potential as aspects of other generic design types in organized action not as a separate entity.

The other type is context scenarios or patterns used to suggest design solutions to 'users' during system use. Autonomous systems suggest embedded predetermined design choices. Design choices are predefined scenarios created by reflective designers, and active designers only have choice to accept or reject context-sensitive design offered. Design choices are inferred from observed user behaviour actions. Context scenarios are akin to business best practice. Context scenarios and patterns are distinct from actual contexts that deferred systems and real systems active designers encounter.

Reflective designers determine predefined systems functionality in autonomous systems, which may be based on requirements specified by 'users'. Operative design principle is autonomy in context. System effectiveness is improved through autonomous design decisions.

Ontology of data, information and knowledge is objective and specified. It is predetermined and does not permit tailoring. Character of knowledge in expert systems is explicit and declarative knowledge. In general, artificial intelligence systems characterise knowledge as explicit knowledge, fixed and knowable. Data and information are similarly characterised. At present, scope for emergent information is theoretical in multi-agent systems.

The autonomous designer is the intelligent agent embedded in autonomous systems, who makes or recommends autonomous design decisions based on pre-determined context. 'The autonomous designer is the artificial intelligence embedded in a system.' (Patel, 2003: 5) Autonomous designer is enabled by reflective designers to recommend design decisions to 'users', for example in office applications. In more sophisticated example, multiple agents collaborate to determine design decisions. They determine what operational functionality or service to perform in situations.

Autonomous systems are suitable for completely knowable and predictable design domains. In the Internet, a completely knowable routing policy is determined for a collection of IP networks and routers and placed under the control of one entity (or sometimes more) making an autonomous system. A prime facet of autonomous systems is artificial machine intelligence. Autonomous systems are the physical embodiment of machine intelligence.

Different levels of synthesis of planned action and emergence result in these four design types for normal organisation and emergent organisation. The design types are generic and equally appli-

able to designing organisations and information systems. Rational strategy formulation, central planning, and information systems development methodologies are examples of specified design. Emergent strategy formulation and sustainable business and education are examples of deferred and real design. Technologically enabled battlefield action and civil air traffic control are examples of real design.

Invoking systems theory, the taxonomy is further analysed into open information systems and closed information systems (depicted in Figure 3 by the horizontal line). Open systems of information are deferred and real information systems because their boundaries are open and variable. These tend to be self-organising systems that require complex adaptive behaviour undertaken by local actors. Crucially, they are *evolving* information systems and knowledge bases. An example is the World Wide Web and in knowledge management similar to the joint UK, Australian and New Zealand governments' effort to construct a knowledge base for teaching and research. (e-framework, 2008). Closed systems of information and knowledge are specified and autonomous because their boundaries are closed and fixed. Changes to such systems require re-design and re-engineering centrally. Most organisational information systems are closed systems.

The deferred action analysis is applicable to any design problem in which humans are an integral part of the designed artefact. Humans and information technology are in symbiotic relationship. Many such design problems are necessarily open systems because organised action occurs in the political, economic and social environment that is subject to emergence.

PROPERTIES OF EMERGENT ARTEFACTS

Structure, Emergence, Space and Time (SEST) are a set of design constructs applicable for designing artefacts that are affected by emergence. SEST are attributes of rational design conducive to actuality. A construct in social science refers to an idea that is invented for specific research or theory-building. Constructs are built from other concepts. Normally, the construct is not directly subject to observation but is deduced from relevant empirical observation. These constructs were created to inform the design of information systems in emergent organization.

An organisation has a structure (hierarchical, flat, network). The unplanned and unexpected events are emergent aspects. The space is the locale in which action takes place. The period over which the action takes place is the time.

The World Wide Web has a dual structure. It is mounted on the Internet and so limited by the structure of the Internet. But it has its content structure which is very complex. The physical structure of the Internet does emerge as more nodes are added, but the content structure is highly emergent. The geographical space covered by the Internet nodes is the space property and the period of time the Web exists is the time property. Similarly, an ERP system has a physical structure its architecture. It is located in the organisational space of a company and operates over time from the time of its inception. Although its functionality is largely pre-specified, aspects of emergent organisation require enhancement to the functionality over the life of the organisation.

Complex adaptive systems can also be characterised as possessing the SEST properties. An ecosystem has the structure of trees, species of birds and mammals, insects and fauna, which compose the structural elements of the system. The emergent property of an ecosystem is the new structure or order resulting from some change like extinction of an animal or plant species, or possibly deforestation, in the system. The geographical area that the ecosystem covers is the space property and the period of time over which the ecosystem exists or changes is the time property.

Environment is the significant factor affecting the system. The SEST properties are determined in the context of the environment. By gaining knowledge of the environment the system adapts itself. Knowledge is an important determinant of the structure and functions of the system.

DEVELOPING DEFERRED SYSTEMS

Deferred system is the deferred information system and deferred system design is the process for developing a deferred system continuously. The development of a deferred system requires a continuous development process. This is termed the deferred systems design process (DSDp). The development process is necessarily continuous because of the emergence effect. The continuous development process is composed of two types of systems design decisions.

Specified design decisions and deferred design decisions are two types of design decisions stemming from normal organisation (predictable) and emergent organisation (unpredictable) respectively. The pre-determined knowable architecture and functions of the system can be specified and these are specified design decisions. These decisions occur at a specific point in time. These are the predictable aspects of the deferred system. The need for new information in new organisational situations is catered for by deferred design decisions. Actors take the deferred decisions in particular organisational situations. These decisions occur over time.

A deferred system is a model driven architecture and it is modelled as an active model. An active model maintains a synchronised link with the domain of the application (Warboys, et al., 1999). They are models of information systems that are linked and synchronised with actuality. The active model enables deferred design decisions.

The architecture and functions of deferred systems should be capable of adapting and, as Tim

Berners Lee (1999) states for the Web, there should be no single point of failure. The basis of adaptation is systemic deferment point analysis in which deferment points are determined. A deferment point is the juncture at which purposeful human action that is formalised in some sense encounters actuality. A formally designed decision support system meets a deferment point when it fails to provide information that decision makers require. The shortcoming is usually the consequence of pre-programmed rigid data processing algorithms. It is the systemic equivalent of deferred action that arises when purposeful human action encounters emergence (Patel, 2005).

In terms of the deferred action analysis, ERP systems are designed and developed as specified systems. However, they are better conceived as deferred systems. Admittedly, in a manufacturing organisation much of the processes and operations can be pre-determined and specified to develop known system functionality. As noted earlier, there are however unknown events that give rise to emergent processes which cannot be pre-specified. For such reasons ERP systems are better modelled as deferred systems (with elements of specified systems).

APPLICATIONS OF DEFERRED ACTION BASED DESIGN

The theory of deferred action and the principle of deferred design decisions are used and applied by researchers in research systems and applied business systems. Various types of knowledge work benefit from the deferred analysis including legal arbitration and organisational learning. This work tends to be of the semi-structured problem type. Two exemplars are given. Both these systems are in the domain of knowledge management.

E-Arbitraton-T System

Elliman and Eatock (2005) developed the online E-Arbitraton-T system capable of handling workflow for *any* legal arbitration case, thus meeting the emergence criteria. The project aimed to develop an online system for Europen SMEs seeking fair dispute resolution in an international forum. The system would be used by many different organizations offering arbitration services but the cost of adapting E-Arbitratio-T to local priorities, including emergent factors, had to be kept low as some organizations had low case loads making high cost unjustifiable. Elliman and Eatock applied the deferred analysis, particularly the

Table 4. Deferred technology implementations

Term	Description
Deferred-action-list; deferred-action function	Used in emacs-development.
Deferred Execution Custom Actions	Used in scripts for Windows installer.
Deferred Procedure Calls	Microsoft uses DPCs to manage hardware interrupts At micro-processor level: Microsoft's response to this problem is to use Deferred Procedure Calls (DPCs). http://www.nematron.com/HyperKernel/index.shtml
Client side deferred action with multiple MAPI profiles	This is a patent at: http://www.patentalert.com/docs/000/Z00002860.shtml
Java deferred classes	Used in the Java computer programming language.

deferred design decisions principle, to manage the open and changing system requirements, making their system an open system. This enabled users to make design choices rather than the system developer.

CoFIND System

The deferred action construct is reflected in deferred learning systems. Dron (2005) invokes deferred systems to design systems that have 'emergent structure', allowing the system to have changing functionality. He developed a self-organised e-learning web-based system called CoFIND. Self-organisation in CoFIND results in emergent structure which the system needs to reflect. It is not designed from requirements but takes shape in response to the actions of the people that use it.

EXPLAINING SYSTEMS PRACTICE AS DEFERRED ACTION

More generally, the theory can be applied to explain the invention of much deferred technology shown in Table 4. These independent inventions serve to cater for emergence in digital applications of information and communications technologies. It is because fixed technological functions are inadequate in emergent situations that the deferred technology is invented. The function of the deferred technology takes form in actual contexts,

contexts which could not be pre-determined by designers and developers.

Open Source Software as Deferred Systems

Open source software is well explained by the theory of deferred action. Open source software is a complex adaptive system that is a deferred system. It has a planning core that determines the direction in which open source software will develop. This is the planned action element of the system. But the actual problems addressed by open source software are determined locally (emergence) by individual software coders (deferred action). This is the emergent aspect of the system. The Linux operating system is an exemplar.

Extant information systems and information technology can be mapped in terms of the four design types, shown in Table 5.

FUTURE DEVELOPMENTS OF THE THEORY

Deeper empirical investigation of the effect of emergence on the rational design of organisations and its information systems is planned. The purpose of the empirical work is manifold. It is necessary to collect data on aspects of the theory that are still tentative such as determining deferment points and converting them into systemic deferment points. There is also a need to

Table 5. Classification of extant systems in terms of deferred action

Deferred System	Real System	Autonomous System	Specified Systems
World Wide Web CoFIND ViPre Dallas Capital	Internet Semantic Web Air traffic control Modern military systems	Intelligent agents	Payroll Sales Product databases

better define the operational principle of deferred design decisions supported with empirical data, which would provide better scientific basis for the principle. The other purpose is to generate new theoretical constructs from the data to improve our understanding of how complexity can be catered for in rational design.

The empirical data will also support further research into developing a design complexity scale for information systems. What is the design complexity of a proposed information systems project and what is the design complexity of the information systems itself? What is its intrinsic complexity? Such questions can be addressed with a design complexity scale based on empirical data.

Measuring complexity is a critical issue in rational design. Empirical data will enable consideration of items of measure, such as count number of data types and data items, number of data retrievals from database, or number of interactions by users with the information systems. Some measure of complexity is necessary to do rational design properly. It is not the intention to measure complexity per se, as this is theoretically not possible. The purpose is the define measures of complexity suitable for rational design of information systems. In physics, a complex system is measured as the length of the description of the system. In general, a system is more complex if the length of its description is longer.

CONCLUSION

This chapter has addressed how to design rationally information systems for emergent organisation. Complexity and emergence are new design problem that constrains rational design. The Theory of Deferred Action is proposed to reconcile rationalism and emergence in information systems design and development. The theory is a synthesis of rationalism and emergence producing the deferred action design construct. Theories on

designing for normal organisation exist but most of them are borrowed from reference disciplines. The Theory of Deferred Action is based in the information systems discipline and is presented as a theory to inform practice to improve the rational design of information systems for emergent organisation. As emergence is a core feature of complexity, complexity theory was invoked as a base theory for developing the Theory of Deferred Action as a design theory. The Theory of Deferred Action explains the effect of emergence on the rational design of information systems. As a theory to inform practice it provides guidance on how to design rationally information systems for emergent organisation.

The theory has the potential to be applied to any kind of artifactual systems designed by humans in which humans are an integral design element. This includes cities, organisations, information systems, and knowledge management systems among others. It is a general theory for the artificial sciences where the system to be designed interacts with humans and the interaction causes the system to be re-designed by actors in the context of the interaction.

Theoretical physicists and experimental physicists both have exalted places in physics. Theories generated by theoretical physicists inform the experiments that experimental physicist set up. Data produced by experimental physicists lead theoretical physicists to support their theories or revise them. If we are to improve the discipline of information systems then the same should happen in our discipline. The status of theoretical researchers of information systems should be acknowledged and valued.

REFERENCES

Baskerville, R., Travis, J., & Truex, D. P. (1992) Systems without method: The impact of new technologies on information systems development projects. In K. E. Kendell, K. Lyytinen, & J. I.

DeGross, (Eds.), *Transactions on the impact of computer supported technologies in information systems development.* Amsterdam: Elsevier.

Berners-Lee T. & Fischetti M. (1999). *Weaving the Web: The original design and ultimate destiny of the World Wide Web by its inventor.* New York: HarperCollins.

Bertuglia, C. S. and Vaio F (2005) *Nonlinearity, chaos and complexity,* Oxford, UK: OUP.

Casti, J. (1986) On system complexity: Identification, measurement, and management. In J. Casti & A. Karlqvist (Eds.), *Complexity, language, and life: Mathematical approaches.* Berlin: Springer-Verlag.

Dasgupta, S. (1996). *Technology and creativity.* New York: Oxford University Press.

Dron, J. (2005). Epimethean information systems: Harnessing the power of the collective in e-learning. *Int. J. Information Teachnology and Management, 4*(4), 392-404.

Elliman, T., & Eatock J. (2005). Online support for arbitration: Designing software for a flexible business process. *Int. J. Information Teachnology and Management, 4*(4), 443-460.

Feldman, M. S. (2000). Organizational routines as a source of continuous change. *Organization Science, 11*(6), 611-629.

Feldman, M. S. (2004). Resources in emerging structures and processes of change. *Organization Science, 15*(3), 295-309.

Gregor, S. (2006). The nature of theory in information systems. *MIS Quarterly, 30*(3), 611-642.

Purao, S. (2002). *Design research in the technology of information systems: Truth or dare* (Working Paper). Atlanta: GSU Department of CIS.

e-Framework. (2008) *The e-framework.* Retrieved from, http://www.e-framework.org

Gell-Mann, M. (1994). *The jaguar and the quark.* New York: W. H. Freeman and Company.

Johnson, J., Zamenopoulos, T., & Alexiou, K. (Eds.). (2005). *Proceedings from the ECCS 2005 Satellite Workshop: Embracing Complexity in Design.* Paris.

Larsen, T. J., Levine, L., & DeGross, J. I. (Eds.). (1998). *Information systems: Current issues and future changes* (pp. 155-174). Laxenberg, Austria: IFIP.

McMillan, E. (2004). *Complexity, organizations and change.* London: Routledge.

Markus, M. L., Majchrzak, A., et al. (2002). A design theory for systems that support emergent knowledge processes. *MIS Quartely, 26,* 179-212.

Parnas, D., & Clements, P. (1986). Rational design process: How and why we fake it. *IEEE Transactions on Software Engineering, 12*(2), 251-257.

Patel, N. V. (2002). Emergent forms of IT governance to support global ebusiness models. *Journal of Information Technology Theory and Application.*

Patel, N. V. (2005). Sustainable systems: Strengthening knowledge management systems with deferred action. *International Journal of Information Technology and Management, 4*(4), 344-365.

Patel, N. V. (2006). *Organization and systems design: Theory of deferred action.* Basingstoke, UK: Palgrave Macmillan.

Patel, N. V., (Ed.). (2003). *Adaptive evolutionary information systems.* Hershey, PA: Idea Group Publishing.

Polanyi, M. (1966). *The tacit dimension.* New York: Harper Torchbooks.

Rittel, H. & Webber, M. (1984). Planning problems are wicked problems. In *Developments in design methodology* (N. Cross ed.) (pp. 135-144). New York: Wiley.

Rosenthal, R., & Rosnow, R. L. (2008). *Essentials of behavioural research*. New York: McGrawHill.

Shannon, C. E. (1948). A mathematical theory of communication. *Bell System Technical Journal, 27*(July, October), 379-423 & 623-656.

Simon, H. A. (1996). *The sciences of the artificial*. Cambridge, MA: The MIT Press.

Stacey, R. D. (2003). *Strategic management and organizational dynamics*. Harlow, UK: Pearson Education Limited.

Suchman, L. (1987). *Plans and situated action*. UK: Cambridge University Press.

Takeda, H., Veerkamp, P., Tomiyama, T., & Yoshikawam, H. (1990). Modeling Design Processes. *AI Magazine* (Winter), 37-48.

Truex, D. P., Baskerville, R., et al. (1999). Growing systems in emergent organisations. *Communications of the ACM, 42*(8).

Truex, D. P., & Klein H. K. (1991). A rejection of structure as a basis for information systems development. In R. K. Stamper, P, Kerola, R. Lee, & K. Lyytinen, (Eds.), *Collaborative work, social communications, and information systems*. Amsterdam: Elsevier.

Von Foerster, H. (2003). *Understanding understanding*. New York: Springer.

Walls, J. G., & Widmeyer, G. R. (1992). Building an information system design theory for vigilant EIS. *Information Systems Journal, 3*(1), 36-59.

Warboys, B., Kawalek, P., Robertson, I., & Greenwood, M. (1999). *Business information systems: A process approach*. The McGraw-Hill Companies.

Zamenopoulos, T., & Alexiou, K. (2005). Linking design and complexity: A review. In J. Johnson, T. Zamenopoulos, & K. Alexiou (Eds.), *Proceedings of the ECCS 2005 Satellite Workshop on Embracing Complexity in Design* (pp. 91-102). Paris: The Open University.

KEY TERMS AND DEFINITIONS

Action Designer: Action designer is someone engaged in organised action, needs scope to design within bounds of specified design of formal organization or system design. Has knowledge of actual action, determines design in actual space and time. They *come* to know and have procedural knowledge, which is stronger than declarative knowledge.

Actuality: The domain of empirical. Present time.

Autonomous Design: Design capability afforded to intelligent machines by reflective designers that becomes autonomous of humans.

Autonomous Design Decisions: Design decision made by intelligent agents or systems.

Autonomous Designer: Intelligent agents or systems.

Autonomous System: Systems behaving independently of its human reflective designers.

Deferred Action: Deferred action is concerned with enabling actual action as interrelation design within formal design. It is synthesis of planned action and actual (deferred) action.

Deferred Design: Deferred design is design by action designers within formal design to cope with unknowable emergence, space and time, 'equivocal reality'.

Deferred Design Decisions: Design decisions enabled by reflective designers but made by action designers in context.

Deferred Organization: Structure designed by reflective designers whose actual operations take shape in context through behaviours determined by action designers.

Deferred System: Systems architecture designed by reflective designers whose actual operational functionality takes shape in context through behaviours determined by action designers.

Design Domain: The planned action notion of an actual organizational problem demarcated for systems design by specification.

Emergence: A term to describe unknowable and unpredictable social action in all its multifarious aspects. Philosophically, it is instrumental in determining being.

Emergent Organization: Social action that is organised but subject to emergence.

Enacting: Enacting is the act of putting design in social action with interrelations design capable of real-time structural and operational functionality design. Enacting enables action designers to make design decisions in response to Complete SEST.

Formal Methods: System of symbols representative of reality and rules for abstraction of things form reality and their composition to form models.

Formalism: Prescribed methods containing precise symbols and rules for creating structural forms to achieve set objectives.

Individual Deferment Points: Junctures in purposeful action within existing formal structures where next steps are indeterminate.

Natural Design: The conscious and unconscious determination of objectives and action leading to its achievement by conscious or unconscious determination of structure and responses to emergence in actual space and time.

Off-Design: In terms of SEST structure is designable by specification. Off-design is the emergent, spatial, temporal aspects of organized action that cannot be specified for design. Off-design is the universal set of natural design. Some structural properties of action cannot be specified either.

Organization: Determination of goal-directed actions leading to structural forms whose actual form is the result of responses to degrees of emergence.

Organizational Deferment Points: Junctures in purposeful organised action within existing formal structures where next steps are indeterminate.

Planned Action: Planned action is prescribed action enacted by design regardless of actuality.

Problem Space: Metamorphic space where human concern is progressively systematised and formalised to derive a solution.

Rational Design: Rational design is conscious event at some point in organized social action to determine the future. It is abstract design because the design objects are some orders removed from actuality.

Real Design: Design of structures and operations by rational design for enactment in emergent actuality and responsive to it in real-time.

Real Design Decisions: Real-time design decisions by action designers in response to emergent events in actuality.

Real Organization: Organizational structure and operations designed and enacted in emergent actuality and in real-time.

Real Systems: Systems architecture and operations designed and enacted in emergent actuality and in real-time.

Reflective Designer: Designers of structural forms containing deferment mechanisms for deferred operational design. Teams of professional organization and systems designers.

SEST: The attributes of rational design conducive to actuality.

Situated Action: Action that is rich in phenomenological attribution.

Specification Formalism: Prescribed methods for creating structural forms and operational detail to achieve set objectives.

Specified Design: Design by reflective designers from specification obtained from users.

Specified Design Decisions: Design decisions by reflective designers separated spatially and temporally from actuality.

Specified Organization: Organizational structure and operations designed by reflective designers for business workers.

Specified System: Systems architecture and operations designed by reflective designers for business workers.

Systemic Deferment Points: Junctures within existing formal systems where operational design (and for real systems structural design) are deferred to action designers.

Systemic Deferred Objects: Representation of real things in systems by deferred design.

Systems Deferment Point Analysis: Technique to determine structural and operational design deferrable to action designers.

Technological Deferment Points: Junctures within technology where operational design (and for real technology structural design) are deferred to action designers.

Section III
Innovation, Adoption and Diffusion

This section has five chapters addressing theoretical issues concerning adoption and diffusion of technological innovations. The first chapter (Chapter XI) integrates the two theories diffusion of innovation and capability theory for understanding adoption of new applications such electronic government in the context of developing country. The next chapter (Chapter XII) aims to establish whether evolutionary diffusion theory (EDT) could offer an instrument for determining acceptance levels of innovative technologies. The chapter suggests that EDT offers remarkable explanatory depth, applicable not only to analyzing the uptake of complex, multi-user technologies in organizational settings but to any e-business investigation requiring a system-wide perspective. The next chapter, Chapter XIII, analyzes four alternative theories (theory of cognitive dissonance, social judgment theory, theory of passive learning, and self-perception theory) in light of the technology acceptance model (TAM) and suggests that these theories provide a reverse relationship in contrast to the traditional attitude-behavior relationship in TAM. The fourth chapter in this section (Chapter XIV) introduces diffusion of innovations (DOI) as a research problem theory applied to examining a business case involving the replacement of enterprise systems by a large risk-averse public sector university in Australasia. Finally, Chapter XV explores the technology acceptance model and other theories of user acceptance.

Chapter XI
Diffusion of Innovation and Capability Theory in the Context of E–Government

Mahmud Akhter Shareef
Carleton University, Canada

Vinod Kumar
Carleton University, Canada

Uma Kumar
Carleton University, Canada

Ahsan Akhter Hasin
Bangladesh University of Engineering & Technology, Bangladesh

ABSTRACT

E-government (EG) enables governments to provide citizens easier and electronic access to information and modernized services through personal computers, kiosks, telephones, and other resources. Information and communication technology (ICT) is the prime driving force of EG. Therefore, before implementing an EG project, it is vital to investigate the capability of developing countries to adopt ICT and research the impact of adopting ICT in that society. The authors argue that the purposes of implementing EG can only be accomplished and the full benefits of EG realized if a majority of the population of developing countries has the ability to adopt ICT, the main driver of EG. Therefore, it is essential for policy makers of developing countries to study the adoption capability of ICT of citizens prior to launching EG. Otherwise, there is the strong possibility that EG projects could not accomplish the purpose of its implementation and could fail to reduce the digital divide, establish equal rights for all citizens, and promote good governance.

INTRODUCTION

Over recent years, information technology (IT) has experienced an unprecedented degree of change, enabling the transformation of the basic mechanisms of public administration and business. This transformation is accelerated and supported by computer-based applications to the management processes (Miers, 1996). The emergence of the Internet as a general communication channel has also opened the opportunity for E-government (EG) and E-commerce (EC) to be globalized. The adoption and extension of IT is now a major concern in many countries. According to Lanvin (1995), the development of global technology infrastructure is imperative to help both developed and developing countries improve the image of business organizations and exploit the global market substantially (Wilson, 2001). It plays a significant role in the present information- and knowledge-based market by planning, generating, managing, and transmitting information in the most effective way. Modern IT provides easy access and availability across the countries and invites potential customers by providing the necessary information through the Internet. Therefore, the global proliferation of technology is the backbone of global EG and EC. However, the sphere of the scope of EG is much wider than EC. Alternatively, EC is only a fragmented part of EG. EG is about complete relationships with both the public and private institutions and the foundation of our next-generation states and communities. Understanding what citizens and businesses want and how government, the private sector, and other institutions will be integrated is the vital function of EG. Transformation and reengineering of public institutions require new discourses about policy issues and political realities and their impact on the satisfaction of different stakeholders (Sakowicz, 2007). The EG model should also encompass the evolution of ICT, the reformation of public administration, and the integration of stakeholders. Therefore, EG has a

much wider, more extensive, and more exhaustive application of ICT than does EC.

EG refers to government's use of IT to provide and exchange information and services with citizens, businesses, and other stakeholders of government. It is a tool to transform and reengineer public sector work through the use of ICT (Schware and Deane, 2003). It enables government to provide citizens with easier and electronic access to information and modernized services from anywhere in the world through personal computers, kiosks, telephones, and other resources (Banerjee and Chau, 2004). This suggests that citizens, for example, no longer need to claim services in person over the counter. EG involves using ICT to deliver public services through digital channels. Throughout the world, governments are realizing the potential of placing traditional government services online. However, varying degrees of complexity, failure, and success in the process have been observed from different parts of the world. Different EG implementation results (Heeks, 2002; Ho, 2002; Moon, 2002) show that strategic development of EG initiatives can be very complex, which demonstrates the difficulties of transition to EG.

Previous experiences also demonstrate that the proper implementation of EG is very complex and depends on many different factors. Moreover, since its main mission is citizen driven, its implementation, development, and performance should be such that it meets the criteria and facilitating factors that enable citizens to adopt this modern technology-driven government system—EG. In this connection, the diffusion of innovation (DOI) theory can be a powerful instrument to investigate the facilitating factors for adoption of ICT-based EG by citizens (Carter and Bélanger, 2005; Moore and Benbasat, 1991; Rogers, 1995; Tornatzky and Klein, 1982). EG should also overcome the initial resistance of citizens, be culturally sensitive, and change the way different stakeholders of EG relate to each other. One potential concern in this aspect is the digital divide. Does a majority of the population in developing countries, which are less advanced in technology diffusion (exceptions are developing countries like India, China, Malaysia, South Korea, Thailand, and Brazil), have the capability to adopt ICT? The capability theory introduced by Nussbaum and Sen (1993) can provide significant insight in conceptualizing the capability to adopt ICT grounded on DOI.

User ability and acceptance of a new technology can be defined as the skill, integrity, and competence of users to learn, use, and adopt a new technology and also capture the functional benefits of that technology, either completely or partially, and demonstrable willingness to employ that technology for the tasks it is designed to support. Thus, acceptance theorists are less concerned with unintended and unplanned uses and more interested in understanding the factors influencing the ability to use and accept technologies as planned by users who have specific intentions to use it. DOI is an IS theory that models how users come to accept and use a technology, and thus technology is diffused throughout the population. The model suggests that when users are presented with a new technology, a number of societal, behavioral, and individual ability factors influence their decision about how and when they will use it. Researchers have investigated a wide range of issues relating to technology diffusion and transfer. These factors include the attitude of a government, the technology absorption capability of citizens, appropriateness of technology, and the management of ICT. Also important are the development and maintenance of technology, cooperation or conflict between government and citizens, and the social and economic benefits of EG through adopting the new IT (Brudney and Sally, 1995; Bugler and Stuart, 1993; Cusumano and Elenkov, 1994; Norris and Moon, 2005).

The strategy and objectives of EG development has technological, social, economic, organizational, marketing, and political aspects. From the technological point of view, different countries strategically implement EG to institutionalize modern ICT in the government, make citizens familiar with ICT, and capitalize on the benefits of this technology. From the social point of view, the implementation strategy of EG focuses on changing social relations between government and citizens, creating more opportunity for citizens to participate in government decision making, and improving living standards. The economic aspects of developing EG lies in boosting national development, keeping a leading position in the global economy, integrating the domestic market, and promoting international investment, which will improve the economic capability at the micro level. From the organizational perspective, EG has as an objective to reform and re-engineer public administration which can be very bureaucratic, corrupt, and stagnant. The marketing aspect of EG is mostly driven by improving the service quality, which ensures its competence with the private sector. This agenda includes efficient, cost effective, dynamic, extensive, easy, and higher quality services of government to citizens and businesses. The political aspect of EG has as its objectives to enhance public participation and access to government information and decision making, promote a cohesive government with all the stakeholders of government, improve transparency and accountability, and, thus, to improve governance.

However, in order to develop a citizen-focused, EG system that provides participants with accessible, relevant information, and quality services that are more expedient than traditional "brick and mortar" transactions, government agencies must first understand the factors that influence citizens' adoption of this innovation. Developing countries are especially vulnerable to adoption of EG, since ICT is the primary driving force of EG. Due to a significant digital divide in developing countries between the urban and rural populations, accomplishing the primary objectives of EG as a nation fundamentally depends on the adoption capability of ICT among the less advanced population. If it is discovered that the impact of implementing ICT at the national level reflects more discrimination and a deeper digital divide in respect to the social, technological, and financial aspects, it is rarely possible to succeed in implementing EG. Numerous studies (Basu, 2004; Dada, 2006; Ndou, 2004) have shown that it is not only the application of EG, but also ICT in general, that have abruptly failed in developing countries. Success stories can be cited in literature, but failures are more frequent (Krishna *et al.*, 2005). Heeks (2003) studied the application of EG theme in developing countries and found that 35 percent were classified as total failures at the outset of the application or immediately afterwards, and 50 percent were termed as partial failures, i.e., the major goals were not attained or there were unexpected and freaky outcomes. Why did this happen or why is it still happening? Several scholarly articles (Bhatnagar, 2002; Dada, 2006; Heeks, 2002; Madu, 1989) noted that IT is still not diffused in developing countries as a means of appropriate communication, and they also observed that it was a subtle mistake to implement the models of ICT in developing countries by copying directly from developed countries. The technology absorption capacity of developing countries and its impact are quite different from developed countries. Before funding and implementing EG in developing countries, it is a challenging issue to identify the generic and distinctive characteristics of developing countries in terms of the overall technology absorption capabilities of citizens and its impact on the digital divide, since ICT is the driving force of EG. Existing literature hardly addresses this aspect comprehensively, because research into issues related to the implementation of EG are at an early stage (Heeks and Bailur, 2007; Titah and Barki, 2005). However, understanding and conceptualizing this issue is very important for researchers, practitioners, and United Nations organizations (Madon, 2004; Madu, 1989). Therefore, the objective of this research is twofold:

1. To identify the prime purposes of EG development as a major sector of ICT and to identify the issues related to accomplishing those purposes.

2. To explore the use of DOI theory to learn the adoption capability of ICT and shed light on the capability theory.

To accomplish the abovementioned objectives, this study is focused on developing countries. Because developed countries like, USA, Canada, UK, Denmark, Finland, Sweden, Japan, Australia, France, Germany, Italy etc. have already shown enormous success in achieving nationwide implementation of EG. However, due to severe digital divide, non-availability of resources in rural areas, scarcity in capital, higher illiteracy rate, less diffusion of ICT (exceptions are developing countries like India, China, Malaysia, South Korea, Thailand, and Brazil); most of the developing countries are substantially struggling to achieve the strategic mission and objective of EG (Shareef *et al.*, 2007). Therefore, revealing EG adoption capability of overall citizens of developing countries is a potential question to be investigated. The next section deals with the strategic objectives of EG and the issues related to accomplishing those purposes. In this connection, special attention is given to a major controversy of ICT adoption, viz., the digital divide along with shedding light on capability theory. The following section addresses and describes the elaborately conceptual paradigms of the DOI theory with brief conceptualization of exogenous and endogenous variables. Then ICT adoption capability is theorized, based on operationalization of DOI constructs. Finally, we reach a conclusion and offer future research direction.

EG: STRATEGIC OBJECTIVE OF IMPLEMENTATION

EG is a new and fast growing area that is being increasingly studied by researchers from many disciplines, who bring with them their various accumulations of concepts. Being new, there has been limited time to develop conceptual paradigms and theories. Governments, especially of developed countries, are increasingly using ICT in their daily operations and businesses and in presenting government system and services. As a consequence, the study of EG has increased in recent years and researchers attempt to develop theoretical and conceptual paradigms to understand and analyze different aspects of EG (Cresswell and Pardo, 2001; Dawes *et al.*, 2004; Fountain, 2001; Gil-García and Pardo, 2005; Gil-García and Martinez-Moyano, 2007; Gupta and Jana, 2003; Moon, 2002). There are several aspects to EG, such as social, technical, economic, political, and public administrative. As a result, different authors define the fundamental concepts and paradigms of EG from different perspectives. However, most dominating concepts of EG arise from the technical perspective. The use of the Internet and ICT has become an essential part of many government organizations to move forward (Steyaert, 2000). This movement of government organizations towards more IT-based service is simply called EG. EG has potential in that it facilitates the delivery of government services in the electronic form, which is fast, dynamic, efficient, and transparent, and this can, in turn, lead to a considerable reduction of service cost and an increase in the satisfaction of its stakeholders (Al-Mashari, 2007). Gil-Garcia and Martinez-Moyano (2007) delineated the concept of EG as the use of ICT in government settings. Evans and Yen (2006) defined EG as the communication between the government and its stakeholders via computers and the Internet. Hernon *et al.* (2002) defined the meaning of EG as using "technology, particularly the Internet, to enhance the access to and delivery of government information and services to citizens, businesses, government employees, and other agencies." From a technical standpoint, EG initiatives usually involve several types of electronic and information systems, including a database, front office and back office storage, computers and networking, multimedia, automation, security systems, and personal identification technologies (Snellen, 2002).

Accomplishment of ICT Adoption Through EG

After the advent of the Internet, IT and electronic communication played a very important role in fulfilling the vision of reforming government in an entirely different way. Innovations in ICT have dramatically transformed organization-customer, government-citizen, and inter-state communications. The Internet gradually has matured into a universally accepted and user-friendly platform for government organizations to communicate directly with citizens and deliver information at any time of day. Therefore, ICT is believed to be conducive to the movement of government reinvention. It has transformed the way government operates. EG is the pragmatic use of ICT to improve the way that government performs its business. It can be seen as a modern government organizational structure operated through ICT to transform and rationalize public sector work so that citizens have easier and electronic access to information and modernized services through personal computers, kiosks, telephones, and other resources (Banerjee and Chau, 2004; Schware and Deane, 2003).

By using the EG structure, both citizens and government can get a competitive advantage. Citizens can receive effective, efficient, and better quality service whereas governments can reduce operation and management costs, increase transparency, and fulfill political commitment to establish good governance. In the USA, the Internal Revenue Service (IRS) saves significant amount of government costs on printing, sorting, and mailing tax materials by offering web access to citizens and business organizations to tax return forms and publications (Warkentin *et al.*, 2002). EG services are cheaper, faster and more readily available from anywhere and at any time. EG also reduces travel and waiting time, introduces

197

more efficient and effective payment methods, improves transparency and accountability of government operations and eventually leads to transformation of good governance (Abanumy *et al.*, 2003; Prattipati, 2003).

However, all the previously mentioned purposes of EG can only be fully realized if its prime stakeholders, viz., citizens, can adopt this system (Carter, & Bélanger, 2004; Kumar *et al.*, 2007; Shareef *et al.*, in press; Warkentin *et al.*, 2002). But, among many other factors, citizens must have the capability to use ICT to adopt the EG system, Therefore, to accomplish these purposes of launching EG, its main driver should be available and accepted among all the citizens. If adoption and use of ICT in EG create a digital divide and discriminate against a majority of the population, its citizens-centric focus service will totally collapse (Evans and Yen, 2006). Certainly, in that case, EG will fail to create equal rights for all of the population, which is the fundamental premise for any good governance (Okot-Uma and Caffrey, 2000). However, since a majority of the population in developing countries lives in rural areas, the main obstacle for EG to accomplish its prime purposes is its low adoption rate among the rural population due to the severe lack of acceptance of ICT by rural people. Several researchers pointed out that the main cause of failure of ICT in developing countries is the digital divide (Bhatnagar, 2002; Dada, 2006; Heeks, 2003). The term digital divide refers to the gap between those people who have available resources to use and get the benefits of information technology and who do not have the right, freedom, ability, or resources available to use information technology. It includes the disparities to adopt and effectively use EG system. Especially in developing countries, a majority of the population has neither access to ICT or the skills needed to use ICT (Wilhelm, 2004). The present adoption rate of EG initiatives by stakeholders in developing countries, especially citizens who are the prime stakeholder of government, is very low. According to a study

conducted by Taylor Nelson Sofres (2002), the average adoption rate globally for EG is still only 30 percent. For developing countries, this adoption rate is lower and among rural people, it is extremely low (Taylor Nelson Sofres, 2002). The prime reasons for this low adoption rate of ICT and, thus, EG, are mostly due to less awareness, the unavailability of resources, and overall lower capability to use it.

Therefore, to realize the full benefits offered or proclaimed by EG, the capability of adoption of ICT by citizens must be enhanced. When more citizens can use ICT, more people will adopt EG, and this will reduce the operation and management costs of EG (Carter and Belenger, 2005). For this reason, we can see from our extensive literature review that the implementation, adoption, and diffusion of an ICT-based public administration system, viz., EG, can be conceptualized and give significant insight into different technology diffusion, acceptance, and transfer theories (Belenger and Carter, 2005; Bretschneider and Wittmer, 1993; Carter and Belenger, 2005; Caudle *et al.*, 1991; Chircu and Lee, 2003; Danziger, 2004; Gefen *et al.*, 2002; Gilbert *et al.*, 2004; Norris and Moon, 2005; Phang *et al.*, 2005; Ventura, 1995; Warkentin *et al.*, 2002). These authors and many others address implementation, adoption, and diffusion of ICT in public and private organizations and show that an incapability to adopt ICT might create severe discrimination among citizens of a country. This is especially true in developing countries where a majority of the citizens do not have the resources and knowledge to be able to adopt ICT (Basu, 2004; Dada, 2006; Heeks, 2003; Ndou, 2004). Consequently, these citizens who are not capable of adopting ICT fail to use EG and, thus, the implementation of EG produces a severe digital divide in society. Therefore, from our thorough literature review, addressing issues such as the implementation, development, and adoption of EG (Carter and Belenger, 2005; Evans and Yen, 2006; Gil-Garcia and Martinez-Moyano, 2007; Heeks, 2003; Heeks and Bailur,

2007, Inkhin, 2007, Jaeger and Thompson, 2003, Kumar *et al.*, 2007; Moon, 2002; Reddick, 2006; Titah and Barki, 2005; Warkentin *et al.*, 2002), we can remark:

1. EG is significantly dominated by ICT.
2. EG operates through ICT and offers benefits and competitive advantage both for governments and citizens.
3. However, the full benefits of EG are still far from expectation.
4. Adoption rates of EG, operated through ICT, for a majority of citizens of developing countries are low due to lack of awareness, inability to use ICT, and unavailability of resources.
5. The prime reason of failure to use EG is the inability to adopt ICT.
6. The inability to adopt ICT and, thus, the failure to use EG will consistently defeat the strategic purpose of implementing EG.
7. Digital divide is a potential issue for extensive implementation of EG.
8. Diffusion of Innovation theory (DOI) can provide deep insight into strategic development of EG in developing countries.

Digital Divide: Capability Theory

EG will not be successful if the users do not have the ability to use the technology to access useful information and services. Linked to this is the lack of skills and training that are required to effectively use an EG system that is mostly available to privileged citizens in developing countries. This problem has been referred to by numerous academics (Ebrahim and Irani, 2005; Ho, 2002; Moon, 2002). Disparity in access to EG and discrimination in facilitating the same scope of opportunity for all stakeholders of EG are potential managerial issues (Bertot, 2003). Gaps in access to and use of EG can be related to a number of aspects, including gender, race, color, political involvement, income level, educational level, language, and disability. The issues of the

digital divide seem to be present across cultures and nations. (Bertot *et al.*, 1999). All communities need the same services available for them. As a government structure, EG should create a level playing field for all of the population; otherwise, EG in the modern world cannot proliferate.

In this context, if we shed light on the capability theory, we can observe that without equal capability, defined by awareness and availability of resources and skill, the scope of the same opportunity cannot either be created or justified. Following Nussbaum and Sen (1993), the capability approach is defined here as the development objective of a government that seeks to enhance the ability of its stakeholders by expanding and procuring modern ICT and to provide good governance by enhancing the freedoms and capabilities of individuals and groups to voluntarily engage in sustainable state development. Depending on this phenomenal concept of welfare economics, we can develop our paradigm that without creating the same capability for all of the population to use ICT, the adoption of EG and the purpose of implementing EG, cannot be accomplished or justified (Gigler, 2004; Harris, 2005). Rather, implementation of EG in developing countries might have the effect of increasing inequality, the digital divide, and discrimination. Therefore, the single most important issue for the policy makers of developing countries is to study the adoption capability of ICT, especially among the rural population, before launching EG where ICT is the main driver (Bhatnagar, 2000; Krishna and Madon, 2003; Madon, 2000). In this regards, DOI is regarded as a powerful tool to investigate the issue of adoption capability of ICT.

CONCEPTUAL PARADIGMS OF DIFFUSION OF INNOVATION THEORY

DOI (Rogers, 1995) is a popular model used in IS research to explain user adoption of new technologies. Although its acronym is DOI, it is alternatively known as Innovation Diffusion Theory (IDT). This theory is extensively used in information systems (IS) literature for finding epistemological and ontological paradigms of endogenous constructs like diffusion of technology, quality of technology, adoption of technology, strategy of implementing ICT in different projects, and the adoption and diffusion of EG and EC. Based on the paradigms of this theory, a researcher generally must conceptualize the exogenous variables, viz., latent constructs, compatibility of technology, complexity of technology, and relative advantage relating to the aforementioned concepts postulated here as endogenous constructs.

The study of DOI is the study of how, why, and at what rate new ideas, concepts, products, and technology spread across communities. Accordingly, "the innovation-decision process is the process through which an individual or other decision-making unit passes, 1) from first knowledge of an innovation, 2) to forming an attitude toward the innovation, 3) to a decision to adopt or reject, 4) to implementation of the new idea, and 5) to confirmation of this decision" (Rogers, 2003, p. 161). The diffusion of innovation and adoption can be defined as the "process by which an innovation is communicated through certain channels over time among the members of a social system" (Rogers, 2003). Rogers (2003) further points out that this innovation decision process "can lead to either adoption, a decision to make full use of an innovation as the best course of action available, or rejection, a decision not to adopt an innovation." Innovation, in turn, is relative to the adopter, being any "idea, practice, or object that is perceived as new by an individual or other unit of adoption". Rogers (1962) theorized that innovations would spread through members of a community in an S curve, as the early adopters accept the technology first, followed by the majority, until a technology or innovation is common. "The speed of technology adoption is determined by two characteristics: p, which is the speed at which adoption takes off, and q, the speed at which later growth occurs" (Rogers, 1962).

However, the full adoption process depends on several factors called variables. Gallivan (1996) suggests that the appropriate adoption process depends on:

1. Individuals' innovativeness
2. Innovation type
3. Innovation attributes
4. Implementation complexity

According to the operationalization of this theory, the rate of diffusion is affected by an innovation's relative advantage, complexity, compatibility, trialability, and observability Rogers (1995). Rogers (1995) addresses relative advantage as "the degree to which an innovation is seen as being superior to its predecessor." For EG, it is the relative advantage (as perceived by the citizens) of presentation of government information, service, and interaction through websites with the use of ICT as compared with the traditional presentation of government physical office functions. Complexity comparable to competence in use is "the degree to which an innovation is seen by the potential adopter as being relatively difficult to use and understand." Compatibility refers to "the degree to which an innovation is seen to be compatible with existing values, beliefs, experiences and needs of adopters." For EG systems, we assume compatibility as the preference of citizens using EG websites that match with the behavioral attitudes of the citizens. Trialability is the "degree to which an idea can be experimented with on a limited basis." And observability is the "degree to which the results of an innovation are visible." Several literature reviews suggest that relative advantage, compatibility, and complexity are the most relevant constructs to determine the adoption characteristics of ICT by citizens (Carter and Bélanger, 2005; Moore and Benbasat, 1991; Rogers, 1995; Tornatzky and Klein, 1982). In addition, Moore and Benbasat (1991) propose that a new construct, Image, should be added to DOI; this construct influences the acceptance and use of an innovation. Image refers to citizens' perceptions of innovation as a status symbol. Interaction with EG systems based on ICT, instead of using a traditional government office, reflects a perception of the superior status of citizens. Several researchers have encountered this theory while identifying the constructs of ICT-based EG adoption (Bretschneider and Wittmer, 1993; Carter and Bélanger, 2005; Gilbert *et al.* 2004; Shareef *et al.*, 2007, Shareef *et al.*, forthcoming; Ventura, 1995).

IMPLEMENTATION OF EG: ICT ADOPTION CAPABILITY

As IS researchers, policy makers, and United Nations organizations have been addressing the challenge of the digital divide and technology failure in developing countries, the strategic implementation of EG-based ICT research has become a prominent issue (Adam and Wood, 1999; Madon, 1991). While researchers and United Nations organizations report on the strategy of implementation of EG, the adoption of ICT to increase the overall capability of a majority of the populations of developing countries is very limited (Meso *et al.*, 2006). In recent years, United Nations, non-government organizations (NGO), and some researchers (Heeks, 2002; Madon, 1997; Sahay and Avgerou, 2002; Sein and Ahmad, 2001; Walsham and Sahay, 2006) have been addressing this issue in scattered ways.

Madon (2003) developed an exploratory framework for assessing the impact of EG projects through empirical study in a developing country, however, it did not account for the pre-implementation perspective, viz, ICT adoption as a general criterion. Many aspects of the initial situation prior to the implementation of EG must be known so that the diffusion of ICT among the population can be evaluated as the condition of the pre-implementation phase of EG (Menou and Potvin, 2007). Therefore, an assessment of

the adoption capability of ICT based EG is a long-term, continuous process that is contingent upon a variety of factors related to the capability of technology adoption.

Therefore, based on literature review and the discourses drawn from the above discussion, this research argues that strategic implementation of EG should be evaluated based on the capability of adoption of ICT by citizens. Otherwise, the fundamental objective of EG might not be achieved and a government could be accused of creating discrimination among citizens by introducing EG. In this regard, the DOI theory can be used to shed light on the capability theory. Before implementing EG extensively in different public organizations at the local, provincial, and federal levels, an ad-hoc study is essential to investigate and determine whether people are ready and capable to adopt ICT. Getting insight from the capability theory, the capability of adoption is defined by this research as the ability of citizens becoming familiar with modern technology, getting availability of resources required to sufficient access and use, achieving skill to use, and perceiving functional benefits of ICT.

From the implied essence of theory of planned behavior and DOI theory, a user will not have an intention to use the ICT system to get a competitive advantage unless the user has the skill, integrity, and competence to learn, adopt, and use it, and perceives the functional benefits of modern ICT. This is especially true for several developing countries that are less advanced in terms of ICT diffusion and usage. A majority of the citizens of these countries are less educated, do not have enough skill, and are unaware of characteristics and functional benefits of ICT. If that majority of the population does not get sufficient skill and knowledge to use it and realize the absolute and relative functional benefits, they will not invest time and money in learning and using ICT (Dixit, 2006; Mansell, 2002; Mansell and When, 1998).

This research argues that since a majority of the citizens of most of the developing countries (some exceptions are developing countries that are very advanced in usage and adoption of ICT such as China, India, Malaysia, Brazil, Mexico, Thailand, Taiwan, Hong King, and South Korea) are less educated and unfamiliar with modern technology, the purpose of implementing EG should be evaluated based on the capability of a majority of the citizens to adopt ICT (Dixit, 2006; Mansell, 2002; Mansell and When, 1998). At the beginning, to create the belief in and intention to use ICT, people must be aware of the characteristics of ICT and its functional benefits. Overall readiness by awareness, ability, intention, and preparation are contributing factors for the capability to absorb ICT and implement EG. EG fails if the users do not have the ability to use the technology to enable access of useful information and services and do not perceive EG as useful.

Due to revolutionary re-engineering of the traditional government system, the perception of the online organizational structure, which is apparently new, is an important aspect to the perceived ability of using the system. Knowledge of technology is important in the ability to use EG. We argue that perceived complexity of DOI theory can successfully capture the ability of citizens of developing countries to adopt ICT-based EG. This construct can be operationalized through the use of perceived ease of use (PEOU) of the technology adoption model (TAM). TAM is a widely referenced theoretical model for predicting the intention to use and the acceptance of IS by individuals. It proposes that PEOU and perceived usefulness (PU) determine the attitude toward adoption of ICT. This attitude, in turn, leads to the intention to use ICT-based projects and the eventual acceptance and adoption of the IT (Bhattacherjee, 2001; Davis, *et al.*, 1989; Lucas and Spitler, 1999; Moon, 2002; Venkatesh, 2000). Davis (1989) defined PEOU as "the degree to which a person believes that using a particular system would be free of effort." PEOU is assumed

to influence the perception of relative advantage, because the easier a system is to use, the more useful it can be. Relative advantage captures the gain and comparative benefits from adopting a new system in comparison with the existing system (Rogers, 1995). At the personal or organizational level, several aspects of benefits can determine its adoption decision, ranging from effectiveness, efficiency, availability, accessibility from anywhere, comfort in use, time savings, cost savings, and convenience. Relative advantage is a matter of perception of relative benefits, which also capture the TAM's emphasis on perception of usefulness. If citizens perceive functional benefits by adopting an EG system, they might be interested in developing the fundamental capability to adopt ICT. Therefore, we argue that the relative advantage construct of DOI and PU of TAM can be used to model the implementation strategy of EG and adoption of ICT. These constructs can be operationalized to capture the relative benefits and usefulness of adopting EG system by the citizens of developing countries in terms of time, money, availability, travel, bureaucracy, corruption, participation, etc, and termed here as the Perceived Functional Benefits (PFB) of EG. This construct has economical, organizational, marketing, behavioral, and social perspectives. Therefore, for adoption of ICT-based EG, PFB is an exogenous variable.

According to information management principles for ICT adoption, creating awareness among the stakeholders, i.e., the end users, about implementation of innovation with regards to factors and issues, basic paradigms of the new system, a comprehensive view of advantages and disadvantages, and the overall security of the system are prime factors for adoption. Awareness is defined by (Okot-Uma and Caffrey, 2000) as "Providing information about the political process, about services and about choices available, the time horizons for the decision-making process and about the exponents of the decision-making process." A majority of the population in most of the developing countries is very unfamiliar with ICT due to unavailability of information, illiteracy, economic scarcity, and insufficient knowledge about the evolution of modern technology; they are also not very aware of this new innovation of the government system. As we learned from the theories of planned behavior and of reasoned action, beliefs about a system turn to attitudes about the system. However, awareness of the system is important at the beginning to develop beliefs. Before developing an attitude to adopt ICT, stakeholders need to be aware of complete characteristics, including functional behavior, strategic benefits, security and privacy, and the legal environment. Spence (1994) advocates awareness as the predominant explanatory factor for adoption of ICT. Several researchers asserted awareness as the significant independent variable to create the attitude to use ICT system (Nedovic-Budic and God-schalk, 1996; Okot-Uma and Caffrey, 2000; Parent *et al.*, 2005; Watson *et al.* 2000). This research conceptualizes awareness as the gaining knowledge, education, and consciousness as much as a user perceived to be sufficient to learn and use ICT and realize its overall characteristics, strategic functionality, and competitive advantage. Depending on the above arguments, we propose that for developing countries, a slight modification of the compatibility construct of DOI represented by the awareness attribute can be a strong predictor of evaluating adoption capability of ICT and developing an implementation strategy of EG. Several researchers use the compatibility construct as the significant predictor of EG adoption in developed countries where a majority of citizens are completely aware of and habituated to use ICT (Carter and Bélanger, 2004; Chen and Thurmaier, 2005; Shareef *et al.*, 2007). However, since, as we stated before, a majority of the population of most of the developing countries are not aware of ICT and EG, the construct compatibility of DOI can be operationalized for predicting ICT adoption capability and EG implementation strategy by the construct Awareness.

Unavailability of resources—including computers, Internet connection, electricity, and telecommunications—is one of the main barriers for a majority of the population of developing countries to learn, adopt, and use ICT (Dada, 2006). Several researchers asserted that the adoption of new technology is closely related to the availability of resources (Kumar *et al.*, 2007; Parent *et al.*, 2005; Titah and Barki, 2005). From the technological, behavioral, economic, and organizational perspectives, it is anticipated that failing to get enough resources using ICT will not create a behavioral attitude among users to adopt the system. Several researchers pointed out that due to scarcity of computers; the Internet with competent features like access, speed, and cost; and government supports like call-center, resource-center, and cyber-café, ICT implementation in public projects in several countries—especially developing countries—could not attain the desired success (Bhatnagar, 2002; Dada, 2006; Heeks, 2002; Madu, 1989). If we look at the capability theory, it stresses that citizens can not achieve capability in using a system unless they can, without any barrier, use that system. Generally, where computers, Internet, and modern ICT are not available, citizens are economically poor, less educated, socially and culturally unaware of modern technology, and not technologically skilled. As a result, they also do not have a belief that they will acquire benefits by using an ICT system. Therefore, there is an obvious relation between availability of resources (AOR) and adoption capability of ICT. We define AOR as the availability and freedom of using computers, the Internet, and ICT with competitive features like access, speed, and cost. We argue that AOR creates a belief in using ICT, which, in turn, creates an attitude to use ICT. Heeks (2003) and Dada (2006) claim that a low adoption rate and, eventually, failure of EG in developing countries are mostly due to a scarcity of resources and, consequently, lack of skill and knowledge of using ICT. Drawing conclusions from these arguments, we propose that in encapsulating capability of adopting ICT and developing strategy for implementation of EG to accomplish fundamental missions of EG, another construct should be included in DOI. This is AOR.

This is a theoretical framework to study the adoption capability of ICT and implementation strategy of EG in developing countries. This will explain the fundamental purposes of EG implementation by operationalizing DOI and shedding light on the capability theory. From the operationalization of the four independent constructs and one dependent construct, we can measure the ICT adoption capability of the population of developing countries. We argue that those four parameters —PEOU, perceived functional benefits, awareness, and availability of resources—can comprehensively measure the ICT adoption capability of developing countries for the strategic implementation of EG as shown in Figure 1.

Therefore, the relation between the two objectives of this study is obvious. As the first objective, we described the purposes of implementing EG and related issues to accomplish those purposes. Different governments set so many citizen-centric purposes for implementing EG. Those purposes can be achieved if its prime stakeholder, viz., the citizen, has the capability to adopt the EG system. However, since ICT is the main driver of EG,

competence in ICT is a vital issue for adopting EG. So, based on DOI and shedding light on the capability theory, we propose here a theoretical framework (as shown in Figure 1) to investigate the adoption capability of ICT of a country's citizens to accomplish the strategic objective of implementing EG and also minimizing the digital divide.

CONCLUSION AND FUTURE DIRECTION

The purpose of this research, as mentioned earlier, is twofold. In the first section, we have attempted to conceptualize the purpose of EG. We also argued that those purposes of EG can only be accomplished and the full benefits of EG realized if most of the citizens have the ability to adopt ICT, the main driver of EG. Then we have developed a theoretical framework to investigate the adoption capability of ICT of most citizens, especially of developing countries, grounded on DOI and shedding light on the capability theory.

Although the purposes of implementing EG may be multi-dimensional, some regard EG as a powerful tool for improving the internal efficiency of government services and the quality of service delivery as well as enhancing public participation, government accountability, and system transpar-

Figure 1. Adoption capability of citizens' of developing countries

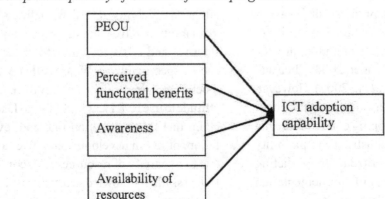

ency (Fountain, 2001). EG is primarily devoted to offering equal and cost-effective service to all of its citizens, including more participation, democracy, transparency, accountability, and good governance through the extensive use of ICT. To capitalize on the full benefits of EG and fulfill the purposes of EG as revealed in this research, different countries, especially developing countries where ICT diffusion and adoption has not achieved significant and extensive progress and where the digital divide is prominent in terms of access and availability of ICT, should conduct empirical studies in the pre-implementation phase of EG to understand the capability of adoption of ICT of a majority of the population. It is the prime motive of policy makers of developing countries to study the adoption capability of ICT of the majority of the citizens prior to launching an EG project. Otherwise, there is a great possibility that EG projects could not accomplish the purpose of their implementation and could abruptly fail to reduce the digital divide, establish equal rights for all citizens, and promote good governance.

In this regard, we have studied DOI theory with a special emphasis on the capability theory. The capability theory provided us a strong paradigm that without getting the capability to adopt modern technology-based public administration, diffusion of technology cannot be possible and EG implementation cannot accomplish its full potential and purpose. Therefore, before implementation of an EG, policy makers of a country should investigate the capability of a majority of the population to determine whether they have the ability to adopt ICT. In this regard, DOI theory might be a powerful tool to explore the adoption capability of majority of the population, especially of developing countries, which is essential for accomplishing EG implementation purposes. Consequently, the constructs of the DOI theory could be recognized and postulated considering the social, cultural, technological, and economic perspectives of a majority of the citizens of developing countries. We identified four constructs from DOI to investigate this theoretical paradigm.

These four constructs are PEOU, perceived awareness, perceived functional benefits, and availability of resources. PEOU is adopted from TAM to visualize the complexity of technology in connection with usage, especially for people who are not very skilled in or familiar with modern ICT. The perceived functional benefit construct targets conceptualizing and revealing absolute and relative benefits that citizens can realize from adopting ICT-based EG system in terms of time, money, availability, travel, bureaucracy, corruption, and participation. This comprises the essence of relative advantage of DOI and includes PU, a construct of TAM. Compatibility is a powerful construct of DOI to evaluate the citizens' social, behavioral, attitudinal, cultural, and technological beliefs to be matched and consistent with technology adoption and usage. However, a majority of the population of developing countries (excluding some developing countries that are very advanced in adopting ICT in private and public organizations) are not familiar with the characteristics, usage, and benefits of ICT. Because of this, a refined form of compatibility, which is denoted by awareness, is introduced here to measure adoption capability of ICT. Finally, since most of the developing countries in Africa and Asia have a shortage of resources in terms of capital, technology infrastructure, computers, Internet, and skilled personnel, a new construct is added in DOI; this is termed as availability of resources to conceptualize the adoption capability of ICT.

This theoretical evaluation has some potential managerial implications for policy makers, academicians, and researchers. For our first objective, as revealed from our literature review, the prime purpose of EG implementation is to provide effective and efficient services to all citizens with equal opportunity and transparency. We can expect that this revolutionary reformation of the traditional government system is implemented to achieve a lower digital divide. However, if the majority of the population of developing countries fails to develop the capability of adopting and using ICT, which is the main driver of EG, the implementation of EG hardly can accomplish its goal. Rather, it will enhance the extreme digital divide. So, at the outset of implementing EG, it is important for developing countries to conduct countrywide empirical studies to address whether the majority of the population has the ability to adopt and use ICT-based public service. In this connection, as our second objective, we have conceptualized DOI shedding light on the capability theory to develop the theoretical paradigm of investigating the capability of adopting ICT, especially in developing countries. Operationalizing the identified four constructs in the light of DOI, developing countries can define and develop their strategy for implementation of EG.

This is a theoretical paradigm for exploring adoption capability for diffusion of ICT and, thus, implementation of EG. However, definite empirical studies are essential for this finding. In different developing countries that are less advanced in usage of ICT, extensive empirical studies could be conducted in identifying the digital divide, the readiness to adopt ICT, the literacy rate in terms of technology, and the resource availability. Also, studies are needed to reveal the mission, objective, and implementation strategy of EG by different countries to conceptualize characteristics of an ICT-based EG system.

REFERENCES

Abanumy, A., Mayhew, P., & Al-Badi, A., (2003). An exploratory study of e-government in two GCC countries. In *Proceedings of the 2003 International Business Information Management Conference*, Cairo, Egypt.

Adam, L., & Wood, F. (1999). An investigation of the impact of information and communication technologies in sub-Saharan Africa. *Journal of Information Science, 25*(4), 307-318.

Al-Mashari, M. (2007). A benchmarking study of experiences with electronic-government. *Benchmarking: An International Journal, 14*(2), 172-185.

Banerjee, P., & Chau, P. (2004). An evaluation framework for analyzing e-government convergence capability in developing countries. *Electronic Government, 1*(1), 29-48.

Basu, S. (2004). E-government and developing countries: An overview. *International Review of Law Computers & Technology, 18*(1), 109-132.

Bhatnagar, S. (2002). E-government: Lessons from implementation in developing countries, regional development dialogue. *UNCRD, 24*(Autumn), 1-9.

Bhatnagar, S. C. (2000). Social Implications of information and communication technology in developing countries: Lessons from Asian success stories. *Electronic Journal of Information Systems for Developing countries, 1*(4), 1-9.

Bhattacherjee, A. (2001). Understanding information systems continuance: An expectation-confirmation model. *MIS Quarterly, 25*(3), 351-370.

Bélanger, F., & Carter, L. (2005). Trust and risk in e-government adoption. In *Proceedings of the 11ᵗʰ Americans Conference on Information Systems*, Omaha, NE, USA.

Bertot, J. C., McClure, C. R., & Owens, K. A. (1999). Universal service in a global networked environment: Selected issues and possible approaches. *Government Information Quarterly, 16*(4), 309-327.

Bertot, J. C. (2003). The multiple dimensions of the digital divide: More than the technology "haves" and "have nots." *Government Information Quarterly, 20*(2), 185-191.

Bretschneider, S., & Wittmer, D., (1993). Organizational adoption of microcomputer technology: The role of sector. *Information Systems Research, 4*(1), 88-108.

Brudney, J., & Sally S. (1995). The adoption of innovation by smaller local governments: The case of computer technology. *American Review of Public Administration, 25*(1), 71-86.

Bugler, D., & Stuart, B. (1993). Technology push or program pull: Interest in new information technologies within public organizations. In B. Bozeman (Ed.), *Public management: The state of the art* (pp. 275–93). San Francisco: Josey-Bass.

Carter, L., & Bélanger, F. (2004). Citizen adoption of electronic government initiatives. In *Proceedings of the 37th Hawaii International Conference on System Sciences*.

Carter, L., & Bélanger, F. (2005). The utilization of e-government services: Citizen trust, innovation and acceptance factors. *Information Systems Journal, 15*, 5-25.

Caudle, S. L., Gorr, W. L., & Newcomer, K.E. (1991). Key information systems management issues for the public sector. *MIS Quarterly, 15*(2), 171-188.

Chen, Y.-C., & Thurmaier, K. (2005). Government-to-citizen electronic services: understanding and driving adoption of online transactions. In *Proceedings of the Association for Public Policy & Management (APPAM) Conference*, Washington, DC.

Chircu, A. M., & Lee, H. D. (2003). Understanding IT investments in the public sector: the case of e-government. In *Proceedings of the 9th Americas Conference on Information Systems* (pp. 792-800).

Cresswell, A. M., & Pardo, T. A. (2001). Implications of legal and organizational issues for urban digital government development. *Government Information Quarterly, 18*, 269-278.

Cusumano, M. A., & Elenkov, D. (1994). Linking international technology transfer with strategy and management: A literature commentary. *Research Policy, 23*, 195-215.

Dada, D. (2006). *The failure of e government in developing countries*. Retrieved 2006, from http://www.lse.ac.uk/collections/informationSystems/iSChannel/Dada_2006b.pdf

Danziger, J. M. (2004). Innovation in innovation? The technology enactment framework. *Social Science Computer Review, 22*(1), 100-110.

Davis, F. (1989). Perceived usefulness, perceived ease of use and user acceptance of information technology. *MIS Quarterly, 13*(3), 319-340.

Dawes, S. S., Pardo, T. A., & Cresswell, A. M. (2004). Designing electronic government information access programs: A holistic approach. *Government Information Quarterly, 21*(1), 3-23.

Dixit, K. (2006). *Does information technology really promote knowledge?* Retrieved 2006, from http://sade.sdnp.undp.org/rc/forums/mgr/sdnpmgrs/msg01283. html

Ebrahim, Z., & Irani, Z. (2005). E-government adoption: Architecture and barriers. *Business Process Management Journal, 11*(5), 589-611.

Evans, D., & Yen, D. C. (2006). E-government: Evolving relationship of citizens and government, domestic, and international development. *Government Information Quarterly, 23*, 207-235.

Fountain, J. E. (2001). *Building the virtual state, information technology and institutional change*. Washington, D.C.: Brookings Institution Press.

Gallivan, M. J. (1996). Strategies for implementing new software processes: An evaluation of a contingency framework. In *Proceedings of the SIGCPR/SIGMIS '96*, Denver, Colorado.

Gefen, D., Pavlou, P. A., Warkentin, M., & Gregory, M. R. (2002). E-government adoption. In *Proceedings of the 8th Americas Conference on Information Systems*.

Gigler, B.-S. (2004). Including the excluded - can ICTs empower poor communities? In *Proceed-*

ings of the *4th International Conference on the Capability Approach*, Italy.

Gilbert, D., Balestrini, P., & Littleboy, D. (2004). Barriers and benefits in the adoption of e-government. *The International Journal of Public Sector Management, 14*(4), 286-301.

Gil-García, J. R., & Pardo, T. A. (2005). E-government success factors: Mapping practical tools to theoretical foundations. *Government Information Quarterly, 22*(2), 187-216.

Gil-Garcia, J. R., & Martinez-Moyano, I. J. (2007). Understanding the evolution of e-government: The influence of systems of rules on public sector dynamics. *Government Information Quarterly, 24*, 266-290.

Gupta, M. P., & Jana, D. (2003). E-government evaluation: A framework and case study. *Government Information Quarterly, 20*(4), 365-387.

Harris, R.W. (2005). Explaining the success of rural Asian telecentres, In R. M. Davison, et al. (Eds.), *Information systems in developing countries: Theory and practice* (pp. 83-100). Hong Kong: City University of Hong Kong Press.

Heeks, R. (2002). information systems and developing countries: Failure, success, and local improvisations. *The Information Society, 18*, 101-112.

Heeks, R. (2003). Most egovernment-for-development projects fail: How can risks be reduced? *iGovernment Working Paper Series.*

Heeks, R., & Bailur, S. (2007). Analyzing e-government research: Perspectives, philosophies, theories, methods, and practice. *Government Information Quarterly, 24*, 243-265

Hernon, P., Reylea, H. C., Dugan, R. E., & Cheverie, J. F. (2002). *United States government information: Policies and sources* (p. 388). Westport, CT: Libraries Unlimited.

Ho, A. T.-K. (2002). reinventing local governments and the e-government initiative. *Public Administration Review, 62*(4), 434-444.

Irkhin, Iu. V. (2007). Electronic government and society: World realities and Russia (a comparative analysis). *Sociological Research, 46*(2), 77-92.

Jaeger, P. T., & Thompson, K. M. (2003). E-government around the world: Lessons, challenges, and future directions. *Government Information Quarterly, 20*, 389-394.

Krishna, S., & Madon, S. (Eds.). (2003). *Digital challenge: Information technology in the development context.* Aldershot, UK: ASHGATE.

Krishna, S., & Walsham, G. (2005). Implementing public information systems in developing countries: Learning from a success story. *Information Technology for Development, 11*(2), 123-140.

Kumar, V., Mukerji, B., Butt, I., & Persaud, A. (2007). Factors for successful e-government adoption: A conceptual framework. *The Electronic Journal of e-Government, 5*(1), 3-76.

Lanvin, B. (1995). Why the global village cannot afford information slums. In *The New Information Infrastructure Strategies for U.S. Policy* (W. J. Drake ed.) (pp. 205-222).

Lucas, H. C., & Spitler, V. K. (1999). Technology use and performance: A field study of broker workstations. *Decision Science, 30*(2), 291-311.

Madon, S. (1991). The impact of computer-based information systems on rural development: A case study in India. In *Imperial College of Science, Technology & Medicine.* London.

Madon, S. (1997). Information-based global economy and socioeconomic development: The case of Bangalore. *Information Society, 13*(3), 227-244.

Madon, S. (2000). The Internet and socio-economic development: Exploring the interaction. *Information Technology & People, 13*(2), 85-101.

Madon, S. (2003). Studying the developmental impact of e-governance initiatives. In *Internationals Federation of Information Processing, IFIP*. Athens, Greece.

Madon, S. (2004). Evaluating the developmental impact of e-governance initiatives: An exploratory framework, *Electronic Journal of Information Systems in Developing Countries*, 20(5), 1-13.

Madu, C. N. (1989). Transferring technology to developing countries – critical factors for success. *Long Range Planning*, 22(4), 115-124.

Mansell, R., & Wehn, U. (1998). *Knowledge societies: Information technology for sustainable development*. New York: Oxford University Press.

Mansell, R. (2002). From Digital divides to digital entitlements in knowledge societies. *Current Sociology*, 50(3), 407-426.

Meso, P., Datta, P., & Mbarika, V. (2006). Moderating information and communication technologies' influences on socioeconomic development with good governance: A study of the developing countries. *Journal of the American Society for Information Science & Technology*, 57(2), 186-197.

Miers, D. (1996). The strategic challenges of electronic commerce. In *Electronic Commerce* (pp. 1-19.). Enix Consulting Limited.

Moon, M. J., (2002). The evolution of e-government among municipalities: Rhetoric or reality. *Public Administration Review*, 62(4), 424-33.

Moore, G., & Benbasat, I. (1991). Development of an instrument to measure the perceptions of adopting an information technology innovation. *Information Systems Research*, 2, 173-191.

Ndou, V. D. (2004). E-government for developing countries: Opportunities and challenges. *Electronic Journal of Information Systems in Developing Countries*, 18(1), 1-24.

Nedovic Dudiec, Z., & Godochalk, D. (1996). Human factors in adoption of geographic information systems, *Public Administration Review*, 56, 554-567.

Norris, D. F., & Moon, M. J. (2005). Advancing e-government at the grassroots: Tortoise or hare? *Public Administration Review*, 65(1), 64-75.

Nussbaum, M., & Sen, A. (Eds.). (1993). *The Quality of Life*. Oxford, UK: Clarendon Press.

Okot-Uma, R. W-O., & Caffrey, L. (Eds.). (2000). Trusted services and public key infrastructure. *Commonwealth Secretariat*, London.

Parent, M., Vandebeek, C. A., & Gemino, A. C. (2005). Building citizen trust through e-government. *Government Information Quarterly*, 22, 720-736.

Phang, C. W., Sutanto, J., Li, Y., & Kankanhalli, A. (2005). Senior citizens' adoption of e-government: In quest of the antecedents of perceived usefulness. In *Proceedings of the 38th Hawaii International Conference on System Sciences*.

Prattipati, S. (2003). Adoption of e-governance: Differences between countries in the use of online government services. *Journal of American Academy of Business*, 3(1), 386-401.

Reddick, C. G. (2006). Information resource managers and e-government effectiveness: A survey of Texas state agencies. *Government Information Quarterly*, 23, 249-266.

Rogers, E. M. (1962). *Diffusion of innovations*. Free Press of Glencoe.

Rogers, E. M. (1995). *Diffusion of innovations*, New York: The Free Press.

Rogers, E. M. (2003). *Diffusion of innovations* (5th ed.). New York: Free Press.

Sakowicz, M. (2007). *How to evaluate e-government? Different methodologies and methods*. Retrieved 2007, from, http://unpan1.un.org/

intradoc/groups/public/documents/NISPAcee/ UNPAN009 486.pdf

Sahay, S., & Avgerou, C. (2002). Introducing the special issue on information and communication technologies in developing countries, *Information Society, 18*(2), 73-76.

Schware, R., & Deane, A. (2003). Deploying e-government program the strategic importance of 'i' before 'e.' *Info, 5*(4), 10-19.

Sein, M., & Ahmad, I. (2001). A framework to study the impact of information and communication technologies on developing countries: The case of cellular phones in Bangladesh. In *Proceedings of BITWORLD 2001*, Cairo, Egypt.

Shareef, M. A., Kumar, U., & Kumar, V. (2007). Developing fundamental capabilities for successful e-government implementation. In *Proceedings of the Administrative Sciences Association of Canada Conference* (pp. 159-177), Ottawa.

Shareef, M. A., Kumar, U., Kumar, V., & Dwivedi, Y. K. (in press). Identifying critical factors for adoption of e-government. *Electronic Government: An International Journal.*

Snellen, I. (2002). Electronic governance: Implications for citizens, politicians and public servants. *International Review of Administrative Sciences, 68*, 183-198.

Spence, W. (1994). *Innovation: The communication of change in ideas, practices and products.* London: Chapman and Hall.

Steyaert, J. (2000). Local government online and the role of the resident. *Social Science Computer Review, 18*, 3-16.

Titah, R., & Barki, H. (2005). E-government adoption and acceptance: A literature review. *HEC Montréal.*

Taylor Nelson Sofres. (2002). *Annual global report on government online an international perspective.* Retrieved from http://unpan1.un.org/

intradoc/groups/public/documents/ APCITY/ UNPAN007044.pdf

Tornatzky, L. G., & Klein, K. J. (1982). Innovation characteristics and innovation adoption-implementation: A meta-analysis of findings. *IEEE Transactions on Engineering Management, EM-29*(1).

Venkatesh, V. (2000). Determinants of perceived ease of use: Integrating control, intrinsic motivation, and emotion into the technology acceptance model. *Information Systems Research, 11*(4), 342-365.

Ventura, S. J. (1995). The use of geographic information systems in local government. *Public Administration Review, 55*(5), 461-467.

Walsham, G., & Sahay, S. (2006). Research on information systems in developing countries: Current landscape and future prospects. *Information Technology for Development, 12*(1), 7-24.

Warkentin, M., Gefen, D., Pavlou, P., & Rose, G. (2002). Encouraging citizen adoption of e-government by building trust. *Electronic Markets, 12*(3), 157-162.

Wilhelm, A. G. (2004). Digital nation: Towards an inclusive information society. *MIT Press,* 133-134.

Wilson, C. (2001). On the scale of global demographic convergence 1950-2000. *Population and Development Review, 27*(1), 155-171.

KEY TERMS AND DEFINITIONS

Adoption of EG: It is the acceptance and use of EG by its stakeholders with satisfaction.

Availability of Resources (AOR) for ICT: It is the availability and freedom of using computers, the Internet, and ICT with competitive features like access, speed, and cost.

Awareness of ICT. It is the gaining knowledge, education, and consciousness as much as a user perceived to be sufficient to learn and use ICT and realize its overall characteristics, strategic functionality, and competitive advantage.

Capability to Adopt ICT: The ability of citizens becoming familiar with modern technology, getting availability of resources required to sufficient access and use, achieving skill to use, and perceiving functional benefits of ICT.

Capability Theory for EG: It can be defined as the development objective of a government that seeks to enhance the ability of its stakeholders by expanding and procuring modern ICT and to provide good governance by enhancing the freedoms and capabilities of individuals and groups to voluntarily engage in sustainable state development.

Developing Countries: A developing country is a country which is not industrially developed and has less economic capacity, per capita income, and lower and inconsistent human development index (HDI).

Diffusion of Innovation (DOI). It can be conceptualized as a systematic process by which an innovation can spread over the members of a society through certain distributing channels. According to the operationalization of this theory, diffusion is measured by an innovation's relative advantage, complexity, compatibility, trialability, and observability.

Digital Divide: The term digital divide refers to the gap between those people who have available resources to use and get the benefits of information technology and who do not have the right, freedom, or resources available to use information technology.

E-Government (EG): EG refers to government's use of IT to exchange information and services with citizens, businesses, and other arms of government. It is the government organizational structure for presentation and delivery of information, service, and function to its users and stakeholders through personal computers, kiosks, telephones, and other network resources.

Chapter XII
Evolutionary Diffusion Theory

Linda Wilkins
RMIT University, Australia

Paula Swatman
University of South Australia, Australia

Duncan Holt
RAYTHEON, Australia

ABSTRACT

Improved understanding of issues affecting uptake of innovative technology is important for the further development of e-business and its integration into mainstream business activities. An explanatory theory that can provide a more effective instrument for determining acceptance levels should therefore be of interest to IS practitioners and researchers alike. The authors aimed to establish whether evolutionary diffusion theory (EDT) could offer such an instrument, developing a set of axioms derived from the EDT literature and applying these to an in-depth review of two e-business implementations: a G2B document delivery system introduced by the Australian Quarantine Inspection Service (AQIS) across a number of industry sectors; and an enterprise-wide system implementation in a local government instrumentality. The authors found EDT offered remarkable explanatory depth, applicable not only to analysing uptake of complex, multi-user technologies in organisational settings but to any e-business investigation requiring a system-wide perspective.

INTRODUCTION

A variety of theoretical frameworks and approaches have been used to study Information Systems (IS) diffusion processes (see, for example, Holbrook and Salazar, 2004; Baskerville and Pries-Heje, 2001; Edquist, 1997). Investigations of a number of these theories and models of Innovative Technology Uptake (ITU) have found that each has only a narrow perspective which tends to capture 'just one part of the story' and only highlights particular areas of interest. No single theory appears uniquely able to explain the circumstances of any particular case (Jones and Myers, 2001 p.1018).

Despite these limitations, influences on uptake and diffusion of IT innovations are of perennial interest to IS researchers. Those attempting to make progress in identifying key issues affecting uptake have had to grapple with the limited explanatory power of recognised diffusion theories over some four decades. The most commonly cited diffusion theory in the IS literature is Rogers' Classical Diffusion of Innovation (DoI) theory, first published in 1961 (Clarke 1999). Rogers originally focused attention on the shape of the diffusion curve, describing innovation as a process that moves through an initial phase of generating variety in technology, to selecting across that variety to produce patterns of change resulting in feedback from the selection process, to the development of further variation (Rogers, 1995).

As a pioneering contribution to conceptualising adoption and diffusion, Classical DoI theory appears to have maintained its iconic status over time and continues to be cited in the IS literature, despite the fact that interest in innovation studies has moved on from the shape of the diffusion curve to a focus on articulating underlying dynamic mechanisms (Lissoni and Metcalfe, 1994; Nelson, 2002). The innovation 'journey' now appears to be more readily understood as a non-linear dynamic system, far less predictable and stable than staged models based on Classical DoI theory represented it to be (see for example Van de Ven et al., 1999). The static orientation of Classical DoI theory, its focus on individual firms and a 'single innovation' perspective has diminished its relevance to the IS field and to the development of online technologies in particular.

The limited explanatory power of Classical DoI theory is well documented in the literature (see, for example, Downes and Mohr, 1976; Moore and Benbasat, 1991; Damsgaard and Lyytinen, 1996; Galliers and Swan, 1999; Clarke, 2002). Seminal

work in the IS field (for example, Orlikowski and Hofman, 1997; Boudreau and Robey, 1999; Reich and Benbasat, 2000) has also clearly established a need for analytical theory in this field which:

- Aligns more closely with the way beliefs, attitudes and understanding of plans and structures are known to influence organisational decision-making
- Can articulate underlying dynamic mechanisms intrinsic to adoption and diffusion processes
- Addresses how complex and networked technologies diffuse
- Acknowledges the uncertainty and surprises that mark the ITU process

The IS field needs a unified theory to identify key influences on uptake of innovative technology that is: appropriate to reviewing open-ended and customisable innovations associated with uptake of e-business technologies; takes into account issues of discontinuing practice or slowing uptake of inappropriate technologies; acknowledges the active role users can play in the innovation process; and allows for changes in an innovation during the adoption and implementation process. Such a theory must also be readily applicable in organisational settings featuring the adoption of complex, multi-user technologies – where the majority of potential applications of diffusion of innovation now occur. An analytical instrument which appears well suited to these requirements is Evolutionary Diffusion Theory.

In this chapter, we begin by exploring the origins and principles underpinning Evolutionary Diffusion Theory, before turning to examine its explanatory strengths. We will make close reference to two case studies that illustrate the relevance of EDT to the field of Information Systems (IS) and, in particular, to the explanation of innovative technology uptake.

EVOLUTIONARY DIFFUSION THEORY (EDT)

The limitations of standard theoretical approaches to analysis of the influences on ITU in the field of Information Systems research have been increased by the fragmentation and minimal 'diffusion' of diffusion research itself. The lack of awareness which the various diffusion research traditions have of one another's work has hindered researchers in their attempts to grasp and frame the ITU problem (Rogers, 1995 p.38). Such communication gaps across the disciplines help to explain why Evolutionary Diffusion Theory does not feature among the analytical instruments referred to in the mainstream IS diffusion literature.

Evolutionary Diffusion Theory: Development and Evolution

Evolutionary Diffusion Theory (EDT) emerged from Evolutionary Economics, a discipline which describes economic phenomena and deals, in particular, with situations of change, open systems and innovation processes (Nelson 1995). As a discipline it has had a major impact on more recent studies of firms, industries, and technical change. The idea of technological advance as an evolutionary process has been developed by scholars operating independently in a variety of different disciplines. These disciplines include, but are not confined to: sociology (Constant, 1980; Bijker, 1995); technological history (Rosenberg, 1969; Mokyr, 1996); and economic modelling (Nelson and Winter, 1982; Saviotti, 1996; Metcalfe, 1994).

Evolutionary Economics—and Evolutionary Diffusion Theory (EDT) in particular—are relatively recent developments, with the bulk of the EDT literature having been published only since the early 1980's. The Nelson-Winter classic evolutionary model of technological change (1982) pioneered a relatively simple conceptual model of Evolutionary Economics which was crucial to the development of Evolutionary Diffusion Theory. The model played a prominent role in defining a paradigm for further research into the conditions which determine industrial concentrations, dynamic competition in alternative technological regimes and the relationship between innovators and imitators (Andersen, 1996). The model demonstrated the possibility of collating a wide diversity of elements and integrating them into an evolutionary process which could then be applied to understanding the uptake of innovative technology. Key elements include: the processes of transmission; variety creation; and selection (Nelson and Winter, 1982, Chs. 4-5).

Nelson and Winter's classic evolutionary model of technological change (1982) was followed by several overviews of Evolutionary Economics (see, for example, key publications by Dosi et al, 1988; Saviotti and Metcalfe, 1991; Dosi and Nelson, 1994; Andersen, 1994; Nelson, 1995). These contributions to the Evolutionary Economics literature share a concept of innovation as a process that moves through an initial phase of generating variety in technology, to selecting across that variety to produce patterns of change resulting in feedback from the selection process, to the development of further variation under continual injections of novelty (Dopfer, 2001). Researchers within this paradigm now apply their attention to enduring issues in innovation studies; and to finding reasons for unexplained outcomes from technology adoption and diffusion.

Instead of the more traditional application of DoI theory to an individual firm, EDT reviews the impact of diffusion theory when applied to the more complex environment of a market (Lissoni and Metcalfe, 1994). Placing theory in a market context raises questions of particular interest to e-business practitioners, such as why all potential users do not immediately adopt innovations which appear to be advantageous compared to existing technology (instead, some firms as potential users adopt later or not at all); and why some agents who can be identified by their spatial location always

Table 1. Features of evolutionary diffusion theory

Evolutionary Diffusion Theory
Explains the innovation process as non-linear and rarely predictable
Explains innovation and diffusion in market environments
Presents the policy maker's role as one of stimulating the building of innovative infrastructure cooperatively with local institutions
Accepts the possibility of human intervention in the process of technology development
Describes the natural trajectory of an unpredictable original selection where the outcome is not always the best one
Stresses the gradualism of internal adoption
Defines a clear role for Government as a policy maker coordinating institutions in innovative systems and seeking solutions which are context specific and sensitive to local path dependencies
Presents adoption of single innovations as part of a greater process of change impacting on organisations and their culture

adopt later than others (Lissoni and Metcalfe, 1994, pp.106, 127).

Table 1 sets out features of EDT frequently cited in the literature and selected for their clear relevance and application to IS research on issues affecting uptake of innovative technology.

We have now outlined the origins and background of Evolutionary Diffusion Theory and provided a synthesis of its key features. The following section of this chapter attends to the explanatory strength of EDT. We will show that EDT is particularly well suited to analysing issues affecting uptake of innovative technology in the e-business context.

Evolutionary Diffusion Theory: Explanatory Strength

Evolutionary Diffusion Theory offers the IS researcher a basis for reviewing innovative technology uptake (Kowol and Kueppers, 2003; Lambooy and Boschma, 2001; Norgren and Hauknes, 1999; Amin, 1998; Lissoni and Metcalfe, 1994; Saviotti and Metcalfe, 1991) which includes:

- A focus on unexplained outcomes
- An emphasis on gradualism of internal adoption

- A concern with development and diffusion of new variety in market environments
- Acceptance of input from a variety of disciplines
- Acceptance of human intervention in technology outcomes
- A clearly defined role for policy makers fostering innovative technology uptake

EDT provides an analytical instrument to examine issues in the uptake of innovative technology in specific cases. The first of two case studies analysed in this chapter features the introduction of EXDOC, an innovative online technology. EXDOC was implemented by the Australian government agency AQIS (Australian Quarantine and Inspection Service) to support the needs of food producers across a number of sectors for access to export documentation. These producers subsequently became the EXDOC community and the population of the case study. Once key features of EDT had been synthesised from the literature and their explanatory strength for the IS/e-commerce context established, it became a matter of deciding how best to apply EDT as the instrument to analyse ITU issues within the case study. The second case study used EDT to review the implementation of an enterprisewide electronic records management solution for a local government authority – an instance of this theoretical approach's relevance to individual organisational analysis, despite its published focus on market-wide innovation.

Four axioms derived from the literature of Evolutionary Diffusion Theory provided the required analytical instrument. Key features of each of the four EDT axioms is described in detail in the following section of this chapter.

An EDT-Based Axiomatic Model

According to the EDT literature, key features of Innovation Diffusion Theory are: the *rejection of optimisation* or the feasibility of determining one 'best' policy; *a focus on systems and markets* rather than individual firms; *the acceptance of human agency* in technology development; and *the role of government as policy maker*. These features are described and explained in some detail as the basis of the four EDT axioms which formed the analytical instrument used to examine the case study data. *Elements* related to each of the four axioms were then drawn from the EXDOC case study.

Figure 1 sets out the four axioms derived from Evolutionary Diffusion theory. The elements describe the features associated with each axiom which are pertinent to understanding influences on the uptake of innovative technology.

Rejection of Optimisation: Innovation Diffusion theory rejects the idea of optimisation or implementing one 'best' policy at both macro and micro levels. At the macro level, rejection of the possibilities of optimising is one of the strongest points of differentiation in the conceptualisations that have emerged from Evolutionary Economics (Metcalfe, 1994). *'If one wants a model in which it is presumed that the actors fully understand the context ... then the formidable challenge facing the 'rational' models let alone a supposedly 'rational' actor is what it means to 'fully understand' the context, whenever the latter depends in some*

complex, non linear ways on the distribution of micro decisions and on chance and is always full of surprises' (Dosi and Nelson 1994, pp.163-164). Instead of optimisation, the Evolutionary Diffusion model presents the idea that a diversity of policies is necessary to allow for a variety of development paths (Amin, 1998). Economists argue that *path dependency*[1] means that systemic technological and innovative capabilities can only be enhanced by openness of competition, lowering barriers to innovative entry; and nurturing interactive learning as a source of innovation (McKelvey, 1997).

Evolutionary Diffusion Theory also rejects the assumptions that: individual firms behave optimally at the micro level; that adoption is a one-off decision; and that uptake of new technology is more or less instantaneous. Innovation processes are described instead as: multi-referential; non-linear; depending on various framing conditions; and rarely predictable (Kowol and Kueppers, 2003). Once diffusion is viewed as a selection process it becomes evident there is no guarantee that more optimistic or better-informed firms will adopt earlier. Successful innovations represent the outcome of multiple and contingent variables and do not always have to be the best ones (Saviotti and Metcalfe, 1991). Models based on Evolutionary Diffusion Theory stress the gradualism of internal adoption between firms and over time. *'Firms called 'adopters' at a given time actually differ in the extent of their commitment to the new technology ... some of them may subsequently reverse their adoption decision'* (Lissoni and Metcalfe, 1994, p.108).

Market Focus: Evolutionary Diffusion Theory is primarily concerned with the development and diffusion of new variety or innovation in an economic system. Evolutionary models serve to extend traditional DoI theory from studies of individual firms to explaining the impact and effects of innovation and patterns of diffusion in the more complex environment of a market (Lissoni and Metcalfe, 1994). A focus on firms alone misses the contributions and investments

Figure 1. Axioms and constituent elements of evolutionary diffusion theory

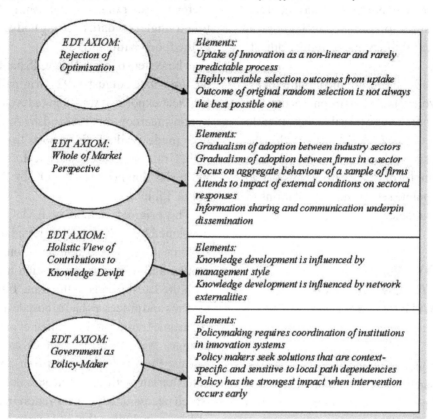

of a wider population of stakeholders into relevant knowledge development. The literature of Evolutionary Diffusion acknowledges the need to encompass these additional sources of information in explaining the diffusion process and thus shifts attention to the aggregate behaviour of a sample of firms, without necessarily relying on explicit modelling of a single firm's decision processes (Nelson and Winter, 1982; Nelson, 1995).

Human Intervention in Economic Processes: Implicit in Evolutionary Diffusion Theory is the assumption that there is a possibility of intervening in the process of technology development; and that the selection of a theory can influence the design of policy. Evolutionary Economics accepts the possibility of human intervention in economic processes where *'users are not exclusively selectors but also involved in the shaping*

of innovations' (Tushman and Rosenkopf, 1992). Once the soft components of technology innovation are recognised, actors must be understood as capable of consciously attempting to change their environment (Nelson, 1995). Evolutionary models draw on a number of reference disciplines to expand the definition of technology to include organisational and cultural elements as well as human artefacts such as machinery and materials. (Lissoni and Metcalfe, 1994.

Government as Policy Maker: The role policy intervention can play and the institutional pressure government can exert to stimulate ITU have been explored by Lissoni and Metcalfe (1994). More recently, the application of EDT to understanding the role of government as policy maker has been extended in work by Lambooy and Boschma (2001) who emphasise the need for ITU solutions to be context-specific and sensitive to local path dependencies. At a regional level, government can use policy measures to stimulate technological and innovative capabilities and minimise adjustment problems.

Clearly, there is no limit to the number of areas to which Evolutionary Diffusion Theory can be applied. It would not be possible, however, to discuss all—or even a sizable sub-set—within the constraints of a single chapter. We have therefore limited our examples of EDT applications to two case studies of public sector implementations of e-business technologies.

CASE STUDY ONE: IMPLEMENTATION OF A G2B DOCUMENTATION SYSTEM (EXDOC)

The Australian Quarantine and Inspection Service (AQIS) developed EXDOC2 to support the preparation of food export documentation by Australian primary producers, who require a health and/or phytosanitary export certificate from AQIS. Health Certificates generated by AQIS are the official means by which the Australian Government certifies to an importing country that a product meets that country's import standards and regulations. The Phytosanitary Certificate is a type of Health documentation testifying to the health status of the certified product. AQIS procedures ensure products meet Australian legislative and importing country standards and requirements; and EXDOC is an integral part of these procedures, providing greater certainty in certification through the standardisation of documentation and the consequently enhanced integrity of Australia's certification systems. The type of product and the destination determine which (if any) certificates are required. In December 2002, the move to harmonisation of regulatory systems and standards gained impetus when. Food Standards Australia New Zealand (FSANZ) assumed responsibility for standards setting in the primary production sector in Australia, so establishing for the first time a single standards-setting body for the whole of the food chain.

The system operated by AQIS has been in production since August 1992. Originally designed for Meat exports, it was then redeveloped for use by non-meat commodities and, by April 2000, had been made available for exports from the Dairy, Fish, Grain and Horticulture sectors. Key events in the development of EXDOC by AQIS are set out in Table 2.

The original version of EXDOC had been developed by 1990. EXDOC relied on open EDI systems at the data communication, application system and document translation levels, in line with the latest trends at the time. Internal AQIS systems and processes had to be redesigned around electronic trading and a number of organisational changes were identified – such as the need to replace the physical signature of an authorised veterinarian with an electronic authorisation – which necessitated process redesign at a number of levels, including that of Human Resources.

In spite of significant problems, the phased implementation of EXDOC survived and developed over time. This AQIS-led project stimulated uptake of new technology, supporting improved food industry supply chain management within and across food sectors and increasing Australian competitiveness on world markets. The case study also revealed that coordination of innovative technology implementations was strongly affected by existing industry culture. Hence it appears that policy maker interventions are most successful where there is a real and recognised need for policy change

A cross-disciplinary review of the literature enabled the authors to synthesise key features of EDT , develop four axioms and then apply them to case study analysis. Table 3 sets out four EDT axioms with their associated elements in order to present a theoretical basis for analysing the AQIS case study data from the EXDOC implementation.

Table 2. Key events in the AQIS Development of EXDOC[3]

EXDOC Development Date	Description of Activity
1990 July:	Development of original EXDOC by AQIS (end date)
1991 Jan:	AQIS Reforms: Commercialisation of Services
1992 August:	EXDOC in production
1997 March:	Development work starts on new EXDOC and extra commodities
1997	The Nairn Report: 109 recommendations on improving quarantine – 'a shared responsibility'
1998 July:	MEAT EXDOC implementation begins
1998 Nov:	DAIRY EXDOC implementation begins
1999 Nov:	FISH EXDOC implementation begins
2000 April:	GRAIN EXDOC & HORTICULTURE EXDOC begin
2002 March:	Minter Ellison Post-Meat Implementation Review reports
2003 June:	WOOL EXDOC & SKINS & HIDES EXDOC begins

(source: N.Scott, EXDOC administrator AQIS, October 2004).

Table 3. Applying EDT Axioms to the AQIS EXDOC implementation

Evolutionary Diffusion Theory	Explanatory Contribution to Case Analysis
Rejection of Optimisation	No predictable pattern of uptake. Unexpected and lengthy delays delay diffusion across sectors after initial swift uptake and industry support Unpredictable (and costly) processes that frequently occur throughout the implementation
Innovation and diffusion from a whole-of-market perspective	Gradualism of internal adoption within firms in a sector Differing rates of uptake across sectors Impact of external conditions on sectoral responses
Holistic View of Contributions to Knowledge Development	Importance of ensuring consistency and compliance with international standards across sectors Need to improve supply chain management across sectors in a globalised environment
Government as policy maker	Plays key role in: Coordinating stakeholder institutions within innovation system Seeking an acceptable business solution to ensure diffusion across sectors Intervening with context specific solutions sensitive to local path dependencies

Analysis of the EXDOC case study confirmed that it was impossible to predict a single 'optimal' policy development path. No single solution or 'magic bullet' emerged for groups of firms targeted for uptake of innovative technology in the AQIS implementation. Uptake and diffusion of

innovative technology in the food industry sectors took unpredictable and non-linear paths. A whole-of-market perspective, however, served to explain the apparently confused and confusing patterns of uptake which occurred during EXDOC's phased implementation. A *holistic view of contributions to knowledge development* and consideration of *the role government can play as policy maker* contributed to the conclusion that rapid dissemination of innovative G2B technology in the Australian food sector depends on compatibility with existing commercial practice, cooperation with local institutions and accommodation of key stakeholders

CASE STUDY TWO: IMPLEMENTATION OF AN ENTERPRISE WIDE DOCUMENT AND RECORDS MANAGEMENT SYSTEM (EDRMS)

In our second case study we move from a cross sectoral document delivery application implemented at Australian federal government level, to a review of an enterprisewide system selected and implemented by a single public sector entity at local government level in South Australia. An Electronic Document and Records Management Systems (EDRMS) implementation with fully scanned records is a type of technology change that affects all users in an organisation, taking them from a manual, self-managed style of work to an organisational systems approach with limited personal customisation. The acceptance required of users is several orders of magnitude greater than in an update of an existing computer-based system, which represents changing "like for like" and hence does not truly test technology acceptance.

Corporate governance requirements and growing pressures for legislative compliance have stimulated national and global uptake of content management systems that can mirror internal corporate approval processes, store information and retrieve it in an accurate and timely manner (Government Exchange, 2004). These external pressures, together with the availability of funding and support for systems underpinning open and accountable government, have resulted in local

government instrumentalities becoming fertile ground for full EDRMS implementations.

The Selection and Implementation of an EDRMS, City of Charles Sturt, South Australia

Local government in Australia consists of 629 Councils and 100 community governments. In South Australia, 68 councils employ around 10,000 people. One of the largest of these councils, covering approximately 10% of metropolitan Adelaide, the state capital, is the City of Charles Sturt (http://www.charlessturt.sa.gov.au/). The City of Charles Sturt (CCS) employs just over 400 full time equivalent staff in 10 business portfolios or departments. Council employs seven Records staff members to register over 300,000 records per annum.

In 2002, the process of replacing the Council's paper records system began with a series of staff workshops designed to examine the issues for staff in moving from paper to electronic documentation. They found that the paper system limited the ability of staff to track and share documentation and the speed at which information could travel through the organisation. The increasing volume and usage of email correspondence in recent times added to these problems. The discussion from this series of workshops culminated in the creation of a *Records Management Strategic Directions* document that clearly established the need for an Electronic Document and Records Management System (EDRMS).

The selection project began with establishing and charging a project team with the responsibility 'to replace the records section of the GEAC TCS and other localized manual and indexed systems used for the same purpose'. The initial document set out six objectives: replacement of the system within a set budget limit, set time frame for implementing the replacement system, work process and efficiency gains, minimized need for new or different hardware and operating systems within the organisation, minimized changeover effects on running the business and ensuring the new system was implemented consistently with the Records Management Strategy. At this stage the size and budget of the project still had to be determined.

In October 2002 the request for tender was advertised; the decision was based on knowledge that the project was now very likely to move forward. A full proposal for the EDRMS was put together in November 2002. Final approval was given by Council in June 2003. Following tender evaluation and demonstrations, TRIM—a product from Tower Software—emerged as the CCS preferred product. By June 2003 the CEO at Council had signed contracts for the purchase of the product.

The EDRMS project team was keenly aware that communication about the project needed planning – otherwise there was likely to be significant resistance from staff when it came to training. Clearly, electronic record-keeping would require a changed understanding of records administration: staff members had to be able to relate the changes to their individual work requirements. Effective communication of these changes was important to project outcomes. Integrating a review of records-keeping with other required topics subsequently led to the vendor's half day training program being extended to a full day.

Around two thirds of the CCS workforce (280 staff members) were involved with the selected EDRMS solution: TRIM. However, unless the EDRMS was fully and formally integrated into business processes, it was likely no one would use the system. The implementation team consequently decided to institute an analysis of all council business processes that touched records. Business process analysis would serve to assist the integration process and also help to identify flagship projects for each area. These flagship projects would champion the benefits of uptake and so accelerate adoption and compliance. Undertaking analysis of well over 100 business processes

required the involvement of many additional staff apart from the members of the three teams. The process accelerated the integration of records with each team's activities, but also ensured that significant communication about the project took place not only within, but across teams.

Moving from paper to TRIM required a number of technology decisions. Containers for records had to be put in the EDRMS. Finding and choosing the containers required considerable fine-tuning. In August 2003, design of the container structures was undertaken by interviewing all business units and ascertaining their needs. Although time-consuming it was important to consult with staff regarding the types of files being used for classification purposes. This process led to the creation of a draft list of containers and the record types that they would hold. The list was distributed to and revised in conjunction with business units in an iterative process.

Workflows in the EDRMS constitute a benefit above and beyond core records management. All business units would use TRIM. The workflow development process was designed to develop the EDRMS as a system people *wanted* - not just one they *had to* use. The aim was to achieve business process gain so business and records would come to be viewed as one process - not two. All new technology and systems needed to be designed around the EDRMS. Otherwise there was a real risk that new information silos would form.

The documentation of business process workflows at CCS began by identifying each business unit and process. An early iteration of this process found some 191 business processes. Each process was then ranked for its suitability for conversion to electronic work flows on TRIM. Ranking was undertaken according to the suitability of workflows to the TRIM system as well as by its priority as assessed by the relevant business unit. Each of the documented workflows was developed over multiple iterations. Whilst feasibility of conversion to TRIM was ultimately an executive decision, there was considerable consultation with staff prior to the final decisions. As part of this exercise interest in specific processes for conversion within individual business units was recorded and ranked. The consultation process proved to be a valuable resource as the rankings were of great assistance to management when it came to selecting 'champions' to promote uptake within a number of CCS business units. Some 10 to 15 of the 191 processes identified as candidates for conversion were then implemented at start-up.

A key challenge facing user acceptance testing early in the development process is the difficulty of conveying to users what a proposed system will consist of in a realistic way. It is at this point that people form general perceptions of a system's usefulness — perceptions that are strongly linked to usage intentions. Hence, introductory training, particularly its perceived relevance and integration with business processes, can have a strong impact on usage intentions (Laeven T, 2005). These intentions are significantly correlated with future acceptance of the system (Davis, Bagozzi and Warshaw, 1989 p.1000). It was vital to ensure that staff understood the meaning of a Record and related procedures once the EDRMS went live. The decision was therefore made to extend the mandatory training for all CCS computer users from the proposed half day to a whole day to cover Records Management procedures. Ten staff members were trained each day over a 7.5 week period.

Continuing steady growth in registration of Council records clearly indicates that processing staff at all levels of the organisation appreciate the benefits of the implementation for finding, searching and viewing documents (Figure 2). Familiarity with the EDRMS at CCS increased staff confidence in using electronic records systems and other software – skills that are increasingly valued in the job market. All records have now been on the TRIM system since 8th March 2004. Staff members understand the system and feel secure. Low compliance remains a problem in certain areas; for example decisions to 'TRIM' (add to records) and the time required entering each item are difficult to resolve in the case of email

The success of systems integration at CCS, achieved for a project budget of $150,000, has been a notable feature of the EDRMS implementation. Transactional integration at CCS has meant that all systems integrate information. Although not part of the original project, the Document Assembly process within TRIM is now widely used for internal forms and document templates. Most importantly, the integration between TRIM, Proclaim One and GIS means that all of these systems can now be viewed at desk level.

The EDRMS replaced a paper-based system that represented a mainstay for staff members' day-to-day operations and one which had been established over many years. For some employees the fact that there is a new baseline for 'business

Figure 2. Year on year registrations 2006 – 2007 (City of Charles Sturt, South Australia)

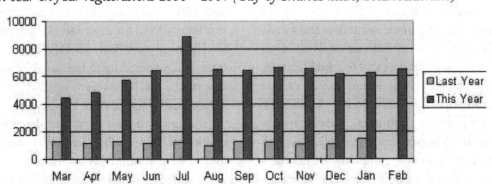

Table 1. Application of EDT Axioms to the EDRMS case study

Evolutionary Diffusion Theory	Explanatory Contribution to Case Analysis
Rejection of Optimisation	Attention to discontinuing ineffective practice & slowing uptake of inappropriate technologies via initial staff workshops
	Decision to articulate dynamic mechanisms underlying uptake of innovation by instituting Business process analysis & documentation of business process work flows
	Recognition that an organisational decision to adopt does not automatically translate into individual or group acceptance without resistance results in use of monthly usage reports by work sectors to stimulate uptake across organisation
	Recognition that subjective norms can be shaped by influence. Hence EDRMS uptake and usage are strongly supported and encouraged by CEO and senior management
Innovation and diffusion from a whole-of-market perspective	N/A
Holistic View of Contributions to Knowledge Development	System wide perspective by management underpins successful integration of EDRMS as indicated by:
	Extra training for all staff to ensure understanding of meaning of a record and so encourage user acceptance of the new system
	Documentation of all business process workflows to encourage identification of business and records as one process and so avoid information silos
	Continual building on the base system to indicate that the EDRMS is a core technology assisting staff become more productive
Government as policy maker	Plays key role in:
	Recognition that subjective norms can be shaped by influences such as pressures for legislative compliance and corporate governance requirements
	Coordinating stakeholder institutions within innovation system by making funding available
	Seeking an acceptable business solution and intervening with context specific solutions sensitive to local path dependencies to ensure diffusion across sectors by providing support for systems underpinning open and accountable government

as normal' continues to be a demanding concept. For any organisation in the public or private sector, new systems integration ultimately means finding ways to maintain the impetus for cultural change (Gregory 2005; Laeven 2005; Maguire 2005; Kotter and Cohen 2002).

The successful outcome of EDRMS uptake in this local government instrumentality has been attributed to a number of factors including:

- The vital role played by senior executive support especially that of the CEO
- The culture of open communication\supportive of staff involvement and risk-taking throughout the project.
- A clear understanding by key players of the benefits of the project and their energy in pursuing outcomes
- The emphasis on consultation from the earliest days of the project

- The pressure for uptake from fellow employees.

Since the initial introduction of TRIM as the EDRMS at the City of Charles Sturt, development has continued in the areas of integration to other systems, complementary smaller software applications to address business issues, work-flow of business records and many other advances associated with the technology. Continual building on the base system clearly demonstrates to staff within CCS that the EDRMS is a core technology and assists them in being more productive. Closely coupled to these on-going advances is sensitivity to the fact that the organisation as a whole must continue to perceive that there is benefit gained for the work that is required to maintain a full EDRMS.

In Table 4 we set out the four axioms we developed from EDT and apply them to this second case study. The four axioms with their associated elements (see Table 1) were applied to analysing our findings from this EDRMS implemented by a local council in South Australia. Table 6 indicates how closely the four axioms could be applied to our single organisation case study analysis.

Understanding the EDT axiom, Rejection of Optimisation provided real insight into how a technology implementation unfolds. It addresses many of the factors that an organisation must deal with when facing technological change such as understanding how choices are made between systems and even whether to choose a system at all. Management appreciation of the importance of the axiom A Holistic View of Contributions to Knowledge underpinned the successful integration of the EDRMS in every aspect of Council business. The new system was deliberately built into every aspect of business undertaken at the City of Charles Sturt, with productivity linked to its success at every opportunity.

The EDT axiom, Government as policy maker also proved highly applicable to the implementation. In many instances, Australian local government has been a leader in implementing EDRMS due in no small part to factors closely associated with government acting in the role of policy maker by exerting pressures for legislative compliance, via corporate governance requirements and the availability of funding for uptake of EDRMS. These three EDT axioms have provided excellent indicators to the project manager and a clear explanation of why the organisation chose a particular path. Only one of the four EDT axioms - Innovation and diffusion from a whole-of-market perspective - was not applicable to our second case study.

CONCLUSION

IS implementation studies lack a widely accepted theoretical framework to satisfactorily explain how complex and networked technologies diffuse in practice. The two detailed case studies described in this chapter applied EDT to analyse how a technology implementation unfolds. We investigated how choices were made between systems or even whether to choose a system at all. EDT provided reliable indicators and an explanation of why the organisation chose a particular path. Three of our EDT axioms *Rejection of Optimisation, A Holistic View of Contributions to Knowledge* and *Government as Policy Maker* offered particularly useful tools for analysing key aspects of both implementations (see Table 6). The only EDT axiom which did not fully apply to our second case study was *Innovation and Diffusion from a Whole-Of-Market Perspective.*

EDT axioms thus proved useful for analyses at both sectoral and organisational levels: they were only marginally less applicable as an analytical tool for investigating a single enterprise wide system implementation. When applied to the AQIS implementation in our first case study, the broader IS investigative approach of Evolutionary Diffusion Theory effectively explained the impact(s) of diffusion in the more complex environment of a market, in a way the more restricted alternative diffusion of innovation theories could not match. Our second case study featured uptake of an enterprise-wide EDRMS solution by a local government entity. Here, EDT provided real assistance in explaining how a single – but complex – organisation can manage a major change in its understanding of activities and sources of information.

Our chapter, therefore, provides not only an introduction to Evolutionary Diffusion Theory, but also sets out how EDT can be effectively applied to explain influences on uptake of innovation in an Information Systems environment. EDT offers an explanatory basis for many of the complex and interrelated issues that apply to instances of e-business uptake in ways which are not matched by either Classical DoI theory, or by the network-based extensions to that approach. We believe that EDT and the axioms we derived from the theory, together offer a richness of analytic approach and a powerful explanatory capability rendering it particularly appropriate to discussing the diffusion of information technology. Since the majority of real world e-business implementations are cross sectoral, confirmation of the validity of EDT for such applications presents exciting possibilities for improved understanding of issues affecting acceptance levels of new technologies in the IS field.

REFERENCES

Andersen, E. S. (1994). *Evolutionary economics: Post-Schumpeterian contributions*. London: Pinter Publishers.

Arthur, W. B. (1994). *Increasing returns and path dependency in the economy*. Ann Arbor, MI: The University of Michigan Press.

Baskerville, R., & Pries-Heje, J. (2001). A multiple-theory analysis of a diffusion of information technology case. *Information Systems Journal,* *11*(3), 181-212.

Bijker, W. B. (1995). *Of bicycles, bakelite and bulbs: Toward a theory of sociotechnical change*. Cambridge, MA: MIT Press.

Boudreau, M-C., & Robey, D. (1999). Organizational transition to enterprise resource planning systems: Theoretical choices for process research. In *Proceedingss. of the Twentieth International Conference on Information Systems*, Charlotte, NC (pp. 291-299).

Clarke, R. (1999, June 7-9). Electronic services delivery: From brochure-ware to entry points. In *Proceedings of the Twelfth International Electronic Commerce Conference*, Bled, Slovenia (pp. 8-9).

Clarke, R. (2001). *Innovation diffusion resources. Open site*. Retrieved September 25, 2005, from http://www.anu.edu.au/people/Roger.Clarke/SOS/InnDiffISW.html

Constant, E. W. (1980). *The origins of the turbojet revolution*. Baltimore: Johns Hopkins University Press.

Damsgaard, J., & Lyytinen, K. (1996). Government Strategies to promote the diffusion of electronic data interchange: What we know and what we don't know. *Information Infrastructure and Policy, 5*(3), 169-190.

Davis, F. D., Bagozzi, R. P., & Warshaw, P. R. (1989). User acceptance of computer technology: A comparison of two theoretical models. *Management Science, 35*(8), 982-1003.

Dopfer, K. (Ed.). (2001). *Evolutionary economics: Program and scope*. Dordrecht, The Netherlands: Kluwer Academic Publishers.

Dosi, G., & Nelson, R. R. (1994). An introduction to evolutionary theories in economics. *Journal of Evolutionary Economics, 4*, 153-172.

Dosi, G., Freeman, C., Nelson, R. R., Silverberg, G., & Soete, L. (Eds.). (1988). *Technological change and economic theory.* London: Pinter Publishers.

Downs, G. W., & Mohr, L. B. (1976). Conceptual issues in the study of innovations. *Administrative Science Quarterly, 21*(Dec), 700-14.

Edquist, C. (Ed.). (1997). *Systems of innovation: Technologies, institutions and organisations.* London: Pinter Publishers.

Fichman, R. G. (1992, December 13-16). Information technology diffusion: A review of empirical research. In *Proceedings of the Thirteenth International Conference on Information Systems (ICIS),* Dallas, TX, USA (pp. 195-206).

Galliers, R. D., & Swan J. A. (1999). Information systems and strategic change: A critical review of business process re-engineering. In W. L. Currie & R. D. Galliers (Eds.), *Rethinking MIS* (pp. 361-387). Oxford, UK: Oxford University Press.

Gregory, K. (2005). Implementing an electronic records management system: A public sector case study. *Records Management Journal, 15,*(2), 80-85.

Holbrook, A., & Salazar, M. (2004). Regional innovation systems within a federation: Do national policies affect all regions equally? *The International Journal of Innovation Research, Commercialization, Policy Analysis and Best Practice, 6*(1), 50-64.

Jones, N., & Myers, M. D. (2001). Assessing three theories of information systems innovation: An interpretive case study of a funds management company. In *Proceedings of the Pacific Asia Conference on Information Systems,* Seoul, Korea (pp. 1005-1019).

Kowol, U., & Küppers, U. (2003). Innovation networks: A new approach to innovation dynamics. In M. van Geenhuizen, D. V. Gibson, & M. V. Heitor (Eds.), *Regional development and conditions for innovation in the network society.* Lafayette, IN: Purdue University Press.

Kotter, J. P., & Cohen, D. S. (2002). *The heart of change: Real-life stories of how people change their organizations.* Boston: Harvard Business School Press.

Kwon, T. H., & Zmud, R. W. (1987). Unifying the fragmented models of information systems implementations. In J. R. Boland & R. Hirschheim (Eds.), *Critical issues in information systems research* (pp. 227-252). New York: John Wiley.

Laeven, T. (2005). Competencies – the asset that counts most: On developing human talents as a prerequisite for successful EDRM changes. In C. Hare & J. McLeod (Eds.), *Managing electronic records* (pp. 129-148). UK: Facet Publishing.

Lambooy, J. G., & Boschma, R. A. (2001). Evolutionary economics and regional policy. *Annals of Regional Science, 35,* 113-131.

Lissoni, F., & Metcalfe, J. S. (1994). Diffusion of innovation ancient and modern: A review of the main themes. In M. Dodgson & R. Rothwell (Eds.), *Handbook of industrial innovation* (pp. 106-144). Cheltenham, UK: Edward Elgar Publishing Limited.

McKelvey, M. (1997). Using evolutionary theory to define systems of innovation. In C. Edquist (Ed.), *Systems of innovation—technologies, institutions and organizations* (pp. 200-222). London: Pinter/Cassell Publishers.

Maguire, R. (2005). Lessons learned from implementing an electronic records management system. *Records Management Journal, 15*(3), 150-157.

Markus, M. L., & Robey, D. (1988). Information technology and organizational change: Causal structure in theory and research. *Management Science, 34*(5), 583-598.

Metcalfe, J. S. (1994). The economics of evolution and the economics of technology policy. *Economic Journal, 104,* 931-944.

Mokyr, J. (1996). Evolution and technological change: A new metaphor for economic history? In R. Fox (Ed.), *Technological change* (pp. 63-83). London: Harwood Publishers.

Moore, G. C., & Benbasat, I. (1991). Development of an instrument to measure the perceptions of adopting an information technology innovation. *Information Systems Research, 2,* 192-222.

Nelson, R. R. (1995). Recent evolutionary theorizing about economic change. *Journal of Economic Literature, 33,* 48-90.

Nelson R. R. (2002). Bringing institutions into evolutionary growth theory, *Journal of Evolutionary Economics, 12*(1/2), 17-29.

Nelson, R. R., & Winter, S. G. (1982). *An evolutionary theory of economic change.* Cambridge, MA: Belknap Press.

Norgren, L., & Hauknes, J. (1999). *Economic rationales of government involvement in innovation and the supply of innovation-related service.* Oslo, Norway: Rise Project, European Commission.

Orlikowski, W. J., & Hofman, J. D. (1997). An improvisational model for change management: The case of groupware technologies. *Sloan Management Review, 38*(2), 11-21.

Reich, B. H., & Benbasat, I. (2000). Factors that influence the social dimension of alignment between business and information technology objectives. *MIS Quarterly, 24*(1), 81-113.

Rogers, E. M. (1995) *The diffusion of innovation* (4th ed.). New York: The Free Press.

Rosenberg, N. (1969). The direction of technological change: Inducement mechanisms and focusing devices. In N. Rosenberg (Ed.), *Economic development and cultural change* (Vol. 18, No. 1, Part 1) (pp. 1-24). Chicago: The University of Chicago Press.

Saviotti, P. P. (1996). Systems theory and technological change. *Futures, Dec.,* 773-785.

Saviotti, P. P., & Metcalfe, J. S. (1991). *Evolutionary theories of economic and technological change: Present status and future prospects.* Reading, UK: Harwood Academic Publishers.

Van de Ven, A. H., Polley, D. E., Garud, R., & Venkatraman, S. (1999). *The innovation journey.* New York: Oxford University Press.

Wilkins, L., Castleman, T., & Swatman P. M. C. (2001). Organisational factors in the diffusion of an industry standard. *Electronic Markets, 11*(4), 222-230.

Wilkins, L., Holt, D., Swatman, P. M. C., & Chan, E. S. K. (2007, June 4-6). Implementing information management strategically: An Australian EDRMS case study. In *Proceedings of the 20th Bled International E-Commerce Conference,* Bled, Slovenia.

Wilkins, L., Swatman, P. M. C., & Castleman, T. (2003). Electronic markets and service delivery: Requisite competencies for virtual environments. In *Proceedings of the 11th European Conference on Information Systems ECIS 2003,* Milan, Italy (pp. 1-13).

Wilkins, L., Swatman, P. M. C., & Castleman, T. (2002). Government sponsored virtual communities and the incentives for buy-in. *International Journal of Electronic Commerce, 7*(1), 121-134.

Wilkins, L., Swatman, P. M. C., & Castleman, T. (2000, June 19-21). Electronic commerce as innovation – a framework for interpretive analysis. In *Proceedings of the 13th Bled International Electronic Commerce Conference,* Bled, Slovenia (pp. 150-121).

KEY TERMS AND DEFINITIONS

Axioms: An axiom is any starting assumption from which other statements are logically derived. An axiom can be a sentence, a proposition, a statement or a rule that forms the basis of a formal system.

Corporate Governance: The system/process by which the directors & officers of an organization are required to carry out & discharge their legal, moral & regulatory accountabilities & responsibilities.

Electronic Document and Records Management System: An EDRMS aims to enable businesses to manage documents throughout the life cycle of those documents, from creation to destruction.

Evolutionary Diffusion Theory: A classic evolutionary model of technological change first developed by Nelson and Winter (1982). The model demonstrates the possibility of collating a wide diversity of elements (including the processes of transmission; variety creation and selection) and integrates them into a process which can then be applied to understanding the uptake of innovative technology.

Market Focus: The development and diffusion of new variety or innovation in an economic system.

Rejection of Optimisation: Evolutionary Diffusion Theory rejects the assumptions that: individual firms behave optimally at the micro level and stress the gradualism of internal adoption of innovative technology between firms and over time. Successful innovations are rarely predictable and represent the outcome of multiple and contingent variables and do not always have to be the best ones.

Rogers' Classical Diffusion of Innovation Theory: Rogers focused attention on the shape of the diffusion curve, describing innovation as a process that moves through an initial phase of generating variety in technology, to selecting across that variety to produce patterns of change resulting in feedback from the selection process, to the development of further variation.

ENDNOTES

[1]   Path dependence is a key concept of Evolutionary Economics, usually explained in association with an industrial process e.g. the QWERTY keyboard. It describes the natural trajectory of an unpredictable original selection where, although many outcomes are possible, under increasing returns the process becomes focused on a particular path (Arthur 1994; Nelson and Winter 1982). Path dependence suggests that it is often costly to change technologies in production processes. When the costs of change are large, it is possible that firms will continue to use sub-optimal technologies.

[2]   A simple overview of the EXDOC system can be accessed at the AFFA website link, under AQIS publications (see http://www. affa.gov.au/content/publications.cfm). This description of the EXDOC system draws on the following sources: an earlier case study of AQIS and EXDOC as part of a major research project on EDI systems integration (Swatman, 1993); the Minter Ellison 2002 Report; and information provided by the EXDOC administrator Mr N Scott 2002/4.

[3]   Aspects of the EXDOC case study have already been reported in the proceedings of BLED 2000, ECIS 2000, ECIS 2003; and in IJEC 2002 and EM 2001 journal articles

Chapter XIII
Contemporary Information Systems Alternative Models to TAM:
A Theoretical Perspective

Ahmed Y. Mahfouz
Prairie View A&M University, USA

ABSTRACT

Based on the theory of reasoned action, the technology acceptance model (TAM) has been one of the most widely used theories in management information systems research. This chapter proposes several alternative theories from the literature to TAM. Four theories are showcased that actually reveal a reverse relationship in contrast to the traditional attitude-behavior relationship in TAM. These four theories are theory of cognitive dissonance, social judgment theory, theory of passive learning, and self-perception theory. Other alternatives to TAM and other popular theories are flow theory, cognitive load theory, capacity information processing theory, and information processing theory. These theories are applicable in e-commerce, online consumer behavior, online shopping, immersive gaming, virtual social interactions, and cognitive research. Pragmatic examples are shown for the theories.

INTRODUCTION AND BACKGROUND

The technology acceptance model or TAM (Davis, 1989; Davis et al., 1989) has been one of the most popular theories utilized in IS research. TAM adoption has been in countless areas, beyond the initial intended application of the theory, technology adoption in organizations. Over 700 citations have been made of the Davis's et al. (1989) article (Bagozzi, 2007). An entire special issue of the *Journal of the Association for Information Systems* (JAIS) in April 2007 was dedicated to TAM, recounting the vast impact of the theory, as well as its shortcomings, such as its simplicity (Bagozzi, 2007; Benbasat and Barki, 2007; Hirschheim, 2007).

This research proposes several alternative theories from the literature to TAM. Instead of the traditional attitude-behavior relationship in TAM, four theories are included to show how the reverse of the relationship, behavior-attitude, is possible: theory of cognitive dissonance, social judgment theory, theory of passive learning, and self-perception theory. TAM (Davis, 1989; Davis et al., 1989) is based on the theory of reasoned action or TRA (Fishbein, 1967; Fishbein and Ajzen, 1975), which was later extended to the theory of planned behavior or TPB (Ajzen, 1991). Table 1 shows a list of attitude-behavior link theories and their reverse link counterparts (Assael, 1998; Davis, 1989; Davis et al., 1989).

Other alternative theories to TAM are flow theory, cognitive load theory, capacity information processing theory, and information processing theory. These theories are relevant in multiple areas in IS, including ecommerce, online consumer behavior, online shopping, immersive gaming, virtual social interactions, and cognitive research. Examples of implementations of the theories are also discussed.

Hence, the objectives of this paper are to provide the following:

- Suggest several alternative theories to TAM from the literature for IS research.
- Propose, specifically, theories that exhibit a reverse relationship to the traditional attitude-behavior link in TAM.

- Discuss more alternative theories, especially flow theory.
- Apply these theories with a discussion and examples.

TAM, THEORIES OF REASONED ACTION, AND PLANNED BEHAVIOR

TAM is based on TRA (Fishbein, 1967; Fishbein and Ajzen, 1975). TRA tries to explain the linkage between attitude and behavior. The influence of attitude towards an actual behavior happens as consciously intended (Davis et al., 1989) or *reasoned* action through the mediating effect of behavioral intention. This mediating effect between attitude and behavior is also called the *sufficiency assumption* (Bettman, 1986). It is more significant to consider users' attitude towards purchasing or using a product than their attitude towards the object or brand itself in predicting their behavior of purchase intention (Fishbein, 1967; Fishbein and Ajzen, 1975). For example, a customer may have a favorable attitude towards a very powerful Dell computer system but an unfavorable attitude toward purchasing it due to cost. The theory was later modified to incorporate beliefs (evaluations of action) and social norms (Fishbein, 1967; Fishbein and Ajzen, 1975). Evaluations of action are a person's beliefs about perceived consequences of one's actions. Social norms are a combination of normative beliefs (perceived expectations of one's family and peers) and motivation to comply with these expectations (Fishbein, 1967; Fishbein and Ajzen, 1975).

Table 1. Attitude-behavior vs. behavior-attitude theories

Attitude-Behavior Theories	Behavior-Attitude Theories
Theory of Reasoned Action	Cognitive Dissonance Theory
Theory of Planned Behavior	Social Judgment Theory
Technology Acceptance Model	Theory of Passive Learning
	Self-Perception Theory

TRA was later extended to the theory of planned behavior (TPB) which includes perceived behavioral control as another determinant of intention and behavior (Ajzen, 1991). Mathieson (1991) compared TAM and TPB in predicting user intentions. TPB is shown in Figure 1. TRA is depicted graphically in Figure 2.

Based on TRA, TAM is a theory that explains user adoption of technology at the organizational level. It is one of the most widely used theories in IS literature. The theory establishes a chain of causality of beliefs about the technology, attitudes towards using the technology, behavioral intentions of use of the system, and behaviors or actual usage of the technology (Heijden et al., 2003), as shown in Figure 3. According to Davis (1989) and Davis et al. (1989), two beliefs (perceived usefulness and perceived ease of use) predict attitudes, which in turn influence intended use of a technology. This intention then consequently impacts behavior of actual system usage. Perceived usefulness is the degree to which a user thinks a

Figure 1. Theory of planned behavior

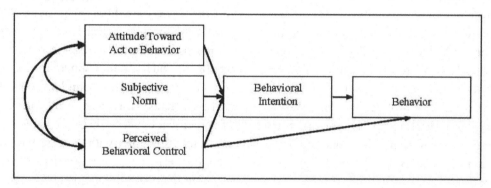

Figure 2. Theory of reasoned action

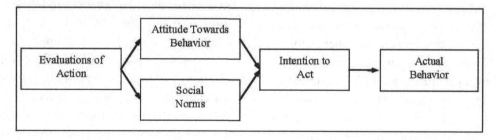

Figure 3. Technology acceptance model

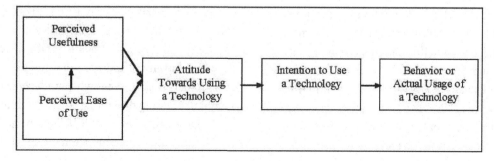

technology would enhance performance or productivity in the workplace. Perceived ease of use is the degree of lack of effort required by the user in adopting a given technology. Perceived ease of use also affects perceived usefulness (Davis, 1989; Davis et al., 1989).

REVERSE RELATIONSHIPS TO TAM: ALTERNATIVE THEORIES OF BEHAVIOR-ATTITUDE

This paper postulates four theories from the literature that could provide alternatives to TAM, as well as explain a reverse relationship in contrast to the traditional attitude-behavior relationship in TAM or TRA. Explaining this reverse relationship, these four theories show how behavior can affect subsequent attitude (such as online attitude postpurchase): cognitive dissonance theory (Festinger, 1957), Sherif's social judgment theory (Sherif et al. 1965), Krugman's theory (1965) of passive learning, and Bem's (1967, 1972) self-perception theory.

Cognitive Dissonance

First, the theory of cognitive dissonance is an example of how behaviors can influence attitudes (Assael, 1998). According to cognitive dissonance theory (Festinger, 1957), a conflict occurs when an individual's attitudes and behaviors are not congruent. The individual tries to reduce this conflict by changing one's opinion to conform to the outcome of one's behavior. For example, if consumers buy an Apple Macintosh computer instead of a PC, they may later have doubts about the purchase when they reevaluate the alternative platform. To reduce this dissonance in cognition or postpurchase conflict, they may extensively highlight the attributes of their current platform to reduce this discrepancy in belief or opinion. Hence, the behavior (purchase) is reinforced and results in more positive feelings (attitude) post-

purchase about the chosen decision. An example of implementing cognitive dissonance theory in systems development, Szajna and Scamell (1993) uncovered an association between realism of users' expectations and their perceptions, but not their actual performance, regarding an information system.

Social Judgment Theory

Second, Sherif's social judgment theory (Sherif et al., 1965) can explain how behavior can impact attitude (Assael, 1998). A recipient's judgment on a persuasive message depends on one's position on the topic. There are three categories of positions: latitude of acceptance (range of acceptable positions), latitude of rejection (range of objectionable positions), and latitude of noncommitment (range of neutral positions). An assimilation effect occurs when recipients of a message exaggerate the degree of agreement between their beliefs and the message, since they agree with the message. However, a contrast effect occurs when the recipients of a message overstate the difference between their beliefs and the message, since they disagree with the message. Small to moderate discrepancies between the recipient's beliefs and the message's position (within the latitude of acceptance and noncommitment) will cause changes in attitude, but large discrepancies (within the latitude of rejection) will not. Simply put, individuals filter in and out messages they agree with or disagree with, respectively, and they will view a message they agree with more positively than it really is, and vice versa.

For example, when expectations regarding a decision or behavior are not met, dissatisfaction (or disconfirmation of expectations) regarding the behavior occurs (Assael, 1998). According to social judgment theory, when users of a web site are dissatisfied somewhat with relatively infrequent but long download times, their attitudes will change slightly (attitude) to accommodate the new expectations (assimilation effect), since they still feel they made the right decision initially by visiting the site (behavior). This occurs since users are accepting and assimilating of the outcome. This only occurs with minor disappointments or changes in expectations. If the users are extremely disappointed for waiting a long time to access the site, a negative attitude forms, and it is likely they overstate this negative change in attitude (contrast effect). Therefore, behavior (visiting the site) results in a change in attitude (negatively, if site visitors are extremely annoyed).

Based on social judgment theory, Nah and Benbasat (2004) examine expert-novice differences in group decision making in a knowledge-based support environment and find that the analyses and explanations provided by knowledge-based systems better support the decision making of novices than experts. Novices are more influenced by the system and find it more useful than experts do. Reagan-Cirincione (1994) suggests Group Decision Support Systems that combine facilitation, social judgment analysis, and information technology should be used to improve the accuracy of group judgment. Interacting groups outperform their most capable members on cognitive conflict tasks (Reagan-Cirincione, 1994).

Passive Learning

Third, Krugman's (1965) theory of passive learning sheds light on how behavior can affect attitude (Assael, 1998). Krugman (1965) realizes that television is a low-involvement, passive medium of learning and advertising since individuals do not actively participate in the communication process. TV viewers have high brand recall but change little in terms of brand attitude. In a low-involvement situation, changes in attitudes may not result in modifications to behavior (Assael, 1998). This is the case with low-involvement products, or items that require little search and decision making on part of the consumer, such as toilet paper. Most TV viewers may actually rate their purchases (behavior) favorably after postpurchase, resulting in more favorable opinions (attitudes) towards the purchase decision or brand.

Self-Perception Theory

Fourth, Bem's (1967, 1972) self-perception theory can be used to explain the reverse relationship of behavior on attitude. It is viewed as an alternative to cognitive dissonance theory. One does not have to experience dissonance to have an attitude change. Instead, individuals have knowledge of their emotions and internal states and reach a certain attitude based on their own overt behavior and the situations in which these behaviors take place just as an outside observer or another person would. In essence, individuals develop their own attitude by observing themselves act in various circumstances. This is especially the case when internal cues are weak or ambiguous that the individual is like an outside observer, relying on external signals to infer an internal state.

MORE THEORIES AS ALTERNATIVES

Below are several theories that serve as additional alternatives to TAM. These theories are flow theory (Csikszentmihalyi, 1975, 1990, 2000), cognitive load theory (Sweller, 1988), limited capacity information processing theory (Lang 1995, 2000), and information processing theory (Miller, 1956). These theories apply to ecommerce, online consumer behavior, online shopping, immersive gaming, virtual social interactions, and cognitive research.

Optimal Experience and Flow

Csikszentmihalyi's flow theory (1975, 1990, 2000) views flow as a state in which individuals are so engaged in an activity that they might be oblivious to the world around them and possibly lose track of time and even of self. Known as *flow experience* or *state of flow*, this state becomes an *optimal experience*, another synonym for flow, when individuals feel they are in control of their actions and in a sense of enjoyment and exhilaration, when the levels of task challenges and their own skills are both equally high. For example, some athletes or people who exercise vigorously report they have *entered the zone* at a peak moment of their game or exercise routine, or are *lost in the experience* for computer-video gamers (Csikszentmihalyi, 1997). In order to facilitate a sense of flow, online sites need to be stimulating and responsive to users. Otherwise, *boredom, anxiety,* and *apathy* experiences materialize (Csikszentmihalyi, 1975, 2000). Boredom results when the interface or site is not challenging enough, while anxiety occurs if the system is too difficult to use. Apathy happens when skills of users and challenges of sites are too low, while a flow experience takes place when both skills and challenges are congruent to one another (Csikszentmihalyi, 1975, 2000). In essence, flow is created when individuals achieve concentration effortlessly and sense joy while carrying out a specific set of objectives that need responses at the workplace, in leisure, or in social engagements (Csikszentmihalyi, 1997).

An important component of this optimal experience is that it is an end in itself or a reward for its own sake, becoming what is called *autotelic*, from the Greek word *auto* or self and *telos* or goal (Csikszentmihalyi, 2000). An autotelic experience is intrinsically interesting and involves establishing goals, becoming absorbed in the activity, paying attention and concentrating on what is happening, and learning to enjoy direct experience. Teaching kids to educate them is not autotelic, but teaching them because one likes to interact with children is autotelic (Csikszentmihalyi, 1990). Ultimately, the line between work and leisure is blurred as they become one whole, which is called life. The German word for experience, *Erlebnis*, is related to the verb *to live* (Schmitt, 1999). Flow experience has been reported in many areas such as rock climbing, chess playing, dancing, surgery,

sports, arts, music compositions, and management, to name a few (Csikszentmihalyi, 1990, 2000). Table 2 lists studies that have utilized or dealt with flow theory in information systems (with a couple in marketing). The Webster and Martocchio (1992) and Agrawal and Karahanna (2000) articles have the distinction of being two of the top 100 cited articles published between 1990-2004 in a combination of *MIS Quarterly, Information Systems Research*, and the IS section of *Management Science* (Lowery et al., 2007). Similarly, Koufaris (2002) is one of the top 100 most cited articles published from 2000 to 2004 (Lowery et al., 2007).

After a flow experience, self becomes more complex in two ways: differentiation and integration (Csikszentmihalyi, 1990). *Differentiation* is a sense of being unique and different from other people. On the contrary, *integration* is a union with others, ideas, and entities outside the individual. For example, customization and personalization of a web site shopping experience is an example of differentiation, but communication with online users in chat rooms and via egroups connected by a common interest is an example of integration.

The Internet facilitates a flow experience (Chen et al., 1999; Novak et al., 2000, 2003), and online activities resulting in flow can be classified as the virtual environment itself, newsgroup discussions, chat rooms, email, and computer games (Chen et al., 1999). User shopping experience, in such contexts as web surfing, online shopping, and playing online computer games, exhibit these characteristics. When users go online, they may have a *clear goal*, such as searching for information on a product or purchasing that item online, and receive *feedback* when the system responds to their search inquiry. They may also entertain themselves through leisurely browsing a site or playing a game with other users on the web. These tasks pose *challenges* and require Internet *skills* to complete them. In essence, users are *carrying out those actions* and *concentrating* on what they are doing. Higher challenge induces increased

Table 2. Sample of studies dealing with flow experience

Relevant Findings	Source
Web site complexity affects flow in online shopping. The study examines a complete model of flow with antecedents.	Guo and Poole (in press)
Using cognitive fit and flow theories, a model and guidelines are developed for establishing a customer decision support system for customized products in online shopping.	Kamis et al. (2008)
Interactivity and site attractiveness impact flow experience, which allows for greater user learning. Users report sensing time distortion, enjoyment, and telepresence while browsing.	Skadberg and Kimmel (2003)
In entertainment and games, in this case an interactive science murder mystery, users achieve a state of flow.	Jennings (2002)
Shopping enjoyment and perceived usefulness of a site are predictors of revisits.	Koufaris (2002)
Cognitive absorption dimensions are temporal dissociation, focused immersion, heightened enjoyment, control, and curiosity.	Agrawal and Karahanna (2000)
Revised model shows skill and control, challenge and arousal, focused attention, and interactivity and telepresence increase flow.	Novak et al. (2000)
Flow is important in improving web site design. Flow includes challenges, control, and feelings of enjoyment.	Chen et al. (1999)
Flow is relevant to sensory, affective, and cognitive experiences.	Schmitt (1999, 2003)
They propose a model that is later revised into Hoffman and Novak's (2000) Model of Flow.	Hoffman and Novak (1996)
12-item flow scale, based on Trevino and Webster's (1992) study, suggests 3 dimensions, combining curiosity and intrinsic interest into one dimension, *cognitive enjoyment*.	Webster et al. (1993)
Four flow measures are control, attention focus, curiosity (sensory and cognitive), and intrinsic interest, as examined in work settings using email and voice mail.	Trevino and Webster (1992)
Computer or cognitive playfulness, involving spontaneous and imaginative interactions with computers, is important in IS.	Webster and Martocchio (1992)

focused attention online (Novak et al., 2000). The users are in *control* of the interface and level of interactivity and manipulate various objects and controls, like buttons and vivid 3D simulations. Experiencing other interactivity features, they customize products to their liking and personalize the experience through user profiles. In interactive 3D games or product simulations, they feel so absorbed in their activities (Swartout and Van Lent, 2003) and may *lose self-consciousness* and *lose track of time*. While browsing and being in a virtual environment and undergoing this sensory, affective, and cognitive experience so far, users feel time distortion, enjoyment, and telepresence, and in turn experience flow (Skadberg and Kimmel, 2003). Those feelings are a consequence of being transported into a virtual world of fantastic games or 3D dressing rooms with virtual models of users or virtual dressing rooms, such as the case

with landsend.com and eddiebauer.com. These experiences of online navigation and playing computer games (Jennings, 2002) become *autotelic* when individuals carry out those activities for their own sake. Table 3 (Csikszentmihalyi and Rathunde, 1993) shows characteristics of such flow dimensions.

McMillan (2002) proposes models of classifications of interactivity in terms of users, documents, and systems. One of those models deals with flow experiences. In the user-to-system interactivity models, as shown in Figure 4 (McMillan, 2002), there are two dimensions: center of control (human vs. computer) and interface (apparent vs. transparent). She gives several examples to illustrate each model next. Computer-based interaction involves such things as users filling in online forms. Human-based interaction includes more user control, such as the case when individuals utilize

Table 3. Flow experience characteristics

Dimension	Details
Clear goals	Task at hand is clear and has *immediate feedback*.
Challenges = skills	Opportunities to act are high, along with one's perceived ability to act.
Merge of action and awareness	One-pointedness of mind
Concentration on task- at-hand	Extraneous input is ignored as worries and concerns are suspended for the time being.
Control	There is a perceived sense of control.
Loss of self-consciousness	Transcendent feelings of belonging to something of greater importance.
Altered sense of time	Sense of time going by faster.
Autotelic experience	When several of the prior conditions exist, the experience is worth the effort just for its own sake.

Figure 4. Four models of user-to-system interactivity (with flow)

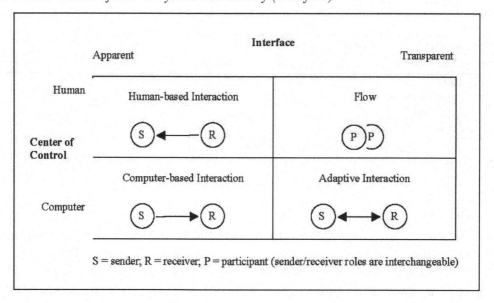

tools setup by programmers, such as spreadsheets and databases. Adaptive communication occurs when the system changes to accommodate users' skills or other characteristics, such as the case with educational systems and computer games (Jennings, 2002). Flow experience emerges when the users are actively interacting with the system, and its interface is virtually transparent since users are concentrating on the task at hand. This state of flow comes about during interactive computer games, online interactions, and virtual reality episodes (Jennings, 2002; Novak et al., 2003).

Webster et al. (1993) show that flow has both affective and cognitive components since users experience control, attention focus, curiosity, and intrinsic interest while interacting with computers. They call the later two *cognitive enjoyment*. In terms of affective shopping experiences, flow includes challenges, control, and feelings of enjoyment (Chen et al., 1999). These feelings of enjoyment and concentration (characteristics of a flow experience) in shopping leads to an increased likelihood of return visits to a web site and changes in behavior, such as purchase intentions (Koufaris, 2002).

Cognitive Load, Limited Capacity and Information Processing Theories

Cognitive load theory (Sweller, 1988) defines cognitive load as the amount of working memory needed to solve a problem. Working memory is short-term memory that stores current information being processed, comparable in function to random access memory (RAM) in computers. According to the theory, whenever individuals learn something new, they build schemata (singular schema), or combinations of elements that combine several elements into a holistic experience. This becomes essentially a knowledge-base from which to draw information. For example, experts are better than novices in solving problems because they have a schema bank over a lifetime of learning that allows them to recognize familiar patterns in problems and solve them quickly. This process of learning can be disrupted if working memory is overloaded failing to digest the new information for proper schema acquisition.

Likewise, limited capacity information processing theory (Lang, 1995, 2000) proposes that proper processing of information is necessary for encoding, storing, and ultimately retrieving this information. However, processing is disrupted either when the recipient allocates fewer resources to the message than necessary, or the message demands more resources than the recipient has to designate to the task.

Both theories draw from a seminal and foundational theory in cognitive psychology, information processing theory (Miller, 1956), which handles *chunking* and short-term memory capacity. According to the theory, short-term memory can handle only seven (or five to nine) pieces of information or chunks at one time. A chunk is a meaningful unit or single element of information.

FUTURE TRENDS

A major area of future research would involve an integrated approach, drawing upon and combining complementary constructs from various relevant theories, in an attempt at unification. The attitude-intention-behavior relationship is a fundamental one that could be a source for this research. Hundreds of studies have utilized TAM, and a relatively newly developed aggregate theory, the Unified Theory of Acceptance and Use of Technology (UTAUT) (Venkatesh et al., 2003) has recently surfaced to incorporate TRA and TAM, as well as six other prominent theories. This aggregation of theories is useful in examining interdisciplinary phenomenon. Combining TAM and flow theory, Koufaris (2003) draws from multiple theories to explain online consumer behavior and conclude that shopping enjoyment and perceived usefulness of a site affect intention to revisit a web site. Skadberg and Kimmel (2004) determine that the indirect effect of flow on attitudinal and behavioral changes is mediated by increased learning about content of a site. These changes include positive attitudes towards the site, site revisits, and a higher propensity to gather more information about the site. Heijden et al. (2003) combine both TRA and TAM to investigate online purchase intentions and conclude that perceived risk and perceived ease of use directly affect attitude towards purchase. Moreover, empirical relationships can also be examined in light of the reverse relationships to TAM discussed above, as in the behavior-attitude vs. attitude-behavior links, based on cognitive dissonance, social judgment theory, theory of passive learning, and self-perception theory.

Furthermore, a significant avenue for future research is to investigate the relationships between attitude and intended or actual behavior, in terms of collaborative experiences in a very narrow context, such as virtual social interactions and immersive online gaming experiences, and how they affect player flow experiences and cognitive skills. Besides the use of flow theory, the cognitive analysis could be explained using the aforementioned theories: cognitive load theory, limited capacity information processing theory, and information processing theory. Combining another possible future research stream (with relational experience), a new study can examine how social norms, such as between peer groups in chat rooms or instant messaging sessions, impact user behavior (e.g. purchase of products online). Such a study can be even more parsimonious in its focus and instead utilize TAM to investigate the same relationships but in the context of information technology in the workplace.

CONCLUSION

This research proposes several alternative theories from the literature to TAM. Instead of the traditional attitude-behavior relationship in TAM, four theories are included to show how the reverse of the relationship, behavior-attitude, are possible: theory of cognitive dissonance, social judgment theory, theory of passive learning, and self-perception theory. Other alternative theories are flow theory, cognitive load theory, capacity information processing theory, and information processing theory. These theories are applicable in many areas in IS: ecommerce, online consumer behavior, online shopping, immersive gaming, virtual social interactions, and cognitive research. Examples of implementations of the theories are also shown.

REFERENCES

Agrawal, R., & Karahanna, E. (2000). Time flies when you're having fun: Cognitive absorption and beliefs about information technology usage. *MIS Quarterly, 24*(4), 665-694.

Ajzen, I. (1991). The theory of planned behavior. *Organizational Behavior and Human Decision Processes, 50*(2), 179-211.

Assael, H. (1998). *Consumer behavior and marketing action.* Cincinnati, OH: South Western College Publishing.

Bagozzi, R. P. (2007). The legacy of the technology acceptance model and a proposal for a paradigm shift. *Journal of the Association for Information Systems, 8*(4), 244-254.

Bem, D. J. (1972). Self-perception theory. In L. Berkowitz (Ed.), *Advances in experimental social psychology* (vol. 6) (pp. 1-62). New York: Academic Press.

Bem, D. J. (1967). Self-perception: An alternative interpretation of cognitive dissonance phenomena. *Psychological Review, 74*(3), 183-200.

Benbasat, I., & Barki, H. (2007). Quo vadis, TAM? *Journal of the Association for Information Systems, 8*(4), 211-218.

Bettman, J. R. (1986). Consumer psychology. *Annual Review of Psychology, 37*, 257-289.

Chen, H., Wigand, R. T., & Nilan, M. S. (1999). Optimal experience of web activities. *Computers in Human Behavior, 15*(5), 585-608.

Csikszentmihalyi, M. (2000). *Beyond boredom and anxiety: Experiencing flow in work and play.* San Francisco: Jossey-Bass Publishers.

Csikszentmihalyi, M. (1975). *Beyond boredom and anxiety: Experiencing flow in work and play.* San Francisco: Jossey-Bass Publishers.

Csikszentmihalyi, M. (1997). *Finding flow: The psychology of engagement with everyday life.* New York: Basic Books.

Csikszentmihalyi, M. (1990). *Flow: The psychology of optimal experience.* New York: Harper and Row, Publishers, Inc.

Csikszentmihalyi, M., & Rathunde, K. (1993). The measurement of flow in everyday life: Toward a theory of emergent motivation. In J. E. Jacobs (Ed.), *Nebraska symposium on motivation 1992* (pp. 57-97). Lincoln, NE: University of Nebraska Press.

Davis, F. D. (1989). Perceived usefulness, perceived ease of use, and user acceptance of information technology. *MIS Quarterly, 13*(3), 319-340.

Davis, F. D., Bagozzi, R. P., & Warshaw, P. R. (1989). User acceptance of computer technology: A comparison of two theoretical models. *Management Science, 5*(8), 982-1003.

Festinger, L. (1957). *A theory of cognitive dissonance*. Stanford, CA: Stanford University Press.

Fishbein, M. (1967). Attitude and the prediction of behavior. In M. Fishbein (Ed.), *Readings in attitude theory and measurement* (pp. 477-492). New York: John Wiley.

Fishbein, M., & Ajzen, I. (1975). *Belief, attitude, intention, and behavior: An introduction to theory and research*. Reading, MA: Addison-Wesley Publishing Company.

Guo, Y., & Poole, M. S. (in press). Antecedents of flow in online shopping: A test of alternative models. *Information Systems Journal*.

Heijden, H., Verhagen, T., & Creemers, M. (2003). Understanding online purchase intentions: Contributions from technology and trust perspectives. *European Journal of Information Systems, 12*(1), 41-48.

Hirschheim, R. (2007). Introduction to the special issue on quo vadis TAM – issues and reflections on technology acceptance research. *Journal of the Association for Information Systems, 8*(4), 203-205.

Hoffman, D. L., & Novak, T. P. (1996). Marketing in hypermedia computer-mediated environments: Conceptual foundations. *Journal of Marketing, 60*(3), 50-68.

Jennings, A. S. (2002). Creating an interactive science murder mystery game: The optimal experi-

ence of flow. *IEEE Transactions on Professional Communication, 45*(4), 297-301.

Kamis, A., Koufaris, M., & Stern, T. (2008). Using an attribute-based decision support system for user-customized products online: An experimental investigation. *MIS Quarterly, 32*(1), 159-177.

Koufaris, M. (2002). Applying the technology acceptance model and flow theory to online consumer behavior. *Information Systems Research, 13*(2), 205-223.

Krugman, H. E. (1965). The impact of television advertising: Learning without involvement. *Public Opinion Quarterly, 29*(3), 349-356.

Lang, A. (1995). Defining audio/video redundancy from a limited-capacity information processing perspective. *Communication Research, 22*(1), 86-115.

Lang, A. (2000). The limited capacity model of mediated message processing. *Journal of Communication, 50*(1), 46-70.

Lowry, P. B., Karuga, G. G., & Richardson, V. J. (2007). Assessing leading institutions, faculty, and articles in premier information systems research journals. *Communications of the Association for Information Systems, 20*(16), 142-203.

Mathieson, K. (1991). Predicting user intentions: Comparing the technology acceptance model with the theory of planned behavior. *Information Systems Research, 2*(3), 173-191.

McMillan, S. J. (2002). Exploring models of interactivity from multiple research traditions: Users, documents, and systems. In L. Lievrouw & S. Livingstone (Eds.), *The handbook of new media* (pp. 163-182). Thousand Oaks, CA: Sage Publications.

Miller, G. A. (1956). The magical number seven, plus or minus two: Some limits on our capacity for processing information. *Psychological Review, 63*(2), 81-97.

Nah, F., & Benbasat, I. (2004). Knowledge-based support in a group decision making context: An Expert-novice comparison. *Journal of the Association for Information Systems, 5*(3), 125-150.

Novak, T. P., Hoffman, D. L., & Duhachek, A. (2003). The influence of global-directed and experiential activities on online flow experiences. *Journal of Consumer Psychology, 13*(1/2), 3-16.

Novak, T. P., Hoffman, D. L., & Yung, Y. (2000). Measuring the customer experience in online environments: A structural modeling approach. *Marketing Science, 19*(1), 22-42.

Reagan-Cirincione, P. (1994). Improving the accuracy of group judgment: A process intervention combining group facilitation, social judgment analysis, and information technology. *Organizational Behavior & Human Decision Processes, 58*(2), 246-270.

Schmitt, B. H. (2003). *Customer experience management: A revolutionary approach to connecting with your customers.* Hoboken, NJ: John Wiley and Sons.

Schmitt, B. H. (1999). *Experiential marketing: How to get customers to sense, feel, think, act, and relate to your company and brands.* New York: The Free Press.

Sherif, C., Sherif, M., & Nebergall, R. (1965). *Attitude and attitude change: The social judgment-involvement approach.* Philadelphia: Saunders.

Skadberg, Y. X., & Kimmel, J. R. (2004). Visitors' flow experience while browsing a web site: Its measurement, contributing factors, and consequences. *Computers in Human Behavior, 20*(3), 403-422.

Swartout, W., & Van Lent, M. (2003). Making a game of system design. *Communications of the ACM, 46*(7), 32-39.

Sweller, J. (1988). Cognitive load during problem solving: Effects on learning. *Cognitive Science, 12*(2), 257-285.

Szajna, B., & Scamell. R. W. (1993). Information system user expectations on their performance and perceptions. *MIS Quarterly, 17*(4), 493-516.

Trevino, L. K., & Webster, J. (1992). Flow in computer-mediated communication, *Communication Research, 19*(5), 539-573.

Venkatesh, V., Morris, M. G., Davis, G. B., & Davis, F. D. (2003). User acceptance of information technology: Toward a unified view. *MIS Quarterly, 27*(3), 425-478.

Webster, J., & Martocchio, J. J. (1992). Microcomputer playfulness: Development of a measure with workplace implications. *MIS Quarterly, 16*(2), 201-226.

Webster, J., Trevino, L. K., & Ryan, L. (1993). The dimensionality and correlates of flow in human-computer interactions. *Computers in Human Behavior, 9*(4), 411-426.

KEY TERMS AND DEFINITIONS

Capacity Information Processing Theory: Proposes that proper processing of information is necessary for encoding, storing, and ultimately retrieving this information. However, processing is disrupted either when the recipient allocates fewer resources to the message than necessary, or the message demands more resources than the recipient has to designate to the task.

Cognitive Load Theory: Defines cognitive load as the amount of working memory needed to solve a problem. Working memory is short-term memory that stores current information being processed. Whenever individuals learn something new, they build schemata, or combinations of elements that combine several elements into a holistic experience. This process of learning can be disrupted if working memory is overloaded failing to digest the new information for proper schema acquisition.

Flow Theory: Views flow as a state in which individuals are so engaged in an activity that they might be oblivious to the world around them and possibly lose track of time and even of self. Individuals feel they are in control of their actions and in a sense of enjoyment and exhilaration, when the levels of task challenges and their own skills are both equally high. It is equated to *entering the zone* (for athletes) or *being lost in the experience* (for computer video gamers).

Information Processing Theory: Is a seminal and foundational theory in cognitive psychology. According to the theory, short-term memory can handle only seven (or five to nine) pieces of information or chunks at one time. A *chunk* is a meaningful unit or single element of information.

Self-Perception Theory: Indicates that individuals have knowledge of their emotions and internal states and reach a certain attitude based on their own overt behavior and the situations in which these behaviors take place just as an outside observer or another person would. In essence, individuals develop their own attitude by observing themselves act in various circumstances.

Social Judgment Theory: Proposes that a recipient's judgment on a persuasive message depends on one's position on the topic. There are three categories of positions: latitude of acceptance, latitude of rejection, and latitude of noncommitment. An assimilation effect occurs when recipients of a message exaggerate the degree of agreement between their beliefs and the message. However, a contrast effect occurs when the recipients of a message overstate the difference between their beliefs and the message. Small to moderate discrepancies between the recipient's beliefs and the message's position will cause changes in attitude, but large discrepancies will not.

Technology Acceptance Model (TAM): Is one of the most widely used theories in IS literature. Two beliefs (perceived usefulness and perceived ease of use) predict attitudes, which in turn influence intended use of a technology. This intention then consequently impacts behavior of actual system usage. Perceived usefulness is the degree to which a user thinks a technology would enhance performance or productivity in the workplace. Perceived ease of use is the degree of lack of effort required by the user in adopting a given technology. Perceived ease of use also affects perceived usefulness.

Theory of Cognitive Dissonance: Suggests a conflict occurs when an individual's attitudes and behaviors are not congruent. The individual tries to reduce this conflict by changing one's opinion to conform to the outcome of one's behavior.

Theory of Passive Learning: Implies that a medium, such as television, is a low-involvement, passive medium of learning and advertising since individuals do not actively participate in the communication process.

Chapter XIV
Diffusion of Innovations Theory:
Inconsistency Between Theory and Practice

Francisco Chia Cua
University of Otago, New Zealand

Tony C. Garrett
Korea University, Republic of Korea

ABSTRACT

The literature review on case study design does not explain how the complex relationships (the issues) in a case study are identified. A top down approach, borrowing from argumentation theory, is a distinct contribution of this chapter which introduces the diffusion of innovations (DOI) as a research problem theory applied to the examination of a business case involving the replacement of enterprise systems by a large risk-averse public sector university in Australasia. The business case document is intended to diffuse the innovation to upper management for funding. But, there is a lack of diffusion study about the business case stage (the process) and the business case document (the outcome) as the construct that affects the innovation and its diffusion. A crucial component of the said diffusion research is designing the case study and mitigating the risks of theory-practice inconsistencies. Critical to mitigating that threat are the complex relationships (issues) that should be thoroughly identified. The context of the research provides experiential practical knowledge and analytical lenses to understand the essential components of a case study and the controversies affecting the rigour in the research design. This makes the top down approach of identifying the issues a good methodological base of designing a single-case study in a particular context. It can be useful to post-graduate and PhD students.

INTRODUCTION

FoxMeyer in United States and Fonterra in New Zealand experienced the unexpected undesirable consequences with regards to replacing enterprise systems. FoxMeyer did not succeed in its Project Delta III which bundled with the SAP R/3 and the Pinnacle warehouse-automation. In Chapter 11 (of the Bankruptcy Code), its gatekeepers claimed that their implementation of the enterprise systems drove them to bankruptcy (Caldwell, 6 July 1998; O'Leary, 2000; Stein, 31 Aug 1998; SAP and Deloitte Sued by FoxMeyer, 27 Aug 1998). They sued SAP and Andersen Consulting for a total of US$1 billion dollars. The dairy giant Fonterra put on hold its global SAP ERP project called Project Jedi (Foreman, 2007). Project Jedi is supposed to standardise its disparate manufacturing systems in line with its new business model of "One Team, One Way of Working" (Jackson, 2006; Ministry of Economic Development, Feb 2004). Fonterra justified the suspension of the project: first to reduce further capital spending and second to provide its farmer-shareholders a slightly higher dividends (Jackson, 2006). It did not escalate Project Jedi despite of the huge sunk costs of about NZ$ 260 million from 2004 to 2006.

These consequences highlight a concern in the business case. In large organisations, upper management generally makes accept-reject decision on the basis of a business case. Corporate governance requires a business case for capital expenditure. The innovation could be strategic to a vision or reactive to a crisis. Their executive sponsor explores all options that best fit his strategic or reactive intention and subsequently develops a business case for approval and funding by the upper management. The business case "sells" the innovation. It attempts to diffuse an innovation to the upper management to make favourable accept-reject decision (aka, adoption decision or strategic investment decision). Good business cases sell while the spectacular ones make the upper management over-commit.

An interesting phenomenon. *A successful diffusion, that is a good business case, is not necessarily good.*

How should the application of the Diffusion of Innovations (DOI) theory be practiced in the context of the business case of replacing enterprise systems? This problem statement has an implication on practice.

Primary problem. *What is the most likely application of the Diffusion of Innovations (DOI) theory when practiced in the context of the business case of replacing enterprise systems?*

Practitioners gave simpler answers. They asked for practical solutions. On the other hand, academics began with certain premises. Replacing enterprise systems is likely about balancing long-term and short-term achievements, ultimately sustaining growth in the end (Burrell & Morgan, 2005; Dettmer, 2003; Hammer, 1996; Trompenaars & Prud'homme, 2004). It is likely a problem-solving intervention (Thull, 2005) that fosters seamless alignment and comes with a VALUE orientation. The assumptions go on but the practitioners may see them as uninteresting. The practitioners are likely to find a simple framework of a business case that they can use. Here exists the concept of dualism, polarity, or differentiation of practice and theory. Embedded in this concept is a threat of theory-practice inconsistency. Also embedded is a teleology of a theory.

According to Clegg, Kornberger, and Rhodes (March 2004), a theory should facilitate the creation of disturbance to the practice so that the organisation will be able to transform itself. This means that a theory should not be simply a tool to understand a practice. It should help the practice create noises and disturbances so that the organisation can transform. A theory should not only be a thinking hat to understand a worm. Rather, it should somehow help that worm to transform itself into a beautiful butterfly. The elements of theory and practice in the primary problem includes this idealism of the butterfly effect.

Primary claim. *The most likely application of the DOI theory is the integration of the business case development as part of the innovation process and the business case document as a form of diffusion of the innovation concerned.*

Purpose

This chapter describes, illustrates, and gives an account of a design process of a single-case study. The research examines a complex phenomenon that is about replacing enterprise systems by University of Australasia (name disguised). A detailed articulation of the research design is a form of discipline (Yin, 1994). It attempts to infuse quality into the research and at the same time mitigates any threats of theory-practice inconsistencies.

Literature review on case study does not show how problem statement, its secondary problems, and their issues are developed. Probably it assumes that the people who will do the case study already know the "how to" knowledge. Even if they do, a different group of researchers attempting to answer the same problem statement and assuming the same primary claim may define the secondary research problem differently and likewise identify the issues and their respective claims differently. The top down approach discussed in this chapter, from the primary problem to the issues, is a distinct contribution.

Furthermore, a good theoretical base and a sound approach to designing a case study can be useful to post-graduate and PhD students who are interested in undertaking case study, especially in the fields of diffusion and innovation. The clarification of the terminologies and concepts can enlighten the novice to the case study.

The chapter utilises Figure 1 as a worldview (Kuhn, 1970) to scrutinise the research design and the research procedure and to mitigate the threats of theory-practice inconsistencies. The diagram[1] helps in fostering awareness of what is out there (the metaphysics) that serves as the basis of knowledge (epistemology) and helps to determine what is right (ethics) and what is the right thing to do (praxis).

Figure 1. Threats (1 to 6) of theory-practice inconsistencies and critical choices ([A] to [E])

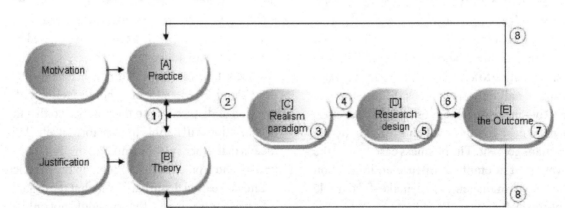

Diagram is adopted, reinterpreted, and modified from Cua & Garrett (2008) and clarified in Endnote 1

Outline and Delimitation

The background section begins by describing the Diffusion of innovations (DOI) theory and clarifying briefly the terms case study, the case, issue, and phenomenon. These terms could be confusing to some. The third section illustrates a top down approach to articulate what is the case. This is followed by the fourth section that answered the epistemological question of what can be learned thoroughly from the One case. The fifth section briefly discussed the research design that can optimise understanding that One case. This chapter attempts to answer only these three questions (see Table 1 below). A section about the future research follows. It ends with a conclusion that summarises the discussions.

A theoretical paradigm[2] comes even **prior** to the ontological and epistemological questions. Without that paradigm in the background, it is not possible to have awareness of what the complex phenomenon is (first question above) and what can be learned thoroughly from that case (third question). This research uses the realism paradigm that allows the researcher to use both objective and subjective evidences. That paradigm is a complex topic excluded in the discussion here.

BACKGROUND

Describing and clarifying the Diffusion of Innovations (DOI) theory and terms such as case study, the case, issues, and phenomenon follow.

The Diffusion of Innovations (DOI) Theory

The mindmap in Figure 2 shows four branches representing the four important constructs of the DOI theory for this research.

Everett M Rogers (1962), in his book entitled *Diffusion of Innovations*, has provided the much needed conceptual framework to evaluate the impact of innovation. In the 1950s, the Iowa State University had a great intellectual tradition in agriculture and rural sociology. George Beal (Rogers' doctoral advisor) and other rural sociologies in Iowa State University were conducting pioneering studies on the diffusion of innovations like the high-yielding hybrid seed corn, chemical fertilizers, and weed sprays. Their questions included why some farmers adopted these innovations while others did not. Naturally, the context of Rogers' theory concerned agricultural products.

Table 1. Ontological, epistemological, and methodological questions

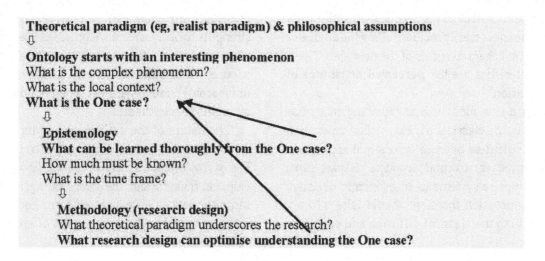

Theoretical paradigm (eg, realist paradigm) & philosophical assumptions
⇩
Ontology starts with an interesting phenomenon
What is the complex phenomenon?
What is the local context?
What is the One case?
⇩
   Epistemology
   What can be learned thoroughly from the One case?
   How much must be known?
   What is the time frame?
   ⇩
      Methodology (research design)
      What theoretical paradigm underscores the research?
      What research design can optimise understanding the One case?

Figure 2. The big picture of diffusion of innovations (DOI) theory

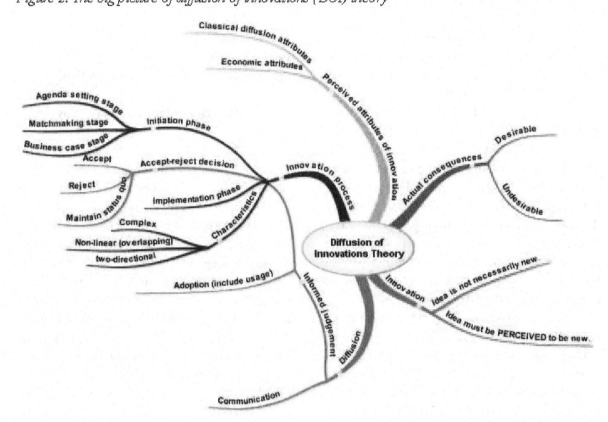

Diffusion is a communication process which goes through through certain channels over a certain period of time among the members of a social system (Rogers, 1962, 2003). The difference between diffusion and communication is the **new idea**—the **innovation**—which diffusion attempts to sell in its communication. Selling the new idea necessarily include selling the unique or important characteristics of the new idea. These characteristics are the **perceived attributes of innovation**[3].

For a new idea, such as replacing enterprise systems, the classical attributes of an innovation is not sufficient because its original application concerned agricultural products. Replacement of enterprise systems is an economic decision. This innovation therefore should take into account both the classical diffusion and economic

(value) attributes of that innovation (Cua & Garrett, in press).

A keyword of perceived attributes of innovation is **perception**. Before perception, there is a need for awareness. After perception comes a personal bias. What matters most in perception is belief. Attributes can be real or imaginary strengths (positives) and weaknesses (negatives) of an innovation. Simply put, the perceived attributes of an innovation result in favorable or unfavorable biases regardless of real or imaginary strengths or weaknesses.

The nature of the innovation and its context account the differences of the diffusion process. For example, the farmers in the 1950s were the decision-makers and the users of agricultural innovations such as hybrid seed corns and chemical fertilisers. For the replacement of enterprise

systems, the executive sponsor and upper manage
ment make the decision while there are the rank
and file personnel using the enterprise systems.
Therefore for the innovation of replacing enterprise systems, there are two sets of stakeholders
and one final **accept-reject decision** to make.
One set (Set 1) concerns the gatekeepers (Rogers,
1962, 2003; Rogers & Shoemaker, 1971). The other
set (Set 2) of stakeholders are the users. There is
also a Set 3, consisting of attributes such as Total
Cost of Owenrship. These three sets are about the
perceived attributes of innovation which lead to
expected consequences (refer to Cua & Garrett, in
press for detail discussion of "justified perceived
attributes of the innovation").

A big branch in Figure 2 shows the actual consequences which may be desirable or undesirable
consequences. Attempting to understand the diffusion process via the "informed judgement" (see
Figure 2) makes DOI theory popular. Attempting
to mitigate the risk of undesirable consequences
(the war stories such as FoxMeyer and Fonterra
above described the branch in Figure 2 about actual consequences to undesirable consequences)
likewise make DOI theory popular.

Innovation process roughly follows certain
steps, namely: being aware of a new idea, forming an attitude toward it, making accept-reject
decision, implementing the innovation, and lastly,
evaluating the decision. These are the five generic
steps of an innovation-decision process model of
Rogers (1962, 2003). The whole process could
be divided into two phases. The initiation phase
(Phase 1) drives the implementation phase (Phase
2). Other authorities break down the innovation
process differently. The innovation process is
akin to escaping from an island prison (Ross &
Vitale, 2000)[4]. Van de Ven *et al.*, (1999, pp 23-25)
uses the metaphor of an innovation journey of
twelve stages in three phases[5]. In general, these
are variants that are more or less similar to the
two process models of Rogers (Cooper & Zmud,
1990; Daft, 1978; Ettlie, 1980; Meyer & Goes,
1988; Ross & Vitale, 2000; Tornatsky & Fleish-

eher, 1990; Van de Ven *et al.*, 1999; Zaltman *et
al.*, 1973). Thus, the composition of the initiation
phase in the mindmap (Figure 2) is a real world
variant applicable to risk-averse large organisation
replacing the enterprise systems.

The Case Study

The terms "case" and "study" defy full specification, according to Stephen Kemmis (1980). He
associates imagination to the case (that is, imagina-
tion⇒ the case) and invention to the study (that is,
invention ⇒ the study). Two concepts are associated to this term. The first, the case, connotes an
abstract object (hereinafter referred to as the **One
case**) that is difficult to understand and that will be
explained in more depth. It is imagined, identified,
and articulated. The second concept concerns the
study, which is the research process that is designed
(invented) to understand the One case. Briefly, the
term case study refers to two components.

Case study (1) = *An abstract **One case** (2) that is
imagined, identified, and articulated + the **study**
(3), the research process, that is invented (designed)
to understand the above abstract One case.*

Authorities agree that a case study, as a research
invention, is effective in (a) exploring a complex
phenomenon and (b) learning the right questions to
ask (Datta, Nov 1990; Hoaglin et al., 1982) confirm
case study to be a good research design for learning the right questions to ask. Datta (Nov 1990)
clarifies. "The product [, the case study report,]
is a sharpened understanding of what might be
[or perceived to be] important *to look at further
in similar situations* and what explains why the
instance happened as it did. Because such inquiry
explores only one situation, it is argued that …
it can contribute *powerfully* to the *invention* of
hypotheses [or the complex issues]." In effect, a
case study is especially effective for exploring a
cave, using Plato's analogy of a cave[6].

Other authorities consider a case study a catch-all name for a method or a methodology (Bassey, 1999; Datta, Nov 1990; Merriam, 1988; Orum *et al.*, 1991; Van Wynsberghe & Khan, 2007; Yin, 1994). In fact, The United States General Accounting Office (GAO) defines a case study as "*a method[ology]* for learning about *a complex instance*, based on *a comprehensive understanding* of that instance obtained by *extensive description and analysis* of that instance taken as a whole and in its context Datta, Nov 1990, p 15)." Robert Stake (2005) defines a case study as "a choice of what is to be studied" and "not a methodological choice." The last phase has an unexpected consequence. Some authorities mistakenly construe that a case study is not a methodology (Van Wynsberghe and Khan, 2007). In reality, case study is a methodology. It is just not a methodological choice. Case study is not only a methodology, it is likewise an outcome of that study (Stake, 2005).

A case study embodies four concepts: the case (the One case), the case study research (the research process), the case study research design (research methodology), and the outcome of a case study research (the case study report).

The One Case

Of those four concepts that refer to the term case study, the most difficult term to understand is the first one. Stake (2005) alternatively refers to "the case" as an individual case (p 443), a single case (p 443), the singular case (p 444), the specific One (p 444), the specific case (p 448), the study (p 449), and the particular case (p 454). Certainly, the single case (without the hyphen) is not necessarily the single-case (with hyphen). It is hereinafter referred to as the **One case** to avoid confusing it with the **single-case**. Emphasis is essential at this point. The One case is abstract. It is a product of imagination, identification, and articulation during the research design. The challenge is not about the

concept of the One case but about articulation of this case.

Issues

Stake (2005, p 446) mentions several types of issues concerning the plan for a case study about Ukraine. Issues are "complex, situated, problematic relationships" (Stake, 2005, p 448). They are the organising themes that deepen the understanding of the One case. Stake clarifies. The key issues bring out the concerns and opportunities for research (Stake, 2005, pp 448-449). A dominant theme is among these key issues. There is likely an issue or two under development. Topical issue pertains to the local setting. Briefly, case study involves a topical dominant issue, other key issues, and an issue or two under development. These issues are not the research questions. However, the research questions are organised around certain issues. Similar to the challenge encountered in articulating the One case, the challenge is **identifying the issues** in order to understand the One case

Issues are complex, contextual, and problematic relationships and themes in a case study that provide the basis for developing the research questions that further bring out the opportunities of the case study. Ultimately, these issues enhance thorough understanding of the One case.

The Complex Phenomenon

A complex phenomenon is a **first choice** in a research. A phenomenon is a state of something at a space-time or an event that changes the state of an object, Ron Weber (2003) clarifies. The state of that object includes its properties and their value in relation to space-time. Presumably, an event triggers the object to evolve at a particular (initial) space-time. The value of its properties changes as a consequence. The initial state, the change event, and actual or the expected subsequent state are the properties of that thing. These properties symbolise the complex phenomenon.

In the parlance of research domain, the complex phenomenon represents the *actual domain*. It has an outer domain which is the natural, the rich local context-sensitive, setting where the phenomenon happens. The contingent conditions of the outer domain makes the change event that happens to the actual domain unique. Beneath the actual domain is an inner layer. It is the the empirical domain where objective facts and subjective experiences can be obtained (Bhaskar, 1978; Outhwaite, 1983; Tsoukas, 1989).

Articulating complex phenomenon demands articulating the three domains (the real, actual, and empirical domains) and the set of assumed, observed, or tentative relationships of the properties of the complex phenomenon. These properties may be about the present state, the change event, and the future state. Constructs or variables are the other words used to signify properties. The statements of relationships are the laws under examination. For this case study, the complex phenomenon is the One case.

Choosing and articulating the complex phenomenon, according to Weber (2003), is the most critical tasks in research. Symbolised by [A] in Figure 1, the two tasks required thorough reflection and understanding of the implications of relevant meta-theoretical assumptions. But, articulating and reflecting the ontological and epistemological assumptions associated to a theoretical paradigm is not a simple task. There exist the relationships between [A], [B], and [C] in Figure 1.

*A **complex phenomenon** has three space-time components and three domains.*

The three space-time components are (a) an initial state (eg, antecedents), (b) a change event (eg, an innovation process), and a subsequent state (eg, actual consequences). The change event influences the change of some or all the properties of the initial state of the phenomenon. The natural or

managed evolution results to a subsequent state. In short, initial state (properties and their values) ⇒ change event ⇒ subsequent state (properties and their values).

The three domains are (a) the real domain, (b) the actual domain, and (c) the empirical domain. A complex phenomenon is itself the actual domain. Its outer domain is the real domain (rich natural setting or the local context-sensitive setting). The inner domain is the empirical domain that embodies objective and subjective evidences. In short, real domain ⇒ actual domain ⇒ empirical domain.

ONTOLOGY: WHAT IS THE ONE CASE?

A series of choices that confront case study (Stake, 2005) start with choosing the complex phenomenon (Weber, 2003).

The Complex Phenomenon

Previously stated, choosing the complex phenomenon, articulating the complex phenomenon, and [justifying the choice] are the most critical tasks in a research (Weber, 2003). A business case influences upper management to be cautious, positive, or overly positive. At one extreme of the continuum is upper management's inability to commit or under-commit. At the other extreme is an over-commitment. Both extremes in the continuum result to unexpected undesirable consequences. **A successful diffusion, that is a good business case, is not necessarily good.** This gives justification to the importance of understanding the complex phenomenon.

As stated above, a complex phenomenon has three space-time components and three domains. The research questions about a complex phenomenon in context form a matrix (Table 2) a matrix of these three components and three domains.

The **complex phenomenon** of this research concerns the replacement of enterprise systems. Replacing enterprise systems is likely a problem-solving intervention to foster seamless alignment (ontological assumption). Thus, its initial state likely contains a condition that triggers the need for the change event with an expected subsequent state in mind. In a risk-averse organisation, the person who is supposed to undertake the change event and the person who approves the change event belong to different organisational hierarchy. The executive sponsor to the innovation agenda is normally a senior manager from the middle management while the people who control the use of resources and who approve the replacement of the enterprise systems belong to the upper management. For the change event to take place, the executive sponsor normally submits a business case which is a document intended to sell his new idea for approval by the upper management. How that business case is written and presented influences the upper management

to be cautious, positive, or overly positive. At one extreme of the continuum is upper management's inability to commit or under-commit. At the other extreme is an over-commitment. Both extremes in the continuum result to unexpected undesirable consequences. Thus, a good business case is not necessarily good after all.

Table 2 and Figure 4 map the relationships of the four constructs: the innovation, the diffusion, the business case, and the perceived attributes of the innovation. At the initial state, the active constructs are the innovation (the new idea in mind), the interactions and the diffusion among the people within and without the social systems (the University of Australasia), the consequences expected by walking the innovation process, the consequences expected by not walking it, and the perceived attributes associated to the innovation. The mindset also includes the supposedly right way to walk the innovation. The process includes

Table 2. Articulating the complex phenomenon by analysing it in terms of the real domain (the local context), the actual domain (the complex phenomenon), and the empirical domain (the issues)

		Initial state	Change event	Subsequent state
Local context		What was the state of the University of Australasia that made the replacement of enterprise systems necessary?	How did the executive sponsor walk the initiation phase that ends with the submission of the business case to the upper management?	What did the executive sponsor expect when he acted on his agenda? What really happened?
Complex phenomenon		What were the dimensions of the innovation (construct 1)? What were the reasons cited to diffuse (that is, to justify; construct 2) the replacement of the enterprise systems? What were the perceived attributes (construct 4)?	How did the executive sponsor convey and sell his intention to replace the enterprise systems in the business case (construct 3)?	Was the executive sponsor successful in selling his innovation? Why? Why not?
Issues		Perceived attributes (issue 3), Decision points (issue 4)	Matchmaking stage (issue 1)	Business case (issue 2)

request for information (RFI), request of proposal (RFP), and a business case submission. The business case construct therefore has two components: a process component and an outcome component. After the business case submission, an accept-reject decision will occur. This critical change event will affect what the subsequent state will look like.

Justifying the complex phenomenon. Real world cases, such as those of FoxMeyer and Fonterra, have highlighted a need to understand the business case in the innovation process. Yet the Diffusion of Innovations (DOI) theory has overlooked the business case as a construct. Likewise, it has overlooked "visioning" (or a view of the future) as a crucial element in walking the innovation. Rogers (2003, p 422) mentions that organisations generally react to problems and thereafter perceives the need for innovation. His two process models clearly indicate that walking the innovation is reactive to a problem and not strategic to a vision. That reactive intention probably leads to an oversight of strategic intention.

The Local Context

The local context of this research concerns the replacement of enterprise systems by the University of Australasia (name disguised). In effect, this research is a single-case study that explores the complex phenomenon articulated in Table 2.

This exploratory single-case study starts with an intrinsic interest on a complex phenomenon. It has just one aim: to explore and understand thoroughly the business case development and the business case document in a context. The aim includes the intention to understand the empirical domain (the four issues in Table 2). It consists of theory and practice dimensions which can be likened to the two sides of a coin. The researcher attempts to identify the domain and put a structure to the business case research using the DOI lens and focusing on the four complex issues (discussed later).

The theory and practice dimensions are the two thinking hats. The academic hat wants to look at the relationships of the DOI constructs that are

Figure 3. The boundary of the complex phenomenon

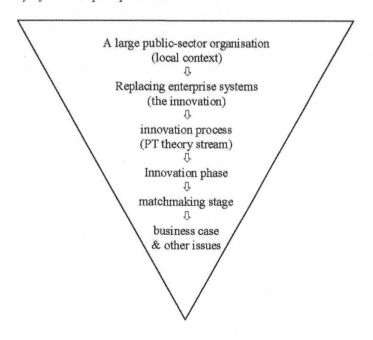

A large public-sector organisation
(local context)
⇩
Replacing enterprise systems
(the innovation)
⇩
innovation process
(PT theory stream)
⇩
Innovation phase
⇩
matchmaking stage
⇩
business case
& other issues

relevant to the business case and the domain of the business case stream of a diffusion research. A business case research should embrace a plurality view toward visualising, mapping, and realising expected consequences. Such a mindset fosters a better understanding of the current state and the perceived needs, the innovation as a solution or a means to an end, the alternative options, the preferred choice of the executive sponsor, a view of the future state, the desirable expected consequences to achieve, the undesirable expected consequences to avoid, and the perceived positive attributes required. The practitioner hat, on the other hand, wants to know more about the business case, noting the caveat that a good business case is not necessarily good for the organisation. A structured approach to develop a business case will be a welcomed resource.

What justifies this context? As a Certified Public Accountant, an Associate Chartered Accountant, and an Oracle Implementation Team Member (Master Level), this researcher is fortunate to gain access to investigate on the replacement of enterprise systems. For the last twenty years, he has had the opportunities to implement many enterprise systems. The systems range from small SBT/ACCPAC accounting systems to big Oracle Financials. In an upgrade *cum* implementation of Oracle Financials, his executive sponsor had a nervous breakdown. The organisation had been forced to upgrade. The old version would not be supported in a near future even if it was meeting the needs. The upgrade was inevitable. The executive sponsor became ambitious. He decided to include several new modules to be implemented simulteneously with the upgrade. Obviously, the account executive was effective in diffusing the idea of a simultaneous upgrade and implementation. The project became huge. The budget skyrocketed. The stress became unbearable, causing a nervous breakdown.

This is a field of research that he is passionate about from both academic and practitioner perspectives. So, the research commenced with an opportunity which he subsequently "exploited". It is without doubt that the University of Australasia is typical of a large public sector risk-averse organisation. Its four campuses, its ranking in the performance-based research fund regime, and its offerings provide adequate contextual uniqueness. So the justification follow the following path:

The researcher availed an opportunity of ACCESS of a complex phenomenon in a large public sector risk-averse organisation.
⇩
This site is not easily accessible. It is critical and extremely unique (Yin, 1994).
⇩
The intrinsic interest (initially on the complex phenomenon and later the One case) justifies the case study (Stake, 2005).
⇩
The lack of research on the business case in a context compels the research to explore this field.
⇩
Exploratory single-case research
⇩
Opportunity exploited

The One Case

Imagine a local context as the outermost layer of a reality (the biggest rectangular box in Figure 4). Beneath it are two inner layers. The second layer is a complex phenomenon under study (the shaded rectangular box that the four constructs). Beneath that complex phenomenon is a third layer consisting of the four issues, their interactions, and the research questions (Table 2). The three layers are respectively the real domain, actual domain, and empirical domain (Bhaskar, 1978).

The four issues of case study research reflect complex relationships of their structural and functional elements. They represent the One case. Their relevance to the One case relies on how these issues have been identified. In turn, the relevance of the One case to the primary problem depends on how relevant the issues are to the one case. There is a chain of relevance and in that chain embeds the justification of the One case.

The process of thinking and developing the issues from the primary problems is not a simple one. It will be thoroughly explained. The rigour and the logic that put into the process serve to justify the relevance of the issues.

Because the research concerns the innovation process of replacing enterprise systems and because the stages in walking an innovation is a variant of the process model of Rogers (2003), another diagram will be useful in validating the relevance of the issues. Figure 5 is consistent to the second model of Rogers where between the initiation phase and the implementation phase is a dotted line which symbolises an accept-reject decision to be made by the upper management.

There is nothing new to the formal structured procurement stages from RFI (request for information) to RFP (request for proposal) to BC (business case). Many organisations, especially the large and risk-averse organisation, imposes this standard operating procedure as part of their governance. The identified four issues in Figure 4 fits perfectly into Figure 5 with the perceived attributes of the innovation (Issue 3 in Figure 5) embedded into the decision points that run across the whole process. This leads to the concept of value.

In a business sense, assessing a business case means justifying that the innovation (that is, replacing the enterprise systems) adds economic value in the medium term as well as in the long term (Copeland *et al.*, 2000; Morin & Jarrell, 2001; Rappaport, 1986; ten Have *et al*, 2003).

Figure 4. The four constructs in the DOI theory and a worldview

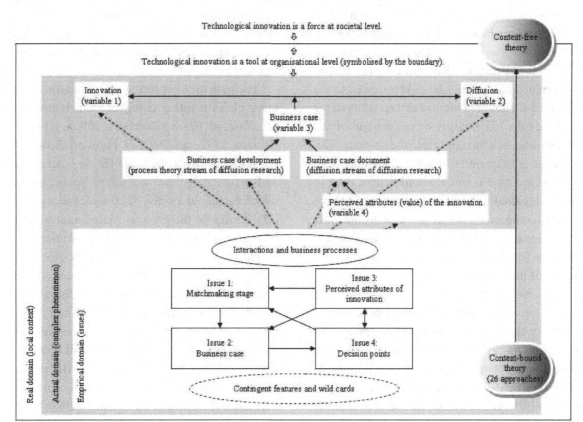

Figure 5. The stages in the initiation phase of replacing the enterprise systems by the University of Australasia

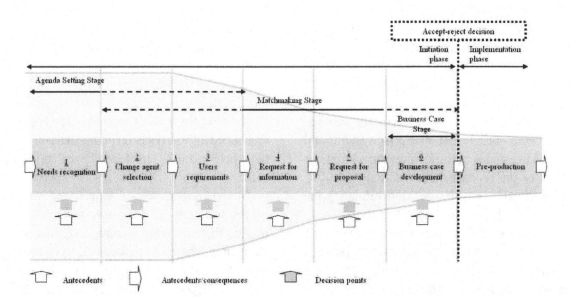

How does an executive sponsor sell that value to the upper management? This brings in the next two questions, which are: What constitutes value? How do enterprise systems help an organisation to create value? Probably, the value could be traced to the enterprise systems. It could be traced to the perceived attributes of the new enterprise systems to replace the old enterprise systems and of the vendors who will be supporting the systems. The challenge is to quantify benefits and value.

The One case is more complex than the big picture depicted in Figure 4 and Figure 5. There are more components to take into account than just the four issues and the boundary visualised in that diagram. Table 3 provides a more comprehensive picture of the One case.

The One case is difficult to conceive at the start. A top down approach starts by articulating a primary claim (❶ in Figure 6) that captures the essence of the primary problem (❷), which is the overriding problem. There should only be one primary claim (❶) to capture the essence of a primary problem (❷). An assertion (the thesis statement) represents that claim. It is a statement that should

be supported by evidences (eg, the experiential data or narrative truth) and argumentation. The result of the argument is epistemology, the processed knowledge, which contributes ultimately to knowledge.

The path to interpreting and evaluating a primary claim is rather complex (Van Eemeren *et al.*, 2002, pp 63-78; Zarefsky, 2005a, pp 86-95; Willard, 1992, pp 239-257). Figure 6 shows how the primary claim (❶) leads (❸) to determining and articulating the secondary problems (❹) which further identifies (❺) the secondary claim (❻). Similar to the primary claim, analysing the secondary claim helps to identify (❼) the issues (❽) which subsequently serve as a basis to further determine (❾) tertiary claims (❿). The secondary claims (❹) and those claims below them (❿), if validly argued, will support the primary claim (❶). It is when the primary claim becomes valid and accepted by the community will there be a contribution to a higher realm of knowledge. That primary claim is a statement that will capture the substance of the primary problem. It is the ultimate

Table 3. Essential components of the One case

1.	Context:	Local context and the complex phenomenon
2.✿	Foreshadowed problem:	The research gap of a theory
3.✿	Issues:	Dominant theme, key issues, and those issues under development
4.✿	Information questions:	Guides to thoroughly understand the issues
5.✿	Assertion (claims)	Evidences from experiential knowledge and argumentation
6.	Visual case study map:	Boundary, structural/functional elements, & their relationships
7.	Triangulation:	Chain of evidences
8.	Ethics:	Ethical considerations and ethical clearance

Figure 6. Relationships among research problems, claims, and issues

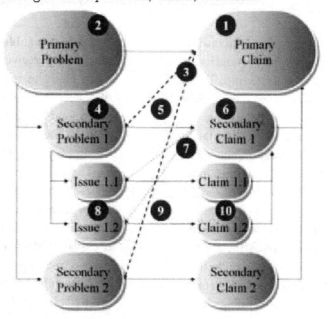

claim in which the judgment is sought.

That top down approach that culminates in Figure 6 satisfies the rule of confirmability (construct validity), which is to break the phenomenon down into components. Literature review on case study design does not show how the problem statement, its secondary problems, and their issues are to be developed. Probably it assumes that the people who will do the case study already know the "how to" knowledge. Even if they do, a different group of researchers attempting to answer the same problem statement and assuming the same primary claim may define the secondary research problem differently and likewise identify the issues and their respective claims differently. Nevertheless, the top down approach imposes a rigour to identifying the issues and their corresponding claims. The systematic way of thinking about the research problem (first level) and breaking down into the issues (third level) inevitably includes interpretive judgment of the researcher. The approach in Figure 6 is subjective, interpretive, somewhat unconventional, but certainly emergent. The four issues—the matchmaking stage, the business case, the perceived attributes of innovation, and decision points—integrate properly into a bigger picture.

EPISTEMOLOGY: WHAT CAN BE LEARNED THOROUGHLY FROM THE ONE CASE?

A thorough examination of the One case indicates the following problems, issues, and claims (also refer to Figure 6 and Appendix) can be learned.

- **Foreshadow problem**. The relationships between innovation (construct 1) and its diffusion (construct 2) are not clear in diffusion research. Furthermore, these relationships have not been investigated in the context of the business case (construct 3) of replacing enterprise systems by large public-sector organisation. Particularly important in the business case are the perceived benefits and value (aka, the perceived attributes of innovation; construct 4) of the alternative courses of action. Given the second, third, and fourth constructs, how do these constructs affect each other? For example, how does the business case influence the perceptions of positive or negative attributes of the alternatives to be explored? What factors (eg, the organizational size and its mindset to risk) affect the perceptions and the diffusion process?
- **Secondary problem 1**. What is the most likely explanation for the importance of the innovation process prior to the accept-reject decision using the Diffusion of Innovations theory?
- **Secondary claim 1 (of secondary problem 1)**. The most likely explanation for the importance of the innovation process prior to the accept-reject decision using the DOI

theory is its description as organisation's exploitation of an opportunity.

- **Issue 1.1 (derived from the secondary claim 1)**. Matchmaking stage
  - o **Claim 1.1 (of issue 1.1)**. The matchmaking stage is likely to embody opportunities for the organisation to establish the right relationships with the right vendor.
- **Issue 1.2 (derived from the secondary claim 1)**. Business case
  - o **Claim 1.2 (of issue 1.2)**. The business case is the most likely form of diffusion to facilitate the selling of an innovation.
- **Secondary problem 2**. Is the concept of classically perceived attributes of innovation more likely to matter to the replacement of enterprise systems? Are there newer theoretical attributes that falsify, replace, or make the classical attributes obsolete?
- **Secondary claim 2 (of secondary problem 2)**. The concept of classical perceived attributes of innovation of the DOI theory is more likely generic and "one-sized" in order to fit all innovations. This strength is inadequate to explain that part of the innovation process prior to making the accept-reject decision of replacing the enterprise systems. It is more likely that there are newer theoretical attributes that make the classical attributes of innovation obsolete.
- **Issue 2.1 (derived from the secondary claim 2)**. Perceived attributes (value) of the innovation
  - o **Claim 2.1 (of issue 2.1)**. Each perceived attribute of innovation likely represents a decision point in the initiation phase of an innovation process. The set of attributes likely varies depending on whether the innovation (that is, the replacement of enterprise systems) is strategic or reactive.
- **Issue 2.2 (derived from the secondary**

claim 2). Decision points

o **Claim 2.2 (of issue 2.2).** The relevance of a perceived attribute of innovation likely depends on where the decision point occurs in the timeline of the innovation process.

How Much Must be Known?

Despite delimiting the One case to the four issues, there is nevertheless a wide range of viewpoints concerning those issues.

Visioning the Outcome of the Case Study

Visioning is a critical part in designing the case. It helps to determine how much must be known from the case. As a preview (Figure 8) which is like that of a whole movie, the vision helps to anticipate and explore plausibly and coherently the ways in which the One case may evolve. Every issue is sufficiently complex. It is a system in itself. It is worth studying. It is a mini case in itself.

Identifying the Research Questions

Research questions that surround the issues have yet to be identified. The top-down approach, that starts with a problem statement and ends with the four issues and their respective claims, does not simply stop there. The research questions concern the individuals, the social systems, their structural and functional elements, and others. They help to understand the One case. Answers could be drawn all at once (Stake, 2005) from sources as Stouffer (1941) has suggested: PEST (political, economic, social, and technological) environments, competitive environment, physical settings, historical background, tasks and processes of the socio-technical system, informants, and other cases.

Integrating the four issues, as illustrated in Figure 4, Figure 5, and Figure 6, leads to the exploration and interpretation of their complex interactions, the context, the possibility of contingent features or wild cards that can change the phenomenon, and the research questions surrounding them. In all these diagrams, the interaction is a dominant logic, loosely adopted from that of C Prahalad & Richard Bettis (1986), that mentally locks the thinking about the new idea and diffusion (communication) into a specific contextual manner.

It should be noted that Diffusion of Innovations theory takes into account the antecedents (❶ in Figure 7) which includes the conditions, the expected consequences, and the perceived attributes (❹) of the innovation, the process which consists of the decision points in that process (❷), and the consequences (❸). This research examines the decision points in the matchmaking stage and the business case stage (Figure 5) as well as their implications. In effect the worldview of Figure 7 complements the worldviews of Figure 4, Figure 5, and Figure 8. These four diagrams are viewpoints of the same complex phenomenon and the One case being examined. The following research questions that have been derived from articulating the complex phenomenon in Table 2 become relevant.

1. **What constitutes VALUE to the organisation on the bases of the vision and objectives the organisation is trying to achieve?** What are the vision and the objectives of the organisation? Explain the innovation. What were the dimensions of this innovation? What is it? Why is it so? What were the key barriers? What were their implications, especially to the executive sponsor?

2. **How did the change event (the innovation process) and how will the new enterprise systems (the innovation) help to achieve that value?** What were the actual or perceived attributes, whether positive or negative, about the innovation that the

Figure 7. Another worldview of the business case stream of diffusion research

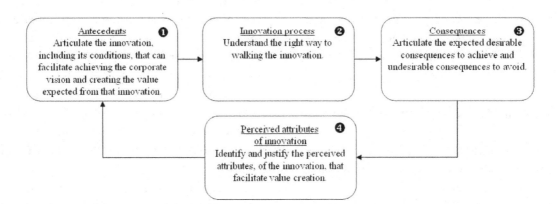

executive sponsor, change agent, and other team members had used to assess alternative options? What were the reasons cited to "sell" the innovation by the executive sponsor to the upper management? How well did the business case document do the selling? What are the relevant information technologies that will enable the organisation to bring in the value? How did the business case document influence the perceptions of positive or negative attributes of the innovation and its options? How successful was the executive sponsor in selling this agenda? Why? Why not? How should the organisation walk the innovation in order to be able to leverage the information technologies? What are the benefits expected? How do those benefits align with the vision, objectives, and value (eg, total value of ownership)?

3. **What or who triggered the change (the innovation)?** Who were the key participants and stakeholders during the initiation phase?

4. How did the initiation phase happen? Why did it happen that way? **Did the process (including the business case submitted) make sense? Why? Why not?** What factors (eg, the size of organisation or the mindset to risk) affect the perceptions and the process?

If each considered attribute of innovation would be regarded as a decision point, what were the decision points along the initiation phase? How relevant was each decision point at that point in time? Was there a time element factor?

5. **Did the timeline matter? Why? Why not?**

METHODOLOGY: WHAT DESIGN CAN OPTIMISE UNDERSTANDING THE ONE CASE?

Case Study as a Research Design

Realism paradigm by default justifies the use of case study. The One case further justifies the use of case study. In fact, the One case is the one and only justification of case study (Stake, 2005).

Certain key characteristics (Table 4) justify the use of case study methodology (Benbasat *et al.*, 2002; Feagin *et al.*, 1991; Flyvbjerg, 2001, 2006; Simon, 1980; Stake, 1995, 2005; Yin, 1993, 1994). A case study attempts to essentially answer the why and how questions about a contemporary phenomenon that is complex. The *essence* does not compel a similar *form*. The primary problem of this research illustrates the point[7].

Figure 8. A preview of the case study

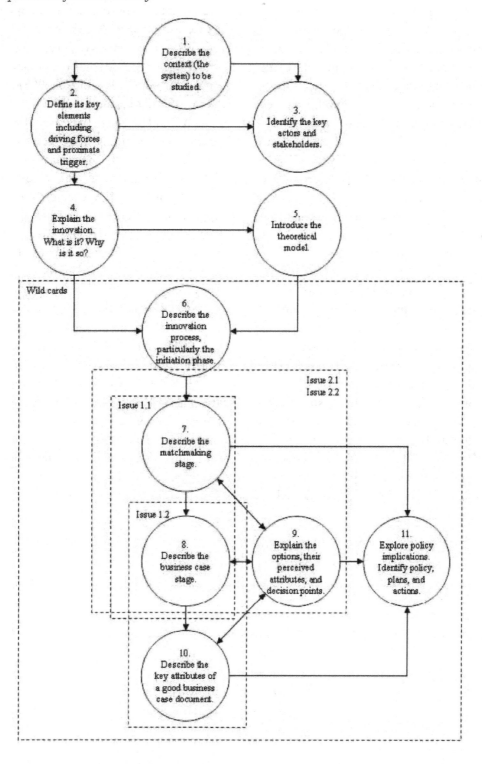

The natural setting provides the rich context for the researcher to examine the unit of analysis intensively. The researcher does not, cannot, and should not undertake experimental controls or other manipulations. The complexity of the phenomenon makes articulation difficult at the start. However the passion and a hundred percent attention committing to the case overcome this difficulty. A third pre-requisite is inherent to the researcher. The outcome of a case study relies heavily on his integrative power because the strength of the case study comes from the triangulation of methods used to gather, to analyse the data, and to theorise. These three conditions justify the use of the case study as a research design.

An interest in the One case can be intrinsic or it can be instrumental. In a majority of case studies, the *intrinsic* interest compels the use of case study design to understand thoroughly the complex phenomenon in its rich local setting. An interest in the case can be *instrumental*. Alternatively, the researcher may use case study as a means to an end. The interest on case study is thus instrumental to an end in mind. According to Yin (1993), a case study can be a means to describe, to explore, or to explain that complex phenomenon. Whether a case study is descriptive, exploratory, or explanatory, it is instrumental to achieve those ends. GAO (Datta, Nov 1990) refers to them as the expected consequences (the applications) of a case study design. Regardless, it is the intrinsic interest or instrumental interest on the One case that triggers the case study (Benbasat *et al.*, 2002; Franz & Robey, 1984; Stake, 2005).

A different reason for choosing a case study design could be due to the dissatisfaction with or a personal bias against quantitative methodology (Benbasat *et al.*, 2002). Quantitative methodology has to have large sample size in order to generalise. Yet, the generalised knowledge could not possibly apply to all practices, especially to those with rich and sensitive contexts. This weakness becomes the strength of case study. It is particularly well suited to generate knowledge for the practitioners. Knowledge learned from the instrumental case study makes practice less complex over time (Baskerville & Pries-Heje, 2001; Benbasat *et al.*, 2002 Christenson, 1976). Even a trial-and-error practice is crucial for knowledge to accumulate (Christenson, 1976). It is especially appropriate to a research area, such as the business case, in which none or few previous studies have been carried out (Benbasat *et al.*, 2002). In short, a case study design facilitates the exploration of a complex phenomenon.

Table 4. Key characteristics of case study as a research design

1.	Overriding theoretical paradigm:	Realism ([C] of Figure 1)
2.	Phenomenon:	Contemporary and complex ([A] of Figure 1)
3.	Context:	Natural setting (University of Australasia)
4.	Questions:	Why and how
5.	Unit of analysis:	Streams of innovation/diffusion research
6.	Application:	Intensive examination of unit of analysis
7.	Motivation of the study:	Intrinsic or instrumental interest ([A] of Figure 1)
8.	Concentration required:	One hundred percent (100%) attention required
9.	Skill of the researcher:	Integrative powers of the researcher

Optimising the Understanding of the One Case

Justifying the Research Problem Theory (DOI Theory) in a Single-Case Study

The seven constructs[8], identified in Figure 2, make the DOI appropriate to understand thoroughly the selling of new enterprise systems through a formal business case document.

However, does DOI theory fit more appropriate to a study of large number of enterprises than a single enterprise? The answer is no, not necessarily. Earlier works of using DOI theory to a single-case study justify the appropriateness of this theory to single case study. One single-case study used DOI theory to identify in advance the complex issues that inhibit or facilitate the radical technological change in a hospital at Uganda[9] (Gladwin *et al*, Jun 2003). Another single-case study found the concept of perceived characteristics of the innovation useful to provide a framework for thinking about the adoption of video conferencing technology[10] (Al-Qirim, 9-11 June 2003).

A third justification concerns the two units of analysis to guide the philosophical inquiry. Diffusion research has several distinct streams[11,12], each with a specified unit of analysis. The critical task[13] of choosing the unit of analysis is not simply picking any or a combination of the five streams. This research uses the DoI and the PT streams after having thoroughly reflected and selected the complex phenomenon and its boundary ([A] in Figure 1), after having conducted a thorough review of the Diffusion of Innovations theory ([B] in Figure 1), and after mapping the constructs and their relationships (Figure 3 and Figure 4) to examine. The business case development is part of the matchmaking stage during the initiation phase of the innovation process. The business case document is likely a form of diffusion. These justify the PT and DoI streams as the units of analysis.

Optimising the Understanding of the One Case means not Generalising the One Case

Does optimising the understanding of the One case mean that nothing follow after understanding the One case? Is theorising the One case is not a part of the purpose of the study?

Case study excludes generalising. *The purpose to understand thoroughly the One case does not include generalising beyond the One case, although a case study is a means, a small step, toward generalisation (Campbell, 1975; Feagin et al., 1991; Flyvbjerg, 2001, 2006; Simon, 1980; Stake, 2005, p 448; Vaughan, 1999; Yin, 1993, 1994). Generalising beyond the case reduces the one hundred percent concentration required by the case study to thoroughly understanding the particulars of the case (Stake, 2005, p 448).*

Therefore understanding the One case and attempting to generalising it is in itself a threat of theory-practice inconsistency because it hinders the 100% attention[14] and the 100% knowledge expected from understanding the One case. This is the reason why the intention to generalise should simply linger during the whole research process (Stake, 2005).

Not Generalising the One Case Does Not Mean Not Theorising the One Case

If optimising the understanding of the One case should not include generalising beyond the One case, then does not generalising the One case mean not theorising the One case? A researcher conducting the case study and attempting to thoroughly understand the One case can nevertheless theorise even if he does not generalise beyond the One case. Understanding what a theory is and differentiating theorising and generalising resolve this confusion.

A **theory** is simply a statement of the **relationships** (eg, the four issues in Figure 4) of the properties, constructs (eg, the four constructs in the same diagram), or variables related to a complex phenomenon (eg, the shaded area in that diagram). Weber (2003, p iv) defines theory as "an *account* that is intended to explain or predict some *phenomena* that we perceive in the world." Thus, a theory is an account of a phenomenon in practice. This account expresses relationships. Metaphor, dualism, category, and concept are statements of the relationships. These are theories, which can be context-bound or context-free. Llewelyn (2003) suggests a five-level structure to what counts as theory (Table 5).

If the context-bound theory (the Level 4 theory) of Llewelyn (2003) and her context-free theory

(Level 5 theory) could be interpreted as a differentiation of two extremes in a continuum and if the metaphor (Level 1 theory), differentiation (Level 2 theory), and conceptual innovation (Level 3 theory) are the theories that reside at any points on the continuum, then it could be said that the Level 1 to Level 3 theories developed through theorising are not the product of generalisation as long as these theories do not reside at the context-free theory side or somewhere near that end. Theorising is therefore not generalising as long as the theory that has been created reside near or somewhere near the end of the context-bound theory.

With this interpretation, it is possible to bring into relevance the theory or theories that result from the thorough understanding of the One case and putting the practice ([A]) either in congruence or paradox to the research problem theory ([B]). Thus, *the purpose of case study is*

Table 5. 5-level structure to what counts as theory

- Opposite to the highest Level 5 grand theory is the lowest **Level 1** metaphor. Giving meaning to form, a metaphor is a concept of what "we live by", state Lakoff & Johnson (1980, p 126). Morgan (1983) clarifies that metaphor is "a basic structural form of experience through which human beings engage, organise, and understand their world."

- **Level 2** theories involve differentiating, comparing, contrasting, categorising, and bridging the dualism. Examples of dualities are black and white, left and right, up and down, presence and absence, objectivity and subjectivity, finite and infinite, private and public, inner and outer, yin and yang, masculine and feminine, micro and macro, and so on. McGregor (2006) differentiates Theory X (the traditional view of direction and control) and Theory Y (the integration of individual and organisational goal). The concept of social construction by Berger & Luckman (1966) bridges the objective and subjective dualism. Level 2 theories cuts up experience, creates meaning and significance, sets up contrasts and layered categories, and bridges dualism.

- A concept belonging to **Level 3** is what Anthony Giddens (1987) associates it as a "conceptual innovation". In this level, there is a certain degree of generalisation and opens up "ways of seeing" (Giddens, 1987). It associates itself a certain unit of analysis and bridges gaps from micro level to meso (organisational) level to macro level.

- **Level 4** is specific to a specific social, organisational, or individual phenomenon in their rich contextual setting.

- **Level 5** grand theory is applicable to all phenomena. The last is a one-size fits all.

the understanding thoroughly the One case. That understanding includes giving accounts of the issues in the form of theories that are context-bound. The following twenty six approaches of Weber (2003) are applicable to theorising (Table 6). A pre-requisite is the identification of the focal constructs (eg, the four constructs of Diffusion of Innovations theory).

Modes of Analysis

Six modes of analysis are relevant to optimise the understanding of the One case. Each mode of analysis ensures a tight coupling of data gathering and data analysis (Myers & Avison, 2002). An underlying principle is the concurrent gathering and analysing of the data. Data will not be gathered and later analyse. Rather, prior to the data gathering phase, there is a contemplation of how

the data will be analysed and subsequently how the data will be collected. This mindset lingers subconsciously as the research design goes on. Here are the six relevant modes of analysis:

1. The simple "noticing, collecting, and thinking" (Seidel, 1998) facilitates the clarification of the data. It is iterative and progressive in a continuous infinite spiral to end when this report is completed.
2. "Little data with lots of brain" limits the code of the data with the use of ALTAS.ti version 5 as little as possible (Agar, 1991, p 194). This mode starts by reading and re-reading the data, noticing a few interesting things, avoiding intensive coding early in the analytic process, collecting one or more of these things, and intensively thinking about them.

Table 6. Types of theory and steps of generating theory

Type 1 theory articulates the constructs of a theory and explains or predicts its value. The theory may be (1) new. The construct may be (2) new to, (3) added to or (4) taken from an existing theory. The existing constructs of an existing theory can be (5) defined more precisely or (6) conceptualised somewhat differently.

Type 2 theory articulates the relationships between or among the constructs of a theory and explains with precision how the value will change based on some sort of law. The relationships and the laws are social constructions. The theory may propose (6) new laws of interaction among the new constructs in a new theory. It may propose (7) a new law, (8) add a law, or (9) remove a law for the existing theory. It may even (10) define an existing law more precisely or (12) conceptualise it somewhat differently.

Type 3 theory articulates the lawful present state of the phenomenon for which the value of the construct holds. The theory may specify more precisely a singular value that a construct (13) holds or (14) cannot hold or a collective values of constructs for which the theory (15) holds or (16) does not hold.

Type 4 theory articulates the lawful change event with (17) unlawful initial state or (18) unlawful subsequent state or (19) both unlawful states. Likewise, the change event may be unlawful with (20) lawful initial or (21) lawful subsequent states or (22) both lawful states.

Type 5 theory, similar to Type 3, articulates the lawful future state of the phenomenon for which the value of the construct holds. The theory may specify more precisely a singular value that a construct (23) will hold or (24) will not hold or the collective values of the constructs for which the theory will (25) hold or will (26) not hold.

3. The "critical narrative truth" tells a story of how University of Australasia walked the innovation until the point Craig submitted his business case. The narration is written in a way that links it to the theory. Effectively, the narration reflects a real-word in relation to the theory about change and innovation. It is therefore informative and, at the same time, critical of the social change to benefit the intended audiences (Chase, 2005, pp 669-671; Clough, 2000; Lincoln, 1997; Rüegg-Stürm, 2005).

4. Hermeneutics and content analysis, the fourth mode, helps to interpret the way the executive sponsor, his project team members, and upper management make the adoption decision meaningful (Boland Jr, 2002). It attempts to form a big picture of what the executive sponsor was trying to convey. But interpreting texts of a document has a problem with "hermeneutic circle" (Gadamar, 1976; Myers & Avison, 2002, p 10). What is true of the parts is probably true to the whole (generalisation). In reverse, what is true for the whole is probably true for the parts (classification). To mitigate that problem of the circle of generalisation and classification, it is essential to interpret the texts individually and collectively. It is likewise essential to understand the subjects from the viewpoints of other people. Examining and appreciating the rich-local setting facilitate perceiving the viewpoints of other people.

5. Argumentation is a form of analysis and thinking. It is thinking per se and "selling" the claim in a way that people will freely assent to that claim. Toulmin's model is a good start. However, it is not complete. So here comes the sixth mode.

6. Clarifying, classifying, and structuring are the first three steps of the seven-step argument analysis of Michael Scriven (McPeck, 1981, pp 87-89; Scriven, 1976; Walton, 2006).

First, clarify a meaning of an argument and its components. Second, identify hidden or stated assumptions. Third, portray the structure.

FUTURE TRENDS

Visioning

Adapting to ever-changing external environments means that an organisation should be able to maintain its stability while moving forward to implement a radical change which can cause disruptions. (Burrell & Morgan, 2005; Dettmer, 2003; Trompenaars & Prud'homme, 2004). An illustration of this is Air New Zealand which outsourced the maintenance of its wide-bodied jets Boeing overseas in order to reduce costs and improve profit, causing job cuts that affected more than six hundred engineers ("Air NZ has no option: Norris", 22-23 Oct 2005; Dearnaley, 2005). Air New Zealand has attempted to manage its profitability and cash flows in the short term and innovation in the long term to be able to sustain itself in the end.

The two crucial elements of innovation include a vision that comes with a time frame and the means of implementing that change as well as its contribution to the vision and the company. (Nadler and Tushman, 2004; Trompenaars & Prud-homme, 2004). Just as people are bound to their self-conscious *image of the future* (Polak, 1973), organisational change can also be bound by the corporate vision. Radical innovation consists of a vision, an innovation that fits that vision, and an innovation process.

A vision is a view of the future. Although "vision" and "future" are not in the index section of the book entitled Diffusion of Innovations written by Rogers (2003), "uncertainty" and "time" are in that section. Rogers has mentioned "vision" and "future" in the discussion of the innovation-development process (Rogers, 2003, pp 136-167), the birth of the laptop computer at Toshiba (Abetti, 1997; Rogers, 2003, p 145), and the fumbling of the future at Xerox PARC (Rogers, 2003, p 153). Vision is a crucial element in walking the innovation. But, that vision is a missing construct in the DOI theory.

A Matrix of a Vertical Continuum and a Horizontal Continuum

The determinism viewpoint of authorities like Karl Marx & Frederick Engels (1973), Marshall McLuhan (1964), Alvin Toffler (1970), Jacques Ellul (1964), George Orwell (1949) defines a technological innovation as a force beyond human control that causes a change in a social system. The instrumentalism viewpoint negates this. It defines technology as a tool that people use to control their destiny and shape their future. Depending on the way it is used, the technological innovation could be good or bad. The deployment or replacement of enterprise systems is used to change a business process (Luftman & Koeller, 2003) Whether the change produces positive or negative results, technological instrumentalism is perceived to be valuable to an organization because of the perceived benefits that comes with it. (MacKenzie & Wajcman, 1999).

The real issue does not lie within the vertical continuum between determinism and instrumentalism, Andrew Feenberg (1991) believes. Instead, it can be found in the innovation, the options it provides, the expected consequences, and the process involved. Other points that should be considered include the vision from which the expected consequences originate and the perceived value of the innovation. which is crucial to the attributes of the innovation that are perceived to be critical. Other authorities, however, believe that the vertical continuum is relevant because the points within it drive the innovation. The origin of an innovation, its diffusion, and other constructs drive an innovation (Lubrano, 1997). The "other constructs" affirm that understanding the social

systems, their relatively unstable components, and their relatively stable structure is essential to understanding the innovation (Toffler, 1970).

A diffusion research about technological innovation can examine a matrix that is formed by the intersection of a vertical line that represents determinism and instrumentalism and the horizontal line that represents the macro and micro view of innovation. With this matrix of Daniel Surry and John Farquhar (May 1997) and Toffler (1970), technological innovation can be seen as a force at societal level and a tool at organisational level. The macro view of determinism consists of a relatively stable societal structure and its effective framework while its micro view includes the process of designing, developing, and evaluating the innovation. The macro view of instrumentalism, on the other hand, shows the unstable political, economic, societal, & technological environments of an organisation. Its micro view represents the perceptions of potential adopters, their needs, and the characteristics of the adoption site.

One to One, One to Many, Many to One, and Many to Many

Although this diffusion research uses the DoI and the PT streams because of their relevance, other streams provide opportunities for future research. Many authorities favour using multiple streams or perspectives in their research. According to Abrahamson (1991), in a period of uncertainty, the fad and fashion models give better explanations than the efficient choice model. Baskerville & Pries-Heje (2001) utilise three process models and show a possibility of mapping one or more models to one or more streams of the diffusion study provided that the model fits the stream of the study. Poole & Van de Ven (1989) illustrate the study of innovation using different perspectives of organisational theory (eg, institutional, rational, and emergent). Thus, the streams of the diffusion research and their models can be utilised in the diffusion research on the basis of one to one, one to many, many to one, or many to many.

CONCLUSION

This chapter has briefly introduced the Diffusion of Innovations (DOI) theory and an overarching framework to understand a complex phenomenon that concerns the business case (construct) of replacing enterprise systems. A business case influences upper management to be cautious, positive, or overly positive. At one extreme of the continuum is upper management's inability to commit or under-commit. At the other extreme is an over-commitment. Both extremes in the continuum result to unexpected undesirable consequences.

To explore this complex phenomenon involving business case, vision, and executive sponsors, this chapter further describes, illustrates, and gives an account of a design process of a single-case study. The eight questions in Table 1 will likely guide the researcher to articulate a case study design and ensure quality in designing the research.

Of the essential components of a case study (Table 3), the most difficult is identifying the issue in the One case. The diagram in Figure 6 shows a top down approach. In this approach, the secondary problems and issues could be determined from the primary problem. Another approach could start from primary claim (similar to hypothesis in quantitative research) that answers the primary problem. From this claim, identifying the secondary problems and their issues is possible. Both of these approaches can be used singularly or collectively. Borrowed from argumentation theory, the top-down approach satisfy the rule of confirmability (construct validity) by breaking down the phenomenon into components.

The realism paradigm is appropriate in a case study. Understanding a complex phenomenon using both objective and subjective viewpoints is practitioner-oriented. Case study is rich, contextually speaking, if the study is able to accept all empirical and experiential evidences from all possible sources.

The complexity of a case study, however, demands a hundred percent attention while the researcher undertakes the study. The study relies on the integrative power of the researcher.

For a case study to be credible to the community in which it is intended, quality must be embedded into its research design.

REFERENCES

Abetti, P. A. (1997). Birth and growth of Toshiba's laptop and notebook computers: A case study in Japanese corporate venturing. *Journal of Business Venturing, 12*, 507-529.

Abrahamson, E. (1991). Managerial fads and fashions: The diffusion and rejection of innovations. *Academy of Management Review, 16*(3), 586-612.

Agar, M. (1991). The right brain strikes back. In N. Fielding & R. Lee (Eds.), *Using computers in qualitative research* (pp. 181-194). Newbury Park, CA: Sage Publications.

Air NZ has no option: Norris. (2005, October 22-23). *Otago Daily Times.*

Baskerville, R. L., & Pries-Heje, J. (2001). A multiple-theory analysis of a diffusion of information technology case. *Information Systems Journal, 11*, 181-212.

Bassey, M. (1999). *Case study research in educational settings.* Buckingham, UK: Open University Press.

Benbasat, I., Goldstein, D. K., & Mead, M. (2002). The case research strategy in studies of information systems. In M. D. Myers & D. Avison (Eds.), *Qualitative research in information systems: A reader* (pp. 79-99). London: Sage Publications.

Berger, P. L., & Luckmann, T. (1966). *The social construction of reality: A treatise in the sociology of knowledge.* New York: Doubleday.

Bhaskar, R. (1970). *A realist theory of science.* Hassocks, Sussex, UK: Harvester Press.

Bhaskar, R. (2002). *From science to emancipation: Alienation and the actuality of enlightenment.* Delhi, India: Sage Publications India Pvt Ltd.

Boland R. J., Jr. (2002). In M. D. Myers & D. Avison (Eds.), *Qualitative research in information systems: A reader* (pp. 225-240). London: Sage Publications.

Burrell, G. & Morgan, G. (2005). *Sociological paradigms and organisational analysis: Elements of the sociology of corporate life.* Ardershot, UK: Ashgate Publishing Limited.

Caldwell, B. (1998, July 6). Andersen sued on R/3. *InformationWeek.*

Campbell, D. T. (1975). Degrees of freedom and the case study. *Comparative Political Studies, 8,* 178-193.

Chase, S. E. (2005). Narrative inquiry. In N. K. Denzin & Y. S. Lincoln (Eds.), *Handbook of qualitative research* (3rd ed.) (pp. 651-679). Thousand Oaks, CA: Sage Publications.

Christenson, C. (1976). Proposals for a program of empirical research into the properties of triangles. *Decision Sciences, 7*(3), 631-648.

Clegg, S. R., Kornberger, M., & Rhodes, C. (Mar 2004). Noise, parasites and translation: Theory and practice in management consulting. *Management Learning, 35*(1), 31-44.

Clough, P. T. (2000). Comments on setting criteria for experimental writing. *Qualitative Inquiry, 6,* 278-291.

Coon, D. (2005). *Psychology: A modular approach to mind and behavior* (10th ed.). Belmont, CA: Thomson Wadsworth.

Cooper, R. B., & Zmud, R. W. (1990). Information technology implementation research: A technological diffusion approach. *Management Science, 36*(2), 123-139.

Copeland, T., Koller, T., & Murrin, J. (2000). *Valuation: Measuring and managing the value of companies* (3rd ed.). New York: John Wiley & Sons.

Cua, F. C., & Garrett, T. C. (2008). Understanding ontology and epistemology in information systems research. In A. Cater-Steel & L. Al-Hakim (Eds.), *Information systems research methods, epistemology and applications,* (pp. 33-56). Hershey, PA: Information Science Reference.

Cua, F. C., & Garrett, T. C. (2009). Analyzing diffusion and value creation dimensions of a business case of replacing enterprise systems. In T. T. Kidd (Ed.), *Handbook of Research on Technology Project Management, Planning and Operation,* (pp. 139-171). Hershey, PA: IGI Publishing.

Daft, R. L. (1978). A dual-core model of organizational innovation. *Academy of Management Journal, 21,* 193-210.

Datta, L. E. (1990, November). *Case study evaluations.* Retrieved February 21, 2008, from http://www.gao.gov/special.pubs/10_1_9.pdf

Dearnaley, M. (2005). Air NZ engineers plead for their jobs. *The New Zealand Herald.*

Dettmer, H. W. (2003). *Strategic navigation: A systems approach to business strategy.* Milwaukee, WI: ASQ Quality Press.

Downs G. W., Jr., & Mohr, L. B. (1976). Conceptual issues in the study of innovation. *Administrative Science Quarterly, 21*(4), 700-714.

Ellul, J. (1964). *The technological society.* New York: Alfred A Knopf, Inc.

Ettlie, J. E. (1980). Adequacy of stage models for decision on adoption of innovation. *Psychological Reports, 46,* 991-995.

Feagin, J. R., Orum, A. M., & Sjoberg, G. (1991). *A case for the case study.* Chapel Hill: University of North Carolina Press.

Feenberg, A. (1991). *Critical theory of technology.* New York: Oxford University Press.

Flyvbjerg, B. (2001). *Making social science matter: Why social inquiry fails and how it can succeed again* (S. Sampson, Trans.). MA: Cambridge University Press.

Flyvbjerg, B. (2006). Five misunderstandings about case-study research. *Qualitative Inquiry, 12*, 219-245.

Foreman, M. (2007). *Fonterra to offshore IT jobs to India?* Retrieved November, 19. 2007, from http://www.zdnet.com.au/news/software/soa/Fonterra-to-offshore-IT-jobs-to-India-/0,130061733,339274389,00.htm

Franz, C. R., & Robey, D. (1984). An investigation of user-led system design: Rational and political perspectives. *Communications of the ACM, 27*(12), 1202-1217.

Gadamer, H. G. (1976). The historicity of undestanding. In P. Connerton (Ed.), *Critical sociology: Selected readings.* Harmondsworth, UK: Penguin Books.

Giddens, A. (1987). *Social theory and modern sociology.* Cambridge, UK: Polity Press.

Gladwin, J., Dixon, R. A., & Wilson, T. D. (Jun 2003). Implementing a new health management information system in Uganda. *Health Policy and Planning, 18*(2), 214-224.

Grant, R. M. (1996). Toward a knowledge-based theory of the firm. *Strategic Management Journal, 17*, 109-122.

Grant, R. M. (1997). The knowledge-based view of the firm: Implications for management practices. *Long Range Planning, 30*(3), 450-454.

Hammer, M. (1996). *Beyond reengineering: How the process-centered organization is changing our work and our lives.* New York: HarperCollins Publishers, Inc.

Hausman, A. (2005). Innovativeness among small businesses: Theory and propositions for future research. *Industrial Marketing Management, 34*(8), 773-782.

Hoaglin, D. C., Light, R. J., McPeek, B., Mosteller, F., & Stoto, M. A. (1982). *Data for decisions: Information strategies for policymakers.* Cambridge, MA: Abt Books.

Hurt, H. T., & Hubbard, R. (1987, May). *The systematic measurement of the perceived characteristics of information technologies: Microcomputers as innovations.* Paper presented at the ICA Annual Conference, Montreal, Quebec.

Jackson, R. (2006). *Fonterra puts SAP project on ice.* Retrieved October 5, 2006, from http://computerworld.co.nz/news.nsf/news/3C182BBD1B82A2C1CC2571F80016AEF1?Opendocument&HighLight=2,fonterra

Jaskyte, K., & Dressler, W. W. (2005). Organizational culture and innovation in nonprofit human service organization. *Administration in Social Work, 29*(2), 23-41.

Kemmis, S. (1980). The imagination of the case and the invention of the study. In H. Simons (Ed.), *Towards a science of the singular* (pp. 93-142). Norwich, UK: University of East Anglia, Center for Applied Research in Education.

Kuhn, T. S. (1970). *The structure of scientific revolutions.* IL: University of Chicago Press.

Lakoff, G., & Johnson, M. (1980). *Metaphors we live by.* IL: The University of Chicago Press.

Lincoln, Y. S. (1997). Self, subject, audience, text: Living at the edge, writing in the margins. In W. G. Tierney & Y. S. Lincoln (Eds.), *Representation and the text: Re-framing the narrative voice* (pp. 37-55). Albany, NY: State University of New York Press.

Llewelyn, S. (2003). What counts as "theory" in qualitative management and accounting research?

Introducting five levels of theorizing. *Accounting, Auditing & Accountability Journal, 16*(4), 662-708.

Lubrano, A. (1997). *The telegraph: How technology innovation caused social change.* New York: Garland Publishing.

Luftman, J., & Koeller, C. T. (2003). Assessing the value of IT. In J. N. Luftman (Eds.), *Competing in the information age: Align in the sand* (2nd ed.) (pp. 77-106). UK: Oxford University Press.

MacKenzie, D., & Wajcman, J. (Eds.). (1999). *The social shaping of technology* (2nd ed.). Buckingham, UK: Open University Press.

Marx, K., & Engels, F. (1973). *Karl Marx: On society and social change.* IL: University of Chicago Press.

McGregor, D. (2006). *The human side of enterprise* (Annotated ed.). New York: The McGraw-Hill Companies, Inc.

McLuhan, M. (1964). The medium is the message. In *Understanding media* (pp. 7-23). London: Routledge and Kegan Paul.

McPeck, J. E. (1981). *Critical thinking and education.* New York: St Martin's.

Melling, D. (1987). *Understanding Plato.* New York: Oxford University Press.

Merriam, S. B. (1988). *Case study research in education: A qualitative approach.* San Francisco: Jossey Bass.

Meyer, A. D., & Goes, J. B. (1988). Organizational assimilation of innovations: A multilevel contextual analysis. *Academy of Management Journal, 31,* 897-923.

Ministry of Economic Development. (2004, February). *Restructuring to accommodate the "new" model.*

Moore, G. C., & Benbasat, I. (1991). Development of an instrument to measure the perceptions of adopting an information technology innovation. *Information Systems Research, 2*(3), 192-222.

Morgan, G. (1983). More on metaphor: Why we cannot control tropes in administrative science. *Administrative Science Quarterly, 28,* 601-607.

Morin, R. A., & Jarrell, S. L. (2001). *Driving shareholder value.* New York: McGraw-Hill.

Myers, M. D., & Avison, D. E. (2002). An introduction to qualitative research in information systems. In M. D. Myers & D. E. Avison (Eds.), *Qualitative research in information systems: A reader* (pp. 3-12). London: Sage Publications Ltd.

Nadler, D. A., & Tushman, M. L. (2004). Implementing new design: Managing organizational change. In M. L. Tushman & P. Andersen (Eds.), *Managing strategic innovation and change: A collection of readings* (2nd ed.). UK: Oxford University Press.

O'Leary, D. E. (2000). Enterprise resource planning systems: Systems, life cycle, electronic commerce, and risk. New York: Cambridge University Press.

Orum, A. M., Feagin, J. R., & Sjoberg, G. (1991). Introduction: The nature of the case study. In J. R. Feagin & A. M. Orum (Eds.), *A case for the case study* (pp. 1-26). Chapel Hill: University of North Carolina Press.

Orwell, G. (1949). *Nineteen eighty-four.* London: Secker.

Outhwaite, W. (1983). Toward a realist perspective. In G. Morgan (Ed.), *Beyond method: Strategies for social research* (pp. 321-330). Beverly Hills, CA: Sage Publications, Inc.

Polak, F. L. (1973). *The image of the future.* Amsterdam: Elsevier.

Poole, M. S., & Van de Ven, A. H. (1989). Toward a general theory of innovation processes. In A. H. Van de Ven, H. L. Angle, & M. S. Poole (Eds.),

Research on the management of innovation: The Minnesota studies. New York: Harper & Row.

Prahalad, C. K., & Bettis, R. A. (1986). The dominant logic: A new linkage between diversity and performance. *Strategic Management Journal, 7,* 485-501.

Rappaport, A. (1986). *Creating shareholder value: A guide for managers and investors.* New York: The Free Press.

Rogers, E. M. (1962). *Diffusion of innovations.* New York: The Free Press of Glencoe.

Rogers, E. M. (2003). *Diffusion of innovations* (5th ed.). New York: Free Press/Simon & Schuster, Inc.

Rogers, E. M. & Shoemaker, F. F. (1971). *Communication of innovations: A cross-cultural approach* (2nd ed.). New York: The Free Press.

Ross, J. W. & Vitale, M. R. (2000). The ERP revolution: Surviving vs thriving. *Information Systems Frontiers, 2*(2), 233-241.

Santas, G. X. (Ed.). (2006). *The Blackwell guide to Plato's Republic.* Malden, MA: Blackwell Publishing Ltd.

SAP and Deloitte Sued by FoxMeyer. (1998, August 27). *The New York Times.* Retrieved February 17, 2007, from http://query.nytimes.com/gst/fullpage.html?res=9A05E7D7123CF934A1575BC0A96E958260

Scriven, M. (1976). *Reasoning.* New York: McGraw-Hill.

Seidel, J. V. (1998). *Qualitative data analysis.* Retrieved December 1, 2005, from www.qualisresearch.com

Simon, E. (Ed.). (1980). *Towards a science of the singular.* Norwich, UK: University of East Anglia.

Smaling, A. (1987). *Methodological objectivity and qualitative research.* Lisse, The Netherlands: Swets & Zeitlinger.

Smith, M. L. (2006). Overcoming theory-practice inconsistencies: Critical realism and information systems research. *Information and Organization, 16,* 191-211.

Stake, R. E. (1995). *The art of case study research.* London: Sage Publications, Inc.

Stake, R. E. (2005). Qualitative case studies. In N. K. Denzin & Y. S. Lincoln (Eds.), *The Sage handbook of qualitative research* (3rd ed.) (pp. 443-466).

Stein, T. (1998, August 31). SAP sued over R/3. *InformationWeek.*

Stouffer, S. A. (1941). Notes on the case-study and the unique case. *Sociometry, 4,* 349-357.

Surry, D. W., & Farquhar, J. D. (1997, May). Diffusion theory and instructional technology. *Journal of Instructional Science and Technology, 2*(1).

Taleb, N. N. (2007). *The black swan: The impact of the highly improbable.* London: Penguin Books Ltd.

ten Have, S., ten Have, W., Stevens, F., van der Elst, M., & Pol-Coyne, F. (2003). *Key management models: The management tools and practices that will improve your business.* Harlow, Essex, UK: Financial Times Prentice Hall/Pearson Education Limited.

Thull, J. (2005). *The prime solution.* Dearborn Trade Publishing.

Toffler, A. (1970). *Future shock.* New York: Bantam Books.

Tornatzky, L. G., & Fleishcher, M. (1990). *The process of technological innovation.* Lexington, MA: Lexington Books.

Tornatzky, L. G., & Klein, K. J. (1982). Innovation characteristics and innovation adoption-implementation: A meta-analysis of findings. *IEEE Transactions on Engineering Management, 29*, 28-45.

Trompenaars, F., & Prud'homme, P. (2004). *Managing change across corporate cultures.* Chichester, UK: Capstone.

Tsoukas, H. (1989). The validity of idiographic research explanations. *Academy of Management Review, 14*(4), 551-561.

Van de Ven, A. H., Polley, D. E., Garud, R., & Venkataraman, S. (1999). *The innovation journey.* New York: Oxford University Press.

Van Eemeren, F. H., Grootendorst, R., & Henkemans, A. F. S. (2002). *Argumentation: Analysis, Evaluation, presentation.* Mahwah, NJ: Lawrence Erlbaum Associates Inc.

van Wynsberghe, R., & Khan, S. (2007). Redefining case study. *International Journal of Qualitative Methods, 6*(2), 1-10.

Vaughan, D. (1999). The dark side of organizations: Mistake, misconduct, and disaster. *Annual Review of Sociology, 25*, 271-305.

Walton, D. (2006). *Fundamentals of critical argumentation: Critical reasoning and argumentation.* New York: Cambridge University Press.

Weber, R. (2003). Editor's comments: Theoretically speaking. *MIS Quarterly, 27*(3), iii-xii.

Willard, C. A. (1992). On the utility of descriptive diagrams for the analysis and criticism of arguments. In W. L. Benoit, D. Hample, & P. J. Benoit (Eds.), *Readings in argumentation: Pragmatics and discourse analysis* (pp. 239-257). Berlin, Germany: Foris Publications.

Wolfe, R. A. (1994). Organizational innovation: Review, critique and suggested research directions. *Journal of Management Studies, 31*(3), 405-431.

Yin, R. K. (1993). *Applications of case study research.* Newbury Park, CA: Sage Publications.

Yin, R. K. (1994). *Case study research: Design and methods* (2nd ed.). London: Sage Publications.

Zaltman, G., Duncan, R., & Holbek, J. (1973). *Innovations and organizations.* New York: John Wiley and Sons.

Zarefsky, D. (2005). *Argumentation: The study of effective reasoning, part 1 of 2.* Chantilly, VA: The Teaching Company.

KEY TERMS AND DEFINITIONS

Business Case is used both to describe a process and a document. Corporate governance generally compels a business case document as a tool to justify a capital investment (a radical innovation). In this report, the exploitation of an agenda by an executive sponsor is considered a form of diffusion. A completed business case document is a formal written document that argues a course of action, which contains a point-by-point analysis that leads to a decision after considering a set of alternative courses of action to accomplish a specific goal. A business case process walks through the initiation phase of the innovation.

Business Case Stream of Diffusion Research embraces a plurality view of visualising, mapping, and realising future consequences. It permits an attempt to understand the perceived needs (the current state), the solution (aka, the innovation), its alternatives (objects of innovation), the preferred choice, a view of the future (the future state), the desirable expected consequences to achieve, the undesirable expected consequences to avoid, and the perceived positive attributes required.

Diffusion is essentially the communication of a new idea (aka, the innovation) within a social system (such as an organisation) with the intention of convincing the audience to adopt or use the innovation.

Diffusion of Innovations (DOI) Theory is a theory of Everett M Rogers (1962) that concerns the study of communicating a new idea to individuals or organisations. It can be defined as the study of how, why, and at what rate the new idea (the innovation) diffuses and its adoption takes place.

Innovation represents a product, a service, or an idea that is perceived or should be perceived by the audience or the market in which this innovation is intended to be new and of value.

Implementation Phase proceeds after the initiation phase of "walking an innovation." For enterprise systems, this phase consists of pre-production, production, and post-production (also known as upgrade and maintenance). Refer to innovation process.

Initiation Phase consists of awareness stage and matchmaking stage, which ends with an accept-reject decision. This phase is the first phase of the innovation process. The second phase that follows is the implementation phase. Refer to innovation process.

Innovation Process starts with an initiation phase through which the individuals or decision-making units move from identifying and understanding the innovation, to forming an attitude toward that innovation. This subsequently leads to the decision to accept or reject it. The awareness stage is an agenda setting stage. The attitude formation stage is the matchmaking stage in which the executive sponsor attempts to match the attributes of the innovation to the requirement. The accept-reject decision terminates the initiation phase. An accept decision continues the innovation process toward the implementation phase, which consists of the pre-production, production, post-production, and confirmation stages.

Perceived Attributes of an Innovation are the Set 1 positive or negative biases that the decision makers have. These attributes may be real or imaginary. However, it is the perception of their presence that matters.

Perceived Attributes of Using an Innovation are the Set 2 positive or negative biases that the users have. Similar to the perceived attributes of an innovation (Set 1), what matters is the perception regardless of whether the attributes (eg, perceived usefulness and perceived ease of use) are real or imaginary.

Risk connotes a possible negative impact to something of value. It symbolises the probability of a loss.

Total Cost of Ownership, also known as TCO, is a rigorous and holistic methodology, which helps in estimating how much an investment will cost to operate over its lifetime. It takes into account all direct and indirect costs. The indirect costs are generally insignificant individually. However, they become very substantial when accumulated over time.

ENDNOTES

[1]   This chapter concerns how to mitigate the threats of theory-practice inconsistencies. One threat exists between theory and practice (❶ in Figure 1). It originates from an attempt to understand a practical problem in theory or an academic theory in practice (Baskar, 2002; Smaling, 1987; Smith, 2006; Taleb, 2007). Another threat resides between philosophical assumptions and the research design (❹). The ontological and epistemological assumptions (❷) influence the awareness of the practice (the complex phenomenon) and theory (the Diffusion of Innovations theory as a research problem theory). The same assumptions affects (❹) the research design (❺) and its reasoning (interpretation) and argumentation (evalu-

ation). In turn, that research design affects (❻) the outcomes (❼) of the research. In turn, those outcomes affect a person's understanding of the reality (❽) as well as the contribution of the research to epistemology (❾). A backward link from the outcome to the research design applies to action research where the outcomes of the study go back to research design. Lastly, there is a threat that is embedded in the research design (❺) itself.

2   A paradigm contributes to knowledge (*epistemology*) by naming and describing certain generative mechanisms (the real domain) that facilitate understanding a complex phenomenon (the actual domain). The understanding leads to the discovery of experiences (the empirical domain) or new knowledge with the use of theoretical reasoning (Bhaskar, 1978; Outhwaite, 1983, p 332; Tsoukas, 1989). The reasoning when combined with *episteme* (a lower realm of knowledge) results to *epistemology* (a higher form of knowledge). It is obvious of the tight coupling of a theoretical paradigm to *ontology* and *epistemology*.

3   The classical perceived attributes of innovation is a crucial concept in DOI (Hurt and Hubbard, 1987; Kwon & Zmud, 1987; Moore & Benbasat, 1991; Rogers, 2003; Tornatzky and Klein, 1982; Van de Ven, 1993).

4   In the design stage, a prisoner executes a plan, carefully considers if he should go through his intentions (vision and expected consequences), and maps out the path to take at the same time. Then, in the implementation stage that follows, he takes a dive off a cliff and toward the bottom of the sea. The third stage is stability. Before running out of breath, he attempts to resurface, hoping that he would not be shot. The fourth stage is improvement. He starts to swim to freedom. The last stage is transformation. If he

succeeds, he transforms himself into a free man.

5   The initiation phase consist of the gestation (stage a), the shocks (stage b), and the planning (stage c). The planning stage is tantamount to the business case stage in which a plan (eg, the business case) is submitted to the top management (the resource controller) to obtain the resources needed to move on to the next phase. In the development phase, one can find the stages of proliferation (stage d), setbacks and mistakes (stage e), changing of goal post (stage f), fluid team composition (stage g), getting continuous support from the top management (stage h), building interorganizational relationships (alliances; stage i), and involving network externalities (stage j). The third phase is implementation phase composing of constant adoption and re-adaptation of old to new (stage k) and visible cultural change (stage l).

6   Plato compares the knowledge-gathering process to a journey through a dark cave, walking through the long tunnel and coming out into the open to view objects under the bright light of day (Melling, 1987; Santas, 2006). The individuals inside the cave can only see the illusions on the wall. They are ignorant of the reality outside the cave. If they successfully walk out into the open and be exposed to the sun for the first time, they will realise the reality outside the cave. They will be enlightened. They will discover a *higher realm* of reality through a long challenging intellectual journey. The reality outside the cave as well as the illusions that they have experienced while inside the cave are both their sources of knowledge. I*n the case study,* Stake (2005) suggests drawing all the information from multiple sources at the same time to learn about the One case (discussed in the chapter) and to answer epistemological questions of the case.

7   The question, "What is the most likely application of the Diffusion of Innovations (DOI) theory when practiced in the context of the business case of replacing enterprise systems?" elicits the primary claim which explains how the DOI theory is applied in this context as a response. The secondary problem, "What is the most likely explanation for the importance of the innovation process prior to the accept-reject decision using the Diffusion of Innovations Theory?" leads to the secondary claim which explains how important the innovation process is to the result of the accept-reject decision.

8   The seven constructs are, namely: the innovation (Construct 1), the diffusion (Construct 2), the business case (Construct 3) which is embedded in the matchmaking stage (Construct 5) of the initiation phase (Construct 6) of the innovation process (Construct 7), and perceived attributes of the innovation (Construct 4).

9   In their single-case study of the planning and implementation a health management information system (HMIS) that was introduced as part of national policy in a low-income African country, Gladwin *et al* (Jun 2003, pp 215, 221) used DOI theory to "identify in advance issues that inhibit or facilitate adoption [that is, the implementation] of a technological change". The DOI theory serves as a thinking hat to identify issues.

10   Al-Qirim (9-11 June 2003).regarded the perceived characteristics of the innovation (eg, relative advantage, etc) in the DOI theory to be appropriate to gain a richer picture of his single-case study of adoption of video conferencing technology (TMVC) for dermatology within Health Waikato in New Zealand.

11   A study that focuses on the new idea itself (the innovation itself or the objects of innovation) belongs to the Diffusion of Innovations (DoI) stream. The organisational innovativeness (OI) stream focuses on the organisation and its innovativeness. The process theory (PT) stream focuses on the stages of the innovation process. The organisational learning (OL) explores the influences of the experiential learning processes of acquiring knowledge about action-outcome relationships in organisations and its effects on innovation performance. The ambidextrous organisation (AO) stream uses organisational design as a unit of analysis. Of these five streams, the first three streams are the thoroughbred of diffusion research.

12   The organisational innovativeness stream of diffusion research is a consequence of the realisation of the limitations of the DoI stream (Wolfe, 1994). It concerns the variables that influence the propensity of an organisation to innovate. Organisational structure is a key variable. Other variables include the adopters, the stakeholders, the concerned organisation(s), and the macro environments (Hausman, 2005). Cultural consensus and organisational value are independent variables (Jaskyte & Dressler, 2005). With organisation itself as a unit of analysis, OI stream of diffusion research purports to discover and understand an organisation's propensity to innovate (Wolfe, 1994, pp 408-409). The research methodology is commonly statistical. However, the way the variables interact with each other hasn't been completely understood (Downs Jr & Mohr, 1976). Making the research context specific might help. Another solution might be to use knowledge-based view of the organisation (Grant, 1996, 1997) as a a post-script to shed light on organisational innovativeness. The OI stream will consequently lead to the examination of the innovation process.

13   Although this section discusses the DoI and the PT streams because of their relevance to this particular research, other streams provide opportunities for future research.

Many authorities favour using multiple streams or perspectives in diffusion research. According to Abrahamson (1991), in a period of uncertainty, the "fad" and "fashion" models give better explanations than the efficient choice model. Baskerville & Pries-Heje (2001) utilise three process models and show a possibility of mapping one or more models to one or more streams of the diffusion study provided that the model fits the stream of the study. Poole & Van de Ven (1989) illustrate the study of innovation using different perspectives of organisational theory (eg, institutional, rational, and emergent). Thus, the streams of the diffusion research and their models can be utilised in the diffusion research based on one to one, one to many, many to one, or many to many relationships.

14

A success factor of case study is a commitment to put a hundred percent concentration (Stake, 2005, p 448). "Attention," a fifteen-century Japanese Zen Buddhist priest Ikkyu responded when his student asked him to summarise the highest wisdom (Coon, 2005, p 213). When asked again, what that word means, he answered gently: "Attention means attention." It is this "attention" or the mindfulness or concentration to thoroughly understand the particular One case that represents the greatest strength of case study.

APPENDIX: FROM PRIMARY PROBLEM TO ISSUES

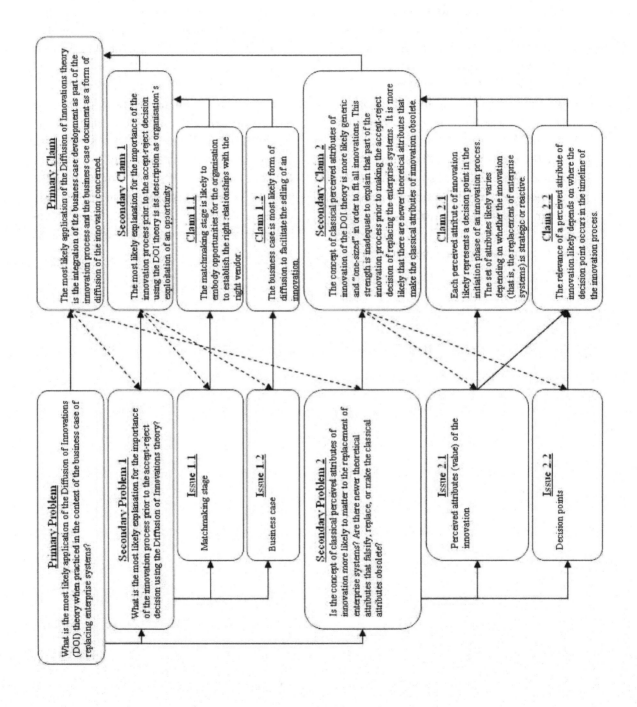

Chapter XV
The Technology Acceptance Model and Other User Acceptance Theories

Joseph Bradley
University of Idaho, USA

ABSTRACT

As global business markets become increasingly competitive, firms look to information technology to manage and improve their performance. Timely and accurate information is a key to gaining performance efficiency. Yet, firms may invest in technology only to find that their users are not willing to accept and use the new technology. This chapter explores the technology acceptance model and other theories of user acceptance.

INTRODUCTION

There is nothing more difficult to plan, more doubtful of success, nor more dangerous to manage than the creation of a new order of things... Whenever his enemies have the ability to attack the innovator, they do so with the passion of partisans, while others defend him sluggishly, so that the innovator and his party alike are vulnerable. (Machiavelli, 1513, from Rogers, E. M., Diffusion of Innovations, 2003)

The above quote from the 16th Century demonstrates that resistance to innovation is not unique to information systems, but has been with us for a long time with any type of innovation. Industry has turned to information systems technology to become more competitive in controlling resource use and costs to face increased global competition. The successful implementation of information systems ranging from simple applications, such as word processing and spreadsheets, to more complicated applications, such as enterprise resource planning systems, requires user acceptance. Yet, users are not always willing to accept the new technology. Academics and practitioners will benefit from a better understanding user acceptance. With this knowledge, user response can be predicted and systems modified to improve acceptance. Davis et al. (1989) propose a model of how users deal with the adoption of new technologies.

Davis et al (1989) developed the Technology Acceptance Model (TAM) based on the Theory of Reasoned Action (Ajzen and Fishbein, 1980). The TAM uses two variables, perceived usefulness (PU) and perceived ease of use (PEOU), as determinants of user acceptance. A key element of the TAM is behavioral intent which leads to the desired action, use of the system.

This article will first look at the theoretical development of the TAM beginning with the Expectancy-Value Theory and the Theory of Reasoned Actions. The TAM is introduced and described. A discussion of the impact of TAM on information systems research follows together with the limitations of the model. Extensions of TAM and alternative theories of user acceptance are then discussed. Lastly, a current discussion of the future of TAM is presented.

BACKGROUND

The theoretical roots of TAM can be found in the expectancy-value model and the theory of reasoned action.

Expectancy-Value Theory

The expectancy value theory was developed to understand motivations underlying the behavior of individuals. Behavioral intent is posited as the immediate precursor of a particular behavior. If we understand the elements that influence intention, we can better predict the likelihood of an individual engaging in a behavior. "Individuals choose behaviors based on the outcomes they expect and the values they ascribe to those expected

outcomes" (Borders, Earleywine & Huey, 2004, p. 539). Expectancy is "the measurement of the likelihood that positive or negative outcomes will be associated with or follow from a particular act" (Mazis, Ahtola & Kippel, 1975, p. 38). The strength of the expectancy and the value attributed to the outcome will determine the strength of the tendency to act (Mazis et al., 1975, p.38). A simple example demonstrated by Geiger and Cooper (1996) is that college students who valued increasing their grades were more willing to increase their effort in the course.

Theory of Reasoned Action

The theory of reasoned action (TRA), found in social psychology literature, improves the predictive and explanatory nature of the Expectancy Value Theory. The TRA explains the determinants of consciously intended behaviors (Fishbein and Ajzen, 1975; Ajzen and Fishbein, 1980). TRA is a general model which posits that an "a person's performance of a specific behavior is determined by his or her behavioral intention (BI) to perform the behavior" (Davis et al., 1989). Eveland (1986) observes that "ultimately, technology transfer is a function of what individuals *think* – because what they *do* depends on those thoughts, feelings and interests" (p. 310).

TRA, shown in Figure 1, posits that a person's beliefs and evaluations lead to their attitude (A) toward the behavior, which in turn leads to behavioral intention (BI). Normative beliefs and motivation affect the subjective norm (SN) which also influences BI. The subjective norm is defined as the influence others will have on the acceptance decision. Beliefs in the model are defined as "the individual's subjective probability that performing the target behavior will result in consequence *i*" (Davis et al., 1989, p. 984). Behavioral intention is determined by the person's attitude (A) and subjective norm (SN) concerning the behavior in question (Davis et al., 1989). Attitude toward behavior is a function of individual's "salient

Figure 1. Theory of reasoned action

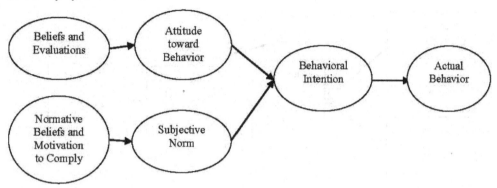

Adapted with permission from Davis, F.D., Bagozzi, R.P., Warshaw, P.R., (1989). User Acceptance of Computer Technology: A Comparison of Two Theoretical Models. Management Science 35(8) 982--1003. Copyright (1989), the Institute for Operations Research and the Management Sciences, 7240 Parkway Drive, Suite 300, Hanover, Maryland 21076. INFORMS is not responsible for errors introduced in the adaption of the original article.

beliefs (b_i) about consequences of performing the behavior multiplied by the evaluation (e_i) of those consequences" (p. 984). Subjective norm (SN) is determined by the user's normative beliefs (nb_i) which are the perceived expectations of specific individuals and groups, and the user's motivation to accept these expectations (mc_i).[1]

TECHNOLOGY ACCEPTANCE MODEL

TAM evolved from the TRA with the goal "to provide an explanation of the determinates of computer acceptance that is general, capable of explaining user behavior across a broad range of end-user computing technologies and user populations, while at the same time being both parsimonious and theoretically justified" (Davis et al., 1989, p. 985). TAM, however, does not contain the subjective norm element of TRA. Davis states that, "It is difficult to disentangle direct effects of SN on BI from indirect effects via A" (p. 986). Like TRA, TAM postulates that actual technology usage is determined by behavioral intent (BI). The model is shown in Figure 2.

The perceived usefulness (PU) is based on the observation that "people tend to use or not use the application to the extent they believe it will help them perform their job better" (Davis, 1989, p. 320). PU directly influences the attitude toward use of the system and indirectly influences behavioral intention to use. Even if an application is perceived as useful, it will only be used if it is perceived as easy to use, that is, benefits of usage outweigh the effort of using the system. PEOU influences attitude toward use of the system. These two determinants, PU and PEOU, directly influence the user's attitude toward using the new information technology, which in turn leads to the user's behavioral intention to use. PEOU influences perceived usefulness (PU). PU also has a direct impact on behavioral intention (BI). Behavioral intention to use leads to actual system use.

The two key variables in TAM are perceived usefulness and perceived ease of use. Perceived usefulness (PU) is defined from the prospective user's point of view. Will the application improve his or her job performance in the organization? Perceived ease of use (PEOU) is a variable that describes the perception of the user that the system will be easy to use. In the model, PU directly

Figure 2. Technology acceptance model

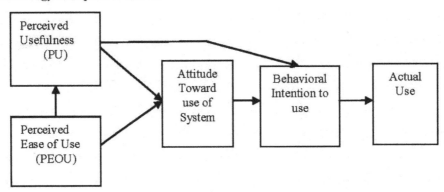

Adapted with permission from Davis, F.D., Bagozzi, R.P., Warshaw, P.R., (1989). User Acceptance of Computer Technology: A Comparison of Two Theoretical Models. Management Science 35(8) 982--1003. Copyright (1989), the Institute for Operations Research and the Management Sciences, 7240 Parkway Drive, Suite 300, Hanover, Maryland 21076. INFORMS is not responsible for errors introduced in the adaption of the original article.

influences both attitude toward using attitude (A) and behavioral intention to use (BI). PEOU influences both PU and A. Davis (1989) develops and validates a scale for these variables.

Theoretical support for the use of these variables can be found in self-efficacy theory, the cost-benefit paradigm and adoption of innovation literature. Bandura (1982) defines self-efficacy as "judgments of how well one can execute courses of action required to deal with prospective situations" (p. 122). Davis (1989) describes self-efficacy as similar to perceived ease of use. Self-efficacy beliefs are theorized as determinants of behavior. This theory does not offer a general measure sought by Davis, but is situationally-specific. Davis et al., (1989) differentiate TAM from TRA with respect to one's salient beliefs. In TRA these beliefs are "elicited anew for each new context" (p. 988). TAM determines these variables for a population resulting in a more generalized view of systems and users. External effects on the model can be separately traced to each of these variables

The cost-benefit paradigm from the behavioral decision literature is also relevant to perceived usefulness and perceived ease of use. The paradigm describes decision-making strategies "in terms of a cognitive trade-off between the effort required to employ the strategy and the quality (accuracy) of the resulting decision" (Davis, 1989, p. 321).

Adoption of innovation literature finds that compatibility, relative advantage and complexity of the innovation are key factors. Rogers and Shoemaker's (1971) definition of complexity is similar to PEOU: "the degree to which an innovation is perceived as relatively difficult to understand and use" (p. 154). Davis (1989) points out the convergence of these and other theories to support the concepts of PU and PEOU.

Gefen and Straub (2000) describe PEOU and PU in terms of intrinsic and extrinsic characteristics. PEOU relates to the "*intrinsic* characteristics of IT, such as the ease of use, ease of learning, flexibility and clarity of its interface" (p. 1). PU results from a user's assessment of IT's "*extrinsic*, i.e., task-oriented, outcomes: how IT helps users achieve task-related objectives, such as task efficiency and effectiveness" (p. 1-2). Using MBA students Gefen and Straub demonstrated that PEOU affects intrinsic tasks, i.e., using a Web site for inquiry, but not extrinsic tasks, i.e., using a Web site to make a purchase.

Impact of TAM

The IS community has found the TAM to be a powerful model. Lee et al. (2003) found that the first two TAM articles, Davis (1989) and Davis et al. (1989), received 698 journal citations through 2003. A Google Scholar search on the term, "Technology Acceptance Model," in June 2008 produced 7,330 hits.

Lee et al. (2003) examined a number of variables related to TAM research, including types of information systems examined, external variables tested, number of publications by year by journal, most prolific researchers, characteristics of research subjects, relationship between major TAM variables, major limitations, and research methodology.

Types of Information Systems Examined

TAM researchers have applied the model to a wide variety of information systems. In the area of communications systems, TAM has been applied in 25 articles to e-mail, v-mail, fax and dial-up systems. General purpose systems were examined in 34 articles, including Windows, PC, internet, workstations, computer resource centers and groupware. Office systems such as word processors, spread sheets, presentation software, database programs and groupware were the sub-

ject of 33 articles. Specialized business systems such as computerized models, case tools, hospital systems, decision support systems, expert support systems and MRP were examined in 30 articles (Lee et al., 2003).

External Variables Tested

Researchers have proposed and examined many external TAM variables. Lee et al. (2003) assembled the following list of external variables in TAM research which is summarized below. See Lee et al. (2003) for definitions, origin and referred articles.

TAM Publications

Lee et al. (2003) found 101 studies involving TAM were published in what they defined as major journals and conferences between 1989 and 2003. *MIS Quarterly* led the group with 19 TAM articles; *Information & Management*, 12; *Information Systems Research* and *Journal of Management Information Systems*, 10 each. The peak of interest in TAM was the period from 1999 to 2001 when 41 articles appeared in a three year period. Subsequent to 2003 the pace of articles appears to have declined. MISQ ran two articles in 2004, one in 2005 and none since. However, a Journal of the Association for Information Systems special issue in April 2007 included eight

Table 1. TAM variables

Accessibility	Anxiety	Attitude
Compatibility	Complexity	Result demonstrability
Perceived enjoyment	End user support	Experience
Facilitating conditions	Image	Job relevance
Managerial Support	Playfulness	Personal Innovativeness
Relative Advantage	Self-Efficacy	Social Influence, Subjective Norms and Social Pressure
Social Presence	Trialability	Usability
Visibility	Voluntariness	

articles assessing the current status of technology acceptance research.

Characteristics of TAM Research Subjects

Research subjects used in the technology acceptance literature cited by Lee et al. (2004) were composed of students (44 studies) and knowledge workers (60 studies). For example, Davis et al. (1989) used 107 students and word processing technology. Taylor and Todd (1995) used 786 students dealing with the use of a university computing center.

Major Limitations of the TAM Model

Lee et al. (2003) found the major limitation of the TAM studies included in their research was self-reported usage. The studies did not measure actual usage, but relied on the research subject to indicate usage. A better approach would have been to employ an independent measure actual use. Another limitation was the use of a single IS system in each research project limiting the generalizability of the conclusions. Student samples were heavily employed raising the questions of how representative this group was to the real working environment. Other limitations discuss in these papers include single subjects (i.e., one organization, one department, one student group, etc.), one-time cross sectional studies, measurement problems (for example, low validity of new measures), single task, low variance scores, and mandatory situations.

Most Published TAM Authors

Lee et al. (2003) found that 11 authors published 4 or more papers accounting for 50 of the 101 articles found in major IS journals. The most prolific TAM authors through 2003 include Viswanath Venkatesh (12), Fred D. Davis (9), Detmar W. Straub (8), Elena Karahanna (6), David Gefen (6), and Patrick Y.K. Chau (6).

Recent TAM Research

Although the appearance of TAM articles in major journal appears to be on a downturn, TAM research continues to appear in the literature. More recent research extends the TAM to ERP implementation (Amoako-Gyampah and Salam, 2004; Bradley and Lee, 2007; Hwang, 2005), cross cultural implementation studies (McCoy, Galleta and King, 2006; McCoy, S., Everard, A., and Jones, B.M., 2005), e-commerce participation among older consumers (McCloskey, 2006), and biometric devices (James et al., 2006). Pijpers and van Montfort (2006) investigate senior executives' acceptance of technology using the TAM and found that gender has no effect on perceived usefulness or perceived ease of use, but also found that gender affects positively actual usage frequency.

Following the introduction of the TAM in 1989 and validation period ranging from 1992 through 1996 and a period of model extension, a model elaboration period ensued "to develop the next generation TAM" model and "to resolve the limitations raised by previous studies" (Lee et al., 2003, p. 757).

TAM MODEL ELABORATIONS

TAM2

Venkatesh and Davis (2000) developed and tested an extension to TAM which "explains the perceived usefulness and usage intentions in terms of social influence and cognitive instrumental processes" (p. 186). In the ten years following the publication of the TAM, empirical studies found that the model explained about 40% of the variance in usage intentions and behavior. In an effort to expand the explanatory impact of the model, TAM2 was developed. Figure 3 shows this model. TAM2 extended the TAM model to include seven additional variables. Five of these new variables directly influence perceived usefulness (PU). TAM2 considers both social influences (subjective norm, voluntariness and image) and cognitive instrumental processes (job relevance, output quality, result demonstrability and perceived ease of use. The expanded model accounts for 60% of the variance in the drivers of user intentions. While less parsimonious than the original TAM, the model is more powerful.

Unified Theory of Acceptance and Use of Technology (UTAUT)

Venkatesh, Morris, Davis and Davis (2003) examine eight competing models of technology acceptance and formulate a unified model that integrates elements of these models. The eight models are: TRA, TAM, motivational model, TPA, TAM/TPB combined, a model of PC uti-

lization, innovation diffusion theory and social cognitive theory. UTAUT includes four variables, performance expectancy, effort expectancy, social influence and facilitating conditions, and up to four moderators of key behaviors, gender, age, experience and voluntariness. In an experiment, the eight models varied in explanatory power from 17 to 53 percent of the variance in user intentions to use information technology. UTAUT was tested on the same data and explained 69 percent of the variance.

Both TAM2 and UTAUT have stronger explanatory power than the original TAM model, but the additional number of variables raises the question of parsimony. What is the balance between the added explanatory power and the complexity introduced by the additional variables?

Figure 3. TAM2-extension of the technology acceptance model

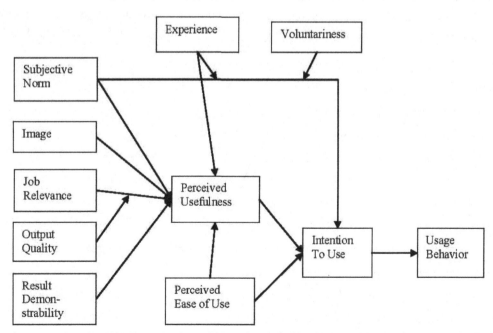

Adapted with permission from Venkatesh, V. and Davis, F.D. (2000). A Theoretical Extension of the Technology Acceptance Model: Four Longitudinal Field Studies, Management Science, 46(2), 186-204. Copyright (1989), the Institute for Operations Research and the Management Sciences, 7240 Parkway Drive, Suite 300, Hanover, Maryland 21076. INFORMS is not responsible for errors introduced in the adaption of the original article.

OTHER THEORIES OF USER ACCEPTANCE

Theory of Planned Behavior (TPB)

The Theory of Planned Behavior (Ajzen 1985, 1991) shown in figure 4 is an extension of the Theory of Reasoned Action (Fishbein and Ajzen, 1975). TPB addresses conditions where users do not have complete behavioral control. It introduces the variable perceived behavioral control (PBC). Behavioral intention (BI) is seen as a weighted function of attitude (A), subjective norm (SN) and perceived behavioral control. Behavior (B), that is actual use, is the weighted function of intention and PBC[2]. Relationships among beliefs are determined using an expectancy-value model.

Decomposed Theory of Planned Behavior (DTPB)

The decomposed theory of planned behavior expands the TPB theory by deconstructing the elements of attitude into three variables: perceived usefulness, ease of use, compatibility (See Fig-

ure 5). The subjective norm is comprised of two variables: peer influence and superior's influence. Perceived behavioral control is influenced by three variables: self-efficacy, resource facilitating conditions and technology facilitating conditions.

Comparison of TAM, TPB and Decomposed TPB

Taylor and Todd (1995) compared the TAM, TPB and Decomposed TPD using student data from a computer resource center with structural equation modeling. In all three models behavioral intention is the primary factor in the desired behavior, the use of technology. It was anticipated that the addition of the subjective norm and perceived behavioral control variables would give the TPB greater explanatory power, contrary to the finding of Davis (et al., 1989). Their results found that TAM explained 52% of the variance in BI while the pure TPB explained 57% of the variance and decomposed TPB explained 60%. The improvement from the social norm and perceived behavior control may be due to the setting of the Taylor and Todd (1995) research. While in this

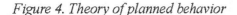

Figure 4. Theory of planned behavior

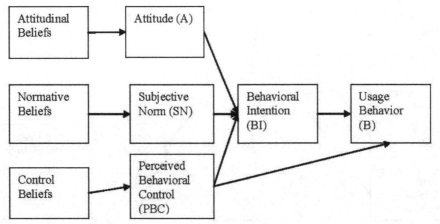

Adapted with permission from Taylor, S., and Todd, P.A. (1995). Understanding Information Technology Usage: A test of Competing Models. Information Systems Research, 6(2), 144-176. Copyright (1995), the Institute for Operations Research and the Management Sciences, 7240 Parkway Drive, Suite 300, Hanover, Maryland 21076. INFORMS is not responsible for errors introduced in the adaption of the original article.

Figure 3. Decomposed theory of planned behavior

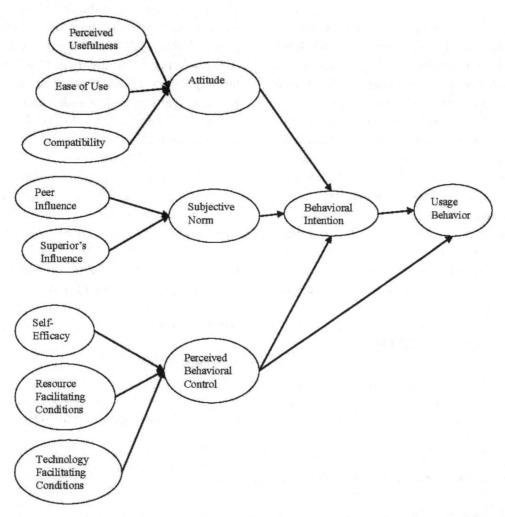

Adapted with permission from Taylor, S., and Todd, P.A. (1995). Understanding Information Technology Usage: A test of Competing Models. Information Systems Research, 6(2), 144-176. Copyright (1995), the Institute for Operations Research and the Management Sciences, 7240 Parkway Drive, Suite 300, Hanover, Maryland 21076. INFORMS is not responsible for errors introduced in the adaption of the original article.

particular research setting the decomposed TPB proved superior in explanatory power, TAM may still be a more parsimonious model. Mulaik et al (1989) recommend as preferable a model that has good predicting power while using the fewest variables. The TAM explains over 50% of variance of BI with two variables. The decomposed TPB requires seven variables to explain 60%.

Innovation Diffusion Theory

Another line of research on the acceptance of new technology is examined by Rogers (1983, 2003). This perspective views such factors as individual user characteristics, information sources and communication channels and innovation characteristics as determinants of IT usage and adoption. Rogers (2003) views the diffusion of innovation as "a social process in which subjectively perceived information about a new idea is communicated person to person" (p. *xx*). Communication channels distribute knowledge of the innovation, contribute to the prospective user forming attitudes about the innovation leading to a decision to accept or reject the innovation.

Knowledge occurs when a potential systems user is exposed to the existence and functionality of the technology. Persuasion is when a user forms an attitude toward the new system. The attitude can be either favorable or unfavorable. The decision step is when a user decided to accept or reject the IS event. Implementation is putting to technology into use. The confirmation step occurs after the technology is in use. The user seeks confirmation and reinforcement of the decision he or she has made.

Task-Technology Fit Model

Dishaw, Strong and Bandy (2002) propose a combination of the TAM and the Task-Technology

Fit (TTF) Model (Goodhue & Thompson, 1995). The combined model is shown in Figure 7. The Task-Technology Fit Model is the "matching of the capabilities of the technology to the demands of the task, that is, the ability of IT to support a task" (p. 1022). The TTF model which is composed of four constructs: Task Characteristics, Technology Characteristics, Task-Technology Fit which leads to either performance or utilization. Task characteristics and

Technology characteristics are related to task-technology fit. Task-technology fit is related to both performance impacts and utilization. Utilization also is directly related to performance impacts. Dishaw et al. (2002) posit that "IT will be used if, and only if, the functions available to the user support (Fit) the activities of the user" (p. 1022). IT without any significant advantage will not be used.

Coping Model

Beaudry and Pinsonneault (2005) explore a coping mode of user acceptance to understand user

Figure 6 - Technology diffusion process

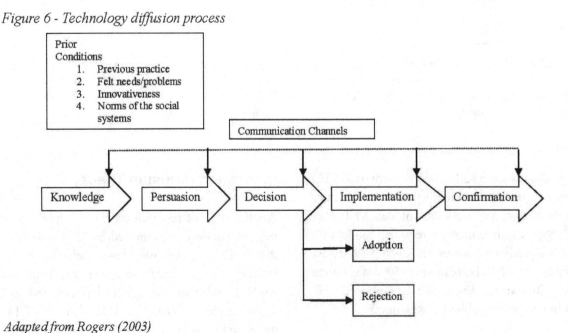

Adapted from Rogers (2003)

responses to information technology changes. User adaptation is defined as *"the cognitive and behavioral efforts exerted by users to manage specific consequences"* (p. 496). The model posits that users apply a variety of coping strategies based on their "assessment of the expected consequences of an IT event (p. 493)" and an assessment of their control over the situation. Users ask (p. 495), "What it at stake for me in this situation?" Four major coping strategies are identified: "benefits maximizing, benefits satisficing, disturbance handling and self-preservation" (p. 493). Applying these coping mechanisms lead to one of three different individual level outcomes: 1) restoring emotional stability, 2) minimizing the perceived threats of the technology, and 3) improving user efficiency and effectiveness.

Beaudry and Pinsonneault (2005) tested the model at two North American banks. The case

studies supported their propositions. Although they observe that the benefits satisficing and self preservation strategies may "first appear suboptimal" (p. 517), the benefits of raising this level of acceptance may be outweighed by the costs. The model provides guidance to managers to understand how users evaluate IT events, which may help them guide users to adaptation strategies.

Elaboration Likelihood Model

Bhattacherjee and Sanford (2006) examine how "external influences shape information technology acceptance among potential users, how such influence effects vary across a user population, and whether these effects are persistent over time" (p. 805). They are critical of prior research, including TAM, TRA, TPB, DTBP and UTAUT, which do not address external influence on user

Figure 7. TAM and TTF model

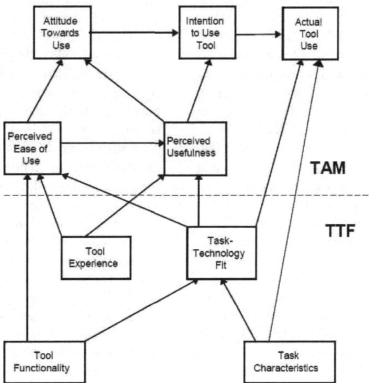

From -Dishaw et al (2002)

Figure 8. Coping model of user adaption

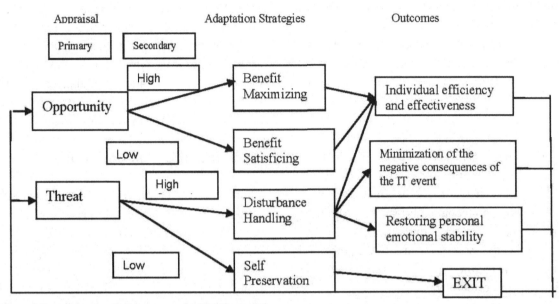

Adapted from Beaudry & Pinsonneault (2005), p. 499

acceptance beyond social norm. Drawing on social psychology literature, Bhattacherjee and Sanford examine dual-process theories "that suggest that external information is the primary driver of attitude change and consequent behavior change" (p. 808). Within these dual process theories, they select the elaboration-likelihood model (ELM) as:"(1) it relates directly to influence processes and their impacts on human perception and behavior and (2) it also explains why a given influence process may lead to differential outcomes across different users in a given user setting" (p. 808). Attitude change can follow either a central or peripheral route, which result in different amounts of information processing by individuals. The central route requires critical thinking about "potential benefits of system acceptance, comparison of alternative systems, availability and quality of system support, and/or costs of and returns from system acceptance" (p. 808). The peripheral route requires less effort, relying on endorsements from prior users and experts

and the likeability of experts. ELM supports the extension of the TAM and other models to include messages of external agents as primary external variables. This model is shown figure 9.

Wixon and Todd (2005) propose an integrated model to reconcile two major streams of research on IS success, technology acceptance literature and user satisfaction literature. This model is similar to the TRA, TAM and UTAUT, but separates the concepts into object-based beliefs, object-based attitudes, behavioral beliefs and behavioral attitudes. Variables of completeness, accuracy, format and currency impact information quality which in turn influence information satisfaction. Information satisfaction influences usefulness which influences both attitude and intention. Reliability, flexibility, integration, accessibility, and timeliness influence systems quality which in turn influence systems satisfaction, ease of use, attitude and intention. Systems satisfaction influences information satisfaction. Ease of use influences usefulness.

FUTURE OF THE TECHNOLOGY ACCEPTANCE MODEL

A special issue of the Journal of the Association for Information Systems in April 2007 focused on *"Quo Vadis* TAM-Issues and Reflections on Technology Acceptance Research."

While acknowledging the significant contribution of the TAM, Benbasat and Barki (2007, p. 212) state:

the intense focus on TAM has led to several dysfunctional outcomes: 1) the diversion of researchers' attention away from important phenomena. First, TAM-based research has paid scant attention to the antecedents of its belief constructs: most importantly, IT artifact design and evaluation. Second, TAM-based research has provided a very limited investigation of the full range of the important consequences of IT adoption, 2) TAM-based research has led to the creation of an illusion of progress in knowledge accumulation, 3) The inability of TAM as a theory to provide a systematic means of expanding and adapting its core model has limited its usefulness in the constantly evolving IT adoption context, 4) The efforts to "patch-up" TAM in evolving IT contexts have not been based on solid and commonly accepted foundations, resulting in a state of theoretical confusion and chaos.

Schwarz and Chin (2007) call for an expansion and broadening of technology acceptance research to include a "wider constellation of behavioral usage and its psychological counterparts" (p.230).

Straub and Burton-Jones (2007) challenge the notion that TAM has been "established 'almost to the point of certainty'" (p. 224). They state that the system usage construct has been understudied. Exploration of usage may open up possibilities to enrich the model. Straub and Burton-Jones (2007) point to a research flaw in TAM studies where respondents self-rated three key variables: PU and PEOU (IV's) and usage level. This methodology results in a common methods bias. They suggest TAM researchers undertake "strenuous effort" to gather usage data independent of the source of PU and PEOU. Straub and Burton-Jones (2007) also challenge the parsimony of TAM. However, in this challenge they do not directly challenge the TAM but move forward in the TAM development stream to the UTAUT claiming that its 10

Figure 9. Elaboration likelihood model

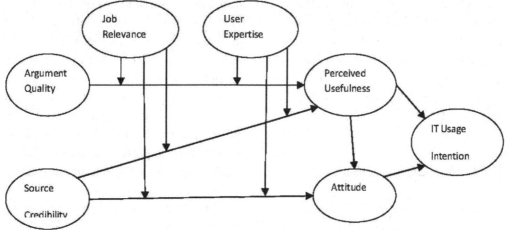

Adapted from Bhattacherjee & Sanford (2006)

Figure 10. Wixon and Todd model

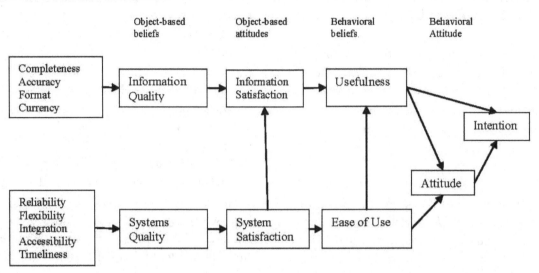

Adapted with permission from Wixom, B.H. and Todd, P. A. (2005). A Theoretical Integration of User Satisfaction and Technology Acceptance. Information Systems Research, 16(1), 85-102. Copyright (2005), the Institute for Operations Research and the Management Sciences, 7240 Parkway Drive, Suite 300, Hanover, Maryland 21076. INFORMS is not responsible for errors introduced in the adaption of the original article.

constructs are not parsimonious. They observe that Lee et al. (2003) enumerate "21 external variables that affect the four central variables in the model" (p. 227).

Silva (2007) examines TAM applying three criteria on what is scientific and what is a theory. He uses the perspective of three science philosophers: Karl Popper, Thomas Kuhn and Imre Lakatos. Popper's principle of falsifiability suggests that "a good theory should 'prohibit' the occurrence of specific phenomena" (p. 264). Using Kuhn's lens, Silva finds TAM to be a typical example of normal science as it provides an easily transferable and verifiable problem solving apparatus.

SUMMARY AND CONCLUSION

Despite the large body of research on this topic, "user acceptance of information technology remains a complex, elusive, yet extremely im-

portant phenomenon" (Venkatesh and Davis, 2000). Organizations invest billions of dollars in new technology each year. If employees are not willing to accept this new technology, the return on this investment will be reduced.

This chapter has surveyed the literature on the development and extension of the technology acceptance model and explored other user acceptance model. The TAM model is widely used and has been validated many times. Researchers have extended the model to encompass the impact of dozens of variables.

A central principle of the TAM model and its extensions is the measurement of behavioral intention to use and user attitude. Yet, most studies rely on self reported measures of this variable which may be unreliable. Straub and Burton-Jones (2007) point out that reliance on self-reported key variables, like attitude and intention, open models based on these variables to significant questions. Researchers need to find more reliable method to measure these variables. Limitations on data gathering need to be addressed.

Other models examined in the chapter do not rely on behavioral intention or attitude. The innovation diffusion model is described as a social process which relys on communication and persuasion. The task technology fit relies on how well the technology fits the uses' tasks. The coping model examines the reaction to new technology as an opportunity or threat.

A promising avenue for future development may be combining the TAM models with other approaches to user acceptance such as the combination of TAM with the task-technology fit model (Dishaw et al., 2002) and the combination of TAM research and user satisfaction research demonstrated in the integrated model developed by Wixom and Todd (2005). Combining the extensive work in user acceptance and user satisfaction with the smaller body of knowledge on user resistance may prove fruitful.

The profession needs to learn more about user acceptance, user resistance and user satisfaction. Research should better inform systems designers on the attributes which will make their products easier for users to accept. Opportunities abound for scholars to take new directions in technology acceptance research.

REFERENCES

Ajzen, I., & Fishbein, M. (1980). *Understanding attitudes and predicting social behavior.* Englewood Cliffs, NJ: Prentice Hall.

Ajzen. I. (1985). From intentions to action: A theory of planned behavior. In J. Kuhl & J. Bechmann (Eds.), *Action control: From cognition to behavior* (pp. 11-39). New York: Springer Verlag.

Ajzen, I. (1991). The theory of planned behavior. *Organizational Behavior and Human Decision Processes, 50*, 179-211.

Amoako Gyampah, K., & Salam, A. F. (2003). An extension of the technology acceptance model in an ERP implementation environment. *Information & Management, 41*, 731-745.

Bandura, A. (1982). Self-efficacy mechanism in human agency. *American Psychologist, 37*(2), 122-147.

Beaudry, A., & Pinsonneault, A. (2005). Understanding user responses to information technology: A coping model of user adaptation. *MIS Quarterly, 29*(3), 493-524.

Benbasat, I., & Barki, H. (2007). Quo vadis, TAM? *Journal of the Association for Information Systems, 8*(4), 211-218.

Bhattacherjee, A., & Sanford, C. (2006). Influence processes for information technology acceptance: An elaboration likelihood model. *MIS Quarterly, 30*(4), 805-825.

Borders, A., Earleywine, M., & Huey, S. (2004). Predicting problem behaviors with multiple expectancies: Expanding expectancy value theory, *Adolescence, 39*, 539-551.

Bradley, J., & Lee, C. C. (2007). ERP training and user satisfaction: A case study. *International Journal of Enterprise Information Systems, Special topic issue on Use of ERP in Education, 3*(4), 33-50.

Davis, F. D. (1989). Perceived usefulness, perceived ease of use, and user acceptance of information technology. *MIS Quarterly, 13*(3), 319-340.

Davis, F. D., Bagozzi, R. P., & Warshaw, P. R. (1989). User acceptance of computer technology: A comparison of two theoretical models. *Management Science, 35*(8), 982-1003.

Dishaw, M. T., Strong, D. M., & Brandy, D. B. (2002). Extending the task-technology fit model of self-efficacy constructs. In R. Ramsower & J. Windso (Eds.), *Proceedings of the 8th Americas Conference on Information Systems*, Dallas, TX (pp. 1021-1027).

Eveland, J. D. (1986). Diffusion, technology transfer, and implementation. *Knowledge: Creation, Diffusion, Utilization, 8*(2), 302-322.

Fishbein, M., & Ajzen, I. (1975). *Belief, attitude, intention and behavior: An introduction to theory and research.* Reading, MA: Addison-Wesley.

Gefen, D., & Straub, D. (2000). The relative importance of perceived ease of use in IS adoption: A study of e-commerce adoption. *Journal of the Association for Information Systems, 1*(8), 1-28.

Geiger, M. A., & Cooper, E. A. (1996). Cross-cultural comparisons using expectancy theory to assess student motivation. *Issues in Accounting Education, 11*(1), 113-129.

Goodhue, D. L., & Thompson, R. L. (1995). Task-technology fit and individual performance. *MIS Quarterly, 19*(2), 213-236.

Hwang, Y. (2005). Investigating enterprise systems adoption: Uncertainty avoidance, intrinsic motivation and the technology acceptance model. *European Journal of Information Systems, 14*, 150-161.

James, T., Pirim, T., Boswell, K., Reithel, B., & Barkhi, R. (2006). Determining the intention to use biometric devices: An application and extension of the technology acceptance model. *Journal of Organizational and End User Computing, 18*(3), 1-24.

Johnson, E. J., & Payne, J. W. (1985). Effort and accuracy in choice. *Management Science, 31*(4), 395-414.

Lee, Y., Kozar, K., & Larsen, K. R. T. (2003). The technology acceptance model: Past, present and future. *Communications of the Association for Information Systems, 12*(50), 752-780.

Mulaik, S., James, L. R., Van Alstine, J., Bennett, N., Lind, S., & Stillwell, C. D. (1989). Evaluation of goodness of fit indices in structural equation models, *Psychological Bulletin, 105*(3), 430-445.

Mazis, M., Ahtola, O., & Kippel, R. (1975). A comparison of four multi attribute models in the prediction of consumer attitudes. *Journal of Consumer Research, 2*, 38-53.

McCloskey, D. W. (2006). The importance of ease of use, usefulness, and trust to online consumers: An examination of the technology acceptance model with older consumers. *Journal of Organizational and End User Computing, 18*(3), 47-65.

McCoy, S., Galleta, D. F., & King, W. R. (2007). Applying TAM across cultures: The need for caution. *European Journal of Information Systems (2007), 16*, 81-90.

McCoy, S., Everard, A., & Jones, B. M. (2005). An examination of the technology acceptance model in Uruguay and the US: A focus on culture. *Journal of Global Information Technology Management, 8*(2), 27-45.

Payne, J. W. (1982). Contingent decision behavior. *Psychological Bulletin, 92*(2), 382-402.

Pijpers, G. G. M., & van Montfort, K. (2006). An investigation of factors that influence senior executives to accept innovations in information technology. *International Journal of Management, 23*(1), 11-23

Rogers, E. M. (2003). *Diffusion of innovations* (5th ed.). New York: Free Press.

Rogers, E. M. (1983). *Diffusion of innovations.* New York: Free Press.

Silva, L. (2007). Post-positivist review of technology acceptance model. *Journal of the Association for Information Systems, 8*(4), 255-266.

Straub, D. W., & Burton-Jones, A. (2007). Veni, vedi, vici: Breaking the TAM logjam. *Journal of the Association for Information Systems, 8*(4), 223-229.

Taylor, S., & Todd, P. A. (1995). Understanding information technology usage: A test of competing models. *Information Systems Research, 6*(2), 144-176.

Venkatesh, V., & Davis, F. D. (2000). A theoretical extension of the technology acceptance model: Four longitudinal field studies. *Management Science, 46*(2), 186-204.

Venkatesh, V., Morris, M. G., Davis, G. B., & Davis. F. D., (2003). User acceptance of information technology: Toward a unified view. *MIS Quarterly, 27*(3), 425-478.

Venkatesh, V., Davis, F. D., & Morris, M. G. (2007). Dead or alive? The development, trajectory and future of technology adoption research. *Journal of the Association for Information Systems, 8*(4), 267-286.

Wixom, B. H., & Todd, P. A. (2005). A theoretical integration of user satisfaction and technology acceptance. *Information Systems Research, 16*(1), 85-102.

KEY TERMS AND DEFINITIONS

Coping Model: Adaptation strategies to significant information systems events consisting of benefits maximizing, benefits satisficing, disturbance handling, and self-preservation. Expected outcomes of these strategies are restoring emotional stability, minimizing the perceived threats of the technology and improving user effectiveness and efficiency (Beaudry and Pinsonneault, 2005).

Decomposed Theory of Planned Behavior: A variation of the theory of planned behavior which breaks down attitudinal, normative and control beliefs into a set of more measureable variables.

Innovation Diffusion Theory: A theory of adoption of new technology based on individual user characteristics, information sources and communications channels, and innovation characteristics (Rogers, 1983).

Perceived Ease of Use (PEOU): One of the two key variables in the technology acceptance model. Perceived ease of use will lead to attitude toward use, behavioral intention to use and actual use. PEOU also influences the second key variable, perceived usefulness.

Perceived Usefulness (PU): One of the two key variables in the technology acceptance model. PU directly influences both attitude toward systems use and behavioral intention to use the system. PU is influenced by perceived ease of use.

Task-Technology Fit Model (TTF): A model of user acceptance that relates actual use to tool functionality and task characteristics (Dishaw et al., 2002).

Technology Acceptance Model (TAM): TAM is a model of user acceptance of information systems technology based on the theory of reasoned action. Two variables perceived usefulness and perceived ease of use lead to attitude toward use, behavioral intention to use and use of the system.

Theory of Planned Behavior (TPB):. A theory which extends the theory of reasoned action to include users who do not have complete control over the use of an innovation. A variable of perceived behavioral control is added to the TRA.

Theory of Reasoned Action (TRA): A theory found in social psychology literature which explains the determinants of consciously intended behaviors (Fishbein and Ajzen, 1975; Ajzen and Fishbein, 1980).

User Acceptance: This term describes the willingness of a user of information systems technology to adopt and accept new IT initiatives.

ENDNOTES

[1]   Behavioral intention can be shown as $BI = A + SN$, attitude can be expressed as $A = \sum b_i e_i$, and subjective norm as $SN = \sum nb_i mc_i$.

[2]   Taylor and Todd (1995) describe this model as: $B = w_1 BI + w_2 PBC$ and $BI = w_3 A + w_4 SN + w_5 PBC$, where w is the weight of each factor.

Section IV
Management Theories

There are five chapters included within this section. The first chapter (Chapter XVI) provides a resource-based perspective on information technology, knowledge management, and firm performance. The second chapter in the section (Chapter XVII) analyses electronic marketplaces by using transaction cost theory. Chapter XVIII presents a conceptual framework in which social networking plays a mediating role in the relationship between IT usage and firm performance. The fourth chapter (Chapter XIX) introduces and illustrates the use of competing commitment theory. Finally, chapter XX presents an integrative theory of dynamic capabilities and institutional commitments.

Chapter XVI
A Resource–Based Perspective on Information Technology, Knowledge Management, and Firm Performance

Clyde W. Holsapple
University of Kentucky, USA

Jiming Wu
California State University–East Bay, USA

ABSTRACT

The resource-based view of the firm attributes superior firm performance to organizational resources that are valuable, rare, non-substitutable, and difficult to imitate. Aligned with this view, the authors contend that both information technology (IT) and knowledge management (KM) comprise critical organizational resources that contribute to superior firm performance. The authors also examine the relationship between IT and KM, and develop a new second-order variable – IT-KM competence – with IT capability and KM performance as its formative indicators. Thus, this chapter contributes not only by investigating the determinants of firm performance but also by broadening our understanding of the relationships among IT, KM, and firm performance.

INTRODUCTION

For the last two decades, the investigation of the return on investments in IT has become a key objective of many studies. In pursuing this objective, researchers have developed two main theoretical frameworks: one asserts that IT has a direct impact on firm performance (Bharadwaj, 2000), while the other proposes that the effect of IT on firm performance is mediated by business process (Tanriverdi, 2005). However, no matter which theoretical framework has been employed, some studies have failed to find a significant correlation between IT and firm performance. Because the return on IT investments seems to be contingent, scholars call for more research into why IT may not benefit business, how to make IT effective, and what are the key determinants of the success of IT (Dehning & Richardson, 2002).

Meanwhile, considerable research attention has been devoted to the importance of KM in the rapidly changing, competitive, and dynamic business environment (Holsapple & Wu, 2008). Modern organizations are turning to KM practices and applications to foster the creation, integration, and usage of knowledge assets that enable them to compete in an increasingly global economy. In light of this, researchers have attempted to provide empirical evidence of the strategic consequences that KM can bring to organizations (Grant, 1996). For example, based on the survey data collected from 177 firms, Chuang (2004) finds that greater KM capabilities are significantly associated with greater competitiveness and that social KM resource has a significant impact on competitive advantage. Similarly, in a survey-based investigation of the link between KM activities and competitiveness, Holsapple and Singh (2005) observe that the KM activities of interest can be performed in ways that improve organizational competitiveness, and can do so in each/all of four ways: enhanced productivity, agility, innovation, and reputation.

Although there exist studies on IT firm performance relationship and on KM-firm performance link, these studies have paid insufficient attention to the full map of relationships among IT, KM, and firm-level return, and have placed relatively less emphasis on the collaborative effect of IT and KM on firm performance (Wu, 2008). Given the inseparability of IT and KM, and the strategic importance of the two, a thorough investigation of both their joint and separate roles in firm performance is necessary. Such investigation would enrich not only the theoretical understanding of the mechanism for competitive advantage, but also the research models investigating determinants of superior firm performance. Thus, the work would be of value not only to practitioners striving to achieve and sustain business success, but also to researchers interested in identifying determinants of better firm performance.

This study contributes to such investigation. More specifically, the purpose of this chapter is to theorize a triangle of relationships among IT, KM, and firm performance, and to develop a theoretical model with testable hypotheses that improve our understanding of the effects of IT and KM on firm performance. The theoretical foundation of this paper is embedded in the resource-based view of the firm and prior work by Holsapple and his colleagues. The current study contributes to the literature in a number of ways. First, this study is among the first to recognize that KM may play an important role in the link between IT and firm performance. Thus, the study may provide a plausible explanation for why some previous research has failed to discover a significant relationship between IT and firm performance. Second, we examine the determinants of firm performance by introducing and employing a new perspective, which focuses on the collective impacts of IT and KM. Such a perspective may broaden our approach to identifying determinants of firm performance. Third, we present methods to measure relevant variables. Therefore, the current chapter is useful and effective in guiding future empirical research in this regard. Finally, this study also investigates the relationship between IT and KM, which has so far received relatively little research attention.

The remainder of the chapter is organized as follows. In the next two sections, we review the state of IT and KM. Then, we present the research model and hypotheses, followed by a section in which we discuss methods for measuring the variables. Finally, we provide a brief summary of the contributions provided by this research.

INFORMATION TECHNOLOGY

Information technology can be defined as covering a broad range of technologies involved in information processing and handling, such as computer hardware, software, telecommunications, and databases (Huff & Munro, 1985). Realizing that IT enables businesses to run efficiently and profitably, organizations around the world have made tremendous investments in it. As estimated by market research organizations, world IT spending in 2000 was about $2 trillion and will reach $3.3 trillion in 2008, with an average growth rate of over 7% in these eight years (WITSA, 2000; Gartner, 2007). It is also estimated that such a growth rate will be sustained for several years after 2008 (InformationWeek, 2007). In the U.S. economy, IT spending now accounts for nearly 40% of overall expenditure on capital equipment, making it the largest line item in American firms' budgets for capital investment (Cline & Guynes, 2001). Not surprisingly, IT spending has already accounted for approximately 4% of U.S. gross domestic product (GDP) (BusinessWeek, 2001).

IT has profoundly changed the way that business gets done in nearly every industry. Using IT, organizations radically redesign their business processes to streamline and simplify operations and remain competitive in a changing environment. With the help of computer-aided design and operational systems, organizations can greatly reduce overall cost and time of developing and manufacturing its products and of providing its services. Key customer-related IT, such as customer relationship management systems, allows organizations to capture and maintain detailed information about customer interactions, thus enabling them to provide quality customer service and to increase sales. As a specific category of IT serving middle-level managers, management information systems summarize and report on a company's basic operations using transaction-level data, and thus help with monitoring, controlling, and decision-making activities (Laudon & Laudon, 2006). Today in the U.S., more than 23 million managers and 113 million workers in the labor force rely on information systems to conduct day-to-day business and to achieve strategic business objectives (Laudon & Laudon, 2006).

Along with the rapid growth and development of IT, the role of IT in business has greatly expanded, ranging from simple back-office functions to enabler of business process reengineering and key driver of competitive advantage. Until the 1960s, IT had played a very simple role in business operation: transaction processing, record-keeping, accounting, and other data processing activities; by the late 1970s, the major role of IT began to shift toward providing managerial end users with ad hoc and interactive support of their decision-making processes; in the 1980s-1990s, IT was mainly employed to support end users to use their own computing resources for job requirements and to assist top executives in easily accessing critical information in their preferred formats; now the primary role of IT is to help develop fast, reliable, and secure Internet, on which e-commerce and Web-enabled enterprise are based (Laudon & Laudon, 2006). Figure 1 shows the expanding role of IT in business and organizational management. Because IT is an area of rapid change and growth, it is important and necessary for organizations and individuals to continually adapt and develop new skills and knowledge.

Figure 1. The expanding role of IT in business (O'Brien & Marakas, 2007)

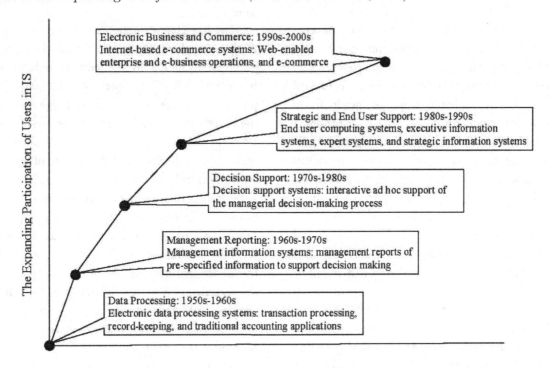

KNOWLEDGE MANAGEMENT

Knowledge refers to a fluid mix of framed experience, values, contextual information, and expert insight that offers a framework for interpreting, assimilating, and integrating new experiences and information (Davenport & Prusak, 1998). Knowledge is highly human-related. More specifically, it is originated from and applied in brains of human beings. From one perspective, knowledge is a product of human reflection and experience emphasizing understanding and sense making (why and how), while information can be considered as a message focusing on the awareness of something (who and what) (Bennet & Bennet, 2003). Others contend that modern computer technology can also make sense of situations, learn from its experiences, and derive/discover new knowledge – in addition to message handling (Holsapple 2005). In this vein, knowledge is something that is conveyed in representations (e.g., linguistic, symbolic, digital, mental,

behavioral, material patterns) that are usable to some processor (e.g., human mind) and can be categorized as being descriptive (characterizations of the state of some system – who, what, when, etc.), procedural (characterizations of how to do something), or reasoning (characterizations of logic or causality). In this view, information is one gradation of descriptive knowledge, but it can be operated on by other types of knowledge (i.e., procedures and logic).

Holsapple and Joshi (2004, p. 593) define knowledge management as "an entity's systematic and deliberate efforts to expand, cultivate, and apply available knowledge in ways that add value to the entity, in the sense of positive results in accomplishing its objectives or fulfilling its purpose." Thus, KM involves any activities of generating new knowledge through derivation or discovery, acquiring valuable knowledge from outside sources, selecting needed knowledge from internal sources, altering the state of knowledge resources, and embedding knowledge into organizational outputs (Holsapple & Joshi, 2004).

KM is becoming increasingly important and prevalent for many reasons. To succeed in today's dynamic global economy, organizations must reduce their cycle times in production, operate with minimum fixed assets and costs, shorten product development time, improve customer service and product quality, enhance employee productivity and performance, provide innovative products and services, modernize and reengineer business process, and increase agility and flexibility (Gupta et al., 2004). All these critical business activities require continued efforts to acquire, create, document, share, and apply knowledge by employees and teams at all organizational levels. Because of the importance of KM to success, organizations have invested heavily in it. According to *IDC*, global business spending on KM was rising from $2.7 billion in 2002 to $4.8 billion in 2007 (Babcock, 2004). The company also estimated that in the United States, KM spending reached $1.4 billion in 2001 and $2.9 billion in 2006, exhibiting an average annual growth rate of over 20% in these five years (Motsenigos & Young, 2002).

KM has also attracted tremendous attention from researchers. Figure 2 exhibits the trend of publications for KM as tracked by Google Scholar from 1995 to 2007. For each year, the number of publications referring to "knowledge management" is shown. Such publications were 513 in 1995, or about 10 per week, and exponentially increased to 12,600 in 2005, or about 243 per week. This indicates that two weeks' publications in 2005 are almost equal to whole year's publications in 1995 and that the average annual growth rate in these 10 years is astonishing –236%! To put this KM trend in perspective, we compare it with the traditional business discipline of operations management (OM), for which Google Scholar reports 1,190 publications in 1995, ramping up to 3,760 in 2005. Figure 2 also shows the trend of publications for OM.

One important research stream in this field focuses on the KM ontology that offers a com-

Figure 2. Publication trends for knowledge management and operations management

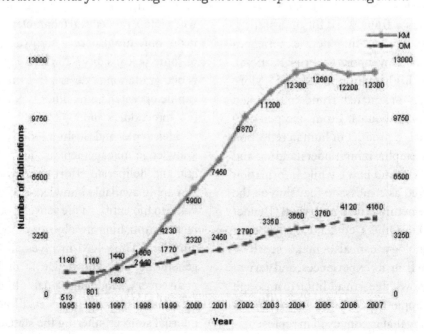

Source: Google Scholar, March 24, 2008

prehensive understanding of KM phenomena (Holsapple & Joshi, 2004). While specifying the conceptualization of the KM domain, the study recognizes three categories of KM influences: managerial, resource, and environmental. The study also identifies five major knowledge manipulation activities: acquisition, selection, generation, assimilation, and emission, as well as four major managerial activities that constituted the managerial influences: leadership, coordination, control, and measurement.

RESEARCH MODEL AND HYPOTHESES

Drawing on the resource-based view (RBV) of the firm and prior empirical findings, we introduce a conceptual model positing that IT and KM both play an important role in predicting firm performance, and that KM performance is highly related to IT capability. As depicted in Figure 3, the model includes a new variable – IT-KM Competence, which is also conceptualized as a key antecedent of firm performance. Below we describe and discuss the new variable and the conceptual links in the research model.

IT Capability and KM Performance

In the last decade, more and more researchers have adopted the notion that IT plays a critical role in shaping firms' efforts for KM. For example, in a study examining the link between KM and computer-based technology, Holsapple (2005) argues that IT is of great importance not only for enabling or facilitating the knowledge flows among knowledge processors (human or computer-based) but also for assisting in the measurement, control, coordination, and leadership of knowledge and the knowledge processors. Thus, he asserts that modern KM is inseparable from a consideration of IT. Similarly, in a study investigating the relationships among IT, KM, and firm performance, Tanriverdi (2005) argues that an IT-based coordination mechanism can increase the reach and richness of a firm's knowledge resources, and enable business units of the firm to learn about knowledge sharing opportunities with each other. Thus, he posits that IT relatedness, which is defined as "the use of common IT infrastructures and common IT management processes across business units," (p. 317) is positively associated with KM capability.

Not surprisingly, previous research also suggests that IT plays an important role in supporting

Figure 3. A conceptual model of IT, KM, and firm performance

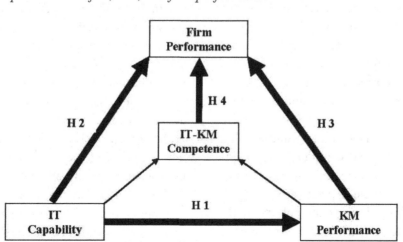

and enhancing aforementioned KM activities: acquisition, selection, generation, assimilation, and emission (Holsapple & Singh, 2003; Jones, 2004). In performing knowledge acquisition activities, an IT-based network system can assist in identifying, evaluating, analyzing, and qualifying external knowledge that needs to be acquired to support the firm's growth (Holsapple & Singh, 2003). An IT-based knowledge selection system can help a firm be more efficient and effective in the process of knowledge selection. For example, Buckman Laboratories uses K'Netix, an IT-based knowledge selection system, to locate, collect, select, and package appropriate knowledge received from 11 resources and transfer it to the person requesting the knowledge (Holsapple & Singh, 2003).

In the activity of knowledge generation, a decision support system may draw on databases and text-bases, plus banks of solvers and/or rule sets to derive knowledge in the sense of expectations, explanations, evaluations, solutions, recommendations, and so forth (Bonczek et al., 1981; Holsapple & Whinston, 1996). In addition, such systems can also help in other knowledge generation activities such as data mining, text mining, and sense-making (Jones, 2004). In the activities of knowledge assimilation, an IT-based organizational memory system can help in modeling, representing, and archiving knowledge, while an IT-based less structured repository (e.g., discussion database and lessons-learned system) can be used to store insights and observations (Jones, 2004). Finally, in the process of knowledge emission, IT-based systems can support users in sharing and transferring knowledge quickly and cost-efficiently. For instance, to enhance knowledge sharing among employees in geographically dispersed locations, Honda has established a full-service international communications network system (called Pentaccord) and a system to manage selected databases (sales, finance, and part ordering) on a global basis (Holsapple & Singh, 2003). In short, the current literature suggests that

KM performance is of particular relevance to IT. Thus, we hypothesize:

H1: *IT capability is positively related to KM performance.*

Here, IT capability refers to an organization's ability to identify IT that meets business needs, to deploy IT to improve business process in a cost-effective manner, and to provide long-term maintenance and support for IT-based systems (Karimi et al., 2007). By KM performance, this chapter means the degree to which KM activities harness organizational resources to achieve the goals or purposes of KM initiatives (Wu, 2008). Through linking IT capability to KM performance, the first hypothesis highlights that KM and IT are inseparable, and can play a communal and collective role in an organization.

The Resource-Based View of the Firm

Rooted in management strategy literature, the RBV of the firm is developed to understand why firms are able to gain and sustain a competitive advantage (Newbert, 2007). RBV states that a firm's performance is mainly determined by a unique set of firm resources that are valuable, rare, non-substitutable, and difficult to imitate. RBV indicates that such resources are often rent-yielding and likely to survive competitive imitation when protected by isolating mechanisms such as resource connectedness, historical uniqueness, and causal ambiguity (Barney, 1991). In short, RBV addresses firm performance differences by using resource asymmetry. That is, the resources needed to achieve strategic business objectives are heterogeneously distributed across firms, and thus are posited to account for the differences in firm performance (Grant, 1991).

Based on the RBV, a resource can be defined as a rare and inimitable firm-specific asset that adds value to firms' operations by enabling them to implement strategies that improve efficiency and effectiveness (Wade & Hulland, 2004). Advocates of RBV tend to characterize resources broadly – including financial capital, physical assets, knowledge, brand image, IT, organizational processes, and so forth (Bharadwaj, 2000). Thus, a resource is an observable but not necessarily tangible asset that can be independently managed, appraised, and even valued (Karmi et al., 2007). RBV suggests that a resource held by a majority of competing firms (i.e., a non-rare resource) may not explain firm performance differences (Newbert, 2007). It also suggests that if a resource held by just a few competing firms is not costly to imitate, the resource is likely to be quickly obtained by competitors, and thus may not explain differences in firm performance, either (Ray et al., 2005).

IT Capability and Firm Performance

As an important firm resource, IT capability plays a key role in firm performance. IT capability enables organizations to design innovative products and services, and to reduce the overall cost and time of developing the products and providing the services. For instance, IT giant Apple developed an innovative product – iPod, which has dominated digital music player sales in the United States and brings the company new sales records and great business success. Continuing to innovate, the company recently released iPhone, an Internet-enabled multimedia mobile phone. Computer-aided design (CAD) systems assist Toyota's designers to create and modify their product specifications much faster than before, and thus achieve cost efficiency. CAD allows a designer to see his or her ideas as they take shape on a monitor display, in addition to clay models. Taking the advantage of CAD, Toyota designs quality into its products.

IT capability is the primary driver of business process reengineering, which integrates a strategy of promoting business innovation with a strategy of making major improvements to business process so that a company can gain and sustain competitiveness (O'Brien & Marakas, 2007). The computation capability, information processing speed, and connectivity of computers and Internet technologies can considerably enhance the efficiency of a business process, as well as communications and collaboration among the people responsible for its management, implementation, and maintenance (Wade & Hulland, 2004). For example, many Fortune 500 companies count on enterprise resource planning (ERP) systems to reengineer, automate, and integrate their marketing, manufacturing, sales, distribution, finance, and human resource business processes (O'Brien & Marakas, 2007).

IT capability used for production and operations can improve performance of companies that must plan, monitor, and control inventories, facilities, and the flow of products and services. Many manufacturing and production systems can efficiently deal with the operation and maintenance of production facilities; the establishment of production goals; the acquisition, storage, and distribution of production materials; and the scheduling of equipment, facilities, materials, and labor required to fulfill an order (Laudon & Laudon, 2006). Thus, computer-integrated (or –aided) manufacturing enables organizations to reduce the cost and time of producing goods by simplifying, automating, and integrating all production and support processes (O'Brien & Marakas, 2007). Moreover, such manufacturing helps companies achieve highest product quality by bridging the gap between the conceptual design and the manufacturing of finished goods.

IT capability is the key to electronic commerce, which refers to the use of digital technology and the Internet to execute major business processes of developing, marketing, selling, delivering, servicing, and paying for products and services (Laudon & Laudon, 2006; O'Brien & Marakas, 2007). Electronic commerce is transforming firms' relationships with customers, employees, suppliers, distributors, retailers, and partners into digital relationships using networks and the Internet (Laudon & Laudon, 2006; Wheeler, 2002). More important, it can dramatically improve firm performance by allowing companies to achieve six major business values: (1) generate new revenue from online sales, (2) reduce costs via online transaction, (3) attract new customers through online marketing and advertising, (4) increase customer loyalty and retention by providing Web-based customer service and support, (5) develop new Web-based markets and distribution channels, and (6) develop and sell digital goods such as music track, video stream, online game, and flight ticket (O'Brien & Marakas, 2007; Wheeler, 2002).

IT capability can be a key enabler of superior firm performance by improving communication and collaboration within an organization. IT, especially network technologies, provides basic infrastructure and platform for communication, coordination, and collaboration among the members of business teams and workgroups. In other words, such IT capability enables employees and/ or managers at all levels to work together more easily and effectively by helping them share information with each other, coordinate their individual efforts and use of resources, and work together cooperatively on joint projects and assignments (O'Brien & Marakas, 2007). For example, knowledge experts, technicians, computer specialists, and R&D engineers may form a virtual team for a KM system development project. The communication, coordination, and collaboration among the team members may rely heavily on IT-based applications such as email, instant messaging, newsgroup, videoconferencing, discussion forum, and a Web-based database for convenient and immediate access to work-in-progress information. Such improved communication and collaboration can significantly increase the quality of the team work.

Adopting the resource-based view of the firm, information systems researchers suggest that IT capability has an impact on firm performance. For example, Mata and colleagues (1995) point out that managerial IT skills are scarce and firm specific, and thus likely to serve as sources of sustained competitive advantage. Focusing on the differential effects of various IT resources on customer service performance, Ray and colleagues (2005) argue that such factors as IT are valuable resources because they enable firms to increase the efficiency or effectiveness of business processes compared to what would be the case if these resources were not exploited. Similarly, Bharadwaj (2000) contends that organizations successful in developing superior IT capability will enjoy superior financial performance by boosting revenues and/or reducing costs. In line with the resource-based view of the firm and the literature, we therefore hypothesize:

H2: *IT capability is positively related to firm performance.*

KM Performance and Firm Performance

As mentioned earlier, the RBV indicates that knowledge is a unique company resource (Grant, 1996). Therefore, KM can also be viewed as such resource important to firm performance because it allows the firm to better leverage its knowledge. KM facilitates organizational learning, which keeps organizations in tune with trends and developments in their business, and thus helps them perform better. Here, organizational learning refers to individual learning, team learning (i.e., learning in small or large groups), or entire organization-level learning (Bennet & Bennet, 2003). All these levels of learning are necessary for an organization eager to possess the requisite knowledge to improve performance. From a KM perspective, organizational learning is critical and should be nurtured and made an integral part of KM strategy. Organizational learning also reflects an organization's capacity to acquire or generate the knowledge necessary to survive and compete in its environment (Bennet & Bennet, 2003).

KM can change an employee's attitude toward learning and its impact on an organization's competitive position (Wu, 2008). Such change is likely to stimulate organizational learning because individuals and teams become to believe that learning can help their company to handle change, uncertainty, and complexity in the ever-changing business environment. KM helps define and specify what should be learned, when it should be learned, and who should be learning it. KM can also create a culture of peer collaboration and open communication, both leading to a setting conducive to organizational learning. Moreover, KM activities of knowledge acquisition and generation promote organizational learning by motivating individuals to obtain new knowledge from external sources or from existing knowledge, and to make it suitable for future use.

KM can improve firm performance not only by facilitating organizational learning but also by encouraging knowledge sharing. A core principle of KM is to make knowledge sharing easier and timely, and to encourage employees and managers to work together in ways that will incorporate knowledge shared among them. Consequently, one important goal of KM is to boost productivity and efficiency by building a set of methods and tools to foster appropriate flows of knowledge. For instance, to align with the strategy of possessing a platform for quick and easy knowledge sharing on global scale, Xerox developed Eureka, an intranet based communication system, in 1996 (Barth, 2000). The system is linked with a corporate database that helps service technicians share repair tips. There are more than 36,000 tips in the system which can be accessed by about 19,000 Xerox technicians via their laptop computers (Barth, 2000). The increasing importance of KM also motivates managers to develop a reward and personnel evaluation structure favoring knowledge sharing activities. Reward and punishment standards help define acceptable behavior. By incorporating desired KM behavior into annual performance evaluation, an organization may improve its own performance by encouraging such critical activities as knowledge sharing and foregoing organizational learning.

KM can strengthen an organization's competitive position by increasing its agility (Holsapple & Singh, 2003). In general, agility refers to an organization's ability to detect changes, opportunities, and threats in its business environment and to provide speedy and focused responses to customers and other stakeholders by reconfiguring resources and processes and/or by developing strategic partnerships and alliances (Mathiyalakan et al., 2005). Thus, agility derives from both the physical ability to act and the intellectual ability to understand appropriate things to act upon (Dove, 2003). KM is recognized as a key success factor for agility because it enables an organization to apply effectively its knowledge of market opportunity, production process, business practice, cutting-edge technology, quality service, management skills, the extent of a threat, and so forth. In a continuously changing and unpredictable business environment, it is crucial for an organization to manage knowledge in a way to quickly absorb new knowledge, fully assimilate it, and effectively exploit it (Holsapple & Wu, 2008). Consequently, an organization with sufficient competencies in KM will be agile enough to deliver leading edge and achieve a better competitive position.

KM can also improve an organization's performance by fostering its innovation. As a subject of research and practice, innovation refers to the ability of creating valuable and useful new product, new services, new technology, or production processes (Liao & Chuang, 2006). Innovation has been recognized as a primary value creator for organizations, in both times of generating revenues and in times of cutting costs. Innovation consists of two important dimensions: magnitude, which reflects the extent or breadth of innovation, and speed, which shows an organization's quickness to adopt an innovation, relative to its competitors

(Liao & Chuang, 2006). KM plays a critical role in the ability of an organization to be innovative because KM initiatives and activities often serve as a key platform for creating new and inventive ideas that will benefit and add value to the organization. More specifically, KM activities such as knowledge generation and sharing can broaden understanding of relevant issues and concepts, and push thinking beyond the constraints of presumption, narrow rationality, and traditional method. Therefore, KM can be an important organizational practice that spurs innovation.

In summary, RBV suggests that a firm can outperform its competitors by taking advantage of its KM. As a unique company resource, KM plays a fundamental role in firm performance because it facilitates organizational learning, encourages knowledge sharing, increases agility, and fosters innovation. Although it is complex to acquire and difficult to leverage KM resources, firms that succeed in doing so are likely to experience learning effects whereby they improve their abilities for creating value. This directly leads to the following hypothesis:

H3: *KM performance is positively related to firm performance.*

IT-KM Competence and Firm Performance

IT-KM competence is defined as a firm's IT and KM ability and resources that are peculiar to achieving and sustaining business success. The new variable is conceptualized as a composite construct with IT capability and KM performance as its two formative indicators. Such conceptualization is in line with prior research and RBV, which suggest that KM and IT are inseparable from each other and both are unique and important firm resources. Thus, the current literature supports the idea to represent IT capability and KM performance by a single composite construct that impacts firm performance. We contend that

such conceptualization can push our thinking beyond current theoretical boundaries and offer a new perspective for investigating determinants of firm performance. Thus, we advance the following hypothesis:

H4: *IT-KM competence is positively related to firm performance.*

MEASURING THE VARIABLES

Firm performance can be measured in a variety of ways, including financial performance, market performance, and business process performance. Financial performance is usually evaluated by means of standard profit and cost ratios, which can be calculated by using accounting data obtained from Standard & Poor's COMPUSTAT. A common way to assess market performance is to use Tobin's q, which can also be calculated by using COMPUSTAT data. However, one factor researchers need to be aware of is that for private firms and not-for-profit organizations, accounting data are not readily available in COMPUSTAT. Perceived business process performance can be evaluated by using a survey questionnaire. Often, researchers can find well-developed survey instruments in the literature and adapt them for their specific needs. In addition, it is very important to address data validity and reliability issues when using survey data to test research hypotheses.

Past research suggests that IT capability can be measured by IT spending/use, survey questionnaire, or results of studies conducted by public independent organizations. IT spending/use data are often available in annual corporate financial reports. *InformationWeek* and *ComputerWorld* are the two publicly available sources of data on corporate IT spending and other measures of IT use. Survey instruments for some constructs related to IT capability have already been developed and applied to practice by prior IS research such as the aforementioned study by Tanriverdi (2005).

Results of independent organizations' studies are also a very valuable source for IT capability data. For example, the IT leader study by *Information-Week* may provide the data useful for measuring an organization's capability to leverage its IT resources on a continuous basis. Past research suggests that KM performance can be measured by survey questionnaire or results of studies conducted by public independent organizations. Tanriverdi (2005) has developed a survey instrument to assess the extent to which an organization creates, transfers, integrates, and leverages related product, customer, and managerial knowledge resources. KM performance data may also be obtained by collecting and analyzing results of relevant studies conducted by independent KM research organizations such as KMWorld (http://www.kmworld.com), and *Teleos* and its *KNOW Network* (http://www.knowledgebusiness.com).

CONCLUSION

Over the past decade, one of the most striking developments in business has been the rapid proliferation of KM. Organizations have launched KM initiatives to consolidate and reconcile knowledge assets that enable them to compete in the dynamic and changing global business environment. Therefore, in parallel to the focus on the relationship between IT and firm performance, the role of KM in firm profitability has also received considerable research attention. Drawing on the RBV of the firm, plus findings from prior research, this chapter argues that both IT capability and KM performance are primary antecedents of firm performance and that IT capability has a significant impact on KM performance. The current chapter also introduces a new composite variable—IT-KM competence—with IT capability and KM performance as its formative indicators. As a result, this chapter broadens our understanding of the relationships among IT, KM, and firm performance by (1) viewing both IT and KM as unique and important firm resources, (2) suggesting that KM can play a mediating role between IT and firm performance, and (3) proposing that IT and KM may be represented by a single composite variable, which might play a more important and effective role in predicting firm performance.

NOTE

Authors are listed alphabetically and have contributed equally to this chapter.

REFERENCES

Babcock, P. (2004). Shedding light on knowledge management. *HR Magazine, 49*(5), 46-50.

Barney, J. (1991). Firm resources and sustained competitive advantage. *Journal of Management, 17*(1), 99-120.

Barth, S. (2000). *Eureka! Xerox has found it.* Retrieved from http://kazman.shidler.hawaii.edu/eurekacase.html

Bennet, A., & Bennet, D. (2003). The partnership between organizational learning and knowledge management. In C. W. Holsapple (Ed.), *Handbook on knowledge management 1: Knowledge matters* (pp. 439-455). Berlin/Heidelberg, Germany: Springer-Verlag.

Bharadwaj, A. S. (2000). A resource-based perspective on information technology capability and firm performance: An empirical investigation. *MIS Quarterly, 24*(1), 169-196.

Bonczek, R., Holsapple, C., & Whinston, A. (1981). *Foundations of decision support systems.* New York: Academic Press.

BusinessWeek. (2001). *How bad will it get?* Retrieved from http://www.businessweek.com/magazine/content/ 01_11/b3723017.htm

Chuang, S. (2004). A resource-based perspective on knowledge management capability and competitive advantage: An empirical investigation. *Expert Systems with Applications, 27*(3), 459-465.

Cline, M. K., & Guynes, C. S. (2001). A study of the impact of information technology investment on firm performance. *Journal of Computer Information Systems, 41*(3), 15-19.

Davenport, T. H., & Prusak, L. (1998). *Working knowledge.* Cambridge, MA: Harvard Business School Press.

Dehning, B., & Richardson, V. J. (2002). Returns on investments in information technology: A research synthesis. *Journal of Information Systems, 16*(1), 7-30.

Dove, R. (2003). Knowledge management and agility: Relationships and roles. In C. W. Holsapple (Ed.), *Handbook on knowledge management 2: Knowledge directions* (pp. 309-330). Berlin/Heidelberg, Germany: Springer-Verlag.

Gartner. (2007). *Gartner says worldwide IT spending to surpass $3 trillion in 2007.* Retrieved from http://www.gartner.com/it/page.jsp?id=529409

Grant, R. M. (1991). The resource-based theory of competitive advantage: Implications for strategy formulation. *California Management Review, 33*(3), 114-135.

Grant, R. M. (1996). Prospering in dynamically-competitive environments: Organizational capability as knowledge integration. *Organization Science, 7*(4), 375-387.

Gupta, J. N. D., Sharma, S. K., & Hsu, J. (2004). An overview of knowledge management. In J. N. D. Gupta, S. K. Sharma (Eds.), *Creating knowledge based organizations* (pp. 1-29). Hershey, PA: Idea Group Inc.

Holsapple, C. W. (2005). The inseparability of modern knowledge management and computer-based technology. *Journal of Knowledge Management, 9*(1), 42-52.

Holsapple, C. W., & Joshi, K. D. (2004). A formal knowledge management ontology: Conduct, activities, resources, and influences. *Journal of the American Society for Information Science and Technology, 55*(7), 593-612.

Holsapple, C. W., & Singh, M. (2003). The knowledge chain model: Activities for competitiveness. In C. W. Holsapple (Ed.), *Handbook on knowledge management 2: Knowledge directions* (pp. 215-251). Berlin/Heidelberg, Germany: Springer-Verlag.

Holsapple, C. W., & Singh, M. (2005). Performance implications of the knowledge chain. *International Journal of Knowledge Management, 1*(4), 1-22.

Holsapple, C., & Whinston, A. (1996). *Decision support systems: A knowledge-based approach.* Minneapolis, MN: West Publishing.

Holsapple, C. W., & Wu, J. (2008). In search of a missing link. *Knowledge Management Research & Practice, 6*(1), 31-40.

Huff, S. L., & Munro, M. C. (1985). Information technology assessment and adoption: A field study. *MIS Quarterly, 9*(4), 327-340.

InformationWeek. (2007). *Global IT spending to reach $1.48 trillion in 2010, IDC says.* Retrieved from http://www.informationweek.com/news/management/outsourcing/showArticle.jhtml;jsessionid=JB4IADNZACBP2QSNDLRSKH0CJUNN2JVN?articleID=196802764&_requestid=885619

Jones, K. G. (2004). *An investigation of activities related to knowledge management and their impacts on competitiveness.* Unpublished doctoral dissertation, University of Kentucky.

Karimi, J. K., Somers, T. M., & Bhattacherjee, A. (2007). The role of information systems resources in ERP capability building and business process outcomes. *Journal of Management Information Systems, 24*(2), 221-260.

Laudon, K. C., & Laudon, J. P. (2006). *Management information systems: Managing the digital firm*. NJ: Prentice Hall.

Liao, C., & Chuang, S. (2006). Exploring the role of knowledge management for enhancing firm's innovation and performance. In *Proceedings of the 39ᵗʰ Hawaii International Conference on System Sciences*.

Mata, F. J., Fuerst, W. L., & Barney, J. B. (1995). Information technology and sustained competitive advantage: A resource-based analysis. *MIS Quarterly, 19*(4), 487-505.

Mathiyalakan, S., Ashrafi, N., Zhang, W., Waage, F., Kuilboer, J., & Heimann, D. (2005, May 15-18). Defining business agility: An exploratory study. In *Proceedings of the 16ᵗʰ Information Resource Management Association International Conference*, San Diego, CA.

Motsenigos, A., & Young, J. (2002). *KM in the U.S. government sector. KMWorld.* Retrieved from http://www.kmworld.com/Articles/Editorial/Feature/KM-in-the-U.S.-government-sector-9397.aspx

Newbert, S. L. (2007). Empirical research on the resource-based view of the firm: An assessment and suggestions for future research. *Strategic Management Journal, 28*(2), 121-146.

O'Brien, J. A., & Marakas, G. (2007). *Introduction to Information Systems* (13ᵗʰ ed.). McGraw-Hill/Irwin.

Ray, G., Muhanna, W. A., & Barney, J. B. (2005). Information technology and the performance of the customer service process: A resource-based analysis. *MIS Quarterly, 29*(4), 625-652.

Tanriverdi, H. (2005). Information technology relatedness, knowledge management capability, and performance of multibusiness firms. *MIS Quarterly, 29*(2), 311-334.

Wade, M., & Hulland, J. (2004). Review: The resource-based view and information systems research: Review, extension, and suggestions for future research. *MIS Quarterly, 28*(1), 107-142.

Wheeler, B. C. (2002). BEBIC: A dynamic capabilities theory for assessing net-enablement. *Information Systems Research, 13*(2), 125-146.

WITSA. (2000). *Digital planet 2000*. Arlington, VA: World Information and Technology Services Alliance.

Wu, J. (2008). *Exploring the link between knowledge management performance and firm performance*. Unpublished doctoral dissertation, University of Kentucky.

KEY TERMS AND DEFINITIONS

Agility: Refers to an organization's ability to detect changes, opportunities, and threats in its business environment and to provide speedy and focused responses to customers and other stakeholders by reconfiguring resources and processes and/or by developing strategic partnerships and alliances (Mathiyalakan et al., 2005).

Information Technology: Can be defined as a broad range of technologies involved in information processing and handling, such as computer hardware, software, telecommunications, and databases (Huff & Munro, 1985).

IT Capability: Refers to an organization's ability to identify IT meeting business needs, to deploy IT to improve business process in a cost-effective manner, and to provide long-term maintenance and support for IT-based systems (Karimi et al., 2007).

IT Relatedness: Is defined as "the use of common IT infrastructures and common IT management processes across business units" (Tanriverdi 2005, p. 317).

IT-KM Competence: Is defined as a firm's IT and KM ability and resources that are peculiar to achieving and sustaining business success.

Innovation: Refers to the ability of creating valuable and useful new product, new services, new technology, or production process (Liao & Chuang, 2006).

Knowledge: Refers to a fluid mix of framed experience, values, contextual information, and expert insight that offers a framework for interpreting, assimilating, and integrating new experiences and information (Davenport & Prusak, 1998).

Knowledge Management: Is "an entity's systematic and deliberate efforts to expand, cultivate, and apply available knowledge in ways that add value to the entity, in the sense of positive results in accomplishing its objectives or fulfilling its purpose" (Holsapple and Joshi 2004, p. 593).

KM Performance: Is the degree to which KM activities harness organizational resources to achieve the goals or purposes of KM initiatives.

A Resource: Can be defined as a rare and inimitable firm-specific asset that adds value to firms' operations by enabling them to implement strategies that improve efficiency and effectiveness (Karmi et al., 2007).

Chapter XVII
Reconfiguring Interaction Through the E–Marketplace:
A Transaction Cost Theory Based Approach

Cecilia Rossignoli
University of Verona, Italy

Lapo Mola
University of Verona, Italy

Antonio Cordella
LSE-London School of Economics and Political Science, UK

ABSTRACT

The aim of this chapter is to analyse electronic marketplaces from an organisational point of view. These marketplaces are considered as a particular form of electronic network and are analysed from the perspective of transaction cost theory. This chapter considers the three classical effects identified by Malone et al. (communication effect, electronic integration effect, electronic mediation effect), and also evaluates a fourth effect on the grounds of empirical evidence; this effect is defined by Wigand as "the strategic electronic network effect." Adopting the case study approach, the chapter describes how ICT affects marketplace organisation, and reshapes relationships among the actors involved in this particular type of electronic network.

INTRODUCTION

This chapter analyses electronic marketplaces as a particular kind of electronic network and studies their characteristics as an organisational form emerging as consequence of the diffusion of ICT (Information and Communication Technology).

We consider e-marketplaces as an ICT based organizational form that mixes market coordination mechanisms (prices) and network coordination mechanisms (trust and common values).

This chapter focusses on three principal aspects. First, how ICTs favour the establishment of more competitive markets; second, how the power exercised by the individual actors in the network chain is redefined within the e-marketplace; finally, what the impact is on organizational boundaries.

Building upon Kallinikos's idea of "Networks as an alternative form of organisations" (Kallinikos, 2003), this study highlights how the network supporting electronic marketplaces is a structure connected by links of a different nature, as opposed to the links of an institutional and social nature which tie together formal organisations and markets.

In fact, these electronic networks can be described as strategic configurations able to support and foster specific economic opportunities in determined contexts of time and space that are contingent to specific decisions. These strategic configurations cannot be considered stable in the long term. The strategic network configurations are aimed at developing e-marketplaces, and are often the result of temporary configurations meant to defend particular economic interests. The strategic nature of these configurations are designed not to last in the medium term, since their survival depends largely on the strategic interests contingency of the agents involved.

These new strategic network organisational configurations are designed to provide a smoother market mechanisms functioning, but they are also modifying the underpinning logic that commonly drives the use of human resources and skills: the driving economic force for the efficient use of resources is substituted by the communication needs configuration designed to satisfy the agents. This change in allocative mechanism logic should be studied to better understand the interests that lead the different actors to participate in the network of exchanges.

The logic that leads economic actors to be part of a network of exchanges is a new perspective, and needs to be better analysed to understand the dynamics that characterise e-marketplaces.

The attention traditionally focused on hierarchical relationships and standard contracts evaluation must be refocussed on those aspects that are more closely related to information production and distribution and on the relative strategic implications.

Refocussing, it becomes clear that different and alternative forms of transaction management can be identified while studying electronic networks and e-marketplaces. These forms emerge from the interaction modalities between the network participants often associated with innovative work organisation and new strategic configurations.

Internet use represents a fundamental element in this reconfiguration of the interactions among agents in the economic system. The internet provides the premise to cross institutional and geographical boundaries, and thus facilitates new forms of collaboration and partnership. This fact requires ICT platforms to be developed to support inter-operational systems based on principles of "electronic mutability". The platforms then become the central element of the new organisational forms based on networks of interaction.

The paper investigates whether the electronic network at the base of electronic marketplaces represents a new organisational form, or whether it is simply a new form of transaction management that tends to modify or replace intra-organisational and inter-organisational relations, which, in turn, are characterised by social relationships that were previously governed by other institutional models. How do the relationships between the participants change? Is it a temporary structure with weak connections or is it a stable and long term configuration?

Transaction cost theory is the reference theory used to interpret this phenomenon (Williamson, 1975; 1981; 1991); it is tangled with the idea of networking as an expression of an emerging organisational phenomenon and a fundamental form of competition in the new global economy (Ernst, 1994; Ciborra, 1993; Cordella 2001).

BACKGROUND

Electronic Networks: Looking for a Theoretical Approach

Despite the existing knowledge on the nature, functions, and rules that regulate markets, there is not yet a dominant theory on the role of electronic networks and how the underpinning strategic configurations are affecting the traditional organisation forms of hierarchy and market.

E-marketplaces have often been explained in literature through Transaction Cost Theory (TCT) (Coase, 1937; Williamson, 1975; 1981).

TCT was first developed by Williamson to explain the inconsistency between economic theories and real business practices. In his paper The Nature of the Firm, Coase investigated the issue of company boundaries. Coase's contribution was then expanded by several authors and, with special reference to Information Technology (IT), was re-examined by Picot in 1991.

In his work, Coase points out how hierarchy represents an alternative to the market's invisible hand in governing exchanges, and that it is related to the need for organizational efficiency.

In literature TCT has been adopeted to analyze the efficient bounderies of buying organizations (Bakos, Kemerer 1992). The TCT approach has been applied in the field of IS to study the consequences of inter organizational systems usage on

firms governance structure (Bakos 1997; Dalton, Brynjolfsson 1997; Choudhury et al. 1998; Ciborra 1993; Gurbaxani and Wang, 1991)

When market marginal use costs are excessively high, the visible management hand (Chandler, 1977) becomes more efficient in transaction coordination. When the costs for using the market exceed the organization use costs, it is more advantageous to change the governance method. The point is that hierarchy economizes on information processing cost, which allows for mitigating uncertainty during the various transaction phases. Coase suggested that, on the one hand, enterprises and market are alternative and complementary governance methods for transactions. On the other hand, the methods used to process information affect the comparative efficiency of organizational forms (Ciborra, 1993).

Following the transactional approach, organizational design is therefore connected with choosing the most efficient form of transactions governance (Grandori, 1984). Market and hierarchy represent two opposite ends of the same continuum, inside which different configurations of quasi-market and quasi-organization can be found. From an organizational design standpoint, the problem lies in the identification of an efficient boundary between interdependent organizations (management of inter-organizational processes) or, within the same organization, between different organizational units (management of intra-organizational processes). The objective is to minimize coordination costs. The choice of the most efficient form of transactions governance therefore is connected with the form that contains both production and transaction costs. Hence, the make (i.e., procure internally) or buy (i.e., procure externally) dilemma.

As a consequence, the decisions on which business activities can be conveniently carried out internally and which should instead be outsourced become extremely meaningful from a theoretical standpoint. In fact, the issue at hand is the definition of the balance governing the transactions within the context of internal hierarchical structures and, at the opposite end of the spectrum, the market structure.

Based on this perspective, the purpose of an organization is to mediate the economic transactions either between its members or with other organizations (Ulrich and Barney, 1984).

Despite the efforts spent attempting to provide a comprehensive explanation of the dualism between markets and hierarchies, the traditional approach to the study of transaction costs does not appear to be sufficient. Insufficient, because it does not highlight, and thus study or evaluate the strategic factors which influence the information exchange processes that characterise those organizational forms chosen by the economic actors in order to manage transactions rather than economic relationships. It is therefore necessary to widen the investigative scope by focusing attention on the relational mechanisms that lead to the proliferation of strategic networks. But is there a true strategic network theory? Kallinikos (Kallinikos, 2003) maintains that there is not.

Strategic network theory originates from Ouchi's work (Ouchi, 1980), which distinguished hierarchical organisational structures into two types: bureaucracies and clans. This distinction is based on the consideration that different uncertainty degrees of exchange and different congruency levels between the objectives pursued by individual persons and organisations require alternative organisational forms to be efficiently managed. The concept of a clan was mainly applied to study intra-company relations, and was conceived as one of the possible organisational structures designed to reduce transaction costs under specific circumstances. Similarly, the same rationale has been followed to study inter-organisational relations, and hence to frame the concept of the networks. According to Thorelli (Thorelli, 1986), networks are "two or more companies that, thanks to the intensity of their interaction, make up a sub-system of one or more markets". Jarillo (Jarillo, 1988), however, defines

long-term links between different organisations as strategic networks. In fact, companies can establish networks of relationships to achieve a competitive advantage over their competitors. Strategic networks are different from vertical integration, because the participating companies are relatively independent.

Strategic network theory enriches transaction cost theory in explaining the emergence of long term relations between various companies. It emphasises the lowering of transaction costs associated to the network's internal coordination effect and those that must be faced when closing a transaction between the network and any external agents. When goal congruency is high, there is a high compatibility of objectives. The collaboration between several companies in a network relationship optimises various activities with a lower total cost than vertical integration. From this point of view, e-marketplaces can also be analysed as strategic networks.

Strategic network theory substantially shifts the analytical focus to the elements that govern the strategic relationship integration, and away from the traditional effects discussed by Malone et al (1987), that is, ICT in terms of communication speed among economic agents.

It is necessary to bear in mind how Thorelli and Jarillo faced the question of strategic networks in an historical-environmental context; the internet did not yet favour the development of new types of electronically mediated relations between companies.

Malone et al (Malone, Yates, Benjamin, 1987) identified the three "famous" ICT effects on transaction costs through examining the ability of organisations to coordinate economic activities:

1. Communication effect: the possibility of transmitting information increasingly more quickly favours a reduction in transaction costs.
2. Electronic integration effect: ICT makes electronic connections between suppliers and buyers closer and easier.

3. Electronic mediation effect: buyers and sellers can compare offers much more easily on the electronic market.

Wigand (Wigand, 1996) adds another effect, called the strategic electronic network effect: ICT allows for the designing and strategically planned formation of links between companies who cooperate to achieve strategic objectives, with the final aim of obtaining competitive advantages (Wigand, 1997). This latter aspect is often underestimated, but becomes fundamental to explain the strategic implications of network relations, not only those involving relations within the network itself, but also those outside the network. This topic will be discussed further when analysing the case of TileSquare.

In, reference to Cohendet and Llerena's studies (Cohendet, Llerena, 1989), Castells underlines how organisational change, which led to the phenomenon of company networks, occurred independently from technological progress; rather, it was a necessary answer to survive and face an increasingly complex environmental context.

When operational feasibility became apparent, the new technologies facilitated or even enhanced the tendency towards networked organisational forms (Boyett, Conn, 1991).

Strategic alliances, sub-supply agreements, and decentralised decisional processes managed by large companies with the support of computer /network based systems are all part of the phenomenon of networking, which has developed progressively since the 1980s. Castells maintains that it was organisational innovation that, to some degree, induced the technological path (Castells, 2000).

By means of a series of empirical analyses, Bar and Borrus (Bar, Borrus, 1993) show how information technology has favoured the establishment of flexible processes of management, production, and distribution, both at an inter-company level and in intra-company relations. Since the late 1990s, the internet has favoured and accelerated the company network phenomenon. In his research, Ernst demonstrates how networking, with the subsequent organisational and technological changes, is only another "fundamental form of competition in the new global economy" (Ernst, 1994).

Participating in a network also means forming an entry barrier for those on the outside as a result of the "strategic electronic network effect" (Wigand, 1996). Castells (2000) raises this theme in terms of network access, a phenomenon that can also be found in the analysis of the case shown below. The purpose of the network is to defend the members from unfair competition and to give them more favourable strategic positions compared to those who are not members of the network. The questions that arise are numerous and do not only concern production costs. The real and fundamental problem is: How high is this barrier to entry? And: What happens if the unfair competitors also implement a much more efficient network? And: What if some participants of the old network also become part of a competing network? The fundamental problem changes and becomes: Is it possible to defend rent seeking positions through the network? The answer is undoubtedly negative. But: Is it possible to create new rent seeking opportunities through the network? Is it only a question of time? How do participant roles and their strategic positions change? What are the implications for the protagonists who are either inside or outside of the network? As can be seen, many questions arise, and this study cannot answer all of them. Here we focus attention on the new challenges and opportunities for the future based on using the new transaction management forms in a more systematic and organised manner, and all of this is strictly connected to the use of ICT.

In any case, the concept of network seems to be the efficient solution to overcome the institutional and strategic restrictions of other organisational forms, such as markets and hierarchies. The network, if studied as an alternative to transaction management, is a form of management where the four previously mentioned effects (communication, brokerage, integration and networking) play new roles and call for a redefinition of relations between the actors involved in the organisational network.

The first marketplaces were open electronic platforms enabling transactions and interactions between several companies (Holzmuller, Schlichter, 2002). The primary purpose of first-generation e-marketplaces was the creation of a more competitive market and friction-free commerce (Bakos, 1997; 1998). They were therefore characterized by large numbers of participants and basic services

With time, for the purpose of creating a more sustainable business model, some e-marketplaces re-oriented their processes to include the management of the entire transaction, from the on-line definition and development of orders to logistics management (Philipps, Meeker, 2000). The technological drive towards increasing the volume of transaction pushed the marketplaces to develop new processes and tools. However, the development of these portals was crippled by the pricy nature of these services, so that in some instances the number of participants was too low to guarantee the survival of the platform. The gist of the problem is that both the business model and the service model required a high number of members to reach critical mass (MacDuffie, Helper, 2003) and this was difficult to obtain because of the pricey services.

Christiaanse and Markus (2003) call collaboration mediators those second generation marketplaces that managed to provide advanced services of process integration. They "act more as purchasing process facilitators, enabling interorganizational systems integration and providing specialized supply chain collaboration capabilities".

The case study analyzed in this paper can be considered a second generation e-marketplace; it provide a good framework for study in detail how, and to what effect, the organisational net-

works, and particularly the e-marketplaces, are closely correlated to the technological variables that sustain the activities concerned.

THE CASE STUDY

The research project required analysing a case study considered significant for the following reasons:

1. The case study is based on a company founded in Italy, but which immediately found international relevance.
2. The electronic marketplace has played a role in the industry since 2001 (more than 7 years). In this same year, the Tilesquare marketplace changed its role in the industry and took several initiatives despite a turbulent context.
3. The number of members in this digital market is particularly high.
4. The significant ICT role in the modification of the "function rules" and the balance of power of the productive sector participants.

The investigation required qualitative data collection, mainly based on interviews of strategic and operational managers, system designers, managers and users of information systems in the marketplaces concerned.

The case study research method was chosen because it is useful for the examination of a phenomenon in its natural settings (Benbasat, 1984). The table below shows the major study phases flow. Case study research can also be an ideal vehicle for developing a deeper understanding of implicit and explicit business processes, and of the roles of people and systems in organisations (Campbell, 1975; Dukes, 1965; Hamel et al., 1993; Lee, 1989; Stake, 1995).

The following case study was qualitatively researched using semi-structured interviews.

The samples were set up by the e-marketplace

Table 1. Major phases of the study

June 2004	Scanning and preliminary investigation
August 2004	Selection of research topic and subject organisation
September 2004 – November 2004	Collection and analysis of secondary data
November 2004 – April 2005	Collection and analysis of primary data
March 2005 – April 2005	Overall assessment
June 2005 – September/October 2005	Preparation of paper preliminary version write-up
June 2007 – January 2008	Updating of data
March 2008 – April 2008	Preparation of paper final version write-up

general managers, the IT managers, and the project managers. The interviewees responded to questions on the development of platforms, project management and organisational impact.

TileSquare

TileSquare was founded as a joint stock company in 2001.

TileSquare is an e-marketplace, a business market that reproduces production modalities in the ceramics sector with the aim of favouring and developing relations between digital market participants. It is ideally designed for operators but also available to final consumers, who have free access to a vast area of goods and services.

The company's mission is to build a reference marketplace for the sector by grouping together organisations with commercial relations in the ceramics field. It does so through the standardisation of more effective and efficient homogeneous procedures designed to support all sector operators, i.e. raw material suppliers, machinery producers, and retailers. These operators are the e-marketplace members; presently there are about one thousand, some of which operate abroad, particularly in East European countries. One of the fundamental aspects of the portal is its neutrality, an indispensable condition for the initiative's own survival. Neutrality means respect for the rules

of the real market with no interference in how the actors do their business. They can act with complete autonomy and with no intrusion in how they conduct their affairs and activities.

As a neutral actor, the first aim of TileSquare was to facilitate communication between the producer and the re-sellers such that the final user service available could be increased. (See Figure 1.)

The company's shares are held by strategic partners, such as InterAge S.r.l., a company which develops Internet sites and portals. This company has consolidated experience in the ceramics field and presently acts as the marketplace coordinator.

The Services Offered by TileSquare

Initially founded as a digital platform for tile producers, over time, the system oriented itself more and more towards assisting retailers with the new requirements. This change in orientation came about due to the use of three-dimensional display software, the 3DWeb system.

This software is available for retailers who join the e-marketplace. It is a sales support programme rather than a real design project instrument. According to retailers with average confidence in IT and computer based applications, the software is extremely easy to use. Moreover, the final user is

Figure 1. The actors involved in the value chain

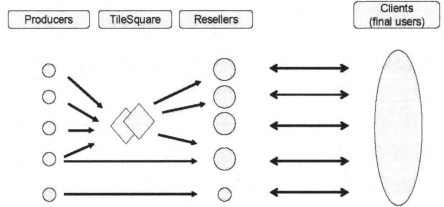

not a designer but a salesperson. The main reason why these final users are attracted to this software is the speed with which an initial approximation of an interior design project can be created.

With 3DWeb, once the materials have been selected and the parameters set, it is possible to have an immediate cost estimate; the program also allows entry of any discount policies that the individual retailer may obtain from the producers. Each individual retailer enjoys particular conditions for which it would be almost impossible to establish management and accounting standards, given the present situation. The hypothetical final transaction, however, is made with the utmost reserve and with no interference whatsoever from the virtual market managers. TileSquare's price policy also tends towards this direction: there is no commission on the effective final transactions; instead there is a fixed cost regime based on the service package the user has requested.

Another peculiarity of the software is that it allows the retailer to suggest a range of goods to his client; this advantage is atypical of the ceramics sector.

The real application strong point is the homogenisation and standardisation of the link between the individual producer and the retailer. There is no longer one software programme for each individual producer, but one single procedure that manages the whole sector upstream from the re-

tailer. Before, there was only an ad hoc programme for each individual product with the inevitable management problems for the retailer.

Furthermore, the portal offers the possibility to update catalogues instantly, to introduce new products, not to mention new lines, and to offer special conditions for end-of-range stock (in the special offers section).

The retailers listed in the e-marketplace can make their clients exclusive offers for certain product series only found in their catalogue. The environment created allows for standard product packages that can be listed and accessed by both the listed retailers (by means of a password) and the final consumers (free access).

Another service that TileSquare offers to its members is the possibility to access the WWW site, the most authoritative on-line magazine in the ceramics sector. WWW guarantees its readers the latest sector news and updated statistical data.

Listed below are a series of "applicative areas" also available within the e-marketplace; they can be personalised and eventually integrated with other projects.

- A directory service for the companies in the portal
- A sophisticated search engine for publishing catalogues and a product database that can be linked with external data sources

- A well-developed content management system to create and review documents and to manage the publication process of data and applications
- An e-learning system, including management and sales courses
- An e-marketing section with efficient instruments to divide, analyse and monitor the target over time
- A community system, a mechanism that puts users of the same company or different companies in contact in order to achieve a goal
- The possibility to add vertical applications, integrating them with the rest of the portal
- e-commerce systems, both B-to-B and B-to-C
- Web services that allow the platform to exchange information with other systems
- A discussion forum

As can be seen from the analysis of the case, widespread alternative forms of transaction management can be compared to the traditional ones. These new forms of transaction management support innovative interaction modalities between network participants and new production organisation modalities. An example is how retailers work: first, they develop their projects and designs with 3D instruments, thus saving on designer costs. Second, they create projects in a matter of minutes rather than days. Another aspect that becomes evident is that retailer collaboration gives rise to the so-called community of peers phenomenon. Lastly, the retailers themselves are able to offer their clients simulations and alternative suggestions, which was not possible before.

DISCUSSION: TILESQUARE: AN IMPROPER STRATEGIC NETWORK

The description of TileSquare's characteristics has presented some food for thought on ceramics industry development trends.

On a worldwide level, some countries have rapidly developed (especially China) and are now able to offer products which are qualitatively very similar to Italian products, but at decidedly lower prices. Since these products are easy to produce, and especially since the technological gap has been breached in these emerging economies, it can be stated that Italian products find themselves in the medium-high market bracket, more due to marketing reasons than a real difference in quality. Asian products cannot find outlets in the internal Italian markets because there are obstacles in the traditional trading venues. These obstacles could stimulate looking for new venues, such as electronic channels or digital markets, which would therefore become real alternative outlets.

Moreover, it has been seen how a portal founded particularly to satisfy producer needs has been particularly successful with retailers. Producers who enjoy competitive advantages in the traditional market generally cannot see the necessity of becoming part of a virtual market. Only marginalized producers understand the advantage of trying to erode market shares away from the stronger producers. The balance of the ceramics market has thus been modified by the establishment of TileSquare, especially since there currently is product excess on the market; the retailer can choose the best combination of quality, quantity and price for his particular needs. The digital market tends to undermine producers in oligopoly positions, thus the retailer is guaranteed the necessary information transparency to make a rational choice.

To date, the TileSquare e-marketplace has not reached its aspired objectives in terms of transactions concluded directly on the digital market. No contract has yet been signed through the Website; traditional channels are still being used. Several conflicting reasons can probably explain this effect. On the one hand, purchases are not made on impulse; the final retailer customer feels the need to physically see the product and to evaluate the various possibilities before finalising the transaction. On the other hand, the presence of the portal itself may be seen as a restriction on virtual market development, particularly in B-to-B. In fact, in some cases, there is no requirement for physical distance between the producer and the seller, so the contract can be concluded in the traditional manner because the parties can meet in person. But this trend is changing. The constant increase in foreign retailers will force TileSquare to offer services aimed also at supporting the final stages of a purchase or sales contract, and will require these services to be increasingly developed. TileSquare could thus become a disruptive channel for introducing foreign goods into Italy, and it is exactly in this environment that it could truly function as a virtual market.

To study the electronic network created by TileSquare, it is wise to consider the three effects highlighted by Malone et al., i.e. the communication effect, the brokerage effect and the integration effect.

- Communication effect: this implies the creation of an efficient information flow. TileSquare definitely makes this effect possible in that the various participants in the ceramics production chain can be seen by everyone else (and therefore generate information). At the same time, they can receive information from other economic actors or access specialised magazines through special links to view sector studies and other areas in the portal.
- Brokerage effect: this implies matching the needs of the buyer to the offers by the sellers. From this point of view, TileSquare potentially offers its clients the possibility to finalise a transaction on-line by means of the RFX method. In truth, this has never happened because the various actors prefer to conduct such operations following traditional methods, particularly by meeting the other parties in person.

- Integration effect: this implies the creation of closer links. TileSquare is definitely one instrument that allows the agents in the ceramics sector to veer away from strictly competitive logic and instead favour the development of collaborative relations, between subjects who hold a different hierarchical position and between those at the same level.

A different but more complete understanding of the consequences associated with the development of the TileSquare marketplace can be found through an analysis of the networking effect as described by Wigand (1996): TileSquare reshapes the relations of the ceramics product market creating a competitive advantage in favour of the retailers that participate the marketplace. The e-marketplace therefore creates rent seeking opportunities for the actors involved. By reducing the transaction costs, the retailers are able to make their offers more competitive on the e-marketplace, thus favouring those within the network rather than those outside of it. All this should urge producers to participate in the e-marketplace, even if Wigand's networking effect causes an increase in the level of industry competition and thus reduces oligopolistic revenues. Should producers decide not to participate, they would theoretically be excluded from the market because the transaction costs for finalising economic activities with non-participants would be higher than the costs retailers would face when finalising transactions with e-marketplace participants.

This transaction cost effect should lead retailers and producers to be more interested in joining the e-marketplace, and would create positive spin offs, which in turn would increase the range of offers within the e-marketplace, thus making it yet more advantageous for the retailers and, at the same time, increasing the disadvantages for those not participating. This virtuous/vicious circle, depending on the point of view, creates a new ceramics product market strategic configuration as a result of the ICT effects on: 1) coordination costs within the network; 2) transaction costs between participating agents and those who interact with them through economical transactions.

In short, TileSquare allows for the creation of an electronic, strategic and improper network.

Tilesquare can be called an improper strategic network since each member is present on the portal and also on the traditional market. If, on the one hand it is useful to be on TileSquare as a channel to access information, on the other, the actual transaction takes place externally. From an organisational point of view, the retailers can install contacts and, for example, form purchase groups through the communication instruments that TileSquare makes available (e.g. direct contact or video-conference).

A brokerage effect is not created inside the network. At the moment there are only collaborative links.

Another interesting aspect which emerges from the TileSquare case is the role played by the network in terms of exceeding the traditional limits of market access for producers and suppliers. TileSquare creates a new electronic market superimposed over the existing one, mainly limited to geographical boundaries, thus permitting the development of new trading activities for the other actors involved in the network. In this case the electronic marketplace can be defined not only as a new organisational form to support relations between the institutional actors directly present on the digital market, but also as a mediation instrument that allows new economic relations to arise between the actors, who, in a market that is not mediated by ICT, certainly could not meet because of high transaction costs. The Chinese producers case is a clear example of this point. TileSquare therefore, not only supports "existing" relations more efficiently, but also allows new relations to be created which would otherwise not have been possible given the high transaction costs: it therefore also plays the part of a market-maker.

CRITICAL NETWORK REMARKS: CONCLUSIONS AND FUTURE OPPORTUNITIES

The research topic of this chapter is to discuss whether:

- E-marketplaces are an organisational network and what role ICT plays in this organisational configuration.
- ICTs favour new and/or alternative organisational forms.
- ICTs change the definition and the nature of organisational boundaries.

From the analysis of the case, it can be seen how ICTs enhance the establishment of more competitive markets because they are more transparent. A particularly important fact is that the power exercised by the individual actors in the network is redefined within the e-marketplace. This fact is very evident in the case of TileSquare. The producers participate in the e-marketplace so that they are not excluded in favour of other producers ready to supply the relative information on their own goods, catalogues and direct on-line warehouses. It is obvious how all of this could, over time, modify competitive relations between medium to large-sized producers and those less known. Unlike the obligation in the brick and mortar market, in the digital market, the latter do not have to make large fixed cost investments to be more broadly visible. Therefore, rent seeking opportunities are reduced, as they are not closely connected to real competitive factors.

Lastly, it becomes easier to widen the organisational boundaries of the virtual market by involving participants from countries that otherwise would find it difficult to integrate through structures with high fixed costs. The digital market presence of member retailers from Eastern countries is a typical case.

Interesting food for thought is therefore presented, particularly with regard to the role played by technology, not only in defining the inter-organisational networks that are at the base of e-marketplaces, but also in the redefinition of traditional organisational boundaries (according to the transaction cost model). The distinct boundaries between markets, electronic markets and traditional hierarchical organisational forms become less clear. Though not the topic of this chapter, but certainly of interest for future study, e-marketplaces are a supporting instrument for traditional markets, electronic markets or relational networks with specific characteristics.

As further directions of this research we wish therefore to continue the study analyzing how through Business Intelligent Systems it is possible to analyze the data on the use of the portal by retailers and in this way provide to manufacturers information that they can use for marketing purposes.

Using empirical evidence from the case presented, this chapter has tried to answer how ICT reshapes relationships among actors. It is obvious how e-marketplaces are a true form of transaction management but have particular characteristics that require looking into more deeply.

In recent years, literature has shown a growing interest in these organisational forms, but we are certainly only at the beginning of a more general phenomenon; organisational planning will be ever more closely correlated to the development of ICT. New organisational paths and new organisational forms cannot ignore the implications that ICTs determine for them. At the same time, there is no point in studying the new technologies without considering the organisational content that every technological decision suggests and implies. The research questions posed by Straub and Watson (Straub, Watson, 2001) on the new ICTs as "facilitators" of new organisational forms or modalities point in this direction.

REFERENCES

Bakos, Y., & Kemerer, C. (1992) Recent applications of economic theory in information technology research. *Decision Support Systems, 8*, 365-388

Bakos, J. Y. (1997) Reducing buyer search costs: Implications for electronic marketplaces. *Management Science, 43*(12), 1676-1692

Bakos, Y., & Brynjolfsson, E., (1997) Information technology incentives, and the optimal number of suppliers. *Journal of Management information Systems, 10*, 35-53

Bakos, J. Y. (1998) The emerging role of electronic marketplaces on the internet. *Communications of the ACM, 41*(8), 35-42

Bar, F., & Borrus, M. (1993). *The future of networking* (BRIE working paper). Berkeley: University of California.

Benbasat, I. (1984). An analysis of research methodologies. In F. W. McFarlan (Ed.), *The information systems research challenges* (pp. 47-85). Boston: Harvard Business School Press.

Boyett, J. H., & Conn, H. P. (1991). *Workplace 2000: The revolution reshaping american business*. New York: Dutton.

Campbell, D. T. (1975). 'Degrees of freedom' and the case study. *Comparative Political Studies, 8*(2), 178-193.

Castells, M. (2000). *The Rise of the Network Society. The Information Age: Economy, Society and Culture*, Vol. 1:. Oxford, UK: Blackwell Publisher Ltd.

Chandler, A. D., Jr. (1977). *The visible hand: The managerial revolution in American business*. Cambridge, MA: Harvard University Press.

Choudhury, V., Hartzel, K., & Konsynski, B. (1998). Uses and consequences of electronic markets: An empirical investigation in the aircraft parts industry. *MIS Quarterly, 22,* 471-507

Christiaanse, E., & Markus, L. (2002 December 18-21). Business to business electronic marketplace and the structure of channel relationships. In *Proceedings of the 23rd International Conference on Information Systems*, Barcelona, Spain.

Christiaanse, E., & Markus, L. (2003). Participation in collaboration electronic marketplaces. In *Proceedings of the Hawaii International Conference on System Science*, Hawaii, USA.

Ciborra, C. (1993). *Teams, markets and system.* Cambridge, UK: Cambridge University Press.

Coase, R. H. (1937). The nature of the firm. *Economica.*

Cohendet P., & Llerena P. (1989). Flexibilité, information et décision. *Economica.* Paris.

Cordella, A. (2001, June 27-29). Does information technology always lead to lower transaction costs? In *Proceedings of the 9th European Conference of Information Systems* (pp. 854-864).

Dukes, W. (1965). N=1. *Psychological Bulletin, 64,* 74-79.

Ernst, D. (1994). *Inter-firms networks and market structure: Driving forces, barriers and patterns of control* (BRIE research paper). Berkeley: University of California.

Grandori, A. (1984). *Teorie organizzative.* Milan, Italy: Giuffrè.

Gurbaxani, V., & Wang, S. (1991). The impact of information systems on organization and markets. *Communications of the ACM, 34,* 59-73

Hamel, J., Dufour, s., & Fortin, D. (1993). *Case study methods.* Beverly Hills, CA: Sage Publications, Inc.

Holzmuller, H., & Schlichter, J. (2002). Delphi study about the future of B2B marketplace in Germany. *Electronic Commerce Research and Application, 1,* 2-19.

Jarillo, J. C. (1988). On strategic networks. *Strategic Management Journal, 9.*

Kallinikos, J. (2003, June 16-21). Networks as alternative forms of organization: Some critical remarks. In *Proceedings of the 11th European Conference on Information Systems*, Naples, Italy.

Lee, A. S. (1989). A scientific methodology for MIS case studies. *MIS Quarterly, 13*(1), 33-52.

MacDuffie, J. P., & Helper, S. (2003). B2B and mode or exchange: Evolutionary and transformative effect. In *The global internet economy.* Cambridge, MA: MIT Press.

Malone, T., Yates, J. E., & Benjamin, R. I. (1987). Electronic markets and electronic hierarchies. *Communications of the ACM, 30*(6).

Ouchi, W. G. (1980). Markets, bureaucracies and clans. *Administrative Science Quarterly, 25.*

Philipps, C., & Meeker, M. (2000). *The B2B internet report: Collaborative commerce.* Morgan Stanley Dean Bitter Research.

Picot, A. (1991). Ein neuer Ansatz zur Gestaltung der Leistungstiefe. *Zeitschrift für betriebswirtschaftliche Forschung, 43,* 336-359.

Rossignoli, C., & Mola, L. (2004, June 21-23). E.M.P. as enabler of new organisational architectures: An Italian case study. In *Proceedings of the 17th Bled eConference, eGlobal,* Bled, Slovenia.

Stake, R. E. (1995). *The art of case study research.* Thousand Oaks, CA: Sage Publications.

Straub, D. W., & Watson R.T. (2001). Research commentary: Transformational issues in researching IS an net-enabled organizations. *Information System Research, 12*(4), 337-345.

Thorelli, H. B. (1986). Networks: Between markets and hierarchies. *Strategic Management Journal, 7.*

Wigand, R. T. (1996, May 23-27). *An overview of electronic commerce and markets.* Paper presented at the Annual Conference of the International Communication Association, Chicago, Illinois.

Wigand, R. T. (1997). Electronic commerce: Definition, theory and context. *The Information Society, 13,* 1-16.

Williamson, O. E. (1975). *Market and hierarchies. Analysis and antitrust implication.* New York: The Free Press.

Williamson, O. E. (1981). The economics of organizations: The transaction cost approach. *American Journal of Sociology, 87,* 548-577.

Williamson, O. E. (1991). Comparative economic organization: The analysis of discrete structural alternatives, *Administrative Science Quarterly, 36,* 269-296.

KEY TERMS AND DEFINITIONS

Brokerage Effect: This implies matching the needs of the buyer to the offers by the sellers. From this point of view, TileSquare potentially offers its clients the possibility to finalise a transaction on-line by means of the RFX method. In truth, this has never happened because the various actors prefer to conduct such operations following traditional methods, particularly by meeting the other parties in person.

Communication Effect: This implies the creation of an efficient information flow. TileSquare definitely makes this effect possible in that the various participants in the ceramics production chain can be seen by everyone else (and therefore generate information). At the same time, they can receive information from other economic actors or access specialised magazines through special links to view sector studies and other areas in the portal.

Electronic Marketplace: Open electronic platforms enabling transactions and interactions between several companies or people. We consider e-marketplaces as an ICT based organizational form that mixes market coordination mechanisms (prices) and network coordination mechanisms (trust and common values)

Integration Effect: This implies the creation of closer links. TileSquare is definitely one instrument that allows the agents in the ceramics sector to veer away from strictly competitive logic and instead favour the development of collaborative relations, between subjects who hold a different hierarchical position and between those at the same level

Strategic Electronic Network Effect: ICT allows for the designing and strategically planned formation of links between companies who cooperate to achieve strategic objectives, with the final aim of obtaining competitive advantages

Strategic Electronic Network: Strategic configurations able to support and foster specific economic opportunities in determined contexts of time and space that are contingent to specific decisions.

Transaction Cost: Are costs incurred in making an economic exchange

Chapter XVIII
Applying Social Network Theory to the Effects of Information Technology Implementation

Qun Wu
University of Arkansas-Little Rock, USA

Jiming Wu
California State University, East Bay, USA

Juan Ling
Georgia College & State University, USA

ABSTRACT

While some studies have found a significant link between information technology (IT) and firm performance, others have observed negative or zero returns on IT investments. One explanation for the mixed findings is that the causal link from IT to firm performance may be mediated. However, previous information system (IS) research has paid relatively little attention to such mediators. In this chapter, we develop a conceptual framework in which social network plays a mediating role in the relationship between IT usage and firm performance. Specifically, IT usage helps organizations strengthen inter- and intra-organizational networks, which, in turn, enhance firm performance.

INTRODUCTION

Today, many organizations are leveraging information technology (IT) to develop innovative products and/or create new business models for generating revenues and engaging consumers. Consequently, strategic use of IT has been viewed as a key driver of organizational success in an increasingly dynamic business environment. Given the great importance of IT, a large body of research has been dedicated to the relationship between IT usage and firm performance. For example, Bharadwaj (2000) argues that IT can be conceptualized as an organizational capability and empirically examines the association between that capability and firm performance. Hitt and Brynjolfsson (1996) suggest that empirical results on IT value may depend heavily on what research questions are being addressed and what data are being used. Drawing on economic theory, they investigate the link between IT spending and business value in terms of productivity, profitability, and consumer value.

While some studies have found a significant link between IT and firm performance, others have observed negative or zero returns on IT investments (Dehning & Richardson, 2002). One explanation for the mixed findings is that the causal link from IT to firm performance is too long and that many studies have ignored key organizational competences that mediate the relationship between IT and firm performance (Tanriverdi, 2005). This chapter proposes a theoretical approach to the exploration of the underlying mechanism through which IT contributes to business success. Specifically, this study is based on social network perspective and delineates the mediating role of such networks in the relationship between IT usage and firm performance.

BACKGROUND

The origin of social network theory can be traced back to the late 1800s. Tönnies (2001) argues that individuals who share values and beliefs are linked by social ties. Durkheim (1997, 1982) models the modern society as "organic solidarity", which emphasizes the role of cooperation between differentiated individuals with independent roles.

In 1900s, the further development of social network analysis has rested on three cornerstones. The first one is sociometric analysis developed by researchers working on small groups with techniques of graph theory. One of the distinguished achievements in the sociometric analysis is made by Moreno (1934), who pioneers the systematic recording and analysis of social interaction in small groups, especially in classrooms and work groups. The second one is the investigation of interpersonal relations conducted by the Harvard researchers in 1930s. One such investigation is known as Hawthorne Studies led by Warner and Mayo. The third one is the examination of community relations in tribal and village societies by the Manchester anthropologist. Gluckman, a central figure at Manchester, makes great contribution to the development of structural approach during his investigation of community networks in southern Africa. In 1960s and 1970s, the three strands of research have been brought together and the contemporary social network analysis has emerged (see Scott, 2000 and Freeman, 2004 for the history of social network analysis).

Social networks have become one of the hot research areas in recent years. The network research has boomed in management as well as in other disciplines (Borgatti & Foster, 2003). A social network is comprised of nodes and ties. Nodes are actors (i.e., individuals, groups, and organizations) in the network, while ties are the relationships between the actors. Social network theory[1] suggests that social networks actors are embedded within ties, which facilitate or hinder their actions and performance.

The literature in management provides consistent evidence of the influence of social networks on performance at different levels. Focusing on the link between micro-level networks and performance, researchers observe that employees' social networks can lead to their career development and performance improvement. For example, Mehra and colleagues (2001) investigate how people shape the networks that constrain or benefit their work performance. Their results indicate that high-self monitors are more likely to occupy central positions than low-self monitors and that self-monitoring and centrality in social networks independently predict individuals' workplace performance. Seibert and colleagues (2001) have employed structural holes theory, weak ties theory, and social resource theory to explicate the effects of social networks on career success. They observe that structural holes and weak ties affect social resources, which in turn influence individuals' salary, promotion, and career satisfaction through access to information, resources, and career sponsorship.

More recently, social network research has been extended to the macro level. McDonald and Westphal (2003) examine how CEOs' networks affect firm performance and strategic change. Based on a sample of 600 CEOs, they find that CEOs of firms with poor performance seek more advice from other firm executives who are their friends, work in the same industry, and have similar functional backgrounds. Their results indicate that such advice seeking is not very helpful to CEOs striving to leverage best practices to enhance business strategies. Ingram and Roberts (2000) posit that managers' friendships with competitors and the cohesiveness of the friendship networks can improve firm performance. The

data collected from 31 general managers in the Sydney hotel industry confirm the proposition and also suggest that cohesiveness of friendships with competitors plays the most important role in firm performance.

SOCIAL NETWORK AS A MEDIATOR

As discussed above, many studies have explored the effects of IT usage on firm performance, but few of them have investigated the mediating role of social network in the relationship between IT usage and firm performance. In this chapter, we propose that IT usage will affect both intra- and inter-organizational networks – the key determinants of firm performance and competitive advantages. Our theoretical model is shown in Figure 1.

Specifically, for intra-organizational network, we mainly focus on internal network closure, and for inter-organizational network, we are primarily interested in external network centrality. Thus, the theoretical framework can be adjusted as shown in Figure 2. Below we describe and discuss the two network constructs and the four conceptual links in the research model.

Internal Network Closure

IT usage can affect organizational performance via internal network closure of that organization.

Figure 1. Theoretical framework

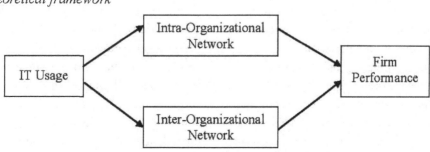

Figure 2. An alternative theoretical framework

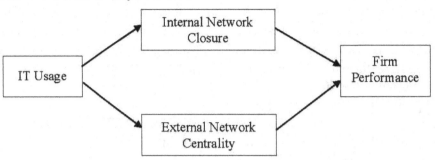

Closure is a network structure where actors are highly interconnected (Burt, 2000). Coleman's (1988) seminal work in social capital is based on the closure argument. He asserts that network closure is the source of social capital. Individuals in a dense, strongly interconnected network build trust, establish effective norms, and share understandings and meanings. When network closure is high, these common norms, meanings, and trust reinforce one another and generate a synergistic influence on the flow of information (Gnyawali & Madhavan, 2001). In this case, information exchange channels are more unblocked; individuals prefer to share good ideas and knowledge, help accelerate information flow, and provide useful feedback. Prior research suggests that information is likely to be distorted as information moves from one to another in a large chain of people. Networks with a high density and more direct connections can alleviate the decrease of information quality in exchange.

In our context, high internal network closure implies that an organization consists of strongly interconnected employees who are embedded within an internal organization network with shared understandings, routines, and norms. IT usage makes connections among employees more robust and their communications more efficient. For example, by connecting users from different locations, instant messaging allows users to communicate in real-time and be aware of online status of coworkers. At Honda, the development of Pentaccord, a full-service communication sys-

tem, makes information and knowledge sharing much easier on a global scale and thus improves efficiency, productivity, and competitiveness.

Specifically, IT can strengthen social networks in the following ways. First, IT leads to more ties, which improve an organization's internal network density or closure (Granovetter, 1982; Coleman, 1988). As Coleman (1990) suggests, network closure is essential for an organization to become more efficient. It will accelerate information flow from one employee to another. Dense network linkages act as conduits for employees to communicate about and share perceptions, interpretations, and norms via IT-based channels (Ibarra & Andrews, 1993).

Second, IT makes an organization more cohesive. Granovetter (1992) puts forward with "structural embeddedness;" that is, employees are embedded within an intra-organizational network and have mutual coworkers so that they have more confidence in cooperation. Furthermore, these employees will build an organizational identity and view themselves as part of the organization. This identity stems from a collective mind, a common language, and a shared organizational culture (Nahapiet & Ghoshal, 1998; Podolny & Baron, 1997; Weick & Roberts, 1993). IT usage improves internal network density, which, in turn, enables employees to have the organizational identity. Employees will consider themselves as important components of the organization and try to make contributions. The collective interests will take precedence over their self interests (Coleman,

1988). For example, employees will be more willing to share information, knowledge, and working experiences. They will cooperate with each other and pay more attention to the cooperative image they present (Burt, 2000).

Third, IT usage enhances tie strength and multiplicity, and thus increases the number of strong ties, which help deal with complex organizational information and knowledge (Hansen, 1999). As mentioned earlier, ties act as conduits through which information, knowledge, and resources flow. The strength of a tie is "a combination of the amount of time, emotional intensity, intimacy, and the reciprocal services that characterize the tie" (Granovetter, 1973, p. 1361). The stronger the ties, the more likely will the focal actors and their contacts share and exchange resources (Lin, 2001). People who possess strong ties with each other often have a history together, so they are highly motivated to cooperate with one another and even provide help (Krackhardt, 1992). Strong ties also provide a base for trust, which is critical to an organization's ability to meet business challenges and handle crisis situations. Krackhardt (1992) points out that the strength of strong ties lies in trust, especially in cases of crisis. Close and frequent interactions provide employees with comfort in the face of uncertainty. Employees with a high cohesion usually trust each other and can respond quickly to a crisis.

Fourth, strong ties based on IT facilitate individuals to develop and share norms of behavior and thus accelerate resource flow. Common norms provide a guideline for employee behavior. Employees share and obey these norms, which increase the ease of interaction and cooperation. More to the point, strong ties enhance the rate of resource flow. Therefore, focal actors can draw on more resources from their contacts. In the context of an organization, the focal actor can be an employee, a project team, or a division. For example, strong ties between an organization's divisions (e.g., production, R&D, sales) enable

timely knowledge integration and make the organization more efficient and effective (Hansen, 1999; Szulanski, 1996). The two-way interaction between the source and the recipient through strong ties allows the two parties to articulate some complex knowledge in detail. Hansen (1999) examines the influence of strong ties on knowledge transfer across organization divisions and finds that weak ties facilitate searching for useful knowledge outside of the divisions, whereas strong ties greatly foster the transfer of complex knowledge within the divisions.

The positive effect of network closure on firm performance has been verified in recent empirical research. For example, Tsai and Ghoshal (1998) argue that shared values and collective visions within an organization encourage its members to trust each another. This perceived trust encourages different organizational units to have resource exchange and combination, which, in turn, results in high firm innovation. Results from 15 units of a multinational electronics company show that common visions and trust are positively related to resource exchange and combination, which significantly influences value creation. Maurer and Ebers (2006) examine the configuration and dynamics of organizational network closure of start-ups and explicate how it affects firm performance. They observe that firms' social capital in terms of network closure, cohesion, and organizational identity is vital to the founding and continued growth of biotechnology start-ups. Ng (2004) finds that strong network closure promotes the sharing of resources, knowledge, and experiences, and that the formation of network closure is positively associated with the social capital, which greatly improves efficiency.

In short, IT usage can improve internal network closure by increasing the number of ties and tie strength, hence affecting firm performance. Our propositions for the relationship between IT usage, internal network, and firm performance are as follows:

P1: *There is a positive relationship between IT usage and internal network closure.*

P2: *There is a positive relationship between internal network closure and firm performance.*

External Network Centrality

In today's global business environment, firms are increasingly embedded into a competitive and cooperative external (or inter-organizational) network. Gnyawali and Madhavan (2001) define an external network as a cooperative relationship among companies that involves flows of assets, information, and status. The role of external network in firm's behavior and performance has been examined from different angles. Fracassi (2008) suggests that a firm's financing policy decisions depend on its position in the network. Walske and colleagues (2007) find that strong-tie venture syndicates increase the likelihood of entrepreneurial firm success. Hochberg and colleagues (2007) observe that better-networked venture capital firms experience significantly better performance. Gompers and colleagues (2005) indicate that entrepreneurial networks play an important role in the foundation of a start-up company. Leitner (2005) develops and empirically tests a network model for financial institutions and finds that social networks or linkages may allow the institutions to obtain some mutual insurance.

The usage of information system such as electronic data interchange (EDI) helps an organization improve its position in an external network. In 1979, Tichy and colleagues appeal that the future research agenda for organizational studies based on network analysis should include external relationships as well as organizations and their boundaries. Position within an overall pattern of external relationships is critical to firm performance (Ibarra, 1992). In this study, we focus on external network centrality, which measures whether an organization occupies a central position in its inter-organizational network (Freeman,

1979). A central organization is more prone to have power or high status (Brass, 1984), and is better positioned to access various information sources and less likely to miss important information (Burt, 1987; Van de Ven, 1986). The more central the organization, the clearer view about external network it can get by accessing to others (Perry-Smith, 2006).

Recently, more and more researchers have investigated the influence of centrality on performance at the inter-organizational level. For example, Palmer and Barber (2001) find that well-networked top managers who are central in elite social networks but relatively marginal with respect to social status are more likely to pursue diversifying acquisitions. Bell (2005) examines the relationship between innovation of 77 mutual fund companies and their centrality in managerial or institutional tie networks. The results show that centrality in the network of managerial ties positively impacts firm innovation.

IT usage helps organizations have high centrality in a network. An organization using a powerful database system may be able to increase network centrality because the system permits the organization's easier and speedier access to important information. A virtual private network (VPN) system may result in a higher centrality of a company through its ability to quickly provide secure information to others. An organization may also reach higher centrality in a social network by implementing online analytical processing (OLAP) technology, which enhances its information-processing capability and allows it to obtain valuable business information. In addition, communication systems can help an organization become more active and attentive in a social network by eliminating the obstacles to participation, such as lack of time and budget for travelling. IT may also help an organization go toward higher centrality by improving organizational learning, which is viewed as a key to knowledge-based organization development.

IT-based systems can connect organizations

to each other, open up opportunities for collaboration, and increase the possibility of resource sharing. Thus, the organizations are likely to develop more and strong ties with other nodes and increase their centrality. In the absence of such systems, some organizations may remain isolated, making it difficult for others to reach them and exchange information with them. Moreover, IT-based systems facilitate organizations to share goals, values, and beliefs, which help engage in inter-organizational relationships and thus lead to higher centrality.

As for the effect of centrality on firms' behavior and performance, we argue that higher centrality can lead to a firm's more aggressive, timely, and complex competitive actions, which result in superior firm performance. This is in line with Ferrier and colleagues' (1999) finding that unaggressive, simple, and slow action explains poor firm performance in terms of market share erosion. Below, we offer more reasons.

First, a central firm can take advantage of great resources to conduct (or initiate) more and aggressive competitive actions (Gnyawali & Madhavan, 2001). The reasons are as follows. With a higher centrality in an inter-organizational network, a firm often has better access to resources including assets, information, and the associated status and power. This superior resource base enables the firm to initiate competitive actions (Chen, 1996). In addition, the central firm usually has earlier and more convenient access to relevant new information and technological developments in the network. Thus, it is in a good position to take actions. Furthermore, after the central firm's initial action, a non-central competitor's response is expected to be delayed or weakened because of their lack of assets, information, and power. Such expectation will further encourage the central firm to initiate competitive actions (Chen, 1996).

Second, a central firm can conduct (or initiate) more timely competitive actions (or responses) due to its information advantage. Within an inter-organizational network, a central firm can

enjoy information advantage in terms of its access to and judgment about competitors' behaviors and motives, and the competitive dynamics in the network. Thus, the central firm can conduct competitive attacks (or responses) more timely and quickly. Action timing, defined as the time elapsed between the actions carried out by a firm and those carried out by a rival, has been widely recognized as a critical factor for firm performance (e.g., Smith et al., 1992; Ferrier et al., 1999).

Third, a central firm can conduct more complex competitive actions. Competitive action complexity is regarded as important in affecting firms' performance because firms with more complex competitive action repertoire are less predictable for rivals (e.g., D'Aveni, 1994) and more likely to capture and sustain a lead (Schumpeter, 1934, 1950). As mentioned earlier, a high centrality offers a firm better access to resources such as assets, information, and the associated status and power. With that resource advantage, a central firm is capable of increasing its action repertoire complexity, hence capturing the competitive advantage and improving performance.

Taken together, we contend that higher centrality leads to superior firm performance due to a central firms' capability to conduct more aggressive, timely, and complex competitive actions achieved through a resource advantage. In short, IT usage can impact firm performance by improving external network centrality. Formally, we propose:

P3: *There is a positive relationship between IT usage and external network centrality.*

P4: *There is a positive relationship between external network centrality and firm performance.*

IMPLICATION

Social network analysis has been increasingly used to explain important phenomena in many fields.

For example, Allen and Babus (2008) suggest that modern financial system can and should be examined from the network perspective because of the high degree of interdependence of financial system. However, very few studies in IS field have paid attention to the social network theory. This chapter tries to fill this gap by proposing a linkage between IT usage and social network.

Applying social network theory to IS field has several important implications for researchers. First, while traditional IS studies have investigated the effect of IT adoption on individual's behavior, they typically ignore its effect on the social network. Such ignorance certainly undermines our understanding of the role of IT in firm performance. This is because increasingly, IT is being used by organizations to build social connections and collaboration, which provide employees with access to knowledge benefiting both individual work and group projects. Second, by examining IT usage from a network perspective, we can construct a bridge between micro- and macro-level effects of IT. Specifically, the perspective may help address the following research questions: (1) Does IT-based network impact individual, team, and firm performance? (2) If so, does it impact them differently? It may also help investigate how IT usage at individual level impacts the development and evolution of an organization-level social network. Third, Granovetter (1982) argues that further development of network ideas should move away from static analysis and toward more systematic accounts of how such systems develop and change. Actually, IT usage is an important driving force for network dynamics. Therefore, IT researchers may make considerable contributions to the development of social network analysis by combining network theory with IT studies. Forth, applying network theory to IT usage may provide IS researchers with a good opportunity to improve and extend current research methodology.

This study also sheds light on some areas that may benefit practitioners. First, this study sends an important message to business managers that they should pay careful attention to IT-based network in the interest of bottom-line performance for their firms. Managers must look broadly and deeply at strengths and weaknesses in their own social network, especially internal network closure and external network centrality. A second key implication for managers relates to the application of IT to the development and improvement of social network. Our research model suggests that IT can play a key role in the network maturity. Thus, managers may purposefully use IT to enhance network closure, increase network density, and boost the number of strong ties.

CONCLUSION

Drawing on a social network perspective, this study explores the underlining mechanism through which IT usage contributes to firm performance. Specifically, we contend that IT usage has a positive effect on firm performance via inter- and intra-organizational networks. That is, IT usage increases an organization's internal network closure and external network centrality, which, in turn, enhance firm performance. The current study makes several contributions. First, this study examines the impact of IT usage on firm performance through inter- and intra-organizational networks. Such impact has so far received insufficient research attention. Second, this study is one of the first to employ social network theory to investigate the effects of IT usage on firm performance. Third, this study contributes to the social network research by identifying IT usage as one of the key drivers of network development and evolution.

REFERENCES

Allen, F., & Babus, A. (2008). *Networks in finance* (working paper). University of Pennsylvania and Erasmus University.

Bell, G. G. (2005). Clusters, networks, and firm innovativeness. *Strategic Management Journal, 26,* 287-295.

Bharadwaj, A. S. (2000). A resource-based perspective on information technology capability and firm performance: An empirical investigation. *MIS Quarterly, 24,* 169-196.

Borgatti, S. P. (2004). The state of organizational social network research today (working paper).

Borgatti, S. P., & Foster, P.C. (2003). The network paradigm in organizational research: A review and typology. *Journal of Management, 29,* 991-1013.

Brass, D. J. (1984). Being in the right place: A structural analysis of individual influence in an organization. *Administrative Science Quarterly, 29,* 518-539.

Burt, R. S. (1987). Social contagion and innovation: Cohesion versus structural equivalence. *American Journal of Sociology, 92,* 1287-1335.

Burt, R. S. (2000). The network structure of social capital. *Research in Organizational Behavior, 22,* 345-423.

Burt, R. S. (2001). Structural holes versus network closure as social capital. In N. Lin, K. S. Cook, & R. S. Burt (Eds.), *Social capital: Theory and research.* Berlin, Germany: Aldine de Gruyter.

Chen, M. (1996). Competitor analysis and interfirm rivalry: Toward a theoretical integration. *Academy of Management Review, 1,* 100-134.

Coleman, J. S. (1988). Social capital in the creation of human capital. *American Journal of sociology, 94,* 95-120.

D'Aveni, R. (1994). *Hypercompetition: Managing the dynamics of strategic maneuvering.* New York: Free Press.

Dehning, B., & Richardson, V. (2002). Returns on investments in information technology: A research synthesis. *Journal of Information Systems, 16,* 7-30.

Durkheim, E. (1982). *Rules of sociological method.* The Free Press.

Durkheim, E. (1997). *The division of labour in society.* The Free Press.

Ferrier, W. J., Smith, K. G., & Grimm, C. M. (1999). The role of competitive action in market share erosion and industry dethronement: A study of industry leaders and challengers. *Academy of Management Journal, 42,* 372-388.

Fracassi, C. (2008). Corporate finance policies and social networks (working paper). University of California, Los Angeles.

Freeman, L. C. (1979). Centrality in social networks: Conceptual clarification. *Social Networks, 1,* 215-239.

Freeman, L. C. (2004). *The development of social network analysis: A study in the sociology of science.* Vancouver, Canada: Empirical Press.

Gnyawali, D., & Madhavan, R. (2001). Cooperative network and competitive dynamics: A structural embedness perspective. *Academy of Management Review, 26,* 431-445.

Gompers, P., Lerner, J., & Scharfstein, D. (2005). Entrepreneurial spawning: Public corporations and the genesis of new ventures, 1986 to 1999. *Journal of Finance, 60,* 577-614.

Granovetter, M. (1973). The strength of weak ties. *American Journal of Sociology, 78,* 1360-1380.

Granovetter, M. (1982). The strength of weak ties. In P. V. Marsden & N. Lin (Eds.), *Social structure and network analysis* (pp. 105-130). Beverly Hills, CA: Sage.

Hansen, M. T. (1999). The search-transfer problem: The role of weak ties in sharing knowledge across organization subunits. *Administrative Science Quarterly, 44,* 82-111.

Hitt, L. M., & Brynjolfsson, E. (1996). Productivity, business profitability, and consumer surplus: Three different measures of information technology value. *MIS Quarterly, 20,*121-142.

Hochberg, Y., Ljungqvist, A., & Lu, Y. (2007). Whom you know matters: Venture capital networks and investment performance. *Journal of Finance, 62,* 251-301.

Ingram, P., & Roberts, P. W. (2000). Friendships among competitors in the Sydney hotel industry. *American Journal of Sociology, 106,* 387-423.

Ibarra, H., & Andrews, S. B. (1993). Power, social influence, and sense making: Effects of network centrality and proximity on employee perceptions. *American Science Quarterly, 38,* 277-303.

Ibarra, H. (1992). Homophily and differential returns: Sex differences in network structure and

access in an advertising firm. *Administrative Science Quarterly, 37,* 422-447.

Podolny, J. M., & Baron, J. N. (1997). Resources and relationships: Social networks and mobility in the workplace. *American Sociological Review, 62,* 673-693.

Krackhardt, D. (1992). The strength of strong ties: The importance of philos in organization. In N. Nohria and R. C. Eccles (Eds.), *Networks and organizations: Structure, form, and action* (pp. 216-239). Boston, MA: Harvard Business School Press.

Leitner, Y. (2005). Financial networks: Contagion, commitment, and private sector bailouts. *Journal of Finance, 60,* 2925-2953.

Lin, N. (2001). *Social capital: A theory of social structure and action.* Cambridge, UK: Cambridge University Press

Mauer, I., & Ebers, M. (2006). Dynamics of social capital and their performance implications: Lessons from biotechnology start-ups. *Administrative Science Quarterly, 51,* 262-292.

McDonald, M., & Westphal, J. (2003). Getting by with the advice of their friends: CEOs' advice networks and firms' strategic responses to poor performance. *Administrative Science Quarterly, 48,* 1-32.

Mehra, A., Kilduff, M., & Brass, D. (2001). The social networks of high and low self-monitors: Implications for workplace performance. *Administrative Science Quarterly, 46,* 121-146.

Moreno, J. (1934). *Who shall survive?* New York: Bacon Press.

Nahapiet, J., & Ghoshal, S. (1998). Social capital, intellectual capital, and the organizational advantage. *Academy of Management Review, 23,* 242-266.

Ng, D. (2004). The social dynamics of diverse and closed networks. *Human Systems Management, 23,* 111-122.

Palmer, D., & Barber, B. M. (2001). Challengers, elites, and owning families: A social class theory of corporate acquisitions in the 1960s. *Administrative Science Quarterly, 46,* 87-120.

Perry-Smith, J. (2006). The role of social relationships in facilitating individual creativity. *Academy of Management Journal, 49,* 85-101.

Schumpeter, J. (1934). *The theory of economic development.* Cambridge, MA: Harvard University Press.

Schumpeter, J. (1950). *Capitalism, socialism, and democracy* (3rd ed.). New York: Harper.

Smith, K., Grimm, G., & Gannon, M. (1992). *Dynamics of competitive strategy.* Newbury Park, CA: Sage.

Scott, J. (2000). *Social network analysis: A handbook* (2nd ed.). Newbury Park, CA: Sage.

Seibert, S. E., Kraimer, M. L., & Liden, R. C. (2001). A social capital theory of career success. *Academy of Management Journal, 44,* 219-237.

Szulanski, G. (1996). Exploring internal sticki-ness: Impediments to the transfer of best practice within the firm. *Strategic Management Journal, 17,* 27-43.

Tanriverdi, H. (2005). Information technology relatedness, knowledge management capability, and performance of multibusiness firms. *MIS Quarterly, 29*(2), 311-334.

Tönnies, F. (2001). Gemeinschaft and gesellschaft: An essay on communism and socialism as histori-cal social systems. In *Community and civil society.* Cambridge, UK: Cambridge University Press.

Tsai, W., & Ghoshal, S. (1998). Social capital and value creation: The role of intrafirm networks. *Academy of Management Journal, 41,* 464-476.

Van de Ven, A. H. (1986). Central problems in the management of innovation. *Management Sci-ence, 32,* 590-607.

Weick, K. E., & Roberts, K. H. (1993). Collective mind in organizations: Heedful interrelating on flight decks. *Administrative Science Quarterly, 38,* 357-381.

KEY TERMS AND DEFINITIONS

IT Usage: Refers to an organization's ability to use IT to meet business needs and improve business process.

Network Centrality: Describes the extent to which the focal actor occupies a strategic posi-tion in the network by virtue of being involved in many significant ties.

Network Closure: Describes the extent to which actors are strongly interconnected (Burt, 2001).

Network Density: Measures "the extent to which all possible relations are actually present" (Scott, 2000, p. 32).

A Social Network: Is comprised of nodes and ties. Nodes are actors (i.e., individuals, groups, and organizations) in the network while ties are the relationships between the actors.

Social Network Theory: Suggests that actors are embedded within the network and an actor' behavior and performance are dependent on its position and relationship in the network.

Strong Tie and Weak Tie: The strength of a tie is "a combination of the amount of time, emotional intensity, intimacy, and the reciprocal services that characterize the tie" (Granovetter, 1973, p. 1361). For example, ties to friends are strong ties whereas ties to acquaintances are weak ties. Strong ties enable individuals to gain more resources from their contacts than weak ties.

Chapter XIX
Competing Commitments Theory

John McAvoy
University College Cork, Ireland

Tom Butler
University College Cork, Ireland

ABSTRACT

Information system development, like information systems adoption, can be considered to be a change process; yet problems arise when change is introduced. Resistance to the change can develop and the reasoning behind the resistance needs to be determined in order to address it. Resistance can be straightforward, where the change threatens a person's job or creates stress for individuals, yet resistance can also be hidden and complex. Individuals may describe themselves as supporting a change, yet they work against that change (even if they are unaware that they are doing so). When this is happening, competing commitments can be at play; a competing commitment is where an individual professes a commitment to a course of action yet works against that commitment in different, usual subconscious, ways. The competing commitments process is a means of identifying why resistance is occurring even though individuals profess support.

INTRODUCTION

Information system (IS) development has been conceptualized as a change process (Lyytinen, 1987); however, the change referred to by Lyytinen refers to the intervention into complex social webs (Kling & Scacchi, 1982) by a project team in the design and implementation of software artifacts for use in organizational IS. Similarly, the seminal article by (Markus & Robey, 1988) looks at the relationship between information technology and change within organisations. The process by which software artifacts are developed is itself subject to change (Beck, 2000), with the behaviours of project team members being one such object of the change. Significantly, Lafleur (1996) maintains that change is a constant in a software project, while in a broader context, several authors have described how projects are often used to bring about change: an example of which would be introducing a new ERP system, or a change of work practice (Alsene, 1999; Boody & Macbeth, 2000; Clarke, 1999; McElroy, 1996; Pellegrinelli, 1997; Turner & Muller, 2003).

Much has changed since the 1990s in terms of IS development practice; however, problems still persist. For example, the Standish Group's Chaos Report of 2004 found that over 53% of software projects were challenged, in that they were either over time, over budget and/or the software artifacts lacked critical features and requirements. Another 18% were failures, with the remaining 29% being deemed a success. In explaining the modest improvement since the 1994 survey, Standish Group Chairman Jim Johnson stated that: "People have become much more savvy in project management. When we first started the research, project management was a sort of black art. People have spent time trying to get it right and that has also been a major step forward" (SoftwareMag.com, 2004). The clear implications from this comprehensive industry-based study is that improvements in project management practice have not delivered the necessary improvements in the process and product of IS development. In addition, new design and development programming languages, methods, and techniques have been introduced since the original Chaos Report in 1994 to help solve the 'wicked problems' that plague software project teams. The obvious question is why haven't these improvements worked? The answer may be that all this change to software development processes and practice may not have been as beneficial as is believed. It is clear from extant research that problems arise when change is introduced to project teams. For example, systems developers endeavor to maintain stability and security in the face of change to design and development processes and procedures (Nader, 1993). They do this because the imposition of change can result in stress and, accordingly, developers endeavor to avoid stressful situations by resisting change (Whitehead, 2001).

This chapter explores the phenomenon of change, and commitment to change, in IS development project teams and theorizes on the underlying factors that shape this complex phenomenon; it then proposes a research method with which to effectively investigate this phenomenon. The goal of this chapter is therefore to identify the difficulties resistance to change brings to many IS projects, and then to describe a method with which to identify the cause of the resistance.

BACKGROUND

The nature of change in IS projects is complex viz. according to Beck (2000, p. 28): "The requirements change. The design changes. The team changes. The business changes. The team members change. The problem isn't change, per se, because change is going to happen; the problem, rather, is the inability to cope with change when it comes". It is clear from Beck that management of change in a software development project is vital. The problem is how is this achieved? Cushway and Lodge (1999) indicate that change is best managed by developing new strategies and structures; they make no mention of the teams and individuals who will effect, and be affected by, change to processes and activities. However, Zmud (1983) argues that trying to implement process change by changing people will lead to resistance: hence, Rainwater (2002) indicates that projects in which the impact of change is not assessed are in danger of running into problems. Clearly, successful change in software development processes and practices in teams will be dependent on several factors (Beck, 2000; Whitehead, 2001). However, if team members resist change, whatever their competences and abilities, then problems ensue.

The concept of resistance to change centering on the reluctance to deviate from group or individual norms is noted in Lewin (1951), and further elaborated in Dent and Goldberg (1999), Asch (1952), and Wren (2005). Argyris (1985) and Robbins and Finlay (1998) argue that resistance to change occurs when an accompanying threat is perceived, as people adopt defensive positions in the face of threats. Individuals also resist when a change is forced upon them. For example, users may resist the change to business processes associated with the adoption of an IS, if there was a low level of participation in the software development project (Cavaye, 1995). In a general context, Mitsufuji (2001) and Venkatesh and Davis (2000) argue that without the consensus of the targeted user group, the diffusion of a new software artifact will probably not be accepted. Without input, the users of the system can feel that they are being forced into using it and their commitment will be reduced (Cavaye, 1995). The significance of commitment to project success can be seen in an exploratory study by Gemmill and Wilemon (1997), who found that sixty-six out of one hundred IT project managers expressed frustration at the lack of commitment from their project team members. From this, we can see the influence, and importance, of commitment to IS projects.

Argyris (1998) describes two types of commitment: external commitment and internal commitment. External commitment arises when compliance is required of the employee, where the goals, tasks, and required behaviours are defined by management. Internal commitment is where the individual is committed to a task, project, or person for personal reasons. Internal commitment derives from having personal preferences in terms of goals and objectives.

Resistance to change can indicate a lack of commitment to the change, but there can be other explanations (Bowe, Lahey, Kegan, & Armstrong, 2003). Software developers provide excellent examples of such resistance to change. In his study of the Microsoft NT Project, Zachary (1994, p. 13) observes that programmers "*like converts to a new religion... often display a destructive closed-mindness bordering on zealotry*", a consequence of which is a high level of resistance to change. In 'Software Development on a Leash', resistance to change is shown to be modulated by other factors and in perspectives that view change being detrimental to a project (Birmingham, 2002); elsewhere, and in the same vein, change is something that must be coped with and its disruptive impact minimized, rather than embraced and fostered (Field & Keller, 1998). Returning to the point made by Bowe *et al.* (2003a), there can be other explanations for resistance to change other than a lack of commitment. Lawrence (1969) believes that this resistance to change can highlight the fact that something is being overlooked, that the change itself has not been thought through and may be sub-optimal. In this scheme of things, resistance to change should not be viewed as being negative, it may be an indicator that the change itself needs further examination. Furthermore, Kegan and Lahey (2001a) propose that some resistance is easy to explain (for example the stress of learning a new skill) but other resistance is not as easily explained. A paradox exists where people show a commitment to, and support for, change yet still resist the change. Robbins and Finley (1998) state that some forms of resistance can be subconscious viz. team members all agree on a new course of action, but then do nothing to implement it. Although individuals may consciously believe that a change would be beneficial, unconscious or latent attitudes may create potent barriers to this change (Patching, 1999; Statt, 2004). This has consequences for practitioners instituting change and researchers studying it. In the latter case, researchers would benefit from the application of a method which would identify and explain the causes for this paradox.

The Open Systems School examines change through organizations and their component subsets. It posits that any change in one subset will impact the others; accordingly, it is necessary to take a holistic view of the organization when implementing change. Boody and Macbeth (2000) add subtly to this by stating that change in one area, needs to be accompanied by (as opposed to 'will cause') changes elsewhere. Take, for example, the introduction of a datamining application in a marketing department. As with the implementation of all new IS, users would have to accept and have a good understanding of technology before they could use it effectively—thus, there is a requirement for training and help during use, which would not have been necessary before the change. Hunt and Thomas (2000) refer to this as an example of a non-orthogonal system, while Birmingham (2002) describes the small changes affecting other areas as having either a ripple effect or cascading effect. In sum, this school of thought argues that a small change in one area, can have both foreseen and unforeseen or unintended consequences in seemingly independent areas or activities.

The Group Dynamics School places emphasis on instituting change by focusing on groups. As individuals work in groups, changes occur through changing a group's norms and practices (Alkire & Denevlin, 2002). Thus, as this paper argues in line with extant thought in the discipline, the implementation of an IS, or changes in IS development process and project team, will ultimately change the norms and practices of the end users and/or the developers (business analysts, designers, programmers etc.). One finding that needs to be considered in all this is that one of the reasons people form into, and attach to, groups is to shield themselves from change – in addition to the commonly held conceptions, a group is also *"an insurance mechanism coping with uncertainties"* (Alkire & Denevlin, 2002, p.21).

We argue herein that researching resistance to change in IS development projects can be problematic. Venkatesh and Davis (2000) maintain that, for a new system to be accepted, its usefulness must be visible to those using it. Visibility is one

thing, but understanding another, as Raghavan and Chand (1989) state that innovations (such as new software development methodologies) can be both misunderstood and misapplied. Ultimately, therefore, something as apparently simple as a misunderstanding could lead to resistance and the emergence of complex problems. It is apparent, however, that the reasons behind resistance may be more complex than just misunderstanding; hence, the latent, as opposed to manifest reasons, can be hidden from researchers, and be so ingrained that those resisting change are unaware of them (McAvoy & Butler, 2005).

Thus resistance to, or problems with, the acceptance of, for example, a new approach to IS development may be overt or covert. For example, deliberate sabotage of an adoption such as an Agile programming methodology is described as a potential concern by Broza (2005) and Schwaber (2002). These problems, though, are often latent or hidden, even from those involved in the process; Edmondson and Moingeon (2003, p.27) refer to these as *"built in impediments"*, while Luecke (2003) refers to 'passive resistors'. Individuals are usually unable to determine the origins of their resistance to change, although they may offer a view of what they consider to be the problem (manifest condition), which may not be the real crux of the issue at hand (latent causes cf. Goleman, 1996; McAvoy and Butler, 2005). Often, resistance to change stems from an emotional reaction rather than a logical reasoning in the consequence of change (Whitehead, 2001). Thus, Veryard (2001) shows how resistance to the diffusion of an innovation can be both logical and ridiculous.

Chris Argyris (1976) captures the essence of such issues in his illustration of how individuals are unable to discern the difference between what they believe in and what they actually do ('espoused theories' versus 'theories in use'). It is clear from Argyris that the inability to discern between, and reflect upon, 'espoused theories' versus 'theories in use' is usually not recognized by those affected by the phenomenon. We argue, therefore that surveys, questionnaires, and other such approaches are unsuitable research methods as a respondent cannot, or may not wish to, identify the differences between their 'espoused theories' and 'theories in use'.

Other organisational psychologists, notably Kegan and Lahey (2001 a,b), elaborate on this paradox, and argue that resistance to change does not imply the inability to commit to a particular course of action, rather the existence of a competing commitment. Competing commitments are not normally visible as conscious utterances or actions; they are observed as energy being unwittingly applied against the manifest commitments already entered into. This resisting force is caused by commitments that act against the initial commitment. For example, while a manager may be initially committed to Business Intelligence in his company, there may be a gradual erosion of commitment to the extent that the manager continually complains that the system does not provide the information he requires. Rather than the manager resisting the change to the use of BI, the manager may actually fear that his role in the organisation is being displaced by technology. So while the manager may imply that he is committed to using only the best information, his competing commitment, not being displaced by the technology, will work against the original commitment. An approach is required to determine why individuals resist the change inherent in IS projects, and to determine if individuals have commitments working against the change. Competing commitment theory explains the change paradox by examining the people involved in the IS project.

It is clear then, that the investigation of the factors that inhibit, or cause resistance to, the adoption of new technologies or techniques may be phenomena that would be normally hidden from, or not observable by, outsiders such as researchers. As indicated above, this situation calls for the application of research approaches that are sensitive to such issues (Jorgensen, 1989).

THE COMPETING COMMITMENTS PROCESS

Previous studies on the commitment concept are underpinned by the assumption that highly committed individuals are high-performance employees that provide positive benefits for an organization with reduced turnover and absenteeism being cited as some of the positive benefits (Mowday, 1998). Mowday illustrates the extent of 'commitment' research and its many dimensions and anomalies, and concludes that its contribution has been positive. Benkhoff (1997, p.114) concludes, however, that "[a]fter 30 years of research on employee commitment the results are disappointing. So far there is no evidence of a systematic relationship between commitment and its presumed consequences – turnover and job performance – even though these links are almost implied by the definition of the concept. Nor do we know very much about the factors that explain the phenomenon." Thus, there appears to something paradoxical with the concept.

IS research, while limited, has picked up on this and has focused on the escalation of commitment in IS development projects (see, for example, Keil, Rai & Mann, 2000). In brief, escalation of commitment is a negative phenomenon that occurs when project managers and teams remain committed to particular courses of action in projects that should change direction or be abandoned (Keil et al., 2000). The other stream of commitments research follows the conventional line and focuses on the benefits of commitment for IS development projects (cf. Newman & Sabherwal, 1996). Inspired by Winograd and Flores' (1987) seminal work, Butler (2003) drew on institutional theory in sociology to illustrate that commitments are shaped by, and are manifested at, several levels: individual, group, organizational, and societal. We now focus on the most interesting anomaly with the concept of commitment, which may help explain its often paradoxical and confusing nature.

Kegan and Lahey (2001a; 2001b) have been instrumental in exploring the paradox of competing commitments. In their scheme of things they prefer the term 'immunity to change' in place of 'resistance to change'. Resistance implies knowingly working against something for reasonably defined objectives. They argue that competing commitments, in which there is a manifest commitment (i.e. an 'espoused theory') and a latent commitment (a 'theory in use') that are not obvious, even to the individuals who possess them. Banerjee (2003, p.74) describes competing commitments as "*self-defeating behaviour.*" Elsewhere, Goleman (1996) refers to 'vital lies' and 'simple truths'. These behaviours, particularly if subconscious, act against change in attitudes and behaviours.

Competing Commitments Theory, also known as the Big Assumptions Theory, proposes a process through which the competing commitments, that negatively effect change, can be surfaced (i.e. made manifest) and identified for what they are. This process was originally proposed in Kegan and Lahey (2001a), and further discussed and demonstrated in Kegan and Lahey (2001b), Sparks (2002), Nash (2002), Bowe *et al.* (2003a; 2003b), and Banerjee (2003). Competing commitments have some similarity with the view of Milgram (1971) who argues that public declarations of adherence to group decisions do not imply that the individual will translate this adherence into action. Kegan and Lahey's competing commitments describe the reasons why this initial acceptance or commitment to change is not acted upon. It should be pointed out, though, that Millgram's experiments showed that adherence to a particular position can translate into desired behaviours and actions.

It is clear from Kegan and Lahey that their theory has wide application. For example, Nash (2002) and Bowe et al. (2003a; 2003b) apply the process in the field of medicine and medical education, while Banerjee (2003) applies it at the organisational level in business enterprises.

We argue that competing commitments theory and method is of particular use at the level of IS development or software project teams, and to investigate change management in IS implementations, from senior management to the end users. Thus, the theory can operate at several levels of analysis. To the best of our knowledge, other researchers have not applied this theory in the IS domain.

The suitability of this approach for Medical Education is identified in Bowe et al. (2003b, p.723) who describe the technique being used to examine why problems arose "*during implementation [of programs] when unanticipated or unaddressed organizational resistance surfaces.*" Nash (2002, p. 592) describes the use of the competing commitments process to go beyond "buy-in". Kegan, in Sparks (2002), describes what Nash refers to as "buy-in" as a short-lived espoused commitment. For example, Bowe *et al.* (2003a, p.715) described the problem with "buy-in" as "*like many new years' resolutions, sincere intent to change may be short lived and followed by a return to old behaviours.*"

Kegan and Lahey (2001a,b) developed a technique to investigate and identify competing commitments. Various authors describe this technique (Bowe et al., 2003a, 2003b; Kegan & Lahey, 2001a, 2001b; Nash, 2002; Sparks, 2002), although it had not been applied it in the IS field. The technique comprises six steps, in the form of questions, although different authors merge some steps. The examples used below are those used in Kegan and Lahey (2001b).

In the example above, the dialogue between the researcher and the manger moved from a complaint by him about a team not keeping the project manager informed, to the 'big assumption' that people will think him incompetent if it is perceived that he cannot solve every problem. The individual publicly states a commitment to full communication, yet the competing commitment—not learning about things the project manager can't control—effectively works against their commitment to full communication.

FUTURE TRENDS

McAvoy and Butler (2005) utilized this process in an investigation into resistance to the adoption of a software development methodology in an IS development team. While the team expressed an initial commitment to the methodology, over time this commitment was watered down and resistance to it developed. Likewise, the developers and the project manager expressed a commitment to effective use of resources in the project. After a short period of use, team members expressed the opinion that the new methodology was a waste of time, and the resources employed could be better used elsewhere. The process followed, on one of the team members, is shown below (table 2.), and follows the steps provided in Kegan and Lahey (2001b), shown in table 1.

The researchers applied the competing commitments process to each individual team member to determine why the change was being resisted. There was uniformity in the competing commitments that were identified; they were each more committed to team unity than the introduction of the new methodology. They felt that team unity was being impacted by the new methodology, so they resisted it. The cause of the resistance was

actually not initially visible to the researchers, in fact those resisting were not aware of the reasons themselves. Simply interviewing the team would have come to the conclusion that the problem was a resource allocation problem. The team had convinced themselves that their problem was with resource allocation; through the competing commitments process they could identify that the real concern was with its impact on the unity of what was a highly cohesive team – cohesion was more important to the individuals than the new methodology.

While the research described above was in the IS development domain and with project teams, the approach here outlined can also be applied in other areas such as management of change around IS adoption. Organisations do not truly reflect on problems surrounding IS adoptions. Weick (1995) argues that sensemaking occurs when individuals make retrospective sense of where they are now, and how they got there. Swanson and Ramiller (2004, p. 554) argue that organisations, which adopt and implement information systems, *"entertain scant reasoning for their moves... deliberative behaviour can be swamped by an acute urgency to join the stampeding herd, notwithstanding the high cost and apparent risk*

Table 1. Determining competing commitments – from Kegan and Lahey (2001b)

Step	Question	Example Response
1	What problem are you experiencing in work – a gripe or complaint?	My team do not tell me what's happening in a project
2	The complaint identifies something about you. What commitment does it imply?	I am committed to maximising the flow of information within the project.
3	What am I doing or not doing that goes against this commitment?	Sometimes I don't go out of my way to find out what is happening.
4	What do you think would happen if you were not doing what you described in question three – if you did the opposite of the undermining behaviour? What would worry you about this?	I might find out things from my team that I can do nothing about, something I can't fix.
5	What does this worry imply that you are committed to?	I am committed to not learning about things I can't control.
6	Inverting the answer from step five, and making it into the beginning of an assumption, complete the sentence. i.e. I assume that if I	I assume that if I learned about thing I couldn't control, people would realise that I am not able to do my job.

Table 2. Sample determination of competing commitments for one team member

Step	Question	Response
1	What is your problem with the new methodology?	It doesn't necessarily add value to the project.
2	The complaint identifies something about you. What commitment does it imply?	I am committed to only doing work that adds value
3	What am I doing or not doing that goes against the commitment to only performing work that adds value?	Chatting with the lads on the team. Long coffee breaks.
4	What do you think would happen if you were not doing what you described in question three – if you did the opposite of the undermining behaviour? What would worry you about this?	Won't get on with the team. Harder to interact with team. Team would be less likely to help me.
5	What does this worry imply that you are committed to?	I am committed to being part of the team, one of the lads. This is more important than the project itself.
6	Inverting the answer from step five, and making it into the beginning of an assumption, complete the sentence. i.e. I assume that if I ….	I assume that if I was not committed to the team then I would be a loner and not part of the group.

involved". It is clear from Swanson and Ramiller's findings that far from being mindful, heedless or mindless behaviour by organisations is the rule, rather than the exception, when it comes to the adoption of Information Systems. One of the major concerns with organizations adopting Information Systems is what Swanson and Ramiller describe as unchallenged assumptions. It is argued herein, that the competing commitments process is a mechanism that can be used to identify and challenge these assumptions.

CONCLUSION

Change is inherent in IS projects, and often problematic. It is argued herein that competing commitments may play a part in the problems in IS change efforts, and that *"without an understanding of competing commitments, attempts to change employee behavior are virtually futile"* (Luecke 2004, p.150). One of the recommendations deriving from this chapter is that team members involved in an IS adoption should not conduct a competing commitments analysis, as we believe that the team member will bring their own biases, even their own competing commitments into the

process. A suitably removed Devil's Advocate would be most effective in this role. Significantly, this runs counter to Swanson & Ramiller's (2004) recommendation of the use of internal experts working in the relevant domain. This would have the paradoxical consequence of a using mindless approach to investigating a mindless adoption.

The use of the competing commitments process is not recommended as a panacea for all research into resistance to change in IS projects. Some resistance occurs because the proposed system or idea is intrinsically flawed or unsuitable (Veryard, 2001). In scenarios such as this, there may be no hidden factors influencing the resistance; the resistance is open rather than latent. Similarly, individuals may be able to readily identify their reasons for resistance without recourse to the competing commitments process – assuming of course though they are genuinely providing a truly reflective answer. There are, though, times when a researcher needs to be able to identify hidden factors behind the resistance to an IS project. Competing commitments theory, on its own, will not solve resistance to change within IS projects; rather it can be the first stage where the cause of the resistance can be identified. Competing commitments theory is therefore a theory to add to the research toolkit, to be used when the research scenario necessitates it.

REFERENCES

Alkire, S., & Denevlin, S. (2002). Individual motivation, its nature, determinants, and consequences for within group behaviour. In J. Heyer, F. Stewart, & R. Thorp (Eds.), *Group behaviour and development* (pp. 51-73). New York: Oxford University Press.

Alsene, E. (1999). Internal changes and project management structures within enterprises. *International Journal of Project Management, 17*(6), 367-376.

Argyris, C. (1976). Single-loop and double-loop models in research on decision making. *Administrative Science Quarterly, 21*(3), 363-375.

Argyris, C. (1985). Defensive routines. In D. Pugh (Ed.), *Organization theory. Third Edition* (pp. 439-454). London: Penguin Books.

Argyris, C. (1998). Empowerment: The emperor's new clothes. *Harvard Business Review, 76*(3), 98-105.

Arrow, H., McGrath, J., & Berdahl, J. (2000). *Small Groups as complex systems*. CA: Sage Publications.

Asch, S. (1952). *Social psychology*. NJ: Prentice-Hall.

Banerjee, R. (2003). Organisational character: Issues, imperatives and practices. *International Journal of Human Resources Development and Management, 3*(1), 72-83.

Beck, K. (2000). *Extreme programming explained. Embrace change*. New York: Addison Wesley.

Benkhoff, B. (1997). Disentangling organizational commitment - the dangers of OCQ for research and policy. *Personnel Review, 26*(1), 114-131.

Birmingham, D. (2002). *Software development on a leash*. NY: Springer-Verlag.

Boody, D., & Macbeth, D. (2000). Prescriptions for managing change: A survey of their effects in projects to implement collaborative working between organizations. *International Journal of Project Management, 18*(5), 297-306.

Bowe, C., Lahey, L., Kegan, R., & Armstrong, E. (2003a). Questioning the big assumptions. Part I: Addressing personal contradictions that impede professional development. *Medical Education, 37*(8), 715-722.

Bowe, C., Lahey, L., Kegan, R., & Armstrong, E. (2003b). Questioning the big assumptions. Part II: Recognizing organizational contradictions that impede organisational change. *Medical Education, 37*(9), 723-733.

Broza, G. (2005). *Early community building: A critical success factor for XP projects*. Paper presented at the Agile Conference, Denver, CO, USA.

Butler, T. (2003). An institutional perspective on the development and implementation of Intranet and Internet-based IS. *Information Systems Journal, 13*(3), 209-232.

Clarke, A. (1999). A practical use of key success factors to improve the effectiveness of project management. *International Journal of Project Management, 17*(3), 139-145.

Coch, L., & French, J. (1968). Overcoming resistance to change. In D. Cartwright & A. Zander (Eds.), *Group dynamics* (pp. 182-191). NY: Harper & Row Publishers.

Cushway, B., & Lodge, D. (1999). *Organization behaviour and design*. London: Kogan Page Ltd.

Dent, E., & Goldberg, S. (1999). Challenging a resistance to change. *Journal of Applied Behavioural Science, 35*(1), 25-41.

Duck, J. (1993). Managing change: The art of balancing. *Harvard Business Review, 71*(6), 109-118.

Edmondson, A., & Moingeon, B. (2003). From organizational learning to the learning organization. In C. Grey & E. Antonacopoulou (Eds.), *Essential readings in management learning* (pp. 21-36). London: Sage Publications.

Festinger, L., & Carlsmith, J. (1959). Cognitive consequences of forced compliance. In E. Coats & R. Feldman (Eds.), *Classic and contemporary readings in social psychology. Third Edition* (pp. 194-203). NJ: Pearson Education.

Field, M., & Keller, L. (1998). *Project management.* London: Thomson Learning.

Gemmill, G., & Wilemon, D. (1997). The hidden side of leadership in technical team management. In R. Katz (Ed.), *The human side of managing technological innovation* (pp. 237-245). New York: Oxford University Press.

Giangreco, A. (2001). *Conceptualisation and operationalisation of resistance to change.* Catellanza, Italy: LIUC Papers.

Goleman, D. (1996). *Vital lies simple truths: The psychology of self-deception.* New York: Simon and Schuster Books.

Harmon-Jones, E. (1998). Towards an understanding of the motivation underlying dissonance effects: Is the production of adverse consequences necessary. In E. Coats & R. Feldman (Eds.), *Classic and contemporary readings in social psychology* (3rd ed.) (pp. 204-213). NJ: Pearson Education.

Herzog, J. (1991). People: The critical factor in managing change. *Journal of Systems Management, 42*(3), 6-11.

Hunt, A., & Thomas, D. (2000). *The pragmatic programmer.* MA: Addison Wesley Longman.

Jennings, D. (2004). Myths about change. *CPA Journal, 74*(4), 12-13.

Jorgensen, D. (1989). Participant observation: A methodology for human studies. CA: Sage Publications.

Kegan, R., & Lahey, L. (2001a). *How the way we talk can change the way we work.* San Francisco: Jossey-Bass.

Kegan, R., & Lahey, L. (2001b). The real reason people won't change. *Harvard Business Review, 79*(10), 85-89.

Keil, M., Mann, J., & Rai, A. (2000). Why software projects escalate: An empirical analysis and test of four theoretical models. *MIS Quarterly, 24*(4), 631-660.

Kling, R., & Scacchi, W. (1982). The web of computing: Computing technology as social organisation. In M. Yovits (Ed.), *Advances in Computers, Vol. 21* (pp. 3-90). New York: Academic Press.

Lafleur, R. (1996). Project management. Getting control and keeping control of complex projects. *American Programmer, 9*(4), 24-28.

Lawrence, P. (1969). How to deal with resistance to change. *Harvard Business Review, 47*(1), 77-86.

Lewin, K. (1951). Frontiers in group dynamics. In D. Cartwright (Ed.), *Field theory in social science* (pp. 188-237). CN: Greenwood Press.

Likert, R. (1978). An improvement cycle for human resource development. *Training and Development Journal, 78*(32), 16-18.

Luecke, R. (2003). *Managing change and transition.* MA: Harvard Business School Press.

Luecke, R. (2004). *Coaching and mentoring: How to develop top talent and achieve stronger performance.* MA: Harvard Business School Press.

Lyytinen, K. (1987). Different perspectives on information systems: Problems and solutions. *ACM Computing Surveys, 19*(1), 5-46.

Markus, M., & Robey, D. (1988). Information technology and organizational change: Causal structure in theory and research. *Management Science, 34*(5), 583-598.

McAvoy, J., & Butler, T. (2005). A paradox of virtual teams and change: An implementation of the theory of competing commitments. *International Journal of e-Collaboration, 2*(3), 1-24.

McElroy, W. (1996). Implementing strategic change through projects. *International Journal of Project Management, 14*(6), 325-329.

Milgram, S. (1971). Group pressure and action against a person. In D. Taylor (Ed.), *Small groups* (pp. 157-170). IL: Markham Publishing Company.

Mitsufuji, T. (2001). A perspective of the innovation-diffusion process. In M. Ardis & B. Marcolin (Eds.), *Diffusing software product and process innovations* (pp. 51-66). MA: Kluwer Academic Publishers.

Mowday, R. (1998). Reflections on the study and relevance of organizational commitment. *Human Resource Management Review, 8*(4), 387-401.

Nader, D. (1993). Concepts for the management of organisational change. In C. Mabey & B. Major-White (Eds.), *Managing change* (2nd ed.) (pp. 5-19). London: Paul Chapman Publishing.

Nash, D. (2002). Beyond buy-in. *P&T Journal, 27*(11), 617-618.

Newman, M., & Sabherwal, R. (1996). Determinants of commitment to information systems development: A longitudinal investigation. *MIS Quarterly, 20*(1), 23-54.

Patching, K. (1999). *Management and organisational development*. London: Macmillian Business.

Pellegrinelli, S. (1997). Programme management: Organising project-based change. *International Journal of Project Management, 15*(3), 141-149.

Raghavan, S., & Chand, D. (1989). Diffusing software-engineering methods. *IEEE Software, 6*(4), 81-90.

Rainwater, J. (2002). Herding cats: A primer for programmers who lead programmers. New York: Springer-Verlag.

Robbins, H., & Finley, M. (1998). *Why change doesn't work*. London: Orion Publishing.

Schelling, T. (1989). The mind as a consuming organ. In D. Bell, H. Raiffa, & A. Tversty (Eds.), *Decision making. Descriptve, normative, and prescriptive interactions* (pp. 343-357). UK: Cambridge University Press.

Schwaber, K. (2002). When and where agile suceeds. *Cutter IT Journal, 15*(9), 22-27.

Sparks, D. (2002). Inner conflicts, inner strengths. *Journal of Staff Development, 23*(3), 66-71.

Statt, D. (2004). *Psychology and the world of work* (2nd ed.). Hampshire, UK: Palgrave Macmillan.

Strebel, P. (1998). Why do employees resist change. In J. Kotter, J. Collins, R. Pascale, K. Duck, J. Porras, & A. Athos (Eds.), *Harvard Business Review on change* (pp. 139-157). MA: Harvard Business School Press.

Swanson, E., & Ramiller, N. (2004). Innovating mindfully with information technology. *MIS Quarterly, 28*(4), 553-583.

Turner, J., & Muller, R. (2003). On the nature of the project as a temporary organization. *International Journal of Project Management, 21*(1), 1-8.

Venkatesh, V., & Davis, F. (2000). A theoretical extension of the technology acceptance model: Four longitudinal field studies. *Management Science, 46*(2), 186-204.

Veryard, R. (2001). The diffusion of components. In M. Ardis & B. Marcolin (Eds.), *Diffusing software product and process innovations* (pp. 131-146). MA: Kluwer Academic Publishers.

Weick, K. (1995). *Sensemaking in organizations.* CA: Sage.

Weinberg, G. (1971). *The psychology of computer programming.* New York: Van Nostrand Reinhold Co.

Whitehead, R. (2001). *Leading a software development team. A developer's guide to successfully leading people and projects.* London: Addison-Wesley.

Winograd, T., & Flores, F. (1987). *Understanding computers and cognition.* MA: Addison Wesley.

Wren, D. (2005). *The history of management thought* (5th ed.). NJ: John Wiley & Sons.

Zachary, G. (1994). *Show-Stopper! The breakneck race to create Windows NT and the next generation at Microsoft.* New York: The Free Press.

Zmud, R. (1983). The effectiveness of external information channels in facilitating innovation within software development groups. *MIS Quarterly, 7*(2), 43-58.

KEY TERMS AND DEFINITIONS

Adoption: The selection and implementation of a new system.

Assumptions: Statements and beliefs accepted as true without proof or demonstration

Commitment: The act of binding yourself (intellectually or emotionally) to a course of action.

Competing Commitments: Energy being unwittingly applied against a commitment already made.

Resistance to Change: The action taken by individuals and groups, both conscious and subconscious, when they perceive that a change is a threat to them.

Chapter XX
Researching IT Capabilities and Resources:
An Integrative Theory of Dynamic Capabilities and Institutional Commitments

Tom Butler
University College Cork, Ireland

Ciaran Murphy
University College Cork, Ireland

ABSTRACT

Recent studies have highlighted the utility of the resource-based view (RBV) in understanding the development and application of IT capabilities and resources in organisations. Nevertheless, IS research has inadvertently carried over several fundamental problems and weaknesses with the RBV from reference disciplines. This chapter proposes an integrative theory, model and research propositions that draws on dynamic capabilities theory from the resource-based view of the firm in institutional economics, and commitment theory in institutional sociology, to explain and understand the process by which IT capabilities and resources are developed and applied in organizations. In so doing, this study addresses the paucity of theory on the role of IT capabilities in building and leveraging firm-specific IT resources. The chapter also addresses the aforementioned problems and weaknesses to build a logically consistent and falsifiable theory, with relatively superior explanatory power, for application in both variance and process-based research, whether positivist or interpretivist in orientation.

INTRODUCTION

Researchers in the IS field have noted that the process by which IT capabilities are created, developed and applied is not well understood. Take, for example, this comment by Bharadwaj (2000): "The underlying mechanisms through which… superior IT-capability leads to improved firm performance…is by no means clear. Additional research is needed to identify the full chain of variables connecting IT-capability to firm performance" (p. 188). Wade and Hulland (2004) contributed to the cumulative body of research in this area by identifying and categorizing capabilities and resources under the headings of (a) managing external relationships, (b) managing internal relationships, and (c) responsiveness to market, (d) IS planning and change management, (e) the processes by which IS are developed, and (f) managing IS operations effectively. However as with Bharadwaj, Wade and Hulland (2004) report that "[considerations] such as how resources are developed, how they are integrated within the firm, and how they are released have been under-explored in the literature" (p.131). While several recent papers have contributed to such an understanding, Bharadwaj's call for a refined theoretical model remains unanswered.

Thus, there is a clear requirement for a rigorous theoretical model and framework to help guide research in the task of understanding the application of business and IT Capabilities in organisations. This chapter proposes a theoretical model that integrates and builds upon prior cumulative research in the IS and reference disciplines to propose specific concepts and identify the relationships between them. Several propositions are derived from the resultant theoretical model by drawing on extant research. Following calls made by Williamson (1998) and Knudsen (1994), the integrative theoretical model proposed herein incorporates a set of descriptive microanalytic attributes that describe a firm's capabilities and resources—core, enabling, and supplemental—while also includ-

ing an intentionality view of behavioural theory that helps explain how organisational knowledge translates into capabilities. The recent work of Teece and Pisano (1998) on the dynamic capabilities of firms is integrated with Philip Selznick's (1949, 1957) concept of commitment to provide the model with its principal theoretical and analytic components. The inclusion of Selznick's theoretical perspective provides this study with normative and cognitive foci to augment the predominantly regulative focus of dynamic capabilities theory in institutional economics and the strategic management literatures. The rationale behind this integrative approach to theory building originates in Scott's (1995) contention that the various schools of institutional thought do not give equal weight to regulative (rules and laws institutionalised as protocols and routines in support of governance and power systems), normative (values and expectations that govern conformity and performance of duty within institutional regimes and authority systems), and cultural-cognitive (symbols, categories and typifications which shape performance programs, scripts and institutional identity) forces that shape institutions and organizations. Rather, researchers have generally stressed one or other as central, while implicitly incorporating others (DiMaggio and Powell, 1983). This study therefore adopts a holistic perspective and adopts a view of organizations and institutions that operates at several levels of analysis and which incorporates a theory of human behaviour that recognizes the primacy of social rationality. This chapter's theoretical model will therefore help researchers examine the development and application of business and IT capabilities and resources as key components of core or distinctive competence in knowledge-intensive firms.

The remainder of this chapter is structured as follows: Section 2 explores the origins of the resource-based view (RBV), which is regulative in its focus; Section 3 builds on this by presenting what is regarded as the most promising view in resource-based theory—the dynamic capabilities perspective; Section 4 presents a normative/cultural-cognitive theory of commitments and distinctive competence, which many argue had a seminal influence on capabilities theory; Section 5 then draws the conceptual strands together and presents theoretical model and several related propositions that should inform future research on IT capabilities and resources; the final section then offers some brief conclusions.

INSTITUTIONALISM AND THE RBV

Institutional theories originate in both sociology and economics (Rowlinson, 1997). Institutional theory in sociology has been employed fruitfully by a number of IS researchers to help explain and understand the development, application and use of IT in organizations (see Noir and Walsham (2007) for examples of previous IS research). Institutional theory in economics (or the New Institutional Economics as Williamson (1998) puts it) has also been applied for IS research, particularly transaction cost economics (see, for examples, Clemons & Hitt, 2004).

In writing on the 'The Personal and Intellectual Roots of Resource-Based Theory', Jay Barney (2004) illustrates the fertile ground in sociology and economics that gave birth to the resource-based view (RBV). Thus, the origins of this theory of the firm are to be found in institutional economics and institutional sociology. Following Scott (1995), however, this chapter views resource-based theory as being chiefly regulative in orientation, as it conceptualizes the firm as a bundle of idiosyncratic resources and related capabilities the interplay of which deliver competitive advantage (Rumelt, 1984). The seminal theories on which the RBV rests supports this perspective. In economics, for example, Penrose (1959) conceives the firm as a collection of competencies that embody its knowledge. Following Hayek (1945), Penrose argues that a firm's competitive position is dependent on the manner in which the experiential knowledge of its personnel is developed and leveraged. Penrose (1959) notes that the services (and products) provided by a firm's resources are of strategic import—not resources *per se*. However, the delivery of firm-specific services is dependent on how resources are employed, which is in turn dependent on the capabilities of organizational actors. Capabilities are thus conceptualized as the efficient and effective application of the experiential knowledge of a firm's personnel.

The view of organisations as *"repositories of productive knowledge"* is expanded upon by Nelson and Winter (1982, p. 175), who maintain that an organization's productive knowledge is to be found in its operational routines. Nelson and Winter argue that routines allow organisations to cope with complexity and uncertainty under the conditions of bounded rationality; in addition, they provide an efficient way of storing an organisation's accumulated experiential knowledge. Nelson and Winter also posit that organizational routines are the basis of a firm's distinctiveness and are, therefore, the source of its competitiveness. Thus, the resource-based view considers the firm as a repository of knowledge, rather than a response to information-related problems, which is the focus of theories such as transaction cost economics, agency theory, and so on (Fransman 1998). It is significant, therefore, that Newbert (2007) asserts that the "resource-based view of the firm (RBV) is one of the most widely accepted theoretical perspectives in the strategic management field" (p. 121).

The resource-based view is attractive to IS researchers because of its theoretical utility in explicating the link between IT resources, the capabilities required to develop and apply them, and the competitive success of enterprises (see, for examples, Mata et al.,1995; Wade & Hulland, 2004; and Wheeler, 2003). The primary argument of this strand of research is articulated by Henderson and Venkatraman (1993), who point out that sophisticated technological functionality does not secure competitive advantage for firms. Rather, sustainable competitive advantage emanates from the application of business and IT capabilities to develop and leverage a firm's IT resource for the purpose of organizational reconfiguration, transformation, integration and learning, all of which underpin the delivery of products and services. However, echoing arguments made by Penrose (1959) and Nelson and Winter (1984), Henderson and Venkatraman argue that business and IT capabilities are embodied in the firm-specific knowledge of organizational actors—which is itself an intangible asset or resource. Thus, the notion that knowledge is the only firm-specific (valuable, unique, and imperfectly mobile) asset or resource was readily accepted in the IS field (see, for example, Andreu & Ciborra, 1996).

Several issues require attention, however, concerning the RBV and its use for research in the IS field. The first of these concerns the inability of IS researchers to fully integrate regulative, normative and cognitive strands of institutional theory in their research so as to understand comprehensively how IT capabilities and resources are created, developed, and applied in organisations. The second issue is articulated by Nanda (1996), who argues that the resource-based view "is in a state of considerable flux .work linking the resource paradigm with intraorganizational processes." For example, Nanda illustrates that researchers employ terms like resources, assets, competencies and capabilities interchangeably in presenting their theoretical arguments or when describing their empirical findings[1]. In addition, several researchers have presented their own idiosyncratic conceptual definitions, while ignoring those articulated in established literature. All of this has occurred at the expense of building an accepted conceptual lexicon. A later critique of the RBV by Priem and Butler (2001) echoed these arguments. Unfortunately, this definitional 'confusion' has also been evident in several IS-based studies cited above. For example, a much-cited conceptual overview of the RBV by Mata

et al. (1995), and, more recently, research by Wheeler (2002) and Wade and Hulland (2004), treat the concepts of capabilities and resources as conceptual synonyms, when clearly they are not. Such incidences of definitional confusion tend to support arguments made by critics of the RBV and those within the IS field who question IS researchers' understanding and use of theory from reference disciplines (see Checkland & Holwell, 1998).

The third problem is articulated by Knudsen (1994) who, echoing Nanda (1996), argues that institutional economists, particularly those responsible for articulating the resource-based view of the firm, fail to adopt a process-based perspective when conducting their research and, instead, focus on outcomes variables, which do little to explain the dynamic nature of capabilities, their creation, and application. In order to address these problems, an integrative theoretical model is proposed, the conceptual components of which have been the subject of debate in economics, sociology, organization theory and strategic management for some time. This task is now undertaken.

DYNAMIC CAPABILITIES FRAMEWORK

In assessing the contribution of the RBV, Williamson (1998) poses the following question: *"[W]hat—in addition to an inventory of its physical assets, an accounting for its financial assets, and a census of its workforce—is needed to describe the capabilities of a firm[?]" (p. 28)*. He (ibid.) argues that this will require the articulation of an "intentionality view…that [incorporates] microanalytic attributes that define culture, communication codes, and routines," he also emphasizes that this "is an ambitious exercise." This section begins the task of describing just such a set of 'microanalytic attributes,' thereby answering to Williamson's call. It is clear from comments made by Richard Nelson (1994) that the dynamic capabilities framework of Teece and Pisano (1998), which builds on that proposed by Teece, Pisano and Shuen (1990), is the most appropriate candidate, as it incorporates extant theory and correctly focuses on the dynamic capabilities of firms (cf. Wheeler, 2002). More recently, the findings of Newbert's (2007) comprehensive meta-analysis of empirical research on the RBV leads him to argue for the empirical fidelity of RBV-based theories that focus on organisational capabilities. He argues that such approaches address Priem and Butler's (2001) reservations on the RBV's inability to account for the processes by which resources lead to improved firm performance.

While the dynamic capabilities perspective has been widely accepted in the literature, recent research by Teece and Pisano (1998) develop it into a conceptual framework that helps capture and describe the nature of a firm's distinctive or core competence. In presenting their framework, Teece and Pisano focus on the development and renewal of internal and external firm-specific capabilities as being of strategic importance to business enterprises. The concept of dynamic capabilities incorporates two valuable observations: first, the shifting character of the economic environment renders it dynamic—for example, decreasing time to market for products, shifting barriers to entry through technological change, globalization of national economies, and environmental uncertainty caused by political strife; second, organizational capabilities lie at the source of competitive success. In elaborating their perspective, Teece and Pisano (1998) state that core capabilities must be *"honed to a user need"*, must be *"unique"*, and *"difficult to replicate"* (p. 195). Enabling capabilities, on the other hand are those deemed necessary for firms to enter the game, while supplemental capabilities are non-proprietary and imitable (Leonard-Barton 1995). In order to understand firm-specific dynamic capabilities, Teece and Pisano present an analytic framework that incorporates a set of descriptive dimensions

or attributes that help researchers and practitioners evaluate and understand the source of such capabilities—these are now delineated.

Organizational and Managerial Processes: These describe the patterns of current practice and learning in a firm, tangible evidence of which is to be found in its routines. For Example, *Integration* processes are concerned with the efficient and effective internal coordination of organizational activities and production. In knowledge intensive firms, integration is also concerned with routines and mechanisms for knowledge sharing. *Learning* processes involve repetition and experimentation to enable tasks to be performed better and more rapidly—this occurs at the level of the individual, group, organizational and interorganisational levels. *Reconfiguration and Transformation* processes relate the capabilities required to evolve a firm's asset structure.

Asset Positions: These include a firm's endowment of technology and intellectual property (as indicated by its difficult–to-trade knowledge assets) as well as its relational assets with partners, customers and suppliers. *Technological Assets*, such as IT, may generally be considered commodities, and confer no strategic advantage; however, if they are highly firm- and task-specific, or if as generic technologies they can be configured to make them unique, then they are of strategic value. Also, if the knowledge which created such assets is also proprietary and firm-specific then this adds a further ring of protection. *Complementary Assets* involve the use of related assets to develop new products and services or the mechanisms by which they are to be delivered. Such assets are considered complementary and typically have uses beyond their immediate function. *Financial Assets* include the state of the balance sheet, a firm's cash position, and degree of financial leverage. Experiential knowledge and skills in financial management may be of strategic value here. Finally, a firm's *Locational Assets* may influence its ability to produce and distribute products and services at low cost. Some locational assets are non-tradable and therefore the source of difficult-to-replicate advantages.

Paths: The strategic alternatives available to a firm are a function of its past activities and positions. A consideration of *Path Dependencies* help us understand exactly how the firm's present market position is a function of its past performance and future possibilities. However, a firm's past investments and present repertoire of productive routines may act to constrain its future behaviour and choice of action. The *Technological Opportunities* presented to a firm are often down to internal and external organizational and institutional structures, collaborations and knowledge links. Quite often it is the idiosyncratic experiential knowledge of firms that guides managers in choosing the most appropriate and feasible of opportunities, and leads to the development of business and IT capabilities that enable them to realize such opportunities.

We argue that Teece and Pisano's (1998) framework helps answer Williamson's call for an 'intentionality view' of the firm; in that it incorporates an organization's culture, communication codes, and routines, in addition to accounting for its assets. However, the framework does not provide a behavioural dimension that would help explain how (and why) organizational actors develop capabilities and apply them in organizational contexts. Implicit as it is in many perspectives in institutional economics, Fransman (1998) maintains that the concept of bounded rationality is inappropriate as a behavioural theory to help explain how (and why) capabilities are developed. In proposing his concept, Simon (1957) argues that humans are limited in their cognitive abilities to acquire, store, recall and process information. Hence, their rationality is 'bounded' by such factors; hence, when involved in decision-making, social agents 'satisfice' on the paths taken to achieve desired objectives. Satisficing in the face of limited cognitive abilities and access to information is said to characterize the behaviour of all organizational actors; hence, individuals

run the risk of making what may be sub-optimal and inefficient choices. These factors, according to Simon, are the key issues that give rise to the existence of human organizations. Therefore organizations provide mechanisms for social actors to cooperate in pooling their cognitive capacities, communicate, and share information in order to transcend their individual bounded rationalities. Perrow (1984) propose an alternative model of rationality—social rationality—to account for factors not encompassed by the theory of bounded rationality. Briefly, social rationality recognizes the cognitive limits on rational choice, but argues that these limits are not entirely responsible for poor choices; in fact, they are viewed as beneficial in many respects as they encourage social bonding, interaction, and collaboration among diverse actors leading to shared learning. Perrow (1984) argues that social rationality better explains the behaviour of organizational actors—hence, the relevance and inclusion of theory from institutional sociology, as outlined in the following section.

THE ROLE OF INSTITUTIONAL COMMITMENTS IN SHAPING DISTINCTIVE COMPETENCE

The concept of distinctive competence was developed by Phillip Selznick's in his seminal work *Leadership in Administration*. Selznick's perspective subsequently informed Hamel and Prahalad's (1994) work on core competence and Leonard-Barton's (1995) treatise on core capabilities. Selznick (1957) argued that it is the various commitments entered into by organisational stakeholders that defines an organisation's character and bestows upon it a *distinctive competence* in the conduct of its affairs. For Selznick, commitment is an enforced component of social action—as such it refers to the binding of an individual to particular behavioural acts in the pursuit of organisational objectives. One of the chief strengths of Selznick's perspective is its emphasis on group and organizational levels of analysis.

The process of institutionalisation gives rise to and shapes the commitments of organizational actors and groupings (Selznick, 1949, 1957). Such commitments in turn define an organization's character for good or ill, thereby bestowing upon it a *distinctive competence*—when commitments are aligned with organizational imperatives—or a *distinctive incompetence*—when commitments are misaligned with organizational imperatives or are dysfunctional in nature. Following Selznick, Leonard-Barton (1992) argues that this gives rise to 'core rigidities' in organizations, which, she argues, are the flip-side of 'core capabilities'. Thus, the process of institutionalization is a double-edged sword, depending on the manner in which commitments are formed. This is an important point, organizational, group, and individual commitments determine whether organizational resources are employed with maximum efficiency and whether organizational capabilities are developed to leverage such resources to attain a competitive advantage (Selznick, 1957).

Several forms of commitment are described by Selznick (1949): their locus of origin range from the social character of individual actors to groups operating on the basis of sectional interests, to those enforced by institutional norms and organisational imperatives, and, finally, to commitments enforced by the external social and cultural environment (see Table 1 for a more detailed account of Selznick's theoretical concepts). Thus, as Selznick (1957) argues, it is through commitment, enforced as it is by a complex web of factors and circumstances, and operating at all levels within an organisation, that social actors influence organisational strategies and outcomes. However, these commitments do not evolve spontaneously, they are shaped by 'critical decisions' that reflect or constitute management policy: as Selznick illustrates, the visible hand of leadership influences the social and technological character of organisations and helps shape *distinctive competence* in them.

Support for Selznick's position comes from several quarters. Knudsen (1994) offers direct support and recommends Selznick's (1957) institutional theory as a suitable process-based perspective to augment the outcome-centric view of organizational competence prevalent in the literature on the RBV. Of import here is Knudsen's

Table 1. A framework and taxonomy for understanding organisational commitments

Type of Commitment	Description
Commitments enforced by uniquely organisational imperatives.	Organisational imperatives, which reflect business objectives, are concerned with reality preservation. They are usually implemented by policy decisions associated with system maintenance; consequently, they ensure that the organisational requirements of order, discipline, unity, defence, and consent are fulfilled.
Commitments enforced by the social character of the personnel.	The personnel, or so-called human capital, in an organisation come to the firm with particular needs, levels of aspiration, training and education, social ideals and class interest; thus, influences from the external environment are directly imported into an organisation through its personnel.
Commitments enforced by institutionalization.	Because organisations are social systems, goals, policies or procedures tend to achieve an established, value impregnated status. Commitment to established or institutionalized patterns is thereby accomplished, restricting choice and enforcing specific behavioural standards.
Commitments enforced by the social and cultural environment.	Organisational policies and outcomes are often influenced and shaped by actors in the external social and cultural environment.
Commitments enforced by the centres of interest generated in the course of action.	Decentralization and delegation of decision making to particular individuals and groups within an organisation runs the risk that policies and programs are influenced by the tangential informal goals of these individuals and sectional interests; as such, they may be unanticipated and incongruent with those of the organisation.

contention that the deficiencies in resource-based perspectives (in adaptionist sociological theory and in equilibrium-based economic theory) are countered by the fact that Selznick's institutional theory captures the dynamics of the continuous exchange and interrelationships between an organization's latent competencies and its structure and processes. Knudsen argues that these are an expression of a firm's accumulated knowledge and are a consequence of human design and 'intentionality' as expressed by the commitments entered into by the organization's stakeholders. Selznick's work therefore provides appropriate behavioural foundations for the resource-based view of the firm, which has hitherto operated from the perspective of bounded rationality. In terms of the design and development of computer-based information systems, Winograd and Flores (1986) highlight the role of commitment in shaping the design of such systems. However, in the field of management, Ulrich (1998) calls for researchers to focus on the relationship between commitment and competence or capability building in organisations.

AN INTEGRATIVE THEORY OF IT CAPABILITIES, RESOURCES, AND COMMITMENTS

Following Wheeler (2003), this chapter argues for the importance of theory in the research process because it acts "to impose order on unordered experiences to increase human understanding and prediction in the real world", (p. 129). In the positivist scheme of things, theory posits relationships between independent and dependent variables or antecedents and outcomes, while also determining what data is to be collected (Wheeler, 2003). From an interpretivist perspective, theory acts to help formulate a pre-understanding or to enrich extant understandings of IS phenomena (Butler, 1998)—the integrative dynamic capability theory presented in this chapter accords well with both positivist and interpretive perspectives.

The kernel of the extended dynamic capabilities theory as articulated in the integrative theoretical model is as follows:

A firm's business and IT capabilities and resources are the product of its past activities and are observable in its organisational and managerial processes (capabilities) and asset positions (resources). The various commitments entered into by organisational stakeholders, in the pursuit of business, social, cultural, sectional and personal objectives, determine how efficiently and effectively valuable services are leveraged from resources through the application of business and IT capabilities. This, in turn, determines whether a firm develops a core capability or distinctive competence in conducting its activities and which help it met its business objectives. Building core capabilities and firm-specific resources is a product of the application of business and IT firm-specific tangible (explicit) and intangible (tacit) knowledge.

Elaborating on this kernel definition, IT capabilities are conceptualised as knowledge in action—that is, the application of experiential and technical knowledge of committed IT professionals to acquire, build and deploy the hardware and software components of a firm's IT architecture. At a fundamental level, core, enabling and supplemental capabilities are applied in IS-related activities such as project management, IS analysis and design, programming, the use of IT-based Integrated Development Environments (IDE), systems administration (Windows 2008, Linux and related workstation/server/networking platforms etc.), telecommunications infrastructure management, and technical support, to name but a few. From an IT capabilities perspective, IT capabilities operate on IT-based resources such as project management tools, IT-based analysis and design technologies, programming paradigms (.NET, J2EE etc.) and development technologies and platforms (Visual Studio, IntelliJ etc.), management of information and communication technology (ICT) infrastructures etc. to produce IT infrastructure resources for business. Of course, IT capabilities arise from, and operate on, the explicit and tacit business and IT meta-, standard technical, industry, technical trade, intraorganisational, and unique knowledge (Nordhaug 1994: cf. Wade and Hulland (2004) on the role of knowledge of the business and IS technical knowledge and skills).

Having introduced the conceptual components of this study's integrative model of business and IT capabilities and resources in some detail in previous sections, this chapter's theoretical model is now presented in Figure 1. Unlike previous conceptualizations, this model is process-based, in that the 'microanalytic attributes' of organizational and managerial processes are further

elaborated by the application of Selznick's (1949, 1957) theory of commitment, thereby capturing the multi-faceted nature of the phenomenon. The role of the explicit and tacit knowledge as the tangible and intangible resources which underpins capability development is also recognized (Nonaka & Takeuchi, 1995; Andreu & Ciborra, 1996; Fransman, 1998). Furthermore, the model's scope and constituent concepts map well onto Benbasat and Zmud's (2003) "view…of the phenomena studied by IS scholars" and its articulation in their conceptualization of the "IT artifact and its immediate nomological net" (p. 186).

As IT hardware and software infrastructures are increasingly being leveraged to deliver superior value propositions and services to internal stakeholders, customers, and business partners

Figure 1. An integrative theoretical model for understanding the development and application of IT capabilities and resources

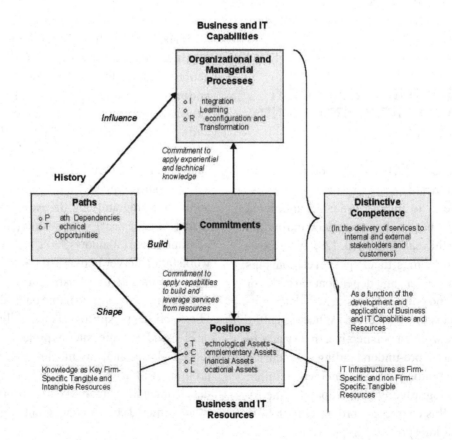

(e.g. in B2B/B2C/B2G etc.), they have acquired the status of firm-specific (i.e., valuable, rare, appropriate, imperfectly imitable, non-substitutable, and imperfectly mobile) resources: accordingly, the IT capabilities that are used to acquire, build, deploy and manage these resources in pursuit of business objectives have become core capabilities for business enterprises. It is important to note therefore that important synergies and relationships exist between business and IT capabilities and resources.

Theoretical Propositions and Analysis

We now present several propositions drawn from this study's theoretical model and based on insights from the literature cited previously. Each proposition is elaborated by empirical examples drawn from extensive research by Butler (2002)[2] and related publications, which assesses the business and IT competence profiles of four organizations: two newspaper company's—News International Newspapers Ltd. and Examiner Publications Ltd. (EPL); microelectronics manufacturer, Analog Devices Inc. (ADI); and Interactive Multimedia Systems Ltd. (IMS), a software company. The propositions are built on the fundamental assumption that a firm's IT capabilities and resources are the product of its history. This assumption indicates the need to study the historical activities and performance of firms: path dependencies, for example, are argued: (a) to influence a firm's organizational and managerial processes; (b) to build commitments; and (c) to shape the formation of asset positions. The theoretical propositions and the associated model therefore prepare the way for future process-based research of an interpretive nature on IT capabilities and resources, while also helping to inform the conduct of variance-based research strategies.

Butler (2002) illustrates the way in which News International Newspapers Ltd. developed its IT capabilities and resources to meet specific

business objectives. It is significant that many component IT resources (both software and hardware) at News International were commodities, while others were industry specific. However, innovative customization and unique recombination of what were supplemental and enabling IT resources through the application of firm-specific IT capabilities made such resources them core or strategic (Butler, 2002; Butler and Murphy, 1999).

Proposition 1: *Three types of capabilities and resources coalesce to form a firm's competitive position: that is, IT capabilities and resources (tangible and intangible) may be core (that is firm-specific, valuable, rare, and inimitable), enabling (industry specific), or supplemental (commodities).*

In all four organisations studied by Butler (2002) the existence of core business and IT capabilities and resources were observed to be a function of the optimal alignment of individual, group/sectional, social and cultural commitments with business objectives, as expressed by commitments to organisational imperatives. In two of the organisations, News International and EPL, core rigidities–that is attachment to outmoded capabilities and resources–were only overcome when the various commitments identified by Selznick (1949) were properly aligned in the pursuance of business objectives.

Proposition 2: *The development and application of IT capabilities and resources are influenced and shaped by the commitments entered into by an organization, its members, and wider institutions.*

Butler (2002) and Butler and Murphy (2008) report that the software development company IMS possessed a range of software capabilities, based on idiosyncratic knowledge of particular technologies (e.g. multimedia and Case-based

Reasoning (CBR)), that enabled it to produce software-based services in the area of learning and knowledge management to customers in the financial services, electronic and real estate sectors. Furthermore, Butler's (2002) case study of Analog Devices Inc. illustrates how IT-literate business managers made all the difference in applying supplemental and enabling IT resources through their in-depth knowledge of their business practices and products. Without such firm-specific capabilities and knowledge, commodity-like IT resources would, in and of themselves, not have delivered valuable services to internal or external stakeholders and customers.

Proposition 3: *IT capabilities operate on resources to produce services that are of value to internal and external stakeholders and customers.*

IT capabilities are, at base, knowledge in action: they are often embedded in the processes, routines and operational procedures of an organisation. Butler (2002) illustrates that the Sales and Marketing Divisions at Analog Devices Inc. possessed a unique blend of business and IT experiential and technical knowledge that saw user-led development of IT-based strategic sales and marketing solutions (Butler, 2003). The case study of News International and EPL described how these companies were leaders in the innovative application of IT to stay ahead of competitors in the newspaper industry. They achieved this through a mixture of experimentation and collaborative partnerships that saw transfers of knowledge within and between suppliers and partners, IT professionals and business staff. Butler and Murphy (2008) also report that IMS' success in developing and applying innovative CBR technologies grew in a similar fashion through pan-European collaborations. These cases revealed that integration, learning and reconfiguration and transformation IT capabilities are the product of systematic, patterned, responsive interaction of committed individuals and groups shape an organization's business and IT capabilities.

Proposition 4: *Valuable IT capabilities will be dynamic in nature and are evidenced by a firm's and/or IS function's integrative capacities, ability to learn, and abilities to transform and reconfigure their operations in response to environmental conditions.*

Butler (2002) and Butler and Murphy (2008) demonstrate the institutional and cultural conditions that are conducive to capability transfers within and between organisations; however, these studies also show that interorganisational knowledge and capability transfers (e.g. in the newspaper industry, where organisation-specific commitments militate against learning) are difficult to achieve (Butler, 1999). Thus we present the following proposition.

Proposition 5: *Firm-specific capabilities will be 'sticky' and difficult to imitate, or replicate, even across 'communities-of-practice' in and across organisations.*

Nordhaug (1994) and Nonaka and Takeuchi (1995) delineate the relationship between explicit and tacit knowledge and capabilities. Tangible and intangible experiential knowledge of the use and deployment of IT artefacts is the differentiating factor across competing firms (Butler, 2002, 2003; Butler and Murphy, 1999, 2008). In the latter studies, it was found that tangible IT resources were sourced from the marketplace and customized using the tangible and intangible experiential knowledge of key social actors.

Proposition 6: *Tangible and Intangible knowledge resources (experiential and technical) underpin all business and IT capabilities.*

These propositions describe at a high level of analysis the central tenets of this paper's elaboration of the RBV and the role of commitment in shaping the development and application of capabilities. The propositions are the product of logical deductions informed by a critical analysis of the different strands of institutional thought that surround the RBV. As such, they address many of the theoretical limitations of the RBV (Nanda, 1996; Priem & Butler, 2002; Newbert, 2007), while also extending and elaborating the theory of dynamic capabilities. They also incorporate a behavioural dimension by applying a theory of commitment that operates on several levels of analysis.

CONCLUSION

This chapter has drawn on old and new institutional thought in economics and sociology in order to posit a theory of business and IT capabilities, resources, and commitments that spans all three pillars or approaches—regulative, normative and cultural-cognitive—to understanding organisational processes and structures (Scott, 1995). In extending and elaborating upon extant treatments of the resource-based view (see, for example, Wheeler, 2002; Wade & Hulland, 2004), this chapter's theoretical model and associated framework presents IS researchers with a comprehensive perspective on the development and application of capabilities and resources in organizations. For example, the model's behavioural theory component views IT professionals and organizational actors as intentional, purposeful entities who commit themselves to particular courses of action as part of socially constructed 'communities-of-practice'. Furthermore, the theoretical model and its associated research framework illustrates that an understanding of the institutional and organisational mechanisms which shape and influence knowledge construction in social contexts, and of the commitments which shape and influence the development and application of such knowledge, is vital if the capabilities of IT professionals—core, enabling and supplemental—that are used to build and leverage IT resources to deliver valuable services are to be fully comprehended and explained.

In conclusion, the outcome of this chapter's integration and elaboration of institutional theory from economics and sociology has, we believe, resulted in a logically consistent theory, model and framework that helps explain better the processes by which IT capabilities and resources are developed and applied in organisations. It therefore provides a foundation for future academic research on this important topic.

REFERENCES

Andreu, R., & Ciborra, C. (1996). Organisational learning and core capabilities development: The role of IT. *Journal of Strategic Information Systems, 5,* 111-127.

Barney, J. B. (2004). Where does inequality come from? The personal and intellectual roots of resource-based theory. In M. A. Hitt & K. G. Smith (Eds.), *Great minds in management* (pp. 280-303). New York: Oxford University Press.

Benbasat, I., & Zmud, R. W. (2003). The identity crisis in the IS field: Defining and communicating the disciplines core properties. *MIS Quarterly, 27*(2), 183-194.

Bharadwaj, A. (2000). A resource-based perspective on information technology capability and firm performance: An empirical investigation. *MIS Quarterly, 24*(1), 169-196.

Butler, T. (1998). Towards a hermeneutic method for interpretive research in information systems. *Journal of Information Technology, 13*(4), 285-300.

Butler, T. (2002). *Building IT resources in post-industrial organizations: Cases on the development and application of IT competencies.* Unpublished doctoral dissertation, University College Cork, Ireland. Retrieved from http://afis.ucc.ie/tbutler/PhD.htm

Butler, T. (2003). An institutional perspective on the development and implementation of intranet- and Internet-based IS. *Information Systems Journal, 13*(3), 209-232.

Butler, T., & Murphy, C. (1999). Shaping information and communication technologies infrastructures in the newspaper industry: Cases on the role of IT competencies. In *An IT Vision of the 21st Century, Proceedings of the 20th International Conference on Information Systems (ICIS)*, Charlotte, NC. (pp. 364-377).

Butler, T., & Murphy, C. (2008). An exploratory study on IS capabilities and assets in a small to medium software enterprise. *Journal of Information Technology, 23*, 330-344.

Checkland, P., & Holwell, S. (1998). *Information, systems and information systems: Making sense of the field*. Chichester, UK: John Wiley and Sons Ltd.

Clemons, E. K., & Hitt, L. M. (2004). Poaching and the misappropriation of information: Transaction risks of information exchange. *Journal of Management Information Systems, 21*(2), 87-107.

DiMaggio, P. J., & Powell, W. W. (1983). The iron cage revisited: Institutional isomorphism and collective rationality in organizational fields. *American Sociological Review, 48*, 47-60.

Fransman, M. (1998). Information, knowledge, vision, and theories of the firm. In G. Dosi, D. J. Teece, & J. Chytry (Eds.), *Technology, organisation, and competitiveness: Perspectives on industrial and corporate change* (pp. 147-192). New York: Oxford University Press Inc.

Hamel, G., & Prahalad, C. K. (1994). *Competing for the future*. Boston: Harvard Business School Press.

Hayek, F. A. (1945). The use of knowledge in society. *American Economic Review, 35*, 519-532.

Henderson, J. C., & Venkatraman, N. (1993). Strategic alignment: Leveraging information technology for transforming organisations. *IBM Systems Journal, 20*(1), 4-16.

Knudsen, C. (1994). The competence view of the firm: What can modern economists learn from Philip Selznick's sociological theory of leadership. In W. R. Scott & S. Christensen (Eds.), *The institutional construction of organisations: International and longitudinal studies* (pp. 135-163). Thousand Oaks, CA: Sage Publications Inc.

Leonard-Barton, D. (1995). *Well-springs of knowledge: Building and sustaining the sources of innovation*. Boston: Harvard Business School Press.

Malone, T. W., Yates, J., & Benjamin, R. I. (1987). Electronic markets and electronic hierarchies. *Communications of the ACM, 30*(6) 485.

Mata, F. J., Fuerst, W. L., & Barney, J. B. (1995). Information technology and sustained competitive advantage: A resource based analysis. *MIS Quarterly, 9*(4), 487-505.

Nanda, A. (1996). Resources, capabilities and competencies. In B. Moingeon & A. Edmondson (Eds.), *Organizational learning and competitive advantage* (pp. 93-120). London: Sage Publications Ltd.

Nelson, R. R. (1994). Why do firms differ and how does it matter? In R. P. Rumelt, D. E. Schendel, & D. J. Teece (Eds.), *Fundamental issues in strategy* (pp. 230-247). Boston: Harvard Business School Press.

Nelson, R. R., & Winter, S. G. (1982). *An evolutionary theory of economic change*. Cambridge, MA: The Belknap Press of Harvard University Press.

Newbert, S. L. (2007). Empirical research on the resource-based view of the firm: An assessment and suggestions for future research. *Strategic Management Journal, 28*, 121-146.

Noir, C., & Walsham, G. (2007). The great legitimizer: ICT as myth and ceremony in the Indian healthcare sector. *Information Technology & People, 20*(4), 313-333.

Nonaka, I., & Takeuchi, H. (1995). *The knowledge creating company.* New York: Oxford Press University.

Nordhaug, O. (1994). *Human capital in organisations: Competence, training and learning.* New York: Oxford University Press.

Penrose, E. (1959). *The theory of the growth of the firm.* London: Basil Blackwell.

Perrow, C. (1984). *Normal accidents: Living with high-risk technologies.* New York: Basic Books.

Priem, R. L., & Butler, J. E. (2001). Is the resource-based 'view' a useful perspective for strategic management research? *Academy Management Review, 26*(1), 22-40.

Rowlinson, M. (1997). *Organisations and institutions.* London: Macmillan Press Ltd.

Rumelt, R. P. (1984). Towards a strategic theory of the firm. In R. B. Lamb (Ed.), *Competitive strategic management* (pp. 556-570). Englewood Cliffs, NJ: Prentice Hall.

Scott, W. R. (1995). *Institutions and organizations.* Thousand Oaks, CA: Sage Publications Ltd.

Selznick, P. (1949). *TVA and the grass roots.* Berkley: University of California Press.

Selznick, P. (1957). *Leadership in administration: A sociological interpretation.* New York: Harper and Row.

Simon, H. A. (1957). *Models of man.* New York: John Wiley & Sons.

Teece, D. J., & Pisano, G. (1998). The dynamic capabilities of firms: An introduction. In G. Dosi, D. J. Teece, & J. Chytry (Eds.), *Technology, organisation, and competitiveness. Perspectives on industrial and corporate change* (pp. 17-66). New York: Oxford University Press Inc.

Teece, D. J., Pisano G., & Shuen, A. (1990). *Firm capabilities, resources and the concept of strategy* (CCC Working Paper No. 90 8). CA: University of California at Berkeley.

Ulrich, D. (1998). Intellectual capital = competence x commitment. *Sloan Management Review, 39*(2), 15-26.

Wade, M., & Hulland, J. (2004). The resource-based view and information systems research: Review, extension and suggestions for future research. *MIS Quarterly, 28*(1), 107-142.

Wheeler, B. C. (2002). NEBIC: A dynamic capabilities theory for assessing net-enablement. *Information Systems Research, 13*(2), 125-146.

Williamson, O. E. (1998). Transaction cost economics and organization theory formation, knowledge, vision, and theories of the firm. In G. Dosi, D. J. Teece, & J. Chytry (Eds.), *Technology, organisation, and competitiveness: Perspectives on industrial and corporate change* (pp. 17-66). New York: Oxford University Press Inc.

Winograd T., & Flores, F. (1986). *Understanding computers and cognition: A new foundation for design.* Norwood, NJ: Ablex Publishing Corporation.

KEY TERMS AND DEFINITIONS

Asset Positions: (Technological, Complementary Financial and Locational Assets) include a firm's endowment of technology and intellectual property, as indicated by its difficult–to-trade knowledge assets as well as its relational assets with partners, customers and suppliers.

Capabilities: Include core capabilities are "honed to a user need", are "unique", and are "difficult to replicate"; enabling capabilities are those deemed necessary for firms to enter the game; and supplemental capabilities are nonproprietary and imitable.

Commitment: Is an enforced component of social action; as such, it refers to the binding of an individual to particular behavioural acts in the pursuit of organisational objectives. It is through commitment, enforced as it is by a complex web of factors and circumstances, and operating at all levels within an organisation, that social actors influence organisational strategies and outcomes.

Distinctive Competence: Is a function of the commitments of organisational groupings and social actors to develop and apply business and IT capabilities and resources to deliver services that are of value to customers.

Dynamic Capabilities: This concept is based on two valuable observations: first, the shifting character of the economic environment renders it dynamic; second, organizational capabilities lie at the source of competitive success.

Organizational and Managerial Processes: Consist of integration processes, learning processes, and reconfiguration and transformation processes.

Paths: Encompass the strategic alternatives available to a firm are a function of its past activities and positions. A consideration of *Path Dependencies* help us understand exactly how the firm's present market position is a function of its past performance and future possibilities. However, a firm's past investments and present repertoire of productive routines may act to constrain its future behaviour and choice of action. The *Technological Opportunities* presented to a firm are often down to internal and external organizational and institutional structures, collaborations and knowledge links.

ENDNOTES

[1] It is important to make a distinction between a competence or capability and the assets or resources which they relate to and operate on. For example, a competence or capability in hammering nails refers to three physical objects or resources/ assets—a hammer, nails, and the object(s) to be nailed. In describing a competence or capability, therefore, it is customary to refer to the object or asset/ resource that one has a competence in using, but not to include it as a competence or capability.

[2] The entire research monograph, including case study narratives and extended analysis is available from http://afis.ucc.ie/tbutler/ PhD.htm

Section V
Marketing Theory

There are two chapters in 'Section V. The first chapter (Chapter XXI) reviews past research around information systems facilitating customer services and identifies the technical and social attributes of IT-enabled customer service systems, as well as the functionalities of customer service systems enabled by these attributes. Finally, chapter XXII presents expectation-confirmation theory (ECT) suggesting that satisfaction is determined by the interplay of prior expectations and perception of delivery. This chapter provides an overview of ECT applications in IS research and demonstrates how polynomial regression analysis allows for a more robust set of models.

Chapter XXI
Toward a Theory of IT–Enabled Customer Service Systems

Tsz-Wai Lui
Cornell University, USA

Gabriele Piccoli
Università di Sassari, Italy

ABSTRACT

As the use of customer service as a tool to create customer value and differentiation continues to increase, the set of customer services that surround the product rather than the product alone will increasingly become a source of competitive advantage and one of the most critical core business processes. However, there is a lack of a strong conceptual foundation for a service economy and a lack of theoretical guidance for optimal customer service systems design. In this chapter, the authors review past research around information systems facilitating customer services and identify the technical and social attributes of IT-enabled customer service systems, as well as the functionalities of customer service systems enabled by these attributes. Moreover, given the key role of customers as co-producers of the customer service experience, the authors address the role of customers' characteristics in IT-enabled customer service systems. Finally, they identify existing research gaps and call for future research in these areas.

INTRODUCTION

Customer service nowadays has become an essential part of product offerings in every industry (Levitt 1972), as it has emerged as a critical source of differentiation and competitive advantages (Bowen et al, 1989; Sheehan, 2006).

While companies have realized the importance of customer service and implemented different service innovation processes to create competitive advantages, there is a lack of a strong conceptual foundation for their work (Chesbrough and Spohrer 2006). Therefore, there is a need to apply research findings in the appropriate management and organizational contexts related to service innovation, design and delivery, and the resulting customer satisfaction and business value. The information systems discipline is at the nexus of the service science literature and can bring a distinct integrative research perspective to this area of study, thus becoming a reference discipline for service science research (Baskerville and Myers 2002). Our main contribution in this chapter is the development of a theoretical framework that integrates the cross-disciplinary research on customer service systems. We draw theories from different disciplines, including information systems, marketing, operations management, and psychology, to abstract an overarching framework about IT-enabled customer service system.

This chapter is organized as follows: we first address the key concepts in the theory of IT-enabled customer service systems in the next section. Then, we present four major components of an IT-enabled customer service system (functionalities of the system, technical and social attributes of the system, and customers' characteristics) and the impact of these components on customer value. Finally, we address the research gaps that call for future research attentions.

BACKGROUND AND DEFINITIONS

Customer Services

We adopt a broad definition of customer service. Service is "a change in the condition of a person, or a good belonging to some economic entity, brought about as a result of the activity of some other economic entity with the approval of the first person or economic entity" (Hill 1977, p.318). This process changes the condition of the customers with the objective of enhancing customer value. An important distinction is between core services and supplementary services. Sometimes, customer services represent the core benefits delivered to the consumer, such as consulting or teaching.

Sometimes, the service is supplementary to the core value proposition and it enables it, such as providing product information on a car manufacturer's website (Lovelock 1994). In this chapter, we focus on supplementary services, because they apply to any industry, not just the service industry, and because they are increasingly IT-enabled.

IT-Enabled Customer Service Systems

The deployment of information technologies in supporting customer service has a long tradition of research in information systems (Ives and Learmonth, 1984; Piccoli et al, 2001; Sawy and Bowles 1997; Ray et al 2005; Orman 2007). The customer service life cycle (Ives and Learmonth, 1984) maps customer needs as they emerge at different stages of the interaction between an organization and its customers.

Drawing from the socio-technical tradition (Bostrom and Heinen 1977), we define a customer service system to encompass both technical and social subsystems. We therefore define IT-enabled customer service systems as the collection of information systems that provide supplementary customer services to fulfill customer needs (Piccoli et al. 2004). This general definition that encompasses any customer service system, from simple ones like a website providing the menu of the local mom and pop restaurant, to complex global systems such as Hilton OnQ (Applegate, Piccoli and Dev 2008), enabling reservations, check-in, check-out, customer relationship management, etc. at over 3,000 hotels in the global Hilton Hotels chain.

Functionalities of Customer Service Systems

Functionality is the particular set of capabilities associated with computer software, hardware, or an electronic device (Webster). Therefore, functionality represents the "purpose" of an entity and the enabler of the act that will change the condition (i.e., performing service). Thus, a functionality of a customer service system allows a service provider or customers (in the case of self-service) to perform the action to change their condition from pre-service (need condition) to after-service (need fulfilled condition) so as to fulfill customer needs. Functionalities, increasingly IT-enabled, represent the nexus of interaction between customers in need of service and the firm providing it.

Customer Value

Customer service systems aim to provide customer value, defined as "customer's perceived performance for and evaluation of those product attributes, attribute performances, and consequences arising from use that facilitates (or block) achieving the customer's goal and purposes in use situations" (Woodruff 1997, p.142). In short, customer value improves either when benefits received by customers increase or when cost required for obtaining the benefits declines (Han and Han 2001). In the context of customer service systems designed to enable supplementary services, customer value is created when the firm is able to better fulfill customers' needs arising throughout the customer service life cycle or it is able to reduce the cost of such need fulfillment for the customer. For example, an airline check-in kiosk enables self-service. For the computer savvy frequent traveler the kiosk creates significant customer value – enabling the traveler to see the plane map and pick the seat she deems most suitable – while reducing the cost of need fulfillment through shorter lines. We theorize that the functionalities of customer service systems are enabled by a blend of the technical and social components of the customer service system. Identifying the components of such systems and designing their optimal blend is predicated on an understanding of both the components and the way in which they interact: in short, a theory of IT-enabled Customer Service Systems.

TOWARD A THEORY OF IT-ENABLED CUSTOMER SERVICE SYSTEMS

In this section, we discuss the technical and social attributes of IT-enabled customer service systems and the functionalities they create. We then address the important role and characteristics of customers, since they are involved in the co-production of the service. Finally, we discuss the impact of these components of a customer service system on customer value represented in Figure 1.

Customer Service Systems Components

Functionalities of IT-Enabled Customer Service Systems

There exists is no widely accepted formal definition or taxonomy of the functionalities of customer service systems. While some studies have used the stages in the customer service life cycle as the functionalities (Lightner 2004; Cenfetelli et al 2008), we consider that these stages are more precisely representative of customer needs, as defined above, rather than system functionalities. Upon review of the interdisciplinary research on customer service we abstracted the following taxonomy:

Sensing Customers' Needs

With complete information about its customers, a business will be able to anticipate customers' needs and requests and be responsive to them (Sisodia 1992). Being able to know customer needs facilitates customers in smooth searching and acquisition of products and services (i.e., the beginning phases of the customer service life cycle) that achieve customers' goals. This functionality also enables the business to react to customers'

Figure 1. Theory of customer service systems

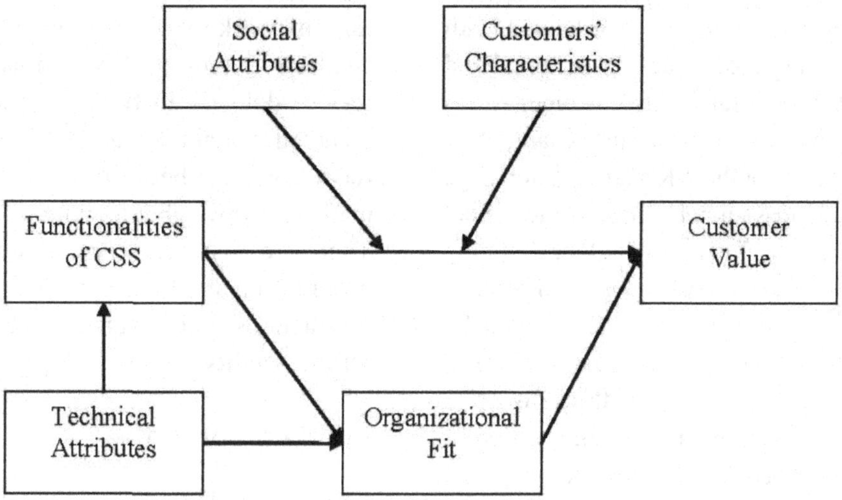

needs and requests promptly and effectively, providing the customer with the knowledge necessary to make a purchase (Dillon and Reif 2004) and consume the products and services (i.e., the third stage of the customer service life cycle). Finally, being able to predict customer needs also helps businesses handle complaints effectively (i.e., the last stage of the customer service life cycle), which in turn enhances service quality (Erevelles et al. 2003).

Providing Information

Organizations can enhance service offerings by disseminating valuable information to their customers (Furey 1991). For example, Ikea, the Swedish furniture store, has installed a kiosk in its stores to offer customers the opportunity to obtain information on the combination of different colors and designs and order a sofa through a touch screen public access terminal (Rowley and Slack 2003). This functionality is even more important when customers purchase products and services over the internet, where they rely on mediated representation of the products and services to acquire information (Dillon and Reif

2004). The ability to inform customers about relevant product alternatives in a timely and accurate fashion will increase the user satisfaction of web-based customer support (Negash et al. 2003; Lin 2007).

Customization and Personalization

Customization, the ability to tailor products, services, and the transactional environment to individual customers, increases the probability that customers will find something they wish to buy (Srinivasan et al., 2002). In this situation, service providers do not just provide product information, but they exchange information with the customers. The customer provides some information about themselves, and customer service systems make recommendations or provide additional information to facilitate the customer's decision making. A personalized product offering showing that the company cares about giving individualized service enhances the service quality.

Moreover, this notion of "Personalization" of the transactional environment is expected to emerge with the evolution of websites when businesses wish to create in-industry differentiation and barriers to imitation (Piccoli et al. 2004). This is especially important in the information age when customers are overloaded with information. Being able to deliver personalized information that accurately fits customer needs will enhance customer satisfaction (Liang et al. 2006). Halifax, one of the UK's largest mortgage lenders, placed kiosks in a Halifax service outlet without a "shop-front" in a large indoor shopping center. The kiosks calculate the costs and benefits of personal loans from the parameters entered by potential customers (Rowley and Slack 2003). A customer will be able to complete the transaction more efficiently when the transactional environment (e.g., the website) is customized, and, as a result, perceives higher service quality.

Facilitating Transactions and Payments

Technology allows service providers to access customers' data in a faster and more accurate fashion so as to increase the customers' confidence in the reliability of the transaction process, reduce waiting time, enhance the responsiveness of the service providers to customers' feedback, ensure the accuracy of the payment process, and give customers individual attention (Sivabrovornvatana et al. 2005).

Flexibility with respect to payment options enhances customer services by providing more means for customers to finish a transaction (Erevelles et al. 2003). For example, kiosks that sell rail tickets at railway stations provide an alternative method of purchasing a rail ticket (Rowley and Slack 2003). As a result, customers will have more access to the resources needed to complete their transaction and payments and experience less frustration when constrained by limited ways of completing the purchase. Another example is the FedEx kiosks, which allow anybody with a credit card or prearranged account number to drop off an overnight letter or small package at a self-service kiosk. All labeling and billing is executed on a touch-screen terminal. The routing

information and billing confirmation is carried out over the private nationwide telecommunications network by which Federal Express already conducts its business. With this new means of service delivery to fulfill transaction and payment functionalities, customers will receive more reliable service because of the reduction of human error through automation (Ramirez 1993). Therefore, customer service systems that provide different means for customers to process their transactions and payments will receive higher service quality scores.

Problem Solving

The functionality that solves customers' problems includes detecting errors and correcting errors, and at the same time minimizes the disruption of consumption of the core products and services (Erevelles et al. 2003). One way to solve customers' problems is to have answers for a set of frequently asked questions. This can solve customers' problems faster than providing solutions through email or online requests. This avoids delays of the service because email and online requests rely on manpower to reply to the customers' requests. Having this functionality can significantly reduce the service cost and provide more efficient and effective customer service (Tseng and Hwang 2007).

Relationship Building

Once a customer has an entry in the database, further records of customer purchases can be added, so that ultimately it is possible to build a profile of an individual customer's purchasing habits. With this information, businesses can provide products and services more appropriate for the customers, and, as a result, enhance customer value with time (Piccoli et al. 2004). Sainsburys, a leading UK food retailer, placed public access kiosks at the entrances of their stores that tie in with the store's loyalty cards. Customers swipe their loyalty card through the card slot and the kiosk provides them with access to special offers and coupons (Rowley and Slack 2003). In summary, customer service systems can provide functionalities that draw people into a community or a relationship with a retailer. These functionalities can enhance relationships and commitment to a retailer through features such as special offers and service enhancements (Rowley 2000).

TECHNICAL ATTRIBUTES OF IT-ENABLED CUSTOMER SERVICE SYSTEMS

The technical components of the customer service infrastructure enable and/or constrain the above functionalities provided by customer service systems (Craig 1986). In this section, we address two important attributes of information systems— data and system quality—and their impact on the functionalities of customer service systems as well as the service delivery channels (i.e., the medium through which service is delivered).

Data Quality

Businesses that learn the preference of individual clients and capture this information can use it to best advantage in fulfilling a client's requirements (Berry and Gresham 1986; Teo et al. 2006) so as to enable several functionalities of the customer service systems. First, with complete customer information gained from market intelligence, businesses can fulfill customers' needs before they ask for the service (Bessen 1993; Berkley and Gupta 1995). That is, business can sense customers' needs in advance and be prepared for them. For example, British Airways installed a software application that allows them to track onboard amenities at 160 airports around the world. Therefore, when travelers fly with British Air, their preferred newspaper, meal or drink will be provided for them without them having to request it more than once (Peppers 1999).

Second, transactional and operational data, service history, and guest complaints data can assist the service agent in responding to individual customers during the service encounter (Berkley and Gupta 1995). After the data is collected, an integrated customer data is needed so the businesses can focus on the customer and treat each customer as an individual across different functional departments, so as to provide personalized service (Delene and Lyth 1989). Therefore, complete customer data enhances the personalized service experience. Third, with a greater level of data completeness and integration, customers are more likely to feel that their needs are understood or will want to build and maintain a long-tern relationship with the company (Ives and Mason 1990; Dev and Ellis 1991; Wells et al 1999; Brohman et al. 2003). Data integration is becoming more and more important as customers may prefer to use different channels at different times for different purposes, and it ensures that the data available through these channels are identical and equally current so as to serve customers' needs, such as providing information or facilitating transactions (Stamoulis et al. 2001).

Finally, the data contained in the customer service systems not only refers to customers' information, but also to information about the company and its products (Berkley and Gupta 1995). This includes instructions for accessing the service, such as hours of operation, information about the behavior expected from the customer, recommendations and warnings, and conditions of access (Bancel-Charensol 1999). Walt Disney World has learned that cast members (as their employees are called) with brooms are five times more likely to be asked a question than the people ostensibly provided for that purpose. Therefore, Disney maintains a complete database of answers to the questions guests might ask. If the cast member does not know the answer to a question, the answer is only a phone call away (Berkley and Gupta 1994). Without this complete database, the cast members would not be able to deliver the functionality of providing information.

In summary, the completeness and integration of data enables functionalities of customer service systems, including providing information, sensing customers' needs, personalizing services, facilitating transactions and building relationships with customers.

System Quality

The quality of information systems has a positive impact on the use of an information system and user satisfaction (DeLone and McLean 1992). Applying this notion to the customer service context, a reliable and responsive customer service system is necessary to provide any kind of functionality of the system, as it ensures the right kind of functionality will be delivered to the right customer through the right channel in a timely manner (Choi et al. 2006). First, system reliability is proven to have a positive impact on service quality through the effects of decision effectiveness and efficiency of task completion (Bharati and Berg 2003). Second, accuracy, another of the measures of system quality that ensures accurate billing and records, is critical in providing functionalities involving transactions and payments (Berkley and Gupta 1994; Zhu et al. 2002). Third, accessibility of the customer service systems, the number of accessible service delivery points that are available when customers need them, also influences service quality (Zhu et al. 2002). Fourth, a flexible customer service system enables firms to implement IT applications to support customer service more efficiently and effectively (Ray et al. 2005) by facilitating rapid development and implementation of IT applications that enhance customer service process performance by enabling the organization to respond swiftly to customer needs and provide functionalities that take advantage of emerging opportunities or neutralize competitive threats. Finally, customers normally expect that their records will remain confidential, especially financial information, such as accounts and credit card use (Berkley and Gupta 1995).

Customers are concerned with their privacy, especially when using IT-based services such as the internet. This concern about the potential invasion of personal information affects customers' willingness to obtain services, especially those involving the functionalities of transaction and payment (Zhu et al. 2002).

Service Delivery Channels

Customers do not evaluate service quality based solely on the outcome of the service, but also on the quality of the service delivery process (Han and Han 2001). Froehle and Roth (2004) have proposed five different customer service channels (Figure 2): (a) technology-free customer contact, (b) technology-assisted customer contact, (c) technology-facilitated customer contact, (d) technology-mediated customer contact, and (e) technology-generated customer contact (self-service). Situations (a), (b), and (c) are "face-to-face" service encounters because the customer and customer service representative are physically co-located. Situations (d) and (e), where the customer and the customer service representative are not co-located, are often referred to as "face-to-screen," because the customer is generally using some sort of visual display and/or audible interface to interact with the service provider.

Different types of service interactions call for different types of interface: people-dominant, machine-dominant, or a hybrid of both (Rayport and Jaworski 2004). That is, different types of interfaces may more appropriately support different kinds of functionalities delivered by the customer service systems. The manner in which a service is delivered may be more important when using personal service (e.g., friendliness of staff), whereas the outcome maybe more important when using self-service technology (e.g., speed of technology) (Beatson, Coote and Rudd 2006). Therefore, a people-dominant interface that is better at conveying empathy and handling exceptions is a better interface in delivery

Figure 2. Types of Service Delivery Channels. Reprinted from Journal of Operations Management, Volume 22, Issue 1, Craig M. Froehle and Aleda V. Roth, Mew Measurement Scales for Evaluating Perceptions of the Technology-Mediated Customer Service Experience, Page 3, 2004, with permission from Elsevier.

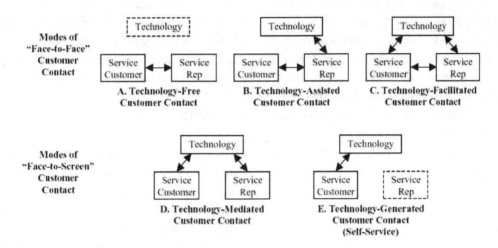

functionalities such as relationship building and problem recovery, while a machine-dominant interface that excels in routine processing is more appropriate for functionalities such as transactions and payments.

However, even if companies distinguish between e-service delivered through self-service vehicles and customer service delivered through customer service representatives, customers themselves do not. People form different attitudes toward different technologies that vary from service to service and, at times, within a single provider's operation (Curran and Meuter 2005). They generally develop separate, distinct attitudes toward the employees and self-service technology, but more global attitudes toward the service firm (Curran et al. 2003). Therefore, organizations must treat all channels as part of a larger customer experience continuum. That is, companies should look for options to integrate self-service channels with personal contact (Selnes and Hansen 2001; Salomann et al. 2007). It is also important to note that the integration of service delivery channels

may be able to provide a higher level of customer service (Li et al. 2003). A customer may start by looking at the company's website to search a product's information, and then go to purchase the products at a physical store. Therefore, the combined effects of different service delivery channels should be considered.

SOCIAL ATTRIBUTES OF IT-ENABLED CUSTOMER SERVICE SYSTEMS

The social attributes of IT-enabled customer service systems include the service-oriented culture of the company, the human assets (i.e., knowledge and skills of the employees), and training.

Service-Oriented Culture

Service climate is defined as "employee perceptions of the practices, procedures and behaviors

371

that are expected, supported and rewarded with regard to customer service and customer service quality" (Schneider et al. 1998, p.151). That is, an organization that shows commitment to customers and has customer satisfaction as a major objective is one with customer-oriented strategies (Levenburg and Klein 2006). With a customer-oriented strategy, the firm focuses more on a commitment to customers and their needs rather than the product itself. In this situation, supplementary service has become a source of customer value in addition to products. Research has shown a positive link between a service-oriented business strategy and company performance (Agnihothri et al. 2002; Ray et al. 2004).

Human Assets

The skills that a customer service representative should acquire are telephone skills, customer service and customer retention, telemarketing, problem-solving capabilities, the ability to maintain customer satisfaction, and the effective use of technology. With the same functionality, employees with different levels of knowledge and skills provide service at different levels of quality. For example, an employee with a higher overall level of knowledge of the service process can make a better judgment at the point of customer contact and provide better service (Berkley and Gupta 1994). While employees' knowledge can be increased by acquiring information from the customer service systems, customer service agents' interpersonal skills remain the major differentiating factor of services, such as the information given to customers, the style of welcome and interactions, the ability to listen and understand the needs of customers, the capacity to personalize the service in real-time, and the skills in handling crisis situations (Meyronin 2004). During the service encounter, successful communication between the customer and customer service agents is essential to ensure successful service delivery. Therefore, the communication

skills of a guest service agent are important to ensure a successful service encounter. This is even more important when computer-mediated communication is playing a larger role in customer service encounters. In summary, with the same functionalities, a guest service representative who has better business knowledge and interpersonal skills can serve customers better and provide higher service quality.

Training

The education content of training programs significantly influences the educational effectiveness and impact of customer service (Lee et al. 2007). Training ensures employees' compliance with the operating procedures so they can deliver the expected service (Torkzadeh et al. 2006). Continuous training and support can affect employee self-efficacy in service delivery (Agnihothri et al. 2003). It is even more important when customer services are becoming more and more complex and customers are becoming more and more demanding. Training ensures that guests will have fewer contacts, interact with more knowledgeable employees and experience fast and personalized service recovery (Brown 1997). Therefore, given the same service encounter involving service recovery, a better trained employee will be able to provide better service quality.

CUSTOMERS' CHARACTERISTICS

One of the key defining characteristics of customer service is the inseparability of production and consumption (Zeithaml et al. 1985). This characteristic "forces the buyer into intimate contact with the production process" (Carmen and Langeard 1980, p.8). Therefore, it is important to discuss how buyers' (i.e., customers') characteristics influence the customer service outcome. Customer characteristics included in this chapter are individual differences (i.e., demographic, inertia personality and need for personal interaction), experience with the technology and company, and technology readiness.

Demographic

The demographic variables include age, income, and education level. Aging is associated with the decline in perceptual skills, working memory, processing speed, and the encoding of information into episodic memory (Hedden and Gabrieli 2004). On the other hand, aging is also associated with cumulative learning processes and an increase in life experience; therefore, the perception of service complexity decreases with age. Therefore, older people are more willing to engage in complex face-to-face communication with service providers, especially when the speed of service is not a key factor for them (Simon and Usunier 2007). A bank customer survey shows that younger customers showed more interest in online banking while older customers preferred traditional branch banking (Milligan and Hayes 1997). Another study on financial service also found a similar result: younger customers are more open to direct means such as phone or online banking and more affluent customers are less likely to need human interaction while acquiring financial services (Lee 2002). People exposed to higher levels of education are likely to perform more comprehensive information gathering and processing efforts than less educated people, and are therefore likely to form a positive attitude toward using self-service technology (Weijters et al. 2007). In summary, younger, more affluent, and higher educated customers will required less time and effort when acquiring service through self-service technology; therefore, the demographic characteristics of customers moderate the relationship between service delivery channels and customer value.

Inertia

Inertia may limit customers' efforts to learn about different technologies and thus reduces their motivation to adopt a new customer service channel. As a result, the customers perceive that they invest more time and energy in adopting a different customer service channel than other non-inertia customers (Meuter et al. 2005). Therefore, this personality moderates the relationship between service delivery channels and customer value.

Need for Personal Interaction

A need for interaction is a desire to retain personal contact with others during service encounters. Cognitive-experiential self-theory (**Epstein 1994**) proposes that people have two parallel interacting modes of information processing: a rational system and an emotionally driven experiential system. Interpersonal interaction relates to the experiential system, whereas reasoning and problem solving mobilize the rational system. People who rely more on the experiential system tend to experience more difficulties in navigating the interface associated with a self-service technology, as they do not perform well when the interaction is logical and sequential. However, they find it easier to follow the transmission of implicit and pragmatic messages during face-to-face communication (Simon and Usunier 2007). A high need for personal interaction will lead to decreased interest in learning how self-service technologies work and increased effort in learning self-service technologies (Meuter et al. 2005).

Moreover, people have different tolerance levels for replacing people with machines (Dabholkar 1996). Those who desire personal attention and social interaction may be less likely to favor IT-based services (Zhu et al 2002; Walker et al. 2002; Curry and Penman 2004). Sometimes, these interpersonal interactions are a valued aspect of service consumption (Curran and Meuter 2005). For example, people dining at a restaurant expect the social element of the experience, including being seated by a host and so forth.

Experience with Technology

Customers' previous experiences with the technology will influence their feelings about using IT-enabled customer service systems (Dabholkar 1992). Experience with the technology may improve customers' confidence and willingness to use it (Walker et al. 2002). Customers are expected to place a higher value on the systems if they feel comfortable using them (Zhu et al. 2002). After customers use the customer service systems for a while, they become skillful with the system and, for routine tasks (e.g., taking money out from an ATM), the effort needed to obtain the service is reduced. Even the previous use of related technology will increase perceptions of self-confidence and guide behavior (Meuter et al. 2005). For example, people who have had more experience using the internet are more likely to adopt the web personalization functionality (Greer and Murtaza 2003).

Technology Readiness

Technology readiness (Parasuraman 2000) refers to people's propensity to embrace and use new technologies to accomplish goals in home life and at work. Most people today are likely to have been exposed to some technological products, such as an ATM, and have formed an attitude toward using such technology. This general attitude influences the evaluation of new but similar situations (Dabholkar 1996). For customers to adopt a new technology, they have to feel positively inclined toward the technology, perceive that they have the ability to use the new channel, and understand what they need to do (Bitner et al. 2002). Consumers who have a positive attitude toward the technology will anticipate positive outcomes from the service encounter and perceive higher service quality, and hence higher customer value

(Curran and Meuter 2007). A customer who is more technologically ready will spend less time and effort when experiencing service in a technology-mediated or technology-generated customer contact situation. Therefore, even with the same service delivery channel, a customer's investment in time and effort to acquire services through this channel may differ from another's. The time and effort a customer needs to invest in order to obtain the service depends on the technology readiness of the customer. As a result, the perceived value will be different.

IMPACT ON CUSTOMER VALUE

Functionalities of IT-Enabled Customer Service Systems

We identify six functionalities of an IT-enabled customer service system from reviewing interdisciplinary research on customer service. These functionalities are enabled and/or constrained by the technical components of the customer service systems currently owned by the businesses (Craig 1986). Data quality is essential to sense customers' needs, to provide personalize service and to build a relationship with customers (Day 1994; Berry and Parasuraman 1997; Zhu and Nakata 2007). Moreover, a reliable and responsive customer service system is necessary in providing any kind of functionalities of the systems as it ensure the right kind of functionality will be delivered to the right customers through the right channel at a timely manner (Zhu et al 2002; Bharati and Berg 2003).

Each of these functionalities has been shown to have a direct positive impact on customer value. As we discussed above, sensing customer needs allow businesses to be prepared and react to these needs more efficiently and more effectively. For example, United Airlines has a system to rebook the passengers on delayed flights to the next available flight and convey this information to them before they leave the first flight (Sisodia 1992). Providing customers with information pertaining to the product or the company enhances service offerings. Extending the notion of IS Success (De-Lone and McLean 1992), we propose that quality of the product and information provided by the company affect customer satisfaction through the increasing service quality, a precursor of customer value (Parasuraman and Grewal 2000).

Customization and personalization enhance customer value by offering better-fitting products and services to customers. Facilitating transactions and payments allows businesses to process transactions in a variety methods according to customers' preferences, and in a more efficient and accurate fashion. As a result, customer value increases as the benefits received by the customers increase. Problem solving provides customers solutions more efficiently with the aid of information technology. Finally, businesses can build long-term relationships with customers with the ability to collect customers' information, such as their preferences and past purchase.

We see that different functionalities impact different aspects of service value: some reducing customers' costs of obtaining the services and others increase the service offerings benefits. When a customer service system provides a new functionality that fulfills the emerging customers' need or enhance the performance of the existing functionality, the customer value will be improved. But functionalities not only have a direct effect on customer value, they also have a mediated effect that is dependent on the degree of organizational fit they have. We discuss this relationship next.

ORGANIZATIONAL FIT

For any information system to have an impact on customer value, there should be a fit or match between a system and its organizational context. Extending this notion of organizational validity

(Markus and Robey 1983), we propose that there should be (a) data fit, (b) user fit, and (c) structure fit. Data fit is defined as a fit between the type of data produced by the customer service system and the functionalities provided by the system, in terms of the user preferences for information content and format that are rooted in personal cognitive styles (Markus and Robey 1983). Not only the content but also the user-friendliness formats of the information are needed to be in accordance with service providers' needs for decision-making. Both are important in the system that assists service providers in planning, analysis, decision-making, and control in the customer service strategy (de Ruyte and Zuurbier 1993).

We define user fit as a fit between a system and the user's cognitive process. Cognitive process refers to "the way people process information" (Markus and Robey 1983, p.208). As mentioned above, there are five different customer service delivery channels. Each represents an interface between the customers and the customer service systems. Providing an interface that fits customers' characteristics at each service encounter is a strategic decision that calls for the consideration of both costs and customer outcomes (Rayport and Jaworski 2004). When choosing the service delivery channel, customers consider the effort involved in using the channel and the complexity of the service delivery process (Zhu et al. 2002). As customer value includes both benefits received and costs invested, customers will consider that using the service delivery channel requiring less time and effort will create higher customer value.

Structure fit is defined as a fit between a system and users' internal needs or motivations (Markus and Robey 1983). A flexible customer service system is more appropriate for an organic organizational structure and decentralized decision-making, while a standardized customer service system is more appropriate for a mechanistic organizational structure and centralized decision making. For example, a dynamic network organization which links, on an as-needed basis, teams of empowered employees, suppliers and customers to solve one-time problems provides personalized customer service and will need an IT infrastructure that is flexible, well-connected, and able to provide needed information at the right time. In summary, both the technical and social attributes of a customer service system should fit well with the organizational context to achieve higher levels of service outcome and create higher customer value.

SOCIAL ATTRIBUTES OF IT-ENABLED CUSTOMER SERVICE SYSTEMS

Businesses with a service-oriented strategy create "benefit bundles" that comprise products and supplementary services, rather than just the value of the product offerings (Homburg et al 2002). Customers often interact with a few front-line employees during a service encounter, and typically develop an overall image of the emotions that members of a given organization will display (Sutton and Rafaeli 1988). A warm emotional front may promote sales when customers expect that it should and will be a central part of a firm's service. Most importantly, even though employees are the ones to provide customer services, management must be committed to its employees and its customers to make it work. With this commitment, management provides training to employees, respects and empowers employees to provide customers with solutions to their problems or needs. Employees can then establish personal relationship with customers when delivering services. As a result, important information about the customers can be obtained through the personal encounters, which can be used to increase the benefits provided to the customer (i.e. customer value) (Beatty et al 1996). Therefore, even with the same functionalities, businesses with a service-oriented strategy and well-trained employees can provide higher

customer value due to more customer information and stronger relationship.

CUSTOMER CHARACTERISTICS

In a series of studies by Meuter et al. (2000, 2005) and Bitner et al. (2002), customers choose to use self-service technologies because they can save money and time. The notion of "service convenience" (Berry et al. 2002) is related to the customer's desire to conserve time and effort. Different service delivery channels will have different level of service convenience, especially access convenience (time and effort needed to order or purchase a service), transaction convenience (perceived time and effort needed to secure the right to use a service) and post-benefit convenience (time and effort needed to reinitiate contact with the firm after the benefit has been received). When customers perceive that they save money and time in obtaining a service, the cost component of customer value decreases; therefore, customers perceive higher customer value.

However, this relationship between IT-enabled customer service systems and customer value is moderated by customer characteristics. As we discussed above, a customer's demographic, inertia personality, need for personal interaction, experience with technology and technology readiness affect the perception of using technology to acquire services. For example, younger, higher-educated, and more affluent individuals will feel that they invest less time and effort when using self-service technologies, and these will therefore result in higher customer value. On the other hand, people who rely more on the experiential system (Epstein 1994) will invest more time and effort in navigating through self-service technologies, which will therefore result in lower customer value. Moreover, when the customers have more accumulated experience in interacting with the technology, they become more skillful and are clearer about the role they play in the service delivery process. As a result, the time and effort needed to put the system to use will decrease with the accumulation of experience with the related technology. In summary, the relationship between the customer service system and customer value is contingent upon the customers' characteristics.

FUTURE TRENDS

As we have summarized in this chapter, the functionalities currently being studied by researchers are the capability to sense customer needs, provide information, personalize service, facilitate transactions and payment processes, solve problems and recover customer complaints and build relationships. However, there has been no formal definition of functionalities of customer service systems. Several researches have used the stages of the customer service life cycle as functionalities. However, we argue that the stages of the customer service life cycle should represent the emerging customer needs throughout the cycle where customers acquire, specify, consume and retire the products, but the functionalities are the capabilities of customer service systems to fulfill these needs throughout the life cycle. Therefore, more work is needed to define the functionalities of customer service systems and explore other functionalities that have not been address by the past literature, such as the capability of helping customers retire old products and acquire new ones.

Also, studies of service delivery channels have focused on a single channel (e.g., self-service). It is important to note that service can be delivered to customers through multiple channels during one transaction. For example, a customer can order a product through a call center, and then check the order status online. It is important to address service delivery channels as integrated service delivery solutions instead of separated solutions. Therefore, both theoretical and empirical research is needed in this area.

Finally, no study to date has directly attempted to evaluate customer service interaction value, the proportion of customer value based on the customer's perception of what he or she contributes during the service encounter and receives in return (Piccoli et al. 2004). However, it is important to separate the customer service interaction value from customer value in general. As presented above, the components of customer value include the benefits derived from the core product offerings as well as from other additional services (e.g., support service, recovery service and other extraordinary service that further satisfies customers). To more precisely evaluate the impact of customer service, it is essential to explore the concept of customer service interaction value in depth.

CONCLUSION

As Levitt (1972) aptly put it over thirty years ago: "There is no such thing as a service industry. There are only industries whose service components are greater or less than those of other industries. Everybody is in service (p.41)." Providing a level of service that differentiates a business from its competitors has become a key to success in competitive market. However, there is no cohesive conceptual foundation for service science. We believe that the information systems discipline, at the nexus of the technical and behavioral aspects of customer service, is the best candidate to provide such foundation. We have therefore reviewed past literature to identify the technical components (data, system and service delivery channel) and the social components (customer service agents and customers) of a customer service system, and have provided an overview of the literature on IT-enabled customer service systems from different disciplines to illustrate the relationship among these components as well as the relationships between these components and customer value. Specifically, the technical attributes, including data quality, system quality and service delivery channels, and social attributes, including a service-oriented culture, human assets and training, of customer service systems should fit well with the organizational context so as to have an impact on customer value. Customers' characteristics, including demographic, inertia, need for personal interaction, experience with technology and technology readiness, moderate the relationship between the functionalities provided by the customer service system and customer value. However, the unclear definition of functionality of customer service systems, the analysis of the combined effect of different customer service delivery channels, and the new concept of customer service interaction value are issues that require academic research to produce useful knowledge for both academia and practitioners.

REFERENCES

Agnihothri, S., Sivasubramaniam, N., & Simmons, D. (2003). Leveraging technology to improve field service. *International Journal of Service Industry Management, 13*(1), 47-68.

Bancel-Charensol, L. (1999). Impacts on information and communication technologies on service production systems. *The Service Industries Journal, 19*(4), 147-157.

Baskerville, R. L., & Myers, M. D. (2002). Information systems as a reference discipline. *MIS Quarterly, 26*(1), 1-14.

Beatson, A., Coote, L. V., & Rudd, J. M. (2006). Determining consumer satisfaction and commitment through self-service technology and personal service usage. *Journal of Marketing Management, 22*(7), 853-882.

Beatson, A., Lee, N., & Coote, L. V. (2007). Self-service technology and the service encounter. *The Service Industries Journal, 27*(1), 75-89.

Beatty, S. B., Mayer, M., Coleman, J. E., Reynolds, K. E., & Lee, J. (1996). Customer-sales associate retail relationships. *Journal of Retailing, 72*(3), 223-247.

Berkley, B. J., & Gupta, A. (1994). Improving service quality with information technology. *International Journal of Information Management, 14*(2), 109-121.

Berkley, B. J., & Gupta, A. (1995). Identifying the information requirements to deliver quality service. *International Journal of Service Industry Management, 6*(5), 16-35.

Berry, L. L., & Parasuraman, A. (1997). Listening to the customer - the concept of a service-quality information system. *Sloan Management Review, 38*(3), 65-76.

Berry, L. L., Seiders, K., & Grewal, D. (2002). Understanding service convenience. *Journal of Marketing, 66*(3), 1-17.

Berry, L. L., & Gresham, L. G. (1986). Relationship retailing: Transforming customers into clients. *Business Horizons, 29*(6), 43-47.

Bessen, J. (1993). Riding the marketing information wave. *Harvard Business Review, 71*(5), 150-160.

Bharati, P., & Berg, D. (2003). Managing information systems for service quality: A study from the other side. *Information Technology & People, 16*(2), 183-201.

Bitner, M. J., Ostrom, A. L., & Meuter, M. L. (2002). Implementing successful self-service technologies. *Academy of Management Executive, 16*(4), 96-108.

Bostrom, R. P., & Heinen, J. S. (1977). MIS problems and failures: A socio-technical perspective. *MIS Quarterly, 1*(3), 17-32.

Bowen, D. E., Siehl, C., & Schneider, B. (1989). A framework for analyzing customer service orientations in manufacturing. *Academy of Management Review, 14*(1), 75-95.

Brohman, M. K., Watson, R., Piccoli, G., & Parasuraman, A. (2003). Data completeness: A key to effective net-based customer service systems. *Communications of the ACM, 46*(6), 47-51.

Brown, S. W. (1997). Service recovery through IT. *Marketing Management, 6*(3), 25-27.

Carmen, J. M., & Langeard, E. (1980). Growth strategies of service firm. *Strategic Management Journal, 1*(1), 7-22.

Cenfetelli, R. T., Benbasat, I., & Al-Natour, S. (2008). Addressing the what and how of online services: Positioning supporting-service functionality and service quality for business to consumer success. *Information Systems Research, 19*(2), 161-181.

Chesbrough, H., & Spohrer, J. (2006). A research manifesto for service science. *Communications of the ACM, 49*(7), 35-40.

Choi, D. H., Kim, C. M., Kim, S., & Kim, S. H. (2006). Customer loyalty and disloyalty in internet retail stores: Its antecedents and its effect on customer price sensitivity. *International Journal of Management, 23*(4), 925-941.

Craig, S. R. (1986). Seeking strategic advantage with technology? -- Focus on customer value! *Long Range Planning, 19*(2), 50-56.

Curran, J. M., & Meuter, M. (2005). Self-service technology adoption: Comparing three technologies. *The Journal of Services Marketing, 19*(2), 103-113.

Curran, J. M., & Meuter, M. L. (2007). Encouraging existing customers to switch to self-service technologies: Put a little fun in their lives. *Journal of Marketing Theory and Practice, 15*(4), 283-298.

Curry, A., & Penman, S. (2004). The relative importance of technology in enhancing customer relationships in banking - a Scottish perspective. *Managing Service Quality, 14*(4), 331-341.

Dabholkar, P. A. (1992). Role of affect and need for interaction in on-site service encounters. *Advances in Consumer Research, 19*(1), 563-569.

Dabholkar, P. A. (1996). Consumer evaluations of new technology-based self-service options: An investigation of alternative models of service quality. *International Journal of Research in Marketing, 13*(1), 29-51.

Day, G. S. (1994). The capabilities of market-driven organizations. *Journal of Marketing, 58*(4), 37-52.

de Ruyter, K., & Zuurbier, J. (1993). Customer information systems: Approaching a new field in information systems from a new perspective. *Information & Management, 24*, 247-255.

Delene, L. M., & Lyth, D. M. (1989). Interactive services operations: The relationships among information, technology and exchange transactions on the quality of the customer-contact interface. *International Journal of Operations & Production Management, 9*(5), 24-32.

DeLone, W. H., & McLean, E. R. (1992). Information systems success: The quest for the dependent variable. *Information Systems Research, 3*(1), 60-95.

Dev, C. S., & Ellis, B. D. (1991). Guest histories: An untapped service resource. *Cornell Hotel And Restaurant Administration Quarterly, 32*(2), 28-37.

Dillon, T. W., & Reif, H. L. (2004). Factors influencing consumers' e-commerce commodity purchases. *Information Technology, Learning, and Performance Journal, 22*(2), 1-12.

Epstein, S. (1994). Integration of the cognitive and the psychodynamic unconscious. *American Psychologist, 49*(8), 709-724.

Erevelles, S., Srinivasan, S., & Rangel, S. (2003).

Customer satisfaction for Internet service providers: An analysis of underlying processes. *Informatioin Technology and Management, 4*(1), 69-89.

Froehle, C. M., & Roth, A. V. (2004). New measurement scales for evaluating perceptions of the technology-mediated customer service experience. *Journal of Operations Management, 22*(1), 1-21.

Furey, T. R. (1991). How information power can improve service quality. *Planning Review, 19*(3), 24-26.

Greer, T. H., & Murtaza, B. (2003). Web personalization: The impact of perceived innovation characteristics on the intention to use personalization. *The Journal of Computer Information Systems, 43*(3), 50-55.

Han, J., & Han, D. (2001). A framework for analyzing customer value of internet business. *Journal of Information Technology Theory and Application, 3*(5), 25-38.

Hedden, T., & Gabrieli, J. D. E. (2004). Insights into the ageing mind: A view from cognitive neoroscience. *Nature Reviews Neuroscience, 5*(2), 87-96.

Hill, T. P. (1977). On goods and services. *Review of Income and Wealth, 23*(4), 315-338.

Homburg, C., Hoyer, W. D., & Fassnacht, M. (2002). Service orientation of a retailer's business strategy: Dimensions, antecedents and performance outcome. *Journal of Marketing, 66*, 86-101.

Ives, B., & Learmonth, G. P. (1984). The information system as a competitive weapon. *Communications of the ACM, 27*(12), 1193-1201.

Ives, B., & Mason, R. (1990). Can information technology revitalize your customer service? *Academy of Management Executive, 4*(4), 52-69.

Judd, R. C. (1964). The case for redefining services.

Journal of Marketing, 28(1), 58-59.

Lee, J. (2002). A key to marketing financial services: The right mix of products, services, channels and customers. *The Journal of Services Marketing, 16*(2/3), 238-258.

Lee, S. M., Lee, H., Kim, J., & Lee, S. (2007). ASP system utilization: Customer satisfaction and user performance. *Industrial Management + Data Systems, 107*(2), 145-165.

Levenburg, N. M., & Klein, H. A. (2006). Delivering customer services online: Identifying best practices of medium-sized enterprises. *Information Systems Journal, 16*(2), 135-156.

Levitt, T. (1972). Production-line approach to service. *Harvard Business Review, 50*(5), 41-52.

Li, Y. N., Tan, K. C., & Xie, M. (2003). Factor analysis of service quality dimension shifts in the information age. *Managerial Auditing Journal, 18*(4), 297-302.

Liang, T., Lai, H., & Ku, Y. (2006). Personalized content recommendation and user satisfaction: Theoretical synthesis and empirical findings. *Journal of Management Information Systems, 23*(3), 45-70.

Lightner, N. J. (2004). Evaluating e-commerce functionality with a focus on customer service. *Communications of the ACM, 47*(10), 88-92.

Lin, H. (2007). The impact of website quality dimensions on customer satisfaction in the B2C e-commerce context. *Total Quality Management & Business Excellence, 18*(4), 363-378.

Lovelock, C. H. (1994). *Product plus: How product + service = competitive advantage.* New York: McGraw-Hill, Inc.

Markus, M. L., & Robey, D. (1983). The organizational validity of management information systems. *Human Relations, 36*(3), 203-266.

Meuter, M. L., Bitner, M. J., Ostrom, A. L., &

Brown, S. (2005). Choosing among alternative service delivery modes: An investigation of customer trial of self-service technologies. *Journal of Marketing, 69*(4), 61-83.

Meuter, M. L., Ostrom, A. L., Bitner, M. J., & Roundtree, R. (2003). The influence of technology anxiety on consumer use and experiences with self-service technologies. *Journal of Business Research, 56*(11), 899-906.

Meyronin, B. (2004). ICT: The creation of value and differentiation in services. *Managing Service Quality, 14*(2/3), 216-225.

Milligan, J. W., & Hayes, T. (1997). What do customers want from you? Everything! *U.S. Banker, 107*(12), 38-45.

Negash, S., Ryan, T., & Igbaria, M. (2003). Quality and effectiveness in web-based customer support systems. *Information & Management, 40*(8), 757-768.

Orman, L. V. (2007). Consumer support systems. *Communications of the ACM, 50*(4), 49-54.

Parasuraman, A. (2000). Technology readiness index (TRI): A multiple-item scale to measure readiness to embrace new technologies. *Journal of Service Research, 2*(4), 307-320.

Parasuraman, A., & Grewal, D. (2000). The impact of technology on the quality-value-loyalty chain: A research agenda. *Journal of the Academy of Marketing Science, 28*(1), 168-174.

Peppers, D. (1999). Capturing customers by computer. *International Journal of Retail & Distribution Management, 27*(5), 198-199.

Piccoli, G., Applegate, L. M., & Dev, C. S. (2008). *Hilton hotels: Brand differentiation through customer relationship management* (Reference No. 9-809-029). Cambridge, MA: Harvard Business Publishing.

Piccoli, G., Brohman, K., Watson, R. T., & Para-

suraman, A. (2004). Net-based customer service systems: Evolution and revolution in web site functionalities. *Decision Sciences, 35*(3), 423-455.

Piccoli, G., Spalding, B. R., & Ives, B. (2001). The customer service lift cycle: A framework for Internet use in support of customer service. *Cornell Hotel and Restaurant Administration Quarterly, 42*(3), 38-45.

Ramirez, A. (1993, March 31). Teller machines inspire a new kiosk business. *The New York Times.*

Ray, G., Muhanna, W. A., & Barney, J. B. (2005). Information technology and the performance of the customer service process: A resource-based analysis. *MIS Quarterly, 29*(4), 625-652.

Rayport, J. G., & Jaworski, B. J. (2004). Best face forward. *Harvard Business Review, 82*(12), 47-58.

Rowley, J. (2000). Loyalty kiosks: Making loyalty cards work. *British Food Journal, 102*(5/6), 390-397.

Rowley, J., & Slack, F. (2003). Kiosks in retailing: The quiet revolution. *International Journal of Retail & Distribution Management, 31*(6/7), 329-339.

Salomann, H., Dous, M., Kolbe, L., & Brenner, W. (2007). Self-service revisited: How to balance high-tech and high-touch in customer relationships. *European Management Journal, 25*(4), 310-319.

Sawy, O. A. E., & Bowles, G. (1997). Redesigning the customer support process for the electronic economy: Insights from storage dimensions. *MIS Quarterly, 21*(4), 457-483.

Schneider, B., White, S. S., & Paul, M. C. (1998). Linking service climate and customer perceptions of service quality: Tests of a casual model. *Journal of Applied Psychology, 83*(2), 150-163.

Selnes, F., & Hansen, H. (2001). The potential hazard of self-service in developing customer loyalty. *Journal of Service Research, 4*(2), 79-90.

Sheehan, J. (2006). Understanding service sector innovation. *Communications of the ACM, 49*(4), 43-47.

Shostack, G. L. (1977). Breaking free from product marketing. *Journal of Marketing, 41*(2), 73-80.

Simon, F., & Usunier, J. (2007). Cognitive, demographic, and situational determinants of service customer preference for personnel-in-contact over self-service technology. *International Journal of Research in Marketing, 24*(2), 163-173.

Sisodia, R. S. (1992). Marketing information and decision support systems for services. *The Journal of Services Marketing, 6*(1), 51-64.

Sivabrovornvatana, N., Siengthai, S., Krairit, D., & Paul, H. (2005). Technology usage, quality management system, and service quality in Thailand. *International Journal of Health Care Quality Assurance, 18*(6/7), 413-423.

Srinivasan, S. S., Anderson, R., & Ponnavolu, K. (2002). Customer loyalty in e-commerce: An exploration of its antecedents and consequences. *Journal of Retailing, 78*(1), 41-50.

Stamoulis, D., Gouscos, D., Georgiadis, P., & Martakos, D. (2001). Revisiting public information management for effective e-government services. *Information Management & Computer Security, 9*(4), 146-153.

Sutton, R. I., & Rafaeli, A. (1988). Untangling the relationship between displayed emotions and organizational sales: The case of convenience stores. *Academy of Management Journal, 31*(3), 461-487.

Teo, T. S. H., Devadoss, P., & Pan, S. L. (2006). Towards a holistic perspective of customer relationship management (CRM) implementation: A case study of the housing and development board, Singapore. *Decision Support Systems,* *42*(3), 1613-1627.

Torkzadeh, G., Chang, J. C., & Hansen, G. W. (2006). Identifying issues in customer relationship management at Merck-Medco. *Decision Support Systems, 42*(2), 1116-1130.

Tseng, J. C. R., & Hwang, G. (2007). Development of an automatic customer service system on the internet. *Electronic Commerce Research and Applications, 6*(1), 19.

Walker, R. H., Craig-Lees, M., Hecker, R., & Francis, H. (2002). Technology-enabled service delivery: An investigation of reason affecting customer adoption and rejection. *International Journal of Service Industry Management, 13*(1), 91-106.

Wang, Y., Lin, H., & Luarn, P. (2006). Predicting consumer intention to use mobile service. *Information Systems Journal, 16*(2), 157-179.

Weijters, B., Rangarajan, D., Falk, T., & Schillewaert, N. (2007). Determinants and outcomes of customers' use of self-service technology in a retail setting. *Journal of Services Research, 10*(1), 3-21.

Wells, J. D., Fuerst, W. L., & Choobineh, J. (1999). Managing information technology (IT) for one-to-one customer interaction. *Information & Management, 35*, 53-62.

Woodruff, R. B. (1997). Customer value: The next source for competitive advantage. *Academy of Marketing Science Journal, 25*(2), 139-153.

Zeithaml, V. A., Parasuraman, A., & Berry, L. L. (1985). Problems and strategies in services marketing. *Journal of Marketing, 49*(2), 33-46.

Zhu, F. X., Wymer, W. J., & Chen, I. (2002). IT-based services and service quality in consumer banking. *International Journal of Service Industry Management, 13*(1), 69-90.

Zhu, X., & Nakata, C. (2007). Reexamining the link between customer orientation and business performance: The role of information systems. *Journal of Marketing Theory and Practice, 15*(3), 187-203.

KEY TERMS AND DEFINITIONS

Cognitive-Experiential Self-Theory: A theory proposing that people have two parallel interacting modes of information processing: a rational system and an emotionally driven experiential system. Interpersonal interaction relates to the experiential system, whereas reasoning and problem solving mobilize the rational system.

Customer Service: A change in the condition of a person, or a good belonging to some economic entity, brought about as a result of the activity of some other economic entity with the approval of the first person or economic entity.

Customer Service Life Cycle: A framework that maps customer needs as they emerge at different stages of the interaction between an organization and its customers

Customer Value: Customer's perceived performance for and evaluation of product attributes, attribute performances, and consequences arising from use that facilitates (or block) achieving the customer's goal and purposes in use situations

IT-Enabled Customer Service Systems: A collection of information systems that are to provide supplementary customer services so as to fulfill customer needs

Organizational Validity: A fit or match between an information system and its organizational context

Service Convenience: Customer's perception in time and effort conservation

Chapter XXII
Expectation–Confirmation Theory:
Capitalizing on Descriptive Power

James J. Jiang
University of Central Florida, USA & National Taiwan University, ROC

Gary Klein
The University of Colorado at Colorado Springs, USA

ABSTRACT

Expectation-confirmation theory (ECT) posits that satisfaction is determined by interplay of prior expectations and perception of delivery. As such, there are many applications in research and practice that employ an ECT model. The descriptive power allows independent investigations manipulating either of the components and a format to examine just why clients are satisfied (or not) with a particular product or service. However, the use of ECT can be impeded by a seeming lack of analysis techniques able to handle the difficulties inherent in the model, restricting information system (IS) researchers to limit the model to less descriptive and analytical accuracy. This chapter provides an overview of ECT applications in IS research and demonstrates how polynomial regression analysis (PRA) allows for a more robust set of models.

INTRODUCTION

The concept behind Expectation-Confirmation Theory (ECT) is simple. Prior to any event, you have an expectation. If that expectation is met in a positive fashion, then you are satisfied. If that expectation is met in a negative fashion, you are dissatisfied. It is this elegant simplicity that makes ECT such a powerful explanatory tool. Customers make a purchase, if the product meets or exceeds performance expectations, the customer is satisfied. If a client enters a contract with a service provider and the client's expectations are exceeded in a positive way, the client is satisfied with the service. If a manager makes a hire and the employee outstrips performance expectations, the manager is satisfied with the employee. If the product, service, or employee fails to meet expectations, then the customer, client, or manager is dissatisfied.

Researchers apply the theory in a multitude of contexts where satisfaction is a variable of interest, either as the dependent, mediator, or moderator variable. This is valuable because the resulting level of satisfaction in a transaction may serve as an indicator of further behavior. It seems only logical that customers are more likely to return after satisfactory transactions, clients will return only if satisfied with previous service, managers will rate the work of employees more highly if satisfied with their performance. However, logic and simplicity have yielded to a debate in the research arena about modeling and testing of models that employ ECT. This is often due to the two component considerations of ECT: prior expectations and posterior perceptions. There are concerns about the measurement of any gap between these components, the true relationships of each unique component to satisfaction, and the binds of analytical methods regarding gap measures.

In this chapter, we will expand on the description of ECT to highlight these and other problems. We will describe several issues that have been raised in the literature and describe how many of the analysis problems can be avoided using individual component scores and polynomial regression analysis (PRA). In addition, we will illustrate an approach that overcomes many of the methodological difficulties in a personnel setting.

BACKGROUND

The origin of Expectation-Confirmation Theory dates back many decades. Military experts have long believed that the fulfillment of expectations lead to positive changes in morale (Spector, 1956). General models of satisfaction have considered a discrepancy between an individual standard and outcome as influential (Locke, 1969). Satisfaction with job performance is considered a function of expectation and deviation from expectation (Ilgen, 1971). In the consumer arena, experiments to test the impact of discrepancies go back to the middle of the previous century (Cardozo, 1965), though more current thought that relates the resulting satisfaction of a discrepancy to future behavior is usually pegged to later work (Oliver, 1980). In each of these, and subsequent, studies, the primary consideration is that both the expectations prior to an event and the subsequent evaluation after the event combine to determine satisfaction with the event. The event in question can be any number of items, but usually concern some kind of product, service, or performance consumption.

Figure 1 shows a basic model of Expectation Confirmation Theory. The four main constructs in the model are: expectation, performance, disconfirmation, and satisfaction. Expectations serve as the comparison anchor in ECT – what consumers use to evaluate performance and form a disconfirmation judgment (Halstead, 1999). Expectations reflect anticipation (Churchill & Suprenant, 1982). They are predictive over product attributes at some point in the future (Spreng, MacKenzie & Olshavsky, 1996). Performance is an evaluation by the individual after the event, such as a perception of product quality. If a product meets or outperforms expectations (confirmation) post-purchase satisfaction will result. If a product falls short of expectations (disconfirmation) the consumer is likely to be dissatisfied (Spreng, et al., 1996). Typically, disconfirmation is often measured directly, or as a difference score between expectation and performance components. How-

Figure 1. Expectation-confirmation theory model

ever, the disconfirmation measure is redundant when expectations and performance are taken directly into satisfaction.

Models using ECT will often use the derived satisfaction as an antecedent to further variables to explain behavior (Oliver, 1980). The logic (or further theory) being that satisfaction, in turn, will lead to an action, such as a repurchase of a product. This should hold for most any event, with a prime focus in the literature on a product, service, or performance. Likewise, models vary in the incorporation of direct links from the two components directly to satisfaction. In other words, each component may directly influence satisfaction in addition to the cognitive comparison process between expectation and performance (Jiang & Klein, 2002; Jiang, Klein, Van Slyke & Cheney, 2003).

In the information systems (IS) literature, ECT models are reported in a variety of contextual settings. Some researchers use the model to test for factors influencing satisfaction (Susarla, Barua & Whinston, 2003). Many focus on particular contexts (McKinney, Yoon & Zahedi, 2002). Some extend the model to consider other influences to satisfaction (Au, Ngai & Cheng, 2002). Many use the resulting satisfaction to determine continued use of a system or system product (Liao, Chen & Yen, 2007). Still others merge ECT with other theories to determine a fuller picture of how satisfaction is derived (Sorebo & Eikebrokk, 2008). Regardless of the exact approach, matching expectations is crucial to practitioners and an important modeling tool for researchers (Nevo & Wade, 2007). Table 1 summarizes a few of the IS research studies that employ ECT.

METHODOLOGICAL ISSUES

The methodological issues of applying ECT lie primarily in measuring "disconfirmation". One choice is a direct measure that captures the disconfirmation with a single construct. However, direct measurement of the score presents cognitive difficulties and lacks valuable information about the true nature of the relationship (DeVellis, 1991; Edwards, 2001). The second is to indirectly measure the (dis)confirmation and elicit both expected levels and levels of perceived performance. Often, for indirect measures, researchers construct a difference score, computed as performance (P) – expectation (E). Difference score constructs often suffer from measurement issues including ambiguity of expectation, unstable dimensionality, low reliability, discriminant validity, and lack of predictive power (Cronbach, 1958; Johns, 1981; Wall & Payne, 1973). In addition, difference scores impose constraints on the relationship between the component measures and the outcome. In a strictly linear relationship, an implicit assumption of difference score is that the components of the difference score have *equal but opposite* effect on the outcome variable, as can be seen from equation 1 and its restatement as equation 2:

$$Satisfaction = b_0 + b_1(P_i - E_i) + e \qquad (1)$$

$$Satisfaction = b_0 + b_1(P_i) - b_1(E_i) + e \qquad (2)$$

Clearly, the effect of performance on satisfaction (b_1) must be equal and opposite to the effect of expectations ($-b_1$). "Like any constraint, this

Table 1. IS Studies of expectation confirmation theory

Report	Context	Conclusion
Au, Ngai & Cheng (2002)	End-user satisfaction	Disconfirmation is a crucial explanatory variable in determining end user satisfaction
Bhattacherjee (2001a)	Information systems continuance	Confirming expectations from prior system use is crucial in explaining satisfaction, which in turn leads to continued use intentions
Bhattacherjee (2001b)	E-commerce continuance decisions	Confirming expectations form initial use is crucial in explaining satisfaction, which in turn leads to continued use intentions
Erevelles, Srinivasan & Rangel (2003)	ISP customer satisfaction	Satisfaction is based on expectations from previous experience and market conditions
Hseih & Wang (2007)	Employee extended use of IS	Confirmation positively impacts satisfaction, perceived usefulness and ease of use
Liao, Chen & Yen (2007)	Continued use of online services	Disconfirmation is related to satisfaction, which in turn impacts continued use
Lin, Wu & Tsai (2005)	Continued use of a web portal	Confirmation increases satisfaction, which in turn impacts continuation
McKinney, Yoon & Zahedi (2002)	Web customer satisfaction	Confirmation of information and system quality lead to satisfaction
Nevo & Wade (2007)	Satisfaction with information systems	The expectations of each stakeholder should be met to improve satisfaction
Sorebo & Eikebrokk (2008)	System use in mandatory environments	Confirmation increases satisfaction, which in turn impacts continuation
Staples, Wong & Seddon (2002)	Perceived benefits of a system	Unrealistically high expectations lead to a lessening of perceived benefits
Susarla, Barua & Whinston (2003)	Satisfaction with Application Service Providers	Disconfirmation leads to less satisfaction

cannot increase the variance explained, and in most cases will decrease it." (Edwards, 1994, p.56). Unfortunately, this implicit assumption in ECT is usually overlooked.

Another implicit assumption is that there is no difference in the relationship at varying magnitudes. A balanced difference will present the same level of the objective value regardless of component magnitude. In other words, the magnitude of the components is lost in taking the difference, so any model implicitly states that a variable dependent on a difference score is independent of the magnitude of the component scores. These are very different than a relationship where the dependent variable is reliant on both components, such as the one in equation 3:

$$\text{Satisfaction} = b_0 + b_1(P_i) - b_2(E_i) + e \qquad (3)$$

Here, component scores are separate predictors of satisfaction, while in equation 1 the difference between the two components is a single predictor term. Equation 1 also restricts the effect to be the same for any magnitude of the components P and E. Unfortunately, this implicit assumption has also been overlooked in studies adopting ECT.

Finally, equation 3 still assumes the relationship to be linear. Could a non-linear relationship exist? In fact, ECT only states that positive disconfirmation (performance exceeds expectations) leads to satisfaction and negative disconfirmation leads to dissatisfaction; however, an exact shape has never been predicted. One may conjecture that ECT could also support an asymptotic shape requiring a nonlinear relationship in certain contexts. Well established concepts as diminishing returns, prospect theory, and utility theory indicate that the relationship may, in fact, be non-linear in nature (Blaug, 1997; Kahneman & Tversky, 1979). The inclusion of a separate disconfirmation variable in ECT is an admission that there must be some form of interaction between expectation and performance that cannot be explained by strict linearity between the components and satisfaction.

In order to avoid difference score methodological issues, one may elect to use categorized comparisons by creating subgroups based on the congruence between two component measures (Church & Waclawski, 1996). With the sub-grouping approach, respondents with self-scores above or below some threshold are classified accordingly. This procedure is tantamount to subtracting another score from self-determined scores and subdividing the resulting difference score. Therefore, classifications created by the sub-grouping approach are difference scores in disguise (Edwards, 2001).

POLYNOMIAL REGRESSION ANALYSIS

To avoid many of the problems with difference scores, yet retain the rich information made available by two distinct components, researchers apply polynomial regression analysis (Edwards, 1994). Successful applications of PRA in the behavioral management literature include fit between stress and work conflicts (Kreiner, 2006), the match between supervisor and employee traits (Glomb & Welsh, 2005), job satisfaction as related to job demands (Hecht & Allen, 2005), and ratings from multiple sources (Antonioni & Park, 2001; Bono & Colbert, 2005). Each of these studies was based on established theory that had empirical questions about the observed, non-linear shape of the relationships.

In essence, polynomial regression replaces the difference score with the component measures in the analysis. Interactions and squared relationships

are included - allowing more complete use of the information collected and incorporating the two components and disconfirmation into a single equation. This approach provides comprehensive tests of relationships that motivate the use of difference scores and examine complexities that linear modeling cannot represent because difference scores severely distort the joint effects of their components on various outcomes (Van Vianen, 2000). Thus, polynomial regression allows relationships that are more complex than simple difference scores, or even linear models of the component scores (Edwards, 1994). One polynomial equation form is:

$$\text{Satisfaction} = b_0 + b_1P + b_2E + b_3P^2 + b_4PE + b_5E^2 + e. \qquad (4)$$

To formally interpret the surfaces implied by equation 4, it is useful to apply response surface analysis (RSA). When the surfaces are planar, interpretation is relatively straightforward and termed a discrepancy surface. When surfaces are curvilinear, the surface can be one of many types, a few of which are a concave or convex U-shape, a saddle relationship where interaction terms are strong, and an asymptotic form where the function approaches a high or low limit.

The shape of the surface along a line can be determined by substituting an appropriate expression into equation (4). The shape of the surface along the $P = E$ line indicates whether an outcome varies when the two components are congruent – an outcome is minimized or maximized along the line of perfect match (where $P - E = 0$). When the dependent variable does not vary by the magnitude of the components, a flat surface along $P = E$ exists as is implicitly expected under the assumption of difference scores. The surface along the $P = E$ line can be obtained by substituting P for E in equation (4), which produces the following equation:

$$\text{Satisfaction} = b_0 + (b_1 + b_2)P + (b_3 + b_4 + b_5)P^2 + e. \tag{5}$$

The curvature of the surface depends on $(b_3 + b_4 + b_5)$ and the slope of the magnitude on $(b_1 + b_2)$. To meet the assumptions of difference scores both must be zero.

The shape of the surface along the P = -E line represents the effects of incongruence on the outcome. If the dependent variable is maximized along the line of perfect congruence, then the surface should be curved "downward" along the P = -E line on both sides. The shape of the surface along the P = -E line can be obtained by substituting –P for E in equation (4), which produces the following equation:

$$\text{Satisfaction} = b_0 + (b_1 - b_2)P + (b_3 - b_4 + b_5)P^2 + e. \tag{6}$$

If the quantity $(b_3 - b_4 + b_5)$ is negative, the surface is curved "downward" from the P= -E line. If the quantity $(b_3 - b_4 + b_5)$ is positive, the surface is curved "upward" from the P= -E line. In other words, when $(b_3 - b_4 + b_5)$ is either positive or negative, congruence is either at a minimum or maximum, respectively. The slope represented by $(b_1 - b_2)$ indicates whether the magnitude of the difference between expectation and perception influences the dependent variable. Table 2 and Figure 2 present a sample of cases that could be present in a data set with accompanying descriptions.

EMPLOYEE JOB SKILLS EXAMPLE

Relationships between job performance satisfaction and the skill levels of information system service providers will serve as an illustration. Past examinations into the interpersonal skills of IS professionals and organizational achievement found no positive relation in spite of theory and garnered wisdom that would lead one to expect

the presence of such skills to be important in the success of a system and eventual contribution to the organization (Byrd & Tuner, 2001). Significant insight into the complexity of the relationship arose from a study that examined a balance of skills between expectations and performance (Wade & Parent, 2002). A balance occurs when the IS employee's level of performance in a skill (P) is approximately equal to the expectation that an employee will have the essential skill (E). An intriguing conceptual argument in recent studies is that a complex *combination* of performance in job skills and skill expectations provides a link to satisfaction of performance (Jiang, et al., 2003; Tesch, Jiang & Klein, 2003).

Conclusions in previous personnel studies were restricted because of the weak statistical results, application of difference scores, and the methodology employed in analysis (Edwards & Harrison, 1993). Early techniques that work around difference scores typically employ an ANOVA analysis that washes out magnitude effects. Sub-groupings for ANOVAs are difference scores in disguise - segmenting scores merely accentuate the loss of information and reduction in explained variance that plague difference scores (Edwards, 2001). Such problems with difference scores can be avoided by using polynomial regression analysis (Edwards, 1994; Edwards & Parry, 1993). This approach can provide additional insights on how "skill expectations" and "skill performance" interact together to influence the evaluators' satisfaction with the IS professional's job performance (Edwards, 1994).

Skill confirmation can be viewed as an ECT model, with the difference between the expectations a manager might have of employee skills and the application of those skills in the performance of the job relating to the satisfaction of performance, where satisfaction is one form of success (Nelson & Cheney, 1987). Early work examined whether the high rate of system development failure was due to IS personnel who were deficient in expected skills (Nelson, 1991; Trauth, Farwell &

Table 2. Examples of polynomial regression coefficients and their shapes

	$(b_3 + b_4 + b_5)$	$(b_1 + b_2)$	$(b_3 - b_4 + b_5)$	$(b_1 - b_2)$	Description
Figure 2a	0	0	0	+	Linear relation, no curvatures, magnitude makes no difference in value of dependent variable, meets difference score implicit assumptions. At any level of expectation the highest satisfaction is achieved by maximizing performance, but it is best to keep expectations as low as possible.
Figure 2b	0	+	0	+	Linear discrepancy relation, no curvatures, magnitude of components matter (slopes downward along P = E line), violates implicit difference score magnitude assumption. Satisfaction is highest when both expectation and performance are high.
Figure 2c	0	0	-	+	Dependent variable maximized at congruence, magnitude of components do not matter, meets difference score implicit assumptions as a U-shaped curve. No matter what the level of expectation, performance should match it.
Figure 2d	+	+	-	+	Saddle Curve where interaction term is large magnitude, meets no implicit assumption, highest at an extreme of congruence. Best to only match expectations. The market should target only high and low end, those in between are at a disadvantage.
Figure 2e	0	+	0	-	One of many possible asymptotic shapes where low satisfaction is the floor for the component scores, meets no implicit assumption. This shows increasing returns of satisfaction as performance grows or performance and satisfaction grow together.

0 represents an insignificant regression coefficient,
+ a significant positive coefficient
- a significant negative coefficient

Lee, 1993). Later studies employed variations of discrepancy theory to find increased satisfaction, as viewed by multiple stakeholders, associated with surplus skills (Tesch, et al., 2003). One study found satisfaction with job performance enhanced when the skills are in "balance," that is skills displayed during job performance being equal to an expectation of usefulness (Wade & Parent, 2002). These studies employ techniques that implicitly or explicitly use a difference between an expectation and performance of skills. This application of a traditional approach to studying the difference assume equal and opposite weights on the two components (expectation and performance). This assumption will be tested using the data sample.

Satisfaction with one's job performance is determined by examining the relationship between what is expected and what is delivered. Discrepancy based theories allow an argument that having too much of a good thing is as detrimental as not having enough. A lack of balance leads to negative outcomes (Wade & Parent, 2002). Previous studies in work related issues find this relationship to hold and promote a shape change so that theory can accommodate observation (Warr, 1994). Two assumptions drive this characterization: (1) satisfaction is maximized at perfect equality, and (2) non-linear relationships hold, such that satisfaction bends downward from the line of equality. Figure 2c shows this type of relation when an additional assumption holds - the level of satisfaction is constant across the absolute levels of skill expectation and achieved performance of those skills – there is no difference in satisfaction as P (or E) varies (Assouline & Meir, 1987). This latter assumption has been questioned in other disciplines; when equality holds, satisfaction is often higher when the components are both high than when both are low (Livingstone, Nelson & Barr, 1997). This implicit assumption is not examined in recent IS skill studies, but will be examined here using our illustrative example.

Figure 2. Example shapes for polynomial relations of satisfaction components

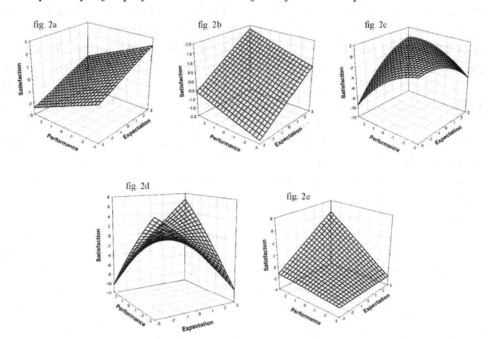

Sample

Data from a published study will serve in this illustrative example (Tesch, et al., 2003). To gain the context of the data we will briefly review the collection and validation of the dataset. A full discussion may be found in the original source (Tesch, et al., 2003). The IS department/division managers from twenty-eight organizations in the South-Central USA were contacted and asked to participate in this study. The organizations were identified from a list of advisory organizations to the information systems program at a major southern university. Seventeen department/division managers agreed to participate. Each of these managers then distributed questionnaires to individual IS project managers. The IS project managers were asked to rate their skill expectations of a particular IS specialist, their perceived performance delivery of each skill by that specialist, and satisfaction with that specialist's job performance. This single respondent approach

for the component and satisfaction measures is crucial in ECT theory as the satisfaction formed is a function of personal expectation and perceived delivery. Table 3 shows demographic characteristics of the sample.

Constructs

There are three measures employed in this study: 1) skill expectation of an IS specialist, 2) perception of skill performance exhibited by the IS specialist, and 3) the IS manager's satisfaction with the specialist's performance. Identical items concerning skill expectation and skill performance were administered to IS managers along with a job performance satisfaction measure. Three categories of skills found in previous studies are considered, including technology management skills, business function skills, and interpersonal skills (Byrd & Turner, 2001; Lee, et al., 1995). An additional category, specialized technology skills, was omitted due to its nature of significant change in meaning across organizations (Byrd & Turner, 2001; Trauth, et al., 1993).

Skill Expectation and Skill Performance Delivery

The IS skill construct is adapted from Lee, et al. (1995). The instrument asks respondents to indicate their expectation for each identified skill as well as their perception of delivery with regard to the indicated skill. A low value (1) means low expectation and/or performance of that particular skill. The items of the skill constructs are listed in Table 4.

Job Performance Satisfaction

The IS employees' job performance satisfaction was self-evaluated by IS employees using a scale

Table 3. Demographics of the sample

Work Experience:	
< 10 years	39
>=10 & < 20	33
>= 20	33
No report	3
Age:	
< 30 years old	9
>= 30 & < 40	33
>=40 & < 50	21
>=50	21
No report	24
Gender:	
Male	72
Female	32
No report	4
Education:	
Graduate Degree	18
Bachelor Degree	58
Less	28
No report	4

developed by Greenhaus, Parasuraman & Wormley (1990). The construct includes items to measure "task" and "relationship" related performance. We used a 5-point scale ranging from "very unsatisfactorily" to "very satisfactorily" and included an additional attribute to capture the IS managers' evaluation of overall job performance. The job satisfaction items are stated in Table 5.

The measurement model was validated using PLS (Chin, 1988). Convergent and discriminant validity for all constructs were examined according to expected standards. In order to control for the independent measurement of skill expectation and performance, correlations between both components were inspected. A moderate level of correlation will occur because of the tendencies for managers to align an individual's skills with their job requirements (French, Caplan & Harrison, 1982). For the purpose of analysis, the measures were scaled by averaging the relevant items and subtracting the scale midpoint (i.e., 3), producing scores that could range from -2 to + 2. Scale-centering reduces multicollinearity between component measures and their associated higher-order terms and facilitates the interpretation of coefficients on first-order terms when higher-order terms are in the equation (Cronbach, 1987). The descriptive statistics before centering are in Table 6.

Data Analysis

To test the algebraic discrepancy effect, regression coefficients from linear regression analysis are examined. The coefficients should be equal magnitude for both skill performance and expectation, but of opposite sign. Three separate regressions were conducted to test this underlying difference score assumption for each skill category. The results in Table 7 indicate all significant skill expectation and performance dimensions have positive signs. The coefficients of skill expectation and skill performance for each dimension,

Table 4. Skill items

Constructs	Items
Technology Management	Ability to learn new technologies
	Ability to focus on technology as a means, not an end
	Ability to understand technological trends
Business functions	Ability to learn about business functions
	Ability to interpret business problems and develop appropriate technical solutions
	Ability to understand the business environment
	Knowledge of business functions
Interpersonal Skill	Ability to plan and execute work in a collaborative environment
	Ability to deal with ambiguity
	Ability to work with customers and maintain productive user/client relationships
	Ability to accomplish assignments
	Ability to teach others
	Ability to be self-directed and proactive
	Ability to be sensitive to the organization's culture/politics

Table 5. Job performance satisfaction items

Construct	Item
Total Job performance satisfaction	Cooperation
	Loyal to organization
	Quality of work
	Interpersonal relationships
	Accuracy
	Responsibility
	Punctuality
	Attitude
	Productivity
	Judgment
	Planning
	Ability
	Promotability
	Job knowledge
	Commitment to organization
	Attendance

however, were not equal, as would be assumed in the difference score regression. These results imply that an individual's job performance satisfaction is indeed determined by both components (i.e., skill expectation and skill performance) as indicated in the IS literature (Wade & Parent, 2002; Tesch, et al., 2003); however, the exact gap functions may not be equally weighted, or perhaps not linear. The R^2 value improves significantly moving from the difference score model to the two component model.

For a quadratic equation, the coefficients on E and P represent the slope of the surface at the mid-point of E and P scales. Table 8 shows the results from a polynomial regression for each skill type. The quantities of $(b_3 + b_4 + b_5)$ and $(b_1 + b_2)$ along the $P = E$ line must all be zeros to show that the relationship is independent of the magnitudes of the components (Edwards and Parry, 1993). Based upon the values in Table 8, we note that the level of job performance satisfaction is independent of the level of skills when in balance (again based on the elemental components being significantly different from zero before addition). Again, note the improvement in R^2 going from the results in table 7 to those in table 8. The improvement is significant at $p < .05$.

Graphical Results

The surface in Figure 3 shows the relationship of job performance satisfaction to expectation and performance and is somewhat "concave". The slope (at point E = 0 and P = 0) is positive along the P= E line. The surface along the P=E line indicates that, given a perfect skill fit (e.g., "balance") condition, the IS manager's job performance satisfaction is higher when expectation and performance are both high. The downward slope in both directions along the E = -P line indicate that a disconfirmation results in lower satisfaction in either direction, a situation that cannot be represented by a continuous linear function – any linear model would provide false results and poor predictive power in this data set. In general, the level of job performance satisfaction is not only determined by technology management skill performance but also the level of technology management skill expectation. Uniquely, even when skill performance exceeds expectations, job performance satisfaction declines, too much of a good thing results in lower performance satisfaction. This could be due to an actual de-

cline in performance through over qualification or simply the employee allowing a bias to enter responses due to a poor job fit (Wade & Parent, 2002). A similar pattern was found for business skills (Figure 4).

Figure 5 shows a variation to the pattern. Job performance satisfaction is still relatively high when both skill components are high. However, the level of satisfaction is higher along much of the entire edge of high skill performance. In this case, there is not the pronounced decline along the E = P line in both directions. It seems that even though high interpersonal skills are not always expected, they are always appreciated. The decline to the right side of the curve shows the usual lack of satisfaction when expectations exceed delivered performance. This approaches an asymptotic shape, where diminishing returns show a declining slope toward a maximum value and steeper relationships on the other extreme.

The implications for practice from an exploration of the graphs include hiring and training concerns. IS personnel must be hired or developed to a level necessary to perform specific IS jobs. IS personnel with a skill deficiency will achieve a significantly lower level of job performance satisfaction than IS personnel with a skill balance (or surplus for interpersonal skills). IS personnel with a skill balance have higher job performance satisfaction than those with a skill balance that is low. This goes hand-in-hand with developing realistic expectations on the part of stakeholders.

Table 6. Descriptive statistics

	Mean	TME	BE	IME	TMP	BP	IMP
Technology Management Expectation	4.38						
Business Functions Expectation	4.30	0.04					
Interpersonal/Management Expectation	4.32	0.33	0.38				
Technology Management Performance	4.03	0.14	0.09	0.25			
Business Functions Performance	3.90	0.15	0.30	0.23	0.72		
Interpersonal/Management Performance	3.95	0.16	0.06	0.22	0.79	0.77	
Total Job Performance Satisfaction	4.16	0.10	0.22	0.06	0.33	0.35	0.38

Table 7. Linear regression analysis

	Difference score		Component scores		
	P-E	R²	Expectation	Performance	R²
Technology Management	0.14	0.02	0.14*	0.07	0.13
Business Skills	0.15	0.02	0.21*	0.17*	0.12
Interpersonal Skills	0.25*	0.06	-0.02	0.15*	0.12
*significant at p<.05					

Table 8. Polynomial regression analyses

	b0	b1	b2	b3	b4	b5	R²
Technology Management	0.12*	0.12*	0.27*	0.03	0.08	-0.18*	.30
Business	0.08	0.18*	0.28*	0.05	0.03	-0.12*	.25
Interpersonal	0.27*	-0.03	0.38*	-0.12*	-0.06	-0.17*	.29

	(b1-b2)	(b3-b4+b5)	(b1+b2)	(b3+b4+b5)
Technology Management	-0.15*	0.03	0.38*	-0.32*
Business	-0.10	0.05	0.46*	-0.20*
Interpersonal	-0.41*	-0.12*	0.35*	-0.46*

* – significant at .05

CONCLUSION

ECT extends our current understanding of satisfaction by comparing an expected level of a delivery to perceived levels received. This concept was illustrated by an example where IS personnel skill impact satisfaction with job performance - as examined with polynomial regression analysis. Skill performance and expectation were not found to be equally weighted nor have a flat response surface. The results also indicate that job performance satisfaction will not be the same for both low versus high performance and expectation.

The richness of ECT becomes evident through this more thorough analysis. By not collapsing skill expectation and skill performance into a single difference score, the more complex relationships allowed by ECT can be explored. Difference scores confound the separate relationships of expectation and performance, impose a restrictive set of constraints that may not be supported, and reduce the inherently three-dimensional relationship between expectation, performance and satisfaction to two dimensions.

FUTURE TRENDS

Expectation Confirmation Theory has tremendous descriptive power by allowing the examination of separate, comparative components to a common measure of success – satisfaction. In information systems, uses of satisfaction as success include user satisfaction, job satisfaction, and service satisfaction (DeLone & McLean, 1992; Tesch, et al., 2003). Satisfaction from other fields could

Figure 3. Technology management skills and job performance satisfaction

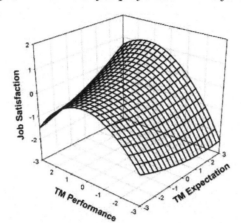

Figure 4. Business skills and job performance satisfaction

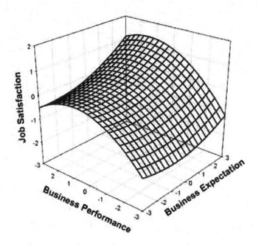

also be applied as long as identifiable expectations and performance exist. Such fields include service quality, customer relationship management, and user co-production.

In addition, ECT allows a multitude of shapes that may be very appropriate under different theoretical assumptions. This can be handled well in exploratory fashion by careful examination of terms and response surfaces or through prior assumptions about shapes (such as those in Figure 2) and subsequent examination of alignment with those shapes. This type of study has already been

found to indicate linear models are representative in the ease of use variable of the Technology Acceptance Model (TAM), but may not be adequate for the usefulness variable (Brown, Venkatesh, Kuruzovich & Massey, 2008). Functional forms are crucial and have significant implications in the application of theory that should not be ignored (Edwards & Cooper, 1990). Just what the forms are in the relationship among expectation, perceived performance, and satisfaction need to be addressed for a variety of contexts and tempered by both observation and theory.

Polynomial regression analysis opens up the

Figure 5. Interpersonal skills and job performance satisfaction

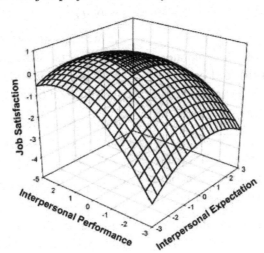

possibility for more studies using ECT and superior interpretation of results. How satisfaction really varies according to differences between expectation and performance open up with the loss of rigid assumptions and increased ability to visualize the relationships through response surface graphing. Predictive models are improved through the inclusion of component variables rather than difference scores (Edwards, 1994). Descriptive models likewise benefit from the improved fit and graphing. Theoretical testing is enhanced with truer representation of relationships and the ability to incorporate the component variables into path models with block variables for non-linear models or congruence modeling when linearity is present (Cheung, 2009; Edwards, 2009; Jagodzinski & Weede, 1981; Marsden, 1982).

REFERENCES

Antonioni, D., & Park, H. (2001). The effects of personality similarity on peer ratings of contextual work behaviors. *Personnel Psychology, 54,* 331-360.

Assouline, M., & Meir, E. I. (1987). Meta-analysis of the relationship between congruence and well-being measures. *Journal of Vocational Behavior, 31,* 319-332.

Au, N., Ngai, E., & Cheng, E. (2002) A critical review of end-user information system satisfaction research and a new research framework. *Omega, 30,* 451-478.

Bhattacherjee, A. (2001a). Understanding information systems continuance: An expectation-confirmation model. *MIS Quarterly, 25,* 351-370.

Bhattacherjee, A. (2001b). An empirical analysis of the antecedents of electronic commerce service continuance. *Decision Support Systems, 32,* 201-214.

Blaug, M. (1997). *Economic theory in retrospect* (5th ed.). UK: Cambridge University Press.

Bono, J. E., & Colbert, A. E. (2005) Understanding responses to multi-source feedback: The role of core self-evaluations, *Personnel Psychology, 58,* 171-203

Brown, S. A., Venkatesh, V., Kuruzovich, J., & Massey, A. P. (2008). Expectation confirmation:

An examination of three competing models. *Organizational Behavior and Human Decision Processes, 105*, 52-66.

Byrd, T. A., & Turner, E. D. (2001). An exploratory analysis of the value of the skills of IT personnel: Their relationship to IS infrastructure and competitive advantage. *Decision Sciences, 32*, 21-54.

Cardozo, R. N. (1965). An experimental study of consumer effort, expectation, and satisfaction. *Journal of Marketing Research, 2*, 244-249.

Cheung, G. W. (2009). Introducing the latent congruence model for assessment of similarity, agreement, and fit in organizational research. *Organizational Research Methods, 12*(1), 6-33.

Chin, W. W. (1988). *The partial least squares approach to structural equation model.* Mahwah, NJ: Lawrence Erlbaum Associates.

Church, A. H., & Waclawski, J. (1996) The effects of personality orientation and executive behavior on subordinate perceptions of workgroup enablement. *International Journal of Organizational Analysis, 4*, 20-51.

Churchill, G. A., & Surprenant, C. (1982) An investigation into the determinants of customer satisfaction. *Journal of Marketing Research, 19*, 491-504.

Cronbach, L. J. (1958). Proposals leading to analytic treatment of social perception scores. In R. Tagiuri & L. Petrullo (Eds.), *Person perception and interpersonal behavior* (pp 353-379). CA: Stanford University Press.

Cronbach, L. J. (1987). Statistical tests for moderator variables: Flaws in analyses recently proposed. *Psychological Bulletin, 102*, 414-417.

DeLone, W. H., & McLean, E. R. (1992). Information systems success: The quest for the dependent variable. *Information Systems Research, 3*(1), 60-95.

DeVellis, R. F. (1991). *Scale development: Theories and applications.* Newbury Park, CA: Sage.

Edwards, J. R. (1994). The study of congruence in organizational behavior research: Critique and a proposed alternative. *Organizational Behavior and Human Decision Processes, 58*, 51-100.

Edwards, J. R. (2001). Ten differences score myths. *Organizational Research Methods, 4*(3), 265-287.

Edwards, J. R. (2009). Latent variable modeling in congruence research: Current problems and future directions, *Organizational Research Methods, 12*(1), 34-62.

Edwards, J., & Cooper, C. (1990) The person-environment fit approach to stress: Recurring problems and some suggested solutions. *Journal of Organizational Behavior, 11*, 293-307.

Edwards, J. R., & Harrison, R. V. (1993). Job demands and worker health: A three-dimensional reexamination of the relationship between person-environment fit and strain. *Journal of Applied Psychology, 78*, 628-648.

Edwards, J. R., & Parry, M. E. (1993). On the use of polynomial regression equations as an alternative to difference scores in organizational research. *Academy of Management Journal, 36*, 1577-1613.

Erevelles, S., Srinivasan, S., & Rangel, S. (2003). Consumer satisfaction for Internet service providers: An analysis of underlying processes. *Information Technology and Management, 4*(1), 69-89.

French, J. R. P., Caplan, R. D., & Harrison, R. V. (1982). *The mechanisms of job stress and strain.* New York: Wiley.

Glomb, T. M., & Welsh, E. T. (2005). Can opposites attract? Personality heterogeneity in supervisor-subordinate dyads as a predictor of subordinate outcomes. *Journal of Applied Psychology, 90*(4), 749-757

Greenhaus, J. H., Parasuraman, S., & Wormley, W. M. (1990). Race effects of organizational experience, job performance evaluations, and career outcomes. *Academy of Management Journal, 33,* 64-86.

Halstead, D. (1999). The use of comparison standards in customer satisfaction research and management: A review. *Journal of Marketing Theory & Practice, 7*(3), 13-26.

Hecht, T. D., & Allen, N. J. (2005). Exploring links between polychronicity and well-being from the perspective of person–job fit: Does it matter if you prefer to do only one thing at a time? *Organizational Behavior and Human Decision Processes, 98*(2), 155-178.

Hsieh, J. J. & Wang, W. (2007) Explaining employees' extended use of complex information systems. *European Journal of Information Systems, 16,* 216-227.

Ilgen, D. R. (1971). Satisfaction with performance as a function of the initial level of expected performance and the deviation from expectations. *Organizational Behavior and Human Performance, 6,* 345-361.

Jagodzinski, W., & Weede, E. (1981). Testing curvilinear propositions by polynomial regression with particular reference to the interpretation of standardized solutions. *Quantity and Quality, 5,* 447-463.

Jiang, J. J., & Klein, G. (2002). A discrepancy model of information system personnel turnover, *Journal of Management Information Systems, 19,* 249-272.

Jiang, J. J., Klein, G., Van Slyke, C., & Cheney, P. (2003). A note on interpersonal and communication skills for IS professionals: Evidence of positive influence. *Decision Sciences, 34,* 799-812.

Johns, G. (1981). Difference score measures of organizational behavior variables: A critique. *Organizational Behavior and Human Performance, 27,* 443-463.

Kahneman, D., & Tversky, A. (1979) Prospect theory: An analysis of decision under risk. *Econometrica, 47,* 263-292.

Kreiner, G. E. (2006). Consequences of work-home segmentation or integration: A person-environment fit perspective. *Journal of Organizational Behavior, 27,* 485-507.

Lee, D. M. S., Trauth, E. M., & Farwell, D. (1995). Critical skills and knowledge requirements of IS professionals: A joint academic/industry investigation. *MIS Quarterly, 19,* 313-340.

Liao, C., Chen, J.-L., & Yen, D. C. (2007). Theory of planning behavior (TPB) and customer satisfaction in the continued use of e-service: An integrated model. *Computers in Human Behavior, 23,* 2804-2822.

Lin, C. S., Wu, S., & Tsai, R. J. (2005). Integrating perceived playfulness into expectation-confirmation model for web portal context. *Information & Management, 42,* 683-693.

Livingstone, L. P., Nelson, D. L., & Barr, S. H. (1997). Person-environment fit and creativity: An examination of supply-value and demand-ability versions of fit. *Journal of Management, 23,* 119-146.

Locke, E. A. (1969). What is job satisfaction? *Organizational Behavior and Human Performance, 4,* 309-336.

Marsden, P. V. (1982). A note on block variables in multi-equation models. *Social Science Research, 11,* 127-140.

McKinney, V., Yoon, K., & Zahedi, F. (2002). The measurement of web-customer satisfaction: An expectation and disconfirmation approach. *Information Systems Research, 13,* 296-315.

Nelson, R. R. (1991). Educational needs as perceived by IS and end-user personnel: A survey of knowledge and skill requirements. *MIS Quarterly, 15,* 502-525.

Nelson, R. R., & Cheney, P. H. (1987). Training end users: An exploratory study. *MIS Quarterly, 11*, 546-559.

Nevo, D., & Wade, M. R. (2007). How to avoid disappointment by design. *Communications of the ACM, 50*(4), 43-48.

Oliver, R. L. (1980). A cognitive model of the antecedents and consequences of satisfaction decisions. *Journal of Marketing Research, 17*, 460-469.

Sorebo, O., & Eikebrokk, T. R. (2008). Explaining IS continuance in environments where usage is mandatory. *Computers in Human Behavior, 24*(5), 2357-2371.

Spector, A. J. (1956). Expectations, fulfillment and morale. *Journal of Abnormal and Social Psychology, 52*, 51-56.

Spreng, R. A., MacKenzie, S. B., & Olshavsky, R. W. (1996). A reexamination of the determinants of consumer satisfaction. *Journal of Marketing, 60*, 15-28.

Staples, D. S., Wong, I., & Seddon, P. B. (2002). Having expectations of information systems benefits that match received benefits: Does it really matter? *Information & Management, 40*, 115-131.

Susarla, A., Barua, A., & Whinston, A. B. (2003). Understanding the service component of application service provision: An empirical analysis of satisfaction with ASP services. *MIS Quarterly, 27*, 91-123.

Tesch, D., Jiang, J. J., & Klein, G. (2003). The impact of information system personnel skill deiscrepancies on stakeholder satisfaction. *Decision Sciences, 34*, 107-129.

Trauth, E., Farwell, D. W., & Lee, D. (1993). The IS expectation gap: Industry expectations versus academic preparation. *MIS Quarterly, 13*, 293-307.

Van Vianen, A. E. M. (2000). Person-organization fit: The match between newcomers' and recruiters' preferences for organizational culture. *Personnel Psychology, 53*, 113-149.

Wade, M. R., & Parent, M. (2002). Relationships between job skills and performance. *Journal of Management Information Systems, 18*, 71-96.

Wall, T. D., & Payne, R. (1973). Are deficiency scores deficient? *Journal of Applied Psychology, 58*, 322-326.

Warr, P. (1994). A conceptual framework for the study of work and mental health. *Work and Stress, 8*(2), 84-97.

KEY TERMS AND DEFINITIONS

Confirmation: An individual's perception of an outcome meets an established expectation.

Difference Score: A single value representation of two distinct instances of a single concept. The instances may be across time, individual, or situation, but each instance must be measured with identical constructs.

Direct Measure: Determining a gap or fit between two distinct concepts with a single value.

Disconfirmation: A difference between a perceived outcome, usually a collection of events or activities, as compared to an established expectation.

Expectation: A belief about the value of a future event, activity, or property rooted in the values of an individual that serve as an anchor for comparison.

Indirect Measure: Determining a gap between two distinct concepts with two component values.

Performance: The perceived level of achievement for an event, activity, or property that has already been conducted or delivered.

Satisfaction: An individual level of approval resulting from experience of an activity, event, or property.

Polynomial Regression Analysis Determining the best relationship in a specific data set between a single dependent variable and one or more independent variables that incorporates interaction and higher order terms of the independent variables.

Section VI
Sociological and Cultural Theories

This section includes five chapters. The first chapter (Chapter XXIII) presents various aspects (including background, premises, key concepts and ideas, and critique) of the prominent sociological theory actor network theory. The next chapter (Chapter XXIV) presents various dimensions of another prominent social theory called social capital theory. Chapter XXV reviews the origins, approaches and roles associated with using cultural historical activity theory in information systems research. The fourth chapter (Chapter XXVI) performs a citation analysis on Hofstede's culture's consequences in IS research to re-examine how IS research has used Hofstede's national culture dimensions. Finally, chapter XXVI introduces and discusses domestication theory and its relevance and importance to information systems research.

Chapter XXIII
Actor Network Theory and IS Research

Amany Elbanna
Loughborough University, UK

ABSTRACT

Actor network theory is a sociological theory that emerged as a useful vehicle to study technology and information systems. This chapter gives the reader some background about the development and emergence of this sociological theory. It reviews some of the premises of the theory and introduces the reader to key concepts and ideas. It also presents some of the critique of the theory, ANT authors' response, and the implication on IS research. This chapter also gives the reader an overview of the application of ANT in different streams of IS research.

INTRODUCTION

Actor Network Theory is one of the emerging theories in IS research. It advocates the intertwining of the social and technical agency to constitute a performing network. This chapter provides a general overview of the premises of the theory and the main ideas of the founding authors. It also reviews the main areas where ANT is criticised in order to indicate the theoretical shortcomings and expected strengths that the theory offers for IS research. The chapter ends with a critical review of ANT's application in the IS field.

BACKGROUND

Actor Network Theory appeared more than two decades ago in the sociology of science, mainly to investigate the emergence of scientific knowledge. One of its earliest landmark publication is Latour and Woolgar's (1979) *Laboratory Life*, which was an immediate success and is said to be "the best known book in science studies" at that time according to Susan Star (Star, 1988). This book documents the creation of a scientific 'fact' through an ethnographic study of a scientific laboratory, which opened the door to a series of laboratory studies and descriptions of 'fact-making' that follow this ethnomethodological approach.

The theory draws on a variety of fields, such as linguistics (specially semiotics), anthropology, and the ethnomethodology tradition in sociology. It consistently argues that scientific knowledge is a product of a network of heterogeneous materials that is partly social, partly technical, and partly natural. Its field of study is extended from investigating the creation of scientific knowledge to studying technology and the construction of technological artefacts. Its focus is also extended from the production of knowledge towards agents, social institutions, machines, economic markets, and organisations to form a comprehensive theory. ANT creates a 'thick description' of the interaction between technology and society involving a wealth of detailed information (Bijker, Hughes, & Pinch, 1987), as well as a distinctive view of the constitution of society.

The development, amendments, and grounding of the theory took place over a relatively long period through the collaborative and cooperative work and discussions of a group of sociologists. Most of them—especially in the 1980s—were associated with, and in several cases located at, the Centre de Sociologie de l'Innovation of the Ecole Nationale Superieure des Mines de Paris. These pioneers of the theory include Bruno Latour, Michel Callon, John Law, Madeleine Akrich, Steven Woolgar, and Michael Serres (Law, 1992). Much literature was generated by this activity; as Collins and Yearley commented in the early 1990s, "It would not be possible to deal with six books, five edited volumes, and about sixty articles in anything less than a Ph.D thesis" (Collins & Yearley, 1992b). Over a decade later, that number has at least been doubled.

ACTOR NETWORK THEORY: CONCEPTS

ANT has passed through constant reviews, extensions, and amendments from its key authors.

The theory's developers have also continuously changed topics, field sites, styles, and concepts in their journey to establish their approach within sociology. This makes it a moving target (Latour, 1999a) and reviewing its concepts is far from a straightforward task. The theory has also changed as it moved from one domain to another and from one researcher to another, in time and place. Law, for example, admits that the form taken by ANT of Paris in the 1980s is quite different than the ANT of the 1990s that is used in different places (Law, 1997).

Although it is possible to identify certain common ANT preoccupations and concerns in the literature, "there is no orthodoxy, no one "right way" of developing the approach. This also means that Actor Network Theory is not a single orthodoxy, a fully consistent body of writing with its holy scriptures" (Centre for Science Studies, 2001). As there is no 'unity' for the theory and both commonalties and differences coexist between ANT authors, it is the researcher's task to decide which part of the theory to review and apply in his study. This section introduces the reader to the ANT concepts of society, network, and translation.

Society

ANT fundamentally reviews the notion of society by arguing that "society is constructed, but not just *socially* constructed" (Latour, 1994b, pg.793; 1999b, pg 198). It suggests that society is constructed through intertwining networks of heterogeneous materials: some of these are human and others are non-human, and their intertwining constitutes 'the social'. This contends that all artefacts incorporate social relations and it is not possible to define a social structure without the integration of non-humans into it, as every human interaction is sociotechnical (Latour, 1994b).

In order to account for humans and non-humans, and to treat both the social and the technical symmetrically, ANT authors developed a distinctive language that is intentionally "neutral" and does not differentiate in principle between them (Law & Callon, 1988). This vocabulary is drawn from semiotics and is intended to avoid the use of terms that assume a distinction between the technical and the social (Akrich & Latour, 1992). Thus, ANT's vocabulary has achieved a kind of metalinguistic formulation into which any sequence of human and non-human actions can be encoded (Lee & Brown, 1994).

Network

ANT uses the notion of 'network' in a way that is fundamentally different from its standard usage in sociology, as it is not primarily concerned with mapping interactions between individuals. Rather, it is concerned with mapping how actors define and distribute roles, and mobilise or invent others to play these roles. Such roles may be social, political, technical, or bureaucratic in character; the objects that are mobilised to fill the roles are also heterogeneous and may take the form of people, organisations, machines, or scientific findings. A network metaphor helps to underline the simultaneously social and technical character of any social arrangements. It is a metaphor for the interconnected heterogeneity that underlies sociotechnical engineering (Law & Callon, 1988).

ANT renders agency to both humans and non-humans and hence adopts the notion of actors or actants from semiotics (Greimas, 1990). Accordingly, an actor could be any entity, human or non-human, involved in a series of actions. Actors are tied together in a certain network through intermediaries. Intermediaries then represent the relationship or transaction that passes between actors or what ties them together.

The actor is seen to be playing two roles: one as an actor in a network that is created by him; the other as being a network, hence the term 'actor network'. An actor network is an actor whose activity is networking heterogeneous elements, and at the same time it is a network that is able to

redefine and transform what it is made of (Michel Callon, 1987, pg. 93; Law, 1992, pg. 93). Thus, an actor network cannot be seen as an actor alone or a sociological network alone. It should be seen as a series of heterogeneous entities that are associated with one another for a certain period of time.

As a result, "action is simply not a property of humans but of an association of actants" (Latour, 1999b). Similarly, the "responsibility of action must be shared among the various actants" (ibid). In principle, this proposition could reveal an endless number of actors and networks if a researcher goes on to de-construct every node (actor) in a network into its constituent actors. This tendency towards de-composition adds a complexity to any study, which is so serious that it may be difficult, or even impossible, to handle. The advised methodological solution (Latour, 1987, 1988b, 1996; Law & Callon, 1988) is to follow the actors in the construction of their network, de-compose what they negotiate and compose, and accept and take for granted what they take for granted; 'black box' entities by treating internally complex network only through its simpler external interfaces. This methodology follows the associations and disassociations wherever they are produced (M. Callon & Latour, 1981). The researcher then needs to understand analytically the logic behind black boxing or punctualising some actors while negotiating and decomposing others.

Translation

'Translation' refers to the dynamics by which an actor recruits others into his project. It is a continuous process and "never a complete accomplishment" (Michel Callon, 1986). By and large, it follows how actors are "bent", "enrolled", "enlisted", "mobilised" in any of the others' plots (Latour, 1999b).

The word 'translation' itself reflects its usual linguistic sense in that it means that one version translates every other (Latour, 1987, pg.121). It does not mean a shift from one vocabulary to another, but it does mean "displacement, drift, invention, mediation, the creation of a link that did not exist before and that to some degree modifies two elements or agents" (Latour, 1994a, pg.32) (Latour, 1999b, pg.179). It also has a "geometric meaning" that is about moving from one place to the other. Translating interests means at once offer new interpretations of these interests and channel people in different directions (Latour, 1987, pg.117) . It was first created and used by Michel Serres (M. Callon & Latour, 1981; Serres, 1974) and its first English publication appears in Callon (1986). Since then, it has been adopted through Callon (1986).

ACTOR NETWORK THEORY: DYNAMICS

The concept of translation presents a dynamic view of the creation and maintenance of an intertwining network of human and non-human. This section reviews the dynamic properties of the concept. It presents the different strategies of translation before reviewing the widely quoted 'moments of translation'.

Strategies of Translation

The translation or recruitment could take place through implementing several strategies. All would lead the actors, whatever they do and whatever their interests, to help the network builders to pursue their interests. Interests in ANT are "what lie between actors and their goals". Latour identifies five translation strategies (Latour, 1987, pg.108-121). The following are four of them, with the fifth described later in this section after the discussion of the tactics of the fourth strategy:

The first is to Tailor the network builder's project in such a way that it caters for the actors' explicit interests. This is considered the easiest way to find people who will immediately believe in the network builder's interests, invest in the

project, or buy the ideas. *The second strategy is to mobilise people towards the network builder's goal* in order to cut off their usual way and to convince, persuade, or betray them that their project is not possible. Then, displace and shift their explicit interests towards adopting the network builder's interests. However, this displacement of explicit interests is rare and might be easier to be achieved through the next strategy. *The third strategy aims to clearly cut off the path being followed* to achieve an actor's interests and projects, then create a favourable detour through the builder's project. This suggests that "you cannot reach your goal straight away, but if you come my way, it will be a short cut so you can reach it faster". Seducing people through such a little detour depends on the road being obviously cut off, the new detour well defined, and the detour appearing to be short. *The Fourth strategy Seeks to do away with explicit interests* so as to increase the actor-network builder's margin for manoeuvre. This suggests that interests and goals can be reshuffled. It differs from the assumption in the above three strategies that explicit goals exist, which actors can express and are largely dependent on the actors' interpretations of their interests and that of the others they enrol.

To achieve translation through the fourth strategy, five tactics could be followed. The first tactic is to *displace goals through problematisation*. When the network builders have a solution, they need to look for a problem for the target actors to position their solution against. In order to do this, they need to shift the target actors' goals slightly, but sufficiently to change their standing. In his much referenced article, Callon (1986) named this process "problematisation" (Michel Callon, 1986). This tactic depends on the network builders' ability to determine a set of actors and define their identity in such a way as to establish the network builders as an 'obligatory passage' point in the network of relationships they are building. Problematisation is therefore a double movement of defining the actors and their goals and of rendering the network builders as indispensable or an obligatory passage point. 'Obligatory passage point' is a military term and is used to mean a strategic placement between an actor's goal and the fulfilment of this goal (Latour, 1987). The second tactic is *to invent completely new goals all together*. As the scope of what interests others is related to, and limited by, their previously adopted goals and their original interests, increasing the margins of this scope requires the creation of new goals. The third tactic is *to invent new groups*. Since the ability of inventing new goals is quite limited by the existence of already defined groups. Thus it would be much better to define new groups that could be endowed with new goals, goals that could be reached by only helping the network builders to pursue their goals and build their network of relationships. In practice, this tactic is the easiest and by far the most efficient strategy. It is about building either literally or conceptually new groups that change the old defined and established groups. This makes it easier to create common interest for the new reordered or new established group. The fourth tactic is *to render the detour invisible*. Although translation is a transitive relation, the final version should not be perceived as a detour, no matter how far it drifts from the actor's original aims and path. On the contrary, it should be seen as the only straight route to realising the initial project. In this sense, translation includes both its linguistic and geometric meaning. It incorporates not only a new interpretation but also a displacement and slow movement from one place to another. Callon calls this process of displacement "mobilisation". The main advantage of such mobilisation is that particular issues are closely tied to the wider issues, to the extent that threatening the former would be perceived threat to the latter. This move is necessary in order to turn the detour into a progressive drift. The enrolled group will then still think that it is going along a straight line, without ever abandoning its own interests. "Subtly woven and carefully thrown, this very fine net can be very useful at keeping groups in its meshes" (Latour, 1987, pg.117).

A final tactic *is to seek to win trials of attribution*. In constructing a network, in principle everyone is as important as everyone else, as each is necessary to contribute to the construction of the network if the network is to perform. Nevertheless, only a few are likely to be pointed at as the lead and the main cause of collective action. This "attribution of responsibility" is called "the secondary mechanism" by Latour (Latour, 1987, pg.118-119), where he refers to the "the primary mechanism" as the principle of everyone being important. He warns that the two mechanisms should not be confused, even when the secondary mechanism prevails and people make some versions more credible than others. This tactic is more about convincing others to contribute to the network and to compromise with them if necessary, at the same time as keeping the attribution of responsibility limited to few people or even one person.

The fifth translation strategy identified by Latour *is to become indispensable*. The previously mentioned strategies and tactics should lead to render the network builder and his path indispensable. The network builders should patiently succeed to make others to follow them through successive translations that move them from the most extreme weakness (that forced the network builders to follow the others) to the greatest strength (that forces all the others to follow the network builders). In doing so, everyone would contribute to the spread of a claim in time and space, which will then become a routine black box in everyone's hands.

Moments of Translation

Callon defines the anatomy of translation in terms of "four moments of translation": "problematisation", "interessement", "enrolment", and "mobilisation" (Michel Callon, 1986). He asserts that these moments are interrelated and could be inseparable in reality.

Problematisation, as the term implies, is concerned with finding a problem for the presented solution to which other entities could subscribe. In order to do this, the 'enunciators' need to define the other actors' identities, what they might possibly want and make themselves or other entities as an obligatory passage point. By becoming the obligatory point of passage, the network builders define the way for the actors to proceed if they to realise their goals.

Interessement is the action of interest building. The term is derived from the Latin *interesse*, "to be situated between". Interessement is therefore the group of actions by which an entity attempts to impose and stabilise the identity of the other actors it defines through its problematisation (Michel Callon, 1986, pg.207-208). Stengers (1997) explains that interesting someone does not necessarily mean either entering into pre-existing interests or gratifying that person's desire for power, money, or fame. From this perspective, to interest someone in something means "to act in such a way that this thing - apparatus, argument, or hypothesis... - can concern the person, intervene in his or her life, and eventually transform it" (Stengers, 1997, pg.83).

As in problematisation, the network builder identifies the other actors (potential allies), their identities, and their goals. Yet these allies are tentatively implicated in the problematisations of other actors. Their identity is consequently defined in other competitive ways. Hence, interessement includes attempts to interest other actors and to build devices that can be placed between them and all other entities that want to define their identities (Latour, 1987, 1988b). This process carries the risk that actors may refuse the identification of their identities and define their identity, goals, projects, motivations, or interests in another manner.

The successful process of problematisation and interessement leads to enrolment, which does not imply, nor does it exclude, pre-established roles. Enrolment designates the device by which a set of interrelated roles is defined and attributed to actors who accept them. Thus, it entails conflict and struggle between entities in order to convince them to play the roles they are ascribed. Actors could be enrolled through seduction, transaction, and consent without discussion (Latour, 1987, 1988a). It also includes efforts to pull entities together towards the enunciator proposal. The last moment of translation is mobilisation. As the word suggests, it is to render mobile those entities that were not so beforehand.

CRITICISMS OF ANT AND THEIR IMPLICATION FOR IS RESEARCH

The fundamental reconsideration of 'the social' introduced by ANT triggered strong reaction, particularly - and not surprisingly - in the sociology field. A landmark seminar organised by Bath School of Sociology that took place in February 1990 crystallised and summarised many of the criticisms at the time and provided actor network theorists with a way forward to extend and develop some of their ideas further (Pickering, 1992). Overall, the criticism of ANT has revolved around a few closely-related issues, grouped here as: symmetrical stance, material agency, and ethics.

Symmetrical Stance

The first criticism attacks the 'symmetrical' stance of ANT. As explained earlier in this chapter, this calls for a similar analytical treatment - using the same semiotic language and without changing repertoire - of all old dichotomies, successes and failures, nature and society, human and non-human entities. ANT suggests that the boundary is an issue of investigation rather than a starting point. The symmetrical view has been problematic for both mainstream sociology and the sociology of scientific knowledge (SSK).

By and large, this stance is the most shocking aspect of ANT for most sociologists as it removes humans from their pivotal role (Collins & Yearley, 1992a). This ontological position of society and things shakes the very ground that mainstream sociology stands on, since sociology in general does not account for non-humans and considers the social only in term of humans as the focus of its studies. Main stream sociology does focus on some social aspects and social relations, such as power, classes, and institutions, but it argues that science is outside the sphere of sociology and should be left to experts. For this reason, the symmetrical view of ANT and its positioning towards seeing non-humans as the glue or cement that holds society together is considered a "structural failure" of the theory to account for the reified social facts, structures, and institutions (Pels, 1995).

The counter argument is that ANT's account of the social structure is quite distinctive, as it goes beyond the duality of structure (Giddens, 1994) towards a sort of mesh of structure with the actors. The notion of network and its nodes embodies a structure within each node, and with the node and its network. In ANT, the structure would therefore be inside and outside the node.

Furthermore, mainstream sociology does not account for science and technology, and only intervenes in this area to identify the socio-psychological causes of cases of error, irrationality and deviation from the proper norms. Apart from this, sociologists can, at best, illuminate the general conditions that encourage or inhibit science. This contrasts sharply with the symmetrical view of ANT that treats the success and failure phenomena with the same analytical lens. For ANT, failure is not the occasion where sociologists intervene to study; rather, it is the way the making of science and the establishment of networks that perform science that concerns ANT.

SSK's sociologists "categorically" deny that ANT can be identified with SSK under a label of 'social constructivism' as "the two approaches are deeply opposed", a comment made in David Bloor's lengthy attack to ANT in general and Latour in particular (Bloor, 1999).

Despite the fact that the two approaches share the same preference for detailed case-studies, Seguin (2000) explains that the object of study is different in the two approaches (Seguin, 2000). SSK is concerned with the role of society in science and technology production particularly with identifying the social factors and providing social explanations of science and technology production. Therefore, it does not render any agency to non-humans and sees the production as an occasion for social explanation.

ANT, on the other hand, focuses on the role of science and technology in building society. As Callon and Latour bluntly put it: "we have never been interested in giving a social explanation of anything, but we want to explain society..." (Michel Callon & Latour, 1992, pg.348). Thus, ANT renders agency to both the social and the technical or humans and non-humans in order to follow the network building and the interweaving of both to constitute what ANT sees as 'the social'. Being a "relationism" theory, it sticks to the empirical task of tracing the establishment of relations (Latour, 1999a) through the co-production of the social and the technical (science and technology). It stresses that neither could be explained in the other's terms and for this reason ANT studies the production of an intertwined relationship between the subject and the object as it follows the association chain that is being established.

Furthermore, SSK considers ANT to be a kind of technological determinism which, as Collins and Yearley (1992a) put it, "once learned to ignore". In this sense, ANT is accused of being concerned with natural realism that embraces the priority of technological descriptions adopted from scientists. Collins and Yearley also argue that the domain for scientific and technological phenomena should be left to experts to describe and talk about, as sociologists lack the scientific credentials (Collins & Yearley, 1992a). They encourage STS sociologists to stand on the social and stick to the "social realists" approach (Collins & Yearly, 1992b).

Responding to the criticism that sociologist should leave the science and technology to experts, Woolgar (1992) argues that this suggestion itself partitions the world into groups and assigns differential positions (capabilities and actions) to these groups. He argues that this contradicts the ethnomethodological roots that stress "any presumption of structured reality is a travesty of a key sociological phenomenon: how are structurings of this kind managed and achieved, for what purposes, by whom, and so on?"(Woolgar, 1992).

ANT's use of similar semiotic language to describe both humans and non-humans was also criticised, for example by Collins and Yearly (1992a), for being hollow and for rendering bizarre intentionality to non-humans (Collins & Yearley, 1992a). In a response article to Collins and Yearly, Callon and Latour (1992) explain that extending symmetry to vocabulary "does not mean that [they] wish to extend intentionality to things, or mechanisms to human (Michel Callon & Latour, 1992).

Material Agency

ANT's granting of agency to material objects – such as man-made things like in the case of technology, machines and artefacts - seems problematic for some. Critics argue that if this is possible for natural living entities, it is not possible for technology (Collins & Yearley, 1992a). Moreover, Schaffer (1991) finds it illegitimate and unnecessary to ascribe will, life, and interests to non-humans, describing it as "heresy of hylozoism" (Schaffer, 1991). He argues that this hylozoism takes the researcher away from looking for the crucial human actors in favour of seeking non-human explanations and therefore "disables understanding". Collins and Yearly (1992a,b) denied the granting of agency to a piece of paper,

a door or any other non-human. They suggest that treating the social and the technical symmetrically leads ANT to attribute capabilities to technology that are properly considered to be human, hence diminishing the potential for human agency (Collins & Yearley, 1992a).

Callon and Latour (1992) addressed this issue by explaining that their "empirical program does not claim either that humans and artifacts are exactly the same or that they are radically different", and that they leave the question of agency open. They argue that the redistribution of "actantial roles" are themselves subject to negotiation, and thus subject to empirical evidence rather than *a priori* determination. They claim it is a matter of empirical evidence to follow the fact builders (scientists, technologists) on their work of constructing these competences. Callon and Latour (ibid) also demonstrate that *a priori* attribution would not only be a methodological mistake but worse, in their opinion, a serious error of political judgment "since differences are so visible, what needs to be understood is their construction, their transformations, their remarkable variety and mobility, in order to substitute a multiplicity of little local divides for one great divide"

Law (1991a, 1992) defends ANT in a similar sense, by contending that it explores the nature of the social through its symmetrical vocabulary. This reveals that the glue holding the society together is achieved by heterogeneous means, and that the social is not social at all. "The social world would not hang together if the natural, the corporeal, the technological, the textual and the topographical were taken away" (Law, 1991). He argues that ANT has a "serious commitment to heterogeneity and in particular to the heterogeneity of the sociotechnical" (ibid).

As indicated earlier, Collins and Yearly (1992b) eventually shifted their position and accepted the importance of the term "actant", although they argued that "the notion of actors is much more important, and the differences between actors and actants are vital" (Collins & Yearley, 1992b).

Ethics

The symmetrical treatment of humans and non-humans raises an ethical concern regarding the equality between man and machine and in viewing humans as machines and machines as humans. Pels (1995) criticises the ideas presented in Latour (1993) by opposing what he called Latour's "radical exaggeration" of the principle of symmetry and the "identitarian drift" of ANT (Latour, 1993). Instead, he argues in favour of weaker asymmetries that preserve some critical boundary between humans and non-humans (Pels, 1995).

In this regard, Callon and Latour (1992) assert that they do not regard these entities as equivalent, but are interested only in the analytical level as they believe that there is no perceptible difference. They clearly claim that "the point is methodological" and that there is a difference between the analytic view and the ethical view of the issue (Michel Callon & Latour, 1992). Latour (1999a) explains that his colleagues and himself aim "to avoid the absurdities of having some entities playing a role and dropping out of the story others" (Latour, 1999a). This notion was well received by Lee and Brown (1994) when they embraced ANT for its "liberal democratic" orientation (Lee & Brown, 1994), in the sense that it liberates the oppressed through enfranchisement and appropriate representation by challenging the usual dichotomy between humans and non-humans.

Law (1991a) jokingly says, "I am not a Nazi, and neither ... do I currently think of myself as a machine" (Law, 1991). He argues that there are two reasons that this division should not carry an analogous explanatory weight. First, humans are heterogeneous networks and hence the product of confused overlaps. Second, the very dividing line between people and machines is variable and negotiable. ANT is concerned with how differences and similarities are constructed and sustained.

IMPLICATION FOR IS RESEARCH

The severe criticism of ANT from mainstream sociology and from SSK researchers has generally little effect on the use of ANT in the IS field, apart from creating awareness and caution around certain points.

In the IS field, ANT's ontological stance is particularly celebrated as information systems researchers witness the constant constitution of performing networks of people and things, of the social and technical. In information systems, ANT has the potential to account for both and to explain how actors construct their heterogeneous world. Also, the stance of not determining *a priori* the boundary between what is social and what is technical, and leaving it as an empirical matter to be decided by the actors, has proved to be useful in IS research. Many authors have found it productive to explore how both the technical and the social are negotiated (Bloomfield & Vurdubakis, 1994; Grint & Woolgar, 1997; Rachel & Woolgar, 1995).

The symmetrical stance of ANT is therefore welcomed in the IS field, in contrast to the mainstream sociology perspective. In IS, this is one of main attractions of ANT since many researchers see its value in accounting for the technology as an actant. Granting agency to systems and technology helps IS researchers to understand the role of technology in a different way from the technology determinism or social construction (SCOT) arguments.

In IS research, the ethical concerns regarding the symmetrical view of ANT seems irrelevant as many IS researchers clearly announce that their use of the symmetrical view serves only an analytical purpose and does not reflect an ethical belief (e.g. Walsham, 1997).

THE APPLICATION OF ANT IN IS RESEARCH

As already indicated, ANT is much celebrated in the IS field, where its philosophical position and methods of inquiry are seen to facilitate its practical application, as well as having much to offer the IS researchers (Walsham, 1997). The clear account given by ANT for non-humans lays sound conceptual grounding for IS research.

The remainder of this section offers a brief review of ANT's application in IS research, showing how its recent use covers both a wide range of topics, from system implementation to development methodologies, and a variety of approaches - from a simple adoption of the ANT vocabulary towards more productive deployments of concepts and methodology. The key areas of ANT outlined below include: systems implementation; organisational change; systems design; IS development methodology; IT infrastructure development, introduction and use; evaluation; and the role of IT consultants.

Some IS researchers apply ANT to conceptualise the implementation process of certain technologies. For example, Vidgen and McMaster study the implementation of an automated access control system for a car park (Vidgen & McMaster, 1996). They focus on how the technology black box was opened by the parties involved and how what was once believed to be a simple installation of a technology opened up to reveal a much more complex web of relations and associations. They adopt the notions of 'quasi object', 'networks', and 'black boxes' to conceptualise the mutual changes that occur to the technology and the organisation, including both humans and non-humans in the stakeholder map. Elbanna (2007) studied the implementation of ERP system in an international organisation. She applied ANT as a critical lens to discuss the notion of integration and unravel the intertwining relationship between the ERP system and its organisational setting (Elbanna, 2007). She also applied the theory in another study to reveal the model of improvisation involved in the implementation of rigid systems such as ERP (Elbanna, 2006).

Lilley also studied the implementation of an Oil Management System that emerged from one of the European sites of a parent company (Lilley, 1998), which went on to extend the system's implementation to several sites around the world. The aim was to implement a site-specific systems built around a common core. Lilley tells the story of this case of network building using Callon's four moments of translation. Interestingly, he tries to account not only for the translation process from the outside viewed by the network builder, but also from the inside viewed by the recruited entities.

McGrath (2001) examined the role of environmental forces on the IS implementation. She applies the vocabulary of Callon's sociology of translation to shed some light on how the environmental forces influenced action during a specific period of organisational change and how actors engaged locally in enrolling and mobilising support for that intervention (McGrath, 2001). She focuses on linking the global and local contexts of the implementation of the new computer system, suggesting that this "mechanism" is available within ANT. McGrath arguably view ANT as a "collection of powerful tools and ideas", as opposed to being a "complete and constraining methodology".

Some IS research applies ANT for conceptualising the development of IT. For example, Bloomfield and others analyse a series of events in the design and development of information systems in the UK National Health Service (NHS) (Bloomfield, Coombs, Knights, & Littler, 1997). They adopt the ANT understanding of system development as the construction of a complex heterogeneous network of humans and non-humans. In the case study, they focus on the analysis following the notion of stabilisation and destabilisation of the actor network.

Klischewski (2000) applies ANT to conceptualise IS development by regarding it as "networking" (Klischewski, 2000) with black boxed commitments (Klischewski, 2001). Being interested in providing a practical guide for systems development, Klischewski makes black boxed commitments a starting point of the analysis and then follows their circulation as immutable mobiles rather than following the construction of each commitment and how it is black boxed and reopened in times of controversies.

Along a similar line, Monteiro (2000) attempts to find a practical use of ANT in systems design (Monteiro, 2000). He defines some guidelines for systems design using ANT. To do this, he appropriated the theory and made arbitrary uses of a simplified version of it that focuses only on a selection of concepts rather than accounting for all of them.

Atkinson (2000) develops a contingency approach for systems development named Soft Information Systems and Technologies Methodology (SISTeM), which stems from Soft System Methodology (SSM) using ANT as an underpinning framework (Atkinson, 2000). He proposes to regard the methodology as a network or a "methodological actor network" in its own right that enrols and mobilises a heterogeneous set of human and non-human actors. At the same time, it is a node or non-human actant in the actor network of the real world. Its use in the real world is therefore shaped by the relationship it has with the other actants in the network into which it has been enrolled. Atkinson also suggests the methodology can be seen as network building in each stage of its application.

Some researchers find ANT useful for accounting for the introduction of a certain technology. For example, Aanestad and Hanseth (2000) explore the introduction of a multimedia technology in a medical surgery, presenting three detailed micro-level snap-shots of local instances of the case being studied (Aanestad & Hanseth, 2000). This usefully reveal the highly complex setting of tech-

nology and work practices, the highly emergent and evolutionary use of multimedia technology, and the complexity of the network of human and non-human alliances that needed to be recruited to use the technology. They show through ANT's conceptualisation how the demands of technology and medical work practice can coexist in a stable network and how they may be in conflict and hence translation is required to align actors and enrol them in a stable network. In the third story, Aanestad and Hanseth describe how the alignment of the network proved to be fragile as it broke apart. They conclude by arguing that the use of ANT offers a suitable and valuable conceptualisation of the use of multimedia technology to cultivate a hybrid of humans and non-humans, technologies and non-technologies.

Knights, Murray, and Willmott draw upon ANT, particularly Callon's notion of the sociology of translation, to study the establishment of an electronic network for the insurance industry (Knights, Murray, & Willmott, 1997). They apply the concepts of problematisation, interessement, enrolment, and mobilisation. Although it is very brief, their description of the case illustrates a sensitive use of ANT. They suggest that the sociology of translation does not account for power/knowledge relations, so chose to complement it by the use of Foucault's understanding of power (Foucault, 1980).

Other researchers are interested in the theory itself and experiment with some of its concepts. Monteiro and Hanseth (1996) examine the relationship between IT and organisations in the light of ANT framework. They argue that ANT provides a firm grasp of the interplay between IT and organisational issues that take "IS quite seriously" (Monteiro & Hanseth, 1996). Comparing ANT with Structuration Theory (Giddens, 1984), they argue in favour of ANT. They find that ANT provides immediate benefits through its language, and that its "overall rationale is geared" towards providing an analysis that goes far beyond "IT enables/constrains actions". In their concern with standards and infrastructure, they attempt to briefly but broadly apply notions like actor-network, translation, alignment, inscription, and irreversibility to understand how standards acquire stability and how they become increasingly "irreversible". Although their study is valuable, it does not provide any detailed or proccessual account of any of the ANT concepts.

Bloomfield and Vurdubakis relate to one of the principles of ANT; that it does not set any *a priori* assumptions concerning the technical and the social, and their boundaries (Bloomfield & Vurdubakis, 1994). Through two case studies, they follow the actors in their negotiations of the boundary between the social and the technical. They conclude that boundary-setting is situated and an *a priori* distinction is far from being appropriate, as the content of the social and the technical is subject to ongoing negotiations between various actors.

Pouloudi and Whitley (2000) address the representation of non-humans, one of the problematic aspects in applying ANT . As ANT views human and non-human entities symmetrically, researchers tend to think that representing the non-human is far more problematic than the straight forward task of representing humans, as the latter can speak for themselves. Pouloudi and Whitley argue that this common concern is not as clear cut as it appears. They study an NHS-wide networking project, following the way two stakeholders were represented in the project: one human (patients) and the other non-human (an encryption algorithm). They show that the two actors that are different in kind (human and non-human) can share the same representation difficulties where many stakeholders seek to represent the actors.

There is also research on IT infrastructure development from a variety of angles. For instance, Hanseth and Braa (1998) apply ANT to understand IT infrastructure development and use in the European fertiliser division of Norsk Hydro (Hanseth & Braa, 1998). They apply ANT to develop a broad account that conceptualises

SAP as a non-human actor which shapes its environment as well as its own future. The authors follow the SAP technology as it builds and changes alliances with others. This assisted understanding of how the addition of an infrastructure gains momentum and influences future developments of that infrastructure.

Hanseth and Monteiro (1997) continue their interest in infrastructure spread and development by studying how it inscribes a certain pattern of use. They focus on the two ANT notions of inscription and translation to help analyse the phenomena more broadly (Hanseth & Monteiro, 1997). In this process, they uncover, through the notion of inscription, the sociotechnical complexity of establishing an information infrastructure. They try to reveal how explicit anticipations of some actors were inscribed into the standards, who inscribe them, how these inscriptions were carried out, and the efforts taken to oppose them or work around them.

Also, Hanseth and Braa (2000) present the story of the evolution of the infrastructure in the Norwegian company Norsk Hydro (Aanestad & Hanseth, 2000). They use ANT to offer an explanation of how the SAP part of the infrastructure drifted from the initial planning towards an almost opposite outcome. They question who is really in control, as people, departments, and divisions who once thought that they controlled SAP and could align it to their interests ended up being aligned, controlled, and locked-in by SAP. Their analysis, however, seems to produce a technologically deterministic stance that they justify by the use of ANT.

Cordella and Simon (2000) study the infrastructure accumulation in Astra Hässle, a Swedish pharmaceutical research company (Cordella & Simon, 2000). They introduce a model for analysing infrastructure implementation based on the notion of inscription adopted from ANT, providing a framework that is a matrix of technology and organisational inscriptions.

There is also research on the evaluation of IT using ANT. For example, Lehoux and others (Lehoux, Sicotte, & Denis, 1999) study the evaluation of a computerised medical record system in four Quebec hospitals. They illustrate and discuss the integration of the two ANT concepts of problematisation and script of use within the evaluation framework employed. They suggest to study: the developers 'problematisation' or initial definition of the roles, tasks, skills and objectives of a large set of actors; and the 'script of use' within the developed innovation, prior to examining the users' confinement to their assumed roles.

The role of IT external consultants has also been studied within the ANT framework. For example, Bloomfield and Danieli (1995) use some of the ANT vocabulary to explore and conceptualise IT consultants' practices in IS development (Bloomfield & Danieli, 1995). They are particularly interested in revealing the ongoing negotiations and conflicts over who has the legitimate voice to speak on behalf of IT and the organisation. They also reveal the consultants' endeavour to overcome resistance and to hold a network of interlocking agreements. However, although they seem to be influenced by the ANT vocabulary and some of its concepts, nearly no direct reference is made to the theory as such.

Bloomfield and Vurdubakis (1997) also use ANT to interpret a consulting document for an NHS projects (Bloomfield & Vurdubakis, 1997). Here, they are concerned particularly with the intermediary role of that document as an attempt to bring together IT and the organisation (doctors, managers, etc.), while at the same time respecting their separation and differences. They build on the assumption that "all forms of administrative, political, and managerial intervention are not reactions to reality as such but to reality socially and discursively constructed within documents". This assumption underestimates other forms of communication within the organisation that contribute to the construction of its social reality.

CONCLUSION

Actor Network Theory provides a rich lens to study information systems. It has been adopted by many researchers in the IS field, in the belief that it could provide a new and valuable insight into the relationship between technology and society. The theory has received a fierce criticism from main stream sociology and sociology of scientific knowledge (SSK). In the IS field, these points of criticism provides useful insight to understand information systems in different settings and should not deter IS researchers from applying the theory in their studies.

REFERENCES

Aanestad, M., & Hanseth, O. (2000, June 10-12). *Implementing open network technologies in complex work practices: A case from telemedicine.* Paper presented at the IFIP 8.2, Aalborg, Denmark.

Akrich, M., & Latour, B. (1992). A Summary of a convenient vocabulary for the semiotics of human and nonhuman assemblies. In W. E. Bijker & J. Law (Eds.), *Shaping technology/building society: Studies in sociotechnical change* (pp. 259-264). Cambridge, MA: The MIT Press.

Atkinson, C. J. (2000). The 'soft information systems and technologies methodology' (SISTeM): An actor network contingency approach to integrated development. *European Journal of Information Systems, 9,* 104-123.

Bijker, W. E., Hughes, T. P., & Pinch, T. J. (Eds.). (1987). *The social construction of technological systems: New directions in the sociology and history of technology.* Cambridge, MA: The MIT Press.

Bloomfield, B. P., Coombs, R., Knights, D., & Littler, D. (Eds.). (1997). *Information Technology and Organizations: Strategies, Networks, and Integration*: Oxford University Press.

Bloomfield, B. P., & Danieli, A. (1995). The role of management consultants in the development of information technology: The indissoluble nature of socio-political and technical skills. *Journal of Management Studies, 32*(1), 23-46.

Bloomfield, B. P., & Vurdubakis, T. (1994). Boundary disputes, negotiating the boundary between the technical and the social in the development of IT systems. *Information Technology & People, 7*(1), 9-24.

Bloomfield, B. P., & Vurdubakis, T. (1997). Paper traces: Inscribing organizations and information technology. In B. P. Bloomfield, R. Coombs, D. Knights, & D. Littler (Eds.), *Information technology and organizations: Strategies, networks, and integration* (pp. 85-111). UK: Oxford University Press.

Bloor, D. (1999). Anti-Latour. *Studies in the History and Philosophy of Science, 30*(1), 81-112.

Callon, M. (1986). Some elements of a sociology of translation: Domestication of the scallops and the fishermen of St Brieuc Bay. In J. Law (Ed.), *Power, action and belief: A new sociology of knowledge* (pp. 196-233). London: Routledge and Kegan Paul.

Callon, M. (1987). Society in the making: The study of technology as a tool for sociological analysis. In W. E. Bijker, T. P. Hughes, & T. Pinch (Eds.), *The social construction of technological systems* (pp. 83-103). Cambridge, MA: The MIT Press.

Callon, M., & Latour, B. (1981). Unscrewing the big leviathan: How actors macro-structure reality and how sociologists help them to do so. In K. Knorr-Cetina, & A. V. Cicourel (Eds.), *Towards an integration of micro- and macro- sociologies* (pp. 277-303). London: Routledge& Kegan Paul.

Callon, M., & Latour, B. (1992). Don't throw the baby out with the bath school!: A reply to Collins and Yearley. In A. Pickering (Ed.), *Science as practice and culture* (pp. 343-368). IL: The University of Chicago Press.

Centre for Science Studies. (2001). *Actor network resources*.

Collins, H. M., & Yearley, S. (1992a). Epistemological chicken. In A. Pickering (Ed.), *Science as practice and culture* (pp. 301-326). IL: The Universty of Chicago Press.

Collins, H. M., & Yearley, S. (1992b). Journey into space. In A. Pickering (Ed.), *Science as practice and culture* (pp. 369-389). IL: The University of Chicago Press.

Cordella, A., & Simon, K. A. (2000). Global and local dynamics in infrastructure deployment: The Astra Hassle experience. In C. U. Ciborra (Ed.), *From control to drift: The dynamics of corporate information infrastructure* (pp. 172-192). UK: Oxford University Press.

Elbanna, A. R. (2006). The validity of the improvisation argument in the implementation of rigid technology: The case of ERP systems. *Journal of Information Technology, 21*, 165-175.

Elbanna, A. R. (2007). Implementing an integrated system in a socially dis-integrated enterprise: A critical view of ERP enabled integration. *Information Technology and People, 20*(2), 121-139.

Foucault, M. (1980). *Power/knowledge: Selected interviews and other writings 1972-1977.* Brighton, UK: The Harvester Press.

Giddens, A. (1984). *The constitution of society: Outline of the theory of structuration.* Cambridge, UK: Polity Press.

Giddens, A. (1994). *The constitution of society: Outline of the theory of structuration.* Cambridge, UK: Polity Press.

Greimas, A. J. (1990). *The social science, a semiotic view* (P. Perron & F. H. Collins, Trans.). Minneapolis: University of Minnesota Press.

Grint, K., & Woolgar, S. (1997). *The machine at work: Technology, work and organization.* Cambridge, UK: Polity Press.

Hanseth, O., & Braa, K. (1998, December 13-16). *Technology as traitor: Emergent SAP infrastructure in a global organization.* Paper presented at the Nineteenth International Conference on Information Systems (ICIS), Helsinki, Finland.

Hanseth, O., & Monteiro, E. (1997). Inscribing behaviour in information infrastructure standards. *Accounting, Management and Information Technology, 7*(4), 183-211.

Klischewski, R. (2000). *Systems development as networking.* Paper presented at the Americas Conference on Information Systems (AMCIS), Long Beach, CA.

Klischewski, R. (2001, June 27-29). *Commitments enabling co-operation in distributed information systems development.* Paper presented at the The 9th European Conference on Information Systems, Bled, Slovenia.

Knights, D., Murray, F., & Willmott, H. (1997). Networking as knowledge work: A study of strategic inter-organizational development in the financial service industry. In B. P. Bloomfield, R. Coombs, D. Knights, & D. Littler (Eds.), *Information technology and organizations: Strategies, networks, and integration* (pp. 137-159). UK: Oxford University Press.

Latour, B. (1987). *Science in action: How to follow scientists and engineers through society.* Cambridge, MA: Harvard University Press.

Latour, B. (1988a). Mixing humans and nonhumans together: The sociology of a door-closer. *Social Problems, 35*(3), 298-310.

Latour, B. (1988b). *The pasteurization of France* (A. Sheridan & J. Law, Trans.). Cambridge, MA: Harvard University Press.

Latour, B. (1993). *We have never been modern.* Cambridge, MA: Harvard University Press.

Latour, B. (1994a). On technical mediation-- philosophy, sociology, genealogy. *Common Knowledge, 3*(2), 29-64.

Latour, B. (1994b). Pragmatogonies. *American Behavioral Scientist, 37*(6), 791-808.

Latour, B. (1996). *Aramis or the love of technology* (C. Porter, Trans.). Cambridge, MA: Harvard University Press.

Latour, B. (1999a). For David Bloor... and beyond: A reply to David Bloor's 'Anti-Latour'. *Studies in the History and Philosophy of Science, 30*(1), 113-129.

Latour, B. (1999b). *Pandora's hope: Essays on the reality of science studies.* Cambridge, MA: Harvard University Press.

Law, J. (1991). Introduction: Monsters, machines and sociotechnical relations. In J. Law (Ed.), *A Sociology of monsters: Essays on power, technology and domination* (pp. 1-23). London: Routledge.

Law, J. (1992). Notes on the theory of the actor-network: Ordering, strategy, and heterogeneity. *Systems Practice, 5*(4), 379-393.

Law, J. (1997). *Traduction/trahison-notes on ANT.* Retrieved November 2, 1999, from http://www.lancs.ac.uk/sociology/stslaw2.html

Law, J., & Callon, M. (1988). Engineering and sociology in a military aircraft project: A network analysis of technological change. *Social Problems, 35*(3), 284-297.

Lee, N., & Brown, S. (1994). Otherness and the actor network. *American Behavioral Scientists, 37*(6), 772-790.

Lehoux, P., Sicotte, C., & Denis, J.-L. (1999). Assessment of a computerized medical record system: Disclosing script of use. *Evaluation and Program Planning, 22*, 439-453.

Lilley, S. (1998). Regarding screens for surveillance of the system. *Accounting, Management and Information Technology, 8*, 63-105.

McGrath, K. (2001, June 27-29). *The golden circle: A case study of organizational change at the London Ambulance Service (case study)*. Paper presented at the The 9th European Conference on Information Systems, Bled, Slovenia.

Monteiro, E. (2000). Monsters: From systems to actor-networks. In K. Braa, C. Sorensen, & B. Dahlbom (Eds.), *Planet Internet*. Lund, Sweden: Studentlitteratur.

Monteiro, E., & Hanseth, O. (1996). Social shaping of information infrastructure: On being specific about the technology. In W. J. Orlikowski, G. Walsham, M. R. Jones, & DeGross, J. I. (Eds.), *Information technology and changes in organizational work* (pp. 325-343). London: Chapman and Hall.

Pels, D. (1995). Have we never been modern? Towards a demontage of Latour's modern constitution. *History of the Human Sciences, 8*(3), 129-141.

Pickering, A. (Ed.). (1992). *Science as practice and culture*. IL: The University of Chicago Press.

Rachel, J., & Woolgar, S. (1995). The discursive structure of the social-technical divide: The example of information systems development. *The Sociological Review, 43*(2), 251-273.

Schaffer, S. (1991). The eighteenth brumaire of Bruno Latour. *Studies in the History and Philosophy of Science, 22*(1), 174-192.

Seguin, E. (2000). Bloor, Latour, and the field. *Studies in the History and Philosophy of Science, 31*(3), 503-508.

Serres, M. (1974). *La traduction*. Paris: Hermes III.

Star, S. L. (1988). Introduction: The sociology of science and technology. *Social Problems, 35*(3), 197-205.

Stengers, I. (1997). *Power and invention: Situating science* (P. Bains, Trans.). Minneapolis: University of Minnesota Press.

Vidgen, R., & McMaster, T. (1996). Black boxes, non-human stakeholders and the translation of IT through mediation. In W. J. Orlikowski, G. Walsham, M. R. Jones, & J. I. DeGross (Eds.), *Information technology and change in organizational work* (pp. 250-271). London: Chapman and Hall.

Walsham, G. (1997). Actor-network theory and IS research: Current status and future prospects. In A. S. Lee, J. Liebenau, & J. I. DeGross (Eds.), *Information systems and qualitative research* (pp. 467-480). London: Chapman and Hall.

Woolgar, S. (1992). Some remarks about positionism: A reply to Collins and Yearley. In A. Pickering (Ed.), *Science as practice and culture* (pp. 327-342). IL: The University of Chicago Press.

KEY TERMS AND DEFINITIONS

Actant: Non-human actor.

Actor: An entity that could be human and non-human that is made to act affect by the support of other actors.

Enrollment: Designates the device by which a set of interrelated roles is defined and attributed to actors who accept them.

Interessement: The action of interest building.

Mobilization: To render mobile those entities

that were not so before the actor network building activities.

Network: A conceptual tool to describe and make sense of actors' worknets.

Problematisation: Finding a problem for the presented solution to which other entities could subscribe.

Translation: Is a mechanism by which actor recruit others into its network.

Chapter XXIV
Social Capital Theory

Hossam Ali-Hassan
York University, Canada

ABSTRACT

Social capital represents resources or assets rooted in an individual's or in a group's network of social relations. It is a multidimensional and multilevel concept which has been characterized by a diversity of definitions and conceptualizations which focus on the structure and/or on the content of the social relations. A common conceptualization of social capital in information systems research consists of a structural, relational and cognitive dimension. The structural dimension represents the configuration of the social network and the characteristics of its ties. The relational dimension represents assets embedded in the social relations such as trust, obligations, and norms of reciprocity. The cognitive dimension represents a shared context which facilitates interactions and is created by shared codes, language and narratives. For a single or multiple members of a network, social capital can be a source of solidarity, information, cooperation, collaboration and influence. Social capital has been and remains a sound theory to study information systems in research areas affected by social relations and the assets embedded in them.

INTRODUCTION

Social capital which represents in a sense the goodwill, such as sympathy, trust and forgiveness, engendered by the fabric of social relations and which could facilitate action, has gained increasing attention from researchers in sociology, political science, economics and organizational science (Adler & Kwon, 2002). This chapter looks at the different and diverse perspectives used to define social capital and its value, sources and characteristics. A popular multi-dimensional model of social capital developed by Nahapiet and Ghoshal (1998) is then explored, followed by a summary of its use in information systems research. This chapter then addresses the issue of social capital levels of analysis and the general benefits and risks social capital can carry along with its potential for future information systems research.

BACKGROUND

The term "Social Capital" originated from the areas of sociology and political science and origi-nally appeared in Hanifan (1916) study of rural schools community centers. It appeared later in community studies where networks of strong personal relationships provided the basis for trust, cooperation and collective action which were key for the survival and functioning of city neighbor-hoods (Jacobs, 1965). Then at the individual level, Loury (1977) studied the resources intrinsic in family relations and community social structure and their role in the development of young children. The concept was then applied to a wide range of social phenomena such as the development of human capital, economic performance of firms, geographic regions, and nations (Nahapiet & Gho-shal, 1998). Now it can be found in a wide range of social science disciplines, such as sociology, political science, and economy (Adler and Kwon, 2002), in addition to organizational and manage-ment sciences (Huysman & Wulf, 2004).

Definitions

Social capital is used to describe relational resources embedded in personal ties, which are useful in the development of individuals in community social organizations and has been conceptualized either as a set of social resources embedded in relationships or more broadly as including, in addition to social relationships, the norms and values associated with them (Tsai & Ghoshal, 1998). An example of definitions which focused on the social resources embedded in relationships is Burt's (1992) who defined social capital as *"friends, colleagues, and more general contacts through whom you receive opportuni-ties to use your financial and human capital"* (p. 9). An example of definition which focused on the norms and values associated with the social relations is Woolcock's (1998) who defined it as *"the information, trust and norms of reciprocity inherent in one's social network"* (p.153).

Adler and Kwon (2002) compiled a list of twenty different definitions for social capital in the key literature, highlighting the diversity in its streams of research. These definitions focus either on the relations an actor maintains with other actors and/or on the structure of relations among actors in a collectivity. They also focus on the social ties and relationships and /or on the characteristics and content of those ties and the assets they represent. Examples of such definitions of social capital include:

- *the ability of actors to secure benefits by virtue of membership in social networks or other social structures* (Portes, 1998, pp.6)
- *features of social organization such as net-work, norms and social trust that facilitate coordination and cooperation for mutual benefits* (Putnam, 1995, pp.67)
- *the sum of the resources, actual or virtual, that accrues to an individual or a group by virtue of possessing a durable network of more or less institutionalized relationships of mutual acquaintance and recognition* (Bourdieu & Wacquant, 1992, pp.119)
- *a variety of different entities, with two elements in common: they all consist of some aspect of social structures , and they facilitate certain actions of actors—whether persons or corporate actors – within the structure* (Coleman, 1988, pp.S98).

The diverse definitions can be synthesized into: *"Social capital is the goodwill available to individuals or groups. Its source lies in the struc-ture and content of the actor's social relations. Its effects flow from the information, influence, and solidarity it makes available to the actor"* (Adler & Kwon, 2002, pp.23).

Despite that most authors agree that the main proposition of social capital theory is that networks of relationships are a valuable resource for social action, social capital does not have a precise and universally accepted definition. This indicates that it is not a unidimensional concept (Putnam, 1995). Agreeing with the belief that social capital has many dimensions, Nahapiet and Ghoshal (1998) defined social capital "*as the sum of the actual and potential resources embedded within, available through, and derived from the network of relationships possessed by an individual or social unit*" (p.243) and identified three dimensions for it: the structural, the relational and the cognitive dimensions of social capital. The adoption of this definition of social capital and its three dimensions has facilitated the conceptualization and measurement of social capital in multiple studies in the area of management and information systems. A detailed description of Nahapiet and Ghoshal's (1998) different dimensions of social capital and their significance follows later in the chapter.

In summary, social capital has a wide range of definitions which focus on two aspects: social networks (e.g. Burt, 1992) and the resources embedded within the networks (e.g. Bourdieu, 1986). *Social capital theory* premise is the benefit an actor, individual or collective, can reap from those social relations and their embedded resources. However, it is important to note that some researchers on that same topic, such as Granovetter (1982), used the term *social network theory* instead of social capital, highlighting the commonality between the two.

Key Literature

A number of seminal researchers have made a significant contribution to the development of the literature on social capital theory and they include: Bourdieu (1986), Burt (1992), Coleman (1988, 1990), Granovetter (1973, 1982), Portes (1998), Putnam (1995), and Woolcock (1998). A couple of highly cited papers in the area of management and information systems (IS) are Nahapiet and Ghoshal's (1998) article which includes a model of dimensions and items of social capital and Adler and Kwon's (2002) article which is a synthesis of the vast and diverse research on social capital.

BASIC CONCEPTS

According to Coleman (1988) social capital is defined by its function and it is not a single entity but a variety of different entities consisting of some aspect of social structures, which facilitate action of individual actors within the structure. Those actors could be persons or corporate. What makes social relations a useful capital resource for individuals are the three forms of social capital: (i) obligations and expectations, (ii) information channels, and (iii) social norms. The first form of social capital, obligations and expectations, depends on two elements, the trustworthiness of the social environment (the chances obligations for previous favors or actions will be repaid), and the extent of obligations held. The differences in these social structures (trustworthiness of social environment and extent of obligations) come from different sources such as the cultural differences in the tendency to ask for or give aid, in the closure of social networks, in the actual needs for help, in the sources for aid and in the degree of affluence. Individual actors in social structures with high level of outstanding obligations have more social capital to draw on. Individuals however differ in the amount of social capital they can draw on. The second value of social capital, or its second form, is the potential for information that is inherent in social relations. Information, which is an important basis for action, is costly and requires attention which is a scarce supply. Information comes from social relations which have been established and maintained for other purposes. Finally, the third form which is the social norms, when they exist and when they are effective, can be a powerful yet fragile form of social capital. A prescriptive norm within a collectivity is where one would forgo self-interest and act in the interest of the collectivity, and is reinforced by social support, status, honor and other rewards. These norms can be supported by either internal or external sanctions and by rewards. All social relations and social structures facilitate some form of social capital, but certain kinds of social structure can be more beneficial for certain forms of social capital. Closure of social networks is one property of social relations, which is necessary but not sufficient for the emergence of effective norms. A closure can de described as actor A having social relations with actors B and C, and actors B and C also linked by a social relation between them. An open structure is when actors B and C have social relations with actors D and E respectively but not between them. In the case of open structure, the lack of relation between B and C, prevents them from combining forces to sanction A. Whereas in the case of closure, B and C can combine forces to provide a collective sanction for A and facilitate the existence of effective social norms. Closure is also important for the trustworthiness of social structure, necessary for the proliferation of obligations and expectations. Closure can facilitate the rise of reputation and collective sanctions that would ensure trustworthiness and prevent defection from an obligation.

Burt (1992) has also focused on the structure of social networks and highlighted the benefits of both closure relationships and bridging relationships. When a set of people are connected by strong direct or short indirect (via a third party) connections, Burt refers to that as a closed network, or cluster. A bridge on the other hand is a relationship for which there is no effective indirect connection through third parties; a bridge is a relation spanning a structural hole (Burt, 2005). A structural hole is the lack of a direct or indirect relationship between clusters of people. A third common characteristics of network relations is the tie strength defined by Granovetter (1973) as the combination of the amount of time, the intimacy, the emotional intensity and the reciprocal services characterizing those ties. According to Burt (2005), a social network characterized by strong ties, high density, and network closure, fosters trust, norms, control, individual relationships, consistency, trustworthiness, availability, accuracy, richness and affordability of informa-

tion, and cooperation (Burt, 2005). On the other hand, a social network characterized by weak internal ties, low density, structural holes, and with a high degree of brokerage (connections to other networks) has access to alternative opinion/ practice, information variation, creativity, and new idea generation.

SOURCES OF SOCIAL CAPITAL

There is a general consensus that social capital is derived from social relations (Adler & kwon 2002). Almost all definitions of social capital include some form of *network of relationships* (Bourdieu, 1986; Nahapiet & Ghoshal, 1998), *friends, colleagues and more general contacts* (Burt, 1992), *social structure* (Coleman, 1990), *social network* (Woolcock, 1998) and other related terms. Without social relations and social networks, social capital does not exist. Most literature on social capital sources hence focus on social relations and can be divided into two main categories; the research that locates social capital in the formal structure of the social network ties, and the research that focuses on the content of the ties. Adler and Kwon (2002) examined the sources of social capital, and for them, social capital is the resource available to actors as a function of their location in the structure of their social relations. They distinguished three forms of social structure, each based on a different type of relation: (i) market relations where goods and services are exchanged for money, (ii) hierarchical relations where obedience to authority is exchanged for material and spiritual security, and (iii) social relations where favors and gifts are exchanged. The social relations represent the social structure dimension where social capital lies. However, the market and hierarchical relations contribute to the emergence of social relations due to the repeated interactions, and thus contributing indirectly to the formation of social capital.

Network structure features include among other things network closure, structural holes and tie strength, while network ties features include for example norms of reciprocity, trust, and shared values and beliefs. According to Adler and Kwon (2002) an actor's social network provides the opportunity, motivation and ability for social capital transactions. The different types of networks with their internal, external, direct, indirect, formal and informal ties create the opportunity for social capital benefits. Even the structure of the network also contributes to the development of social capital. Network closure, (Coleman 1988) provides the internal cohesiveness within a community or organization, while structural holes (Burt 1992), or the sparse network with few redundant ties, provide access to cost effective external resources, hence both yielding benefit (Adler & Kwon, 2002). The motivation for actions which would enhance social capital transactions, such as helping others, comes from trust and shared norms such as collective goals, obligations, and reciprocity. Finally, ability represents the competencies and resources that actors mobilize via their social relations (Adler & Kwon, 2002).

CHARACTERISTICS

Social capital is not characterized as a property of an individual but as embedded in the relationship with others (Burt 1997). It is relation specific, neither fully interchangeable (Coleman, 1988), nor easily transferable (Nahapiet & Ghoshal, 1998). It increases with use instead of decreasing (Adler & Kwon, 2002) and deteriorates when the social relationships it is based on are not developed or maintained (Nahapiet & Ghoshal, 1998). Like other types of capital, it is considered a productive resource (hence being called capital), helping individuals achieve career success (Burt, 1992; Podolny & Baron, 1997), helping workers find jobs (Granovetter, 1973, 1995; Lin et al., 1981), facilitating a firm's business operations (Burt,

1992; Coleman, 1990; Tsai & Ghoshal, 1998), and enhancing intellectual capital in a firm (Nahapiet & Ghoshal, 1998). Once developed, it can be exchanged for other capital, such as economic and human capital (Bourdieu, 1986).

DIMENSIONS AND MEASUREMENT

In their comprehensive review of social capital, Adler and Kwon (2002) developed a conceptual model of social capital. In that model, the sources of social capital lie in the social relations, located in the ties' structure and content. The structure features could be closure or structural holes and tie contents most commonly are shared norms and beliefs, and abilities. Social relations provide the opportunity, motivation and ability to create social capital. Narayan and Cassidy (2001) developed another framework to measure social capital in their survey in Ghana and Uganda. Their measurements were based on the World Values Survey, the New South Wales Study, the Barometer of Social Capital, Columbia, and the Index of National Civic Health, USA. Their dimensions of social capital are group characteristics, generalized norms, togetherness, everyday sociability, neighborhood connections, volunteerism, and trust. Other examples of social capital measures are Putnam's (2000) which include organization of society, citizen's involvement in society actions, voluntary actions, informal socializing, and social trust.

A widely used social capital framework or model was the one developed by Nahapiet and Ghoshal (1998) to study the impact of social capital on the creation of intellectual capital. Their model was developed based on the notion of resources available in the network of relationships (Bourdieu, 1986), the concept of "weak ties" (Granovetter, 1973), and social status (Burt, 1992). Nahapiet and Ghoshal identified three clusters of social capital, which they labeled "dimensions" of social capital: the structural, the relational and the cognitive dimensions of social capital (Figure 1).

Each dimension incorporates a number of features. The structural dimension refers to social capital as the social network of relationships; its features include network ties and network configuration. The network ties represent the actual dyadic relationship between two nodes, and could represent a friendship, business relationship, or other social relationships. It also represents the medium across which the relationship exists, such as face-to-face, telephone, e-mail and so on. According to the authors, it refers to the *"overall pattern of connections between actors"* or *"who you can reach and how you can reach them"* (pp.244) and its most important facets are the presence or absence of network ties, the network configuration, and the pattern of linkages in terms of density, connectivity, and hierarchy. Nahapiet and Ghoshal (1998) also included appropriable organization as an additional facet of the structural dimension, or the use of an existing network for another purpose than the one it was created for. The relational dimension refers to the assets rooted in the relationships such as trust, trustworthiness, sanctions, norms, expectations, obligations, identity and identification. This dimension refers to those *"assets created and leveraged through relationships"* (p.244) and a history of interactions. The cognitive dimension reflects the common understandings that consist of shared codes and language and shared narratives. It captures what Coleman (1990) calls the "public good aspect of social capital". It includes shared vision and common values in an organization. According to Nahapiet and Ghoshal (1998) this dimension refers to the *"resources providing shared representations, interpretations, and systems of meaning among parties"* (p.244). Among the three dimensions, the cognitive dimension is the least discussed in the mainstream literature and least included in empirical studies on social capital however its inclusion is valuable in the context of knowledge sharing and transfer. Despite being separately identified with distinct facets, the three dimensions are highly interrelated.

Figure 1. Social capital dimensions (adapted from Nahapiet & Ghoshal, 1998)

(A) Structural Dimension
- Network ties
- Network configurations
- Appropriable organization

(B) Cognitive Dimension
- Shared codes and language
- Shared narratives

(C) Relational Dimensions
- Trust
- Norms
- Obligations
- Identification

SOCIAL CAPITAL MODELS IN INFORMATION SYSTEMS RESEARCH

Compared to the other models, the one developed by Nahapiet and Ghoshal, has the advantage of being simple with three clear key dimensions and with flexibility in the selection of features. It has been adapted and used in multiple IS empirical studies. Tsai and Ghoshal (1998) used it to evaluate the value creation (product innovation) at a large multinational electronics company. Liao and Welsch (2003, 2005) used it to study entrepreneurship and venture creation. Levin and Cross (2004) used a modified version of it, replacing the cognitive dimension with knowledge, to study the mediating role of trust in knowledge transfer. Wasko and Faraj (2005) used to examine individual motivation, social capital and knowledge contribution. Chou et al (2006) used it to study IT outsourcing decisions. Kankahalli et al (2005) found a positive relation between reciprocity and electronic knowledge repositories use. Yli-Renko et al (2001) studied the relation between social interaction and relationship quality and knowledge acquisition. Chiu et al (2006) examined the relation between multiple dimensions of social capital and quantity and quality of knowledge sharing. Each of these studies was based on some dimensions of Nahapiet and Ghoshal's framework, but each one measured the items or characteristics particular to the context and goal of their study. Some studies have also measured social capital based on other models and dimensions. A sample list of information systems or management related

empirical studies measuring social capital, its dimension(s), item(s) and dependent variable(s) can be found in table 1.

LEVELS OF ANALYSIS

Social capital has been conceptualized and operationally defined at many different levels of analysis (Tsai & Ghoshal, 1998), including individual (e.g. Burt 2005; McFadyen & Canella, 2004; Perry-Smith, 2006) and collective, such as family (e.g. Coleman, 1988), organizational units (e.g. Hansen, 1999), organization (e.g. Burt, 1992; Chou et al., 2006; Nahapiet & Ghoshal

Table 1. Sample of empirical studies measuring social capital

Study	Social Capital Dimension(s)	Items	Dependent Variable(s)
Nahapiet & Ghoshal (1998)	Structural (S), cognitive (C) and relational (R)	S: Network ties (access, timing, referrals), network configuration (density, connectivity, hierarchy), appropriable social org C: shared codes and language, shared narratives R: trust, norms, obligations & expectations, identification	New intellectual capital (+ 4 full mediators: access to parties, anticipation of value and motivation to combine/exchange intellect cap and combination capability)
Walker et al. (1997)	Structural equivalence	Same relationships between firms in a network	Formation of an industry network
Patnayakuni et al. (2006)	Structural (S), cognitive (C) and relational (R)	S: digitization, relational asset specificity & cross-functional application integration. C: relational interaction routines and data consistency. R: long term orientation	Supply chain integration (full mediator) then organizational performance
Arling & Subramani (2005)		Face-to-face prominence, face-to-face information diversity, computer-mediated prominence, computer-mediated diversity	Social capital
McFadyen & Cannella (2004)	Structural	Number of relations and strength of relations	Knowledge created (citations)
Brookes et al. (2006)		Conductivity (interactions), trust, respect, longetivity (age of relation), common experience, wider social context (outside project)	Project social capital

continued on following page

Table 1. continued

Study	Social Capital Dimension(s)	Items	Dependent Variable(s)
Wasko & Faraj (2005)	Structural (S), cognitive (C) and relational (R) and individual motivation (IM)	S: Centrality C: self rated expertise and tenure in field R: commitment and reciprocity IM: reputation and enjoying helping	Knowledge contribution in electronic network of practice
Huang & DeSanctis (2005)	Structural	Closeness (and interactions) and centrality	Knowledge sharing (messages in forum)
Sherif et al. (2006)	Structural (S), cognitive (C) and relational (R) (case study)	S: Network ties connectivity and density R: social norms, obligations, expectations, trust & identity C: common language and shared narrative	Social capital
Tsai & Ghoshal (1998)	Structural (S), cognitive (C) and relational (R)	S: Social interaction ties C: Shared vision R: trust and trustworthiness	Resource exchange and combination (full mediator) and product innovation
Borgatti & Cross (2003)	Social network	Knowing area of expertise, positive evaluation, having access to, cost, physical proximity	Information seeking (learning)
Chiu et al. (2006)	Structural (S), cognitive (C) and relational (R)	S: Social interaction ties R: trust, norms of reciprocity and identification C: shared language and vision	Quality of knowledge sharing and knowledge quality
Levin & Cross (2004)		Tie strength Benevolence- and competence-based trust (mediators)	Receipt of useful info
Hansen (1999)		Inter-unit tie strength and type of knowledge	Knowledge sharing (Project completion time)
Hansen (2002)	"Knowledge network"	Network path length, number of network connections	Knowledge sharing (Quantity of knowledge and project completion time)
Kankanhalli et al. (2005)		Cost (loss of knowledge power, codification effort), extrinsic benefit (org reward, image, reciprocity), intrinsic benefits (knowledge self-efficacy, enjoyment in helping others), context (pro-sharing norms, generalized trust, identification)	Electronic knowledge repository (EKR) use
Yli-Renko et al. (2001)		Social interaction, relationship quality, customer network ties	Knowledge acquisition (full mediator) and knowledge exploitation (new product dev, tech distinctiveness, sales cost)
Chou et al. (2006)	Structural (S), cognitive (C) and relational (R) (case study)	S: Technical source and funding ties, human capital tie, business interdependencies tie R: trust (reputation, experience, pre-existing relationship C: prior knowledge and experience	IT outsourcing decision
Newell et al. (2004)	Structural (case study)	External bridging and internal bonding	Knowledge integration
Perry-Smith (2006)	Structural (S)	Network ties (weak), network centrality, closeness.	Individual creativity
Liao & Welsch (2003)	Structural (S), cognitive (C) and relational (R)	S: Number of ties C: Recognition R: Support	Entrepreneurial growth aspirations

1998), inter-organizational arrangement (e.g. Baker, 1990), inter-firm networks (Uzzi, 1997), community (e.g. Coleman, 1988; Putnam 2000), society (e.g. Putnam, 1995), country (e.g. Knack & Keefer, 1997) and geographic region (e.g. Cooke, 2007; Fukuyama, 1995). The different levels of analysis are also evident in information systems research where social capital has been conceptualized and studied at the individual level (e.g. Wasko & Faraj, 2005), team level (e.g. Arling et al., 2005) and firm level (e.g. Patnayakuni et al., 2006). Few key researchers however directly addressed the question of whether social capital is an individual or collective concept. Putnam said that it is both an individual and collective property which has a private and public face and which can be simultaneously a private and a public good, while Portes defined it as being individual, and Bourdieu recognized individual social capital as a collective resource used for individual purposes (Yang 2007). This divergence can be resolved by treating social capital as the *"properties of a collective entity that an individual member can make use for advancing his or her own interests"* (Yang, 2007, pp.21).

Although many researchers take it for granted that social capital is collective since social relations between multiple actors is a necessary condition for its existence, many social surveys in fact measured social capital implicitly at the individual level (Yang 2007). Some researchers, for example Reagans and Zuckerman (2001) who wanted to study social capital at the R&D team level, have aggregated individual level social capital items or measures into a collective one. Similarly, Leana and Van Buren (1999) definition of organizational social capital includes the characteristics of individual social relations within the firm, along with members' levels of collective goal orientation and shared trust, leading to successful collective action. This discrepancy is due to the difficulty of measuring a collective construct and the need to collect data at the individual level, such as employee or manager and aggregating the result

to a collective level, such as team or network of organizations.

POTENTIAL BENEFITS AND RISKS

It is important to note that social capital, like any other type of capital, carries benefits and risks, the former being more emphasized in the literature than the latter. According to Adler and Kwon (2002), social capital has three direct benefits. The first is information from a broader source of information with quality, relevance and timeliness. The second is that it is a source of influence, control and power. The third benefit is solidarity. Nahapiet and Ghoshal (1998) highlighted two main consequences of social capital for action. The first is that it increases the efficiency of action by reducing the costs of transactions and second, it encourages cooperative behavior which facilitates the development of new forms of association and innovation, leading to the development of intellectual capital. Moreover, social capital facilitates the resolution of collective problems since it facilitates cooperation and information dissipation (Putnam, 2000).

However, social capital can carry certain risks. The investment in establishing and maintaining social relationships may be cost inefficient. The ingroup solidarity or embeddedness may reduce the flow of new ideas into a group, causing parochialism and inertia (Gargiulo & Bernassi, 1999). Tight-knit communities may create free-riding problems and obstruct entrepreneurship (Portes, 1998). Strong identification with the smaller group may result in fragmentation of the broader whole (Adler & Kwon, 2002). Effective norms, which are a powerful form of social capital facilitate certain actions but constraint others; they can prevent innovativeness in an area, such as deviant actions that harm others but also deviant actions that can benefit everyone (Coleman, 1988).

To weigh the benefits and cost of social capital on an organization, there is need to focus mainly on the net impact on the structural dimension of social capital, which is the key dimension in the Nahapiet and Ghoshal (1998) model. On one hand, a social network characterized by strong ties, high density, and network closure (relational embeddedness), fosters trust, norms, control, individual relationships, consistency, trustworthiness, availability, accuracy, richness and affordability of information, and cooperation (Burt, 2005). On the other hand, a social network characterized by weak internal ties, low density, structural holes, and with a high degree of brokerage has access to alternative opinion/practice, information variation, creativity, and new idea generation (Burt, 2005).

FUTURE TRENDS

As a socio-technical domain, information systems research has and will benefit from adopting the social capital theory. This theory has been applied in multiple information systems research areas which include knowledge sharing (e.g. Levin & Cross, 2004; Wasko & Faraj, 2005), knowledge acquisition and exploitation (Yli-Renko et al., 2001), supply chain integration (e.g. Patnayakuni et al, 2006), project management (Brookes et al, 2006), innovation (e.g. Ahuja, 2000) and others. However there is still a great potential for IS research to adopt social capital as a theory. Balijepally at al (2004) identified four general information systems research areas where social capital is a sound potential theoretical basis for studies and they are: IS outsourcing, software development, IT-based interorganizational linkages and organizational knowledge management. According to Balijepally at al (2004) social capital can be the basis for analyzing outsourcing relationships and partner selection and governing structures. Business process outsourcing and offshore outsourcing are two emerging phenomena which would benefit from social capital research. Moreover, in the area of software development where the shift is to team-based collaborative approaches, reflected in the agile software development methodologies, social capital can be used to study the resources embedded in the social relations between agile project team members such as trust and shared norms and their impact on the project success. Social capital with its induction of cooperative behavior and reduction in transaction cost can be studied as an asset in IT-based interorganizational linkages. Finally, organizational knowledge management research can benefit from the study of social networks, which are a major conduit for information and knowledge along with the role of shared narratives and language, trust and obligations as resources for knowledge sharing. A currently emerging information systems area where social capital is a suitable theoretical lens is social computing or web 2.0. The structural dimension of social capital can be used for example to study the impact of online social networking tools on online and offline social relations (Ellison et al, 2007) while the relational dimension can be used to study the motivation for participation in online communities (Parameswaran & Whinston, 2007).

CONCLUSION

In this chapter there was an attempt to synthesis seminal research on social capital and focus on the relevant literature for information systems research. A summary of key concepts was introduced and a framework developed by Nahapiet and Ghoshal (1998) was presented. It was followed by an inventory of information systems research which has conceptually and empirically relied on the social capital theory to explore the relation between information technology and relevant concepts like collaboration, knowledge sharing, creativity and technology use. Given that most literature focus on the potential benefits of social capital, it was important to point out the embedded risks that it can carry. The contention about whether social capital is an individual or collective entity was briefly addressed along with the different levels of analysis, highlighting that social capital can be treated as a collective entity with collective benefits or a collective entity used by individual members of a social network for their own benefits. At the group level however, social capital is mainly measured at the individual level and then aggregated. Finally, social capital theory does not only provide a theoretical perspective for information systems research, but can also be used to study practical implications of technology.

Implications for Information Systems Research

Social capital theory presents itself as a sound perspective for studying any information system related topic affected by social relations and the resources embedded in them. It has been effectively used to study the relation between information and communication technology (ICT) and its effects on social network and relationships between individuals, teams, business units and even firms. It also provides a lens to study the assets embedded inside those social networks such as trust, reciprocity, mutuality and support and the benefits they can generate. Social capital theory is valuable in research areas with a focus on communication, collaboration and information flow such as knowledge creation, knowledge sharing and innovation.

Implications for Practice

Social capital can be a valuable asset for organizations and managers should try to foster it by encouraging social interactions between employees, business units, regional offices and even with business partners. However, as discussed earlier, managers should consider the value of the two key characteristics of the social network structure or the structural dimension of social capital: bonding or network closure and bridging or structural holes given that each one has a different contribution to the organizational goal and each requires a different type of investments (Adler & Kwon, 2002). Managers can use information technology such as online social networks, virtual communities, chat rooms, videoconferencing and other technologies to create the opportunity for social interactions. Finally, technology can be used to map internal and external social networks at individual or collective levels and provide managers a better understanding of how information, knowledge and other assets can be flowing.

REFERENCES

Adler, P. S., & Kwon, S.-W. (2002). Social capital: Prospects for a new concept. *The Academy of Management Review, 27*(1), 17.

Arling, P., & Subramani, M. (2005). Being there versus being wired: The effect of colocation on social capital in distributed teams. In *Proceedings of The Twenty-Sixth International Conference on Information Systems*. Las Vegas, NV.

Baker, W. E. (1990). Market networks and corporate behavior. *American Journal of Sociology, 96*(3), 589.

Borgatti, S. P., & Cross, R. (2003). A relational view of information seeking and learning in social networks. *Management Science, 49*(4), 432-445.

Bourdieu, P. (1986). The forms of social capital. In J. G. Richardson (Ed.), *Handbook of theory and research for the sociology of education* (pp. 241-258). Westport, CT: Greenwood Press.

Bourdieu, P., & Wacquant, L. (1992). *An invitation to reflexive sociology*. Chicago: University of Chicago Press.

Brookes, N. J., Morton, S. C., Dainty, A. R. J., & Burns, N. D. (2006). Social processes, patterns and practices and project knowledge management: A theoretical framework and an empirical investigation. *International Journal of Project Management, 24*(6), 474-482.

Burt, R. S. (1992). *Structural holes: The social structure of competition.* Cambridge, MA: Harvard Business Press.

Burt, R. S. (1997). The contingent value of social capital. *Administrative Science Quarterly, 42*(2), 339-365.

Burt, R. S. (2005). *Brokerage and closure: An introduction to social capital.* New York: Oxford University Press.

Chiu, C.-M., Hsu, M.-H., & Wang, E. T. G. (2006). Understanding knowledge sharing in virtual communities: An integration of social capital and social cognitive theories. *Decision Support Systems, 42*(3), 1872-1888.

Chou, T.-C., Chen, J.-R., & Pan, S. L. (2006). The impacts of social capital on information technology outsourcing decisions: A case study of a Taiwanese high-tech firm. *International Journal of Information Management, 26*(3), 249-256.

Coleman, J. S. (1988). Social capital in the creation of human capital. *The American Journal of Sociology, 94*, S95-S120.

Coleman, J. S. (1990). *Foundations of social theory.* Cambridge, MA: Harvard University Press.

Cooke, P. (2007). Social capital, embeddedness, and market interactions: An analysis of firm performance in UK regions. *Review of Social Economy, 65*(1), 79-106.

Fukuyama, F. (1995). *Trust: The social virtues and the creation of prosperity.* New York: Free Press.

Gargiulo, M., & Bernassi, M. (1999). The dark side of social capital. In A. J. L. S. M. Gabbay (Ed.), *Corporate social capital and liability* (pp. 298-322). Boston, MA: Kluwer.

Granovetter, M. S. (1973). The strength of weak ties. *The American Journal of Sociology, 78*(6), 1360-1380.

Granovetter, M. S. (1982). The strength of weak ties: A network theory revisited. In P. V. Marsden & N. Lin (Eds.), *Social structure and network analysis* (pp. 105-130). Beverly Hills, CA: Sage.

Granovetter, M. S. (1995). *Getting a job: A study of contacts and careers* (2nd ed.). Chicago: University of Chicago Press.

Hanifan, L. J. (1916). The rural school community center. *Annals of the American Academy of Political and Social Sciences, 67*, 130-138.

Hansen, M. T. (1999). The search-transfer problem: The role of weak ties in sharing knowledge across organization subunits. *Administrative Science Quarterly, 44*(1), 82-111.

Hansen, M. T. (2002). Knowledge networks: Explaining effective knowledge sharing in multiunit companies. *Organization Science, 13*(3), 232-248.

Huang, S., & DeSanctis, G. (2005). Mobilizing informational social capital in cyber space: Online social network structural properties and knowledge sharing. In *Proceedings of the Twenty-Sixth International Conference on Information Systems.* Las Vegas, NV.

Huysman, M., & Wulf, V. (2004). *Social capital and information technology.* Cambridge, MA: The MIT Press.

Jacobs, J. (1965). *The death and life of great American cities.* London: Penguin Books.

Kankanhalli, A., Tan, B. C. Y., & Kwok-Kee, W. (2005). Contributing knowledge to electronic knowledge repositories: An empirical investigation. *MIS Quarterly, 29*(1), 113-143.

Knack, S., & Keefer, P. (1997). Does social capital have an economic payoff? A cross-country investigation. *Quarterly Journal of Economics, 112*(4), 1251.

Leana, C. R., & Van Buren III, H. J. (1999). Organizational social capital and employment practices. *Academy of Management Review, 24*(3), 538-555.

Levin, D. Z., & Cross, R. (2004). The strength of weak ties you can trust: The mediating role of trust in effective knowledge transfer. *Management Science, 50*(11), 1477-1490.

Liao, J., & Welsch, H. (2003). Social capital and entrepreneurial growth aspiration: A comparison of technology- and non-technology-based nascent entrepreneurs. *Journal of High Technology Management Research, 14*(1), 149.

Liao, J., & Welsch, H. (2005). Roles of social capital in venture creation: Key dimensions and research implications. *Journal of Small Business Management, 43*(4), 345-362.

Lin, N., Ensel, W. M., & Vaughn, J. C. (1981). Social resources and strength of ties: Structural factors in occupational status attainment. *American Sociological Review, 46*(4), 393-405.

Loury, G. C. (1977). A dynamic theory of racial income differences. In P. A. Wallace & A. M. LaMonde (Eds.), *Women, minorities and employment discriminations*. Lexington, MA: Lexington Books.

McFadyen, M. A., & Cannella, A. A., Jr. (2004). Social capital and knowledge creation: Diminishing returns of the number and strength of exchange relationships. *Academy of Management Journal, 47*(5), 735-746.

Nahapiet, J., & Ghoshal, S. (1998). Social capital, intellectual capital, and the organizational advantage. *Academy of Management Review, 23*(2), 242-266.

Narayan, D., & Cassidy, M. F. (2001). A dimensional approach to measuring social capital: Development and validation of a social capital inventory. *Current Sociology, 49*(2), 59-102.

Newell, S., Tansley, C., & Huang, J. (2004). Social capital and knowledge integration in an ERP project team: The importance of bridging and bonding. *British Journal of Management 15*, S43-S57.

Patnayakuni, R., Seth, N., & Rai, A. (2006). Building social capital with IT and collaboration in supply chains: An empirical investigation. In *Proceedings of the Twenty-Seventh International Conference on Information Systems*, Milwaukee, Wisconsin.

Perry-Smith, J. E. (2006). Social yet creative: The role of social relationships in facilitating individual creativity. *Academy of Management Journal, 49*(1), 85-101.

Podolny, J. M., & Baron, J. N. (1997). Resources and relationships: Social networks and mobility in the workplace. *American Sociological Review, 62*(5), 673-693.

Portes, A. (1998). Social capital: Its origins and applications in modern sociology. *Annual Review of Sociology, 24*, 1-24.

Putnam, R. D. (1995). Bowling alone: America's declining social capital. *Journal of Democracy, 6*(1), 65.

Putnam, R. D. (2000). *Bowling alone: The collapse and revival of American community*. New York: Simon and Schuster.

Reagans, R., & Zuckerman, E. W. (2001). Networks, diversity, and productivity: The social capital of corporate r&d teams. *Organization Science, 12*(4), 502-517.

Sherif, K., Hoffman, J., & Thomas, B. (2006). Can technology build organizational social capital? The case of a global IT consulting firm. *Informa-*

tion & Management, 43(7), 795-804.

Tsai, W., & Ghoshal, S. (1998). Social capital and value creation: The role of intrafirm networks. *Academy of Management Journal, 41*(4), 464.

Uzzi, B. (1997). Social structure and competition in interfirm networks: The paradox of embeddedness. *Administrative Science Quarterly, 42*(1), 35-67.

Walker, G., Kogut, B., & Shan, W. (1997). Social capital, structural holes and the formation of an industry network. *Organization Science, 8*(2), 109-125.

Wasko, M. M., & Faraj, S. (2005). Why should I share? Examining social capital and knowledge contribution in electronic networks of practice. *MIS Quarterly, 29*(1), 35-57.

Woolcock, M. (1998). Social capital and economic development: Towards a theoretical synthesis and policy framework. *Theory and Society, 27,* 151-208.

Yang, K. (2007). Individual social capital and its measurement in social surveys. *Survey Research Methods, 1*(1), 19-27.

Yli-Renko, H., Autio, E., & Sapienza, H. J. (2001). Social capital, knowledge acquisition, and knowledge exploitation in young technology-based firms. *Strategic Management Journal, 22*(6/7), 587.

KEY TERMS AND DEFINITIONS

Cognitive Dimension: Represents the shared context and understanding necessary for sharing information in a social network

Network Closure: A social network characterized by a high number of ties between nodes

Open Structure: A social network characterized by a low number of ties between nodes

Relational Dimension: Represents the assets rooted in the social network such as trust and reciprocity.

Social Capital: Resources found in social relations that would benefit individuals and communities in the form of support, solidarity, access to information and influence.

Social Network: The network of ties which represent relationships between individuals (nodes) in the form of friendship, business relationships or other social relations.

Structural Dimension: Represents the configuration and characteristics of the ties of a social network

Tie Strength: Defined by the amount of time, the intimacy, the emotional intensity and the reciprocal services between two network nodes

Chapter XXV
Cultural Historical Activity Theory

Faraja Teddy Igira
University of Oslo, Norway & Institute of Finance Management, Tanzania

Judith Gregory
Institute of Design, IIT, USA

ABSTRACT

This chapter reviews the origins, approaches and roles associated with the use of cultural historical activity theory (CHAT) in information systems (IS) research. The literature is reviewed and examples are discussed from IS and related fields of human-computer interaction (HCI), computer supported co-operative work (CSCW) and computer supported collaborative learning (CSCL), to illustrate the power of CHAT in IS research as well as its link to appropriate research methods. After explicating the value of its use, the chapter concludes by discussing theoretical and methodological implications of applications of CHAT in examining real-world problems in IS research.

INTRODUCTION

The mission of information systems (IS) research is to study the technological, human, social and organizational aspects of IS. The extant IS research literature shows that all aspects of any IS are shaped and in turn shape a highly complex and constantly changing social context (e.g. Avgerou, 2001; Walsham, 1993). The nature of the object of study in IS research has thus led to the need for theoretical frameworks to provide a basis for research into complex and dynamic socio-technical contexts into which IS and IT enter.

Cultural historical activity theory (CHAT) has the potential to provide a robust meta-theoretical framework for understanding and analyzing many areas of IS research and practice. The strengths of CHAT are grounded both in its long historical roots and extensive contemporary use. CHAT offers a philosophical and cross-disciplinary perspective for analyzing diverse human practices as development processes in which both individual and social levels are interlinked (Engeström, 1999b; Kuutti, 1996). With its recent emphasis on networks, interactions and boundary-crossings between activity systems, CHAT helps in exploring and understanding interactions in their social context, multiple contexts and cultures, and the dynamics and development of particular activities.

This chapter explores the descriptive, analytical and interpretive power of CHAT for IS research. We begin by introducing CHAT's philosophical and conceptual background. The concreteness of our own grasp of CHAT's theoretical ideas is grounded in our own intervention research within health care organizations. Applications of CHAT in IS research and the related fields of human-computer interaction (HCI), computer supported cooperative work (CSCW) and computer supported collaborative learning (CSCL) are discussed. Empirical examples of the research approaches, methods of data collection, and modes of analysis that are appropriate within a CHAT framework are also presented. The relations between CHAT's methodological endeavors and other theories are briefly discussed. We conclude with an outline of theoretical and methodological implications regarding the application of CHAT in examining real-world research problems in IS research.

CULTURAL HISTORICAL ACTIVITY THEORY (CHAT)

Cultural historical activity theory (CHAT) or Activity Theory as it is also known, traces its roots from the Soviet Union in the 1920s as part of the socio-historical school of Russian psychology.

Its basic foundations were laid by the insights of Russian psychologists Vygotsky, Leont'ev and Luria into the dynamics of thought and consciousness (e.g. Leont'ev, 1978; Luria, 1976; Vygotsky, 1978). Their arguments arose in response to the need to transcend prevailing understandings of psychology, child development and learning studies that were then dominated by behaviorism (Skinner) on one hand, and psychological theories that they regarded as individually oriented rather than socioculturally oriented on the other hand, including Piaget's developmental theory and psychoanalysis (Engeström, 1987). In doing so, they sought to go beyond the individual to the social. Engeström (2001), a leading contemporary theorist of CHAT, describes the theoretical tradition of CHAT as passing through three generations or phases: the first phase focused on mediated action, the second phase focused on the individual in collective activity, and the third phase which currently focuses on multiple, interacting activity systems and boundary-crossings between them. We provide a brief introduction to 'three generations of activity theory' in the following subsections.

First Generation Activity Theory: Mediated Action

The culturally mediated nature of human activity is one of the most important concepts of CHAT. Vygotsky (1978) introduced the elementary concept of *mediation*: the idea that humans' interactions with their environment cannot be direct but are instead always mediated through the use of tools and signs. Vygotsky particularly criticized the dominant psychological theory of behaviorism that attempted to explain consciousness or the development of the human mind by reducing 'mind' to a series of atomic components or structures associated primarily with the brain as 'stimulus – response' processes, a perspective that set the metaphor for early theories of communication as well as behaviorist psychology.

Vygotsky argued that the explanatory principle for the human mind must be sought in society and culture as they evolve historically rather than in the human brain or individual mind unto itself. To Vygotsky, consciousness emerges from mediated human activity. Mediation occurs through the use of different types of tools and material, semiotic and ideational artifacts that include culture and language (Vygotsky, 1978). On this basis, Vygotsky posited that there must always be an 'intermediate link' – *mediation* - between stimulus and response. Thus 'the conditioned direct connection between stimulus (S) and response (R) was transcended by "a complex, mediated act"' (Figure 1A). Vygotsky's idea of cultural mediation of actions is commonly expressed as the triad of subject, object and mediating artifact (Figure 1B) (Engestrom, 2001, p. 133-134 citing Vygotsky, 1978). The term 'mediating artifacts' is understood as encompassing tools, signs and all types of material, semiotic and conceptual artifacts.

In mediated action, the *subject* refers to a person engaged in an activity; an *object* (in the sense of motive or motivation towards a future-oriented objective) is held by the subject and motivates the existence of activity, giving it a specific direction. Mediating artifacts are used by the subject to effect a change in the object of the activity; they expand the subject's possibility to manipulate and transform the object, but also restrict what can be done within the limitation of available tools, which in turn often motivates improvements to existing tools or invention of new means (Verenikina & Gould, 1998). In this process, the tools also exert reciprocal influence on the minds and actions of the persons using them. This means that the transformative aspect of human activity is not only a tool-mediated transformation of material things, but also the transformation of the subject him/herself. In Vygotsky's model, the unit of analysis remained individually focused: mediation by and with other human beings and social relations was not theoretically integrated (Engeström, 2001). Leont'ev and Engeström extended the Vygotsky's fundamental concept of mediated action from the individual to collective activity.

Second Generation Activity Theory: From Individual to Collective Activity

In recognition of the importance of the collective aspect of human activity, Leont'ev (1978, 1981) expanded Vygotsky's concept to provide a distinction between an 'individual action' and 'collective activity'. This distinction is evident in his analysis

Figure 1. (1A) Vygotsky's model of mediated action and (1B) its common reformulation as a triad of subject, object and mediating artifact (adapted from Engeström 2001, p. 134). (© 2001, Yrjö Engeström, Journal of Education and Work, 14(1). Used with permission.).

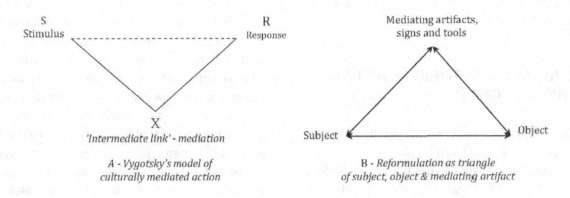

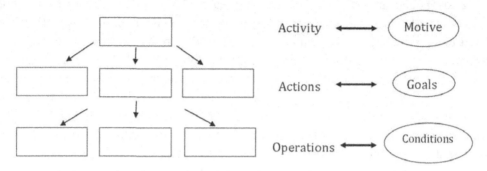

of the structure of activity and its hierarchical levels (see Figure 2) in which activities consist of goal-oriented *actions* that are completed through *operations* determined by specific *conditions*. An activity is defined by a motive (the object of activity) and develops over time and historically in social praxis. Actions are consciously planned towards specific goals and occur in a limited time span; actions are not meaningful in themselves unless they are part of an activity. Operations do not have their own goals; rather they provide means for execution and adjustment of actions to particular situations.

Incorporating Vygotsky's model of mediated action, we illustrate Leont'ev's expansion to depict collective activity by using an example of interaction during a doctor's consultation with a patient. A doctor (*subject*) is engaged in an *activity*, for example, diagnosing a patient. An object – the patient and her/his sickness - confronts the doctor and *motivates* his/her activity, giving it a specific direction. The object requires actions including understanding the patient's illness through to recording the patient's information for keeping his/her medical history. To achieve the object, these goal-oriented *actions* are taken by the doctor with mediating artifacts that include tools, instruments and the history-taking interview with the patient. Different actions and strategies may be

taken to achieve the same goal, such as asking the patient about how long s/he has experienced pain (if any), incidence of chronic disease in the family, and listening to the patient's heartbeats. More than one goal may be achieved by the same action. For example, asking the patient's family health history can result, at the same time, in revealing the relationship between the patient's current illnesses with a particular chronic disease in the family and the patient's historical health-related information. On the level of operations, the doctor may routinely use his/her stethoscope to hear the patient's heartbeats, and a computer or pen and paper (or both) to record the patient's information.

Leont'ev's model of the structure of activity helps to conceptualize the inter-relatedness of levels of mediated action oriented by specific goals that constitute an activity dynamically, and how they are linked to the shared object of that activity. Leont'ev's model was subsequently criticized for its emphasis on the 'what' side of activity (what is being done) and insufficient attention to the 'who' and 'how' side of the activity (by those engaged in carrying out the activity) (see e.g. Davydov, 1999). Leont'ev's depiction of the structure of an activity does not indicate the roles and responsibilities of individuals involved in carrying out the collective activity.

Drawing on the works of Vygotsky (1978) and Leont'ev (1978; 1981), among others, Engeström (1987) developed his concept of an *activity system* for understanding how people are embedded in a sociocultural context with which they continuously interact. The complex interactions of individuals with and in their working and learning environments can be examined using a historically evolving collective activity system. An activity system comprises the *object of activity*, the *subject* involved in the activity, *tools* and *artifacts* relevant to the activity, *rules* and *procedures* that shape participation in the activity, the *community* relevant to the activity and the *division of labor* entailed in carrying out the activity. In Engeström's conceptualization, Figure 3 depicts the core features of an activity system.

In an activity system, a *subject* may be an individual or a collective subject such as a team whose agency is motivated towards the solution of a problem or purpose (an *object* or object of activity). As in the earlier models of Vygotsky and Leont'ev, the *object* thus refers to the 'raw material' or 'problem space' toward which the subject's activity is directed; the object is transformed through activity into *outcomes*. The relations between the subject and the object are mediated by *tools, artifacts, rules, procedures, the division of labor* and the *community*. *Tools* or *artifacts* refer to culturally produced means for changing the environment and achieving goals. The *division*

of labor refers to both the horizontal actions and interactions among the members of the community and to the vertical division of power, resources and status. The *community* refers to the participants who share the common *object* that shapes and gives direction to individual actions and the shared activity at hand. Within any community engaged in collective activity, there are *formal* as well as *informal rules* and regulational *norms* and relational *values,* each of which afford and constrain the internal dynamics, accomplishments and development of an activity system.

The elements of an activity system are not static; they do not exist in isolation from one another. Rather, they are dynamic; their continuous interactions with each other constitute the activity system as a whole (Barab, Barnett, Yamagata-Lynch, Squire & Keating, 2002). Accordingly, the analysis of any activity system must consider the dynamics amongst its constitutive elements. Each element of an activity system (Figure 3) relates to other elements and aspects with tensions and contradictions between them. Contradictions serve as motive forces for transformative change within the activity system itself (Cole & Engeström, 1993). The analysis of contradictions in an activity system helps practitioners to focus their efforts on the roots and causes of tensions and problems. Doing so can give rise to rethinking the object itself, redesign of technological systems and/or design of new tools and other

Figure 3. The structure of a human activity system (adapted from Engeström, 1987, p. 78). (© 1987, Yrjö Engeström, Orienta Konsultit. Used with permission.).

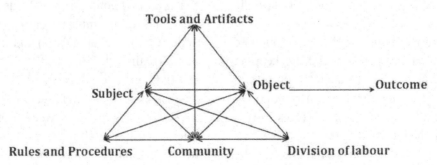

mediating artifacts, and reformulation of rules or divisions of labor. Activity systems change and develop by resolving their historically evolving internal contradictions. In these regards, CHAT elaborates a conceptual apparatus for understanding and contributing to developmental processes of organizations and practices.

Third Generation Activity Theory: Multiple Interacting Activity Systems

The third generation of activity theory aims to exploit and challenge the latent potentialities of CHAT by building on and expanding upon the previous two generations. It goes beyond the limits of a single activity system and takes as its unit of analysis the plurality of different activity systems that mutually interact, promoting multiple perspectives and voices, dialogues, networks and collaboration between activity systems (Yamazumi, 2006) and boundary-crossings between activity systems (Tuomi-Gröhn & Engeström, 2003). Engeström (2001) initially models these perspectives in a network of minimally two interacting activity systems (Figure 4); that is to say, two activity systems comprise the minimum unit of analysis. For example, in relation to a doctor's consultation with a patient, the object moves from an initial state of unreflected, situationally given 'raw material' (object-1, the problem of the patient) to a collectively meaningful object constructed by the activity system (object-2, an outlook on the patient's multiple problems), and toward the emergence of a shared object that is jointly constructed between multiple activity systems (object-3, a collaboratively constructed understanding about the patient's life situation and care plan). Figure 4 highlights the emerging shared object between the minimum unit of analysis of two activity systems A and B (there may be more), showing how inter-organizational expansive learning can occur.

The fact that activity systems interact and overlap with other activity systems implies that

the elements of an activity system are always produced by some other activity. Likewise, the outcomes of an activity are usually intended for one or more other activities, either as means, objects or as new subjects of the latter (Korpela, Mursu, Soriyan & Eerola, 2002). In health care work practices, for example, there are always at least two interacting and overlapping activity systems: the activity system of health care services delivery and that of the health information system (HIS). The two activity systems interact and overlap in the sense that the health care services delivery system produces data that are to be collected through and in HIS, and both activity systems involve overlapping subjects (e.g. doctors and nurses). However, the interactions and overlaps between health care services delivery and HIS contribute to contradictions within and between the elements of each activity system as well as between the interacting activity systems. These contradictions carry historically accumulating structural tensions that emerge in the execution of day-to-day tasks and provide impetus for people to change their activities and simultaneously change themselves (Engeström, 2001).

Seeing each person as a full participant in his or her activity contexts, CHAT aims at reconstructing contexts in practice so that individuals, their collaborative partners, and the activities in which they are jointly engaged are continually transforming and developing in mutually integrative ways. In the same manner, communities and contexts are constantly changing and being changed, which results in changed opportunities for development. This approach differentiates CHAT from other studies of context, for example, cultural or cross-cultural studies in which culture and context are seen as variables that influence development (Robbins, 2005). From the CHAT perspective, context is not simply a situationally created space; context is conceptualized as an entire activity system, integrating the subjects, the object of activity, the tools, the community, its rules and norms, and divisions of labor into a

Figure 4. A shared object emerges between two or more interacting activity systems engaged in inter-organizational learning (adapted from Weber, 2003, p. 171). (© Emerald Group Publishing Limited 2003, Used with permission.).

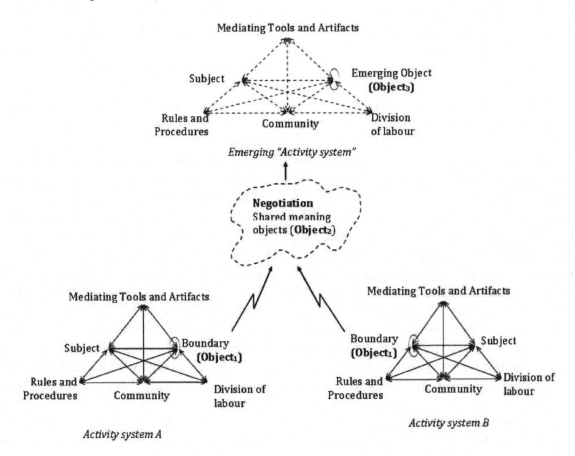

unified whole. Thinking of context this way has led to specific theoretic-empirical methodologies such as developmental work research (DWR) and the Change Laboratory, an application of CHAT in work, technology and organizations (Engeström, 1991, 2005).

Developmental Work Research

Developmental Work Research (DWR) is a CHAT-based interventionist methodology that is specified for studying change and development in work practices and the organization of human labor. The approach is particularly oriented to understanding collective work practices that are undergoing processes of change (Miettinen, 2005). DWR combines active and reflective participation of workers in the analysis of problems and formulation and prototyping of new models with research monitoring of the change interventions over time; ideally, evaluation is carried out jointly by local participants and researchers. In applying general CHAT principles specifically to work practices. DWR incorporates the central proposition that the historical development of activity systems proceeds in 'expansive cycles of learning' instigated by cycles of disturbance, emergence, transformation and resolution of the internal contradictions within and between activity systems (Engeström, 1999c).

An expansive learning cycle entails six stages of generating change (see Figure 5). The *first* stage is engagement of participants in an activity system in questioning and criticizing aspects of existing practice (praxis). The *second* is an analysis of the situation to identify systemic tensions or contradictions within and between activity systems. One type of analysis is historical, which seeks to explain the situation by tracing its origins and evolution. Another type of analysis is empirical, which seeks to explain the situation by constructing a picture of its inner systemic relations. The analysis serves as a basis for planning a solution toward the contradictions in present praxis. The *third* is modeling a new approach (an interven-

tion or prototype) to address the problems and tensions identified in stages one and two. Such modeling involves sketching the zone of proximal development (ZPD) for the collective activity system (see discussion below). The *fourth* stage involves an examination and testing of the model to establish its potential and limitations. The *fifth* is the implementation of the model (prototype) in order to concretize its application in practice. The *sixth* stage involves evaluation and reflection upon the intervention and a consolidation process where the outcomes of the model become a new form of practice. Figure 5 highlights the iterative phases of expansive learning cycles.

Figure 5. The iterative phases of an expansive learning cycle (adapted from Gay & Hembrooke, 2004, p. 12). (© Gay, Geraldine, and Helene Hembrooke, Activity-Centered Design: An Ecological Approach to Designing Smart Tools and Usable Systems, page 12 © 2004, Massachusetts Institute of Technology, by permission of the MIT Press.)

The phases of an expansive cycle do not follow each other automatically. On the contrary, the phases represent possibilities that can only be realized through active developmental research interventions and conscious learning activity. The model helps to surpass the narrow view of change as a step from one organizational or work practice *status quo* to a targeted new state and to grasp the continual qualitative change of the activity system (Virkkunen & Ahonen, 2004). Accordingly, the expansive learning cycle is a tool for understanding the developmental dynamics of an activity.

Zone of Proximal Development

The zone of proximal development known as ZPD is a core CHAT concept that is especially related to transformational learning. Vygotsky (1978) described the ZPD as the difference between what a person can accomplish when acting alone and what the same person can accomplish when acting with support from someone else and with culturally produced artifacts. Vygotsky put forward the concept of ZPD in the context of mass education and literacy campaigns in Russia in the 1920s for children and adults learning 'higher scientific concepts.' Consequently, many researchers have narrowly construed the concept of the ZPD as being primarily concerned with interaction between an expert and novices in which the novices' state of knowledge is advanced through social interaction with the expert (Lantolf, 2000). Yet at the heart of the ZPD, Vygotsky emphasized the *transformation of knowledge* that occurs when someone internalizes concepts, in contrast to notions of 'transfer' or 'transmission' in rote learning. Subsequently, Kuutti (1996) and Engeström (1999b), among others, advocated for a broader understanding of the scope of the ZPD to include peer-to-peer and multi-disciplinary learning beyond expert-to-novice and apprentice-novice modes of learning.

ZPD "is more appropriately conceived of as the collaborative construction of opportunities for individuals to develop their abilities" (Lantolf, 2000, p. 17). Even in those learning situations between experts and novices, as in IS design and implementation processes, novices do not merely copy the expert's ability and knowledge; rather, the knowledge offered by experts are transformed by novices as they appropriate it. During this process the IS design and implementation activities are focused not on the transfer of skills from the expert to the novices (learner) but on collaboration between the expert and the learner that enables the learner to participate in changing IS practices. Constructing a zone of proximal development and/or creating the conditions for a zone of proximal development to emerge is an essential conceptual, analytic and practical step in CHAT methodologies for enhancing formal and informal learning environments and in DWR.

CHAT IN DIVERSE FIELDS WITH RELEVANCE FOR IS RESEARCH

CHAT has been taken up by researchers in diverse fields that have relevance for information systems research. In this section, we briefly discuss some of the recent approaches to research using CHAT as a focus within the HCI, CSCW, CSCL and IS fields, ending with CHAT in studies of pedagogy and technology-enhanced learning. Each of these fields has relevance for IS research.

CHAT was introduced in HCI research in the 1980s (e.g. Bødker, 1989). Since then, CHAT's ideas have provided viable means for analyzing the context and practice of the use of technologies in workplaces (e.g. Kaptelinin & Nardi, 2006; Korpela, Soriyan & Olufokunbi, 2000; Nardi, 1996). HCI is a field concerned with the design, implementation and evaluation of interactive computing systems for human use and with the study of the ways humans interact with these systems (Gilmore, 1995). Considering the shift from 'command line' computer interfaces to graphical user interfaces (GUI), researchers within the HCI field recognized the importance and relevance of CHAT as a theoretical framework for describing and understanding the individual user's and collective users' context, situation and practice for the purpose of design and evaluation of computer systems (e.g. Bødker, 1991; Kaptelinin, 1992; Kuutti, 1992; Nardi, 1996). In general, the use of CHAT perspectives in HCI research enhance and extend the practical concerns of tool usage by linking the design solutions to sociocultural and psychological aspects of the tool user in his/her context (Mwanza, 2001).

Researchers within the fields of CSCW and CSCL strive to address how collaborative activities and their coordination can be supported by means of computer systems (Beaudouin-Lafon, 1999). Kuutti (1991b) proposed CHAT as a basis for CSCW research. Since then, many studies following or influenced by CHAT have been conducted (e.g. Bardram, 1997; Blackler, 1995; deSouza & Redmiles, 2003). CHAT helps to understand collaborative activities from a sociocultural perspective in which the concept of activity is used to generate a tentative definition of the basic units of the work practice to be supported (Convertino, Farooq, Rosson, Carroll & Meyer, 2007). In addition, CHAT has proved to be helpful in analyzing organizational situations in order to locate places where new CSCW and CSCL applications could be used (Kuutti & Arvonen, 1992).

CHAT has been used widely in studies of learning and pedagogy in the context of schools and other educational institutions (e.g. Engeström, 1987; Sue, 1993). Recent studies of education have employed CHAT to examine technology-supported learning environments (e.g. Basharina, 2007; Mwanza & Engeström, 2005; Resta, 2008). Basharina (2007) used CHAT to analyze and describe contradictions that emerged in a WebCT bulletin board collaboration among English learners from different countries and cultures. The analysis laid the basis for devising strategies towards making online interaction more user-friendly. In a study on the task of managing content in e-learning environments, Mwanza & Engeström (2005) used CHAT to examine ways in which teaching and learning activities shape and are shaped by relationships, mediators, motives, and sociocultural influences from the environments in which content is created and used. They developed an activity-centered approach to abstracting contextually and pedagogically-enriched metadata descriptions of educational content and interactions with 'learning objects' that are mediating artifacts (tools, instruments, conceptual frames or scaffolding) in learning. Resta (2008) used CHAT for understanding the complex interactions and issues in the implementation of a laptop initiative in teacher education.

Because a primary purpose of IS is to facilitate work activities, Kuutti (1991a) advocated that the object of analysis in IS should be work activity systems in all their aspects and dynamics. Since then, CHAT has been employed as an underlying framework in IS research for understanding use contexts, interactions, practices and disparate logics in order to deepen design for future-oriented change (e.g. Crawford & Hasan, 2006; Gregory, 2000; Igira, 2008a; Igira, 2008b; Korpela et al., 2002). The main achievement of using CHAT from the point of view of information systems research is the formation of a collectively shared comprehensive perspective, which guides the long-term development of tools as integral components of the activity system in realizing the potentials of its zone of proximal development.

Nardi (1996) suggests that the basic principles and vocabulary of CHAT offer valuable resources for describing human activity. As CHAT is meta-theoretical and philosophical perspective, CHAT concepts and principles have been interpreted and applied in a variety of ways in different contexts. Several IS research groups employing CHAT have formalized particular methodological approaches: The Change Laboratory (Engeström et al., 1996), the Activity Checklist (Kaptelinin, Nardi & Macaulay, 1999), Activity Analysis and Development (ActAD) (Korpela et al., 2000), and the Activity-Oriented Design Method (AODM) (Mwanza, 2002). In addition to specified programmatic approaches, researchers also constitute theoretical, philosophical and methodological frameworks based on CHAT perspectives for specific research studies. We briefly present these approaches in the following subsections.

The Change Laboratory

The Change Laboratory (CL) implements cycles of expansive learning and development of social practices in carrying out developmental work research (DWR) in specific work settings (Engeström, 2007; Engeström, Virkkunen, Helle, Pihlaja & Poikela, 1996). The Change Laboratory was developed in 1996, as a condensed way to carry out DWR methodology *in situ*. In a particular workplace, a Change Laboratory constitutes a forum for cooperation between expert interventionists and local practitioners. The purpose of a Change Laboratory is to help a work team or members of an organization to encounter the problems they face in their work practices and systematically analyze the systemic causes of these problems and design and implement a new form (a new model) - for the activity to overcome the root cause of daily problems. Participants typically meet during working hours in the context of an intensive workshop.

The Change Laboratory methodology involves arranging a space on a shopfloor in which a rich set of instruments are provided for analyzing contradictions in the work activity and for constructing new models for the analyzed work practice (Engeström et al., 1996). The central tool for the CL is a 3x3 set of surfaces for representing the work activity, building on Vygosky notion of *dual stimulus* (Vygotsky, 1978). The first stimulus is provided by showing the participating practitioners 'mirror data' from their everyday work.

The second stimulus focuses on producing a new model of activity for which a zone of proximal development (ZPD) is defined for potential transformational learning. These processes are supported through the use of a range of devices and procedures such as templates, diagrams, diaries and calendars (to summarize important events), maps (to depict the key parties, roles and places involved), video recorders (to facilitate the documentation and review of critical events in subsequent sessions), and a projector (for displaying video documentation and other visual materials). The CL has been applied in health care services in Finland (e.g. Engeström, 1999c), in projects for integration of ICTs in schools (e.g. Engeström, Engeström & Suntio, 2002) and in telecommunications companies (e.g. Virkkunen & Ahonen, 2004).

The Activity Checklist

Kaptelinin, Nardi & Macaulay (1999) developed an Activity Checklist that makes concrete the conceptual perspectives of CHAT for early phases of systems design and for evaluating existing systems. Accordingly, there are two slightly different versions of the checklist: the "evaluation version" and the "design version." Each version provides a guideline intended to elucidate important contextual factors of human-computer interaction, which researchers, designers or practitioners should pay attention to when trying to understand the context for which the information system is being designed, will be used or is in use. With strong emphasis on IS as tool mediation, the checklist reflects five basic principles of CHAT: *object-orientedness, hierarchical structure of activity, internalization and externalization, mediation, and development*.

An Activity Checklist is structured in four sections, which correspond to four main perspectives on the target technology (Kaptelinin, Nardi & Macaulay, 1999, pp. 33-39). The first perspective concerns *means and ends* – the extent to which the technology facilitates and constrains the attainment of users' goals and its impact on provoking or resolving conflicts between goals. The second concerns *social and physical aspects of the environment* – the integration of the target technology with requirements, tools, resources, and social rules of the environment. The third is focused on *learning, cognition and articulation* – distinguishing internal and external aspects of activity and support of their mutual transformations with target technology. The fourth focuses on *development* – developmental transformation of the foregoing activity and its context as a whole.

When conducting systems design and evaluation using the Activity Checklist, researchers and practitioners need to consider the following. First, use of the checklist should be combined with other methods such as interviews and observations. Second, rather than using the four checklist sections in a linear manner participants should look for patterns of related items both within the same section and between different sections. Third, participants should familiarize themselves with the checklist by making use of it during the various phases of the design and evaluation processes. Fourth, in order to be able to focus on relevant items and ignore irrelevant ones, potential users of the checklist should clearly understand why and how they are using the checklist in their particular context.

Examples of the application of the Activity Checklist can be found in the design and evaluation of web-based information systems (e.g. Gould & Verenikina, 2003), evaluation of the use of a tangible user interface (TUI) developed to facilitate collaboration between a group of designers and planners (e.g. Fjeld, Morf & Krueger, 2004), and the analysis of empirical data gathered by means of ethnographic research (e.g. Maier, 2005).

Activity Analysis and Development: ActAD

Activity Analysis and Development (ActAD) was developed by Korpela (1997, 1999) based on Engeström's expansive cycle of learning (Figure 5). ActAD provides a methodology for examining sociocultural features that can inform the development of IS and work practices. It is recommended for several uses such as for user teams who want to develop their own work practices, for IS developers facilitating change in people's work practices and for IS and other researchers as a research methodology at the level of work practices.

The ActAD methodology details five steps. The first step involves the identification of the constituitive elements, components and relations of the activity system to be supported by the IS, e.g. the shared objects of work and jointly produced outcomes of the activity for which information and communication technologies are being designed. The second step provides a checklist of questions to guide a structural analysis of the activity system components and aspects that have been identified. This analysis involves understanding the linkages between the components, between the identified activity and other activities, and/or between the identified activity and the wider context in which it takes place. The third step involves developmental analysis in which participants focus on how the central activity should be improved. *Developmental analysis* involves three phases: *History* - how has the central activity and its network emerged and developed up to that moment? *Problems* – what kind of weaknesses, deficiencies and imbalances are there within and between each of it constituitive elements, components and relations? *Potential* – what kind of strengths and emerging new possibilities are there in the internal dynamics of the activity and within and between the components of the activity, other activities and activity systems in the broader social-historical context? The fourth step is the development of new tools required for improvement of processes based on the information elicited and analyzed in the previous steps. The fifth step involves disseminating the results, evaluating the process and initiating a possible new start.

The ActAD method has been further developed and used as a research methodology for studying IS development work itself as an activity. For example, Korpela et al. (2000) used ActAD as a lens for rapid analysis of the work and services activity chain by nurses in general practitioners' offices in a local health centre. Mursu (2002) used ActAD as an analytical tool regarding IS development practices and problems. ActAD was used by Soriyan (2004) to analyze a hospital software development project in a university HIS research environment. Taking ActAD methodology further, Mursu, Luukkonen, Toivanen and Korpela (2007) developed the Activity Driven Model, an analytic model based on ActAD, activity theory and participatory design. The Activity Driven Model contributes to an integrated analysis of work activity at multiple levels: individual, group, organization and global. While the highest level -- global -- serves as a map to and from which lower level descriptions are traced and reflected, the model is designed to enable zooming in and out between the four levels, as is always necessary. For example, a contextually detailed Activity Driven Model can be used to explore how changes in individual work processes may affect the organizational level.

Activity-Oriented Design Method: AODM

The Activity-Oriented Design Method (AODM) was developed by Mwanza (2001, 2002) based on Engeström's expanded model of human activity (Figure 3). The AODM is intended to support the processes of gathering, analyzing and communicating early systems design requirements focusing on HCI research and practice. It consists of four methodological tools that are applied iteratively in

a six-stage process. The first stage is an eight-step model consisting of eight questions that guide the analysis of the activity system and its constituitive elements and internal dynamics. In the second stage, Engeström's activity system triangle is used to model the work practices of the situation being investigated based on the information obtained in the first stage. The third stage entails the use of an 'activity notation' tool to decompose the activity system analysis produced in the second stage, into sub-activity systems with which IS designers then work. The fourth stage involves the generation of research questions based on the sub-activity systems developed in the third stage. These questions can be used to support data gathering, analysis and systems evaluation phases. The fifth stage comprises a detailed investigation guided by the research questions generated in the fourth stage. The sixth and final stage involves the interpretation and communication of the findings to a broader community of stakeholders, by re-modeling the activity system of the situation undergoing analysis for HCI design.

Examples on the application of the AODM can be found in studies carried out by Mwanza and Engeström for the design and evaluation of an e-Learning environment (Mwanza & Engeström, 2005), and research analyzing interactions among various stakeholder groups involved in e-Learning courses (Greenhow & Belbas, 2007).

CHAT Frameworks in Specific Studies

In addition to the four methodological approaches discussed above, researchers have employed CHAT as a framework for elaborating research in a variety of ways in specific studies (e.g. Jonassen & Rohrer-Murphy, 1999; Martins & Daltrini, 1999). Jonassen and Rohrer-Murphy devised a CHAT-based process for determining the components of an activity system that can be modeled in constructivist learning environments (CLEs). Their framework consists of six steps that provide sample questions and actions that can be taken. The first step is to clarify the purpose (object) of the CLE as an activity system. The second step is to analyze the CLE activity system following Engeström's triangular activity system model (Engeström, 1987). The third step involves decomposing the CLE activity system into actions and operations to describe its structure. The description of the activity system's structure comprises the interrelationships of all of the conscious and unconscious thought and performances that are focused on the object of the activity (its motive and purposes). The fourth step involves the analysis of tools and mediators (e.g. instruments, signs, procedures, machines, methods, languages, formalisms, laws, etc.) that have been used and their transformations over time. The fifth step concerns the analysis of the context within which the CLE activity system occurs, and aims to elicit information about how learning and related activities are accomplished in the particular context. The sixth step involves analyzing the dynamics of the activity system to assess how its constituitive tools, mediators and participants affect each other, with the aim to discern what other resources are needed to enhance the relations between the constituitive aspects of the CLE.

Martins and Daltrini (1999) describe a CHAT-based framework for software requirements elicitation, consisting of three steps. The first step is to identify procedures performed in the activities of the system engaged in IS research and development. The next step is to identify the subject(s), tool(s), object(s), community, rules, divisions of labor and outcome(s) of the target activity system (following Engeström, 1987). The third step is to decompose the activities into actions and operations based on Leont'ev's model of the individual and collective activity (Figure 2). The actions and operations that are identified expand the basis for deriving requirements for IS system design and development.

CHAT IN RELATION TO OTHER THEORIES AND METHODOLOGIES

Cultural Historical Activity Theory holds several methodological foci and concerns in common with actor network theory (ANT), structuration theory and action research methodology. CHAT, ANT and structuration theory share foci on everyday and historically evolving design, use and continuous adaptation of artifacts and technologies; critical reflection on the production and reproduction of relations between people, things and nature; continuous learning and knowledge and potential for transformation through our interactions and practices; an appreciation of the particularities and contingencies of social contexts and configurations of human-machine and other human and non-human collectives; and design for negotiation between the multiplicities of objects, activities, logics and systems. CHAT and action research share commitments to co-development of interventions for change in organizations and communities.

Among contemporary discussions of the differences and similarities between CHAT and ANT, see for example, Engeström & Escalante (1996), Berg (1997), Bratteteig & Gregory (1999), Miettinen (1999, 2001) and Kaptelinin & Nardi (2006). Comparative discussions between CHAT and structuration theory are offered by Bratteteig and Gregory (1999) and Widjaja and Balbo (2005). As in action research methodologies, CHAT-based developmental work research (DWR) comprises cycles of research, mutual learning and change; yet there are differences between the two methodological approaches (see e.g. Engeström, 1999a; Nilsson, 2000). Considering the different histories and theoretical standpoints between these four theoretical traditions that are actively circulating in IS research, their distinctive perspectives provide contrasting and complementary points of view that offer the basis for fruitful critical dialogue (Miettinen, 1997).

CONCLUDING REMARKS

In this chapter we have reviewed the origins, approaches and roles associated with the use of Cultural Historical Activity Theory in IS research. It is our hope that our discussion demonstrates not only how CHAT has been taken up as a theoretical framework and a repertoire of theoretic-methodological analytical tools for IS research, but also suggests areas in the IS field where CHAT-based approaches can add insights. The thoughtful construction and use of a CHAT framework can orient IS researchers' attention especially toward aspects of the context of an IS as part of a work activity system in organizational and sociocultural context. CHAT provides a comprehensive, holistic and dynamic analytical framework that makes it possible to analyze the complex inter-related factors that shape and are shaped by people, technology and context, which are central to current IS research.

CHAT can be used to model, design and prototype new practices and IS to respond to changing needs and constraints. The integration of multiple dimensions of work processes in the concept of an activity system moves 'from the abstract to the concrete' towards prospective design insights that can thus facilitate change. Cultural-historical and sociocultural theory is also useful in proposing and iteratively generating research questions. An application of CHAT, however, requires an IS research and development timeframe that is long enough to understand activity systems, including changes in objects of activity over time, and their relations to other activity systems. This is of particular importance to the IS field in which research into the complex and dynamic social context of IS is an area that requires further exploration.

Activity theoretical approaches and methodologies in IS research are still emerging. The practical implication of this, put in theoretical terms, is that as future development of information and communication systems and IS tools and their wide and diverse applications require new ideas and knowledge, evolving trends in activity theoretical research on the design, implementation and use of such methods and tools may prove to be a central contribution.

REFERENCES

Avgerou, C. (2001). The significance of context in information systems and organisational change. *Information Systems Journal, 11*(1), 43-63.

Barab, S. A., Barnett, M., Yamagata-Lynch, L., Squire, K., & Keating, T. (2002). Using activity theory to understand the systemic tensions characterizing a technology-rich introductory astronomy course. *Mind, Culture, and Activity, 9*(2), 76-107.

Bardram, J. E. (1997). Plans as situated action: An activity theory approach to workflow systems. In W. Prinz, T. Rodden, & K. Schmidt (Eds.), *Proceedings of the Fifth European Conference on Computer Supported Cooperative Work* (pp. 17-32). Norwell, MA: Kluwer Academic Publishers.

Basharina, O. K. (2007). An activity theory perspective on student - reported contradictions in international telecollaboration. *Language Learning & Technology, 11*(2), 82-103.

Beaudouin-Lafon, M. (Ed.). (1999). *Computer supported co-operative work*. Chichester, UK: John Wiley & Sons Limited.

Berg, M. (1997). On distribution, drift and the electronic medical record: Some tools for a sociology of the formal. In W. Prinz, T. Rodden, & K. Schmidt (Eds.), *Proceedings of the Fifth European Conference on Computer Supported Cooperative Work* (pp. 141-156). Norwell, MA: Kluwer Academic Publishers.

Blackler, F. (1995). Activity theory, CSCW and organizations. In A. Monk & N. Gilbert (Eds.),

Perspectives on HCI - diverse approaches (pp. 223 - 248). London, UK: Academic Press.

Bratteteig, T., & Gregory, J. (1999). Human action in context: A discussion of theories for understanding the use IT. In T. Käkölä (Ed), *Proceedings of the 22nd Information Systems Research Seminar in Scandinavia (IRIS 22): Enterprise Architectures for Virtual Organisations* (pp. 161-182). Jyväskylä, Finland: University of Jyväskylä.

Bødker, S. (1989). A human activity approach to user interfaces. *Human Computer Interaction, 4*(3), 171-195.

Bødker, S. (1991). *Through the interface: A human activity approach to user interface design.* Mahwah, NJ: Lawrence Erlbaum Associates.

Cole, M., & Engeström, Y. (1993). A cultural-historical approach to distributed cognition. In G. Salomon (Ed.), *Distributed cognitions: Psychological and educational considerations* (pp. 1-46). UK: Cambridge University Press.

Convertino, G., Farooq, U., Rosson, M. B., Carroll, J. M., & Meyer, B. J. F. (2007). Supporting intergenerational groups in computer-supported cooperative work (CSCW). *Behaviour & Information Technology, 26*(4), 275-285.

Crawford, K., & Hasan, H. (2006). Demonstrations of the activity theory framework for research in information systems. *Australasian Journal of Information Systems 13*(2), 49-68.

Davydov, V. V. (1999). The content and unsolved problems of activity theory. In Y. Engeström, R. Miettinen, & R.-L. Punamäki (Eds.), *Perspectives on activity theory* (pp. 39-52). UK: Cambridge University Press.

deSouza, C. R. B., & Redmiles, D. F. (2003, September). *Opportunities for extending activity theory for studying collaborative software development.* Paper presented at the 8th European Conference of Computer-Supported Cooperative Work (ECSCW'03): Workshop on applying activity theory to CSCW research and practice, Helsinki, Finland.

Engeström, Y. (1987). *Learning by expanding: An activity theoretical approach to developmental research.* Helsinki, Finland: Orienta Konsultit.

Engeström, Y. (1991). Developmental work research: Reconstructing expertise through expansive learning. In M. I. Nurminen & G. R. S. Weir (Eds.), *Human jobs and computer interfaces* (pp. 265-290). Amsterdam: Elsevier Science Publishers (North Holland).

Engeström, Y. (1999a). Activity theory and individual and social transformation. In Y. Engeström, R. Miettinen, & R. L. Punamäki (Eds.), *Perspectives on activity theory* (pp. 19-38). New York: Cambridge University Press.

Engeström, Y. (1999b). Expansive visibilization of work: An activity-theoretical perspective. *Computer Supported Cooperative Work: Special issue on a web on the wind: The structure of invisible work, 8*(1-2), 63-93.

Engeström, Y. (1999c). Innovative learning in work teams: Analyzing cycles of knowledge creation in practice. In Y. Engeström, R. Miettinen, & R. L. Punamäki (Eds.), *Perspectives on activity theory* (pp. 377-402). New York: Cambridge University Press.

Engeström, Y. (2001). Expansive learning at work: Toward an activity theoretical reconceptualization. *Journal of Education and Work, 14*(1), 133-156.

Engeström, Y. (2005). *Developmental work research: Expanding activity theory in practice.* Berlin: Lehmanns Media.

Engeström, Y. (2007). Putting Vygotsky to work: The change laboratory as an application of double stimulation. In H. Daniels, M. Cole, & J. V. Wertsch (Eds.), *The Cambridge companion to Vygotsky* (pp. 363-382). New York: Cambridge University Press.

Engeström, Y., Engeström, R., & Suntio, A. (2002). From paralyzing myths to expansive action: Building computer-supported knowledge work into curriculum from below. In G. Stahl (Ed.), *Proceedings of computer support for collaborative learning: Foundations for a CSCL community* (pp. 318-325). NJ: Lawrence Erlbaum Associates, Inc.

Engeström, Y., & Escalante, V. (1996). Mundane tool or object of affection? The rise and fall of the Postal Buddy. In B. A. Nardi (Ed.), *Context and consciousness: Activity theory and human-computer interaction* (pp. 325 - 373). Cambridge, MA: The MIT Press.

Engeström, Y., Virkkunen, J., Helle, M., Pihlaja, J., & Poikela, R. (1996). The change laboratory as a tool for transforming work. *Lifelong Learning in Europe, 1*(2), 10-17.

Fjeld, M., Morf, M., & Krueger, H. (2004). Activity theory and the practice of design: Evaluation of a collaborative tangible user interface. *International Journal of Human Resources Development and Management (IJHRDM), 4*(1), 94-116.

Gay, G., & Hembrooke, H. (2004). *Activity-centered design: An ecological approach to designing smart tools and usable systems.* Cambridge, MA: The MIT Press.

Gilmore, D. J. (1995). Interface design: Have we got it wrong? In K. Nordby, P. H. Helmersen, D. J. Gilmore, & S. A. Arnesen (Eds.), *Proceedings of INTERACT 95 - IFIP TC13 Fifth International Conference on Human-Computer Interaction* (pp. 173-178). London: Chapman & Hall.

Gould, J., & Verenikina, 1. (2003). An activity theory framework for computer interface design. In L. Budin, V. Lužar-Stiffler, Z. Bekić, & V. H. Dobrić (Eds.), *Proceedings of the 25th International Conference on Information Technology Interfaces (ITI 2003)* (pp. 301-307). University of Zagreb, Croatia: SRCE University Computing Centre.

Greenhow, C., & Belbas, B. (2007). Using activity-oriented design methods to study collaborative knowledge-building in e-learning courses within higher education. *Computer-Supported Collaborative Learning, 2*(4), 363-391.

Gregory, J. (2000). *Sorcerer's apprentice: Creating the electronic health record: Re-inventing medical records and patient care.* Unpublished doctoral dissertation, Department of Communication, University of California at San Diego, La Jolla, CA.

Igira, F. T. (2008a). The situatedness of work practices and organizational culture: Implications for information systems innovation uptake. *Journal of Information Technology, 23*(2), 79-88.

Igira, F. T. (2008b). *The interplay between transformation in everyday work practices and IS design and implementation processes: Empirical experiences from the health information system in Tanzania.* Unpublished doctoral dissertation, Department of Informatics, University of Oslo, Oslo, Norway.

Jonassen, D. H., & Rohrer-Murphy, L. (1999). Activity theory as a framework for designing constructivist learning environments. *Educational Technology Research and Development, 47*(1), 61-79.

Kaptelinin, V. (1992). *Human computer interaction in context: The activity theory perspective.* Paper presented at the East-West International Conference on Human-Computer Interaction, St. Petersburg, Russia.

Kaptelinin, V., & Nardi, B. A. (2006). *Acting with technology: Activity theory and interaction design.* Cambridge, MA: The MIT Press.

Kaptelinin, V., Nardi, B. A., & Macaulay, C. (1999). Methods & tools: The activity checklist: A tool for representing the "space" of context. *Interactions, 6*(4), 27-39.

Korpela, M. (1997). *Activity analysis and develop-*

ment in a nutshell. Retrieved May 12, 2008, from http://www.uku.fi/tike/actad/nutshell-97.html

Korpela, M. (1999). *Activity analysis and development in a nutshell*. Retrieved May 12, 2008, from http://www.uku.fi/tike/actad/nutshell.html

Korpela, M., Mursu, A., Soriyan, A., & Eerola, A. (2002). Information systems research and information systems practice in a network of activities. In Y. Dittrich, C. Floyd, & R. Klischewski (Eds.), *Social thinking software practice* (pp. 287-308). Cambridge, MA: The MIT Press.

Korpela, M., Soriyan, H. A., & Olufokunbi, K. C. (2000). Activity analysis as a method for information systems development: General introduction and experiments from Nigeria and Finland. *Scandinavian Journal of Information Systems, 12*(1-2), 191-210.

Kuutti, K. (1991a). Activity theory and its applications to information systems research and development. In H.-E. Nissen, H. K. Klein, & R. Hirschheim (Eds.), *Information systems research: Contemporary approaches & emergent traditions* (pp. 529-549). Amsterdam: Elsevier Science Publishers (North-Holland).

Kuutti, K. (1991b). The concept of activity as a basic unit of analysis for CSCW research. In L. Bannon, M. Robinson, & K. Schmidt (Eds.), *Proceedings of the Second European Conference on Computer-Supported Cooperative Work, EC-SCW'91* (pp. 249-264). London: Kluwer Academic Publishers.

Kuutti, K. (1992). HCI research debate and activity theory position. In J. Gornostaev (Ed.), *Proceedings of the 2nd East-West Conference on Human-Computer Interaction, EWHCI'92* (pp. 13-22). Moscow: International Centre for Scientific and Technical Information (ICSTI).

Kuutti, K. (1996). Activity theory as a potential framework for human-computer interaction research. In B. A. Nardi (Ed.), *Context and consciousness: Activity theory and human-computer interaction* (pp. 17- 44). Cambridge, MA: The MIT Press.

Kuutti, K., & Arvonen, T. (1992). Identifying potential CSCW applications by means of activity theory concepts: A case example. In *Proceedings of the 1992 ACM conference on Computer-supported cooperative work* (pp. 233-240). New York: ACM Press.

Lantolf, J. P. (2000). Introducing sociocultural theory. In J. P. Lantolf (Ed.), *Sociocultural theory & second language learning* (pp. 1-26). UK: Oxford University Press.

Leont'ev, A. N. (1978). *Activity, consciousness, and personality*. Englewood Cliffs, NJ: Prentice-Hall.

Leont'ev, A. N. (1981). *Problems of the development of mind*. Moscow, Russia: Progress Publishers.

Luria, A. R. (1976). *Cognitive development its cultural and social foundations*. Cambridge, MA: Harvard University Press.

Maier, E. (2005). Activity theory as a framework for accommodating cultural factors in HCI studies. In *Workshop-Proceedings der 5. fachübergreifenden Konferenz Mensch und Computer* (pp. 69-79). Wien: Oesterreichische Computer Gesellschaft.

Martins, L. E. G., & Daltrini, B. M. (1999). Activity theory: An approach to software requirements elicitation using precepts from activity theory. In A. Rawlinson (Ed.), *Proceedings of the 14th IEEE international conference on automated software engineering* (pp. 15-23). Washington, DC: IEEE Computer Society.

Miettinen, R. (1997). *The concept of activity in the analysis of heterogenuous networks in innovation processes*. Paper presented at the Centre for Social Theory and Technology (CSTT) Workshop on Actor Network Theory and After, Keele University, UK. Retrieved May 13, 2008, from http://communication.ucsd.edu/MCA/Paper/Reijo/Reijo.html

Miettinen, R. (1999). The riddle of things: Activity theory and actor-network theory as approaches to studying innovations. *Mind, Culture, and Activity, 6*(3), 170-195.

Miettinen, R. (2001). Artifact mediation in Dewey and in cultural-historical activity theory. *Mind, Culture, and Activity, 8*(4), 297-308.

Miettinen, R. (2005). Object of activity and individual motivation. *Mind, Culture, and Activity, 12*(1), 52-69.

Mursu, A. (2002). *Information systems development in developing countries: Risk management and sustainability analysis in Nigerian software companies.* Unpublishd doctoral dissertation, University of Jyväskylä, Kuopio, Finland.

Mursu, A., Luukkonen, I., Toivanen, M., & Korpela, M. (2007). Activity theory in information systems research and practice: Theoretical underpinnings for an information systems development model. *Information Research, 12*(3).

Mwanza, D. (2001). Where theory meets practice: A case for an activity theory based methodology to guide computer system design. In M. Hirose (Ed.), *Proceedings of the 8ᵗʰ TC13 IFIP International Conference on Human-Computer Interaction, INTERACT'01* (pp. 342-349). Amsterdam: IOS Press.

Mwanza, D. (2002). *Towards an activity-oriented design method for HCI research and practice.* Unpublishd doctoral dissertation, Open University, Milton Keynes, UK.

Mwanza, D., & Engeström, Y. (2005). Managing content in e-learning environments. *British Journal of Educational Technology, 36*(6), 453-463.

Nardi, B. A. (Ed.). (1996). *Context and consciousness: Activity theory and human-computer interaction.* Cambridge, MA: The MIT Press.

Nilsson, M. (2000). *Organizational development as action research, ethnography, and beyond.* Paper presented at the Annual Meeting of the American Educational Research Association (AERA), New Orleans, LA.

Resta, P. (2008). Activity theory framework for implementation of a laptop initiative in teacher education. In K. McFerrin, R. Weber, R. Carlsen, & D. A. Willis (Eds.), *Proceedings of Society for Information Technology and Teacher Education International Conference 2008* (pp. 2203-2209). Chesapeake, VA: AACE.

Robbins, J. (2005). Contexts, collaboration, and cultural tools: A sociocultural perspective on researching children's thinking. *Contemporary Issues in Early Childhood, 6*(2), 140-149.

Soriyan, H. A. (2004). *A conceptual framework for information systems development methodology for educational and industrial sectors in Nigeria.* Unpublished doctoral dissertation, Obafemi Awolowo University, IleIfe, Nigeria.

Sue, G. (1993). Mature students learning statistics: The activity theory perspective. *Mathematics Education Research Journal, 5*(1), 34-49.

Tuomi-Gröhn, T., & Engeström, Y. (Eds.). (2003). *Between school and work. New perspectives on transfer and boundary-crossing.* Amsterdam: Pergamon/Elsevier Science.

Verenikina, I., & Gould, E. (1998). Cultural-historical psychology and activity theory. In H. Hasan, E. Gould, & P. Hyland (Eds.), *Information systems and activity theory: Tools in context* (pp. 7-18). Wollongong, Australia: University of Wollongong Press.

Virkkunen, J., & Ahonen, H. (2004). Transforming learning and knowledge creation on the shop floor. *International Journal of Human Resources Development and Management, 4*(1), 57-72.

Vygotsky, L. S. (1978). *Mind and society.* Cambridge, MA: Harvard University Press.

Walsham, G. (1993). *Interpreting information systems in organizations*. Chichester, UK: Wiley.

Weber, S. (2003). Boundary-crossing in the context of intercultural learning. In T. Tuomi-Gröhn & Y. Engeström, (Eds.), *Between school and work: New perspectives on transfer and boundary crossing* (pp. 157-178). Amsterdam: Pergamon/ Elsevier Science.

Widjaja, I., & Balbo, S. (2005). Structuration of activity: A view on human activity. In *Proceedings of the 19th conference of the Computer-Human Interaction Special Interest Group (CHISIG) of Australia on Computer-human interaction, Citizens online: considerations for today and the future* (pp. 1-4). Narrabundah, Australia: Computer-Human Interaction Special Interest Group (CHISIG) of Australia.

Wilson, T. D. (2006). A re-examination of information seeking behaviour in the context of activity theory. *Information Research, 11*(4).

Yamazumi, K. (2006). *Learning for critical and creative agency: An activity-theoretical study of advanced network of learning in new school project* (CHAT Technical Reports No. 01).

KEY TERMS AND DEFINITIONS

Activity System and Activity: An activity system is a collective formation with a complex mediational structure that serves as the primary unit of analysis in cultural historical activity theory. An activity is the engagement of individuals toward a certain goal or objective. Activities are not short-lived events or actions; rather, activities 'are systems that produce events and actions and evolve over lengthy periods of sociohistorical time' (Engeström 1987).

Artifacts, Mediating Artifacts: *Artifacts* and *mediating artifacts* encompass tools, instruments, signs and all types of material, semiotic and conceptual means for accomplishing human activity.

Contradictions: Contradictions refer to tensions and disturbances that arise within and between constituents of activities, between different activities or different developmental phases of an activity, and within and between activity systems as they evolve over time. Analysis of contradictions is 'a key to understanding the sources of trouble as well as the innovative and developmental potentials and transformations of activity' (Engeström 2008, p. 5).

Cultural Historical Activity Theory (CHAT): Cultural historical activity theory offers a meta-theoretical philosophical basis and transdisciplinary perspective for analyzing diverse human practices in socio-cultural context and across multiple contexts and networks, as developmental processes in which individual, organizational, societal and cultural levels are dynamically inter-related.

Expansive Learning: Expansive learning is defined by Engeström as follows: 'Expansive learning is initiated when some individuals involved in a collective activity take the action of transforming an activity system through reconceptualization of the object and the motive of activity embracing a radically wider horizon of possibilities than in the previous mode of activity' (Engeström 2003, pp. 30-31).

Information Systems: An information system is defined comprehensively as the use of information technology (manual or computer-based) in a collective work activity, either as a means of work or of co-ordination and communication (Mursu et al. 2007).

Mediated Action, Mediation: The concepts of *mediated action* and *mediation* are grounded in the conceptual view that humans do not interact directly with their environments; rather their interactions are always mediated through the use of different types of tools, signs and material, semiotic and ideational artifacts that include culture and language and that are evolved over time.

Object of Activity and Object-Oriented Activity: 'Objects of activities are prospective outcomes that motivate and direct activities, around which activities are coordinated, and in which activities are crystallized in a final form when the activities are complete' where is the start of the quote (Kaptelinin & Nardi 2006, p. 66). Object-orientedness characterizes all human activity in the sense of motive or desire, whether the object of activity is material or psychological, individual or collective.

Social Context: The social context passes an entire activity system in which the information systems (IS) operate. It includes the integration of the subject, the object, the tools, the community, rules and division of labor.

Social Practice and Praxis: Praxis, understood as practical wisdom that is grounded in particular, perceptual and concrete experience (phronesis), is inseparably complementary to theory, understood as scientific knowledge that is generalizable, conceptual and abstract (episteme). Research regarding social practice encompasses two senses — scientific focus on activity and interventive meaning related to developing the practice; these are understood as simultaneous and complementary.

Zone of Proximal Development (ZPD): The zone of proximal development refers to transformational learning. Vygotsky (1978, p. 86) defined the zone of proximal development as 'the distance between the actual developmental level as determined by independent problem-solving and the level of potential development as determined through problem-solving in collaboration with more capable peers' and with culturally produced artifacts.

Chapter XXVI
Hofstede's Dimensions of National Culture in IS Research[1]

Dianne P. Ford
Memorial University of Newfoundland, Canada

Catherine E. Connelly
McMaster University, Canada

Darren B. Meister
University of Western Ontario, Canada

ABSTRACT

In this chapter, the authors do a citation analysis on Hofstede's Culture's Consequences in IS research to re-examine how IS research has used Hofstede's national culture dimensions. They give a brief history of Hofstede's research, and review Hofstede's cultural dimensions and the measurement of them. The authors then present the results from their original citation analysis (which included years 1994-1999) from Ford, Connelly and Meister (2003) and their follow-up citation analysis (years 2000-2005). The authors examine the extent to which Hofstede's national culture dimensions inform IS research, what areas of IS research have used them, and what changes have occurred since the original citation analysis. They then discuss the implications for IS research.

INTRODUCTION

Globalization continues to challenge organizations by restructuring organizational boundaries, increasing competition, and creating new manage-rial concerns, ranging from having employees in different countries, to the structure of international alliances. Globalization is important for IS practitioners and researchers, because national differences may affect the use, implementation,

---

[1] This chapter is based on and extends a previous article: Ford, Connelly & Meister (2003) Information Systems Research and Hofstede's *Culture's Consequences*: An Uneasy and Incomplete Partnership. *IEEE Transactions in Engineering, 50*(1), 8-25

structure, and characteristics of information systems in many international settings (Abdul-Gader, 1997; Day, Dosa, & Jorgensen, 1995; Dustbar & Hofstede, 1999; Ferratt & Vlahos, 1998; M. Martinsons, 1991). Factors such as a country's infrastructure (e.g., the preponderance of wireless technology in South Korea, versus a heavier reliance on fiber-optic technologies in North America), the political and economic situations (e.g., a factor in the Digital Divide, Cronin, 2002), and the physical environment (e.g., in some parts of Africa where the temperature can become so high that computers simply will not work in the environment, De Vreede, Jones, & Mgaya, 1998-99), and cultural dynamics (e.g., norms, values, and languages) have been shown to be relevant. These studies, among others, have led to several calls for more research to integrate the IS and national culture domains (Gallupe & Tan, 1999; Nelson & Clark Jr., 1994; R.T. Watson, Ho, & Raman, 1994).

National culture has a rich research tradition. While there are several competing conceptualizations of national culture, Hofstede's dimensions of national culture are very commonly used. These dimensions allow national-level analysis, and are standardized to allow multiple country comparisons. Furthermore, Hofstede's dimensions have often been employed by researchers when "international" or "national culture" issues are discussed within IS. However, it is not clear whether the IS field been able to build strong theory and generalizable managerial practices from this framework.

In 2003, we examined how IS researchers have used Hofstede's cultural dimensions. We analyzed the impact of Hofstede's work, based on a citation analysis of the IS literature up to 1999 (see Ford, Connelly, & Meister, 2003). At that point in time, we concluded that the IS literature did not strongly integrate Hofstede's work. Many papers cited Hofstede incidentally as they mentioned national culture, many more adopted the dimension scores without considering regional or organizational

impacts on the dimension scores. Finally, very few papers contributed to the broader literature on the conceptualization or effects of national culture. Generally, it appeared that much work remained to be done.

In this chapter we re-examine how Hofstede's work has contributed to IS research. As with our original paper, it should be noted that it is not our contention that Hofstede's measure and national culture dimensions are the best approach to study issues relating to national culture. Rather, it is the purpose of this chapter to understand how Hofstede's national culture dimensions have added value to IS research, and what role these dimensions should play in future IS research. Our focus in this chapter is primarily on the body of IS research that has been published since our last analysis.

This chapter begins by reviewing the cultural dimensions proposed by Hofstede. The results of the citation analysis are presented next; the citations are classified according to the IS classification schema developed by Barki, Rivard and Talbot (1993) and classified according to the extent of their integration of Hofstede's national culture dimensions and IS research. The paper then identifies the degree to which IS research has been informed by this research. Summaries of major findings as well as opportunities and approaches for future research, which will encourage a more cumulative tradition in this area, will also be discussed.

HOFSTEDE'S CULTURAL DIMENSIONS

Hofstede (1980a) pioneered the construct of "national culture". His argument was that in order to be able to act together, people must understand and be aware of the differences between cultures. He defined culture as "the collective programming of the mind which distinguishes the members of one human group from another" (p. 25). Members of the same culture were said to view the world similarly. Building on this definition, Hofstede was able to contribute to the field by developing a taxonomy of culture.

Many articles have established Hofstede's dimensions' usefulness in theory development, and have found support for its contributions (Carpenter & Fredrickson, 2001; Carter, 2000; Merritt, 2000; Moenaert & Souder, 1996; Png, Tan, & Wee, 2001). Furthermore, in a major citation analysis, Hofstede's work was identified as having one of the most significant impacts, of all research, on the field of International Business studies (Chandy & Williams, 1994). Hofstede (1980a; 1980b) conducted two surveys of virtually every employee at IBM (1967-1969 and 1971-1973) resulting in a data bank of 116,000 questionnaires. His purpose was to determine the main criteria by which national cultures differ (Hofstede, 1980b). Subsequently, the survey was administered to a group of 400 international managers from a variety of organizations. Finally, the results were used to develop hypotheses, which were then tested using data from national economic and social indicators and public opinion polls.

Four dimensions of national culture were defined: Individualism-Collectivism, Power Distance, Uncertainty Avoidance and Masculinity-Femininity. The dimensions are measured by the Values Survey Module, and then the scores are converted into indices using a standardized formula provided by the VSM Manual (Hofstede, 1994). The original index scores are presented in Hofstede's original book (Hofstede, 1980a), and more up-to-date indices are available in the latest version (Hofstede, 2001). Hofstede defines these dimensions as follows (Hofstede, 1980a, 1980b, 1991).

The first dimension, Individualism-Collectivism, represents a continuum: high index scores on this dimension indicate an individualistic culture and low index scores indicate a collectivistic culture. An individualist culture is one in which the ties between individuals are loose. On the other hand, a collectivist society finds people integrated into strong, cohesive groups. Cultures high in Individualism will value personal time, personal accomplishments. Whereas cultures high in Collectivism will value the group's well-being more than individual desires; the belief is that it is best for the individual if the group is cohesive (Hofstede, 1980a).

The second defining dimension is Power Distance, which is the extent to which the less powerful members of institutions and organization within a country expect and accept that power is distributed unequally. Cultures that are high in Power Distance (indicated by a high index score) are illustrated by decisions being made by superiors without consultation with subordinates (and subordinates preferring this practice), and employees being fearful of disagreeing with their superiors (Hofstede, 1980a); whereas cultures that are low in Power Distance (indicated by a low index score) will have a more participative and egalitarian relationship between superiors and subordinates. In other words, Power Distance has been defined by Mulder (1977) and adopted by Hofstede (2001) as:

The power distance between a boss B and a subordinate S in a hierarchy is the difference between the extent to which B can determine the behavior of S and the extent to which S can determine the behavior of B (p.83).

Uncertainty Avoidance, defined as the extent to which the members of a culture feel threatened by uncertain or unknown situations, is the third dimension, measured from weak to strong. Uncertainty Avoidance is "related to anxiety, need for security, and dependence upon experts" (Hofstede, 1980a, p. 110). A culture that is high in Uncertainty Avoidance (i.e., high index score) would exhibit a rule orientation, prefer employment stability, and exhibit stress (Hofstede, 1980a) as the members of the culture try to explain, mitigate, and minimize the uncertainty that is inherent to life.

Finally, the fourth dimension is Masculinity-Femininity; high index scores indicate masculine cultures, low index scores indicate feminine cultures. This is possibly the most controversial dimension in Hofstede's taxonomy, and perhaps the most misunderstood. Initially, it had been defined in terms of social gender roles, and the distinctions made. Highly Masculine cultures had very distinct gender roles, where "men are supposed to be assertive, tough, and focused on material success; women are supposed to be more modest, tender, and concerned with the quality of life" (Hofstede et al., 1998, p. 6). Both men and women being concerned about quality of life characterized feminine cultures. The more popular view of this dimension is to view the Masculine and Feminine culture in terms of emphasis of competitiveness and material success versus nurturance and quality of life, rather than in terms of gender roles for the sexes.

The distinction between these two definitions of the Masculinity-Femininity dimension is the application of the cultural dimension. When Masculinity-Femininity is applied to the national culture as a whole, the gender roles view (social roles for the different sexes) is the appropriate interpretation. However, when the Masculinity-Femininity dimension is applied to the workplace, the following interpretation is appropriate, "Masculine countries stressed pay security, and job content; feminine countries stressed relationships and physical conditions" (Hofstede, 2001, p. 313).

In addition to these four characteristics, Hofstede and Bond (1988) subsequently defined a fifth characteristic, Long Term Orientation or 'Confucian Dynamism'. Long Term Orientation cultures value virtues oriented toward future rewards, in particular perseverance and thrift. Short Term Orientation stands for the fostering of virtues related to the past and present, in particular, respect for tradition, preservation of 'face', and fulfilling social obligations. This dimension is associated with Confucian Dynamism (i.e., Confucius' teach-

ings); however, Hofstede named it Long Term Orientation because, as he explains, "Michael Bond and I [Hofstede] got perfectly meaningful scores on it from countries that had never heard of Confucius" (Hodgetts, 1993, p. 54).

Hofstede's work is cited in many disciplines. From 1980 to 2005, Hofstede's original book (1980a) was cited approximately 2,800 times in the Social Science Citation Index (SSCI) and frequently by IS researchers. However, there are those within the IS field who have questioned this reliance on Hofstede's dimensions and characterization of culture (Igbaria, Iivari, & Maragahh, 1995; Kamel & Davison, 1998; L.-H. Lim, Raman, & Wei, 1994; Myers & Tan, 2002; Straub, 1994). There are several major concerns regarding Hofstede's taxonomy of culture. Hofstede's dimensions assume culture falls along national boundaries, and that the cultures are viewed as static over time (Myers & Tan, 2002). National culture is assumed to be homogenous; sub-cultures are often assumed to not exist in the use of Hofstede's taxonomy (Myers & Tan, 2002). The level of analysis implied by the dimensions and subsequent uses of the dimensions is also problematic; the five dimensions are national-level measures, but several studies apply this national measure to groups or individuals (Igbaria, Iivari et al., 1995; Kamel & Davison, 1998; L.-H. Lim et al., 1994; Straub, 1994).

However, these criticisms are often targeted at research that uses the national level results of Hofstede's work without either replication or consideration of individual responses. Hofstede has stated that "if the questionnaire is used to compare responses from individuals, from occupations, from employers, or from other categories other than nations or regions, the answers should be studied question by question and not combined into the five dimensions." (Hofstede, 1994, p. 3). The theme that runs throughout these criticisms focuses on the way that researchers have *used* the dimensions, not on the theoretical construct itself. Such criticisms are properly directed at the employed research methodology. We should emphasise that the goal of this chapter is not to critique Hofstede's theory; rather, we investigate the use of this theory in IS research.

Aside from the above-mentioned concerns regarding Hofstede's taxonomy of culture, there has been a call for a more theoretical approach to studying culture (Myers & Tan, 2002; Straub, Loch, Evaristo, Karahanna, & Srite, 2002). Straub et al.'s (2002) approach (i.e., the saliency of culture) enables IS researchers to have a theoretical framework for studying culture at an individual level. They caution IS researchers that individuals may or may not identify with the national culture; the researcher should not assume that they necessarily do. In short, it provides a complimentary research perspective, not necessarily a competing one.

As noted, Hofstede's original work defined four dimensions of national culture, but a fifth dimension (Long Term Orientation) was added several years later. However, most references to Hofstede's work cite the original 1980 book where the four dimensions were initially defined. Therefore, in order to provide a reasonable and consistent scope to this research project, our citation analysis followed the 1980 book, and its subsequent editions.

METHOD

In our citation analysis, the goal was to find IS research articles that were published in peer-reviewed journals. To accomplish this, a three-stage process was employed: the articles were located; they were classified according to their content; and then they were classified according to their use of the national culture dimensions. This was done initially for the years 1994 to 1999 (Ford et al., 2003). In this chapter we present results that include the original analyses, along with the IS research articles that were published between 2000 and 2005.

Article Identification

The first stage of the article identification was to find the IS research articles that referenced Hofstede (1980a; 2001). While it was unlikely that all articles would be found, a thorough search was likely to find a substantial and representative portion. (See Ford et al., 2003 for information on the article identification.) For the articles published between 1999 and 2005, we used the following search engines: Business Source Complete and WebSpirs citation index. As a result, an additional 53 articles were found for inclusion in our analysis. These search engines also included the *Journal of Global Information Management*, so a hard copy search was not completed for this journal as it had been in the original paper. Together, these searches produced 57 articles from 22 journals in the original search (Ford et al., 2003), and 53 articles from 26 journals in the 1999-2005 search.

Coding

The purpose of the coding process was to categorize the articles according to the relevant topics and how Hofstede was cited. The first coding was done using the Barki *et al.* (1993) classification scheme. This classification scheme was originally developed in 1983 through an extensive search of the IS literature and it provides keywords to describe IS research topics in a standardized and concise manner. The resulting classification scheme divided the IS field into eight main categories and gave each a letter code (A - Reference Disciplines, B - External Environment, C - Information Technology, D - Organizational Environment, E - IS Management, F - IS Development and Operations, G - IS Usage, and H - Information Systems). For each of these categories, more specific sub-categories were developed (e.g., EL – IS Management Issues; GB – Users).

This classification scheme has been adopted by several journals, including MIS Quarterly, and has been updated by the authors twice since the original publication. For this chapter, we used the most recent version of the classification scheme (Barki et al., 1993). Our analysis focused on categories D, E, F, G, H as these were the salient categories for our purposes.

All articles were also coded as to how Hofstede was cited. Five possible codes were defined prior to coding.

1. Incidental: These citations mentioned Hofstede briefly.
2. Defining or describing culture: Hofstede's theory and dimensions were used either to define the construct of culture or to describe the context of the study.
3. Developing hypotheses or propositions: Hofstede's theory and dimensions were used to assist in the development of the hypotheses or propositions.

These first three codes are mutually exclusive. Two other ways of using Hofstede were included, that could be used in conjunction with one of the prior codes.

4. Post-hoc explanation: Hofstede's dimensions of "national culture" were mentioned as a possible factor in the interpretation of the results.
5. Contributing to Hofstede's theory: The study contributes to Hofstede's theory, such as by illustrating its validity (or lack thereof).

As with the original paper, the coding process for this chapter followed an iterative consensus procedure of initial independent work followed by a consensus building stage. Initially, two researchers coded both sets of characteristics for the articles independently. The two researchers then met and checked for agreement. When necessary, differences in coding were resolved by discussion and consultation with the third researcher.

RESULTS

Areas of Research

In order to determine the IS research topics most influenced by Hofstede's work, the high-level (Table 1) and secondary-level (Table 2) analyses were considered. For ease of reference, the original analyses are identified in the column marked 1994-1999, and the current follow-up analysis in the column marked 2000-2005. In our original analysis, Category E – IS Management was the prevalent category, with H – Information Systems as the next largest category; similarly, in the current analysis, Category E – IS Management was the most used category, but this time G- IS Usage and H – Information Systems were the next largest classifications. In addition, H – Information Systems, dropped from 17 articles to 9 articles as the primary focus of the paper. A Chi-square test of independence indicates that the classifications did not change significantly across the two timeframes ($\chi^2 = 3.495$, df = 6, p = 0.752). In other words, IS research that has used Hofstede's dimensions has focused on managerial aspects of IS, rather than technical or implementation issues. While this high-level analysis shows some significant differences in focus, the secondary-level analysis allowed for richer analysis. One reason was that multiple categories for a single article (e.g., EL – IS Management Issues and HA – Types of Information Systems) were allowed.

Table 2 shows the distribution of the secondary-level classifications. Articles were included in their three most relevant classifications; therefore, the counts are greater than the number of articles coded. In the original analysis (1994-1999), the majority of the articles focused on EL – IS Management Issues, and HA – Types of Information Systems, with the prevalence of HA due to the number of studies on cross-cultural effects with Group Decision Support Systems (GDSS) (Aiken, Hwang, & Martin, 1996; Aiken, Kim, Hwang, & Lu, 1995; Aiken, Martin, Shirani, & Singleton,

Table 1. Summary of high level analysis

Category Label	Frequency		Examples of Topics
	1994-1999	2000-2005	
B. External Environment	0	0	
C. Information Technology	0	0	
D. Organizational Environment	3	5	1994-1999: BPR; Small business implementation; IT alignment with business 2000-2005: Organizational culture and KM, Tools development context, Cultural differences and code systems; organizational and national culture for IT; Reexamination of culture;
E. IS Management	27	26	1994-1999: MIS in specific countries or regions; Global IS; IS workers' work perceptions; teams and transfer of research information; IS planning in small business; attitudes to computers; technology adoption; technology transfer; IS professional and gender, evaluation, career; IS success; technology environment fit; IS design; IS implementation 2000-2005: Adoption; Acceptance; IS use; IS Security/Spyware; IT services management; Critical issues for IS personnel; Developers' values; Software project management; IS specialists' roles; IS evaluation; Global IT; IS Risks and IS Failures; IT sourcing; S/W Project Risks; Piracy
F. IS Development and Operations	4	4	1994-1999: IS Implementation and power; CASE Tool implementation; IS design 2000-2005: IS development strategies; Systems development life cycle; S/W project development; Requirements engineering.
G. IS Usage	6	9	1994-1999: CMC and virtual teams; end user characteristics; LDC and IS; CIO perception of IM; global strategy 2000-2005: Users of mobile commerce/access; Managers'/users needs; User behavior; Online shopping; Virtual teams; User attitudes (innovativeness).
H. Information Systems	17	9	1994-1999: GDSS; EDI impact; Videoconferencing; Internet 2000-2005: MAIS, AMT systems; Website designs and characteristics; ERP components; Decision Support System based on web services; E-market systems; Scheduling systems characteristics; GSS; Internet portals.

1994; Griffith, 1998; B. Tan, Watson, & Wei, 1995; R.T. Watson et al., 1994; Williams & Wilson, 1997). Other categories that contained several articles were IS Implementation, and Users.

From 2000 to 2005, the top three secondary-level classifications were: HA – Type of Information Systems, GB – Users, and EL – IS Management. The largest change was the increase on focus of Users; however, this may reflect a change in the coders' sensitivity to user issues. The other change of note is the introduction of more diverse research topics within the classification: Task Characteristics, Organizing IS, IS Security, IS Development Strategies, IS Life Cycle Activities,

IS Operations, Type of IS Access, IS Applications Areas, Components of IS, and IS Characteristics. A Chi-squared test suggests that the classifications changed significantly across the two timeframes ($\chi^2 = 39.346$, df = 22, p = 0.013).

Because there were a large number of articles about EL – IS Management Issues, a more detailed analysis was done on this category. Table 3 provides a detailed breakdown of category, (EL – IS Management Issues). This analysis was done with the keywords provided for EL - IS Management Issues (Barki et al., 1993). IS Technology Transfer, which includes the Technology Acceptance Model (TAM) (Davis, 1989), was the largest group for

Table 2. Summary of secondary level analysis

Detailed Level Classification	Frequency		Citations
	1994-1999	2000-2005	
DA. Organizational Characteristics	2	5	1994-1999: (Thong, Yap, & Raman, 1996; Ward & Peppard, 1996) 2000-2005: (Corbitt, Peszynski, Inthanond, Hill, & Thanasankit, 2004; Davison, 2002; Gallivan & Strite, 2005; Myers & Tan, 2002; Thatcher, Stepina, Srite, & Liu, 2003)
DC. Task Characteristics	0	1	1994-1999: N/A 2000-2005: (Thatcher et al., 2003)
DD. Organizational Dynamics	1	0	1994-1999: (M. Martinsons & Hempel, 1998) 2000-2005: N/A
EE. IS Project Management	1	7	1994-1999: (Tractinsky & Jarvenpaa, 1995) 2000-2005: (Gordon & Gordon, 2002; Hayne & Pollard, 2000; Keil et al., 2000; M. G. Martinsons & Cheung, 2001; Mursu, Lyytinen, Soriyan, & Korpela, 2003; Schmidt, Lyytinen, Keil, & Cule, 2001; R. T. Watson et al., 2005)
EF. IS Planning	6	3	1994-1999: (Abdul-Gader, 1997; Doukidis, Lybereas, & Galliers, 1996; Kamel & Davison, 1998; Nelson & Clark Jr., 1994; Shore & Venkatachalam, 1995; van den Hoven, van Valkenburg, & Heng, 1994) 2000-2005: (Gordon & Gordon, 2002; Hayne & Pollard, 2000; Okazaki & Rivas, 2002)
EG. Organizing IS	0	1	1994-1999: N/A 2000-2005: (Akgun, Byrne, Keskin, Lynn, & Imamoglu, 2005)
EH. IS Staffing	5	6	1994-1999: (Bryan, McLean, Smits, & Burn, 1995; Holmes, 1998; Hunter & Beck, 1996; Igbaria, Meredith, & Smith, 1995; McLeod et al., 1997) 2000-2005: (Hayne & Pollard, 2000; Kankanhalli, Tan, Wei, & Holmes, 2004; M. G. Martinsons & Cheung, 2001; Rao, 2004; Rutkowski & van de Walle, 2005; R. T. Watson et al., 2005)
EI. IS Evaluation	2	5	1994-1999: (Igbaria & Zviran, 1996; Kim, Peterson, & Kim, 1999) 2000-2005: (Calhoun, Teng, & Cheon, 2002; Mursu et al., 2003; Peterson & Kim, 2003; Tung & Quaddus, 2002; Vlahos, Ferratt, & Knoepfle, 2004)
EK. IS Security	0	2	1994-1999: N/A 2000-2005: (Freeman & Urbaczewski, 2005; S. K. Shin, Gopal, Sanders, & Whinston, 2004)
EL. IS Management Issues	25	24	1994-1999: (Abdul-Gader, 1997; Al-Khaldi & Olusegun Wallace, 1999; Day et al., 1995; Doukidis et al., 1996; Gefen & Straub, 1997; Harris & Davison, 1999; Hasan & Ditsa, 1999; Hill, Lock, Straub, & El-Sheshai, 1998; Hu, Chau, Liu Sheng, & Yan Tam, 1999; Igbaria, Iivari et al., 1995; Jensen & Scheraga, 1998; Kumar, van Dissel, & Bielli, 1998; Lally, 1994; M. Martinsons & Westwood, 1997; Montealegre, 1998; Nelson & Clark Jr., 1994; Peppard, 1999; Phelps & Mok, 1999; Robichaux & Cooper, 1998; Seror, 1996; Steinwachs, 1999; Straub, 1994; Straub, Keil, & Brenner, 1997; Tractinsky & Jarvenpaa, 1995; Ward & Peppard, 1996) 2000-2005: (Akgun et al., 2005; Akmanligil & Palvia, 2004; Bunker, 2001; Caldeira & Ward, 2003; Calhoun et al., 2002; Chudoba, Wynn, Lu, & Watson-Manheim, 2005; De Angeli, Athavankar, Joshi, Coventry, & Johnson, 2004; Gefen, Rose, Warkentin, & Pavlou, 2005; Huang, Lu, & Wong, 2003; Hwang, 2005; Karahanna, Evaristo, & Srite, 2005; Keil et al., 2000; Koeszegi, Vetschera, & Kersten, 2004; J. Lim, 2003; Mahmood, Bagchi, & Ford, 2004; M. G. Martinsons & Cheung, 2001; Palvia, Palvia, & Whitworth, 2002; Peterson & Kim, 2003; Rao, 2004; Robbins & Stylianou, 2001, 2003; Shoib & Nadhakumar, 2003; Tung & Quaddus, 2002; Walsham, 2002)
FA. IS Development Strategies	0	3	1994-1999: N/A 2000-2005: (Akmanligil & Palvia, 2004; Kankanhalli et al., 2004; Mursu et al., 2003)

continued on following page

Table 2. continued

FB IS Life Cycle Activities	0	2	1994-1999: N/A 2000-2005: (Brugha, 2001; Thanasankit, 2002)
FC IS Development Methods and Tools	1	4	1994-1999: (Iivari, 1996) 2000-2005: (Brugha, 2001; Kankanhalli et al., 2004; Thanasankit, 2002; R. T. Watson et al., 2005)
FD IS Implementation	4	1	1994-1999: (Cavaye & Christiansen, 1996; Cooper, 1994; Shore & Venkatachalam, 1995; Thong et al., 1996) 2000-2005: (Peterson & Kim, 2003)
FE IS Operations	0	1	1994-1999: N/A 2000-2005: (Gordon & Gordon, 2002)
GA. Organizational Use of IS	2	9	1994-1999: (Jarvenpaa & Leidner, 1998; Palvia, 1997) 2000-2005: (Akgun et al., 2005; Alavi, Kayworth, & Leidner, 2005; Caldeira & Ward, 2003; Chudoba et al., 2005; Kambayashi & Scarbrough, 2001; Mahmood et al., 2004; Olson & Olson, 2000; Paul, Samarah, Seetharaman, & Mykytyn, 2004; Zahir, Dobing, & Hunter, 2002)
GB. Users	6	26	1994-1999: (Al-Khaldi & Olusegun Wallace, 1999; Furst, Blackburn, & Rosen, 1999; Gefen & Straub, 1997; Harris & Davison, 1999; Hu et al., 1999; Igbaria, Iivari et al., 1995) 2000-2005: (Alavi et al., 2005; Blake, Neuendorf, & Valdiserri, 2003; Bunker, 2001; Caldeira & Ward, 2003; Calhoun et al., 2002; Choe, 2004; Chudoba et al., 2005; Corbitt et al., 2004; Cyr & Trevor-Smith, 2004; Freeman & Urbaczewski, 2005; Gefen et al., 2005; Huang et al., 2003; Hwang, 2005; S. L. Jarvenpaa, K. R. Lang, Y. Takeda, & V. K. Tuunainen, 2003; Kambayashi & Scarbrough, 2001; Karahanna et al., 2005; Koeszegi et al., 2004; J. Lim, 2003; Mahmood et al., 2004; Olson & Olson, 2000; Paul et al., 2004; Rao, 2004; B. Shin & Higa, 2005; Thanasankit, 2002; Thatcher et al., 2003; Vlahos et al., 2004)
GC. Type of IS Support	2	0	1994-1999: (McLeod et al., 1997; van den Hoven et al., 1994) 2000-2005: N/A
GD. Type of IS Access	0	1	1994-1999: N/A 2000-2005: (S. Jarvenpaa, K. R. Lang, Y. Takeda, & V. K. Tuunainen, 2003)
HA. Types of Information Systems	18	27	1994-1999: (Aiken et al., 1996; Aiken et al., 1995; Aiken et al., 1994; Burn, 1995; Chung & Adams, 1997; Dustbar & Hofstede, 1999; Ferratt & Vlahos, 1998; Furst et al., 1999; Johnston & Johal, 1999; Kamel & Davison, 1998; L.-H. Lim et al., 1994; Niederman, 1999; Robichaux & Cooper, 1998; Straub, 1994; B. Tan et al., 1995; B. Tan, Wei, Watson, & Walczuch, 1998; R.T. Watson et al., 1994; Williams & Wilson, 1997) 2000-2005: (Akgun et al., 2005; Akmanligil & Palvia, 2004; Alavi et al., 2005; Blake et al., 2003; Bunker, 2001; Choe, 2004; Davison, 2002; De Angeli et al., 2004; Freeman & Urbaczewski, 2005; Gefen et al., 2005; Huang et al., 2003; Hwang, 2005; S.L. Jarvenpaa et al., 2003; Karahanna et al., 2005; Koeszegi et al., 2004; Kwon, 2003; J.Lim, 2003; Okazaki & Rivas, 2002; Olson & Olson, 2000; Paul et al., 2004; Robbins & Stylianou, 2001, 2003; Rutkowski & van de Walle, 2005; B. Shin & Higa, 2005; Tung & Quaddus, 2002; Vlahos et al., 2004; Zahir et al., 2002)
HB. IS Applications Areas	0	1	1994-1999: N/A 2000-2005: (Choe, 2004)
HC. Components of IS	0	3	1994-1999: N/A 2000-2005: (Cyr & Trevor-Smith, 2004; Rutkowski & van de Walle, 2005; B. Shin & Higa, 2005)
HD. IS Characteristics	0	6	1994-1999: N/A 2000-2005: (Cyr & Trevor-Smith, 2004; De Angeli et al., 2004; Kwon, 2003; Okazaki & Rivas, 2002; Robbins & Stylianou, 2001, 2003)

Table 3. EL – IS management issues subcategories analysis

Subcategory	Frequency		Citations
	1994-1999	2000-2005	
Marketing of MIS	0	1	1994-1999: N/A 2000-2005: (Gefen et al., 2005)
IS Problems	1	3	1994-1999: (Kumar et al., 1998) 2000-2005: (Keil et al., 2000; Palvia et al., 2002; Peterson & Kim, 2003)
IS Success	0	4	1994-1999: N/A 2000-2005: (Akgun et al., 2005; Akmanligil & Palvia, 2004; Peterson & Kim, 2003; Tung & Quaddus, 2002)
IS Evolution	3	0	1994-1999: (Doukidis et al., 1996; Steinwachs, 1999; Ward & Peppard, 1996) 2000-2005: N/A
IS Technology Transfer (Adoption)	13	10	1994-1999: (Al-Khaldi & Olusegun Wallace, 1999; Day et al., 1995; Doukidis et al., 1996; Gefen & Straub, 1997; Harris & Davison, 1999; Hasan & Ditsa, 1999; Hill et al., 1998; Hu et al., 1999; Igbaria, Iivari et al., 1995; Jensen & Scheraga, 1998; Phelps & Mok, 1999; Robichaux & Cooper, 1998; Seror, 1996; Straub, 1994; Straub et al., 1997) 2000-2005: (Bunker, 2001; De Angeli et al., 2004; Gefen et al., 2005; Huang et al., 2003; Hwang, 2005; Karahanna et al., 2005; Koeszegi et al., 2004; J. Lim, 2003; Mahmood et al., 2004; Shoib & Nadhakumar, 2003)
IS Integration	1	0	1994-1999: (Lally, 1994) 2000-2005: N/A
Outsourcing of IS	0	3	1994-1999: N/A 2000-2005: (Akmanligil & Palvia, 2004; M. G. Martinsons & Cheung, 2001; Rao, 2004)
IS Risk Management	0	0	1994-1999: N/A 2000-2005: N/A
Globalization of IS	6	8	1994-1999: (Abdul-Gader, 1997; M. Martinsons & Westwood, 1997; Montealegre, 1998; Nelson & Clark Jr., 1994; Peppard, 1999; Tractinsky & Jarvenpaa, 1995) 2000-2005: (Akmanligil & Palvia, 2004; Bunker, 2001; Calhoun et al., 2002; Chudoba et al., 2005; Karahanna et al., 2005; Rao, 2004; Robbins & Stylianou, 2001, 2003)
IS Downsizing	0	0	1994-1999: N/A 2000-2005: N/A

both time periods. This is not surprising given the popularity of TAM research in IS (King & He, 2006). However, the other keywords showed some change. For example, the popularity of IS Success, Outsourcing and Globalization of IS increased, while IS Evolution decreased.

Integration

To analyze how Hofstede was cited, a cross-tabulation of the high-level categories with the levels of citation use is presented (see Tables 4a,

b). A Chi-square test for independence showed no significant difference in usage between the high-level categories for 1994-1999 ($\chi^2 = 5.641$, df $= 16$, $p \approx 0.997$), and for 2000-2005 ($\chi^2 = 19.595$, df $= 16$, $p = 0.239$). Incidental usage of Hofstede is quite common, and indeed it is the modal coding for each high-level research category. Furthermore, relatively few articles contributed to Hofstede's theory, although it appears as though there might be an increase from the 1994-1999 timeframe to the 2000-2005 timeframe. However, the level of citation is independent from the two timeframes ($\chi^2 = 5.391$, df $= 4$, $p = 0.249$).

Again, the category E – IS Management and the subcategories of EL were divided into a finer level of detail (Tables 5a, b). For both time periods, IS Technology Transfer was the most frequently studied topic. However, for 1994-1999, the most common uses of Hofstede were incidental, but for 2000-2005, the most common use of Hostede was to derive hypotheses or theory, although these were not statistically significant differences. For IS Technology Transfer, only two articles used Hofstede incidentally (Caldeira & Ward, 2003; Shoib & Nadhakumar, 2003). Across the other categories and keywords, there was no significant change over time.

Finally, Table 6 summarizes the detailed contributions of each dimension, nested by category, as previously described. While the focus of this paper is on Hofstede's original dimensions, findings relevant to Long Term Orientation have been included when they were part of an article included in the analysis. Each of these summaries were derived from the individual studies that specified the relationships between the specific dimensions and the IS topic. No summaries were

Table 4a. Analysis of citation level and MIS categories 1994-1999

Primary MIS Category	Incidental Citation	Define or Describe Culture	Derive Hypotheses or Theory	Post-Hoc Discussion	Contribution to Hofstede's Theory	N
D – Organizational Environment	(Ward & Peppard, 1996)	(Thong et al., 1996)	(M. Martinsons & Hempel, 1998)	(Thong et al., 1996)		4
E – IS Management	(Doukidis et al., 1996; Harris & Davison, 1999; Hill et al., 1998; Kumar et al., 1998; Montealegre, 1998; Peppard, 1999; Phelps & Mok, 1999; Seror, 1996; Tractinsky & Jarvenpaa, 1995)	(Al-Khaldi & Olusegun Wallace, 1999; Day et al., 1995; Hu et al., 1999; Hunter & Beck, 1996; Igbaria, Iivari et al., 1995; Igbaria, Meredith et al., 1995; Jensen & Scheraga, 1998; Nelson & Clark Jr., 1994; van den Hoven et al., 1994)	(Abdul-Gader, 1997; Bryan et al., 1995; Hasan & Ditsa, 1999; Holmes, 1998; Kim et al., 1999; Lally, 1994; M. Martinsons & Westwood, 1997; Steinwachs, 1999; Straub et al., 1997)	(Bryan et al., 1995; Hu et al., 1999; Igbaria, Iivari et al., 1995; Kumar et al., 1998; Phelps & Mok, 1999; Tractinsky & Jarvenpaa, 1995)	(Holmes, 1998; Hunter & Beck, 1996)	35
F – IS Development and Operations	(Cavaye & Christiansen, 1996; Cooper, 1994)	N/A	(Shore & Venkatachalam, 1995)	(Cavaye & Christiansen, 1996; Iivari, 1996)		5
G – IS Usage	(Furst et al., 1999; Palvia, 1997)	(McLeod et al., 1997)	(Gefen & Straub, 1997; Igbaria & Zviran, 1996; Jarvenpaa & Leidner, 1998)	(McLeod et al., 1997)	(Gefen & Straub, 1997)	8
H – Information Systems	(Aiken et al., 1996; Aiken et al., 1994; Chung & Adams, 1997; Kamel & Davison, 1998; Niederman, 1999; Williams & Wilson, 1997)	(Aiken et al., 1995; Ferratt & Vlahos, 1998; L.-H. Lim et al., 1994; Straub, 1994)	(Dustbar & Hofstede, 1999; Johnston & Johal, 1999; Robichaux & Cooper, 1998; B. Tan et al., 1995; B. Tan et al., 1998; R.T. Watson et al., 1994)	(Chung & Adams, 1997; Ferratt & Vlahos, 1998; Straub, 1994; Williams & Wilson, 1997)	(Johnston & Johal, 1999)	21
Total	20	16	20	14	4	74

Table 4b. Analysis of citation level and MIS categories 2000-2005

Primary MIS Category	Incidental Citation	Define or Describe Culture	Derive Hypotheses or Theory	Post-Hoc Discussion	Contribution to Hofstede's Theory	N
D – Organizational Environment	(Alavi et al., 2005)	(Corbitt et al., 2004; Gallivan & Strite, 2005; Myers & Tan, 2002)	(Bunker, 2001)	(Alavi et al., 2005)	(Corbitt et al., 2004; Gallivan & Strite, 2005; Myers & Tan, 2002)	9
E – IS Management	(Akgun et al., 2005; Caldeira & Ward, 2003; Freeman & Urbaczewski, 2005; Hayne & Pollard, 2000; M. G. Martinsons & Cheung, 2001; Palvia et al., 2002; Peterson & Kim, 2003; Shoib & Nadhakumar, 2003)	(Koeszegi et al., 2004; Rao, 2004; Schmidt et al., 2001; S. K. Shin et al., 2004; Walsham, 2002)	(Calhoun et al., 2002; De Angeli et al., 2004; Gefen et al., 2005; Gordon & Gordon, 2002; Huang et al., 2003; Hwang, 2005; Kankanhalli et al., 2004; Keil et al., 2000; J. Lim, 2003; Okazaki & Rivas, 2002; Robbins & Stylianou, 2001; R. T. Watson et al., 2005)	(Akgun et al., 2005; Freeman & Urbaczewski, 2005; Koeszegi et al., 2004; M. G. Martinsons & Cheung, 2001; Vlahos et al., 2004)	(Huang et al., 2003; Robbins & Stylianou, 2001; Walsham, 2002)	33
F – IS Development and Operations	(Akmanligil & Palvia, 2004; Brugha, 2001)		(Thanasankit, 2002)	(Mursu et al., 2003)		4
G – IS Usage	(Blake et al., 2003; Chudoba et al., 2005; S. L. Jarvenpaa et al., 2003; Mahmood et al., 2004; Olson & Olson, 2000)		(Kambayashi & Scarbrough, 2001; Paul et al., 2004; Thatcher et al., 2003)	(Olson & Olson, 2000)	(Karahanna et al., 2005)	10
H – Information Systems	(Davison, 2002; Kwon, 2003)		(Choe, 2004; Cyr & Trevor-Smith, 2004; Robbins & Stylianou, 2003; Rutkowski & van de Walle, 2005; B. Shin & Higa, 2005; Zahir et al., 2002)		(Robbins & Stylianou, 2003)	9
Total	18	8	23	8	8	65

included unless there was explicit discussion of these relationships, either through propositions, or conclusions. For instance, in the Types of Information Systems section, under Uncertainty Avoidance, it was proposed that countries high in UAI might want formal rules for videoconferencing meetings (Dustbar & Hofstede, 1999).

Summary

This section has reported on the results of the citation analysis. It shows that Hofstede's work has contributed to the IS research but that there is considerable variation in how researchers have used it. The following section will discuss some of the possible reasons for this, and some

Table 5a. Analysis of citation level and secondary categories for E – IS management for 1994-1999

Detailed E Category	Incidental Citation	Define or Describe Culture	Derive Hypotheses or Theory	Post-Hoc Discussion	Contribution to Hofstede's Theory	N
EE – IS Project Management	(Tractinsky & Jarvenpaa, 1995)					1
EF – IS Planning	(Doukidis et al., 1996; Kamel & Davison, 1998)	(Nelson & Clark Jr., 1994; van den Hoven et al., 1994)	(Abdul-Gader, 1997; Shore & Venkatachalam, 1995)			6
EH – IS Staffing		(Hunter & Beck, 1996; Igbaria, Meredith et al., 1995; McLeod et al., 1997)	(Bryan et al., 1995; Holmes, 1998)	(Bryan et al., 1995)	(Holmes, 1998; Hunter & Beck, 1996)	8
EI – IS Evaluation			(Igbaria & Zviran, 1996; Kim et al., 1999)			2
EL – IS Management Issues						
IS Problems	(Kumar et al., 1998)			(Kumar et al., 1998)		2
IS Evolution	(Doukidis et al., 1996; Ward & Peppard, 1996)		(Steinwachs, 1999)			3
IS Technology Transfer (Adoption)	(Doukidis et al., 1996; Harris & Davison, 1999; Hill et al., 1998; Phelps & Mok, 1999; Seror, 1996; Ward & Peppard, 1996)	(Al-Khaldi & Olusegun Wallace, 1999; Day et al., 1995; Hu et al., 1999; Jensen & Scheraga, 1998)	(Gefen & Straub, 1997; Hasan & Ditsa, 1999; Robichaux & Cooper, 1998; Straub, 1994; Straub et al., 1997)	(Hu et al., 1999; Igbaria, Iivari et al., 1995; Phelps & Mok, 1999))		18
IS Integration			(Lally, 1994)			1
Globalization of IS	(Montealegre, 1998; Peppard, 1999)	(Nelson & Clark Jr., 1994)	(Abdul-Gader, 1997; M. Martinsons & Westwood, 1997)	(Tractinsky & Jarvenpaa, 1995)		6
Total	14	10	15	6	2	47

** Total count for this analysis is 47 (12 more than the general E category count). This is not an error, rather a result of the multiple relevant codes for these articles.

opportunities for further theoretical integration. In addition, there has not been much change over the time period of 1994-2005.

DISCUSSION

Our analyses indicate that there has not been a lot of change in the way IS researchers have used Hofstede's work. Specifically, it appears as though there is still a tendency to use it incidentally, although there may be a slight shift towards using fewer incidental citations and more hypothesis development. Overall, there does appear to be more IS research in 2000-2005 that informs the culture literature; the frequency of this type of research has recently doubled, from 7% (4 out of 57) to 15% (8 out of 54) of the IS research that cites

Table 5b. Analysis of citation level and secondary categories for E — IS management for 2000-2005

Detailed E Category	Incidental Citation	Define/ Describe Culture	Derive Hypotheses or Theory	Post-Hoc Discussion	Contribution to Hofstede's Theory	N
EE – IS Project Management	(Hayne & Pollard, 2000; M. G. Martinsons & Cheung, 2001)	(Schmidt et al., 2001)	(Gordon & Gordon, 2002; Keil et al., 2000; R. T. Watson et al., 2005)	(M. G. Martinsons & Cheung, 2001)		7
EF – IS Planning	(Hayne & Pollard, 2000)		(Gordon & Gordon, 2002; Okazaki & Rivas, 2002)			3
EG -	(Akgun et al., 2005)			(Akgun et al., 2005)		2
EH – IS Staffing	(Hayne & Pollard, 2000; M. G. Martinsons & Cheung, 2001)	(Rao, 2004)	(Kankanhalli et al., 2004; R. T. Watson et al., 2005)	(M. G. Martinsons & Cheung, 2001)		6
EI – IS Evaluation	(Peterson & Kim, 2003)		(Calhoun et al., 2002)	(Vlahos et al., 2004)		3
EK – IS	(Freeman & Urbaczewski, 2005)	(S. K. Shin et al., 2004)		(Freeman & Urbaczewski, 2005)		3
EL – IS Management Issues						
IS Marketing			(Gefen et al., 2005)			1
IS Problems	(Palvia et al., 2002; Peterson & Kim, 2003)		(Keil et al., 2000)			3
IS Success	(Akgun et al., 2005; Caldeira & Ward, 2003; Peterson & Kim, 2003)			(Akgun et al., 2005)		4
IS Technology Transfer (Adoption)	(Caldeira & Ward, 2003; Shoib & Nadhakumar, 2003)	(Koeszegi et al., 2004; Walsham, 2002)	(De Angeli et al., 2004; Gefen et al., 2005; Huang et al., 2003; Hwang, 2005; J. Lim, 2003)	(Koeszegi et al., 2004)	(Huang et al., 2003; Walsham, 2002)	12
Outsourcing of IS	(M. G. Martinsons & Cheung, 2001)	(Rao, 2004)		(M. G. Martinsons & Cheung, 2001)		3
Globalization of IS		(Rao, 2004)	(Calhoun et al., 2002; Robbins & Stylianou, 2001)		(Robbins & Stylianou, 2001)	4
Total	16	7	17	8	3	51

** Total count for this analysis is 49 (16 more than the general E category count). This is not an error, rather a result of the multiple relevant codes for these articles.

Hofstede's work. Furthermore, two recent articles critiqued Hofstede's work and the measurement and incorporation of culture in IS research (Gallivan & Strite, 2005; Myers & Tan, 2002). Thus, one can see a subtle shift towards more engagement with fundamental issues regarding national culture and IS.

Coverage

In our original analysis, it appeared as though Hofstede's national culture dimensions had not been applied in equal measures to all areas of IS research. Indeed, the bulk of the research was focused on issues related to E - IS Management and

Table 6. Summary of dimensions and the categories

Category	Summary of Cultural Impacts
D – Organizational Environment	*Power Distance:* As Power Distance increases, top-down directives increase for BPR (M. Martinsons & Hempel, 1998). *Uncertainty Avoidance:* For countries higher in Uncertainty Avoidance, top management's role in implementation is decreased (and employees' responsibility increased) (Thong et al., 1996). For BPR, as UAI increases companies are less likely to view challenges as problems that require solving (M. Martinsons & Hempel, 1998). *Individualism-Collectivism:* Countries lower in Individualism may be more willing to take risks with IS (Thong et al., 1996). For BPR and countries lower in Individualism, there is easier initiation of BPR, and more difficult implementation of it (M. Martinsons & Hempel, 1998).
E – IS Management	
EE – IS Project Management	*Uncertainty Avoidance:* Cultures lower in UAI have a stronger negative relationship between risk propensity and risk perception for software projects than cultures higher in UAI (Keil et al., 2000). *Individualism-Collectivism:* Individualism may decrease the need to centralize the setting and enforcing of standards (Gordon & Gordon, 2002); however, results were not specifically analyzed along this dimension.
EF – IS Planning	*Power Distance:* In countries with higher PDI, participative IS development may not be appropriate. *Uncertainty Avoidance:* Countries higher in UAI, may experience the following: higher resistance to applications; higher traditionalism, therefore, IS should be tied to cultural traditions (Montealegre, 1998); and there may be less long term goals for IS plans and less detailed plans *Individualism-Collectivism:* Individualism-Collectivism is reflected in the frequency of individualistic values in Japanese MNC Web marketing communications according to the target country (Okazaki & Rivas, 2002). *Long Term Orientation:* Korean IS development is more focused on short and intermediate term goals (Kim et al., 1999).
EH - IS Staffing	*Power Distance:* There are gender differences for IS professionals, such that men prefer consultative management (Holmes, 1998). Countries higher in PDI emphasize professionalism and expertise; whereas countries lower in PDI emphasize abilities to enhance client participation in IS development (Hunter & Beck, 1996). *Individualism-Collectivism:* Women are more collectivistic than men IS professionals (Holmes, 1998). Individualism is positively related to economic, technical and sociopolitical values for IS developers (Kankanhalli et al., 2004). *Masculinity-Femininity:* Male IS professionals rate higher in Masculinity than female IS professionals - this relates to different professional goals (Holmes, 1998). Masculinity is positively related to economic, technical and sociopolitical values for IS developers (Kankanhalli et al., 2004).
EL - IS Problems	*Masculinity:* IS implementation may fail if the IS does not match the culture (e.g., self-efficacy and competitiveness in Prato) (Kumar et al., 1998).
EL - IS Evolution	None of the dimensions are explicitly related to issues of IS Evolution.
EL - IS Technology Transfer (Adoption)	*Power Distance:* In countries with higher PDI, adoption of power reducing technologies is limited (Straub et al., 1997). For ATM adoption, class in a high PDI country (India) is powerful predictor, as ATM seem to be for the "rich, educated people living business lives" whereas for the lower class, ATM's might be preferred because writing is not required, avoids face-to-face contact with individuals of higher status and individuals of the opposite sex (De Angeli et al., 2004). In cultures high in PDI, the effect of subjective norms on perceived usefulness for email is moderated by PDI, such that email removes cues of reverence to superiors and thus is likely to seen as less appropriate by subordinates (Huang et al., 2003). *Uncertainty Avoidance:* As UA increases, TAM may not be appropriate, and there is limited adoption of technologies that are limited in social presence and information richness (Straub et al., 1997). Uncertainty Avoidance is positively related to perceived ease of use for ERP systems (Hwang, 2005). *Individualism-Collectivism:* As Individualism decreases, the importance of voluntarism increases in adoption (Igbaria, Iivari et al., 1995), and technologies that are low in SPIR, will have limited adoption (Straub et al., 1997). Collectivism decreases the need for ATM due to a social network for borrowing/obtaining money, and it alters the use of ATMs (sharing cards, sharing accounts) and decreases the social space at the ATM (De Angeli et al., 2004). In an individualistic culture (e.g., USA), trust is associated with an increase in perceived usefulness of e-voting; whereas, in collectivistic cultures (e.g., South Africa) trust does not play a role (Gefen et al., 2005). *Long Term Orientation:* Cultures with a LTO (i.e., India) impacts adoption of ATMs as 'saving time' is not seen as a selling point for the middle class (De Angeli et al., 2004).
EL - IS Integration	*Individualism-Collectivism:* Countries higher in Individualism will have more varied IS infrastructures and applications than countries higher in Collectivism (Lally, 1994).

continued on following page

Table 6. continued

Category	Summary of Cultural Impacts
EL - Globalization of IS	*Power Distance:* For countries high in PDI, the paternalism of management, decreases the use of IT for decentralization (M. Martinsons & Westwood, 1997).
F – IS Development and Operations	*Power Distance:* As PDI increases, the participation of end users decreases in IS development, the more the project is controlled from management, and the there is less distributed architecture (Shore & Venkatachalam, 1995). In high PDI culture (i.e., Thai) the requirements engineering process is affected in terms of the level of communication, criticism and feedback that is given, which also decreases performance and increases frustration for the systems analysts (Thanasankit, 2002). *Uncertainty Avoidance:* As Uncertainty Avoidance increases, IS projects will focus more on automation, outsourcing IS development will increase, and access to systems will become more limited (Shore & Venkatachalam, 1995).
G – IS Usage	*Power Distance:* Higher PDI is associated with a higher preference for and higher practice of hierarchical use of IT (e.g., Japan vs. Britain) (Kambayashi & Scarbrough, 2001). *Uncertainty Avoidance:* For countries higher in Uncertainty Avoidance, high context IT is preferred, and will alter how IT is used (Jarvenpaa & Leidner, 1998). UAI is negatively associated with personal innovativeness with IT (Thatcher et al., 2003). *Individualism-Collectivism:* Individualism is associated with a higher preference and higher practice of individualistic use of IT (Kambayashi & Scarbrough, 2001). Collectivism helps to enhance the level of collaborative conflict management styles in global virtual teams (Paul et al., 2004). *Masculinity-Femininity:* For women, there is an increase in relevance of SPIR, perceived usefulness, and perceived ease of use, but no difference of use (Gefen & Straub, 1997).
H – Information Systems	*Power Distance:* Countries with higher PDI would experience a greater equalizing influence of GDSS (in anonymous applications) than those with lower PDI (B. Tan et al., 1995; R.T. Watson et al., 1994). Higher PDI is associated with avoidance conflict management styles with GSS (Tung & Quaddus, 2002). Global corporate websites reflect PDI; high PDI is associated with the presence of biographies of top leaders and a corporate message from the CEO (Robbins & Stylianou, 2003). PDI is associated with types of services and information available on Internet portals (Zahir et al., 2002). *Uncertainty Avoidance:* Countries high in UAI may want formal rules for videoconference meetings (Dustbar & Hofstede, 1999). Countries higher in UAI will also prefer a more rich communication media. With high levels of advanced manufacturing technology, cultures high in uncertainty avoidance may need more information (e.g., financial performance information, advanced cost control information and traditional cost control information) (Choe, 2004). Lower UAI is associated with integrative conflict management style; moderate UAI is associated with more conflict being identified in GSS (Tung & Quaddus, 2002). Global corporate websites reflect UAI; low UAI is associated with list of job openings, career and job opportunity descriptions (Robbins & Stylianou, 2003). UAI is associated with types of services and information available on Internet portals (Zahir et al., 2002). *Individualism-Collectivism:* GDSS will decrease the power and status differentials in countries that low in Individualism (individuals living in a collectivist country will seek cues from the high status individuals to create group harmony) (B. C. Y. Tan, Wei, Watson, Clapper, & McLean, 1998); they may also have less satisfaction for meetings that are geographically disperse and without non-verbal cues support (Dustbar & Hofstede, 1999). Collectivism is associated with less conflict being identified in a GSS context, and individualism is associated with more issue-based conflict (Tung & Quaddus, 2002). High individualistic cultures (e.g., Australia) are associated with high team-based performance measures under a high level of task interdependence (Choe, 2004, p. 676). Global corporate websites reflect Ind/Coll, which is associated with the use of cookies, privacy policy statements, and the capacity for secure communication (Robbins & Stylianou, 2003). Ind/Coll is associated with types of services and information available on Internet portals (Zahir et al., 2002). *Masculinity-Femininity:* Countries high in Masculinity will have more conflict within the discussions (Dustbar & Hofstede, 1999). Countries high in Masculinity will also benefit from an increase in participation with GDSS's parallel entry due to a reduction in time domination. Countries high in Femininity will benefit from an increase in participation with anonymous entry with GDSS due to a decrease in conflict avoidance (Robichaux & Cooper, 1998). Global corporate websites reflect Masc/Fem; Masculinity is associated with the reporting of the Annual Report and financial indicators, Femininity is associated with presence of cultural sensitivity (Robbins & Stylianou, 2003). In a high collectivism culture (Hong Kong), face-to-face and email scheduling are preferred and F2F is seen more efficient to automatic scheduling, even though the automatic scheduling system produces fewer schedule conflicts (B. Shin & Higa, 2005). *Long Term Orientation:* Countries, which are more Short Term orientation, will be more concerned with saving face than achieving objectives (Dustbar & Hofstede, 1999). Global corporate websites reflect LTO, which is associated availability of a search engine, FQA, press releases, and presence of corporate history (Robbins & Stylianou, 2003). ***Internet*** – One article applied the four original dimensions to the Internet to determine the Internet's culture (Johnston & Johal, 1999).

H - Information Systems, which was unsurprising due to the popularity of these topics (Eom, 1995; Pervan, 1998). In the 2000-2005 analysis, much of the research is still about E – IS Management, and at the primary level, F – IS Development and Operations, and G – IS Usage still received little attention. However, at the secondary-level, F – IS Development and Operations and G – IS Usage did show an increase since the original analysis.

Interestingly, where a single type of technology (Group Decision Support Systems) dominated the research in 1994-1999, in 2000-2005, the technologies studied were more varied with the favored technologies being ERP and the Internet. We had anticipated there would have been more interest in KMS (Knowledge Management Systems) (Ford et al., 2003), which does not seem to have occurred within the 2000-2005 timeframe. This is somewhat surprising as knowledge creation, capture, transfer and storage often considered to be influenced by cultural influences (e.g., Alavi et al., 2005; Ford & Chan, 2003).

The E - IS Management category may continue to be so popular for cross-cultural research using Hofstede's cultural dimensions because certain topics, such as IS technology transfer, and IS planning both lend themselves quite easily to research on national culture because they each deal very explicitly with human factors. National culture aside, these are also popular areas of research. For example, in the 1990s, nearly 500 articles have been published that discuss TAM and its implications (Venkatesh & Davis, 2000).

In our original paper, we had mentioned that a new development in the cultural-IS research is the suggestion that perhaps the Internet, itself, might be considered as a separate culture (Johnston & Johal, 1999) that transcends national boundaries; much more research is needed to investigate this claim more fully. This would extend Hofstede's framework from national borders to supranational organizations. In our current analysis, we did find some papers that examined the characteristics of Internet portals for different countries (Zahir et

al., 2002), website characteristics for multinational corporations (Okazaki & Rivas, 2002), and website characteristics in general for different countries (Cyr & Trevor-Smith, 2004; Robbins & Stylianou, 2001, 2003). These studies have found that there are cultural clusters within the Internet that reflect distinctive national cultures (or cultural clusters) as opposed to a single "Internet culture" (Cyr & Trevor-Smith, 2004; Okazaki & Rivas, 2002; Robbins & Stylianou, 2001, 2003; Zahir et al., 2002).

As with our original paper in which we suggested that the classification system (Barki et al., 1993) used could be updated, the current analysis suggests similar shortcomings. The broader IS categories (e.g. E, F, H) are useful and still apply well to most IS articles, as do most of the subcategories, with two exceptions. Information Systems HA – Types of Information Systems, and HB – IS Application Areas, are somewhat outdated. Some of the articles in our sample did not fit under the specific keywords listed in these subcategories (e.g., Internet, Web-based systems, E-Commerce, M-Commerce). This is not surprising, because the (Barki et al., 1993) classification scheme was previously updated after five years, and it has not been updated in the last 13 years.

Implications for Researchers

In writing this chapter, our goal was to examine how the use of Hofstede's framework has changed over the past six years. In this regard, it may be useful to revisit our 2003 paper, and consider the research that has been published since then. In our original paper we proposed the following primary suggestions for researchers.

First, we noted that researchers must have strong theoretical reasons for including Hofstede's national culture dimensions in any study prior to using them. An examination of more recent research in our current analysis suggests that researchers have begun to integrate the dimensions more directly into their theoretical discussions.

While the increase in the proportion of papers using the dimensions either *a priori* or *post hoc* in theoretical development and discussions is not statistically significant, there is an important trend that bears further scrutiny over time. Stronger theoretical grounding is a positive development, as it contributes to a cumulative tradition.

Second, we noted that researchers should include Hofstede's actual measures (in survey research) in order to evaluate changes in national culture that may have arisen over the previous 30 years. However, in our current analysis, it is apparent that researchers are still not including these survey items. This continued omission is problematic, as reliance on Hofstede's results from nearly 40 years ago potentially ignores changes in national culture that may be quite significant. For example, in the early 1970s China was amidst the Cultural Revolution, but today this country has the world's largest income disparity amongst its citizens. The potential for significant change in each country's scores along each of Hofstede's dimensions must be recognized and incorporated into IS research, if it is to remain relevant and rigorous. Hofstede (2001) provides a 20-item questionnaire and method that can be used to measure the five dimensions. The questionnaire is available in several languages, for research purposes, for a reasonable copyright fee, from the Institute for Research on Intercultural Cooperation at Tilburg University.

Third, we had suggested that a reasonable approach to improving cross-cultural research would be to introduce national culture, as operationalized by Hofstede, as independent variables to the model. Our current analysis suggests that this seems to be an area where little has changed. There are some practical concerns that we may have understated in our original work. For example, if a data set is drawn from a relatively small number of countries, the observations are not strictly independent. Therefore, this creates problems for regression-based techniques such as structural equation modeling due to multi-collinearity. However, newer techniques such Hierarchical Linear Modeling allow researchers to model these groupings in an appropriate fashion.

Fourth, we had suggested that another way in which Hofstede's dimensions could be introduced would be to hypothesize a moderating role. In our review, it does not appear that this has occurred; additional research in this area is certainly warranted. For example, one could expect Individualism-Collectivism to influence several predictor weightings. In a culture that was more Individualistic, we would expect the relative weighting of subjective norm to decrease and the weightings of attitude toward the behavior and perceived behavioral control to increase, as an individual's opinions are more important to that individual in such a culture.

Fifth, we also suggested, in our 2003 paper, that the national culture dimensions should be considered key control variables, as are traditional demographic variables such as age and sex. Based on our updated review of the literature, this does not appear to be happening. One possible explanation is that there seem to be growing concerns in the research community about the length of survey instruments. While these concerns are often legitimate, especially given the above-mentioned call to include direct measures of the dimensions of national culture (rather than simply using the country of origin as a proxy) we would suggest continued consideration of this suggestion, where appropriate.

Finally, in our 2003 paper, we expected that Knowledge Management Systems (KMS) would become a hot topic (Ford & Chan, 2003; Yoo, Ginzberg, & Ahn, 1999) following the pattern of GDSS in the early 1990s. This does not seem to have occurred in the body of research that we examined (1999-2005). Although a substantial body of KMS research has been published (including Special Issues of journals such as *MIS Quarterly*), our citation analysis suggestions that specific focus on technology has declined when considering national culture. It is not clear if this is a positive or negative development. Obviously, for IS research, there should be a focus on the technology itself as that artifact is central to our research. However, it appears that the shift has come from increased theorizing about how national culture affects IS management and usage. The latter is also central to our field and therefore at worst this seems to be a neutral trend.

CONCLUSION

Hofstede's dimensions enable IS researchers to understand the difficult concept of "culture". Although it would be unwise to solely rely on Hofstede's concept of culture there is a need in our field for an understanding of how national culture affects how information systems are developed, used, and managed. As Hofstede (2001) contends, "phenomena on all levels (individuals, groups, organizations, society as a whole) and phenomena related to different aspects (organization, polity, exchange) are potentially relevant" (p. 20). We hope that additional research at the national (or sub-cultural) level will assist in furthering our understanding.

NOTE

* This chapter is based on and extends a previous article: Ford, Connelly & Meister (2003) Information Systems Research and Hofstede's *Culture's Consequences*: An Uneasy and Incomplete Partnership. *IEEE Transactions in Engineering, 50*(1), 8-25

REFERENCES

Abdul-Gader, A. H. (1997). Information systems strategies for multinational companies in Arab Gulf countries. *International Journal of Information Management, 17*(1), 3-12.

Aiken, M., Hwang, H., & Martin, J. (1996). A Japanese group decision support system. *International Journal of Computer Applications in Technology, 9*(5/6), 233-238.

Aiken, M., Kim, D., Hwang, C., & Lu, L.-C. (1995). A Korean group decision support system. *Information & Management, 28*(5), 303-310.

Aiken, M., Martin, J., Shirani, A., & Singleton, T. (1994). A group decision support system for multicultural and multilingual communication. *Decision Support Systems, 12*(2), 93-96.

Akgun, A. E., Byrne, J., Keskin, H., Lynn, G. S., & Imamoglu, S. Z. (2005). Knowledge networks in new product development projects: A transactive memory perpsective. *Information & Management, 42*(8), 1105-1120.

Akmanligil, M., & Palvia, P. C. (2004). Strategies for global information systems development. *Information & Management, 42*(1), 45-59.

Al-Khaldi, M., & Olusegun, W. R. (1999). The influence of attitudes on personal computer utilization among knowledge workers: The case of Saudi Arabia. *Information & Management, 36*, 185-204.

Alavi, M., Kayworth, T. R., & Leidner, D. E. (2005). An empirical examination of the influence of organizational culture on knowledge management practices. *Journal of Management Information Systems, 22*(3), 191-224.

Barki, H., Rivard, S., & Talbot, J. (1993). A keyword classification scheme for IS research literature: An update. *MIS Quarterly, 17*(2), 209-226.

Blake, B. F., Neuendorf, K. A., & Valdiserri, C. M. (2003). Innovativeness and variety of Internet shopping. *Internet Research - Electronic Networking Applications and Policy, 13*(3), 156-169.

Brugha, C. M. (2001). Implications from decision science for the systems development life cycle in information systems. *Information Systems Frontiers, 3*(1), 91-105.

Bryan, N. B., McLean, E. R., Smits, S. J., & Burn, J. M. (1995). Work perceptions among Hong Kong and United States I/S workers: A cross-cultural comparison. *Journal of End User Computing, 7*(4), 22-29.

Bunker, D. (2001). A philosophy of information technology and systems (IT & S) as tools: Tool development context, associated skills and the global technology transfer (GTT) process. *Information Systems Frontiers, 3*(2), 185-197.

Burn, J. (1995). The new cultural revolution: The impact of EDI on Asia. *Journal of Global Information Management, 3*(3), 16-23.

Caldeira, M. M., & Ward, J. M. (2003). Using resource-based theory to interpret the successful adoption and use of information systems and technology in manufacturing small and medium-sized enterprises. *European Journal of Information Systems, 12*(2), 127-141.

Calhoun, K. J., Teng, J. T. C., & Cheon, M. J. (2002). Impact of national culture on information technology usage behaviour: An exploratory study of decision making in Korea and the USA. *Behaviour & Information Technology, 21*(4), 293-302.

Carpenter, M. A., & Fredrickson, J. W. (2001). Top management teams, global strategic posture, and the moderating role of uncertainty. *Academy of Management Journal, 44*(3), 533-545.

Carter, C. R. (2000). Ethical issues in international buyer-supplier relationships: A dyadic examination. *Journal of Operations Management, 18*(2), 191-208.

Cavaye, A., & Christiansen, J. (1996). Understanding IS implementation by estimating power of subunits. *European Journal of Information Systems, 5*, 222-232.

Chandy, P. R., & Williams, T. G. E. (1994). The impact of journals and authors on international business. *Journal of International Business Studies, 25*(4), 715.

Choe, J. M. (2004). The consideration of cultural differences in the design of information systems. *Information & Management, 41*(5), 669.

Chudoba, K. M., Wynn, E., Lu, M., & Watson-Manheim, M. B. (2005). How virtual are we? Measuring virtuality and understanding its impact in a global organization. *Information Systems Journal, 15*(4), 279-306.

Chung, I., & Adams, C. (1997). A study on the characteristics of group decision making behaviour: Cultural difference perspective of Korea versus United States. *Journal of Global Information Management, 5*(3), 18-29.

Cooper, R. B. (1994). The inertial impact of culture on IT implementation. *Information & Management, 27*, 17-31.

Corbitt, B. J., Peszynski, K. J., Inthanond, S., Hill, B., & Thanasankit, T. (2004). Cultural differences, information and code systems. *Journal of Global Information Management, 12*(3), 65-85.

Cronin, B. (2002). The digital divide. *Library Journal, 127*(3), 48.

Cyr, D., & Trevor-Smith, H. (2004). Localization of Web design: An empirical comparison of German, Japanese, and United States Web site characteristics. *Journal of the American Society for Information Science and Technology, 55*(13), 1199-1208.

Davis, F. D. (1989). Perceived usefulness, perceived ease of use, and user acceptance of information technology. *MIS Quarterly, 13*(3), 319-340.

Davison, R. (2002). Cultural implications of ERP. *Communications of the ACM, 45*(7), 109-111.

Day, D., Dosa, M., & Jorgensen, C. (1995). The transfer of research information within and by multicultural teams. *Information Processing & Management, 31*(1), 89-100.

De Angeli, A., Athavankar, U., Joshi, A., Coventry, L., & Johnson, G. I. (2004). Introducing ATMs in India: A contextual inquiry. *Interacting with Computers, 16*(1), 29-44.

De Vreede, G., Jones, N., & Mgaya, R. J. (1998-99). Exploring the application and acceptance of group support systems in Africa. *Journal of Management Information Systems, 15*(3), 197-234.

Doukidis, G., Lybereas, P., & Galliers, R. (1996). Information systems planning in small business: A stages of growth analysis. *The Journal of Systems and Software, 33*(2), 189-201.

Dustbar, S., & Hofstede, G. J. (1999). Videoconferencing across cultures - a conceptual framework for floor control issues. *Journal of Information Technology, 14*, 161-169.

Eom, S. B. (1995). Decision support systems research: Reference disciplines and a cumulative tradition. *Omega: International Journal of Management Science, 23*(5), 511-523.

Ferratt, T., & Vlahos, G. (1998). An investigation of task-technology fit for managers in Greece and the US. *European Journal of Information Systems, 7*, 123-136.

Ford, D. P., & Chan, Y. E. (2003). Knowledge sharing in a multi-cultural setting: A case study. *Knowledge Management Research & Practice, 1*(1), 11-27.

Ford, D. P., Connelly, C. E., & Meister, D. B. (2003). Information systems research and Hofstede's culture's consequences: An uneasy and incomplete partnership. *IEEE Transactions on Engineering Management, 50*(1), 8-25.

Freeman, L. A., & Urbaczewski, A. (2005). Why do people hate spyware? *Communications of the ACM, 48*(8), 50-53.

Furst, S., Blackburn, R., & Rosen, B. (1999). Virtual team effectiveness: A proposed research agenda. *Information Systems Journal, 9*, 249-269.

Gallivan, M., & Strite, M. (2005). Information technology and culture: Identifying fragmentary and holistic perspectives of culture. *Information & Organization, 15*(4), 295-338.

Gallupe, R. B., & Tan, F. (1999). A research manifesto for global information management. *Journal of Global Information Management, 7*(3), 5-18.

Gefen, D., Rose, G. M., Warkentin, M., & Pavlou, P. A. (2005). Cultural diversity and trust in IT adoption: A comparison of potential e-voters in the USA and South Africa. *Journal of Global Information Management, 13*(1), 54-78.

Gefen, D., & Straub, D. (1997). Gender differences in the perception and use of e-mail: An extension to the technology acceptance model. *MIS Quarterly, 21*(4), 389-400.

Gordon, J. R., & Gordon, S. R. (2002). Information technology service delivery: An international comparison. *Information Systems Management, 19*(1), 62-70.

Griffith, T. L. (1998). Cross-cultural and cognitive issues in the implementation of new technology: Focus on group support systems and Bulgaria. *Interacting with Computers, 9*(4), 431-447.

Harris, R., & Davison, R. (1999). Anxiety and involvement: Cultural dimensions of attitudes toward computers in developing societies. *Journal of Global Information Management, 6*(1), 26-38.

Hasan, H., & Ditsa, G. (1999). The impact of culture on the adoption of IT: An interpretive study. *Journal of Global Information Management, 7*(3), 5-15.

Hayne, S. C., & Pollard, C. E. (2000). A comparative analysis of critical issues facing Canadian information systems personnel: A national and global perspective. *Information & Management, 38*(2), 73-86.

Hill, C., Lock, K., Straub, D., & El-Sheshai, K. (1998). A qualitative assessment of Arab culture and information technology transfer. *Journal of Global Information Management, 6*(3), 29-38.

Hodgetts, R. (1993). A conversation with Geert Hofstede. *Organizational Dynamics, 21*, 53-62.

Hofstede, G. (1980a). *Culture's consequences: International differences in work-related values.* Beverly Hills, CA: Sage Publications.

Hofstede, G. (1980b). Motivation, leadership and organization: Do American theories apply abroad. *Organizational Dynamics, 8*(Summer), 42-63.

Hofstede, G. (1991). *Cultures and organizations: Software of the mind.* New York: McGraw-Hill.

Hofstede, G. (1994). *Values survey module manual.* Tilburg, The Netherlands: IRIC.

Hofstede, G. (2001). *Culture's consequences: Comparing values, behaviors, institutions, and organizations across nations* (2nd ed.). Thousand Oaks, CA: Sage Publications.

Hofstede, G., Arrindell, W., Best, D., De Mooij, M., Hoppe, M., Van de Vliert, E., et al. (1998). *Masculinity and femininity: The taboo dimension of national cultures.* Thousand Oaks, CA: SAGE Publications.

Hofstede, G., & Bond, M. H. (1988). Confucius & economic growth: New trends in culture's consequences. *Organizational Dynamics, 16*(4), 4-21.

Holmes, M. (1998). Comparison of gender differences among information systems professionals: A cultural perspective. *Journal of Computer Information Systems, 38*(4), 78-86.

Hu, P., Chau, P., Liu Sheng, O., & Yan Tam, K. (1999). Examining in technology acceptance model using physician acceptance of telemedicine technology. *Journal of Management Information Systems, 16*(2), 91-110.

Huang, L. J., Lu, M. T., & Wong, B. K. (2003). The impact of power distance on email acceptance: Evidence from the PRC. *Journal of Computer Information Systems, 44*(1), 93-101.

Hunter, M. G., & Beck, J. E. (1996). A cross-cultural comparison of "excellent" systems analysts. *Information Systems Journal, 6*, 261-281.

Hwang, Y. (2005). Investigating enterprise systems adoption: Uncertainty avoidance, intrinsic motivation, and the technology acceptance model. *European Journal of Information Systems, 14*(2), 150-161.

Igbaria, M., Iivari, J., & Maragahh, H. (1995). Why do individuals use computer technology? A Finnish case study. *Information & Management, 29*, 227-238.

Igbaria, M., Meredith, G., & Smith, D. (1995). Career orientations of information systems employees in South Africa. *Journal of Strategic Information Systems, 4*(4), 319-340.

Igbaria, M., & Zviran, M. (1996). Comparison of end-user computing characteristics in the US, Israel and Taiwan. *Information & Management, 30*, 1-13.

Iivari, J. (1996). Why are CASE tools not used? *Communications of the ACM, 39*(10), 94-103.

Jarvenpaa, S., Lang, K. R., Takeda, Y., & Tuunainen, V. K. (2003). Mobile commerce at crossroads. *Communications of the ACM, 46*(12), 41-44.

Jarvenpaa, S., & Leidner, D. (1998). An information company in Mexico: Extending the resource-based view of the firm to a developing country context. *Information Systems Research, 9*(4), 342-361.

Jarvenpaa, S. L., Lang, K. R., Takeda, Y., & Tuunainen, V. K. (2003). Mobile commerce at crossroads. *Communications of the ACM, 46*(12), 41-44.

Jensen, O., & Scheraga, C. (1998). Transferring technology: Costs and benefits. *Technology in Society, 20,* 99-112.

Johnston, K., & Johal, P. (1999). The Internet as a "virtual cultural region": Are extant cultural classification schemes appropriate? *Internet Research, 9*(3), 178-186.

Kambayashi, N., & Scarbrough, H. (2001). Cultural influences on IT use amongst factory managers: A UK-Japanese comparison. *Journal of Information Technology, 16*(4), 221-236.

Kamel, N., & Davison, R. (1998). Applying CSCW technology to overcome traditional barriers in group interactions. *Information & Management, 34*(4), 209-219.

Kankanhalli, A., Tan, B. C. Y., Wei, K. K., & Holmes, M. C. (2004). Cross-cultural differences and information systems developer values. *Decision Support Systems, 38*(2), 183-195.

Karahanna, E., Evaristo, J. R., & Srite, M. (2005). Levels of culture and individual behavior: An integrative perspective. *Journal of Global Information Management, 13*(2), 1-20.

Keil, M., Tan, B. C. Y., Wei, K.-K., Saarinen, T., Tuunainen, V., & Wassenaar, A. (2000). A cross-cultural study on escalation of commitment behavior in software projects. *MIS Quarterly, 24*(2), 299-325.

Kim, C., Peterson, D., & Kim, J. (1999). Information systems success: Perceptions of developers in Korea. *Journal of Computer Information Systems, 40*(2), 90-95.

King, W. R., & He, J. (2006). A meta-analysis of the technology acceptance model. *Information & Management, 43*(6), 740-755.

Koeszegi, S., Vetschera, R., & Kersten, G. (2004). National cultural differences in the use and perception of Internet-based NSS: Does high or low context matter? *International Negotiation, 9*(1), 79-109.

Kumar, K., van Dissel, H. G., & Bielli, P. (1998). The merchant of Prato - revisited: Toward a third rationality of information systems. *MIS Quarterly, 22*(2), 199-226.

Kwon, O. B. (2003). Meta Web service: Building web-based open decision support system based on web services. *Expert Systems with Applications, 24*(4), 375-389.

Lally, L. (1994). The impact of environment on information infrastructure enhancement: A comparative study of Singapore, France, and the United States. *Journal of Global Information Management, 2*(3), 5-12.

Lim, J. (2003). A conceptual framework on the adoption of negotiation support systems. *Information and Software Technology, 45*(8), 469-477.

Lim, L.-H., Raman, K., & Wei, K.-K. (1994). Interacting effects of GDSS and leadership. *Decision Support Systems, 12*(3), 199-221.

Mahmood, M. A., Bagchi, K., & Ford, T. C. (2004). On-line shopping behavior: Cross-country empirical research. *International Journal of Electronic Commerce, 9*(1), 9-30.

Martinsons, M. (1991). Management philosophy and IT assimilation: The east-west divide. *Journal of Technology Management, 18,* 207-218.

Martinsons, M., & Hempel, P. (1998). Chinese business process re-engineering. *International Journal of Information Management, 18*(6), 393-407.

Martinsons, M., & Westwood, R. (1997). Management information systems in the Chinese business culture: An explanatory theory. *Information & Management, 32,* 215-228.

Martinsons, M. G., & Cheung, C. (2001). The impact of emerging practices on IS specialists: Perceptions, attitudes and role changes in Hong Kong. *Information & Management, 38*(3), 167-183.

McLeod, R., Kim, C., Saunders, C., Jones, J., Scheel, C., & Estrada, M. (1997). Information management as perceived by CIO's in three Pacific Rim countries. *Journal of Global Information Management, 5*(3), 5-16.

Merritt, A. (2000). Culture in the cockpit - do Hofstede's dimensions replicate? *Journal of Cross-Cultural Psychology, 31*(3), 283-301.

Moenaert, R. K., & Souder, W. E. (1996). Context and antecedents of information utility at the r&d/marketing interface. *Management Science, 42*(11), 1592-1610.

Montealegre, R. (1998). Managing information technology in modernizing "against the odds": Lessons from an organization in a less-developed country. *Information & Management, 34*(2), 103-116.

Mulder, M. (1977). *The daily power game.* Leiden, The Netherlands: Martinus Nijihoff.

Mursu, A., Lyytinen, K., Soriyan, H. A., & Korpela, M. (2003). Identifying software project risks in Nigeria: An international comparative study. *European Journal of Information Systems, 12*(3), 182-194.

Myers, M., & Tan, F. (2002). Beyond models of national culture in information systems research. *Journal of Global Information Management, 10*(1), 24-32.

Nelson, K., & Clark, T., Jr. (1994). Cross-cultural issues in information systems research: A research program. *Journal of Global Information Management, 2*(4), 19-29.

Niederman, F. (1999). Global information systems and human resource management: A research agenda. *Journal of Global Information Management, 7*(2), 33-39.

Okazaki, S., & Rivas, A. A. (2002). A content analysis of multinationals' Web communication strategies: Cross-cultural research framework and pre-testing. *Internet Research - Electronic Networking Applications and Policy, 12*(5), 380-390.

Olson, G. M., & Olson, J. S. (2000). Distance matters. *Human-Computer Interaction, 15*(2-3), 139-178.

Palvia, P. C. (1997). Developing a model of the global and strategic impact of information technology. *Information & Management, 32*, 229-244.

Palvia, P. C., Palvia, S. C. J., & Whitworth, J. E. (2002). Global information technology: A meta-analysis of key issues. *Information & Management, 39*(5), 403-414.

Paul, S., Samarah, I. M., Seetharaman, P., & Mykytyn, P. P. (2004). An empirical investigation of collaborative conflict management style in group support system-based global virtual teams. *Journal of Management Information Systems, 21*(3), 185-222.

Peppard, J. (1999). Information management in the global enterprise: An organizing framework. *European Journal of Information Systems, 8*, 77-94.

Pervan, G. (1998). A review of research in group support systems: Leaders, approaches and directions. *Decision Support Systems, 23*(2), 149-159.

Peterson, D. K., & Kim, C. (2003). Perceptions on IS risks and failure types: A comparison of designers from the United States, Japan and Korea. *Journal of Global Information Management, 11*(3), 19.

Phelps, R., & Mok, M. (1999). Managing the risks of intranet implementation: An empirical study of user satisfaction. *Journal of Information Technology, 14*, 39-52.

Png, I. P. L., Tan, B. C. Y., & Wee, K. L. (2001). Dimensions of national culture and corporate adoption of IT infrastructure. *IEEE Transactions on Engineering Management, 48*(1), 36-45.

Rao, M. T. (2004). Key issues for global IT sourcing: Country and individual factors. *Information Systems Management, 21*(3), 16-21.

Robbins, S. S., & Stylianou, A. C. (2001). A study of cultural differences in global corporate web sites. *Journal of Computer Information Systems, 42*(2), 3.

Robbins, S. S., & Stylianou, A. C. (2003). Global corporate web sites: An empirical investigation of content and design. *Information & Management, 40*(3), 205-212.

Robichaux, B., & Cooper, R. (1998). GSS participation: A cultural examination. *Information & Management, 33*(6), 287-300.

Rutkowski, A. F., & van de Walle, B. (2005). Cultural dimensions and prototypical criteria for multi-criteria decision support in electronic markets: A comparative analysis of two job markets. *Group Decision & Negotiation., 14*(4), 285-306.

Schmidt, R., Lyytinen, K., Keil, M., & Cule, P. (2001). Identifying software project risks: An international Delphi study. *Journal of Management Information Systems, 17*(4), 5-36.

Seror, A. (1996). Action research for international information technology transfer: A methodology and a network model. *Technovation, 16*(8), 421-429.

Shin, B., & Higa, K. (2005). Meeting scheduling: Face-to-face, automatic scheduler, and email based coordination. *Journal of Organizational Computing and Electronic Commerce, 15*(2), 137-159.

Shin, S. K., Gopal, R. D., Sanders, G. L., & Whinston, A. B. (2004). Global software piracy revisited. *Communications of the ACM, 47*(1), 103-107.

Shoib, G., & Nadhakumar, J. (2003). Cross-cultural IS adoption in multinational corporations. *Information Technology for Development, 10*(4), 249-260.

Shore, B., & Venkatachalam, A. (1995). The role of national culture in systems analysis and design. *Journal of Global Information Management, 3*(3), 5-14.

Steinwachs, K. (1999). Information and culture - the impact of national culture on information processes. *Journal of Information Science, 25*(3), 193-204.

Straub, D. (1994). The effect of culture on IT diffusion: E-mail and FAX in Japan and the US. *Information Systems Research, 5*(1), 23-47.

Straub, D., Keil, M., & Brenner, W. (1997). Testing the technology acceptance model across cultures: A three country study. *Information & Management, 33*, 1-11.

Straub, D., Loch, K., Evaristo, R., Karahanna, E., & Srite, M. (2002). Toward a theory-based measurement of culture. *Journal of Global Information Management, 10*(1), 13-23.

Tan, B., Watson, R., & Wei, K.-K. (1995). National culture and group support systems: Filtering communication to dampen power differentials. *European Journal of Information Systems, 4*, 82-92.

Tan, B., Wei, K.-K., Watson, R., & Walczuch, R. (1998). Reducing status effects with computer-mediated communication: Evidence from two distinct national cultures. *Journal of Management Information Systems, 15*(1), 119-141.

Tan, B. C. Y., Wei, K. K., Watson, R. T., Clapper, D. L., & McLean, E. R. (1998). Computer-mediated communication and majority influence: Assessing the impact in an individualistic and a collectivistic culture. *Management Science, 44*(9), 1263-1278.

Thanasankit, T. (2002). Requirements engineering: Exploring the influence of power and Thai values. *European Journal of Information Systems, 11*(2), 128.

Thatcher, J. B., Stepina, L. P., Srite, M., & Liu, Y. M. (2003). Culture, overload and personal innovativeness with information technology: Extending the nomological net. *Journal of Computer Information Systems, 44*(1), 74-81.

Thong, J., Yap, C.-S., & Raman, K. (1996). Top management support, external expertise and information systems implementation in small businesses. *Information Systems Research, 7*(2), 248-267.

Tractinsky, N., & Jarvenpaa, S. (1995). Information systems design decisions in a global versus domestic context. *MIS Quarterly, 19*(4), 507-534.

Tung, L. L., & Quaddus, M. A. (2002). Cultural differences explaining the differences in results in GSS: Implications for the next decade. *Decision Support Systems, 33*(2), 177-199.

van den Hoven, P., van Valkenburg, F., & Heng, M. (1994). Managing information systems within Japanese companies in Europe: An empirical study. *Information & Management, 27*, 315-325.

Venkatesh, V., & Davis, F. D. (2000). A theoretical extension of the technology acceptance model: Four longitudinal field studies. *Management Science, 46*, 186-204.

Vlahos, G. E., Ferratt, T. W., & Knoepfle, G. (2004). The use of computer-based information systems by German managers to support decision making. *Information & Management, 41*(6), 763-779.

Walsham, G. (2002). Cross-cultural software production and use: A structurational analysis. *MIS Quarterly, 26*(4), 359-380.

Ward, J., & Peppard, J. (1996). Reconciling the IT/business relationship: A troubled marriage in need of guidance. *Strategic Information Systems, 5*, 37-65.

Watson, R. T., Boudreau, M. C., Greiner, M., Wynn, D., York, P., & Gul, R. (2005). Governance and global communities. *Journal of International Management, 11*(2), 125-142.

Watson, R. T., Ho, T. H., & Raman, K. S. (1994). Culture: A fourth dimension of group support systems. *Communications of the ACM, 37*(10), 44-55.

Williams, S. R., & Wilson, R. L. (1997). Group support systems, power and influence in an organization: A field study. *Decision Sciences, 28*(4), 911-937.

Yoo, Y., Ginzberg, M., & Ahn, J. H. (1999). A cross-cultural investigation of the use of knowledge management systems. *ACM Website*.

Zahir, S., Dobing, B., & Hunter, M. G. (2002). Cross-cultural dimensions of Internet portals. *Internet Research - Electronic Networking Applications and Policy, 12*(3), 210-220.

KEY TERMS AND DEFINITIONS

Confucian Dynamism: Also known as Long Term Orientation is a national culture dimension which describes the extent to which individuals within the culture focus on the short-term and immediate consequences versus take a long-term focus.

Individualism-Collectivism: A national culture dimension, which reflects the ties between individuals and groups.

IS Research Classifications: The IS Research Classifications is a classification system that defines all the different areas of IS research and was developed by Barki, Rivard and Talbot (1993).

Masculinity-Femininity: A national culture dimension, which was initially described as the extent to which sex roles were defined.

National Culture: National culture is the shared values and assumptions held by individuals within the nation.

Power Distance: A national culture dimension, which is the extent to which the less powerful members of institutions and organizations expect and accept that power is distributed unequally.

Uncertainty Avoidance: A national culture dimension, which is the extent to which the members of a culture feel threatened by uncertain or unknown situations, is the third dimension.

Chapter XXVII
What Use is Domestication Theory to Information Systems Research?

Deirdre Hynes
Manchester Metropolitan University, UK

Helen Richardson
University of Salford, UK

ABSTRACT

This chapter introduces and discusses domestication theory—essentially about giving technology a place in everyday life—and its relevance and importance to information systems (IS) research. The authors discuss domestication within the context of the social shaping of technology and critique use and adoption theories more widely found in IS studies. The authors illustrate how domestication theory underpins studies of how Irish households find ways of using computers (or not) in their everyday life and research into the use of ICTs in UK gendered households. In conclusion they outline how developments in domestication theory can contribute to future IS research.

INTRODUCTION

In this chapter we discuss domestication theory, its origin in the reference discipline of sociology and potential/undiscovered importance to Information Systems (IS) research. The relationship between technology and everyday life (and implicit in this construction is the prevalence of users) is a matter of increasing concern for many academics in a wide range of disciplines. Disciplines like IS may claim *ownership* for the study and treatment of the end-users of computer systems, for example terming the field *Human Factors of Computing* or *Human Computer Interaction.* Yet, although examining the interaction between people and the technological artefact and the systems running on it, little attention is often paid to the social constructs in which computer use actually takes place, and how if at all, this influences how computers are acquired, used and made sense of.

Domestication, essentially, is about giving technology a place in everyday life. The concept catches the practical, temporal, spatial place, but most importantly, it underlines how this is mixed with the cultural as an expression of lifestyles and values.

According to Haddon (2006), the very first outlines of the Domestication framework emerged in the early 1990s. Two major strands of domestication literature can be detected – the UK strand (for example Silverstone *et al.*, 1989, 1992, 1994) and the Norwegian strand (for example Sørenson *et al.* 1996). Silverstone and his collaborators focused their version of domestication within the household setting and on media technologies, while Sørenson and his collaborators widened their interest in domestication to contexts outside of the home and on other technologies, such as the car and 'smart-houses'.

In the IS field, it is crucial to understand domestication theory as IS research begins to engage with the concept of ubiquitous computing in everyday life beyond engineering or design issues and the organisational setting for system implementation. In this chapter we therefore aim to showcase significant studies that illustrate domestication theory as an approach and discuss research strategies in the method adopted. The majority of IS research focus on computer usage in settings other than the household (and indeed the construct of everyday life). Organisational, educational, institutional contexts are and have been prioritized over the household setting or the realm of everyday life. IS has not been solely guilty of this obvious neglect but so too the fields of media studies, audience studies, computer

studies and so on, that is until the 1990s with the emergence of the Domestication concept set within a social shaping of technology framework. It is first important to define and discuss this theoretical framework before we can fully appreciate the value of Domestication as a concept.

The chapter will proceed by placing the concept of Domestication in the context of the development of theory related to the social shaping of technology. Then we critically analyze other approaches to the study of adoption and use of technology more widely used in IS research. We explain how Domestication theory is an important alternative to our understanding of technology in everyday life and we illustrate our arguments with examples of how IS researchers have utilized Domestication theory in their research. Finally we draw conclusions and suggest the likely future developments of Domestication theory.

DOMESTICATION THEORY IN CONTEXT

In this section we focus on theories that underpin domestication of ICTs and that help to understand technologies in everyday life. These theories are discussed under the umbrella term – the social shaping of technology.

Social Shaping of Technology

Social research, studies of technological use and ways of thinking about technology have tended to focus on the effects of technology on society: its impact, its implications, and so on. A 'social shaping' or 'constructivist' approach to technology means to locate the technology as something social, or a product of social interaction. Wajcman (2004) explains that technology must be understood as part of the social fabric that holds society together; it is never merely technical or social. Rather, technology is always a socio-material product, 'a seamless web or network combining artefacts, people, organizations, cultural meanings and knowledge' (2004:106).

Studies emerged from more sociological-related disciplines examining the social context of use and agency of technology in everyday life. The social shaping perspective emerged during the mid-1980s through influential writings from MacKenzie and Wacjman (1985, 1999), Bijker *et al.* (1987) and Bijker (1995). This way of looking at technology in society crossed the boundaries of many disciplines including audience & media studies, cultural studies, anthropological treatments of objects in everyday life and so on. Cockburn and Ormrod (1993) for example discuss how in western culture, 'technology' is surrounded in mystique neglecting everyday meanings involved in the knowledge and practice of doing, making and producing. The common link between these studies is the rejection of technological imperatives on the emergence, use and transformatory effects of technology in society, namely techno-logical determinist accounts.

Technologically determinism suggests views of the world that assume that technology can 'fix' social problems (van Dijk 2005), are decisive 'agents' of social change yet are somehow 'aloof' from the social world despite having enormous social effects (Webster 2002). Technology then is viewed as autonomous, coercing and determining social and economic relationships. Technology is a complex term embracing the physical artefact (including how it is designed and configured); it forms part of a set of human activities and also incorporates what people know as well as what they do (MacKenzie and Wajcman 1985). Moreover history shows us that technologies do not emerge without active involvement of users who have to accept them as relevant and useful in their everyday lives (Silverstone 2005) and in these terms what technologies we have and how they are used are not inevitable. Domestication challenges a dominant viewpoint of the essentialist assumptions held about technologies and those that consume them.

This differs substantially from the dominant understanding of technology which perceives technology as distinct from social life, but with the ability to radically change our lives in a utopian or dystopian manner. This remains a powerful and prevalent way of thinking about technology. According to this determinist view, the potential for change lies in the invention of technology. This view of technology has until recently dominated academic research. Technology has been viewed as determining the development of social structures. A social shaping of technology (SST) perspective, in contrast, radically reverses the views advanced by technological determinism advocates, emphasising that technologies are embedded in the social (see Mackenzie & Wajcman 1985, 1999). SST studies have shown that technology does not develop to an inner technical logic, but is instead a social product, patterned by the conditions of its creation and use. SST theory seeks to grasp the complexity of socio-economic, cultural and political processes involved in technological innovation and use, and to move beyond narrow technical considerations. It is becoming increasingly common as a way of interpreting technology in IS research (Wilson and Howcroft 2005).

Within the SST approach, one particular theory addressing the relationship between technology and society is of interest here: Social Construction of Technology (SCOT), developed by Wiebe Bijker and Trevor Pinch (Bijker, 1995; Bijker *et al.*, 1987; Bijker & Kline, 1999). SCOT sought to open up the technological artifact to sociological analysis with respect to not just usage but also design and technical content (Wajcman 2000). This theory focuses on a very significant point namely 'interpretive flexibility'. This refers to the way in which different groups of people involved with a technology (different 'relevant social groups', in Bijker and Pinch's terminology) can have very different understandings of the technology, including different understandings of its technical characteristics (McKenzie & Wajcman, 1999:21).

Users can then radically alter the meanings and deployment of technologies (Wajcman 2000). The notion of relevant social groups makes SCOT very useful as a theory. Relevant social groups play a vital role in the development of a technological artefact and are defined as groups who share a meaning of the artefact. This meaning can then be used to explain particular developmental pathways. Typical groups might include engineers, advertisers, consumers, and so on. These groups are not static, and newly emergent groups can also be identified within SCOT. Although relevant social groups share a meaning of the artefact, for example, young boys viewing computers as games machines (Haddon, 1992), they may also share other group characteristics. However, interpretive flexibility does not continue forever. 'Closure' and 'stabilisation' occur, such that some artefacts appear to have fewer problems becoming embedded in society. These can become the dominant form of technology. The trend of technological determinist studies predominantly in the IS field led to utilisation of models that tended to be more technology-focused.

Modeling the Adoption and Use of ICTs

In this section we analyze deterministic models of ICT adoption and use. We particularly offer a critique of the Technology Acceptance Model (TAM) given its widespread take-up in IS research. Depending on the academic field, deterministic theoretical concepts range from linear accounts to more user focused adoption and use studies. The technology diffusion model for example, developed by Rogers (1995) focuses on profiles of users and expects the technology to diffuse as it is. This method typically uses the survey method to gain quantitative and statistical data. In this way, groups of people are packaged into easily managed categories. In Rogers' model from *Diffusion of Innovation* (1995) we have five distinct categorizations of users: 'innovators', 'early adopters',

'early majority', 'late majority' and 'laggards'. What is interesting here is that users appear to be privileged while non-users or informed rejecters are spoken about in terms of 'missing out on something' and lagging behind those who have followed the trend and 'accepted' the technology – a deficiency model of ICT adoption. We now explore this theme in relation to TAM.

Technology Acceptance Model

Davis (1989) developed a model to explain computer-usage behaviour. The Technology Acceptance Model (TAM) sought to explain the determinants of computer acceptance and to explain user behaviour across a broad range of end-user computing technologies. The model contains two key sets of constructs: (1) perceived usefulness (PU) and perceived ease of use (PEOU) and (2) user attitude. The basic hypothesis is that acceptance of a technology is determined by his or her voluntary intentions towards using the technology. Further, attitudes tend to relate to perceptions of its usefulness (Yousafzai et al 2007). TAM utilizes social cognition theories such as the 'Theory of Planned Behaviour' and the 'Theory of Reasoned Action'. Yet a useful critique of such social cognition models has been provided by Ogden (2003). She agrees that they are pragmatic tools but essentially flawed in their conceptual basis. The models focus on analytical 'truths' and may create or change conditions and behaviour rather than describe them.

Davis (1989) considered the strength of the belief-attitude-intention-behaviour relationship in order to predict actual behaviour and so PU is influenced by PEOU. PU was initially applied to organisational settings and how performance with new IS may be affected (Yousafzai et al 2007). Later the model was used outside the organisation in studies related to e-shopping and so on. Yousafzai et al (2007) have analyzed 145 TAM based studies in detail and compared conclusions and interpretations of data collected. They note that in the papers they analyzed, over 70 external variables have been considered alongside PU and PEOU.

TAM research generally draws on behavioural and social psychology literature and is mainly quantitatively based. Technology use and adoption can therefore mean that the whole process of technology adoption and usage is rooted in individual psychology 'obviating the need to consider the social structures within which individuals necessarily operate' (Adam et al 2004). In their meta-analysis for example, Yousafzai et al (2007) reveal that 41% of the TAM studies were conducted with a student group and over 19% were lab based.

One issue that is clear is that TAM is weakened by its lack of focus on how perceptions are formed or how they can be manipulated. The model was developed for organisational contexts and is constrained in its consideration of social and cultural factors and influences. Although from the TAM model, the MATH (Model of Adoption of Technology in Households) (for example see Venkatesh and Brown 2001) emerged, yet both have been criticized as being one-dimensional and limiting based on 'rationalistic causal models' (Cushman and Klecun 2005). The models are unhelpful in understanding what technologies and services mean to people and how they are experienced in everyday life (Haddon 2006), particularly void of analyzing household interactions, gender and other socially constructed relations. Green and Adam (1998) have noted how little is considered about the way in which ICTs impact on everyday life in the home and in particular they observe the gendered social relation of domesticity which surround the use of ICTs and the negotiation involved.

Technology acceptance is not necessarily a voluntary activity, choice may not enter the relationship and thus in an organisational setting, analysis of inequalities in power relations is needed. In particular Adam et al (2004) criticize the use of the TAM model in studies that comment on gender difference in use and attitudes (see for example Venkatesh and Morris's (2000) study of attitudes towards the employment of a new software system). They suggest such studies are problematic without reference to the widespread literature analysing gender and technology as cultural constructs and variables that should be theorized and considered. Further criticism is also of essentialism, with a strong tendency of 'making men's and women's character and behaviour seem, fixed and pre-determined, reproducing and reinforcing well-known stereotypes' (Adam et al 2004). Cushman and Klecun (2005) further critique the tendency of TAM to rely on supposed rational decisions made by agents with the notion of people as passive consumers. Individuals appear seemingly unchanged by adoption and use of technology rather than viewing the relationship as a social engagement.

Domestication Theory: An Alternative View

Domestication theory offers an alternative to these models and is essentially about giving technology a place in everyday life. The domestication concept enables researchers initially to understand media technology use in the complex structures of everyday life settings, with attention to interpersonal relationships, social background, changes and continuities, but also to the increasingly complex interconnection between different media, and the convergence of different media technologies and media texts.

Domestication traces the creation of meaning in media from its inception (when the producers and advertisers create certain meanings for new media) to its later use (or non-use) and the meanings that emerge. Thus, the emphasis is on consumption as well as use. Domestication, both as a metaphor and as an analytical concept, is used to find the crossover where technologies and people adjust to each other and find (or do not find) a way to co-exist. Central to the domestication process is the often unconscious attempt to make technologies fit into their surroundings in a way that makes them invisible or taken for granted. This requires mutual adjustment on behalf of both the users and the technology, and is where social shaping comes in to play. In essence, the person shapes the technology to fit into his or her life.

Haddon (2006) gives a useful overview of the use of domestication theory suggesting that it has been concerned with research into adoption and non-adoption of ICTs, time and space constraints (e.g. see Richardson 2004), symbolic dimensions of ICTs, the social consequences of ICTs and understanding trade-offs between what is gained and lost, social and cultural capital (Hynes, 2005; Hynes and Rommes 2006) and the social shaping of technology.

Hynes (2005) illustrates Silverstone *et al's* four aspects or 'non-discrete elements' used to describe and analyse this system where the 'moral economy' plays a central role: appropriation, objectification, incorporation and conversion. In the **appropriation** phase, possession and ownership are central. The acquisition of the technology is the main activity or concern. A technology gets appropriated as it is sold and then owned or possessed by a household. That is the point at which a commodity crosses the threshold between public and private, beginning its new life as a domestic object. **Objectification** tries to capture how values, tastes or styles are expressed through the display of the new technology. It involves both a spatial aspect (where it is placed in the house), and a temporal aspect (how it is fitted in the time structure). However, the spatial aspect is more central in this phase, '…physical artefacts, in their arrangement and display, as well as…in the creation of the environment for their display, provide an objectification of the values, the aesthetic and…cognitive universe, of those who feel comfortable or identify with them' (Silverstone et al., 1992:22–23). The **incorporation** phase emphasises how ICTs are used, and the temporal aspect is more central in the incorporation phase.

Silverstone et al. (1992) suggest that for an artefact to be incorporated it has to be actively used, such as in the performance of a task. The **conversion** phase is concerned with the relations between the households' internal affairs and the public domain or outside world.

Throughout, the users play a role in how the technology is adopted, not only into the household as a physical space, but also into the everyday routines of the household members and their perception of the technologies. The overall process is not a linear or closed one, 'domestication is practice, it involves human agency, it requires effort and culture and it leaves nothing as it is' (Silverstone 2005:231) Re-negotiations are common and assessments and uses can change over time. Roger Silverstone has spoken about the 'double and interdependent character of the meaningfulness of the mass media', arguing that we need to address, on the one hand, responses to particular texts or genres brought to us by the media and, on the other hand, the significance of media technologies themselves in our daily lives. He writes: 'There is meaning in the texts of both hardware and software' (1991:189). This plays an important role in the ways the technology is conceptualised. Sonia Livingstone (2007) and Maren Hartmann (2006) provide useful analyses of the concept of double and even triple articulation of media technologies.

At the time of its first formulation, the domestication concept within the media studies framework quite crucially shifted the emphasis away from a concentration on texts and reception, but instead focused on the practices of use. This was an important step in recognising and researching the embeddedness of media consumption in wider social practices, in everyday lives. The domestication concept also embraced the engagement with the whole media environment and not just one medium or even one text. Like other theories in media studies that emphasise the partial power of the audience in the interpretation of media content (for example, Ang, 1991; Morley, 1992, 2000), domestication adds a similar element of partial (and ambivalent) power to the user of technologies in general (and shifts the emphasis from the content to the technology). The theory thus adds perceptions concerning the artefact in question to the process of appropriation and use of technologies (including the idea that sometimes only parts of the technology are adopted or rejected, even after the acquisition).

Silverstone *et al.* (1992) stress how meanings of ICTs in formal and public life are actively transformed and translated through negotiations in the practices of everyday life in households. Domestication of technology may be defined as 'the family's capacity to incorporate and control technological artefacts into its own technological culture, to render them more or less 'invisible' within the daily routines of family life' (Silverstone et al., 1989:24).

As Silverstone and Hirsch (1992) have pointed out, the household is a complex social, economic and political space that powerfully affects both the way technologies are used and their significance. We know little about the economic or social context of the use of technologies in the home and how ICTs are appropriated and consumed in households, including the gender dimensions of this and the negotiation involved (Green 2001). Generally what findings there are suggest that gender politics and sexual division of labour impact strongly on the use of domestic technologies and the appropriation of electronic leisure (Green and Adam 1998). Indeed:

The new debates on household technologies have begun to engage not only with issues of power and economics, but also with the issues of moralities, choices and strategies within the nexus of family and personal relationships (Habib and Cornford 2002:338)

The key challenge is the attempt to conceptualise how ICTs are culturally transformed to fit in with the household's own understanding of itself.

The aspect of family culture that technologies are fitted into comprises what Silverstone et al. (1989) call the "moral economy" of the family. This concept is the starting point for a way of analysing how technologies become part of the household's value system. 'moral economy' refers more explicitly to:

... these families' own way of working with the social, economic and technological opportunities which frame their world, and which depend on, contribute to and sometimes compromise the ongoing structural forces for change which can be observed and analysed on a macro-sociological scale (Silverstone et al., 1989:1–2).

This implies that the uses and interpretations of media texts or technologies in domestic contexts will be negotiable – depending upon the material and discursive resources which are accessed by households and their members.

The acceptance, use and meaning of ICTs in the context of everyday life of households is central. The incorporation of ICTs into household activities and routines, and thus into the social organisation of the household, shapes and may change the everyday life of these households. At the same time, there is a clear impact of the technologies on households themselves; patterns of ICT acceptance, use and meaning construction are shaped by the way people have organised their everyday lives.

While the use of Domestication as an analytical and methodological concept is well suited to the domestic sphere and in particular in consideration of personal engagement with technologies, it has still yet to be tested on mass organisational levels or extended to groups. Domestication continues to be developed and applied to new contexts there is still more work to do to make it an attractive concept to broadly positivist analysts seeking to quantify on a mass scale the impact of the adoption of technologies.

METHODOLOGY AND APPROACHES TO DOMESTICATION RESEARCH

While the diffusion process is useful in the ways it explains how technologies are appropriated, the domestication process is more valuable in the ways it provides insights into the intricate processes whereby the user assigns meaning and significance to the artefact, and how this is experienced by domestic users during the acquisition and consumption of the technology. Meaning attribution is seen as a continuous process whereby such meanings can experience renegotiation, and even change altogether.

Methodologically studies have been mainly qualitative – unsurprising given the centrality of understanding the significance of ICTs to people as well as ambiguities and contradictions (Haddon 2006). Skepticism tends to be built into the domestication approach (Silverstone 2005) involving challenging industry assumptions and highlighting implications of decisions as well as presumptions of rationality and efficiency within discourses of 'consumer needs'. In IS research therefore Domestication theory tends to fit with the critical paradigm that aims to critique the status quo and expose deep-seated structural contradictions within social systems. It involves a critical stance against 'taken-for-granted' assumptions and a dialectical analysis to reveal the historical and ideological contradictions within social practices.

Although a neglected area of research, nevertheless there are indications that Domestication theory is being used by IS researchers. For example, Hynes (2005) found that Irish households engage in a complex justification process to rationalize the purchase of the computer (and internet). The main motivations were educational purposes (both adult and children), peer pressures and wider social pressures from official and commercial sources. Using Domestication as methodological and analytical tool, Hynes found

that users (and even non-users) design their own domestication process, no two experiences are the same bringing about an overall rejection of the 'one size fits all' adage so easily applied by technological determinist hyperbole. This study rejects the notion that computer users can be seen as a homogeneous group but instead many social, cultural, economic and political factors shape the use of and engagement with computer and internet technologies in everyday life.

Hynes and Rommes (2006) and Hynes (2003) found that public IT courses were an important factor that played a significant role in the domestication processes of users. It was found that the design of the courses served as a catalyst in the overall Domestication process when course-participants could easily translate the course curriculum and relate the material to their everyday lives. IT Courses therefore needed to address both the material and symbolic capital course participants brought with them to IT courses.

Hynes (2007) found that the application of the domestication model resulted in quite diverse negotiations of users' domestication experiences. In addition, the increased functionality of new media and computing technologies brought about renegotiations of those meanings that had been previously ascribed to them. This research showed that domestication is a fluid and dynamic process unlike competing adoption and use models which are rational, harmonious, liner and fixed. Furthermore, Hynes (2007) argued that domestication can be applied as an analytical model which produces rich, lived realities of the everyday experience of living with technologies.

Richardson (2006; 2005a; 2005b) has found that the approach has also been useful for feminist research, since it focuses attention on the under-researched domestic context. With a lens on the UK gendered household, she conducted a five-year longitudinal study of ICT use in households and family life detailing time and space constraints and gendered domestic leisure that impacted on motivational, material, skills and usage access.

Women maintain primary responsibility for the smooth running of the home and for the reproduction of domestic order and comfort. This means, among other things, that domestic leisure remains heavily gendered (Morley 2000). Green's (2001) studies of women's leisure continue to show time synchronization and time fragmentation dominating most women's lives leading them to find 'snatched' spaces for leisure and enjoyment. The research showed that a striking feature of everyday lives is how little leisure time people have or perceive themselves to have (Richardson 2006).

In these terms Richardson (2006) draws on an aspect of the social shaping of technology identified as underpinning Domestication theory, that of the co-construction of gender and technology in understanding use of ICTs in a domestic setting. In early gender and technology studies the core argument was that technology is a key source of men's power and a defining feature of masculinity (Wajcman 2004:6). Faulkner (2000) has summarized the gender and technology arguments to involve how technology is gendered because the 'key specialist actors' are men, that is those who design new technologies. There is also a strong gender division of labour based on a link being specified between the idea of masculinity and technical skill. Technical artifacts can also be seen as being gendered both materially and symbolically, though it is important to appreciate that there is considerable flexibility in use, so technology is shaped by users and as such often have usage not intended by the designers. Finally the cultural image of technology is strongly associated with hegemonic masculinity despite the mismatch between image and reality.

These issues were linked to analysis that did not take the family as a gendered institution for granted and further placed the research within the dominant discourse of the 'digital divide' which in the UK centered on engagement with ICTs in a 'meaningful way' as defined by government. This research challenged the technological determinism of corporate and governmental visions of

the future. It gave voice in particular to women's experiences in the home.

The research undertaken by Richardson (2006; 2005a; 2005b) showed that technologies and the gender structures which contribute to the shaping of women's work in the public sphere and 'consumption work' in the home are therefore mutually constitutive - neither is autonomous, immutable or determinate. Webster (1995) discusses how women come to perform tasks which carry an imprint of their socially constructed roles both within the family and workplace. Hynes (2005) adds another dimension in terms of how the routines and habits of everyday life are shaped by the use of technology and how in turn the technology is shaped by everyday life and indeed often the gender dimension is ignored here. So the concept of domestication is seen as expressing a process of shaping a technology to an acceptable form within the family (Hynes 2005). Domestication theory therefore helped understand the household as a site of consumption, reproduction of labour power and formation of gender relations.

In conclusion to how the domestication concept can be used effectively in IS research it provides a frame to contextualize studies and is a tool to understand the perspective and environment of empirical data. It does not take technology for granted and allows multiple interpretations for a more in-depth and rich understanding of technology use in everyday life.

CONCLUSION

This chapter has contributed to a neglected area of information systems research namely applying the concept of domestication to understand socio-economic change where it matters and is taken for granted 'in the intimate spaces of the home and household' (Silverstone 2005:231). In practice the era of ubiquitous computing involves much more than the spheres of design, development or end-user implementation. ICTs involve dynamic, mutually shaping relations and application of domestication theory means giving technology a place in everyday life.

We have placed Domestication theory in the context of the Social Shaping of Technology originating in the IS reference discipline of Sociology. We then offered a critique of other approaches to the use and adoption of technology more popular as a theoretical model for IS researchers. The TAM model for example is clearly growing in its use by Information Systems researchers. We provide evidence from Yousafzai et al (2007) for example, who provide a meta-analysis discussing 145 papers published on TAM. Systematic critiques of this model are rare (see Cushman & Klecun 2005 and Adam et al 2004 for exceptions). Yet we have argued that it is important to apply more than a deficiency model of ICT adoption for academic study to offer in-depth and consequential research to this important area. Application of TAM in IS research in our view has led to essentialist analysis of who does what and why with technology and a lack of analysis of power relations associated with technology usage.

Domestication research highlights a dominant viewpoint of the essentialist assumptions held about technologies and those that consume them. The future and what technologies we have and how they are used is not inevitable and critical interpretation means a shift in focus from what appears to be self-evident, natural and unproblematic on the one hand and what can be interpreted as the freezing of social life, irrational and changeable on the other (Alvesson and Skoldberg 2000). Moore (2003) describes the corporate versions that seek to produce corporate identities presenting a future that is ultimately knowable through expertise resting on the valued endpoint of competitive advantage. She continues to highlight the inexorable logic of future-orientated technological determinism.

Domestication theory is one of the only theoretical approaches that explores the complex processes of adoption and especially the use of technologies into and in everyday life. New developments suggest that the domestication framework considers interactions with wider networks outside the home and also is increasingly discussing 'professional domestication' for example through telework and home working (Pierson, 2006). This is important as the boundaries between home and work are increasingly blurred with the need to understand how ICTs fit into (or not) existing work patterns (Haddon 2006).

A recurrent theme among advocates of technological deterministic perspectives that imbibe notions of a culture of consumption is that consumers and users are 'passive dupes' and 'impotent, malleable consumers, unthinking and unprotesting in the face of media technology' (Heap et al 1995). Hynes (2005) also notes that study of consumption of ICTs is often a number-crunching exercise and 'quantitative discourse' pervades - in other words trying to profile a typical user buying a particular brand in a 'technology-driven strategy'. Bourdieu (1998) suggests that these analyses are a submission to the values of the economy where a return to individualism means not only blaming the victim for their own misfortune but also an attempt to destroy any notion of collective responsibility lest this may interfere with commercial interests. This represents an essentialist view of people, households and technologies and their use and the specific contexts, dynamics and dimensions of inclusion or exclusion thus remains under researched. We conclude that the household has such a central role in our lives that there is a great need to document, analyse and understand changes that are occurring in the ways in which people consume technologies in the domestic setting through their everyday lives (Hynes 2005). Not to do so is to give into the corporate version and vision of the future.

REFERENCES

Adam, A., Howcroft, D., & Richardson, H. (2004). A decade of neglect: Reflecting on gender and IS. *New Technology Work and Employment, 19*(3).

Alvesson, M., & Skölberg, K. (2000). *Reflexive Methodology*. London: SAGE.

Ang, I. (1991) Desperately seeking the audience. London; New York: Routledge.

Bijker, W. E., Hughes, T. P. and Pinch, T. (eds) (1987) *The Social Construction of Technological Systems*. Cambridge, MA: MIT Press

Bijker, W. E. (1995). *Of Bicycles, bakelites, and bulbs: Towards a theory of sociotechnical change*. Cambridge, MA: MIT Press.

Bourdieu, P. (1998). *Acts of resistance. Against the new myths of our time*. UK: Polity Press

Cockburn, C., & Ormrod, S. (1993). *Gender and technology in the making*. London: SAGE.

Cushman, M., & Klecun, E. (2005). *How (can) non-users perceive usefulness: Bringing in the digitally excluded* (Penceil Paper 7). London School of Economics.

Davis, F. D. (1989). Perceived usefulness, perceived ease of use, and user acceptance of information technology. *MIS Quarterly, 13*(3), 319-340.

Faulkner, W. (2000, June) the technology question in feminism. A view from feminist technology studies. In *Proceedings of the Women's Studies International Forum*.

Green, E. (2001). Technology, leisure and everyday practices. In E. Green & A. Adam (Eds.), *Virtual gender. Technology, consumption and identity matters*. New York: Routledge.

Green, E., & Adam, A. (1998). On-line leisure. Gender and ICT's in the home. *Information, Communication and Society, 1*(3), 291-312.

Habib, L., & Cornford, T. (2002). Computers in the home: Domestication and gender, *Information Technology & People, 15*(2). 159-174.

Haddon, L. (1992) Explaining ICT Consumption: The Case of the Home Computer, in Silverstone, R. and Hirsch, E. (eds.) Consuming Technolo-gies: Media and Information in Domestic Spaces, London Routledge.

Haddon, L. (2006). The contribution of domesti-cation research to in-home computing and media consumption. *The Information Society, 22*(4). 195-203.

Hartmann, M. (2006). The triple articulation of ICTs. Media as technological objects, symbolic environments and individual texts. In T. Berker, M. Hartmann, Y. Punie, & K. J. Ward (Eds.), *The domestication of media and technology* (pp. 80-102). Maidenhead, UK: Open University Press.

Heap, N. Thomas, R. Einion, G. Mason, R. Mackay, H (eds) (1995) Information Technology and Society: a reader London; Thousand Oaks, Calif: Sage Publications in association with the Open University.

Hynes, D. (2003). The role of computer courses in the domestication of the computer. In *Case study for the strategies of inclusion: Gender and the information society project (SIGIS)*.

Hynes, D. (2005). *Digital multimedia use & con-sumption in the household setting*. Unpublished doctoral dissertation, Dublin City University, Ireland.

Hynes, D. (2007). Applying domestication: How the Internet found its place in the home. In M. Khosrow-Pour (Ed.), *Managing worldwide operations and communications with informa-tion technology* (pp. 799-801). Hershey, PA: IGI Publishing.

Hynes, D., & Rommes, E. (2006). Fitting the In-ternet into our lives. In T. Berker, M. Hartmann, Y. Punie, & K. Ward (Eds.), *Domestication of media and technologies*. UK: Open University Press.

Livingstone, S. (2007). On the material and the symbolic: Silverstone's double articulation of research traditions in new media studies. *New media and society, 9*(1), 16-24.

MacKenzie, D., & Wajcman, J. (1985). *The social shaping of technology.* London: Open University Press.

Morley, D (1992) Television Audiences and Cultural Studies, London New York: Routledge

Morley, D. (2000), Home Territories (London; New York: Routledge).

Moore, K. (2003). *Versions of the future in relation to mobile communication technologies.* Unpublished doctoral dissertation, University of Surrey, UK.

Ogden, J. (2003). Some problems with social cognitions models: A pragmatic and conceptual analysis. *Health Psychology, 22*(4), 424-428.

Pierson, J. (2006). Domestication at work in small businesses. In T. Berker, M. Hartmann, Y. Punie, & K. Ward (Eds.), *Domestication of media and technologies.* UK: Open University Press.

Richardson, H. (2005a). Consuming passions in the global knowledge economy. In D. Howcroft & E. Trauth (Eds.), *Handbook of critical research in information systems* (pp. 272-299). Cheltenham, UK: Edward Elgar.

Richardson, H. (2005b, December 11-14). *Making the links: Domestication of ICT's in the global knowledge economy.* In D. Avison, D. Galletta, & J. I. DeGross (Eds.), *Proceedings of the 26ᵗʰ International Conference on Information Systems,* Las Vegas, Nevada.

Richardson, H. (2006, July). Space invaders: Time raiders: Gendered technologies in gendered UK households'. In J. Kendall, D. Howcroft, E. Trauth, T. Butler, B. Fitzgerald, & J. I. DeGross (Eds.), *Social inclusion: Societal and organisational implications for information systems.* Springer-Verlag.

Rogers, E. M. (1995). *Diffusion of innovations.* New York: The Free Press.

Silverstone, R. and Haddon, L. (1996), 'Design and the Domestication of Information and Communication Technologies: Technical Change and Everyday Life', in Communication by Design: the Politics of Information and Communication Technologies, (ed.) R. Silverstone and R. Mansell (Oxford: Oxford University Press).

Silverstone, R. (Ed.). (2005). *Media, technology and everyday life.* Aldershot, UK: Ashgate.

Silverstone, R., Hirsch, E. and Morley, D. (1992), 'Information and communication', in Information and Communication Technologies, pp.44-74 (Oxford: Oxford University Press).

Silverstone, R. and Hirsch, E. (eds.) (1992), Consuming Technologies: Media and Domestic Practices (London: Routledge).

Silverstone, R., Morley, D., Dahlberg, A. and Livingstone, S. (1989), 'Families, Technologies and Consumption: the household and information and communication technologies', CRICT discussion paper (Uxbridge, Middlesex: Centre for Research into Innovation, Culture and Technology).

Silverstone, R. (1994), Television and Everyday Life London: Routledge.

Van Dijk, J. (2005). *The deepening divide.* Thousand Oaks, CA: SAGE.

Venkatesh, V., & Brown, S. A. (2001). A longitudinal investigation of personal computers in homes: Adoption determinants and emerging challenges. *MIS Quarterly, 25*(1), 71-98.

Wajcman, J. (2000). Reflections on gender and technology studies. In what state is the art? *Social Studies of Science, 30*(3), 447-464.

Wacjman, J. (2004), Technofeminism Wiley-Blackwell. Webster, F. (2002). *Theories of the information society.* London: Routledge.

Wilson, M., & Howcroft, D. (2005). Power, politics and persuasion in IS evaluation: A focus on 'relevant social groups'. *Journal of Strategic Information Systems, 14,* 17-43.

Yousafzai, S. Y., Foxall, G. R., & Pallister, J. G. (2007). Technology acceptance: A meta-analysis of the TAM: Part 1. *Journal of Modeling in Management, 2*(3), 251-280.

KEY TERMS AND DEFINITIONS

Domestication Theory: A theory developed by Silverstone et al (1994) to interpret how technologies become part of everyday life.

Feminist Research: Field of research examining women's political, cultural, social and economic experiences

Gender: Social construction of identity and roles based on normative values

Social Shaping of Technology: This approach argues that the emergence and development of technology is a social process and people and their social arrangements are the crucial factors in promoting change. This approach argues against intrinsic characteristics inherent in technologies determining their effect and use.

TAM: The Technology Acceptance Model seeks to explain the determinants of computer acceptance and user behaviour across a broad range of end-user computing technologies. The model contains two key sets of constructs: (1) perceived usefulness (PU) and perceived ease of use (PEOU) and (2) user attitude. The basic hypothesis is that acceptance of a technology is determined by his or her voluntary intentions towards using the technology.

Technological Determinism: This approach places technology as the pivotal factor in bringing about social change. Technologies are seen as autonomous inventions that have direct effects on social life.

Section VII
Psychological and Behavioral Theories

The final section on psychological and behavioral theories includes four chapters. The first chapter (Chapter XXVIII) outlines personal construct theory as a psychological theory and discusses current applications of methodologies based in the theory. It also explores the positioning of the theory within a broader taxonomy of IS theory. The next chapter (Chapter XXIX) presents coping theory, its underlying assumptions and inherent components, discusses its application, highlights the complementarities with existing models and theories currently used in IS research, and provides several areas for future research. Chapter XXX uses and tests vocational theory and personality traits of information technology professionals. Finally, Chapter XXXI describes and illustrates the use of the theory of planned behavior and the theory of reasoned action for predicting technology adoption behavior.

Chapter XXVIII
Personal Construct Theory

Peter Caputi
University of Wollongong, Australia

M. Gordon Hunter
University of Lethbridge, Canada

Felix B. Tan
Auckland University of Technology, New Zealand

ABSTRACT

The development of any discipline is related to the strength of its underpinning theoretical base. Well-established disciplines have a diversity of clearly stated and competing theoretical frameworks to describe and explain theoretical constructs. Information systems (IS) is a relatively new discipline; many well-known IS theories (such as the technology acceptance model, theory of reasoned action and theory of planned behaviour) are borrowed from disciplines such as economics and psychology. This chapter outlines personal construct psychology, a psychological theory. Current applications of methodologies based in personal construct theory are discussed, and the positioning of the theory within a broader taxonomy of IS theory is explored.

INTRODUCTION

It is interesting that despite the volume of research in computer-based information systems, there is no commonly agreed definition of what is an information system (IS) (Paul, 2007). However, a number of common elements emerge from these definitions. Computer-based IS are associated with information technologies, involving software and hardware components. These systems are then used by people. They use IS in particular ways and follow established rules of usage (what Paul [2007] would call formal processes), and quite often adapt or modify formal procedures in order to ensure that tasks are completed (or informal processes [Paul, 2007]). In other words, when trying to understand what one means by IS, one needs to consider the interactivity of users, the technologies and the usage processes (Paul, 2007).

A good theory not only describes the phenomena of interest, it also explains why those phenomena occur. Explanation and prediction are, therefore, key defining features of a theory. It follows that (good) theories or models of computer-based IS should describe and explain relevant phenomena associated with the IS. Moreover, if the interactivity of user, technologies and process is a defining characteristic of an IS, then this interaction needs to be considered in any theory or model of IS. The user (the person), then, is a stakeholder in theories of IS. The role of 'user' and usage behaviour is important in IS theory.

Good theory should also have practical application. As Burr and Butt (1992) point out, "A good theory is a useful theory" (p.v). Good theory informs practice and in turn is informed by practice. This point is particularly relevant to the IS discipline. The development and application of IS theory should happen in tandem with, and not separately from IS practice (Mathias, Caputi & Vella, 2008).

A perusal of the prominent models of IS adoption and usage reveals the important role of psychological or behavioural variables. Concepts such as perceived playfulness (Moon & Kim, 2001; Chung & Tan, 2004) have been discussed in the IS literature. In addition, the motivation (both extrinsic and intrinsic) to use IS has also been examined in the literature (e.g., Davis, Bagozzi & Warshaw, 1992; Lee, Cheung & Chen, 2003). Behavioural intention models of usage such the Technology Acceptance Model (Davis, 1993) posits that an individual is more likely to express an intention to use technology if that technology is perceived to be useful and easy to use. Perceived usefulness and ease of use are individualised experiences; they reflect the views of an individual and how the individual will eventually behave.

Furthermore, theories such as the Theory of Planned Behaviour (Ajzen, 1991) attempt to account for social influence by including variables that capture social influences to comply or behave in a certain way. In other words, these theories are social- psychological in nature.

The influence of psychological concepts is evident in models of IS usage. A psychological theory that has received little attention in the IS domain is George Kelly's (1955/1991) Personal Construct Theory. Ironically, methods such as the repertory grid, an assessment tool developed by Kelly (1955/1991), have been used extensively in IS research (see Tan & Hunter, 2002), but independent from the theory. The objective of this chapter is to explore and articulate how Personal Construct Theory can be applied to Information Systems research. This objective will be addressed in the following sections of this chapter. The next section discusses Psychological theories that have been applied in information systems research. Then an overview is presented regarding Personal Construct Theory. The following section includes a review of methods employed with the purview of Personal Construct Theory. Then issues surrounding the use of Personal Construct Theory to conduct research into information systems are discussed. Finally, examples are presented about the use of Personal Construct Theory in practice.

"PSYCHOLOGICAL" THEORIES IN IS RESEARCH

The number of models and theories in the IS literature is voluminous. The "Theories in IS research Wiki" maintained at the University of York by Scott Schneberger and Mike Wade (http://www.fsc.yorku.ca/york/istheory/wiki/index.php/Main_Page) illustrates this point with well over 70 theories listed. In this section we limit our discussion to theories of IS adoption and usage. Table 1 presents a summary of some models and

Table 1. Some psychological/behavioural theories to consider

Theory	Examples	Key variables/constructs
Cognitive dissonance theory/ Expectancy confirmation theory	Bhattacherjee (2001). Staples, Wong & Seddon (2002).	Expectations, confirmation
Adaptive structuration theory	Orlikowski (2000)	Users, work practices, work structures.
Contingency theory	Teo & Pian (2003)	Technology compatibility, adoption, business strategy, management support.
Diffusion of innovations	Agarwal & Prasad (1997)	Innovation characteristics including compatibility, result demonstrability, image, relative advantage; current and future use.
Social Cognitive theory	Compeau, Higgins & Huff (1999)	Self-efficacy, outcome expectations, usage
Technology Acceptance Model	Davis (1989)	Perceived ease of use, perceived usefulness, behavioural intention
Theory of Planned Behavior	Mathieson (1991)	Attitude, perceived behavioural control, subjective norms, intention.
Theory of Reasoned Action	Davis, Bagozzi & Warshaw (1989)	Attitude, subjective norms, intention.
Unified Theory of Acceptance and Use of Technology	Venkatesh et al (2003).	Performance expectancy, effort expectancy, social influence, facilitating conditions, experience.

(source: www.fsc.yorku.ca/york/istheory/wiki/index.php/Main_Page)

theories used in IS adoption and usage research based on the list generated by Schneberger and Wade (http://www.fsc.yorku.ca/york/istheory/wiki/index.php/Main_Page). A subset of these theories have generated three important streams of research output in the IS literature, namely, models focused on behavioural intention, socio-cognitive theories and research influenced by Diffusion of Innovation theory (Kufafka, Johnson, Linfante & Allegrante, 2003). The discussion that follows is not intended to be comprehensive or detailed; rather the intention is to highlight the "psychology" implicit in such theories. Before presenting a brief discussion of these models it may be useful to digress and consider the distinction between theory and model.

In many disciplines, including IS, the terms model and theory are sometimes used interchangeably. However, having the terms refer to similar things is problematic (Valentine, 1982). Theories are abstract; theories explain phenomena and enable predictions to be made. Models are narrower in scope; they are analogies or representations that assist in describing and conveying the central principles or ideas of a theory. Importantly, models are not theories (Valentine, 1982). Models assist in explaining a theory; they do not replace theory (Valentine, 1982).

Behavioural Intention Models

A subset of the models listed in Table 1 can be classified as behavioural intention models. These models focus on behavioural intention as an important predictor of technology usage (Kufafka, et al., 2003). The Theory of Reasoned Action (TRA), the Theory of Planned Behaviour (TPB), the Technology Acceptance Model (TAM), and the Unified Theory of Acceptance and Use of Technology (UTAUT) are included in this stream of research. Put simply, these models explain why people behave the way they do in relation to usage they do when engaging with an IS. Each model specifies theoretical variables or factors that predict the determinants of that behaviour. Some factors are theorised to influence behaviour directly; other factors influence behaviour via mediating variables. Venkatesh et al. (2003) summarised the conceptual framework of intention-based models as follows: Intention to use and actual usage are impacted by people's reaction to using technology; intention to use influences behaviour; however, actual usage, in turn, influences how people will react to technology in the future. Researchers such as Riemenschneider, Harrison and Mykytyn (2003) point out that the TAM and the TRA, and TPB that preceded the TRA, are well established intention models grounded in a large body of research (Rawstorne, 2005).

Certain implicit assumptions underlie the behavioural intention models. Rawstorne (2005) highlights that rationality and rational decision making are important meta-theoretical assumptions that underpin these models. Further, these assumptions are also able to explain social behaviour (that is, how the opinions and views of others may influence individual actions). This chapter is not intended to argue whether these assumptions are valid. Rather, Rawstorne's (2005) observations highlight the important role of the individual in these theories. Moreover, implicit in these assumptions is the notion that, within the context of IS adoption/acceptance and usage, the individual actively engages in processes related to acceptance and usage.

The Technology Acceptance Model (TAM: Davis, 1989) is seen by many researchers (e.g., Karahanna et al., 2002, Gefen et al., 2003) to be the most widely used theoretical framework for investigating technology acceptance and usage (Rawstorne, 2005). The TAM originally proposed by Davis (1986) posits that behaviour (such as IS usage) was directly influenced by attitude toward the behaviour (usage). In turn, attitude toward the behaviour was influenced by about the extent to which the IS is perceived to be useful and easy to use. Davis (1989) revised his original model by dropping attitude as a mediating variable and replacing it with behaviour intention, although there are variants of the TAM that include both attitudes and intentions as explanatory variables.

Conceptually, the TAM is derived from Fishbein and Ajzen's (1975) TRA and Ajzen's (1985, 1991) TPB. The TRA posits that behavioural intention is determined by attitudes towards a specific behaviour and the endorsement by others of the behaviour (or social norms). Thus, the determinants of intention are both personal (attitude) and social (social norms) in nature (Ajzen & Fishbein, 1980). In turn, attitudes towards behaviour are influenced by an interaction of behavioural beliefs and outcome evaluations, while the social influence component of the model reflects the interaction of normative beliefs and the degree of motivation to comply (Rawstorne, 2005).

Ajzen (1985, 1991) expanded the TRA to include the variable Perceived Behavioural Control (PBC) as a way of accounting for behaviours that are non-volitional. Both behaviour intention and behaviour are directly influenced by PBC. The resultant model is known as the Theory of Planned Behaviour. Perceived behavioural control refers to an individual's perception of how much control he or she has when completing a task or behaving in a certain way. This perception may be influenced by external factors relating to control such as availability and quality of training, or internal or person-oriented factors such as beliefs in one's abilities to perform a task (Taylor & Todd, 1995). The latter influence is closely related to the construct of self efficacy, which is discussed in section 2.2.

Socio-Cognitive Models

One can argue that the TRA, TPB, and the TAM and its derivatives and elaborations are cognitive or socio-cognitive in nature (Rawstorne, 2005). However, other theories also fall under this classification. Information systems research has drawn on elements of Social Learning Theory (Bandura, 1977), notably, the theoretical constructs of self-efficacy and reciprocal determinism (Kukafka et al., 2003). In the context of IS usage, self efficacy refers to beliefs about one's ability to perform tasks associated with the IS or IT, and is seen as an antecedent to use (Compeau, Higgins & Huff, 1999).

Reciprocal determinism is also an important construct in Bandura's (1977) social learning theory. Bandura (1977) maintained that people's actions could be explained by considering the interaction between the action that person makes, the cognitions that are associated with that actions, and the context or environment in which that action is made. This reciprocal and dynamic interaction can also be used to explain learning, and in the context of IS, how beliefs about IS influence behaviour. Despite widespread use of social learning theory, it has not generated the same amount of research interest as models such as the TAM (Rawstorne, 2005).

Diffusion of Innovations

Rogers' (1995) Diffusion of Innovation Theory has initiated another stream of research that has proven fruitful in understanding IS adoption and usage. Diffusion based models describe and explain how innovations spread within organisations and the community at large (Rogers, 1995).

An important premise of these models is that the uptake and use of technologies is influenced by individuals, the communities or social groups that individuals are part of, and characteristics of the technology itself (Rawstorne, 2005). In terms of individual characteristics, diffusion of innovation theory posits that individuals adopt innovations at different rates, with Rogers identifying five types of adopters, innovators, early adopters, early majority, late majority and laggards. In addition to the characteristics of the adopters, diffusion models also consider the characteristics of the technologies or innovations. Variables such as relative advantage, comparability, complexity, trialability and observability are salient in diffusion models. The general observation is that increasing complexity of a technology is associated with negative perceptions /attitudes, which in turn influences adoption rate. On the other hand, positive perceptions of relative advantage, comparability, trialability and observability have a positive influence on uptake (Rawstorne, 2005).

Unifying Theory

Venkatesh et al (2003) proposed a unified view after reviewing all the models used in the field of user acceptance research. This model is known as the Unified Theory of Acceptance and Use of Technology (UTAUT) model; it represents "a definitive model that synthesizes what is known and provides a foundation to guide future research in this area" (Venkatesh et al., 2003, p. 425). Within this model, three factors (performance expectancy, effort expectancy, social influence) are deemed to be direct determinants of intention to use; while IS usage is determined by intention to use and facilitating conditions. The relationship between predictor variables and outcomes is mediated by demographic factors (sex and age of user), experience with the IS or technology and the extent to which usage is deemed to be voluntary.

Performance expectancy refers to "the degree to which an individual believes that using the system will help him or her to attain gains in job performance" (Venkatesh et al., 2003, p.447). This construct is comprised of five variables, perceived usefulness, job fit, extrinsic motivation, outcome expectation and relative advantage. Effort expectancy is the degree to which the system is easy to use. Therefore, variables such as complexity and ease of use are associated with this construct. Social influence, as the name suggests, refers to the strength of beliefs users holds that salient others want them to use a particular technology. Social norms, therefore, would be associated with social influence. The construct, facilitating conditions, refers to the extent to which users believe there are support systems in place (at say an organisational level) to assist in using the technology. Variables such as perceived behavioural control would be a component of this construct (Ventatesh et al., 2003).

OVERVIEW OF PERSONAL CONSTRUCT THEORY

Personal Construct Theory focuses on how individuals make sense of the experiences, events, and people in their world. George Kelly presented the theory in 1955 in two volumes titled *The Psychology of Personal Constructs*. He was a clinical psychologist and, in many ways, the two volumes acted as a practitioner manual for his students. But these works represented far more. Kelly presented a unique and original theory of human behaviour. Many (e.g., Bruner, 1956) have tried to classify Personal Construct Theory as a personality or cognitive theory. Kelly, himself, argued against the latter (Walker & Winter, 2007). In essence, Personal Construct Theory is a psychological theory that explains how people engage with the world they inhabit. Kelly uses the metaphor of person-as-scientist (a naïve scientist at that) to explicate how a person makes sense

of his or her environment and experiences. But for Kelly, the site of decision making is not just within the individual; Personal Construct Theory also includes a social psychology. People engage with their environment, with other people. They come to understand and make predictions about their world on the basis of this (social) interaction with others (Walker, 1996).

The first volume of *The Theory of Personal Constructs* presents Kelly's ideas quite formally. The theory is structured so that there is a fundamental postulate and 11 supporting colloraries (see Appendix 1, section 8). However, the foundation stone of Kelly's ideas is the concept of constructive alternativism, which asserts that "all of our present interpretations of the universe are subject to revision or replacement" (Kelly, 1955, p.15). In other words, our current view of things is open to revision; we can always look at things differently. This idea is not new; Kelly acknowledges the influence of Vaihinger's (1924) concept of "*as if*" in his work, the view that it is possible to interpret (or indeed re-interpret) an event *as if* it were correct. This position is consistent with the metaphor of person-as-scientist. Although the notion of *as if* is one of make-believe, it is nonetheless also about experimentation and hypothesis (Warren, 1998, p.47). Moreover, it is this invitational mood, as Kelly also refers to it, that is conducive for experimentation and 'doing science' in one's everyday life.

Central to Kelly's theory is the process of *construing*. We make sense of the world and our experiences by engaging in a process of discriminating and differentiating between objects, things and people that "make up" our world. A feature of these discriminations is that they are bipolar in nature. If I say I *dislike* aspects of mobile telephony, I can only do so by being aware of aspects that I *like*. The dichotomous construct *dislike-like* allows me to makes sense of my interaction with mobile phones, why and how I use them. It should be noted that poles of constructs are not necessarily logical opposites. For instance, the construct *dislike-accept* could equally apply in the previous example.

In addition, Kelly posited that construing is anticipatory. We anticipate events by "construing their replications". The process of construing allows us to provide meaning to repeated themes or observations in our world. An obvious process that repeats is day and night, it's a cyclic process. The emergence and presence of the sun is known as 'day', while the absence of the sun and the emergence of the moon is known as 'night' (Kelly, 1955/1991). Moreover, most of our activities are influenced by this cyclical, repetitive process. We work and go to school through the day, while we usually sleep and rest at night.

Our lives are filled with varied experiences. It follows that we would have a network of constructs in order to deal with these experiences. This network or system of construing allows us to "describe the process of actively developing a personal world" (Scheer & Sewell, 2006, p.8). The metaphor of a network is chosen deliberately in this explication of Kelly's theory. A network conjures up a vision of interconnectedness or interrelatedness. Moreover, Kelly posited that constructs are organised hierarchically. Some constructs (referred to as superordinate) are abstract in nature and can be applied more widely, while others (known as subordinate) more concrete and represent a specific application (Walker & Winter, 2007, p.454). In other words, superordinate constructs are applicable to a wider range of experiences than subordinate constructs (Walker & Winter, 2007, p.456). The hierarchical nature of construing can also be understood in terms of implications among constructs; some constructs imply other constructs; some constructs are implied by others. Hinkle (1965) redefined the relationship among constructs in terms of implications. Consequently, superordinate constructs have a greater number of implicative relations than do subordinate constructs. Those constructs with a greater network of implications are therefore more meaningful (Walker & Winter, 2007, p.456).

Construing is an individual process. Kelly (1955, p.55) argued that "Persons differ from each other in their construction of events". For example, two friends may view the same movie and leave the cinema with quite differing interpretations of the film. Similarly, the same email system may be viewed as "wonderful" by some users, and yet, loathed by others. Personal Construct Theory provides a way of understanding these differences. The differences in email user perceptions and attitudes, and ultimately how they behave, can be explained in terms of the different ways these users view the situation; the different ways in which they construe aspects of the email system.

However, groups of people may also share common perspectives on experiences. This degree of similarity in thinking is addressed by Kelly's (1955) Commonality Corollary which states that "To the extent that one person employs a construction of experience which is similar to that employed by another, his [sic] psychological processes are similar to those of the other person" (p.90). Consequently, the apparent streamlined adoption of a safety reporting information system in a manufacturing company may be attributed to the shared attitudes users have toward safety issues in general. Within a Personal Construct framework, these shared attitudes on safety can be understood in terms of similar constructions of experiences held by the users, and this shared construing results in the users behaving in a similar way, that is, successfully adopting a safety reporting information system. However, commonality of construing is only a necessary condition for behaving in a similar way. Individuals may have similar constructs but use or apply those constructs in different ways. A middle manger in an organisation may make sense of IS using the construct *efficient-inefficient*. A fellow manager may have an identical construct, but the range and scope of experiences that the construct has been applied to may vary markedly between managers. The process of construing then is also defined by (i) the range and scope of experiences that the construct is applied to (what Kelly referred to as range of convenience), and (ii) the context within which the construct is applied.

Commonality of construing is one aspect of what can be considered as the social psychology that is embedded in Personal Construct Theory. Kelly's theorising acknowledges that construing does not occur in isolation. We interact with our environment, our world and people who are part of our realm of existence. We are social beings. Personal Construct Theory captures this sociality. Kelly (1955) proposed that "to the extent that one person construes the construction processes of another he [sic] may play a role in a social process involving the other person". Within this framework, social interactions are explained in terms of construing, specifically a person trying to construe the constructions of another person. This process does not just involve an attempt at replicating someone's constructions. Rather, it also involves the construing (interpreting, making sense of) of that person's construct systems (Fransella & Bannister, 1977, p.8). The process of construing is a social act. It involves a person interacting and trying to understand his or her environment or what Walker (1996) refers to as person-in-relation. The act of construing the construct system of another is a social action and the basis of relationships.

Personal Construct Theory lends itself to understanding why some people embrace change and others resist it. The question of how constructs develop is also related to understanding change. The elements or structures that facilitate or hinder change are present in the definition of a construct. The bipolar construing process is one of discrimination and differentiation that allows one to make sense of experiences, such that a person discriminates between things that are similar and different from others. Constructs then reflect contrasts and comparisons. Walker and Winter (2007, p.454) point out that "Contrasts are central to an understanding of change in that

the contrast (or opposite pole) to the current way of seeing the world is the most readily available alternative, and changed behavior will reflect this, at least initially".

Hinkle's (1965) Theory of Implications also provides an explanation of change and the possibility for change. Each construct has both superordinate and subordinate implications; there are constructs (specifically poles of constructs) that are implied by other construct poles, and conversely there are construct poles that imply other construct poles. We noted earlier that the range of implications of a construct can be used as a measure of the extent to which that construct is meaningful. "Constructs functioning at a higher level of superordination in a hierarchical context will show a greater relative resistance to slot change than constructs functioning at a low level" (Hinkle, 1965, p.29). Put simply, the more meaningful a construct (in terms of range of implications), the more likely that construct is to be resistant to change.

How constructs change can also be understood in terms of various cycles of experience and action. One such cycle is Kelly's (1955) Validation Cycle. He posited that "validation represents the compatibility (subjectively construed) between one's prediction and the outcome he observes" (p. 158). If the prediction is disconfirmed by observation then invalidation eventuates. Constructs can develop and change through a process of predicting or anticipating what could happen, testing that prediction against the "real world" and then revising one's construing on the basis of the outcome of testing. This, Kelly argued, is how we make sense of our world. We propose or predict, we test these propositions and see whether there is evidence (in the world) for supporting or refuting the prediction. Implicit in this notion is the metaphor of person-as-scientist. Kelly argued that psychological functioning can be best understood using this metaphor. The person is not an effective scientist; rather "his proposal is more about a person as an incipient (potential) scientist"

(Walker, Oades, Caputi, Stevens & Crittenden, 2000, p.102). In other words, we don't always get it right; we make mistakes and our endeavours may not also be 'good science'.

The Validation Cycle is one of several processes that Kelly identified as offering an explanation of how and why people change their construing. Kelly also argued that a person's meaning-making can also develop through a process of successive loose and tight construing. Loose construing allows the person to come with new ideas by allowing elements (the objects, events, people etc that are construed to) to shift from construct pole to construct pole (Winter, 1992). These new ideas or predictions can then be tested, but in order to do so the person needs to tighten construing by fixing the allocation of elements (Winter, 1992).

How and why we behave can be best appreciated by what Kelly (1955) referred to as the Experience Cycle. When faced with any event, we go through a process of anticipating an outcome, engaging in that anticipation, experiencing that event and acting, evaluating the outcome (was the prediction supported or refuted?), and finally re-evaluating or revising the predictions (one's construing) in order to make sense of it all! Caputi and Warren (2007) argued that the Experience cycle may be useful to understand the process whereby an IS user might exhibit resistant behaviour and/or how decisions to accept or reject IS are made.

REVIEW OF PERSONAL CONSTRUCT THEORY-BASED METHODS

Personal Construct Theory is based on the premise that people construe their world. But how can the process of construing be assessed? In response to this question, Kelly's theory has spawned a variety of assessment tools. The repertory grid is one of many techniques used for assessing the content and structure of personal construct systems. Walker and Winter (2007) distinguish between grid and non-grid based techniques. This review is structured using this distinction.

Known originally as the role construct repertory test, Kelly's repertory grid technique is widely used in Personal Construct research. Neimeyer, Baker and Neimeyer (1990) reported that over 90% of research in Personal Construct Theory is repertory grid based. The repertory grid has also been applied to diverse research settings such as clinical psychology, tourism and information systems (Walker & Winter, 2007).

In spite of the range of application of grid-based methods, Bell (1988) reminds us, quite correctly, that the repertory grid technique is theory-based and not independent of Personal Construct Theory. Bell (2003) points out that Kelly's (1955) Fundamental Postulate underpins the repertory grid. The Postulate states "a person's processes are psychologically channelized by the ways in which he anticipates events". "The *ways* are the constructs of a repertory grid, and the *events* are the elements" (Bell, 2003, p.95). The literature on repertory grid use is vast, and a detailed treatment of repertory grids is beyond the scope of this chapter. For more detailed accounts of repertory grids, methods of analysis of grid data and issues relating to their application, the reader is directed to texts such as Fransella, Bell, and Bannister (2004) and Jankowicz (2003).

What then is a repertory grid? Put simply, a repertory grid is a matrix of elements, constructs and a relation that defines how constructs discriminate among the elements. Recall that elements are objects, events, people, things defined within a particular context. Imagine you are interested in why people prefer certain Websites for online shopping. A person who shops online may identify three sites they use regularly and three sites they use infrequently. The six sites identified are the elements. We may also ask this person to consider any three sites, and consider how two sites are similar yet different from the third. This is known as the triadic elicitation process. If he states that the two similar sites are reliable while the third is unreliable, our respondent has identified a bipolar construct *reliable-erratic*. The task can be repeated with three other Websites, this time identifying a second construct, say *easy to use-complicated*. These bipolar constructs are ways of discriminating the online shopping Websites. Within the context of our questioning, these constructs represent how our respondent makes sense of online shopping, and why (s)he prefers to return to some and not others.

Let us examine how the constructs *reliable-erratic* and *easy to use-complicated* are applied in the online shopping example. We can ask the respondent to consider each Website in turn and, using a rating scale of say 1 to 7 where 1 is most like the left hand pole of the each construct and 7 is like the right hand side of each construct, rate each Website on the constructs *reliable-erratic* and *easy to use-complicated*. A rating of an element on a construct defines the *relation* between that element and construct. This task results in a matrix of element-construct ratings - a repertory grid. The repertory grid captures (within a context – online shopping in the previous example) how (the constructs – e.g., *reliable-erratic*) the individual is making sense of events (the elements – the particular Websites). A unique and distinguishing feature of the repertory grid as an assessment tool is that it provides both qualitative and quantitative data (Bell, 2003). The constructs and elements can be interpreted qualitatively, while data such as ratings of elements along construct dimensions lend themselves to quantitative investigation (Bell, 2003, p.96).

Walker and Winter (2007) refer to repertory grids as *construct-element grids*, but they also identify two additional classes of grids. With a repertory grid, the axes of the grid refer to elements and constructs. A variation of this basic structure is that have constructs define the grid axes, resulting in a *construct-construct grid*; alternatively, the axes of the grid can be formed by elements, resulting in an *element-element grid* (Walker & Winter, 2007). Hinkle's implication grid typifies

construct-construct grids. There are procedural variations of implication grids (see Fransella, 1972), however, essentially, an individual is asked to consider whether poles of constructs imply other construct poles. Alternatively, if a person was to change from one pole to another pole of a construct, would this result in a change in other constructs in the grid? The implication grid is also grounded in theory in that it captures the central feature of Kelly's (1955) Organisation Corollary which states that constructs are hierarchically related.

Kelly's (1955) situational resources grid (also known as the dependency grid) is an example of an element-element grid. This grid involves asking an individual to consider a list of resources, say people, and identify to whom they might go to for help in various situations. It provides a mapping of how dependencies are dispersed across the situations (Walker, Ramsey, & Bell, 1988).

A number of non-grid based methods have also been developed from Personal Construct Theory. For the purposes of this review, we will discuss the more commonly used non-grid based techniques, namely, laddering and pyramiding, self-characterisation, and content analysis of text. Kelly (19955/1991) argued constructs do not sit in isolation but are related hierarchically to each other. Laddering is an interviewer-based approach that can be used to explore the hierarchical nature of systems of constructs. It is used to elicit constructs that are increasingly more abstract and superordinate in nature (Hinkle, 1965; Fransella, 2003). The interviewer begins by eliciting a construct and asking the respondent to identify the pole of that construct that he or she prefers. The respondent is then asked why he or she prefers that pole. The response to this question results in eliciting a new construct pole. The respondent is asked to identify the contrast pole of the new construct pole. The process and steps outlined are repeated until the respondent can not elicit any additional constructs (Fransella, 2003). The laddering technique is based on the assumption that a series of 'why' questions will elicit super-ordinate constructs (Fransella, 2003).

The technique known as pyramiding (Landfield, 1971) is assumed to elicit more concrete, subordinate constructs using 'how' and 'what' questions. For example, a person may be asked to think of a trainer who has recently provided training for the implementation of a new IS system. A user may identify that the trainer is a 'good trainer'. We may ask "How would you describe someone who is not a 'good trainer'?" "Someone who is a 'poor trainer'". "What sort of person is a 'good trainer'?" "Someone who is organised". "What sort of person is a 'poor trainer'?" "Someone who is disorganised". (This example is adapted from one provide by Fransella, 2003, p.118). This line of questioning then continues until construct elicitation is exhausted or the respondent prefers to stop.

One of the more inventive and creative qualitative assessment tools developed by Kelly (1955) is the self-characterisation sketch. This technique involves asking an individual to write a character sketch about her or himself, as if they were a character in a play. However, the individual writes the sketch in the third person from the perspective of a friend or someone who knows her or him very well and sympathetically. The resulting script can then be analysed to identify emergent construct poles. Self-characterisations are based on an important premise in Personal Construct Theory. If we are to understand why a person behaves in a particular way we need to suspend our own belief systems and preconceptions of how we might interpret his or her actions. Kelly argued that you want to find out something about a person, why not ask them! In doing so, however, you need to be open and accepting of what the individual tells you. You need to adopt what Kelly referred to as the 'credulous attitude or approach'.

The self-characterisation sketch generates textual information. There are numerous approaches to analysing text with a Personal Construct Theory framework. Content analysis scales have been applied to text generated from interview questions such as "I would like you to think of X. Tell me the good things and the bad things about X" (Viney & Caputi, 2005). In addition, various methods for categorising constructs by themes have been developed (Feixas, et al., 2002; Green, 2004).

How have some of these constructivist assessment methods been applied in IS research? Perhaps the most commonly used method in IS research is the repertory grid. It has also been used to address diverse research questions. In their review paper, Tan and Hunter (2002) noted the importance of cognitive approaches in understanding organisation in IS research; however, they highlighted the lack of a specific methodology for investigating this issue. They put forward the repertory grid technique as a method that can be used to study cognition in IS research. Tan and Hunter (2002) highlighted studies that have previously used repertory grids in IS. They noted the application of repertory grids to understanding how information system analysts are perceived (Hunter, 1997), and how the concept of "excellent" systems analysts is perceived cross-culturally (Hunter & Beck, 2000). Tan and Hunter also identified work by Moynihan (1996), Lattta and Swigger (1992) and Phythian and King (1992) as studies that have used repertory grids. Moynihan (1996) used grid methodology to explore factors influencing risk in systems projects. Moynihan (1996) noted the utility of construct elicitation techniques in IS research. Latta and Swigger (1992) asked students to complete grids on online retrieval systems to examine the degree of shared construing. Their findings provided support for the use of grid methodology for modelling shared knowledge. Phythian and King (1992) developed an expert support system for tender decisions using rules based on findings from repertory grids and laddering.

Repertory grid methodology has been used to examine the alignment of business and IS, and in particular, the shared understanding of business and IS executives (Tan & Gallupe, 2006). Likewise, Davis and Hunagel (2004) argued that repertory grid methods provided a framework for testing the existence of shared cognitive schema or what Davis and Hunagel refer to as work motifs, and how these work motifs influence how knowledge workers react to the implementation of an IS. This type of research also highlights the applicability of Kelly's (1955) notion of commonality and individuality. Tan and Tung (2003) used repertory grid methodology to identify criteria that Web designers use for Website evaluation. In addition, repertory grids have also been used in cross-cultural IS research (Hunter & Beck, 2000).

Kelly's (1955) methodologies have also been applied to IS development and requirements analysis (for example, Guiterrez, 1989; Darke & Shanks, 1997; Jain, Vitharana & Zahedi, 2003). Lee and Truex (2000) investigated how formal IS development methods would impact the cognitions (i.e., cognitive complexity) of novice developers.

The utility of Hinkle's laddering technique in IS research is also discussed in the literature. Rugg, Eva, Mahmood, Rehman, Andrews and Davies (2002) provide a description of the technique and how it may be applied to eliciting knowledge about organisational culture. They cite examples of the application of laddering in knowledge acquisition (Rugg & McGeorge, 1995) and a procedure for the acquisition of requirements (Maiden & Rugg, 1996). The laddering technique underpins means-end chain theory (Reynolds & Gutman, 1988). Means-end analysis has also been applied to the IS literature. For example, Chiu (2005) used the approach for eliciting user requirements for a Web-based document management system being developed. Moreover, Chiu (2005) also demonstrated how the means-end chain theory could be integrated with the TAM.

PERSONAL CONSTRUCT THEORY AND IS THEORIES

Researchers in IS (or any other discipline for that matter) must address issues pertaining to theory and methods for addressing empirical questions that emerge from that theory. Relative to other disciplines, IS is in its infancy, with researchers borrowing from other disciplines (Gregor, 2005). As such, there is a recognition that theory development within the discipline is also at its infancy and continues to be a challenge for IS researchers (Grover, Lyytien, Srinivasan & Tan, 2008). Moreover, there is the added recognition that "aspiring authors propose something in their manuscript as a theory when it is not" (Grover et al., 2008, p.42).

As a way of addressing the theoretical challenges of the IS discipline, Gregor (2002, 2006) proposed a meta-theoretical examination of theory in IS and presented a taxonomy of theory types in IS. She distinguishes between five theory types. Each type is defined in terms of its goals; these goals are either to describe and analyse, to explain, to predict or to prescribe (Gregor, 2006). Gregor distinguishes between the theory types in terms of pivotal questions addressed by each type. Theory of *analysis and description* address question of "what is"; these theory types do not seek to predict or explain phenomena. In addition to "what is" questions, *explanatory* theory types also ask "how", "why", "when" and "where" questions. Gregor notes that these theories provide explanation of phenomena but they do not provide testable propositions or hypotheses. Theory types can be *predictive*. These types are the questions "what is" and "what will be". They generate hypotheses or propositions that are testable. However, given the absence of an explanatory goal, causal statements are not a feature of predictive theories. Theory types that are both *predictive and explanatory* do provide causal explanations. These types provide answers to "what is", "how", "why", "when", "where" and "what will be". The final theory type of Gregor's taxonomy is *design and action*. These theory types are prescriptive; they provide statements on "how to do something". These theory types are "about the methodologies and tools used in the development of information systems" (Gregor, 2002, p. 11).

So where is Personal Construct Theory located in Gregor's taxonomy? In order to answer this question we need to revisit what is meant by theory. Warren (1998), citing O'Connor (1957), notes the term theory can have four distinct meanings. "One refers to a body of related problems or questions (as in the epistemology as 'the theory of knowledge'). A second refers to a conceptual framework that might be abstract and quite removed from practical activity; mathematical theory is a case in point. A third is a more common-sense meaning which contrasts theory from practice (not itself a straightforward concept) where it refers to procedures, precepts or rules pertaining to a craft or activity. The fourth is the more formal sense where a theory is a logically interconnected set of confirmed hypotheses" (Warren, 1998, p.51). Warren adds that Kelly referred to "personal construct psychology as a theory in the first and fourth senses…"(p.51). This assertion implies that Personal Construct Theory is more than just a descriptive account. Indeed, Warren (1998) elegantly articulates the links between Personal Construct Theory and philosophy; for instance, Kelly openly acknowledges the influence of Dewey's pragmatism and Vaihinger's philosophy of 'as if'; while some of the underlying philosophical dimensions underpinning Personal Construct Theory include existentialism and phenomenology (Warren, 1998). The observation that Personal Construct Theory is a theory in the formal sense implies that it is propositional in nature, and that these propositions are testable. For instance, testing the assumption that construing is bipolar has received particular attention (Walker & Winter, 2007). Personal Construct Theory allows one to propose testable hypotheses; Personal Construct Theory

provides explanation of human behaviour. This view suggests that Personal Construct Theory can be categorised within Gregor's theory of explanation and prediction.

As discussed in section 4, Kelly's Personal Construct Theory not only articulates a theoretical framework for understanding human behaviour, it also provides researchers with methodology. Furthermore, these methods are not isolated from theory. At times, the theory suggests an approach to research. The interplay between theory and method is best exemplified with Kelly's notion of constructive alternativism. Personal Construct Theory is a way of understanding why people do and do not change; constructive alternativism can be used to understand change. But the notion of "as if" is central to methods such as self-characterisation. From this perspective, Personal Construct Theory also has elements of Gregor's fifth categorisation of design and action.

We have demonstrated that Personal Construct Theory can be located within Gregor's (2006) a taxonomy of theory types in IS. But how does Personal Construct Theory extend theorising in the IS domain? Personal Construct Theory reminds IS researchers of the centrality of the person, and the importance of person in any explanation of IS usage. The theory provides both a theoretical framework and a methodology for adding to current IS research. IS research based on Personal Construct Theory would acknowledge results that are grounded in relevant experience. These experiences can be derived from individuals, groups, work units or indeed companies. The next section examines how the theory can be applied to research issues in the IS domain.

PERSONAL CONSTRUCT THEORY AND IS RESEARCH

How might Personal Construct Theory be applied to an IS research issues? To illustrate, let us consider the influence of personal choice in IS adoption/acceptance. The IS literature provides models and theories for understanding IS adoption and usage. In Section 2, we reviewed the more prominent models of IS usage and adoption. Models such as the UTAUT (Venkatesh et al., 2003) consider (either implicitly or explicitly) why people choose to use an IS. The UTAUT, for instance, includes variables such as voluntariness and social influence. Users may choose to use the system as infrequently as possible, or in the manner not intended. These are choices that users make; particularly if they wish to retain a sense of control of how to use an IS in say a mandated setting.

Caputi and Warren (2007) demonstrated how personal choice in IS usage could be understood using the Experience Corollary. In particular, the Experience Cycle is useful in understanding the process whereby an IS user might exhibit resistance to IS usage. As discussed in Section 3, the Experience Cycle has five phases or components; anticipation, investment, encounter, confirmation/ disconfirmation, and constructive revision. Anticipation within the Experience Cycle involves prediction of a outcome in return for an action after considering what might be possible outcomes given the construct system held by an individual (Kelly, 1970). Caputi and Warren (2007) highlighted that anticipation is not foreign to the models of IS adoption. The TRA posits the influence of beliefs in decision making. Committing to an action is influenced by relevant belief sets held by an individual; these beliefs enable the individual to anticipate outcomes before committing to an action (Fishbein & Azjen, 1975). In this context, the Experience Cycle is useful for examining the underlying processes in using these beliefs to commit to an action, and the role of anticipation in those processes.

The anticipated outcome of an action has some level of associated investment or commitment. In a mandated usage setting, an individual may be more committed to retaining freedom of choice than to complying with IS use in a particular way. In this case, the user may resist, and react in order to restore the option of making a choice by not using the IS as it was intended to be used, or avoiding to use the system whenever possible (Caputi & Warren, 2007).

Actions are also evaluated; anticipations are either confirmed or disconfirmed. Caputi and Warren (2007) noted that this confirmatory/ disconfirmatory phase is evident in current IS models, such as Rogers' (1995) Diffusion of Innovations, in which users evaluate the results of usage. Usage has influenced how IT is perceived. However, Rogers' model does not delineate how evaluation of use leads to future decisions about usage. Whereas, within a Personal Construct Theory framework, a person who predicts that he or she can use a new module of a system based on a construct of say, 'having mastery of IS use' and then has that outcome confirmed or validated will be more likely to decide to continue to use the new module (Caputi & Warren, 2007).

The final phase of the Experience Cycle is constructive revision. In this phase, an individual examines the outcome of testing his or her anticipations, and if necessary, re-construes in light of the outcome. For instance, an office worker may predict that a new email system will be difficult to use. This conclusion may be based on the individual's poor mastery of technology. Upon trialing the new system, our user may find the system is not as difficult to use as anticipated. As a consequence, may revise their notion of poor mastery. Current models of IS adoption and usage focus on external factors that influence usage. Little attention is given to internal processes that may influence attitudes, beliefs and intentions, and how revisions of any of these variables may impact subsequent IS usage (Caputi & Warren, 2007). The notion of constructive revision may be useful in understanding these under-researched internal processes.

CONCLUSION

Good theory, in any domain, strives to describe, explain and predict. In particular, good theory explains core theoretical constructs. In this chapter, we have argued that users and user behaviour plays an important role in IS theory. As such, IS theories should account for the "psychology" of IS usage. A number of theories described in the IS literature deal with psychological variables. The TAM and the extensions of the TAM are examples of theories that describe and account for psychological variables. Typically, such theories are limited in explaining psychological processes that individuals experience when using information systems. We have argued that Kelly's (1955 /1991) Theory of Personal Constructs can be applied to information systems in accounting for the phenomenology of IS usage. Personal Construct Theory provides an internally consistent theoretical framework for describing, explaining and predicting IS usage. Moreover, Personal Construct Theory also provides a set of theoretically rooted methodologies that can be adapted for use in IS research. Some of these methodologies, notably the repertory grid technique and laddering, have been applied to IS research. However, these techniques have been used outside of the theory from which they were derived. Future research is warranted to examine the utility of Personal Construct Theory and methods in IS research.

REFERENCES

Ajzen, I. (1985). From intentions to actions: A theory of planned behaviour. In J. Kuhl & J. Beckman (Eds.), *Action-control:From cognition to behaviour* (pp. 11-39). Heidelberg, Germany: Springer.

Ajzen, I. (1991). The theory of planned behaviour. *Organizational Behaviour and Human Decision Processes, 50,* 179-211.

Ajzen , I., & Fishbein, M. (1980). *Understanding attitudes and predicting social behaviour.* NJ: Prentice Hall.

Bandura, A. (1977). *Social learning theory.* NJ: Prentice Hall.

Bell, R. C. (1988). Theory-appropriate analysis of repertory grid data. *International Journal of Personal Construct Psychology, 1,* 101-118.

Bell, R. C. (2003). The repertory grid technique. In F. Fransella (Ed.), *International handbook of personal construct psychology.* Chicester, UK: Wiley.

Bruner, J. S. (1956). A cognitive theory of personality. *Contemporary Psychology, 1,* 355-357.

Burr, V., & Butt, T. (1992). *Invitation to personal construct psychology.* London: Whurr Publishers.

Caputi, P., & Warren, C. (2007, July). *Exploring the process of how individuals decide to use mandatory information systems.* Paper presented at the XXth Congress of Personal Construct Psychology, Brisbane.

Chiu, C. (2005). Applying means-end chain theory to eliciting system requirements and understanding users perceptual orientations. *Information & Management, 42,* 455-468.

Chung, J., & Tan, F. B. (2004). Antecedents of perceived playfulness: An exploratory study on user acceptance of general information-searching Websites. *Information & Management, 41,* 869-881.

Compeau, D., Higgins, C. A., & Huff, S. (1999). Social cognitive theory and individual reactions to computing technology: A longitudinal study. *MIS Quarterly, 23,* 145-158.

Darke, P., & Shanks, G. (1997). User viewpoint modeling: Understanding and representing user viewpoints during requirements definition. *Information Systems Journal, 7,* 213-239.

Davis, C. J., & Hunagel, E. M. (2004). *Implementing information systems to support knowledge work: An exploration of work motifs*. Retrieved from http://is2.lse.ac.uk/asp/aspecis/

Davis, F. D. (1986). A technology acceptance model for empirically testing new end-ser information systems: Theory and results. Unpublished doctoral dissertation, Sloan School of Management, Massachusetts Institute of Technology.

Davis, F. D. (1989). Perceived usefulness, perceived ease of use, and user acceptance of information technology. *MIS Quarterly, 13*, 319-339.

Davis, F .D., Bagozzi, R. P., & Warshaw. P. R. (1992). Extrinsic and intrinsic motivation to use computers in the workplace. *Journal of Applied Social Psychology, 22*, 1111-1132.

Davis, F. D. (1993). User acceptance of information technology: System characteristics, user perceptions and behavioral impacts. *International Journal of Man-Machine Studies, 38*, 475-487.

Feixas, G., Geldschlager, H., & Neimeyer, R. A. (2002). Content analysis of personal constructs. *Journal of Constructivist Psychology, 15*, 1-20.

Fishbein, M., & Ajzen, I. (1975). *Belief, attitude, intention and behaviour: An introduction to theory and research*. Reading, MA: Addison-Wesley.

Fransella, F. (1972). *Personal Change and Reconstruction: Research on a Treatment of Stuttering*. Academic Press: London.

Fransella, F. (2003). Some tools and skills for personal construct practitioners. In F. Fransella (Ed). *International Handbook of Personal Construct Psychology*. Chicester: UK Wiley.

Fransella, F. & Bannister, D. (1977). *A manual for Repertory Grid Technique*. Academic Press: London.

Fransella, F., Bell, R., & Bannister, D. (2004). *A manual for Repertory Grid Technique*. Chicester: UK Wiley, 2nd Ed.

Gefen, D. E., Karahanna, E., & Straub, D.W. (2003). Trust and TAM in Online shopping: An integrated model. *MIS Quarterly, 27*, 51-90.

Green, B. (2004). *Personal construct psychology and content analysis. Personal construct theory & practice*. Retrieved from http://www.pcp-net.org/journal/pct04.pdf

Gregor, S. (2002). A theory of theories in information systems. In *Information systems foundation: Building the theoretical base* (pp. 1-20). Canberra, Australia: Australian National University. Retrieved from http://dsi.esade.edu/theorybuilding/papers/Gregor%20ISF-theory-paper-final-t.pdf

Gregor, S. (2005). The struggle towards an understanding of theory in information systems. In D. Hart & S. Gregor (Eds.), *Information systems foundations: Constructing and criticising* (pp. 3-12). Canberra, Australia: Australian National University. Retrieved from http://epress.anu.edu.au/info_systems/part-ch01.pdf

Gregor, S. (2006). The nature of theory in information systems. *MIS Quarterly, 30*, 611-642.

Grover, V., Lyytinen, K., Srinivasan, A., & Tan, B. C. (2008). Contributing to rigorous and forward thinking explanatory theory. *Journal of the Association for Information Systems, 9*, 40-47.

Guiterrez, O. (1989). Experimental techniques for information requirements analysis. *Information & Management, 16*, 31-43.

Hinkle, D. N. (1965). *The theory of personal constructs from the viewpoint of a theory of construct implications*. Unpublished doctoral dissertation, Ohio State University.

Hunter, M. G. (1997). The use of repgrids to gather interview data about information system analysts. *Information Systems Journal, 7*, 67-81.

Hunter, M. G., & Beck, J. E. (2000). Using repertory grids to conduct cross-cultural information systems research. *Information Systems Research, 11*, 93-101.

Jain, H., Vitharana, P., & Zahedi, F. (2003). An assessment model for requirements identification in component-based software development. *The DATA BASE for Advances in Information Systems, 34*, 48.

Jancowicz, D. (2003). *The easy guide to repertory grids*. London: Wiley.

Karahanna, E., Ahuja, M., Srite, M., & Galvin, J. (2002). Individual differences and relative advantage: The case of GSS. *Decision Support Systems, 32*, 327-341.

Kelly, G. A. (1955/1991). *The psychology of personal constructs*. New York: Norton.

Kukafka, R., Johnson, S. B., Linfante, A., & Allegrante, J. P. (2003). Grounding a new information technology implementation framework in behavioural science: A systematic analysis of the literature on IT use. *Journal of Biomedical Informatics, 36*, 218-227.

Landfield, A. (1971). *Personal construct systems in psychotherapy*. Chicago: Rand McNally.

Latta, G. F., & Swigger, K. (1992). Validation of the repertory grid for use in modelling knowledge. *Journal of the American Society for Information Science, 43*, 115-129.

Lee, J., & Truex, D. P. (2000). Exploring the impact of formal training in ISD methods on the cognitive structure of novice information systems developers. *Information Systems Journal, 10*, 347-367.

Maiden, N. A. M., & Rugg, G. (1996). ACRE: Selecting methods for requirements acquisition. *Software Engineering Journal, 11*, 183-192.

Mathias, T. M., Caputi, P., & Vella, S. C. (2008). *Information systems implementation and the scientist-practitioner model*. Unpublished manuscript, University of Wollongong.

Moon, J., & Kim, Y. (2001). Extending the TAM for a world-wide-Web context. *Information &*

Management, 38, 217-230.

Moynihan, T. (1996). An inventory of personal constructs for information systems project risk researchers. *Journal of Information Technology, 11*, 359-371.

Neimeyer, R. A., Baker, K. D., & Neimeyer, G. J. (1990). The current status of personal construct theory: Some scientometric data. In R. A. Neimeyer & G. J Neimeyer. (Eds.), *Advances in personal construct psychology* (vol 1) (pp. 3-22). Greenwich, CT: JAI.

Paul, R. J. (2007). Editorial: Challenges to information systems: Time to change. *European Journal of Information Systems, 16*, 193-195.

Phythian, G. J., & King, M. (1992). Developing an expert system for tender enquiry evaluation: A case study. *European Journal of Operational Research, 56*, 15-29.

Rawstorne, P. R. G. (2005). *A systematic analysis of the theory of reasoned action, the theory of planned behaviour and the technology acceptance model when applied to the prediction and explanation of information systems use in mandatory usage contexts*. Unpublished doctoral dissertation, University of Wollongong.

Reynolds, T. J., & Gutman, J. (1988). Laddering theory, method, analysis and interpretation. *Journal of Advertising Research, 28*, 11-31.

Riemenschneider, C. K., Harrison, D. A., & Mykytyn, P. P. (2003). Understanding IT adoption decisions in small business: Integrating current theories. *Information & Management, 40*, 269-285.

Rogers, E. M. (1995). *Diffusion of innovations*. (4th ed). New York: The Free Press.

Rugg, G., Eva, M., Mahmood, A., Rehman, N., Andrews, S., & Davies, S. (2002). Eliciting information about organizational culture via laddering. *Information Systems Journal, 12*, 215-229.

Rugg, G., & McGeorge, P. (1995). Laddering. *Expert Systems, 12,* 339-346.

Scheer, J. W., & Sewell, K. W. (Eds.). (2006) *Creative construing: Personal constructions in the arts.* Giessen, Germany: Psychosozial-Verlag.

Tan, F. B., & Hunter, M. G. (2002). The repertory grid technique: A method for the study of cognition in information systems. *MIS Quarterly, 26,* 39-57.

Tan, F. B., & Gallupe, R. B. (2006). Aligning business and information systems thinking: A cognitive approach. *IEEE Transactions on Engineering Management, 53,* 223-237.

Tan, F. B., & Tung, L. L. (2003). Exploring Website evaluation criteria using the repertory grid technique: A Web designer's perspective. In *Proceedings of the Second Annual Workshop on HCI Research in MIS,* Seattle, WA.

Taylor, S., & Todd, P. A. (1995). Understanding information technology usage: A test of competing models. *Information Systems Research, 6,* 144-176.

Valentine, E. R. (1982). *Conceptual issues in psychology.* London: George Allen & Unwin.

Ventatesh, V., Morris, M. G., Davis, G. B., & Davis, F. D. (2003). User acceptance of information technology: Toward a unified view. *MIS Quarterly, 27,* 425-478.

Viney, L. L., & Caputi, P. (2005). The origin and pawn, positive affect, psychosocial maturity and cognitive affect scales: Using them in counselling research. *Measurement & Evaluation in Counseling Development, 34,* 115-26.

Walker, B. M. (1996). A psychology for adventurers: An introduction to personal construct psychology from a social perspective. In D. Kalekin-Fishman & B. M. Walker. (Eds.), *The construction of group realities: Culture, society and personal construct psychology* (pp. 7-26).

Malabar, FL: Krieger.

Walker, B. M., Ramsey, F. L., & Bell, R. C. (1988). Dispersed and undispersed dependency. *International Journal of Personal Construct Psychology, 1,* 63-80.

Walker, B. M., Oades, L. G., Caputi, P., Stevens, C. D., & Crittenden, N. (2000). Going beyond the scientist metaphor: From validation to experience cycles. In J. W. Scheer (Ed.), *The person in society: Challenges to a constructivist theory.* Giessen, Germany: Psychosozial-Verlag.

Walker, B. M., & Winter, D. A. (2007). The elaboration of personal construct psychology. *Annual Review of Psychology, 58,* 453-477.

Warren, B. (1998). *The philosophical dimensions of personal construct psychology.* London: Routledge.

Winter, D. A. (1992). *Personal construct psychology in clinical practice: Theory, research and applications.* London: Routledge.

KEY TERMS AND DEFINITIONS

Computer-Based Information Systems: A computer-based information system involves information technologies that used by people according to set rules and protocols.

Constructive Alternativism: The proposition that a person is not limited to just one way of making sense of the world. People have the capacity to revise how they understand and interpret the world, or construe new ways of making sense of their worlds.

Personal Construct Theory: A theory developed by George Kelly (1955) which focuses on how individuals make sense of the experiences, events, and people in their world, and how these constructions are tested against reality.

Repertory Grid: A repertory grid is a matrix of elements (these can be objects, people, events experienced in a person's world), constructs (these are the attributes and characteristics that can be used to describe or make sense of elements) and a relation that defines how constructs discriminate among the elements. For example, each element can be rated on each construct using a Likert-type rating scale.

Theory: A set of laws, propositions, hypotheses that describes, explains and predicts phenomena of interest.

APPENDIX A: FUNDAMENTAL POSTULATE AND ELEVEN COROLLARIES OF KELLY'S PERSONAL CONSTRUCT THEORY.

Fundamental Postulate: A person's processes are psychologically channelized by the ways in which he anticipates events.

Construction Corollary: A person anticipates events by construing their replications.

Dichotomy Corollary: A person's construction system is composed of a finite number of dichotomous constructs.

Individuality Corollary: Persons differ from each other in their construction of events.

Organisation Corollary: Each person characteristically evolves, for his convenience in anticipating events, a construction system embracing ordinal relationships between constructs.

Choice Corollary: A person chooses for himself that alternative in a dichotomised construct through which he anticipates the greater possibility for extension and definition of his system.

Range Corollary: A construct is convenient for the anticipation of a finite range of events only.

Experience Corollary: A person's construction system varies as he successively construes the replications of events.

Modulation Corollary: The variation in a person's construction system is limited by the permeability of the constructs within whose ranges of convenience the variants lie.

Fragmentation Corollary: A person may successively employ a variety of construction subsystems which are inferentially incompatible with each other.

Commonality Corollary: To the extent that one person employs a construction of experience which is similar to that employed by another, his psychological processes are similar to those of the other person.

Sociality Corollary: To the extent that one person construes the construction processes of another he may play a role in a social process involving the other person.

Chapter XXIX
Coping with Information Technology

Anne Beaudry
Concordia University, Canada

ABSTRACT

New information technology implementations, as major modifications to existing ones, bring about changes in the work environment of individuals that trigger an important adaptation process. Extant research on the adaptation process individuals go through when a new IT is implemented in their working environment is rather limited. Furthermore, variance theories and models useful to explain IT adoption and use are not well suited to study the dynamics underlying the adaptation process. Coping theory, because it links antecedents, adaptation behaviors, and outcomes altogether, provides a rich lens through which we can study individuals' IT-related adaptation process. A better understanding of this process will enable researchers and practitioners to understand and predict IT acceptance and related behaviors and thus to better manage them. This chapter presents coping theory, its underlying assumptions and inherent components, discusses its application, highlights the complementarities with existing models and theories currently used in IS research, and provides several avenues for future research in this area.

INTRODUCTION

The extant literature suggests a growing interest in how users behave when new information technologies (IT) are implemented in their work environment (Barki, Titah, & Boffo, 2007; Beaudry & Pinsonneault, 2005; Majchrzak, Rice, Malhotra, King, & Ba, 2000; Poole & DeSanctis, 1990; Tyre & Orlikowski, 1994; 1996). This growing interest comes from the acknowledgement that current variance theories and models, while useful to explain antecedents of IT adoption and use, do not contribute to explain the adaptation process through which individuals go when a new

IT is implemented in their working system and disturbs their work routine.

Psychologists have been studying individual adaptation to disruptive events in various contexts for decades (Lazarus, 2000). Coping theory (Lazarus, 1966) has been developed to explain the dynamics underlying individuals' appraisal and reactions to disruptive episodes in their life. It has since been used to understand individuals' responses to a large array of events ranging from natural disasters (Baum, Fleming, & Singer, 1983), injuries (Billings & Moos, 1984), deadly disease and mourning (Folkman, Lazarus, Gruen, & DeLongis, 1986; Folkman & Moskowitz, 2000), to disruptions in organizational contexts such as layoffs (Leana, Feldman, & Tan, 1998), organizational downsizing (Shaw & Barrett-Power, 1997), and firms' mergers and acquisitions (Cartwright & Cooper, 1996b).

The overall objective of this chapter is to provide a broad understanding of coping theory and its applicability in IS research. In this perspective, a description of the theory and its inherent components will be followed by a review of IS studies that have used coping theory. This stream of research will next be linked to current research approaches used in the field highlighting their complementarity. The chapter ends on a discussion of several avenues for future research.

COPING THEORY

In psychology, there are three main models of coping (Folkman, 1992). The ego-psychology perspective considers coping as an unconscious adaptive defense mechanism that manages instinct and affect, reduces tension, and restores an individual's psychological equilibrium (White, 1974). Defense mechanisms are structured hierarchically in terms of their maturity, and coping is one of the most mature adaptive processes along with sublimation, suppression, and humor. In the personality perspective, coping is a personality trait that reflects an ability to effectively face environmental challenges (Grasha & Kirschenbaum, 1986). Therefore, an individual's coping behavior can be predicted by one's coping trait, disposition, or style (Folkman, 1992). Examples of research in this stream include innovativeness (Kirton, 1976) and locus of control (Rotter, 1966). Both models, although useful for understanding some individual behaviors, have important limitations and have received, over the years, mixed support from empirical studies[1].

The contextual model of coping, which is the one discussed in this chapter, has received most attention and is widely used and accepted in psychology. In this perspective, coping is defined as "the cognitive and behavioral efforts exerted to manage (reduce, minimize, or tolerate) specific external and/or internal demands that are appraised as taxing or exceeding the resources of the person" (Folkman et al., 1986; Lazarus & Folkman, 1984). Internal demands are personal desires or requirements that the environment must meet such as an individual's desire to get challenging work versus the challenges that a specific job effectively carries (French, Rodgers, & Cobb, 1974). External demands emanate from the environment and must be met by individuals. They are related to the roles one has to play in a given environment (e.g., organization, society), such as a secretarial position requiring a typing speed of 50 words per minutes versus the effective typing ability of a candidate. Coping serves two main functions: managing the issue that is causing the discomfort and maintaining a psychological and emotional equilibrium (Folkman, 1992; Lazarus & Folkman, 1984; Mechanic, 1974). In the contextual perspective, coping is studied in relation to particular situations or events, perceived as positive or negative, occurring in the individual's environment. This allows for a wide range of patterns as individuals can interpret similar situations differently or different situations similarly and also because an individual's coping acts can vary in different contexts and over time. Hence, in this model, coping responses are not a stable feature of personality or unconscious defense mechanisms, but rather, they are what a person thinks and does in response to changes in a given situation (Folkman, 1992).

Coping theory is well suited to study the individual adaptation process triggered by a new IT implementation because it shares three fundamental characteristics with extant user adaptation studies. First, both, studies of user adaptation and coping theory, deal with how individuals respond to important changes that occur in their environment (e.g. Leonard-Barton, 1988; Majchrzak, Rice, Malhotra, King, & Ba, 2000; Tyre & Orlikowski, 1994). Adaptation studies typically focus on users' responses to the implementation of a new technology as they can potentially involve important consequences in organizations. As with stressors in coping theory, IT-induced changes can be perceived positively or negatively and they can generate significant stress and strain (Cartwright & Cooper, 1996a; Louis & Sutton, 1991). Second, both coping theory and user adaptation studies focus on similar components of the individual-environment relationship. Both deal with acts related to the self (e.g. learning new skills, psychological distancing) and to the environment (e.g. confronting or convincing others, modifying one's working procedures, customizing applications) (e.g. Poole & DeSanctis, 1990; Tyre & Orlikowski 1994; 1996). In addition, both coping and user adaptation acts can be oriented toward managing the issue at hand such as adapting a new technology to make it fit with one's own preferences or work routines (e.g. Goodhue & Thompson, 1995; Kraut, Dumais, & Koch, 1989; Pentland, 1989; Vessey & Galletta, 1991); or they can be oriented toward restoring emotional stability such as avoidance and denial (e.g. Beaudry & Pinsonneault, 2005; Zuboff, 1988). Third, both are interested in the vast array of potential outcomes of the adaptation/ coping process ranging from solving the problem at hand, increasing one's productivity, restoring emotional stability, to maintaining one's sense of well-being (e.g. Patrickson, 1986; Zuboff, 1988). Prior adaptation studies, although very insightful, have however shed light on the phenomenon in a non-integrated manner. Coping Theory provides a well established and empirically validated theoretical system to further examine and deepen our understanding of the phenomenon.

The Coping Process

Coping Theory (Lazarus, 1966) depicts the coping process as made of two key components which continuously influence each other: appraisal, the cognitive evaluation of a particular situation or event, and coping, the cognitive and behavioral efforts exerted to manage the given situation. The process begins with appraisal, which is realized in two steps. In the primary appraisal, the nature of the particular event and its personal importance and relevance are assessed. In other words, when a disruption occurs, one first asks: "What is at stake for me in this situation?" The paramount issue for the individual is to determine what consequences this event is likely to have and what the personal significance of the disruption is (Folkman, 1992). While a multitude of events exist, Coping Theory suggests that disruptive events can be categorized into three main types: challenge, threat, or loss (Folkman, 1992; McCrae, 1984). Empirical studies have however shown that the concepts of "threat" and "loss" tend to be confused by people (McCrae, 1989). In fact, factor analyses indicate that a clear distinction exist between a challenge, which is often associated to events that can have positive consequences, and threat/loss, which are related to events expected to have negative consequences (Carpenter, 1992; McCrae, 1989). The theory states that events are multifaceted and are usually appraised as comprising both dimensions (i.e. challenge and threat) but that their perceived relative importance varies across individuals and situations. In the second step, called secondary appraisal, individuals evaluate the coping options available to them. They determine the level of control they exert over the situation and what they feel they can do about it given the coping resources available to them (Lazarus & Folkman, 1984). Here, "resources" is used in a general sense and includes financial, material, physical, psychic, and social resources as well as specific knowledge, skills, and attitudes. While some argue that controllability may not be independent of the type of stressor (Carpenter, 1992), empirical evidence indicates that they are separate dimensions (Felton & Revenson, 1984). Individuals have been found to perceive some level of control even in situations where the stressor was essentially uncontrollable (Folkman & Moskowitz, 2000; Taylor, Helgeson, Reed, & Skokan, 1991). In those situations, control is regained by relinquishing original goals that are no longer attainable for new, realistic ones (Folkman & Moskowitz, 2000).

The second component of the process, coping, follows the two-step appraisal. Lazarus' Coping Theory accounts for two main types of coping acts: problem-focused and emotion-focused, both of which include cognitive and behavioral acts (Folkman, 1992; Lazarus & Folkman, 1984; Stone et al., 1992). Problem-focused coping acts aim at managing the disruptive issue itself. They are oriented toward solving the problem or taking advantage of a given opportunity perceived as associated with it. Problem-focused coping acts can be directed at changing the environment, such as altering or alleviating environmental pressures, barriers, resources, or procedures; and they can be oriented inward, at the self, such as developing new standards of behavior, shifting levels of aspiration, finding new channels of gratification, and learning new skills or procedures (Lazarus & Folkman, 1984). Emotion-focused coping acts are oriented toward the self and aim at regulating personal emotions and tensions, restoring a sense of stability, and reducing emotional distress (Lazarus & Folkman, 1984). This can be accomplished through numerous cognitive and behavioral efforts. One can change his/her perception

of a situation by minimizing the consequences or threats (e.g., maintaining hope and optimism, refusing to acknowledge the negative side of the event), positive comparison (i.e., comparing one's situation with others that are worse off), situation redefinition, and passive acceptance. Other emotion-focused acts include avoidance (e.g., escaping the situation), self-deception and denial (e.g., denying the facts and their implications and acting as if the event never happened), selective attention, distancing, doing physical activities to get one's mind off, venting anger, and seeking psychological or emotional support (Lazarus & Folkman, 1984).

Individuals use both types of coping acts in most situations but the amount of efforts invested in each type and the specific coping acts performed depend on one's appraisal of the situation (Folkman, 1992; Lazarus & Folkman, 1984). Perceived likely consequences (i.e., primary appraisal) and perceived controllability (i.e., secondary appraisal) together influence the extent to which one relies on problem- or emotion-focused acts (Folkman, 1992; Folkman & Lazarus, 1985; McCrae, 1984; Oakland & Ostell, 1996; Patterson et al., 1990; Stone et al., 1992). Emotion-focused coping efforts occur mainly when individuals feel that they do not have much control over a threatening situation whereas problem-focused coping occurs mainly when individuals feel that they do have some control over the situation (Folkman & Moskowitz, 2000; Folkman, 1992; Folkman et al., 1986; Lazarus & Folkman, 1984). This can be explained by the fact that in response to disruptive events, individuals tend to choose the coping strategy that promises the greater chances of success[2], thus restoring a sense of well-being (Begley, 1998). By over-relying on problem-focused acts in an unchangeable situation, individuals engage in a process that is likely to result in frustration and distress, while not solving the problem at hand (Begley, 1998; Cohen et al., 1986; Folkman 1992). Conversely, relying solely on emotion-focused acts in a changeable situation, instead of undertaking actions that could potentially solve the problem or issue at hand, would also likely result in frustration (Begley, 1998; Folkman, 1992). Extreme cases, when an event is appraised as negative and insurmountable or too demanding given the control/resources one has, can lead an individual to withdraw from the situation. Here, the coping strategy consists of consciously escaping from the disruptive event altogether and removing oneself from a threatening situation. Such a strategy may imply, for example, asking for a transfer, quitting a job, or retiring (Begley, 1998).

Because the coping process varies from one individual to the other, its related outcomes also vary. Problem-focused acts, if successful, may lead to solving the problem at hand, reducing the effective negative consequences, increasing one's related knowledge and skills, or decreasing uncertainty. On the other hand, emotion-focused acts may lead to restoring one's emotional stability, reducing stress and strain, positive reappraisal, or avoidance of various psychosomatic disorders. The coping acts and their outcomes may also lead one to reappraise the situation and perform another wave of coping acts.

Coping Theory in IS Research

Major organizational changes are recognized as significant stressors in organizational life associated with negative outcomes such as job loss, reduced status, conflicts at work and home, and threats to the psychological well-being of individuals (Judge, Pucik, & Welbourne, 1999). Coping Theory has been used to study individual reactions to a variety of organizational changes such as layoffs due to firm closures (Leana et al., 1998), firms' reorganizations and downsizing (Ashford, 1988; Judge et al., 1999; Shaw & Barrett-Power, 1997), and firms' mergers and acquisitions (Cartwright & Cooper, 1996b; Judge et al., 1999).

Organizational transitions are often strategic in nature and imposed from the top down, meaning that most employees have little influence over the nature of the change or the manner and timing of its implementation. Ashford (1988) suggested that adopting an avoidance strategy may enable individuals to reduce stress as they consciously focus their energies elsewhere or simply try to avoid thinking about the events to come. By opposition to avoidance, a major component of problem-focused coping is information seeking. Obtaining information enhances the predictability of a situation; this is thought to help individuals avoid future difficulties, deal with present ones, and increase their sense of control and confidence (Ashford, 1988). Individuals can also cope with new IT implementation by relieving emotional discomfort through affect regulation, resigned acceptance, and emotional discharge (Ashford, 1988).

Judging from the extant literature in IS (e.g. Leonard-Barton, 1988; Poole & DeSanctis, 1990; Tyre & Orlikowski, 1994; 1996), new IT implementation, and major changes to existing ones, are significant events in the life of organizational actors. Still, we do not know much about the adaptation process that inevitably follows (Ashford, 1988; Leonard-Barton, 1988; Tyre & Orlikowski, 1994). Having been tested numerous times in various settings, Coping Theory offers sound directions to examine the individual IT-related adaptation process. It also provides insights with regard to the most relevant antecedents and outcomes of the IT-related adaptation process. In IS, Coping Theory has been used to study how IT managers cope with rapid IT changes (Benamati & Lederer, 2001), users' reactions toward software restrictions (Yang & Teo, 2007), IT professionals strategies to deal with the stress associated with having to constantly update their technical skills (Tsai, Compeau & Haggerty, 2007), and users' reactions to new IT implementation in their work environment (Beaudry & Pinsonneault, 2005).

Benamati & Lederer (2001) investigated the coping mechanisms used by IT managers to reduce the problems associated with rapid changes in IT. Thirty-six various coping mechanisms were identified from sixteen interviews with IT managers. Results from a survey of 246 IT managers indicate that each of these 36 mechanisms was employed and successfully used by multiple respondents. Results from a factor analysis of the 36 mechanisms revealed five factors labeled: consultant support, education & training, vendor support, internal procedures, and endurance (Benamati & Lederer, 2001). While the first four factors can be labeled as problem-focused acts directed either at the IT, the working system, or the implementation procedure, the fifth factor is clearly an emotion-focused factor comprising items conveying avoidance. Interestingly, endurance (emotion-focused) was the second most used coping strategy among respondents (Benamati & Lederer, 2001).

Yang & Teo (2007) designed a longitudinal field experiment to study the coping behaviors triggered by free software trial restriction and their impact on participants' willingness to buy the full version. They argue that coping acts are crucial intermediaries connecting the negative disconfirmation that restrictions impose on time and functionality and subsequent purchase decision making. Yang & Teo's results suggest that negative disconfirmation on time limit expectation is positively related to controlling negative emotions toward trial restrictions whereas negative disconfirmation on functionality restrictions is related to action coping (i.e. problem-focused coping acts) which is, in turn, related to users' willingness to pay a premium for the software.

Tsai et al. (2007) conducted interviews with 14 IT professionals in order to investigate how they perceive and cope with the stress associated with constantly having to update their technical skills. Their results suggest that IT professionals rely on six coping strategies (3 problem-focused and 3 emotion-focused) to reduce the distress associated with the threat of skills obsolescence. Furthermore, their results suggest that the higher the level of distress felt by respondents, the more

numerous the coping acts, both problem- and emotion-focused, performed. Tsai et al conclude that individuals relying on a balance of problem- and emotion-focused coping seem to experience lower stress as a result.

Drawing on Coping Theory, Beaudry & Pinsonneault (2005) propose the Coping Model of User Adaptation (CMUA) to examine how and why individuals adapt to the implementation of a new IT in their work environment (Figure 1). Beaudry & Pinsonneault (2005) define user adaptation as "the cognitive and behavioral efforts exerted by individuals to manage the specific consequences associated with a significant IT event occurring in their work environment". In line with Coping Theory, this definition implies that 1) both "visible" and "invisible" adaptation acts can be performed by the individual as part of his/her adaptation process; 2) adaptation acts will vary from one individual to another depending on one's interpretation of the potential positive and negative consequences that the new IT will bring about; 3) the adaptation acts one performs are also related to one's perceived control over the management of the consequences.

Beaudry & Pinsonneault (2005) suggest that the personal and professional consequences one associates with a new IT can be perceived as being monolithically an opportunity or a threat or as involving both opportunities and threats. This primary appraisal coupled with one's assessment of the level of control one has over the new IT (i.e. secondary appraisal) are said to be the main determinants of one's adaptation strategy. The adaptation strategy will most likely comprise both types of coping acts (i.e. emotion- and problem-focused) but their relative importance will vary according to one's appraisal of the situation (e.g. Foldman, 1992). While emotion-focused acts aim at the self only by restoring one's sense of equilibrium (e.g. comparing one's situation to others who are worse off; venting anger against the new IT or it's developers; convincing oneself that the new IT will not change one's job that much),

Figure 1. Coping model of user adaptation (CMUA) (Beaudry & Pinsonneault, 2005) Copyright © 2005, Regents of the University of Minnesota. Used with permission.

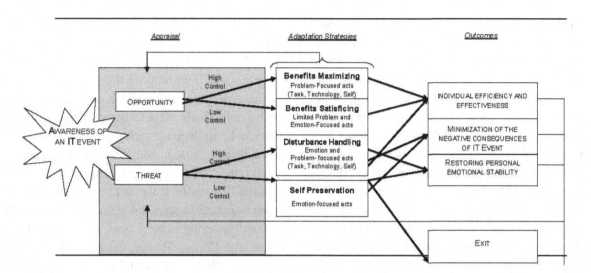

problem-focused coping can be directed at the self (e.g. learning new skills; convincing oneself that the new IT will be easy to use), at the technology (e.g. customizing the application; changing personal settings), or at the work environment (e.g. modifying working procedures; acquiring new furniture such as ergonomic rests).

Beaudry & Pinsonneault put forth four "pure" adaptation strategies derived by combining the two extreme cases from both types of appraisal (i.e. opportunity and threat with high and low control). As can be seen in Figure 1, CMUA suggests that when the IT-related expected consequences are interpreted as an opportunity, one will follow a "Benefits Maximizing" if one feels he/she has a high level of control over the situation whereas a "Benefits Satisficing" strategy will be adopted if one thinks he/she only has limited control over the situation. The Benefits Maximizing strategy, comprising mainly problem-focused adaptation acts, is likely to be related to increased individual efficiency and effectiveness at work. The Benefits Satisficing strategy, implying only limited adaptation acts, is expected to be related to increased, but limited, work efficiency and effectiveness.

By opposition, when the expected consequences of the new IT are perceived as a threat, one will adopt a "Disturbance Handling" strategy if one feels he/she has a significant level of control over the situation whereas a "Self-Preservation" strategy will be adopted if one thinks he/she only has very limited control over the situation. Because one feels threatened, emotion-focused adaptation acts are expected to be performed leading to the minimization of the perceived negative consequences and the restoration of one's emotional stability. Nevertheless, because the individual also thinks he/she has some control over the situation, the Disturbance Handling strategy also implies the performance of problem-focused acts which may eventually lead to some increase in individual efficiency and effectiveness. The Self-Preservation strategy, comprising only emotion-focused acts, will most likely result either in the restoration of one's emotional stability or in withdrawal from the situation in extreme cases.

As can be seen from Figure 1, the adaptation process is iterative with appraisal and adaptation strategies constantly influencing each other. The performance of adaptation acts and their outcomes lead individuals to reappraise the situation and either keep up with their initial adaptation strategy or follow a new one (Beaudry & Pinsonneault, 2005). This explains why a new IT implementation initially negatively appraised might be more positively reappraised after an initial round of adaptation acts.

Because it provides insights as to what triggers individual action, a parallel can be made between CMUA and other behavioral theories such as the Theory of Reasoned Action (TRA) and the Theory of Planned Behavior (TPB). Coping theory however goes a step further because it takes into account the dynamics pertaining to the adaptation process (the feedback loops). Furthermore, CMUA provides insights as to what the likely outcomes of the process are. In that sense, it can be viewed as a complementary perspective to the variance models widely used in IS research.

FUTURE TRENDS

Judge et al (1999) reviewed the personality literature in search of the dispositional variables most likely to be related to coping with change. Their results suggest that seven personality variables: locus of control, self-efficacy, self-esteem, positive affectivity, openness to experience, tolerance for ambiguity, and risk aversion, are related to successful coping with change with tolerance for ambiguity and positive affectivity being the most consistent. Judge et al (1999) suggest that individuals who can successfully cope in an organization undergoing high degrees of change should be more satisfied and committed to the organization. Their results further indicate that coping mediates most relations between dispositional factors, job satisfaction and organizational commitment. Future research should investigate the role of individual coping in reaction to new IT implementation on these two very important outcomes for organizations.

Dispositional factors such as personality traits, accounted for in disciplines such as education, management, organizational behaviour, and psychology, are left largely unexplored in the IS literature. Thatcher & Perrewe (2002) argue that in order to gain a better understanding of the role of personality in IT-related behaviours, research is needed to examine how different stable traits, both broad and situation-specific, relate to constructs that influence eventual computer use (Thatcher & Perrewe, 2002). Traits theorists argue that people possess broad predispositions, called traits, which cause them to behave in a particular way (Lin et al., 2001). After several decades of replication, researchers converged upon the Big-5 factors of personality, also called the Five-Factor Model of personality (FFM) (Costa & McCrae, 1988), as the premiere framework of personality. The Big-5 factors of personality (i.e. neuroticism, extraversion, openness, conscientiousness, and agreeableness) have been found to be significantly related to job performance (Barrick & Mount, 1991), job satisfaction (Judge et al., 1997), performance motivation (Judge & Ilies, 2002), and job acceptance behaviour (Wooten, 1991). McElroy et al's (2007) results indicate a significant relationship between the Big-5 factors and Internet usage.

Despite some attempts to study individual characteristics with respect to IT adoption models such as TAM, the study of individual characteristics and their relationship with IT-related behaviours is still wide opened. As personality traits are thought to be relatively stable characteristics of individuals that influence cognition and behaviour, their specific study warrants inclusion in IT-related user adaptation research.

Feelings of control or mastery play an important role among coping resources (Ashford, 1988). Moos & Billings (1992) argue that people with high feelings of self-efficacy are more active and persistent in their efforts to handle threatening situations. Such individuals are thought to be more likely to view situations as learning experiences and opportunities to demonstrate skill rather than as threats. Ashford (1988) argues that what matters most is the individuals' beliefs about their ability to control a given situation; not their actual ability to master it. Furthermore, results from Jex & Bliese (1999) and Jex et al., (2001) indicate that self-efficacy moderates the appraisal – coping relationship. IS researchers have studied the role of computer self-efficacy (one's belief about his/her ability to use a computer) as an antecedent to IT adoption and use. Further research is needed to investigate its potential moderating role in the coping process of individuals when a new IT is implemented in their work environment.

Beaudry & Pinsonneault (2005) have proposed four "pure" types of IT-related coping strategies. Further research is needed to develop a complete repertoire of IT-related coping profiles and strategies, identify their antecedents, both individual and organizational, and study their outcomes. Furthermore, each of their coping strategies unquestionably comprises more coping acts than they could identify in one particular setting. Future research should aim at putting together a more comprehensive inventory of IT-related coping acts and at identifying their specific antecedents and outcomes.

The relationship between users' coping process and acceptance of and resistance to IT should also be investigated. Coping theory offers a complementary perspective to the more techno centric models such as the Technology Acceptance Model (TAM) and allows for studying the dynamics underlying users reactions to new IT in a way that is unattainable with more static models. Relying on Coping Theory to supplement more techno-centric and static models and theories, IS researchers can contribute to further our understanding of IT-related behaviors and provide practitioners with most required guidance in managing them.

CONCLUSION

Variance models and theories have been most helpful in helping furthering our understanding of individual adoption and use of new information technologies. Coping Theory enables researchers to move a step further and investigate the adaptation process that inevitably follows the disruption that new IT implementation brings in the work environment of individuals. By taking into account the individual interpretation of the positive and negative consequences that new IT will have on them and their work, and by examining related overt and covert cognitive and emotional adaptation acts performed by individuals, we will reach a deeper understanding of IT-related reactions and of their individual and organizational outcomes. Examples from extant literature relying on the concepts of Coping Theory have been presented in this chapter along with many suggestions for further research in this area. Hopefully, this chapter will trigger such research work.

REFERENCES

Ashford, S. J. (1988). Individual strategies for coping with stress during organizational transitions. *The Journal of Applied Behavioral Science, 24*(1), 19-36.

Barki, H., Titah, R., & Boffo, C. (2007). Information system use-related activity: An expanded behavioral conceptualization of individual-level information system use. *Information Systems Research, 18*(2), 173-192.

Barrick, R., & Mount, M. K. (1991). The big five personality dimensions and job performance: A meta-analysis. *Personnel Psychology, 44*, 1-26.

Baum, A., Fleming, R., & Singer, J. E. (1983). Coping with technological disaster. *Journal of Social Issues, 39*, 117-138.

Beaudry, A., & Pinsonneault, A. (2005). Understanding user responses to information technology: A coping model of user adaptation. *MIS Quarterly, 29*(3), 493-524.

Begley, T. M. (1998). Coping strategies as predictors of employee distress and turnover after an organizational consolidation: A longitudinal analysis. *Journal of Occupational and Organizational Psychology, 71*, 305-329.

Benamati, J., & Lederer, A. L. (2001). Rapid information technology change, coping mechanisms, and the emerging technologies group. *Journal of Management Information Systems, 17*(4), 183-202.

Billings, A. G., & Moos, R. H. (1984). Coping, stress, and resources among adults with unipolar depression. *Journal of Personality and Social Psychology, 46*, 877-891.

Carpenter, B. (1992). Issues and advances in coping research. In B. Carpenter (Ed.), *Personal coping: Theory, research, and application* (pp. 1-14). Westport, CT: Praeger.

Cartwright, S., & Cooper, C. L. (1996a). Coping in occupational settings. In M. Zeidner & N. S. Endler (Eds.), *Handbook of coping: tTheory, research, applications* (pp. 202-220). New York: John Wiley & Sons.

Cartwright, S., & Cooper, C. L. (1996b). The psychological impact of merger and acquisition on the individual: A study of building society managers. *Human Relations, 46*(3), 327-347.

Cohen, S., Evans, G. W., Stokols, D., & Krantz, D. S. (1986). *Behavioral, health, and environmental stress.* New York: Plenum.

Costa, P. T., & McCrae, R. R. (1988). Personality in adulthood: A six-year longitudinal study of self-reports and spouse ratings on the NEO personality inventory. *Journal of Personality and Social Psychology, 54*, 853-863.

Felton, B. J., & Revenson, R. A. (1984). Coping with chronic illness: A study of illness controllability and the influence of coping strategies on psychological adjustment. *Journal of Consulting and Clinical Psychology, 52*, 343-353.

Folkman, S. (1992). Making the case for coping. In B. N. Carpenter (Ed.), *Personal coping: Theory, research, and application* (pp. 31-46). Westport, CT: Praeger.

Folkman, S., & Lazarus, R. S. (1985). If it changes it must be a process: Study of emotion and coping during three stages of a college examination. *Journal of Personality and Social Psychology, 48*(1), 150-170.

Folkman, S., Lazarus, R. S., Gruen, R. J., & DeLongis, A. (1986). Appraisal, coping, health status and psychological symptoms. *Journal of Personality and Social Psychology, 50*(3), 571-579.

Folkman, S., & Moskowitz, J. T. (2000). Positive affect and the other side of coping. *American Psychologist, 55*(6), 647-654.

French, J. R. P. Jr., Rodgers, W., & Cobb, S. (1974). Adjustment as person-environment fit. In G. V. Coelho, D. A. Hamburg & J. E. Adams (Eds.), *Coping and adaptation* (pp. 316-333). New York: Basic Books.

Goodhue, D. L., & Thompson, R. L. (1995). Task-technology fit and individual performance. *MIS Quarterly, 19*(2), 213-236.

Grasha, A. F., & Kirschenbaum, D. S. (1986). *Adjustment and competence: Concepts and applications.* Saint-Paul, MN: West.

Jex, S. M., & Bliese, P. D. (1999). Efficacy beliefs as a moderator of the effects of work-related stressors: A multilevel study. *Journal of Applied Psychology, 84*, 349-361.

Jex, S. M., Bliese, P. D., Buzzel, S., & Primeau, J. (2001). The impact of self-efficacy on stressor-strain relations: Coping style as an explanatory mechanism. *Journal of Applied Psychology, 86*(3), 401-409.

Judge, T. A., & Ilies, R. (2002). Relationship of personality to performance motivation: A meta-analytic review. *Journal of Applied Psychology, 87,* 797-807.

Judge, T. A., Locke, A. E., & Durham, C. C. (1997). The dispositional causes of job satisfaction: A core evaluation approach. In L. L. Cummings & B. M. Staw (Eds.), *Research in organizational behavior* (pp. 151-188). Greenwich, CT: JAI Press.

Judge, T. A., Thoresen, C. J., Pucik, V. P., & Welbourne, T. M. (1999). Managerial coping with organizational change: A dispositional perspective. *Journal of Applied Psychology, 84*(1), 107-122.

Kirton, M. (1976). Adaptors and innovators: A description and measure. *Journal of Applied Psychology, 61*(5), 622-629.

Kraut, R., Dumais, S., & Koch, S. (1989). Computerization, productivity, and quality of work-life. *Communications of the ACM, 32*(2), 220-238.

Lazarus, R. S. (1966). *Psychological stress and the coping process.* New York: McGraw-Hill.

Lazarus, R. S. (2000). Toward better research on stress and coping. *American Psychologist, 55*(6), 665-673.

Lazarus, R. S., & Folkman, S. (1984). *Stress, appraisal, and coping.* New York: Springer Publishing Company.

Leana, C. R., Feldman, D. C., & Tan, G. Y. (1998). Predictors of coping behavior after a layoff. *Journal of Organizational Behavior, 19,* 85-97.

Leonard-Barton, D. (1988). Implementation as mutual adaptation of technology and organization. *Research Policy, 17,* 251-267.

Lin, N. P., Chiu, H. C., & Hsieh, Y. C. (2001). Investigating the relationship between service providers' personality and customers' perceptions

of service quality across gender. *Total Quality Management, 12*(1), 57-67.

Louis, M. R., & Sutton, R. I. (1991). Switching cognitive gears: From habits of mind to active thinking. *Human Relations, 44,* 55-76.

Majchrzak, A., Rice, R. E., Malhotra, A., King, N., & Ba, S. (2000). Technology adaptation: The case of a computer supported inter-organizational virtual team. *MIS Quarterly, 24*(4), 569-600.

McCrae, R. R. (1989). Age differences and changes in the use of coping mechanisms. *Journal of Gerontology, 44,* 161-169.

McCrae, R. R. (1984). Situation determinants of coping responses: Loss, threat, and challenge. *Journal of Personality and Social Psychology, 46,* 919-928.

McElroy, J. C., Hendrickson, A. R., Townsend, A. M., & DeMarie, S. M. (2007). Dispositional factors in Internet use: Personality versus cognitive style. *MIS Quarterly, 31*(4), 809-820.

Mechanic, D. (1974). Social structure and personal adaptation: Some neglected dimensions. In G. V. Coelho, D. A. Hamburg, & J. E. Adams (Eds.), *Coping and adaptation.* New York: Basic Books.

Moos, R. H., & Billings, A. G. (1992). Conceptualizing and measuring coping resources and processes. In L. Goldberger & S. Breznitz (Eds.), *Handbook of stress* (pp. 212-230). New York: The Free Press.

Oakland, S., & Ostell, A. (1996). Measuring coping: A review and critique. *Human Relations, 49*(2), 133-155.

Patrickson, M. (1986). Adaptation by employees to new technology. *Journal of Occupational Psychology, 59,* 1-11.

Pentland, B. T. (1989). Use and productivity in personal computing: An empirical test. In *Proceedings of the tenth International Conference on*

Information Systems, Boston, (pp. 211-222).

Poole, M. S., & DeSanctis, G. (1990). Understanding the use of group decision support systems: The theory of adaptive structuration. In J. Fulk & C. Steinfield (Eds.), *Organizations and communication technology* (pp. 173-193). Newbury Park, CA: Sage Publications.

Rotter, J. B. (1966). Generalized expectancies for internal versus external control of reinforcement. *Psychological Monographs: General and Applied, 80*(609).

Shaw, J. B., & Barrett-Power, E. (1997). A conceptual framework for assessing organization, work group, and individual effectiveness during and after downsizing. *Human Relations, 50*(2), 109-127.

Stone, A. A., Kennedy-Moore, E., Newman, M. G., Greenberg, M., & Neale, J. M. (1992). Conceptual and methodological issues in current coping assessments. In B. N. Carpenter (Ed.), *Personal coping: Theory, research, and application* (pp. 15-39). Westport, CT: Praeger.

Taylor, S. E., Helgeson, V. S., Reed, G. M., & Skokan, L. A. (1991). Self-generated feeling of control and adjustment to physical illness. *Journal of Social Issues, 47*, 91-109.

Thatcher, J. B.. & Perrewe, P. L. (2002). An empirical examination of individual traits as antecedents to computer anxiety and computer self-efficacy. *MIS Quarterly, 26*(4), 381-396.

Tsai, H. Y., Compeau, D., & Haggerty, N. (2007). Of races to run and battles to be won: Technical skill updating, stress, and coping of IT professionals. *Human Resources Management, 46*(3), 395-409.

Tyre, M. J., & Orlikowski, W. J. (1994). Windows of opportunity: Temporal patterns of technological adaptation in organizations. *Organization Science, 5*(1), 98-118.

Tyre, M. J., & Orlikowski, W. J. (1996). The episodic process of learning by using. *International Journal of Technology Management, 11*(7/8), 790-798.

Vessey, I., & Galletta, D. (1991). Cognitive fit: An empirical study of information acquisition. *Information Systems Research, 2*(1), 63-84.

White, R. W. (1974). Strategies of adaptation: An attempt at systematic description. In G. V. Coelho, D. A. Hamburg, & J. E. Adams (Eds.), *Coping and adaptation* (pp. 47-68). New York: Basic Books.

Wooten, W. (1991). The effects of self-efficacy on job acceptance behavior among American college students. *Journal of Employment Counseling, 28*, 41-48

Yang, X., & Teo, H. H. (2007). How do user cope with trial restrictions? A longitudinal field experiment on free trial software. In *Proceedings of the twenty-eight International Conference on Information Systems*, Montreal, QC, Canada, (pp. 1-18).

Zuboff, S. (1988). *In the age of the smart machine: The future of work and power*. New York: Basic Books.

KEY TERMS AND DEFINITIONS

Appraisal: "The cognitive evaluation of a particular situation or event" (Lazarus, 1966). The appraisal is realized in two steps labeled primary and secondary appraisals.

Coping: "The cognitive and behavioral efforts exerted to manage (reduce, minimize, or tolerate) specific external and/or internal demands that are appraised as taxing or exceeding the resources of the person" (Folkman, Lazarus, Gruen, & DeLongis, 1986; Lazarus & Folkman, 1984).

Coping Process: Coping Theory (Lazarus, 1966) depicts the coping process as made of two key components which continuously influence each other: appraisal and coping.

Emotion-Focused Coping: Cognitive and behavioral acts performed in the aim of restoring a sense of stability (i.e. regulating emotions and reducing tensions).

Primary Appraisal: First step of the appraisal where one assesses the importance and relevance of a given event/situation. At this stage, one determines the likely consequences of the event.

Problem-Focused Coping: Cognitive and behavioral acts performed in the aim of managing the situation (i.e. solving the problem or taking advantage of it).

Secondary Appraisal: Second step of the appraisal where one assesses the level of control one has over the situation and what can be done.

ENDNOTES

[1] Space limitation does not allow discussing this issue in further details. Readers can consult Folkman (1992) and Lazarus and Folkman (1984) for an extensive discussion of the three perspectives and their respective limitations and strengths.

[2] The contextual perspective of coping suggests that an individual will adopt a different coping strategy and will thus perform various coping acts depending on the situation at hand. By opposition, the personality perspective of coping implies that an individual, having a coping style or preferred way of coping, will perform similar coping acts in any situation.

Chapter XXX
Holland's Vocational Theory and Personality Traits of Information Technology Professionals

John W. Lounsbury
University of Tennessee, Knoxville & eCareerFit.Com, USA

R. Scott Studham
Oak Ridge National Laboratory, USA

Robert P. Steel
University of Michigan-Dearborn, USA

Lucy W. Gibson
eCareerFit.com & Resource Associates, USA

Adam W. Drost
eCareerFit.com, USA

ABSTRACT

Drawing on Holland's (1985, 1996) vocational theory and based on a sample of 9,011 IT professionals, two research questions were investigated. On what personality traits do IT professionals differ from other occupations and which of these are also related to their career satisfaction? Five traits met both these criteria—Emotional Resilience, Openness, Tough-Mindedness, and Customer Service—for which IT professionals had higher scores, and conscientiousness, for which they had lower scores. IT career satisfaction was also positively related to E xtraversion, Agreeableness/Teamwork, Assertiveness, Optimism, Tough-Mindedness, Work Drive, and Visionary Style. Results are discussed in terms of the fit of these traits with IT work and the value of these insights for personnel-management functions like selection, training, professional development, and career planning.

PERSONALITY TRAITS AND CAREER SATISFACTION OF INFORMATION TECHNOLOGY PROFESSIONALS

The purpose of this chapter is to apply Holland's (1985; 1996) vocational theory to the occupational field of Information Technology (IT) using a large, empirical sample of IT professionals. Original findings are presented on key personality traits of IT professionals and implications of these results are discussed.

John L. Holland is, arguably, one of the most eminent and influential vocational theorists of our time. He is famous for his psychological theory of careers, including career choice, vocational preference, and a taxonomy of personality types for occupations. Holland's vocational theory has several main premises. First, people can be characterized by their resemblance to basic personality attributes. In his view, the key personality attributes are what he terms "types" which have historically been assessed as vocational interests (Holland, 1985). However, as will be explained below, accumulating evidence convincingly shows that personality traits may be effectively substituted for vocational interests in explications of the main tenets of Holland's theory.

The six main vocational interest themes in Holland's model are: Realistic, Investigative, Artistic, Social, Enterprising, and Conventional (The Career Key, 2008). Another major premise of Holland's vocational theory is that jobs, occupations, and work environments can also be viewed in terms of their resemblance to these basic personality types. The final major premise of Holland's theory is that the correspondence or fit between persons and work environments on these personality types leads to important vocational outcomes, including satisfaction, tenure, and performance. Holland summarized the essence of his vocational theory as follows:

Studies show that people flourish in their work environment when there is a good fit between their personality type and the characteristics of the environment. Lack of congruence between personality and environment leads to dissatisfaction, unstable career paths, and lowered performance. (Holland, 1996, p. 397).

There are two logical corollaries of Holland's fit model which have been generally verified by subsequent research and are germane to the present study. 1) There are differences in average scores on personality characteristics associated with occupations which help determine fit; and 2) higher scores on these personality characteristics are related to higher levels of satisfaction. Thus, for example, under the Holland model artists tend to have higher mean scores on the Artistic vocational interest scale and higher artistic scores are associated with greater job satisfaction of artists (Holland, 1985; 1996). Making a similar extension of Holland's taxonomy to the IT professions, computer programmers and IT workers have typically (e.g., O*NET, 2008) been considered as exemplifying three of the Holland dimensions—Investigative, Realistic, and Conventional--reflecting, respectively, the profession's scientific-research orientation, its emphasis on practical concerns including working with machinery and equipment, and its penchant for working in a structured, office setting.

Although research has been conducted on a variety of topics related to psychological characteristics and the functioning of IT workers—including work values (Prasad, Enns, & Ferratt, 2007), best management practices (Major, Davis, Germano, Fletcher, Sanchez-Hucles, & Mann, 2007), precursors of voluntary turnover (Rouse, 2001), self-efficacy and well-being (Beas & Salanova, 2006), anomie (Shankar, 2007), burnout (Hetland, Sandal, & Johnsen, 2007), and work-nonwork conflict (Messersmith, 2007)—research on the vocational interests of IT workers is much more limited. The few extant studies in this literature mainly focus on topics like programmer gender differences (Rosenbloom, Ash, Dupont, & Coder, 2008), IT vocational interests and job satisfaction (Perry, 1967), and the distinctive vocational interests of IT workers compared to other occupations (Perry & Cannon, 1968). For instance, using a sample of 1378 computer programmers, Perry and Cannon (1968) showed that, compared with other occupations, male programmers had greater interest in problem solving, mathematics, and mechanical pursuits and less *interest* in people.

An alternative approach to the study of careers and occupations involves the use of personality traits (which are relatively enduring characteristics of individuals that are relatively consistent over time and across situations). In recent years a broad-based consensus has emerged that all normal personality traits can be parsimoniously described by five traits, termed the *Big Five* model of personality (Agreeableness, Conscientiousness, Emotional Stability, Extraversion, and Openness) (De Raad, 2000). The Big Five personality traits have been replicated across a wide range of settings (e.g., De Raad, 2000), and they have been validated against many different criteria, including job performance (Salgado, 1997), job satisfaction (Judge, Heller, & Mount, 2002), career success (Judge, Higgins, Thoresen, & Barrick, 1999), life satisfaction (DeNeve & Cooper, 1998), and academic performance (Lounsbury, Sundstrom, Loveland, & Gibson, 2003).

More recently, some researchers have argued that the Big Five taxonomy is too broad and that more narrow-scope personality constructs may augment their ability to predict behavior. These arguments have received verification in work and academic domains (e.g., Lounsbury, Sundstrom et al., 2003; Paunonen & Ashton, 2001). As a case in point, Lounsbury, Loveland, Sundstrom, Gibson, Drost, and Hamrick (2003), found that six narrow traits (Assertiveness, Customer Service Orientation, Optimism, Image Management, Intrinsic Motivation, and Work Drive) were positively

related to career satisfaction for individuals in various occupational fields.

There has been some work attempting to logically map personality traits onto various occupational classes (see, for example, O*NET, 2008), but an empirically-validated personality trait profile for IT professionals has not, as yet, been developed. Using judgments provided by subject matter experts, O*NET links the following personality traits to computer programmers: attention to detail, dependability, initiative, achievement, flexibility, independence, integrity, persistence, and cooperation. However, there is currently no empirical evidence showing that any of these traits reliably differentiate IT professionals from members of other occupational groups, nor is there evidence that possession of these traits by IT professionals results in enhanced career satisfaction.

Returning to the goals of the present study, the following research questions were examined:

RQ1: On which personality traits do IT professionals differ from other occupations? *This research question is based directly on Holland's vocational theory. Scores on traits important for an occupation should differ in magnitude from scores on the same traits obtained from other occupations. The personality traits assessed were the Big Five personality traits and a set of narrow-scope traits studied previously by Lounsbury, Loveland et al. (2003).*

RQ2: Which personality traits are related to career satisfaction for IT professionals? *This question is also derived from Holland's vocational theory, which indicates that salient traits for an occupation will be related to satisfaction with that occupation.*

Under Holland's vocational theory, personality traits that differentiate IT professionals from other occupational groups and relate to career satisfaction provide a theoretical perspective for understanding the psychological makeup of IT professionals. This knowledge may also assist organizational decision makers performing such functions as career planning, selection, counseling, and succession planning for IT professionals. It may also help to inform interventions designed to optimize person-environment fit for IT professionals.

The following sections describe the methodology and results of this study, followed by a discussion of the meaning of the results, both in terms of theoretical and practical implications.

Method

Overview

Data for this study were extracted from an archival database generated by *eCareerfit.com*, an organization which offers online, personality-based career assessments to companies for transition services, outplacement, career development, succession planning, coaching, mentoring, and leadership development. Data were collected over the period March of 2003 to January of 2008.

Participants

The sample was comprised of a total of 9011 IT professionals employed in a large number of different jobs with many different companies in the United States. Respondents provided their job titles which resulted in the following breakdown: Analyst—4%, Application Developer—2%, Computer Programmer—7%, Computer Analyst--6%, Computer Engineer—5%, Database Administrator—3%, Developer—2%, IT—7%, IT Consultant—1%, IT project manager—2%, IT manager 3%, LAN Administrator—1%, Network Administrator-1%, Network Engineer—1%, Oracle DBA—1%, Programmer—3%, Programmer Analyst 6%, Project Manager—5%, SAP—Consultant—1%, Senior Analyst—2%, Software Analyst—1%, Software Engineer—5%, Solutions

Consultant—1%, Systems Administrator—4%, Systems Analyst 4%, Tech. Support—2%, Test Engineer—1%, UNIX System Administrator—1%, and Web Developer—2%. All told, the database included over 2,000 unique job titles. Of the total sample, 69% were male and 31% were female. Participation rates by age group were as follows: under 30—8%; 30-39—31%; 40-49—36%, 50 and over—25%. Race/ethnic data were not available. Respondents came from many different industries and organizational sectors, including technology services (33%), financial services (11%), telecommunications (11%), manufacturing (7%), professional services (5%), printing (3%), communications (3%), retail (3%), health care (2%), consumer products (2%), science and technology (1%), non-profit organizations and charities (1%), entertainment (1%), automotive (1%), airlines (1%), education (1%), and "other" (14%).

Personality Factors

The personality instrument used in the current study was the Resource Associates' *Personal Style Inventory (PSI)*, a work-based personality measure comprising the Big Five as well as narrow personality traits. The PSI has been used in a variety of organizational settings, mainly for career development and pre-employment screening purposes, for which there is extensive evidence of criterion-related and construct validity (Lounsbury, Gibson, & Hamrick, 2004; Lounsbury, Gibson, Sundstrom, Wilburn, & Loveland, 2003; Lounsbury, Loveland, et al., 2003; Lounsbury, Park, Sundstrom, Williamson, & Pemberton, 2004; Williamson, Pemberton, & Lounsbury, 2005). All of the PSI items had five-point response scales with bipolar verbal anchors. Following is a sample item from the Optimism scale.

A brief description of each of the personality and managerial style measures used in the present study are presented below along with the number of items in each scale and the coefficient alpha for

When the future is uncertain, I tend to anticipate positive outcomes.	1	2	3	4	5	When the future is uncertain, I tend to anticipate problems.

the total sample. For each scale, an average score was obtained by taking the mean of the scores on the individual items, so that the minimum possible score in each case was 1.0 and the maximum possible score was 5.0.

Big Five Personality Traits

- **Agreeableness/Teamwork**-- propensity for working as part of a team and functioning cooperatively on work group efforts (6 items; coefficient alpha = .82).
- **Conscientiousness**—dependability, reliability, trustworthiness, and inclination to adhere to company norms, rules, and values (8 items; coefficient alpha = .75).
- **Emotional Resilience**--overall level of adjustment and emotional resilience in the face of job stress and pressure (6 items; Coefficient alpha = .85).
- **Extraversion**—tendency to be sociable, outgoing, gregarious, expressive, warm-hearted, and talkative (7 items; coefficient alpha = .84).
- **Openness**—receptivity/openness to change, innovation, novel experience, and new learning (9 items; coefficient alpha = .79).

Narrow Personality Traits

- **Assertiveness**—a person's disposition to speak up on matters of importance, expressing ideas and opinions confidently, defending personal beliefs, seizing the initiative, and exerting influence in a forthright, but not aggressive, manner (8 items; coefficient alpha = .81).
- **Customer Service Orientation**—striving to provide highly responsive, personalized, quality service to (internal and external)

customers; putting the customer first; and trying to make the customer satisfied, even if it means going above and beyond the normal job description or policy (7 items; coefficient alpha = .71).

- **Intrinsic Motivation**—a disposition to be motivated by intrinsic work factors, such as challenge, meaning, autonomy, variety and significance (6 items; coefficient alpha = .84).
- **Image Management**—reflects a person's disposition to monitor, observe, regulate, and control the self–presentation and image s/he projects during interactions with other people (6 items; coefficient alpha = .80).
- **Optimism**-- having an upbeat, hopeful outlook concerning situations, people, prospects, and the future, even in the face of difficulty and adversity; a tendency to minimize problems and persist in the face of setbacks (8 items; coefficient alpha = .88).
- **Tough-Mindedness**—appraising information, drawing conclusions, and making decisions based on logic, facts, and data rather than feelings, values and intuition; disposition to be analytical, realistic, objective, and unsentimental (7 items; coefficient alpha = .79).
- **Visionary Style**—focusing on long-term planning, strategy, and envisioning future possibilities and contingencies (8 items; coefficient alpha = .84).
- **Work Drive**—disposition to work for long hours (including overtime) and an irregular schedule; investing high levels of time and energy into job and career, and being motivated to extend oneself, if necessary, to finish projects, meet deadlines, be productive, and achieve job success (8 items; coefficient alpha = .82).

Career Satisfaction

A five-item scale was used to measure career satisfaction (Lounsbury, Moffitt, Gibson, Drost, & Stevenson, 2007), with items tapping satisfaction with career progress and trajectory, career advancement, future career prospects, and career as a whole. Career satisfaction items were framed on a five-point response scale with verbally opposing anchors at each end (e.g., "I am very satisfied with the way my career has progressed so far" versus "I am very dissatisfied with the way my career has progressed so far". Coefficient alpha for the career satisfaction scale = .82. The career satisfaction measure was added three years ago to the inventory on which the database was derived; thus, the sample size for statistics involving career satisfaction was smaller (n = 1059) than the sample size for the personality traits.

RESULTS

Our first research question focused on personality factor differences between IT professionals and individuals in other occupations. For these analyses we used a one-sample *t* test to compare the mean scores of IT professionals against normative statistics derived from over 200,000 individuals representing all non-IT occupations in the database collected over the course of an eight year period. The mean scores for the IT professionals are presented in Table 1 grouped by whether they were found to be significantly higher, lower, or undifferentiated from the normative mean scores.

Compared to all other occupations, IT professionals had significantly higher mean scores on five personality traits—Customer Service Orientation, Tough-Mindedness, Intrinsic Motivation, Openness, and Emotional Resilience. The mean scores were below norm for three traits—Conscientiousness, Visionary Style, and Image Management. The mean scores for IT professionals were not

significantly different from the norm group on five traits—Optimism, Agreeableness/Teamwork, Assertiveness, Extraversion, and Work Drive.

The second research question examined the relationships between career satisfaction and the personality traits of IT professionals. Pearson correlation coefficients were computed to examine relationships between career satisfaction and the study's personality measures. Results are displayed in Table 2. Career satisfaction was positively and significantly related to all of the Big Five traits—with correlations ranging from r = .46 (p < .01) for Emotional Resilience to r = .12 (p < .01) for Conscientiousness. Career satisfaction was significantly related to all but two (Image Management and Intrinsic Motivation) of eight narrow-scope traits, with correlations ranging from r = .38 (p < .01) for Optimism to r = .05 (p > .05) for Visionary Style.

DISCUSSION

Using Holland's (1985, 1996) theory of vocational choice as a conceptual point-of-departure, we attempted to determine whether scores on Big Five and narrow-scope personality traits could differentiate IT professionals from other occupational groups. We also assessed whether these traits were related to the career satisfaction of IT professionals. Based on the results of over 9,000 IT employees in a wide variety of job titles from a broad range of organizations, five traits met both of these criteria. Specifically, IT workers had above-norm average scores on four traits which were also positively related to career satisfaction—Emotional Resilience, Tough-Mindedness, Openness, and Customer Service Orientation. They had below-norm scores on Conscientiousness, which was also positively related to career satisfaction.

Considering each of these traits individually, we consider first those traits which met two criteria drawn from Holland's vocational theory: (1) mean

Table 1. Mean scores on personality traits for IT professionals grouped by comparisons to all other occupations

Dimensions on which IT professionals have higher mean scores than the norm for all occupations	
Dimension	Mean Score
Customer Service	4.65
Tough-Mindedness	3.73
Intrinsic Motivation	3.61
Openness	3.57
Emotional Resilience	3.33
Dimensions on which IT professionals have similar mean scores than the norm for all occupations	
Dimension	Mean Score
Optimism	3.23
Agreeableness/Teamwork	3.22
Assertiveness	3.12
Extraversion	3.09
Work Drive	2.98
Dimensions on which IT Professionals Have Lower Mean Scores than the Norm for all Occupations	
Dimension	Mean Score
Conscientiousness	2.77
Visionary Style	2.36
Image Management	2.26

Note: For IT Professionals n = 9,011.

scores which were significantly different (either higher or lower) from the norm for all occupations and (2) significant correlations with career satisfaction. First, Emotional Resilience was higher among IT professionals than other occupations and was the trait most highly correlated with career satisfaction in our sample. One possible explanation for the importance of Emotional Resilience is that high levels of stress are inherent in many IT jobs (Jepson, 2004). Individuals who work in IT often face schedule pressure, demands from multiple constituencies in their employing organizations, and, typically, an "impossible workload" (Savvas, 2004). Similarly, as noted by Major, Davis, Germano, Fletcher, Sanchez-Hucles, and

Mann (2007), IT workers experience numerous sources of stress that are universal across occupations and work environments. As consumer electronics continue to exponentially mature, non-IT employees are pressuring IT employees to improve enterprise services at a similar rate. Meanwhile information assurance and computer security place IT staff in the situation of having to limit the use of consumer technology. These two countervailing forces (consumer electronics and enterprise security) often place IT staff in the difficult situation of having to limit the desired pace of change in the non-IT lines of business. IT professionals with higher levels of Emotional Resilience are better able to handle the chronic

Table 2. Correlations of personality traits with career satisfaction

	Correlations With Career Satisfaction
Big Five-Related Traits	
Conscientiousness	.12**
Emotional Resilience .	46**
Extraversion	.27**
Openness	.26**
Agreeableness/Teamwork	.21**
Narrow Traits	
Assertiveness	.31**
Customer Service Orientation	.22**
Image Management	-.01
Intrinsic Motivation	.04
Optimism	.38*
Tough-Mindedness	.18**
Work Drive	.29**
Visionary Style	.05

$n = 1059$
$*p < .05;$ $**p < .01$

stress associated with their work. As Weinberg (1972) concludes in his landmark book on *The Psychology of Computer Programming*"... we can probably say with assurance that someone without the ability to tolerate stressful situations for a period of a week or more is not good programmer material-given the realities of programming work today." The importance of Emotional Resilience is likely to increase in the future for IT professionals given current trends toward consumer electronics, greater outsourcing of work, limitations caused by enterprise IT security, increased competition from programmers in other countries, and continual technological innovation (for a review of extra-job factors influencing the career environment, see Storey, 2000).

Openness was also higher for IT professionals in our sample, and it was positively correlated with career satisfaction. Higher levels of Openness enable individuals to adapt to change and facilitate personal discovery, new learning, and professional development. The field of IT is continually changing due to new technology and innovations in software, information systems, and arrangements for integrating IT with other organizational units and functions. IT staff need to be nimble and flexible. Technology launches in the last 2-3 years have doubled the complexity when compared against all prior technology combined. IT staff that enjoy openly learning and sharing information flourish in this type of environment. IT staff often drive the business adoption of collaboration technologies such as instant messenger and virtual web meetings. Most enterprises are constantly assessing the need to retrain or replace the IT workforce. The IT workers that openly stay abreast of new technologies and openly share them with their peers tend to flourish. In fact, the Association of Information Technology Professionals (AITP) lists the following conduct standards for all members:

In recognition of my obligation to management I shall: keep my personal knowledge up- to-date and insure that proper expertise is available when needed. (AITP, 2006, para. 2).

In recognition of my obligation to my employer I shall: make every effort to ensure that I have the most current knowledge and that the proper expertise is available when needed. (AITP, 2006, para. 5).

The IT field should continue to expand and become more differentiated with respect to areas of specialization and expertise. Thus, Openness will continue to be critical to the success and psychological well-being of IT professionals. In fact, it is difficult to imagine an IT employee who is closed to new ideas and resists change being effective in any IT job or deriving satisfaction from this work.

Two other traits were also of higher magnitude and were positively correlated with career satisfaction for IT professionals—Tough-Mindedness and Customer Service Orientation. Qualities like tough-mindedness have often been seen as an important qualification for working in the IT profession. For example, Exforsys (2008) states that "the first trait which computer programmers should possess is an analytical mind" and CareerOverview.Com (2008) avers that "the most qualified applicants for programming jobs will have analytical and logical thinking skills...". Also, the Myers-Briggs Thinking dimension (which involves using a logical thinking style and basing decisions on facts and data rather than feelings) has been described as characteristic of computer programmers, systems analysts and computer specialists (BSM Consulting, 2008). In addition, "being logical and factual" has been associated with computer programmers (careerpath. com, 2008). Given the relatively limitless options in technology and the rapid pace of change, IT staff need to be willing to make a decision and stick with it. Their decisions need to be grounded

in a rigorous analysis of integration with other information systems, but reviews must be done quickly. IT staff need to be tough-minded enough to stick with a grounded decision.

The results for Customer Service Orientation are consistent with studies showing a positive relationship between the career satisfaction of IT employees and the IT service orientation (Jiang, Klein, & Ballou, 2001). Most IT departments in organizations have service level agreements to provide timely, quality service to internal customers. Then, too, more effective IT performance has been found to have a positive impact on the satisfaction of external customers within the company (Karimi, Somers, & Gupta, 2001). The importance of customer service for IT workers is at the cornerstone of their drive to expand services to additional internal customer groups (e.g. marketing and sales departments) and integrate IT with other organizational functions (Lee, Trauth, & Farwell, 1995). This customer service drive to standardize IT services often results in cost savings as services become consistent across the enterprise. If the IT organization can align with external facing lines of business (sales, marketing, etc), the IT staff's alignment with Customer Service Orientation can be used to directly benefit the business by supporting technologies such as new marketing and service activities increases, such as personalized marketing, self-service sales, podcasts, instant product presentation, real-time customer intelligence. (Gogan, 1998).

One personality trait which was positively related to career satisfaction but for which IT professionals had, on average, below-norm scores was Conscientiousness. The latter result is not surprising given the generally unstructured nature of IT work and the freedom and discretion IT professionals have in how they solve problems and perform their work (see O*NET, 2008). The current findings of below-norm Conscientiousness for IT professionals are consistent with results from a recent investigation by Ash, Rosenbloom, Coder, and Dupont (2008). They found that non-IT professionals had higher Conscientiousness scores than IT professionals. Similarly, a study by Mastor and Ismael (2004) observed slightly below-norm Conscientiousness scores for IT majors. Interestingly, however, Witt and Burke (2008) found that Conscientiousness is positively related to the job performance of IT professionals.

Considered as a whole, the above findings for Conscientiousness and IT work are complex and do not lend themselves to simple interpretations. While higher levels of Conscientiousness may be desirable from the standpoint of career satisfaction and the job performance of IT professionals, IT professionals generally score lower on Conscientiousness than individuals in other occupations. This may be to due to a self-selection bias in that individuals lower on Conscientiousness gravitate toward IT work for any number of reasons. Like all of the Big Five traits, Conscientousness is a broadband construct. It subsumes personal qualities like attention to detail and quality consciousness in the same way that it embraces qualities like conformity and rule-boundedness. The conformity and rule-boundedness aspects of Conscientousness may be incongruent with the noncomformist, unconventional personalities often attracted to IT work. Such individuals prefer more informal and less structured work environments, relaxed dress codes and personal appearance requirements, greater discretion and less standardization in how the work is accomplished; and, in some cases, more schedule freedom. From the organization's standpoint, based on the above results, it would be desirable to recruit and hire IT candidates with higher levels of Conscientiousness and to emphasize Conscientiousness-enhancing training and development programs (such as time management, safety and security issues, and organizational citizenship).

Two other traits on which IT professionals had below-norm scores, but which were not significantly related to career satisfaction were Visionary Style and Image Management. The former finding is understandable given that IT

work, with its emphasis on details and many small, interlocking steps in task completion, typically involves the opposite of visionary thinking style. As summarized by Walling (2008):

I have never, ever, ever seen a great software developer who does not have amazing attention to detail.

As for a relative under-emphasis on Image Management, very little IT work requires careful monitoring of one's own image and trying to project a smooth, polished, self-presentation in interpersonal settings. As an anonymous blogger put it, "in my experience, computer programmers don't *care* that much about being popular or good looking—they are skilled craftsmen with a solid work ethic" (Half Sigma, 2008).

Although each was positively related to career satisfaction, there were no significant differences in mean scores between IT and other occupations on five traits: Assertiveness, Extraversion, Optimism, Agreeableness/Teamwork, and Work Drive. Regarding the importance of Assertiveness, while it might not be listed in most inventories of key attributes of IT employees, Schneider (2002) lists it as one of the key personality attributes for IT consultants, noting that "you need to be assertive...You need to make sure people don't walk over you. You also need to be able to stick up for yourself without coming across as too aggressive." Similarly, Weinberg (1972) contends that a critical personality trait for programmers is "...assertiveness, or force of character. A programmer's job is to get things done, and getting things done sometimes requires moving around obstacles, jumping over them, or simply knocking them down." The field of Information Technology changes at such an incredible rate that staff who find themselves without the ability to drive a solution quickly find themselves lacking current skills and unable to perform effectively.

Optimism is another trait which is unlikely to appear in any IT job description. However, it is the second most highly correlated trait with career satisfaction for IT professionals. This is similar to Lounsbury, Loveland, et al.'s (2003) finding that Optimism was one of the top two correlates of Career Satisfaction for occupations in general. The importance of Optimism for IT work may be due to the benefits for problem-solving associated with having a positive mindset and persisting toward solutions despite setbacks, and the attendant satisfaction that comes from successful task completion. Nearly all important IT work is fraught with difficulties and challenges for which an optimistic frame of mind would be an advantage (cf. Seligman, 1990). Perhaps that is why Walling (2008) concludes that in the case of software development, "...all great developers are optimistic...". In many cases software programmers must embark on programming efforts without a complete understanding of how the programming will be done. For Optimistic IT staff, this can be an exciting time that contributes to career satisfaction.

As for the importance of Work Drive, having a strong work ethic is frequently listed as a requisite factor for success in computer programming or other types of IT work (e.g., Liberty, 1999). Given the multiple, continual demands placed on IT workers and the often high-stakes nature of successful IT project completion, it makes sense to argue that those with high levels of Work Drive may be better suited for such work. They would also be more likely than their less hard-working peers to receive the organizational rewards and recognition that, over the long term, leads to higher levels of career satisfaction. The field of information technology changes so frequently that most IT staff have a healthy sense of "Retool", "Retrain" or "Replace". Those with a consistent Work Drive tend to provide value to the organization by constantly retraining themselves with little effort from management.

IT work is widely regarded as being mainly the domain of introverts with two-thirds of computer professionals estimated as being introverted, (e.g.,

Institute for Management Excellence, 2006). However, in the present study there were no significant differences between our sample of IT professionals and other occupations as a whole on this dimension. Moreover, the average IT-worker score represented about an equal emphasis on Introversion and Extraversion. Also, Extraversion was positively correlated with IT career satisfaction in the present study. How can such observations be reconciled? The answer may be that Extraversion leads to more satisfying experiences over the course of a career, perhaps because it results in more acquaintanceships and friendships, greater personal communication with coworkers and bosses, or even a more positive reception by others at work. Such dynamics would produce a positive correlation between Extraversion and career satisfaction. Regardless, the present results should be considered by those individuals engaged in career planning, vocational development, job counseling, and others who help individuals choose an occupation and might be inclined to not recommend IT for extraverts. From the standpoint of career satisfaction, one would encourage more extraverted individuals to go into IT work. On the other hand, the current findings are consistent with recommendations that interpersonal skills and communication should be emphasized in IT professional training and development (Lee et al., 1995). In addition, since Extraversion is related to higher levels of career satisfaction, organizations may want to consider offering IT employees more opportunities to socialize, fraternize, and interact with other employees through, for example, company-sponsored luncheons, picnics, recreation programs, outings, and other activities that promote extraversion-related behaviors.

Regarding teamwork, in the present sample IT professionals did not differ from other occupations, which is at variance with the traditional view of IT employees working independently (cf. U. S. Dept. of Labor, 1991). Teamwork was, however, positively correlated with career satisfaction in the current study. One reason for this is that IT departments usually have to coordinate and collaborate with other organizational units to achieve successful information systems. IT professionals are increasingly involved in cross-organizational teaming, and internal IT teaming has become more the norm with the advent of team-based or agile programming (Beck 1999). As noted by Schneider (2002) in his research on factors contributing to the success of IT projects, "... teamworking and motivation are more important than technical competence or formal training." Additionally, Major et al. (2007) list as best practices for managing IT employees using teams for general problem-solving, knowledge-sharing, and peer learning. In terms of practical implications, based on the present results, individuals who are more teamwork-oriented would be more likely to enjoy careers in IT. However, the Occupational Information Network (O*NET), which is one of the premiere sources of occupational planning information, lists the opposite of Teamwork—Independence—as a key Work Style and Work Value for IT occupations (O*NET, 2008). Further research is needed to clarify which of these attributes is more important for successful and satisfying IT careers.

As previously noted, an empirically-based personality profile of IT professionals has yet to be developed. The current study is an important first step in that direction. Holland's theoretical framework characterizes IT professionals as having mainly investigative, realistic, and conventional interests. While consistent with Holland's vocational theory, the current study goes beyond such interest-based depictions by showing that, compared to other occupations, IT professionals are more: tough-minded and analytic, more open to new experiences and learning, emotionally resilient, customer-oriented, and intrinsically motivated. They are also less: conscientious, concerned with image management, and less visionary in their thinking style. Moreover, we found higher magnitude and positive correlations with career satisfaction for the traits of Emotional Resilience, Optimism, Assertiveness, Work Drive, Extraversion, and Openness. In summary, the Holland vocational theory is very germane for the field of IT and there appear to be multiple personality pathways to career satisfaction for IT professionals.

REFERENCES

Association of Information Technology Professionals. (2008). *Standard of conduct.* Retrieved October 8, 2008, from http://www.aitp.org/organization/about/conduct/conduct.jsp

Ash, R. A., Rosenbloom, J. L., Coder, L., & Dupont, B. (2008). *Gender differences and similarities in personality characteristics for information technology professionals.* Retrieved June 16, 2008, from http://www.ipsr.ku.edu/~ipsr/ITWorkforce/pubs/GenderDifferences.shtml

BSM Consulting. (2008). *Careers for INTJ personality types.* Retrieved June 16, 2008, from *http://www.personalitypage.com/INTJ_car.html*

Beas, M. I., & Salanova, M. (2006). Self-efficacy beliefs, computer training and psychological well-being among information and communication technology workers. *Computers in Human Behavior, 22*(6), 1043-1058.

Beck. K. (1999). *Extreme programming explained: Embrace change.* Boston: Addison -Wesley.

CareerPath.Com. (2008). *Does your personality hold the key to the perfect job?* Retrieved June 16, 2008, from http://www.careerpath.com/advice/194357-does-your-personality-hold-key-to-the-perfect-job

CareerOverview.Com. (2008). *Computer programming careers, jobs, and training.* Retrieved June 16, 2008, from *http://www.careeroverview.com/computer-programming-careers.html*

De Raad, B. (2000). *The big five personality fac-*

tors (the psycholexical approach to personality). Seattle, WA: Hogrefe & Huber.

DeNeve, K. M., & Cooper, H. (1998). The happy personality: A meta-analysis of 137 personality traits and subjective well-being. *Psychological Bulletin, 95,* 542-575.

Exforsys Inc. (2008). *The role of a computer programmer.* Retrieved June 16, 2008, from http://www.exforsys.com/career-center/career-tracks/the-role-of-a-computer-programmer.html

Gogan, K. (1998). Build customer satisfaction using real-time intelligence. *Marketing News, 32*(11), 13.

Half Sigma. (2008). *Not enough women majoring in computer science?* Retrieved June 16, 2008, from http://www.halfsigma.com/2007/04/not_enough_wome.html

Hetland, H., Sandal, G. M., & Johnsen, T. B. (2007). Burnout in the information technology sector: Does leadership matter? *European Journal of Work and Organizational Psychology, 16*(1), 58-75.

Holland, J. L. (1985). *Making vocational choices: A theory of vocational personalities and work environments.* Odessa, FL: Psychological Assessment Resources.

Holland, J. L. (1996). Exploring careers with a typology: What we have learned and some new directions. *American Psychologist, 51*(4), 397-406.

Institute for Management Excellence. (2006). *Differences between "computer" folks and the general population.* Retrieved April 14, 2006, from http://www.itstime.com/jul2003.htm

Jepson, K. (2004). Stress and IT. *Credit Union Journal, 14.*

Jiang, J. J., Klein, G., & Ballou, J. L. (2001). The joint impact of internal and external career anchors on entry-level IS career satisfaction. *Information & Management, 39*(1), 31-39.

Judge, T. A., Heller, D., & Mount, M. K. (2002). Five-factor model of personality and job satisfaction: A meta-analysis. *Journal of Applied Psychology, 87*(3), 530-541.

Judge, T. A., Higgins, C. A., Thoresen, C. J., & Barrick, M. R. (1999). The big five personality traits, general mental ability, and career success across the life span. *Personnel Psychology, 52*(3), 621-652.

Karimi, J., Somers, T. M., & Gupta, Y. P. (2001). Impact of information technology management practices on customer service. *Journal of Information Management, Systems, 17*(4), 125-158.

Koscho, G. R. (2003). President's message. *Information Executive, 7*(2), 1.

Lee, D. M. S., Trauth, E. M., & Farwell, D. (1995). Critical skills and knowledge requirements of IS professionals: A joint academic industry investigation. *MIS Quarterly, 19*(3), 313-340.

Liberty, J. (1999). *The complete idiot's guide to a career in computer programming.* Indianapolis, IN: Que Press.

Lounsbury, J. W., Gibson, L. W., & Hamrick, F. L. (2004). The development of a personological measure of work drive. *Journal of Business and Psychology, 18*(4), 347-371.

Lounsbury, J. W., Gibson, L. W., Sundstrom, E., Wilburn, D., & Loveland, J. (2003). An empirical investigation of the proposition that "school is work": A comparison of personality-performance correlations in school and work settings. *Journal of Education and Work, 17*(1), 119-131.

Lounsbury, J. W., Loveland, J. M, Sundstrom, E. D., Gibson, L. W., Drost, A. W., & Hamrick, F. L. (2003). An investigation of personality traits in relation to career satisfaction. *Journal of Career Assessment, 11,* 287-307.

Lounsbury, J. W., Moffitt, L., Gibson, L. W.,

Drost, A. W., & Stevenson, M. W. (2007). An investigation of personality traits in relation to the job and career satisfaction of information technology professionals. *Journal of Information Technology, 22*, 174-183.

Lounsbury, J. W., Park, S. H., Sundstrom, E., Williamson, J., & Pemberton, A. (2004). Personality, career satisfaction, and life satisfaction: Test of a directional model. *Journal of Career Assessment, 12*, 395-406.

Lounsbury, J. W., Sundstrom, E., Loveland, J. M., & Gibson, L. W. (2003) Intelligence, "big five" personality traits, and work drive as predictors of course grade. *Personality and Individual Differences, 35*, 1231-1239.

Major, D. A., Davis, D. D., Germano, L. M., Fletcher, T. D., Sanchez-Hucles, J., & Mann, J. (2007). Managing human resources in information technology: Best practices of high-performing supervisors. *Human Resource Management, 46*(3), 411-427.

Mastor, K. A. & Ismael, A. H. (2004). Personality and cognitive style differences among matriculation engineering and information technology students. *World Transactions on Engineering and Technology Education, 3*(1), 101-105.

Messersmith, J. (2007). Managing work-life conflict among information technology workers. *Human Resource Management, 46*(3), 429-451.

O*NET. (2008). *Occupational information network. O*NET online.* Retrieved January 20, 2006, from http://online.onetcenter.org/

Paunonen, S. V., & Ashton, M. C. (2001). Big five factors and facets and the prediction of behavior. *Journal of Personality and Social Psychology, 81*(3), 524-539.

Perry, D. K. (1967). Vocational interests and success of computer programmers. *Personnel Psychology, 20*(4), 517-524.

Perry, D. K., & Cannon, W. M. (1968). Vocational interests of female computer programmers. *Journal of Applied Psychology, 52*(1), 31-35.

Prasad, J., Enns, H. G., & Ferratt, T. W. (2007). One size does not fit all: Managing IT employees' employment arrangements. *Human Resource Management, 46*(3), 349-372.

Rosenbloom, J. L., Ash, R. A., Dupont, B., & Coder, L. (2008). Why are there so few women in information *technology?* Assessing the role of personality in career choices. *Journal of Economic Psychology, 29*(4), 543-554.

Rouse, P. D. (2001). Voluntary turnover related to information technology professionals: A review of rational and instinctual models. *International Journal of Organizational Analysis, 9*(3), 281-290.

Salgado, J. F. (1997). The five factor model of personality and job performance in the European Community. *Journal of Applied Psychology, 82*(1), 607-620.

Savvas, A. (2004). Work stress at record high. Computer Weekly, 4.

Schneider, K. (2002). Non-technical factors are key to ensuring project success. *Computer Weekly.*

Seligman, M. E. P. (1990). *Learned optimism.* New York: Pocket Books.

Shankar, D. R. (2007). Anomie among information technology employees. *Journal of Indian Psychology, 25*(1-2), 101-107.

Storey, J. A. (2000). 'Fracture lines' in the career environment. In A. Collin & R. A. Young (Eds.), *The future of career.* UK: Cambridge University.

The Career Key. (2008). *Holland's six personality types.* Retrieved Jun 10, 2008, from http://www.careerkey.org/asp/your_personality/hollands_6_personalitys.asp

United States Department of Labor Employment and Training Administration. (1991). *Dictionary of occupational titles*. Indianapolis, IN: JIST Works.

Walling R. (2008). *Personality traits of the best software developers*. Retrieved June 16, 2008, from http://www.softwarebyrob.com/2006/08/20/personality-traits-of-the-best-software-developers/

Weinberg, G. M. (1972). Critical personality traits. In *The psychology of computer programming*. Retrieved June 16, 2008 from, *http://www.dorsethouse.com/features/excerpts/expsych8.html*

Williamson, J. W., Pemberton, A. E., & Lounsbury, J. W. (2005). An investigation of career and job satisfaction in relation to personality traits of information professionals. *Library Quarterly, 75*(2), 122-141.

Witt, L. A., & Burke, L. A. (2008). Using cognitive ability and personality to select information-technology professionals. In M. Mahmood (Ed.), *Advanced topics in end user computing, Volume 2* (pp. 1-17). Hershey, PA: Idea Group Publishing.

KEY TERMS AND DEFINITIONS

Big Five Model: An extensively researched, conceptual model of normal personality proposing five basic traits—Openness, Conscientiousness, Extraversion, Agreeableness, and Emotional Stability—that characterize individual differences in personality. Also known as the Five-Factor Model.

Career Choice: Process of choosing a career path which can involve choices regarding education and training for a given career.

Career Satisfaction: Overall feelings of accomplishment and fulfillment a person has regarding his or her career as a whole, which can represent 80,000-100,000 hours of work for the typical American.

Holland's Vocational Theory: John L. Holland's basic vocational theory contends that people flourish in jobs and careers in which there is a good fit between their personality and characteristics of the work environment. Better fit leads to higher levels of satisfaction, productivity, and longevity.

Information Systems Careers: Careers in the information systems or information technology professions

Personal Style Inventory (PSI): A normal personality inventory developed by Resource Associates that measures broad and narrow traits which have been contextualized for work as well as academic settings.

Personality Traits—Broad and Narrow: Broad personality traits, such as Extraversion and Conscientiousness, are global constructs representing relatively enduring characteristics of individuals consistent over time and across situations. Narrow personality traits, such as Optimism or Tough-mindedness, are more conceptually specific constructs, often components of broad traits, that are consistent over time and across situations.

Person-Environment Fit: Degree of correspondence between a person and his or her environment, usually viewed as the alignment between the personality of the individual and the demands of an environment, as in person-job fit.

Vocational Choice-Information Systems: Process of choosing information systems as a career.

Vocational Interests: Characteristic likes or dislikes a person has regarding different occupations or types of work, usually conceptualized as a small set of basic dimensions, such as Holland's six-fold taxonomy of Realistic, Investigative, Artistic, Social, Enterprising, and Conventional vocational interests.

Chapter XXXI
Theory of Planned Behavior and Reasoned Action in Predicting Technology Adoption Behavior

Mahmud Akhter Shareef
Carleton University, Canada

Vinod Kumar
Carleton University, Canada

Uma Kumar
Carleton University, Canada

Ahsan Akhter Hasin
Bangladesh University of Engineering & Technology, Bangladesh

ABSTRACT

Research related to the impact of individual characteristics in their acceptance of online systems driven by information and communication technology (ICT) observed that dissimilarities among individuals influence their adoption and use of the systems. Thus, research streams investigating this issue generally follow the traditions of the theory of reasoned action (TRA) or the theory of planned behavior (TPB). Research reveals that individual characteristics, mediated by beliefs, affect attitudes, which affect intentions and behaviors. These two major behavioral theories related to technology acceptance and the intention to use technology might provide significant theoretical paradigms in understanding how online system adoption and diffusion, driven by information technology, can vary globally. In this study, the authors' first objective is to understand TRA and TPB as they study ICT-based online adoption and diffusion globally. Then, based on that theoretical framework, their second objective focuses on developing a theory of ICT adoption and diffusion as an online behavior.

INTRODUCTION

Evolution, which may denote a variety of concepts, is most generally defined as the accumulation of historically acquired information in an organized fashion (Bandura, 1986). Technological evolution seems to refer to natural forces not dissimilar to the forces of natural selection. The technological stage of evolution is characterized by the development and expansion of technology and information from generation to generation and by intensification of competition between human groups. On the other hand, technological development implies complete control over the process. This controlled process of technology development, diffusion, disruption, and adoption has cultural, behavioral, and social aspects (Kumar *et al,* 2008).

The adoption and extensive use of ICT-based online systems in public and private organizations has expanded dramatically. The Internet has become, within a very short time, one of the basic media of modern society to accept ICT. Many countries now consider understanding online systems and mastering the basic skills and concepts of ICT as part of the paradigms of market development. It is the single most powerful tool for participating in global markets, promoting political accountability, improving the delivery of and cost cutting in basic services, developing efficiency in operations of public and private organizations, and enhancing local development opportunities. Researchers indicate that, from the last decade, about 50 percent of all new capital investment in organizations has been in information technology (IT)-based online systems (Westland and Clark 2000). This huge investment in online systems and ICT can only be realized if its full potential is achieved. For ICT to achieve its full potential, it must be accepted and used by employees of organizations internally and by citizens externally. Explaining user acceptance of new technology is often regarded as a research area of great potential in contemporary ICT literature (Hu *et al.* 1999). Organizational theorists, IT professionals,

psychologists, sociologists, economists, market researchers, policy makers, and academics are all keenly interested in analyzing different aspects of the IT-intensive online system adoption from their own fields. The globalization of the market economy is extremely helpful in understanding technology diffusion and adoption in developed countries as well as in some developing countries regarded as Asian giants—such as Singapore, Hong Kong, Taiwan, Malaysia, South Korea, China, Singapore, Thailand, and India. However, the diffusion of ICT and acceptance of online systems do not follow a single track for all countries. In each country, the different economic and government policies and differences in social, cultural, and behavioral aspects are very significant and prominent. This paper mainly concentrates on evaluating ICT-based online system adoption and diffusion criteria based on the previously mentioned perspectives. Researchers also argue that the cultural, social, and behavioral attitudes in adopting online systems are strongly affected by some external attributes arising from political, economic, and marketing issues (AL-Shehry *et al.*, 2006; Damodran *et al.*, 2005). However, before going into further analysis regarding those aspects, we should examine brief definition of IT. Information technology (IT), also known as information and communication(s) technology (ICT) is concerned with the use of modern computer-based technology in managing, organizing, diffusing, and processing information in different public and private sectors.

The fundamental opportunity offered by an online system is for suppliers, developers, and sellers (i.e., providers of ICT) to gain direct access to different stakeholders without the development and maintenance costs associated with the physical distribution channels. In the electronic medium, competitors can emerge from anywhere in the world with significant differences in attitude, especially toward adopting new ICT. As a result, national and also global cultural attributes show significant disparities in the behavioral intention and attitudes of users of online systems. A society produces some values, ideas, intentions, and speculations about the human personality. These perceived psychological phenomena depend on rules, regulations, relationships, religious and political views, values, culture, tradition, etc. Depending on cultural and social factors, the behavioral intention to adopt online system operated through ICT can be affected substantially (Engel *et al.*, 1993). Based on the literature reviews (Chase and Tansik, 1978; Donthu and Boonghee, 1998; Furrer *et al.*, 2000; Kale and Sudharshan, 1987; Kettinger *et al.*; 1995; Kogut and Singh, 1988; Li, 1994; Liu *et al.*, 2001), the importance of those social values for determining adoption factors of online system is evident. Social values generate attitudes and beliefs that lead to the stakeholders' behavior of using certain objects, viz., IT (Shareef *et al.*, 2008). Therefore, studies of behavioral intentions and culture have a significant place in the development of an adoption framework of ICT-based online system.

Research related to the impact of individual characteristics observed that dissimilarities among individuals influence their adoption and use of online systems (Titah and Barki, 2005). A research stream (Carter and Bélanger, 2005; Gilbert *et al.*, 2004; Phang *et al.*, 2005; Titah and Barki, 2005) investigating the influence of individual characteristics on online system adoption that generally follows the tradition of the TRA and TPB (Fishbein and Ajzen, 1975) reveals that individual characteristics mediated by beliefs affect attitudes, which affect intentions and behaviors. These two major behavioral theories related to technology acceptance and the intention to use technology might provide significant theoretical paradigms of understanding how IT-intensive online system adoption and diffusion can vary globally. Technology Acceptance Model (TAM) by Davis *et al.*, (1989) is also an information system theory that models how users come to accept and use a technology. However, TAM has used TRA to conceptualize its paradigms of modeling.

Rogers (1995) Diffusion of Innovation Theory is also a powerful theory in predicting technology diffusion and adoption. However, in this study since our prime focus is to investigate human behavior, attitude, and belief in accepting ICT, we have focused primarily on TRA and TPB. Here, our first objective is to understand TRA and TPB as we study ICT-based online adoption and diffusion globally. Then, based on that theoretical framework, our second objective focuses on developing a theoretical framework of ICT adoption and diffusion as an online behavior.

In the next section, we will investigate basic concepts of TRA and TPB with a background synopsis and briefly illustrate their utility in identifying ICT-based online acceptance behavior. The next section develops conceptual paradigms of ICT-based online system acceptance. The conclusion explains the usage of TRA and TPB in relation to online system acceptance behavior grounded on the proposed theoretical framework. Finally, future research direction is suggested.

THEORETICAL FRAMEWORK OF TRA AND TPB

Behavioral attitude is dependent on some external and internal factors including experience, personality, and social values (Engel *et al.*, 1993). Behavioral intention has significant implications in assessing adoption determinants. Service literature has incorporated behavioral intention in their models for a long time to identify dimensions that create the intention to accept certain systems (Azjen and Fishbein, 1980; Bellizzi and Hite, 1992; Cox and Rich, 1964; Davis *et al.*, 1989). Nevertheless, IT service designers have not given enough priority to social characteristics of different stakeholders, like behavior, personality, attitude, belief, values etc., as an antecedent of the adoption framework (Damodaran *et al.*, 2005). Several authors intended to use the frameworks of TRA and TPB to postulate the fundamental paradigms of different acceptance characteristics of information technology (Davis, 1989; Treiblmaier *et al.*, 2004; Warkentin *et al.*, 2002).

In 1980, Ajzen and Fishbein formulated the TRA. This resulted from attitude research using the Expectancy Value Models (Fishbein, 1968). They formulated the TRA after trying to estimate the discrepancy between attitude and behavior. The fundamentals of the TRA come from the field of social psychology. Social psychologists attempt, among other things, to explain how and why attitude affects behavior. That is, how and why people's beliefs change the way they act. The study of the ways attitude influences behavior began in 1872 with Charles Darwin. Darwin defined attitude as the external expression of an emotion. In the 1930s psychologists defined attitude as an emotion or thought with a behavioral component. This behavior could be non-verbal such as body language, signals, signs, or vocally expressed. Psychologists argued about what should make up the term attitude. Social psychologists suggest that attitude includes behavior and cognition, and that attitude and behavior are positively correlated.

TRA has three general constructs: (1) behavioral intention, (2) attitude, and (3) subjective norm. Ajzen and Fishbein (1980) proposed that a person's behavior is determined by the person's intention to perform the behavior and that this intention is, in turn, a function of the person's attitude toward the behavior. One of the potential reflectors of possible behavioral outcome is intention. Intention is the cognitive representation of a person's readiness to perform an intended behavior, and it is considered to be the immediate indicator of behavior. Behavioral intention measures the relative strength of a person's likelihood to perform an anticipated behavior. It comprises motivational or attitudinal factors that capture how persons are engaging to perform the intended behavior (Ajzen 1991). So, TRA conjectures that behavioral intention is the most influential predictor of behavior. In a meta analysis of 87 studies, an average correlation of

.53 was observed between intentions and behavior (Sheppard *et al.* 1988).

For different contexts, the magnitude of beliefs, which in turn affect attitude, differs. So, these constructs will be evaluated by a person's valuation of the weight of these consequences. One might have the belief that adopting modern ICT is good for one's professional career. It enhances efficiency and also effectiveness. However, it is time consuming to learn and resources are also not always available. Each of these beliefs can be weighted based on one's perception of the merits of those beliefs. Subjective norm is regarded as a combination of perceived expectations from relevant individuals or groups along with the intention to comply with these expectations. It is considered as the person's belief that individuals or groups associated with that person expect that the person should or should not perform the behavior and the person's expectation to comply with the specific references (Fishbein and Ajzen, 1975). Associates of one individual might have engaged in ICT-based projects. They have enough skill and are advancing their professional career by adopting ICT. These associates have explicit and implied influence on that individual's intention to learn ICT. However, at the same time that individual's brother might have had adverse consequences in trying to adopt ICT in professional life. That brother may have devoted much time, money, and efforts to learn IT and, ultimately, could not pay back these investments. So, he might discourage that person from learning ICT. This circumstance might have a negative impression on that individual's decision making about learning ICT. The beliefs of these people, weighted by the importance of the individual attitude to each circumstance/opinion, might influence the person's behavioral intention to use ICT, which in turn will affect that person's behavior to learn or not learn ICT in a professional career. So, a person's intention toward a specific behavior is affected by the person's attitude toward that behavioral outcome and the attitude a person perceives other people would have towards the performance of that behavior. A person's attitude, combined with subjective norms, forms the person's behavioral intention. From the review of TRA, we get the essence that behavioral intention, a function of both attitudes toward a behavior and subjective norms toward that behavior can predict actual behavior. A person's attitudes about learning ICT in professional life combined with the subjective norms about learning ICT in professional life, each with their own weight, will determine intention of learning ICT in professional life (or not), which will then lead to the actual behavior.

Fishbein and Ajzen asserted that attitudes and norms are not weighted equally in predicting a specific behavior. Most important is context-based measurement, i.e., issue or subject related measurement. "Indeed, depending on the individual and the situation, these factors might be very different effects on behavioral intention; thus a weight is associated with each of these factors in the predictive formula of the theory. For example, you might be the kind of person who cares little for what others think. If this is the case, the subjective norms would carry little weight in predicting your behavior" (Miller, 2005, pp. 127). TRA has been tested in numerous studies across many areas—including dieting (Sejwacz *et al.*, 1980), using condoms (Greene, Hale, and Rubin, 1997), consuming genetically engineered foods (Sparks *et al.*, 1995), and limiting sun exposure (Hoffman *et al.*, 1999). ICT literature incorporated this theory to define attitudes, behavioral intention, and cultural differences on the way to adopting online systems (George, 2000; Collier and Bienstock, 2006). This theory can be extended to conceptualize the human behavioral pattern in the decision-making strategy and, ultimately, to design the application of ICT, whether it is E-commerce (EC) and E-government (EG), looking at global behavioral attitudes.

The validity of the TRA is extensive within some conditions; however, under circumstances where internal and external factors might control or affect the motivation of the outcome of behavior, TRA is a relatively poor or partial predictor of those types of behaviors. For actual behavioral outcome, it appears not to be completely voluntary and under control; this resulted in the addition of certain external or internal factors, termed as perceived behavioral control. With this addition, the theory was called the TPB. TPB is a theory that predicts intended and rational behavior, because behavior can be deliberative, organized, and planned. Thus, TPB, which is an extension of TRA, was developed to incorporate behavioral control factors in predicting behavior. This theory extends the incomplete concept of TRA in predicting an actual behavior under the influence of certain stimuli that intended behaviors are also controlled by some uncertainty. Therefore, performing a behavior depends not only on intention but also on some external or internal factors that may interfere with the motivational behavior. Behavioral control is conceptualized as one's perception of the context of performing a behavior. This construct reflects a person's perception of the presence or absence of external favoring or non-favoring resources and opportunities to perform a behavior of interest (Barnett and Presley, 2004). It is a product of belief of availability of external pursuing factors multiplied by a perception of importance of those factors to the achievement of behavioral outcome. Based on the context of behavioral outcome, this behavioral control needs a significant insight from the researchers to identify the related factors. For example, external or internal factors, which can control the outcome of a behavior, can influence an actual behavior (Netemeyer *et al.*, 1990).

In this theory, the main dependent construct is behavioral intention/conduct and the main independent construct(s)/factor(s) are attitudes toward that behavior, subjective norms, and perceived behavioral control. The theory explains that individual behavior is driven by behavioral intentions where behavioral intentions are a function of an individual's attitude toward the behavior, the subjective norms surrounding the performance of the behavior, and the individual's perception of the ease with which the behavior can be performed (behavioral control). Although Ajzen (1991) has suggested that the link between behavior and behavioral control outlined in the model should be between behavior and actual behavioral control, rather than perceived behavioral control, the difficulty of assessing actual control has led to the use of perceived control as a dummy variable. This theory has a significant implication in identifying differences in the users' perception of the intention to adopt an ICT-based online system. These are characterized by cultural differences, security perceptions from the local external environment, and a disposition of trust as a behavioral control (Robey and Sahay, 1996; Warkentin *et al.*2002). TPB provides useful information for the development of communication strategies and consumer behavior. This theory is also used in evaluation studies like ICT adoption and diffusion, predicting online behavior toward, for example, EC and EG. In the IS literature, this theory has been used in identifying users' behaviors and attitudes in issues relating to Internet use, online purchase, household computer use, and online privacy, security, and trust. It is also frequently used in predicting user acceptance of word processing technology, user intentions to use microcomputers and IS, and organizational judgments in evaluating employees motivation towards job schedule (Ajzen, 1991; Albarracin *et al.*, 2001; Barnett and Presley, 2004; Bernadette, 1996; Brown and Venkatesh, 2005; Kraut *et al.*, 1998; Mathieson, K., 1991; Newburger, 1999; Pavlou and Fygenson, 2006; Vijayan *et al.*, 2005). This model can also be used in other fields like, for predicting citizens' voting behavior, disease prevention behavior, biological behavior etc. (Jaccard and Davidson, 1972).

CONCEPTUAL PARADIGMS OF ICT ADOPTION

This section of research is organized to identify and figure out theoretical perspectives of adoption framework of ICT-based online systems as behavioral outcome grounded on TRA and TPB. Therefore, in this study our dependent variable is actual behavior towards adoption of ICT-based online systems. This research, first attempts to investigate the prime aspects of online system adoption by individuals. Then, after analyzing those prime aspects of ICT adoption driven by ICT, successively, this research attempts to recognize and postulate the plausible explanatory variables for adoption. While investigating and revealing the prime perspectives of independent variables of online system adoption, this research explores the literature that addresses ICT-based online system adoption, implementation, characteristics, and related issues and the fundamental essences of TRA and TPB as derived in the previous section. Then, by comparing, adjusting, and integrating views collected from those studies, this research illustrates the design perspectives of ICT-based online system adoption for investigating explanatory variables.

Ventura (1995), in his early work on adoption of ICT-based online systems, argued that the integrative view of the ICT adoption paradigm should investigate technical, organizational, and institutional factors simultaneously to reveal a comprehensive concept. Drawing a reference from a study by Chwelos *et al.* (2001) on electronic data interchange (EDI) adoption, Tung and Rieck (2005) postulated that an online system adoption framework can be investigated from three interrelated perspectives: the technological, organizational, and inter-organizational aspects. The technological aspect deals with perceived characteristics of ICT; the organizational aspect reveals organizational characteristics of ICT users in multi-levels, whereas the inter-organizational perspective encompasses factors relating to the actions of other organizations and collaboration between the public and private sectors. Al-adawi *et al.* (2005) and Chwelos *et al.* (2001) conceptualized an online adoption model from the perspectives of technology and trust. Heeks and Bailur (2007) looked at both technological and social aspects to formulate the impacts of ICT-intensive systems, like EC and EG. In the light of the Socio-technical theory, Damodran *et al.* (2005) also formulated online system adoption concepts based on social, organizational, and technical perspectives. Anthopoulos *et al.* (2007), while developing the design of EG, emphasized that ICT strategic plans are political. The online paradigm emphasized internal networking, external collaboration, and globalization through adoption of technology, by putting services and information that public organizations offer online for stakeholders so that these services and information can be easily reached (Dunleavy, 2002; Moon, 2002).

However, different researchers (AL-Shehry *et al.*, 2006) emphasized that online system adoption is more than a technological matter, as it is influenced by many factors, such as organizational, behavioral, economic, social, and cultural issues. These are important forces, and they relate to the pattern and functions of public and private organizations, as well as government itself and good governance (Carter and Belanger, 2004; Holtham, 1992; Moon and Norris, 2005). Chen and Thurmaier's (2005) model includes technological, cultural, economic, behavioral, and organizational perspectives to design an adoption framework of ICT-based systems. Steyaert (2004) adopted a marketing perspective to formulate technology performance. He proposed an EC-based performance model to evaluate EG performance in terms of citizen satisfaction. Parent *et al.* (2005) and Warkentin *et al.* (2002) investigated the effect of trust on adoption of ICT projects. They suggested that trust in online systems, an antecedent of adoption, has political, organizational, and behavioral perspectives. Gilbert *et al.* (2004) proposed integration of the service quality, technology, and behavioral aspects of the technology adoption framework.

Consistent with practices in the IS research literature, Wang (2002), in studying the adoption of electronic tax filing, argued that individual differences refer to user factors that include traits such as personality and demographic variables. Also important are situational and contextual variables that account for differences attributable to circumstances, such as experience, prior knowledge, learning, and training, as aspects to be investigated in an adoption framework. Titah and Barki (2005) extensively reviewed adoption literature of EG and they suggested that technological, organizational, social, cultural, behavioral, and economic aspects should be considered in a comprehensive framework of ICT system adoption. Other researchers also postulated that the use of online systems is overwhelmingly influenced by several behavioral, cultural, marketing, economic, social, and organizational aspects (Barnett and Presley, 2004; Brown and Venkatesh, 2005; Karahanna *et al.*, 1999; Pavlou and Fygenson, 2006; Straub *et al.*, 1995; Venkatesh and Davis, 2000; Vijayan *et al.*, 2005). Therefore, from our literature review, we perceive that technological, behavioral, social, cultural, organizational, economic, political, and marketing aspects might provide important insights while investigating explanatory variables for ICT-based online system adoption, especially for investigating perceived behavioral control.

Now to delineate the theoretical paradigms and examine theoretical discourses that we observed from TRA and TPB, this research, at the outset of this present section, looks at Contingency Theory. The perspective originated with the work of Woodward (1965), who argued that technologies directly determine differences in such organizational attributes as organizational control, multilevel interactions, system of work, centralization of authority, and the formalization of rules and procedures. Environmental change and uncertainty, technology, different stakeholders, culture, behavioral differences, and different organizational attributes are all identified as environmental factors impacting the effectiveness of different organizational forms.

If we translate the core doctrine of Sociotechnical Theory (Trist and Bamforth, 1951) and Complementary Theory (Massini and Pettigrew, 2003), which explains the social aspects of people and society and technical aspects of information, communication, and technology, we get deep insights into integrating the social, organizational, and technological aspects of the ICT adoption framework. These theories refer to the interrelatedness of social, cultural, organizational, marketing, political, economic, and technical aspects. The discursive discourses of these theories explain the systems consisting of social and organizational elements as well as technical elements, and emphasizes that successful systems require the integrative interaction of technical, organizational, and social aspects of the system (Damodaran *et al.*, 2005). This doctrine of integrating all the aspects related to online system characteristics is also supportive of ideas from the Complementary theory, which several researchers of online system investigated. This theory suggests that in developing and conceptualizing the framework of ICT implementation, variables influencing the complete process at different phases should be considered as part of an integrated system of factors that are mutually reinforced (Massini and Pettigrew, 2003; Whittington and Pettigrew, 2003). Drawing inferences from all the previously mentioned paradigms, culture plays a significant role in conceptualizing adoption of an online system by developing perceived behavioral control, one of the important antecedents of behavioral intention.

A fundamental paradigm of TRA from an online ICT perspective is its assertion that any other factors that influence behavior do so only indirectly by influencing attitude and subjective norms in presence of certain external and internal factors as behavioral control. Such variables would

include, among others things, the system design characteristics, communication styles, behavioral characteristics and perception of trust and security, social and cultural values (including cognitive styles and other personality variables), and work related properties (Vijayan *et al.*, 2005). So TRA is quite appropriate in the context of predicting the behavior of using online systems. Further, TPB gives a new outlook on external facilities, which have a direct effect on intention for a behavior and behavioral outcome. Mathieson (1991) used the TPB as well as the Technology Acceptance Model (TAM) to predict user's intentions. As a general model, it is designed to explain most human behaviors (Ajzen, 1991). Hence, it is reasonable to conjecture that a TPB-based model could effectively explain ICT-based online adoption behavior (Pavlou and Fygenson, 2006; Sheppard *et al.*, 1988;). TPB includes three distinct categories of external beliefs related to attitudinal, normative, and control aspects— the antecedents of behavioral intention. These beliefs are context and situation specific and cannot be generalized a priori. Hence, for each new behavior, one must explore several explicit beliefs that have specific context (Ajzen and Fishbein 1980).

According to information management principles for online adoption, a prime factor for adoption is creating awareness among the prospective users. This means informing the end users about the implementation of innovation, important factors and issues, basic paradigms of the new system, comprehensive information about advantages and disadvantages, and the overall security of the system. Awareness is a relative concept. The public may be partially aware or completely aware of the strategic functionality of ICT. Awareness provides the retrospective material from which prospective users develop cues, concepts, or subjective ideas about their experience. As we learned from TRA and TPB, beliefs about a system turn to the attitude of using the system. However, awareness of the system is important at the beginning to develop beliefs.

Before developing an attitude to adopt an online system, prospective users need to be aware of its complete characteristics, including functional behavior, strategic benefits of the system, the safety and legal environment, etc. So we categorize this predicted variable for adoption as antecedents of beliefs to use, since awareness is the primary stimulus of creating attitudinal, normative, and behavioral control beliefs. This research defines Perceived Awareness (PA) as having and acquiring knowledge as much as a user perceived to be sufficient to learn the characteristics of online system and interact through perception or by means of information about ICT.

TAM is a widely referenced theoretical model for predicting the intention to use and the acceptance of IS by individuals. It proposes that perceived ease of use (PEOU) and perceived usefulness (PU) determine the attitude toward adoption of ICT. The attitude, in turn, leads to the intention to use ICT and the eventual acceptance (Bhattacherjee, 2001; Davis *et al.*, 1989; Lucas and Spitler, 1999; Moon, 2002; Venkatesh, 2000). Several researchers strongly predicted that these two constructs develop attitudinal belief and perceived behavioral control (PBC) in adopting ICT-based systems (Chau and Hu, 2001; Davis, 1989; Pavlou and Fygenson, 2006; Vijayan *et al.*, 2005). We can borrow the same definitional concepts for these two constructs of beliefs from TAM. PU has marketing, economic, and organizational aspects. PEOU is assumed to influence PU, because the easier a system is to use, the more useful it can be. A system will not be accepted if users do not perceive the system both useful and easy to use (Davis, 1989). Several scholarly articles (Brown and Venkatesh, 2005; Collier and Bienstock, 2006; Loiacono *et al.*, 2002; Udo, 2001; Wolfinbarger and Gilly, 2003; Yoo and Donthu, 2001) reveal that, for online interaction, communication quality, technical and design quality, and informational quality help to measure the constructs PU and PEOU for online adoption by citizens and business organizations.

Agency theory also asserted those behavioral aspects (Eisenhardt, 1989).

Several online researchers accepted two constructs— compatibility and image— from diffusion of innovation theory (DOI) as the creator of normative beliefs. When a person observes that close, important individuals have adopted and are using an online system frequently; this may create motivational beliefs in that person to also use, or not use, this online system. Compatibility is also responsible for imparting attitudinal beliefs for a person's behavior to comply with a virtual system. Compatibility has cultural, behavioral, and social aspects. It is dependent on individual characteristics, such as avoiding personal interaction and social influence. Several researchers indicated that specific characteristics of online systems that allow users to avoid personal interaction might create the perception of compatibility among users to adopt an online system (Gilbert *et al.*, 2004). Shedding light on TRA and TPB, the compatibility of an online system with adopters' beliefs, values, and attitudes reflects the behavioral aspect. From the socio-technical and complementary theories, beliefs and attitudes of adopters of a new technology system also have social and cultural aspects. Several researchers use this construct as the significant predictor of online adoption (Brown and Venkatesh, 2005; Carter and Bélanger, 2004; Chen and Thurmaier, 2005; Pavlou and Fygenson, 2006; Shareef *et al.*, 2007). Image, as proposed by Moore and Benbasat (1991), influences the acceptance and use of an innovation according to the DOI theory. Image refers to the perceptions that prospective users have of innovation as a status and prestige symbol. Interaction with online systems reflects a perception of superior status, which creates normative beliefs. So, several researchers included this construct in their proposed model of online adoption (Gefen *et al.*, 2002; Gilbert *et al*, 2004; Pavlou and Fygenson, 2006; Phang *et al*, 2005; Tung and Rieck, 2005; Vijayan *et al.*, 2005). Since adoption of online systems might reflect the adopter's familiarity with modern technology, higher level of education, competence in using the computer and Internet, and perception of modernism, these phenomena impart some degree of social values and prestige to adopters. Therefore, this research argues that image has social, behavioral, and also cultural aspects. Superior perception of using online has cultural ingredients. It also depends on personal behavioral ideology. Both compatibility and image constructs can be conceptualized from original DOI theory.

Socio-technical theory has great implications in evaluating the success of IT. According to this theory, it is essential for the technical system to be properly synthesized with the social-cultural aspect and the organizational environment in which the technical system must operate (Damodaran *et al.*, 2005; Finkelstein and Dowell, 1996; NAO, 1999). Based on this theory, looking at the online behavior of consumers for adopting an ICT-based online system reveals that in the virtual environment ICT adoption is significantly affected by trust disposition attitude as well as beliefs which have technological, behavioral, social, cultural, and organizational perspectives. Many consumers do not trust online systems due to their technology beliefs and behavioral characteristics. A disposition and attitude of trust towards online systems can be fundamentally described by normative beliefs and motivation to comply with the specific characteristics of the online environment. It is also dependent on institutional based beliefs (private organizations for EC and public organizations for EG). TRA suggests that trusting attitudes or beliefs significantly affect behavior. This trust disposition attitude is in turn characterized by cultural effects. Hofstede (1994) defined culture as "the collective programming of the mind". Hofstede's (1994) findings strongly suggest that cultural differences and social values differentiate customers in terms of their disposition and attitude of trust that, in turn, influence the perception and expectation of adopting online systems. However, adoption of an online system by

influential members of a person's nearby associates also affects that person's motivational belief towards online acceptance (Brown and Venkatesh, 2005). So, disposition and beliefs of trust can affect attitude and subjective norm constructs. We define this belief, i.e., trust disposition attitude, here as the general belief of an individual toward human beings, society, organizations, i.e., toward any object. This belief is also characterized by normative values of society and culture.

The control beliefs incorporated into different online system adoption models account for factors that may inhibit or encourage performance and behavior, such as lack/availability of resources, influence of external surrounding systems, knowledge, or social opportunity or barriers for engaging in that behavior (Ajzen 1985, 1991; Ajzen and Madden 1986; Taylor and Todd, 1995). In this connection, researchers have investigated a wide range of issues— including the attitude of a government, technology absorption capability, appropriateness of technology, and management of ICT. Other topics of investigation have been development and maintenance of technology, cooperation and conflict between government and citizens, and the social and economic benefits of online systems by adopting new IT (Brudney and Sally, 1995; Bugler and Stuart, 1993; Cusumano and Elenkov, 1994; Norris and Moon, 2005).

Many researchers have asserted that adoption of the new technology is closely related to knowledge and experience of that system and also availability of resources (Al-adawi *et al.*, 2005; AL-Shehry *et al.*, 2006; Carter and Bélanger, 2004; Chen and Thurmaier, 2005; Parent *et al.*, 2005; Tung and Rieck, 2005; Warkentin *et al.*, 2002). Users can secure and achieve traditional service without prior knowledge of modern ICT or availability of resources— including computers, Internet connection, call-center, and access. However, the adoption of online systems implies acceptance, use, and adoption of the Internet, virtual environment, software, and computers. From TPB, DOI, and Transaction Cost Analysis

(TCA), a user will not arrive at an intention to use an online system, which requires computer knowledge to get a competitive advantage, unless the user has competence from experience in the use of modern ICT. From technological, behavioral, economic, and organizational perspectives, it is anticipated that failing to get practical experience of technology will not create a user's behavioral intention to adopt the system. Also, in the absence of computer knowledge, a user can not perceive the economic advantages of online, which is largely due to extensive use of the computer and the Internet. So the availability of resources and knowledge of resources are important criteria for prospective users of the online system. In general, prior research has suggested a positive relationship among availability of resources; knowledge of and prior experience with ICT, Internet, and computers; and an attitude to use the system (Levin and Gordon, 1989; Wang, 2002).

Technology availability and computer self-efficacy have been examined in the IS literature (Compeau and Higgins, 1995; Wang, 2002). Continuing research efforts on availability of resources and knowledge, published in recent IS studies (Agarwal *et al.*, 2000), confirmed the critical role that resource availability and experience play in understanding individual responses to online system adoption. Wang (2002) investigated the relation of technology availability and computer self-efficacy with behavioral intention to adopt online tax filling system and observed a positive relation. The proposed relationship between computer availability and knowledge and attitudinal intention to use an online system is based on the theoretical framework proposed by Davis (1989) and Davis *et al.* (1989). Based on the social cognitive theory (Bandura, 1986), technology availability and technology self-efficacy affect an individual's perception of ability to use a computer, which, in turn, has an impact on creating a positive attitude toward using a technology intensive system. Bandura (1986) defined computer self-efficacy in general as: "People's judgments of

their capabilities to organize and execute courses of action required to attain designated types of performances. It is concerned not with the skills one has but with judgments of what one can do with whatever skills one possesses."

A society produces some values, ideas, intentions, and speculations on human personality. These values depends on several factors such as, rules, regulations, relationships, culture, tradition, etc. Online adoption can be affected extensively by different influences from the social environment (Engel *et al.*, 1993). Based on the literature reviews (Chase and Tansik, 1978; Donthu and Boonghee, 1998; Furrer *et al.*, 2000; Kale and Sudharshan, 1987; Kogut and Singh, 1988; Kettinger *et al.*, 1995; Li, 1994; Liu *et al.*, 2001), it is evident that those social values, which generate a pre-trust disposition or security concerns on the adopters' part, are very important for determining PBC. Perceived local environmental security is strongly based on experience from the surroundings, society, culture, local values, and state-wide rules and regulations, and it is affected by both extrinsic and intrinsic motivations (Davis *et al.*, 1992). Customers' perception of high uncertainty from the status of the society/country environment would dissuade them from choosing an uncertain situation and insist that they avoid uncertainty through risk aversion behavior (Nakata and Sivakumar, 1996). Therefore, customers perceiving high uncertainty from the surrounding environment have higher trust expectation compared with customers having low uncertainty perceptions (Donthu and Boonghee, 1998). Actually, the importance of a social, institutional, judicial, and state structure, that regulates law and orders, increases in the absence of personal relationships between service providers and customers (Shapiro, 1987). Such local structural assurances provide the perceived environmental security that ultimately contributes toward perceived trustworthiness in global operations like an online system. Depending on the above arguments, this research assumes that the perceived local environmental security perception of users can create PBC beliefs. Therefore, this paper defines the variable perceived local environmental security as, the degree to which a person perceives overall security assurance from the local environment (where he/she belongs) towards human beings, society, organizations, i.e., toward interrelations. This general security concern of individuals is based on cognitive experiences about security gathered from the country, government, society, local market, shopping, organizations, and interpersonal interaction.

Now, the light shed by our previous analyses on technology, psychology, sociology, organizational behavior, and marketing theories and literature review, we propose the theoretical frame of TRA and TPB for online adoption behavior that is shown in Figure 1. The prime characteristic of this model is that we have introduced perceived awareness as the antecedent of technology beliefs, i.e., perceived awareness of technology causes beliefs on technology acceptance. In addition we have identified theoretically different attributes of technology usage beliefs which in turn affect

attitude, subjective norm, and behavioral control of online technology acceptance. These three factors affect behavioral intention to accept ICT-based online system which leads to actual behavior regarding acceptance of online system.

CONCLUSION

The proposed theoretical framework of ICT-based online adoption, grounded in TRA and TPB under the virtual environment context, has significant implications for technology adoption behavior for global users. We have also investigated TAM, TCA, DOI, Socio-technical Theory and Complementary Theory to reveal different attributes of technology beliefs and to develop the final theoretical framework for predicting behavior related to adoption of ICT-based online system based on TPB and TRA. Several researchers have attempted to describe and develop this behavior. Nevertheless, prospective users' behavior in global context has been largely ignored. However, global users differ significantly, particularly in attitudes

Figure 1. ICT-based online acceptance framework

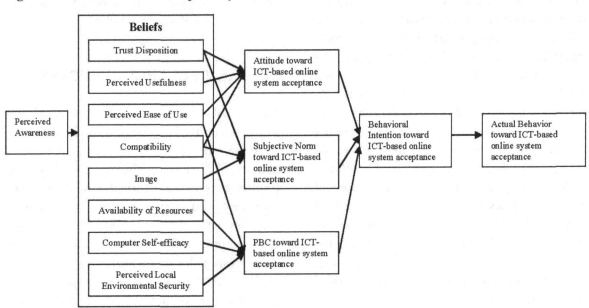

and behavioral control beliefs. These differences arise from differences in technological diffusion, government policies, perceived environmental security concerns, organizational aspects, economic phenomena, and social and cultural values. Individuals' perception of and expectation from an ICT-based online system significantly depend on cultural diversity (Tsikriktsis, 2002; Shareef *et al.*, 2008). Culture contains standards, ideology, values, and expectations that develop personal attitudes and characteristics (Lemme, 1999). Expectations and perceptions are not homogeneous across customers of all countries. For the last couple of decades, several models have been developed to provide an approach for the comparative analysis of different cultures (Hofstede, 1980). Although each of the articles developed cultural models that employed somewhat different terminologies and conceptual paradigms, the core concept generated offer sufficient convergence to provide support for their universality. Over the past decades, the validity of these findings has been confirmed in studies exploring consumer attitude, consumer acceptance, consumer trust disposition, and consumer decision making. A fundamental problem encountered in any attempt to study and analyze culture is based on the fact that concept of culture is very complex and always has relative sense. It is only useful in explaining differences. The proposed theoretical framework, integrating different technology adoption and diffusion and social and cultural theories, successfully incorporated social and cultural beliefs for global intentions of online users. Therefore, this theoretical framework can be used to predict online adoption behavior of global consumers. To validate our judgment, we have focused on cultural differences of global consumers and incorporated some exploratory attributes like Perceived Local Environmental Security, Trust Disposition Attitude, and Availability of Resources to include characteristics of beliefs towards technology adoption of all consumers—either from developed or developing countries.

PU, PEOU, compatibility, trust disposition, and computer self-efficacy are widely used in predicting ICT-based online acceptance behavior. However, from the theoretical aspects, this research paper finds philosophical underpinnings that the availability of resources and perceived environmental security are two strong beliefs for perceived behavioral control in the global context. It also conjectured that image might be a strong predictor for creating normative beliefs.

However, the prime implication of this research is to develop its paradigm for extension of TRA and TPB that beliefs have also an antecedent for the majority of the global population who are unfamiliar with and unaware of ICT-based online systems. Without awareness of the characteristics, components, perceived functional benefits, and a usage of ICT-based online system, behavioral intention and actual use of online systems cannot be developed. Therefore, the fundamental paradigm of this theoretical framework for predicting ICT-based online acceptance behavior of global prospective users is based on the argument that perceived awareness is the primary predictor of developing beliefs to use online systems; perceived awareness should be used as the antecedent of attitudinal, normative, and perceived behavioral control beliefs in the ICT-based online acceptance framework based on TRA and TPB.

FUTURE RESEARCH DIRECTION

This is a theoretical framework for predicting ICT-based online acceptance behavior for global consumers developed as an extended form of TRA and TPB. However, this extended theoretical framework is a general form. For different countries, perceived awareness might have different conjoint relationships with this model. Also, other attributes of attitudinal, normative, and behavioral control, especially those which are incorporated to capitalize on the global users phenomena— viz., perceived environmental security, image, and availability of resources have different inherent properties based on country contexts. So future research to operationalize those constructs can be conducted in different countries that differ significantly in social, cultural, economic, political, and technological aspects. Future research can also be carried on to contrast online system diffusion in private and public sector and the ICT-based online system acceptance grounded on the proposed framework in different countries. These types of studies can give proper insights into how those global attributes and beliefs can affect online diffusion and acceptance.

REFERENCES

Agarwal, R., Sambamurthy, V., & Stair, R. M. (2000). Research report: The evolving relationship between general and specific computer self-efficacy—an empirical assessment. *Information Systems Research, 11*(4), 418-430.

Ajzen, I., & Fishbein, M. (1980). *Understanding attitudes and predicting social behavior.* Englewood Cliffs, NJ: Prentice-Hall Inc.

Ajzen, I. (1985). From intentions to actions: A theory of planned behavior. In J. Kuhl & J. Beckman (Eds.), *Action control: From cognition to behavior* (pp. 11-39). New York: Springer Verlag.

Ajzen, I., & Madden, T. J. (1986). Prediction of goal-directed behavior: Attitudes, intentions, and perceived behavioral control. *Journal of Experimental Social Psychology, 22*, 453-474.

Ajzen, I. (1991). The theory of planned behavior. *Organizational Behavior and Human Decision Processes, 50*(2), 179-221.

Albarracin, D., Johnson, B. T., Fishbein, M., & Muellerleile, P. A. (2001). Theories of reasoned action and planned behavior as models of condom use: A meta-analysis. *Psychological Bulletin, 127*(1), 142-161.

Al-adawi, Z., Yousafzai, S., & Pallister, J. (2005). Conceptual model of citizen adoption of e-government. In *Proceedings of The 2nd International Conference on Innovations in Information Technology (IIT'05).*

Anthopoulos, L. G., Siozos, P., & Tsoukalas, L. A. (2007). Applying participatory design and collaboration in digital public services for discovering and re-designing e-government services. *Government Information Quarterly, 24*, 353-376.

Bandura, A. (1986). *Social foundations of thought and action.* Englewood Cliffs, NJ: Prentice-Hall.

Barnett, W., & Presley, A. (2004). Theory of planned behavior model in electronic learning: A pilot study. *Journal of Issues in Information Systems, V*(1), 22-28.

Bellizzi, J. A., & Hite, R. E. (1992). Environmental color, consumer feelings, and purchase likelihood. *Psychology & Marketing, 9*(5), 347-363.

Bernadette, S. (1996). Empirical evaluation of the revised technology acceptance model. *Management Science, 42*(1), 85-93.

Bhattacherjee, A. (2001). Understanding information systems continuance: An expectation-confirmation model, *MIS Quarterly, 25*(3), 351-370.

Brown, S. A., & Venkatesh, V. (2005). Model of adoption of technology in the household: A baseline model test and extension incorporating household life cycle. *MIS Quarterly, 29*, 399-426.

Brudney, J., & Sally S. (1995). The adoption of innovation by smaller local governments: The case of computer technology. *American Review of Public Administration, 25*(1), 71-86.

Bugler, D., & Stuart, B. (1993). Technology push or program pull: Interest in new information technologies within public organizations. In B. Bozeman (Ed.), *Public management: The state of the art* (pp. 275-293). San Francisco: Jossey-Bass.

Carter, L., & Bélanger, F. (2004). Citizen adoption of electronic government initiatives. In *Proceedings of the 37th Hawaii International Conference on System Sciences.*

Carter, L., & Bélanger, F. (2005). The utilization of e-government services: Citizen trust, innovation and acceptance factors. *Information Systems Journal, 15,* 5-25.

Chase, R. B., & Tansik, D. A. (1978). The customer contact model for organization design. *Management Science, 29*(9), 673-687.

Chau, P. Y. K., & Hu, P. J.-H. (2001). Information technology acceptance by individual professionals: A model comparison approach. *Decision Sciences, 32*(4), 699-719.

Chen, Y.-C., & Thurmaier, K. (2005, November 3-6). Government-to-citizen electronic services: Understanding and driving adoption of online transactions. In *Proceedings of the Association for Public Policy & Management (APPAM) conference,* Washington, D.C.

Chwelos, P., Benbasat, I., & Dexter, A. S. (2001). Research report: Empirical test of an EDI adoption model. *Information Systems Research, 12*(3), 304-321.

Collier, J. E., & Bienstock, C. C. (2006). Measuring service quality in e-retailing. *Journal of Service Research, 8*(3), 260-275.

Compeau, D. R., & Higgins, C. A. (1995). Computer self-efficacy: Development of a measure and initial test. *MIS Quarterly, 19*(2), 189-211.

Cox, D. F., & Rich, S. U. (1964). Perceived risk and consumer decision making - the case of telephone shopping. *Journal of Marketing Research, 1*(4), 32-39.

Cusumano, M. A., & Elenkov, D. (1994). Linking international technology transfer with strategy and management: A literature commentary. *Research Policy, 23,* 195-215.

Damodaran, L., Nicholls, J., & Henney, A. (2005). The contribution of sociotechnical systems thinking to the effective adoption of e-government and the enhancement of democracy. *The Electronic Journal of e-Government, 3*(1), 1-12.

Davis, F. D. (1989). Perceived usefulness, perceived ease of use and user acceptance of information technology. *MIS Quarterly, 13*(3), 319-340.

Davis, F. D., Bagozzi, R. P., & Warshaw, P. R. (1989). User acceptance of computer technology: A comparison of two theoretical models. *Management Science, 35*(8), 982-1003.

Donthu, N., & Boonghee, Y. (1998). Cultural influences on service quality expectations. *Journal of Service Research, 1*(2), 178-186.

Dunleavy, P. (2002). *Better public services through e-government* (Report by Comptroller and Auditor General, HC 704-1). London, National Audit Office Press.

Eisenhardt, M, K. (1989). Agency theory: An assessment and review. *Academy of Management Review, 14*(1), 57.

Engel, J. F., Blackwell, R. D., & Miniard, P. W. (1993). *Consumer behavior* (7th ed.). USA: The Dryden Press, Harcourt Brace Jovanovich.

Finkelstein, A., & Dowell, J. (1996). A comedy of errors: The London ambulance service case study. In *Proceedings of the 8th International Workshop on Software Specification & Design IWSSD-8* (pp. 2-4). IEEE CS Press.

Fishbein, M., & Ajzen, I. (1975). *Beliefs, attitude, intention, and behavior: An introduction to theory and research.* Reading, MA: Addison-Wesley.

Fishbein, M. (1968). An investigation of relationships between beliefs about an object and the attitude towards that object. *Human Relationships, 16,* 233-240.

Furrer, O., Liu, B. S.-C., & Sudharshan, D. (2000). The relationships between culture and service quality perceptions: Basis for cross-cultural market segmentation and resource allocation. *Journal of Service Research, 2*(4), 355-371.

Gefen, D., Pavlou, P. A., Warkentin, M., & Gregory, M. R. (2002). E-government adoption. In *Proceedings of the 8th Americas Conference on Information Systems.*

George, J. F. (2000). The effects of Internet experience and attitudes toward privacy and security on Internet purchasing. In *Proceedings of the 8th European Conference in Information Systems (ECIS),* (pp. 1053-1058). Austria: Vienna University of Economics and Business Administration.

Gilbert, D., Balestrini, P., & Littleboy, D. (2004). Barriers and benefits in the adoption of e-government. *The International Journal of Public Sector Management, 14*(4), 286-301.

Greene, K., Hale, J. L., & Rubin, D. L. (1997). A test of the theory of reasoned action in the context of condom use and AIDS. *Communication Reports, 10,* 21-33.

Hale, J. L., Householder, B. J., & Greene, K. L. (2003). The theory of reasoned action. In J. P. Dillard & M. Pfau (Eds.), *The persuasion handbook: developments in theory and practice* (pp. 259-286). Thousand Oaks, CA: Sage.

Heeks, R. B., & Bailur, S. (2007). Analyzing e-government research: Perspectives, philosophies, theories, methods, and practice. *Government Information Quarterly, 24,* 243-265.

Hoffmann, R. G., Rodrigue, J. R., & Johnson, J. H. (1999). Effectiveness of a school-based program to enhance knowledge of sun exposure: Attitudes toward sun exposure and sunscreen use among children. *Child Health Care, 28,* 69-86.

Hofstede, G. (1980). *Culture's consequences: International differences in work-related values.*

Beverly Hills, CA: Sage.

Hofstede, G. (1994). Management scientists are human. *Management Science, 40*(1), 4-13.

Holtham, C. (1992). Developing local and wide area networking to improve academic efficiency and effectiveness. In B. C. William & A. H. S. Nicholson (Eds.), *Management Education, Proceedings of the 3rd Annual Conference,* Bradford, Norwich, UK.

Hu, P. J., Chau, P. Y. K., Sheng, O. R. L., & Tam. K. Y. (1999). Examining the technology acceptance model using physician acceptance of telemedicine technology. *Journal of Management Information Systems, 6*(2), 91-112.

Jaccard, J. J., & Davidson, A. R. (1972). Toward an understanding of family planning behaviors: An initial investigation. *Journal of Applied Social Psychology, 2,* 228-235.

Kale, S. H., & Sudharshan, D. (1987). A strategic approach to international segmentation. *International Marketing Review, 4*(4), 60-70.

Karahanna, E., Straub, D. W., & Chervany, N. L. (1999). Information technology adoption across time: A cross-sectional comparison of pre-adoption and post-adoption beliefs. *MIS Quarterly, 23*(2), 183-213.

Kettinger, W. J., Lee, C. C., & Lee, S. (1995). Global measures of information service quality: A cross-national study. *Decision Sciences, 26*(5), 569-588.

Kogut, B., & Singh, H. (1988). The effect of national culture on the choice of entry mode. *Journal of International Business Studies, 19*(3), 411-432.

Kraut, R., Mukhopadhyay, T., Szczypula, J., Kiesler, S., & Scherlis, W. (1999). Communication and information: Alternative uses of the Internet in households. In *Proceedings of the Conference on Human Factors in Computing Systems* (pp.

368-375).

Kumar, U., Kumar, V., & Shareef, M. A. (2008, May 24-27). E-government development: Understanding impact of information and communication technology in developing countries. In *Proceedings of the Administrative Sciences Association of Canada Conference,* Halifax, Canada.

Lemme, B. H. (1999). *Development in adulthood* (2nd ed.). Needham Heights, MA: Allyn & Bacon.

Levin, T., & Gordon, C. (1989). Effect of gender and computer experience on attitudes towards computers. *Journal of Educational Computing Research, 5*(1), 69-88.

Li, J. (1994). Experience effects and international expansion: Strategies of service MNCs in the Asia-Pacific region. *Management International Review, 34*(3), 217-234.

Liu, B. S.-C., Furrer O., & Sudharshan, D. (2001). The relationships between culture and behavioral intentions toward services. *Journal of Service Research, 4*(2), 118-129.

Loiacono, E. T., Watson, R. T., & Goodhue, D. L. (2002). WEBQUAL: A measure of website quality. In K. Evans & L. Scheer (Eds.), *Proceedings of the Marketing Educators' Conference: Marketing Theory and Applications* (pp. 432-437).

Massini, S., & Pettigrew, A. M. (2003). Complementarities in organizational innovation and performance: Empirical evidence from the INNFORM survey. In A. M. Pettigrew, R. Whittington, L. Melin, C. Sanchez-Runde, F. Van den Bosch, W. Ruigrock, & T. Numagami (Eds.), *Innovative forms of organizing, international perspectives.* Thousand Oaks, CA: SAGE Publications.

Mathieson, K. (1991). Predicting user intentions: Comparing the technology acceptance model with theory of planned behavior. *Information Systems Research, 2*(2), 173-191.

Miller, K. (2005). *Communications theories: Perspectives, processes, and contexts.* New York: McGraw-Hill.

Moon, M. J. (2002). The evolution of e-government among municipalities: Rhetoric or reality? *Public Administration Review, 62*(4), 424-433.

Moon, M. J., & Norris, D. F. (2005). Does managerial orientation matter? The adoption of reinventing government and e-government at the municipal level. *Information Systems Journal, 15,* 43-60.

Nakata, C., & Sivakumar, K. (1996). National culture and new product development: An integrative review. *Journal of Marketing, 60*(1), 61-72.

NAO (National Audit Office). (1999). *The passport delays of summer 1999.* London: Stationary Office.

Netemeyer, R., Johnston, M., & Burton, S. (1990). Analysis of role conflict and role ambiguity in a structural equations framework. *Journal of Applied Psychology, 75,* 400-410.

Newburger, E. C. (1999). *Computer use in the United States: October 1997* (Report No. PPL-114). Atlanta, GA: U.S. Department of Commerce, U.S. Census Bureau.

Norris, D. F., & Moon, M. J. (2005). Advancing e-government at the grassroots: Tortoise or hare? *Public Administration Review, 65*(1), 64-75.

Parent, M., Vandebeek, C. A., & Gemino, A. C. (2005). Building citizen trust through e-government. *Government Information Quarterly, 22,* 720-736.

Pavlou, P. A., & Fygenson, M. (2006). Understanding and predicting electronic commerce adoption: An extension of the theory of planned behavior. *MIS Quarterly, 30*(1), 115-143.

Phang, C. W., Sutanto, J., Li, Y., & Kankanhalli, A. (2005). Senior citizens' adoption of e-government:

In quest of the antecedents of perceived usefulness. In *Proceedings of the 38th Hawaii International Conference on System Sciences.*

Robey, D., & Sahay, S. (1996). Transforming work through information technology: A comparative case study of geographic information systems in county government. *Information Systems Research, 7*(1), 93-110.

Rogers, E. (1995). *Diffusion of innovations.* New York: The Free Press.

Sejwacz, D., Ajzen, I., & Fishbein, M. (1980). Predicting and understanding weight loss. In I. Ajzen & M. Fishbein (Eds.), *Understanding attitudes and predicting social behavior* (pp. 101-112). Englewood-Cliffs, NJ: Prentice-Hall.

Shapiro, S. P. (1987). The social control of impersonal trust. *American Journal of Sociology, 93*(3), 623-658.

Shareef, M. A., Kumar, U., & Kumar, V. (2007), Developing fundamental capabilities for successful e-government implementation. In *Proceedings of the Administrative Sciences Association of Canada Conference,* Ottawa, Canada (pp. 159-177).

Shareef, M. A., Kumar, U., & Kumar, V. (2008). Role of different electronic- commerce (EC) quality factors on purchase decision: A developing country perspective. *Journal of Electronic Commerce Research, 9*(2), 92-113.

Sheppard, B. H., Hartwick, J., & Warshaw, P. (1988). The theory of reasoned action: A meta-analysis of past research with recommendations for modifications and future research. *Journal of Consumer Research, 15*(3), 325-343.

Sparks, P., Shepherd, R., & Frewer, L. J. (1995). Assessing and structuring attitudes toward the use of gene technology in food production: The role of perceived ethical obligation. *Basic and Applied Social Psychology, 16*, 267-285.

Steyaert, J. C. (2004). Measuring the performance of electronic government services. *Information & Management, 41*(3), 369-375.

Straub, D., Limayem, M., & Karahanna-Evaristo, E. (1995). Measuring system usage: Implications for IS theory testing. *Management Science, 41*(8), 1328-1342.

Taylor, S., & Todd, P. A. (1995). Decomposition and crossover effects in the theory of planned behavior: A study of consumer adoption intentions. *International Journal of Research in Marketing, 12*, 137-156.

Titah, R., & Barki, H. (2005). E-government adoption and acceptance: A literature review. *HEC Montréal.*

Treiblmaier, H., Pinterits, A., & Floh, A. (2004). Antecedents of the adoption of epayment services in the public sector. In *Proceedings of the 25th International Conference on Information Systems.*

Trist, E. L., & Bamforth K. W. (1951). Some social and psychological consequences of the longwall methods of coal-getting. *Human Relations, 14*, 3-38.

Tsikriktsis, N. (2002). Does Culture influence website quality expectations? An empirical study. *Journal of Service Research, 5*(2), 101-112.

Tung, L. L., & Rieck, O. (2005). Adoption of electronic government services among business organizations in Singapore. *Journal of Strategic Information Systems, 14*, 417-440.

Venkatesh, V. (2000). Determinants of perceived ease of use: Integrating control, intrinsic motivation, and emotion into the technology acceptance model. *Information Systems Research, 11*(4), 342-365.

Venkatesh, V., & Davis, F. (2000). A theoretical extension of the technology acceptance model: Four longitudinal field studies. *Management Science, 46*(2), 186-204.

Ventura, S. J. (1995). The use of geographic information systems in local government. *Public Administration Review, 55*(5), 461-467.

Vijayan, P., Perumal, V., & Shanmugam, B. (2005). Multimedia banking and technology acceptance theories. *The Journal of Internet Banking and Commerce, 10*(1), 1-7.

Wang, Y.-S., (2002). The adoption of electronic tax filing systems: An empirical study. *Government Information Quarterly, 20*, 333-352.

Warkentin, M., Gefen, D., Pavlou, P., & Rose, G. (2002). Encouraging citizen adoption of e-government by building trust. *Electronic Markets, 12*(3).

Westland, J. C., & Clark, T. H. K. (2000). *Global electronic commerce: Theory and case studies.* Cambridge, MA: MIT Press.

Whittington, R., & Pettigrew, A. M. (2003). *Complementarities thinking.* In A. M. Pettigrew, R. Whittington, L. Melin, C. Sanchez-Runde, F. Van den Bosch, W. Ruigrock, & T. Numagami (Eds.), *Innovative forms of organizing, international perspectives.* Thousand Oaks, CA: SAGE Publications.

Wolfinbarger, M., & Gilly, M. C. (2003). eTailQ: Dimensionalizing, measuring, and predicting etail quality. *Journal of Retailing, 79*(3), 183-98.

Woodward, J. (1965). *Industrial organization: Theory and practice.* London: Oxford University Press.

Yoo, B., & Donthu, N. (2001). Developing a scale to measure the perceived quality of an Internet shopping site (sitequal). *Quarterly Journal of Electronic Commerce, 2*(1), 31-46.

KEY TERMS AND DEFINITIONS

Adoption of Online System: The term can be viewed as the acceptance and use of, and satisfaction with ICT-based online system.

Attitude: Attitude can be defined as human beings' personal evaluation or approach towards any course of action. It is derived from personal characteristics.

Beliefs: It is psychological and behavioral perception about any action to be happened or not happened.

Information Technology (IT): IT can be defined as the use of modern computer-based technology in managing and processing information in different public and private sectors.

Perceived Awareness (PA): This term can be conceptualized as having and acquiring knowledge as much as a user perceived to be sufficient to learn the characteristics of online system and interact through perception or by means of information about ICT.

Perceived Local Environmental Security: The term can be viewed as the degree to which a person perceives general security from the local environment (where he/she belongs) towards human beings, society, organizations, i.e., toward any object. This general security concern of individuals is based on cognitive experiences about security gathered from the country, government, society, local market, shopping, organizations, and inter-personal interaction.

Trust: It is the general belief of an individual toward human beings, society, organizations, i.e., toward any object. This belief is also characterized by normative values of society and culture.

Compilation of References

3G.co.uk. (2004, December 15). *3G adoption a few more years*. Retrieved December 3, 2005, from http://www.3g.co.uk/PR/December2004/8830.htm

Aarts, J., et al. (2004). Understanding implementation: The case of a computerized physician order entry system in a large dutch university medical center. *J Am Med Inform Assoc, 11*(3), 207-216.

Abanumy, A., Mayhew, P., & Al-Badi, A., (2003). An exploratory study of e-government in two GCC countries. In *Proceedings of the 2003 International Business Information Management Conference*, Cairo, Egypt.

Abdul-Gader, A. H. (1997). Information systems strategies for multinational companies in Arab Gulf countries. *International Journal of Information Management, 17*(1), 3-12.

Abetti, P. A. (1997). Birth and growth of Toshiba's laptop and notebook computers: A case study in Japanese corporate venturing. *Journal of Business Venturing, 12*, 507-529.

Abrahamson, E. (1991). Managerial fads and fashions: The diffusion and rejection of innovations. *Academy of Management Review, 16*(3), 586-612.

Ackroyd, S., & Fleetwood, S. (Eds.). (2000). *Realist perspectives on management and organisations*. London: Routledge.

Adam, A., Howcroft, D., & Richardson, H. (2004). A decade of neglect: Reflecting on gender and IS. *New Technology Work and Employment, 19*(3).

Adam, L., & Wood, F. (1999). An investigation of the impact of information and communication technologies in sub-Saharan Africa. *Journal of Information Science, 25*(4), 307-318.

Adler, P. S., & Kwon, S.-W. (2002). Social capital: Prospects for a new concept. *The Academy of Management Review, 27*(1), 17.

Afifi, A. A., & Elashoff, R. M. (1966). Missing observations in multivariate statistics: I. Review of the literature. *Journal of the American Statistical Association, 61*(315), 595-604.

Agar, M. (1991). The right brain strikes back. In N. Fielding & R. Lee (Eds.), *Using computers in qualitative research* (pp. 181-194). Newbury Park, CA: Sage Publications.

Agarwal, R., Sambamurthy, V., & Stair, R. M. (2000). Research report: The evolving relationship between general and specific computer self-efficacy—an empirical assessment. *Information Systems Research, 11*(4), 418-430.

Agnihothri, S., Sivasubramaniam, N., & Simmons, D. (2003). Leveraging technology to improve field service. *International Journal of Service Industry Management, 13*(1), 47-68.

Agrawal, R., & Karahanna, E. (2000). Time flies when you're having fun: Cognitive absorption and beliefs about information technology usage. *MIS Quarterly, 24*(4), 665-694.

AIHW. (2006). *Chronic disease and associated risk factors in Australia, 2006*. Canberra: Australian Government, Department of Health and Ageing.

Aiken, M., Hwang, H., & Martin, J. (1996). A Japanese group decision support system. *International Journal of Computer Applications in Technology, 9*(5/6), 233-238.

Aiken, M., Kim, D., Hwang, C., & Lu, L.-C. (1995). A Korean group decision support system. *Information & Management, 28*(5), 303-310.

Aiken, M., Martin, J., Shirani, A., & Singleton, T. (1994). A group decision support system for multicultural and multilingual communication. *Decision Support Systems, 12*(2), 93-96.

Air NZ has no option: Norris. (2005, October 22-23). *Otago Daily Times.*

Ajzen, I., & Fishbein, M. (1980). *Understanding attitudes and predicting social behavior.* NJ: Prentice Hall.

Ajzen, I. (1985). From intentions to actions: A theory of planned behaviour. In J. Kuhl & J. Beckman (Eds.), *Action-control: From cognition to behaviour* (pp. 11-39). Heidelberg, Germany: Springer.

Ajzen, I. (1991). The theory of planned behavior. *Organizational Behavior and Human Decision Processes, 50*(2), 179-211.

Ajzen, I., & Madden, T. J. (1986). Prediction of goal-directed behavior: Attitudes, intentions, and perceived behavioral control. *Journal of Experimental Social Psychology, 22*, 453-474.

Akgun, A. E., Byrne, J., Keskin, H., Lynn, G. S., & Imamoglu, S. Z. (2005). Knowledge networks in new product development projects: A transactive memory perpsective. *Information & Management, 42*(8), 1105-1120.

Akmanligil, M., & Palvia, P. C. (2004). Strategies for global information systems development. *Information & Management, 42*(1), 45-59.

Akrich, M., & Latour, B. (1992). A Summary of a convenient vocabulary for the semiotics of human and nonhuman assemblies. In W. E. Bijker & J. Law (Eds.), *Shaping technology/building society: Studies in sociotechnical change* (pp. 259-264). Cambridge, MA: The MIT Press.

Al-adawi, Z., Yousafzai, S., & Pallister, J. (2005). Conceptual model of citizen adoption of e-government. In *Proceedings of The 2nd International Conference on Innovations in Information Technology (IIT'05).*

Alavi, M., Kayworth, T. R., & Leidner, D. E. (2005). An empirical examination of the influence of organizational culture on knowledge management practices. *Journal of Management Information Systems, 22*(3), 191-224.

Albani, A., & Dietz, J. L. G. (2006). The benefit of enterprise ontology in identifying business components. In D. Avison, S. Elliot, J. Krogstie, & J. Pries-Heje (Eds.), *The past and future of information systems: 1976–2006 and beyond* (Vol. 214/2006, pp. 243-254). Boston: Springer.

Albarracin, D., Johnson, B. T., Fishbein, M., & Muellerleile, P. A. (2001). Theories of reasoned action and planned behavior as models of condom use: A meta-analysis. *Psychological Bulletin, 127*(1), 142-161.

Albrecht, A. J. (1979). Measuring applications development productivity. In *Proceedings of the IBM Application Development* (pp. 83-92).

Al-Khaldi, M., & Olusegun, W. R. (1999). The influence of attitudes on personal computer utilization among knowledge workers: The case of Saudi Arabia. *Information & Management, 36*, 185-204.

Alkire, S., & Denevlin, S. (2002). Individual motivation, its nature, determinants, and consequences for within group behaviour. In J. Heyer, F. Stewart, & R. Thorp (Eds.), *Group behaviour and development* (pp. 51-73). New York: Oxford University Press.

Allen, F., & Babus, A. (2008). *Networks in finance* (working paper). University of Pennsylvania and Erasmus University.

Allison, P. D. (2003). Missing data techniques for structural equation modeling. *Journal of Abnormal Psychology, 112*(4), 545-557.

Allwood, J. (1977). A critical look at speech act theory. In Ö. Dahl (Ed.), *Logic, pragmatics and grammar* (pp. 53-99). Lund, Sweden: Studentlitteratur.

Al-Mashari, M. (2007). A benchmarking study of experiences with electronic-government. *Benchmarking: An International Journal, 14*(2), 172-185.

Alonso, G., Casati, F., Kuno, H., & Machiraju, V. (2004). *Web services: Concepts, architectures and applications.* Berlin: Springer-Verlag.

Alsene, E. (1999). Internal changes and project management structures within enterprises. *International Journal of Project Management, 17*(6), 367-376.

Alter, S. (2002). The work systems model and its role for understanding information systems and information systems research, *Communications of the Association for Information Systems, 9,* 90-104.

Alter, S. (2002). Sidestepping the IT artifact, scrapping the IS silo and laying claim to "systems in organizations". *Communications of the Association for Information Systems, 12,* 494-526.

Alter, S. (2003). 18 reasons why IT-reliant work systems should replace "the IT artifact" as the core subject matter of the IS field. *Communications of the Association for Information Systems, 12*(23), 366-395.

Alter, S. (2004). A work system view of DSS in its fourth decade, *Decision Support Systems, 38*(3), 319-327.

Alter, S. (2004). Desperately seeking systems thinking in the information systems discipline, In *Proceedings of the Twenty Fifth ICIS Conference (pp.* 757-769).

Alter, S. (2006). Work systems and IT artifacts: Does the definition matter? *Communications of the Association for Information Systems, 17*(14), 299-313.

Alter, S. (2006). Pitfalls in analyzing systems in organizations. *Journal of Information Systems Education, 17*(3), 295-303

Alter, S. (2006). *The work system method: Connecting people, processes, and IT for business results.* Larkspur, CA: Work System Press.

Alter, S. (2007). Could the work system method embrace systems concepts more fully? *Information Resource Management Journal, 20*(2), 33-43.

Alter, S. (2008). Service system fundamentals: Work system, value chain, and life cycle. *IBM systems journal, 47*(1).

Alter, S., & Browne, G. (2005). A broad view of systems analysis and design: Implications for research. *Communications of the Association for Information Systems, 16*(50), 981-999.

Alvesson, M., & Skö1berg, K. (2000). *Reflexive Methodology.* London: SAGE.

Amoako-Gyampah, K., & Salam, A. F. (2003). An extension of the technology acceptance model in an ERP implementation environment. *Information & Management, 41,* 731-745.

AMWAC. (2005). *The general practice workforce in Australia: Supply and requirements to 2013.* Australian Medical Workforce Advisory Committee.

Andersen, E. S. (1994). *Evolutionary economics: Post-Schumpeterian contributions.* London: Pinter Publishers.

Anderson, J. C., & Gerbing, D. W. (1984). The effect of sampling error on convergence, improper solutions, and goodness-of-fit indices for maximum likelihood confirmatory factor analysis. *Psychometrika, 49*(2), 155-173.

Anderson, J. C., & Gerbing, D. W. (1988). Structural equation modeling in practice: A review and recommended two-step approach. *Psychological Bulletin, 103*(3), 411-423.

Andreu, R., & Ciborra, C. (1996). Organisational learning and core capabilities development: The role of IT. *Journal of Strategic Information Systems, 5,* 111-127.

Annells, M. (1996). Grounded theory method: Philosophical perspectives, paradigm of inquiry, and postmodernism. *Qualitative Health Research, 6*(3), 379-393.

Anthopoulos, L. G., Siozos, P., & Tsoukalas, L. A. (2007). Applying participatory design and collaboration in digital public services for discovering and re-designing e-government services. *Government Information Quarterly, 24,* 353-376.

Antoniol, G., Lokan, C., Caldiera, G., & Fiutem, R. (1999, September). A function point-like measure for object-oriented software. *Empirical Software Engineering, 4*(3), 263-287.

Antonioni, D., & Park, H. (2001). The effects of personality similarity on peer ratings of contextual work behaviors. *Personnel Psychology, 54,* 331-360.

Archer, M. S. (1979). *Social origins of educational systems.* London: Sage.

Archer, M. S. (1995). *Realist social theory: The morphogenetic approach.* Cambridge, UK: Cambridge University Press.

Archer, M. S. (2007). Morphogenesis/morphostatis. In M. Hartwig (Ed.), *Dictionary of critical realism* (p. 319). London: Routledge.

Archer, M., Bhaskar, R., Collier, A., Lawson, T., & Norrie, A. (Eds.). (1998). *Critical realism: Essential readings.* London: Routledge.

Argyris, C. (1976). Single-loop and double-loop models in research on decision making. *Administrative Science Quarterly, 21*(3), 363-375.

Argyris, C. (1985). Defensive routines. In D. Pugh (Ed.), *Organization theory. Third Edition* (pp. 439-454). London: Penguin Books.

Argyris, C. (1998). Empowerment: The emperor's new clothes. *Harvard Business Review, 76*(3), 98-105.

Argyris, C., & Schon, D. (1978). *Organizational learning.* Englewood Cliffs, NJ: Prentice-Hall.

Arling, P., & Subramani, M. (2005). Being there versus being wired: The effect of colocation on social capital in distributed teams. In *Proceedings of The Twenty-Sixth International Conference on Information Systems.*

Arnott D., & Pervan, G. (2005). A critical analysis of decision support systems research. *Journal of Information Technology, 20*, 67-87

Arrow, H., McGrath, J., & Berdahl, J. (2000). *Small Groups as complex systems.* CA, USA: Sage Publications.

Arthur, W. B. (1994). *Increasing returns and path dependency in the economy.* Ann Arbor, MI: The University of Michigan Press.

Asch, S. (1952). *Social psychology.* NJ, USA: Prentice-Hall.

Ash, R. A., Rosenbloom, J. L., Coder, L., & Dupont, B. (2008). *Gender differences and similarities in personality characteristics for information technology professionals.* Retrieved June 16, 2008, from http://www.ipsr.ku.edu/~ipsr/ITWorkforce/pubs/GenderDifferences.shtml

Ashford, S. J. (1988). Individual strategies for coping with stress during organizational transitions. *The Journal of Applied Behavioral Science, 24*(1), 19-36.

Assael, H. (1998). *Consumer behavior and marketing action.* Cincinnati, OH: South Western College Publishing.

Association of Information Technology Professionals. (2008). *Standard of conduct.* Retrieved October 8, 2008, from http://www.aitp.org/organization/about/conduct/conduct.jsp

Assouline, M., & Meir, E. I. (1987). Meta-analysis of the relationship between congruence and well-being measures. *Journal of Vocational Behavior, 31*, 319-332.

Atkinson, C. J. (2000). The 'soft information systems and technologies methodology' (SISTeM): An actor network contingency approach to integrated development. *European Journal of Information Systems, 9*, 104-123.

Au, N., Ngai, E., & Cheng, E. (2002) A critical review of end-user information system satisfaction research and a new research framework. *Omega, 30*, 451-478.

Audet, A. M., et al. (2004). Information technologies: When will they make it into physicians' black bags? *MedGenMed, 6*(2).

Auramaki, E., Lehtinen, E., & Lyytinen, K. (1988). A speech-act-based office modeling approach. *ACM Transactions on Information systems (TOIS), 6*(2), 126-152.

Austin, J. L. (1962). *How to do things with words.* Cambridge, MA: Harvard University Press.

Australian Institute of Health Policies Studies, & VicHealth. (2008). *A platform for advancing the health of all Australians.* Australian Institute of Health Policies Studies, Melbourne, Australia.

Avgerou, C. (2000). IT and organizational change: An institutionalist perspective. *Information Technology & People, 13*(4), 234.

Avgerou, C. (2001). The significance of context in information systems and organisational change. *Information Systems Journal, 11*(1), 43-63.

Babchuk, W. (1996, October 17-19). *Glaser Or Strauss?: Grounded theory and adult education.* Paper presented at the Proceedings of Midwest Research-to-Practice Conference in Adult, Continuing, and Community Education, University of Nebraska-Lincoln.

Babcock, P. (2004). Shedding light on knowledge management. *HR Magazine, 49*(5), 46-50.

Bach, K., & Harnish, R. M. (1979). *Linguistic communication and speech acts.* Cambridge, MA: MIT Press.

Bacharach, S. B. (1989). Organizational theories: Some criteria for evaluation. *Academy of Management Review, 14*(4), 496-515.

Bagozzi, R. P. (2007). The legacy of the technology acceptance model and a proposal for a paradigm shift. *Journal of the Association for Information Systems, 8*(4), 244-254.

Bagozzi, R. P., Yi, Y., & Phillips, L. W. (1991). Assessing construct validity in organizational research. *Administrative Science Quarterly, 36*(3), 421-458.

Bajaj, A., Batra, D., Hevner, A., Parsons, J., & Siau, K. (2005). Systems analysis and design: Should we be researching what we teach? *Communications of the AIS, 15*, 478-493.

Baker, W. E. (1990). Market networks and corporate behavior. *American Journal of Sociology, 96*(3), 589.

Bakos, J. Y. (1997) Reducing buyer search costs: Implications for electronic marketplaces. *Management Science, 43*(12), 1676-1692

Bakos, J. Y. (1998) The emerging role of electronic marketplaces on the internet. *Communications of the ACM, 41*(8), 35-42

Bakos, Y., & Brynjolfsson, E., (1997) Information technology incentives, and the optimal number of suppliers. *Journal of Management information Systems, 10*, 35-53

Bakos, Y., & Kemerer, C. (1992) Recent applications of economic theory in information technology research. *Decision Support Systems, 8*, 365-388

Bancel-Charensol, L. (1999). Impacts on information and communication technologies on service production systems. *The Service Industries Journal, 19*(4), 147-157.

Bandura, A. (1977). *Social learning theory.* NJ: Prentice Hall.

Bandura, A. (1982). Self-efficacy mechanism in human agency. *American Psychologist, 37*(2), 122-147.

Bandura, A. (1986). *Social foundations of thought and action.* Englewood Cliffs, NJ: Prentice-Hall.

Banerjee, P., & Chau, P. (2004). An evaluation framework for analyzing e-government convergence capability in developing countries. *Electronic Government, 1*(1), 29-48.

Banerjee, R. (2003). Organisational character: Issues, imperatives and practices. *International Journal of Human Resources Development and Management, 3*(1), 72-83.

Bar, F., & Borrus, M. (1993). *The future of networking* (BRIE working paper). Berkeley, University of California.

Barab, S. A., Barnett, M., Yamagata-Lynch, L., Squire, K., & Keating, T. (2002). Using activity theory to understand the systemic tensions characterizing a technology-rich introductory astronomy course. *Mind, Culture, and Activity, 9*(2), 76-107.

Barclay, D., Higgins, C., & Thomson, R. (1995). The partial least squares approach (PLS) to causal modeling, personal computer adoption and use as an illustration. *Technology Studies, 2*(2), 285-309.

Bardram, J. E. (1997). Plans as situated action: An activity theory approach to workflow systems. In W. Prinz, T. Rodden, & K. Schmidt (Eds.), *Proceedings of the Fifth European Conference on Computer Supported Cooperative Work* (pp. 17-32). Norwell, MA: Kluwer Academic Publishers.

Barki, H., Rivard, S., & Talbot, J. (1993). A keyword classification scheme for IS research literature: An update. *MIS Quarterly, 17*(2), 209-226.

Barki, H., Titah, R., & Boffo, C. (2007). Information system use-related activity: An expanded behavioral conceptualization of individual-level information system use. *Information Systems Research, 18*(2), 173-192.

Barley, S. R. (1986). Technology as an occasion for structuring: Evidence from observations of CT scanners and the social order of radiology departments. *Administrative Science Quarterly, 31*(1), 78.

Barnett, W., & Presley, A. (2004). Theory of planned behavior model in electronic learning: A pilot study. *Journal of Issues in Information Systems, V*(1), 22-28.

Barney, J. (1991). Firm resources and sustained competitive advantage. *Journal of Management, 17*(1), 99-120.

Barney, J. B. (2004). Where does inequality come from?

The personal and intellectual roots of resource-based theory. In M. A. Hitt & K. G. Smith (Eds.), *Great minds in management* (pp. 280-303). New York: Oxford University Press.

Barrett, M., & Walsham, G. (1999). Electronic trading and work transformation in the London insurance market. *Information Systems Research, 10*(1), 1-21.

Barrick, R., & Mount, M. K. (1991). The big five personality dimensions and job performance: A meta-analysis. *Personnel Psychology, 44,* 1-26.

Barth, S. (2000). *Eureka! Xerox has found it.* Retrieved from http://kazman.shidler.hawaii.edu/eurekacase.html

Bartunek, J. M. (1984). Changing interpretive schemes and organizational structuring: The Example of a religious order. *Administrative Science Quarterly, 29,* 355-372.

Bartunek, J. M., & Moch, M. (1987). First order, second order, and third order change and organization development interventions: A cognitive approach. *Journal of Applied Behavior Science, 23*(4), 483-500.

Basharina, O. K. (2007). An activity theory perspective on student - reported contradictions in international telecollaboration. *Language Learning & Technology, 11*(2), 82-103.

Baskerville, R. L., & Myers, M. D. (2002). Information systems as a reference discipline. *MIS Quarterly, 26*(1), 1-14.

Baskerville, R. L., & Pries-Heje, J. (2001). A multiple-theory analysis of a diffusion of information technology case. *Information Systems Journal, 11,* 181-212.

Baskerville, R., Travis, J., & Truex, D. P. (1992) Systems without method: The impact of new technologies on information systems development projects. In K. E. Kendell, K. Lyytinen, & J. I. DeGross, (Eds.), *Transactions on the impact of computer supported technologies in information systems development.* Amsterdam: Elsevier.

Bassey, M. (1999). *Case study research in educational settings.* Buckingham, UK: Open University Press.

Basu, S. (2004). E-government and developing countries: An overview. *International Review of Law Computers & Technology, 18*(1), 109-132.

Bates, D. W. (2000). Using information technology to reduce rates of medication errors in hospitals. *British Medical Journal, 320,* 788-791.

Bates, D. W. (2005). Physicians and ambulatory electronic health records. *Health Affairs, 24*(5), 1180-1189.

Bates, D. W., et al. (1995). Incidence of adverse events and potential adverse drug events: Implications for preventions. *JAMA, 274,* 29-34.

Baum, A., Fleming, R., & Singer, J. E. (1983). Coping with technological disaster. *Journal of Social Issues, 39,* 117-138.

Beas, M. I., & Salanova, M. (2006). Self-efficacy beliefs, computer training and psychological well-being among information and communication technology workers. *Computers in Human Behavior, 22*(6), 1043-1058.

Beatson, A., Coote, L. V., & Rudd, J. M. (2006). Determining consumer satisfaction and commitment through self-service technology and personal service usage. *Journal of Marketing Management, 22*(7), 853-882.

Beatson, A., Lee, N., & Coote, L. V. (2007). Self-service technology and the service encounter. *The Service Industries Journal, 27*(1), 75-89.

Beatty, S. B., Mayer, M., Coleman, J. E., Reynolds, K. E., & Lee, J. (1996). Customer-sales associate retail relationships. *Journal of Retailing, 72*(3), 223-247.

Beaudouin-Lafon, M. (Ed.). (1999). *Computer supported co-operative work.* Chichester, UK: John Wiley & Sons Limited.

Beaudry, A., & Pinsonneault, A. (2005). Understanding user responses to information technology: A coping model of user adaptation. *MIS Quarterly, 29*(3), 493-524.

Beck. K. (1999). *Extreme programming explained: Embrace change.* Boston, MA: Addison -Wesley.

Beeson, I., & Green, S. (2003, April 9-11). *Using a language action framework to extend organizational process modelling.* Paper presented at the UK Academy for Information systems (UKAIS) Conference, University of Warwick.

Begley, T. M. (1998). Coping strategies as predictors of employee distress and turnover after an organizational consolidation: A longitudinal analysis. *Journal of Occupational and Organizational Psychology, 71*, 305-329.

Bélanger, F., & Carter, L. (2005). Trust and risk in e-government adoption. In *Proceedings of the 11ᵗʰ Americans Conference on Information Systems*, Omaha, NE, USA.

Bell, G. G. (2005). Clusters, networks, and firm innovativeness. *Strategic Management Journal, 26*, 287-295.

Bell, R. C. (1988). Theory-appropriate analysis of repertory grid data. *International Journal of Personal Construct Psychology, 1*, 101-118.

Bell, R. C. (2003). The repertory grid technique. In F. Fransella (Ed.), *International handbook of personal construct psychology*. Chicester, UK: Wiley.

Bellizzi, J. A., & Hite, R. E. (1992). Environmental color, consumer feelings, and purchase likelihood. *Psychology & Marketing, 9*(5), 347-363.

Bem, D. J. (1967). Self-perception: An alternative interpretation of cognitive dissonance phenomena. *Psychological Review, 74*(3), 183-200.

Bem, D. J. (1972). Self-perception theory. In L. Berkowitz (Ed.), *Advances in experimental social psychology* (vol. 6) (pp. 1-62). New York: Academic Press.

Benamati, J., & Lederer, A. L. (2001). Rapid information technology change, coping mechanisms, and the emerging technologies group. *Journal of Management Information Systems, 17*(4), 183-202.

Benbasat, I. (1984). An analysis of research methodologies. In F. W. McFarlan (Ed.), *The information systems research challenges* (pp. 47-85). Boston, MA: Harvard Business School Press.

Benbasat, I., & Barki, H. (2007). Quo vadis, TAM? *Journal of the Association for Information Systems, 8*(4), 211-218.

Benbasat, I., & Zmud, R. W. (2003). The identity crisis within the IS discipline: Defining and communicating the discipline's core properties. *MIS Quarterly, 27*(2), 183-194.

Benbasat, I., Goldstein, D. K., & Mead, M. (2002). The case research strategy in studies of information systems.

In M. D. Myers & D. Avison (Eds.), *Qualitative research in information systems: A reader* (pp. 79-99). London: Sage Publications.

Benkhoff, B. (1997). Disentangling organizational commitment - the dangers of OCQ for research and policy. *Personnel Review, 26*(1), 114-131.

Bennet, A., & Bennet, D. (2003). The partnership between organizational learning and knowledge management. In C. W. Holsapple (Ed.), *Handbook on knowledge management 1: Knowledge matters* (pp. 439-455). Berlin/Heidelberg, Germany: Springer-Verlag.

Bentler, P. M. (1990). Comparative fit indexes in structural models. *Psychological Bulletin, 107*(2), 238-246.

Bentler, P. M., & Chou, C. P. (1987). Practical issues in structural modeling. *Sociological Methods and Research, 16*, 78-117.

Bentler, P. M., & Dijkstra, T. (1985). Efficient estimation via linearization in structural models. In R. Krishnaiah (Ed.), *Multivariate analysis VI* (pp. 9-42). Amsterdam: North Holland.

Berg, M. (1997). On distribution, drift and the electronic medical record: Some tools for a sociology of the formal. In W. Prinz, T. Rodden, & K. Schmidt (Eds.), *Proceedings of the Fifth European Conference on Computer Supported Cooperative Work* (pp. 141-156). Norwell, MA: Kluwer Academic Publishers.

Berger, P. L., & Luckmann, T. (1967). *The social construction of reality: A treatise on the sociology of knowledge*. Garden City, NY: Anchor.

Berkley, B. J., & Gupta, A. (1994). Improving service quality with information technology. *International Journal of Information Management, 14*(2), 109-121.

Berkley, B. J., & Gupta, A. (1995). Identifying the information requirements to deliver quality service. *International Journal of Service Industry Management, 6*(5), 16-35.

Bernadette, S. (1996). Empirical evaluation of the revised technology acceptance model. *Management Science, 42*(1), 85-93.

Berners-Lee T. & Fischetti M. (1999). *Weaving the Web: The original design and ultimate destiny of the World Wide Web by its inventor*. New York: HarperCollins.

Bernstein, R. (1983). *Beyond objectivism and relativism: Science, hermeneutics, and Praxis*. Philadelphia: University of Pennsylvania Press.

Berry, L. L., & Gresham, L. G. (1986). Relationship retailing: Transforming customers into clients. *Business Horizons, 29*(6), 43-47.

Berry, L. L., & Parasuraman, A. (1997). Listening to the customer - the concept of a service-quality information system. *Sloan Management Review, 38*(3), 65-76.

Berry, L. L., Seiders, K., & Grewal, D. (2002). Understanding service convenience. *Journal of Marketing, 66*(3), 1-17.

Bertalanffy, L. V. (1962). General system theory - a critical review. *General Systems, 7*, 1-20.

Bertot, J. C. (2003). The multiple dimensions of the digital divide: More than the technology "haves" and "have nots." *Government Information Quarterly, 20*(2), 185-191.

Bertot, J. C., McClure, C. R., & Owens, K. A. (1999). Universal service in a global networked environment: Selected issues and possible approaches. *Government Information Quarterly, 16*(4), 309-327.

Bertuglia, C. S. and Vaio F (2005) *Nonlinearity, chaos and complexity*, Oxford, OUP.

Bessen, J. (1993). Riding the marketing information wave. *Harvard Business Review, 71*(5), 150-160.

Bettman, J. R. (1986). Consumer psychology. *Annual Review of Psychology, 37*, 257-289.

Bharadwaj, A. (2000). A resource-based perspective on information technology capability and firm performance: An empirical investigation. *MIS Quarterly, 24*(1), 169-196.

Bharati, P., & Berg, D. (2003). Managing information systems for service quality: A study from the other side. *Information Technology & People, 16*(2), 183-201.

Bhaskar, R. (1978). *A realist theory of science*. Sussex, UK: Harvester Press.

Bhaskar, R. (1989). *Reclaiming reality: A critical introduction to contemporary philosophy*. London: Verso.

Bhaskar, R. (1991). *Philosophy and the idea of freedom*. Oxford, UK: Basil Blackwell.

Bhaskar, R. (1998). *The possibility of naturalism* (3rd ed.). London: Routledge.

Bhaskar, R. (2002). From science to emancipation: Alienation and the actuality of enlightenment. Delhi, India: Sage Publications India Pvt Ltd.

Bhaskar, R. (2002). *Reflections on meta-reality: Transcendence, enlightenment and everyday life*. London: Sage.

Bhatnagar, S. (2002). E-government: Lessons from implementation in developing countries, regional development dialogue. *UNCRD, 24*(Autumn), 1-9.

Bhatnagar, S. C. (2000). Social Implications of information and communication technology in developing countries: Lessons from Asian success stories. *Electronic Journal of Information Systems for Developing countries, 1*(4), 1-9.

Bhattacherjee, A. (2001). Understanding information systems continuance: An expectation-confirmation model. *MIS Quarterly, 25*(3), 351-370.

Bhattacherjee, A. (2001). An empirical analysis of the antecedents of electronic commerce service continuance. *Decision Support Systems, 32*, 201-214.

Bhattacherjee, A., & Sanford, C. (2006). Influence processes for information technology acceptance: An elaboration likelihood model. *MIS Quarterly, 30*(4), 805-825.

Bijker, W. E. (1995). *Of Bicycles, bakelites, and bulbs: Towards a theory of sociotechnical change*. Cambridge, MA: MIT Press.

Bijker, W. E., & Law, J. (1992). *Shaping technology/building society: Studies in socio-technical change*. Cambridge, MA: MICT Press.

Bijker, W. E., Hughes, T. P., & Pinch, T. J. (Eds.). (1987). *The social construction of technological systems: New directions in the sociology and history of technology*. Cambridge, MA: The MIT Press.

Billings, A. G., & Moos, R. H. (1984). Coping, stress, and resources among adults with unipolar depression. *Journal of Personality and Social Psychology, 46*, 877-891.

Birmingham, D. (2002). *Software development on a leash*. NY, USA: Springer-Verlag.

Bitner, M. J., Ostrom, A. L., & Meuter, M. L. (2002). Implementing successful self-service technologies. *Academy of Management Executive, 16*(4), 96-108.

Bjørn-Andersen, N., & Davis, G. B. (Eds.). (1988). *Information systems assessment: Issues and challenges.* Amsterdam: North-Holland.

Black, F. (1987, August). Goldman Sachs and Company. *Essays of an Information Scientist, 10*(33), 16.

Black, F., & Scholes, M. (1973, May-June). The pricing of option and corporate liabilities. *The Journal of Political Economy, 81*(3), 637-654.

Blackler, F. (1995). Activity theory, CSCW and organizations. In A. Monk & N. Gilbert (Eds.), *Perspectives on HCI - diverse approaches* (pp. 223 - 248). London, UK: Academic Press.

Blake, B. F., Neuendorf, K. A., & Valdiserri, C. M. (2003). Innovativeness and variety of Internet shopping. *Internet Research - Electronic Networking Applications and Policy, 13*(3), 156-169.

Blalock, H. M. (1969). *Theory construction: From verbal to mathematical formulations.* Englewood Cliffs, NJ: Prentice-Hall.

Blalock, H. M. (1971). Causal models involving unobserved variables in stimulus-response situations. In H. M. Blalock (Ed.), *Causal models in the social sciences* (pp. 335-347). Chicago: Aldine.

Blaug, M. (1997). *Economic theory in retrospect* (5th ed.). Cambridge, UK: Cambridge University Press.

Bloomfield, B. P., & Danieli, A. (1995). The role of management consultants in the development of information technology: The indissoluble nature of socio-political and technical skills. *Journal of Management Studies, 32*(1), 23-46.

Bloomfield, B. P., & Vurdubakis, T. (1994). Boundary disputes, negotiating the boundary between the technical and the social in the development of IT systems. *Information Technology & People, 7*(1), 9-24.

Bloomfield, B. P., & Vurdubakis, T. (1997). Paper traces: Inscribing organizations and information technology. In B. P. Bloomfield, R. Coombs, D. Knights, & D. Littler (Eds.), *Information technology and organizations: Strat-*

egies, networks, and integration (pp. 85-111). Oxford, UK: Oxford University Press.

Bloomfield, B. P., Coombs, R., Knights, D., & Littler, D. (Eds.). (1997). *Information Technology and Organizations: Strategies, Networks, and Integration:* Oxford University Press.

Bloor, D. (1999). Anti-Latour. *Studies in the History and Philosophy of Science, 30*(1), 81-112.

Blumer, H. (1969). *Symbolic interactionism: Perspective and method.* Englewood Cliffs, NJ: Prentice-Hall.

Bodenheimer, T. (1999). The American health care system; The movement for improved quality in health care. *N Engl J Med, 340,* 488-492.

Bødker, S. (1989). A human activity approach to user interfaces. *Human Computer Interaction, 4*(3), 171-195.

Bødker, S. (1991). *Through the interface: A human activity approach to user interface design.* Mahwah, NJ: Lawrence Erlbaum Associates.

Boehm, B., & Turner R. (2004). *Balancing agility and discipline - a guide for the perplexed.* Boston, MA: Addison–Wesley.

Boland R. J., Jr. (2002). In M. D. Myers & D. Avison (Eds.), *Qualitative research in information systems: A reader* (pp. 225-240). London: Sage Publications.

Bollen, K. L. (1989). *Structural equations with latent variables.* New York: John Wiley.

Bollen, K., & Lennox, R. (1991). Conventional wisdom on measurement: A structural equation perspective. *Psychological Bulletin, 110*(2), 305-314.

Bonczek, R., Holsapple, C., & Whinston, A. (1981). *Foundations of decision support systems.* New York: Academic Press.

Bono, J. E., & Colbert, A. E. (2005) Understanding responses to multi-source feedback: The role of core self-evaluations, *Personnel Psychology, 58,* 171-203

Booch, G. (1993). *Object-oriented analysis and design with applications* (2nd ed.). Indianapolis, IN: Addison-Wesley Professional.

Boody, D., & Macbeth, D. (2000). Prescriptions for managing change: A survey of their effects in projects to implement collaborative working between organizations. *International Journal of Project Management, 18*(5), 297-306.

Boomsma, A. (1982). The robustness of LISREL against small sample sizes in factor analysis models. In K. G. Joreskog & H. Wold (Eds.), *Systems under indirect observation: Causality, structure, prediction* (pp. 149-173). Amsterdam: North Holland.

Boomsma, A. (2000). Reporting analyses of covariance structures. *Structural Equation Modeling, 7*, 461-483.

Borders, A., Earleywine, M., & Huey, S. (2004). Predicting problem behaviors with multiple expectancies: Expanding expectancy value theory, *Adolescence, 39*, 539-551.

Borgatti, S. P. (2004). The state of organizational social network research today (working paper).

Borgatti, S. P., & Cross, R. (2003). A relational view of information seeking and learning in social networks. *Management Science, 49*(4), 432-445.

Borgatti, S. P., & Foster, P.C. (2003). The network paradigm in organizational research: A review and typology. *Journal of Management, 29*, 991-1013.

Bostrom, R. P., & Heinen, J. S. (1977). MIS problems and failures: A socio-technical perspective. *MIS Quarterly, 1*(3), 17-32.

Boudreau, M-C., & Robey, D. (1999). Organizational transition to enterprise resource planning systems: Theoretical choices for process research. In *Proceedingss. of the Twentieth International Conference on Information Systems*, Charlotte, NC (pp. 291-299).

Bougnon, et al. (1977). Cognition in organizations: An analysis of the Utrecht Jazz Orchestra. *Administrative Science Quartely, 22*(4), 606-639.

Bourdieu, P. (1977). *Outline of a theory of practice.* Cambridge, MA: Cambridge University Press.

Bourdieu, P. (1986). The forms of social capital. In J. G. Richardson (Ed.), *Handbook of theory and research for the sociology of education* (pp. 241-258). Westport, CT: Greenwood Press.

Bourdieu, P. (1998). *Acts of resistance. Against the new myths of our time.* UK: Polity Press

Bourdieu, P., & Wacquant, L. (1992). *An invitation to reflexive sociology.* Chicago: University of Chicago Press.

Bowe, C., Lahey, L., Kegan, R., & Armstrong, E. (2003). Questioning the big assumptions. Part I: Addressing personal contradictions that impede professional development. *Medical Education, 37*(8), 715-722.

Bowe, C., Lahey, L., Kegan, R., & Armstrong, E. (2003). Questioning the big assumptions. Part II: Recognizing organizational contradictions that impede organisational change. *Medical Education, 37*(9), 723-733.

Bowen, D. E., Siehl, C., & Schneider, B. (1989). A framework for analyzing customer service orientations in manufacturing. *Academy of Management Review, 14*(1), 75-95.

Bowers, J. (1992). The politics of formalism. In M. Lea (Ed.), *Contexts of computer-mediated communication* (pp. 232-261). New York: Harvester Wheatsheaf.

Boyett, J. H., & Conn, H. P. (1991). *Workplace 2000: The revolution reshaping american business.* New York: Dutton.

Bradley, J., & Lee, C. C. (2007). ERP training and user satisfaction: A case study. *International Journal of Enterprise Information Systems, Special topic issue on Use of ERP in Education, 3*(4), 33-50.

Brass, D. J. (1984). Being in the right place: A structural analysis of individual influence in an organization. *Administrative Science Quarterly, 29*, 518-539.

Bratteteig, T., & Gregory, J. (1999). Human action in context: A discussion of theories for understanding the use IT. In T. Käkölä (Ed), *Proceedings of the 22nd Information Systems Research Seminar in Scandinavia (IRIS 22): Enterprise Architectures for Virtual Organisations* (pp. 161-182). Jyväskylä, Finland: University of Jyväskylä.

Brealey, R. A., & Myers, S. C. (2003). Principles of corporate finance (7th ed.). McGraw Hill.

Bretschneider, S., & Wittmer, D., (1993). Organizational adoption of microcomputer technology: The role of sector. *Information Systems Research, 4*(1), 88-108.

Britt, H. (2007). The quality of data on general practice: A discussion of BEACH reliability and validity. *Australian Family Physician, 36*(1/2).

Brohman, M. K., Watson, R., Piccoli, G., & Parasuraman, A. (2003). Data completeness: A key to effective net-based customer service systems. *Communications of the ACM, 46*(6), 47-51.

Brooke, C. (2002). What does it mean to be `critical' in IS research? *Journal of Information Technology, 17*(2), 49-57.

Brookes, N. J., Morton, S. C., Dainty, A. R. J., & Burns, N. D. (2006). Social processes, patterns and practices and project knowledge management: A theoretical framework and an empirical investigation. *International Journal of Project Management, 24*(6), 474-482.

Brown, S. A., & Venkatesh, V. (2005). Model of adoption of technology in the household: A baseline model test and extension incorporating household life cycle. *MIS Quarterly, 29*, 399-426.

Brown, S. A., Venkatesh, V., Kuruzovich, J., & Massey, A. P. (2008). Expectation confirmation: An examination of three competing models. *Organizational Behavior and Human Decision Processes, 105*, 52-66.

Brown, S. W. (1997). Service recovery through IT. *Marketing Management, 6*(3), 25-27.

Broza, G. (2005). *Early community building: A critical success factor for XP projects.* Paper presented at the Agile Conference, Denver, CO, USA.

Brudney, J., & Sally S. (1995). The adoption of innovation by smaller local governments: The case of computer technology. *American Review of Public Administration, 25*(1), 71-86.

Brugha, C. M. (2001). Implications from decision science for the systems development life cycle in information systems. *Information Systems Frontiers, 3*(1), 91-105.

Bruner, J. S. (1956). A cognitive theory of personality. *Contemporary Psychology, 1*, 355-357.

Bryan, N. B., McLean, E. R., Smits, S. J., & Burn, J. M. (1995). Work perceptions among Hong Kong and United States I/S workers: A cross-cultural comparison. *Journal of End User Computing, 7*(4), 22-29.

Bryant, A. (2001). A constructive/ist response to Glaser. *Forum: Qualitative Social Research, 4*(1). Retrieved from http://www.qualitative-research.org/fqs-texte/1-03/1-03bryant-e.pdf

Bryant, A. (2002). Re-grounding grounded theory. *The Journal of Information Technology Theory and Application, 4*(1), 25-42.

Bryman, A. (2001). *Social research methods.* Oxford, UK: Oxford University Press.

BSM Consulting. (2008). *Careers for INTJ personality types.* Retrieved June 16, 2008, from *http://www.personalitypage.com/INTJ_car.html*

Bugler, D., & Stuart, B. (1993). Technology push or program pull: Interest in new information technologies within public organizations. In B. Bozeman (Ed.), *Public management: The state of the art* (pp. 275–93). San Francisco: Josey-Bass.

Bunker, D. (2001). A philosophy of information technology and systems (IT & S) as tools: Tool development context, associated skills and the global technology transfer (GTT) process. *Information Systems Frontiers, 3*(2), 185-197.

Burn, J. (1995). The new cultural revolution: The impact of EDI on Asia. *Journal of Global Information Management, 3*(3), 16-23.

Burr, V., & Butt, T. (1992). *Invitation to personal construct psychology.* London: Whurr Publishers.

Burrell, G. & Morgan, G. (2005). *Sociological paradigms and organisational analysis: Elements of the sociology of corporate life.* Ardershot, UK: Ashgate Publishing Limited.

Burt, R. S. (1987). Social contagion and innovation: Cohesion versus structural equivalence. *American Journal of Sociology, 92*, 1287-1335.

Burt, R. S. (1992). *Structural holes: The social structure of competition.* Cambridge, MA: Harvard Business Press.

Burt, R. S. (1997). The contingent value of social capital. *Administrative Science Quarterly, 42*(2), 339-365.

Burt, R. S. (2000). The network structure of social capital. *Research in Organizational Behavior, 22*, 345-423.

Burt, R. S. (2001). Structural holes versus network closure as social capital. In N. Lin, K. S. Cook, & R. S. Burt (Eds.), *Social capital: Theory and research*. Berlin, Germany: Aldine de Gruyter.

Burt, R. S. (2005). *Brokerage and closure: An introduction to social capital*. New York: Oxford University Press.

Burton-Jones, A., & Gallivan, M. J. (2007). Toward a deeper understanding of system usage in organizations: A multilevel perspective. *MIS Quarterly, 31*(4), 657-679.

BusinessWeek. (2001). *How bad will it get?* Retrieved from http://www.businessweek.com/magazine/content/01_11/b3723017.htm

Butler, T. (1998). Towards a hermeneutic method for interpretive research in information systems. *Journal of Information Technology, 13*(4), 285-300.

Butler, T. (2002). *Building IT resources in post-industrial organizations: Cases on the development and application of IT competencies*. Unpublished doctoral dissertation, University College Cork, Ireland. Retrieved from http://afis.ucc.ie/tbutler/PhD.htm

Butler, T. (2003). An institutional perspective on the development and implementation of Intranet and Internet-based IS. *Information Systems Journal, 13*(3), 209-232.

Butler, T., & Murphy, C. (1999). Shaping information and communication technologies infrastructures in the newspaper industry: Cases on the role of IT competencies. In *An IT Vision of the 21st Century, Proceedings of the 20th International Conference on Information Systems (ICIS)*, Charlotte, NC. (pp. 364-377).

Butler, T., & Murphy, C. (2008). An exploratory study on IS capabilities and assets in a small to medium software enterprise. *Journal of Information Technology, 23*, 330-344.

Byrd, T. A., & Turner, E. D. (2001). An exploratory analysis of the value of the skills of IT personnel: Their relationship to IS infrastructure and competitive advantage. *Decision Sciences, 32*, 21-54.

Byrne, B. M. (2006). *Structural equation modeling with EQS* (2nd ed.). Mahwah, New Jersey: Lawrence Erlbaum Associates.

Caldeira, M. M., & Ward, J. M. (2003). Using resource-based theory to interpret the successful adoption and use of information systems and technology in manufacturing small and medium-sized enterprises. *European Journal of Information Systems, 12*(2), 127-141.

Caldwell, B. (1998, July 6). Andersen sued on R/3. *InformationWeek*.

Calhoun, K. J., Teng, J. T. C., & Cheon, M. J. (2002). Impact of national culture on information technology usage behaviour: An exploratory study of decision making in Korea and the USA. *Behaviour & Information Technology, 21*(4), 293-302.

Callon, M. (1986). Some elements of a sociology of translation: Domestication of the scallops and the fishermen of St Brieuc Bay. In J. Law (Ed.), *Power, action and belief: A new sociology of knowledge* (pp. 196-233). London: Routledge and Kegan Paul.

Callon, M. (1987). Society in the making: The study of technology as a tool for sociological analysis. In W. E. Bijker, T. P. Hughes, & T. Pinch (Eds.), *The social construction of technological systems* (pp. 83-103). Cambridge, MA: The MIT Press.

Callon, M., & Latour, B. (1981). Unscrewing the big leviathan: How actors macro-structure reality and how sociologists help them to do so. In K. Knorr-Cetina, & A. V. Cicourel (Eds.), *Towards an integration of micro- and macro- sociologies* (pp. 277-303). London: Routledge & Kegan Paul.

Callon, M., & Latour, B. (1992). Don't throw the baby out with the bath school!: A reply to Collins and Yearley. In A. Pickering (Ed.), *Science as practice and culture* (pp. 343-368). Chicago: The University of Chicago Press.

Campbell, D. T. (1975). 'Degrees of freedom' and the case study. *Comparative Political Studies, 8*(2), 178-193.

Campbell, D. T., & Fiske, D. W. (1959). Convergent and discriminant validation by the multi trait multi method matrix. *Psychological Bulletin, 56*(2), 81-105.

Caputi, P., & Warren, C. (2007, July). *Exploring the process of how individuals decide to use mandatory information systems*. Paper presented at the XXth Congress of Personal Construct Psychology, Brisbane.

Carbone, D. (2008). Information systems in general practice: A framework to implement the management and prevention of chronic diseases. Unpublished doctoral dissertation, Victoria University.

Cardozo, R. N. (1965). An experimental study of consumer effort, expectation, and satisfaction. *Journal of Marketing Research, 2*, 244-249.

CareerOverview.Com. (2008). *Computer programming careers, jobs, and training.* Retrieved June 16, 2008, from *http://www.careeroverview.com/computer-programming-careers.html*

CareerPath.Com. (2008). *Does your personality hold the key to the perfect job?* Retrieved June 16, 2008, from http://www.careerpath.com/advice/194357-does-your-personality-hold--key-to-the-perfect-job

Carlsson S. A., Henningsson, S., Hrastinski, S., & Keller, C. (2008, May 7-9). Towards a design science research approach for IS use and management: Applications from the areas of knowledge management, e-learning and IS integration. In *Proceedings of the Third International Conference on Design Science Research in Information Systems & Technology* (DESRIST 2008), Atlanta, GA.

Carlsson, S. A. (2003). Advancing information systems evaluation (research): A critical realist approach. *Electronic Journal of Information Systems Evaluation, 6*(2), 11-20.

Carlsson, S. A. (2004). Using critical realism in IS research. In M. E. Whitman & A. B. Woszczynski (Eds.), *The handbook of information systems research* (pp. 323-338). Hershey, PA:IGI Global Publishing.

Carlsson, S. A. (2006): Towards an information systems design research framework: A critical realist perspective. In *Proceedings of the First International Conference on Design Science in Information Systems and Technology (DESRIST 2006)*, (pp. 192-212).

Carlsson, S. A. (2009). Design science in information systems: A critical realist approach. In A. Hevner & S. Chatterjee (Eds.), *Design science research in information systems*. New York: Springer.

Carlsson, S. A., Leidner, D. E., & Elam, J. J. (1996). Individual and organizational effectiveness: Perspectives on the impact of ESS in multinational organizations. In P.

Humphreys, L. Bannon, A. McCosh, P. Migliarese & J. C. Pomerol (Eds.), *Implementing systems for supporting management decisions: Concepts, methods and experiences* (pp. 91-107). London: Chapman & Hall.

Carmen, J. M., & Langeard, E. (1980). Growth strategies of service firm. *Strategic Management Journal, 1*(1), 7-22.

Carpenter, B. (1992). Issues and advances in coping research. In B. Carpenter (Ed.), *Personal coping: Theory, research, and application* (pp. 1-14). Westport, CT: Praeger.

Carpenter, M. A., & Fredrickson, J. W. (2001). Top management teams, global strategic posture, and the moderating role of uncertainty. *Academy of Management Journal, 44*(3), 533-545.

Carter, C. R. (2000). Ethical issues in international buyer-supplier relationships: A dyadic examination. *Journal of Operations Management, 18*(2), 191-208.

Carter, L., & Bélanger, F. (2004). Citizen adoption of electronic government initiatives. In *Proceedings of the 37th Hawaii International Conference on System Sciences.*

Carter, L., & Bélanger, F. (2005). The utilization of e-government services: Citizen trust, innovation and acceptance factors. *Information Systems Journal, 15*, 5-25.

Cartwright, S., & Cooper, C. L. (1996a). Coping in occupational settings. In M. Zeidner & N. S. Endler (Eds.), *Handbook of coping: fTheory, research, applications* (pp. 202-220). New York: John Wiley & Sons.

Cartwright, S., & Cooper, C. L. (1996b). The psychological impact of merger and acquisition on the individual: A study of building society managers. *Human Relations, 46*(3), 327-347.

Casey, D., & Brugha, C. (2005). From fighting fires to building bridges: The role of metaphor in systems requirements. In *Proceedings of the International Professional Communication Conference, 2005. IPCC 2005.*

Castells, M. (2000). *The Rise of the Network Society. The Information Age: Economy, Society and Culture*, Vol. 1:. Oxford, UK: Blackwell Publisher Ltd.

Casti, J. (1986) On system complexity: Identification, measurement, and management. In J. Casti & A. Karlqvist (Eds.), *Complexity, language, and life: Mathematical approaches*. Berlim, Germany: Springer-Verlag.

Caudle, S. L., Gorr, W. L., & Newcomer, K. E. (1991). Key information systems management issues for the public sector. *MIS Quarterly, 15*(2), 171-188.

Cavaye, A., & Christiansen, J. (1996). Understanding IS implementation by estimating power of subunits. *European Journal of Information Systems, 5*, 222-232.

Cecez-Kecmanovic, D., & Webb, C. (2000). Towards a communicative model of collaborative Web-mediated learning. *Australian Journal of Educational Technology, 16*(1), 73-85.

Celler, B. G., et al. (2003). Using information technology to improve the management of chronic disease. *MJA, 179*(5), 242-246.

Cenfetelli, R. T., Benbasat, I., & Al-Natour, S. (2008). Addressing the what and how of online services: Positioning supporting-service functionality and service quality for business to consumer success. *Information Systems Research, 19*(2), 161-181.

Centre for Science Studies. (2001). *Actor network resources*.

Chan, D. (1998). Functional relations among constructs in the same content domain at different levels of analysis: A typology of composition models. *Journal of Applied Psychology, 83*(2), 234-246.

Chandler, A. D., Jr. (1977). The visible hand: The managerial revolution in American business. Cambridge, MA: Harvard University Press.

Chandy, P. R., & Williams, T. G. E. (1994). The impact of journals and authors on international business. *Journal of International Business Studies, 25*(4), 715.

Charmaz, K. (2000). Grounded theory: Objectivist and constructivist methods. In N. K. Denzin & Y. S. Lincoln (Eds.), *Handbook of qualitative research* (2nd. ed.) (pp. 509-535). Thousand Oaks, CA: Sage.

Chase, R. B., & Tansik, D. A. (1978). The customer contact model for organization design. *Management Science, 29*(9), 673-687.

Chase, S. E. (2005). Narrative inquiry. In N. K. Denzin & Y. S. Lincoln (Eds.), *Handbook of qualitative research* (3rd ed.) (pp. 651-679). Thousand Oaks, CA: Sage Publications.

Chau, P. Y. K., & Hu, P. J.-H. (2001). Information technology acceptance by individual professionals: A model comparison approach. *Decision Sciences, 32*(4), 699-719.

Chaudhry, B., et al. (2006). Systematic review: Impact of health information technology on quality, efficiency, and costs of medical care. *Annals of Internal Medicine, 144*(10).

Checkland, P. (1999). *Systems thinking, systems practice*. Chichester, England: Wiley.

Checkland, P., & Holwell, S. (1998). *Information, systems and information systems: Making sense of the field*. Chichester, UK: John Wiley & Sons.

Chen, H., Wigand, R. T., & Nilan, M. S. (1999). Optimal experience of web activities. *Computers in Human Behavior, 15*(5), 585-608.

Chen, M. (1996). Competitor analysis and interfirm rivalry: Toward a theoretical integration. *Academy of Management Review, 1*, 100-134.

Chen, W., & Hirschheim, R. (2004). A paradigmatic and methodological examination of information systems research. *Information Systems Journal, 14*(3), 197-235.

Chen, Y.-C., & Thurmaier, K. (2005, November 3-6). Government-to-citizen electronic services: Understanding and driving adoption of online transactions. In *Proceedings of the Association for Public Policy & Management (APPAM) conference*, Washington, D.C.

Cherns, A. (1976). The principles of sociotechnical design. *Human Relations, 29*(8), 783-792.

Chesbrough, H., & Spohrer, J. (2006). A research manifesto for service science. *Communications of the ACM, 49*(7), 35-40.

Cheung, G. W. (2009). Introducing the latent congruence model for assessment of similarity, agreement, and fit in organizational research. *Organizational Research Methods, 12*(1), 6-33.

Chin, R., & Benne, K. (1969). The planning of change. In *General strategies for effecting changes in human systems* (2nd ed.) (Vol. 1). New York: Holt, Rinehart & Winston.

Chin, W. W. (1988). *The partial least squares approach to structural equation model.* Mahwah, NJ: Lawrence Erlbaum Associates.

Chin, W. W. (1998). The partial least squares approach to structural equation modeling. In G. A. Marcoulides (Ed.), *Modern methods for business research* (pp. 295-336). Mahwah, NJ: Lawrence Erlbaum Associates.

Chin, W. W., Gopal, A., & Salisbury, W. D. (1997). Advancing the theory of adaptive structuration: The development of a scale to measure faithfulness of appropriation. *Information SystemsResearch, 8*(4), 342-367.

Chircu, A. M., & Lee, H. D. (2003). Understanding IT investments in the public sector: the case of e-government. In *Proceedings of the 9th Americas Conference on Information Systems* (pp. 792-800).

Chiu, C. (2005). Applying means-end chain theory to eliciting system requirements and understanding users perceptual orientations. *Information & Management, 42*, 455-468.

Chiu, C.-M., Hsu, M.-H., & Wang, E. T. G. (2006). Understanding knowledge sharing in virtual communities: An integration of social capital and social cognitive theories. *Decision Support Systems, 42*(3), 1872-1888.

Choe, J. M. (2004). The consideration of cultural differences in the design of information systems. *Information & Management, 41*(5), 669.

Choi, D. H., Kim, C. M., Kim, S., & Kim, S. H. (2006). Customer loyalty and disloyalty in internet retail stores: Its antecedents and its effect on customer price sensitivity. *International Journal of Management, 23*(4), 925-941.

Chou, T.-C., Chen, J.-R., & Pan, S. L. (2006). The impacts of social capital on information technology outsourcing decisions: A case study of a Taiwanese high-tech firm. *International Journal of Information Management, 26*(3), 249-256.

Choudhury, V., Hartzel, K., & Konsynski, B. (1998). Uses and consequences of electronic markets: An empirical investigation in the aircraft parts industry. *MIS Quarterly, 22*, 471-507

Christenson, C. (1976). Proposals for a program of empirical research into the properties of triangles. *Decision Sciences, 7*(3), 631-648.

Christiaanse, E., & Markus, L. (2002 December 18-21). Business to business electronic marketplace and the structure of channel relationships. In *Proceedings of the 23rd International Conference on Information Systems,* Barcelona, Spain.

Christiaanse, E., & Markus, L. (2003). Participation in collaboration electronic marketplaces. In *Proceedings of the Hawaii International Conference on System Science,* Hawaii, USA.

Chuang, S. (2004). A resource-based perspective on knowledge management capability and competitive advantage: An empirical investigation. *Expert Systems with Applications, 27*(3), 459-465.

Chudoba, K. M., Wynn, E., Lu, M., & Watson-Manheim, M. B. (2005). How virtual are we? Measuring virtuality and understanding its impact in a global organization. *Information Systems Journal, 15*(4), 279-306.

Chung, I., & Adams, C. (1997). A study on the characteristics of group decision making behaviour: Cultural difference perspective of Korea versus United States. *Journal of Global Information Management, 5*(3), 18-29.

Chung, J., & Tan, F. B. (2004). Antecedents of perceived playfulness: An exploratory study on user acceptance of general information-searching websites. *Information & Management, 41*, 869-881.

Church, A. H., & Waclawski, J. (1996) The effects of personality orientation and executive behavior on subordinate perceptions of workgroup enablement. *International Journal of Organizational Analysis, 4*, 20-51.

Churchill, G. A. (1979). A paradigm for developing better measures of marketing constructs. *Journal of Marketing Research, 16*(1), 64-73.

Churchill, G. A., & Surprenant, C. (1982) An investigation into the determinants of customer satisfaction. *Journal of Marketing Research, 19*, 491-504.

Churchman, C. W. (1979). *The systems approach.* New York: Dell.

Chwelos, P., Benbasat, I., & Dexter, A. S. (2001). Research report: Empirical test of an EDI adoption model. *Information Systems Research, 12*(3), 304-321.

Ciborra, C. (1993). *Teams, markets and system.* Cambridge, UK: Cambridge University Press.

Ciborra, C. (1999). Notes on improvisation and time in organizations. *Accounting, Management & Information Technologies, 9*(2), 77-94.

Ciborra, C., & Willcocks, L. (2006). The mind or the heart? It depends on the (definition of) situation. *Journal of Information Technology, 21*(3), 129-140.

Cigola, M., & Peccati, L. (2005, March). On the comparison between the APV and the NPV computed via the WACC. *European Journal of Operational Research, 161*(2), 377-385.

Clarke, A. (1999). A practical use of key success factors to improve the effectiveness of project management. *International Journal of Project Management, 17*(3), 139-145.

Clarke, A. E. (2003). Situational analyses: Grounded theory mapping after the postmodern turn. *Symbolic Interaction, 26*(4), 553-576.

Clarke, R. (1999, June 7-9). Electronic services delivery: From brochure-ware to entry points. In *Proceedings of the Twelfth International Electronic Commerce Conference*, Bled, Slovenia (pp. 8-9).

Clarke, R. (2001). *Innovation diffusion resources. Open site.* Retrieved September 25, 2005, from http://www.anu.edu.au/people/Roger.Clarke/SOS/InnDiffISW.html

Clausen, C., & Koch, C. (1999). The role of space and occasions in the transformation of information technologies - lessons from the social shaping of ICT systems for manufacturing in a Danish context. *Technology Analysis and Strategic Management, 11*(3), 463-482.

Clegg, C. W. (2000). Sociotechnical principles for systems design. *Applied Ergonomics, 31*, 463-477

Clegg, S. R., Kornberger, M., & Rhodes, C. (Mar 2004). Noise, parasites and translation: Theory and practice in management consulting. *Management Learning, 35*(1), 31-44.

Clemons, E. K., & Hitt, L. M. (2004). Poaching and the misappropriation of information: Transaction risks of information exchange. *Journal of Management Information Systems, 21*(2), 87-107.

Cline, M. K., & Guynes, C. S. (2001). A study of the impact of information technology investment on firm performance. *Journal of Computer Information Systems, 41*(3), 15-19.

Clough, P. T. (2000). Comments on setting criteria for experimental writing. *Qualitative Inquiry, 6*, 278-291.

Coase, R. H. (1937). The nature of the firm. *Economica.*

Coch, L., & French, J. (1968). Overcoming resistance to change. In D. Cartwright & A. Zander (Eds.), *Group dynamics* (pp. 182-191). NY, USA: Harper & Row Publishers.

Cockburn, C., & Ormrod, S. (1993). *Gender and technology in the making.* London: SAGE.

Cockburn, J. (2004). Adoption of evidence into practice: Can change be sustainable? *MJA, 180*, S66-S67.

Cohen, I. J. (1989). *Structuration theory: Anthony Giddens and the constitution of social life.* New York: St Martin's Press.

Cohen, J., Cohen, P., West, S. G., & Aiken, L. S. (2003). *Applied multiple regression/correlation analysis for the behavioral sciences* (3rd ed.). Mahwah, NJ: Lawrence Erlbaum Associates.

Cohen, S., Evans, G. W., Stokols, D., & Krantz, D. S. (1986). *Behavioral, health, and environmental stress.* New York: Plenum.

Cohendet P., & Llerena P. (1989). Flexibilité, information et décision. *Economica.* Paris.

Cole, M., & Engeström, Y. (1993). A cultural-historical approach to distributed cognition. In G. Salomon (Ed.), *Distributed cognitions: Psychological and educational considerations* (pp. 1-46). Cambridge, UK: Cambridge University Press.

Coleman, J. S. (1988). Social capital in the creation of human capital. *American Journal of sociology, 94*, 95-120.

Coleman, J. S. (1990). *Foundations of social theory.* Cambridge, MA: Harvard University Press.

Collier, J. E., & Bienstock, C. C. (2006). Measuring service quality in e-retailing. *Journal of Service Research, 8*(3), 260-275.

Collins, H. M., & Yearley, S. (1992a). Epistemological chicken. In A. Pickering (Ed.), *Science as practice and culture* (pp. 301-326). Chicago: The Universty of Chicago Press.

Collins, H. M., & Yearley, S. (1992b). Journey into space. In A. Pickering (Ed.), *Science as practice and culture* (pp. 369-389). Chicago: The University of Chicago Press.

Colombetti, M., & Verdicchio, M. (2002). *An analysis of agent speech acts as institutional actions.* Paper presented at the International Conference on Autonomous Agents, Bologna, Italy.

Compeau, D. R., & Higgins, C. A. (1995). Computer self-efficacy: Development of a measure and initial test. *MIS Quarterly, 19*(2), 189-211.

Compeau, D., Higgins, C. A., & Huff, S. (1999). Social cognitive theory and individual reactions to computing technology: A longitudinal study. *MIS Quarterly, 23*, 145-158.

Connors, D. T. (1992). Software development methodologies and traditional and modern information systems. *ACM SIGSOFT Software Engineering Notes, 17*(2), 43-49.

Constant, E. W. (1980). *The origins of the turbojet revolution.* Baltimore: Johns Hopkins University Press.

Convertino, G., Farooq, U., Rosson, M. B., Carroll, J. M., & Meyer, B. J. F. (2007). Supporting intergenerational groups in computer-supported cooperative work (CSCW). *Behaviour & Information Technology, 26*(4), 275-285.

Cook, T. D., & Campbell, D. T. (1979). *Quasi-experimentation: Design and analysis issues for field settings.* Boston, MA: Houghton Mifflin Company.

Cooke, P. (2007). Social capital, embeddedness, and market interactions: An analysis of firm performance in UK regions. *Review of Social Economy, 65*(1), 79-106.

Coon, D. (2005). *Psychology: A modular approach to mind and behavior* (10th ed.). Belmont, CA: Thomson Wadsworth.

Cooper, R. B. (1994). The inertial impact of culture on IT implementation. *Information & Management, 27*, 17-31.

Cooper, R. B., & Zmud, R. W. (1990). Information technology implementation research: A technological diffusion approach. *Management Science, 36*(2), 123-139.

Copeland, T., & Tufano, P. (2004, March). A real-world way to manage real options. *Harvard Business Review, 82*(3), 90-99.

Copeland, T., Koller, T., & Murrin, J. (2000). *Valuation: Measuring and managing the value of companies* (3rd ed.). New York: John Wiley & Sons.

Corbitt, B. J., Peszynski, K. J., Inthanond, S., Hill, B., & Thanasankit, T. (2004). Cultural differences, information and code systems. *Journal of Global Information Management, 12*(3), 65-85.

Cordella, A. (2001, June 27-29). Does information technology always lead to lower transaction costs? In *Proceedings of the 9th European Conference of Information Systems* (pp. 854-864).

Cordella, A., & Simon, K. A. (2000). Global and local dynamics in infrastructure deployment: The Astra Hassle experience. In C. U. Ciborra (Ed.), *From control to drift: The dynamics of corporate information infrastructure* (pp. 172-192). Oxford, UK: Oxford University Press.

Costa, P. T., & McCrae, R. R. (1988). Personality in adulthood: A six-year longitudinal study of self-reports and spouse ratings on the NEO personality inventory. *Journal of Personality and Social Psychology, 54*, 853-863.

Cox, D. F., & Rich, S. U. (1964). Perceived risk and consumer decision making - the case of telephone shopping. *Journal of Marketing Research, 1*(4), 32-39.

Cox, J. C., Ross, S. A., & Rubinstein, M. (1979, September). Options pricing: A simplified approach. *Journal of Financial Economics, 7*(3), 229-264.

Cox, S., Dulfer, R., Han, D., Ruiz, U., & Alter, S. (2002). TDG engineering: Do we need really another upgrade? *Communications of the Association for Information Systems, 8*, 232-250

Craig, S. R. (1986). Seeking strategic advantage with technology? -- Focus on customer value! *Long Range Planning, 19*(2), 50-56.

Crawford, K., & Hasan, H. (2006). Demonstrations of the activity theory framework for research in information systems. *Australasian Journal of Information Systems 13*(2), 49-68.

Cresswell, A. M., & Pardo, T. A. (2001). Implications of legal and organizational issues for urban digital government development. *Government Information Quarterly, 18*, 269-278.

Cronbach, L. J. (1958). Proposals leading to analytic treatment of social perception scores. In R. Tagiuri & L. Petrullo (Eds.), *Person perception and interpersonal behavior* (pp 353-379). Stanford, CA: Stanford University Press.

Cronbach, L. J. (1987). Statistical tests for moderator variables: Flaws in analyses recently proposed. *Psychological Bulletin, 102*, 414-417.

Cronbach, L. J., & Meehl, P. E. (1955). Construct validity in psychology tests. *Psychological Bulletin, 52*(4), 281-302.

Cronen, V. (2001). Practical theory, practical art, and the pragmatic-systemic account of inquiry. *Communication theory, 11*(1).

Cronin, B. (2002). The digital divide. *Library Journal, 127*(3), 48.

Csikszentmihalyi, M. (1975). *Beyond boredom and anxiety: Experiencing flow in work and play*. San Francisco: Jossey-Bass Publishers.

Csikszentmihalyi, M. (1990). *Flow: The psychology of optimal experience*. New York: Harper and Row, Publishers, Inc.

Csikszentmihalyi, M. (1997). *Finding flow: The psychology of engagement with everyday life*. New York: Basic Books.

Csikszentmihalyi, M. (2000). *Beyond boredom and anxiety: Experiencing flow in work and play*. San Francisco: Jossey-Bass Publishers.

Csikszentmihalyi, M., & Rathunde, K. (1993). The measurement of flow in everyday life: Toward a theory of emergent motivation. In J. E. Jacobs (Ed.), *Nebraska symposium on motivation 1992* (pp. 57-97). Lincoln, NE: University of Nebraska Press.

Cua, F. C., & Garrett, T. C. (2009). Understanding ontology and epistemology in information systems research. In A. Cater-Steel & L. Al-Hakim (Eds.), *Information systems research methods, epistemology and applications*. Hershey, PA: Information Science Reference.

Cua, F. C., & Garrett, T. C. (in press). Analyzing diffusion and value creation dimensions of a business case of replacing enterprise systems. In T. T. Kidd (Ed.), *Handbook of Research on Technology Project Management, Planning and Operation*. New York: IGI Publishing.

Curbera, F., Nagy, W. A., & Weerawarana, S. (2001). *Web services: Why and how*. Paper presented at the Workshop on Object-Oriented Web services held with the ACM Conference on Object-Oriented Programming, Systems, Language and Applications (OOPSLA), Tampa, Florida, USA.

Curran, J. M., & Meuter, M. (2005). Self-service technology adoption: Comparing three technologies. *The Journal of Services Marketing, 19*(2), 103-113.

Curran, J. M., & Meuter, M. L. (2007). Encouraging existing customers to switch to self-service technologies: Put a little fun in their lives. *Journal of Marketing Theory and Practice, 15*(4), 283-298.

Curry, A., & Penman, S. (2004). The relative importance of technology in enhancing customer relationships in banking - a Scottish perspective. *Managing Service Quality, 14*(4), 331-341.

Cushman, M., & Klecun, E. (2005). *How (can) non-users perceive usefulness: Bringing in the digitally excluded* (Penceil Paper 7). London School of Economics.

Cushway, B., & Lodge, D. (1999). *Organization behaviour and design*. London, UK: Kogan Page Ltd.

Cusumano, M. A., & Elenkov, D. (1994). Linking international technology transfer with strategy and management: A literature commentary. *Research Policy, 23*, 195-215.

Cusumano, M. A., & Elenkov, D. (1994). Linking international technology transfer with strategy and management: A literature commentary. *Research Policy, 23,* 195-215.

Cyr, D., & Trevor-Smith, H. (2004). Localization of Web design: An empirical comparison of German, Japanese, and United States Web site characteristics. *Journal of the American Society for Information Science and Technology, 55*(13), 1199-1208.

D'Aveni, R. (1994). *Hypercompetition: Managing the dynamics of strategic maneuvering.* New York: Free Press.

Dabholkar, P. A. (1992). Role of affect and need for interaction in on-site service encounters. *Advances in Consumer Research, 19*(1), 563-569.

Dabholkar, P. A. (1996). Consumer evaluations of new technology-based self-service options: An investigation of alternative models of service quality. *International Journal of Research in Marketing, 13*(1), 29-51.

Dada, D. (2006). *The failure of e-government in developing countries.* Retrieved 2006, from http://www.lse.ac.uk/collections/informationSystems/iSChannel/Dada_2006b.pdf

Daft, R. L. (1978). A dual-core model of organizational innovation. *Academy of Management Journal, 21,* 193-210.

Dalrymple, J. (2005, September 9). Quark adopts new corporate identity. *MacWorld.* Retrieved November 20, 2005, from http://www.macworld.com/news/2005/09/09/quarkchange/index.php

Damodaran, L., Nicholls, J., & Henney, A. (2005). The contribution of sociotechnical systems thinking to the effective adoption of e-government and the enhancement of democracy. *The Electronic Journal of e-Government, 3*(1), 1-12.

Damsgaard, J., & Lyytinen, K. (1996). Government Strategies to promote the diffusion of electronic data interchange: What we know and what we don't know. *Information Infrastructure and Policy, 5*(3), 169-190.

Danziger, J. M. (2004). Innovation in innovation? The technology enactment framework. *Social Science Computer Review, 22*(1), 100-110.

Darke, P., & Shanks, G. (1997). User viewpoint modeling: Understanding and representing user viewpoints during requirements definition. *Information Systems Journal, 7,* 213-239.

Dasgupta, S. (1996). *Technology and creativity.* New York: Oxford University Press.

Datta, L. E. (1990, November). *Case study evaluations.* Retrieved February 21, 2008, from http://www.gao.gov/special.pubs/10_1_9.pdf

Davenport, T. H., & Prusak, L. (1998). *Working knowledge.* Cambridge, MA: Harvard Business School Press.

Davenport, T. H., & Pursak, L. (2001). Information ecology: Mastering the information and knowledge environment. *Business History Review, 3*(75), 15-61.

Davidson, E. (2002). Technology frames and framing: A socio-cognitive investigation of requirements determination. *MIS Quarterly, 26*(4), 329-358.

Davis, C. J., & Hunagel, E. M. (2004). *Implementing information systems to support knowledge work: An exploration of work motifs.* Retrieved from http://is2.lse.ac.uk/asp/aspecis/

Davis, D. A., et al. (2004). Solving the information overload problem: A letter from Canada. *MJA, 180,* S68-S71.

Davis, F .D., Bagozzi, R. P., & Warshaw. P. R. (1992). Extrinsic and intrinsic motivation to use computers in the workplace. *Journal of Applied Social Psychology, 22,* 1111-1132.

Davis, F. D. (1986). A technology acceptance model for empirically testing new end-ser information systems: Theory and results. Unpublished doctoral dissertation, Sloan School of Management, Massachusetts Institute of Technology.

Davis, F. D. (1989). Perceived usefulness, perceived ease of use and user acceptance of information technology. *MIS Quarterly, 13*(3), 319-340.

Davis, F. D., Bagozzi, R. P., & Warshaw, P. R. (1989). User acceptance of computer technology: A comparison of two theoretical models. *Management Science, 35*(8), 982-1003.

Davis, F. D. (1993). User acceptance of information technology: System characteristics, user perceptions and behavioral impacts. *International Journal of Man-Machine Studies, 38*, 475-487.

Davis, G. B., & Olson, M. H. (1984). *Management information systems: Conceptual foundations, structure, and development* (2nd ed.). New York: McGraw-Hill.

Davison, R. (2002). Cultural implications of ERP. *Communications of the ACM, 45*(7), 109-111.

Davydov, V. V. (1999). The content and unsolved problems of activity theory. In Y. Engeström, R. Miettinen, & R.-L. Punamäki (Eds.), *Perspectives on activity theory* (pp. 39-52). Cambridge, UK: Cambridge University Press.

Dawes, S. S., Pardo, T. A., & Cresswell, A. M. (2004). Designing electronic government information access programs: A holistic approach. *Government Information Quarterly, 21*(1), 3-23.

Dawson, P., et al. (2000). Political processes in management, organization and the social shaping of technology. *Technology Analysis and Strategic Management, 12*(1) 5-15.

Day, D., Dosa, M., & Jorgensen, C. (1995). The transfer of research information within and by multicultural teams. *Information Processing & Management, 31*(1), 89-100.

Day, G. S. (1994). The capabilities of market-driven organizations. *Journal of Marketing, 58*(4), 37-52.

De Angeli, A., Athavankar, U., Joshi, A., Coventry, L., & Johnson, G. I. (2004). Introducing ATMs in India: A contextual inquiry. *Interacting with Computers, 16*(1), 29-44.

De Michelis, G., & Grasso, M. A. (1994). *Situating conversations within the language/action perspective: the Milan conversation model.* Paper presented at the ACM conference on Computer supported cooperative work, Chapel Hill, North Carolina, United States.

De Michelis, G., Dubois, E., Jarke, M., Matthes, F., Mylopoulos, J., Papazoglou, M. P., et al. (1997). Cooperative information systems: A manifesto. In M. P. Papazoglou & G. Schlageter (Eds.), *Cooperative information systems: Trends & directions.* Academic Press.

De Raad, B. (2000). *The big five personality factors (the psycholexical approach to personality).* Seattle, WA: Hogrefe & Huber.

de Ruyter, K., & Zuurbier, J. (1993). Customer information systems: Approaching a new field in information systems from a new perspective. *Information & Management, 24*, 247-255.

De Vaujany F.-C. (2008). Capturing reflexivitiy modes in IS: A critical realist approach. *Information and Organization, 18*, 51-71.

De Vreede, G., Jones, N., & Mgaya, R. J. (1998-99). Exploring the application and acceptance of group support systems in Africa. *Journal of Management Information Systems, 15*(3), 197-234.

Dean, K., Joseph J., & Norrie, A. (2005). Editorial: New essays in critical realism. *New Formations, 56*, 7-26.

Dearnaley, M. (2005). Air NZ engineers plead for their jobs. *The New Zealand Herald.*

Dehning, B., & Richardson, V. (2002). Returns on investments in information technology: A research synthesis. *Journal of Information Systems, 16*, 7-30.

Delene, L. M., & Lyth, D. M. (1989). Interactive services operations: The relationships among information, technology and exchange transactions on the quality of the customer-contact interface. *International Journal of Operations & Production Management, 9*(5), 24-32.

DeLone, W. H., & McLean, E. R. (1992). Information systems success: The quest for the dependent variable. *Information Systems Research, 3*(1), 60-95.

DeLone, W. H., & McLean, E. R. (2003). The DeLone and McLean model of information systems success: A ten-year update. *Journal of Management Information Systems, 19*(4), 9-30.

DeNeve, K. M., & Cooper, H. (1998). The happy personality: A meta-analysis of 137 personality traits and subjective well-being. *Psychological Bulletin, 95*, 542-575.

Dent, E., & Goldberg, S. (1999). Challenging a resistance to change. *Journal of Applied Behavioural Science, 35*(1), 25-41.

Denzin, N. K., & Lincoln, Y. S. (2005). Introduction: The discipline and practice of qualitative research. In N. K. Denzin & Y. S. Lincoln (Eds.), *The Sage handbook of qualitative research* (3rd ed.) (pp. 1-32). Thousand Oaks, CA: Sage.

Department of Health and Aged Care. (2003). *Practice incentive payments*. Retrieved November, 2003, from http//: www.health.gov.au/pip/index.htn

DeSanctis, G., & Poole, M. S. (1994). Capturing the complexity in advanced technology use: Adaptive structuration theory. *Organization Science, 5*(2), 121-147.

deSouza, C. R. B., & Redmiles, D. F. (2003, September). *Opportunities for extending activity theory for studying collaborative software development*. Paper presented at the 8th European Conference of Computer-Supported Cooperative Work (ECSCW'03): Workshop on applying activity theory to CSCW research and practice, Helsinki, Finland.

Dettmer, H. W. (2003). *Strategic navigation: A systems approach to business strategy*. Milwaukee, WI: ASQ Quality Press.

Dev, C. S., & Ellis, B. D. (1991). Guest histories: An untapped service resource. *Cornell Hotel And Restaurant Administration Quarterly, 32*(2), 28-37.

DeVellis, R. F. (1991). *Scale development: Theories and applications*. Newbury Park, CA: Sage.

Dewey, J. (1938). *Logic: The theory of inquiry*. New York: Henry Holt.

Dey, I. (1999). *Grounding grounded theory*. San Diego, CA: Academic Press.

Dickinson, J. (2002). General practice. *MJA, 176*(1), 17.

Dietz, J. L. G. (1994). *Business modeling for business redesign*. Paper presented at the Hawaii International Conference on System Sciences (HICSS), Maui, Hawaii.

Dietz, J. L. G. (2001). Coherent, consistent and comprehensive modeling of communication, information, action and organzation. In M. Rossi & K. Siau (Eds.), *Information modeling in the new milennium* (pp. 9-33). Hershey, PA: Idea Group Publishing.

Dietz, J. L. G. (2002). *The atoms, molecules and matter of organizations*. Paper presented at the International Working Conference on the Language-action perspective on Communication Modelling (LAP).

Dietz, J. L. G. (2003). The atoms, molecules and fibers of organizations. *Data & Knowledge Engineering, 47*(3), 301-325.

Dietz, J. L. G., Rijst, N. B. J. v. d., & Stollman, F. L. H. (1996). *The specification and implementation of a DEMO supporting CASE-Tool*. Paper presented at the International Workshop on Communication Modeling - The Language/Action Perspective (LAP), Tilburg, The Netherlands.

Dillon, T. W., & Reif, H. L. (2004). Factors influencing consumers' e-commerce commodity purchases. *Information Technology, Learning, and Performance Journal, 22*(2), 1-12.

DiMaggio, P. J., & Powell, W. W. (1983). The iron cage revisited: Institutional isomorphism and collective rationality in organizational fields. *American Sociological Review, 48*, 47-60.

Dishaw, M. T., Strong, D. M., & Brandy, D. B. (2002). Extending the task-technology fit model of self-efficacy constructs. In R. Ramsower & J. Windso (Eds.), *Proceedings of the 8th Americas Conference on Information Systems*, Dallas, TX (pp. 1021-1027).

Dixit, K. (2006). *Does information technology really promote knowledge?* Retrieved 2006, from http://sade.sdnp.undp.org/rc/forums/mgr/sdnpmgrs/msg01283. html

Dobson, P. J. (2001). The philosophy of critical realism—an opportunity for information systems research. *Information Systems Frontier, 3*(2), 199-201.

Dobson, P., Myles, J., & Jackson, P. (2007). Making the case for critical realism: Examining the implementation of automated performance management systems. *Information Resources Management Journal, 20*(2), 138-152.

DoHA. (2008). National primary care collaboratives. Retrieved April 28, 2008, from http://www.npcc.com.au/

Donabedian, A. (1988). The quality of care. How can it be assessed? *JAMA, 260*, 1743-1748.

Donthu, N., & Boonghee, Y. (1998). Cultural influences on service quality expectations. *Journal of Service Research, 1*(2), 178-186.

Doolin, B. (1998). Information technology as disciplinary technology: Being critical in interpretive research on information systems. *Journal of Information Technology, 13*(4), 301-311.

Doolin, B., & Lowe, A. (2002). To reveal is to critique: Actor-network theory and critical information systems research. *Journal of Information Technology, 17*(2), 69-78.

Dopfer, K. (Ed.). (2001). *Evolutionary economics: Program and scope.* Dordrecht, The Netherlands: Kluwer Academic Publishers.

Dosi, G., & Nelson, R. R. (1994). An introduction to evolutionary theories in economics. *Journal of Evolutionary Economics, 4*, 153-172.

Dosi, G., Freeman, C., Nelson, R. R., Silverberg, G., & Soete, L. (Eds.). (1988). *Technological change and economic theory.* London: Pinter Publishers.

Doty, D. H., & Glick, W. H. (1994). Typologies as a unique form of theory building: Toward improved understanding and modeling. *Academy of Management Review, 19*(2), 230-251.

Doukidis, G., Lybereas, P., & Galliers, R. (1996). Information systems planning in small business: A stages of growth analysis. *The Journal of Systems and Software, 33*(2), 189-201.

Dove, R. (2003). Knowledge management and agility: Relationships and roles. In C. W. Holsapple (Ed.), *Handbook on knowledge management 2: Knowledge directions* (pp. 309-330). Berlin/Heidelberg, Germany: Springer-Verlag.

Downs G. W., Jr., & Mohr, L. B. (1976). Conceptual issues in the study of innovation. *Administrative Science Quarterly, 21*(4), 700-714.

Dron, J. (2005). Epimethean information systems: Harnessing the power of the collective in e-learning. *Int. J. Information Teachnology and Management, 4*(4), 392-404.

Duck, J. (1993). Managing change: The art of balancing. *Harvard Business Review, 71*(6), 109-118.

Dukes, W. (1965). N=1. *Psychological Bulletin, 64*, 74-79.

Dumay, M., Dietz, J., & Mulder, H. (2005). *Evaluation of DEMO and the language/action perspective after 10 years of experience.* Paper presented at the International Working Conference on the Language-action perspective on Communication Modelling (LAP), Kiruna, Sweden.

Dunleavy, P. (2002). *Better public services through e-government* (Report by Comptroller and Auditor General, HC 704-1). London, National Audit Office Press.

Dupuit, J. (1844). De la mesure de l'utilité des travaux publics. *Annales de Ponts et Chaussées, 8*(2).

Durkheim, E. (1982). *Rules of sociological method.* The Free Press.

Durkheim, E. (1997). *The division of labour in society.* The Free Press.

Dustbar, S., & Hofstede, G. J. (1999). Videoconferencing across cultures - a conceptual framework for floor control issues. *Journal of Information Technology, 14*, 161-169.

Ebrahim, Z., & Irani, Z. (2005). E-government adoption: Architecture and barriers. *Business Process Management Journal, 11*(5), 589-611.

Eden, C. (1992). On the nature of cognitive maps. *Journal of Management Studies, 29*(3), 261-265.

Edmondson, A., & Moingeon, B. (2003). From organizational learning to the learning organization. In C. Grey & E. Antonacopoulou (Eds.), *Essential readings in management learning* (pp. 21-36). London: Sage Publications.

Edquist, C. (Ed.). (1997). *Systems of innovation: Technologies, institutions and organisations.* London: Pinter Publishers.

Edwards, J. R. (2009). Latent variable modeling in congruence research: Current problems and future directions, *Organizational Research Methods, 12*(1), 34-62.

Edwards, J. R. (1994). The study of congruence in organizational behavior research: Critique and a proposed alternative. *Organizational Behavior and Human Decision Processes, 58*, 51-100.

Edwards, J. R. (2001). Multidimensional constructs in organizational behavior research: An integrative analytical framework. *Organizational Research Methods, 4*(2), 144-192.

Edwards, J. R. (2001). Ten differences score myths. *Organizational Research Methods, 4*(3), 265-287.

Edwards, J. R., & Bagozzi, R. P. (2000). On the nature and direction of relationships between constructs and measures. *Psychological Methods, 5*(2), 155-174.

Edwards, J. R., & Harrison, R. V. (1993). Job demands and worker health: A three-dimensional reexamination of the relationship between person-environment fit and strain. *Journal of Applied Psychology, 78*, 628-648.

Edwards, J. R., & Parry, M. E. (1993). On the use of polynomial regression equations as an alternative to difference scores in organizational research. *Academy of Management Journal, 36*, 1577-1613.

Edwards, J., & Cooper, C. (1990) The person-environment fit approach to stress: Recurring problems and some suggested solutions. *Journal of Organizational Behavior, 11*, 293-307.

e-Framework. (2008) *The e-framework*. Retrieved from, http://www.e-framework.org

Eisenhardt, K. M. (1989). Building theories from case study research. *Academy of Management Review, 14*(4), 532-550.

Eisenhardt, M, K. (1989). Agency theory: An assessment and review. *Academy of Management Review, 14*(1), 57.

Elbanna, A. R. (2006). The validity of the improvisation argument in the implementation of rigid technology: The case of ERP systems. *Journal of Information Technology, 21*, 165-175.

Elbanna, A. R. (2007). Implementing an integrated system in a socially dis-integrated enterprise: A critical view of ERP enabled integration. *Information Technology and People, 20*(2), 121-139.

Elliman, T., & Eatock J. (2005). Online support for arbitration: Designing software for a flexible business

process. *Int. J. Information Teachnology and Management, 4*(4), 443-460.

Ellram, L. M. (1993). A framework for total cost of ownership. *The International Journal of Logistics Management, 4*(2), 49-60.

Ellul, J. (1964). *The technological society*. New York: Alfred A Knopf, Inc.

Engel, J. F., Blackwell, R. D., & Miniard, P. W. (1993). *Consumer behavior* (7th ed.). USA: The Dryden Press, Harcourt Brace Jovanovich.

Engeström, Y. (1987). *Learning by expanding: An activity theoretical approach to developmental research*. Helsinki, Finland: Orienta Konsultit.

Engeström, Y. (1991). Developmental work research: Reconstructing expertise through expansive learning. In M. I. Nurminen & G. R. S. Weir (Eds.), *Human jobs and computer interfaces* (pp. 265-290). Amsterdam: Elsevier Science Publishers (North Holland).

Engeström, Y. (1999). Activity theory and individual and social transformation. In Y. Engeström, R. Miettinen, & R. L. Punamäki (Eds.), *Perspectives on activity theory* (pp. 19-38). New York: Cambridge University Press.

Engeström, Y. (1999). Expansive visibilization of work: An activity-theoretical perspective. *Computer Supported Cooperative Work: Special issue on a web on the wind: The structure of invisible work, 8*(1-2), 63-93.

Engeström, Y. (1999c). Innovative learning in work teams: Analyzing cycles of knowledge creation in practice. In Y. Engeström, R. Miettinen, & R. L. Punamäki (Eds.), *Perspectives on activity theory* (pp. 377-402). New York: Cambridge University Press.

Engeström, Y. (2001). Expansive learning at work: Toward an activity theoretical reconceptualization. *Journal of Education and Work, 14*(1), 133-156.

Engeström, Y. (2005). *Developmental work research: Expanding activity theory in practice*. Berlin: Lehmanns Media.

Engeström, Y. (2007). Putting Vygotsky to work: The change laboratory as an application of double stimulation. In H. Daniels, M. Cole, & J. V. Wertsch (Eds.), *The Cambridge companion to Vygotsky* (pp. 363-382). New York: Cambridge University Press.

Engeström, Y., & Escalante, V. (1996). Mundane tool or object of affection? The rise and fall of the Postal Buddy. In B. A. Nardi (Ed.), *Context and consciousness: Activity theory and human-computer interaction* (pp. 325 - 373). Cambridge, MA: The MIT Press.

Engeström, Y., Engeström, R., & Suntio, A. (2002). From paralyzing myths to expansive action: Building computer-supported knowledge work into curriculum from below. In G. Stahl (Ed.), *Proceedings of computer support for collaborative learning: Foundations for a CSCL community* (pp. 318-325). New Jersey, USA: Lawrence Erlbaum Associates, Inc.

Engeström, Y., Virkkunen, J., Helle, M., Pihlaja, J., & Poikela, R. (1996). The change laboratory as a tool for transforming work. *Lifelong Learning in Europe, 1*(2), 10-17.

Eom, S. B. (1995). Decision support systems research: Reference disciplines and a cumulative tradition. *Omega: International Journal of Management Science, 23*(5), 511-523.

Epstein, S. (1994). Integration of the cognitive and the psychodynamic unconscious. *American Psychologist, 49*(8), 709-724.

Erevelles, S., Srinivasan, S., & Rangel, S. (2003). Consumer satisfaction for Internet service providers: An analysis of underlying processes. *Information Technology and Management, 4*(1), 69-89.

Ernst, D. (1994). *Inter-firms networks and market structure: Driving forces, barriers and patterns of control* (BRIE research paper). Berkeley, University of California.

Ettlie, J. E. (1980). Adequacy of stage models for decision on adoption of innovation. *Psychological Reports, 46*, 991-995.

Evans, D., & Yen, D. C. (2006). E-government: Evolving relationship of citizens and government, domestic, and international development. *Government Information Quarterly, 23*, 207-235.

Eveland, J. D. (1986). Diffusion, technology transfer, and implementation. *Knowledge: Creation, Diffusion, Utilization, 8*(2), 302-322.

Exforsys Inc. (2008). *The role of a computer programmer*. Retrieved June 16, 2008, from http://www.exforsys.com/career-center/career-tracks/the-role-of-a-computer-programmer.html

Faulkner, W. (2000, June) the technology question in feminism. A view from feminist technology studies. In *Proceedings of the Women's Studies International Forum*.

Fay, B. (1996). *Contemporary philosophy of social science: A multicultural approach*. Oxford, UK: Blackwell.

Feagin, J. R., Orum, A. M., & Sjoberg, G. (1991). *A case for the case study*. Chapel Hill, NC: University of North Carolina Press.

Feenberg, A. (1991). *Critical theory of technology*. New York: Oxford University Press.

Feixas, G., Geldschlager, H., & Neimeyer, R. A. (2002). Content analysis of personal constructs. *Journal of Constructivist Psychology, 15*, 1-20.

Feldman, M. S. (2000). Organizational routines as a source of continuous change. *Organization Science, 11*(6), 611-629.

Feldman, M. S. (2004). Resources in emerging structures and processes of change. *Organization Science, 15*(3), 295-309.

Feldman, M. S., & Pentland, B. T. (2003). Reconceptualizing organizational routines as a source of flexibility and change. *Administrative Science Quarterly, 48*, 94–118.

Felton, B. J., & Revenson, R. A. (1984). Coping with chronic illness: A study of illness controllability and the influence of coping strategies on psychological adjustment. *Journal of Consulting and Clinical Psychology, 52*, 343-353.

Ferratt, T. W., Gorman, M. F., Kanet, J. J., & Salisbury, W. D. (2007). IS journal quality assessment using the author affiliation index. *Communications of the Association for Information Systems, 17*, 710-724.

Ferratt, T., & Vlahos, G. (1998). An investigation of task-technology fit for managers in Greece and the US. *European Journal of Information Systems, 7*, 123-136.

Ferrier, W. J., Smith, K. G., & Grimm, C. M. (1999). The role of competitive action in market share erosion and industry dethronement: A study of industry leaders and challengers. *Academy of Management Journal, 42*, 372-388.

Festinger, L. (1957). *A theory of cognitive dissonance.* Stanford, CA: Stanford University Press.

Festinger, L., & Carlsmith, J. (1959). Cognitive consequences of forced compliance. In E. Coats & R. Feldman (Eds.), *Classic and contemporary readings in social psychology. Third Edition* (pp. 194-203). NJ, USA: Pearson Education.

Fichman, R. G. (1992, December 13-16). Information technology diffusion: A review of empirical research. In *Proceedings of the Thirteenth International Conference on Information Systems (ICIS),* Dallas, TX, USA (pp. 195-206).

Field, M., & Keller, L. (1998). *Project management.* London: Thomson Learning.

Fieser, J., & Dowden, B. (2008). *Deductive and inductive arguments.* Retrieved from http://www.iep.utm.edu/

Finin, T., Labrou, Y., & Mayfield, J. (1994). *KQML as an agent communication language.* Paper presented at the International Conference on Information and Knowledge Management (CIKM), Gaithersburg, MD, USA.

Finkelstein, A., & Dowell, J. (1996). A comedy of errors: The London ambulance service case study. In *Proceedings of the 8ᵗʰ International Workshop on Software Specification & Design IWSSD-8* (pp. 2-4). IEEE CS Press.

FIPA-ACL. (2002, December 06). *FIPA ACL message structure specification.* Retrieved February 2, 2007, from http://www.fipa.org/specs/fipa00061/

Fishbein, M. (1967). Attitude and the prediction of behavior. In M. Fishbein (Ed.), *Readings in attitude theory and measurement* (pp. 477-492). New York: John Wiley.

Fishbein, M. (1968). An investigation of relationships between beliefs about an object and the attitude towards that object. *Human Relationships, 16*, 233-240.

Fishbein, M., & Ajzen, I. (1975). *Belief, attitude, intention and behavior: An introduction to theory and research.* Reading, MA: Addison-Wesley.

Fithgerald, P. (2002). General practice corporatisation: The half-time score. *MJA, 177*(2), 90-92.

Fitzgerald, B. (1997). The use of systems development methodologies in practice: A field study. *Information Systems Journal, 7*(3), 201-212.

Fjeld, M., Morf, M., & Krueger, H. (2004). Activity theory and the practice of design: Evaluation of a collaborative tangible user interface. *International Journal of Human Resources Development and Management (IJHRDM), 4*(1), 94-116.

Flanagan, J. C. (1954). The critical incident technique. *Psychological Bulletin, 51*(4), 327-358.

Fleetwood, S. (2002). Boylan and O'Gorman's causal holism: A critical realist evaluation. *Cambridge Journal of Economics, 26*, 27-45.

Fleetwood, S., & Ackroyd, S. (Eds.). (2004). *Critical realist applications in organisation and management studies.* London: Routledge.

Flood, R. L. (1999). *Rethinking the fifth discipline: Learning within the unknowable.* New York: Routledge.

Flores, F., & Ludlow, J. (1980). Doing and speaking in the office. In G. Fick & R. H. Sprague (Eds.), *Decision support systems: Issues and challenges* (Vol. 11, pp. 95-118). New York: Pergamon Press.

Flores, F., Graves, M., Hartfield, B., & Winograd, T. (1988). Computer systems and the design of organizational interaction. *ACM Transactions on Office Information systems (TOIS), 6*(2), 153-172.

Flyvbjerg, B. (2001). *Making social science matter: Why social inquiry fails and how it can succeed again* (S. Sampson, Trans.). Cambridge, MA: Cambridge University Press.

Flyvbjerg, B. (2006). Five misunderstandings about case-study research. *Qualitative Inquiry, 12*, 219-245.

Folkman, S. (1992). Making the case for coping. In B. N. Carpenter (Ed.), *Personal coping: Theory, research, and application* (pp. 31-46). Westport, CT: Praeger.

Folkman, S., & Lazarus, R. S. (1985). If it changes it must be a process: Study of emotion and coping during three stages of a college examination. *Journal of Personality and Social Psychology, 48*(1), 150-170.

Folkman, S., & Moskowitz, J. T. (2000). Positive affect and the other side of coping. *American Psychologist, 55*(6), 647-654.

Folkman, S., Lazarus, R. S., Gruen, R. J., & DeLongis, A. (1986). Appraisal, coping, health status and psychological symptoms. *Journal of Personality and Social Psychology, 50*(3), 571-579.

Ford, D. P., & Chan, Y. E. (2003). Knowledge sharing in a multi-cultural setting: A case study. *Knowledge Management Research & Practice, 1*(1), 11-27.

Ford, D. P., Connelly, C. E., & Meister, D. B. (2003). Information systems research and Hofstede's culture's consequences: An uneasy and incomplete partnership. *IEEE Transactions on Engineering Management, 50*(1), 8.

Foreman, M. (2007). *Fonterra to offshore IT jobs to India?* Retrieved November, 19. 2007, from http://www.zdnet.com.au/news/software/soa/Fonterra-to-offshore-IT-jobs-to-India-/0,130061733,339274389,00.htm

Fornell, C. (1983). Issues in the application of covariance structure analysis. *Journal of Consumer Research, 9*, 443-448.

Fornell, C., & Bookstein, F. L. (1982). Two structural equation models: LISREL and PLS applied to consumer exit-voice theory. *Journal of Marketing Research, 19*(4), 440-452.

Foucault, M. (1980). *Power/knowledge: Selected interviews and other writings 1972-1977.* Brighton, UK: The Harvester Press.

Fountain, J. E. (2001). *Building the virtual state, information technology and institutional change.* Washington, D.C.: Brookings Institution Press.

Fracassi, C. (2008). Corporate finance policies and social networks (working paper). University of California, Los Angeles.

Fransella, F. & Bannister, D. (1977). *A manual for Repertory Grid Technique.* Academic Press: London.

Fransella, F. (1972). *Personal Change and Reconstruction: Research on a Treatment of Stuttering.* Academic Press: London.

Fransella, F. (2003). Some tools and skills for personal construct practitioners. In F. Fransella (Ed). *International Handbook of Personal Construct Psychology.* Chicester: UK Wiley.

Fransman, M. (1998). Information, knowledge, vision, and theories of the firm. In G. Dosi, D. J. Teece, & J. Chytry (Eds.), *Technology, organisation, and competitiveness: Perspectives on industrial and corporate change* (pp. 147-192). New York: Oxford University Press Inc.

Franz, C. R., & Robey, D. (1984). An investigation of user-led system design: Rational and political perspectives. *Communications of the ACM, 27*(12), 1202-1217.

Freeman, L. A., & Urbaczewski, A. (2005). Why do people hate spyware? *Communications of the ACM, 48*(8), 50-53.

Freeman, L. C. (1979). Centrality in social networks: Conceptual clarification. *Social Networks, 1*, 215-239.

Freeman, L. C. (2004). *The development of social network analysis: A study in the sociology of science.* Vancouver, Canada: Empirical Press.

French, J. R. P. Jr., Rodgers, W., & Cobb, S. (1974). Adjustment as person-environment fit. In G. V. Coelho, D. A. Hamburg & J. E. Adams (Eds.), *Coping and adaptation* (pp. 316-333). New York: Basic Books.

French, J. R. P., Caplan, R. D., & Harrison, R. V. (1982). *The mechanisms of job stress and strain.* New York: Wiley.

Froehle, C. M., & Roth, A. V. (2004). New measurement scales for evaluating perceptions of the technology-mediated customer service experience. *Journal of Operations Management, 22*(1), 1-21.

Fukuyama, F. (1995). *Trust: The social virtues and the creation of prosperity.* New York: Free Press.

Fulk, J. (1993). Social construction of communication technology. *Academy of Management Journal, 36*(5), 921-951.

Furey, T. R. (1991). How information power can improve service quality. *Planning Review, 19*(3), 24-26.

Furrer, O., Liu, B. S.-C., & Sudharshan, D. (2000). The relationships between culture and service quality perceptions: Basis for cross-cultural market segmentation and resource allocation. *Journal of Service Research, 2*(4), 355-371.

Furst, S., Blackburn, R., & Rosen, B. (1999). Virtual team effectiveness: A proposed research agenda. *Information Systems Journal, 9*, 249-269.

Gable, G. (1994). Integrating case study and survey research methods: An example in information systems. *European Journal of Information Systems, 3*(2), 112-126.

Gadamer, H. (1975). Hermeneutics and social science. *Cultural Hermeneutics, 2*(4).

Gadamer, H. G. (1976). The historicity of understanding. In P. Connerton (Ed.), *Critical sociology: Selected readings*. Harmondsworth, UK: Penguin Books.

Galal, G. H., & McDonnell, J. T. (1997). Knowledge-based systems in context: A methodological approach to the qualitative issues. *AI & Society, 11*(1-2), 104-121.

Galliers, R. D., & Swan J. A. (1999). Information systems and strategic change: A critical review of business process re-engineering. In W. L. Currie & R. D. Galliers (Eds.), *Rethinking MIS* (pp. 361-387). Oxford, UK: Oxford University Press.

Gallivan, M. J. (1995). Contradictions among stakeholder assessments of a radical change initiative: A cognitive frames analysis. In W. J. Orlikowski, et al. (Eds.), *Information technology and changes in organizational work*. London: Chapman and Hall.

Gallivan, M. J. (1996). Strategies for implementing new software processes: An evaluation of a contingency framework. In *Proceedings of the SIGCPR/SIGMIS '96*, Denver, Colorado.

Gallivan, M., & Strite, M. (2005). Information technology and culture: Identifying fragmentary and holistic perspectives of culture. *Information & Organization, 15*(4), 295-338.

Gallupe, R. B., & Tan, F. (1999). A research manifesto for global information management. *Journal of Global Information Management, 7*(3), 5-18.

GAO. (2003). *Information technology: Benefits realized for the selected health care functions*. Report to the Ranking Minority Member. US Senate.

Gargiulo, M., & Bernassi, M. (1999). The dark side of social capital. In A. J. L. S. M. Gabbay (Ed.), *Corporate social capital and liability* (pp. 298-322). Boston, MA: Kluwer.

Gartner. (2007). *Gartner says worldwide IT spending to surpass $3 trillion in 2007*. Retrieved from http://www.gartner.com/it/page.jsp?id=529409

Gasson, S. (1999). The reality of user-centered design. *Journal of End User Computing, 11*(4), 3-13.

Gasson, S. (2003). Rigor in grounded theory research: An interpretive perspective on generating theory from qualitative field studies. In M. Whitman & A. Woszczynski (Eds.), *Handbook for information systems research*. Hershey, PA: IGI Publishing.

Gay, G., & Hembrooke, H. (2004). *Activity-centered design: An ecological approach to designing smart tools and usable systems*. Cambridge, MA: The MIT Press.

Gefen, D. E., Karahanna, E., & Straub, D.W. (2003). Trust and TAM in Online shopping: An integrated model. *MIS Quarterly, 27*, 51-90.

Gefen, D., & Straub, D. (1997). Gender differences in the perception and use of e-mail: An extension to the technology acceptance model. *MIS Quarterly, 21*(4), 389-400.

Gefen, D., & Straub, D. (2000). The relative importance of perceived ease of use in IS adoption: A study of e-commerce adoption. *Journal of the Association for Information Systems, 1*(8), 1-28.

Gefen, D., Pavlou, P. A., Warkentin, M., & Gregory, M. R. (2002). E-government adoption. In *Proceedings of the 8th Americas Conference on Information Systems*.

Gefen, D., Rose, G. M., Warkentin, M., & Pavlou, P. A. (2005). Cultural diversity and trust in IT adoption: A comparison of potential e-voters in the USA and South Africa. *Journal of Global Information Management, 13*(1), 54-78.

Gefen, D., Straub, D. W., & Boudreau, M.-C. (2000). Structural equation modeling and regression: Guidelines for research practice. *Communications of the Association Information Systems, 4*(7), 1-77.

Geiger, M. A., & Cooper, E. A. (1996). Cross-cultural comparisons using expectancy theory to assess student motivation. *Issues in Accounting Education, 11*(1), 113-129.

Gell-Mann, M. (1994). *The jaguar and the quark.* New York: *W. H. Freeman and Company.*

Gemmill, G., & Wilemon, D. (1997). The hidden side of leadership in technical team management. In R. Katz (Ed.), *The human side of managing technological innovation* (pp. 237-245). NY, USA: Oxford University Press.

George, J. F. (2000). The effects of Internet experience and attitudes toward privacy and security on Internet purchasing. In *Proceedings of the 8th European Conference in Information Systems (ECIS),* (pp. 1053-1058). Vienna: Vienna University of Economics and Business Administration.

Giangreco, A. (2001). *Conceptualisation and operationalisation of resistance to change.* Catellanza, Italy: LIUC Papers.

Giddens, A. (1984). *The constitution of society: Outline of the theory of structuration.* Cambridge, UK: Polity Press.

Giddens, A. (1987). *Social theory and modern sociology.* Cambridge, UK: Polity Press.

Giddens, A. (1989). A reply to my critics. In D. Held & J. B. Thompson (Eds.), *Social Theory of Modern Societies: Anthony Giddens and His Critics* (pp. 249-305). Cambridge, MA: Cambridge University Press.

Giddens, A. (1990). *The consequences of modernity.* Stanford, CA: Stanford University Press.

Giddens, A., & Pierson, C. (1998). *Conversations with Anthony Giddens; Making sense of modernity.* Cambridge, MA: Polity Press.

Gigler, B.-S. (2004). Including the excluded - can ICTs empower poor communities? In *Proceedings of the 4th International Conference on the Capability Approach,* Italy.

Gilbert, D., Balestrini, P., & Littleboy, D. (2004). Barriers and benefits in the adoption of e-government. *The International Journal of Public Sector Management, 14*(4), 286-301.

Gil-Garcia, J. R., & Martinez-Moyano, I. J. (2007). Understanding the evolution of e-government: The influence of

systems of rules on public sector dynamics. *Government Information Quarterly, 24,* 266-290.

Gil-García, J. R., & Pardo, T. A. (2005). E-government success factors: Mapping practical tools to theoretical foundations. *Government Information Quarterly, 22*(2), 187-216.

Gilmore, D. J. (1995). Interface design: Have we got it wrong? In K. Nordby, P. H. Helmersen, D. J. Gilmore, & S. A. Arnesen (Eds.), *Proceedings of INTERACT 95 - IFIP TC13 Fifth International Conference on Human-Computer Interaction* (pp. 173-178). London: Chapman & Hall.

Gladwin, J., Dixon, R. A., & Wilson, T. D. (Jun 2003). Implementing a new health management information system in Uganda. *Health Policy and Planning, 18*(2), 214-224.

Glaser, B. G. (1978). *Advances in the methodology of grounded theory: Theoretical sensitivity.* Mill Valley, CA: The Sociology Press.

Glaser, B. G. (1992). *Basics of grounded theory analysis: Emergence vs. forcing.* Mill Valley, CA: The Sociology Press.

Glaser, B. G. (2002). Constructivist grounded theory? *Forum: Qualitative Social Research, 3*(3).

Glaser, B. G., & Strauss, A. L. (1967). *The discovery of grounded theory: Strategies for qualitative research.* Chicago: Aldine Publishing.

Glasser, M. (1964). Linear regression analysis with missing observations among the independent variables. *Journal of the American Statistical Association, 59*(307), 834-844.

Glomb, T. M., & Welsh, E. T. (2005). Can opposites attract? Personality heterogeneity in supervisor-subordinate dyads as a predictor of subordinate outcomes. *Journal of Applied Psychology, 90*(4), 749-757

Gnyawali, D., & Madhavan, R. (2001). Cooperative network and competitive dynamics: A structural embedness perspective. *Academy of Management Review, 26,* 431-445.

Goetzmann, W. N. (2003, October). *Fibonacci and the financial revolution* (Working Paper N° 03-28). Yale International Center for Finance.

Goffman, I. (1974). *Frame analysis*. New York: Harper and Row.

Gogan, K. (1998). Build customer satisfaction using real-time intelligence. *Marketing News, 32*(11), 13.

Goldkuhl, G. (1996). *Generic business frameworks and action modelling*. Paper presented at the International Working Conference on the Language-action perspective on Communication Modelling (LAP).

Goldkuhl, G. (1998). *The six phases of business processes - business communication and the exchange of value*. Paper presented at the International Telecommunications Society (ITS) Conference - Beyond Convergence: Communication into the Next Millennium, Stockholm, Sweden.

Goldkuhl, G. (2000). *The validity of validity claims: An Inquiry into communication rationality*. Paper presented at the International Workshop on the Language-action perspective on Communication Modelling (LAP), Aachen, Germany.

Goldkuhl, G. (2005). *The many facets of communication – a socio-pragmatic conceptualisation for information systems studies*. Paper presented at the International Workshop on Communication and Coordination in Business Processes, Kiruna, Sweden.

Goldkuhl, G., & Ågerfalk, P. J. (2000). *Actability: A way to understand information systems pragmatics*. Paper presented at the International Workshop on Organisational Semiotics, Staffordshire University, Stafford, UK.

Goldkuhl, G., & Lind, M. (2002). *Continuing the dialogue: Generic layer for business interaction*. Paper presented at the International Working Conference on the Language-action perspective on Communication Modelling (LAP).

Goldkuhl, G., & Lyytinen, K. (1982). A language action view of information systems. In *Proceedings of the International Conference on Information Systems*.

Goldkuhl, G., & Lyytinen, K. (1984). Information system specification as rule reconstruction. In T. A. Bemelmans (Ed.), *Beyond productivity - information systems for organizational effectiveness* (pp. 79-95). New York: North-Holland.

Goleman, D. (1996). *Vital lies simple truths: The psychology of self-deception*. NY, USA: Simon and Schuster Books.

Gompers, P., Lerner, J., & Scharfstein, D. (2005). Entrepreneurial spawning: Public corporations and the genesis of new ventures, 1986 to 1999. *Journal of Finance, 60*, 577-614.

Goodhue, D. L., & Thompson, R. L. (1995). Task-technology fit and individual performance. *MIS Quarterly, 19*(2), 213-236.

Gopal, A., & Prasad, P. (2000). Understanding GDSS in symbolic context: Shifting the focus from technology to interaction. *MIS Quarterly, 24*(3), 509-546.

Gordon, J. R., & Gordon, S. R. (2002). Information technology service delivery: An international comparison. *Information Systems Management, 19*(1), 62-70.

Gottschalk, K., Graham, S., Kreger, H., & Snell, J. (2002). Introduction to Web services architecture. *IBM Systems Journal, 41*(2), 170-177.

Gould, J., & Verenikina, I. (2003). An activity theory framework for computer interface design. In L. Budin, V. Lužar-Stiffler, Z. Bekić, & V. H. Dobrić (Eds.), *Proceedings of the 25th International Conference on Information Technology Interfaces (ITI 2003)* (pp. 301-307). University of Zagreb, Croatia: SRCE University Computing Centre.

GPDV & GPT. (2007). *Outcomes of the CQI in information management workshop*. Melbourne: General Practice Victoria and General Practice Tasmania.

Grandori, A. (1984). *Teorie organizzative*. Milan, Italy: Giuffrè.

Granovetter, M. (1982). The strength of weak ties. In P. V. Marsden & N. Lin (Eds.), *Social structure and network analysis* (pp. 105-130). Beverly Hills, CA: Sage.

Granovetter, M. S. (1973). The strength of weak ties. *The American Journal of Sociology, 78*(6), 1360-1380.

Granovetter, M. S. (1995). *Getting a job: A study of contacts and careers* (2nd ed.). Chicago: University of Chicago Press.

Grant, R. M. (1991). The resource-based theory of competitive advantage: Implications for strategy formulation. *California Management Review, 33*(3), 114-135.

Grant, R. M. (1996). Prospering in dynamically-competitive environments: Organizational capability as knowledge integration. *Organization Science, 7*(4), 375-387.

Grant, R. M. (1996). Toward a knowledge-based theory of the firm. *Strategic Management Journal, 17*, 109-122.

Grant, R. M. (1997). The knowledge-based view of the firm: Implications for management practices. *Long Range Planning, 30*(3), 450-454.

Grasha, A. F., & Kirschenbaum, D. S. (1986). *Adjustment and competence: Concepts and applications.* Saint-Paul, MN: West.

Green, B. (2004). *Personal construct psychology and content analysis. Personal construct theory & practice.* Retrieved from http://www.pcp-net.org/journal/pct04.pdf

Green, E. (2001). Technology, leisure and everyday practices. In E. Green & A. Adam (Eds.), *Virtual gender. Technology, consumption and identity matters.* New York: Routledge.

Green, E., & Adam, A. (1998). On-line leisure. Gender and ICT's in the home. *Information, Communication and Society, 1*(3), 291-312.

Greene, K., Hale, J. L., & Rubin, D. L. (1997). A test of the theory of reasoned action in the context of condom use and AIDS. *Communication Reports, 10*, 21-33.

Greenhaus, J. H., Parasuraman, S., & Wormley, W. M. (1990). Race effects of organizational experience, job performance evaluations, and career outcomes. *Academy of Management Journal, 33*, 64-86.

Greenhow, C., & Belbas, B. (2007). Using activity-oriented design methods to study collaborative knowledge-building in e-learning courses within higher education. *Computer-Supported Collaborative Learning, 2*(4), 363-391.

Greer, T. H., & Murtaza, B. (2003). Web personalization: The impact of perceived innovation characteristics on the intention to use personalization. *The Journal of Computer Information Systems, 43*(3), 50-55.

Gregor, S. (2002). A theory of theories in information systems. In *Information systems foundation: Building the theoretical base* (pp. 1-20). Canberra, Australia: Australian National University. Retrieved from http://dsi.esade.edu/theorybuilding/papers/Gregor%20ISF-theory-paper-final-t.pdf

Gregor, S. (2005). The struggle towards an understanding of theory in information systems. In D. Hart & S. Gregor (Eds.), *Information systems foundations: Constructing and criticising* (pp. 3-12). Canberra, Australia: Australian National University. Retrieved from http://epress.anu.edu.au/info_systems/part-ch01.pdf

Gregor, S. (2006). The nature of theory in information systems. *MIS Quarterly, 30*(3), 611-642.

Gregory, J. (2000). *Sorcerer's apprentice: Creating the electronic health record: Re-inventing medical records and patient care.* Unpublished doctoral dissertation, Department of Communication, University of California at San Diego, La Jolla, CA.

Gregory, K. (2005). Implementing an electronic records management system: A public sector case study. *Records Management Journal, 15*,(2), 80-85.

Greimas, A. J. (1990). *The social science, a semiotic view* (P. Perron & F. H. Collins, Trans.). Minneapolis, MN: University of Minnesota Press.

Griffith, T. L. (1998). Cross-cultural and cognitive issues in the implementation of new technology: Focus on group support systems and Bulgaria. *Interacting with Computers, 9*(4), 431-447.

Grimshaw, J., et al. (2004). Effectiveness and efficiency of guideline dissemination and implementation strategies. *Health Technol Assess.*

Grint, K., & Woolgar, S. (1997). *The machine at work: Technology, work and organization.* Cambridge, UK: Polity Press.

Groff, R. (2004). *Critical realism, post-positivism and the possibility of knowledge.* London: Routledge.

Grol, R. (2000). Implementation of evidence and guidelines in clinical practice: A new field of research? *International Journal for Quality in Health Care, 12*(6), 455-456.

Grol, R., & Grimshaw, J. (2003). From best evidence to best practice: Effective implementation of change. *Lancet, 362*, 1225-1230.

Grol, R., & Wensing, M. (2004). What drives change? Barriers to and incentives for achieving evidence-based practice. *MJA, 180*, S57-S60.

Grol, R., et al. (1998). Attributes of clinical guidelines that influence use of guidelines in general practice: Observational study. *British Medical Journal, 315*, 418-421.

Gross, P. F., et al. (2003). Australia confronts the challenge of chronic disease. *MJA, 179*(5), 233-234.

Grover, V., Lyytinen, K., Srinivasan, A., & Tan, B. C. (2008). Contributing to rigorous and forward thinking explanatory theory. *Journal of the Association for Information Systems, 9*, 40-47.

Guest, G., Bunce, A., & Johnson, L. (2006). How many interviews are enough? An experiment with data saturation and variability. *Field Methods, 18*(1), 59-82.

Guiterrez, O. (1989). Experimental techniques for information requirements analysis. *Information & Management, 16*, 31-43.

Guo, Y., & Poole, M. S. (in press). Antecedents of flow in online shopping: A test of alternative models. *Information Systems Journal*.

Gupta, J. N. D., Sharma, S. K., & Hsu, J. (2004). An overview of knowledge management. In J. N. D. Gupta, S. K. Sharma (Eds.), *Creating knowledge based organizations* (pp. 1-29). Hershey, PA: Idea Group Inc.

Gupta, M. P., & Jana, D. (2003). E-government evaluation: A framework and case study. *Government Information Quarterly, 20*(4), 365-387.

Gurbaxani, V., & Wang, S. (1991). The impact of information systems on organization and markets. *Communications of the ACM, 34*, 59-73

Habermas, J. (1984). *The theory of communicative action: Reason and the rationalization of society* (T. McCarthy, Trans. Vol. 1). Boston: Beacon Press.

Habib, L., & Cornford, T. (2002). Computers in the home: Domestication and gender, *Information Technology & People, 15*(2). 159-174.

Haddon, L. (2006). The contribution of domestication research to in-home computing and media consumption. *The Information Society, 22*(4). 195-203.

Haigh, T. (2001). Inventing information systems: The systems men and the computer, 1950-1968. *Business History Review, 3*(75), 15-61.

Haines, A., & Donald, A. (1998). Getting research findings into practice: Making better use of research findings. *British Journal of General Practice, 317*(7150), 72-75.

Hair, J. F., Black, W.C., Babin, B., Anderson, R. E., & Tathem, R. L. (2006). *Multivariate data analysis* (6th ed.). Upper Saddle River, NJ: Prentice Hall.

Hale, J. L., Householder, B. J., & Greene, K. L. (2003). The theory of reasoned action. In J. P. Dillard & M. Pfau (Eds.), *The persuasion handbook: developments in theory and practice* (pp. 259-286). Thousand Oaks, CA: Sage.

Half Sigma. (2008). *Not enough women majoring in computer science?* Retrieved June 16, 2008, from http://www.halfsigma.com/2007/04/not_enough_wome.html

Hall, C. S., & Lindzey, G. (1957). *Theories of personality*. New York: Wiley.

Halstead, D. (1999). The use of comparison standards in customer satisfaction research and management: A review. *Journal of Marketing Theory & Practice, 7*(3), 13-26.

Halstead, M. H., Elshoff, J. L., & Gordon, R. D. (1976). On software physics and GM's PL/I programs. *GM Research Publication GMR-2175, 26*.

Hamel, G., & Prahalad, C. K. (1994). *Competing for the future*. Boston, MA: Harvard Business School Press.

Hamel, J., Dufour, s., & Fortin, D. (1993). *Case study methods*. Beverly Hills, CA: Sage Publications, Inc.

Hammer, M. (1996). *Beyond reengineering: How the process-centered organization is changing our work and our lives*. New York: HarperCollins Publishers, Inc.

Han, J., & Han, D. (2001). A framework for analyzing customer value of internet business. *Journal of Information Technology Theory and Application, 3*(5), 25-38.

Hanifan, L. J. (1916). The rural school community center. *Annals of the American Academy of Political and Social Sciences, 67*, 130-138.

Hansen, B. H., & Kautz, K. (2005). *Grounded theory applied - studying information systems development methodologies in practice.* Paper presented at the 38th Hawaii International Conference on System Sciences (HICSS 2005). Retrieved from http://csdl2.computer.org/comp/proceedings/hicss/2005/2268/08/22680264b.pdf

Hansen, M. T. (1999). The search-transfer problem: The role of weak ties in sharing knowledge across organization subunits. *Administrative Science Quarterly, 44*(1), 82-111.

Hansen, M. T. (2002). Knowledge networks: Explaining effective knowledge sharing in multiunit companies. *Organization Science, 13*(3), 232-248.

Hanseth, O., & Braa, K. (1998, December 13-16). *Technology as traitor: Emergent SAP infrastructure in a global organization.* Paper presented at the Nineteenth International Conference on Information Systems (ICIS), Helsinki, Finland.

Hanseth, O., & Monteiro, E. (1997). Inscribing behaviour in information infrastructure standards. *Accounting, Management and Information Technology, 7*(4), 183-211.

Harmon-Jones, E. (1998). Towards an understanding of the motivation underlying dissonance effects: Is the production of adverse consequences necessary. In E. Coats & R. Feldman (Eds.), *Classic and contemporary readings in social psychology* (3rd ed.) (pp. 204-213). NJ, USA: Pearson Education.

Harris A. L, Lang, M., Oates B., & Siau, K. (2006). Systems analysis & design: An essential part of IS education, *Journal of Information Systems Education, 17*(3), 241-248.

Harris, R., & Davison, R. (1999). Anxiety and involvement: Cultural dimensions of attitudes toward computers in developing societies. *Journal of Global Information Management, 6*(1), 26-38.

Harris, R.W. (2005). Explaining the success of rural Asian telecentres, In R. M. Davison, et al. (Eds.), *Information systems in developing countries: Theory and practice* (pp. 83-100). Hong Kong: City University of Hong Kong Press.

Hartmann, M. (2006). The triple articulation of ICTs. Media as technological objects, symbolic environments and individual texts. In T. Berker, M. Hartmann, Y. Punie, & K. J. Ward (Eds.), *The domestication of media and technology* (pp. 80-102). Maidenhead, UK: Open University Press.

Hartwig, M. (Ed.). (2007). *Dictionary of critical realism.* London: Routledge.

Hasan, H., & Ditsa, G. (1999). The impact of culture on the adoption of IT: An interpretive study. *Journal of Global Information Management, 7*(3), 5-15.

Hassan, N. (2006). *Is information systems a discipline? A Foucauldian and Toulminian analysis.* Paper presented at the 27th International Conference on Information Systems, Milwaukee, WI.

Hausman, A. (2005). Innovativeness among small businesses: Theory and propositions for future research. *Industrial Marketing Management, 34*(8), 773-782.

Hayek, F. A. (1945). The use of knowledge in society. *American Economic Review, 35*, 519-532.

Hayes, M. (2001, August). Payback time: Making sure ROI measures up. *InformationWeek.* Retrieved October 1, 2005, from http://www.informationweek.com/showArticle.jhtml;?articleID=6506422

Hayne, S. C., & Pollard, C. E. (2000). A comparative analysis of critical issues facing Canadian information systems personnel: A national and global perspective. *Information & Management, 38*(2), 73-86.

HealthConnect. (2005). *About HealthConnect.* Retrieved June 04, 2005, from http://www7.health.gov.au/health-connect/about/index.htm

HealthConnectSA. (2007). *GP change management strategy: Engagement with general practice.* South Australian Department of Health.

Hearts, J. (2002, November 25). Can 3G adoption gather pace? *IT-Director.* Retrieved December 3, 2005, from http://www.it-director.com/article.php?articleid=3377

Hecht, T. D., & Allen, N. J. (2005). Exploring links between polychronicity and well-being from the perspective of person–job fit: Does it matter if you prefer to do only one thing at a time? *Organizational Behavior and Human Decision Processes, 98*(2), 155-178.

Heckley, P. H. (2004). Evidence-based medicine in 2006: A survey of health plan leaders identifies current and emerging stratgies. *Healtcare Informatics,* (April 2004).

Hedden, T., & Gabrieli, J. D. E. (2004). Insights into the ageing mind: A view from cognitive neoroscience. *Nature Reviews Neuroscience, 5*(2), 87-96.

Heeks, R. (2002). Information systems and developing countries: Failure, success, and local improvisations. *The Information Society, 18*, 101-112.

Heeks, R. (2003). Most egovernment-for-development projects fail: How can risks be reduced? *iGovernment Working Paper Series.*

Heeks, R. B., & Bailur, S. (2007). Analyzing e-government research: Perspectives, philosophies, theories, methods, and practice. *Government Information Quarterly, 24*, 243-265.

Heijden, H., Verhagen, T., & Creemers, M. (2003). Understanding online purchase intentions: Contributions from technology and trust perspectives. *European Journal of Information Systems, 12*(1), 41-48.

Henders, R. A. (1998). An evolutionary approach to application development with object technology. *IBM Systems Journal, 37*(2).

Henderson, J. C., & Venkatraman, N. (1993). Strategic alignment: Leveraging information technology for transforming organisations. *IBM Systems Journal, 20*(1), 4-16.

Hendy, J., et al. (2005). Challenges to implementing the national programme for information technology (NPfIT): A qualitative study. *BMJ, 331*, 331-336.

Henin, P.-Y. (1986). Desequilibria it the present day. In *macrodynamics: A study of the economy in equilibrium and disequilibrium* (pp. 404). Routledge Kegan Paul.

Heracleous, L., & Barrett, M. (2001). Organizational change as discourse: Communicative actions and deep structures in the context of information technology implementation. *Academy of Management Journal, 44*(4), 755-778.

Heracleous, L., & Marshak, R. J. (2004). Conceptualizing organizational discourse as situated symbolic action. *Human Relations, 57*(10), 1285-1312.

Hernon, P., Reylea, H. C., Dugan, R. E., & Cheverie, J. F. (2002). *United States government information: Policies and sources* (p. 388). Westport, CT: Libraries Unlimited.

Herzlinger, R. E., & Ricci, R. J. (2002). Dr. know: Can physicans share their experience? *Think Leadership Magazine from IBM.*

Herzog, J. (1991). People: The critical factor in managing change. *Journal of Systems Management, 42*(3), 6-11.

Hetland, H., Sandal, G. M., & Johnsen, T. B. (2007). Burnout in the information technology sector: Does leadership matter? *European Journal of Work and Organizational Psychology, 16*(1), 58-75.

Hevner, A. R., March, S. T., Park, J., & Ram, S. (2004). Design science in information systems research. *MIS Quarterly, 28*(1), 75-105.

Hevner, A. R., March, S. T., Park, J., & Ram, S. (2004). Design science in information systems research. *MIS Quarterly, 28*(1), 75-105.

Hill, C., Lock, K., Straub, D., & El-Sheshai, K. (1998). A qualitative assessment of Arab culture and information technology transfer. *Journal of Global Information Management, 6*(3), 29-38.

Hill, T. P. (1977). On goods and services. *Review of Income and Wealth, 23*(4), 315-338.

Hillestad, R., et al. (2005). Can electronic medical record systems transform health care? Potential health benefits, savings and costs. *Health Affairs, 24*(5), 1103-1117.

Hinkle, D. N. (1965). *The theory of personal constructs from the viewpoint of a theory of construct implications.* Unpublished doctoral dissertation, Ohio State University.

Hirschheim, R. & Klein, H. K. (2003). Crisis in the IS field? A critical reflection on the state of the discipline. *Journal of the Association of Information Systems, 4*(5), 237-293.

Hirschheim, R. (2007). Introduction to the special issue on quo vadis TAM – issues and reflections on technology acceptance research. *Journal of the Association for Information Systems, 8*(4), 203-205.

Hirschheim, R., Iivari, J., & Klein, H. K. (1997). A comparison of five alternative approaches to information systems development. *Australian Journal of Information Systems, 5*(1), 3-29.

Hirschheim, R., Klein, H. K., & Lyytinen, K. (1995). *Information systems development and data modeling: Conceptual and philosophical foundations.* Cambridge, UK: Cambridge University Press.

Hirschheim, R., Klein, H. K., & Lyytinen, K. (1996). Exploring the intellectual structures of information systems development: A social action theoretic analysis. *Accounting, Management and Information Technologies (AMIT), 6*(1/2), 1-64.

Hitt, L. M., & Brynjolfsson, E. (1996). Productivity, business profitability, and consumer surplus: Three different measures of information technology value. *MIS Quarterly, 20*,121-142.

Ho, A. T.-K. (2002). reinventing local governments and the e-government initiative. *Public Administration Review, 62*(4), 434-444.

Hoaglin, D. C., Light, R. J., McPeek, B., Mosteller, F., & Stoto, M. A. (1982). *Data for decisions: Information strategies for policymakers.* Cambridge, MA: Abt Books.

Hochberg, Y., Ljungqvist, A., & Lu, Y. (2007). Whom you know matters: Venture capital networks and investment performance. *Journal of Finance, 62*, 251-301.

Hodgetts, R. (1993). A conversation with Geert Hofstede. *Organizational Dynamics, 21*, 53-62.

Hoffman, D. L., & Novak, T. P. (1996). Marketing in hypermedia computer-mediated environments: Conceptual foundations. *Journal of Marketing, 60*(3), 50-68.

Hoffmann, R. G., Rodrigue, J. R., & Johnson, J. H. (1999). Effectiveness of a school-based program to enhance knowledge of sun exposure: Attitudes toward sun exposure and sunscreen use among children. *Child Health Care, 28*, 69-86.

Hofstede, G. (1980). *Culture's consequences: International differences in work-related values.* Beverly Hills, CA: Sage.

Hofstede, G. (1980). Motivation, leadership and organization: Do American theories apply abroad. *Organizational Dynamics, 8*(Summer), 42-63.

Hofstede, G. (1991). *Cultures and organizations: Software of the mind.* New York: McGraw-Hill.

Hofstede, G. (1994). Management scientists are human. *Management Science, 40*(1), 4-13.

Hofstede, G. (1994). *Values survey module manual.* Tilburg, The Netherlands: IRIC.

Hofstede, G. (2001). *Culture's consequences: Comparing values, behaviors, institutions, and organizations across nations* (2nd ed.). Thousand Oaks, CA: Sage Publications.

Hofstede, G., & Bond, M. H. (1988). Confucius & economic growth: New trends in culture's consequences. *Organizational Dynamics, 16*(4), 4-21.

Hofstede, G., Arrindell, W., Best, D., De Mooij, M., Hoppe, M., Van de Vliert, E., et al. (1998). *Masculinity and femininity: The taboo dimension of national cultures.* Thousand Oaks, CA: SAGE Publications.

Holbrook, A., & Salazar, M. (2004). Regional innovation systems within a federation: Do national policies affect all regions equally? *The International Journal of Innovation Research, Commercialization, Policy Analysis and Best Practice, 6*(1), 50-64.

Holland, J. L. (1985). *Making vocational choices: A theory of vocational personalities and work environments.* Odessa, FL: Psychological Assessment Resources.

Holland, J. L. (1996). Exploring careers with a typology: What we have learned and some new directions. *American Psychologist, 51*(4), 397-406.

Holmes, M. (1998). Comparison of gender differences among information systems professionals: A cultural perspective. *Journal of Computer Information Systems, 38*(4), 78-86.

Holsapple, C. W. (2005). The inseparability of modern knowledge management and computer-based technology. *Journal of Knowledge Management, 9*(1), 42-52.

Holsapple, C. W., & Joshi, K. D. (2004). A formal knowledge management ontology: Conduct, activities, resources, and influences. *Journal of the American Society for Information Science and Technology, 55*(7), 593-612.

Holsapple, C. W., & Singh, M. (2003). The knowledge chain model: Activities for competitiveness. In C. W. Holsapple (Ed.), *Handbook on knowledge management 2: Knowledge directions* (pp. 215-251). Berlin/Heidelberg, Germany: Springer-Verlag.

Holsapple, C. W., & Singh, M. (2005). Performance implications of the knowledge chain. *International Journal of Knowledge Management, 1*(4), 1-22.

Holsapple, C. W., & Wu, J. (2008). In search of a missing link. *Knowledge Management Research & Practice, 6*(1), 31-40.

Holsapple, C., & Whinston, A. (1996). *Decision support systems: A knowledge-based approach.* Minneapolis, MN: West Publishing.

Holtham, C. (1992). Developing local and wide area networking to improve academic efficiency and effectiveness. In B. C. William & A. H. S. Nicholson (Eds.), *Management Education, Proceedings of the 3rd Annual Conference*, Bradford, Norwich, UK.

Holzmuller, H., & Schlichter, J. (2002). Delphi study about the future of B2B marketplace in Germany. *Electronic Commerce Research and Application, 1*, 2-19.

Homburg, C., Hoyer, W. D., & Fassnacht, M. (2002). Service orientation of a retailer's business strategy: Dimensions, antecedents and performance outcome. *Journal of Marketing, 66*, 86-101.

Horak, J. B. (2001). Dealing with human factors and managing change in knowledge management: A phased approach. *Topics in Health Information Management, 21*(3), 8-17.

Howell, R. D., Breivik, E., & Wilcox, J. B. (2007). Reconsidering formative measurement. *Psychological Methods, 12*(2), 205-218.

Hrastinski, S., Keller C., & Carlsson, S. A. (2007, May 13-15). Towards a design theory for synchronous computer-mediated communication in e-learning environments. In *Proceedings of the 2nd nternational Conference on Design Science Research in Information Systems & Technology (DESRIST 2007)*, Pasadena.

Hsieh, J. J. & Wang, W. (2007) Explaining employees' extended use of complex information systems. *European Journal of Information Systems, 16*, 216-227.

Hu, L., & Bentler, P. M. (1998). Fit indices in covariance structure modeling: Sensitivity to under-parameterized model misspecification. *Psychological Methods, 3*(4), 424-453.

Hu, P. J., Chau, P. Y. K., Sheng, O. R. L., & Tam. K. Y. (1999). Examining the technology acceptance model using physician acceptance of telemedicine technology. *Journal of Management Information Systems, 6*(2), 91-112.

Huang, L. J., Lu, M. T., & Wong, B. K. (2003). The impact of power distance on email acceptance: Evidence from the PRC. *Journal of Computer Information Systems, 44*(1), 93-101.

Huang, S., & DeSanctis, G. (2005). Mobilizing informational social capital in cyber space: Online social network structural properties and knowledge sharing. In *Proceedings of the Twenty-Sixth International Conference on Information Systems.*

Huber, G. P. (1990). A theory of the effects of advanced information technologies on organizational design, intelligence, and decision making. *Academy of Management Review, 15*(1), 47-71.

Huff, S. L., & Munro, M. C. (1985). Information technology assessment and adoption: A field study. *MIS Quarterly, 9*(4), 327-340.

Hughes, J., & Wood-Harper, A. T. (1999). Systems development as a research act. *Journal of Information Technology, 14*(1), 83-94.

Hull, J. (1992). *Options, futures and other derivatives* (2nd ed.). Prentice Hall.

Humber, M. (2004). National programme for information technology. *British Medical Journal, 328*, 1145-1146.

Hummers-Pradiera, E., et al. (2008). Simply no time? Barriers to GPs' participation in primary health care research. *Family Practice*, 1-8.

Hunt, A., & Thomas, D. (2000). *The pragmatic programmer.* MA, USA: Addison Wesley Longman.

Hunter, M. G. (1997). The use of repgrids to gather interview data about information system analysts. *Information Systems Journal, 7*, 67-81.

Hunter, M. G., & Beck, J. E. (1996). A cross-cultural comparison of 'excellent' systems analysts'. *Information Systems Journal, 6*(4), 261-281.

Hunter, M. G., & Beck, J. E. (2000). Using repertory grids to conduct cross-cultural information systems research. *Information Systems Research, 11*, 93-101.

Hurt, H. T., & Hubbard, R. (1987, May). *The systematic measurement of the perceived characteristics of information technologies: Microcomputers as innovations*. Paper presented at the ICA Annual Conference, Montreal, Quebec.

Huysman, M., & Wulf, V. (2004). *Social capital and information technology*. Cambridge, MA: The MIT Press.

Hwang, Y. (2005). Investigating enterprise systems adoption: Uncertainty avoidance, intrinsic motivation, and the technology acceptance model. *European Journal of Information Systems, 14*(2), 150-161.

Hynes, D. (2003). The role of computer courses in the domestication of the computer. In *Case study for the strategies of inclusion: Gender and the information society project (SIGIS)*.

Hynes, D. (2005). *Digital multimedia use & consumption in the household setting*. Unpublished doctoral dissertation, Dublin City University, Ireland.

Hynes, D. (2007). Applying domestication: How the Internet found its place in the home. In M. Khosrow-Pour (Ed.), *Managing worldwide operations and communications with information technology* (pp. 799-801). Hershey, PA: IGI Publishing.

Hynes, D., & Rommes, E. (2006). Fitting the Internet into our lives. In T. Berker, M. Hartmann, Y. Punie, & K. Ward (Eds.), *Domestication of media and technologies*. UK: Open University Press.

Ibarra, H. (1992). Homophily and differential returns: Sex differences in network structure and

Ibarra, H., & Andrews, S. B. (1993). Power, social influence, and sense making: Effects of network centrality and

proximity on employee perceptions. *American Science Quarterly, 38*, 277-303.

Igbaria, M., & Zviran, M. (1996). Comparison of end-user computing characteristics in the US, Israel and Taiwan. *Information & Management, 30*, 1-13.

Igbaria, M., Iivari, J., & Maragahh, H. (1995). Why do individuals use computer technology? A Finnish case study. *Information & Management, 29*, 227-238.

Igbaria, M., Meredith, G., & Smith, D. (1995). Career orientations of information systems employees in South Africa. *Journal of Strategic Information Systems, 4*(4), 319-340.

Igira, F. T. (2008a). The situatedness of work practices and organizational culture: Implications for information systems innovation uptake. *Journal of Information Technology, 23*(2), 79-88.

Igira, F. T. (2008b). *The interplay between transformation in everyday work practices and IS design and implementation processes: Empirical experiences from the health information system in Tanzania*. Unpublished doctoral dissertation, Department of Informatics, University of Oslo, Oslo, Norway.

Iivari, J. (1996). Why are CASE tools not used? *Communications of the ACM, 39*(10), 94-103.

Iivari, J., Hirschheim, R. & Klein, H. (2004). Towards a distinctive body of knowledge for information systems experts: Coding ISD process knowledge in two IS journals. *Information Systems Journal, 14*, 313-342.

Iivari, J., Parsons, J., & Hevner, A. R. (2005). Research in information systems analysis and design: introduction to the special theme papers. *Communications of the AIS, 16*, 810-813.

Ilgen, D. R. (1971). Satisfaction with performance as a function of the initial level of expected performance and the deviation from expectations. *Organizational Behavior and Human Performance, 6*, 345-361.

InformationWeek. (2007). *Global IT spending to reach $1.48 trillion in 2010, IDC says*. Retrieved from http://www.informationweek.com/news/management/outsourcing/showArticle.jhtml;jsessionid=JB4IAD NZACBP2QSNDLRSKH0CJUNN2JVN?articleI D=196802764&_requestid=885619

Ingelse, K. (1997). *Theoretical frameworks*. Retrieved January 6, 2008, from http://jan.ucc.nau.edu/~kmi/nur390/Mod2/theoretical/lesson.html

Ingram, P., & Roberts, P. W. (2000). Friendships among competitors in the Sydney hotel industry. *American Journal of Sociology, 106*, 387-423.

Institute for Management Excellence. (2006). *Differences between "computer" folks and the general population*. Retrieved April 14, 2006, from http://www.itstime.com/jul2003.htm

Introna, L. D. (1996). Commentary on the intellectual structures of information systems development by Hirschheim, Klein and Lyytinen. *Accounting, Management and Information Technologies (AMIT), 6*(1/2), 87-97.

Irkhin, Iu. V. (2007). Electronic government and society: World realities and Russia (a comparative analysis). *Sociological Research, 46*(2), 77-92.

Ives, B., & Learmonth, G. P. (1984). The information system as a competitive weapon. *Communications of the ACM, 27*(12), 1193-1201.

Ives, B., & Mason, R. (1990). Can information technology revitalize your customer service? *Academy of Management Executive, 4*(4), 52-69.

Jaccard, J. J., & Davidson, A. R. (1972). Toward an understanding of family planning behaviors: An initial investigation. *Journal of Applied Social Psychology, 2*, 228-235.

Jackson, R. (2006). *Fonterra puts SAP project on ice*. Retrieved October 5, 2006, from http://computerworld.co.nz/news.nsf/news/3C182BBD1B82A2C1CC2571F80016AEF1?Opendocument&HighLight=2,fonterra

Jacobs, J. (1965). *The death and life of great American cities*. London: Penguin Books.

Jaeger, P. T., & Thompson, K. M. (2003). E-government around the world: Lessons, challenges, and future directions. *Government Information Quarterly, 20*, 389-394.

Jagodzinski, W., & Weede, E. (1981). Testing curvilinear propositions by polynomial regression with particular reference to the interpretation of standardized solutions. *Quantity and Quality, 5*, 447-463.

Jain, H., & Zhao, H. (2003). *A conceptual model for comparative analysis of standardization of vertical industry languages*. Paper presented at the MIS Quartely Special Issue Workshop on: Standard Making - A Critical Research Frontier for Information systems.

Jain, H., Vitharana, P., & Zahedi, F. (2003). An assessment model for requirements identification in component-based software development. *The DATA BASE for Advances in Information Systems, 34*, 48.

James, T., Pirim, T., Boswell, K., Reithel, B., & Barkhi, R. (2006). Determining the intention to use biometric devices: An application and extension of the technology acceptance model. *Journal of Organizational and End User Computing, 18*(3), 1-24.

Jancowicz, D. (2003). *The easy guide to repertory grids*. London: Wiley.

Jarillo, J. C. (1988). On strategic networks. *Strategic Management Journal, 9*.

Jarvenpaa, S. L., Lang, K. R., Takeda, Y., & Tuunainen, V. K. (2003). Mobile commerce at crossroads. *Communications of the ACM, 46*(12), 41-44.

Jarvenpaa, S., & Leidner, D. (1998). An information company in Mexico: Extending the resource-based view of the firm to a developing country context. *Information Systems Research, 9*(4), 342-361.

Jarvis, C. B., Mackenzie, S. B., & Podsakoff, P. M. (2003). A critical review of construct indicators and measurement model misspecification in marketing and consumer research. *Journal of Consumer Research, 30*(2), 199-218.

Jaskyte, K., & Dressler, W. W. (2005). Organizational culture and innovation in nonprofit human service organization. *Administration in Social Work, 29*(2), 23-41.

Jasperson, J., Carter, P. E., & Zmud, R. W. (2005). A comprehensive conceptualization of post-adoptive behaviors associated with information technology enabled work systems, *MIS Quarterly, 29*(3), 525-557.

Jennings, A. S. (2002). Creating an interactive science murder mystery game: The optimal experience of flow. *IEEE Transactions on Professional Communication, 45*(4), 297-301.

Jennings, D. (2004). Myths about change. *CPA Journal, 74*(4), 12-13.

Jensen, O., & Scheraga, C. (1998). Transferring technology: Costs and benefits. *Technology in Society, 20,* 99-112.

Jepson, K. (2004). Stress and IT. *Credit Union Journal,* 14.

Jex, S. M., & Bliese, P. D. (1999). Efficacy beliefs as a moderator of the effects of work-related stressors: A multilevel study. *Journal of Applied Psychology, 84,* 349-361.

Jex, S. M., Bliese, P. D., Buzzel, S., & Primeau, J. (2001). The impact of self-efficacy on stressor-strain relations: Coping style as an explanatory mechanism. *Journal of Applied Psychology, 86*(3), 401-409.

Jiang, J. J., & Klein, G. (2002). A discrepancy model of information system personnel turnover, *Journal of Management Information Systems, 19,* 249-272.

Jiang, J. J., Klein, G., & Ballou, J. L. (2001). The joint impact of internal and external career anchors on entry-level IS career satisfaction. *Information & Management, 39*(1), 31-39.

Jiang, J. J., Klein, G., Van Slyke, C., & Cheney, P. (2003). A note on interpersonal and communication skills for IS professionals: Evidence of positive influence. *Decision Sciences, 34,* 799-812.

Johannesson, P. (1995). Representation and communication - a speech act based approach to information systems design. *Information systems, 20*(4), 291-303.

Johns, G. (1981). Difference score measures of organizational behavior variables: A critique. *Organizational Behavior and Human Performance, 27,* 443-463.

Johnson, E. J., & Payne, J. W. (1985). Effort and accuracy in choice. *Management Science, 31*(4), 395-414.

Johnson, J., Zamenopoulos, T., & Alexiou, K. (Eds.). (2005). Proceedings from the ECCS 2005 Satellite Workshop: *Embracing Complexity in Design.* Paris.

Johnston, K., & Johal, P. (1999). The Internet as a "virtual cultural region": Are extant cultural classification schemes appropriate? *Internet Research, 9*(3), 178-186.

Jonassen, D. H., & Rohrer-Murphy, L. (1999). Activity theory as a framework for designing constructivist learning environments. *Educational Technology Research and Development, 47*(1), 61-79.

Jones, K. G. (2004). *An investigation of activities related to knowledge management and their impacts on competitiveness.* Unpublished doctoral dissertation, University of Kentucky.

Jones, M. (1999). Structuration theory. In W.L. Currie & B. Galliers (Eds.), *Rethinking management information systems* (pp 103-135). Oxford, UK: Oxford University Press.

Jones, M. P. (1996). Indicator and stratification methods for missing explanatory variables in multiple linear regression. *Journal of the American Statistical Association, 91*(433), 222-230.

Jones, M. R., & Karsten, H. (2008). Giddens's structuration theory and information systems research. *MIS Quarterly, 32*(1), 127-157.

Jones, N., & Myers, M. D. (2001). Assessing three theories of information systems innovation: An interpretive case study of a funds management company. In *Proceedings of the Pacific Asia Conference on Information Systems,* Seoul, Korea (pp. 1005-1019).

Joreskog, K. G., & Sorbom, D. (1996). *LISREL 8: User's reference guide.* Chicago: Scientific Software International.

Joreskog, K. G., & Wold, H. (1982). The ML and PLS techniques for modeling with latent variables: Historical and comparative aspects. In K. G. Joreskog & H. Wold (Eds.), *Systems under indirect observation: Causality structure and prediction* (Vol. 1, pp. 263-270). Amsterdam: North Holland.

Jorgensen, D. (1989). Participant observation: A methodology for human studies. CA, USA: Sage Publications.

Judd, R. C. (1964). The case for redefining services. *Journal of Marketing, 28*(1), 58-59.

Judge, T. A., & Ilies, R. (2002). Relationship of personality to performance motivation: A meta-analytic review. *Journal of Applied Psychology, 87,* 797-807.

Judge, T. A., Heller, D., & Mount, M. K. (2002). Five-factor model of personality and job satisfaction: A meta-analysis. *Journal of Applied Psychology, 87*(3), 530-541.

Judge, T. A., Higgins, C. A., Thoresen, C. J., & Barrick, M. R. (1999). The big five personality traits, general mental ability, and career success across the life span. *Personnel Psychology, 52*(3), 621-652.

Judge, T. A., Locke, A. E., & Durham, C. C. (1997). The dispositional causes of job satisfaction: A core evaluation approach. In L. L. Cummings & B. M. Staw (Eds.), *Research in organizational behavior* (pp. 151-188). Greenwich, CT: JAI Press.

Judge, T. A., Thoresen, C. J., Pucik, V. P., & Welbourne, T. M. (1999). Managerial coping with organizational change: A dispositional perspective. *Journal of Applied Psychology, 84*(1), 107-122.

Kahneman, D., & Tversky, A. (1979) Prospect theory: An analysis of decision under risk. *Econometrica, 47,* 263-292.

Kale, S. H., & Sudharshan, D. (1987). A strategic approach to international segmentation. *International Marketing Review, 4*(4), 60-70.

Kallinikos, J. (2003, June 16-21). Networks as alternative forms of organization: Some critical remarks. In *Proceedings of the 11ᵗʰ European Conference on Information Systems,* Naples, Italy.

Kambayashi, N., & Scarbrough, H. (2001). Cultural influences on IT use amongst factory managers: A UK-Japanese comparison. *Journal of Information Technology, 16*(4), 221-236.

Kamel, N., & Davison, R. (1998). Applying CSCW technology to overcome traditional barriers in group interactions. *Information & Management, 34*(4), 209-219.

Kamis, A., Koufaris, M., & Stern, T. (2008). Using an attribute-based decision support system for user-customized products online: An experimental investigation. *MIS Quarterly, 32*(1), 159-177.

Kankanhalli, A., Tan, B. C. Y., & Kwok-Kee, W. (2005). Contributing knowledge to electronic knowledge repositories: An empirical investigation. *MIS Quarterly, 29*(1), 113-143.

Kankanhalli, A., Tan, B. C. Y., Wei, K. K., & Holmes, M. C. (2004). Cross-cultural differences and information systems developer values. *Decision Support Systems, 38*(2), 183-195.

Kaplan, B., & Duchon, D. (1988). Combining qualitative and quantitative methods in information systems research: A case study. *MIS Quarterly, 12*(4), 571-586.

Kaptelinin, V. (1992). *Human computer interaction in context: The activity theory perspective.* Paper presented at the East-West International Conference on Human-Computer Interaction, St. Petersburg, Russia.

Kaptelinin, V., & Nardi, B. A. (2006). *Acting with technology: Activity theory and interaction design.* Cambridge, MA: The MIT Press.

Kaptelinin, V., Nardi, B. A., & Macaulay, C. (1999). Methods & tools: The activity checklist: A tool for representing the "space" of context. *Interactions, 6*(4), 27-39.

Karahanna, E., Ahuja, M., Srite, M., & Galvin, J. (2002). Individual differences and relative advantage: The case of GSS. *Decision Support Systems, 32,* 327-341.

Karahanna, E., Evaristo, J. R., & Srite, M. (2005). Levels of culture and individual behavior: An integrative perspective. *Journal of Global Information Management, 13*(2), 1-20.

Karahanna, E., Straub, D. W., & Chervany, N. L. (1999). Information technology adoption across time: A cross-sectional comparison of pre-adoption and post-adoption beliefs. *MIS Quarterly, 23*(2), 183-213.

Karimi, J. K., Somers, T. M., & Bhattacherjee, A. (2007). The role of information systems resources in ERP capability building and business process outcomes. *Journal of Management Information Systems, 24*(2), 221-260.

Karimi, J., Somers, T. M., & Gupta, Y. P. (2001). Impact of information technology management practices on customer service. *Journal of Information Management, Systems, 17*(4), 125-158.

Karyda, M., Kiountouzis, E., & Kokolakis, S. (2005) Information systems security policies: A contextual perspective. *Computers & Security, 24*(3), 246-255.

Kautz, K., Hansen, B. H., & Jacobsen, D. (2004). The utilization of information systems development methodologies in practice. *Journal of Information Technology Cases and Applications, 6*(4), 1-20.

Kazi, M. A. F. (2003). *Realist evaluation in practice*. London: Sage.

Kegan, R., & Lahey, L. (2001). *How the way we talk can change the way we work*. CA, USA: Jossey-Bass.

Kegan, R., & Lahey, L. (2001). The real reason people won't change. *Harvard Business Review, 79*(10), 85-89.

Keil, M., Mann, J., & Rai, A. (2000). Why software projects escalate: An empirical analysis and test of four theoretical models. *MIS Quarterly, 24*(4), 631-660.

Keil, M., Tan, B. C. Y., Wei, K.-K., Saarinen, T., Tuunainen, V., & Wassenaar, A. (2000). A cross-cultural study on escalation of commitment behavior in software projects. *MIS Quarterly, 24*(2), 299-325.

Kelly, G. A. (1955/1991). *The psychology of personal constructs*. New York: Norton.

Kemmis, S. (1980). The imagination of the case and the invention of the study. In H. Simons (Ed.), *Towards a science of the singular* (pp. 93-142). Norwich, UK: University of East Anglia, Center for Applied Research in Education.

Kendall, M. G. (1953). The analysis of economic time series – part I: Prices. *Journal of the Royal Statistical Society, 96*, 11-25.

Kettinger, W. J., Lee, C. C., & Lee, S. (1995). Global measures of information service quality: A cross-national study. *Decision Sciences, 26*(5), 569-588.

Khalaf, R., Mukhi, N., & Weerawarana, S. (2003). *Service-oriented composition in BPEL4WS*. Paper presented at the International World Wide Web Conference (WWW), Budapest, Hungary.

Kim, C., Peterson, D., & Kim, J. (1999). Information systems success: Perceptions of developers in Korea. *Journal of Computer Information Systems, 40*(2), 90-95.

Kimbrough, S. O., & Moore, S. A. (1997). On automated message processing in electronic commerce and work support systems: Speech act theory and expressive felicity. *ACM Transactions on Information systems (TOIS), 15*(4), 321-367.

King, J. L., & Schrems, E. L. (1978, March). Cost-benefits analysis in information systems development and operation. *ACM Computing Surveys, 10*(1), 19-34.

King, W. R., & He, J. (2006). A meta-analysis of the technology acceptance model. *Information & Management, 43*(6), 740-755.

Kirton, M. (1976). Adaptors and innovators: A description and measure. *Journal of Applied Psychology, 61*(5), 622-629.

Klein, H. K. K., & Myers, M. (1999). A set of principles for conducting and evaluating interpretive field studies in information systems. *MIS Quarterly, 23*(1), 67-94.

Klein, H. K., & Huynh, M. Q. (2004). The critical social theory of Jürgen Habermas and its implications for IS research. In J. Mingers & L. Willcocks (Eds.), *Social theory and philosophy for information systems* (pp. 157 - 237). West Sussex, England: John Wiley and Sons Ltd.

Klein, K. J., Tosi, H., & Cannella, A. A., Jr. (1999). Multilevel theory building: Benefits, barriers, and new developments. *Academy of Management Review, 24*(2), 243-248.

Kline, R. B. (2005). *Principles and practice of structural equation modeling* (2nd ed.). New York: The Guilford Press.

Kling, R., & Scacchi, W. (1982). The web of computing: Computing technology as social organisation. In M. Yovits (Ed.), *Advances in Computers, Vol. 21* (pp. 3-90). NY, USA: Academic Press.

Klischewski, R. (2000). *Systems development as networking*. Paper presented at the Americas Conference on Information Systems (AMCIS), Long Beach, CA.

Klischewski, R. (2001, June 27-29). *Commitments enabling co-operation in distributed information systems development*. Paper presented at the The 9th European Conference on Information Systems, Bled, Slovenia.

Knack, S., & Keefer, P. (1997). Does social capital have an economic payoff? A cross-country investigation. *Quarterly Journal of Economics, 112*(4), 1251.

Knights, D., Murray, F., & Willmott, H. (1997). Networking as knowledge work: A study of strategic inter-organizational development in the financial service industry. In B. P. Bloomfield, R. Coombs, D. Knights, & D. Littler (Eds.), *Information technology and organizations: Strategies, networks, and integration* (pp. 137-159). Oxford, UK: Oxford University Press.

Knudsen, C. (1994). The competence view of the firm: What can modern economists learn from Philip Selznick's sociological theory of leadership. In W. R. Scott & S. Christensen (Eds.), *The institutional construction of organisations: International and longitudinal studies* (pp. 135-163). Thousand Oaks, CA: Sage Publications Inc.

Koch, C. (2000). Collective influence on information technology in virtual organizations – emancipatory management of technology. *Technology Analysis and Strategic Management, 12*(3), 357-368.

Koeszegi, S., Vetschera, R., & Kersten, G. (2004). National cultural differences in the use and perception of Internet-based NSS: Does high or low context matter? *International Negotiation, 9*(1), 79-109.

Kogut, B., & Singh, H. (1988). The effect of national culture on the choice of entry mode. *Journal of International Business Studies, 19*(3), 411-432.

Korpela, M. (1997). *Activity analysis and development in a nutshell.* Retrieved May 12, 2008, from http://www.uku.fi/tike/actad/nutshell-97.html

Korpela, M., Mursu, A., Soriyan, A., & Eerola, A. (2002). Information systems research and information systems practice in a network of activities. In Y. Dittrich, C. Floyd, & R. Klischewski (Eds.), *Social thinking software practice* (pp. 287-308). Cambridge, MA: The MIT Press.

Korpela, M., Mursu, A., Soriyan, A., Eerola, A., Häkkinen, H., & Toivanen, M. (2004). Information systems research and development by activity analysis and development: Dead horse or the next wave? In B. Kaplan, D. P. Truex III, D. Wastell, A. T. Wood-Harper, J. I. DeGross (Eds.), *Information systems research. Relevant theory and informed practice* (pp. 453-471). Boston, MA: Kluwer Academic Publishers.

Korpela, M., Soriyan, H. A., & Olufokunbi, K. C. (2000). Activity analysis as a method for information systems development: General introduction and experiments from Nigeria and Finland. *Scandinavian Journal of Information Systems, 12*(1-2), 191-210.

Koscho, G. R. (2003). President's message. *Information Executive, 7*(2), 1.

Kotter, J. P., & Cohen, D. S. (2002). *The heart of change: Real-life stories of how people change their organizations.* Boston, MA: Harvard Business School Press.

Koufaris, M. (2002). Applying the technology acceptance model and flow theory to online consumer behavior. *Information Systems Research, 13*(2), 205-223.

Kowol, U., & Küppers, U. (2003). Innovation networks: A new approach to innovation dynamics. In M. van Geenhuizen, D. V. Gibson, & M. V. Heitor (Eds.), *Regional development and conditions for innovation in the network society.* Lafayette, IN: Purdue University Press.

Krackhardt, D. (1992). The strength of strong ties: The importance of philos in organization. In N. Nohria and R. C. Eccles (Eds.), *Networks and organizations: Structure, form, and action* (pp. 216-239). Boston, MA: Harvard Business School Press.

Kraut, R., Dumais, S., & Koch, S. (1989). Computerization, productivity, and quality of work-life. *Communications of the ACM, 32*(2), 220-238.

Kraut, R., Mukhopadhyay, T., Szczypula, J., Kiesler, S., & Scherlis, W. (1999). Communication and information: Alternative uses of the Internet in households. In *Proceedings of the Conference on Human Factors in Computing Systems* (pp. 368-375).

Kreiner, G. E. (2006). Consequences of work-home segmentation or integration: A person-environment fit perspective. *Journal of Organizational Behavior, 27,* 485-507.

Krishna, S., & Madon, S. (Eds.). (2003). *Digital challenge: Information technology in the development context.* Aldershot, England: ASHGATE.

Krishna, S., & Walsham, G. (2005). Implementing public information systems in developing countries: Learning from a success story. *Information Technology for Development, 11*(2), 123-140.

Krugman, H. E. (1965). The impact of television advertising: Learning without involvement. *Public Opinion Quarterly, 29*(3), 349-356.

Kuhn, T. S. (1970). *The structure of scientific revolutions.* Chicago: University of Chicago Press.

Kukafka, R., Johnson, S. B., Linfante, A., & Allegrante, J. P. (2003). Grounding a new information technology implementation framework in behavioural science: A systematic analysis of the literature on IT use. *Journal of Biomedical Informatics, 36,* 218-227.

Kumar, K. (1990, February). Post implementation evaluation of computer-based information systems: Current practices. *Communications of the ACM, 33*(2), 203-212.

Kumar, K., van Dissel, H. G., & Bielli, P. (1998). The merchant of Prato - revisited: Toward a third rationality of information systems. *MIS Quarterly, 22*(2), 199-226.

Kumar, U., Kumar, V., & Shareef, M. A. (2008, May 24-27). E-government development: Understanding impact of information and communication technology in developing countries. In *Proceedings of the Administrative Sciences Association of Canada Conference,* Halifax, Canada.

Kumar, V., Mukerji, B., Butt, I., & Persaud, A. (2007). Factors for successful e-government adoption: A conceptual framework. *The Electronic Journal of e-Government, 5*(1), 3-76.

Kuutti, K. (1991). Activity theory and its applications to information systems research and development. In H.-E. Nissen, H. K. Klein, & R. Hirschheim (Eds.), *Information systems research: Contemporary approaches & emergent traditions* (pp. 529-549). Amsterdam: Elsevier Science Publishers (North-Holland).

Kuutti, K. (1991). The concept of activity as a basic unit of analysis for CSCW research. In L. Bannon, M. Robinson, & K. Schmidt (Eds.), *Proceedings of the Second European Conference on Computer-Supported Cooperative Work, ECSCW'91* (pp. 249-264). London, UK: Kluwer Academic Publishers.

Kuutti, K. (1992). HCI research debate and activity theory position. In J. Gornostaev (Ed.), *Proceedings of the 2nd East-West Conference on Human-Computer Interaction, EWHCI'92* (pp. 13-22). Moscow: *International* Centre for Scientific and Technical Information (ICSTI).

Kuutti, K. (1996). Activity theory as a potential framework for human-computer interaction research. In B. A. Nardi (Ed.), *Context and consciousness: Activity theory and human-computer interaction* (pp. 17- 44). Cambridge, MA: The MIT Press.

Kuutti, K., & Arvonen, T. (1992). Identifying potential CSCW applications by means of activity theory concepts: A case example. In *Proceedings of the 1992 ACM conference on Computer-supported cooperative work* (pp. 233-240). New York: ACM Press.

Kwon, O. B. (2003). Meta web service: Building web-based open decision support system based on web services. *Expert Systems with Applications, 24*(4), 375-389.

Kwon, T. H., & Zmud, R. W. (1987). Unifying the fragmented models of information systems implementations. In J. R. Boland & R. Hirschheim (Eds.), *Critical issues in information systems research* (pp. 227-252). New York: John Wiley.

Labrou, Y., Finin, T., & Peng, Y. (1999). Agent communication languages: The current landscape. *IEEE Intelligent Systems and Their Applications, 14*(2), 45-52.

Laemmel, A., & Shooman, M. (1977). Statistical (natural) language theory and computer program complexity (Tech. Rep. POLY/EE/E0-76-020). Brooklyn, New York: Department of Electrical Engineering and Electrophysics, Polytechnic Institute of New York.

Laeven, T. (2005). Competencies – the asset that counts most: On developing human talents as a prerequisite for successful EDRM changes. In C. Hare & J. McLeod (Eds.), *Managing electronic records* (pp. 129-148). UK: Facet Publishing.

Lafleur, R. (1996). Project management. Getting control and keeping control of complex projects. *American Programmer, 9*(4), 24-28.

Lakoff, G., & Johnson, M. (1980). *Metaphors we live by.* Chicago: The University of Chicago Press.

Lally, L. (1994). The impact of environment on information infrastructure enhancement: A comparative study of Singapore, France, and the United States. *Journal of Global Information Management, 2*(3), 5-12.

Lambooy, J. G., & Boschma, R. A. (2001). Evolutionary economics and regional policy. *Annals of Regional Science, 35,* 113-131.

Lammy, D. (2008). *David Lammy -Leitch and healthcare*. Retrieved April 28, 2008, from http://www.dius.gov.uk/speeches/lammy_leitch_020408.html

Land, F. (Ed.). (2000). *Evaluation in a socio-technical context*. Boston: Kluwer Academic Publishers.

Landfield, A. (1971). *Personal construct systems in psychotherapy*. Chicago: Rand McNally.

Lang, A. (1995). Defining audio/video redundancy from a limited-capacity information processing perspective. *Communication Research, 22*(1), 86-115.

Lang, A. (2000). The limited capacity model of mediated message processing. *Journal of Communication, 50*(1), 46-70.

Lantolf, J. P. (2000). Introducing sociocultural theory. In J. P. Lantolf (Ed.), *Sociocultural theory & second language learning* (pp. 1-26). Oxford, UK: Oxford University Press.

Lanvin, B. (1995). Why the global village cannot afford information slums. In *The New Information Infrastructure Strategies for U.S. Policy* (W. J. Drake ed.) (pp. 205-222).

Lapointe, L., & Rivard, S. (2005) A multilevel model of resistance to information technology implementation. *MIS Quarterly, 29*(3), 461-491.

Larsen, T. J., Levine, L., & DeGross, J. I. (Eds.). (1998). *Information systems: Current issues and future changes* (pp. 155-174). Laxenberg, Austria: IFIP.

Latour, B. (1987). *Science in action: How to follow scientists and engineers through society*. Cambridge, MA: Harvard University Press.

Latour, B. (1988). Mixing humans and nonhumans together: The sociology of a door-closer. *Social Problems, 35*(3), 298-310.

Latour, B. (1988). *The pasteurization of France* (A. Sheridan & J. Law, Trans.). Cambridge, MA: Harvard University Press.

Latour, B. (1993). *We have never been modern*. Cambridge, MA: Harvard University Press.

Latour, B. (1994). On technical mediation-- philosophy, sociology, genealogy. *Common Knowledge, 3*(2), 29-64.

Latour, B. (1994). Pragmatogonies. *American Behavioral Scientist, 37*(6), 791-808.

Latour, B. (1996). *Aramis or the love of technology* (C. Porter, Trans.). Cambridge, MA: Harvard University Press.

Latour, B. (1999). For David Bloor... and beyond: A reply to David Bloor's 'Anti-Latour'. *Studies in the History and Philosophy of Science, 30*(1), 113-129.

Latour, B. (1999). *Pandora's hope: Essays on the reality of science studies*. Cambridge, MA: Harvard University Press.

Latta, G. F., & Swigger, K. (1992). Validation of the repertory grid for use in modelling knowledge. *Journal of the American Society for Information Science, 43*, 115-129.

Laudon, K. C., & Laudon, J. P. (2006). *Management information systems: Managing the digital firm*. NJ: Prentice Hall.

Law, J. (1991). Introduction: Monsters, machines and sociotechnical relations. In J. Law (Ed.), *A Sociology of monsters: Essays on power, technology and domination* (pp. 1-23). London: Routledge.

Law, J. (1992). Notes on the theory of the actor-network: Ordering, strategy, and heterogeneity. *Systems Practice, 5*(4), 379-393.

Law, J. (1997). *Traduction/trahison-notes on ANT*. Retrieved November 2, 1999, from http://www.lancs.ac.uk/sociology/stslaw2.html1

Law, J., & Callon, M. (1988). Engineering and sociology in a military aircraft project: A network analysis of technological change. *Social Problems, 35*(3), 284-297.

Lawrence, C. (2005). From Milan to Mann Gulch: Reflections on the intellectual contributions of Professor Claudio Ciborra. *European Journal of Information Systems, 14*(5), 484-495.

Lawrence, P. (1969). How to deal with resistance to change. *Harvard Business Review, 47*(1), 77-86.

Layder, D. (1993). *New strategies in social research*. Cambridge, UK: Polity Press.

Layder, D. (1998). *Sociological practice: Linking theory and social research*. London: Sage.

Lazarus, R. S. (1966). *Psychological stress and the coping process*. New York: McGraw-Hill.

Lazarus, R. S. (2000). Toward better research on stress and coping. *American Psychologist, 55*(6), 665-673.

Lazarus, R. S., & Folkman, S. (1984). *Stress, appraisal, and coping*. New York: Springer Publishing Company.

Leana, C. R., & Van Buren III, H. J. (1999). Organizational social capital and employment practices. *Academy of Management Review, 24*(3), 538-555.

Leana, C. R., Feldman, D. C., & Tan, G. Y. (1998). Predictors of coping behavior after a layoff. *Journal of Organizational Behavior, 19*, 85-97.

Lee, A. (2000). Systems thinking, design science, and paradigms: Heeding three lessons from the past to resolve three dilemmas in the present to direct a trajectory for future research in the information systems field. *Keynote Address at the 11th International Conference on Information Management*, Taiwan. Retrieved from, http://www.people.vcu.edu/aslee/ICIM-keynote-2000

Lee, A. S. (1989). A scientific methodology for MIS case studies. *MIS Quarterly, 13*(1), 33-52.

Lee, A. S. (1991). Integrating positivist and interpretative approaches to organizational research. *Organization Science, 2*(4), 342-365.

Lee, A. S., Liebenau, J., & DeGross, J. (Eds.)(1997). *Information systems and qualitative research*. London: Chapman & Hall.

Lee, D. M. S., Trauth, E. M., & Farwell, D. (1995). Critical skills and knowledge requirements of IS professionals: A joint academic industry investigation. *MIS Quarterly, 19*(3), 313-340.

Lee, J. (2002). A key to marketing financial services: The right mix of products, services, channels and customers. *The Journal of Services Marketing, 16*(2/3), 238-258.

Lee, J., & Truex, D. P. (2000). Exploring the impact of formal training in ISD methods on the cognitive structure of novice information systems developers. *Information Systems Journal, 10*, 347-367.

Lee, N., & Brown, S. (1994). Otherness and the actor network. *American Behavioral Scientists, 37*(6), 772-790.

Lee, S. M., Lee, H., Kim, J., & Lee, S. (2007). ASP system utilization: Customer satisfaction and user performance. *Industrial Management + Data Systems, 107*(2), 145-165.

Lee, Y., Kozar, K., & Larsen, K. R. T. (2003). The technology acceptance model: Past, present and future. *Communications of the Association for Information Systems, 12*(50), 752-780.

Lehoux, P., Sicotte, C., & Denis, J.-L. (1999). Assessment of a computerized medical record system: Disclosing script of use. *Evaluation and Program Planning, 22*, 439-453.

Leidner, D. E., & Carlsson, S. A. (1998). Les bénéfices des systèmes d'information pour dirigeants dans trois pays. *Systèmes d'Information et Management, 3*(3), 5-27.

Leidner, D. E., & Elam, J. J. (1995). The impact of executive information systems on organizational design, intelligence, and decision making. *Organization Science, 6*(6), 645-665.

Leidner, D. E., Carlsson, S. A., Elam, J. J., & Corrales, M. (1999). Mexican and Swedish managers' perceptions of the impact of EIS on organizational intelligence, decision making, and structure. *Decision Sciences, 30*(3), 633-658.

Leitner, Y. (2005). Financial networks: Contagion, commitment, and private sector bailouts. *Journal of Finance, 60*, 2925-2953.

Lemme, B. H. (1999). *Development in adulthood* (2nd ed.). Needham Heights, MA: Allyn & Bacon.

Leonard-Barton, D. (1988). Implementation as mutual adaptation of technology and organization. *Research Policy, 17*, 251-267.

Leonard-Barton, D. (1995). *Well-springs of knowledge: Building and sustaining the sources of innovation*. Boston, MA: Harvard Business School Press.

Leont'ev, A. N. (1978). *Activity, consciousness, and personality*. Englewood Cliffs, NJ: Prentice-Hall.

Leont'ev, A. N. (1981). *Problems of the development of mind*. Moscow, Russia: Progress Publishers.

Levenburg, N. M., & Klein, H. A. (2006). Delivering customer services online: Identifying best practices of medium-sized enterprises. *Information Systems Journal, 16*(2), 135-156.

Levin, D. Z., & Cross, R. (2004). The strength of weak ties you can trust: The mediating role of trust in effective knowledge transfer. *Management Science, 50*(11), 1477-1490.

Levin, T., & Gordon, C. (1989). Effect of gender and computer experience on attitudes towards computers. *Journal of Educational Computing Research, 5*(1), 69-88.

Levina, N., & Vaast, E. (2008). Innovating or doing as told? Status differences and overlapping boundaries in offshore collaboration. *MIS Quarterly, 32*(2), 307-332.

Levitt, T. (1972). Production-line approach to service. *Harvard Business Review, 50*(5), 41-52.

Lewin, K. (1951). Frontiers in group dynamics. In D. Cartwright (Ed.), *Field theory in social science* (pp. 188-237). CN, USA: Greenwood Press.

Li, J. (1994). Experience effects and international expansion: Strategies of service MNCs in the Asia-Pacific region. *Management International Review, 34*(3), 217-234.

Li, Y. N., Tan, K. C., & Xie, M. (2003). Factor analysis of service quality dimension shifts in the information age. *Managerial Auditing Journal, 18*(4), 297-302.

Liang, T., Lai, H., & Ku, Y. (2006). Personalized content recommendation and user satisfaction: Theoretical synthesis and empirical findings. *Journal of Management Information Systems, 23*(3), 45-70.

Liao, C., & Chuang, S. (2006). Exploring the role of knowledge management for enhancing firm's innovation and performance. In *Proceedings of the 39ʰ Hawaii International Conference on System Sciences.*

Liao, C., Chen, J.-L., & Yen, D. C. (2007). Theory of planning behavior (TPB) and customer satisfaction in the continued use of e-service: An integrated model. *Computers in Human Behavior, 23*, 2804-2822.

Liao, J., & Welsch, H. (2003). Social capital and entrepreneurial growth aspiration: A comparison of technology- and non-technology-based nascent entrepreneurs.

Journal of High Technology Management Research, 14(1), 149.

Liao, J., & Welsch, H. (2005). Roles of social capital in venture creation: Key dimensions and research implications. *Journal of Small Business Management, 43*(4), 345-362.

Liberty, J. (1999). *The complete idiot's guide to a career in computer programming.* Indianapolis, IN: Que Press.

Liehr, P., & Smith, M. (2001). Frameworks for research. Retrieved January 6, 2008, from http://homepage.psy.utexas.edu/homepage/class/Psy394V/Pennebaker/Reprints/Liehr%20Class.doc

Lightner, N. J. (2004). Evaluating e-commerce functionality with a focus on customer service. *Communications of the ACM, 47*(10), 88-92.

Likert, R. (1978). An improvement cycle for human resource development. *Training and Development Journal, 78*(32), 16-18.

Lilley, S. (1998). Regarding screens for surveillance of the system. *Accounting, Management and Information Technology, 8*, 63-105.

Lim, J. (2003). A conceptual framework on the adoption of negotiation support systems. *Information and Software Technology, 45*(8), 469-477.

Lim, L.-H., Raman, K., & Wei, K.-K. (1994). Interacting effects of GDSS and leadership. *Decision Support Systems, 12*(3), 199-221.

Lin, C. S., Wu, S., & Tsai, R. J. (2005). Integrating perceived playfulness into expectation-confirmation model for web portal context. *Information & Management, 42*, 683-693.

Lin, H. (2007). The impact of website quality dimensions on customer satisfaction in the B2C e-commerce context. *Total Quality Management & Business Excellence, 18*(4), 363-378.

Lin, N. (2001). *Social capital: A theory of social structure and action.* Cambridge, UK: Cambridge University Press

Lin, N. P., Chiu, H. C., & Hsieh, Y. C. (2001). Investigating the relationship between service providers' personality and customers' perceptions of service quality across gender. *Total Quality Management, 12*(1), 57-67.

Lin, N., Ensel, W. M., & Vaughn, J. C. (1981). Social resources and strength of ties: Structural factors in occupational status attainment. *American Sociological Review, 46*(4), 393-405.

Lincoln, Y. S. (1997). Self, subject, audience, text: Living at the edge, writing in the margins. In W. G. Tierney & Y. S. Lincoln (Eds.), *Representation and the text: Reframing the narrative voice* (pp. 37-55). Albany, NY: State University of New York Press.

Lincoln, Y. S., & Guba, E. G. (2000). Paradigmatic controversies contradictions and emerging confluences. In N. K. Denzin & Y. S. Lincoln (Eds.), *The handbook of qualitative research* (pp. 163-188). Beverly Hills, CA: Sage Publications.

Lind, M., & Goldkuhl, G. (2001). Generic layered patterns for business modelling. In *Proceedings of the International Working Conference on the Language-action perspective on Communication Modelling (LAP)*.

Lind, M., & Goldkuhl, G. (2006). How to develop a multi-grounded theory: The evolution of a business process theory. *Australasian Journal of Information Systems, 13*(2), 69-86.

Lissoni, F., & Metcalfe, J. S. (1994). Diffusion of innovation ancient and modern: A review of the main themes. In M. Dodgson & R. Rothwell (Eds.), *Handbook of industrial innovation* (pp. 106-144). Cheltenham, UK: Edward Elgar Publishing Limited.

Little, R. J. A., & Rubin, D. A. (1987). *Statistical analysis with missing data*. New York: John Wiley & Sons.

Little, T. D., Lindenberger, U., & Nesselroade, J. R. (1999). On selecting indicators for multivariate measurement and modeling with latent variables: When "good" indicators are bad and "bad" indicators are good. *Psychological Methods, 4*(2), 192-211.

Littlejohns, P., et al. (2003). Evaluating computerised health information systems: Hard lessons still to be learnt. *British Medical Journal, 326*, 860-863.

Liu, B. S.-C., Furrer O., & Sudharshan, D. (2001). The relationships between culture and behavioral intentions toward services. *Journal of Service Research, 4*(2), 118-129.

Livingstone, L. P., Nelson, D. L., & Barr, S. H. (1997). Person-environment fit and creativity: An examination of supply-value and demand-ability versions of fit. *Journal of Management, 23*, 119-146.

Livingstone, S. (2007). On the material and the symbolic: Silverstone's double articulation of research traditions in new media studies. *New media and society, 9*(1), 16-24.

Ljungberg, J., & Holm, P. (1997). Speech acts on trial. In *Computers and design in context* (pp. 317-347). Cambridge, MA: MIT Press.

Llewelyn, S. (2003). What counts as "theory" in qualitative management and accounting research? Introducting five levels of theorizing. *Accounting, Auditing & Accountability Journal, 16*(4), 662-708.

Locke, E. A. (1969). What is job satisfaction? *Organizational Behavior and Human Performance, 4*, 309-336.

Loiacono, E. T., Watson, R. T., & Goodhue, D. L. (2002). WEBQUAL: A measure of website quality. In K. Evans & L. Scheer (Eds.), *Proceedings of the Marketing Educators' Conference: Marketing Theory and Applications* (pp. 432-437).

Long, J. S. (1983). *Covariance structure models: An introduction to LISREL*. Beverly Hills, CA: Sage.

Longshore Smith, M. (2006). Overcoming theory-practice inconsistencies: Critical realism and information systems research. *Information and Organization, 16*(3), 191–211.

Lòpez, J., & Potter, G. (Eds.). (2001). *After postmodernism: An introduction to critical realism*. London: Athlone.

Lorenzi, N. (2003). *Strategies for creating successful local health information infrastructure initiatives*. Tennessee: Dept of Biomedical Informatics, Vanderbilt University.

Louis, M. R., & Sutton, R. I. (1991). Switching cognitive gears: From habits of mind to active thinking. *Human Relations, 44*, 55-76.

Lounsbury, J. W., Gibson, L. W., & Hamrick, F. L. (2004). The development of a personological measure of work drive. *Journal of Business and Psychology, 18*(4), 347-371.

Lounsbury, J. W., Gibson, L. W., Sundstrom, E., Wilburn, D., & Loveland, J. (2003). An empirical investigation of the proposition that "school is work". A comparison of personality-performance correlations in school and work settings. *Journal of Education and Work, 17*(1), 119-131.

Lounsbury, J. W., Loveland, J. M, Sundstrom, E. D., Gibson, L. W., Drost, A. W., & Hamrick, F. L. (2003). An investigation of personality traits in relation to career satisfaction. *Journal of Career Assessment, 11*, 287-307.

Lounsbury, J. W., Moffitt, L., Gibson, L. W., Drost, A. W., & Stevenson, M. W. (2007). An investigation of personality traits in relation to the job and career satisfaction of information technology professionals. *Journal of Information Technology, 22*, 174-183.

Lounsbury, J. W., Park, S. H., Sundstrom, E., Williamson, J., & Pemberton, A. (2004). Personality, career satisfaction, and life satisfaction: Test of a directional model. *Journal of Career Assessment, 12*, 395-406.

Lounsbury, J. W., Sundstrom, E., Loveland, J. M., & Gibson, L. W. (2003) Intelligence, "big five" personality traits, and work drive as predictors of course grade. *Personality and Individual Differences, 35*, 1231-1239.

Loury, G. C. (1977). A dynamic theory of racial income differences. In P. A. Wallace & A. M. LaMonde (Eds.), *Women, minorities and employment discriminations.* Lexington, MA: Lexington Books.

Lovelock, C. H. (1994). *Product plus: How product + service = competitive advantage.* New York: McGraw-Hill, Inc.

Lowe, A. (1996). *An explanation of grounded theory.* Swedish School of Economics and Business Administration.

Lowry, P. B., Karuga, G. G., & Richardson, V. J. (2007). Assessing leading institutions, faculty, and articles in premier information systems research journals. *Communications of the Association for Information Systems, 20*(16), 142-203.

Lubrano, A. (1997). The telegraph: How technology innovation caused social change. New York: Garland Publishing.

Lucas, H. C., & Spitler, V. K. (1999). Technology use and performance: A field study of broker workstations. *Decision Science, 30*(2), 291-311.

Luecke, R. (2003). *Managing change and transition.* MA, USA: Harvard Business School Press.

Luecke, R. (2004). *Coaching and mentoring: How to develop top talent and achieve stronger performance.* MA, USA: Harvard Business School Press.

Luftman, J., & Koeller, C. T. (2003). Assessing the value of IT. In J. N. Luftman (Eds.), *Competing in the information age: Align in the sand* (2nd ed.) (pp. 77-106). Oxford, UK: Oxford University Press.

Luria, A. R. (1976). *Cognitive development its cultural and social foundations.* Cambridge, MA: Harvard University Press.

Lyytinen, K. (1987). Different perspectives on information systems: Problems and solutions. *ACM Computing Surveys, 19*(1), 5-46.

Lyytinen, K. (2004). *The struggle with the language in the IT – why is LAP not in the mainstream?* Paper presented at the International Working Conference on the Language-action perspective on Communication Modelling (LAP), New Brunswick, NJ.

Lyytinen, K. (2008, May 7-9): Design: "shaping in the wild". Keynote speech at the *Third International Conference on Design Science Research in Information Systems & Technology (DESRIST 2008)*, Atlanta, GA.

Lyytinen, K., Lehitnen, E., & Auramäki, E. (1987). SAMPO: A speech-act based office modelling approach. *ACM SIGOIS Bulletin, 8*(4), 11-23.

MacCallum, R. C. (1986). Specification searches in covariance structure modeling. *Psychological Bulletin, 100*(1), 107-120.

MacCallum, R. C., Roznowski, M., & Necowitz, L. B. (1992). Model modifications in covariance structure analysis: The problem of capitalization on chance. *Psychological Bulletin, 111*(3), 490-504.

MacDuffie, J. P., & Helper, S. (2003). B2B and mode or exchange: Evolutionary and transformative effect. In *The global internet economy.* Cambridge, MA: MIT Press.

MacKenzie, D., & Wajcman, J. (Eds.). (1999). *The social shaping of technology* (2nd ed.). Buckingham, UK: Open University Press.

Madon, S. (1991). The impact of computer-based information systems on rural development: A case study in India. In *Imperial College of Science, Technology & Medicine*. London.

Madon, S. (1997). Information-based global economy and socioeconomic development: The case of Bangalore. *Information Society, 13*(3), 227-244.

Madon, S. (2000). The Internet and socio-economic development: Exploring the interaction. *Information Technology & People, 13*(2), 85-101.

Madon, S. (2003). Studying the developmental impact of e-governance initiatives. In *Internationals Federation of Information Processing, IFIP*. Athens, Greece.

Madon, S. (2004). Evaluating the developmental impact of e-governance initiatives: An exploratory framework, *Electronic Journal of Information Systems in Developing Countries, 20*(5), 1-13.

Madu, C. N. (1989). Transferring technology to developing countries – critical factors for success. *Long Range Planning, 22*(4), 115-124.

Magretta, J., & Stone, N. (2002, April). *What management is: How it works and why it's everyone's business* (1st ed.). Simon & Schuster Adult Publishing Group.

Maguire, R. (2005). Lessons learned from implementing an electronic records management system. *Records Management Journal, 15*(3), 150-157.

Mahmood, M. A., Bagchi, K., & Ford, T. C. (2004). On-line shopping behavior: Cross-country empirical research. *International Journal of Electronic Commerce, 9*(1), 9-30.

Maiden, N. A. M., & Rugg, G. (1996). ACRE: Selecting methods for requirements acquisition. *Software Engineering Journal, 11*, 183-192.

Maier, E. (2005). Activity theory as a framework for accommodating cultural factors in HCI studies. In *Workshop-Proceedings der 5. fachübergreifenden Konferenz Mensch und Computer* (pp. 69-79). Wien: Oesterreichische Computer Gesellschaft.

Majchrzak, A., Rice, R. E., Malhotra, A., King, N., & Ba, S. (2000). Technology adaptation: The case of a computer supported inter-organizational virtual team. *MIS Quarterly, 24*(4), 569-600.

Major, D. A., Davis, D. D., Germano, L. M., Fletcher, T. D., Sanchez-Hucles, J., & Mann, J. (2007). Managing human resources in information technology: Best practices of high-performing supervisors. *Human Resource Management, 46*(3), 411-427.

Malone, T. W., Yates, J., & Benjamin, R. I. (1987). Electronic markets and electronic hierarchies. *Communications of the ACM, 30*(6) 485.

Mansell, R. (2002). From Digital divides to digital entitlements in knowledge societies. *Current Sociology, 50*(3), 407-426.

Mansell, R., & Wehn, U. (1998). *Knowledge societies: Information technology for sustainable development.* New York: Oxford University Press.

Marcoulides, G. A., & Saunders, C. (2006). PLS: A silver bullet? *MIS Quarterly, 30*(2), iii-ix.

Markus, M. L., & Robey, D. (1983). The organizational validity of management information systems. *Human Relations, 36*(3), 203-266.

Markus, M. L., & Robey, D. (1988). Information technology and organizational change: Causal structure in theory and research. *Management Science, 34*(5), 583-598.

Markus, M. L., & Saunders, C. (2007). Looking for a few good concepts…and theories…for the information systems field. *MIS Quarterly, 31*(1), 3-6.

Markus, M. L., Majchrzak, A., et al. (2002). A design theory for systems that support emergent knowledge processes. *MIS Quartely, 26*, 179-212.

Marsden, P. V. (1982). A note on block variables in multi-equation models. *Social Science Research, 11*, 127-140.

Marsh, H. W., Hau, K.-T., & Wen, Z. (2003). In search of golden rules: Comment on hypothesis-testing approaches to setting cutoff values for fit indexes and dangers in overgeneralizing Hu and Bentler's (1999) findings. *Structural Equation Modeling, 11*(3), 320-341.

Marshall, A. (1920). *Principles of economics* (8th ed.). Macmillan and Co., Ltd. Retrieved October 1, 2005, from http://www.econlib.org/library/Marshall/marP.html

Martins, L. E. G., & Daltrini, B. M. (1999). Activity theory: An approach to software requirements elicitation using precepts from activity theory. In A. Rawlinson (Ed.), *Proceedings of the 14th IEEE international conference on automated software engineering* (pp. 15-23). Washington, DC: IEEE Computer Society.

Martinsons, M. (1991). Management philosophy and IT assimilation: The east-west divide. *Journal of Technology Management, 18*, 207-218.

Martinsons, M. G., & Cheung, C. (2001). The impact of emerging practices on IS specialists: Perceptions, attitudes and role changes in Hong Kong. *Information & Management, 38*(3), 167-183.

Martinsons, M., & Hempel, P. (1998). Chinese business process re-engineering. *International Journal of Information Management, 18*(6), 393-407.

Martinsons, M., & Westwood, R. (1997). Management information systems in the Chinese business culture: An explanatory theory. *Information & Management, 32*, 215-228.

Marx, K., & Engels, F. (1973). *Karl Marx: On society and social change.* Chicago: University of Chicago Press.

Massini, S., & Pettigrew, A. M. (2003). Complementarities in organizational innovation and performance: Empirical evidence from the INNFORM survey. In A. M. Pettigrew, R. Whittington, L. Melin, C. Sanchez-Runde, F. Van den Bosch, W. Ruigrock, & T. Numagami (Eds.), *Innovative forms of organizing, international perspectives.* Thousand Oaks, CA: SAGE Publications.

Mastor, K. A. & Ismael, A. H. (2004). Personality and cognitive style differences among matriculation engineering and information technology students. *World Transactions on Engineering and Technology Education, 3*(1), 101-105.

Mata, F. J., Fuerst, W. L., & Barney, J. B. (1995). Information technology and sustained competitive advantage: A resource-based analysis. *MIS Quarterly, 19*(4), 487-505.

Mathias, T. M., Caputi, P., & Vella, S. C. (2008). *Information systems implementation and the scientist-practitioner model.* Unpublished manuscript, University of Wollongong.

Mathieson, K. (1991). Predicting user intentions: Comparing the technology acceptance model with the theory of planned behavior. *Information Systems Research, 2*(3), 173-191.

Mathiyalakan, S., Ashrafi, N., Zhang, W., Waage, F., Kuilboer, J., & Heimann, D. (2005, May 15-18). Defining business agility: An exploratory study. In *Proceedings of the 16th Information Resource Management Association International Conference*, San Diego, CA.

Mauer, I., & Ebers, M. (2006). Dynamics of social capital and their performance implications: Lessons from biotechnology start-ups. *Administrative Science Quarterly, 51*, 262-292.

Mayer, J. D., Roberts, R. D., & Barsade, S. G. (2008). Human abilities: Emotional intelligence. *Annual Review of Psychology, 59*(1), 507-536.

Mazis, M., Ahtola, O., & Kippel, R. (1975). A comparison of four multi attribute models in the prediction of consumer attitudes. *Journal of Consumer Research, 2*, 38-53.

Maznevski, M., & Chudoba, K. M. (2000). Bridging space over time: Global virtual team dynamics and effectiveness. *Organization Science, 11*(5), 473-492.

McAvoy, J., & Butler, T. (2005). A paradox of virtual teams and change: An implementation of the theory of competing commitments. *International Journal of e-Collaboration, 2*(3), 1-24.

McCabe, T. J. (1976). A complexity measure. In *Proceedings of the 2nd International Conference on Software Engineering (ICSE '76)* (p. 407).

McCloskey, D. W. (2006). The importance of ease of use, usefulness, and trust to online consumers: An examination of the technology acceptance model with older consumers. *Journal of Organizational and End User Computing, 18*(3), 47-65.

McCoy, S., Everard, A., & Jones, B. M. (2005). An examination of the technology acceptance model in Uruguay and the US: A focus on culture. *Journal of Global Information Technology Management, 8*(2), 27-45.

McCoy, S., Galleta, D. F., & King, W. R. (2007). Applying TAM across cultures: The need for caution. *European Journal of Information Systems (2007), 16*, 81-90.

McCrae, R. R. (1984). Situation determinants of coping responses: Loss, threat, and challenge. *Journal of Personality and Social Psychology, 46*, 919-928.

McCrae, R. R. (1989). Age differences and changes in the use of coping mechanisms. *Journal of Gerontology, 44*, 161-169.

McDonald, M., & Westphal, J. (2003). Getting by with the advice of their friends: CEOs' advice networks and firms' strategic responses to poor performance. *Administrative Science Quarterly, 48*, 1-32.

McDonald, R. P., & Ho, M.-H. R. (2002). Principles and practice in reporting structural equation analyses. *Psychological Methods, 7*, 64-82.

McElroy, J. C., Hendrickson, A. R., Townsend, A. M., & DeMarie, S. M. (2007). Dispositional factors in Internet use: Personality versus cognitive style. *MIS Quarterly, 31*(4), 809-820.

McElroy, W. (1996). Implementing strategic change through projects. *International Journal of Project Management, 14*(6), 325-329.

McFadyen, M. A., & Cannella, A. A., Jr. (2004). Social capital and knowledge creation: Diminishing returns of the number and strength of exchange relationships. *Academy of Management Journal, 47*(5), 735-746.

McGrath, K. (2001, June 27-29). *The golden circle: A case study of organizational change at the London Ambulance Service (case study)*. Paper presented at the The 9th European Conference on Information Systems, Bled, Slovenia.

McGregor, D. (2006). *The human side of enterprise* (Annotated ed.). New York: The McGraw-Hill Companies, Inc.

McKay, J., & Marshall, P. (2005, November 29–December 2) A review of design science in information systems. In *Proceedings of the 16ᵗʰ Australasian Conference on Information Systems*, Sydney.

McKelvey, M. (1997). Using evolutionary theory to define systems of innovation. In C. Edquist (Ed.), *Systems of innovation—technologies, institutions and organizations* (pp. 200-222). London: Pinter/Cassell Publishers.

McKinney, V., Yoon, K., & Zahedi, F. (2002). The measurement of web-customer satisfaction: An expectation and disconfirmation approach. *Information Systems Research, 13*, 296-315.

McLeod, R., Kim, C., Saunders, C., Jones, J., Scheel, C., & Estrada, M. (1997). Information management as perceived by CIO's in three Pacific Rim countries. *Journal of Global Information Management, 5*(3), 5-16.

McLoughlin, I., et al. (2000). Rethinking political process in technological change: Socio-technical configurations and frames. *Technology Analysis and Strategic Management, 12*(1), 17-37.

McLuhan, M. (1964). The medium is the message. In *Understanding media* (pp. 7-23). London: Routledge and Kegan Paul.

McMillan, E. (2004). *Complexity, organizations and change*. London: Routledge.

McMillan, S. J. (2002). Exploring models of interactivity from multiple research traditions: Users, documents, and systems. In L. Lievrouw & S. Livingstone (Eds.), *The handbook of new media* (pp. 163-182). Thousand Oaks, CA: Sage Publications.

McPeck, J. E. (1981). *Critical thinking and education*. New York: St Martin's.

Mead, G. H. (1934). *Mind, self and society*. Chicago: University of Chicago Press.

Mechanic, D. (1974). Social structure and personal adaptation: Some neglected dimensions. In G. V. Coelho, D. A. Hamburg, & J. E. Adams (Eds.), *Coping and adaptation*. New York: Basic Books.

Medina-Mora, R., Winograd, T., Flores, R., & Flores, F. (1992). *The action workflow approach to workflow management technology*. Paper presented at the ACM conference on Computer-supported cooperative work, Toronto, Ontario, Canada.

Mehra, A., Kilduff, M., & Brass, D. (2001). The social networks of high and low self-monitors: Implications for workplace performance. *Administrative Science Quarterly, 46*, 121-146.

Melling, D. (1987). *Understanding Plato.* New York: Oxford University Press.

Merriam, S. B. (1988). *Case study research in education: A qualitative approach.* San Francisco: Jossey Bass.

Merritt, A. (2000). Culture in the cockpit - do Hofstede's dimensions replicate? *Journal of Cross-Cultural Psychology, 31*(3), 283-301.

Meso, P., Datta, P., & Mbarika, V. (2006). Moderating information and communication technologies' influences on socioeconomic development with good governance: A study of the developing countries. *Journal of the American Society for Information Science & Technology, 57*(2), 186-197.

Messersmith, J. (2007). Managing work-life conflict among information technology workers. *Human Resource Management, 46*(3), 429-451.

Metcalfe, J. S. (1994). The economics of evolution and the economics of technology policy. *Economic Journal, 104*, 931-944.

Meuter, M. L., Bitner, M. J., Ostrom, A. L., & Brown, S. (2005). Choosing among alternative service delivery modes: An investigation of customer trial of self-service technologies. *Journal of Marketing, 69*(4), 61-83.

Meuter, M. L., Ostrom, A. L., Bitner, M. J., & Roundtree, R. (2003). The influence of technology anxiety on consumer use and experiences with self-service technologies. *Journal of Business Research, 56*(11), 899-906.

Meyer, A. D., & Goes, J. B. (1988). Organizational assimilation of innovations: A multilevel contextual analysis. *Academy of Management Journal, 31*, 897-923.

Meyronin, B. (2004). ICT: The creation of value and differentiation in services. *Managing Service Quality, 14*(2/3), 216-225.

Miers, D. (1996). The strategic challenges of electronic commerce. In *Electronic Commerce* (pp. 1-19.). Enix Consulting Limited.

Miettinen, R. (1997). *The concept of activity in the analysis of heterogenuous networks in innovation pro-*

cesses. Paper presented at the Centre for Social Theory and Technology (CSTT) Workshop on Actor Network Theory and After, Keele University, UK. Retrieved May 13, 2008, from http://communication.ucsd.edu/MCA/Paper/Reijo/Reijo.html

Miettinen, R. (1999). The riddle of things: Activity theory and actor-network theory as approaches to studying innovations. *Mind, Culture, and Activity, 6*(3), 170-195.

Miettinen, R. (2001). Artifact mediation in Dewey and in cultural-historical activity theory. *Mind, Culture, and Activity, 8*(4), 297-308.

Miettinen, R. (2005). Object of activity and individual motivation. *Mind, Culture, and Activity, 12*(1), 52-69.

Miles, M. B., & Huberman, A. M. (1994). *Qualitative data analysis.* Newbury Park, CA: Sage Publications.

Milgram, S. (1971). Group pressure and action against a person. In D. Taylor (Ed.), *Small groups* (pp. 157-170). IL, USA: Markham Publishing Company.

Miller, G. A. (1956). The magical number seven, plus or minus two: Some limits on our capacity for processing information. *Psychological Review, 63*(2), 81-97.

Miller, K. (2005). *Communications theories: Perspectives, processes, and contexts.* New York: McGraw-Hill.

Milligan, J. W., & Hayes, T. (1997). What do customers want from you? Everything! *U.S. Banker, 107*(12), 38-45.

Mingers, J. (2003). A critique of statistical modelling from a critical realist perspective. In *Proceedings of the 11th European Conference on Information Systems.*

Mingers, J. (2004). Re-establishing the real: Critical realism and information systems. In J. Mingers & L. Willcocks (Eds.), *Social theory and philosophy for information systems* (pp. 372-406). Chichester, UK: Wiley.

Ministry of Economic Development. (2004, February). *Restructuring to accommodate the "new" model.*

Ministry of Health. (2007). *How to monitor for population health outcomes: Guidelines for developing a monitoring framework.* Wellington, New Zealand: Ministry of Health.

Miranda, S. M., & Bostrom, R. P. (1993-1994). The impact of group support systems on group conflict and conflict management. *Journal of Management Information Systems, 10*(3), 63-95.

Mitchell, T. R., & James, L. R. (2001). Building better theory: Time and the specification of when things happen. *Academy of Management Review, 26*(4), 530-547.

Mitsufuji, T. (2001). A perspective of the innovation-diffusion process. In M. Ardis & B. Marcolin (Eds.), *Diffusing software product and process innovations* (pp. 51-66). MA, USA: Kluwer Academic Publishers.

Moenaert, R. K., & Souder, W. E. (1996). Context and antecedents of information utility at the r&d/marketing interface. *Management Science, 42*(11), 1592-1610.

Mohr, L. B. (1982). *Explaining organizational behavior.* San Francisco: Jossey-Bass.

Mokyr, J. (1996). Evolution and technological change: A new metaphor for economic history? In R. Fox (Ed.), *Technological change* (pp. 63-83). London: Harwood Publishers.

Montealegre, R. (1997). The interplay of information technology and the social milieu. *Information Technology and People, 10*(2), 106-131.

Montealegre, R. (1998). Managing information technology in modernizing "against the odds": Lessons from an organization in a less-developed country. *Information & Management, 34*(2), 103-116.

Monteiro, E. (2000). Monsters: From systems to actor-networks. In K. Braa, C. Sorensen, & B. Dahlbom (Eds.), *Planet Internet*. Lund, Sweden: Studentlitteratur.

Monteiro, E., & Hanseth, O. (1996). Social shaping of information infrastructure: On being specific about the technology. In W. J. Orlikowski, G. Walsham, M. R. Jones, & DeGross, J. I. (Eds.), *Information technology and changes in organizational work* (pp. 325-343). London: Chapman and Hall.

Moon, J., & Kim, Y. (2001). Extending the TAM for a world-wide-web context. *Information&Management, 38*, 217-230.

Moon, M. J. (2002). The evolution of e-government among municipalities: Rhetoric or reality? *Public Administration Review, 62*(4), 424-433.

Moon, M. J., & Norris, D. F. (2005). Does managerial orientation matter? The adoption of reinventing government and e-government at the municipal level. *Information Systems Journal, 15*, 43-60.

Moore, G. C., & Benbasat, I. (1991). Development of an instrument to measure the perceptions of adopting an information technology innovation. *Information Systems Research, 2*(3), 192-222.

Moore, K. (2003). *Versions of the future in relation to mobile communication technologies*. Unpublished doctoral dissertation, University of Surrey, UK.

Moore, S. A. (2001). A foundation for flexible automated electronic communication. *Information systems Research, 12*(1), 34-62.

Moos, R. H., & Billings, A. G. (1992). Conceptualizing and measuring coping resources and processes. In L. Goldberger & S. Breznitz (Eds.), *Handbook of stress* (pp. 212-230). New York: The Free Press.

Mora, M., Gelman, O., Forgionne, G., Petkov D., & Cano, J. (2007). Integrating the fragmented pieces in IS research paradigms and frameworks – a systems approach. *Information Resource Management Journal, 20*(2), 1-22.

Mora, M., Gelman, O., Frank, M., Paradice, D., Cervantes, F., & Forgionne, G. A. (2008). Towards an interdisciplinary engineering and management of complex IT intensive organizational systems: A systems view. *International Journal on Information Technologies and the Systems Approach, 1*(1), 1-24.

Moreno, J. (1934). *Who shall survive?* New York: Bacon Press.

Morgan, G. (1983). More on metaphor: Why we cannot control tropes in administrative science. *Administrative Science Quarterly, 28*, 601-607.

Morgeson, F. P., & Hofmann, D. A. (1999). The structure and function of collective constructs: Implications for multilevel research and theory development. *Academy of Management Review, 24*(2), 249-265.

Morin, R. A., & Jarrell, S. L. (2001). *Driving shareholder value*. New York: McGraw-Hill.

Morton P. (2006). Using critical realism to explain strategic information systems planning. *Journal of Information Theory and Application, 8*(1), 1-20.

Motsenigos, A., & Young, J. (2002). *KM in the U.S. government sector. KMWorld.* Retrieved from http://www.kmworld.com/Articles/Editorial/Feature/KM-in-the-U.S.-government-sector-9397.aspx

Mowday, R. (1998). Reflections on the study and relevance of organizational commitment. *Human Resource Management Review, 8*(4), 387-401.

Moynihan, T. (1996). An inventory of personal constructs for information systems project risk researchers. *Journal of Information Technology, 11*, 359-371.

Mulaik, S., James, L. R., Van Alstine, J., Bennett, N., Lind, S., & Stillwell, C. D. (1989). Evaluation of goodness of fit indices in structural equation models, *Psychological Bulletin, 105*(3), 430-445.

Mulder, H., & Reijswoud, V. v. (2003). *Three ways of talking business and IT design: Similarities and differences between three approaches.* Paper presented at the The World Multi-Conference on Systemics, Cybernetics and Informatics, Orlando, USA.

Mulder, M. (1977). *The daily power game.* Leiden, The Netherlands: Martinus Nijihoff.

Mumford, E. (2003). *Redesigning human systems.* Hershey, PA: IRM Press.

Mumford, E. (2006a). Researching people problems: Some advice to a student. *Information Systems Journal, 16*(4), 383-389.

Mumford, E. (2006b). The story of socio-technical design: Reflections on its successes, failures and potential. *Information Systems Journal, 16*(4), 317-342.

Mursu, A. (2002). *Information systems development in developing countries: Risk management and sustainability analysis in Nigerian software companies.* Unpublishd doctoral dissertation, University of Jyväskylä, Kuopio, Finland.

Mursu, A., Luukkonen, I., Toivanen, M., & Korpela, M. (2007). Activity theory in information systems research and practice: Theoretical underpinnings for an information systems development model. *Information Research, 12*(3).

Mursu, A., Lyytinen, K., Soriyan, H. A., & Korpela, M. (2003). Identifying software project risks in Nigeria: An international comparative study. *European Journal of Information Systems, 12*(3), 182-194.

Mutch, A. (2002). Actors and networks or agents and structures: Towards a realist view of information systems. *Organizations, 9*(3), 477-496.

Mwanza, D. (2001). Where theory meets practice: A case for an activity theory based methodology to guide computer system design. In M. Hirose (Ed.), *Proceedings of the 8th TC13 IFIP International Conference on Human-Computer Interaction, INTERACT'01* (pp. 342-349). Amsterdam: IOS Press.

Mwanza, D. (2002). *Towards an activity-oriented design method for HCI research and practice.* Unpublishd doctoral dissertation, Open University, Milton Keynes, UK.

Mwanza, D., & Engeström, Y. (2005). Managing content in e-learning environments. *British Journal of Educational Technology, 36*(6), 453-463.

Myers, M. D., & Avison, D. E. (2002). An introduction to qualitative research in information systems. In M. D. Myers & D. E. Avison (Eds.), *Qualitative research in information systems: A reader* (pp. 3-12). London: Sage Publications Ltd.

Myers, M., & Tan, F. (2002). Beyond models of national culture in information systems research. *Journal of Global Information Management, 10*(1), 24-32.

Myers. M. (2009). *Qualitative research in business & management.* London: Sage.

Nader, C. (2007, November 9). Expert warn of a health 'tsunami'. *The Age.*

Nader, D. (1993). Concepts for the management of organisational change. In C. Mabey & B. Major-White (Eds.), *Managing change* (2nd ed.) (pp. 5-19). London: Paul Chapman Publishing.

Nadler, D. A., & Tushman, M. L. (2004). Implementing new design: Managing organizational change. In M. L. Tushman & P. Andersen (Eds.), *Managing strategic innovation and change: A collection of readings* (2nd ed.). Oxford, UK: Oxford University Press.

Nah, F., & Benbasat, I. (2004). Knowledge-based support in a group decision making context: An Expert-novice comparison. *Journal of the Association for Information Systems, 5*(3), 125-150.

Nahapiet, J., & Ghoshal, S. (1998). Social capital, intellectual capital, and the organizational advantage. *Academy of Management Review, 23*, 242-266.

Nakata, C., & Sivakumar, K. (1996). National culture and new product development: An integrative review. *Journal of Marketing, 60*(1), 61-72.

Nanda, A. (1996). Resources, capabilities and competencies. In B. Moingeon & A. Edmondson (Eds.), *Organizational learning and competitive advantage* (pp. 93-120). London: Sage Publications Ltd.

NAO (National Audit Office). (1999). *The passport delays of summer 1999*. London: Stationary Office.

Narayan, D., & Cassidy, M. F. (2001). A dimensional approach to measuring social capital: Development and validation of a social capital inventory. *Current Sociology, 49*(2), 59-102.

Nardi, B. A. (Ed.). (1996). *Context and consciousness: Activity theory and human-computer interaction*. Cambridge, MA: The MIT Press.

Nash, D. (2002). Beyond buy-in. *P&T Journal, 27*(11), 617-618.

Ndou, V. D. (2004). E-government for developing countries: Opportunities and challenges. *Electronic Journal of Information Systems in Developing Countries, 18*(1), 1-24.

Nedovic¢-Budic¢, Z., & Godschalk, D. (1996). Human factors in adoption of geographic information systems, *Public Administration Review, 56*, 554-567.

Negash, S., Ryan, T., & Igbaria, M. (2003). Quality and effectiveness in web-based customer support systems. *Information & Management, 40*(8), 757-768.

Neimeyer, R. A., Baker, K. D., & Neimeyer, G. J. (1990). The current status of personal construct theory: Some scientometric data. In R. A. Neimeyer & G. J Neimeyer. (Eds.), *Advances in personal construct psychology* (vol 1) (pp. 3-22). Greenwich, CT: JAI.

Nelson R. R. (2002). Bringing institutions into evolutionary growth theory, *Journal of Evolutionary Economics, 12*(1/2), 17-29.

Nelson, K., & Clark, T., Jr. (1994). Cross-cultural issues in information systems research: A research program. *Journal of Global Information Management, 2*(4), 19-29.

Nelson, R. R. (1991). Educational needs as perceived by IS and end-user personnel: A survey of knowledge and skill requirements. *MIS Quarterly, 15*, 502-525.

Nelson, R. R. (1994). Why do firms differ and how does it matter? In R. P. Rumelt, D. E. Schendel, & D. J. Teece (Eds.), *Fundamental issues in strategy* (pp. 230-247). Boston, MA: Harvard Business School Press.

Nelson, R. R. (1995). Recent evolutionary theorizing about economic change. *Journal of Economic Literature, 33*, 48-90.

Nelson, R. R., & Cheney, P. H. (1987). Training end users: An exploratory study. *MIS Quarterly, 11*, 546-559.

Nelson, R. R., & Winter, S. G. (1982). *An evolutionary theory of economic change*. Cambridge, MA: The Belknap Press of Harvard University Press.

Nelson, R. R., Todd, P. A., & Wixom, B. H. (2005). Antecedents of information and system quality: An empirical examination within the context of data warehousing. *Journal of Management Information Systems, 21*(4), 199-235.

Netemeyer, R., Johnston, M., & Burton, S. (1990). Analysis of role conflict and role ambiguity in a structural equations framework. *Journal of Applied Psychology, 75*, 400-410.

Nevo, D., & Wade, M. R. (2007). How to avoid disappointment by design. *Communications of the ACM, 50*(4), 43-48.

Newbert, S. L. (2007). Empirical research on the resource-based view of the firm: An assessment and suggestions for future research. *Strategic Management Journal, 28*(2), 121-146.

Newburger, E. C. (1999). *Computer use in the United States: October 1997* (Report No. PPL-114). Atlanta, GA: U.S. Department of Commerce, U.S. Census Bureau.

Newell, S., Tansley, C., & Huang, J. (2004). Social capital and knowledge integration in an ERP project team: The importance of bridging and bonding. *British Journal of Management 15*, S43-S57.

Newman, M., & Sabherwal, R. (1996). Determinants of commitment to information systems development: A longitudinal investigation. *MIS Quarterly, 20*(1), 23-54.

Ng, D. (2004). The social dynamics of diverse and closed networks. *Human Systems Management, 23*, 111-122.

Ngwenyama, O. N. (1998). Groupware, social action and organizational emergence: On the process dynamics of computer mediated distributed work. *Accounting, Management and Information Technology, 8*, 127-146.

Nicholson, B., & Sahay, S. (2001). Some political and cultural issues in the globalization of software development: Case experience from Britain and India. *Information and Organization, 11*, 25-43.

Nickols, F. (2006). *Change management 101: A primer*. Retrieved March 29, 2008, from http://home.att.net/~nickols/change.htm

Niederman, F. (1999). Global information systems and human resource management: A research agenda. *Journal of Global Information Management, 7*(2), 33-39.

Nilsson, M. (2000). *Organizational development as action research, ethnography, and beyond*. Paper presented at the Annual Meeting of the American Educational Research Association (AERA), New Orleans, LA.

Noir, C., & Walsham, G. (2007). The great legitimizer: ICT as myth and ceremony in the Indian healthcare sector. *Information Technology & People, 20*(4), 313-333.

Nonaka, I., & Takeuchi, H. (1995). *The knowledge creating company*. New York: Oxford Press University.

Nordhaug, O. (1994). *Human capital in organisations: Competence, training and learning*. New York: Oxford University Press.

Norgren, L., & Hauknes, J. (1999). *Economic rationales of government involvement in innovation and the supply of innovation-related service*. Oslo, Norway: Rise Project, European Commission.

Norris, D. F., & Moon, M. J. (2005). Advancing e-government at the grassroots: Tortoise or hare? *Public Administration Review, 65*(1), 64-75.

Novak, T. P., Hoffman, D. L., & Duhachek, A. (2003). The influence of global-directed and experiential activities on online flow experiences. *Journal of Consumer Psychology, 13*(1/2), 3-16.

Novak, T. P., Hoffman, D. L., & Yung, Y. (2000). Measuring the customer experience in online environments: A structural modeling approach. *Marketing Science, 19*(1), 22-42.

Nunnally, J. C., & Bernstein, I. H. (1994). *Psychometric theory* (3rd ed.). New York: McGraw-Hill, Inc.

Nussbaum, M., & Sen, A. (Eds.). (1993). *The Quality of Life*. Oxford, UK: Clarendon Press.

Nwana, H. S. (1996). Software agents: An overview. *Knowledge Engineering Review, 11*(2), 205-244.

O*NET. (2008). *Occupational information network. O*NET online*. Retrieved January 20, 2006, from http://online.onetcenter.org/

O'Brien, J. A., & Marakas, G. (2007). *Introduction to Information Systems* (13th ed.). McGraw-Hill/Irwin.

O'Leary, D. E. (2000). Enterprise resource planning systems: Systems, life cycle, electronic commerce, and risk. New York: Cambridge University Press.

Oakland, S., & Ostell, A. (1996). Measuring coping: A review and critique. *Human Relations, 49*(2), 133-155.

Ogden, J. (2003). Some problems with social cognitions models: A pragmatic and conceptual analysis. *Health Psychology, 22*(4), 424-428.

Okazaki, S., & Rivas, A. A. (2002). A content analysis of multinationals' Web communication strategies: Cross-cultural research framework and pre-testing. *Internet Research - Electronic Networking Applications and Policy, 12*(5), 380-390.

Okot-Uma, R. W-O., & Caffrey, L. (Eds.). (2000). Trusted services and public key infrastructure. *Commonwealth Secretariat*, London.

Olesen, K., & Myers, M. D. (1999). Trying to improve communication and collaboration with information technology: An action research project which failed. *Information Technology and People, 12*(4), 317-332.

Oliver, R. L. (1980). A cognitive model of the antecedents and consequences of satisfaction decisions. *Journal of Marketing Research, 17*, 460-469.

Olson, G. M., & Olson, J. S. (2000). Distance matters. *Human-Computer Interaction, 15*(2-3), 139-178.

Oreskes, N., Shrader-Frechette, K., & Belitz, K. (1994). Verification, validation, and confirmation of numerical models in the earth sciences. *Science, 263*(5147), 641-646.

Orlikowski, W. J. & Gash, D. C. (1994). Technological frames: Making sense of information technology in organizations. *ACM Transactions on Information Systems, 12*(2), 174-207.

Orlikowski, W. J. & Yates, J. (1994). Genre repertoire: The structuring of communicative practices in organizations. *Administrative Science Quarterly, 39*(4), 541-574.

Orlikowski, W. J. (1991). Integrated information environment or matrix of control? The contradictory implications of information technology. *Accounting, Management and Information Technology, 1*(1), 9-42.

Orlikowski, W. J. (1992). The duality of technology: Rethinking the concept of technology in organizations. *Organization Science, 3*(3), 398-427.

Orlikowski, W. J. (1993). CASE tools as organizational change: investigating incremental and radical changes in systems development. *MIS Quarterly, 17*(3), 309-340.

Orlikowski, W. J. (1996). Improvising organizational transformation over time: A situated change perspective. *Information Systems Research, 7*(1), 63-92.

Orlikowski, W. J. (2000). Using technology and constituting structures: A practice lens for studying technology in organizations. *Organization Science, 11*(4), 404-428.

Orlikowski, W. J., & Hofman, J. D. (1997). An improvisational model for change management: The case of groupware technologies. *Sloan Management Review, 38*(2), 11-21.

Orlikowski, W. J., & Iacono, C. S. (2001). Research commentary: Desperately seeking "IT" in IT research - a call to theorizing the IT artifact. *Information Systems Research, 12*(2), 121-134.

Orman, L. V. (2007). Consumer support systems. *Communications of the ACM, 50*(4), 49-54.

Orum, A. M., Feagin, J. R., & Sjoberg, G. (1991). Introduction: The nature of the case study. In J. R. Feagin & A. M. Orum (Eds.), *A case for the case study* (pp. 1-26). Chapel Hill, NC: University of North Carolina Press.

Orwell, G. (1949). *Nineteen eighty-four*. London: Secker.

Ouchi, W. G. (1980). Markets, bureaucracies and clans. *Administrative Science Quarterly, 25*.

Outhwaite, W. (1983). Toward a realist perspective. In G. Morgan (Ed.), *Beyond method: Strategies for social research* (pp. 321-330). Beverly Hills, CA: Sage Publications, Inc.

OutSystems. (n.d.). Retrieved November 20, 2005, from http://www.outsystems.com

Palmer, D., & Barber, B. M. (2001). Challengers, elites, and owning families: A social class theory of corporate acquisitions in the 1960s. *Administrative Science Quarterly, 46*, 87-120.

Palvia, P. C. (1997). Developing a model of the global and strategic impact of information technology. *Information & Management, 32*, 229-244.

Palvia, P. C., Palvia, S. C. J., & Whitworth, J. E. (2002). Global information technology: A meta-analysis of key issues. *Information & Management, 39*(5), 403-414.

Papazoglou, M. P. (2003). Web services and business transactions. *World Wide Web, 6*(1), 49-91.

Papazoglou, M. P., & Georgakopoulos, D. (2003). Service oriented computing. *Communications of the ACM, 46*(10), 24-28.

Parasuraman, A. (2000). Technology readiness index (TRI): A multiple-item scale to measure readiness to embrace new technologies. *Journal of Service Research, 2*(4), 307-320.

Parasuraman, A., & Grewal, D. (2000). The impact of technology on the quality-value-loyalty chain: A research agenda. *Journal of the Academy of Marketing Science, 28*(1), 168-174.

Parent, M., Vandebeek, C. A., & Gemino, A. C. (2005). Building citizen trust through e-government. *Government Information Quarterly, 22*, 720-736.

Parnas, D., & Clements, P. (1986). Rational design process: How and why we fake it. *IEEE Transactions on Software Engineering, 12*(2), 251-257.

Patching, K. (1999). *Management and organisational development*. London: Macmillian Business.

Patel, N. V. (2002). Emergent forms of IT governance to support global ebusiness models. *Journal of Information Technology Theory and Application*.

Patel, N. V. (2005). Sustainable systems: Strengthening knowledge management systems with deferred action. *International Journal of Information Technology and Management, 4*(4), 344-365.

Patel, N. V. (2006). *Organization and systems design: Theory of deferred action*. Basingstoke, England: Palgrave Macmillan.

Patel, N. V., (Ed.). (2003). *Adaptive evolutionary information systems*. Hershey, PA: Idea Group Publishing.

Patnayakuni, R., Seth, N., & Rai, A. (2006). Building social capital with IT and collaboration in supply chains: An empirical investigation. In *Proceedings of the Twenty-Seventh International Conference on Information Systems*, Milwaukee, Wisconsin.

Patrickson, M. (1986). Adaptation by employees to new technology. *Journal of Occupational Psychology, 59*, 1-11.

Patton, M. Q. (2002). *Qualitative evaluation and research methods*. Thousand Oaks, CA: Sage Publications.

Paul, R. J. (2007). Editorial: Challenges to information systems: Time to change. *European Journal of Information Systems, 16*, 193-195.

Paul, S., Samarah, I. M., Seetharaman, P., & Mykytyn, P. P. (2004). An empirical investigation of collaborative conflict management style in group support system-based global virtual teams. *Journal of Management Information Systems, 21*(3), 185-222.

Paunonen, S. V., & Ashton, M. C. (2001). Big five factors and facets and the prediction of behavior. *Journal of Personality and Social Psychology, 81*(3), 524-539.

Pavlou, P. A., & Fygenson, M. (2006). Understanding and predicting electronic commerce adoption: An extension of the theory of planned behavior. *MIS Quarterly, 30*(1), 115-143.

Pawson, R. (2006). *Evidence-based policy: A realist perspective*. London: Sage.

Pawson, R., & Tilley, N. (1997). *Realistic evaluation*. London: Sage.

Payne, J. W. (1982). Contingent decision behavior. *Psychological Bulletin, 92*(2), 382-402.

Peirce, C. S. (1958). Collected papers. In C. Hartshorne & P. Weiß (Eds.), (pp. 1931-1935). Cambridge, MA: Harvard University Press.

Pellegrinelli, S. (1997). Programme management: Organising project-based change. *International Journal of Project Management, 15*(3), 141-149.

Pels, D. (1995). Have we never been modern? Towards a demontage of Latour's modern constitution. *History of the Human Sciences, 8*(3), 129-141.

Penrose, E. (1959). *The theory of the growth of the firm*. London: Basil Blackwell.

Pentland, B. T. (1989). Use and productivity in personal computing: An empirical test. In *Proceedings of the tenth International Conference on Information Systems*, Boston, MA, (pp. 211-222).

Pentland, B. T., & Feldman, M. S. (2005). Organizational routines as a unit of analysis. *Industrial and Corporate Change, 14*, 793-815.

Pentland, B. T., & Feldman, M. S. (2007). Narrative networks: Patterns of technology and organization. *Organization Science. 18*(5), 781-797.

Penwell, L. W., & Nicholas, J. M. (1995, September). From the first pyramid to space station - an analysis of big technology and mega-projects. In *Proceedings of the AIAA Space Programs and Technologies Conference*.

Peppard, J. (1999). Information management in the global enterprise: An organizing framework. *European Journal of Information Systems, 8*, 77-94.

Peppers, D. (1999). Capturing customers by computer. *International Journal of Retail & Distribution Management, 27*(5), 198-199.

Perrow, C. (1984). *Normal accidents: Living with high-risk technologies.* New York: Basic Books.

Perry, D. K. (1967). Vocational interests and success of computer programmers. *Personnel Psychology, 20*(4), 517-524.

Perry, D. K., & Cannon, W. M. (1968). Vocational interests of female computer programmers. *Journal of Applied Psychology, 52*(1), 31-35.

Perry-Smith, J. (2006). The role of social relationships in facilitating individual creativity. *Academy of Management Journal, 49*, 85-101.

Perry-Smith, J. E. (2006). Social yet creative: The role of social relationships in facilitating individual creativity. *Academy of Management Journal, 49*(1), 85-101.

Pervan, G. (1998). A review of research in group support systems: Leaders, approaches and directions. *Decision Support Systems, 23*(2), 149-159.

Pescovitz, D. (2005). HOWTO write a theory of everything. Retrieved April 2, 2005, from http://www.boingboing.net/2005/08/04/howto-write-a-theory.html

Peterson, D. K., & Kim, C. (2003). Perceptions on IS risks and failure types: A comparison of designers from the United States, Japan and Korea. *Journal of Global Information Management, 11*(3), 19.

Petersson, J (2005). Aren't the fundamental concepts of work systems about actions? In *Proceedings of the Fifth Conference for the Promotion of Research in IT at New Universities and University Colleges in Sweden,* Borlänge.

Petkov, D., & Petkova, O. (2008). The work system model as a tool for understanding the problem in an introductory IS project. *Information Systems Education Journal, 6*(21).

Petkov, D., Edgar-Nevill, D., Madachy, R., & O'Connor, R. (2008), Information systems, software engineering and systems thinking – challenges and opportunities. *International Journal on Information Technologies and the Systems Approach, 1*(1), 62-78.

Petter, S., Straub, D., & Rai, A. (2007). Specifying formative constructs in information systems research. *MIS Quarterly, 31*(4), 623-656.

Pettigrew, A. M. (1985). Contextualist research and the study of organizational change processes. In E. Mumford, et al. (Eds.), *Research methods in information systems.* New York: North Holland.

Pettigrew, A. M. (1987). Context and action in the transformation of the firm. *Journal of Management Studies, 24*(6), 649-670.

Pettigrew, A. M. (1990). Longitudinal field research on change: Theory and practice. *Organization Science, 1*(3), 267-292.

Phang, C. W., Sutanto, J., Li, Y., & Kankanhalli, A. (2005). Senior citizens' adoption of e-government: In quest of the antecedents of perceived usefulness. In *Proceedings of the 38th Hawaii International Conference on System Sciences.*

Phelps, R., & Mok, M. (1999). Managing the risks of intranet implementation: An empirical study of user satisfaction. *Journal of Information Technology, 14*, 39-52.

Philipps, C., & Meeker, M. (2000). *The B2B internet report: Collaborative commerce.* Morgan Stanley Dean Bitter Research.

Phythian, G. J., & King, M. (1992). Developing an expert system for tender enquiry evaluation: A case study. *European Journal of Operational Research, 56*, 15-29.

Piccoli, G., Applegate, L. M., & Dev, C. S. (2008). *Hilton hotels: Brand differentiation through customer relationship management* (Reference No. 9-809-029). Cambridge, MA: Harvard Business Publishing.

Piccoli, G., Brohman, K., Watson, R. T., & Parasuraman, A. (2004). Net-based customer service systems: Evolution and revolution in web site functionalities. *Decision Sciences, 35*(3), 423-455.

Piccoli, G., Spalding, B. R., & Ives, B. (2001). The customer service lift cycle: A framework for Internet use in support of customer service. *Cornell Hotel and Restaurant Administration Quarterly, 42*(3), 38-45.

Pickering, A. (Ed.). (1992). *Science as practice and culture.* Chicago: The University of Chicago Press.

Picot, A. (1991). Ein neuer Ansatz zur Gestaltung der Leistungstiefe. *Zeitschrift für betriebswirtschaftliche Forschung, 43*, 336-359.

Pierson, J. (2006). Domestication at work in small businesses. In T. Berker, M. Hartmann, Y. Punie, & K. Ward (Eds.), *Domestication of media and technologies*. UK: Open University Press.

Pijpers, G. G. M., & van Montfort, K. (2006). An investigation of factors that influence senior executives to accept innovations in information technology. *International Journal of Management, 23*(1), 11-23

Pinch, T. F., & Bijker, W. E. (1984). The social construction of facts and artifacts: Or how the sociology of science and the sociology of technology might benefit each other. In W. E. Bijker, et al. (Eds.), *The social construction of technology systems. New directions in the sociology and history of technology*. The MICT Press.

Piterman, L. (2000). Methodological/ethical issues and general practice research. *Australian Family Physician, 29*(9), 890-891.

Pitt, J., Guerin, F., & Stergiou, C. (2000). *Protocols and intentional specifications of multi-party agent conversions for brokerage and auctions*. Paper presented at the International Conference on Autonomous Agents, Barcelona, Spain.

Png, I. P. L., Tan, B. C. Y., & Wee, K. L. (2001). Dimensions of national culture and corporate adoption of IT infrastructure. *IEEE Transactions on Engineering Management, 48*(1), 36-45.

Podolny, J. M., & Baron, J. N. (1997). Resources and relationships: Social networks and mobility in the workplace. *American Sociological Review, 62*(5), 673-693.

Polak, F. L. (1973). *The image of the future*. Amsterdam: Elsevier.

Polanyi, M. (1966). *The tacit dimension*. New York: Harper Torchbooks.

Poole, M. S., & DeSanctis, G. (1990). Understanding the use of group decision support systems: The theory of adaptive structuration. In J. Fulk & C. Steinfield (Eds.), *Organizations and communication technology* (pp. 173-193). Newbury Park, CA: Sage Publications.

Poole, M. S., & Van de Ven, A. H. (1989). Toward a general theory of innovation processes. In A. H. Van de Ven, H. L. Angle, & M. S. Poole (Eds.), *Research on the management of innovation: The Minnesota studies*. New York: Harper & Row.

Popper, K. (1979). *Objective knowledge - an evolutionary approach*. Oxford.

Popper, K. R. (1992). *The logic of scientific discovery*. New York: Routledge.

Porter, M. E. (1985). The value chain and competitive advantage. In *Competitive advantage: Creating and sustaining superior performance* (pp. 33-61). Free Press.

Portes, A. (1998). Social capital: Its origins and applications in modern sociology. *Annual Review of Sociology, 24*, 1-24.

Power, D. J. (2003). The maturing IS discipline: Institutionalizing our domain of inquiry. *Communications of AIS, 2003*(12), 539-545.

Pozzebon, M. (2004). The influence of a structurationist perspective on strategic management research. *Journal of Management Studies, 41*(2), 247-272.

Pozzebon, M., & Pinsonneault, A. (2005). Challenges in conducting empirical work using structuration theory: Learning from ICT research. *Organization Studies, 26*(9), 1353-1376.

Pozzebon, M., Titah, R., & Pinsonneault, A. (2006). Combining social shaping of technology and communicative action theory for understanding rhetorical closure in IT. *Information Technology & People, 19*(3), 244-271.

Prahalad, C. K., & Bettis, R. A. (1986). The dominant logic: A new linkage between diversity and performance. *Strategic Management Journal, 7*, 485-501.

Prasad, J., Enns, H. G., & Ferratt, T. W. (2007). One size does not fit all: Managing IT employees' employment arrangements. *Human Resource Management, 46*(3), 349-372.

Prattipati, S. (2003). Adoption of e-governance: Differences between countries in the use of online government services. *Journal of American Academy of Business, 3*(1), 386-401.

Priem, R. L., & Butler, J. E. (2001). Is the resource-based 'view' a useful perspective for strategic management research? *Academy Management Review, 26*(1), 22-40.

Pries-Heje, J. (1992). Three barriers for continuing use of computer-based tools in information systems development: A grounded theory approach. *Scandinavian Journal of Information Systems, 4,* 119-136.

Purao, S. (2002). *Design research in the technology of information systems: Truth or dare* (Working Paper). Atlanta: GSU Department of CIS.

Putnam, R. D. (1995). Bowling alone: America's declining social capital. *Journal of Democracy, 6*(1), 65.

Putnam, R. D. (2000). *Bowling alone: The collapse and revival of American community.* New York: Simon and Schuster.

Quinn, R. E., Faerman, S. R., Thompson, M. P., & McGrath, M. R. (1996). *Becoming a master manager* (2nd ed.). New York: John Wiley & Sons.

Rachel, J., & Woolgar, S. (1995). The discursive structure of the social-technical divide: The example of information systems development. *The Sociological Review, 43*(2), 251-273.

Raghavan, S., & Chand, D. (1989). Diffusing software-engineering methods. *IEEE Software, 6*(4), 81-90.

Rains, E. (1991). Function points in an ADA object-oriented design? *ACM SIGPLAN OOPS Messenger, 2*(4), 23-25.

Rainwater, J. (2002). Herding cats: A primer for programmers who lead programmers. NY, USA: Springer-Verlag.

Ramiller, N. C. (2005). Animating the concept of business process in the core course in information systems. *Journal of Informatics Education Research, 3*(2).

Ramirez, A. (1993, March 31). Teller machines inspire a new kiosk business. *The New York Times.*

Ranson, S., Hinings, B., & Greenwood, R. (1980). The structuring of organizational structures. *Administrative Science Quarterly, 25,* 1-17.

Rao, M. T. (2004). Key issues for global IT sourcing: Country and individual factors. *Information Systems Management, 21*(3), 16-21.

Rappaport, A. (1986). Creating shareholder value: A guide for managers and investors. New York: The Free Press.

Rawstorne, P. R. G. (2005). *A systematic analysis of the theory of reasoned action, the theory of planned behaviour and the technology acceptance model when applied to the prediction and explanation of information systems use in mandatory usage contexts.* Unpublished doctoral dissertation, University of Wollongong.

Ray, G., Muhanna, W. A., & Barney, J. B. (2005). Information technology and the performance of the customer service process: A resource-based analysis. *MIS Quarterly, 29*(4), 625-652.

Rayport, J. G., & Jaworski, B. J. (2004). Best face forward. *Harvard Business Review, 82*(12), 47-58.

Reagan-Cirincione, P. (1994). Improving the accuracy of group judgment: A process intervention combining group facilitation, social judgment analysis, and information technology. *Organizational Behavior & Human Decision Processes, 58*(2), 246-270.

Reagans, R., & Zuckerman, E. W. (2001). Networks, diversity, and productivity: The social capital of corporate r&d teams. *Organization Science, 12*(4), 502-517.

Reddick, C. G. (2006). Information resource managers and e-government effectiveness: A survey of Texas state agencies. *Government Information Quarterly, 23,* 249-266.

Reed, M.I. (1997). In praise of duality and dualism: rethinking agency and structure in organizational analysis. *Organization Studies, 18*(1), 21-42.

Reich, B. H., & Benbasat, I. (2000). Factors that influence the social dimension of alignment between business and information technology objectives. *MIS Quarterly, 24*(1), 81-113.

Reijswoud, V. E. v., Mulder, H. B. F., & Dietz, J. L. G. (1999). Communicative action-based business process and information systems modelling with DEMO. *Information Systems Journal, 9*(2), 117-138.

Resta, P. (2008). Activity theory framework for implementation of a laptop initiative in teacher education. In K. McFerrin, R. Weber, R. Carlsen, & D. A. Willis (Eds.), *Proceedings of Society for Information Technology and Teacher Education International Conference 2008* (pp. 2203-2209). Chesapeake, VA: AACE.

Reynolds, T. J., & Gutman, J. (1988). Laddering theory, method, analysis and interpretation. *Journal of Advertising Research, 28,* 11-31.

Richards, B., et al. (1999). *Information technology in general practice: A monograph commissioned by the general practice branch of the Commonwealth Department of health and Ageing.* Commonwealth Department of Health and Ageing.

Richardson, H. (2005). Consuming passions in the global knowledge economy. In D. Howcroft & E. Trauth (Eds.), *Handbook of critical research in information systems* (pp. 272-299). Cheltenham, UK: Edward Elgar.

Richardson, H. (2005, December 11-14). *Making the links: Domestication of ICT's in the global knowledge economy.* In D. Avison, D. Galletta, & J. I. DeGross (Eds.), *Proceedings of the 26th International Conference on Information Systems,* Las Vegas, Nevada.

Richardson, H. (2006, July). Space invaders: Time raiders: Gendered technologies in gendered UK households'. In J. Kendall, D. Howcroft, E. Trauth, T. Butler, B. Fitzgerald, & J. I. DeGross (Eds.), *Social inclusion: Societal and organisational implications for information systems.* Springer-Verlag.

Riemenschneider, C. K., Harrison, D. A., & Mykytyn, P. P. (2003). Understanding IT adoption decisions in small business: Integrating current theories. *Information & Management, 40,* 269-285.

Rittel, H. & Webber, M. (1984). Planning problems are wicked problems. In *Developments in design methodology* (N. Cross ed.) (pp. 135-144). New York: Wiley.

Robbins, H., & Finley, M. (1998). *Why change doesn't work.* London: Orion Publishing.

Robbins, J. (2005). Contexts, collaboration, and cultural tools: A sociocultural perspective on researching children's thinking. *Contemporary Issues in Early Childhood, 6*(2), 140-149.

Robbins, S. S., & Stylianou, A. C. (2001). A study of cultural differences in global corporate web sites. *Journal of Computer Information Systems, 42*(2), 3.

Robbins, S. S., & Stylianou, A. C. (2003). Global corporate web sites: An empirical investigation of content and design. *Information & Management, 40*(3), 205-212.

Robey, D., & Sahay, S. (1996). Transforming work through information technology: A comparative case study of geographic information systems in county government. *Information Systems Research, 7*(1), 93-110.

Robichaux, B., & Cooper, R. (1998). GSS participation: A cultural examination. *Information & Management, 33*(6), 287-300.

Robson, C. (2002). *Real world research* (2nd ed.). Oxford, UK: Blackwell.

Rogers, E. M. & Shoemaker, F. F. (1971). *Communication of innovations: A cross-cultural approach* (2nd ed.). New York: The Free Press.

Rogers, E. M. (2003). *Diffusion of innovations* (5th ed.). New York: Free Press/Simon & Schuster, Inc.

Ropohl, G. (1999). Philosophy of socio-technical systems. In *Society for philosophy and technology* (Vol. 4).

Rosenberg, N. (1969). The direction of technological change: Inducement mechanisms and focusing devices. In N. Rosenberg (Ed.), *Economic development and cultural change* (Vol. 18, No. 1, Part 1) (pp. 1-24). Chicago: The University of Chicago Press.

Rosenbloom, J. L., Ash, R. A., Dupont, B., & Coder, L. (2008). Why are there so few women in information *technology?* Assessing the role of personality in career choices. *Journal of Economic Psychology, 29*(4), 543-554.

Rosenthal, R. (1979). The "file drawer problem" and tolerance for null results. *Psychological Bulletin, 86*(3), 638-641.

Rosenthal, R., & Rosnow, R. L. (2008). *Essentials of behavioural research.* New York: McGrawHill.

Ross, J. W. & Vitale, M. R. (2000). The ERP revolution: Surviving vs thriving. *Information Systems Frontiers, 2*(2), 233-241.

Rossignoli, C., & Mola, L. (2004, June 21-23). E.M.P. as enabler of new organisational architectures: An Italian case study. In *Proceedings of the 17th Bled eConference, eGlobal,* Bled, Slovenia.

Rotter, J. B. (1966). Generalized expectancies for internal versus external control of reinforcement. *Psychological Monographs: General and Applied, 80*(609).

Rouse, P. D. (2001). Voluntary turnover related to information technology professionals: A review of rational and instinctual models. *International Journal of Organizational Analysis, 9*(3), 281-290.

Rowley, J. (2000). Loyalty kiosks: Making loyalty cards work. *British Food Journal, 102*(5/6), 390-397.

Rowley, J., & Slack, F. (2003). Kiosks in retailing: The quiet revolution. *International Journal of Retail & Distribution Management, 31*(6/7), 329-339.

Rowlinson, M. (1997). *Organisations and institutions.* London: Macmillan Press Ltd.

Rugg, G., & McGeorge, P. (1995). Laddering. *Expert Systems, 12*, 339-346.

Rugg, G., Eva, M., Mahmood, A., Rehman, N., Andrews, S., & Davies, S. (2002). Eliciting information about organizational culture via laddering. *Information Systems Journal, 12*, 215-229.

Rumelt, R. P. (1984). Towards a strategic theory of the firm. In R. B. Lamb (Ed.), *Competitive strategic management* (pp. 556-570). Englewood Cliffs, NJ: Prentice Hall.

Rutkowski, A. F., & van de Walle, B. (2005). Cultural dimensions and prototypical criteria for multi-criteria decision support in electronic markets: A comparative analysis of two job markets. *Group Decision & Negotiation., 14*(4), 285-306.

Rymer, J. R., & Moore, C. (2007, September). *The dynamic business applications imperative.* Forrester Research.

Sacks, H. (1995). *Lectures on conversation.* Hoboken, NJ: Blackwell.

Sahay, S. (1998). Implementation of GIS technology in India: Some issues of time and space. *Accounting, Management and Information Technologies, 8*(2-3), 147-188.

Sahay, S., & Avgerou, C. (2002). Introducing the special issue on information and communication technologies in developing countries, *Information Society, 18*(2), 73-76.

Sahay, S., & Robey, D. (1996). Organizational context, social interpretation, and the implementation and consequences of geographic information systems. *Ac-counting, Management and Information Technology, 6*(4), 255-282.

Sakowicz, M. (2007). *How to evaluate e-government? Different methodologies and methods.* Retrieved 2007, from, http://unpan1.un.org/intradoc/groups/public/documents/NISPAcee/UNPAN009 486.pdf

Salgado, J. F. (1997). The five factor model of personality and job performance in the European Community. *Journal of Applied Psychology, 82*(1), 607-620.

Salomann, H., Dous, M., Kolbe, L., & Brenner, W. (2007). Self-service revisited: How to balance high-tech and high-touch in customer relationships. *European Management Journal, 25*(4), 310-319.

Santas, G. X. (Ed.). (2006). *The Blackwell guide to Plato's Republic.* Malden, MA: Blackwell Publishing Ltd.

SAP and Deloitte Sued by FoxMeyer. (1998, August 27). *The New York Times.* Retrieved February 17, 2007, from http://query.nytimes.com/gst/fullpage.html?res=9A05E7D7123CF934A1575BC0A96E958260

Sarker, S., Sarker, S., & Sidorova, A. (2006). Actor-networks and business process change failure: An interpretive case study. *Journal of Management Information Systems, 23*(1), 51-86.

Sassone, P. G. (1988, April). Cost benefit analysis of information systems: A survey of methodologies. In Proceedings of the Conference Sponsored by ACM SIGOIS and IEEECS TC-OA on Office information systems (Vol. 9, pp. 126-133).

Satorra, A. C., & Bentler, P. M. (1988). *Scaling corrections for chi-square statistics in covariance structure analysis.* Paper presented at the Proceedings of the Business and Economics Sections, Alexandria, VA.

Saviotti, P. P. (1996). Systems theory and technological change. *Futures, Dec.,* 773-785.

Saviotti, P. P., & Metcalfe, J. S. (1991). *Evolutionary theories of economic and technological change: Present status and future prospects.* Reading, UK: Harwood Academic Publishers.

Savvas, A. (2004). Work stress at record high. *Computer Weekly,* 4.

Sawy, O. A. E., & Bowles, G. (1997). Redesigning the customer support process for the electronic economy: Insights from storage dimensions. *MIS Quarterly, 21*(4), 457-483.

Sayer, A. (1992). *Method in social science: A realist approach* (2ⁿᵈ ed.). London: Routledge.

Sayer, A. (2000). *Realism and social science*. London: Sage.

Schaffer, S. (1991). The eighteenth brumaire of Bruno Latour. *Studies in the History and Philosophy of Science, 22*(1), 174-192.

Scheer, J. W., & Sewell, K. W. (Eds.). (2006) *Creative construing: Personal constructions in the arts*. Giessen, Germany: Psychosozial–Verlag.

Schelling, T. (1989). The mind as a consuming organ. In D. Bell, H. Raiffa, & A. Tversty (Eds.), *Decision making. Descriptve, normative, and prescriptive interactions* (pp. 343-357). Cambridge, UK: Cambridge University Press.

Schmidt, R., Lyytinen, K., Keil, M., & Cule, P. (2001). Identifying software project risks: An international Delphi study. *Journal of Management Information Systems, 17*(4), 5-36.

Schmitt, B. H. (1999). *Experiential marketing: How to get customers to sense, feel, think, act, and relate to your company and brands*. New York: The Free Press.

Schmitt, B. H. (2003). *Customer experience management: A revolutionary approach to connecting with your customers*. Hoboken, NJ: John Wiley and Sons.

Schneberger, S., & Wade, M. (2006). *Theories used in IS research*. Retrieved from http://www.istheory.yorku.ca

Schneider, B., White, S. S., & Paul, M. C. (1998). Linking service climate and customer perceptions of service quality: Tests of a casual model. *Journal of Applied Psychology, 83*(2), 150-163.

Schneider, K. (2002). Non-technical factors are key to ensuring project success. *Computer Weekly*.

Schoop, M. (2001). An introduction to the language-action perspective. *ACM SIGGROUP Bulletin, 22*(2), 3-8.

Schoop, M. (2003). A language-action approach to electronic negotiations. In *Proceedings of the International Working Conference on the Language-action perspective on Communication Modelling (LAP)*.

Schoop, M., & Kethers, S. (2000). *Habermas and Searle in University: Teaching the language-action perspective to undergraduates*. Paper presented at the International Workshop on the Language-action perspective on Communication Modelling (LAP).

Schoop, M., Jertila, A., & List, T. (2003). Negoisst: A negotiation support system for electronic business-to-business negotiations in e-commerce. *Data & Knowledge Engineering, 47*(3), 371-401.

Schultze, U., & Leidner, D. E. (2003). Studying knowledge management in information systems research: Discourses and theoretical assumptions. *MIS Quarterly, 26*(3), 213-242.

Schumpeter, J. (1934). *The theory of economic development*. Cambridge, MA: Harvard University Press.

Schumpeter, J. (1950). *Capitalism, socialism, and democracy* (3ʳᵈ ed.). New York: Harper.

Schuster, D. M., et al. (2003). Involving users in the implementation of an imaging order entry system. *American Medical Informatics Association, 10*(4), 315-321.

Schutz, A. (1970). *On phenomenology and social relations*. Chicago: University of Chicago Press.

Schwaber, K. (2002). When and where agile suceeds. *Cutter IT Journal, 15*(9), 22-27.

Schwandt, T. A. (1994). Constructivist, interpretivist approaches to human inquiry. In N. K. Denzin & Y. S. Lincoln (Eds.), *Handbook of qualitative research* (pp. 118-137). Newbury Park, CA: Sage.

Schware, R., & Deane, A. (2003). Deploying e-government program the strategic importance of 'i' before 'e.' *Info, 5*(4), 10-19.

Scott, J. (2000). *Social network analysis: A handbook* (2ⁿᵈ ed.). Newbury Park, CA: Sage.

Scott, J. E. (1995, February). The measurement of information systems effectiveness: evaluating a measuring instrument. *Data Base Advances, 26*(1), 43-61.

Scott, W. R. (1995). *Institutions and organizations.* Thousand Oaks, CA: Sage Publications Ltd.

Scriven, M. (1976). *Reasoning.* New York: McGraw-Hill.

Searle, J. R. (1969). *Speech acts: An essay in the philosophy of language.* Cambridge, England: Cambridge University.

Searle, J. R., & Vanderveken, D. (1985). *Foundations of illocutionary logic.* Cambridge, England: Cambridge University Press.

Seguin, E. (2000). Bloor, Latour, and the field. *Studies in the History and Philosophy of Science, 31*(3), 503-508.

Seibert, S. E., Kraimer, M. L., & Liden, R. C. (2001). A social capital theory of career success. *Academy of Management Journal, 44,* 219-237.

Seidel, J. V. (1998). *Qualitative data analysis.* Retrieved December 1, 2005, from www.qualisresearch.com

Sein, M., & Ahmad, I. (2001). A framework to study the impact of information and communication technologies on developing countries: The case of cellular phones in Bangladesh. In *Proceedings of BITWORLD 2001,* Cairo, Egypt.

Sejwacz, D., Ajzen, I., & Fishbein, M. (1980). Predicting and understanding weight loss. In I. Ajzen & M. Fishbein (Eds.), *Understanding attitudes and predicting social behavior* (pp. 101-112). Englewood-Cliffs, NJ: Prentice-Hall.

Seligman, M. E. P. (1990). *Learned optimism.* New York: Pocket Books.

Selnes, F., & Hansen, H. (2001). The potential hazard of self-service in developing customer loyalty. *Journal of Service Research, 4*(2), 79-90.

Selznick, P. (1949). *TVA and the grass roots.* Berkley, CA: University of California Press.

Selznick, P. (1957). *Leadership in administration: A sociological interpretation.* New York: Harper and Row.

Seror, A. (1996). Action research for international information technology transfer: A methodology and a network model. *Technovation, 16*(8), 421-429.

Serres, M. (1974). *La traduction.* Paris: Hermes III.

Shankar, D. R. (2007). Anomie among information technology employees. *Journal of Indian Psychology, 25*(1-2), 101-107.

Shannon, C. E. (1948). A mathematical theory of communication. *Bell System Technical Journal, 27*(July, October), 379-423 & 623-656.

Shapiro, S. P. (1987). The social control of impersonal trust. *American Journal of Sociology, 93*(3), 623-658.

Shareef, M. A., Kumar, U., & Kumar, V. (2007), Developing fundamental capabilities for successful e-government implementation. In *Proceedings of the Administrative Sciences Association of Canada Conference,* Ottawa, Canada (pp. 159-177).

Shareef, M. A., Kumar, U., & Kumar, V. (2008). Role of different electronic- commerce (EC) quality factors on purchase decision: A developing country perspective. *Journal of Electronic Commerce Research, 9*(2), 92-113.

Shareef, M. A., Kumar, U., Kumar, V., & Dwivedi, Y. K. (in press). Identifying critical factors for adoption of e-government. *Electronic Government: An International Journal.*

Sharma, S. (1996). *Applied multivariate techniques.* New York: John Wiley & Son, Inc.

Shaw, J. B., & Barrett-Power, E. (1997). A conceptual framework for assessing organization, work group, and individual effectiveness during and after downsizing. *Human Relations, 50*(2), 109-127.

Sheehan, J. (2006). Understanding service sector innovation. *Communications of the ACM, 49*(4), 43-47.

Sheppard, B. H., Hartwick, J., & Warshaw, P. (1988). The theory of reasoned action: A meta-analysis of past research with recommendations for modifications and future research. *Journal of Consumer Research, 15*(3), 325-343.

Sherif, C., Sherif, M., & Nebergall, R. (1965). *Attitude and attitude change: The social judgment-involvement approach.* Philadelphia: Saunders.

Sherif, K., Hoffman, J., & Thomas, B. (2006). Can technology build organizational social capital? The case of a global IT consulting firm. *Information & Management, 43*(7), 795-804.

Shin, B., & Higa, K. (2005). Meeting scheduling: Face-to-face, automatic scheduler, and email based coordination. *Journal of Organizational Computing and Electronic Commerce, 15*(2), 137-159.

Shin, S. K., Gopal, R. D., Sanders, G. L., & Whinston, A. B. (2004). Global software piracy revisited. *Communications of the ACM, 47*(1), 103-107.

Shoib, G., & Nadhakumar, J. (2003). Cross-cultural IS adoption in multinational corporations. *Information Technology for Development, 10*(4), 249-260.

Shore, B., & Venkatachalam, A. (1995). The role of national culture in systems analysis and design. *Journal of Global Information Management, 3*(3), 5-14.

Shostack, G. L. (1977). Breaking free from product marketing. *Journal of Marketing, 41*(2), 73-80.

Siau, K., Sheng, H., & Nah, F. (2004). The value of mobile commerce to customers, In *Proceedings of the Pre ICIS SIGCHI Symposium.*

Silva, L. (2007). Post-positivist review of technology acceptance model. *Journal of the Association for Information Systems, 8*(4), 255-266.

Silver, M., Markus, M. L., & Beath, C. (1995). The information technology interaction model: A foundation for the MBA core course. *MIS Quarterly, 19*(3), 361-390.

Silverstone, R. (Ed.). (2005). *Media, technology and everyday life.* Aldershot, UK: Ashgate.

Simon, E. (Ed.). (1980). *Towards a science of the singular.* Norwich, UK: University of East Anglia.

Simon, F., & Usunier, J. (2007). Cognitive, demographic, and situational determinants of service customer preference for personnel-in-contact over self-service technology. *International Journal of Research in Marketing, 24*(2), 163-173.

Simon, H. A. (1957). *Models of man.* New York: John Wiley & Sons.

Simon, H. A. (1996). *The sciences of the artificial.* Cambridge, MA: The MIT Press.

Sisodia, R. S. (1992). Marketing information and decision support systems for services. *The Journal of Services Marketing, 6*(1), 51-64.

Sivabrovornvatana, N., Siengthai, S., Krairit, D., & Paul, H. (2005). Technology usage, quality management system, and service quality in Thailand. *International Journal of Health Care Quality Assurance, 18*(6/7), 413-423.

Skadberg, Y. X., & Kimmel, J. R. (2004). Visitors' flow experience while browsing a web site: Its measurement, contributing factors, and consequences. *Computers in Human Behavior, 20*(3), 403-422.

Smaling, A. (1987). *Methodological objectivity and qualitative research.* Lisse, The Netherlands: Swets & Zeitlinger.

Smit, J., & Bryant, A. (2000). *Grounded theory method in IS research: Glaser vs. Strauss* (Working Paper IMRIP 2000-7). Retrieved from http://www.leedsmet.ac.uk/inn/2000-7.pdf

Smith, K., Grimm, G., & Gannon, M. (1992). *Dynamics of competitive strategy.* Newbury Park, CA: Sage.

Smith, M. L. (2006). Overcoming theory-practice inconsistencies: Critical realism and information systems research. *Information and Organization, 16*, 191-211.

Snellen, I. (2002). Electronic governance: Implications for citizens, politicians and public servants. *International Review of Administrative Sciences, 68*, 183-198.

Sorebo, O., & Eikebrokk, T. R. (2008). Explaining IS continuance in environments where usage is mandatory. *Computers in Human Behavior, 24*(5), 2357-2371.

Soriyan, H. A. (2004). *A conceptual framework for information systems development methodology for educational and industrial sectors in Nigeria.* Unpublished doctoral dissertation, Obafemi Awolowo University, Ile Ife, Nigeria.

Sparks, D. (2002). Inner conflicts, inner strengths. *Journal of Staff Development, 23*(3), 66-71.

Sparks, P., Shepherd, R., & Frewer, L. J. (1995). Assessing and structuring attitudes toward the use of gene technology in food production: The role of perceived ethical obligation. *Basic and Applied Social Psychology, 16*, 267-285.

Spector, A. J. (1956). Expectations, fulfillment and morale. *Journal of Abnormal and Social Psychology, 52*, 51-56.

Spence, W. (1994). *Innovation: The communication of change in ideas, practices and products.* London: Chapman and Hall.

Spitzer, F. (2001, January). *Principles of random walk* (2nd ed.). Springer.

Spreng, R. A., MacKenzie, S. B., & Olshavsky, R. W. (1996). A reexamination of the determinants of consumer satisfaction. *Journal of Marketing, 60*, 15-28.

Srinivasan, S. S., Anderson, R., & Ponnavolu, K. (2002). Customer loyalty in e-commerce: An exploration of its antecedents and consequences. *Journal of Retailing, 78*(1), 41-50.

Stacey, R. D. (2003). *Strategic management and organizational dynamics.* Harlow, England: Pearson Education Limited.

Stake, R. E. (1995). *The art of case study research.* Thousand Oaks, CA: Sage Publications.

Stake, R. E. (2005). Qualitative case studies. In N. K. Denzin & Y. S. Lincoln (Eds.), *The Sage handbook of qualitative research* (3rd ed.) (pp. 443-466).

Stal, M. (2002). Web services: Beyond component-based computing. *Communications of the ACM, 45*(10), 71-76.

Stamoulis, D., Gouscos, D., Georgiadis, P., & Martakos, D. (2001). Revisiting public information management for effective e-government services. *Information Management & Computer Security, 9*(4), 146-153.

Stamper, R. (1996). Signs, information, norms and systems. In B. Holmqvist, P. B. Andersen, H. Klein, & R. Posner (Eds.), *Signs of work: Semiotics and information processing in organisations* (pp. 349-397). Berlin, Germany: Walter de Gruyter & Co.

Staples, D. S., Wong, I., & Seddon, P. B. (2002). Having expectations of information systems benefits that match received benefits: Does it really matter? *Information & Management, 40*, 115-131.

Star, S. L. (1988). Introduction: The sociology of science and technology. *Social Problems, 35*(3), 197-205.

Statt, D. (2004). *Psychology and the world of work* (2nd ed.). Hampshire, UK: Palgrave Macmillan.

Steiger, J. H. (1990). Structural model evaluation and modification: An interval estimation approach. *Multivariate Behavioral Research, 25*(2), 173-180.

Stein, T. (1998, August 31). SAP sued over R/3. *InformationWeek*.

Steinwachs, K. (1999). Information and culture - the impact of national culture on information processes. *Journal of Information Science, 25*(3), 193-204.

Stengers, I. (1997). *Power and invention: Situating science* (P. Bains, Trans.). Minneapolis, MN: University of Minnesota Press.

Steyaert, J. (2000). Local government online and the role of the resident. *Social Science Computer Review, 18*, 3-16.

Steyaert, J. C. (2004). Measuring the performance of electronic government services. *Information & Management, 41*(3), 369-375.

Stone, A. A., Kennedy-Moore, E., Newman, M. G., Greenberg, M., & Neale, J. M. (1992). Conceptual and methodological issues in current coping assessments. In B. N. Carpenter (Ed.), *Personal coping: Theory, research, and application* (pp. 15-39). Westport, CT: Praeger.

Storey, J. A. (2000). 'Fracture lines' in the career environment. In A. Collin & R. A. Young (Eds.), *The future of career.* Cambridge, UK: Cambridge University.

Stouffer, S. A. (1941). Notes on the case-study and the unique case. *Sociometry, 4*, 349-357.

Straub, D. (1994). The effect of culture on IT diffusion: E-mail and FAX in Japan and the US. *Information Systems Research, 5*(1), 23-47.

Straub, D. W., & Burton-Jones, A. (2007). Veni, vedi, vici: Breaking the TAM logjam. *Journal of the Association for Information Systems, 8*(4), 223-229.

Straub, D. W., & Watson R.T. (2001). Research commentary: Transformational issues in researching IS an net-enabled organizations. *Information System Research, 12*(4), 337-345.

Straub, D., Boudreau, M.-C., & Gefen, D. (2004). Validation guidelines for IS positivist research. *Communications of the Association for Information Systems, 13*(24), 380-427.

Straub, D., Keil, M., & Brenner, W. (1997). Testing the technology acceptance model across cultures: A three country study. *Information & Management, 33*, 1-11.

Straub, D., Limayem, M., & Karahanna-Evaristo, E. (1995). Measuring system usage: Implications for IS theory testing. *Management Science, 41*(8), 1328-1342.

Straub, D., Loch, K., Evaristo, R., Karahanna, E., & Srite, M. (2002). Toward a theory-based measurement of culture. *Journal of Global Information Management, 10*(1), 13-23.

Strauss, A. L. (1978). A social world perspective. In N. K. Denzin (Ed.), *Studies in symbolic interaction* (Vol. 1, pp. 119-128). Greenwich, CT: Jai Press Inc.

Strauss, A. L. (1983). *Continual permutations of action.* New York: Aldine de Gruyter.

Strauss, A. L., & Corbin, J. M. (1998). *Basics of qualitative research: Techniques and procedures for developing grounded theory.* Thousand Oaks, CA: Sage.

Strebel, P. (1998). Why do employees resist change. In J. Kotter, J. Collins, R. Pascale, K. Duck, J. Porras, & A. Athos (Eds.), *Harvard Business Review on change* (pp. 139-157). MA, USA: Harvard Business School Press.

Stufflebeam, D. L. (2001). Evaluation models. *New Directions for Evaluation, 89*(Spring), 7-98.

Sturnberg, J., et al. (2003). Rethinking general practice for the 21st century: The patient counts! *Australian Family Physician, 32*(12), 1028-1031.

Su, S. Y. W., Lam, H., Lee, M., Bai, S., & Shen, Z.-J. M. (2001). *An information infrastructure and e-services for supporting Internet-based scalable e-business enterprises.* Paper presented at the IEEE International Enterprise Distributed Object Computing Conference (EDOC).

Suchman, L. (1987). *Plans and situated action.* Cambridge, England: Cambridge University Press.

Suchman, L. (1994). Do categories have politics? The language/action perspective reconsidered. *Computer Supported Cooperative Work (CSCW), 2*(3), 177-190.

Sue, G. (1993). Mature students learning statistics: The activity theory perspective. *Mathematics Education Research Journal, 5*(1), 34-49.

Surry, D. W., & Farquhar, J. D. (1997, May). Diffusion theory and instructional technology. *Journal of Instructional Science and Technology, 2*(1).

Susarla, A., Barua, A., & Whinston, A. B. (2003). Understanding the service component of application service provision: An empirical analysis of satisfaction with ASP services. *MIS Quarterly, 27*, 91-123.

Sutton, R. I., & Rafaeli, A. (1988). Untangling the relationship between displayed emotions and organizational sales: The case of convenience stores. *Academy of Management Journal, 31*(3), 461-487.

Sutton, R. I., & Staw, B. M. (1995). What theory is not. *Administrative Science Quarterly, 40*(3), 371-384.

Swanson, E. B., & Dans, E. (2000). System life expectancy and the maintenance effort: Exploring their equilibration. *MIS Quarterly, 24*(2), 277-297.

Swanson, E., & Ramiller, N. (2004). Innovating mindfully with information technology. *MIS Quarterly, 28*(4), 553-583.

Swartout, W., & Van Lent, M. (2003). Making a game of system design. *Communications of the ACM, 46*(7), 32-39.

Sweller, J. (1988). Cognitive load during problem solving: Effects on learning. *Cognitive Science, 12*(2), 257-285.

Szajna, B., & Scamell. R. W. (1993). Information system user expectations on their performance and perceptions. *MIS Quarterly, 17*(4), 493-516.

Szulanski, G. (1996). Exploring internal stickiness: Impediments to the transfer of best practice within the firm. *Strategic Management Journal, 17*, 27-43.

Takeda, H., Veerkamp, P., Tomiyama, T., & Yoshikawam, H. (1990). Modeling Design Processes. *AI Magazine* (Winter), 37-48.

Taleb, N. N. (2007). *The black swan: The impact of the highly improbable.* London: Penguin Books Ltd.

Tan, B. C. Y., Watson, R. T., & Wei, K.-K. (1995). National culture and group support systems: Filtering communication to dampen power differentials. *European Journal of Information Systems, 4*, 82–92.

Tan, B. C. Y., Wei, K. K., Watson, R. T., Clapper, D. L., & McLean, E. R. (1998). Computer-mediated communication and majority influence: Assessing the impact in an individualistic and a collectivistic culture. *Management Science, 44*(9), 1263-1278.

Tan, B., Watson, R., & Wei, K.-K. (1995). National culture and group support systems: Filtering communication to dampen power differentials. *European Journal of Information Systems, 4*, 82-92.

Tan, B., Wei, K.-K., Watson, R., & Walczuch, R. (1998). Reducing status effects with computer-mediated communication: Evidence from two distinct national cultures. *Journal of Management Information Systems, 15*(1), 119-141.

Tan, F. B., & Gallupe, R. B. (2006). Aligning business and information systems thinking: A cognitive approach. *IEEE Transactions on Engineering Management, 53*, 223-237.

Tan, F. B., & Hunter, M. G. (2002). The repertory grid technique: A method for the study of cognition in information systems. *MIS Quarterly, 26*, 39-57.

Tan, F. B., & Tung, L. L. (2003). Exploring website evaluation criteria using the repertory grid technique: A web designer's perspective. In *Proceedings of the Second Annual Workshop on HCI Research in MIS*, Seattle, WA.

Tan, M. T. K., & Hall, W. (2007). Beyond Theoretical and methodological pluralism in interpretive IS research: The example of symbolic interactionist ethnography. *Communications of AIS, 2007*(19), 589-610.

Tanriverdi, H. (2005). Information technology relatedness, knowledge management capability, and performance of multibusiness firms. *MIS Quarterly, 29*(2), 311-334.

Taylor Nelson Sofres. (2002). *Annual global report on government online an international perspective.* Retrieved from http://unpan1.un.org/intradoc/groups/public/documents/ APCITY/UNPAN007044.pdf

Taylor, S. E., Helgeson, V. S., Reed, G. M., & Skokan, L. A. (1991). Self-generated feeling of control and adjustment to physical illness. *Journal of Social Issues, 47*, 91-109.

Taylor, S., & Todd, P. A. (1995). Decomposition and crossover effects in the theory of planned behavior: A study of consumer adoption intentions. *International Journal of Research in Marketing, 12*, 137-156.

Taylor, S., & Todd, P.A. (1995). Understanding information technology usage: A test of competing models. *Information Systems Research, 6*(2), 144-176.

Teece, D. J., & Pisano, G. (1998). The dynamic capabilities of firms: An introduction. In G. Dosi, D. J. Teece, & J. Chytry (Eds.), *Technology, organisation, and competitiveness: Perspectives on industrial and corporate change* (pp. 17-66). New York: Oxford University Press Inc.

Teece, D. J., Pisano G., & Shuen, A. (1990). *Firm capabilities, resources and the concept of strategy* (CCC Working Paper No. 90 8). CA: University of California at Berkeley.

ten Have, S., ten Have, W., Stevens, F., van der Elst, M., & Pol-Coyne, F. (2003). *Key management models: The management tools and practices that will improve your business.* Harlow, Essex, UK: Financial Times Prentice Hall/Pearson Education Limited.

Teo, T. S. H., Devadoss, P., & Pan, S. L. (2006). Towards a holistic perspective of customer relationship management (CRM) implementation: A case study of the housing and development board, Singapore. *Decision Support Systems, 42*(3), 1613-1627.

Tesch, D., Jiang, J. J., & Klein, G. (2003). The impact of information system personnel skill deiscrepancies on stakeholder satisfaction. *Decision Sciences, 34*, 107-129.

Thanasankit, T. (2002). Requirements engineering: Exploring the influence of power and Thai values. *European Journal of Information Systems, 11*(2), 128.

Thatcher, J. B., Stepina, L. P., Srite, M., & Liu, Y. M. (2003). Culture, overload and personal innovativeness with information technology: Extending the nomological net. *Journal of Computer Information Systems, 44*(1), 74-81.

Thatcher, J. B.. & Perrewe, P. L. (2002). An empirical examination of individual traits as antecedents to computer anxiety and computer self-efficacy. *MIS Quarterly, 26*(4), 381-396.

The Career Key. (2008). *Holland's six personality types*. Retrieved Jun 10, 2008, from http://www.careerkey.org/asp/your_personality/hollands_6_personalitys.asp

The Standish Group International, Inc. (1995). *The CHAOS report*. The Standish Group International, Inc.

The Standish Group International, Inc. (2001). *Extreme CHAOS report*. The Standish Group International, Inc.

Thong, J., Yap, C.-S., & Raman, K. (1996). Top management support, external expertise and information systems implementation in small businesses. *Information Systems Research, 7*(2), 248-267.

Thorelli, H. B. (1986). Networks: Between markets and hierarchies. *Strategic Management Journal, 7*.

Thull, J. (2005). *The prime solution*. Dearborn Trade Publishing.

Titah, R., & Barki, H. (2005). E-government adoption and acceptance: A literature review. *HEC Montréal*.

Toffler, A. (1970). *Future shock*. New York: Bantam Books.

Tönnies, F. (2001). Gemeinschaft and gesellschaft: An essay on communism and socialism as historical social systems. In *Community and civil society*. Cambridge, UK: Cambridge University Press.

Torkzadeh, G., Chang, J. C., & Hansen, G. W. (2006). Identifying issues in customer relationship management at Merck-Medco. *Decision Support Systems, 42*(2), 1116-1130.

Tornatzky, L. G., & Fleishcher, M. (1990). *The process of technological innovation*. Lexington, MA: Lexington Books.

Tornatzky, L. G., & Klein, K. J. (1982). Innovation characteristics and innovation adoption-implementation: A meta-analysis of findings. *IEEE Transactions on Engineering Management, 29*, 28-45.

Tractinsky, N., & Jarvenpaa, S. (1995). Information systems design decisions in a global versus domestic context. *MIS Quarterly, 19*(4), 507-534.

Traum, D. R. (1999). Speech acts for dialogue agents. In M. Wooldridge & A. Rao (Eds.), *Foundations of rational agency* (Vol. 14, pp. 169 - 202). Kluwer Academic Publishers.

Trauth, E., & Jessup, L. (2000). Understanding computer-mediated discussions: Positivist and interpretive analyses of group support system use. *MIS Quarterly, 24*(1), 43-79.

Trauth, E., Farwell, D. W., & Lee, D. (1993). The IS expectation gap: Industry expectations versus academic preparation. *MIS Quarterly, 13*, 293-307.

Trauth, E. M., (Ed.). (2001). *Qualitative research in IS: Issues and trends*. Hershey, PA: Idea Group Publishing.

Treiblmaier, H., Pinterits, A., & Floh, A. (2004). Antecedents of the adoption of epayment services in the public sector. In *Proceedings of the 25th International Conference on Information Systems*.

Trevino, L. K., & Webster, J. (1992). Flow in computer-mediated communication, *Communication Research, 19*(5), 539-573.

Trist, E. L., & Bamforth K. W. (1951). Some social and psychological consequences of the longwall methods of coal-getting. *Human Relations, 14*, 3-38.

Trompenaars, F., & Prud'homme, P. (2004). *Managing change across corporate cultures*. Chichester, UK: Capstone.

Truex, D. P., & Klein H. K. (1991). A rejection of structure as a basis for information systems development. In R. K. Stamper, P, Kerola, R. Lee, & K. Lyytinen, (Eds.), *Collaborative work, social communications, and information systems*. Amsterdam: Elsevier.

Truex, D. P., Baskerville, R., et al. (1999). Growing systems in emergent organisations. *Communications of the ACM, 42*(8).

Tsai, H. Y., Compeau, D., & Haggerty, N. (2007). Of races to run and battles to be won: Technical skill updating, stress, and coping of IT professionals. *Human Resources Management, 46*(3), 395-409.

Tsai, W. T. (2005). *Service-oriented system engineering: A new paradigm*. Paper presented at the International Workshop on Service-Oriented System Engineering (SOSE).

Tsai, W., & Ghoshal, S. (1998). Social capital and value creation: The role of intrafirm networks. *Academy of Management Journal, 41*(4), 464.

Tseng, J. C. R., & Hwang, G. (2007). Development of an automatic customer service system on the internet. *Electronic Commerce Research and Applications, 6*(1), 19.

Tsikriktsis, N. (2002). Does Culture influence website quality expectations? An empirical study. *Journal of Service Research, 5*(2), 101-112.

Tsoukas, H. (1989). The validity of idiographic research explanations. *Academy of Management Review, 14*(4), 551-561.

Tung, L. L., & Quaddus, M. A. (2002). Cultural differences explaining the differences in results in GSS: Implications for the next decade. *Decision Support Systems, 33*(2), 177-199.

Tung, L. L., & Rieck, O. (2005). Adoption of electronic government services among business organizations in Singapore. *Journal of Strategic Information Systems, 14*, 417-440.

Tuomi-Gröhn, T., & Engeström, Y. (Eds.). (2003). *Between school and work. New perspectives on transfer and boundary-crossing.* Amsterdam: Pergamon/Elsevier Science.

Turner, J., & Muller, R. (2003). On the nature of the project as a temporary organization. *International Journal of Project Management, 21*(1), 1-8.

Tyre, M. J., & Orlikowski, W. J. (1994). Windows of opportunity: Temporal patterns of technological adaptation in organizations. *Organization Science, 5*(1), 98-118.

Tyre, M. J., & Orlikowski, W. J. (1996). The episodic process of learning by using. *International Journal of Technology Management, 11*(7/8), 790-798.

Ulrich, D. (1998). Intellectual capital = competence x commitment. *Sloan Management Review, 39*(2), 15-26.

Umapathy, K. (2007). *A study of language-action perspective as a theoretical framework for Web services.* Paper presented at the IEEE Congress on Services, Salt Lake City, Utah, USA.

Umapathy, K., & Purao, S. (2004). *Service-oriented computing: An opportunity for the language-action perspective?* Paper presented at the International Working Conference on the Language-action perspective on Communication Modelling (LAP).

Umapathy, K., & Purao, S. (2007a). A theoretical investigation of the emerging standards for Web services. *Information Systems Frontiers, 9*(1), 119-134.

Umapathy, K., & Purao, S. (2007b). *Towards a theoretical foundation for Web services - the language-action perspective (LAP) approach.* Paper presented at the IEEE International Conference on Services Computing (SCC), Salt Lake City, Utah, USA.

United States Department of Labor Employment and Training Administration. (1991). *Dictionary of occupational titles.* Indianapolis, IN: JIST Works.

Urquhart, C. (1999). Themes in early requirements gathering: The case of the analyst the client and the student assistance scheme. *Information Technology and People, 12*(1), 44-70.

Urquhart, C. (2001). An encounter with grounded theory: Tackling the practical and philosophical issues. In E. M. Trauth (Ed.), *Qualitative research in IS: Issues and trends.* Hershey, PA: Idea Group Publishing.

Urquhart, C. (2001). Analysts and clients in organisational contexts: A conversational perspective. *The Journal of Strategic Information Systems, 10*(3), 243-262.

Urquhart, C. (2002). Regrounding grounded theory? - Or reinforcing old prejudices? A brief reply to Bryant. *The Journal of Information Technology Theory and Application, 4*(3), 43-54.

Uzzi, B. (1997). Social structure and competition in interfirm networks: The paradox of embeddedness. *Administrative Science Quarterly, 42*(1), 35-67.

Valentine, E. R. (1982). *Conceptual issues in psychology.* London: George Allen & Unwin.

Van Aken, J. E. (2004) Management research based on the paradigm of design sciences: The quest for field-tested and grounded technological rules. *Journal of Management Studies, 41*(2), 219-246.

Van de Ven, A. H. (1986). Central problems in the management of innovation. *Management Science, 32*, 590-607.

Van de Ven, A. H., Polley, D. E., Garud, R., & Venkatraman, S. (1999). *The innovation journey.* New York: Oxford University Press.

van den Hoven, P., van Valkenburg, F., & Heng, M. (1994). Managing information systems within Japanese companies in Europe: An empirical study. *Information & Management, 27*, 315-325.

Van Dijk, J. (2005). *The deepening divide*. Thousand Oaks, CA: SAGE.

Van Eemeren, F. H., Grootendorst, R., & Henkemans, A. F. S. (2002). *Argumentation: Analysis, Evaluation, presentation*. Mahwah, NJ: Lawrence Erlbaum Associates Inc.

Van Maanen, J., Sorensen, J. B., & Mitchell, T. R. (2007). The interplay between theory and method. *Academy of Management Review, 32*(4), 1145-1154.

Van Vianen, A. E. M. (2000). Person-organization fit: The match between newcomers' and recruiters' preferences for organizational culture. *Personnel Psychology, 53*, 113-149.

van Wynsberghe, R., & Khan, S. (2007). Redefining case study. *International Journal of Qualitative Methods, 6*(2), 1-10.

Vaughan, D. (1999). The dark side of organizations: Mistake, misconduct, and disaster. *Annual Review of Sociology, 25*, 271-305.

Venkatesh, V. (2000). Determinants of perceived ease of use: Integrating control, intrinsic motivation, and emotion into the technology acceptance model. *Information Systems Research, 11*(4), 342-365.

Venkatesh, V., & Brown, S. A. (2001). A longitudinal investigation of personal computers in homes: Adoption determinants and emerging challenges. *MIS Quarterly, 25*(1), 71-98.

Venkatesh, V., & Davis, F. (2000). A theoretical extension of the technology acceptance model: Four longitudinal field studies. *Management Science, 46*(2), 186-204.

Venkatesh, V., Davis, F. D., & Morris, M. G. (2007). Dead or alive? The development, trajectory and future of technology adoption research. *Journal of the Association for Information Systems, 8*(4), 267-286.

Venkatesh, V., Morris, M. G., Davis, G. B., & Davis, F. D. (2003). User acceptance of information technology: Toward a unified view. *MIS Quarterly, 27*(3), 425-478.

Venkatraman, N. (1989). Strategic orientation of business enterprises: The construct, dimensionality, and measurement. *Management Science, 35*(8), 942-962.

Ventura, S. J. (1995). The use of geographic information systems in local government. *Public Administration Review, 55*(5), 461-467.

Verenikina, I., & Gould, E. (1998). Cultural-historical psychology and activity theory. In H. Hasan, E. Gould, & P. Hyland (Eds.), *Information systems and activity theory: Tools in context* (pp. 7-18). Wollongong, Australia: University of Wollongong Press.

Verharen, E., Dignum, F., & Weigand, H. (1996). A language/action perspective on cooperative information agents. In *Proceedings of the First International Workhshop on Communication Modeling*.

Veryard, R. (2001). The diffusion of components. In M. Ardis & B. Marcolin (Eds.), *Diffusing software product and process innovations* (pp. 131-146). MA, USA: Kluwer Academic Publishers.

Vessey, I., & Galletta, D. (1991). Cognitive fit: An empirical study of information acquisition. *Information Systems Research, 2*(1), 63-84.

Vessey, I., Ramesh, V., & Glass, R. L. (2002). Research in information systems: An empirical study of diversity in the discipline and its journals. *Journal of Management Information Systems, 19*(2), 129-174.

Vidgen, R., & McMaster, T. (1996). Black boxes, non-human stakeholders and the translation of IT through mediation. In W. J. Orlikowski, G. Walsham, M. R. Jones, & J. I. DeGross (Eds.), *Information technology and change in organizational work* (pp. 250-271). London: Chapman and Hall.

Vijayan, P., Perumal, V., & Shanmugam, B. (2005). Multimedia banking and technology acceptance theories. *The Journal of Internet Banking and Commerce, 10*(1), 1-7.

Viney, L. L., & Caputi, P. (2005). The origin and pawn, positive affect, psychosocial maturity and cognitive affect scales: Using them in counselling research. *Measurement & Evaluation in Counseling Development, 34*, 115-26.

Virkkunen, J., & Ahonen, H. (2004). Transforming learning and knowledge creation on the shop floor. *International Journal of Human Resources Development and Management, 4*(1), 57-72.

Vlahos, G. E., Ferratt, T. W., & Knoepfle, G. (2004). The use of computer-based information systems by German managers to support decision making. *Information & Management, 41*(6), 763-779.

Volkoff, O., Strong, D. M., & Elmes, M. B. (2007). Technological embeddedness and organizational change. *Organization Science, 18*(5), 832-848.

Von Foerster, H. (2003). *Understanding understanding.* New York: Springer.

Vygotsky, L. S. (1978). *Mind and society.* Cambridge, MA: Harvard University Press.

Wade, M. R., & Parent, M. (2002). Relationships between job skills and performance. *Journal of Management Information Systems, 18,* 71-96.

Wade, M., & Hulland, J. (2004). Review: The resource-based view and information systems research: Review, extension, and suggestions for future research. *MIS Quarterly, 28*(1), 107-142.

Wade, M., & Hulland, J. (2004). The resource-based view and information systems research: Review, extension and suggestions for future research. *MIS Quarterly, 28*(1), 107-142.

Wajcman, J. (2000). Reflections on gender and technology studies. In what state is the art? *Social Studies of Science, 30*(3), 447-464.

Waldt, D., & Drummond, R. (2005). *EBXML - the global standard for electronic business.* Retrieved February 19, 2005, from http://www.xml.org/xml/waldt_ebxml_global_standard_ebusiness.pdf

Walker, B. M. (1996). A psychology for adventurers: An introduction to personal construct psychology from a social perspective. In D. Kalekin-Fishman & B. M. Walker. (Eds.), *The construction of group realities: Culture, society and personal construct psychology* (pp. 7-26). Malabar, FL: Krieger.

Walker, B. M., & Winter, D. A. (2007). The elaboration of personal construct psychology. *Annual Review of Psychology, 58,* 453-477.

Walker, B. M., Oades, L. G., Caputi, P., Stevens, C. D., & Crittenden, N. (2000). Going beyond the scientist metaphor: From validation to experience cycles. In J.

W. Scheer (Ed.), *The person in society: Challenges to a constructivist theory.* Giessen, Germany: Psychosozial-Verlag.

Walker, B. M., Ramsey, F. L., & Bell, R. C. (1988). Dispersed and undispersed dependency. *International Journal of Personal Construct Psychology, 1,* 63-80.

Walker, G., Kogut, B., & Shan, W. (1997). Social capital, structural holes and the formation of an industry network. *Organization Science, 8*(2), 109-125.

Walker, R. H., Craig-Lees, M., Hecker, R., & Francis, H. (2002). Technology-enabled service delivery: An investigation of reason affecting customer adoption and rejection. *International Journal of Service Industry Management, 13*(1), 91-106.

Wall, T. D., & Payne, R. (1973). Are deficiency scores deficient? *Journal of Applied Psychology, 58,* 322-326.

Walling R. (2008). *Personality traits of the best software developers.* Retrieved June 16, 2008, from http://www.softwarebyrob.com/2006/08/20/personality-traits-of-the-best-software-developers/

Walls, J. G., & Widmeyer, G. R. (1992). Building an information system design theory for vigilant EIS. *Information Systems Journal, 3*(1), 36-59.

Walls, J. G., Widemeyer, G. R., & El Sawy, O. A. (2004). Assessing information system design theory in perspective: How useful was our 1992 initial rendition? *Journal of Information Technology Theory and Application, 6*(2), 43-58.

Walsham, G. (1993). *Interpreting information systems in organizations.* Cambridge, MA: John Wiley and Sons.

Walsham, G. (1997). Actor-network theory and IS research: Current status and future prospects. In A. S. Lee, J. Liebenau, & J. I. DeGross (Eds.), *Information systems and qualitative research* (pp. 467-480). London: Chapman and Hall.

Walsham, G. (2002). Cross-cultural software production and use: A structurational analysis. *MIS Quarterly, 26*(4), 359-380.

Walsham, G., & Chun, K. H. (1991). Structuration theory and information systems research. *Journal of Applied Systems Analysis, 17,* 77-85.

Walsham, G., & Sahay, S. (1999). GIS for district-level administration in India: Problems and opportunities. *MIS Quarterly, 23*(1), 39-56.

Walsham, G., & Sahay, S. (2006). Research on information systems in developing countries: Current landscape and future prospects. *Information Technology for Development, 12*(1), 7-24.

Walton, D. (2006). Fundamentals of critical argumentation: Critical reasoning and argumentation. New York: Cambridge University Press.

Wand, Y., & Weber, R. (2002). Research commentary: Information systems and conceptual modeling – a research agenda. *Information Systems Research, 13*(4), 363-376.

Wang, Y., Lin, H., & Luarn, P. (2006). Predicting consumer intention to use mobile service. *Information Systems Journal, 16*(2), 157-179.

Wang, Y.-S., (2002). The adoption of electronic tax filing systems: An empirical study. *Government Information Quarterly, 20*, 333-352.

Warboys, B., Kawalek, P., Robertson, I., & Greenwood, M. (1999). *Business information systems: A process approach*. The McGraw-Hill Companies.

Ward, J., & Peppard, J. (1996). Reconciling the IT/business relationship: A troubled marriage in need of guidance. *Strategic Information Systems, 5*, 37-65.

Ward, M. H. (2003). What's happening with IT in general practice? *GPEA*, 6-7.

Warkentin, M., Gefen, D., Pavlou, P., & Rose, G. (2002). Encouraging citizen adoption of e-government by building trust. *Electronic Markets, 12*(3), 157-162.

Warr, P. (1994). A conceptual framework for the study of work and mental health. *Work and Stress, 8*(2), 84-97.

Aanestad, M., & Hanseth, O. (2000, June 10-12). *Implementing open network technologies in complex work practices: A case from telemedicine*. Paper presented at the IFIP 8.2, Aalborg, Denmark.

Warren, B. (1998). *The philosophical dimensions of personal construct psychology*. London: Routledge.

Wasko, M. M., & Faraj, S. (2005). Why should I share? Examining social capital and knowledge contribution in electronic networks of practice. *MIS Quarterly, 29*(1), 35-57.

Watson, R. T., Boudreau, M. C., Greiner, M., Wynn, D., York, P., & Gul, R. (2005). Governance and global communities. *Journal of International Management, 11*(2), 125-142.

Watson, R. T., Ho, T. H., & Raman, K. S. (1994). Culture: A fourth dimension of group support systems. *Communications of the ACM, 37*(10), 44-55.

Weber, R. (2003). Editor's comments: Theoretically speaking. *MIS Quarterly, 27*(3), iii-xii.

Weber, R. (2003). Theoretically speaking. *MIS Quarterly, 27*(3), iii-xii.

Weber, S. (2003). Boundary-crossing in the context of intercultural learning. In T. Tuomi-Gröhn & Y. Engeström, (Eds.), *Between school and work: New perspectives on transfer and boundary crossing* (pp. 157-178). Amsterdam: Pergamon/Elsevier Science.

Webster, F. (2002). *Theories of the information society*. London: Routledge.

Webster, J., & Martocchio, J. J. (1992). Microcomputer playfulness: Development of a measure with workplace implications. *MIS Quarterly, 16*(2), 201-226.

Webster, J., Trevino, L. K., & Ryan, L. (1993). The dimensionality and correlates of flow in human-computer interactions. *Computers in Human Behavior, 9*(4), 411-426.

Weick, K. (1993). The collapse of sensemaking in organizations: The Mann Gulch disaster. *Administrative Science Quarterly, 38*(4), 268-282.

Weick, K. (1995). *Sensemaking in organizations*. CA, USA: Sage.

Weick, K. E. (1995). What theory is not, theorizing is. *Administrative Science Quarterly, 40*(3), 385-390.

Weick, K. E., & Roberts, K. H. (1993). Collective mind in organizations: Heedful interrelating on flight decks. *Administrative Science Quarterly, 38*, 357-381.

Weigand, H. (2003). The language/action perspective. *Data & Knowledge Engineering, 47*(3), 299-300.

Weigand, H. (2006). Two decades of the language-action perspective: Introduction. *Communications of the ACM, 49*(5), 44-46.

Weigand, H., & Hasselbring, W. (2001). An extensible business communication language. *International Journal of Cooperative Information systems, 10*(4), 423-441.

Weigand, H., & Heuvel, W.-J. v. d. (1998). *Meta-patterns for electronic commerce transactions based on FLBC.* Paper presented at the Hawaii International Conference on System Sciences (HICSS).

Weigand, H., Heuvel, W.-J. v. d., & Dignum, F. (1998). *Modelling electronic commerce transaction - a layered approach.* Paper presented at the International Workshop on the Language Action Perspective on Communication Modelling (LAP), Stockholm.

Weijters, B., Rangarajan, D., Falk, T., & Schillewaert, N. (2007). Determinants and outcomes of customers' use of self-service technology in a retail setting. *Journal of Services Research, 10*(1), 3-21.

Weinberg, G. (1971). *The psychology of computer programming.* NY, USA: Van Nostrand Reinhold Co.

Weinberg, G. M. (1972). Critical personality traits. In *The psychology of computer programming.* Retrieved June 16, 2008 from, *http://www.dorsethouse.com/features/excerpts/expsych8.html*

Wells, J. D., Fuerst, W. L., & Choobineh, J. (1999). Managing information technology (IT) for one-to-one customer interaction. *Information & Management, 35*, 53-62.

Westland, J. C., & Clark, T. H. K. (2000). *Global electronic commerce: Theory and case studies.* Cambridge, MA: MIT Press.

Wheeler, B. C. (2002). NEBIC: A dynamic capabilities theory for assessing net-enablement. *Information Systems Research, 13*(2), 125-146.

White, R. W. (1974). Strategies of adaptation: An attempt at systematic description. In G. V. Coelho, D. A. Hamburg, & J. E. Adams (Eds.), *Coping and adaptation* (pp. 47-68). New York: Basic Books.

Whitehead, R. (2001). *Leading a software development team. A developer's guide to successfully leading people and projects.* London: Addison-Wesley.

Whitman, M. E., & Woszczynski, A. B. (eds.) (2004). *Handbook for information systems research.* Hershey, PA: Idea Group Publishing.

Whittington, R., & Pettigrew, A. M. (2003). *Complementarities thinking.* In A. M. Pettigrew, R. Whittington, L. Melin, C. Sanchez-Runde, F. Van den Bosch, W. Ruigrock, & T. Numagami (Eds.), *Innovative forms of organizing, international perspectives.* Thousand Oaks, CA: SAGE Publications.

WHO. (2008). *What works: The evidence for action.* Retrieved January 8, 2008, from http://www.who.int/chp/chronic_disease_report/part3_ch2/en/index13.html

Widjaja, I., & Balbo, S. (2005). Structuration of activity: A view on human activity. In *Proceedings of the 19th conference of the Computer-Human Interaction Special Interest Group (CHISIG) of Australia on Computer-human interaction, Citizens online: considerations for today and the future* (pp. 1-4). Narrabundah, Australia: Computer-Human Interaction Special Interest Group (CHISIG) of Australia.

Wigand, R. T. (1996, May 23-27). *An overview of electronic commerce and markets.* Paper presented at the Annual Conference of the International Communication Association, Chicago, Illinois.

Wigand, R. T. (1997). Electronic commerce: Definition, theory and context. *The Information Society, 13*, 1-16.

Wilhelm, A. G. (2004). Digital nation: Towards an inclusive information society. *MIT Press*, 133-134.

Wilkins, L., Castleman, T., & Swatman P. M. C. (2001). Organisational factors in the diffusion of an industry standard. *Electronic Markets, 11*(4), 222-230.

Wilkins, L., Holt, D., Swatman, P. M. C., & Chan, E. S. K. (2007, June 4-6). Implementing information management strategically: An Australian EDRMS case study. In *Proceedings of the 20th Bled International E-Commerce Conference*, Bled, Slovenia.

Wilkins, L., Swatman, P. M. C., & Castleman, T. (2000, June 19-21). Electronic commerce as innovation – a framework for interpretive analysis. In *Proceedings of the 13th Bled International Electronic Commerce Conference*, Bled, Slovenia (pp. 150-121).

Wilkins, L., Swatman, P. M. C., & Castleman, T. (2002). Government sponsored virtual communities and the incentives for buy-in. *International Journal of Electronic Commerce, 7*(1), 121-134.

Wilkins, L., Swatman, P. M. C., & Castleman, T. (2003). Electronic markets and service delivery: Requisite competencies for virtual environments. In *Proceedings of the 11th European Conference on Information Systems ECIS 2003*, Milan, Italy (pp. 1-13).

Willard, C. A. (1992). On the utility of descriptive diagrams for the analysis and criticism of arguments. In W. L. Benoit, D. Hample, & P. J. Benoit (Eds.), *Readings in argumentation: Pragmatics and discourse analysis* (pp. 239-257). Berlin, Germany: Foris Publications.

Williams, R. (1997). Universal solutions or local contingencies? Tensions and contradictions in the mutual shaping of technology and work organization. In I. McLoughlin & M. Harris (Eds.), *Innovation, organization change and technology* (pp. 170-185). International Thomson Business Press.

Williams, S. R., & Wilson, R. L. (1997). Group support systems, power and influence in an organization: A field study. *Decision Sciences, 28*(4), 911-937.

Williamson, H. (2002). *Research methods for students, academics and professionals: Information management and systems* (2nd ed.). Wagga Wagga, Australia: Charles Sturt University.

Williamson, J. W., Pemberton, A. E., & Lounsbury, J. W. (2005). An investigation of career and job satisfaction in relation to personality traits of information professionals. *Library Quarterly, 75*(2), 122-141.

Williamson, O. E. (1975). *Market and hierarchies. Analysis and antitrust implication.* New York: The Free Press.

Williamson, O. E. (1981). The economics of organizations: The transaction cost approach. *American Journal of Sociology, 87*, 548-577.

Williamson, O. E. (1991). Comparative economic organization: The analysis of discrete structural alternatives, *Administrative Science Quarterly, 36*, 269-296.

Williamson, O. E. (1998). Transaction cost economics and organization theory formation, knowledge, vision, and theories of the firm. In G. Dosi, D. J. Teece, & J. Chytry (Eds.), *Technology, organisation, and competitiveness: Perspectives on industrial and corporate change* (pp. 17-66). New York: Oxford University Press Inc.

Wilson, C. (2001). On the scale of global demographic convergence 1950–2000. *Population and Development Review, 27*(1), 155-171.

Wilson, M., & Greenhill, A. (2004): Theory and action for emancipation: Elements of a critical realist approach. In B. Kaplan, D. Truex III, D. Wastell, T. Wood-Harper & J. DeGross (Eds.), *Information systems research: Relevant theory and informed practice* (pp 667-675). Amsterdam: Kluwer.

Wilson, M., & Howcroft, D. (2005). Power, politics and persuasion in IS evaluation: A focus on 'relevant social groups'. *Journal of Strategic Information Systems, 14*, 17-43.

Wilson, T. D. (2006). A re-examination of information seeking behaviour in the context of activity theory. *Information Research, 11*(4).

Winograd T., & Flores, F. (1986). *Understanding computers and cognition: A new foundation for design.* Norwood, NJ: Ablex Publishing Corporation.

Winograd, T. (2006). Designing a new foundation for design. *Communications of the ACM, 49*(5), 71-74.

Winter, D. A. (1992). *Personal construct psychology in clinical practice: Theory, research and applications.* London: Routledge.

Wirth, U. (1998). Abductive inference. In P. Bouissac (Ed.), *Encyclopedia of semiotics.* Oxford, UK: Oxford University Press.

Wirth, U. (2008). What is abductive inference? from http://user.uni-frankfurt.de/~wirth/inferenc.htm

WITSA. (2000). *Digital planet 2000.* Arlington, VA: World Information and Technology Services Alliance.

Witt, L. A., & Burke, L. A. (2008). Using cognitive ability and personality to select information technology professionals. In M. Mahmood (Ed.), *Advanced topics in end user computing, Volume 2* (pp. 1-17). Hershey, PA: Idea Group Publishing.

Wixom, B. H., & Todd, P. A. (2005). A theoretical integration of user satisfaction and technology acceptance. *Information Systems Research, 16*(1), 85-102.

Wixom, B. H., & Watson, H. J. (2001). An empirical investigation of the factors affecting data warehousing success. *MIS Quarterly, 25*(1), 17-41.

Wold, H. (1982). Soft modeling: The basic design and some extensions. In K. G. Joreskog & H. Wold (Eds.), *Systems under indirect observation* (pp. 1-47). New York: North Holland.

Wolfe, R. A. (1994). Organizational innovation: Review, critique and suggested research directions. *Journal of Management Studies, 31*(3), 405-431.

Wolfinbarger, M., & Gilly, M. C. (2003). eTailQ: Dimensionalizing, measuring, and predicting etail quality. *Journal of Retailing, 79*(3), 183-98.

Wolverton, R. W. (1974, June). The cost of developing large-scale software. *IEEE Transactions on Computers, 23*(6), 615-636.

Woodruff, R. B. (1997). Customer value: The next source for competitive advantage. *Academy of Marketing Science Journal, 25*(2), 139-153.

Woodward, J. (1965). *Industrial organization: Theory and practice*. London: Oxford University Press.

Woolcock, M. (1998). Social capital and economic development: Towards a theoretical synthesis and policy framework. *Theory and Society, 27*, 151-208.

Wooldridge, M. (2002). *An introduction to multiagent systems*. Chichester, England: John Wiley & Sons.

Woolgar, S. (1992). Some remarks about positionism: A reply to Collins and Yearley. In A. Pickering (Ed.), *Science as practice and culture* (pp. 327-342). Chicago: The University of Chicago Press.

Wooten, W. (1991). The effects of self-efficacy on job acceptance behavior among American college students. *Journal of Employment Counseling, 28*, 41-48

Wren, D. (2005). *The history of management thought* (5th ed.). NJ, USA: John Wiley & Sons.

Wu, J. (2008). *Exploring the link between knowledge management performance and firm performance*. Unpublished doctoral dissertation, University of Kentucky.

XML. (2006, September 29). *Extensible markup language (XML) 1.0*. Retrieved February 2, 2007, from http://www.w3.org/TR/REC-xml/

Yamazumi, K. (2006). Learning for critical and creative agency: An activity-theoretical study of advanced network of learning in new school project (CHAT Technical Reports No. 01).

Yang, K. (2007). Individual social capital and its measurement in social surveys. *Survey Research Methods, 1*(1), 19-27.

Yang, X., & Teo, H. H. (2007). How do user cope with trial restrictions? A longitudinal field experiment on free trial software. In *Proceedings of the twenty-eight International Conference on Information Systems*, Montreal, QC, Canada, (pp. 1-18).

Yates, J., & Orlikowski, W.J. (1992). Genres of organizational communication: A structurational approach to studying communication and media. *Academy of Management Review, 17*(2), 299-336.

Yetim, F. (2002). *Designing communication action patterns for global communication and cooperation: A discourse ethical approach*. Paper presented at the European Conference on Information systems (ECIS), Information systems and the Future of the Digital Economy, Gdansk, Poland.

Yetim, F. (2006). Acting with genres: Discursive-ethical concepts for reflecting on and legitimating genres. *European Journal of Information Systems, 15*(1), 54-69.

Yetim, F., & Bieber, M. P. (2003). *Towards a language/action theoretic approach to relationship analysis*. Paper presented at the European Conference on Information systems (ECIS), Naples, Italy.

Yin, R. K. (1993). *Applications of case study research*. Newbury Park, CA: Sage Publications.

Yin, R. K. (1994). *Case study research: Design and methods* (2nd ed.). London: Sage Publications.

Yli-Renko, H., Autio, E., & Sapienza, H. J. (2001). Social capital, knowledge acquisition, and knowledge exploitation in young technology-based firms. *Strategic Management Journal, 22*(6/7), 587.

Yoo, B., & Donthu, N. (2001). Developing a scale to measure the perceived quality of an Internet shopping site (sitequal). *Quarterly Journal of Electronic Commerce, 2*(1), 31-46.

Yoo, Y., Ginzberg, M., & Ahn, J. H. (1999). A cross-cultural investigation of the use of knowledge management systems. *ACM Website.*

Yoshioka, T., Yates, J., & Orlikowski, W.J. (1994). Community-based interpretive schemes: Exploring the use of cyber meetings within a global organization. *AMJ Best Papers.*

Yousafzai, S. Y., Foxall, G. R., & Pallister, J. G. (2007). Technology acceptance: A meta-analysis of the TAM: Part 1. *Journal of Modeling in Management, 2*(3), 251-280.

Zachary, G. (1994). *Show-Stopper! The breakneck race to create Windows NT and the next generation at Microsoft.* NY, USA: The Free Press.

Zahir, S., Dobing, B., & Hunter, M. G. (2002). Cross-cultural dimensions of Internet portals. *Internet Research - Electronic Networking Applications and Policy, 12*(3), 210-220.

Zaltman, G., Duncan, R., & Holbek, J. (1973). *Innovations and organizations.* New York: John Wiley and Sons.

Zamenopoulos, T., & Alexiou, K. (2005). Linking design and complexity: A review. In J. Johnson, T. Zamenopoulos, & K. Alexiou (Eds.), *Proceedings of the ECCS 2005 Satellite Workshop on Embracing Complexity in Design* (pp. 91-102). Paris: The Open University.

Zarefsky, D. (2005). *Argumentation: The study of effective reasoning, part 1 of 2.* Chantilly, VA: The Teaching Company.

Zeithaml, V. A., Parasuraman, A., & Berry, L. L. (1985). Problems and strategies in services marketing. *Journal of Marketing, 49*(2), 33-46.

Zhu, F. X., Wymer, W. J., & Chen, I. (2002). IT-based services and service quality in consumer banking. *International Journal of Service Industry Management, 13*(1), 69-90.

Zhu, X., & Nakata, C. (2007). Reexamining the link between customer orientation and business performance: The role of information systems. *Journal of Marketing Theory and Practice, 15*(3), 187-203.

Zipf, G. K. (1949). *Human behaviour and the principle of least effort.* Cambridge, MA: Addison-Wesley.

Zmud, B. (1998). MISQ: Editor's coments. *MIS Quarterly, 22*(2), 1-3.

Zmud, R. (1983). The effectiveness of external information channels in facilitating innovation within software development groups. *MIS Quarterly, 7*(2), 43-58.

Zuboff, S. (1988). *In the age of the smart machine: The future of work and power.* New York: Basic Books.

About the Contributors

Yogesh K. Dwivedi is a lecturer in the School of Business and Economics at Swansea University in the UK. He was awarded his MSc and PhD by Brunel University in the UK, receiving a *Highly Commended* award for his doctoral work by the European Foundation for Management and Development. His research focuses on the adoption and diffusion of ICT in organisations and in addition to authoring a book and numerous conference papers, has co-authored papers accepted for publication by journals such as *Communications of the ACM,* the *Information Systems Journal,* the *European Journal of Information Systems,* and the *Journal of the Operational Research Society.* He is senior editor of *DATABASE for Advances in Information Systems,* assistant editor *of Transforming Government: People, Process and Policy* and a member of the editorial board/review board of a number of other journals, and is a member of the Association of Information Systems, IFIP WG8.6 and the Global Institute of Flexible Systems Management, New Delhi. He can be reached at ykdwivedi@gmail.com.

Banita Lal is a lecturer in the Nottingham Business School, Nottingham Trent University, UK. She obtained her PhD and MSc in information systems from the School of Information Systems, Computing and Mathematics, Brunel University. Her research interests involve examining the individual and organizational adoption and usage of ICTs and technology-enabled alternative forms of working. She has published several research papers in internationally refereed journals such as *Industrial Management and Data Systems, Information Systems Frontiers, Electronic Government, International Journal of Mobile Communications,* and *Transforming Government: People, Process and Policy,* and has presented several papers at several international conferences. She can be reached at banita.la.@ntu.ac.uk

Michael D. Williams is a professor in the School of Business and Economics at Swansea University in the UK. He holds a BSc from the CNAA, an MEd from the University of Cambridge, and a PhD from the University of Sheffield. He is a member of the British Computer Society and is registered as a Chartered Engineer. Prior to entering academia Professor Williams spent twelve years developing and implementing ICT systems in both public and private sectors in a variety of domains including finance, telecommunications, manufacturing, and local government, and since entering academia, has acted as consultant for both public and private organizations. He is the author of numerous fully refereed and invited papers within the ICT domain, has editorial board membership of a number of academic journals, and has obtained external research funding from sources including the European Union, the Nuffield Foundation, and the Welsh Assembly Government. He can be reached at m.d.williams@swansea.ac.uk

Scott L. Schneberger is a professor and the dean of academics at Principia College, Elsah, IL., most recently at the Walker College of Business at Appalachian State University where he was an associate professor and co-executive director of the Center for Applied Research in Emerging Technologies. Schneberger has also taught business information systems courses at the Richard Ivey School of Business at the University of Western Ontario, and the Robinson School of Business at Georgia State University. He has taught undergraduate and graduate students, MBAs, and executive MBAs, PhDs, and delivered executive education information systems courses to corporations. Schneberger has published in numerous academic research journals, presented at leading conferences, published business teaching cases, and authored information systems books. Before entering academia, Schneberger served twenty years in the U.S. Navy as an intelligence officer, retiring at the rank of Commander. He is a combat veteran, and served in ships, submarines, and aircraft. His last naval position was Head of Plans and Policy, Information Systems, for the Director of Naval Intelligence in The Pentagon. He can be reached at Scott.Schneberger@prin.edu

Michael R. Wade is an associate professor of Management Information Systems at the Schulich School of Business, York University, Toronto, where he also holds the position of associate director of the International MBA Program. He received a PhD from the Ivey Business School at the University of Western Ontario. Professor Wade has worked extensively with public and private sector organizations to further an understanding of the strategic use of information systems for sustainable competitive advantage. He has lived and worked in seven countries across four continents and consulted for top international organizations including Cisco Systems, and IBM. His research has appeared in journals such as *MIS Quarterly, Strategic Management Journal,* and the *Communications of the ACM.* Professor Wade is co-author of the textbook *Information Systems Today: Canadian Edition,* and has co-authored two e-commerce casebooks. He can be reached at MWade@schulich.yorku.ca

* * *

Hossam Ali-Hassan is a PhD candidate at the Schulich School of Business, York University, in Toronto, Canada. He is expected to get his degree in the summer of 2009. Before starting his PhD he worked for many years as a practitioner and consultant in the areas of computer networking and IS project management and also as a part-time instructor. His research interest is in social computing (popularly known as Web 2.0) and mobile computing in an organizational context. He is currently studying the newly emerging class of tools known as social computing, and its use by organizations. He is interested in identifying the impact of social computing on social capital among teams and the subsequent benefit to individuals, teams and organizations in the form of collaboration, knowledge sharing and knowledge creation in organizations.

Anne Beaudry is an associate professor at the John Molson School of Business, Concordia University. She earned her PhD at HEC-Montreal. Her research interests include IT-related behaviors, user acceptance, and impacts of IT use. Her work has been presented at international conferences and published in *Communications of the AIS, International Journal of Information and Operation Management Education, International Journal of Knowledge Management, and MIS Quarterly.*

Joseph Bradley is an assistant professor of accounting at the University of Idaho. He received his BA from Claremont McKenna College and his EMBA and PhD from Claremont Graduate University. His teaching interests include accounting information systems, cost accounting, managerial accounting, strategy and management. Dr. Bradley's research focuses on ERP implementation issues. His research has been published in the *International Journal of Enterprise Information Systems, Issues in Information Systems* and the *International Journal of Accounting Information Systems*. His book chapters have appeared in the *Encyclopedia of Information Science and Technology,* the *Handbook of Research for Enterprise Systems* and *Global Implications in Modern Enterprise Information Systems*. He has presented his research at the Information Resource Management Association International Conference, Americas' Conference on Information Systems and the International Research Symposium on Accounting Information Systems. Prior to his academic career Dr. Bradley spent 30 years in industry in various executive positions in accounting and general management.

Tom Butler is a senior lecturer in business information systems, University College Cork, Ireland. Before joining academia, Tom had an extensive career as an IT practitioner in the telecommunications industry. From 2003-2006 he focused conducted two major action research and applied R&D projects on knowledge management systems (KMS). Building on this body of research, he has since 2005 been working with a small-to-medium software enterprise on the design and implementation of Environmental Compliance Knowledge Management Systems. Currently he is applying institutional theory to help understand the implications for the IS field of environmental compliance and Green IT. Tom has published his research the *Information Systems Journal,* the *Journal of Strategic Information Systems,* the *Journal of Organizational and End User Computing,* the *Journal of Information Technology* and in the *Proceedings of ICIS, ECIS, IFIP 8.2 and 8.6.*

Peter Caputi is an associate professor in the School of Psychology at the University of Wollongong, Australia. He is internationally known for his work in personal construct theory and method. He has published extensively in repertory grid methodology and theory, and measurement issues in personal construct theory. Dr. Caputi also has a research interest in psychological determinants of IS usage. He has published in *Behaviour & Information Technology, Computers in Human Behaviour, British Journal of Educational Technology* as well as other journals and refereed conference proceedings.

Daniel Carbone is a lecture/research coordinator for the Rural Health Academic Network (RHAN), University of Melbourne; where he facilitates research capacity in health care settings across north-western state of Victoria, Australia. He is also a health information systems consultant at Central Highlands General Practice Network where he facilitates general practices to adopt relevant information system to improve patient care outcomes. Carbone is also completing a PhD in information systems at Victoria University which focuses on systematic approaches to chronic conditions care models and has been training nurses and doctors in computer and information literacy for over ten years.

Sven Carlsson is professor of informatics at School of Economics and Management, Lund University. Research interests include: IS-supported management processes, knowledge management, enterprise systems, e-business processes in high-velocity environments, and the use of critical realism in IS-research. He has held visiting positions at universities in Europe, Australia, USA, and Singapore. He is a regional editor for *Knowledge Management Research and Practice*. He has published more than

100 peer-reviewed journal articles, book chapters, and conference papers and his work has appeared in journals like *JMIS*, *Decision Sciences*, *Information & Management*, *Knowledge Management Research & Practice*, and *Information Systems and e-Business Management*.

Rodrigo Castelo is a product manager at OutSystems and has been with the company since 2004. Castelo's main focus is managing the strategy, market, customer and user requirements into the OutSystems Agile Platform product. Castelo holds a five-year degree in information systems and computer engineering, with a major in programming and information systems, from Instituto Superior Técnico (IST), Lisbon, Portugal. He also joined an MsC program in the same university, where he conducted practical and theoretical research in the fields of real options, value-based pricing, product segmentation, organizational engineering, and knowledge management, among others.

Catherine E. Connelly, PhD, is an assistant professor of organizational behavior and human resources management in the DeGroote School of Business at McMaster University, Hamilton, Canada. Her main areas of research focus on workers with "non-standard" employment contracts, knowledge sharing, and knowledge hiding in organizations. Her work has appeared in several edited volumes including the *Handbook of Organizational Behavior* and *Research in Personnel and Human Resource* Management. Her articles have appeared in several journals including the *Journal of Management Information Systems*, the *Journal of Applied Psychology*, *Human Resources Management Journal*, the *Journal of Management*, *IEEE Transactions in Engineering Management*, and the *Journal of Vocational Behavior*.

Antonio Cordella is lecturer in information systems at the London School of Economics and Political Science. His research interests and publications cover the areas of e-government, economic theories of information systems, and the social studies of information systems

Francisco C. Cua is a PhD candidate in the Department of Marketing at the University of Otago, New Zealand. He has more than thirty years of experience in accountancy, enterprise systems, consultancy, and teaching. During the writing of this chapter, he was a senior lecturer at the School of Applied Business, Otago Polytechnic, New Zealand. He has worked internationally in Hong Kong, Shanghai, and Beijing as a consultant of Asian Development Bank's project and taken part in various projects as a business analyst, functional analyst, systems manager, and Oracle systems administrator in New Zealand. Diffusion of information systems, business models, supply chain, innovation, and entrepreneurship are his research areas of interest.

Miguel Mira da Silva is professor of information systems at Instituto Superior Técnico (IST) in Lisbon, Portugal. Miguel is also senior researcher at INESC-ID, an academic research institute, and director at INOV, a technical innovation institute that works closely with companies. Both INESC-ID and INOV are private non-profit organizations of the INESC holding, partly owned by IST. Miguel also colaborates directly with several companies, not only as consultant in the area of IT management but also supervising applied PhD and master thesis.

Eduardo Diniz, *Fundaçao Getulio Vargas, Brazil*, electronic engineer, MSc and PhD in business administration, focus in information systems management, visiting scholar in at University of California, Berkeley from 1996 to 1998, and at HEC Montreal in 2007. Professor at FGV-EAESP, Sao Paulo,

Brasil since 1999, is member of the GVcia, Center for Studies in Applied Information Systems at FGV and coordinator of the Technology and Automation Group of CEB (Center for Excellence in Banking) also at FGV. Has researched on banking technology since 1991 and published several papers and articles on the same subject.

Adam W. Drost, is president of eCareerFit.Com (eCF). As a co-founder of eCareerFit.com (eCF), his leadership energized a start up from dust with one assessment in one language to 9 assessments in nine languages versions, which have been distributed in over 30 countries. All eCF growth was organic, needing no debt or venture capital. Prior to eCareerFit.com, Drost developed his leadership skills as president of the Internet Enterprise Group at DBM, a global human resource consulting organization; director of Global/National Accounts at Norrell Corporation, a human resource outsourcing and staffing company; and marketing representative at IBM. Drost is a graduate of the University of Illinois, Champaign/Urbana, with a BS in mathematics and minor in psychology. He participates in numerous community organizations including Habitat for Humanity, The Knights of Columbus and the Peter F. Drucker Foundation.

Amany R. Elbanna is a lecturer in information systems at the Business School of Loughborough University. She holds PhD in information systems from London School of Economics and Political Science. She also holds MBA and MSc in analysis, design, and management of information systems. Elbanna has applied ANT in several studies of ERP implementation and presented her work in several conferences including ECIS, IFIP 8.6, and Bled conferences. Her research interest include IS-based organisational innovation, IS implementation and project management, and Agile software development. Elbanna could be reached by e-mail at: a.elbanna@lboro.ac.uk

Dianne P. Ford, PhD, is an assistant professor of organizational behavior and management information systems in the Faculty of Business Administration at Memorial University of Newfoundland, St.John's, Canada. Her research interests focus at areas that utilize her double major in MIS/OB and include: knowledge management, perceived value of knowledge, trust, and cross-cultural implications for MIS and KM. Ford has published articles in *IEEE: Transactions in Engineering Management, Journal of Knowledge Management Research & Practice, International Journal of Knowledge Management, Handbook on Knowledge Management: 1 Knowledge Matters,* and has presented papers at various conferences.

Brent Furneaux is a doctoral candidate in information systems at York University's Schulich School of Business. His current research interests include the processes surrounding individual and organizational decision making, the strategic management of organizational knowledge, and questions related to the end of the information system life. He is currently pursuing dissertation research that seeks to better understand the factors that drive and constrain organizational decisions to discontinue their use of information systems. Furneaux has published in the areas of knowledge management and requirements engineering as well as on a number of theoretical issues in the field. He is a graduate of the University of Western Ontario and the University of Toronto's Rotman School of Management.

Tony Garrett is a member Korea University Business School in Seoul. Prior to this he was senior lecturer in marketing at the University of Otago (New Zealand). His PhD examined national culture and group dynamics in new product development, with a specific focus on Singapore and New Zealand. Research interests include innovation, qualitative research methodologies and service development, with a focus on the encouragement of entrepreneurial and innovative behavior within established organizations. He has published a number of chapters and refereed articles, Prior to his academic career he had business experience in the development of international brands in the New Zealand market.

Susan Gasson is associate professor in the iSchool at Drexel University. She obtained an MBA and PhD at Warwick Business School in the UK. Her research interests focus on IS design processes and wicked problem-solving, in groups that span knowledge-domain boundaries. The majority of her research studies employ a grounded theory approach. She teaches a doctoral seminar in qualitative research methods and publishes regularly on the topic of interpretive and Grounded Theory approaches to research. Dr. Gasson has extensive experience in IS Group management, process improvement, systems architecture design, and systems analysis. Dr. Gasson is the recipient of a five-year Career Award from the US National Science Foundation and was awarded an Emerald Literati Network Outstanding Paper Award in 2008.

Lucy W. Gibson, PhD, is executive vice president of Resource Associates, Inc. Dr. Gibson is a licensed industrial/organizational psychologist who has over twenty years of experience in the areas of test development, test validation, and implementation of selection testing programs. In addition to helping publish many research articles on Resource Associates' products, she has taught research methods, statistics, program evaluation and human resource management at both the University of Tennessee and Tusculum College. Dr. Gibson's work is focused on selection test development, validation of selection testing programs, and working with client companies to develop tailored employee selection testing..

Judith Gregory, PhD, is on the research faculty of The Institute of Design, Illinois Institute of Technology (IIT) and co-coordinator of the Doctor of Philosophy in Design Program. She holds a PhD in Communication from the University of California-San Diego. Dr. Gregory is active in international discussions concerning activity theory, design of information systems, participatory design and science and technology studies. She is a specialist in qualitative human-centered approaches to technology design. Previously, Dr. Gregory served as Co-PI in the Electronic Health Record iterative prototyping project of Kaiser Permanente (1993-98) and as associate professor in informatics, University of Oslo (2001-05). While at University of Oslo, she was a core faculty member in the dual International MSc-Informatics and Master in Public Health programs that are ongoing capacity-building collaborations between the medical and computer science faculties of Norway and leading universities in Tanzania, Mozambique, Tanzania, Ethiopia and India among additional developing countries.

Varun Grover is the William S. Lee (Duke Energy) distinguished professor of information systems at Clemson University. He has published extensively in the information systems field, with over 180 publications in refereed journals. Six recent articles have ranked him in the top four in research productivity in the top six Information Systems journals in the past decade. Dr. Grover is currently senior editor for *MIS Quarterly*, the *Journal of the AIS* and *Database*. He is currently working in the areas of IT value, system politics, and process transformation.

Ahsan Akhter Hasin is a professor of industrial and production engineering of Bangladesh University of Engineering & Technology, Dhaka, Bangladesh. He received his Master's and PhD degree from the Asian Institute of Technology (AIT), Bangkok, Thailand. Dr. Hasin is a well known expert sought in the field of production engineering and quality management. He has published over 50 papers in refereed journals and proceedings. He has also published 5 reputed books on quality management issues. He is a certified and internationally recognized quality consultant. He was the recipient of more than 15 academic awards including a Best Research Paper Award in the UK.

Clyde Holsapple holds the University of Kentucky's Rosenthal Endowed Chair in MIS. His research focuses on supporting knowledge work, particularly in decision-making contexts. Publication credits include 200 research articles and many books, such as the basic reference works *Handbook on Knowledge Management* and *Handbook on Decision Support Systems*. He is editor-in-chief of the *Journal of Organizational Computing and Electronic Commerce.*

Duncan Holt is a business manager who has worked in many roles ranging from his own technology business to local government and multi-national commercial entities. Most of his roles have involved using technology to improve business operations and information management. With an original core discipline in electronics and computer system hardware he then moved to business analysis and software design before further studies allowed him to move into general management roles in the corporate services field. A highlight of the highly successful programme of business change at the City of Charles Sturt, where he was the IT Manager, was the much reported fully integrated and well used Electronic Document and Records Management System. This system has since been used as a benchmark for many government department and councils.

M. Gordon Hunter is a professor of information systems in the Faculty of Management at The University of Lethbridge, Alberta, Canada. Hunter has previously held academic positions at universities in Canada, Singapore, and Hong Kong. He has held visiting positions at universities in Australia, Monaco, Germany, New Zealand, and USA. Hunter has published articles in *MIS Quarterly, Information Systems Research, The Journal of Strategic Information Systems, The Journal of Global Information Management, Information Systems Journal,* and *Information, Technology and People.* He has conducted seminar presentations in Canada, USA, Europe, Hong Kong, Singapore, Taiwan, New Zealand, and Australia. Hunter's research approach takes a qualitative perspective employing personal construct theory and narrative inquiry to conduct in depth interviews. He applies qualitative techniques in interdisciplinary research such as multi-generation small business, recruitment and retention of physicians, and cross-cultural investigations. His current research interests in the information systems (IS) area include the effective development and implementation of IS with emphasis on the personnel component; the role of Chief Information Officers; and the use of IS by small business.

Deirdre Hynes is a senior lecturer in the Department of Information and Communications in Manchester Metropolitan University, UK. She joined MMU in 2004 from Dublin City University, Ireland, where she conducted her doctoral studies. Her research focuses on how media and computing technologies become part of everyday life and what factors influence this process. She has published in the field of IS, computing, communication studies, educational technologies and the narratives and discourses of ICTs.

Faraja Igira is a faculty member of the Computing and Information Technology Department at the Institute of Finance Management, Dar es Salaam, Tanzania. Her areas of expertise include software engineering and systems analysis and design. Faraja has been actively involved in studying and implementing health information systems in Tanzania (since 2002 to current) and Mozambique (2002 to 2003). During these studies and implementation activities, she participated in general discussions on the design and implementation of health information systems that are ongoing within a network of developing countries including South Africa, Mozambique, Tanzania, Malawi, India, and Vietnam. Faraja is currently undertaking a PhD in information systems at the University of Oslo, Norway. Her interest is on researching organizational and cultural issues in the design and implementation of information systems in which she has been using cultural historical activity theory (CHAT) as a theoretical lens.

Martin Jayo holds a degree in economics and an MSc in media and communications, and is currently a PhD student at Fundação Getulio Vargas, Brazil. His research interests are in ICT for socio-economic development, particularly focusing on banking technology applied to microfinance.

James Jiang is professor of management information systems at the University of Central Florida and the Honorary Sun Yat-Sen Management professor at National Sun Yat-Sen University, Taiwan. He obtained his PhD in information systems at the University of Cincinnati. His research interests include IS project management and IS service quality management. He has published over one hundred and forty academic articles in these areas in journals such as *Decision Sciences, Journal of Management Information Systems, Communications of ACM, IEEE Transactions on Systems Men & Cybernetics, IEEE Transactions on Engineering Management, Journal of AIS, Decision Support Systems, Information & Management, European Journal of Information Systems,* and *the MIS Quarterly.* Currently, he serves as associate editor at *MIS Quarterly.*

Gary Klein is the Couger professor of Information Systems at the University of Colorado in Colorado Springs. He obtained his PhD in management science from Purdue University. Before that time, he served with the company now known as Accenture in Kansas City and was director of the Information Systems Department for a regional financial institution. His research interests include project management, technology transfer, and mathematical modeling, with over 140 academic publications in these disciplines. He is Ddirector of education for the American Society for the Advancement of Project Management and vice president of Member Services for the AIS SIG on Information Technology Project Management. He is a fellow of the Decision Sciences Institute and serves that organization as a vice-president at large. He was a founding co-editor and current co-editor-in-chief of *Comparative Technology Transfer and Society.*

Vinod Kumar is a professor of Technology and Operations Management of the Sprott School of Business (Director of School, 1995–2005), Carleton University. He received his graduate education from the University of California, Berkeley and the University of Manitoba. Vinod is a well known expert sought in the field of technology and operations management. He has published over 150 papers in refereed journals and proceedings. He has won several Best Paper Awards in prestigious conferences, Scholarly Achievement Award of Carleton University for the academic years 1985–1986 and 1987–1988, and Research Achievement Award for the year 1993 and 2001.

Uma Kumar is a full professor of management science and technology management and director of the Research Centre for Technology Management at Carleton University. She has published over 120 papers in journals and refereed proceedings. Ten papers have won best paper awards at prestigious conferences. She has won Carleton's prestigious Research Achievement Award and, twice, the Scholarly Achievement Award. Recently, she won the teaching excellence award at the Carleton University.

Juan Ling is an assistant professor of management at Georgia College & State University. She earned her PhD degree in management at the University of Kentucky, USA. Her research interests include social networks, leadership, and team dynamics. Her coauthored paper, *Aesthetic properties and message customization: Navigating the dark side of Web recruitment*, was published in the *Journal of Applied Psychology*. She has also presented her research projects in many conferences, including the Intro-Organization Networks Conference, Southern Management Association Conference, and Mid-west Management Association Conference. Her teaching interests include principles of management, human resource management, organizational behavior, and compensation and benefits.

John W. Lounsbury, PhD is professor of psychology, University of Tennessee, Knoxville, vice president, eCareerfit.com, and president of Resource Associates, Inc. He is a fellow in the American Psychological Association and a licensed industrial-organizational psychologist. Dr. Lounsbury teaches courses on testing, personality assessment, research methods, psychometrics, and human resources management. He has chaired over 60 doctoral dissertations and has written numerous articles on personality traits, career development, scale validation, life and career satisfaction, and work-nonwork relationships. He has consulted with more than 100 national and international companies in the areas of test development, personality assessment, pre-employment, selection testing, program validation, and career planning.

Tsz-Wai Lui is a PhD candidate at the School of Hotel Administration at Cornell University. Her research interest is in IT-enabled customer service systems. She has participated as a chapter author in the Global Text Project, which is to create electronic textbooks that will be freely available from a Website; and has also recently published in The DATABASE for Advances in Information Systems.

Ahmed Y. Mahfouz, PhD, is an assistant professor of management information systems (MIS) in the Department of Accounting, Finance, and MIS at Prairie View A&M University, Prairie View, Texas. He has a PhD in information and operations management (MIS track) from Texas A&M University, College Station, Texas, USA. He has an MBA and a Bachelor of Science in management science from Virginia Polytechnic Institute and State University (Virginia Tech), Blacksburg, Virginia. His research interests include electronic commerce, online consumer behavior, flow theory, IS strategy, research methodology, and interdisciplinary IS research and education. Dr. Mahfouz' research appears in peer-reviewed journals, books, and conference proceedings, such as *Computers in Human Behavior* and *Journal of Internet Commerce*; IGI Global books, such as, *Inquiring Organizations: Moving from Knowledge Management to Wisdom*, and *Internet Management Issues: A Global Perspective*.

John McAvoy is a lecturer in business information systems at the University College Cork, Ireland. Prior to lecturing, McAvoy had a variety of roles in the Information Systems field, ranging from systems administration to managing software development teams. His research interests are in the areas of software development methodologies, primarily the role played by small teams of software developers.

Darren B. Meister, PhD, is an associate professor of Information Systems in the Richard Ivey School of Business at the University of Western Ontario, London, Canada. His interests focus on the role of technology in enhancing organizational effectiveness, specifically as it concerns innovation processes. He investigates this question primarily within three settings: technology adoption, knowledge management and interorganizational systems. His work has appeared in *Management Science, MIS Quarterly* and other leading journals and conferences.

Ram B. Misra is a full professor of management and information systems at Montclair State University, Montclair, NJ, USA. Dr. Misra has published in *IEEE Transactions,* the *International Journal of Management Research,* the *International Journal of Production Research,* the *Naval Logistics Review,* the *Decision Sciences Journal of Innovative Education,* the *Journal of IT Cases and Applications,* the *Journal of Information Technology and Applications,* the *International Journal of Pharmaceutical and Healthcare Marketing,* the *i-Manager's Journal of Management,* the *Information Technology Journal,* the *Journal of Issues in Informing Science and Information Technology* and the *Journal of Information Technology Research.*

Lapo Mola is lecturer in organization science at the University of Verona, where he holds courses in organization science, and information systems. His research interests cover the area of organizational impacts of ICT.

Ciaran Murphy is Bank of Ireland professor of BIS at University College Cork and is director of the university's Financial Services Innovation Centre at. He has over 20 years of research and commercial experience, and has acted as a consultant to a wide variety of organizations in Ireland and internationally. Murphy was organizing and programme committee chair of the 1997 European Conference on Information Systems. Coauthor of *A Manager's Guide to Current Issues in Information Systems,* he has published widely, including articles in the *Information Systems Journal, the Journal of Strategic Information Systems, Decision Support Systems,* the *Journal of Decision Systems,* the *Journal of Information Technology,* and in the proceedings of ICIS and ECIS conferences.

Nandish Patel has constructed the theory of deferred action as an 'action and design theory' to inform the design and development of organisations and IT systems. This is a theory to inform the practice of organisation design, IT systems design, and integrated organisation and IT systems design in emergent organisation. As well as informing practice, the theory also explains these phenomena of organisation design, IT systems design, and information management in emergent business organisation. It draws on complexity theory to explain emergence and self-organisation. The theory is used by other researchers and has been applied by practitioners. Present research is focused on developing multi-agent models based on the theory.

Doncho Petkov is a full professor and coordinator of the BIS program at Eastern Connecticut State University, USA. He is a deputy editor (USA) for systems research and behavioral science and senior area editor (Software Engineering) of IJITSA . His publications have appeared in the *Journal of Systems and Software, Decision Support Systems, Telecommunications Policy,* IRMJ, *International Journal on Technology Management,* IJITSA, JITTA, JISE, JITCA, South African Computing Journal and elsewhere.

Olga Petkova is a full professor in MIS at Central Connecticut State University, USA. Previously she has taught at several universities in South Africa and Zimbabwe and worked at the Bulgarian Academy of Sciences in Sofia. Her publications are in software development productivity, systems thinking and information systems education. They have appeared in *Decision Support Systems, Journal of Information Technology Theory and Applications* (JITTA), *Journal of Informatics Education Research*, JISE, JITCA and elsewhere.

Gabriele Piccoli is associate professor of information Ssystems at the University of Sassari (Italy). His research, teaching and consulting expertise is in strategic information systems and the use of network technology to support customer service. He is an associate editor of the *MIS Quarterly* and his research has appeared in *MIS Quarterly, Decision Sciences Journal, MIS Quarterly Executive, Communications of the ACM, Harvard Business Review, The DATABASE for Advances in Information Systems, The Cornell Hospitality Quarterly*, as well as other academic and applied journals. He has recently authored the book *Information Systems for Managers: Text and Cases*, published by John Wiley & Sons and serves on the editorial board of the *Cornell Hospitality Administration Quarterly*.

Marlei Pozzebon (PhD in management, McGill University) is associate professor and director of GRESI (research group of information systems) at HEC Montréal. Her research interests are the social, political and cultural aspects of ICT implementation and use, and the use of practice-based theoretical frames and qualitative methods in IS research. Some keywords of her research are structuration theory, critical discourse analysis, local and sustainable development and global-local negotiation. Professionally, she specializes in training and consultancy in the business intelligence area. Pozzebon has published her articles at *Organization Studies, Journal of Management Studies, Information Technology and People, Journal of Information Technology, Journal of Strategic Information Systems*, among others.

Helen Richardson is a senior lecturer in information systems (IS) and joined the University of Salford, UK in 1998 after a varied career including working in the field of social care and running a Research and Training Unit promoting Positive Action for Women at Work. She works in the Research Centre for People, Work and Organization and is engaged in Critical Research in IS including issues of gender and the ICT labour market, the domestication of ICTs and the global location of service work.

Nicholas Roberts is a PhD candidate at the College of Business & Behavioral Science, Clemson University. He worked for several years as an IT project manager prior to re-entering academe. His current research focuses on how firms can use information technology to enhance their agility, competitive activity, and overall performance.

Cecilia Rossignoli is associate professor in organization science at the University of Verona, where she holds courses in organization science, organization science and information systems and strategic role of IS in financial institutions. She is author of several books and papers. She participated at several European projects. Her research interests cover the area of IS and organizational change, the role of IS in inter-organizational information systems, electronic markets and the impact of Business Intelligence Systems within the organizations. Her latest works were published in the *Journal of Electronic Commerce Research* and in the *Journal of Information Systems and e-business Management*.

Mahmud A. Shareef is currently a PhD candidate in management of the Sprott School of Business, Carleton University, Ottawa, Canada. He received his graduate degree from the Institute of Business Administration, Dhaka, Bangladesh in business administration and Carleton University, Ottawa, Canada in civil engineering. His research interest is focused on quality management of e-commerce and e-government. He has published more than 30 papers addressing adoption and quality issues of e-commerce and e-government in different refereed conference proceedings and international journals. He has also published 2 reputed books on quality management issues. He was the recipient of more than 10 academic awards including 2 Best Research Paper Awards in the UK and Canada.

Robert P. Steel, PhD, is a professor of human resource management at the University of Michigan-Dearborn. He received his PhD in industrial-organizational psychology from the University of Tennessee. Professor Steel has published widely in the academic literature. He currently serves on the editorial board of the *Journal of Management* and as associate editor of *Human Resource Management Review*. His research interests include personnel turnover, employee absenteeism, career choice, and work attitudes.

R. Scott Studham is the chief information officer for Oak Ridge National Laboratory (ORNL) and is responsible for planning and executing a coordinated information technology strategy from the desktop to high-performance computing. Studham has broad national laboratory, federal, and corporate experience in managing and delivering information technology services, including recent appointments as chief technology officer for the Center for Computational Sciences at ORNL, associate director for Advanced Computing at PNNL, and Information Technology Project Manager for IBM at the National Weather Service. He has been the program manager or architect for one of the world's top ten supercomputers six times in his career. Studham earned a Bachelor's degree in chemistry from Washington State University and holds a Master's degree in computer science and an MBA from the University of Tennessee. He has published widely on high-end computing, storage, and Linux systems.

Paula Swatman is chair of information systems at the University of South Australia and has researched and taught in ICT and e-business for 25 years. She recently completed a fixed-term appointment as State Records of SA/Fuji Xerox/State Library of SA Chair of Business Information Management, where she led a multidisciplinary, cross-institutional team of experts in designing a suite of leading-edge graduate teaching programs – and will now be spearheading research and academic leadership into the Digital Economy. From 2001-2003 she held the chair of eBusiness at the University of Koblenz-Landau in Germany, where she was foundation director of the Institute for Management and initiated the multidisciplinary, multi-lingual Bachelor/Master of Science in Information Management and where she remains an Emeritus professor. Before moving to Germany, she was Foundation Innovation professor in e-Commerce at RMIT University in Melbourne and Director of RMIT's Interactive Information Institute. She has published widely, producing more than 170 refereed journal articles and conference papers.

Felix B Tan is professor of information systems, director of research mManagement and head of the University Research Office at AUT University, New Zealand. He serves as the editor-in-chief of the *Journal of Global Information Management* and is also the editor of the *EndNote Resources* page on AISWorld Net. He served on the Council of the Association for Information Systems from 2003-2005 and is a fellow of the Information Resources Management Association and the New Zealand Computer

Society. Dr. Tan is internationally known for his work in the global IT field. Dr. Tan's current research interests are in electronic commerce, global information management, business-IT alignment, and the management of IT. He actively uses cognitive mapping and narrative inquiry methods in his research. Dr. Tan has published in *MIS Quarterly, Information & Management, Journal of Information Technology, IEEE Transactions on Engineering Management, Information Systems Journal* as well as other journals and refereed conference proceedings.

Karthikeyan Umapathy is currently working as assistant professor of Information Systems at the School of Computing, University of North Florida. He received his PhD in information sciences and Technology from the Pennsylvania State University. His research interests are interoperability among information systems, service-oriented computing, web services, systems integration, and IT standardization. His research works are published in various conferences such as Americas Conference on Information Systems (AMCIS), Conceptual Modeling (ER), Hawaii International Conference on System Sciences (HICSS), International Conference on Web Services (ICWS), Service Computing Conference (SCC), and Workshop on Information Technologies and Systems (WITS); and journals such as *European Journal of Information Systems* (EJIS), *Information Systems Frontier* (ISF), and *Journal of Computing and Information Science in Engineering* (JCISE).

Michael R. Wade is an associate professor of management information systems at the Schulich School of Business, York University, Toronto. He received a PhD from the Ivey Business School at the University of Western Ontario. Professor Wade has worked with many top international organizations including Cisco Systems, Microsoft and IBM. His research has appeared in journals such as *MIS Quarterly, Strategic Management Journal,* the *Journal of Management Information Systems,* and the *Communications of the ACM.* Professor Wade is co-author of the textbook *Information Systems Today: Canadian Edition,* and has co-authored two e-commerce casebooks. His current research focuses on the strategic use of information systems for sustainable competitive advantage.

Linda Wilkins is educational designer in the School of Business Information Technology, RMIT University. Her background includes experience as an educator, course designer and project manager in engineering, technology and business settings. She was project manager of the Telstra Home Team at RMIT's Interactive Information Institute (1999-2001) awarded the national BHERT award for successful collaboration between researchers and industry. She was subsequently commissioned as researcher and author for the Australian Federal Government funded Creator-2-Consumer Project (2001-2002).She has been an invited lecturer at a number of international institutions including the Asian Institute of Technology, Bangkok and a UNESCO sponsored course leader at the International School of Engineering Lodz, Poland and the Australian Centre for Education, Budapest in 1995. Her research publications focus on issues affecting the uptake of innovative e-technology.

Jiming Wu is an assistant professor in the Department of Management at California State University East Bay. He received his PhD from the University of Kentucky. His research interests include knowledge management, Internet-based business applications and IT acceptance, and computer and network security. His research has been accepted for publication in such journals as *The DATA BASE for Advances in Information Systems, Knowledge Management Research & Practice, Journal of Electronic Commerce Research,* and *Journal of International Technology and Information Management.*

Qin Wu is an assistant professor of finance at the University of Arkansas-Little Rock. He obtained his PhD in finance from the University of Kentucky, USA. His research interests are mainly in corporate finance and investments, including the application of social network theory to finance studies. He has publications in both Chinese and English. One of his coauthored research papers, *"Analysts Get SAD Too: The Effect of Seasonal Affective Disorder on Stock Analyst*s' *Earnings Estimates,"* is forthcoming in the *Journal of Behavioral Finance*. He has extensive experience in teaching different levels of corporate finance, international finance, international business, and business management.

Index